CHINA
in the
POST-UTOPIAN AGE

CHINA
IN THE
POST-UTOPIAN AGE

Christopher J. Smith

University of Albany
State University of New York

Westview Press
A Member of the Perseus Books Group

Copyright © 2000 by Westview Press, A Member of the Perseus Books Group

Published in 2000 in the United States of America by Westview Press, 5500 Central Avenue, Boulder, Colorado 80301-2877, and in the United Kingdom by Westview Press, 12 Hid's Copse Road, Cumnor Hill, Oxford OX2 9JJ

Find us on the World Wide Web at www.westviewpress.com

Library of Congress Cataloging-in-Publication Data

Smith, Christopher J.
    China in the Post-Utopian Age / by Christopher J. Smith.
        p.   cm.
    Includes bibliographical references and index.
    ISBN 0-8133-1986-2 (hc)
    1. China—Social conditions—1976–   . 2. China—Economics conditions—1976–   .
    3. China—Social life and customs—1976–   . I. Title.
HN733.5 .S598   2000
306'095—dc21   99-057687

The paper used in this publication meets the requirements of the American National Standard for Permanence of Paper for Printed Library Materials Z39.48–1984.

10   9   8   7   6   5   4   3   2   1

CONTENTS

PART 3
THE FOUR MODERNIZATIONS:
CHINA'S ECONOMIC AND SPATIAL TRANSITION

PART 4
CONTESTED LIVES AND LANDSCAPES IN
CONTEMPORARY CHINA

PART 5
STATE AND SOCIETY IN CHINA AT THE
END OF THE MILLENNIUM

ACRONYMS

APC	agricultural producer cooperative
AR	Autonomous Region
CCP	Chinese Communist Party
CDP	China Democracy Party
CPCC	Chinese People's Consultative Conference
DPP	Democratic Progressive Party (Taiwan)
EPBs	Environmental Protection Bureaus (1979)
EPC	Environmental Protection Commission (1984)
EPD	Environmental Protection Office (1974)
FDI	foreign direct investment
GDI	Gender Development Index (UNDP)
GDP	gross domestic product
GEM	Gender Empowerment Measure (UNDP)
GNP	gross national product
GVAO	gross value of agricultural output
HDI	Human Development Index (UNDP)
HKSAR	Hong Kong Special Administrative Region
HRS	household responsibility system
IUD	Intrauterine Devices (birth control)
KMT	the Kuomintang, or Nationalist Party
NEPA	National Environmental Protection Administration
NIE	newly industrializing economy
NPC	National People's Congress
OECD	Organization for Economic Cooperation and Development
PLA	People's Liberation Army
PRC	People's Republic of China
ROC	Republic of China (Taiwan)
SEZ	Special Economic Zone
SOE	state-owned enterprise
SRB	sex ratio at birth
TVE	township and village enterprise
UNFPA	United Nations Fund for Population Activities
USAID	United States Agency for International Development
UNDP	United Nations Development Program

ILLUSTRATIONS

Photos

Maps

Figures

PART 1

Introduction

1

China in the Post-Utopian Age

瓦瓦瓦瓦瓦瓦瓦瓦瓦瓦瓦瓦瓦瓦瓦瓦瓦瓦瓦瓦瓦瓦瓦瓦瓦瓦瓦

The utopian mentality ... is withering away. Its intellectual status has sunk to the level of a pathetic adolescent gibberish surviving in leftist sects; in the established communist ideologies the utopian language and utopian imagery have been less and less noticeable throughout the last decades.

—Leszek Kolakowski, *Modernity on Endless Trial* (1990)[1]

Introduction: China's New Great Transformation

Beginning in the late 1970s China launched a program of reform to restructure its industry, agriculture, science and technology, and defense capabilities. The phrase originally used to describe this project—the Four Modernizations—is hardly ever spoken anymore in China, yet over the years there have been few significant changes in the reforms' trajectory. What began as a program of limited, almost haphazard reform evolved gradually into a powerful force that has changed almost every facet of life in China.

Political scientists suggest that a reform program turns into a revolutionary process if (or when) the balance of power between state and society shifts significantly in favor of society.[2] In China the evidence to date demonstrates that only a partial shift in this direction has occurred, and very little of that has been in the realm of political liberalization. What has occurred in China is the expansion of economic freedom and the widespread development of private economic resources. Revolution or not, to keep the reform program moving ahead China's leaders have had to abandon virtually all of their orthodox Marxist ideology; unlike their counterparts in many other parts of the socialist world, however, they have not been forced to give up power.

One goal of this book is to put China's modernization project into the larger context of the transitions away from socialism that began in the late 1980s. The rapid demise of socialism in the former Soviet Union and in Eastern and Central European nations called forth comparisons with what Karl Polanyi has described as the "great transformation"—the nineteenth-century establishment and consolidation of a new civilization that was fundamentally different from anything that preceded it. Some observers are now referring to the swift removal of so many socialist regimes as the "second," or "new," great transformation.[3] In institutional terms the transformations are large-scale events involving entire states and national economies, which are increasingly interacting in the global economic and political communities. In theoretical terms the new transformations can be interpreted as either the final victory for capitalist modernity (symbolized by the demise of socialism and the victory of the market over the plan) or as the twilight of socialist modernity (illustrating the total failure of modernist ideas and rational planning, with states and economies spiraling out of control in a postmodern free-for-all).[4] Although forces operating at these levels are crucial to understanding the events associated with China's new great transformation, this book also attempts to investigate the way such forces play out on the

3

ground, that is, in a multitude of local-scale events and the minutiae of everyday life.[5]

China's Search for Modernity

As part of a determined effort to catch up with the most advanced regions of the modern world, China's Four Modernizations project has considerable historical precedent. In his book *The Search for Modern China*, Jonathan Spence observed that the pursuit of modernity reaches far into the past, but an important landmark was encountered in the middle of the nineteenth century, when China first started to address the threat of Western imperialism.[6] The search continued in the first decades of the twentieth century, when a campaign was launched to rid the Chinese people of their "feudal" past with the widespread introduction of education and the creation of a modern literary canon.[7] The socialist reconstruction that began in the 1950s was clearly another milestone on the road to modernity, and for his role in that process Mao Zedong has been identified as one of the twentieth century's foremost modernists.[8]

After Mao's death China's search for modernity took a quantum leap forward, and the Four Modernizations project represents China's unique version of the search for progress through economic development. To achieve the goals of the Four Modernizations, China's leaders were forced to de-emphasize the importance of class and class struggle, which had dominated political life in China for much of the first three decades after the 1949 revolution. With the gradual introduction of market economics, and with mainland Chinese territory opening up to global capital, the Party-state tied its future legitimacy almost exclusively to the goal of raising China's level of economic development.[9]

In his evaluation of the Four Modernizations project, Gordon White noted that "to the extent . . . the economic reforms were the spearhead of an attempt to resuscitate the political fortunes of Chinese state socialism, they can be judged to be a dismal failure."[10] Most outside observers tend

to agree with White, suggesting that what currently exists in China is so much at odds with the original goals of Chinese socialism that the term "socialism" should be dropped altogether (indeed, by the end of the 1990s that was becoming the case). Kenneth Lieberthal has argued that the publicized statements indicating a commitment to socialism are now little more than "hollow slogans";[11] in addition, there is no longer any link with the larger international socialist movement. Lieberthal in fact has predicted that references to socialism as a goal will soon disappear, to be replaced by unconditional references to such terms as "market development," "modernizing the economy," and "enhancing personal well-being and national strength."[12]

China's Unique Route Out of Socialism

Beginning in the 1980s many socialist regimes began to initiate reforms as a result of economic or political crises that had caused the regimes' legitimacy to be called into question. The transition literature suggests a number of possible routes that regimes can follow in such situations, the two most important outcomes being either political (democratization) or economic (marketization).[13] Because of the unique circumstances they encountered, China's leaders elected not to push along both those fronts simultaneously, and the decision was made to begin with economic reform, leaving the thorny issues of pluralism and democracy for a later date. Deng Xiaoping, usually considered the architect of these reforms, felt that China simply was not ready for democracy in the 1980s: "The conditions are now immature in a huge country like ours, where the population is so large, interregional forces so enormous, and nationalities so numerous. . . . We cannot afford to have a Western two-house system . . . a Western multi-party system. . . . Even public opinion in the West agrees that . . . many things will be impossible without a center to lead the nation."[14]

China's reforms began in 1978 with the radical restructuring and decollectivization of agriculture, but by the mid-1980s the major emphasis had switched more toward urban industrial development, with a particular focus on the production of goods for export.[15] The program was successful in many areas, and the economic benefits experienced by the Chinese people provided what amounted to a cushion effect that counteracted the declining political legitimacy of the regime.[16]

In addition to considering China's basic focus on economic rather than political change, when interpreting the nature of China's reform process it is helpful to consider the differences from events in the former Soviet Union and Eastern Europe.[17] In 1978, when the reform process began, China's political and economic systems were already considerably more decentralized than was ever the case in the Soviet Union; in fact the short thirty years of Chinese Stalinism—what one scholar has called the "socialist detour"—did not significantly alter the ancient traditions of decentralized power in China.[18] Central planning in China was always considerably less inclusive and more primitive than in the Soviet Union, and a substantial share of economic activity had always occurred outside the national plan, administered at the provincial or county level.[19] There was never a

massive push toward privatization in China, at least not until very recently, and then only in some of the coastal areas. And in no way can China's reform process be described as the outcome of a logical, well-planned strategy; in fact it is better described as pragmatic and incremental.[20] Put simply, China elected not to board the fast train to capitalism, preferring a gradualist approach rather than the all-or-nothing ("big bang") strategies adopted elsewhere (see Photo 1.1).[21]

The success of China's reforms was an enigma to the international economists who were advising societies making the transition from socialism. Many of them believed that market socialism would work only if three conditions were met simultaneously: the establishment of clearly defined property rights; the complete freedom of prices from government control; and full integration of the domestic economy into the global economy.[22]

Throughout the reform period a solid stance has been maintained by the Chinese Communist Party (CCP), which proclaimed that public ownership, state planning, and "socialist" values remained central to socioeconomic life. Thus by the end of the 1990s the Chinese modernization project continues to combine the strengths

PHOTO 1.1   China's fast train to capitalism? A billboard in Beijing.

and virtues of both the market and the plan. This stands in sharp contrast to events in many parts of Europe and the former Soviet Union, where the role of the state in the economy was viewed with hostility from the moment the ruling communist parties were ousted.[23]

By the start of the twenty-first century China was certainly the most successful of the socialist states in adjusting to capitalism, with "success" being measured in statistical terms and, more simply, by the fact that the regime has survived despite the demise of so many other socialist states. Socialism remains in place in China, but it is the socialism of flexible production, a curious amalgam created when market mechanisms were introduced into the planned economy. Power in China is still monopolized by the Communist Party, which maintains tight restrictions on civil liberties and the development of trade unions, independent newspapers, and professional associations.

This combination of market reform policies, maintained by a traditionally strong and repressive Party-state, represents what Marc Blecher has referred to as "market Stalinism." Though the definition of "market" needs no explanation, Blecher admits that the reference to "Stalinism" is more of a reach: "Insofar . . . as Stalinism evokes some of the major structural outlines of politics and the state in Dengist China—monopolistic rule by a Leninist-style Communist party, strictures against civil liberties and civil society . . . and the use of political repression in the service of the overriding goal of rapid economic development—the 'Stalinist' part of the term . . . can [also] be advanced."[24]

The Human Consequences of China's Modernization

This book focuses on the transformations that have occurred in China during the leaderships of Deng Xiaoping and Jiang Zemin throughout the 1980s and 1990s. It attempts to ascertain what has changed and what has stayed the same during two extraordinary decades, as well as to evaluate which groups have gained and lost as a result of the reforms. With a different focus in each chapter, we examine some of the ways the accelerated quest for modernity has impacted China's places and peoples. One obvious impact has been the dramatic transformation of China's human geography and the emergence of a new layer of highly uneven landscapes.[25] Spatial inequality has widened between the coastal provinces and the interior and, more generally, between the city and the countryside. Social inequality has also expanded with the emergence of a newly rich middle class in cities and rural areas that has opened even greater gaps between rich and poor.[26]

Another way to address the human impact of China's search for modernity is to focus on the ways in which people think about and represent their experiences over the past two decades. Outsiders express amazement when they view for the first time what has been achieved since Mao Zedong's death. Geographer Joshua Muldavin has suggested that the new China has become "all things to all people," implying that it now has a dazzling hybrid quality allowing us to think about it as "a cross between a newly industrialized country, a Soviet-style industrialization model, an export-led growth model, an import-substitution model [and] a sweat shop/subcontractor to the world's corporations."[27]

More important than outsiders' opinions is what Chinese people themselves think about the current era of reform. Modernity should be thought of as more than just a set of policies or practices or even the changes associated with such practices; it is, as Lisa Rofel has observed, a story that "people tell themselves about themselves in relation to others."[28] In China's case the push for socialist modernity after 1949 provided its people with a powerful story that offered a clear picture of their identity and a reasonably legible map of the future. For a time at least—usually defined as the 1950s and parts of the 1960s and 1970s—China's version of socialism appeared to offer its people a viable and radically different worldview, as well as a set of blueprints for economic development based on something other than capitalism. During the reform era, however, most of that has been cast aside in the rush to embrace capitalism.[29] Thus life in turn-of-the-century China seems to be much more complicated, and the stories people tell about themselves have become conceptually more open and complex.[30]

China has not been alone in making the transition out of socialism; in fact similar events were occurring in many socialist states at roughly the same time. The main difference has been that in China the widespread introduction of capitalism (i.e., economic reform) has not been accompanied by democratization (i.e., political reform); in fact the communist regime is intact, and the state continues to dominate society. The implications of this are enormous, as China's people are now living within two distinct, seemingly paradoxical structural forces: One is the combination of single-party rule and state domination that has effectively strangled the emergence of a fully functioning and independent civil society; the other is the nation's all-out pursuit of economic superpower status, which has brought uneven prosperity and well-being.

Some observers (and probably the regime's leadership as well) believe that the economic liberation in China more than compensates for the lack of political pluralism and liberalization. The evidence to support that claim is clear: Witness, for example, the greedy relish with which some sectors of society have welcomed China's version of "market triumphalism" after the terrible scarcity and deprivation of the Maoist years.[31] Thomas Rawski, for example, described how the reforms propelled China to the top of the world's growth charts, with rapid, uninterrupted expansion among all indicators of economic and social development, concluding that the reforms "have produced no readily identifiable groups of losers whose income and material welfare have declined."[32]

Although Rawski's assertion may be technically accurate, it is misleading to suggest there are no losers in contemporary China. In light of this sort of economic imperialism, it is impor-

tant to question the narrative of success that has accompanied China's modernization project, based on the observations about capitalism's power to consume cultures, destroy environments, upset population dynamics, and remake local economies. In terms of geographical coverage capitalism is obviously the most desirable global development strategy, yet there is increasing evidence that only some places and some people in China are reaping the benefits of the capitalist revolution.[33]

The revolution that began in 1949 reached middle age as the People's Republic of China (PRC) celebrated its fiftieth anniversary in October 1999. The rest of the world has certainly had enough time to become accustomed to China's presence, but the continuing Chinese anachronism—a Leninist party-state managing a capitalist revolution—leaves outsiders mystified about what might happen in the future.[34] In the simplest terms, it is possible to imagine three scenarios: The reforms prove to be too successful for too long; the reforms fail almost entirely to deliver the goods; or the reforms are accompanied by some combination of irreversible damage to Chinese lives and landscapes.

The first scenario played out in the late 1980s, when material successes and economic freedoms associated with the reforms prompted widespread calls for political change. As we know, in 1989 the democracy movement was crushed on the streets of Beijing (the infamous events at Tiananmen Square) and in many other cities around the country; for the time being there are no signs of its revival. The second scenario assumes the reforms are (or will become) unsuccessful, unable to provide the sorts of benefits needed to stave off political challenge. This has not come to pass in China, although some pundits predict such an event is imminent (see below). The third scenario assumes that despite the palpable achievements thus far recorded, the wisdom of the reforms and the narratives of success will need to be comprehensively examined; and based on the evidence of some serious externality effects that are considered to be over and above the price worth paying, an entirely new development strategy will be called for.

All three scenarios revolve around the material impacts—both positive and negative—of the reform policies; but there is another important consideration that is much less tangible: The Four Modernizations project has been accompanied by the demise of traditional socialist ideology, and for the most part that is surely a plus. For example, it has meant the abolition of highly stigmatizing class labels and the continuing focus on class conflict, but it also represents the loss of a powerful organizing principle in Chinese society.[35] As Mark Elvin has pointed out in *Changing Stories of the Chinese World*, Chinese communism was a still "a 'living faith,' it provided the people with a solid story to tell."[36] Without a sense of belonging to a larger whole or community (a class, an urban work unit, a rural production brigade), the people may now have difficulty organizing for collective action in the everyday struggle to get by. These struggles appear to be increasingly polarized in contemporary China; the primary aspirations for the majority of poor people are focused on different ways of simply surviving, whereas at the other extreme rich people seem to be concerned only with getting richer. With the state writing itself out of the picture in both sets of circumstances, it is reasonable for those in the West to ask questions about how the struggles will eventually be resolved.

Is China Losing Its Way at the End of the Millennium?

In the closing years of the twentieth century, the adulation of Mao and his aphorisms has been replaced by nihilism and a loss of faith. An escalating crime rate, increased levels of corruption, the aimlessness and desperation of the "blind flow" of [the] unemployed, and the political instability in the transition to post-Deng China are manifestations of the moral vacuum and sense of insecurity under the surface of the economic success.

—Kate Saunders, *Eighteen Layers of Hell: Stories from the Chinese Gulag* (1996)[37]

In this quotation Kate Saunders rather sweepingly characterizes some of the recent problems in China, but more restrained scholars were also expressing their concern, and in the mid-1990s some even predicted that economic collapse would precipitate political collapse and disintegration within several years. Such predictions were based on the observation that the regime had self-consciously tied its own legitimacy to the success of the economic reforms and would be hoisted upon its own petard if the reforms went awry.[38] As it turned out, such predictions have so far been proved wrong, but it certainly has not been a smooth passage for the Chinese leadership in the post-Mao era. In October 1992, for example, the Fourteenth Party Congress decided the economy desperately needed to cool down.[39] The problem—and many countries would probably be delighted to inherit such a problem—was that China's reforms had started working again too successfully after the post-1989 slump.[40]

By comparison, the early 1990s was a period of relative calm in the realm of domestic politics. There had been little discussion of political reform throughout the period; in fact there was a further curtailment of civil rights in 1995 when Wei Jinsheng, who had been jailed in 1978 after the Democracy Wall movement, was first released, then imprisoned again, along with another roundup of known dissidents. In 1996 all established places of worship were required to register with the government, which might suggest the Party-state felt a need to flex its muscles and tighten up on society.[41] Such ups and downs notwithstanding, the Chinese state has survived, and its support has primarily been due to the successful economy—as Deng Xiaoping always said it would. By 1996 economic growth had slowed down to a more reasonable rate. The succession question had also been settled, with the announcement that Jiang Zemin was to take over at the top.[42]

In spite of the outward confidence China's leaders exuded throughout the 1990s, there are signs of strain. Deep cleavages are evident in the political system between the booming coastal areas and the lagging periphery and, more generally, between the urban centers and the rural localities. In the economic realm conflicts have emerged over issues of finance, trade and investment, economic authority, and resource allocation. But the most explosive situation of all, as Marc Blecher has noted, is the continuing tension between "an increasingly restive society and the state that has kept the lid tightly over it since 1989."[43] There were, in addition, some serious social problems that started to emerge in the early 1990s, involving what Richard Baum labeled the "beggaring" of the peasantry and a series of demonstrations and riots in various parts of the countryside.[44] Many reporters and pulp journalists were writing about a general decline in social order and rising crime rates, and by the middle of the 1990s many of China's social indicators had plummeted, as Baum observed:

> The coexistence of high industrial and commercial growth rates alongside swelling armies of impoverished rural floaters descending on crime-plagued cities gave the country an unsettled, schizophrenic appearance that lent added poignancy to the fading cries of alarm sounded by China's few remaining conservatives. Since 1979, party old-timers had warned anyone who would listen of capitalism's boom and bust nature and polarizing tendencies, bitterly decrying the noxious socio-cultural by-products of bourgeois liberalization. Now that their prophecy appeared in some measure to be coming true, their voices were no longer audible.[45]

In 1994 a book entitled *Viewing China Through a Third Eye*—purportedly written by a conservative CCP cadre—made a highly negative assessment of Deng Xiaoping's legacy. The book predicted the collapse of the regime following the waves of rampant rural lawlessness, blaming the rising discontent on Deng's decision to open up rural China to markets and out-migration, which had turned both the cities and the countryside into an "active volcano." Although the book was dismissed by many as lightweight and journalistic, it struck a

chord at the time because many different sets of commentators—Chinese and foreign—were predicting further chaos leading to inevitable disaster in China.[46]

In another book, published in 1998 under the title *Zhongguo de xianjing* (China's Pitfall), economist He Qinglian leveled an even more devastating critique, arguing that the reforms have had far more negative than positive effects and that by 1997 income growth was slowing significantly and the rural-urban income gap was rising steadily.[47] He's book is a chronicle of the ills brought to China through the reform policies; in fact in her opinion it is a travesty to refer to it as a process of "reform," when in fact it has been "a process in which power holders and their hangers-on [have] plundered public wealth" in the forms of state and collective property.[48] What has taken place, He suggests, has mainly involved the transfer rather than the production of wealth, with the whole process being supported by massive infusions of foreign investment and huge loans from China's state banks. She argues that China does not really have a market economy; rather there is a "simulated" market in which "the actual competition is political" and where "power determines the allocation of resources but has no need to see their efficient use."[49]

China's Pitfall focuses on the events that have been responsible for rising tensions in all corners of Chinese society. Both peasants and workers have been made to suffer the ignominy of late and partial payments from the state and even IOUs on wages owed; and in the spring of 1998 an estimated 12 million state workers were laid off, with another 10 million scheduled to be cut by that year's end.[50] The situation is thought to be even worse in the banking system, because the state regularly bails out inefficient state-owned enterprises (SOEs) with loans that are rarely repaid (being written off as "bad debt"). Officially, 20 percent of all loans are said to be "nonperforming," but He reckons the figure is closer to 40–60 percent.[51]

In spite of its negative tone the book was a moderate best-seller, with the first printing of 100,000 selling out in less than two weeks; five pirated editions sold another 300,000 copies. Liu Binyan and Perry Link, in their review of He's book, have suggested that its popularity was a result of the author's courage in saying what so many people believed but had not been bold enough to say publicly: that the Dengist strategy of fast economic reform with no political change has been a huge and socially costly mistake, the proportions of which are impossible to comprehend from the outside. The rest of the world, according to He, has been strangely willing to believe in the "China miracle," in part, she thinks, because of the official propaganda and statistical manipulation.[52]

Perhaps the most serious side effect of the Four Modernizations project, according to He, is the almost ubiquitous decline in public morality. Ordinary people hear so much about corruption in the higher echelons of political life that some have simply given up trying to toe the line morally. Everyone is attempting to *zia* (literally: slaughter) everyone else, *zia* being a word that Liu and Link suggest corresponds in both sense and tone to the familiar verb "rip off," which "involves an almost complete collapse of ethics, and a total lack of values."[53] At the same time we hear reports that economic corruption and bribery are now endemic throughout the corridors of power in China, to the extent that a truly honest official is nowadays viewed as a "rare and quaint anachronism."[54]

In addition, we have this rather sobering note: From the mid-1990s onward China's leaders have been shifting toward aggressive nationalism. As Kenneth Lieberthal suggests, nationalist appeals are often linked with ideas about the new global openness and inclusiveness and with talk of an assertion of pride (*huaren* or *xiaren*) associated with being Chinese. This implies a broad cultural notion of Chinese identity that includes an array of transnational Chinese populations, both in Asia and globally. Yet there is a more sinister side to rising Chinese nationalism, involving a more statist definition of Chineseness and the exaltation of the Chinese state (*Zhongguo*) as a sovereign entity. In this guise the Party-state has

issued many statements, often disseminated with bluster and assertiveness, about the numerous disputes on China's borders, especially those regarding the "other" Chinas: Taiwan and Hong Kong. Such statements have included accusations of treachery among potential enemy states whose vital interests are tied up with those offshore Chinese territories, the villains usually being identified as the United States and Great Britain.[55]

In light of all this, outsiders are more than curious about how or whether Jiang Zemin will cope with the system that Deng Xiaoping created. Some are fairly pessimistic; for example Perry Link and Liu Binyan have concluded that contemporary China is politically "more bewildered than it has been for a long time."[56] Other groups, more optimistically, argue that the current problems being reported are little more than growing pains associated with the transition out of socialism. He Qinglian's book can in fact be interpreted in this light as the beginning of a moral crusade, launched as the first part of an inquiry into what has gone wrong in reform-era China and how it should be corrected.[57]

During the early 1990s some reporters and academics were making worried comparisons between China and the Balkan states. They predicted that Deng's death (which seemed imminent as early as 1993) would trigger a crisis of disintegration similar to that in Yugoslavia following Marshal Tito's death.[58] As we review the events in China in the 1990s, the similarities with events in parts of Eastern and Central Europe and the former Soviet Union are striking. Katherine Verdery in *What Was Socialism, and What Comes Next?* has insisted that rather than moving along a trajectory from socialism toward democracy, civil society, and a market economy, many states have experienced a transition from socialism to "feudalism."[59] Verdery also observes that socialist regimes have a tendency to think of themselves as responsible for ushering in a radiant future and bringing about the final stages of human happiness. As a result they have tended to classify all human history into "a gigantic sequence with themselves at its apex," and precisely because of that teleological orientation such regimes "became vulnerable to the terrible disappointment of their wards [when they were] betrayed by the system's shortcomings."[60]

Another transition scholar, Vladimir Tismaneanu, has developed this line of reasoning even farther in an analysis of the postsocialist era. He describes conditions in Europe similar to those being reported in China throughout the 1990s, but he is not willing to write off such trends simply as the growing pains of transition. In fact Tismaneanu suggests that what was happening in Russia and Eastern Europe in the late 1990s was the "bewildering, often terrifying territory on which political mythologies make a return."[61] He fears that widespread economic and social disarray characteristic of the postsocialist era has become a potential breeding ground for the emergence of sinister political movements.

Optimists—most significantly the Party-state—can reply that nothing of the sort is likely to occur in China, where it has been possible to steer a middle course throughout the transition period, the result of which is that the Chinese people have not experienced anything like the "terrible disappointments" Verdery has written about in Europe. But pessimists, like He Qinglian, remain convinced that a meltdown in China is already under way.[62] Whether we side with the optimists or the pessimists, erstwhile socialist states in which regimes have been ousted and replaced can provide useful analogies for events in China. As a preliminary exercise, therefore, we will compare the situation in China since the Tiananmen tragedy in 1989 to situations in Russia and Eastern and Central Europe during the same period. China is now one of the few remaining states in which the Communist Party has been able to cling to power, but much of the everyday discourse, both within China and internationally, is based on the assumption either that the Party-state will soon be removed or that it is already being dismissed and ignored.[63] Although the regime remained intact at the turn of the century, most individual and group activities, especially in the realm of economics, are occurring outside the orbit and beyond the reach of the Party-state.

Comparative Postsocialisms: Life in the Post-Utopian Age

At the very core of Marxism one finds a millennialist mythology, a social dream about a perfect world where the ancient conflicts between man and society, between essence and existence, would have been transcended. [But] now that the Leninist order has been overthrown, the moral landscape of post-communism is marred with moral confusion, venomous hatreds, unsatisfied desires, and endless bickerings.

—Vladimir Tismaneanu,
Fantasies of Salvation (1998)[64]

There is general consensus among academics and journalists that the former socialist states of the Soviet Union and Europe have been drifting on dangerous waters. Seemingly commonplace are widespread malaise and a sense of dissatisfaction with the status quo, often combined with severe economic crisis, rising inequality, and the emergence of a newly rich capitalist class. The worst-case scenario appears to be emerging in Russia, where all of this and more has been accompanied by the loss of its empire.[65] In addition to Russia's disastrous economic situation, there have been some disturbing political trends in the 1990s, including the rising popularity of ideologues with vicious campaign messages that threaten to snuff out the fledgling Russian democracy.[66]

The demise of socialism in the former Soviet Union and Eastern Europe was greeted with great expectations, in part because it signaled the end of a system that was based on the "dictatorship over human needs, memories, and hopes, and the almost complete control of the party/police state over human activities."[67] Yet, as Tismaneanu suggests above, something was also in danger of being lost in the rush to sweep away all vestiges of socialism. With the old state systems dismantled, it has proved difficult for the people to re-create stable images with which to identify. For a while they had believed (or they were told to believe) they were part of a widespread utopian strategy to create a better world, one in which there could be everlasting human fraternity and equality. Although attempts to realize socialist utopias have produced what Leszek Kolakowski has described as "the most malignant project[s] ever devised,"[68] holding on to such ideas promised a combination of satisfaction, happiness, and fraternity—all of which proved to be a powerful and not easily replaced opiate for the masses.

In this new era, which can be referred to as the "post-utopian age," the former socialist states have proved to be at their most vulnerable, and Tismaneanu suggests they have become a vacuum or a repository of sorts, into which a multitude of new and reconstituted political myths have been deposited. Many of these new ideas and movements—he refers to them as "fantasies of salvation"—appear to be opposed to any principles of difference, especially among groups that champion pro-Western ideas and pluralist goals. Some of the movements want to bring back collectivist organization in the countryside; some are intent on glorifying and defending the national community; others are noisily scapegoating and demonizing minority groups (which in Russia, Romania, and elsewhere in this region implies Jews and Gypsies). Tismaneanu also points out that in spite of the widespread dissatisfaction with the old socialist regimes the picture today is even more depressing than the one it replaced. As he suggests, adventurers and gangsters have emerged to supplant the dull party members who used to hold power. Even worse is the realization that in many cases the new racketeers are the same people—born again in the form of the loathsome "nomenklatura capitalists."[69]

In such circumstances it is understandable that we can discern a widespread nostalgia for the security and social predictability associated with socialist states. In the post-utopian age there seems to be no sense of purpose, no ideology, no plans for the future, and none of the feelings of fraternity and solidarity associated

with the old days. The people have managed to rid themselves of the authoritarian communist institutions, but they have not been able to purge their need for such institutions: to provide jobs, housing, and schools for the poor and unemployed; and to feed the hungry, treat the sick, and care for the elderly. As a result, people are now held hostage to their memories and fears. In spite of the newfound freedom, what is missing from their lives is the all-embracing presence of socialist paternalism:

> There is nobody to take care of them, to plan their futures, and protect them against what they perceive as threatening, uncontrollable forces. . . . The old paradigms are exhausted [but] the new ones are still inchoate. On the one hand there is a longing for calm and normalcy. On the other, there is nervousness and exasperation with the all-pervasive corruption, cliquishness, and political fragmentation. . . . It is as if there is a *yearning* for a new figure of the future, an expectation of a true revolution that would put an end to all the current ordeals and anxieties.[70]

To Western observers the most disturbing aspect of such yearnings—and the movements emerging to cater to them—is their blatant antimodernity. Among the ideas floating around are searches for sacred symbols, some of which harken to ancient foundation myths; religious revivalisms and the creation of parables about providential saviors; attempts to exhume and revitalize images of the bitter socialist past, including the phenomenon of people lovingly placing flowers on Nicolae Ceausescu's grave in Romania, marching with Stalinist flags in Russia, and reviving Mao imagery and memorabilia in China. It is unlikely that such phenomena signify the reemergence of Ceausescuism, Stalinism, and Maoism, but they can be interpreted as symbolic of a deeply felt disaffection with the contemporary era. There is a widely held view that the new freedoms are not as beneficial as had been anticipated. Some people become anxious as their lives appear to be going nowhere—even if they are making money. Others are repelled by the chaos, anarchy, poverty, political decadence, and moral decrepitude they see around them—the "landscapes of disenchantment" that appear to be pervasive in the post-utopian age.[71]

Events occurring in China under the Four Modernizations share some common features with what has been happening in other socialist states around the world. In the political realm it is difficult to pinpoint the extent of the similarities to the former socialist states, primarily because most attempts to establish official political groups are stifled before they can get off the ground. It is apparent, however, that in the economic and social spheres there are some parallels between events in Eastern and Central Europe and those in contemporary China: the growing level of income inequality, the reemergence of rural and urban capitalist classes, and pervasive corruption.

As noted earlier, the reform process in China amounts to a new great transformation, and exploring that theme will require analysis of macro-level forces at work, both domestically and globally. In addition (and more important) are the thousands and, in China's case, millions of daily, micro-level transformations that are under way. A more disaggregated analysis of events allows a focus on what happens when structural policy decisions and market forces coincide with issues of everyday life in ordinary places. As anthropologists Michael Burawoy and Katherine Verdery have suggested, within transitioning societies "the economy is . . . thoroughly embedded in a variety of noneconomic [cultural and political] practices";[72] it is thus evident that much can be learned by investigating the way individuals and communities respond to and struggle against the transformations associated with the transition.

To interpret and evaluate such reactions will require a focus on such processes as "selective appropriation," "evasive improvisation," and "explicit resistance,"[73] and for that reason Burawoy and Verdery make a strong case for adopting an ethnographic approach to the process of transition. In their view such an approach

allows one to look at the ways in which the "unfolding uncertainties of macro-institutions affect practices within micro worlds and also how family, work, and community are refashioning themselves—often in opposition to what governments intend."[74] As we shall explore in Chapter 2, implicit here is the emergence of new terrains of struggle that provide an opportunity for geographical analysis. It is apparent that the transition process comprises situations in which political power and administered economies (i.e., structures) begin to break down, creating different categories of social and physical space for humans (i.e., agents) to produce multiple responses.

This book will explore some of these newly defined and contested spaces and will consider the outcome of the new life chances being made possible by the reforms.[75] We shall be investigating situations in which people are increasingly left to their own devices, especially in the realm of production and distribution (in China, in both urban and rural areas). We shall also examine some of the ways in which Chinese people have interacted with new markets and market-induced phenomena, for example: in their everyday consumption practices; in buying new homes; in taking care of their health; in exploring and championing their ethnic identity; and in the business of finding jobs and services—all of which can now be conducted independent of the state. Most important, we shall observe some of the ways in which people take on or challenge the power of the state, sometimes victoriously, as in the case of the peasant-led agrarian reforms; although there are countless examples where courageous people have met with much less success.

Burawoy and Verdery also recommend—in the context of Eastern and Central Europe at least—that the postsocialist transitions should not necessarily be conceived of as being either rooted in the past or tied to an imagined future. As they observe, the transition process does not necessarily move forward in a unilinear fashion from one stage to the next, as might be anticipated in the goal-setting phase of neoliberal economic planning. From all accounts it appears that transitioning states are likely to move along multiple, sometimes contradictory pathways, and more often than not transition policies fail to achieve any significant degree of success.[76] As we have seen in Europe—and especially in Russia—there are in fact some distressing cases of regressive dynamics, even involution in which entire regions crumbled into subsistence and large segments of the population have been left to eke out meager existences. To some extent similar events have been reported in China, and we shall examine some of those contradictions.[77]

An Outline of the Book

Part 1 includes this chapter as well as Chapter 2, which explores some of the geographical imperatives operating in China; it continues with a brief exposition of some of the ideas currently circulating within what might be called the "new human geography."[78] Part 2 considers some of the structural influences on everyday life in contemporary China, especially the relationships between society and the state, beginning with an introduction to the overarching influence of culture (Chapter 3) and political economy (Chapter 4). Both chapters illustrate some of the ways Chinese lives and landscapes have been shaped by such influences over the centuries—with an obvious bias toward events occurring since 1978. Chapter 5 addresses the critical problem of China's demographics, describing and interpreting the recent population policies and evaluating some of their consequences. Chapter 6 offers an assessment of the changes that have occurred in the delivery of health care services during the economic reform era, focusing on the implications for issues of life and death in contemporary China. As we shall discover, how well a group of people lives, and how long they live, are shaped largely by where they live and what they do to make a living.

Part 3 focuses on the spatial organization of economic and social life in China during the Four Modernizations. The discussions include the transformation of production, distribution, and consumption activities, first in the agrarian realm (Chapter 7), then more generally within the contexts of the economic reforms and China's transition from plan to market (Chapter 8). These two chapters highlight some of the positive and negative impacts of the reforms on everyday life in China in the 1980s and 1990s; both chapters are pivotal, because much of the discussion in the subsequent chapters follows from the analysis of the impacts of the economic reforms. Part 3 also deals with the restructuring of space in China, both at the city level (Chapter 9) and at the regional level (Chapter 10); both chapters include accounts of the material impacts of the reform policies on China's people and places. Chapter 11 provides an overview of recent events in China's two most significant offshore territories: Hong Kong, which has now been returned to Chinese sovereignty after nearly two decades of debate and anxiety; and Taiwan, which has a much more uncertain future in terms of its relationship with the mainland. During the 1990s the tone of the China-Taiwan relationship has ranged from cordial and cooperative (the early 1990s), to extremely tense (1996), and back again to cooperative and then hostile (turn of the century).[79]

Part 4 narrows the analysis to focus on specific aspects of everyday life in China, exploring some contested issues, between society and the state, between market forces and the plan, and between established city residents and new migrants from the countryside. Chapter 12 addresses China's ethnic minority groups, who have experienced varying fortunes since the 1949 revolution. For the most part ethnic identification is currently being supported by the state, but the fact that some minority groups are actively pursuing policies of separatism is making the regime understandably nervous, bearing in mind some of the traumatic events associated with nationalism and secession in Eastern Europe and the former Soviet Union since the 1989–1991 democratic revolutions. Chapter 13 considers the gender issue, focusing on women and their place in contemporary

China. There is some disturbing evidence that in spite of the booming economy the quality of life for many women, particularly in poorer parts of the countryside, appears to have worsened during the latter part of the 1990s rather than improving. Chapters 14 and 15 focus on China's rapid urbanization during the Four Modernizations, investigating some of the ways market forces have been shaping lives and landscapes in and around the cities. Chapter 14 reflects on the issues of consumption, service delivery, and the quality of life in China's cities, with a focus on the emergence of commodity housing as a policy solution to China's long-standing housing crisis. Chapter 15 considers the causes and consequences of the new population mobility in China, focusing on the emergence of the so-called floating populations in the cities. This phenomenon is part of a trend that some observers are calling the largest migration stream in human history. As China's economy settles and slows down, we can anticipate serious conflicts between migrants and city natives as they compete for jobs, services, and housing in the already overcrowded cities.

Part 5 serves as a conclusion, offering thoughts on issues critical to China's future. This opens with a consideration of environmental degradation in contemporary China (Chapter 16). At the turn of the century the current regime in China and the rest of the world are in agreement as to the seriousness of China's environmental crisis. Some outside experts are convinced that the crisis is practically insoluble given the current economic policies and demographic trajectories we have considered in this book. Chapter 17 reviews some of the most significant economic issues that were making their presence felt in the late 1990s; Chapter 18 contains a parallel discussion of recent political issues. The concluding remarks in Chapter 19 include a brief analysis of the current debates regarding the prospects for civil society and democracy in China. The 1989 events in Tiananmen Square sent a clear message from the people to the government: Unless real progress is made on the issues of freedom and democracy, the economic gains of the last decade will have amounted to nothing. At the time of writing (late 1999) the streets of China's cities are relatively free of visible dissent; in fact Hong Kong was the only city in which there was an organized demonstration associated with the ten-year anniversary of the Tiananmen Square incident (June 4, 1999). Yet despite enforced political silence, the streets are anything but quiet at the turn of the century; in fact the noise of construction and of people making and spending money is practically deafening. Such political silence may symbolize a future in which the Chinese become even more focused on material wealth—but then again it might simply represent the calm before the next storm.

2

China and the Geographical Imagination

Feelings of national identity have expressed themselves in open hostility to the Chinese state and hatred of the Han people. The most obvious examples of this have been in the late 1980s among the Tibetans and in the early 1990s in Xinjiang [but] in most minority areas . . . outright secession is not on the agenda of the overwhelming majority of minority people. Most would regard it as both impracticable and undesirable.

—Colin Mackerras, *China's Minorities* (1994)[1]

Introduction: Geographical Imperatives in Contemporary China

Geography has been shaping the pattern of human settlement and the conduct of everyday life in China for centuries. From the outside we see a physically huge country, yet with a transportation system so rudimentary that distance becomes a major constraint to social interaction. The population is enormous, so the demand for resources almost everywhere outstrips available supplies. Regional variations have also produced a captivating mosaic of human and physical characteristics. Most important, China's people have over centuries developed a strong sense of place based on an almost fanatical attachment to native soil.

Five decades of socialism have altered the character of such geographical imperatives, but for the most part the same forces remain at work. In the first thirty years after the revolution, peasants were tied more strongly to the land than had ever been the case in the past, the result of Mao Zedong's forced collectivization. The restrictions on migration and the nature of work in the new collectives meant that most of China's peasants were legally bound for life to residing in their tiny production units. They

were not allowed to leave, and if they did, their food supply would be jeopardized. For all intents and purposes the peasants were imprisoned in what Mark Selden has referred to as "a community of destiny that structures [their] life opportunities and incomes."[2] A visitor to China today cannot avoid noticing how much has changed in the cities as well as the countryside. One of the most dramatic changes has been the appearance of huge transient populations in many cities. With the agrarian reforms, the end of collectivization, and the loosening of migration restrictions, peasants became free to leave the countryside. They have done just that in massive numbers, heading directly for the nearest town or the bigger cities, where they expect to find jobs.

Geography thus has relevance to the processes of describing and interpreting events in contemporary China, yet this book does not argue for the primacy of spatial factors over social and historical factors. To appreciate current events in China it is still important to be aware of the dominant role of culture and politics in shaping almost all aspects of everyday life. This was certainly true during the 1970s and 1980s, and it was still true at the end of the 1990s; now, however, it is necessary to consider the importance of another dominant force:

economics. Outsiders returning to China today after a ten- or fifteen-year hiatus are surprised to see how thoroughly commerce has penetrated every aspect of life. Thus, although it is reasonable to conclude that geographical factors are important to understanding contemporary China, they should be considered in conjunction with cultural, political, and economic forces. The vicissitudes of physical geography have markedly influenced human activities in China over the centuries, dictating where people could live and what they could grow.[3] The more abstract properties of geography, such as distance and accessibility, have also helped to shape the course of regional development over time. And as we shall see later in this chapter, the roles of place and space in the development of human agency and identity are undeniable.

Geography exerts a powerful force; in fact it may constitute or even determine human activity. But in most instances geography works in more subtle and less direct ways, constraining or mediating human activities. Finding a place for geography, then, is easy to do in a study of China, but at no time in this book is geography elevated to a point where other important social science perspectives are not considered. For that reason this book is clearly not a geography *of* contemporary China; it is an interdisciplinary book *about* China, in which the web of everyday lives and landscapes is interpreted through the eyes of a human geographer.[4] This chapter details aspects of this interpretation. First, however, it is important to identify some geographical factors relevant to any discussion of contemporary China.

In painting their comprehensive and objective pictures of a specific place, academic writers usually feel a need to offer a battery of facts and figures to present all possible sides of each issue.[5] In a country as large and as complex as China, a place where change is occurring so rapidly, it is difficult to determine all the facts, let alone what they tell us. Much of the official data provided by the Chinese government are unreliable and impossible to evaluate. Even if we were reasonably confident about how the numbers are collected and what they mean, the facts themselves may tend to obfuscate rather than illuminate, making it difficult to see the forest for the trees. There is also the important issue of representation, in the sense that different individuals and groups tend to interpret the facts from their own perspectives. Melvyn Goldstein illustrates this point in his discussion of modern Tibet, suggesting that in the recent past "Tibet" has been largely a discursive construction, shaped primarily by the way it has been used by opposing groups to represent their own best interests:

> Because the Tibetan exile government has as one of its main political goals the reunification of all Tibetan areas in China into a single "Greater Tibet," it commonly uses the term "Tibet" to represent events in both ethnographic and political Tibet, fostering the appearance that "Greater Tibet" existed in the recent past. Thus, even though political Tibet was invaded [by China] in October 1950, the Tibetan exile government states that Tibet was invaded in 1949, when Chinese forces "liberated" the ethnographic Tibetan areas of Qinghai, Sichuan and Gansu provinces. Similarly, to create the impression that Tibet was part of China in the 1930s and 1940s, the Chinese government states that Tibetan delegates participated in Chinese governmental meetings, implying that they were sent from Lhasa, whereas they were actually from ethnographic Tibet.[6]

This book contains many facts, some of which may change or become outdated even before the book is published. It is important to stress, therefore, that the facts included herein are intended to illustrate topics and issues, and the reader is encouraged to develop a critical view of them. Survey data collected by Chinese and foreign social scientists have some clear limitations, and official statistics are equally likely to be suspect—but for different reasons. In reading this book, then, consider the facts per se as secondary to the underlying concepts, whether geographical, cultural, political, or economic. That being said, it is useful at the outset to consider a small set of the geographical "facts of life" that are impossible to ignore. For that reason—and bearing in mind that geography is not privileged over other approaches—these facts of life are offered as geographical imperatives.

The first geographical imperative is China's regional context within East Asia and, more generally, the Pacific Rim. China is encircled by mountains and deserts to the west and north and by the vast expanse of the Pacific Ocean to the east (see Map 2.1). As a result, China remained in virtual isolation until the middle of the nineteenth century, trading only occasionally with the outside world and caring little about the opinions and values of foreigners. The Chinese have always considered their country to be the Middle Kingdom (*Zhong guo*), which by definition relegates all other countries to the periphery, their residents to the status of barbarians.[7]

Over the centuries the Chinese became somewhat complacent about their self-sufficiency and overconfident of their supremacy. The intellectual stirrings of the Renaissance bypassed China completely, and the Industrial Revolution, which swept Europe and North America during the eighteenth and nineteenth centuries, had virtually no impact on China. In spite of its isolation China was able to cultivate a rich civilization of its own, as demonstrated by the early development of art and philosophy and the long list of technological innovations and inventions usually attributed to the Chinese. The result, in the words of John King Fairbank, was that "China achieved a cultural superiority over all other East Asian regions, the after-effects of which have lasted to this day."[8] Fairbank believed that this sense of superiority made it especially difficult for the Chinese to suffer their lack of development in modern times. Moreover, the loathsome interference of foreign powers—throughout much of the second half of the nineteenth century and the first half of the twentieth century—has contributed to the aggressive displays of nationalism that we see in the contemporary era.[9]

Size is a second geographical imperative. Everything about China is large: land area, population, resource base, landforms, and, today, even its rate of economic growth. Distances are immense, and they have worked historically to hinder spatial and social interaction between China's regions. China is the third largest country in the world, stretching well over 5,000 kilometers from north to south and east to west. China is larger than the United States, spanning lines of latitude from the frozen north to the subtropical south. Overlaying a map of China onto a map of North America, we would see that the most northerly point (in Heilongjiang Province) corresponds to the vicinity of James Bay in Canada, whereas the southernmost point (in Hainan Province) would be close to Jamaica (see Map 2.3).

China's location is another geographical imperative. Like the United States, much of China lies in the middle latitudes; hence both countries possess the physical attributes needed to support large populations, especially the moisture to grow crops abundantly and the moderate temperatures that make life tolerable; both also have access to a warm-water sea. But the major geographical difference between the two countries is that China has no equivalent to California, which serves both as a seedbed of innovation and as the major food producer. Instead of an ocean on its western flank, China is separated from the rest of Asia by inaccessible mountains and inhospitable deserts.

China's population is an imperative that is impossible to ignore. As of 1996 official Chinese sources placed the population at 1,223,890,000, which represents more than 20 percent of the world's total.[10] Some Chinese provinces, if they were independent countries, would be among the world's largest. Sichuan, with 114 million people, is more populous than Bangladesh, which has the ninth largest population in the world; Shandong, with more than 87 million people, is larger than Mexico.[11] To support all these people China possesses less than 15 percent of the world's land area; more important, it has only about 7 percent of the world's cultivable land. The obvious outcome is

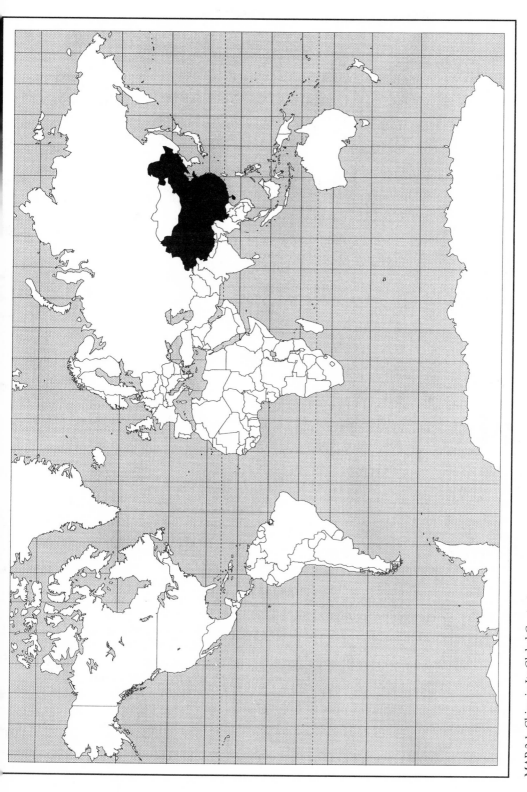

MAP 2.1 China in Its Global Context

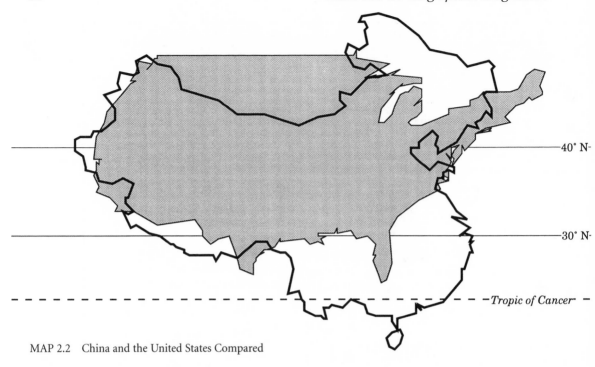

MAP 2.2   China and the United States Compared

a tremendous conflict over space and the way it should be used. During Deng Xiaoping's Four Modernizations project, the lands being used to build roads, houses, shops, and factories are necessarily taken out of cultivation, which ultimately threatens the food supply.

One final geographical imperative is the astonishing amount of diversity among the regions of China. A climate map shows startling variations in rainfall, from the moisture-deficient areas in the northwest to the lush tropical wetlands in the southeast. From west to east the land descends in a series of steps from the Tibetan Plateau to the low-lying plains at the eastern edge of the Yangtze Basin. The spatial variations in China's physical geography are matched by the variations in its human geography. There are more than 73 million minority (non-Han) people in China, representing fifty-plus officially recognized ethnic groups.[12] In terms of language groups and ethnic practices, no two parts of China are alike, which can be not only a blessing (e.g., for the tourist) but also

a frustration (e.g., for those who must interact with others to make a living).

Space, Place, and the Geographical Imagination

In addition to the general geographical imperatives outlined above, I offer what for some readers might be a new way of thinking about China and the consequences of the current transformations. Wherever possible I shall approach contemporary China from the perspective of what Derek Gregory calls the geographical imagination, or "a sensitivity towards the significance of place, space, and landscape in the constitution of social life."[13] At the most general level—and this example works best by thinking about economic issues—the restructurings associated with China's transition out of socialism have involved two groups of people and places: those that are directly involved in the restructuring processes, in the sense that they

are already plugged in to the new global economy; and the others, the people and places forgotten or deliberately avoided by capitalism.[14]
Looking at the presence or absence of transformative processes of this type from the perspective of human geography begins with a
consideration of the space-time settings and
sequences of human activity involved; such an
interpretation attempts to identify relationships
of coexistence, connection, and togetherness
between people and the places they inhabit.

It is important at this point to provide some
definitions. "Space" is generally thought of as
the territory that separates human phenomena.
It is an abstract and general concept, because all
phenomena are located in space and can therefore be defined in spatial, or geographical,
terms. In addition to having unique physical
characteristics, space is usually inscribed by
human occupancy; in other words, the people
who live in a particular space tend to alter it in
their own unique way, so a place is commonly
considered to be that portion of geographical
space that is occupied and lived in by a person
or persons. It is, in other words, humanized
space; so China—the place—is that portion of
the earth's territory occupied by the Chinese
(see Map 2.3).[15] A Chinese village can be
described as a space either by its latitudinal and
longitudinal coordinates (absolute location) or
by its distance from the capital city (relative
location). The spatial coordinates tell us little
about the village, other than providing a rough
idea of climate and indicating some broad
regional characteristics. A description of it as a
place, however, as the home of residents
through the ages, tells us infinitely more about
the village and its people.

Most of the habitable space in China (i.e.,
space that is not too mountainous, wet, dry, or
frozen to inhabit) has been occupied for centuries and transformed by manifold human
activities. The ground has been trampled on
and humanized by millions of people over the
centuries, and although there are older lands in
other parts of the world, none boasts "a more
mature adjustment between man and environment" than China.[16] As the process of human-
ization evolves, "spaces" gradually become
forged into "places." From an abstract point of
view, then, a piece of territory becomes a center
of meaning—a place where humans live. Thus
the essential importance of a place is not its
location or the functions the location serves but
rather the meaning it has for the individual.[17]

It has been suggested that the tendency for
humans to identify with their home place has
been stronger in China than in most other parts
of the world. That is impossible to verify, but
there is certainly evidence that Chinese people
are strongly rooted to their place of birth, no
matter how far they might roam. For peasants
such intense localism has not been a matter of
choice. Their traditional position on the bottom rung of the social ladder has consigned
them to spend most of their working lives
engaged in agricultural production to provide
sustenance for themselves but, more important,
to support the landed elite. After the 1949 revolution they were equally if not more tied to the
land by the collectivization system; and until
the 1980s most peasants simply did not have
the time, money, and energy to move beyond
their village and its immediate marketing area,
let alone travel to other regions. Over the centuries such parochiality has produced extreme
isolation and backwardness in many parts of
China.[18]

The strength of the attachment to one's home
place is illustrated by the desire among many
Chinese to be buried in native soil. In most cities
during the late imperial times, there were associations of "sojourners" from different parts of
China, many of which maintained cemeteries so
that people who were unable to go back home to
die could at least be buried in familiar soil and
close to others from their home districts.[19]
Notwithstanding that strong connection to
home place, people who moved involuntarily often worked hard to connect in some way to the
new place. In their book *Chinese Lives*, Zhang
Xinxin and Sang Ye tell the story of a woman who
lives in a tiny village in a remote corner of Shanxi
Province. She moved there in a marriage swap
arranged by her parents, and when she arrived
she was distressed to find her new home was not

MAP 2.3   China: Provinces and Major Cities

even marked on a 1:100,000 map. It had no water, no electricity, no paved roads. Nevertheless, as she said stoically, "People are like grass. They grow where the seed drops and that is where they belong."[20] We may assume that after the seed has taken root, it is almost as if the meaning of a home place is stamped indelibly in a person's brain, to such an extent that separation becomes a painful experience.[21] Over the centuries the occupants of any patch of land in China impress their values and beliefs onto the landscape, and in this way the fields and villages are manicured in a unique fashion. Some people believe that different cultures are able to leave a permanent signature, or "inscription," on the landscape, something that can be reproduced wherever they go.[22]

Spatial Organization

Many outsiders have remarked on the enormity of the administrative tasks to be undertaken in a country as large and technologically underdeveloped as China. How do the Chinese—with so many people and such vast distances to cover—collect their taxes, maintain law and order, and make sure that everyone is fed? How does the government operate to satisfy the needs of so many people over such vast expanses of territory?[23] Viewed from the macro level, evidence indicates that for the most part there is, or at least there was in the collective era (1949–1976), a form of organization that seemed to work well. In his magisterial work *Age of Extremes: The Short Twentieth Century*, British historian Eric Hobsbawm reviewed this period and marveled at the way the Chinese Communist Party was able to forge a nationwide organization capable of delivering government policy from the capital to the remotest villages in the periphery. As Hobsbawm noted, "Organization, rather than doctrine, was the chief contribution of Lenin's Bolshevism to changing the world."[24]

In China after 1949, administration in both the city and the countryside operated through an all-encompassing pattern of spatial organization. As we shall see in Chapter 7 (on agriculture)

and Chapter 14 (on urban service provision), the enormously complex business of food distribution and the execution of a vast assortment of campaigns and service-delivery projects—some of which were highly unpopular—were facilitated by the spatial organization of administrative territory in urban and rural areas (see Figure 2.1). This made possible the enormous number of face-to-face interactions that are required with so many people involved, and it also helped in the local administration of complex policies mandated at the national and regional levels.

The spatial organization of Chinese society during the Maoist era was characteristic of other socialist societies (especially the Soviet Union), in which the key element of organization is the principle of verticality, in which power flows downward from the core to the periphery, or from the state to the society. In China the administrative goal was to ensure that each individual and social group was incorporated into a hierarchically organized system, as opposed to being connected horizontally to individuals and groups in other localities. At the local level this system was centered on the all-important work unit (*danwei*) in both the city and the countryside and, to a lesser extent, in residential neighborhoods.[25] Work units controlled people's lives in most spheres of activity, and the system of verticality produced what sociologists call "social encapsulation," with individuals virtually cloistered inside geographic units, for the most part unable to live or work anywhere else.[26] As Michael Dutton has observed, the work unit was originally meant to function as the basic unit of accounting, allowing central planners to calculate the totality of productive society. Dutton noted, however, that in fact the work unit began to take on a life of its own, mainly because it provided stability in a potentially chaotic world. To be without a unit was "to be without a home and, to be without this, one is robbed of one's roots, and simultaneously, devoid of any sense of obligation."[27]

Such spatial structures have also provided the mechanisms for close surveillance, which seriously constrains the likelihood of individual

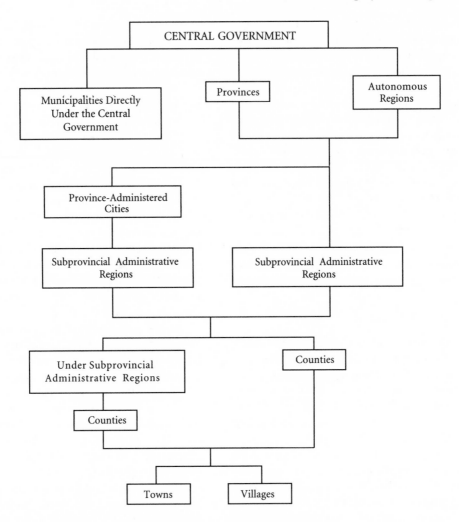

FIGURE 2.1   The Spatial Organization of Urban and Rural Territory in China
   SOURCE: R. Kokimo, 1987, "Urbanization and Urban Problems in China (Tokyo: Institute of Developing Economies, Occasional Paper Series No. 22), pp. 102–103. Reprinted by permission.

acts of noncompliance and deviance from norms. Not surprisingly, the pervasiveness of administrative structures was unpopular with the Chinese people as a rule, as the state was able to use them to infiltrate and dominate everyday lives.[28] With the introduction of economic reforms in the 1980s and their continuation through the 1990s, much of China's production, distribution, and consumption was and is today organized by the imperatives of the market; that has been accompanied by the diminished power and gradually the disman-

tling of the spatial structures operating at both the work-unit and residential levels. The spread of market relations in the economy means that an increasing amount of interaction now takes place along horizontal rather than vertical lines. Private and community-owned enterprises, and to an increasing extent state enterprises as well, are experiencing a proliferation of horizontal ties as they reach out to increasingly autonomous enterprises located outside their existing sphere of geographical activity. As we shall see throughout this book, the new emphasis on horizontal relationships has been accompanied by what Gordon White calls a "flowering of associational life" in many different spheres of society.[29] In the absence of significant political reform in China, such activity can be seen as an embryonic attempt to create a space that is relatively independent from the state, with individuals and groups reaching out horizontally to form and join all manner of economic, cultural, and recreational organizations.

Spatiality and Subjection

To evaluate the ways China's people have been impacted by the Four Modernizations the human geographer attempts to recapture the flow of human agency, which involves "a series of situated events in space and time."[30] From this perspective human activity is defined as that which figuratively and literally takes place, and as that happens "the 'place' itself becomes a process."[31] This process has been referred to by some geographers recently as "spatiality," the geographical corollary of history's temporality and sociology's sociality.[32] Geographers observe with some degree of pique that space has not traditionally been accorded the same status as history and society in the great debates about social theory. Yet they are equally eager to argue that within the last decade this situation appears to be changing.[33] The term "spatiality" is used in different ways, as shown in Figure 2.2, but the most general definition describes it as "socially produced space . . . the created forms and relations of a broadly defined human geography."[34]

A human geographer would use the term "spatiality" to describe how human actions leave their mark, as it were, on the landscape (i.e., as signatures or inscriptions). In addition to providing richly informative detail about people and places, this allows us to understand the distribution of power in everyday life. French philosopher Michel Foucault suggested that "constellations of power and knowledge" are inscribed in space, and in this way "particular subject positions are constituted."[35] This suggests that the human geographer can investigate places and landscapes to find out what

they tell us about how identities are constructed and about the hierarchy of power relationships among the inhabitants of such places. In the Chinese countryside that would have involved the struggles between peasants and landlords during prerevolutionary times and those between peasants and the state after 1949. According to Foucault, such struggles, in which the strong (read: hegemonic powers) are lined up against the weak, involve human reactions to domination, exploitation, and subjection.[36]

Throughout this book we focus, to a greater or lesser degree, on the lives of ordinary people in China, including peasants in the countryside, workers in the cities, students and intellectuals, women, and members of minority groups. As China has steamed ahead with the Four Modernizations it became clear that members of those groups were exposed to two obvious sources of subjection: The first emanates from the logic and demands of China's capitalist revolution; the other, almost perversely, arises from the requirements and dictates of the state. Lisa Rofel has expressed this succinctly in her discussion of modernity, which, she argues, "enfolds and explodes by means of global capitalist forms of domination in conjunction with state techniques for normalizing its citizens."[37] Power in contemporary China is located wherever there is wealth and capital; but power is also very much still lodged in the long arms and the hands of the state. In their interactions and dealings with these two sources of power, the major population subgroups respond in different ways, based on variations along lines of class, ethnicity, and gender. We would expect to find some of these differences manifested or inscribed in space or spatiality.

The best material examples during the economic reform era are the landscapes of uneven development associated with the reassertion of capitalism in many parts of China. As some areas get richer, others are left farther behind. Similarly, among the people the newly rich are clearly differentiated from the permanently poor; the majority people (the Han) are, in most cases, much better off and better educated than the minority people; and as a group

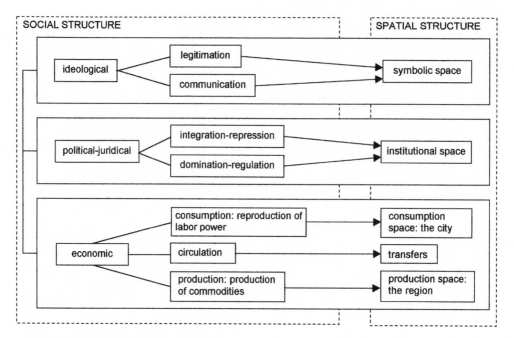

FIGURE 2.2 Spatiality

women are certainly doing worse than men according to most social and economic indicators. In prereform China, socialist ideology would have been at work to diminish such patterns of spatial and social inequality (although as we shall see this was not always the case). In the reform years the assumption of egalitarianism has been cast to the wind, and by the end of the twentieth century that produced some clearly identifiable winners and losers.

The notion of spatiality challenges the conventional separation among ideas about space and society and, most important, the assumption that space has little role to play in the determination of social events. As illustrated in Figure 2.2, spatiality can be used to identify the correspondence between social structure and spatial structure, and at each level of the mode of production such correspondence has its own topography of power (to use Foucault's terminology). The economic space depicted in Figure 2.2 represents the material landscapes of production and consumption. In the post-Mao era, reform policies have dramatically transformed such landscapes, in both urban and rural areas;

indeed entirely new hybrid spaces have been emerging in formerly rural areas between existing cities (see Chapter 9, on the urbanization issue). There is also a political-juridical realm superimposed onto the economic realm, which does not produce material landscapes but represents a form of social or political space. In the Chinese case we can think about that as the space the state allows (or does not allow) individuals and groups to operate in independently, acting to some extent at least as an incipient form of civil society (see Chapter 19). In Mao's China such space was virtually nonexistent, but it has been expanding slowly and in fits and starts throughout the reform years. Figure 2.2 also portrays a realm of ideological space, operating at the highest level of abstraction.[38] The reform era, in sharp contrast to the previous three decades, has been notable for the total abandonment of traditional socialist ideology; in fact the Deng and Jiang regimes have publicly announced that the new ideology (to the extent it can be called such) is centered on the achievement of specific goals for economic development and modernization.

Modern Human Geography and the Condition of Postmodernity

As noted earlier, contemporary human geographers have argued that in discussions about society and social theory, space should be considered to be at least as important as the dominant concepts from history and sociology.[39] It is important to point out that most theories of modernity, including Marxism, have subordinated and even ignored the role of space. One reason is that a concern for space is often considered to be a parochial and premodern characteristic. Modernity is generally associated with movement and international concerns, whereas focusing on a specific locality implies immobility and tradition; in that sense concern for one's locality (sometimes referred to as the "sense of place") is considered to be provincial and narrow-minded. In traditional as well as Maoist China the peasants and the periphery were thought of as quintessentially premodern for all of these reasons; it was only in the urban areas—and then only in the coastal provinces—where modernity, in the sense of internationalization, could be discerned.

Another reason for ignoring the importance of space was Marx's prediction that in the course of capitalist development space would most likely be "annihilated" by time.[40] Implied here is that capitalism expands and reproduces regardless of specific localities; in fact the places where economic development originally emerges are often destroyed or left behind as grotesque reminders of the past (as when old factories, indeed entire industrial areas, are abandoned during the process of deindustrialization). In light of modernity's scant treatment of space, the argument for reinstating and even privileging space can perhaps best be made under the umbrella of postmodernity. Throughout this book we will touch on the proposition that some parts of China and Chinese ways of life have been changed so dramatically in the rush toward modernity that they might now be described as "postmodern." In Chapter 3, for example, we look briefly at the extraordinary proliferation of new cultural forms in contemporary China, focusing on the emergence of different strands of popular culture and the development of postmodern art and poetry; likewise, Chapter 9 examines the nature of China's postmodern urban landscapes, especially in the southeastern coastal provinces and the biggest cities.

Geographers like David Harvey, along with other social and cultural theorists, have long been drawing attention to the so-called condition of postmodernity, the features of which are "excessive ephemerality and fragmentation in the political . . . private [and] social realm."[41] Harvey has argued that the current situation is simply an exaggerated example of the way capitalism has, since the middle of the nineteenth century, destroyed places and left them behind (implied in the "annihilation" of space by time).[42] Yet almost simultaneously new places are being created to better serve the interests of capital. Some of the results of this process—in China and elsewhere—may appear to be distressing to outside observers, for example in the reproduction of identical retail outlets in every shopping mall around the world and the abandonment of once-proud industrial zones and the residential areas that supported them.

This postmodern turn, then, is often construed as a negative trend associated with the loss of old ways of life and past landscapes, carrying foreboding connotations of anonymity and the disorienting features of an ever-shifting and materialistic world. In this vein one school of postmodernist thinkers (the so-called postmodern skeptics) do little more than apocalyptically pronounce the dire state of the modern world; indeed there is no shortage of apocalyptic statements about contemporary China, including predictions of the imminent collapse of the entire reform economy.[43] Yet the postmodernity critique offers a vehicle for analyzing (and critiquing) the forces of dehumanization associated with advanced global capitalism.[44] There are postmodernists, for example, who question and criticize the modernist project and its outcomes, but they are also open, perhaps even willing, to participate in attempts to liberate those groups who suffer most from the depredations of capital.

Theorists in this group—the so-called affirmative postmodernists—offer some useful clues for approaching a discussion of events in contemporary China. Affirmative, or radical, postmodernity brings with it a strongly liberating appeal, because it is associated with a concern for and about "otherness" and the challenge it (i.e., postmodernity) offers to modernity's assumptions about who is able to speak for "others." A postmodern stance, as an oppositional critique, would argue that all groups have a right to speak for themselves, and in post-Mao China there are any number of others acting as individuals and groups attempting to bring their own agency to bear. The implication (referring back to the Mackerras epigraph starting this chapter) is that instead of the author speaking for China's minority people they should be speaking for themselves. It also suggests that in postmodern China there may be millions of people actively wanting and trying to carve out new identities. They may be attempting to generate some political space, or their efforts may be manifested in a search for secure moorings in specific geographical places. That implies the refreshing possibility that human agency, in the face of capitalism's tendency to eradicate local uniqueness and produce an endless array of vapidly homogenous landscapes, is actively at work resisting such forces.[45]

The issue is well illustrated in anthropologist Lisa Rofel's participant-observer fieldwork in a Chinese silk factory. Rofel helped illuminate some of the ways women workers speak on their own behalf, as well as the way they identify and create space for themselves in a contemporary Chinese workplace. In retelling and analyzing their stories, Rofel demonstrated she was able to assess how women workers respond to their subjection, which results from combined gender-class discrimination. From her observations Rofel concluded that there are three general sets of responses, roughly corresponding to the era in which the women had come of age as factory workers. Each cohort began working during distinct, dramatic eras, and although all of the eras were situated within what was still nominally a socialist society, each appears to have influenced the women in different ways. The older workers react to events occurring in post-Mao China by recalling and referring back to what they experienced during the early days after the socialist revolution. As Rofel noted, "The retelling and thus remaking of history, for them, was a crucial site for negotiating new forms of power."[46] Their memories focused primarily on their earlier heroism as revolutionary women undergoing extraordinary hardships. A second group of women workers defined themselves as the Cultural Revolution generation, and their responses to current events and their subordination were shaped largely by their memories and reconstructions of overt challenges to authority that were the norm for that era of chaos and lawlessness.

The youngest workers in the factory responded in markedly different ways, in that they expressed desires to be modern women, yet their ideas of modernity are miles apart from those of their older colleagues. The youngest women have grown up entirely in the post-Mao era, so they have no collective memories of an earlier time. Women in this group, not surprisingly, found neither labor nor the politics of authority to be meaningful or useful in their identity formation. As a result, "They turned to a politics of the body in which they embraced ideas about innate femininity, marriage, and motherhood that explicitly reject the practices of womanhood they saw in the two older cohorts."[47] In contemporary China there are multiple discourses on gender and gender issues. Some of the official (i.e., state) discourses work to repress women's sexual desires and channel them into family-based reproduction, whereas others induce a more implicitly personal interest in matters of love and sexual relationships. Rofel's work indicates that for young female workers those sorts of interests move them beyond any meaningful engagement either with labor—which appears to represent drudgery rather than heroism—or with politics, which they prefer to ignore in the current ideology-free era. As Rofel concludes, "In the place of 'labor' or 'politics,' the post-Mao imaginary of modernity makes 'bodies'—their fecundity, their management, their interiority, their sexual pleasures—the site for constructing modern subjects."[48] As we shall see in Chapter 13, further contributing to sexual yearnings among modern working Chinese women is the commodification of desire in the new market economy, fueled by the romance novels, soap operas, and sexually explicit movies entering China by the bushel from Hong Kong and Taiwan.

Spaces of Resistance: Contested Lives and Landscapes in Contemporary China

Lisa Rofel's work suggests that (on the shop floor at least) it is a part of human nature to resist the forces that act as a source of oppression.[49] Throughout this book we shall examine many situations where different groups in Chinese society have faced a mountain of subjection, some of which may even have threatened their survival. Thus, for example, we will view the industrialization of the countryside from the perspectives of the new jobs it has created (Chapters 7 and 8), as well as the environmental damage to land and lives (Chapter 16). We look at the situation of women in the new China, focusing on the achievements made since the 1949 revolution, as well as the continued refusal of the state to consider implementing legislation that would fundamentally alter the patriarchal structures of Chinese society (Chapter 13). We look at the state's relationships with minority peoples, noting some of the impressive achievements that have been registered in the reform era, considering as well the state's attempts to discipline and in some cases crush the rights of groups threatening to take control of their own futures (Chapter 12).

At the core of the postmodern critique, then, is the politics of difference and resistance. But unlike the traditional politics of modernity those differences are no longer reified into opposition groups that presuppose fixed and binary subject positions: individual versus the state; worker versus peasant; majority versus ethnic minority; men versus women.[50] In an affirmative postmodern narrative there is a call for new ideas, new strategies, new social movements capable of contesting the status quo. This form of politics will, it is hoped, be able to acknowledge—in social, cultural, and economic terms—the multiple, contradictory, and complex positions people come to occupy because of their differences.[51] For example, in Chapter 11 we examine the ways that Chinese people in Taiwan and Hong Kong have worked, with some degree of success, to fashion such a politics in their struggle to emerge from an era of political oppression and silence. By contrast, we shall see that similar efforts on the mainland have thus far been suppressed by state power (see Chapters 4, 18, and 19).

This book can only begin to explore the nature of such politics, looking at the ways certain groups attempt to resist the forces that work to oppress them. The starting point for the analysis, then, is the observation that China's current push toward modernity has produced some obvious negative externality effects, the most visible of which are associated with uneven development and an unequal distribution of wealth.[52] We shall thus examine how the ordinary people—whether they be peasants, women, students, workers, or minorities—work for themselves and on behalf of the places they inhabit, either to live with or to resist the encroachments of new forces. To simplify matters it is possible to think about three alternative strategies for such individuals and groups:

1. Focus on their otherness to make their voices heard in mounting a campaign of resistance. This is still a dangerous proposition in communist China, and even in the late 1990s individuals attempting to legally register the new China Democratic Party have been sentenced to lengthy prison terms.

2. Leave their problems behind and move elsewhere in an effort to improve life's chances. This would include the millions

of peasant migrants who have left the desperation of rural life to take their chances in the cities as temporary workers, the so-called floating populations (Chapter 15), as well as the predicament of the nearly 2 million people whose homes and ways of life will be submerged by the flooding of the Yangtze River after the completion of the Three Gorges Dam (Chapter 16).

3. Attempt to reproduce themselves or rewrite their own histories. In this regard we shall examine the efforts made by migrants and resettled peoples to create new homes and communities for themselves, as in the case of the "ethnic" migrant enclaves beginning to emerge in China's largest cities (Chapter 15), as well as the struggle of minority nationalities to establish some real measure of autonomy from the Chinese state (Chapter 12).

In Figure 2.2 these three processes are seen as spaces of production, spaces of transfer, and spaces of consumption or reproduction. Each response is inherently geographical in nature, representing individual and collective reactions to the forces of wealth and power that produce the patterns of inequality and subjection. The specific places in which these patterns emerge provide both the catalyst for and the location of ongoing resistance, which will be conducted either to hold on to power and wealth (hegemonic struggles) or to resist the status quo (counterhegemonic struggles).

Standing Up or Keeping Silent?

Before concluding this discussion it is useful to consider whether there is an alternative to the three strategies of resistance outlined above. It would appear that there is, but it is a nonresponse, in which the people remain silent. In China that has been observed in the recent past, when people stood aside silently, too afraid to utter a word in the face of extreme subjection. Zhang Xianliang, who was sentenced to a lengthy prison term for speaking out to the oppressors, was scornful of those who continue to choose silence. As he noted in his book *Half of Man Is Woman*:

> If the Chinese people don't stand up and speak, if they don't move to the front line of struggle themselves, then one billion people will no longer have the right to live on the globe. We will have been the most stupid, good for nothing, weak, despicable race on earth. . . . We've been played with . . . used like guinea pigs in an experiment—we've been cheated and tricked. Can it be that when the experiment has utterly failed and we are on the verge of death, we don't even have the guts to shout out, "It hurts?" People who are so numb they can't even yell "It hurts" are people who are really better off dead.[53]

Perhaps silence indicates satisfaction with the way things are, but I suspect such is not the case. In 1989 there was a massive uprising of students, supported by some workers, who did summon up what it took to yell "It hurts!" Unlike similar movements in the socialist world at roughly the same time, that movement failed, in part because other groups, especially people from the countryside, were either too apathetic or not sufficiently aggrieved to join their urban counterparts. As we shall see in Chapters 7–10, the levels of discontent in some parts of rural and urban China have been rising, perhaps to such a degree that peasants may be willing to throw their weight into the ring during the next round—if indeed there is a next round.

PART 2

Space, Society, and the State in China

3

Culture Change in Contemporary China

The 1990s saw the emergence of a new, commercialized Mao cult. T-shirts, key rings, cigarette lighters and even karaoke videos bearing Mao's picture have sold by the million. His image can now be used as an expression of nostalgia, a joke, a national icon, or a good luck talisman. Perhaps this reprocessing of the Chairman's image is the ultimate dismissal of what Mao stood for.

—Delia Davin, *Mao Zedong* (1997)[1]

Introduction: Mao Zedong Makes a Comeback

To outsiders, one of the most extraordinary turn of events during the reform era has been the revival of the cult associated with Mao Zedong. From the late 1980s through roughly the mid-1990s there was a nationwide resurgence of interest in Mao Zedong, which became known popularly as *Maore* (the MaoCraze). It had begun inauspiciously, when people started hanging laminated images of the Chairman from the rearview mirrors of taxis, buses, and trucks.[2] The MaoCraze was different in a number of ways from the personality cult that existed during the Cultural Revolution, in that the renewed interest in Mao (who died in 1976) had little to do with class struggle and politics. Here there was a massive renewal of interest in Mao's life and works. All manner of Mao representations appeared: His face was portrayed on badges, clothes, photographs, jewelry, dishes, vases, and sculpture; songs and music associated with his life were rerecorded and released on tapes and compact discs; versions of the *Little Red Book* were reissued; and all sorts of new works about Mao began to appear in operas, art shows, television series, movies, and plays. Some of the items to appear for sale were genuine antiques—retrieved from attics, basements, and store-

rooms—but the majority was new and mass-produced to cater to the huge domestic demand.

As Geremie Barmé has pointed out, this phenomenon was one of several crazes sweeping China in the late 1980s. Some focused on intellectuals like Sigmund Freud and Jean-Paul Sartre;[3] others involved new recreational and quasireligious activities such as *qigong*.[4] To some extent, therefore, the renewed level of interest in Mao Zedong was a sign of the times, but other explanations for the emergence of the MaoCraze in the late 1980s are worth considering. The most persuasive account attributes it to the fervor of the reform era for producing and marketing anything and everything imaginable. Other accounts suggest that the craze was a cunning ploy engineered by the Chinese Communist Party to counter widespread disaffection among the populace after the Tiananmen Square crisis of 1989. Barmé argued that the former argument is only partly true, and he rejected the latter argument totally. Instead he suggests that the MaoCraze was part of widespread nostalgia among many Chinese people for a simpler, more satisfying past—associated with Mao's leadership—when China was perceived as more stable and egalitarian and possessing a more focused sense of national purpose.

Barmé's suggestion is consistent with the discussion contained in Chapter 1 of this book, namely, that widespread disenchantment seems to have characterized the societies going through the transition out of socialism. In this sense the fetishization of Mao, according to Barmé, reflected a growing resentment associated with many of the by-products of the economic reforms: rising inflation; widespread corruption; egregious nepotism within the Party; and the general air of alienation and dissatisfaction within contemporary Chinese life. In the middle of so many rapid changes and social dislocations, it is plausible to suggest that the "rediscovery of Mao . . . was for many . . . a grounding act of self-affirmation."[5] At the end of what had been a frenetic decade the Chinese people were anxious about many things: fear of national collapse after the 1989 tragedy; ongoing suppression of dissidents by the Party-state; and the fall of communism in Europe and the Soviet Union—all of which might have played a part in the emerging Mao cult. Barmé thus echoes Vladimir Tismaneanu (see Chapter 1), when he (Barmé) argued that "when people face economic uncertainty and social anomie, old cultural symbols, cults, practices, and beliefs are spontaneously revived to provide a framework of cohesion and meaning to a threatening world. To many, Mao was representative of an age of certainty and confidence, of cultural and political unity, and, above all, of economic equality and probity."[6]

The enthusiasm for Mao Zedong and the Maoist era is interesting (though puzzling) to outsiders for two main reasons. First, it represents a stark contrast from the general level of ennui associated with the Dengist present; in fact both Deng Xiaoping and Jiang Zemin are seen as gray and colorless characters in comparison to the larger-than-life (reconstructed and re-created) images of Mao. It is important to point out, however, that it was only with the economic freedoms made possible by Deng that the MaoCraze could have taken off the way it did. In addition, eulogizing Mao in this fashion required people to ignore the savagery and destructiveness of many of his policies.[7] Second, Barmé suggests that the MaoCraze was allowed, even encouraged, by the Party-state because it did not represent any real threat to

the status quo. It was, in other words, an acceptable form of resistance to the current traumas. It was also true that many Chinese people genuinely felt that Mao, for all his faults, was an unwavering patriot who led the nation out of centuries of oppression and humiliation.

By analyzing the form and content of the MaoCraze we gain some valuable insight into what Mao might have meant to the Chinese people. After reviewing a vast amount of material in many different contexts, Barmé concluded that Mao was in fact many things to many people, including: patriotic leader; philosopher-king; poet; calligrapher; wily politician and in-fighter; and rebel chieftain. Contrasting these generally favorable representations are other, less positive ones, including the disturbing revelations of Li Zhisu, Mao's private physician. Among other things, Doctor Li claimed that Mao was sexually hyperactive with women and men until late in his life.[8] Barmé takes this into consideration when he suggests—perhaps with tongue firmly in cheek—that to some extent Mao became a "love object" to or for the Chinese people. He is seen as a bisexual or omnisexual hero figure, even though in reality Mao "was a wrinkled, green-toothed, slack-jawed old man."[9]

In some of the more avant-garde wings of the MaoCraze, artists began to include images of Mao in their paintings and sculptures, which were often humorous and satirical. It is difficult to know if this was meant to be overly political or whether it was just the superficial images of China's new fascination with pop culture. Floral-patterned pictures of Mao were mass-produced as curtains, bedspreads, and wallpaper. In all probability this was little more than postmodern playfulness, which is generally not intended to be taken seriously. Perhaps the ultimate frivolity was Mao's appearance on the wall of Beijing's Hard Rock Café, his photograph opposite those of the Sex Pistols and Chuck Berry. A sign beneath the photograph, presumably a direct quote from the Chairman, read "Love All, Serve All."[10]

What can we conclude from the MaoCraze? Barmé has claimed that the level of enthusiasm associated with the rehashed images of the Great Leader is evidence of how pathetically thin Chinese cultural resources have become in the 1990s. It can also be interpreted, perhaps, as a barometer of anxiety and sense of cultural emptiness, what one scholar described (in referring to Russia) as "totalitarian nostalgia."[11] In a more positive light, the pop-culture aspect of the MaoCraze can be seen as an attempt to create ironic inversions of Mao Zedong in popular culture, maybe with the goal of symbolizing the thorough rejection of Maoist-style thought and practice (see Davin's quote in the epigraph to this chapter). In the end, Barmé accepted that all these views have some merit, yet he concluded that the MaoCraze—and the other cults of that era—were functional during a time when China appeared to be losing its value system and sense of purpose in its headlong rush toward modernity.

With this caveat in mind, we shall examine the changing pattern of cultural values in contemporary China. One of the goals of this chapter is to examine some of the differences between the Chinese ("them") and Westerners ("us"). Why, for example, is it so important for Chinese people to control their emotions? And why is there disagreement between us and them on the importance of "being an individual"? Here we examine whether traditional outsider views of Chinese cultural values—for example, that the Chinese are able to hide their emotions and prefer to be members of collectives rather than groups—have any merit in the present, or whether those views are little more than resilient stereotypes from the past, probably incorrect, not to mention offensive to the Chinese. We shall also inquire into the way Chinese behave toward one another, their homes, their country, and the world around them. Another question—one that is central to the theme of this book—asks whether Chinese values during the latter years of the twentieth century changed much in response to modernization pressures and, if they have, whether the age-old differences between us and them are finally disappearing amid a widespread process of cultural convergence. As we shall see, in at least one

sense—the proliferation of popular culture and the corresponding erosion of China's traditional cultural forms—this hypothesis about converging cultures can be supported. Before considering such events, however, we begin with a discussion of an ancient Chinese custom that has influenced social relationships and cultural practices for centuries and has, to a degree, transcended the effects of economic reform and the convergence of cultures.

Guanxi and Gift-Giving in China: The Resilience of an Ancient Custom

First class people get gifts delivered to the door;
second class people go through the back door;
third class people rely on others;
fourth class people can only fume.[12]

China is a relation-based society, which implies that the focus for human interaction is not on any particular individual or group but on the nature of the relationships between individuals. To understand how such societies work, it is important to focus on the way people interact with each other. In China, as in many other societies, both traditional and modern, that can include looking at the flow of gifts between people. Gift-giving plays a major role in the social life of a relational society by creating, reproducing, and modifying interpersonal relationships. Surprisingly, although gift-giving was a feature of traditional China (the "feudal" era, as the Communists would say), it has survived into the modern era in both the socialist and market-socialist phases.

Yunxiang Yan attempted to understand the longevity of gift-giving and recently reported on her fieldwork in Xiajia village in Heilongjiang Province in northeastern China.[13] Yan argued that gift-giving is closely related to two other notions: *guanxi* (personal networks and particularistic ties between people)[14] and *renqing* (moral norms and human feelings).[15] In everyday life *guanxi* refers to a system in which an individual develops a series of acquaintances for whom favors are done, in the expectation of returned favors at some time in the future. Having "good" *guanxi* has always proved to be an extremely useful way of getting things done in a resource-scarce environment, and in China *guanxi* is manifested in many ways. At the lowest level, it includes perfectly legal "string-pulling," which requires giving small gifts and doing favors; but it also includes outright corruption, including bribery and other criminal acts at all levels of power.

Gift-giving in Xiajia village is one of the most important ways in which villagers maintain and extend their *guanxi* networks, with the gift acting as a sign of or a vehicle for conveying *renqing* to those who receive it. In addition to having symbolic value, gifts are material objects that generally have some monetary value; in Xiajia village, for example, there is an endless exchange of gifts—including banquets and family ceremonies—that constitutes a "gift economy" (see Table 3.1).

As this example indicates, the system of gift-giving is based on the interpersonal relationships that exist within the village, and it helps to sustain the order and security of village life.[16] Gift-giving and *guanxi* also have other essential roles in village life, however, including the business of developing and manipulating one's *guanxi* (*guanxixue*). In the language of contemporary sociology, this process represents a way of culturally constructing oneself, a process that has been evolving over a long period in China's countryside.[17]

In the Maoist era, *guanxi*, and having good *guanxi*, became even more important than ever. The ultraleftists within the CCP (including the so-called Gang of Four) strongly discouraged any bourgeois emphasis on consumption, and it had become standard practice to tighten all controls over sources of goods and services. For ordinary citizens, therefore, it was essential to develop regular channels of access to goods and services. Everything was in short supply, and to acquire anything beyond bare essentials one needed to have a wide network of connections. In this sort of milieu, it is not surprising to find

that acquaintances were selected for purely instrumental purposes. What was happening was a new affirmation of the traditional Chinese custom of "going through the backdoor" to develop ties based on *guanxi*.

As Mayfair Yang has pointed out, *guanxi* means, literally, a "relationship" that exists between objects or persons; but in reference to human relationships it can also imply "social connections."[18] Once *guanxi* has been established between two people, each feels at liberty to ask the other for a favor, in the understanding that the debt incurred will be repaid sometime in the future. Yang has described some of the most common ways in which *guanxi* is used in contemporary China. They include:

- obtaining goods that are in short supply, of better quality, or at lower prices;
- acquiring employment, job transfers, and promotions;
- enabling geographical mobility, overcoming the *hukou* problem of not having an urban registration card;
- maintaining good health by securing access to doctors and hospitals;
- procuring better or more spacious housing;
- promoting political security and advancement;
- facilitating transportation, which was generally very difficult to arrange;
- getting a better education, improving access to nurseries, schools, and evening classes; and
- enjoying recreational activities, which might include getting tickets to movies and other cultural events.[19]

From the traditional perspective of Confucianist morality, using *guanxi* implies a lack of respect for societal rules and regulations. Making use of one's *guanxi* is, in other words, almost the complete opposite of abiding by *li*—the prescribed set of rituals to be followed to ensure virtuous behavior.[20] Yet *guanxi* no doubt works for those who know how to use it, and it is usually much more efficient than playing

TABLE 3.1   One Individual's Record of Outgoing Gifts in Xiajia Village, Heilongjiang, January–June 1991

Recipient's Relationship to the Individual	Gift-Giving Occasion	Value (RMB yuan)
1. Sister's husband	Daughter's wedding	100
2. Wife's mother's cousin	Son's wedding	10
3. Wife's patrilineal cousin	Son's wedding	10
4. Sister's husband's brother	Daughter's wedding	10
5. Wife's cousin's husband	Wife's sterilization	20
6. Brother's wife's brother	Mother's funeral	20
7. Mother's sister's son	Daughter's wedding	20
8. Father's sister's son	Father's funeral	10
9. Mother's sister's husband	Son's wedding	40
10. Mother's fictive sister's son	Son's engagement	40
11. Close friend	Son's wedding	40
12. Friend	Daughter's wedding	20
13. Friend	Son's engagement	10
14. Fellow villager	House construction	10
15. Friend	House construction	20
16. Fellow villager	House construction	10
17. Fellow villager	Father's funeral	10
18. Friend	House construction	20
19. Friend	Wife's sterilization	20
20. Friend and neighbor	Wife's sterilization	20
21. Fellow villager	Wife's sterilization	20
22. Friend	Wife's sterilization	20
23. Fellow villager	Wife's sterilization	10
24. Fellow villager	Wife's sterilization	10
25. Fellow villager	Wife's sterilization	10
26. Fellow villager	Wife's sterilization	10
27. Fellow villager	Wife's sterilization	10

SOURCE: Adapted from Yan (1996), p. 84.

strictly by the rules. To many Chinese the use of *guanxi* itself is not considered to be illegal; in fact the only crime is to be caught doing something that looks, from the outside, like outright bribery. In a society where virtually everything was in short supply—certainly the case during the Cultural Revolution and for much of the Maoist era—the *guanxi* network offered what amounted to an alternative economy. The people who controlled the distribution of scarce resources—the drivers of work-unit vehicles, ticket-sellers, shopkeepers, shop stewards, and office managers—become enormously powerful within their own social units.[21]

Still, there was a counteracting tendency at work during the socialist transformation period (1959–1976), during which major

efforts were made to eliminate the traditional (read: feudal) practices of the past. In this period the tradition of gift-giving was sharply curtailed, and in line with the ascetic principles associated with the CCP, gifts were reduced in value and ceremonies cut back accordingly. But as Yan noted, in Xiajia village the locals managed to adjust their behavior and network cultivation in response to the new events they were encountering and the sociopolitical changes that were affecting everyday village life. This is particularly the case for marriage transactions, which have changed considerably during the reform era. As we shall see in Chapter 13, during the last two decades there has been a significant resurgence of prerevolutionary patterns of gift-giving at marriages, with far more expensive gifts being demanded and supplied than was ever the case.[22]

In addition to the reaffirmation of ancient customs, some new gift-giving rituals emerged that were thoroughly the creations of the socialist state. One involved abortions and female sterilizations, made necessary by the new birth control laws (see Table 3.1). It is traditionally believed that when a woman undergoes sterilization she experiences an outflowing of *qi*, her bodily essence. As such, it causes a great deal of anxiety and discontent, and compensatory gift-giving rituals have emerged. New ceremonies have also appeared surrounding such events as childbirth, which is now less common than it was in the past, and the building of a new house.[23] In recent years it has also become common for villagers to pay more attention to developing networks beyond the village as a way of greasing the skids for existing and future business transactions. To cope with four decades of socialism, Xiajia villagers have consistently adopted new patterns of gift-giving, redefined their perception of *guanxi* networks, and adjusted their methods of "conforming to *renqing* ethics."[24] Another function of gift-giving and *guanxi*, which is especially important in the contemporary era of market socialism, involves relationships with the outside world. As Yan points out, "When villagers encounter outsiders, they tend to use what they know best, that is, *renqing* ethics and *guanxi* networks."[25] This helps to expand existing *guanxi* networks and create new ones, most of which are built entirely on instrumental terms.[26]

Over and above these economically and socially useful functions, *guanxi* has some more explicitly political functions. In her 1994 book, *Gifts, Favors, and Banquets: The Art of Social Relationships in China*, Mayfair Yang argues that *guanxi* networks constitute a system of informal local power that represents opposition to the overwhelming power of the state. According to Yang: "The art of *guanxi* arose as a way to defuse and subvert the elaborate regulations and restrictions that the state redistributive economy has imposed on everyday life. It is in this engagement with the state that the art of

guanxi becomes more instrumental, hardened, cynical, and politicized. . . . In addition, the *guanxi* gift economy has also served in many ways as a substitute for market relations."[27]

The *guanxi* system works because gift-givers find ways to coerce the recipients to provide favors (or gifts) in return, which generates useful resources. In the context of Xiajia village, for example, this version of *guanxi* operates as a form of local redistribution, but at the same time it creates what Yang calls a set of "relational ethics" that are more attuned to local needs than to the dominant set of universalistic (read: collective) ethics of the socialist state. In other words, the *guanxi* network acts as a form of local resistance, in the sense that it "exerts a subversive effect on the microtechniques of administrative power."[28] As such it provides an alternative, or "oppositional," route to resources and power. Yang also argues that the *guanxi* network can serve as the foundation for a Chinese version of a civil society (*minjiang*), by which she means "a realm of people-to-people relationships which is non-governmental or separate from formal bureaucratic channels."[29] The rise of the nation-state has played an extremely important role in China's modernization, and the search for an autonomous realm of human activity—involving *guanxi* and *renqing* relationships—is needed now more than ever to provide an effective counterbalance to state power. Although Yang's argument makes good sense, she may be stepping out on a limb in suggesting that *guanxi* may provide the important raw material from which to build new forms of grassroots-level social movements. As she argues, it will not be long before "every person in the whole society will become locked into one another and their relationships will ramify and spread outward, so that out of formlessness will emerge a sort of organization."[30]

Locating the Chinese Cross-Culturally

It might be reasonable to expect the Chinese to have developed, after almost 2,000 years of immersion in Confucian values and codes of behavior, an identifiable cluster of cultural values that dominates social and cultural life. Many outside observers and visitors to China comment on the gulf between Chinese cultural values and those that dominate life elsewhere in the world. Those differences are revealed in all aspects of publicly observable behavior, particularly in relationships between the sexes.[31] Many Americans who visited China for the first time in the 1970s, especially those who spent any time with young people, reported with some degree of surprise that there was almost a total absence of "focus on intimate feelings [and] virtually no pressure for pairing off, and little sexual game playing."[32] In the last two decades, however, visitors have started to observe major changes in this respect. Lynn Pan, for example, writing in the mid-1980s, noticed a far greater consciousness with sex in Chinese public life, films, novels, and newspapers. Classes on sex education were being added to school curricula, and clinics were opening to counsel couples on ways to improve their sex lives. In spite of all this activity, Pan concluded that most young people in China still had "only a dim notion of sex [and] wide-eyed innocence characterizes the general approach to lovemaking."[33]

The colorful and perceptive accounts of Chinese social life written by travelers and journalists have been supplemented by scientific works conducted by social scientists. Although these accounts generally make for dull reading, they probably come closest to accurately depicting the major dimensions of social relationships in China.[34] The literature identifies five themes considered to be "prototypically Chinese characteristics"[35] (see Table 3.2).

Those characteristics appear to have persisted over time and across space; in other words they are common to Chinese people living in the PRC as well as to overseas Chinese living in Hong Kong, Singapore, Taiwan, and elsewhere in the world. They are traits that have been modified but not significantly changed by political systems and by travel to faraway lands. In a body of literature that has been growing rapidly (especially as mainland-based Chinese social scientists have entered the field), numerous attempts have been made, in studies using Chinese respondents, to quantify such traits.[36] To some extent the studies have validated the stereotypes about Chinese characteristics.[37] Psychological testing conducted in the PRC, for example, has shown that the Chinese, in comparison to Westerners, tend to be "emotionally more reserved, introverted, fond of tranquillity, overly considerate, socially overcautious [and] habituated to self-restraint."[38]

Bearing in mind the hazards of generalizing across cultures, it is apparent that there are empirically identifiable and distinct aspects of national character. The results of a study conducted by G. Hofstede in the early 1980s, using more than 100,000 respondents in fifty-three countries, suggest that there are groups of values that can be associated with specific countries.[39] Two such clusters were strongly associated with Chinese personality traits: One is power distance, which measured the extent to which individuals accept that power in society is distributed unequally; the second is individu-

TABLE 3.2   The Dominant Characteristics of Chinese Personality and Social Relationships

1. An overriding sense of duty and responsibility to the family as the fundamental unit of society;

2. The development and maintenance of very close bonds between parents and their children;

3. The overwhelming importance of other people and relationships within the social network, as opposed to individualism;

4. The ability to control or to hide emotions and feelings, and the cultivation of high moral standards;

5. A strong, almost fanatical emphasis on education and achievement for the children.

SOURCE: Modified from Chu (1985).

alism, which expresses a preference for individualistic over collectivistic social structures. Both dimensions appear to be conceptually related to age-old Confucian values; as one might expect the Chinese respondents scored high on the power-distance dimension and low on the individualism dimension.[40]

In a follow-up study a group of international scholars, calling itself the Chinese Culture Connection, attempted to reproduce these findings.[41] To minimize the Western bias inherent in all such studies, the researchers used a set of values generated by Chinese respondents. Again the results produced dimensions that were able to identify unique sets of national characteristics. One of the most interesting was Confucian work dynamism, which measured the extent to which people agreed that the world of work should be one in which there is a definite ordering, or hierarchy, of relationships by status. At the country level scores on this dimension were strongly correlated with economic growth. In other words, countries possessing high Confucian work dynamism had been economically successful during the 1970s and 1980s.[42] In this respect Asian capitalist societies like Japan, South Korea, Hong Kong, Taiwan, and Singapore could be clearly distinguished from other capitalist societies such as England, Australia, New Zealand, Canada, and the United States. Here we have some empirical support for the once widely held belief that there is an "Oriental" work ethic that helped to account for economic success in the so-called newly industrializing economies (NIEs) in Asia. The results of this study supported a post-Confucian hypothesis of economic development,[43] suggesting that inhabitants of the NIEs share similar cultural values in their approaches to work. In a conclusion quite typical in works of this sort, we are told that "the Confucian ethic—the creation of dedicated, motivated, responsible, and educated individuals and the enhanced sense of commitment, organizational identity, and loyalty to various institutions— will result in all neo-Confucian societies having at least potentially higher growth rates than other cultures."[44]

Researchers concluded from such studies that cultural values can effectively be mapped on a global scale, which demonstrates that there could well be a geography of national character. Some of the characteristics associated with centuries-old Confucianism remain evident in Asian societies today, in spite of vast differences in economic, social, and political systems and the sweeping changes that have occurred during the twentieth century. In the 1990s follow-ups to both the Hofstede and the Chinese Culture Connection, studies have been conducted by Shalom Schwartz and his colleagues, utilizing extensive and sophisticated multicultural surveys.[45] After considerable field-testing and theoretical consideration, Schwartz and his coresearchers identified seven "culture-level types": conservatism; harmony; egalitarian commitment; intellectual autonomy; affective autonomy; mastery; and hierarchy.[46] The mainland Chinese respondents scored high on hierarchy, which emphasizes power and ranking in social affairs and distribution of resources; low on egalitarian commitment, which suggests a transcendence of egocentric concerns and a belief in social principles; and moderately on conservatism, which emphasizes collective values over self-interests. Somewhat surprisingly, Chinese respondents also scored high on mastery, which emphasizes energetic self-assertion to control the social and physical environments. Schwartz concluded from these results that "China is not a prototypical 'collectivist' society [but] the notion of China as a culture that legitimizes hierarchical differentiation is supported; and the major hallmark of this culture is an emphasis on entrepreneurship within highly regulated relationships."[47]

With the economic reforms well into their second decade and the collective structure of Chinese society long since dismantled, these results are close to what might be expected. Interestingly, although China is not considered to be prototypically collectivist, Singapore certainly is, at least if one judges by the high scores on both the hierarchy and conservatism dimensions, which emphasize stable in-group relationships with the role of the self embedded in a collectivity. Although there were no identifiable constellations of values that were common to all of the Chinese groups (Singapore, Taiwan, Hong Kong, and the PRC), at the cultural level Schwartz concluded that Chinese societies can be characterized as those that still place a high value on hierarchy and mastery.[48]

Although it is important not to overstress the results of such studies, there is still some reasonably solid evidence that the mainland Chinese world is dominated by social relationships, which over the centuries may have colored Chinese attitudes toward the physical environment. Many Westerners are surprised by the starkness, even ugliness, of much of the built environment in urban and rural China, and they tend to assume that Chinese people hardly notice their surroundings, although there appears to be no empirical support for such a notion. To some extent an ability to ignore or block out such factors could be based on the force of circumstances, in the sense that when there are barely enough resources to make ends meet there is little left over to beautify the landscape. In addition, during the Maoist era beautification for its own sake—whether of the environment, one's home, or even oneself—was officially considered to be a bourgeois concern.[49]

Modernization and Culture Change

In spite of the potential for excessive environmental determinism, it is worthwhile to explore how the unique set of Chinese character traits has been forged out of the ecological, social, economic, and cultural crucible that has existed in China for such an extended period.[50] From the literature that is available on the topic it is possible to pinpoint three sets of influences:

- the constraints and demands placed on society of an agriculturally based economy operating at best only marginally above subsistence level;
- the dominant moral and religious (and quasireligious) thoughts and doctrines,

such as Confucianism, Taoism, and Buddhism; and

- genetic traits—morphological, physiological, and behavioral—of the ancient Chinese people.[51]

Over the centuries these influences have combined to produce a social structure with the characteristic features we have already noted: a hierarchical structuring of society based on age and seniority; a collectivist organization at the village and neighborhood levels, with individuals subservient to the larger group; and a tightly knit social network, with a strong emphasis on the extended family. These, in turn, are assumed to have influenced the socialization practices unique to traditional China, including the emphasis on characteristics such as dependency, conformity, modesty, self-suppression, self-contentment, and parent-centeredness; as well as the relational characteristics so familiar to Confucianism and Chinese social life such as the orientation toward others and submissiveness.

In this century, and especially since 1949, modernization has produced some important changes in these personality traits. The quintessentially "Chinese" traits, such as the need for deference, the need to seek social approval, and the preference for social restraint and self-control, today are significantly less evident. Other traits, typically identified as "non-Chinese," have become more noticeable: a need for autonomy and achievement; a preference for self-indulgence and sensuous enjoyment; and an inclination toward individual relationships. One might be tempted to conclude there has been a significant cultural convergence between Chinese societies and the West, in other words that "they" are becoming more like "us." This would suggest that the drive toward modernization "makes the Chinese become gradually more like people in a modern industrialized society such as the United States, where the individually-oriented type of achievement motivation prevails."[52]

In *Handbook of Chinese Psychology* (1996), D. Yang reviewed and updated the work he and others conducted on this topic.[53] Here Yang argues that there is now further evidence to support earlier suggestions that the characteristics usually associated with "traditionality" among the Chinese are decreasing and those associated with "modernity" are increasing. In other words, Chinese people now appear to have a lower need for "social-oriented achievement; and a higher need for individual achievement."[54] Other studies contain evidence that Chinese respondents are now more likely to emphasize the present (rather than the past); the notion of mastery over nature (rather than vice-versa); and the importance of economic and social values (rather than aesthetic concerns). Yang thus concludes that his respondents in the 1990s "assigned more importance to a comfortable life, a world at peace, and freedom, and less to ambition and obedience" than was the case in his 1980s work; this is consistent with the trends being reported about the widespread level of interest in television soap operas that are based almost entirely on everyday life issues (see further discussion, below).[55]

In his ongoing work Yang is continuing to explore the impact of social and economic modernization on the characteristics of Chinese people. He has tentatively concluded that "as a result of modernization Chinese people [tend] to be less socially oriented and more individually oriented."[56] More interesting, this recent work tackles one of the major criticisms directed at modernization studies, namely, that they tend to polarize traditionality and modernity—in other words, a person is assumed to be all of one or the other rather than a mix of the two. In his own work Yang identified five independent dimensions, or factors, of traditionality, and five of modernity; he found that in a number of cases measures of traditionality actually coexist with measures of modernity. Put simply, this means that Chinese people may be able to shed some of the values associated with traditionalism while taking on some values of modernization. More specifically, Yang now believes that collectivism and individualism do not necessarily form the opposite poles of one continuum of values. This has allowed

him to begin work on a "revised theory of psychological convergence and divergence" resulting from modernization. He is suggesting that as Chinese society modernizes, some aspects of traditional values are shed or lost, others are retained; the same goes for values associated with modernization.[57]

The Four Modernizations and the Commodification of Personal Relationships

Since 1978 and the introduction of the Four Modernizations project there has been a concerted effort to shift the Chinese economy into high gear. This was partly to keep China moving forward in the quest for modernity, but it was also an effort to right the wrongs of the Cultural Revolution by improving the lot of the Chinese people. By increasing production and generating an economic surplus, it was hoped that the *guanxi* system would no longer be needed and become little more than a distant memory from an austere past. Most important, the new reforms were seen as part of the attempt by the Party-state to improve people's living standards, thereby enhancing its own legitimacy.

A detailed discussion of the economic reforms is contained in Part 3 of this book, so here it is sufficient to say only that the reforms represented a dismantling of the collective efforts of the previous three decades and the introduction of market principles and enterprise into the economy. This would begin in a small way, mainly in the countryside, spreading after the mid-1980s into the cities. Efforts were made to raise human productivity and increase competitiveness on the farms, in the factories, even in the streets. With economic freedom came a certain amount of personal autonomy: People were now able to make and to keep a monetary surplus. Large parts of the economy were to be run on a strictly for-profit basis, operating on the simple premise that "some people must get rich before others," to use a pet phrase of Deng Xiaoping.[58] As Orville Schell pointed out in his 1984 book, *To Get Rich Is Glorious*, across China there were countless examples of the new breed of capitalists showing how it could be done.[59] From that time on, through the 1980s and 1990s, journalists, tourists, and academics have been bringing back different versions of the same story. Schell himself, for example, wrote another book in 1994: *Mandate of Heaven: A New Generation of Entrepreneurs, Dissidents, Bohemians, and Technocrats Lays Claim to China's Future*; since then numerous books have been written about China's runaway economy.[60]

One of the most significant impacts of the reforms was to negate what little success the government had won in trying to foster a new level of caring and socially responsible behavior among Chinese people. Rather than fading from view, however, the instrumentality of the *guanxi* system has made sure that it would become more important than ever in the cash-based economy.[61] The new private ethic in China means that an increasing proportion of social relationships are now being conducted through a cash nexus.[62] This is especially true in the countryside, where higher levels of agricultural productivity have allowed many households to increase their profits. Today, with the contract responsibility system, the sky is the limit: The farmer and his family unit are on their own, and their personal relationships are now more than ever guided by considerations of profit.[63]

There are other trends in contemporary China that provide further evidence of the pervasive shift toward the commodification of personal relationships. One is the increasingly mercenary attitude toward marriage (see Chapter 13). Brides are once again demanding comprehensive wedding gifts, and many young women are looking at prospective husbands from a purely instrumental perspective.[64] In his book *The Garlic Ballads*, Mo Yan related the following story, which can be an allegory for the new China:

An old man calls his three sons to his deathbed. "I'm going to die soon. How do you boys plan to dispose of my body?" The eldest son says,

"Dad, we're so poor we can't afford a decent coffin, so I say we buy a cheap pine box, put you in it, and bury you. How does that sound?" "No good," his father says, shaking his head, "no good at all." "Dad," the second son says, "I think we ought to wrap you in an old straw mat and bury you that way. How's that?" "No good," his father says, "no good at all." The third son says, "Dad, here's what I recommend: we chop you into three pieces, skin you, and take everything to market, where we palm you off as dogmeat, beef, and donkey. What do you think of that?" Their father smiles and says, "Number Three knows his father's mind. Now don't forget to add a little water to the meat to keep the weight up."[65]

Many observers feel that the dominance of market forces is one of the major causes of the erosion of moral standards in China. Importantly, the well-publicized economic corruption and crime are not all that is cited as evidence of this trend; there is also widespread concern about public, street-level morality. All of this further sounds the death knell for the sort of comradeship that was expected to be dominant after the socialist revolution.[66] As Thomas Gold has observed, China has "re-established and is reinforcing the material basis and private ethic for relations based on instrumentalities, the cash nexus and particularistic commitment to family, friends and fellow party members." Gold explains that under these circumstances it is not surprising to find that "the only common goal [is not comradeship but] individual wealth [with] everyone enjoying a 'bit of prosperity.'"[67]

In effect the clock has been turned back as ancient characteristics start to resurface in contemporary China. Most noticeably these include:[68]

- a renewed reliance on family ties, made necessary by the fear of overextending oneself socially and economically;
- a recommodification of marriage;
- a greater deference to authority and a marked lack of civility; and
- a pervasive atmosphere of corruption.

One final example of the commodification of social life in the reform era involves the massive trend toward popular culture that has recently swept China. Jianying Zha, in her book *China Pop: How Soap Operas, Tabloids, and Bestsellers Are Transforming a Culture*, attempts to survey the activities, productions, and outcomes of the new Chinese culture industry. As she observes:

> Popular culture has been the spearhead of the explosive cultural changes that have taken place in post-Tiananmen China. . . . Some see hope in a fast growing, depoliticizing commercial culture [and] emphasize pop culture's positive function in building a more open, relaxed, and pluralist atmosphere. To these optimists, commercial pop culture . . . has broken the Communist Party's cultural monopoly by creating a range of new spaces and forms for both social and personal expression. . . . Others, who consider such hopes naive, perceive it as a new form of mass cultural tyranny and political apathy. . . . In their view, the future of Chinese culture does not look bright, with, on the one side, communist authorities learning to control and manipulate commercial culture and, on the other side, the invasion of China by global capitalist mass culture from the United States, Hong Kong, and Taiwan.[69]

Zha thus argues that China is experiencing a cultural transition, claiming that her goal in writing the book is "to chronicle how cultural productions are being commercialized and professionalized in a semi-communist, third world country, and how such processes have complicated, profound implications for the future of Chinese society."[70] She observes that many of the people who were intellectuals and/or dissidents in the 1980s (especially during the 1989 Tiananmen Square demonstrations) have now gone into business and that many serious novelists and poets now write solely for television sitcoms or write not at all.

As Zha notes, the people are constantly exhorted to "look ahead" and get on with the business of modernization, but she notes that in contemporary China what most people are looking forward to "has turned out to be a large dollar sign."[71] She argues that the tragic events of 1989 produced an almost "schizophrenic" combination in contemporary China, "with a totalitarian government on the one hand, and a runaway free market on the other hand."[72] All of this has had the effect of producing "a half-baked, sheepish, defensive, cynical, masked, stealthy, and often comic atmosphere in which China's reform zigzags ahead."[73] The old structures have experienced a slow erosion, rather than the sudden collapse of those in Eastern Europe and Russia, which gives the impression of "an impure, junky, hybrid quality to nearly all spheres of . . . Chinese life."[74]

It is easy for outsiders to reach the conclusion that the economic reforms have resulted in an unseemly new China, full of selfishness, corruption, vulgarity, and injustice. As noted in Chapter 1, however, at the start of the 1990s Chinese people, as so many others in states transitioning out of socialism, faced very real problems and anxieties. Many felt a deep sense of loss; others struggle even today to find their bearings in the furious activity of commerce, trade, and industry. The fear of *luan* (chaos) is still in many people's thoughts, and such fear may be manifested as inactivity and seclusion, as it was in the Cultural Revolution; but in the 1990s it was producing a new set of outwardly oriented energies and initiatives.

Within two years of the Tiananmen Square massacre, a dramatic shift in China's cultural landscape became evident. Once the economic reforms were back on track China scholars started to notice a marked change in what Chinese people were doing, watching, and reading in their leisure time.[75] During the 1990s China has witnessed a striking rise of multimedia popular culture, including domestic and imported productions of soap operas, sitcoms, radio talk shows, tabloid newspapers, mass-market books, pop music, and action movies. These trends suggest a huge increase in the popularity and production of lowbrow popular culture, which implies a sharp break with both the traditional elite cultural forms of China, including landscape paintings and calligraphy, as well as the state-approved culture that became de rigueur in the Maoist era (see Table 3.3). In the cultural realm such energies have let in a breath of fresh air: New ideas are being tested and innovative projects are being launched, producing what amounts to an era of economic and cultural hybridization. Some critics point out that the new China, forged in such peculiar circumstances, has an inherently unformed and inchoate nature.

Others argue, more pragmatically, that it is important to have peace and that as unsatisfactory as the current era may be, it is better than continuing to fight for an impossible revolutionary dream. As Zha has written, "China will probably remain a '*sibuxiang*' for a long time, a bizarre, hybrid animal neither horse nor donkey, neither here nor there."[76] What now exists is a limited and compromised freedom. The state has backed off somewhat, and although there is a long way to go, it is a start. What this has encouraged is a surge of imported pop culture and consumer products. Arguably, this is little more than a transitional phase, in which there is a new sensibility, especially among the younger generation, that is focused increasingly on money, lifestyle, and professional success.[77] Young people today speak a lot about being able to *qifei* (take off and fly), and for some that is becoming a real possibility.

Some critics feel that in China's headlong rush into business and trade, traditional culture and the arts have suffered seriously, in the sense that state support and funding have largely been withdrawn. Culture has effectively been depoliticized, leaving its production and marketing almost entirely to market forces. Rock singer Cui Jian (once referred to as China's Bob Dylan) has suggested that the basic problem today is not political or economic but cultural. He is implying that the old China still haunts the Chinese, in that there is still too much Confucian dependency and deference to authority. Some argue that radical changes are needed in the "cultural soil" of China.[78] What form this new development might take is not yet obvious. As we shall see in Chapter 18 there are hopeful signs for the emergence of a civil society in contemporary China; and in Chapter 12 we investigate the evidence suggesting a new era of ethnic and cultural diversity.[79]

New Cultural Trends in China

There is certainly not much evidence in contemporary China of the "comradeship" Ezra Vogel wrote about almost a quarter-century ago. The socialist goal of transforming interpersonal relationships into a new utopia, charac-

TABLE 3.3 Classification of Art and Culture in China

	Elite Art/Culture	*Popular-Mass Culture*
Traditional	—ink painting —landscapes —classical poetry —calligraphy —seal carving	—New Year's paintings —opera —novels —handicrafts
Contemporary	—oil painting —symphonies —ballet —spoken drama —avant-garde poetry and painting	—pin-ups —Hong Kong/Taiwan popular music —sex and violence —family life potboilers —disco —television and video —karaoke

SOURCE: Adapted from Kraus (1995), Table 7.1, p. 182.

terized by universal morality and mutual trust, has clearly not come to pass. Arguably the shift back to some of the traditional values has brought with it the worst of both worlds wherein the negative aspects of Confucianism—old hierarchies, authoritarianism, and the commodification of human relationships— have returned untempered by the positives of Confucianism—the emphasis on morality, humane behavior, and the importance of virtue.

In a survey conducted in the early 1990s a group of Chinese American researchers attempted to define what they assumed would be a set of values corresponding to the traditional teachings of Confucius, then tested for their existence among samples of respondents drawn from China and the United States.[80] They were not successful; in fact they concluded that "not only were there rather feeble endorsements of major Confucian precepts, but the key cornerstones of Confucian teachings . . . were actually rejected by a majority of the Chinese respondents."[81] Surprisingly, they also concluded that the Chinese responses more closely resembled those in the United States than those in two other purportedly Confucian societies: Taiwan and South Korea. As they discovered, the latter were "much more clearly Confucian in their general support for the traditional value items."[82] To help account for these findings, the researchers suggest that contemporary China is in a transitional state, not necessarily converging with the West but going its own way. They also note that several decades of anti-Confucian propaganda by the Party-state machinery might have suppressed scores for some items.

Chinese values have certainly been changing in recent years, and nowhere is this more apparent than in relationships between the sexes. The surveys have shown that it is on matters of sexuality and sexual relationships that Chinese and American respondents differ most, although the differences are not always as expected. Overall, Chinese respondents were less accepting of the concept of equal status for men and women; Americans appeared to be considerably

more permissive about premarital sex than were Chinese respondents. Yet ideas about chastity in one's chosen spouse and the need for wifely obedience appear to be essentially similar in China and the United States, which suggests that significant change has occurred on the mainland.[83]

Further support for this apparent decline in Confucian values in China is provided in *Handbook of Chinese Psychology*.[84] One contributor to the volume reported a marked decline in the last two decades in filial attitudes between generations, as well as a "radical change in the Chinese definition of intergenerational relationships, leading to a liberalization of traditional constraints on the development of individuality."[85] This researcher also suggested that individuals having "authoritarian-moralistic personalities," who have been inculcated with filial precepts since childhood, will find it difficult to accept this erosion of filial respect. He may be referring obliquely here to the last cohort of China's gerontocracy within the Party leadership, which now finds itself at odds with the cultural preferences of a huge segment of the populace.

As we already noted, these observations about human relationships in China are paralleled by similar developments in the material culture. The new popular culture certainly reflects China's entry into the global economy, but it also provides evidence of a wave of public fatigue and indifference toward politics, as well as having the state be the sole arbitrator of cultural practice. There is fairly widespread agreement that in contemporary China we are witnessing "a new generation more interested in lifestyle than revolution."[86] As a result of the economic reforms many individuals now have the money to imbibe in popular culture as consumers. More important, perhaps, the new economics now provides the financial incentives for entrepreneurs to produce artifacts of that culture on a massive scale. It has been documented recently that leisure time and the private sphere in general have expanded significantly in China in the 1980s and 1990s.[87] This phenomenon may be as much a result of societal forces nibbling away at the state as it is a deliberate retreat by the state. Yet it would seem that the state has learned to take a back-seat, allowing people more space and free time. In addition to its depoliticization, leisure time has become increasingly commercialized. In fact as one Chinese scholar concluded, "Profit has [now] replaced ideology [as] the primary concern for most providers of recreational products."[88]

All of this is great news for ordinary Chinese people who simply seek entertainment at the end of the workday. The popularity of the television show *Kewang* (Yearning) illustrates this. *Kewang* is a fifty-part soap opera first screened in the early 1990s, focusing on ordinary family life and cultural values, with almost nothing to say about politics, whether dissident or of the center. It was not attempting to cater to the highbrow demands of educated Chinese people—in fact the elite evaluation writes off the show as lightweight fluff. Some observers suggest that for this very reason the huge popularity of *Kewang* is a metaphor for contemporary China, in the sense that it deals primarily with nothing more sophisticated than everyday lives and the quotidian concerns of ordinary people.

A caveat: Even though anything can now be turned into a commodity and sold for profit in the reform era, it is clear that not all forms of art and culture are successful. If we think, for example, of four categories of art and culture, divided along two axes—elite and popular/mass audiences on the one axis, traditional and contemporary on the other axis—it is evident that the only category currently in high-output mode is the production of contemporary popular/mass culture and art (see Table 3.3). It is here where the demand for new products is close to insatiable, and it is here where the potential rewards for performers and producers are greatest. The other side of this story is that the economic reform era has been accompanied by a sharp decline in state subsidies for producers of elite art and culture. As Richard Kraus observed, "High-minded novelists now have more difficulty finding publishers; ballet and spoken drama troupes and symphony orches-

tras are forced to cut their payrolls."[89] As Kraus has also pointed out, it is no longer true to say that the major problem for artists in contemporary China is conflict with a repressive and culturally myopic state, as during much of the Maoist era. Today it is much more likely that the market will determine the nature and content of the art and culture being produced and distributed. Kraus has portrayed this as not an entirely satisfactory trend, because a commodity culture encourages passive arts consumers, not mobilized activists. With the Party-state's abandonment of the arts, it now seems unlikely that there will be any significant development in art that moves people to social and political action.

The recent history of poetry in China provides a good example of this trend. After 1949 the only acceptable form of poetry was that which intended to contribute to Maoist views of developmentalism and socialist realism. This has been described as the "first wave" of poetry, which amounted to a Berlin Wall in the sense that mandated ideas of political correctness blocked meaningful innovation in the content and techniques of poetry.[90] Gradually, the Berlin Wall was pulled down and replaced by the "second wave" that became known as "Misty" poetry. Here there was a shift from verse that reflected political fervor to verse that was more obviously concerned with aesthetics and personal emotions. As S. Wei and W. Larson described it, "Misty poetry represented the 'self,' not redefined as the origin of revolutionary emotions . . . but as a complex and often contradictory place for all kinds of emotions and beliefs."[91] This was the advent of modernity in Chinese poetry. Predictably it has been challenged in recent years by the "third wave" of postmodern poetry, in which the principal message is that "all existing norms, in context, form, or otherwise, should be despised, and that any edifice—spiritual, emotional, or institutional—that implied a stable norm was gone."[92]

The bottom line for Chinese poetry in the 1990s, as with most other forms of elite and cosmopolitan art and culture, is that very few people (other than poets) read it. To some extent this was mandated by the postmodern (and, many would argue, unreadable) nature of the third wave of poetry in China. Verse had become something only for the informed reader, someone who knew about and understood how it was written. To qualify as a modern intellectual in China one need not read or have knowledge of poetry. Thus postmodern culture has forced many art forms, especially poetry, to two poles: "intellectual culture, on the one hand, and popular song lyrics, on the other."[93]

In the world of painting and art, there has been a parallel evolution, from the officially sanctioned works of the Maoist era to the avant-garde art of the 1980s.[94] But during the 1990s the intellectualized art of the previous decade gave way largely to the demands of popular works that could easily find a market. The Chinese art scene today is dominated by a concern for commercial success, to the point that almost all other criteria are discounted. Most of the better avant-garde artists, receiving neither critical recognition nor financial support, have found themselves with no public outlets for their work; many have emigrated.

There has also been some development of a new form of writing—postmodern realism, if one can use that phrase—which attempts to describe, in allegorical form, some of the chaos and nightmarish quality of life in contemporary China. Can Xue, one of a number of such Chinese writers, is at the forefront of the new literary trends in China—and at the center of debates surrounding them. Her 1989 volume of short stories, *Dialogues in Paradise*, can be read as "part political allegory, part poetry, part literary illusion, and part analysis of real human conflict that ranges from somber to playful."[95] The stories are far different from traditional Chinese social realism and thus have more in common with European and American surrealism than with classical Chinese literature.[96] Although such writing may be more concerned with style than substance, in Can Xue's case she may also be speaking about contemporary China in her strangely distorted writings. In one of the novellas, *Yellow Mud Street*, the characters of Yellow Mud Street insult each other in the following way:

> The sun was as red as a pig's lungs. The sky was dusty. Gray ash fell like snowflakes. People said a comet was going to collide with the earth. The end of the world was coming. Every family was cooking good things. Rumor spread that their days were numbered. Eat now or never. Then people felt bloated from overeating. Bloated stomachs in turn led to the shouting of insults in the street. Across the street, across the yellow water, people cursed each other, stamping their feet and shitting at the same time. One man cursed while trying to hold up his pants. At the height of their enthusiasm, they would raise a night stool full of shit and hurl it towards the opposite attic. This action was reciprocated immediately by those across the way. Of course, no excrement really landed on anyone. This was only a way of boosting morale. Several days passed in such hubbub. But then people fell into moaning and complaining again.[97]

It is tempting to conclude that contemporary Chinese people have precious little to believe in anymore, but that would be an impossible statement for an outsider to defend. It would seem, however, that although the goals of a universal socialist morality have been suspended, nothing has emerged to take its place. There is no religion to speak of, no moral principles of Confucianism to cling to.[98] It is plausible to suggest, therefore, that many people might feel they have been left floundering, searching for something in their lives to hang on to. This was evident in the stories Anne Thurston reported in her powerful book *Enemies of the People*, based on conversations with intellectuals who were badly treated during the Cultural Revolution. As one of Thurston's respondents told her, "There is an identity crisis in China now. . . . Norms have been shattered, and there are no substitutes so we are facing a period of anomie, especially the younger generation. People are not sure what they are after, what they want. They want change, but as to what kind of change is adequate, they are not so sure."[99]

As we saw in the case of the MaoCraze, in the early 1990s some older Chinese began reflecting fondly on days of old, when revolutionary zeal offered a sense of purpose and something to believe in. In those days "the young thought they were the vanguard of a revolutionary movement that would sweep the world," but in the new era of competition for economic wealth this is no longer the case. As a former Red Guard put it, "For the revolution we could die [but] how could we die for a refrigerator?"[100] This turned out to be a prophetic statement, because by the late 1980s some of China's youth had indeed found a cause they could believe in. The difference was that this time they were sharply at odds with the leadership, and they were talking about (but not demanding) political changes the Party was not ready to make. The result was that in the summer of 1989 many of them indeed died for their beliefs. Others, in numbers we can only guess at, have disappeared: executed, forced underground, exiled abroad, or sent to the Chinese gulag.

4
China's Political Economy and the Transition out of Socialism

᠗᠗᠗᠗᠗᠗᠗᠗᠗᠗᠗᠗᠗᠗᠗᠗᠗᠗

Only a ruler of virtue is able to make people obedient to him with a liberal government. A comparison may be made with the severe ruler. Fire is fierce, and people fear at the sight of it. So they seldom die of it. Water, on the other hand, is gentle, so that people are inclined to play in it. As a result, many of them drown. For this reason we say that it is very difficult to have a liberal but successful government.

—Ancient Chinese maxim[1]

Introduction: China's Transition

Events in China since 1978, under the reform umbrella of the Four Modernizations, share common features with events in socialist states elsewhere in the world. During the 1980s many socialist states experienced the need to initiate reforms as a result of economic-political crises that caused the regimes' legitimacy to be called into question.[2] Yet more than a decade after the Tiananmen Square tragedy the Chinese Communist Party remains in firm control, although some political scientists would argue that the prolonged success of China's economic reforms will continue to generate enough resistance to eventually pressure the regime into allowing even more political openness.[3] As we have already pointed out, a program of limited reform—which is how the Four Modernizations started–can be transformed into a revolutionary process if the balance of power between state and society shifts significantly toward the latter.[4] It is important to stress, therefore, that China's revolution (if we can call it that) has been carried out primarily from below, that is, by societal forces, and through the operation of the market economy. Some China scholars argue that this was definitely not what the Party-state envisioned

when the first seeds of reform were planted.[5] The preferred and considerably more conservative course of events was for market forces to develop only within the context of the planned economy. This represents the familiar bird-cage analogy, in which the "bird" (the market) is not allowed to fly outside the "cage" (the planned economy). By the late 1980s, however, it was obvious that the bird could no longer be caged, and throughout the 1990s market forces came to dominate and transform the Chinese economy.[6] China's reforms have produced a major crisis for the Party-state, because the course of the reforms has shifted dangerously away from the regime's original vision and because economic performance has effectively replaced communist ideology as the basis of political legitimacy in China. To meet such an assault would require some flexible and creative responses by the leadership.

China's Marxism

Deng Xiaoping had been branded a "capitalist roader" many times during his long career in the Party; in fact he used to make a joke about his deviation from the Party line: "Marx sits up in heaven, and he is very powerful. He sees what we are doing, and he doesn't like it. So he has punished me by making me deaf."[7] Neither Marx nor Mao would have approved of Deng's economic policies in the 1980s, so Deng's deafness can be interpreted either as punishment or more simply as his way of turning his back to Marx and Mao—turning a deaf ear, so to speak.

The 1949 socialist revolution in China was not predicted by Marx, who believed that a successful revolution could be spearheaded only by an urban-based industrial proletariat. That meant revolution must follow a prolonged period of industrial capitalism, in which the proletariat had become sufficiently alienated to seek major changes in the political system. Lenin, for his part, did not completely agree with this, but Lenin, who came to power in the twentieth century, had an advantage in hindsight that Marx did not enjoy. It was clear to Lenin, then, that a revolution in China could not be led by an urban proletariat because industrial capitalism was still in its infancy. Thus to some extent, at least, Mao Zedong was more Leninist than Marxist.[8]

For China to experience a successful revolution, Mao argued, it would have to be based in the countryside, supported by the peasant masses. Here Mao diverged sharply from the majority of Soviet political thinkers, including Lenin. Mao judged the Chinese peasants to be hopelessly naive and utterly unprepared for revolution, yet he was convinced that they could be educated and forged into revolutionary action. The standard wisdom among the Soviets was much less sanguine about the role of the peasants. Even Leon Trotsky, who himself came from humble rural origins, agreed with Marx that peasants would and should never be able to lead a revolution. Marx had generally been scornful of peasants, even describing them as "the class that represents barbarism without civilization."[9] Such antipathy came to a head during Stalin's bloody purges of the kulaks, the wealthy farmers who resisted collectivization and paid dearly for that.[10] Stalin never really took the CCP seriously because of its domination by peasants; in fact in 1944 he described the Chinese as "margarine Communists" who would never amount to very much.[11]

Time proved that Mao, rather than Marx or the Soviets, had a better feel for the revolutionary potential of the Chinese peasants. In the formative years of the CCP, however, Mao was not a very important figure. In fact, until 1927 the CCP was not a revolutionary party at all, and it had chosen to ally itself with the bourgeois Nationalist Party (the Kuomintang, or KMT) led by Chiang Kai-shek. Lenin had approved of that alliance because he felt that in the absence of an urban proletariat the CCP had few other options. He also felt that the KMT, during its anti-imperialist phase, was a reasonable surrogate for a revolutionary (i.e., vanguard) party. Trotsky, in contrast, was violently opposed to the CCP-KMT alliance. For the Communists to join forces with Chiang Kai-shek was, in Trotsky's opinion, like making a pact with the devil.[12]

Trotsky's jaundiced view proved valid, for in 1927 Chiang Kai-shek double-crossed the Communists and nearly wiped them out in Shanghai.[13] At about this time Mao's voice was also becoming a stronger force within the Party. He had been arguing for a break with the KMT and suggested that the Communists move their base of operations away from the cities and into the countryside. Mao's thoughts on the revolutionary potential of the peasant masses were most clearly expressed in the report he wrote about the uprising in his home province of Hunan. In a moment of wishful thinking Mao predicted that there would soon be a successful but violent uprising in the Chinese countryside:

In a very short time, in China's central, southern and northern provinces, several hundred million peasants will rise like a mighty storm, like a hurricane, a force so swift and violent that no power, however great, will be able to hold it back. They will smash all the trammels that bind them and rush forward along the road to liberation. They will sweep away all the imperialists, warlords, corrupt officials, local tyrants and evil gentry into their graves.[14]

In Mao's view, then, the revolution would be powered largely by the peasant masses. This meant that China did not need to wait for the urban proletariat to organize the revolution, and in fact Mao strongly believed that China's cities were centers of bourgeois conservatism that would continually stand in the way of the revolution (see Chapter 9).

Mao's views on revolution also differed from the traditional Marxist emphasis on internationalism. Instead of situating the revolution within the broader context of worldwide socialism—as Lenin and Trotsky had attempted to do—Mao appealed solely to popular Chinese sentiments. In a country that had been humiliated by foreign intruders for more than a century, this turned out to be a popular and realistic choice, and in fact Mao viewed the upcoming revolution as a war for national independence as much as a Marxist-guided struggle for class upheaval.[15] It was not only Mao's politics that were iconoclastic, however: The version of socialist economics he advocated represented a significant break with the economic traditions of feudal (i.e., prerevolutionary) China, as well as with the cultural traditions of Confucian China. It is instructive, therefore, to examine some of the ways that the Maoist political economy signaled a break with the Chinese past—especially the alternative it provided to capitalism.

The basic system of any capitalist economy is one of minimal government interference in the marketplace. Such official nonintervention allows all individuals in society—whether they are entrepreneurs, workers, or consumers—to pursue self-interests freely. In terms of production this implies that actions are driven primarily by the profit motive; for consumption it means that individuals are able to shop around until they maximize overall utility. At the global scale capitalism has been amazingly successful, and the seductive power of material incentive has allowed millions of people to raise their living standards to previously unimaginable levels. According to theory, that happens, almost miraculously, as a result of the workings of the "invisible hand" of market forces. Yet even in the most laissez-faire economies the state inter-

venes to some degree (as in the case of Hong Kong; see Chapter 11). The factors of production are used efficiently, output increases, and national wealth expands almost inexorably. At the end of the twentieth century capitalism is marching around the world triumphantly, with contemporary China offering almost a textbook definition of the prospects, as well as the problems, facing a transition economy.

In China traditional petty capitalism, which had been in place for some 2,000 years, was poorly adapted to the requirements of the first decades in the twentieth century.[16] Although a bourgeois class began to emerge by the 1930s and 1940s, it was unable to establish the financial and technical infrastructures needed for the successful development of capitalism.[17] By then China suffered from some of the same centrifugal tendencies that had threatened to tear the country apart for centuries, and the bourgeois class appeared unable to replace the chaos of feuding regional warlords with a nationally unified government.

In the countryside, poverty, misery, and starvation were endemic.[18] What made the poverty even worse was the total inability of the peasants to do anything to alter their own situations. High rates of illiteracy in the countryside; lethargy born of constant malnutrition; centuries of blind Confucian acceptance of the status quo; and the tendency to seek refuge in spiritual explanations of adversity—all contributed to an acceptance of the way things were. It was clear, then, that only a cataclysmic force would awaken the peasantry, make them aware of their oppression, and give them the confidence needed to challenge the elite groups. Centuries of passivity and a chronic lack of organization would need to be swept away.

Mao's version of Marxism appeared to offer such a solution to the Chinese peasant masses. By radically restructuring rural society the Communists offered the peasants a chance to overcome their powerlessness and bring about real changes in the centuries-old patterns of inequality. The way to achieve that was initially through land reform, which had already been carried out in the old communist base areas before the revolution. The goal was to heighten the class struggle and mobilize the masses. It began by educating the peasants about their rights to the land; getting them to denounce their landlords and, if necessary, dispose of them; and then taking possession of the land.

The essential first step in this process was a careful study of class relationships in order to identify the poor peasants who would then have a crucial role to play in the revolution. According to Mao's definitions, the poor peasantry represented about 70 percent of the rural population, and it was targeted as the vanguard of the revolution. Some of the peasants owned land, but often there was barely enough to provide food at even subsistence level. Most were tenants, small handcrafters, shop assistants, peddlers, and beggars. They were the marginal groups in the Chinese countryside, "whose only hope of improved living conditions lay in the complete remolding of the social and economic order."[19]

The primary goal of land reform was to raise the level of human potential in the Chinese countryside, with a focus on all people rather than merely the best and most productive. At the grassroots level that would require fundamental changes in the human character, beginning with the abandonment of the passivity traditional among the peasants. Mao believed that the Chinese people would have to sacrifice greatly to bring about permanent change, which meant committing to many years of hard work and self-denial. He hoped that the new "communist man" (and woman) would, through frugal living and constant struggle, eventually be able to work miracles, as the hero had in a traditional folktale, "The Foolish Old Man Who Removed the Mountain."[20]

Marx himself considered the dominance of such ascetic values to be inherently repressive. Although he realized that self-sacrifice would be necessary for the revolutionary proletariat during the early stages of capitalist industrialization, in the long run Marx hoped such sacrifices could be dispensed with as the communist

utopia was achieved. This suggests another fundamental divergence between Maoism and Marxism, in that Mao's new "communist man" had what amounted to bourgeois values that Marx assumed would have been "relegated to the 'dustbin of history' with the transition to a socialist society."[21] In Mao's revolution this did not happen; in fact Mao wanted the ascetic values of the spiritually remolded person to continue (rather than disappear) to set an example for the masses by demonstrating the value of "plain living and hard work."[22]

The CCP was violently opposed to the traditional Confucian value system in China, and at various times after 1949 the Party launched virulent anti-Confucius campaigns. At one level the campaigns were symbolically directed at political moderates within the top leadership (like Zhou Enlai), but at another level they also involved fundamental attacks on Confucian values. Mao felt that the Five Constant Virtues were symbolic of the rigid class system that existed in feudal China.[23] The Communists also felt that excessive loyalty to the family, although traditionally Chinese, detracted somewhat from loyalty to the Party and the state. Mao also considered the Confucian education system to be fundamentally unjust, giving unfair advantages to intellectuals and book-learning. As the self-educated son of a peasant, he was eager to break down the centuries-old Confucian meritocracy and to reward manual labor at an equal if not higher rate than mental labor. The true Maoist hero would be the educated youth who goes to the countryside to learn from the peasants. If successful, such a person would emerge "with a dark skin and a red heart,"[24] which is proof that he or she valued hard work in the fields, and, most important, was politically reliable.[25]

The frequent attacks launched on Confucianism by the CCP proved to be only partially successful, as we saw in Chapter 3. In fact Confucian values have refused to die in postrevolutionary China, and to some extent they have even reemerged during the reform era. Critics of communism argue that this was so because no consistent set of social or moral values emerged as a viable alternative to Confucianism in post-1949 China. It is also apparent that during the Maoist era there was not enough development in the material base to support the emerging values of socialism, so, as Mao predicted, the struggle and hard work would have to continue into the foreseeable future.[26]

The Maoist utopia—in which there would be no class divisions, no differentiation between city and country, and equality between men and women—had clearly not been achieved by the end of the 1970s. From the vantage point of the late 1990s, that vision looks like a quaint anachronism. There were still hierarchies in Maoist China, but they were based on political savvy rather than on Confucian learning; the hierarchies in Dengist and post-Dengist China are based more on economic than political power.

What may be most surprising to the outside world is that Chinese leaders, as late as 1998, were still speaking about the reform era as part of the ongoing socialist transformation—in spite of its obvious capitalist characteristics. In the next section of this chapter, therefore, we shall briefly explore the different phases of the five decades of struggle to bring about that socialist transformation in China, from the glory days of the socialist revolution, to the desperation of the late 1980s, to the capitalist triumphalism of the late 1990s. The human impacts of these changes were enormous, and the people were required to transform themselves and their behaviors accordingly, as illustrated in this peasant proverb:

> In the fifties we helped each other,
> In the sixties we killed each other,
> In the seventies we feared each other,
> In the eighties each one thinks for himself.[27]

Before launching into an account of the transformations, however, it is necessary to introduce some of the key elements of Chinese political economy since the communist takeover in 1949.

Political Economy and the Socialist Transformation in China

The fundamental difference between socialist and capitalist economies is reflected in the ownership of the means of production. Until the 1980s the vast majority of the productive forces in China were owned and operated by the state or by the collectives, which are subgroups of the population and include production teams, neighborhoods, communes, and even counties. Most of the heavy industry was state-owned, but light industry was usually collectively owned and operated, and in recent years it is increasingly likely to be owned privately, either by specialized households, by new economic cooperatives, or by joint commercial ventures involving foreigners and their capital (see Chapter 8).

To Mao Zedong, one of the most important issues after 1949 was the relationship between the cities and the rural areas. Persistent efforts were made to introduce industry into the countryside, to such an extent that in some places it was difficult to differentiate between urban and rural landscapes. Small towns in the countryside all over China were bristling with industry; in fact in 1983 rural collectives were responsible for more than three-quarters of China's industrial enterprises, making up over one-fifth of total industrial output.[28] By building up rural industries, jobs and incomes were created for the people who were not needed on the land. In addition, rural industry helped to supply some of the manufactured inputs needed by the agricultural sector, such as farm machinery and fertilizer, thereby reducing transportation costs and increasing local self-sufficiency. The rapid growth and economic success of the township and village enterprises (TVEs) in the 1980s and 1990s, many of which are located in what used to be the agricultural land between cities and the countryside (i.e., the suburbs), have continued the industrialization of the Chinese countryside to such an extent that in some parts there is virtually unbroken industrial, commer-

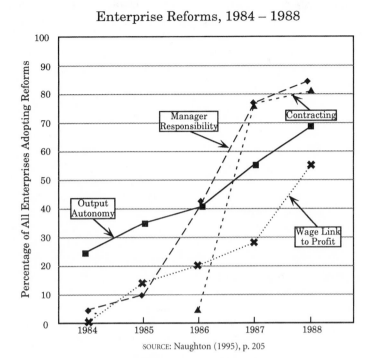

FIGURE 4.1   Enterprise Reforms in China, 1984–1988

cial, and residential development for hundreds of square miles.[29]

Another feature of the socialist economy until the late 1970s was the highly centralized system of state control over all economic decisionmaking. This was most evident immediately after liberation in 1949, when decisions came directly from the center all the way down to local farms and enterprises. Since those early years the Chinese Communists have experimented several times with a more decentralized decisionmaking system. This began during the Great Leap Forward in 1958, when control of much of the country's light industry was shifted down to the provincial level, with the state dealing only with defense industries and the basics, such as steel and coal mining. After reverting to a more centralized planning system in the early 1960s, the Chinese economy was thrust into turmoil during the Cultural Revolution (1966–1976), and the struggle to win control over industry became highly politicized. It was

not until the era of economic reforms after 1978 that the first significant attempts to decentralize down to the enterprise level were made (see Figure 4.1).

At the center of any socialist economy there is typically a regulated price system. Floating prices could obviously create havoc for a country where the major emphasis is on capital accumulation rather than private consumption. It was also important for a socialist government to be able to guarantee the people access to basic commodities and services at reasonable prices. In the cities, cheap food was made available by pricing agricultural products significantly lower than industrial output. This represents the infamous "scissors effect," about which Chinese farmers complained bitterly, as it favored industry (the cities) at the expense of agriculture (the countryside).[30]

After the initial transformation to socialism from what Mao called "semifeudal capitalism," the ultimate goal of the CCP was to steer a course toward communism. In preparing for that transformation the state needed to develop its economic base, which comprises the forces of production and the relations of production.[31] The focus on those two components in postrevolutionary China, as well as their relative importance, changed over time as different theories were embraced by the leadership. During prerevolutionary days and immediately after 1949 the Communists set about dismantling the existing relations of production in the countryside, which they accomplished by dispossessing landlords and giving their lands to peasants. Thus it initially appeared that all they had done was replace one form of private landownership with another (albeit more democratic) form.[32] After this process was successfully completed it became possible to focus on the forces of production in the countryside by trying to increase agricultural output through collective production methods. This is what Mao Zedong meant by "putting politics in command." In other words, a necessary condition for developing the economy by building up the forces of production was the need to launch (and win) the class struggle, that is, developing the relations of production.

The most difficult aspect of the transformation—indeed before the political struggle could even be contested—was raising the consciousness of the peasants. That process began even before the revolution in the communist-controlled parts of rural China, where the new Red Army (the Eighth Route Army) worked diligently to instill revolutionary zeal into the peasants, using a combination of education and propaganda backed by force. Some accounts indicate that the Red Army was different from any other army that had ever roamed the Chinese countryside. The peasants were encouraged to speak out about their oppression for probably the first time ever, in the so-called speak bitterness campaigns. With the army behind them, the peasants could realistically envision a new future for themselves—and for the whole of China. The Red Army, in other words, was not so much an army as "a people in arms." To millions of peasants, soldiers, and civilians the Red Army brought the immediate promise of a new life and liberation from the evils of the old society.[33]

The Communists realized that before the system of landownership could be changed it was necessary to alter the way the peasants thought about themselves and their ability to challenge the status quo. That would require fundamentally altering the society's superstructure, or the dominant ideology, systems of thought, and institutions that legitimated the existing form of government.[34] Changing a society's superstructure is a process rather than a single event; as Mao predicted, the struggle to reform the superstructure would probably continue indefinitely.[35] To describe the flow of events and the process of political change in China after the revolution in 1949, it is helpful to outline three major phases of the socialist transformation, namely, the Stalinist, or Soviet, era (1949 to roughly 1957); the Maoist era (1958–1976); and the Dengist and then Jiangist eras (1978 to the present).[36]

Immediately following the revolution the CCP was faced with the overwhelming task of developing the national economy. To do that it was necessary to put in abeyance much of the prerevolutionary politics that had helped the CCP win support from peasants in the Communist-held base areas. The pragmatic solution was to follow the model of their close allies in the Soviet Union. At this point, the major objective was to develop the forces of production in order to jump-start the economy. Thus, in 1953 a series of Five Year Plans was adopted, focusing on the development of heavy industry. The capital to be used for investment funds during this period was to be generated by squeezing the agricultural sector; in fact critics of the Five Year Plans argue that China's early industrialization was financed largely at the expense of agriculture. This, then, was a highly centralized command economy, largely dependent on Soviet finance, technology, and personnel.

In economic terms this phase of development has been judged highly successful: Between 1953 and 1957 industrial production grew at an average annual rate that exceeded 25 percent.[37] Agricultural production grew at a much slower rate, perhaps as little as 5 percent or less each year during this period, not surprising in light of the relative lack of investment in the agricultural sector.[38] The Chinese adopted the Soviet model of development because they had few other choices in the 1950s, but it is likely that some of the leaders, especially Mao Zedong, did so with considerable feelings of ambivalence. The focus on heavy industry in the existing centers of economic strength, accompanied by the relative lack of focus on agriculture, was sharply discordant with the Maoist goals for geographical equality among regions, between city and countryside, and, most important, between industry and agriculture. It was not surprising, therefore, that by the late 1950s a marked shift to the political left was observable, and a set of economic policies more closely aligned to Mao's political thought emerged.

In spite of the successes of the First Five Year Plan Mao believed that the task of building socialism called for a return to some of the principles that had led the Communist Party to victory in 1949. Mao felt that the centralized economic and political system developed during the First Five Year Plan was much too conservative and needed an injection of dynamism and a greater level of participation by the masses. In recommending a change of strategy Mao was arguing that economic development was a dialectical rather than a scientific process; in other words it needed to be tinkered with as situations changed. The transformation to socialism in China had produced its own set of contradictions, and when those occurred radical changes in strategy were sometimes needed. To some of Mao's critics, his economic development strategies were not so much a set of well-designed plans as a process of discovery or, more accurately, a process of trial and error.[39]

What Mao advocated in the late 1950s was in some ways a swing back toward the successful mass-mobilization campaigns conducted in the prerevolutionary communist base areas. Mao argued for a gigantic collective effort in which individuals would be exhorted to "serve the people" and, by doing so, also serve themselves. This began with the Great Leap Forward (1958–1960) and the continuing efforts to collectivize Chinese agriculture on a vast scale (see Chapter 7). In contrast to the Five Year Plan era, heavy industry would to some extent be de-emphasized and agricultural development privileged. Mao stressed that the economy needed to learn how to "walk on two legs," emphasizing industry and agriculture roughly equally. He had been dreaming of a new basis for the spatial organization of agriculture and industry—the people's communes—which in his words were "the best organizational form for carrying out the two transitions, from socialist . . . to all-embracing public; and from all-embracing public to communist ownership."[40] In this era the emphasis had shifted again from the forces of production to the relations of production. The prerevolutionary emphasis on class struggle was now to be renewed; the last vestiges of private ownership were to be purged from the landscape; and Mao's new "communist man" would be exhorted to lead the way. The Great Leap Forward, beginning in 1958, was intended to bring about a major transformation toward socialism and economic modernization.

With the advantage of hindsight, most commentators agree that the Great Leap failed because it was based too heavily on the radical politics of the prerevolutionary base areas (in Chapter 7 we shall consider its tragic consequences).[41] Such strategies had worked well when China was struggling to repel the Japanese and the Communists were embroiled in a bitter civil war with the Nationalists, but they were not realistic for peacetime. By the late 1950s China was relatively secure from foreign occupation, and the people were desperate to experience some major improvements in their material living standards. They were already tiring of the revolutionary struggle, and most were probably not looking forward to the prospect of prolonged austerity that Mao predicted.[42]

In the early 1960s there was a retreat from the extreme radicalism of the Great Leap, which helped somewhat with the economic recovery from the so-called three disastrous years (1959–1961). Mao Zedong was temporarily diverted from his radical course, and he interpreted this period as one in which the Party was essentially backpedaling from socialism. To prevent this Mao set out to launch an all-out campaign to revitalize the class struggle by enhancing the revolutionary consciousness of the peasants and workers. Using the terminology introduced earlier in this chapter, this meant that Mao was trying to shift the focus of the nation's political economy in an attempt to alter China's superstructure, which at this time he felt was a prerequisite for changing the relations of production.

The result was the so-called Great Proletariat Cultural Revolution (known simply as the Cultural Revolution), which began in 1966. Mao was concerned with reviving what he considered to be a faltering revolution by changing the thinking of those who favored the capitalist road to economic development (Deng Xiaoping among them). To outsiders (and indeed to many Chinese people) the Cultural Revolution was a baffling and chaotic era. What grabbed the headlines was the clash between the leftist thoughts of the Maoists and the rightist thoughts of Mao's opponents, who were usually characterized as the followers of Premier Liu Shaoqi. The Cultural Revolution degenerated into a mass movement in which Mao and his supporters, including the infamous Red Guards, struggled to remove opponents from power. Not surprisingly, very little progress was made during this period to steer China's economy in the direction of communism.[43]

In more ways than one the year 1976 was a traumatic one for China. In January the people mourned the death of their beloved premier, Zhou Enlai; in the summer the old revolutionary army veteran Zhu De died; and in September Mao himself died. There had also been a devastating earthquake in Tangshan, killing a quarter-million people. The struggle for Mao's successor heated up after 1976, and four Mao supporters (the Gang of Four, which included his wife, Jiang Qing) were arrested, awaiting what would become the most comprehensive

and controversial trial held in the PRC up to that time.

The changing winds of fortune in Chinese politics meant that Deng Xiaoping had already been purged twice for his rightism—and then rehabilitated twice. In 1978 he was called upon again, this time to open up a new era in China's history. Deng quickly seized on a theme that had been introduced by Zhou Enlai, the Four Modernizations, involving an ambitious plan to turn China into a powerful socialist country by the beginning of the twenty-first century, with modern agriculture, industry, national defense, and science and technology.

The new strategy was adjusted time and again as circumstances dictated, but the general course of events became fairly clear by the mid-1980s (for details of the economic reforms, see Chapters 7 and 8). To return to the themes introduced earlier, the emphasis during the reform phase has clearly shifted from the relations of production and back toward development of the forces of production. This was to be achieved by a combination of market mechanisms working within an overall state plan, something that has been described as a combination of plan and market but that can also be interpreted, in the long run, as a transition "from plan to market."[44] The new strategies have emphasized more autonomy for production units at the local level; made possible much greater levels of material reward; and allowed higher levels of personal consumption than was ever the case since 1949.

Taking the capitalist road in this fashion allowed some individuals and households to get rich quickly, which threatened to reopen the inequality gap after three decades of egalitarianism. In 1988 confused outsiders were speculating as to how the CCP would respond if it suddenly decided that the push toward market forces had gone too far and that the entire reform process needed to be halted. In fact this would happen several times during the late 1980s and early 1990s in a series of policy zigzags, but the retrenchments never represented major policy shifts in the opposite direction. As we saw clearly in the early summer of

1989, the leadership was willing to go to extreme measures to halt any movement considered to be contrary to its own best interests. The sails of the emerging democracy movement were sharply trimmed, and it was apparent that at any time throughout the 1990s the Party might well decide to shift gears on the economic reforms and move toward a more hard-line, or leftist, stance on economic development. Although most Western economists would contend that China can ill afford to abandon its impressive reform agenda, it is apparent that the CCP will, as usual, continue to steer its own course.

The Tiananmen tragedy of 1989 emphasized the close relationship between issues of economic and political reform in China. It is reasonable to suggest that the loosening of China's economy during the 1980s helped generate calls for political reform, which in turn led to the Beijing Spring.[45] After the brutal clampdown of the democracy movement, China was facing an economic crisis even greater than the one it had encountered in 1988 (the year of hyperinflation). The people who had gone out on a limb and taken the capitalist road could not be certain that the government would continue to support their actions through the 1990s. In addition, confidence among China's trading partners was at an all-time low, and the threat of investment withdrawals was real. As we now know (with the benefit of hindsight), the Chinese government demonstrated that it was in the reform business for the long haul, and nothing would be able to get it off the tracks.

When evaluating this period, outsiders tend to be highly critical of the current regime, one of only a handful of Communist-controlled systems still in existence. Clearly, the regime's economic record is many miles ahead of any of its political achievements. Rulers and regimes around the world have discovered that their people cannot be kept quiet forever, as suggested in the following ancient Chinese maxim:

To forbid people's criticism is more dangerous than to dam a river. The obstructed water will certainly burst with the collapse of the dam, and many will be killed as a result. To stop people criticizing will result in the same. Therefore, a successful hydraulic engineer will dredge rivers instead of damming them, and a successful ruler will encourage his people to speak out.[46]

Many governments have learned, as the good engineer does, that dredging the river is the best policy; but by the end of the 1990s China's leaders are still refusing to accept that argument and are insistent about building dams (see Chapter 16).

It is difficult to be precise in evaluating the success of the socialist economy in postliberation China, partly because of the shortage of useful indicators, and partly because of political bias among the observers. In historical terms, however, there is little doubt that Chinese socialism brought an end to the destitution of the 1930s and 1940s. By the 1980s China was able to feed, clothe, and shelter its people considerably better than many of the world's poor countries.[47] The growth of gross domestic product (GDP) in China during the 1980s and 1990s has been higher than virtually every other country in the world. Even more startling, China's growth has outstripped growth in the newly industrializing economies of South Korea, Taiwan, Singapore, and Hong Kong (see Table 4.1).

The indicators in Table 4.1 show that China has significantly outperformed the other Asian developing countries in a number of ways. The birthrate in China is far lower than average for a developing country and as low as birthrates in some of the NIEs. On another measure of the overall quality of life—the per capita availability of doctors—China is better placed than all the other counties, with the exception of Japan. Yet in comparison to the NIEs China lags far behind in important areas, most notably in average income; the proportion of the workforce engaged in service occupations; and infant mortality.[48]

It is a safe bet that Mao, much like the CCP leaders in 1989, would not have tolerated the scenes that were broadcast worldwide from Tiananmen Square that April and May. No

TABLE 4.1　Economic Growth in Asia and Selected Western Countries

Country	GNP Per Capita (1993 US$)	Average Annual Growth Rate of GNP (%) 1980–1993	Average Annual Growth Rate of Exports 1970–1980	Average Annual Growth Rate of Exports 1980–1993	Gross Domestic Savings as % of GNP 1965	Gross Domestic Savings as % of GNP 1989
China	490	8.2	8.7	11.5	25	36
Asian NIEs						
Hong Kong	18,060	5.4	9.9	15.8	29	35
Taiwan	10,200[1]	6.9[2]	19.0	12.7[3]	29	27[4]
South Korea	7,660	8.2	22.7	12.3	8	37
Singapore	19,850	6.1	4.7	12.7	10	43
Developed Asia						
Japan	31,490	3.4	9.2	4.2	30	34
Developing Asia						
India	340	3.0	5.9	7.0	15	21
Bangladesh	220	2.1	−2.4	9.8	8	1
Philippines	850	−0.6	7.2	3.4	21	18
Indonesia	740	4.2	6.5	6.7	8	37
Malaysia	3,140	3.5	3.3	12.6	24	34
Thailand	2,110	6.4	8.4	15.5	19	29
Other Developed Countries						
United States	24,740	1.7	7.0	5.1	12	13
Canada	19,970	1.4	4.5	5.6	20	23
United Kingdom	18,060	2.3	4.3	4.0	12	18

SOURCE: *World Development Report,* 1995, Tables 1 (pp. 162–163) and 13 (pp. 186–187). Savings data for 1991, *World Development Report,* Table 7 (pp. 206–207).

NOTES:
[1] Statistics for 1991 (estimated).
[2] Statistics for 1965–1986.
[3] Statistics for 1980–1986.
[4] Statistics for 1986.

doubt he would have evaluated his old adversary, Deng Xiaoping, very negatively for his part in the reform process, although he would probably have approved of the hard-line solution to the student demonstrations. Such speculations about the past provide an important way of putting current activities into their historical context. Obviously we will never know what Mao would have thought about Deng, but we do not have to speculate about what Deng and his colleagues at the top of the CCP have thought about Mao since his death; most is a matter of public record and has been published in different formats over the past decade.[49]

Politics and Reform in Post-Mao China

From our end-of-the-millennium vantage point, there are obvious shifts in the way power in China has been exercised since 1949. One of the most notable has been a shift from political logic—with ideological concerns uppermost— to a situation in which economics is very much in command, in the sense that greater emphasis has been given to such issues as profits and comparative advantage. Superimposed onto this fundamental political-economic dynamic are shifts in the scale or structural location of

TABLE 4.2   *Fang-shou* Cycles in the First Decade of the Reform Era

Year/Phase	Key Events
First Round (1978–1979)	
1978 (fang)	"Criterion of Truth" debate
	Democracy Wall
	Third Plenum of the 11th Central Committee
1979 (shou)	The arrest of Wei Jinsheng
	Reassertion of the Four Cardinal Principles
Second Round (1980–1981)	
1980 (fang)	Gengshen reforms
	Local elections
1981 (shou)	Economic readjustment
	Bai Hua criticized
Third Round (1982–1983)	
1982 (fang)	Constitution revised
	"Humanism" and "Alienation" Debated
1983 (shou)	Antispiritual Pollution Campaign
Fourth Round (1984–1985)	
1984 (fang)	Urban reform and "open cities"
	Cultural and artistic freedom
1985 (shou)	Economic retrenchment
	Critique of bourgeois liberalization
Fifth Round (1986–1987)	
1986 (fang)	Revival of Gengshen reforms
	Student demonstrations
1987 (shou)	Hu Yaobang dismissed
	Campaign against "bourgeois liberalization"
Sixth Round (1988–1989)	
1988 (fang)	Neo-authoritarianism (late 1987)
	Administrative reform
1989 (shou)	Economic reforms frozen (late 1988)
	Post–Tiananmen Square crackdowns

SOURCE: Modified from Baum (1997), p. 6.

emphasis, alternating between centralized planning and policymaking to more decentralized periods, when power and authority transferred downward, either to regions (including provinces, cities, and counties) or to enterprises (as was the case after 1978).[50]

Closer analysis reveals shorter policy cycles, which appear to be related to a deep-seated desire to maintain social stability and keep the peace. As Richard Baum has pointed out, during the reform era the state, which seeks the benefits of modernization without the destabilizing effects of social mobilization, has "tended to follow each new round of liberalizing reform with an attempt to retain, or regain control."[51] During the 1980s, for example, that produced a series of shifts from periods of *fang* (letting go) to *shou* (tightening up), which have resulted in an "oscillating pattern of policy initiative and response," as different phases of the reforms alternated between liberalization and retrenchment (see Table 4.2).[52]

Susan Shirk has suggested that these policy shifts were the manifestations of political and ideological cleavages among rival factions within the leadership. At times, when the factional struggles became too intense, the "paramount leader" (Deng Xiaoping) would be forced to intervene, usually by letting the air out of the reform pressures, with an attendant shift backward in the direction of leftism and Leninist orthodoxy.[53]

During the interregnum between the leadership of Mao Zedong and Deng Xiaoping (1976–1978), Hua Guofeng was in power, but his ascendancy rested on a fragile base of support. According to Baum, Hua "wrapped himself in the cloak of Maoist infallibility," coupled with an attempt to develop a personality cult of his own.[54] The ideology during this period is generally referred to as "whateverism," in the sense that Hua and his supporters appeared to believe in, and wanted to implement, whatever Mao had done and said. Lined up against Hua, and soon to replace him, Deng by 1979 had put together a group with quite divergent ideologies, ranging from arch-conservatives and political reactionaries (Chen Yun and Wang Zhen), to reform-minded pragmatists (Zhao Ziyang and Wan Li), to political liberals (Hu Yaobang). Deng's supporters appeared to have little in common with one another, apart from their Lazarus-like qualities; in fact Deng remarked that his group was the "rehabilitated cadres faction," held together by the common experience of public humiliation during the Cultural Revolution and by their opposition to Hua's whateverism. Above all else, Deng's group was committed to restoring order and social stability, as well as economic vitality. They

became known as the "practice faction," with a platform that touted reform and rejected the rigid dogmas of both leftism and rightism.[55] At this time Deng's two principal reformist protégés were Hu Yaobang and Zhao Ziyang, both of whom played major roles in the events leading up to the Tiananmen Square tragedy.[56]

Throughout the 1980s Deng had made attempts (at least four) to overhaul what Baum calls China's "overcentralized, ossified leadership system," but on all occasions he had to abort the projects as a result of the intense factional infighting that characterized the reform era.[57] Twice he had attempted to leave office, but his two handpicked heirs (Hu and Zhao) were rejected by the hardliners. On at least three occasions (see Table 4.2) Deng had attempted to introduce wide-ranging structural reforms (1979, 1984, and 1988), but they were subsequently scuttled by a combination of inflation, rising social unrest, and growing factional strife. Deng could find no effective way to solve the *fang-shou* cyclical character of the 1980s, and he was unable to transfer power over to someone who would eventually be his successor. Baum suggests that as a result Deng was often forced to rely solely on his personal prestige and authority to maintain political stability. This was usually a positive factor, but it also detracted from Deng's oft-stated goal of trying to make the Chinese political system more "routinized" and "rationalized." The great paradox of the Dengist era, in other words, was that the more he attempted to lead China out of the feudal autocracy of the Maoist era toward a more institutionalized political and legal system, the more he was obliged to intervene, using a highly personalized system of control and contradicting his avowed aversion to the Maoist style of cult leadership.

Most scholars agree that Deng Xiaoping had no real blueprints for the reforms, whether economic or political. He was a pragmatist and improviser, implementing a series of piecemeal ad hoc measures that were "designed to facilitate smooth, orderly change."[58] Deng adopted a series of expedient policies, many of which were originally intended to be stopgaps. For example, his implementation of food and housing subsidies in the late 1980s was intended to assuage city dwellers suffering from inflation associated with a too-rapid reform of the pricing system.[59] In this and many other cases, what had originally been intended as stepping-stones became permanent fixtures, effectively deferring more substantial reforms to a later date. In effect the need to bargain and compromise with conservatives worked to prevent more significant reforms and diluted the impact of what was achieved—all of which gave Deng's opponents more cause for optimism.[60]

Deng is remembered most for authorizing the actions to terminate the insurrection in Tiananmen Square in June 1989. It is useful, therefore, to summarize that situation to highlight some of the causes of the crisis, as well as Deng's role in the events.[61] By the beginning of 1989 the stresses of the reform era had heated to the boiling point. Both the economy and the society appeared to be "stalled midway between plan and market, between bureaucrats and entrepreneurs, between *shou* and *fang*."[62] In some ways this was a crisis of "incomplete reform" in which China suffered from the worst effects of the old system without enjoying the benefits of the new system.[63] When the crisis was eventually terminated, Deng's carefully constructed coalition had fallen apart: Several of his more liberal supporters had either died or been dismissed or exiled. A wave of repression, recrimination, and regimentation washed over China. Deng's piecemeal reforms had weakened the old system, which had been efficient at distributing scarce resources equitably; but the new system was not yet efficient enough to generate widespread prosperity.[64] This meant that the stability and predictability of the past had been replaced by crisis events: inflation, panic buying, hoarding of goods, and runs on the banks.

All this exacerbated existing policy conflicts within the leadership, who in turn reinforced popular doubts about whether the Party-state was competent enough to manage either the economy or the political system. Deng and his leadership clique had staked their legitimacy on the ambitious reform program, but after an excellent beginning (lasting until 1985; see Chapter 7), problems associated with the reforms began to overshadow the benefits. By this time it was simply not possible for the state to order a massive retrenchment and restructuring, because too many new reform constituencies had been created.[65] Marc Blecher has argued that the boldness of the student protesters in 1989 was rooted in their perceptions of indecisiveness at the top level.[66] That indecisiveness had become apparent the previous year, when no really firm grip was placed on the economic issues that were starting to backfire, especially the price reforms. The students added other concerns to their agenda, the most serious being rampant corruption, one of the unintended consequences of the half-reformed economy.

Other economic concerns were heaped onto this already unstable base: stagnating productivity; rising state deficits; cyclical overheating and austerity; growing inequality and deteriorating living standards; and a range of emerging social problems. It is important to note that in 1989 there was widespread discontent in China, and the students were supported by many urban groupings. The old assumption—that the Chinese are politically apathetic, especially in the face of what Blecher refers to as "consumerist hedonism and alienated self-absorption"—has clearly proved inaccurate, particularly in the countryside, where numerous revolts and demonstrations were reported in the late 1980s (and would continue into the 1990s).[67] It is also evident that the divisions in Chinese society, so apparent in 1989, are present more than a decade later. Given the mounting evidence of the peasants' willingness to take matters into their own hands, the Chinese state should certainly not get too complacent.[68] Deng declared publicly that the Tiananmen insurgency was "the inevitable result of the domestic microclimate and the international macroclimate," by which he meant that domestic instability was influenced (and perhaps instigated) by events associated with China's new relationships with the outside world, especially the United States.[69]

This issue added to and complicated some of the more basic political problems China faced in the late 1980s: the question of Deng's successor; the conflicts between the central government and the localities;[70] the rapidly changing nature of Chinese society, especially the emergence of new middle-class groups in both city and countryside (see Chapters 7 and 8); and rising expectations among the Chinese, many of whom were unable to keep up with newly rich fellow citizens. It was also obvious that clearheaded decisionmaking about future reforms was necessary and that regardless of which policies were implemented—either further liberalizations or more retrenchments—some groups would inevitably feel more pain than others. In 1989 the state was required to respond to all of these changes and had to find a way to either suppress or incorporate the demands of the emerging groups in the new China.[71] Joseph Fewsmith summarized this well in suggesting that Tiananmen marked an upheaval along "three interrelated fault lines" between the conservatives (leftists) and reformers within the Party; between the Party-state and the emerging forces of society; and between China and the outside world.[72]

When the dust had settled after Tiananmen, many observers offered interpretations of the events. Looking back more than a decade, however, the most salient question remains how the Party-state in China managed to avoid the fates that befell other regimes around the world during that period (especially those in Eastern and Central Europe). The regime in China had (and in many cases still has) a number of obvious advantages compared to regimes elsewhere in the world:

- State socialism in China, unlike socialism in most of Eastern Europe and Central Asia, was associated with national liberation rather than national subjection—in other words it was a homegrown rather than a Soviet-installed communist regime;[73]
- Nationalism was not a major issue, which meant there was no single unifying theme around which a comprehensive challenge to the regime could be launched;

- There was a real sense of fear among Chinese people of embarking on a series of events that were likely to provoke widespread political chaos, social disorder, and a return to prerevolutionary warlordism and internecine struggles;[74]
- There had never been any real development of a "civil society," any meaningful distinction between the public and private spheres, and, at best, a rudimentary notion of individual autonomy as separate from the state;[75]
- The CCP, in spite of its reputation for corruption as well as its declining moral and political authority, was able to act decisively and brutally against the opposition, which was unable to offer concrete suggestions for the future other than challenging the leadership and demanding Party reforms;
- The cumulative benefits of more than a decade of reform-induced economic growth created a safety cushion for the regime and gave many Chinese people a visible stake in seeing the status quo—and the present regime—survive;[76]
- The armed forces showed loyalty and obedience to the civilian command of the CCP, especially at the crucial moment in June 1989; and
- There appeared (at least in hindsight) to be important schisms within the student movement over the means and ends of their struggle and an apparent refusal of some of the student leaders to cooperate fully with factory workers and other potential allies; as scholars later reported it appears that a radical faction within the student leadership led by Chai Ling finally persuaded the students to stay in Tiananmen Square in late May rather than retreat.[77]

In the end Deng Xiaoping became known as the "Butcher of Beijing" for his actions at Tiananmen Square. He never apologized for or allowed a reconsideration of the events; in fact he lobbied hard in the 1990s to make certain that the "counterrevolutionary" label not be removed from the list of public enemies associated with the Tiananmen incident.[78]

Deconstructing Deng Xiaoping and His Legacy

The people ... will have to pass judgement [on Deng]. Most of them will see blemishes on his record ... more black than white. But the majority are likely to see more white than black, if only for having lifted them to a standard of life unknown, and undreamed of, by their parents.

—Richard Evans, *Deng Xiaoping and the Making of Modern China* (1995)[79]

In his biography of Deng Xiaoping, Richard Evans, who was British ambassador to China from 1984 to 1988, reached the conclusion that Deng's legacy, on balance, would be a positive one. Richard Baum would agree with that assessment, yet both believe Deng's will be a tarnished legacy, "laced with contradiction and paradox."[80] Deng combined pragmatism with opportunism, as exemplified by his two most quoted sayings: The first exhorted Chinese people to "seek truth from facts" rather than falling back on outmoded ideology and dogma; the second was his famous statement about "black cats and white cats"—and which was best at getting the job done. Deng was willing to experiment in the economic sphere, leading him where no Chinese (or communist) leader had ever dared go before, uncoupling the notion of market competition (considered to be good) from the stigma of capitalist exploitation (considered bad). Deng threw open China's doors to fast-track capitalism and modernization. As he did, however, Deng always liked to keep his options open, which some outsiders interpret as indecisiveness, others as opportunism: "While pressing hard with one foot on the developmental accelerator, Deng kept the other foot firmly on the political brake. The resulting disjunctive stress—marked by periodic overheating, episodic repression, and spasmodic

forward progress—brought the system perilously close to the point of breakdown in 1989."[81]

After the events at Tiananmen Square, indeed for much of 1990 and 1991, the economy was deliberately retrenched. By the end of 1992, however, economic reforms were being cranked up again—yet there were still no prospects for political reform.[82] In fact new laws and regulations restricting demonstrations were promulgated; ideological campaigns for "socialist spiritual civilization" and against "bourgeois liberalization" were renewed; and there were ominous overtones that the liberalizers might be labeled "class enemies" again—a term that had almost disappeared by 1989.[83]

The crackdowns helped to achieve two years of political quiescence, allowing the Party-state to risk reopening the economic reforms by 1992.[84] Economic austerity was officially announced to be over, and that announcement was followed by reports of Deng Xiaoping's now famous "tour" of southern China (*nanxun*). Deng liked what he saw and was full of praise for the reformers, especially in Guangdong Province, encouraging a deepening of the reforms. Displaying his famous pragmatism, he made the announcement while pointing out that markets per se ought not to be equated with capitalism, reminding his followers that "socialism's real nature is to liberate [the] productive forces."[85] In the new round of economic reforms, the city of Shanghai was to be included; in fact it was to play a key role in China's modernization campaign, which certainly helped Deng to increase his support among the powerful individuals and factions from Shanghai (including Jiang Zemin and Zhu Rongji).

What Deng Xiaoping was able to achieve after Tiananmen appears now to be a skillful mix of relatively passive policies emphasizing social stability, promoting economic development, and relaxing ideological fervor—all of which made good sense and were guaranteed to offend as few people as possible.[86] As Deng said at the time, "stability overrides everything," and he called for "doing some things to satisfy the people." For example, he launched an attack on corrupt cadres and their families.[87] A potential challenge to his leadership, especially bearing in mind his advancing years and apparent poor health, was the news of the conservative coup d'état launched against the Party-state in the former Soviet Union in 1991. When that coup collapsed after only three days, conservative leaders in China were deflated after being buoyed by the original news and a faint prospect that a sharp move back to the left was still possible. In the aftermath, however, even Deng appeared to be worried about what to do next: Should the Party try to preserve its own rule by emphasizing socialist ideology (leftism), or should it continue with the aggressive reform project (rightism)? Chen Yun, one of Deng's oldest foes, was always arguing for the former course of action and had warned people about Deng's reformist economic czar, Zhu Rongji (who Chen referred to as "China's Yeltsin").

Deng's answer was swift and determined: He advocated a strong push for continued reform, although still firmly adhering to "the socialist course and uphold[ing] the dominant role of public ownership."[88] A top Party official announced that all other work must be subordinate to and serve economic construction and that the Party must not allow its "attention to be diverted or turned away" from economic construction, which signaled a clear rebuke to the leftist faction.[89] From this point on, Deng and his followers were able to distance themselves from and enjoy victories over Party leaders on the left. Deng continually emphasized that there could only be "one center" within the party—that associated with the push toward continued economic development. His opponents, chiefly the aging Chen Yun, believed there should be two centers: one focusing on "economic construction," the other on "ideological construction."[90]

Chen and Deng, the two old soldiers whose careers had run along parallel tracks for decades, were in full competition for more than two years on these issues, which were settled in the winter of 1992, after Deng's tour of the southlands. After the tour the competition

between Deng and Chen seemed to be over: Deng had won, and a bandwagon effect set in as more and more former conservatives and fence-sitters fell into line and declared their support for Deng's theory of one center. At this time those who had been largely bystanders in the ongoing struggle, including Li Peng and Qiao Shi, joined Deng's coalition.[91] Jiang Zemin, correctly perceiving which way the wind was blowing, publicly rejected his own earlier stance, stating that he now believed China must continue its drive to economic development, which would mandate the use of "all the social productive forces and all the excellent cultural achievements made in capitalist society."[92] Deng had directed most of his criticism at the leftists within the Party; in fact he warned his compatriots to "watch out for the Right, but mainly defend against the Left," which neatly negated Chen's dictate to do exactly the opposite. Deng's argument was based on his belief that the left was at that time more dangerous because it had more power. He was thinking about such individuals as Deng Liqun, Li Ximing, and Song Ping, in addition to Chen Yun. Deng Xiaoping is quoted as saying: "Some theorists and politicians have used serious charges to intimidate people. . . . To them, it seems that being Leftist is equal to being revolutionary. [They] denounce reform and openness for introducing and developing capitalism, and hold that the main danger of peaceful evolution comes from the economic field. This is Leftism."[93]

The leftists blamed the reforms (and the reformers) for the problems that had occurred throughout the 1980s (including Tiananmen) and into the 1990s, arguing that recentralization of Party and government controls was needed to counteract some of the menacing trends associated with the reforms. On the other side, the rightist reformers wanted to see even more reform, arguing that the problems were caused by the incomplete nature of what had been done thus far.[94] At this time most of the issues being debated were either political or economic, but there were also some breakthroughs in the cultural realm, with public recognition of what was becoming increasingly obvious, namely, that art and literature should no longer be used as weapons of political indoctrination. Such things, in other words, could now simply be devoted to entertainment and aesthetics (see Chapter 3).[95]

The usual calculus when referring to Deng's legacy is to match the positives against the negatives. The positives are obvious and include the extraordinary growth of China's economy. Deng's era was also relatively tranquil, both domestically and internationally, except for the Tiananmen tragedy. The negatives, if we are to believe He Qinglian and others (see Chapter 1), are considerable. There has certainly been, as Richard Baum suggests, "a deep erosion of traditional ideological norms and social controls [that] produced a situation high in raw entrepreneurial energy but low in institutionalized immunity to a wide variety of potential systemic disorders, ranging from rising regional inequality and uncontrolled rural emigration to a nationwide epidemic of crime, corruption, and popular cynicism."[96]

The anonymous author of the *Third Eye* book (see Chapter 1) argued that long before Deng's death (in fact in 1993) the reforms were careening out of control, with a dangerous situation brewing from the increasing inequality that some observers felt might culminate in a social explosion; this fear was starting to boil again at the end of the century.[97] In this sense, then, it would be reasonable to expect Premier Jiang Zemin to attempt to arrest such trends, perhaps following the lead of neoconservative critics calling for a restoration of central authority, which would require some newly inspired unifying ideology. If Mao represented the first generation of communist leaders, those who created the theory of revolutionary socialism; and Deng and his followers were the second generation, attempting to build "socialism with Chinese characteristics"; then Jiang and his supporters represent the third generation, who will

be called upon to make some critical decisions about ideology and policy, perhaps even to save the Party from the dustbin of history.

Joseph Fewsmith suggests that Deng's most serious failing was his inability either to recognize or address obvious fundamental flaws in the Chinese political system.[98] Most notably, no attempt was made during Deng's reign to change the belief that China must be governed by a regime in which political power is unified, monistic, and indivisible.[99] As Fewsmith observed, "Instead of political conflicts being resolved through bargaining and compromise, they become part of a game to 'win all.'"[100] Deng was, however, responsible for de-emphasizing (abandoning, in fact) the importance of class and class struggle. For Deng, what was or was not "socialist" should be decided not through polemical argument but through practice. Deng was impatient with ideology and debate; he wanted, and he assumed that most Chinese people desired, to return to (or create) normal patterns of life, so he worked hard to steer a path between the extreme right and left sides of the Party and to build a coalition that could see China through the tumultuous years of transition. In broad terms, he was able to do just that, thereby temporarily bridging the deep fissures among the leadership. Although a short-run solution had been found, the rules of political conflict and the methods by which such conflicts were solved did not change in the least. The upshot is that Deng handed over a political system essentially unchanged in terms of conflicts within the Party as well as those between the Party-state and society. The question to ask, then, in assessing Deng's legacy, is whether he was able to create "conditions that will allow the next generation of leaders to tackle the problems of China's political system that he himself did not resolve." Fewsmith concluded that after nineteen years Deng had accomplished many things, but institution-building was not among them.[101]

5

China's Population: Resistance, Compliance, and the National Interest

If we let the population grow without effectively controlling it, the realization of the second step strategic goal for China's modernization drive will be directly affected, and the efforts to further improve the people's living standards will be thwarted. This will create heavier pressure on economic and social development in the next century, further reduce China's per capita resources, worsen its environment, and bring endless misery to our posterity.

—Xinhua News Agency (April 28, 1991)[1]

Introduction: The Politics of Reproduction

When the Communists took power in 1949, demographers in the West were convinced that drastic measures were needed to slow the growth rate of the Chinese population. Mao Zedong, however, was not convinced of that; in fact he was dismissive of such advice, referring to it as "bourgeois" Malthusian propaganda. In what would later become one of his better-known public pronouncements, Mao observed in 1949 that

> of all things in the world, people are the most precious. Under the leadership of the Communist Party, as long as there are people, every kind of miracle can be performed. We believe that revolution can change everything, and that before long there will arise a new China with a big population and a great wealth of products, where life will be abundant and culture will flourish. All pessimistic views are utterly groundless.[2]

With statements like this Mao effectively put a damper on the incipient birth control movement in China. After the arduous struggle against the Japanese, followed by the long civil war against the Nationalists, Mao felt that to implement birth control policies would be a cruel punishment for the long-suffering Chinese people. He felt it would be unfair, in a purportedly egalitarian society, to punish the poor for having too many children, and in his opinion birth control was little more than "a means of killing off the Chinese people without shedding blood."[3] Mao reasoned that the Chinese masses were a major component of the productive forces, and in fact they represented the only component that was in a healthy condition after the revolutionary struggles. For a few years Mao's views went unchallenged, and despite great debate over birth control policies, the official party line was that China's population should continue to grow. Mao was not worried about China having too many people because, as he put it in one of his pithy sayings, "every stomach comes with two hands attached."[4] The effects of this decision—or rather nondecision—can be seen in the population growth rates recorded into the 1970s (see Table 5.1).

In 1956 the greatly revered Chinese premier, Zhou Enlai, had publicly announced his sup-

TABLE 5.1   Major Demographic Statistics for China, 1950–1966

Year	Total Population (millions)	Birthrate (per 1,000)	Death Rate (per 1,000)	Natural Growth Rate (per 1,000)	Total Fertility Rate
1950	552	37.00	18.00	19.00	5.81
1955	615	32.60	12.30	20.30	6.26
1960	662	20.90	25.40	-4.50	4.02
1965	725	37.88	9.50	28.38	6.08
1970	830	33.43	7.60	25.83	5.81
1975	924	23.01	7.32	15.69	3.57
1980	987	18.21	6.34	11.87	2.24
1985	1,059	21.04	6.78	14.26	2.20
1990	1,114	21.06	6.67	14.39	2.31
1991	1,158	19.68	6.70	12.98	—
1992	1,171	18.24	6.64	11.60	1.96[1]
1993	1,185	18.09	6.64	11.45	—
1994	1,195	17.70	6.49	11.21	—
1995	1,211	17.12	6.52	10.55	—
1996	1,224	16.98	6.56	10.42	1.80[2]

SOURCES: Adapted from Goldstein, 1996, Table 1.1, p. 6; 1991–1996 data from *China Statistical Yearbook, 1997*, Table 3-2, p. 69; and also Table 3-1, p. 69.

NOTES:

[1] The TFR statistic reported for 1992 (1.65) is based on a survey conducted by the State Family Planning Commission, but Feeney and Yuan (1994) have argued that this was an artificially low estimate and have recalculated it as 1.96.

[2] The estimate for 1996 is taken from *China Population Today*, quoted in Riley and Gardner (1997), p. 11.

port for the concept of planned parenthood, and it seemed likely that a policy change was impending. Even Mao himself was heard to waver on the issue, in 1956, when he wrote: "We have this huge population. It is a good thing, but of course it also has difficulties. . . . Steps must therefore be taken to keep our population for a long time at a stable level, say, of 600 million. A wide campaign of explanation and proper help must be undertaken to achieve this aim."[5] For the next two decades the Chinese government provided such "help" through a series of voluntary measures, including education campaigns and attempts to encourage the use of contraception.[6] The goals of family planning at this time can be broadly described by the three terms *wan* (late), *xi* (thin), and *shao* (fewer). It was hoped that the Chinese people would defer childbirth by marrying later; by spacing out their offspring in intervals of at least four years; and by having fewer children overall.

Until the late 1970s the population policy remained essentially voluntary, and in 1975 the average fertility rate (the number of live births per woman) was between three and four (see Table 5.1). Demographers predicted, if the rate continued, that China would have a population close to 1.5 billion by the year 2000. Even if the fertility rate stayed at the 1978 level, around 2.3, the population would rise to 1.28 billion by that time. This was a frightening prospect in a country so desperately short of land and resources, and to make matters worse a baby boom was expected in the early 1980s as a result of high birthrates in the mid-1960s.[7]

Mao has been criticized since his death on several fronts, including his reluctance to take a firmer stand on the issue of birth control. China's population grew by more than 75 percent between 1949 and 1978, and it was becoming clear to demographers and politicians alike that drastic measures were needed. At this time China had already begun its heralded drive toward the Four Modernizations, the goal of which was to transform China into a powerful and modern socialist society by developing four sectors of the economy: agriculture, industry, science and technology, and national defense.

These modernization reforms emphasized the importance of production and the need to develop the overall skills and professional abilities of the Chinese labor force. There was to be a new emphasis on the profitability of urban and rural enterprises, with a relatively lucrative system of material incentives designed to increase and speed production.

New in China at this time was the first real attempt to link the efforts to increase industrial and agricultural production with the efforts to reduce the growth of the population. It was obvious to some leaders that a population increase of the magnitude experienced during the 1960s and 1970s would become a major barrier to accumulating the capital needed for the modernization drive. As a result the government essentially redefined "production" to include both the production of material goods and the reproduction of human beings. The Chinese people were asked to "grasp these two kinds of production" and to help keep the population down as an integral part of developing the economy.[8] The economic policymakers at this time felt that Mao Zedong had not fully grasped the nature of the link between production and reproduction, hence his decision not to consider implementing any coercive form of population policy. To correct the situation specific targets were laid out in a series of Five Year Plans for both production and reproduction. The goal was to quadruple the gross value of industrial and agricultural production by the year 2000 and to keep the population down to about 1.2 billion by achieving zero population growth at the turn of the century. To do that it was essential to make major changes in China's population control policies.

After extensive deliberation it was decided that a cap would be placed on the number of children each Chinese family was allowed to produce. It was recommended that most families should limit themselves to one child only. There were few consistent official statements regarding the birth of a second child, but there was to be an almost total prohibition on a third child. The slogans in urban areas and among official circles clearly advocated "no second

child," but in the countryside and for certain subgroups the rule was "no more than two." No national standards were set for the official size of families, leaving such judgments to provincial and municipal authorities, who, it was argued, would have the most accurate picture of what was required in their localities.

To sweeten the pill—and to provide this shocking new policy some teeth—incentives encouraged couples with one child to sign a pledge promising to have no more children; penalties would come to those who refused to comply. In Beijing in 1979, for example, it was announced that parents who signed a pledge would receive a Y5 (Chinese yuan) monthly subsidy, in addition to preferential access to nurseries and kindergartens, priority medical care, and the promise of favored treatment in the educational and employment spheres. The family would also receive additional housing space (or a larger plot of land if in the countryside). Punitive economic sanctions were established for families who refused to sign a pledge or failed to adhere to local plans. If the family broke the pledge, it would have to return the subsidy and was in danger of losing all of the other benefits. If a third child was born the family would pay a fine equal to roughly 10 percent of annual income until the child turned fourteen.[9]

China's demographers had calculated that to slow down population growth a drastic reduction in family size was needed. In the attempt to reach zero population growth by the year 2000, the "one-child" policy was considered to be the only viable course of action (see Table 5.2). Most everyone involved was aware of how difficult it would be to implement such a policy: There were more than 240 million women of childbearing age, and producing large families had been the cultural norm for centuries.[10]

A Brief Population Geography

It is possible only to make rough estimates of China's population size and distribution. In addition to numerous boundary changes throughout China's history, its sheer size and

TABLE 5.2   China's Projected Population Increases in Next Thirty Years Under the One-Child Policy, 1985

Year	Population Size (billions)	Number of Women of Childbearing Age (millions)	Births (millions)	Deaths (millions)	Population Growth (per 1,000)	Average Age of Population
1985	0.94	—	16.5	7.4	3.50	29.1
1990	1.02	279	10.2	7.0	3.02	31.7
1995	1.04	299	11.3	8.2	2.95	33.8
2000	1.05	300	10.8	8.9	1.87	35.9
2005	1.05	280	9.1	9.5	−0.39	38.0
2010	1.04	270	7.0	9.7	−2.63	40.5
2015	1.03	240	5.6	9.7	−4.06	43.2

SOURCE: Adapted from *New World Press* (1983), p. 48.

the great distances meant central government rarely had a decent estimate of how many people lived in each province. Reporting rates were inaccurate as a result of deliberate attempts to conceal births, generally to avoid paying taxes, which were based on head counts. From the estimates available, it appears that there may have been just less than 60 million people in the year A.D. 2 (during the Han Dynasty), but from that time on estimates fluctuate wildly.[11] For example, there was an estimated population of only 7.6 million during the Three Kingdoms period (A.D. 220–280), but during the Tang Dynasty (around A.D. 742) the figure reached 50 million. Most scholars agree that China's population remained low, relative to its total land area, for several centuries thereafter, with an overall growth pattern similar to that in Europe.[12] By the end of the fifteenth century China's population may have been less than 100 million, kept low by a combination of natural disasters, famines, and nearly constant warfare.

After 1750 a population explosion occurred in China, and by the start of the twentieth century there were more than 426 million people; by 1949 the count stood at 549 million. The tremendous population growth during the Qing Dynasty has been partly attributed to the prolonged period of relative peace in China, and partly to the introduction of new crops and an increase in lands under cultivation.[13] During the early 1980s China's population passed the 1 billion mark, almost a quarter of the world

total. By the end of the 1980s China's population was increasing by almost 14 million each year, and between 1990 and 1995 the increase averaged more than 13 million annually—this despite two decades of official (some would say draconian) birth control policy.

In the late 1970s concern was expressed by Chinese demographers about two additional demographic facts of life in China. Thanks to the rapid growth rates during the 1950s, 1960s, and 1970s, by 1980 more than 50 percent of the population was younger than twenty-one. This meant some 10 million people became age-eligible to marry each year, and even at a population growth rate of about twelve per 1,000 (see Table 5.1), China's population was projected to grow to more than 1.3 billion by the year 2000. The other concern was that China's population had grown without much increase in the amount of cultivable land; in fact in 1979 there was half as much land per capita (0.1 hectare per person) compared to 1949 (0.2 hectare).[14] This declining hectare-per-person ratio thus became one of the most crucial concerns for Chinese leaders, and in part it accounts for the sharp reversals in agricultural policies since 1978, as well as the all-out attempts to increase agricultural productivity.[15]

It is important to point out that the pressures placed on the land in China have never been equal across China; in fact the vast majority of the population is concentrated in a few low-lying areas where sufficient rainfall and good

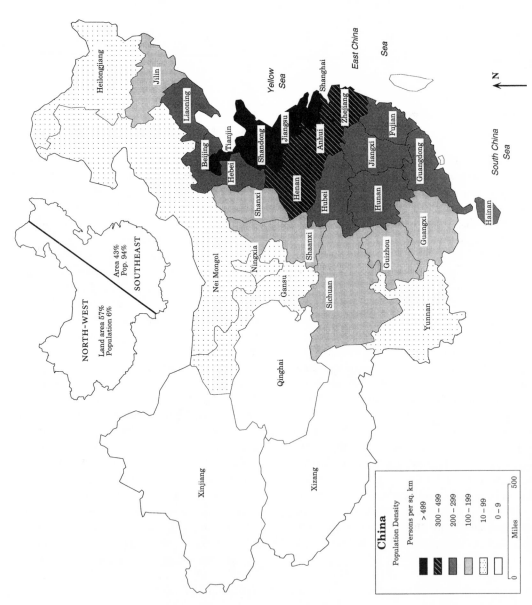

MAP 5.1   China's Population Density and Distribution

soils support intensive agriculture. As Map 5.1 depicts, the major population concentrations are in the North China Plain (Hebei, Shandong, and Henan Provinces); the middle and lower Yangtze Valley; the Pearl River Delta of the Xi (West) River valley in southern China; and the Sichuan Basin.[16]

By contrast, in much of Outer China (e.g., Tibet, Inner Mongolia, Qinghai, Xinjiang, and Heilongjiang) populations are sparsely distributed, principally the result of climate and topography. What becomes apparent from viewing this population map is not so much that China has too many people but that it has too little cultivable land. Today more than 90 percent of the Chinese population lives on about one-sixth of China's total land area. As the late New Zealand geographer Keith Buchanan has observed, "There are few areas in the world where gradients of population density are as steep as they are in China." The contrast between the empty and the filled lands is instantly noticeable "between the closely settled meticulously cultivated flatlands and the empty ravaged upland."[17] Buchanan also pointed out that these patterns have for the most part remained stable over the centuries. As the population of the most desirable land increased, the density would rise, until in some areas "500–600 people . . . were . . . living on an area equal to that of an American family farm supporting 5–6 people."[18]

Implementing the One-Child Policy: A Description

The bigger your family the bigger the fine. . . . This boy of mine worked out at 1300 [yuan]. . . . I paid cash on the nail. If I hadn't they'd have taken out the furniture.

—Big Sister Zheng[19]

At the end of the 1970s China was embarking on an ambitious program of rural and urban economic reform, and it was feared that the benefits of the program—indeed the very success of the reforms—were being threatened by the impending population crisis.[20] This was not the only demographic concern for the Chinese at the time. Improving economic circumstances, as well as some remarkable developments in health care delivery, meant that China's death rate had plummeted since the 1960s. Although everyone was happy that people lived longer, healthier lives, it was feared that the rapid aging of the population would eventually pose problems. These two trends occurring at either end of the demographic spectrum—the falling birthrate and the falling death rate—were beginning to interact with each other to cause concern for many Chinese families by the end of the twentieth century. Because there were fewer children and because people were living longer, there was a concern whether there would be enough adult children to care for aging parents. This concern was especially acute in rural China, as there is little in the way of guaranteed pensions and social security benefits. For centuries, care for aging parents was provided by children, but as the Chinese looked toward the twenty-first century, many feared that tradition, perhaps even the fabric of society, would be difficult to preserve.[21] (In a later section of this chapter we focus on China's elderly population, looking at likely future trends and their implications for Chinese society.)

The one-child population policy was and is one of the most controversial and unpopular policies adopted during the five decades of the PRC. Still, between 1971 and 1985 the net growth rate had been halved, and 21 percent of all couples of childbearing age had only one child. In a country as geographically diverse as China, it should come as no surprise that the success of the new birth control policies varied considerably. In general the best results were seen in urban areas, especially along the eastern coast, with Shanghai, China's most modern city, having the lowest fertility rate (1.32; see Map 5.2). Fertility otherwise increased with distance from the coast, reaching its highest levels in Guizhou Province (4.36) and Ningxia Autonomous Region (4.12). Clearly, the policy was being resisted, even rejected, in some parts of China; in the following sections we explore the

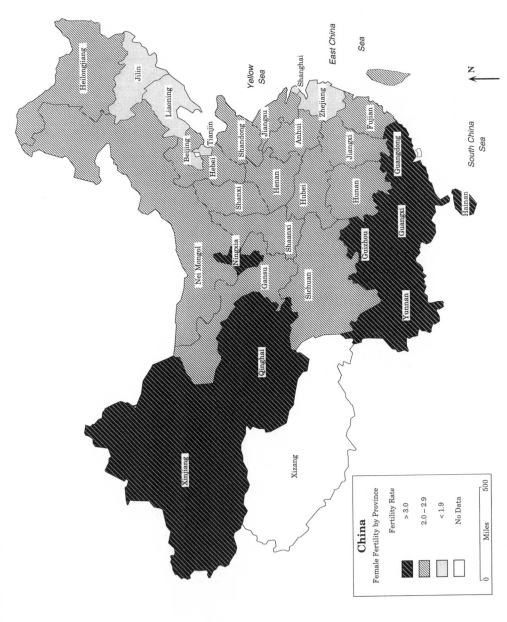

China

Female Fertility by Province

Fertility Rate

- > 3.0
- 2.0 – 2.9
- < 1.9
- No Data

Miles
0   500

MAP 5.2   The Geography of Fertility, 1981

nature and geographical patterns of that resistance.

To explain how such an unpopular policy could have been implemented at all, we need only consider China's political system, as well as the spatial organization of administration that was introduced into the cities and countryside during the 1950s. As noted in Chapter 2, the Chinese government has consistently launched mass campaigns in which the people were required to participate. As for family planning, campaigns were introduced to educate families on the need to lower the birthrate and the means to achieve such an end. Compared to more democratic political systems, in China it was relatively easy to enforce new policies and impress upon the public the consequences of noncompliance. Moreover, the organizational structures in both city and countryside were instrumental in administering the new birth control policies. Through the extensive and virtually all-embracing hierarchy of the organizational units, birth control propaganda was disseminated from the top all the way down to the street and the farm levels. More important, the organization facilitated close surveillance of individuals to make sure they understood the reasons for the policy and to guarantee cooperation.

Using this existing spatial hierarchy, the State Council's Office of Family Planning was able to enforce state policies down to the lowest levels. In rural communes and urban districts all activities were coordinated by a family planning committee. This included distribution of contraceptives; organization of study groups to explain the need for family planning; establishment of strategies to persuade or to force compliance; and, as always, constant surveillance to monitor actual and potential deviations. In the cities such work was performed either in the *danwei* or in the residents' neighborhood-based

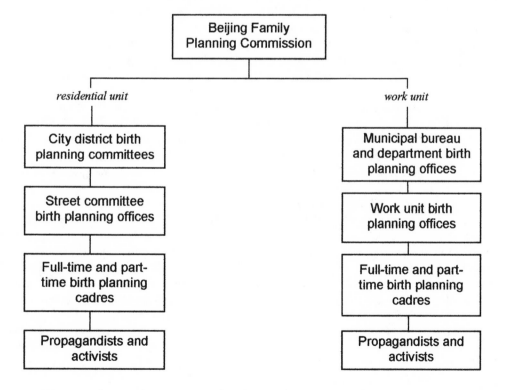

FIGURE 5.1   The Spatial Organization of Birth Control Planning in Beijing

committee, where detailed records were kept on all women of childbearing age (see Figure 5.1).

The norm is for face-to-face contact between families and trained medical and paramedical personnel, their advice being reinforced by nonspecialist neighborhood and *danwei* leaders. In addition there was constant pressure on individuals, from workmates and neighbors, to conform to the policy, not only because it would benefit China as a whole but also because most people, especially the local leaders, realized that noncompliance at the unit level reflected poorly on all members.

It was rumored that in the 1980s birth control cadres were required to reinforce policies at any cost, in the knowledge that they would be the ones to suffer if birth quotas were exceeded. This was especially important in the countryside, where the desire for extra children has always been greater than in the cities. Even a recalcitrant like Big Sister Zheng in Sichuan sometimes felt sorry for local family planning cadres: "They were just doing their job. . . . I hear the township fines the district party secretary and the Family Planning commissioner a lot of money if even one baby more than they're allowed gets born. . . . It has to come out of their own pockets! When they get fined at the end of each year they're in tears."[22] With equal parts of efficiency and intimidation, the spatial organization of Chinese society helped spread the technology of birth control and educate people as to why it was necessary. Most important, it provided a remarkably efficient way of implementing the new policies, particularly by making sure that people comply or, if they do not comply, that they are fully aware of the consequences.[23]

In geographical terms the success of the one-child policy has been uneven to say the least, with compliance highest in the cities and lowest in the remotest parts of the countryside. In the 1982 sample census, for example, the birthrate was estimated to be 14.5 per 1,000 in urban areas, compared to 22.4 in rural areas.[24] Several plausible geographical hypotheses can explain differences in urban and rural growth rates since the new policies were put in force. Certainly greater access to family planning clinics

in the cities is one explanation, as well as a far lower perceived need to bear children for the additional labor they supply. It seems, however, that most of the spatial variation is the result of differences in implementing the one-child policy at local levels. Reports from around the country demonstrate that there have been numerous legal exemptions from the one-child policy, allowing what amounts to second-child births "in conformity with the plan." Such exemptions are granted at the provincial and municipal levels and are intended to shape reproduction plans to local circumstances.

The most notable exemptions arise in the Autonomous Regions (ARs), where many of China's ethnic minority people live.[25] In Ningxia Hui in northwestern China, an area populated by Muslims, minority families are allowed to have two children in the cities, three in the rural areas. As we shall explore in Chapter 12, the relaxation of the policy in the Autonomous Regions has been part of the government's overall attempt to provide social and economic benefits to China's minority populations.[26] In provinces with predominantly Han populations there generally have been fewer exemptions, but again the geographical differences are considerable.[27]

Most people living in rural areas were expected to observe the one-child rule, but if they wanted a second child they could apply to their local birth control authorities for an exemption. Permission was granted to couples who qualified in any of four categories or if their first child was a girl. Most observers agree that the preference for boys is evident all across China, but it is traditionally strongest in the rural areas.[28] In most cases the preference for sons is inversely correlated with the usual indicators of modernization; it tends to be relatively low in the cities and among better-educated families. The actual extent of son preference varies from place to place. For example, there is a slight preference for girls in Beijing, but in Jilin Province there is a 14 percent difference in favor of boys (see Map 5.3).[29]

The primary reason families prefer sons is economic, that is, to generate income and to

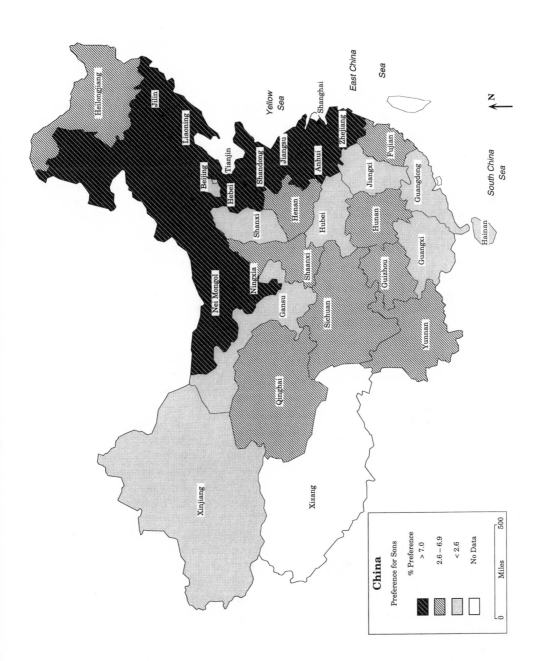

MAP 5.3   Preference for Sons by Province, 1982

provide security for elderly parents. Only a small percentage of China's peasants are entitled to a pension, and the traditional so-called Five Guarantees of the welfare state (covering costs for food, clothing, fuel, burial, and raising children) are rarely adequate. Because of the tradition of exogamy in most parts of China, women generally leave home to marry. Faced with that prospect, parents are convinced that having sons is the best way to ensure someone will be there to support them in the future. Hence only a son will satisfy many parents, whereas the birth of a daughter is often considered to be only a "small happiness."

Exemptions from the one-child policy are possible for couples experiencing "true difficulties" that make it vital for them to have a larger family; as might be expected, the definition of "difficulties" varies considerably from one place to another.[30] In spite of all the exemptions and legal loopholes, however, the majority of second-child and subsequent births have occurred "outside the plan"; in other words it is the result of families not complying with the one-child policy. Data from the 1982 One-per-Thousand Fertility Survey provide some evidence of the extent of noncompliance and suggest some plausible explanations. In one study, comparing rural areas in four provinces, the percentage of families signing a one-child certificate varied from 24 percent to 76 percent, mainly as a result of differences in the intensity of the local campaigns.[31] Of the couples who signed the pledge, 6 percent reneged within a year, with rates varying from a low of less than 1 percent in urban Beijing to a high of 18 percent in rural Henan Province. In general very few urban couples had another child, but the violation rates in the rural areas varied from 11.3 percent in Henan to 26.8 percent in Hebei. In some areas there were no instances of families breaking the pledge, whereas in others all eligible couples had a second child.[32]

There are many claims, and even some evidence, that the one-child policy has contributed to a resurgence in the odious practice of female infanticide in China. Although the practice is officially illegal in China, the abnormally high ratio of males to females among children in many parts of the country implies that local officials may be turning a blind eye (see Chapter 13). As much as the authorities would like to deny the existence of female infanticide, there are suspicions that it still occurs in many parts of rural China.[33]

Resisting the One-Child Policy: An Evaluation

To determine whether the one-child policy has been successful, it is necessary to ask three related questions. Were the program's initial goals met? Did the program actually result in lower rates of fertility? In light of its costs and benefits, was the program worthwhile? In answering the first question, if we look only at statistics it is possible to conclude that the goals of the program were more or less attained. Total fertility rates dropped from a high of 6.47 in 1952 to 2.31 in 1990 (see Table 5.1). In the 1950s and 1960s the net growth of China's population had always been in excess of 20 per 1,000, and in 1971 it stood at 23.4 per 1,000. By 1980 the growth rate had been more than halved, to 11.87 per 1,000.[34] By 1983 56 percent of all births in China were first births and only 19 percent were third births, a remarkable turnaround from the figures in 1970 (20 percent and 62 percent respectively).[35] Although not all of these achievements resulted directly from the one-child policy per se, it now seems that total population by the year 2000 will be on the order of 1,272,400,000 (based on the 1996 total of 1,217,600,000, with a 1.1 percent per annum natural growth rate). This is consistent with the "about" 1.2 billion population goal set in 1984.

As for the second question (fertility rates), it is difficult to reach a clear-cut conclusion. The one-child policy was implemented at the beginning of 1979, but the statistics clearly show that China's total fertility rate was already dropping by that date; in fact it fell from almost 6 per woman/family in the early 1950s to 2–3 by 1979 (the first year the program was implemented). This had been achieved under the auspices of the old ("voluntary") birth control policies. As critics of the new policies pointed out, fertility barely declined at all during the 1980s, the first decade of the one-child program.[36] Except for the first year, the policy seems to have had little effect in reducing the fertility rate.[37] On balance, then, over a two-decade period the fertility decline in China was larger and faster than probably anywhere else in the world, yet the one-child policy was only partly—and sporadically—responsible for the decline in fertility.[38]

In rural China resistance to the one-child policy was widespread, and in the mid-1980s more than 90 percent of rural women were still having two or more (second-order) births.[39] The failure—in statistical terms—of the one-child policy in the countryside is often a result of the local birth control offices being short-handed and overworked. In some of the more remote areas it is also clear that education and knowledge about the program and its potential benefits were seriously lacking. This was certainly the case in Hubei Province, where one study reported that out of more than 1,200 women with two or more children only 5 percent had even heard about their local family planning program; 27 percent had never read about it; and 44 percent said they had never considered birth control measures before getting pregnant. Very few women had any knowledge of contraception over and above the use of intrauterine devices (IUDs) and sterilization. It was also evident that in this particular study (which could reflect situations in countless other remote rural areas in China) actual knowledge about birth control and contraception was rudimentary at best, even among program administrators and officials.

As for the third question—was it worthwhile?—there is also room for doubt, primarily because of the enormous psychological and physical suffering the one-child program has meant for Chinese women. In Chapter 13 we shall detail the issue of "missing" women in China—those millions who either are not born or do not survive, in large part because of the strictures of the one-child policy. There is significant evidence that women who "fail" to give

birth to boys are routinely abused, both mentally and physically. In addition it is clear that women's bodies have become the sites of both compliance with and resistance to the birth control program and that both strategies can have disastrous consequences for women.[40] Many women decide to remove their IUDs in an attempt to get pregnant, then have them reinserted after birth. More than four-fifths of women who resist the program by "illegally" removing their IUDs become pregnant within three months. Reports from various parts of rural China have described the mostly squalid and dangerous conditions under which birth control procedures are performed. Having additional children and tampering with IUDs put women's bodies at risk due to poor local care and inadequate facilities. It is also likely that women who resist the program are labeled as troublemakers and marked for harsh treatment in the future. In another context, women who resist the exhortation to abort "illegal" (i.e., above-quota) pregnancies early on often face the prospect of being coerced into much more dangerous late-term abortions.[41]

The relative lack of success of the one-child policy in rural China has meant that the long-cherished goal of 1.2 billion people and zero population growth by the year 2000 was not attainable.[42] What may have seemed like a minor change in 1987—when the population target was altered from 1.2 billion to "about" 1.2 billion—in fact signified government flexibility on the birth control issue.[43] In spite of the impressive achievements associated with the fertility transition in China, the rate of progress slowed considerably during the late 1980s; in fact in 1986, population growth increased for the first time since the implementation of the new policies, largely as a result of rising birthrates in the middle and late 1980s (see Table 5.1), which produced a net growth rate of 14.26 for 1985 compared to 11.87 in 1980.[44]

A contributing factor to rising birthrates after 1985 was the official relaxation of the one-child policy at the central level. In 1984 and again in 1986 the Party's Central Committee issued documents intended to produce greater flexibility within the policy itself.[45] Coercion was to be phased out in favor of more systematic birth control efforts (thereby ruling out crash programs based on quotas for either births or abortions). As many observers of the program have contended, the state has not been able to alter in any significant way the demands of rural families to have additional children, especially boys,[46] so by the end of the 1980s it was obvious that the time had come to reorient the program. The new thrust was to move away from the simplistic (but enormously difficult to achieve) focus on quantitative measures such as birthrates and fertility, to focus instead on providing better education and living standards for women in the countryside, as well as on offering safer and more effective reproductive health care.[47]

The reliance on inflexible methods of birth control (sterilization and IUDs) was to be switched to more voluntary methods, and educational propaganda was to replace the emphasis on economic sanctions and rewards that had previously been the mainstay of the one-child program. The changes thus indicated three major policy shifts:

1. administrative improvements, which were intended to base policies on the "scientific" study of local conditions, and the introduction of more efficient styles of management;
2. strategic improvements, or a shift from focusing on changing people's ideas about having additional children to improving local socioeconomic conditions to reduce the perception that having more children is an economic necessity; and
3. political improvements, or a shift from the assumption that people can be ordered what to do toward a greater reliance on persuasion and an understanding of geographical variations in social and cultural characteristics.

The impact of these changes was felt almost immediately in the countryside, where many peasant families were allowed a second child, often with the stipulation that a certain length of time had elapsed since the birth of the last child—effectively reverting birth control policy to that which existed during the 1960s and 1970s. In spite of this shift the Party took great pains to point out that the policy was far too important to be dismantled and that the relaxations did *not* herald a major change in direction, merely that it was time to improve the implementation of the policies.[48]

It is important to put the achievements and failures of the one-child policy into a broader historical-geographical context. The data reviewed here suggest that China experienced its demographic transition in record time compared to most other countries. The normal phases of such a transition are: a premodernization phase, when both birth and death rates are high; a modernization phase, in which death rates begin to fall but birthrates remain relatively high; and a postmodernization phase, in which both birthrates and death rates are low. Natural population growth is usually extremely high in the first phase, moderately high in the second phase, and low in the final phase. For most societies modernization *precedes* a significant fall in birthrates, mainly because it takes many decades of education and improved living conditions before families are convinced it is in their best interests to limit their reproduction rate. In China this was clearly not the case, and the birthrate fell very rapidly *before* modernization (for example, in 1953 it was 37 per 1,000, but it was significantly below 20 per 1,000 in 1985). If we compare China's demographic statistics in 1988 to those in other parts of the world (see Table 5.3), we see that the birthrate was lower than the global average, approaching that of developed countries.

Compared to birthrates in other developing countries China's was extremely low (21 as opposed to 35 per 1,000). In fact China's death rate was actually slightly lower than in developed countries (7 per 1,000 as opposed to 9 per 1,000) and was significantly lower than in most developing countries (for example, 17 in Bangladesh and 23 in Chad; the developing

TABLE 5.3   China's Population and Comparisons to Other Countries, 1988

	Birth-rate per 1,000	Death Rate per 1,000	Natural Increase % p.a.	Infant Mortality per 1,000 Live Births	Fertility (# of children per Woman 15–49 yrs).	Life Expec-tancy (yrs.)	Urban Pop. %	GNP Per Capita (1982 US$)
China	21	7	1.4	44	2.4	66	41	300
World	28	10	1.7	77	3.6	63	45	3,010
Developed	15	9	0.6	15	1.9	73	73	10,700
Less Developed Excl. China	35	12	2.4	96	4.8	57	35	780
Sweden	12	11	0.1	5.9	1.8	77	83	13,170
Japan	11	6	0.5	5.2	1.7	78	77	12,850
United States	16	9	0.7	10.9	1.8	75	74	17,500
Canada	15	7	0.7	7.9	1.7	76	76	14,100
Australia	15	7	0.8	9.8	1.9	76	86	11,910
United Kingdom	13	12	0.2	9.5	1.8	75	91	8,920
New Zealand	16	8	0.8	10.8	2.0	74	84	7,110
Bangladesh	43	17	2.7	135	5.8	50	16	160
India	33	13	2.0	104	4.3	54	25	270
Haiti	41	13	2.8	117	5.7	54	25	330
Chad	43	23	2.0	143	5.3	39	27	100
Ethiopia	46	15	3.0	118	7.0	50	10	120
Mali	50	22	2.9	175	6.7	43	18	170

SOURCE: Population Reference Bureau (1988), *World Population Data Sheet.*

country average was 12 per 1,000).[49] As we shall investigate in Chapter 6, the reduction in death rates can be attributed primarily to public health measures that represent part of the "medical revolution" that was put into place in China after 1949.[50]

As a result, the average Chinese person in the mid-1980s could expect to live much longer than was the case before liberation and significantly longer than people in most other developing countries. Chinese parents can reasonably expect a baby to survive beyond the first year; in fact a comparison of infant mortality rates in developing countries is startling (44 per 1,000 live births in China, compared to 135 in Bangladesh, 175 in Mali, and 96 in developing countries worldwide). All these improvements—higher living standards, more effective public health measures, longer life expectancy,

reduced infant mortality—have been welcomed in city and countryside alike, but from the perspective of China's population planners, lowering the death rate puts even more pressure on the state to reduce the birthrate.

Compliance with the One-Child Policy: An Interpretation

One puzzling question remains, namely, how has it been possible to convince families in China's cities to comply with the one-child policy? This was a policy that was universally unpopular from the beginning, and so its success in the cities requires some explanation. Cecilia Milwertz, in her book *Accepting Population Control* (1997), argues, probably controversially, that although the majority of urban

Chinese women would prefer to have more than one child, they came to accept the government policy. No doubt this is at least partly based on fear, but Milwertz suggests that many urban women understand and agree with the state's rationale for implementing the program and have learned to accept the moral legitimacy of the policy. Milwertz quotes one of her respondents: "Giving birth to children is a family matter [but] it is also even more a national matter."[51]

Milwertz conducted in-depth interviews and questionnaire surveys in Beijing and Shenyang. She found that 50 percent of respondents thought the one-child policy benefits the child; 70 percent thought it benefits the mother; and almost 90 percent thought it benefits the nation. In spite of their preferences for having two children (83 percent of respondents said they thought it best to have two), most of the women interviewed told Milwertz they had accepted the state policy. As one respondent said, "Two children is better [but] from the perspective of the nation, population numbers are too large, and one child is a benefit to future development. To the nation there are definite advantages in having only one child."[52] It is thus no surprise that among her respondents 83 percent agreed that China has had no choice but "to adopt a policy to control population"; and 85 percent of them agreed that the individual must "voluntarily submit to the policy."[53]

The intriguing question is whether such acceptance is merely compliance backed by indoctrination, repression, and the fear of coercion, as some observers have suggested.[54] Milwertz rejects that idea and develops the argument that acceptance is gradually constructed within the context of control. In other words control, despite the sinister implications, is actually exerted in the best interests of the individual woman. Control in this sense is a form of "caring" by the state, in that the state uses its power of control to achieve compliance with the policy while care and concern are expressed for women. Implied here is that representatives of the state—in this case local birth control officials—heed and respond to the concerns of

the women under their surveillance, trying to make sure they receive the best care available. As Milwertz noted, "Providing care is an integral aspect of the [family planning] work to ensure policy compliance, in the sense that the motive for providing care is to ensure policy compliance."[55] Milwertz thus concluded that "control" equals "care" only if several conditions are met:

- Monitoring and surveillance of all women are taken for granted, as part of everyday life;
- women know and accept that the birth control workers are only doing their job and must answer to their superiors;
- there is the assumption of reciprocity, in the sense that the woman's work unit will "take care" of her needs; and
- the exact same policy is applied equally to all city residents.

According to Milwertz the last two are the most crucial for ensuring that each woman interprets control as caring, yet it is precisely those two requirements that are the least likely to be satisfied in contemporary Chinese cities. Until fairly recently, most city dwellers could reasonably expect their *danwei* to take care of them by providing the normal entitlements associated with having an urban registration (*hukou*). This would traditionally include subsidized housing, food, education, and health care (including birth control). Unfortunately (for many city residents today, as well as for Milwertz's argument) service provision of this type is rapidly being eroded as work units attempt to increase efficiency and lower costs by offering fewer worker benefits. At the end of the 1990s it is also clear that the work units most likely to provide comprehensive services to their workers—the state-operated enterprises—are either being sold off or radically restructured and downsized in efforts to make them more competitive in the modern economy. In the immediate future the dominant form of enterprise is more likely to be collectively or privately owned, and in such units worker benefits (the reciprocal "care" Milwertz refers to) are rarely provided.

It is also becoming obvious to many urban women that despite the state's intent to apply the birth control policy to all women equally, in reality such is not the case—and is rapidly becoming less so. Private entrepreneurs, for example, are usually not subjected to the same controls as those working in state-operated units; in addition, if their enterprise is successful they will be able to absorb, even ignore, the financial sanctions put in place to ensure compliance; moreover if they are well paid they will be able to absorb any fines and penalties that are levied. This may also prove to be the case for another large and growing group of city dwellers, the new transients (migrants and the floating populations), who are also living outside the gaze of the state's birth control apparatus and, at least in the eyes of the permanent city dwellers, are more likely to ignore family planning laws with impunity.[56]

The argument here is that urban Chinese women accept the one-child program, but their acceptance is not necessarily "voluntary" in the English-language sense of that word. What Milwertz is referring to assumes some degree of self-control and is related somehow to political consciousness. She uses the term "conscientious acceptance" to explain her theory; it appears to be a form of compliance that has a higher purpose and is not necessarily seen as negative. She insists that most urban women do not seriously question the ideology of the population policy and are somehow moved to act selflessly and in deference to the greater demands of the community and state. That may be the case, but making such an assumption treads close to the reinvocation of Confucian traditions. People are still expected, in other words, to "sacrifice the little me to complete the big me," to utilize a traditional Chinese homily.[57] It could well be that such expectations are no longer reasonable in contemporary Chinese cities and that the thoroughly modern Chinese woman might have quite different standards for her own behavior.

Milwertz also suggests that urban women who do comply with the rules—which is the majority—are able to cope with the consequences of their decision by trying to cultivate the "perfect child" to compensate, as it were, for the sacrifice they have made by having only one. She also suggests that another compensatory strategy among women is to strive to become more "virtuous" wives and mothers. What Milwertz is suggesting here is not, at present, backed by substantive evidence; in fact it may be interpreted by those same women as ridiculous, even demeaning. In defense of Milwertz, it is perhaps plausible that women who feel they have been forced to break with Chinese tradition (by not having more children) feel the need to fulfil their traditional roles in other ways, such as trying to be perfect wives and mothers. But surely it is equally likely that urban women might want to celebrate their freedom by focusing more time and energy on themselves and their needs. It would seem to be a step back for urban women—set free from their traditional roles by the new birth control policies—to imprison themselves in other, equally traditional roles.

Side Effects of the One-Child Policy

In addition to the three-part evaluation set forth here, it is evident that the one-child policy has carried with it visible side effects, some of which have added to the program's unpopularity. One of these is the effect on future support for the elderly, but before examining that issue it is important to consider some of the other consequences.[58]

Increasing the Demographic Divide Between City and Countryside

One obvious result of the one-child policy is a dramatic split in the composition of families in cities compared to rural areas. Data from the *Chinese Statistical Yearbook*, for example, show that the average family size in China's largest cities in 1996 was just over 3 (3.08 in Beijing;

3.11 in Shanghai), compared to 4.45 and 4.30 in Qinghai and Guangdong Provinces.[59] This is reflected in (or is a result of) sharp differences in birthrates, which averaged (in 1996) 14.47 per 1,000 in cities, 18.02 in rural areas. Interestingly, official data show a considerable drop—more than 25 percent—in birthrates in rural areas since 1989, when the figure stood at 23.27. Based on such evidence, one might be tempted to conclude that the combination of improving economic circumstances and the continuation of the birth control policies (operated in more humane ways) is paying dividends in terms of lower fertility and birthrates in rural areas.

Exacerbating the "Onlies" Phenomenon

Another side effect already being felt impacts the children themselves—that is, the only child, or "onlies." In general it has been demonstrated that single-child parents are satisfied with their family situation[60] and that fathers are more likely to become involved in family activities (though mothers remain the most involved in all child-related activities). Single-child families also appear more child-centered in attitudes and behaviors than is traditionally the case in China, and research shows that parents invest more hope, time, and family resources into the child.[61] In spite of this, one survey found very few differences between families with one child and larger families in terms of personality characteristics and measures of childhood adjustment.[62] In this sense the research results are remarkably similar to findings in like studies conducted in the West. The only significant difference between onlies and children with siblings was in academics; onlies demonstrated higher scores on intelligence and achievement tests, presumably because they receive more one-on-one quality time with parents.[63] Interestingly, that educational advantage was not evident among rural families, perhaps because parents in the countryside are generally not as well educated and rural children rarely go to preschool, which may be related to higher academic achievements.

Orphaned Girls and China's "Dying Rooms"

One of the unsavory implications of China's one-child policy is child abandonment. This issue has been widely publicized in the West and was, in fact, internationalized by the portrayal of horrifying conditions found by Western journalists in some of China's orphanages. One of the most powerful examples of this was the harrowing BBC documentary *The Dying Rooms*, first televised in June 1995. The Chinese government issued official denials, stating that "the so-called 'dying rooms' do not exist in China at all. . . . Those reports are vicious fabrications."[64] The reality, however, is that such orphanages do exist, and the conditions in them are often atrocious. In a lengthy document prepared by Human Rights Watch/Asia, much of this evidence is presented, most of it coming from official Chinese sources, eyewitnesses, and reporters.

As shocking and gruesome as the conditions are in some orphanages, the report, entitled *Death by Default*, suggests that the problem of orphanages is only the tip of the iceberg. As a side effect of the one-child policy, hundreds of thousands of babies, most of them girls, are abandoned every year in China. The vast majority never make it into an orphanage, as bad as they are. Their whereabouts are simply unknown, and we can only assume the worst. The policy on domestic adoptions makes it virtually impossible for Chinese couples to adopt children unless they are childless and older than thirty-five. In other words, the adoption policy has been incorporated into the family planning laws, which means there are serious restrictions on who can adopt and who can be adopted. It is also extremely difficult for anyone to adopt a child who has been abandoned. The reason is again related to birth control laws, as it is assumed that abandoned babies were born "illegally" (they are usually referred to as "black registrations") and therefore are not classified as "genuine" orphans, whose parents have died and who were probably born "within the plan."

Abortion in China

In an interview with the French news agency (Agence France-Press), the minister of China's Family Planning Commission spoke about the need to convince some women to consider abortion. The problem, as Minister Peng pointed out, is that "you can't tie her up and make her do it," but she (the minister) added that officials should create a "general mood" favoring abortion in their communities and bring pressure to bear to "mobilize" the woman. "If it doesn't work the first time, the woman must be mobilized a few more times. It may take dozens of tries at persuasion for some."[65] One of the major indicators of the success of local programs to implement birth control policies is the prevalence of abortion. This is a controversial subject in China, as it is in other parts of the world, but many urban women report they have had at least one abortion. As more use is made of the voluntary and flexible forms of contraception, local authorities have tried to reduce abortion rates, partly because of the physical and emotional trauma involved and partly to reduce overall costs. In Sichuan Province a low abortion rate is used as one of the standards to judge the effectiveness of local family planning activities, but to achieve a low rate it has often been necessary to relax the one-child rule. For couples who wish to avoid both sterilization and abortion, contracts can sometimes be made allowing a second child but pledging not to have a third.[66]

At the other extreme, much has been made of the excessive and coercive use of abortion to help implement the one-child policy, and that has brought the wrath of foreign governments and so-called right-to-life organizations, especially in the United States.[67] In 1985 the U.S. Agency for International Development (U.S. AID) refused to contribute $25 million Congress had approved for the United Nations Fund for Population Activities (UNFPA) because UNFPA, it was claimed, had supported the program of coercive abortion and involuntary sterilization in China.[68] The congressional hearing conducted on coercive population control methods in 1995 was scheduled in part as a response to U.S. President Bill Clinton's decision to restore funding to UNFPA.[69]

In response to intense scrutiny and criticism, Chinese authorities admitted that some coercion had occurred at the local level, partly in response to overzealous attempts to meet single-child quotas. Although birth control planners deny vehemently that forced abortion is or has ever been official policy, some damaging stories have been reported of "abortion quotas," representing attempts to terminate all third and subsequent pregnancies.[70] Horrifying tales have also been leaked to the press, for example, in Huidong, Guangdong Province: Public security forces used armed guards to search out and publicly label "delinquent" women, or those who were pregnant but refused to consider abortion. According to the report, those women were taken "directly to the hospital to undergo an abortion, the privileged ones by car, the others simply in chairs . . . in lorries surrounded by iron bars that were usually used to transport pigs."[71]

As always the issue of abortion is highly charged. A U.S. congressional delegation to China in 1986 reported that such situations were not typical, that local officials were working hard to stamp out coercive tactics and severely penalizing offenders.[72] What facts there are, unfortunately, do not help to clarify the situation. The 1982 fertility survey reported a national average abortion rate of 21 percent for all pregnancies, which was actually lower than those in the United States (43 percent), Bulgaria (98.5 percent), Sweden (36.5 percent), and Hungary (57 percent).[73] It seems reasonable to assume, however, that the abortion rate measured in a self-reporting survey will usually be undercounted. Yet "official" abortion rates, based on the data collected from the registration reports of local administrative bodies, are likely to overcount. The official abortion rate in China for 1981 was reported at 50 percent, rising to 75 percent in 1983, then falling again to 50 percent in 1984 (see Map 5.4).[74]

Very little research has been conducted on the pattern of abortion rates in China, but what little there is seems to support the probability

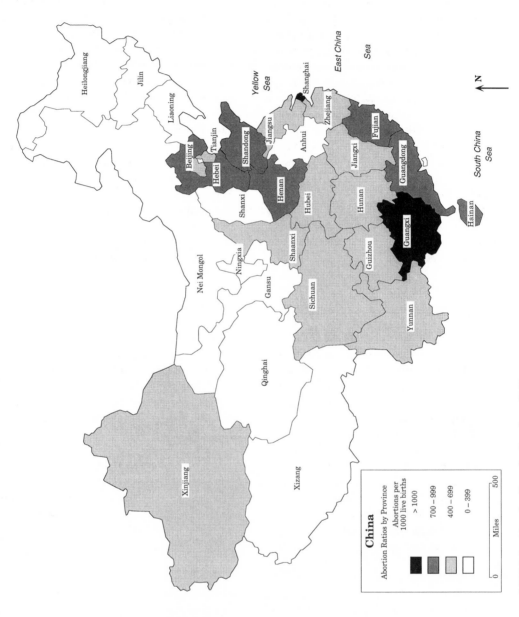

China

Abortion Ratios by Province

Abortions per
1000 live births

■ > 1000

■ 700 – 999

□ 400 – 699

□ 0 – 399

0   Miles   500

MAP 5.4   Abortion Rates by Province, 1990

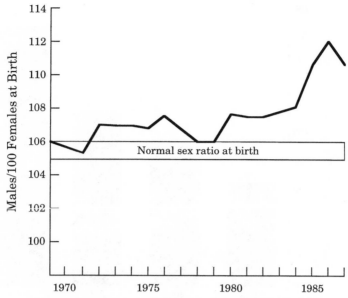

SOURCE: Sten Johansson and Ola Nygren, "The Missing Girls of China:
A New Demograhic Account," *Population and Development Review 17*, no. 1
(March 1991) p. 39

FIGURE 5.2   Sex Ratios at Birth, China 1970–1987

that abortion increases sharply with birth par-ity. Abortion is extremely unlikely for first births, but it rises to close to 100 percent after two births. It is also clear that abortion rates are higher for women with a living son. As we shall see in Chapter 13, it is strongly suspected that sex-selective abortion is used in many parts of rural China as a way of ensuring that the babies born are boys. Although this is vehemently denied by authorities, it is one of the few logical explanations for the growing male bias in sex ratios at birth being recorded in contemporary China (see Figure 5.2).

The New Elderly and Rising Dependency in Contemporary China

At present China is judged, in international terms, to have a relatively young population. In 1990, for example, the proportion of elderly people remained significantly lower than in many Western societies.[75] It is clear, however, that aging is occurring rapidly in China and that the demographic structure will soon catch

up with those in more modernized societies; in addition, because of China's vast population, the absolute size of the elderly sector is huge, with more than 66 million people already older than sixty-five (more than the combined popu-lations of California, Texas, New York, and Florida).[76] By the year 2020, the United Nations estimates, China's elderly population will reach 167 million, which is based on a calculation that there will be on the order of 4.5 million additional elderly each year during the 2010s.[77] According to the sample population census conducted in 1996, there were more than 86 million people aged sixty-five or older in China (see Figure 5.3).[78]

The most important implication of the new aging phenomenon will be dependency, that is, the changing proportion of the working to non-working population. In the mid-1990s China experienced a phase generally referred to as "moderate aging," with the proportion of peo-ple over sixty approaching 10 percent (see Table 5.4).[79] Although the proportion of older people is increasing, the drop in fertility in China means

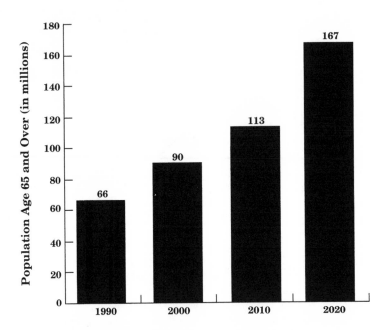

SOURCE: United Nations, *The Sex and Age Distribution of Populations*, the 1990 Revision (New York: UN, 1991), pp. 132–133.

FIGURE 5.3   China's Elderly Population, 1990–2000

that the proportion of children under fourteen should decline from 33 percent to 25 percent between 1982 and 2000, which would result in a drop in the dependency ratio. This means that the economic impacts of the aging phenomenon will be relatively insignificant.

This picture could change dramatically in the new millennium as a result of two phenomena. First, the decline in fertility that occurred during the 1970s, combined with continued efforts to reduce the birthrate, means that the overall percentage of elderly people will increase; second is the rise in life expectancy, a result of the drop in mortality rates.[80] The first two decades of the twenty-first century, therefore, will be characterized by a "quickening aging phase," in which China will shift from being what the gerontologists call a "young-old" society to an "old-old" society. It has been estimated that the proportion of elderly could reach 20 percent by 2025 (see Table 5.4); combined with the reduced population of those under fourteen, this would mean that roughly 35 percent of the

population would be nonworking. The two subsequent decades could be characterized as an era of "super aging," in which the elderly percentage reaches 25 percent—more than 60 percent of them being older than seventy—and the dependency ratio reaching as high as 50 percent.

The obviously pressing impacts are both social and economic as the growing number of elderly people find themselves with an ever smaller number of children to care for them during their later years. In most developing countries it has been recognized that the motivation behind high fertility rates is to make sure that more children are born to provide for aging parents. In China, with the adoption of the one-child policy, it appears that the typical households, especially in urban areas, will be a married couple supporting four elderly parents and one child (the so-called 4–2–1 dilemma; see Figure 5.4). This explains, in part, why so many peasant households have refused to comply with the one-child policy, as a family with

TABLE 5.4   High, Medium, and Low Predictions of Demographic Structure in China, 1990–2050

	Low Prediction (%) Age			Medium Prediction (%) Age			High Prediction (%) Age		
Year	0–14	15–59	60+	0–14	15–59	60+	0–14	15–59	60+
1990	20	65	9	26	65	9	25	65	9
2000	26	64	10	25	64	10	24	65	11
2010	23	65	12	22	65	13	19	67	13
2020	21	64	15	19	64	16	18	64	18
2030	21	59	20	19	58	23	17	58	25
2040	20	58	22	17	57	25	16	55	28
2050	20	59	21	18	57	25	16	54	30

SOURCE: Adapted from Harper (1994), Table 4.5, p. 60.

more children means more protection for the elderly.[81]

The problem is compounded in rural China by the obvious lack of a comprehensive pension scheme for the elderly. This has been a tradition in the Chinese countryside, where children have always taken care of their parents as they grow older, with the state (villages and the communes) providing a safety net for those with no children, no jobs, and no income (the so-called three no's). At present, given the trend toward private enterprise, the shrinking of state responsibilities for welfare provision and the declining importance of collective services will place an increasing burden on a smaller group of adult children to provide for parents for longer periods.[82]

Of course, the impacts of aging are likely to be experienced differently in different locations. In the booming cities of the eastern and southeastern coastal provinces, for example, extremely low fertility rates will impact the ability of existing households to care for parents. By one estimate elderly women would make up 36 percent of China's population by 2000, 40 percent of them living alone.[83] Although rural areas have not experienced such a sharp reduction in fertility, other factors paint a burdensome picture for families. One is the sharp increase in out-migration to the cities, the result of urban employment opportunities and city living, as well as the surplus of rural labor resulting from the agricultural reforms (see Chapter 15). Already being reported in many villages

FIGURE 5.4   China's 4–2–1 Dilemma

throughout the countryside is the emergence of a new family form: grandparents caring for grandchildren while their adult children live and work in cities on a semipermanent basis.

Aggravating this situation is the lack of pension schemes in rural China. There has been discussion about the need for such a system, but at present no systematic action has been taken; what programs do exist involve high monthly premiums and fairly minimal coverage. In the meantime fewer rural elderly receive support from the Five Guarantees (food, fuel, housing, medical treatment, and burial).[84] In addition to the extra burden of support this will place on children, it will widen the already large gap in living standards between urban and rural people. In the cities, although there has been some reduction in comprehensiveness and higher premiums, lifetime pensions have generally been the norm for workers in state units, an entitlement simply not available in the countryside.[85]

In the high tide of collectivism during the Great Leap Forward, there was a brief experiment in providing institutional care for the elderly; in 1958 more than 2 million elderly were placed in 100,000 homes all over the country. This scheme proved to be far too costly and cumbersome, and by 1960 it had been for the most part dismantled. During the reform era there has been a new emphasis on providing homes to elderly who have no one to care for them. Still, there is a tendency to reserve homes, especially better ones, for the urban elite, including former military personnel and high-ranking Party officials.[86]

During the late 1980s and early 1990s there was an extensive debate about the issue of socializing health care benefits and pensions for China's elderly. This would represent a turnabout from the trends toward shrinking state responsibilities and increasing privatization that have accompanied the economic reforms. It is obvious that for the foreseeable future the family will still be expected to provide the bulk of support to the elderly. Thus what is needed is a gradual shift away from the problem-oriented approach to service delivery. That would

involve moving from the current situation, in which the specific needs of the elderly are addressed, toward a more general recognition that all elderly people have certain needs and that the best way to provide for them is to support efforts by family members to offer care. This represents, in other words, a comprehensive, joint effort to combine the activities of the state *and* the family.

The debate about how to provide for the elderly is continuing, and a number of experimental programs have been launched. In 1991, for example, the Ministry of Civil Affairs drafted a proposal for county-level provision of social security–type insurance. A trial implementation began the following year, the idea being to have individual contributions, low premiums, and universal coverage supplemented by insurance coverage from local communities and enterprises. It was also proposed to encourage people to save more for the future. Basic plans of this sort have taken hold in some areas, for example, in Shandong Province, where considerable progress was reported. By the end of 1992 twenty counties in six provinces had introduced pension plans for more than 5 million elderly people. Although this represents a drop in the ocean in light of the demographic realities, it represents a good start. For the vast majority of rural elderly, however, "family care [will continue to be] the norm in the absence of appropriate public arrangements."[87]

Population Policy in the Future: Reducing Coercion, Solving Contradictions

China's fertility rate dropped during the 1990s, although it appears that there was some considerable underreporting of births, possibly caused by sampling and questionnaire errors and (more likely) by the pressure placed on birth control officials to report continuing declines.[88] Yet fertility probably did drop to slightly below replacement level in 1992, thanks in part to the push to gain higher compliance with the laws. But the drop can also be ascribed in part to the large-scale rural out-migration of young people who, instead of having children at home, are either delaying marriage or having children elsewhere (presumably in the cities).[89] A study conducted in three villages in central Shaanxi Province, for example, reported that fertility dropped significantly during the early 1990s, primarily as a result of three sets of factors (all working in conjunction with the existing birth control policies): improved local economic conditions; a reduction in the number of local women of childbearing age, partly due to out-migration; and a 50 percent reduction in the number of women having second births (with third births almost disappearing).

Enormous effort and resources are going into birth control, with considerably less coercion and threats than in the past. Increasing funds were made available for birth control–related surgery; extra money was allocated to families who agreed to comply with limits; higher salaries were paid to birth control workers; and local women were being monitored more closely and given mandatory gynecological examinations. The aforementioned study concluded that roughly 60 percent of the fertility decline could be attributed to the birth control program and local economic improvements; the remaining 40 percent was attributed to demographic factors: overall reduction in mortality, declining number of women having children, and out-migration. It also emphasized that the Party-state retains strong control over both production and reproduction, as well as over all means of local communication, and it is this total package that is responsible for the significant reductions in fertility: "Even in an era of market reform and political loosening, the demographic reach of the Chinese state can be formidable."[90]

If we are to consider the one-child policy a success, it should satisfy two other basic conditions: First, it must not conflict with basic family desires to have two or more surviving children, one of whom is a boy; second, the state must compensate families for the likely negative consequences of having smaller families. Clearly the first condition did not hold, at least throughout the 1980s, and most rural families chose not to comply. As they became wealthier they were even less likely to comply (being more willing to pay the required fines). In the cities, by contrast, only 20 percent of women who have one child go on to have a second (in the countryside 94 percent do). As Milwertz observed, most urban families decided (or were convinced by education and propaganda) that a second child was not absolutely essential. For those who were compensated by state or collective subsidies, that was an acceptable trade-off. Still, in the countryside neither condition was met: The state was unable to convince peasants to accept the policy, and it did not support rural families even as it asked them to reduce family size.

For many Westerners the most unpalatable part of the new birth control policy has always been the increased level of state intervention in internal family affairs. By the end of the 1970s it had become obvious to China's leaders that family plans could no longer be open to negotiation. The new policy represented an attempt almost unique in history to control family decisionmaking. There is no doubt that the Chinese family planning programs have many opponents in the West, especially in the United States. As noted earlier, in 1995 a hearing was conducted in the U.S. House of Representatives on coercive population control in China.[91] At the hearing extensive testimony was presented by two well-chosen demographers, whose opposition to China's birth control policies was a matter of public record.[92] The emotive tone of the hearing was elevated by testimony from several Chinese women appealing for asylum in the United States. They sought U.S. protection based on a fear of returning to China, where, they contended, they were likely to face "coercive" birth control measures, which implies forced abortion and sterilization.

As loathsome as those practices are—and the 1995 testimony added vividly to the already huge body of evidence—it is worthwhile to point out that not all Westerners approach the issue as an obvious violation of human rights.

It is plausible, for example, to argue that our aversion to the excessive zeal and surveillance tactics of the birth control officials (quite apart from the coercive practices) is based on Western values on such issues as privacy and the role of the state. Two well-known anthropologists working in China, for example, are convinced that disagreements between the state and families that resist the one-child policy are not necessarily based on coerciveness and the invasion of privacy.[93] It could well be that in the minds of many Chinese people the state *does* have the right to be invasive. If that indeed is the case, then, state intervention in birth decisions can be interpreted as legitimate by the families, even if they do not agree with them. The dispute centers on the number of children they should have, and many families, especially urban families, support the one-child policy because they have come to appreciate the need to balance resources and population. This is the line (whether one calls it education or propaganda) that authorities have preached on birth control, and many Chinese people accept it.[94]

Taking this argument to its extreme, Ann Anagnost recently offered an interesting hypothesis about the one-child program.[95] She suggests that the need to address the population problem is seen by many people as a sign of modernity, as something crucial to China's cultural and political survival. China must control its population, according to the argument, if it is to assume its rightful place in the modern world. In this sense, then, the birth control policy may not be related to the demographic crisis per se (that is, assuming such a crisis exists). In Anagnost's words, it really is not an issue of children and birth; it is "a test of national will, a race against time and history."[96]

A particularly awkward problem for the CCP has been the apparent conflict between population policy and the economic reforms under the Four Modernizations. The population growth rate had effectively been halved during the 1970s, but as we have seen, the birthrate increased again after the mid-1980s. Much of the increase has taken place in China's rural areas, where births were occurring above the quota set by the state family planning agencies. It was at this time that the economic reform policies had started to take hold in both rural and urban areas. The introduction of new responsibility systems in the countryside allowed individual families much greater leeway to raise incomes by increasing productivity (see Chapter 7). In the low-tech environment that predominates in the countryside, both industrial and agricultural, one of the few ways that can be achieved is by increasing the labor supply; many families believed that the only way to get rich was to have more hands tending the fields and working in the factories.[97]

In sharp contrast to the reproduction policies, the production responsibility system has been very popular among Chinese peasants. In addition to taking some sting out of the economic sanctions imposed for having larger families, the responsibility system began to forge a new set of relationships between individual families and the larger collectives to which they had been tied. Now that a large part of the economic decisionmaking had reverted to the family unit—and with it the life-and-death issues related to the distribution of food, income, and resources—it proved much more difficult for collectives to administer unpopular policies authoritatively from the top down. Individual families realized they liked making their own decisions, and they naturally wanted to extend that newfound freedom to birth control. In the ebb and flow of everyday lives, Chinese people today, whether in rural or urban areas, are reporting fewer and fewer interactions with the state and its agents.[98]

During the 1990s the Chinese government remained firmly committed to the one-child policy, although some relaxation has been allowed at times. Caution was the order of the day, however, because it was felt that a major increase in population growth rates would hold back the drive toward modernization. According to some observers, the state did in fact toughen the one-child policies at various times throughout the 1990s, with visible results.[99] In 1992 China announced that its total fertility rate had dropped to a record low of around

1.56, which meant that population growth had fallen well below replacement level. Several Western demographers were quick to pounce on this startling announcement, contending (and sometimes demonstrating) that a huge underreporting of births during the early 1990s must have produced the sharp drop in fertility. Nevertheless, as a result of continuing efforts at all levels within the birth control hierarchy, China managed to reduce its fertility rate significantly.[100]

One solution to the apparent production-reproduction contradiction is to allow families to hire labor as an alternative to having more children of their own.[101] The willingness to consider this solution indicates how determined the Chinese were in sticking to the basic principles of the one-child policy, for the very concept of hired labor runs counter to the principles of China's economic and social system. Yet the government promised publicly that if the populace strictly adhered to a combined one- and two-child policy for the rest of the twentieth century—or at least until the 1960s baby boom generation passed marriage age—then the policy would be gradually relaxed as the overall growth rate declined. Optimists hoped at the time that the predictions of some demographers would come true in China during the 1990s, that continued modernization and economic prosperity would gradually reduce the desire of Chinese families to have children.[102] As long as China continues to develop its economy and emphasizes education, it should become easier with every passing year, without having to resort to drastic and unpopular measures, to encourage families to limit the number of children. This would give the government considerably more time and breathing space to think through realistic alternatives to current policy.

The policy in the early 1990s was basically a one-child plan with modifications, but according to some demographers viable policy alternatives existed that would have allowed China to reach reasonable population goals without coercion.[103] In 1985, for example, two U.S. demographers produced population projections that showed the implications of three policy packages: The first was a "do-nothing" alternative; the second was a return to voluntary policies in use prior to 1979; the third was rigid adherence to the one-child policy.[104] Based on their projections, the demographers favored the second package, which could work, they argued, if all couples were allowed to have two children (but no more); if they were at least twenty-five years old upon the birth of the first child; and if they allowed a sizeable age gap between the first and second child. In 1987 the same demographers produced seven projections, again based on a series of policy combinations. They showed that continuing with the existing policies, assuming a fertility rate of 1.94 (which has been attained in the 1990s), would result in a total population of 1.24 billion by the year 2000, and 1.44 billion by 2025 (see Table 5.5). Three of the alternative policies described therein (alternatives D, E, and F) would incorporate the desire of most Chinese people to have two children but would also, if implemented with effective "delaying" and "spacing" strategies, result in significantly lower total populations for the twenty-first century.

Other observers have suggested that China would be best advised to move away entirely from controlling and coercive birth control policies. Gale Johnson, for example, has strongly advocated three fundamental changes in policies that could potentially have a huge (though indirect) influence on birthrate and fertility, namely:[105]

- Improve education standards for rural girls and women, who may then be able to make more informed decisions about marriage, work, and family size;
- Change the current policy of land distribution in rural areas (in which the amount of land allocated is based on family size), which would remove one of the obvious advantages of having a larger family; and
- Improve and increase the level of social services and pensions for old people, especially in rural areas, which would reduce the expectation that children will be required to provide for the elderly.

TABLE 5.5   Projected Population Size in 2000 and 2025 Under Current and Alternative Birth Control Policies

Policy	Total Fertility Rate, 1995–2000	Population Size (billions)	
		2000	2025
A. Current Policy	1.94	1.24	1.44
B. One Child Only	1.00	1.09	1.16
C. Two Children	1.76	1.21	1.34
D. Two Children, with Delays and Spacing[1]	1.68	1.11	1.17
E. Two Children, Spaced[2]	1.72	1.17	1.27
F. *Mixture of One and Two*			
Child Policies Cities (stop at one)	1.00	1.15	1.23
Rural Areas (two and space)	1.72	—	—

SOURCE: Adapted from Greenhalgh and Bongaarts (1987), Tables 1 and 2, p. 1169.

NOTES:

[1] This is the so-called 27–4 option, with a minimum age at first childbearing of twenty-seven and a four-year spacing between the two children.

[2] No restrictions on the time of first birth, but a minimum age of thirty for the second birth, necessitating longer spacings of up to eight or ten years.

Programs like these—and the bold policy initiatives discussed earlier in this chapter—will be necessary if China is to be able to deal effectively and equitably with its demographic problems. It is also clear that in thinking about demographic issues, especially those that impact China's families and the issue of childbearing, it will be necessary for policymakers to take bold steps in the near term. As most observers of China's controversial birth control policies agree, the impact falls, and will continue to fall, on women. In theory a one-child policy and smaller families would liberate women, but, as we have seen, the external effects carried disastrous consequences for women. And instead of improving over time, such consequences became worse as policy evolved. In 1985, for example, a provision was made to allow peasant families to have more children if they currently had only one or more girls. Although that represented a major relaxation in the policy, it was also an *official* legitimization of the traditional bias against girls in China, which is a direct contravention of the Chinese constitution. Thus a huge backward step had been taken, because for the foreseeable future "son preference moved from being a peasant value [deeply embedded in social institutions] to becoming a component of informal reproduction policy in the villages."[106] The wretched truth is that under the one-child policy, simply by being born "a daughter prevents her parents from producing and thus acquiring something more precious than herself."[107]

China is a nation seemingly desperate to assume its rightful place in the world. It is a nation searching for modernity. But surely these events suggest that China has lost its way and that it is badly in need of a road map to the future.

6

Life, Death, and the Commodification of Health Care in China

It is always dangerous to bring about radical and sudden . . .
changes, because the complexity of interrelationships in the living
world inevitably makes for unforeseen consequences, often with
disastrous results.

—Rene Dubos, *Mirage of Health* (1959)[1]

Introduction: The Health Care a Society Deserves?

The way in which health care is delivered to citizens in any modern society is shaped largely by the dominant economic values of that society. It would not be at all surprising, then, to find that China's transition from command economics to market socialism would cause some change within the health care system. The pattern of delivery established in postrevolutionary China was greatly admired by outsiders, because it seemed able to provide quality care to the masses without the enormous cost increases experienced in the West. Practitioners and academics worldwide have studied and praised different aspects of the Chinese delivery system, particularly its focus on preventive care, the innovative employment of nonprofessionals, and the elimination of infectious diseases through mass-mobilization campaigns.[2] It looked as though the Chinese were achieving what had previously been an impossible dream for developing nations: a health care system that was both effective and egalitarian.[3]

Throughout the 1980s and 1990s the delivery of health care in China changed dramatically, and as a result outsiders often remark upon the similarities and not the differences between China's system and those in the West.[4]

In this chapter we analyze changes in the Chinese health care system during the reform era. The reforms have brought meaningful benefits to many Chinese, yet they have also carried some of the "unforeseen consequences" that Rene Dubos forewarned in the epigraph just above.

The People's Medicine: Health Care in the Maoist Era

Mao Zedong was concerned about how best to improve the health of the Chinese people, and providing health care was always an important concern for the Chinese Communist Party, even during its formative years. In the remote rural areas (from which the Communists launched their military operations during the civil war), it was essential for the CCP to be able to field an army fit enough to march and fight. It was equally important to be able to guarantee those in the newly liberated areas access to universal health care after the conflict ended.[5] Better health care would extend the longevity and improve quality of life for Chinese peasants, but the concern for health went far deeper than simple humanitarian sentiments. In addition to contributing to the fighting force, providing effective health care was an important component in developing the productive forces, in both city and countryside (see Chapter 4).

Mao's approach to social policy issues was guided in part by his views on the contradictions associated with the drive toward socialist modernization.[6] Although there is little in his writings about health care per se, Mao thought and wrote about three specific contradictions that were crucial to providing health care. These contradictions can be restated as questions:

- Was it possible to balance economic and social development in rural and urban areas, bearing in mind the egregious spatial inequality that had persisted in China for centuries?
- To what extent was it necessary and desirable to replace traditional Chinese medicine with new ways that would be difficult and costly to implement?
- What was the best way to deal with the conflict between professionalism and political reliability in the field of health care?

Spatial Inequality and the Urban-Rural Dichotomy

A key element of Mao's rhetoric in domestic policy was the issue of spatial egalitarianism.[7] Mao thought and wrote extensively about the need to reduce the long-standing dichotomy in living standards between the countryside and the city. He thought the best way to bring that about was to improve the life chances of the peasants: improving diets; increasing wealth; and providing access to low-cost health care. This had become clear to Mao long before the revolution; in fact as early as 1934 he had written that "the revolutionary war is a war of the masses; it can be waged only by mobilizing . . . them."[8] As a result the CCP paid close attention to the everyday concerns of the peasants. As Mao and many others before him were aware, an army moved "on its stomach," so the Party was careful to provide whatever was needed to cater to everyday needs.[9]

Sympathetic observers have argued that Mao's focus on egalitarianism produced singu-lar improvements in the material conditions of the peasants and that this represents one of the most lasting achievements of Chinese communism.[10] In recent years revisionists have challenged that view, arguing that Mao's policies were neither peasant-oriented nor egalitarian in nature; in fact a strong counterargument has been made suggesting that Mao and the CCP consistently exhibited a cynical disregard for the peasantry.[11] As critics have observed, despite the egalitarian rhetoric the countryside became increasingly segregated from the cities during the Maoist era (1949–1976).[12] Such segregation was a direct result of specific Maoist development policies, in which agricultural surplus value was consistently siphoned off to finance industrial growth, most of which was located in the cities.[13] The peasants were not allowed to develop their own commodity economy, and any movement to the cities to search for jobs was prohibited after 1959. The result is that the gap between the cities and the countryside increased rather than decreased during the Maoist era.[14]

The Conflict Between Old and New

In his desire to wrench the backwardness from China, Mao staked his claim as one of the foremost modernists of the twentieth century.[15] The modernist label is misleading, however, because in some policy areas Mao was cautious, even conservative. As for health care he was dismayed by the nonscientific nature of traditional Chinese medicine. In the first decade after the revolution traditional practitioners continued working their trade in the countryside, but their status remained low compared to doctors trained in Western medicine.[16] In light of the problems facing the CCP after 1949—particularly poverty and the population pressures—Mao gradually accepted that it would not be possible to modernize the entire health care system. It was impractical to sweep away everything old; in fact traditional practices of prevention and healing provided a rudimentary care system that was cheap and effective. In 1965, however, Mao launched a campaign to integrate the old and the new in the field of health care. Training schools were opened for traditional practitioners, and the new Western-trained doctors were instructed in some of the more useful remedies that had been passed down through the ages.[17]

Political Reliability or Qualifications: Being "Red" or "Expert"?

Mao was strongly opposed to creating a constituency of highly trained and politically independent professionals, particularly lawyers and doctors.[18] In the domain of medicine he preferred, rather than Western-trained medical doctors, a workforce of individuals whose political loyalties were beyond reproach. Such a strategy made sense economically because a majority of the medical workforce could be trained on site. That was a much cheaper option than building new training hospitals, and it also ensured that some of the providers were familiar to local people and knowledgeable about local areas. To slow down the emergence of a professional medical elite, then, in the first decade after the revolution a licensing system was never established. A practitioner's status was determined primarily on the basis of his or her political reliability, partly on proven ability in the field, not professional credentials. In the egalitarian tradition there was also a push to minimize salary differences among

medical workers throughout the delivery system. The net effect was that doctors in China did not come to enjoy the salaries and status of their counterparts in the West.

The training of the "barefoot doctors" in the countryside was also part of the attempt to stem the tide of rising professionalism in health care delivery. It was an effective way to develop human capital at the local level, which was consistent with Mao's belief that development potential in the countryside should be built upon the principle of geographical self-reliance.[19] When applied to providing health care, this meant that the delivery system should not be dominated by large urban or regional hospitals; in fact the core of the delivery system was focused at the local level. In the countryside barefoot doctors were responsible for virtually all the medical needs of the peasants. They administered the widespread vaccination campaigns, collected medical histories, launched sanitation drives, and trained their own assistants. The health stations from which they operated were usually built by the peasants themselves, using local materials and funds.[20]

Health Care Delivery

Different patterns of delivery emerged during the 1960s and 1970s, depending on local circumstances, but the geography of health care in

TABLE 6.1   The Spatial Organization of Health Care Delivery in Rural China

Spatial Unit	Catchment Area	Medical Facilities and Personnel
Province or Autonomous Region (twenty-eight in China)	Approximately 1–50 million	**Provincial-level hospitals**—subspecialists, Western and traditional practitioners, bureau of public health
County (2,000 +)	Up to 1 million	**County hospitals**—specialists, Western and traditional doctors
Commune (27,000 +)	Up to 60,000	**Commune hospitals and clinics**—Western and traditional doctors, assistant doctors, nurses
Production Brigades (5–20 per commune)	500–3,000	**Brigade health stations**—barefoot doctors, health aides
Production Teams (10–30 per brigade)	50–300	**Barefoot doctors**—health aides

SOURCE: Adapted from Sidel and Sidel (1975b), p. 41.

postrevolutionary China can be described by the adherence to two basic principles.[21] The first was the concern to create an integrated spatial system of service delivery, which means that in both the cities and the countryside providing health care became an integral part of the new spatial organization of administration as described in Chapter 2. The new structures were established from the top down, the specific intent being to create a fully integrated network of administrative structures at all levels in the hierarchy. In the health care sector this meant that even the smallest jurisdictions were connected to higher-level structures, all the way up to the Ministry of Health in Beijing (see Table 6.1). This organizational principle was well suited to a totalitarian system of government because it provided the infrastructure for maintaining law and order, disseminating polit-

ical propaganda, and executing strategic campaigns. It also proved to be highly functional for delivering health care services and implementing health policies at the local level.[22]

In the countryside service delivery followed the administrative hierarchy almost exactly: Hospitals were provided at the county level, clinics at the commune level, and health stations at the production brigade level; the barefoot doctors and other public health workers operated at the lowest level in the villages (see Figure 6.1a). In the cities essentially the same hierarchy was established, with the addition of the hospitals and clinics provided by the *danwei*, to which many urban residents were closely tied for employment and services (see Figure 6.1b).[23] The key to the delivery system in both rural and urban areas was the grassroots worker. Barefoot doctors in the countryside and

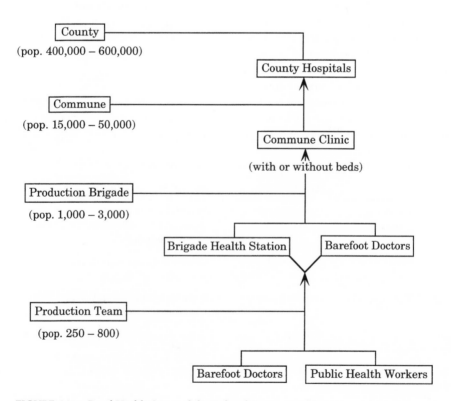

FIGURE 6.1a   Rural Health Care and the Referral System in China

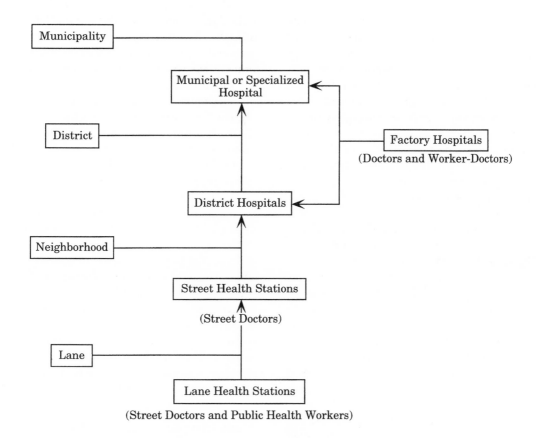

FIGURE 6.1b   Urban Health Care and the Referral System in China

so-called red medical workers in the cities were responsible for most treatment on a daily basis. The more serious cases were referred to facilities at higher levels in the hierarchy, meaning the clinics in the commune headquarters or the urban hospitals.

The goal of the system was to leave no person and no place unserved; comprehensiveness, decentralization, and accessibility were the key concepts. Funding was provided at the collective level (the production brigade in villages and the *danwei* in cities). In rural China brigades were almost entirely responsible for financing, staffing, and operating their own clinics, which sometimes meant that quality varied according to the wealth of the locality. As a result in the richest agricultural areas—where

more surplus funds were generated—collective services were more comprehensive and generally superior to those in poorer areas.[24] Thus even during the supposedly egalitarian Maoist years the quantity and quality of health care provision mirrored the geography of inequality in the Chinese countryside (see Chapter 10).

The second principle of the new health care delivery system was an emphasis on preventive services. During the civil war the CCP began to install a medical care system that was largely curative in nature. That suited the demands of war, but during the peace after 1949 the emphasis shifted toward disease prevention. In a country as large as China the most expedient strategy was to provide preventive treatment to ambulatory patients, either in homes or local clinics rather than in regional hospitals. Only under exceptional circumstances would patients be admitted to a hospital, and in all but the largest hospitals the care provided was rudimentary and the conditions Spartan (at best). Chinese health care, then, was a pragmatic, low-tech adaptation of Western medicine, with traditional Chinese healing methods used as appropriate. The vast majority of time and effort was expended in grassroots-style prevention, which included, for example, campaigns to eliminate pests in the countryside and mass-immunization programs.[25]

This combination of socialist-style illness prevention campaigns and mass provision of basic health services contributed to a sharp decline in mortality rates from most infectious diseases.[26] For financial and ideological reasons the CCP had consciously opted not to allocate resources to high-tech tertiary care, and Western-style medical education was provided only on a limited basis. The emphasis in the countryside was on the development of a network of clinics for disease prevention and stations focusing on children's health issues. Such a system proved effective in combating major health problems prevalent among a population that was still more than 80 percent rural; in statistical terms the positive effects of these efforts quickly became evident. The average life expectancy in China almost doubled, from 35 in the mid-1960s to 68.9 at the beginning of the 1980s. Infant mortality fell to under 30 per 1,000 live births in the early 1980s (it was 200 before 1949).[27] It is important to note, however, that these statistics represent national averages and tend to conceal the reality in remote and poor locations. Not surprisingly, maps depicting traditional health indicators show again that there were significant spatial inequalities (see Maps 6.1a and 6.1b).

The focus on prevention was consistent with Mao's belief in the importance of harnessing human resources creatively. In the public health field it was assumed that the necessary work was everyone's responsibility and that all able-bodied citizens would volunteer their time. A small number of individuals were selected and trained for specific leadership positions, both as officials within the new administrative structures and as providers. Their training was multifunctional, which got the job done cheaply and gave people important functions within the new system. This was particularly important for women (both urban and rural), who for virtually the first time in Chinese history were given meaningful responsibilities outside the home.[28]

Most components of the health care delivery system in rural China had been put into place during the civil war. In the early 1940s, well before their 1949 victory, the Communists developed plans to eliminate the worst aspects of the feudal habits of the past, which they believed tied peasants to a life of passivity. In addition to improving the health status of the peasants, the Party hoped this would raise their collective consciousness in preparing to overthrow their oppressors, the landlords. After the revolution, health care provision was still a primarily political activity, in the sense that efforts to reduce morbidity and mortality also built a constituency supporting the new regime.[29]

Evaluating Maoist Public Health

Health and health care delivery in China during the Maoist era cannot be evaluated in isolation from the political and economic aspects of the socialist revolution. During the struggle to defeat the colonial powers and the Nationalists a radical consciousness was forged, and a highly developed sense of class struggle emerged among the CCP leadership and its supporters. And even though the revolutionary struggle continued after 1949, for practical reasons the focus shifted to the more mundane business of economic reconstruction. Thus during the mid-1950s the new system of spatial organization in the countryside was introduced.[30] It is important to stress that the improvements in health of the Chinese were made possible largely by the radical reorganization of agriculture during the first two decades after 1949 (see Chapter 7). Although forced collectivism in the countryside was generally unpopular, the majority of the peasants were getting more to

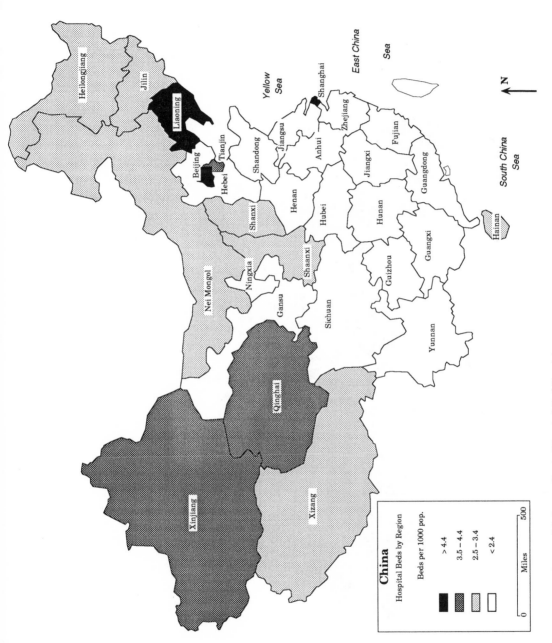

MAP 6.1a   Geographic Inequality in Hospital Bed Provision

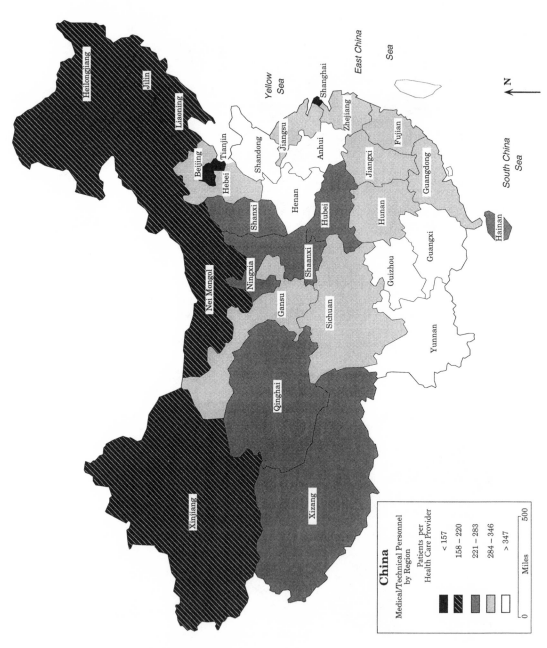

China

Medical/Technical Personnel
by Region

Patients per
Health Care Provider

■	< 157
▨	158 – 220
▦	221 – 283
▧	284 – 346
□	> 347

Miles

0   500

MAP 6.1b   Geographic Inequality in Medical-Technical Personnel

eat than at any time in the past.[31] The agricultural reorganization also influenced the health of China's peasantry by providing the degree of spatial organization needed to implement and administer health care innovations on a larger scale, which probably could not have been achieved through piecemeal measures. All across China, but most notably in the countryside, providing mass public health services became a routine part of the new administrative system. The vast majority of peasants had access to comprehensive health care services that were basic yet cheap and effective. In material terms, therefore, health care delivery was an integral part of the developing infrastructure of production; in ideological terms it was an important contributor to the emerging socialist consciousness.[32]

The achievements of China's health care system in the first two decades after the revolution have been well documented by Western observers.[33] The consensus of opinion was that the newly transformed system had been successful in stemming urgent short-term medical problems in the wake of the revolution. The low-tech aspect of Chinese medicine was well suited to the principle of maximizing access to health care for ambulatory patients, and a delivery system staffed largely by nonprofessionals could respond effectively to the needs of a population threatened chiefly by infectious diseases.

Despite such considerable achievements, by the end of the 1970s it was apparent that China's health care delivery system was already an anachronism and poorly positioned to respond to future medical challenges. China was beginning to experience a sort of epidemiological transition, with the swift elimination of infectious diseases being accompanied by a significant increase in the incidence of chronic diseases.[34] This meant that an ever larger proportion of medical resources would need to be directed toward expensive, high-tech, hospital-based care. The public health model of service delivery during the Maoist era—focusing on immunization campaigns, sanitation drives, pest cleanups, and well-baby clinics—had been highly effective throughout the 1950s and 1960s, yet the very success of such programs virtually guaranteed their demise in the 1970s and beyond. Through organization and hard work the structure of disease in China had been altered, primarily by reducing the incidence of infectious and contagious diseases. Yet at the same time the population had been aging, and the increasing incidence of chronic diseases required changes in the way health care was provided, with a higher demand for hospital beds, longer hospital stays, and greater use of medicines and expensive treatment.

Despite the features Westerners had admired, serious geographical inequalities had become apparent. Outside the most advanced hospitals in the biggest cities, medical equipment was in short supply. In rural areas many of the local paraprofessionals were poorly trained, and for the most part they were unprepared for the rising incidence of chronic diseases. The amateurish philosophy underlying the system also inhibited the flow of medical technology and know-how, both internally, from well-developed urban areas to less developed rural areas, and externally, from overseas into China. In statistical terms spatial inequality, particularly measured at the urban-rural level, was glaringly evident. At the national level the urban-rural ratio for hospital beds per 1,000 persons was 3.4:1 in 1978, and for doctors it was 4.1:1.[35] At the provincial level similar inequalities were apparent. In Guangdong Province, for example, the ratio of doctors to population in the city of Guangzhou (Canton) was approximately 1:6,000; it was around 1:10,000 in the adjacent rural counties.[36] The number of doctors per 1,000 varied from 4.17 in Liaoning in the northeast to 1.79 in the central province of Henan; for hospital beds the range was from 3.13 in Liaoning to 1.46 in Guizhou in the southwest.[37] The most significant predictors of this spatial variation were urbanization and level of economic development, so it is not surprising to find that the population of China's three special municipalities (Beijing, Shanghai, and Tianjin) had far better access to doctors and hospitals.

In attempting to account for geographic inequalities in health care, it is important to look closely at the principles underlying the distribution of social services generally during the Maoist era. Access to the best social services in communist China had always depended more on politics than on considerations of need.[38] At the individual level job status mattered the most, and at the collective level access to health care was determined mainly by the perceived political importance of a particular enterprise or agency.[39] In comparison to the productive (and otherwise privileged) sectors of the economy, most notably the Party units and the Red Army, social service agencies such as hospitals, clinics, and schools were treated as second-class institutions. If surplus funds were needed to boost output levels, social services were traditionally the first to be cut, usually starting with housing, education, and then health care.[40] This attitude represents a long-time tendency to earmark welfare benefits as rewards to individuals for service within a particular work environment. As one observer concluded, "the best quality services [are allocated] to the most highly ranked employees."[41] That observation underscores the highly politicized and personalized nature of the workplace in communist China.[42] Until the reform era there was little separation between politics and the economy, or between the state and society, as there is in most Western countries. Under such circumstances it is not surprising to find that the allocation of benefits was idiosyncratic and not determined by established rules and policy guidelines. As one critic described the situation:

Since individual bureaucrats . . . possess no private property . . . since surplus extraction is collectivized through the state, and since the surpluses . . . are redistributed among the ruling class by political assignment . . . each cadre's access to the social surplus, security of position, chances for career advancement, and much else [including housing, travel opportunities and so forth] depends on [his or her] place or formal rank in the party-bureaucratic hierarchy (the nomenklatura system) and, no

less importantly, upon his or her informal relations of "guanxi" (connections), especially with superiors.[43]

In reality, then, Maoist China was probably nowhere near as egalitarian as the picture was painted by Western enthusiasts.[44] Inequality persisted, and in many instances even increased, throughout the Maoist era.[45] A recent analysis of the central government's patterns of public expenditures has provided additional support for these observations.[46] Compared to most industrialized nations in the West (as well as Japan), China's central government allocated only a small portion of resources to social welfare, education, and health care, as opposed to industrial and military development.[47] In China responsibility for health care and other social services was placed largely in the hands of local governments and enterprises, and as a result the service level varied sharply from one place to another, according to the strength of the local economy. It was clear, therefore, that by the end of the 1970s, despite past successes, China's health care system was in need of reform.

Medicine and Reform: Health Care Concerns in the Dengist Era

Under Deng Xiaoping's leadership the Party-state embarked on the Four Modernizations, the program of rapid economic restructuring. Agricultural efficiency was disastrously low, and incomes and food intake in the countryside had barely increased since the 1950s. After more than a decade of economic stagnation and social and political chaos during the Cultural Revolution, the government realized that in the interests of maintaining its own legitimacy major economic reform was essential. The general consensus has been that in economic terms the reforms produced a number of benefits for rural and urban Chinese citizens. The reforms also influenced the health status of the Chinese people, directly and indirectly. As noted in Chapters 7, 8, and 9 the reforms have altered the structure of opportunity and well-being in China. They have also contributed to a major restructuring in the delivery of health care services.[48] The most meaningful impacts on the health and well-being of the Chinese people have resulted from:

- a marked trend toward privatization and professionalization in the medical delivery system, as well as rapid technology transfers from the West;
- a widespread commodification of Chinese medicine and health care;
- a fundamental shift in the dietary habits of the Chinese people, particularly in the countryside; and
- the persistence of abject poverty in some parts of rural China.

The reforms allowed many peasants to increase their incomes significantly. Rising wealth in the countryside has been associated with higher levels of consumption of all goods and services, including a growing demand for private housing and private schooling. In the health care field the new era of consumption and the luxury of being able to buy better health care have contributed to the rapid emergence of private services. As early as 1984 almost a third of rural health clinics were operating as private, fee-for-service agencies, and by 1989 the figure had increased to almost 60 percent.[49] By the end of the 1980s the trend toward privatization in the countryside had produced a new system of health care delivery, to the extent that doctors were competing for patients and incompetent providers were forced out of business.[50] Such trends have been driven by the desire for greater efficiency, but there has also been a fear that the traditional emphasis on communitywide public health measures has been jeopardized by the move toward private health care and the demise of the collective system. One study reported, for example, that several local immunization programs had been interrupted.[51] Concern has also been raised about the consequences for preventive child health services in the countryside. In some areas well-baby clinics and the regular

monitoring of infants have been de-emphasized in favor of providing more direct and profitable services.[52]

Without guaranteed free (or heavily subsidized) health care at the collective level, many fear that market mechanisms may leave the poorest places and people underserved. In addition, with health care provision now classified primarily as an economic issue, it is likely that the demands of economic efficiency and the desire for higher incomes will favor curative over preventive medical practices, simply because there is more money to be made from the sale of services, medicine, and equipment. Critics of the reforms have pointed out that the withdrawal of preventive services and the relative lack of health care in the poorest areas will put high-risk individuals in even greater peril. It is feared that in rural areas the old, young, disabled, and women generally will be particularly vulnerable in this respect.[53]

Two other radical departures (radical, that is, for China) are apparent: the emergence of highly trained professionals in the delivery system, and the transfer into China of high-tech machinery and expertise from Japan and the West. The benefits of increasing professionalization in the health care delivery system had an almost immediate effect, with better training at all levels and more rigorous standards being set for examinations.[54] The 1980s bore witness to a rapid technology transfer into much of Chinese society generally, and the medical system has been at the forefront of that process. Many well-funded hospitals in urban areas have been able to upgrade their equipment as a result of government investment. And again, in light of prevailing geographic inequities, it is no surprise that as a rule rural hospitals and clinics benefited hardly at all from the technology transfer. Even within cities there are glaring inequalities in technological capabilities. The economic reforms have made it possible for some enterprises, particularly those in the coastal provinces and the new Special Economic Zones (SEZs), to benefit enormously from international trade and investment opportunities, and hospitals attached to such enterprises tend to be better equipped with high-tech medical equipment.[55] In the spirit of the new era such hospitals can now charge market rates for diagnosis and treatment, which allows them to purchase even more equipment.

Privileged Chinese hospitals have also benefited from Western and Japanese investment in recent years. In an analysis of the distribution of CT scanners in China, for example, it was found that a third of the 170 scanners in operation were in hospitals located in China's four largest cities.[56] Such hospitals are likely to be the most attractive to foreign investors; they generally receive more government funds; and they are able to hire well-qualified physicians, especially those trained abroad. The acquisition of an expensive piece of equipment such as a CT scanner is desirable on status grounds alone, but it also worked to establish a hospital's reputation as a high-tech institution, which in turn allowed administrators to raise fees for diagnostic testing and thereby increase revenues. In addition to attracting domestic patients from among the newly rich in the reform era, such hospitals can compete for other cash customers, particularly overseas Chinese from Taiwan, Hong Kong, and elsewhere who come to the mainland for cheap medical care, as well as other foreigners living in China as tourists, diplomats, and entrepreneurs (see Photos 6.1a, 6.1b, and 6.1c).

The increasing professionalization of Chinese medicine and the rapid diffusion of Western equipment should benefit the Chinese population overall, but the rapid changes represent a dramatic shift in the basic philosophy underlying medicine and health care in China.[57] In a relatively short period the Chinese appear to have cast aside centuries of wisdom embodied in traditional medicine and abandoned the grassroots public health model of the Maoist era. Instead there is a more scientific, hospital-based system of medical care dominated by the Western (biomedical) model of treatment; as this shift continues, important principles underpinning the earlier health care system will be sacrificed. Perhaps most alarming is the transfer of decisionmaking power from

humans to machines. In the high-tech world of the new Chinese hospital, this permanently alters the basic character of health care: Providers are now "removed from the patient by diagnostic and treatment technology"; as a result social and medical factors tend to be ignored in the technical process of treatment decisionmaking.[58]

During the Maoist era medical care had clearly been defined as a collective service provided by the state, but in the 1980s it was increasingly being treated as a commodity.[59] Experience in the West has shown that medical care is relatively easy to commodify because drugs and therapeutic procedures generate considerable profits, and also because consumers are prepared to pay large sums to ensure access to decent health care. The shift toward market forces throughout the Chinese economy has been paralleled in the health care system, where the cash nexus has become the primary operating and organizing mechanism. The collective system put in place in the early 1950s to provide universal care has now almost disappeared, and by the end of the 1980s fewer than 10 percent of China's peasants had access to collective medical care;[60] as many as 40 percent had no insurance at all.[61] Wealthier peasants can now travel to clinics and hospitals of their choosing, in other villages or nearby cities, but those with limited resources have no such choice available to them.

The most dramatic changes have been occurring in the hospitals themselves. In many, a modified version of the responsibility system has now been introduced,[62] with new rules emphasizing the personal obligations of hospital and clinic staffs. In one case it was stated that "the tasks of each kind of personnel are clearly defined; the quality and quantity of working standards are issued; if performance is above the working standard, personnel will get economic rewards; below it they will be fined."[63] Providers are now exhorted to work harder and more efficiently, with the added incentive of bonuses and higher salaries; some medical workers have been able to supplement their incomes by as much as 50 percent.

PHOTO 6.1a
The "overseas" Chinese wing
of Nanfang hospital in
Guangzhou.

PHOTO 6.1b
Patients arriving at the
hospital.

PHOTO 6.1c
The check-in desk for
"overseas" Chinese patients.

Attempts have been made to streamline administrative, financial, and organizational practices in China's hospitals. Costs have been held down by limiting reimbursements for hospital treatment and by standardizing subsidies provided to hospitals.[64] Some hospitals have been forced to be creative in finding ways to generate new revenues, employing tactics that sound familiar to Western observers, including processing more patients, raising registration fees, charging more for patient visits, and increasing charges for medicine and new diagnostic techniques.[65] The most troublesome issue in the debate about the commodification of medical services, however, is the quality of medical care, and the concern is that cost rather than quality has become the primary consideration. In one of the few studies on this topic, it was reported that clients receiving fee-for-service treatment were generally more dissatisfied with the quantity and quality of care.[66] They spent less time with doctors and had to travel farther than had been the case during the era of collective health care.[67] In the absence of such studies it is difficult to evaluate the new trends because there are no easily quantifiable ways to assess the pros and cons of a health care system undergoing radical restructuring.[68]

There is evidence that some dubious practices have emerged as a consequence of the commodification of medicine in China. One is the ghoulish business of selling body parts associated with the rise in the arrangement of organ transplants for cash-paying customers, including wealthy expatriates from Hong Kong and Taiwan. A hospital in Nanjing reportedly offered kidney transplants for US$12,800, including round-trip airfare. There are troubling rumors about such practices, including ones that organs are provided voluntarily by the desperately poor to raise cash and involuntarily by executed criminals and dying patients as a method of generating scarce foreign-exchange reserves for local health care agencies. In keeping with the profiteering spirit of the times, there has been a steady growth of unauthorized practitioners and quacks in the countryside. In 1989, for example, more than 2,000 unregistered doctors and unlicensed medicine dealers were discovered in Guanxi Autonomous Region alone.[69]

At times the Chinese press will denounce the corruption and racketeering in the field of medicine, and the government has tried to stay vigilant of the most egregious cases. Even so, attempts to hold down health care costs by subsidizing the supply of medicine and medical services have fallen victim to the corrupt practitioners. In a 1990 report the Hong Kong–based journal *China News Analysis* blew the whistle on a number of practices familiar to Westerners: "For cash-minded medical practitioners, the government's free medical services provide golden opportunities for making money. Physicians prescribe expensive medicine without necessity, increase the number of items covered by public funds, and raise their fees."[70]

The diet of the Chinese populace is another issue impacted by the reforms. Despite much-heralded gains achieved during the Maoist era, it was not until the reform era that the average supply of food energy and protein availability reached levels attained during the 1950s.[71] This was partly a result of the widespread poverty and famine that followed the so-called three disastrous years and the chaos brought about by Mao's abortive Great Leap Forward. Collectivization in the countryside brought some significant gains during the rest of the 1960s and throughout the 1970s, but by 1980 there was a significant gap between the diets of urban and rural residents.[72] After the onset of the reforms one of the earliest impacts was a marked improvement in eating habits among rural citizens. As early as 1983 grain consumption per capita had surpassed that in the cities, and meat consumption had more than doubled from its prereform level.

In many parts of rural China, the reforms meant that peasants were experiencing a greater food surplus than at almost any other time in their history, and naturally such dietary improvements were welcomed. Some medical practitioners, however, have warned about nutritional consequences associated with increased consumption of "luxury" foodstuffs, especially meat and dairy products.[73] It has been suggested that the new consumption patterns represent a departure from a centuries-old dietary tradition. The food intake of peasants was dominated by grains and vegetables, supplemented by small amounts of whatever protein was locally available. The orthodox view in the West is that this type of diet is healthy, and a deviation from it might result in serious nutritional side effects. The agricultural reforms beginning in the 1980s ensured that the supply of more exotic foodstuffs will be met, because under the responsibility system farmers are allowed to produce whatever brings them the maximum return in the marketplace. Newly rich consumers in the cities and the countryside are willing and able to buy such items, which provides the effective demand to reinforce structural shifts in food production prac-

tices. In short, statistics on food consumption during the 1980s indicate some major changes in diet in the countryside (see Table 6.2).

The consumption of grains and vegetables has leveled or declined, but sharp increases in the consumption of cooking oils, meat (especially beef and mutton), dairy, and other sources of protein, such as poultry and fish, have been observed. And beginning in the 1980s Chinese peasants have shown significant increases in the consumption of other food and drink items associated with or symbolic of changing times: beer, liquor, milk, sugar, and, of most concern, tobacco. Sugar intake more than doubled during the 1980s, and liquor consumption rose 4.5 times. In a summary of Chinese newspaper reports, *China News Analysis* focused on these trends and their potential impacts.[74] The story reported that between 1985 and 1989 meat production increased 55 per-

TABLE 6.2   Per Capita Annual Consumption of Major Food Commodities, China's Urban and Rural Households, 1981–1996 (in kilograms)

Urban Residents' Consumption of:	*1981*	*1985*	*1996*	*1996 as % of 1981*
Grain	145.44	134.8	94.7	65.1
Vegetables	152.34	144.4	118.5	77.8
Cooking Oils	4.80	5.8	7.1	147.9
Pork	16.92	16.7	17.1	101.1
Beef and Mutton	1.78	16.7	3.3	185.4
Poultry	1.92	2.0	4.0	208.3
Eggs	5.22	6.8	9.6	183.9
Fish and Shrimp	7.26	7.1	9.3	128.1
Sugar	2.88	2.5	1.7	59.0
Liquor	4.38	9.8	9.7	221.5

Rural Residents' Consumption of:	*1978*	*1985*	*1996*	*1996 as % of 1978*
Grain	247.8	257.5	256.2	103.4
Vegetables	141.5	131.1	106.3	75.1
Cooking Oils	1.97	4.0	6.1	309.6
Pork, Beef, Mutton	5.76	11.0	12.9	223.9
Poultry	0.25	1.03	1.93	772.0
Eggs	0.80	2.1	3.4	425.0
Fish and Shrimp	0.84	1.6	3.4	404.8
Sugar	0.73	1.5	1.4	191.8
Liquor	1.22	4.4	7.1	581.9

SOURCE: *China Statistical Yearbook, 1997,* Table 9-6, p. 295 (urban data); Table 9-24, p. 321 (rural data).

cent, eggs 66 percent, and milk 71 percent; these trends have continued upward throughout the booming 1990s.

Given the data currently available it is impossible to be definitive about the consequences of these new dietary trends, but we know that recent mortality statistics in China demonstrate a shift toward chronic Western-style diseases. By the early 1990s the major causes of death in China were cerebrovascular disorders, heart disease, and cancers, which together accounted for close to 60 percent of all deaths in the cities and more than 40 percent in the countryside (with respiratory diseases associated with smoking accounting for a further 25 percent). A comparison to the situation just four decades ago is alarming: Infectious diseases at that time were the largest single cause of death, but they now account for less than 2 percent of all deaths in China (see Table 6.3).

It is tempting to connect these two trends, that is, the rising incidence of chronic diseases and changing diet patterns in the Chinese countryside. It is generally accepted that a rising mortality rate from chronic diseases is correlated with overeating, particularly with excess consumption of fatty foods and sugar.[75] In the spirit of the public health movement, the Chinese government has moved rapidly to warn people about the dangers of a rapid shift in diet, and a team of nutrition experts even suggested that China should avoid following in the dietary footsteps of the West.[76]

Some evidence from epidemiological studies is starting to accumulate.[77] In those parts of China that have benefited most from the economic reforms—the cities, particularly in the eastern coastal provinces—cholesterol levels were found to be rising rapidly throughout the 1980s.[78] Data collected in a major epidemiological study conducted in sixty-five rural counties also indicated that cancer mortality rates tended to be highest in the areas with the most advanced economies.[79] The data in question allow only ecological (county-level) correlations, but some evidence suggests a connection between rising wealth and higher levels of cholesterol and cancer mortality. The newfound wealth has given many people in the Chinese countryside greater access to a range of foodstuffs and consumer items never before available, something that clearly enhances the quality of life in the countryside. Yet Chinese medical professionals are disturbed to find that cholesterol counts are increasing most rapidly in the wealthiest parts of the countryside. Paradoxically, therefore, the economic reforms may be putting some of China's people at greater risk.

Poverty, Disease, and Death in the Rural Periphery

Although the evidence is somewhat contradictory, it appears that mortality rates have stabilized or risen slightly throughout the 1980s and

TABLE 6.3   Mortality from Infectious and Chronic Disease in China, 1959–1996 (in percentages of all deaths)

Disease Category	1959	1987		1996	
		Cities	Countryside	Cities	Countryside
Infectious and Contagious Diseases	13.6	1.32	2.04	<1.00	1.41[1]
Heart Disease and Stroke	14.1	36.7	27.9	40.7	26.7
Cancers	3.1	21.6	14.2	21.7	16.2
(Respiratory Disease)	—	—	—	15.3	25.2

SOURCES: 1959 data from Henderson (1989); 1987 data from State Statistical Abstract, *China Statistical Yearbook, 1988*, p. 866; State Statistical Bureau (1993), p. 732; 1996 data from *China Statistical Yearbook, 1997*, Tables 19.21, 19.22, pp. 732–733.
NOTE:[1] Excluding TB.

into the 1990s.[80] Economist Amartya Sen fueled the debate by suggesting that the decline of barefoot doctors and a general shortage of government funds for collective health care in the countryside might have contributed to this leveling-off.[81] That argument is difficult to prove, however, and there have been differing opinions. Sen suggested that the death rate had reached its low by 1979, so further reduction was unlikely. In a major critique of Sen's hypothesis, Cambridge economist Peter Nolan contended that Sen misread the evidence and that some reductions in the level of health care in rural areas were necessary because the system was being overused.[82] In addition, many villages grew wealthier during the reform era, which allowed them to provide more and better-quality services, offsetting the reduction in collective health care. The likely effect was greater geographical variability in the quality of health care, with the more prosperous able to offer the best and most comprehensive services.

Rising rural wealth has thus become a double-edged sword as to health status and mortality. On the one hand the quantity and quality of services is raised, the amount of disposable income available to purchase health care is increased, and dietary practices are enhanced. On the other hand increasing income inequality may have worked to raise the mortality rate in two ways: by increasing the prevalence of more "modern" consumption-related diseases associated with excess consumption and new habits; and also by increasing illness susceptibility and decreasing health care access in the poorest sectors of society.[83] This is of greatest concern in the relatively large pockets of poverty that still exist in rural China. A study conducted in Yunnan Province in 1989, for example, showed that the infant mortality rate in a remote minority area approached 100 per 1,000 births (compared to the national average, which is in the 30s, and the rate in Shanghai, which is 11).[84]

To complicate matters, free health care is now a thing of the past.[85] Probably more than half of all rural clinics are now privately owned, and many others are operated under contracts with rural enterprises. The government has recognized the dangers of all-out privatization (in terms of cost and quality), and it has accepted the fact that some health services should return to government control. After reviewing the options, the Ministry of Public Health is now committed to a modified version of the cooperative system, with localities being asked to allocate as much as 80 percent of total revenues to health services. Critics have suggested that this is too large an investment for many villages, likely to perpetuate inequalities in service delivery.[86]

A World Bank report on poverty in the early 1990s looked into the health and health care implications of enduring poverty in the Chinese countryside. One of the major concerns was high infant mortality associated with inadequate or nonexistent care before, during, and after birth. Another concern was variation in the incidence of malnutrition, which averaged 38 percent in preschool children in the poorest rural counties, compared to 10–20 percent for rural areas generally. The malnutrition rate varied from 19 percent to 78 percent in the poorest regions and was generally highest among minority children (see Chapter 12); it was also highly correlated with poverty and lack of education. The World Bank also reported increases in morbidity rates from infectious diseases in the poorest parts of the countryside. Immunization rates for the major diseases varied significantly between urban and rural areas, from 60 percent for children aged under six in the cities to about 30 percent in rural areas, although there have been reports of significant improvements in the poverty areas in recent years.[87]

With the persistence of poverty in rural China, the shrinking of the collective system represents a significant problem. The cost of medical care, especially for hospitalization and medication, prevents poor people from seeking the help they need.[88] For most households going to the hospital is the last resort, and to complicate matters the reforms have eroded health care infrastructures in many townships and villages. Many health centers and hospitals simply closed down in the face of competition from county-level facilities, with a corresponding loss of staff and facilities. In some of the poorest areas there are no health centers at all, and there has been a steady decline in the number of salaried rural health care workers at all levels throughout the 1980s, with barefoot doctors and rural midwives especially hard-hit.[89] Reviewing all this evidence, the World Bank researchers concluded in 1992 that "the health status of the absolute poor appears to be at least as miserable at present as it was in late 1970s." [90]

Catastrophic illness can take a huge toll on poor rural families,[91] and households often have to go into debt. As Elisabeth Croll found, "In a Yunnan Village . . . the very poorest households . . . had all suffered chronic disease, premature death, or mental incapacity. Health profiles revealed that few households had escaped illness and death."[92] Many peasants rightly feel they have been passed over by the reforms. They now pin hopes not on the rejuvenation of local agriculture or on the introduction of new enterprises but on government poverty alleviation programs. Croll noted that one village in Yunnan had benefited from an outside investment, which paid for a new well. By comparison, in another of her study areas, in Guangxi Autonomous Region, located amid the backdrop of spectacularly steep-sided mountains and populated mainly by Zhuang and Yao minority people, villagers have lost all hope of making significant improvements in local wealth and have come to rely almost entirely on the redistributional poverty programs. In the Guangxi village, without the optimism afforded by the outside investment "there seemed little activity to break the eerie 'stillness' of the bare and timeless cycle of poverty and death."[93] In fact some villagers told Croll that the destiny of the sick was death. There were no clinics, no health workers, and no medicine in the village. She concluded: "The doctors were too poor to provide them [clinics and] the villagers were too poor to pay for them and the village had no funds with which to provide a subsidy."[94] Even peasants who travel far to seek treatment find they must pay a deposit upon arriving at a facility that contains only a stethoscope and thermometer. Not surprisingly, few people seek out

health care and most of the peasants in the remote and poor villages had never received any treatment beyond their village health worker. For most of the poor villagers going to the hospital was associated only with death, either their own or that of a relative.[95]

Health Care in the Dengist Era: An Evaluation

The restructuring of China's health care system during the 1980s was one dimension of the drive toward modernization. Although reforms have benefited health and health care in China, some of the gains have been compromised, including the spatially integrated character of the hierarchical delivery system; the comprehensiveness of treatment settings; the focus on accessibility to local services; the ability to keep user costs to a minimum; the utilization of indigenous human capital in service provision; and the emphasis on preventive health care. To some extent, and depending largely on local circumstances, these principles have been sacrificed in the move toward privatized, commodified, professionalized health care. Rising inequality is merely another addition to this list of negatives.[96]

Although evidence of economic success is widespread, many areas have not benefited appreciably from agricultural reform. The poorer localities, particularly in remote regions like Tibet, Xinjiang, and Inner Mongolia, as well as the loess plateau regions in Gansu, Ningxia Hui AR, and Shaanxi and Shanxi Provinces, have fallen farther behind and have experienced widening income inequality.[97] This inequality means there is now even more spatial variability than was the case in the Maoist era, and this exacerbates the impacts of dismantling the communes and abandoning collective responsibility.[98] In short, the new poor no longer have a guaranteed safety net or a minimum level of health care.

Some rural areas have benefited from the economic reforms, generally those adjacent to the largest cities, particularly in the coastal provinces of eastern and southeastern China.[99] Access to health care is thus greater near and in the cities, and official data sources indicate the gap widened throughout the 1980s.[100] During the first few years of the economic reform period, state funding for hospitals in rural areas declined by about a third (that is, between 1975 and 1984);[101] but during the same period funding for city hospitals increased threefold.[102] After a decade of the economic reforms the amount of the Health Services Fund allocated by the government for health care was more than four times higher in China's cities than in the rural areas, and the urban-rural disparity was evident in all of the other standard indicators of health care services and resources (see Table 6.4).[103]

The urban-rural gap in service provision has been reinforced by two other trends in the reform era: the natural preference among trained medical personnel to live and work in cities rather than in rural areas; and the tendency for individuals who might otherwise have trained to be paraprofessional medical workers to choose more profitable and prestigious lines of employment. The economic reforms opened up new opportunities for China's peasants, to put it mildly, and by the mid-1980s there were many ways to get rich, including moving to the nearest city in search of work; working in local factories; opening up a small enterprise; and becoming cash-croppers in the new household responsibility system.

Being a barefoot doctor had been a respectable career choice during the Maoist era, but it was considerably less rewarding during the reform era, and not surprisingly the number of peasants wanting to pursue that line of work declined sharply.[104]

Added to this equation is the evidence that illness can quickly bankrupt all but the wealthiest households[105] and that medical expenses have been rising more rapidly than peasant incomes—and it is no surprise to hear calls for returning to some form of the old system of collective insurance in all of China's rural areas.[106]

In the cities rising inequality has also influenced access to health care facilities. The growth of private enterprise has meant that increasing numbers of city residents do not have access to the collective health services that were formerly provided by work units. For private entrepreneurs who have been successful this has not presented a serious problem, because they have numerous private health care options as long as they can afford to pay. By comparison, employees in small enterprises, as well as the millions of construction workers and transients in the growing cities, are unlikely to receive any health coverage at all. This is also the case for the burgeoning class of city residents who now work for themselves as traders and service providers. Cutting down on health care coverage, or cutting it out completely, is one of the few avenues open to such entrepreneurs during lean times.[107]

TABLE 6.4   Urban and Rural Disparities in Health Resources and Service Usage (1987 data unless noted otherwise)

Item	Rural Areas	Urban Areas	Urban-Rural Ratio
Health Services Fund (yuan per capita)	2.26	9.80	4.34
Hospital Beds (per thousand)	1.57	4.23	2.69
Hospital Beds, 1992 (per thousand)	1.44	4.71	3.27
Doctors (per thousand)	0.98	3.01	3.07
Doctors, (1992) (per thousand)	0.90	3.22	3.58
Annual # Visits (per patient)	3.0	4.0	1.33
# Hospital Days (per patient)	0.48	1.34	2.79
Health Services Expenses (yuan per capita)	18.62	52.13	2.80

SOURCES: Adapted from Liu and Wang (1991), p. 111 (Table 1); 1992 data from *State Statistical Yearbook, 1993,* p. 726, Table 1.

It is important to stress that inequality is not a product of the Dengist reform era alone. Inequality was also a feature of the Maoist era, when spatial disparities in wealth and health care were apparent. Peasant incomes had been suppressed for years by the government's decision to keep food prices low, a policy that effectively subsidized city dwellers by guaranteeing them cheap food.[108] It is no surprise, then, to discover that income disparity was reflected in health-related measures. Yet even under the best of circumstances, health care can only scratch the surface of structural problems contributing to the prevalence of ill health and disease where poverty endures. As one author writing in an official newspaper observed, "Poverty and disease always cause one another: the poorer the place the more serious and widespread the diseases; the more serious and widespread the diseases, the poorer the place."[109] It must be distressing for the Chinese government to learn that despite the glittering economic successes recorded in some of their eastern cities and provinces, chronic poverty and endemic disease continue in many of the more remote places. In 1985 and 1986, for example, outbreaks of bubonic plague were recorded in more than fifty counties across the country.[110]

In addition to the problem of poverty-related disease, there is reason for concern about the relationship between wealth and disease in China. The rising prevalence of "new" Western-style chronic diseases was expected, but the evidence suggests that some of the "old" diseases are also starting to reappear. The Chinese government boasted to the world that it had eliminated venereal diseases in the 1950s and 1960s, but the minister of public health admitted recently that such diseases were returning at a growth rate of 300 percent per year, spreading from Hong Kong and the rich coastal regions to the interior. There are now more than 250 million tobacco smokers in China, their number increasing roughly 10 percent per year.[111] Some of China's cities, Shanghai in particular, already have the highest death rate from lung cancer in the world (see Photo 6.2).[112]

In addition, there has been a dramatic increase in the prevalence of environmental pollution associated with rapid economic growth and industrialization during the reform era, especially in the countryside close to the largest urban centers. It is feared that pollution in these areas, especially of the air and the drinking water, has already had an adverse effect on the health of the Chinese people, causing a significant increase in the incidence of respiratory diseases (see Chapter 16).[113]

Enduring Contradictions in China's Health Care System

The drive toward modernization since 1978 has highlighted a number of important contradictions in China's health care system that will require immediate attention. In some respects these contradictions are similar to the ones Mao Zedong encountered after 1949. There is still a conflict between the new ways and the old in the field of medicine. On the one hand we have witnessed the emergence of high-tech, Western-style medicine in China, but there is still a long tradition of public health–oriented preventive care more characteristic of earlier times. In political terms the new medicine will generate (and has been pioneered by) experts and professionals, some of whom are returning to China after extensive training in the West. As the medical system becomes dominated by highly trained and professional workers, the new elites will challenge the Party leadership at all levels of the hierarchy.

Geographical contradictions have also accompanied the restructuring of China's health care system. The market-driven reforms have widened the gaps in the spatial provision of health care services, and some areas have experienced a net loss of access to quality health care. In spite of the decidedly capitalist flavor of the economic reforms, some within the CCP leadership still espouse the traditionally socialist rhetoric as to social services. Publicly the government continues to promise access to decent health care for all Chinese, regardless of

PHOTO 6.2   Catholic cemetery in Hong Kong.

location, wealth, and ethnic background.[114] Throughout the 1980s and into the new millennium such a promise stands in direct conflict with the government's avowed intent to stop being the primary service provider. This portends a serious contradiction between the traditional, socialist view of health care as a human right to be provided by the state and the capitalist view of medicine as a commodity to be purchased in the marketplace.

This chapter has documented the convergence of health care systems in China and Western societies. The convergence hypothesis allows one to interpret and evaluate some of the changes during the era of economic restructuring. At present it is not possible to back up all aspects of the argument empirically, but with the evidence that is currently available, the following general observations can be made:

- There is a trend within the Chinese health care system toward hospital-based as opposed to ambulatory care;
- the health care delivery system is now dominated by a mix of private and private-public practitioners;
- hospital and clinic treatment is increasingly being provided by professional and highly trained medical personnel, using expensive, high-tech medical equipment and embracing the Western model of medicine;
- there is a concern that the delivery system has become preoccupied with the cost of care, perhaps more so than quality or comprehensiveness; and
- the patterns of morbidity and mortality among the Chinese are becoming more similar to those in the West.[115]

Rising inequality in access to health care has been one of the negative side effects of economic restructuring in post-Mao China, but it would be a mistake to conclude that the reforms have created a new era of neglect.[116] The reality is that neglect of the people and their needs has long been a feature of the Chinese Communist Party, despite the rhetoric of egalitarianism. It would also be incorrect to argue that the post-Mao government has deliberately launched campaigns to dismantle the social service infrastructure during the reform era. The major difference at the turn of the century, after more than two decades of economic restructuring, is that a new tier of privilege—the new rural and urban well-to-do—has been inserted into the social hierarchy. Although the newly rich are not necessarily favored by the government, their economic success allows them freedom of choice, greater access to services, and higher levels of consumption. Those are directly a result of the new policies implemented during the reform era, and to that extent they (the newly rich) are the latest in a long line of recipients of government largesse.

In the general area of social service provision, it is too simplistic to characterize recent developments in China as a shift from the old (Maoist) emphasis on equality to a new (Dengist and Jiangist) emphasis on inequality. Despite the Maoist rhetoric, specific policies in the pre-1978 era worked largely to support the economic and social status quo rather than enhancing the well-being of the poor.[117] During that period access to health care and other social services was anything but egalitarian, so the reform-era trend toward rising inequality represents not so much a reversal as a continuation and extension of existing trends.

The economic reforms have helped to create a new stratum of wealth in China: individuals who can purchase health care services in the private market. Although it is likely that some individuals who were poor during the Maoist era are now relatively rich, on balance the opportunities in the reform era have favored those who already had a comparative advantage, either in terms of location, productivity, or political connections. The result is that the new wealth has effectively widened the gap between the rich and the poor in China, and the changes in the health care delivery system have worked to reinforce patterns of inequality.[118]

PART 3

The Four Modernizations: China's Economic and Spatial Transition

7

Agrarian Reform in China: Feeding the Billion-Plus

ಅಅಅಅಅಅಅಅಅಅಅಅಅಅಅಅಅಅಅಅ

Even to this day I cannot memorize any quotations from Mao Zedong. But I did have class feelings, and I knew that we did not have enough people to do all the work that needed to be done. We had to get together and we had to work together. And when we did that we transformed our lives.

—Chen Yong-Gui, leader of the Dazhai Brigade[1]

Introduction: The Great Famine, 1958–1961

Our rural areas have suffered from serious natural calamities in the last two years [but] there has never been famine. [The Chinese are] fully capable of overcoming temporary difficulties caused by these calamities.

—The Chinese Red Cross Society, February 10, 1961[2]

This chapter does not begin with an analysis of the land reforms that followed the 1949 revolution; instead it opens with events a decade later, during the so-called Great Leap Forward. Over a three-year period beginning at the end of the 1950s the Chinese people experienced one of the worst famines in human history. The message from the Chinese Red Cross quoted just above was in the form of a telegram to the League of Red Cross Societies in Geneva, declaring China's refusal to accept humanitarian food aid from any country or international organization. In spite of the rumors that had leaked from the few foreign correspondents then covering China, the government insisted there was no cause for panic. The official reason for the shortage of food, they said, was a series of *tianzai* (heavenly calamities) that precipitated three consecutive years of poor harvests—the so-called three disastrous years (1958–1961).

This was as close as the Chinese would come to admitting there had been a significant food shortage—known as the Great Famine—until the end of the 1980s. Foreign-based China experts and journalists had been visiting the country at the time, but few reported evidence of serious problems. Some were unable to see through the government's propaganda; others were temporarily blinded by ideological enthusiasm for the Maoist regime. One was Edgar Snow, the American journalist who had written an enormously influential book, *Red Star over China*. Snow was touring the countryside at the time, but reported nothing out of the ordinary. Other friends of China reached the same conclusion, including noted British historian Joseph Needham, Swiss economist Gilbert Etienne, Swedish academic Gunnar Myrdal, and New Zealand poet Rewi Alley. Anna Louise Strong, a journalist whose book, *China's Fight for Grain*, was published in 1963, repeated the government's claim that China had suffered the worst natural disasters in a century. Strong insisted that the commune system, established with breathtaking speed by Mao Zedong in 1958, had in fact saved the Chinese from famine. As we would later discover, however, nothing could have been farther from the truth.

Some journalists and China experts were not as easily misled and managed to send back stories describing the onset of famine conditions in China. Washington columnist Joseph Alsop noted that the average quantity of food being consumed per day had dropped to 600 calories, which would normally cause a person to lose about twenty pounds per month. Alsop concluded that "the population of China is starving. The starvation is methodical and rationed but it is not even very slow starvation."[3] Alsop's reports were strongly denied by the government, and for almost thirty years nobody in China spoke in public about the Great Famine. In 1989 the long silence seemed to be over, when the Chinese government approved the publication of a handbook, "How to Record the Annals of Place," intended to instruct officials how to rewrite Chinese history more realistically than was the case during the Maoist era.[4] A series of natural disasters was no longer to be used as an excuse, and there was a recognition that a famine had indeed occurred. Although the evidence is somewhat contradictory, data on droughts and floods compiled by the national meteorological office show there were no abnormally bad stretches of weather between 1958 and 1962. Only 120 meteorological sites reported droughts in 1960—which was below the yearly average—and only eight events were classed as "serious."

The Party line by the end of the 1980s was that the famine was primarily a result of human error, but it was considered to be an economic rather than a political miscalculation.[5] China now admits there had been no increase in food production during the 1958–1961 period.[6] The official handbook recognized that the famine was a result of "an error in the process of socialist construction of our economy which was solved by readjustment."[7] The "error" lasted only three years, after which it was quickly corrected by a change in policy. With breathtaking brazenness the government, after thirty years of pretending the tragedy never happened, was now attempting to sweep under the table the human impacts of what must be one of the greatest human-induced tragedies of all time.

As Jasper Becker has noted in his book *Hungry Ghosts* (1996), by recasting the famine as a problem of economic policy the Chinese Party-state felt it was not necessary to provide details regarding the loss of human lives. This is a usual practice for Chinese officials; in fact Becker notes that "economic losses are always calculated while reporting disasters [but] similar care is never taken in counting lives lost."[8] The rewriting of history in this fashion would be little more than an amusing sidebar were it not for the scale of the suffering involved and the grotesque nature of the official policies responsible for the famine. Among the most egregious practices were anti–grain-hiding campaigns, whereby state officials forcibly seized whatever grain they could from the peasants on the mistaken assumption they had been hoarding. Where no grain was forthcoming—because it had either not been grown or had already been taken—the peasants were punished and their possessions appropriated.

Although the partial admission of the existence of the famine represents a break with the past, it is still largely taboo to speak about it publicly, which perhaps explains why so few works on the disastrous effects of the Great Leap Forward have been published in China to date.[9] No individual or group has ever been punished or even blamed for the tragedy. Most outsiders lay the blame squarely at the feet of Mao Zedong, but inside China even peasants who lost family members in the famine are still reluctant to condemn Mao, preferring to believe that he was being deceived by false reports of bumper harvests sent from the countryside by aspiring local officials eager to pander to the leaders.[10] There is now incontrovertible evidence that there was a famine, and the only debate seems to be over the number of lives lost.

A veil of secrecy was drawn across all of China's economic statistics and demographic data until the mid-1980s, so an assessment of the period in question was possible only after Mao's death and after Deng Xiaoping had launched the modernization drive, exhorting the Party, the state, and the people to "seek truth from facts." Once the Chinese published or made available the demographic records (the "facts"), Western scholars set off in search of the "truth," reaching conclusions that are almost impossible to comprehend. U.S. demographer Judith Banister has carefully concluded that there were at least 30 million excess deaths in the three-year period;[11] some scholars put the figure even higher, with estimates of more than 32 million deaths in just four provinces (Henan, Anhui, Shandong, and Sichuan).[12]

In his efforts to speed up China's development, Mao Zedong was espousing a philosophy (Marxism) that was based on rationalism and modern Western thought. In place of centuries of myth, feudalism, and emperor worship, Mao promised his people scientific modernization in the immediate future. He was genuinely convinced that "scientific" farming, combined with collectivization, could successfully transform China's agriculture and create the basis for a new, dynamic rural economy. It now appears that Mao was deluding himself about the success of collectivization in the Soviet Union, and he seems to have ignored (or refused to believe) the immense cost in human life that Stalin had wrought with similar actions.

Mao remained an avid believer in Stalin and his achievements, including the "miracles" of Soviet agricultural practices, which he then attempted to introduce in China. Stalin's pseudo-scientists, most notably Trofim Lysenko, had convinced Soviet leaders that major productivity breakthroughs were possible in agriculture. Lysenko thought he could make the steppe lands fertile without using chemical fertilizers and herbicides. Nikita Khrushchev's attempts to apply Lysenko's ideas in the 1950s had ended in disaster rather than a bonanza of food, and evidence of this was available by the time Mao tried to adopt some of the same principles in China. Mao was convinced, however, that his version of utopia was just around the corner. Leaders and the people merely had to work hard to apply the new scientific agricultural practices in the communes. If they followed the rules and were willing to make some early sacrifices, China's people were promised a glut of food, something beyond their wildest dreams.[13]

When the new principles were initially implemented in China, some good early harvests and successes were reported from different parts of the countryside. The information Mao received—which Becker suggests was a roughly equal mix of exaggeration and lies—convinced him that the new methods were successful. Reports started to come in from the countryside of outstanding agricultural yields; fields that had always averaged about 300 pounds of grain per mu of land were reported to be producing in excess of 50,000 pounds (a mu is one-fifteenth of a hectare, or 0.165 of an acre). There were reports of a food glut in 1958, and in some areas food was plentiful by the summertime. The peasants were told they could eat as much as they wanted in the new communal dining halls, but by the winter of 1958–1959 food supplies in many areas were virtually depleted.

At this time, flushed with the spirit of success, Mao and other leaders started refusing to believe there was a food shortage, accusing peasants of hiding grain. Convinced that he was right, Mao called for an increase in grain exports, which doubled between 1958 and 1961; imports were cut off, presumably because Mao thought they were no longer needed.[14] Mao was obsessed with the idea of applying this new version of pseudo-science in the collectives, which he felt would enable China to pass Great Britain in terms of grain production within fifteen years, a figure he reduced to only two years after seeing (or being told about) some of the early results.

Against the advice of some advisers Mao pushed through the new program of forced collectivization, and things began to go wrong almost immediately. The peasants were promised a cornucopia, and in an almost feverish panic of expectant greed they began to gorge, eating much of the seed grain that should have been saved for next year's planting. Many of the draught animals were killed and eaten rather than dividing them up or reallocating them in the communes. Food production had in fact not increased on anything like the scale being reported, and in fact in many areas it had gone down. But even as output declined, the state, still convinced that production was or ought to be rising, began to exact larger quotas of grain from the communes.

Apparently the leaders—taken in by their own enthusiasm and encouraged by local officials' padded output figures—were demanding ever more grain in the following year's production cycle, assuming that the production trends could not only be reproduced but exceeded. The peasants, of course, were unable to meet the mandated harvests, and that is when the authorities accused them of hoarding and hiding food. Stories of food shortages began to circulate in the winter months of 1958–1959, yet Mao remained convinced that like kulaks in the Soviet Union the Chinese peasants were lying in order to extract more help from the state. As one reporter put it, "For the crime of being hungry, the peasants were sentenced to political terror; throughout the countryside, 'anti-hoarding' campaigns applied brutal tortures to uncover non-existent caches of secret food."[15] In *Hungry Ghosts* Becker describes in horrifying detail how events played out in Henan and several other provinces.[16]

Most of Henan Province was poor, and the famine there was severe. It was in Henan that some of the most grisly events would occur over a three-year period in 1958–1961. Although the province had a lower grain target for 1959, based on drought-reduced harvests in the previous year, overzealous local officials determined to impress Beijing with their loyalty and efficiency declared harvests for 1959 that may have been as much as double the actual figure. Grain levies by the state had been set at 30 percent of the harvest, but they subsequently shot up to nearly 90 percent. When the county officials within the prefecture were unable to collect the mandated amount of grain, they launched a brutal campaign that amounted to a war between peasants and local cadres, with the former being accused of suffering from "ideological problems" and not being politically ready to accept socialism.[17] Mass rallies were scheduled to intimidate the peasants, with some being publicly beaten to demonstrate the leaders' commitment to the cause. Fake searches were performed to demonstrate that some peasants had indeed been hiding grain. If local cadres were convinced the peasants had not been hiding grain, they would take chickens, ducks, pigs, and other animals in lieu; then other possessions were requisitioned, including quilts, farm tools, and clothes.[18] At the provincial level a crackdown on the "three obstacles" was announced targeting peasants who declared there was no grain left; peasants who tried to flee in response to their hunger; and peasants who called for the closure of the communal kitchens and dining halls that had become de rigueur in the collectivization drive.

From his collection of archival materials and interviews with survivors, Becker has described some of the atrocities associated with the campaign to locate the missing food. Entire families were beaten and killed in particularly gruesome ways. For crimes involving the "sabotage of production," offenders were routinely beaten to death: "Cadres in Xiangyang Deng commune in Pingyu county ordered the culprits to be dressed in mourning. Some had their noses pierced and wire pulled through their nostrils. They were then forced to pull a plough in the field like an ox. Others were stripped naked and beaten, an oxhide still covered in fresh blood was tied around them. When the hide dried, it was torn off, ripping the victim's skin with it."[19]

In most cases cadres found that no grain was being hidden, and the real tragedy was that all through the campaign of terror, which lasted for more than two years, it appears that some of the state granaries remained well stocked with food that could have kept alive many of those who died of hunger. By early 1960, with nothing left to eat, people started to die en masse, and many families were convinced their only salvation was to leave for the nearest cities or other places where they thought there might be food. Entire villages starved to death; some people resorted to cannibalism, forced to eat their own children who had died from starvation. There were stories of peasants slipping out in the night to carve off a little meat from the corpses of newly dead neighbors.[20]

Based on his case studies, Becker argued that in many localities officials can be blamed directly for their insistence on pushing and punishing the peasants; but ultimately, according to Becker, Mao Zedong should have borne the brunt of the criticism. Mao had personally sanctioned the violence that began in Henan, which subsequently became a model for the rest of the country. It has been claimed that Mao received letters from starving peasants, telling him what was really happening; and he heard stories about officials who refused to administer the official policies. Still, he refused to believe that his dream was falling apart. The famine in Henan finally ended in 1961, when the People's Liberation Army (PLA) was ordered to occupy Xinyang prefecture and commanded to distribute food from the state granaries. Unbelievably, at this time Mao not only took credit for ending the crisis (which he had started) but also officially blamed the rightists for the famine, calling them counterrevolutionaries and class enemies. His argument was a familiar one: The "bad class elements" (including rich peasants and the "stinking" intellectuals) had not been thoroughly purged, so they remained untouched by the revolutionary fervor, making them likely to spread counterrevolutionary ideas.

Stepping back from the repulsive reality of events that have only recently come to light, it is possible to document some of the most likely causes of the famine. The most obvious explanation is that food production dropped drastically, with some estimates suggesting there were more than 50 million tons of grain *less* in 1960 than there had been in 1957.[21] Harvest failures did occur, but they were mainly a result of mismanagement and poor husbandry in the hurriedly created and often chaotically organized collectives. A number of factors, occurring more in some areas than others, conspired to lower productivity in the new communes: the abolition of private property, including land, farm equipment, and draught animals; the universal unpopularity of the communal dining rooms; the reduced incentives associated with the policy of rewarding each person according

to needs rather than work done or productivity; the abolition of private plots that might ordinarily have been used to produce lifesaving food supplies; and the closing of all local markets. The morale of the peasants was low, there were few incentives to work harder, and there were no possibilities to enhance income and food supplies by farming private plots.

The new agricultural techniques created more problems than they solved. As one China scholar has explained, "These experiments took place within the collective system, under which the peasants lost the right to their means of production and their private family life. Systems of economic exchange broke down, and famine left no-one untouched."[22] Grain production was falling, yet local cadres refused to report that to county-level superiors; instead they often made bloated claims, which higher-ups accepted as the truth. For example, Premier Zhou Enlai announced that total grain production had increased from 185 million tons in 1957 to 375 million tons in 1958. With a doubling of output, the central government (in its disinformed state) decided to raise the target for the next year to 525 million tons.

We can only speculate on how a deception of such magnitude could have occurred in a society where the existing regime had risen to power in the countryside with the active support of the peasants. It is possible that the leadership had become mesmerized by inflated production figures they badly wanted to believe. Mao Zedong and his followers had convinced themselves that the agricultural sector "was capable not only of delivering vast quantities of grain to the state granaries but also of making huge sacrifices of land and labor."[23] It also appears that there was a reduction in the agricultural labor force, on the order of 20 percent from 1957 to 1958, as a result of the demand for labor from the massive industrialization associated with the urban component of the Great Leap Forward. Farm animals had either been killed for food or were too weak to work during the famine years. There was a 50 percent drop in the pig population, for example, which meant a huge loss not only of animal protein but also of a valuable source of organic fertilizer. The production problem was exacerbated by a reduction in grain acreage that was announced for 1959, based on the false claims for grain production in 1958, amounting to a drop of more than 20 million hectares in 1959.[24]

The Great Leap Forward thus brought long-term consequences to rural society. There was extensive internal migration, which began as peasants fled to areas they hoped would have more food. Families were broken up by such migrations, and there are even reports of wives being shared with other families or being sold to generate money for food.[25] Children often bore the brunt of the tragedy: Some were sold for money or food; others were left to die when household food supplies ran out. As one peasant described the situation in his village, children were left by the roadside in the hope someone else would take care of them:

> Parents thought their children had a better chance of surviving if they were adopted. . . . The road from the village to the neighboring province was strewn with bodies, and piercing wails came from holes on both sides of the road. . . . You could see the tops of the heads of children who were abandoned. . . . The holes were just deep enough so that the children could not get out to follow [their parents] but could be seen by passers-by who might adopt them.[26]

One lingering question is why the peasants did not take matters into their own hands to resist what were clearly erroneous policies and immoral tactics. There were some reports of peasant rebellions, most often involving attacks on state granaries or trains reported to be transporting food across the country. Some peasants went to Beijing in an attempt to publicize their situation, and others refused to turn over food to the authorities. But in most cases the peasants were simply too weak to offer serious opposition, in addition to which they had no weapons or, in fact, any possessions left in their own care.

It seems that Mao's absolute power resulted in a world of delusion, with officials pandering to the fantasies of the Great Leader. Many Chinese now agree that Mao must have known the reality but either did not care or chose to do nothing until too late. Jasper Becker believes that Mao was punishing the peasants for clinging to feudal habits and beliefs rather than grasping the realities of modernization. That does not explain why so many others in the power hierarchy were willing to deceive, torture, and kill the peasants, and one is tempted to conclude that it had something to do with the fundamental animosity that educated, urban people harbored for centuries toward peasants. For their part, many peasants were seemingly willing slaves and were trusting enough to support, or not to oppose, the state's actions.[27] Perhaps they simply could not conceive that authorities would let them starve; maybe they realized that death on the land was inevitable; or perhaps they became resigned to death as more desirable than stealing from the state granaries. Many peasants continued to believe, up until their deaths, that Mao had not personally caused their peril and that he would, sooner or later, emerge to save them. With almost childlike faith and optimism, peasants "dragged themselves to the top of the nearest mountain, faced the direction of Beijing and called out loud for Mao to help them."[28]

Some scholars have used the evidence of events during the Great Leap Forward to lay blame at the feet of Chinese culture, which had enslaved people for so long that they had become passive, unable to help themselves as the famine evolved. Just as they had done for more than 2,000 years, they remained willing to obey the commands of the emperor. Blaming the past may partly explain why Mao and the peasants acted the way they did, but it may be only a partial explanation. Becker has claimed that nothing can really explain what happened but that it could only have occurred in a closed and shrouded society, where people were encouraged to lie and cheat and where the "facts" were impossible to ascertain due to distortion or concealment. Once a course of action had been boldly pursued, who would be brave (or foolish) enough to stand up to oppose it? Maoist China had become not only a secretive society, caught in the vicelike grip of a pervasive network of informers and spies; it was also an unrelentingly cruel society, and in "a world of distorting mirrors, it became hard to grasp that such senseless cruelty could really be taking place."[29]

The Spatial Organization of Chinese Agriculture, 1949–1976

From the outside it seems obvious that any attempt to develop and modernize China's agriculture after 1949 would be hampered by cultural and geographical constraints that had existed for centuries. The sheer vastness of the country, coupled with the rudimentary transportation system, would continue to favor local self-reliance in food production rather than encouraging the development of highly specialized cash crops in specific regions. Over the centuries the enormous cultural differences across the Chinese landscape, in addition to the constraints of topography and climate, had produced a mosaic of agricultural practices finely tuned to local conditions. Those adaptations were harmonious at the local level, but it was clear that what worked in one area would not necessarily work elsewhere. There was always some doubt, in other words, about the wisdom of trying to superimpose a uniform organizational structure onto this ancient but brilliantly adapted agricultural mosaic (see Photo 7.1).

Critics also argued that collectivization would slow down the country's economic development.[30] In spite of such counterarguments it was "politics first" in the countryside until Mao's death, and colossal efforts were made to restructure Chinese agriculture according to utopian socialist goals. What looked from the outside like a monolithic policy for agriculture concealed a marked lack of consensus about the desirability of collectivization within the uppermost ranks of the CCP.[31] Only after long, bitter struggles between opposing factions within the Party were

PHOTO 7.1   Farm in the mountains near Xian.

Mao's plans for the socialist construction of agriculture implemented.[32] It was also apparent that Chinese agriculture would never fully be able to shake off its own past. What happened at any one time was the result of a blend or, more often, a hodgepodge of different policies superimposed onto the same landscape, mixed in with all the traditions of an ancient past. None of this could be wiped out by simple decree. It is clear, in other words, that agricultural developments are very much path-dependent and should be interpreted in their historical context. In its extreme form, this argument implies that old habits are extremely difficult to break, which helps explain the reemergence of class differences in the Chinese countryside during both the Maoist and the Dengist eras. Mao predicted, in fact, that residual class differences that were never totally eliminated in some parts of the countryside would (and did) account for some of the failures of the collectivization drive.[33]

It is important to keep the tragic events of the Great Famine in mind as we review the socialist transformation of Chinese agriculture after 1949. As remarkable as the achievements were in places like Dazhai, where socialist Chen Yong-Gui had cut his teeth, they should be evaluated in light of the human sacrifices that paved the way for a socialist utopia in the countryside.[34] The basic premise of the CCP's approach to agriculture was that only by shifting from individual to collective work could the peasants emerge successfully from centuries of poverty. In addition to the oppressive domination by the landlords, China had always suffered from a shortage of good cultivable land. As a result of the country's topography, only about a tenth of the land has been suitable for intensive agriculture through the ages, which explains why every available square inch seems to be under cultivation. The climate has only added to the burden: The monsoon often brings too much rain in summer and not enough in winter; worse still is the variability in rainfall from one year to the next.

Since 1949 the Party-state has employed a range of strategies to improve China's ability to feed its population. In the second and third decades of the PRC there was a strong push to collectivize Chinese agriculture, a phase that lasted, with some interruptions, until the early 1970s. During the drive toward collectivization the Chinese tried everything possible to increase the amount of land available for agriculture. To some extent they were successful, through the reclamation of land in peripheral regions; field consolidations; and the removal of grave sites, which occupied as much as 3 percent of cultivable land in some areas. By 1963 such efforts had helped increase the supply of cultivable land by close to 12 percent, from 94 million hectares in 1949 to 110.6 hectares in 1963.[35] Since that time the gains have been more than offset by the loss of agricultural land to urban and industrial uses, the creation of new lakes and dams to conserve water and control flooding, and the afforestation of marginal farmlands.[36] By 1978 the total amount of cultivable land had fallen again to less than 100 million hectares, a 10 percent reduction since 1963, during which time the population had risen to more than 950 million.[37]

The first stage of the socialist transformation of Chinese agriculture was land reform, a process that had already begun in the "liberated" areas of China before 1949. The typical procedure began with the formation of the local Land Reform Work Team, its job to raise the consciousness of the peasants. These teams prepared the groundwork for mass meetings at which landlords would be publicly accused, their holdings revealed, and the extent of their past exploitations exposed. The property in question would then be seized and redistributed among the peasants. Overall the land reform program was highly successful, and by 1952 106 million acres of land had been redistributed to 300 million peasants. The share of China's cropland held by the tiny landlord class fell from 29 percent to 2 percent, whereas that held by the poor peasants and hired laborers (who represented 57 percent of households) increased from 24 percent to 47 percent of cultivated land.[38]

Land reform was accompanied by substantial increases in agricultural production, but in reality the major gains were political rather than economic. The primary goal of land reform was to set the peasants free from the shackles of China's feudal landownership system, and in that sense it was more of a social movement than a production system. The landlord class was essentially destroyed, but, more important, a new source of political leadership emerged at the grassroots level and a new set of local political institutions was established, including associations of poor peasants, peasant militias, women's associations, and youth leagues. In this sense the revolutionary action itself was helping to revolutionize the revolutionaries (as Marx would have predicted), not only by dispossessing the dominant class of its major source of power (land) but also by successfully challenging their political control over the peasantry. Two thousand years of Confucian submissiveness had reinforced in the peasantry a pervasive sense of helplessness, but in mass meetings held all over the countryside there was now visible evidence of an entirely new order emerging.

Land reform, in spite of its successes, created problems that would contribute to a call for the next phase in the socialist transformation. Although the tenant-landlord relationship had been broken forever, the nature of the individual farming economy had not been significantly changed. Most peasants still had too little land to do much more than subsist. This also stymied large-scale investments in rural infrastructure, such as new roads and irrigation schemes, and the use of large machinery. Land reform also specifically protected and even encouraged the richer peasants. Individuals who owned land were guaranteed the so-called four freedoms to help them develop the countryside: the freedom to buy, sell, and rent land; to hire labor for wages; to lend money at interest; and to set up private enterprises for profit. In the spirit of a slogan popular at the time, the newly landed peasants were given the opportunity to "enrich themselves," which allowed and even reinforced social and geographical inequalities within the rural population. Some families prospered, but the majority continued

to struggle. As William Hinton reported, "If some families bought land other families must sell. If some families hired labor others must hire out. . . . For every family that went up the economic ladder, several must go down."[39]

The landlord class was a thing of the past, but China now faced the prospect of a new class struggle, with the "poor" and "middle" peasants lining up in opposition to an emerging class of "rich" peasants. In truth, many peasant families were happy that the revolution and the struggles associated with it were over, and they were ready to "bury their heads in production."[40] In at least one significant way China's land reform process produced a situation similar to that in Russia during the 1930s: the development of a rich peasant (kulak) class that, according to Mao Zedong, was an obstacle to socialist transformation. Unlike Stalin's brutal solution to the kulak problem, Mao's plan was for the poor peasants to organize themselves into mutual aid teams for production purposes—the next logical stage in the agrarian transformation. A team usually consisted of six or seven households in a permanent collective (see Table 7.1). They shared labor, tools, and farm animals, but each of the contributing families took home their own crops. Later on, these would become full-fledged cooperatives, in which crops and the resulting income were pooled and redistributed equally.[41]

By the mid-1950s Mao had convinced his opponents that it was time to combat further class inequality by eliminating what was left of the rich peasantry—what amounted to a rapid drive toward full collectivization. In spite of the existing gains, Mao was worried that a relapse into capitalist agriculture was a distinct possibility. As he argued, "The spontaneous forces of capitalism have been steadily growing . . . with new rich peasants springing up everywhere [while] many poor peasants are still living in poverty."[42] Mao set a target for the creation of 1.3 million cooperatives within the first year (1955), but even his wildest dreams were exceeded, and by 1956 92 percent of all peasant households belonged to elementary, or "lower stage," agricultural producer cooperatives

TABLE 7.1   Growth of Collective Rural Institutions in China, 1950–1959 (in thousands)

Year	Mutual Aid Teams		APCs		Advanced APCs		People's Communes	
1950	2,724	(4.2)	18[1]	(10.4)	1[1]	(32)	—	—
1951	4,765	(5.0)	129[1]	(12.3)	1[1]	(30)	—	—
1952	8,026	(5.7)	4	(15.7)	10[1]	(184)	—	—
1953	7,450	(6.1)	15	(18.1)	15[1]	(137)	—	—
1954	9,931	(6.9)	114	(20.0)	0.2	(59)	—	—
1955	7,174	(8.5)	633	(26.7)	0.5	(76)	—	—
1956	85	(12.3)	216	(48.2)	540	(194?)	—	—
1957	—	—	36	(.5)	753	(157)	—	—
1958	—	—	—	—	—	—	26.63	(5,423)
1959	—	—	—	—	—	—	25.45	(5,008)

SOURCE: Modified from Yang (1996), Table 1, p. 23; the figures in parentheses represent the average number of households in each collective.

NOTE[1] Actual numbers, not in thousands.

(APCs). These co-ops usually contained about thirty households, corresponding wherever possible to existing hamlets or rural neighborhoods (see Table 7.1). The APCs were much larger than the mutual aid teams, and all of the members' productive resources were pooled.

In spite of the successful diffusion of the cooperative system throughout the countryside, Mao considered it to be only a "semisocialist" system because some families still owned unequal shares (if they had brought more into the cooperative than others). Partly as a result of dissatisfaction with this situation and partly because of a wave of contagious enthusiasm for the new cooperatives, the idea of higher-stage cooperatives soon caught on. Initially apprehensive, richer peasants realized that if they did not join quickly, people would start to suspect their class backgrounds, branding them as possible counterrevolutionaries or capitalist-roaders.[43]

It should come as no surprise that the forced drive toward full collectivization produced mixed emotions in the countryside. The peasants were required to give up the land they had been given after the revolution, land they had long dreamed of owning and struggled to acquire. In fact they had *never* owned their land, but in the cooperatives they essentially surrendered even the right to decide how their land would be used. For many families this was

a real blow. They were truly nostalgic about their land and could hardly believe they were losing it again after so short a time. One villager in Long Bow complained that after his bitter struggle to *fanshen* (stand up), he had been thrust right back into feudalism. As he complained, "My donkey works for everyone and here I am laboring in the fields with nothing at all just as I did in the past."[44]

The opponents of collectivization pointed out that the loss of the peasants' land and decisionmaking powers was unprecedented in China.[45] The higher-stage cooperatives were in some ways like Soviet collective farms, in that the peasants had become little more than agricultural wage earners, although many had been able to keep a small "private" plot of land on which to grow a few vegetables. It was clear that Mao had succeeded over his opponents, although his success was to be short-lived. With nearly 800,000 higher-stage cooperatives in China, populated by as few as 150 to as many as 700 (see Table 7.1), the early stages of socialist construction were almost completed by 1957. The landlords and the rich peasants had been removed or co-opted, and the organization of agricultural production had been radically restructured. There had been much local enthusiasm for the cooperatives, but at the national level not everything was going as smoothly. As usual the problems were largely political, but there was also evidence of structural problems in the long-term production capabilities of Chinese agriculture.[46]

The major problems facing Chinese agriculture at this time were low labor productivity and chronic underemployment; there were simply too many mouths to feed and too many hands to keep busy. Although local agricultural practices over the centuries had produced a relatively efficient system of production, yields could not be increased significantly without the introduction of vast inputs of modern technology. Chinese agriculture was still essentially premodern, and the supporters of collectivization felt that output levels could not be increased until Chinese agriculture was able to use new technology, then just starting to diffuse from the West.

At the political level, factional infighting continued among the CCP leadership, and the deterioration of Sino-Soviet relations created great uncertainty about the future. Mao's opponents favored the continuation of a development strategy based on the Soviet model, which would essentially favor the development of heavy industry with a lesser emphasis on agricultural growth. Mao and his supporters, in contrast, were ready to make a clean break with the Soviets, allowing the Chinese economy to walk on two legs—an equal emphasis on industry and agriculture. He hoped to eliminate the distinction between city and country so that the agricultural inputs for the green revolution—the chemical fertilizers and machinery, for example—could be produced locally rather than imported from abroad or transported from other parts of China. He also wanted to see China rely more on its major asset—labor—rather than on capital and technology, which were expensive and in short supply. To achieve all this Mao envisioned massive mobilization campaigns across the nation and a shift away from centralized to local-level decision-making.

In the countryside Mao's dreams were to be put into effect by merging the cooperatives into the new people's communes. At first there was some genuine enthusiasm for communes at the grassroots level, especially after a moderately good harvest in 1958 and the obvious successes of many of the higher-stage cooperatives. The communes were originally intended to be much larger than the cooperatives, at first averaging about 5,000 households; then in 1959 the average size was reduced to about 1,600 households, still roughly ten times larger than the co-ops (see Table 7.1). The plan called for the communes to take over all aspects of political, social, and economic life; provide local social services such as health care and education; and build their own factories to produce agricultural inputs and small machinery.

There was a brief courtship in 1958 with a truly pristine form of collective living, complete with communal kitchens and dining rooms, which was probably the closest China ever came to true communism. But by 1960 the norm had shifted back toward smaller communes with a three-tier structure: production brigades, which corresponded roughly to the higher-stage cooperatives; production teams, which were about the same size as the lower-stage cooperatives; and work groups at the lowest level. The principle of distribution was now fully socialist, with rewards allocated according to work done.[47] Socialism had changed many aspects of the Chinese agricultural landscape, but in some ways very little had changed. From a historical perspective, for example, even in the communes the spatial organization of administration and production remained at the local (village) level, where it had been for centuries.

With the benefit of hindsight, the late 1950s proved to be the zenith of radical socialism in China. By the end of the decade there were more than 70,000 communes covering most parts of the Chinese countryside. Rural industry was humming, and mass-mobilization campaigns began to construct large infrastructure projects such as dams and irrigation ditches. It was a time of genuine enthusiasm and high hopes, with new horizons opening on all fronts, as many peasants gained their first experience outside farming or outside the narrow confines of the village of their birth.[48] As we have seen, such great hopes would soon be dashed, and the enthusiasm of the times often overtook the realities of production—with disastrous results. In production terms grain output declined by an average of 26 percent per year between 1958 and 1961, and there was an annual decline of 71 percent in meat production.[49] Because of the size of the communes and the organizational greenness of the new cadres, production efficiency in many communes was far behind the goals that had been set in the new plans. In addition to their basic food rations, the peasants were being paid collectively, in the form of free services, and according to the critics this was seriously damaging the incentive system. Again the specter of spatial inequality came back to haunt the communes, which in many areas had amalgamated both poor and rich cooperatives. The people from poorer villages naturally felt they were protected by the security blanket provided by the richer areas; those from richer areas saw little point in working hard only to subsidize poorer neighbors. The net effect was that agricultural productivity fell to an all-time low in 1960.[50]

After the catastrophic effects of the Great Leap Forward, it was time for a searching evaluation of the policies that had created it. Retrenchment was the order of the day, and to boost agricultural production the most significant change was a return to local-level decision-making. The power to organize production, manage accounts, and share income was given back to the production teams, which were effectively the lower-stage cooperatives (twenty to thirty families). The larger brigades still undertook important infrastructure projects, organized health care and social activities, and provided political leadership. The brigades (roughly corresponding to the old villages) became more fully integrated with government at the regional and national levels. In terms of production, however, control had shifted markedly downward, which threatened some of the economies of scale possible only in the much larger communes. By 1973 there were about 50,000 communes in China, covering more than 90 percent of available land, more

than twice the number in 1964. The average commune could vary from twenty-five to 130 square kilometers, with an average of 15,000 members, although this varied anywhere from eight to 80,000 depending on the nature of the terrain and the richness of the soils. The commune was the lowest level of central government (in that it was the most localized), but it was also the highest level of spatial organization in the countryside. All the administration functions for the commune were concentrated in the market towns, where the commune's banking, tax collection, buying, and distribution activities were headquartered.

In the 1960s there was a resurgence of social and spatial inequality in rural China. Some of the more efficient peasant families, including those in the formerly rich peasant class, were still critical of the collectivization drive, and they showed production could best be served by following their example. Inequality within the same commune (i.e., at the team level) was now seen in a more positive light than during more radical days. Differences in wealth could now serve the useful purpose of providing incentives to the entire team to work harder, thereby earning more for everyone. It is not surprising, then, that the persistence of these and other spontaneous "capitalist" tendencies in the countryside worked to keep alive the smoldering feud between Mao and his opponents (notably Liu Shaoqi and Deng Xiaoping) over how best to guide China's future agricultural development.

As a result of improvements in farming methods and the spatial reorganization of production in the countryside associated with collectivization, some significant increases in grain harvests were recorded. Output increased from 161 million tons in 1952 to 305 million tons in 1978 (although output fell as much as 25 percent during the Great Leap Forward).[51] The primary factor accounting for the higher yields was the striking increase in inputs, particularly machinery, fertilizer, and irrigation power. This was, in effect, the Chinese version of the so-called green revolution, representing the first widespread employment of modern factors of production in agriculture.[52]

Impressive as those statistics are, they should be considered in conjunction with the growth in China's population during the same period. In addition, throughout the collective era industry consistently performed significantly better than agriculture. Farm output increased by 2.4 times in the first three decades after liberation, compared to a nineteenfold increase for light industry and a ninetyfold increase for heavy industry. This reflects the Soviet-style emphasis on industry-led development in the 1950s, with agriculture taking a backseat. The ratio of investment in agriculture compared to industry fluctuated between 1:4 and 1:6 during the 1950s, and the sluggish performance of agriculture—not to mention the disasters of the Great Famine—was used as ammunition by Mao Zedong's opponents within the CCP, who argued that the move toward collectivization had been too hasty and that the gains of a system based largely on moral incentives were too meager.[53]

In spite of such criticisms (and again with the huge exception of the Great Famine), by the end of the 1970s China's leaders were confident that the age-old problem of famine was a thing of the past. The overall achievements in the agricultural sector can be assessed by comparing China's per capita nutrient availability with that of other countries around the world. China still lagged behind the most developed countries but was significantly ahead of many developing countries, especially in grain availability and protein per capita.[54] Yet during this period of "high collectivism" (1963–1978) several intractable problems continued to plague commune officials all over the countryside. Although the commune was responsible for the collective provision of services and benefits such as education, health care, and welfare, it was evident that material incentives were needed at the local level to encourage peasants to work harder. In many areas small private plots of land had been reallocated to the peasants, so in Mao's terms this stage should not be considered fully socialist. This would continue to be a bone of contention within the Party leadership, but by the end of the 1970s (Mao

Zedong having died in 1976) there would be a dramatic shift back in the direction of individual household agriculture and a virtual dismantling of collective structures in the countryside.

Privatizing Agriculture: China's Agrarian Reforms

The critics of collectivism argued that the state's interference with the production process kept local entrepreneurship in the countryside at an artificially depressed level, which resulted in consistently low rural incomes (incomes had increased by only Y10.5 between 1965 and 1976).[55] In addition to collectivization, there were other factors contributing to the poor performance of China's agricultural economy at this time, most notably Mao Zedong's excessive emphasis on growing grain at the expense of the production of specialized crops in certain areas. The strong central control over rural markets and the restrictions on commercial trading between production teams also worked to lower the incentives of the peasants, because there was no promise of financial reward for working harder and producing more. In spite of such counterarguments it was the collectives themselves that received the brunt of criticism from the new leadership after Mao's death, mainly because they symbolized the old Maoist egalitarianism that was no longer in vogue. Once the agricultural reforms were introduced after 1978 and productivity and incomes started to rise, there was a bandwagon effect, with additional criticism being heaped onto the collective system in general.

During the 1980s (in fact, from 1978 to 1990) systematic attempts were made to dismantle the structure of agricultural administration that had been painstakingly erected in the countryside since the early 1950s. The transformation is best interpreted as neither socialist nor capitalist but as a combination of the two. As a result of the agricultural reforms peasants were able to contract with the collective for land; although they were not typical capitalist contracts—in many cases collectives specified the crops to be grown—they were not drawn up at market values and the peasants did not own the land. Notwithstanding these differences, peasants were in fact allowed to behave like minor capitalists in a number of ways: They could own capital equipment like trucks and tractors; after a few years they were allowed to hire labor and start up businesses; and they could sell surplus produce on the free market for a profit.[56]

The critics of Maoist agricultural policies argued that reform was essential by the late 1970s to return to the peasants what collectivization had taken from them, namely, *quan* (power), *ze* (responsibility), and *li* (payoff).[57] Under the new guidelines output and land were to be contracted out to individual production units, usually households. It is possible to argue that the new arrangements, at least in the beginning, were simply intended as a more efficient way to organize collective agriculture rather than as an outright rejection of collectivization. The most significant criticism of large-scale collectivization was based on the observation that the relations of production (membership in the collectives) were far ahead of the forces of production (see Chapter 4). This meant that the level of development in agriculture was considered to be too low to justify such a radical shift in ownership from individual to collective farming. Mao, however, was not in the mood to listen to such criticisms at the time and persisted with the collectivization drive, hurling invective at those who argued for a slower pace, likening them to "women with bound feet." Ironically, in the late 1970s Mao's critics were able to turn his metaphor around, suggesting that collectivization had forced agriculture to "put on shoes that were too big so that she [agriculture] couldn't move." It was now high time, the critics argued, to find "shoes that fit."[58]

The agricultural reforms can be divided into two categories, although they are closely interrelated. In the first set there was a legitimation of household-based contracting (the household responsibility system, or HRS), which signaled the return to "private" landownership and family-based farming in the countryside. The second set of reforms, made necessary by the first, have proved to be much more controversial and far more difficult to implement: a series of attempts to allow market forces to regulate the distribution of China's agricultural produce. This started in 1979 with a 20 percent increase in grain prices for the summer harvest; a 50 percent increase for all sales above the quota; and an average price rise for all agricultural produce of 22 percent.[59] In 1984 it was announced that the state's thirty-year-old monopoly over the buying and selling of agricultural products would be gradually abolished, thereby allowing market forces, rather than state intervention, to influence the distribution of foodstuffs as well as the production.[60]

Beginning as early as 1978 attempts were made in some parts of the country to introduce the HRS into Chinese agriculture. The basic idea was to allow the peasants—either as individuals, families, or groups of families—to sign contracts with the collectives that would increase their incentives to expand output. Under the socialist guise of "to each according to his work," peasant households would be able to accumulate a surplus by working harder and raising productivity.[61] Households were allowed to dispose of their output however they wished, that is, after they handed over their prearranged quota to the state, paid taxes, and contributed to the collective's fund for investment and welfare programs. In addition to giving the households de facto control of their land, these reforms enabled them to contract for all of the farm inputs (machinery and animals). The production team, in other words, now retained control only in a few areas, for example, in overall planning and setting sales quotas for individual households. In 1983 households were allowed even more freedoms, including the option of buying their own vehicles and machinery and transporting produce for sale across prefectural and provincial boundaries. By 1984 almost all of China's production teams had adopted some form of the household responsibility system, mostly of the type described here (*baogan daohu*).[62]

Peasant households could now choose to produce whatever they could grow and sell most efficiently. Not surprisingly, this resulted in a huge increase in crop diversification, greater productivity, and a corresponding rise in family incomes. Many families branched out into sideline activities such as poultry farming or fish hatching; others got out of agriculture altogether and started up small businesses in catering, construction, or manufacturing. New farmer-entrepreneur families known as "specialized households" began to appear, and many of them reported significant gains in income. In Daqing Township, Liaoning Province, for example, there were forty such households (out of a total of 2,500) by 1983, with total incomes that were four times higher than the local average.[63]

The HRS should be interpreted as one of a broader set of policies intended to restructure the operation of Chinese agriculture rather than as a way to merely increase the incomes of China's long-suffering peasants. It was hoped that the new system would combine the best of collective and individual endeavors while leaving responsibility for overall planning and management tasks, welfare programs, and large-scale infrastructure projects at the collective level. In many parts of China, however, collective work broke down entirely within the first decade of the reforms or was replaced by that of new producer cooperatives or specialized households. In 1982 the people's communes ceased to exist formally, and their political and administrative functions were returned to the townships and the villages.

Although the peasants did not own the land for which they contracted, there was effectively a privatization of property rights under the new arrangements (although such "ownership" was not guaranteed for life). In addition, although the original intent of the reforms was to maintain collective ownership of the forces of production other than land, there was in fact an official sanction of private ownership in the 1980s, which was strengthened by the extension of bank credit to individual households. By 1983 most of China's farm machinery was either owned outright or was leased and operated by private households.

In light of the evidence it is difficult to avoid the conclusion that the reforms broke with the three-decade drive toward collective ownership of the forces of production. Although there were similarities to what occurred in the mutual aid teams and the lower-stage producer cooperatives, the major difference was that during the 1950s "private" landownership was seen as a transitional stage in a transformation toward a more advanced form of collectivization. The Dengist reforms could not be interpreted in the same light, and were, in fact, heralded by the political left as a step back in history, making China a rural economy dominated by rich peasants and bourgeois households (much like the kulaks in Soviet Russia).

The HRS produced what was similar in some ways to a tenant farming system, in which the collective is nominally the landlord, only now playing a minor role. The "rent" paid by households to the collectives was fixed (agricultural taxes plus contributions to investment and welfare funds), but what they could earn by selling their surplus was limited only by the peasants' willingness to work hard, their farming skills, and the productivity of their land. The result was that the new system was far removed from the traditional socialist principal of "to each according to his work." As Deng Xiaoping had suggested, some people would be allowed, even encouraged, to become wealthy under the new regulations. It was anticipated that this greater wealth would benefit the whole community and ultimately the entire country, as the benefits presumably trickled down from the new wealthy class to other groups in society.

Domestic journalists, joined by others from around the world, began to file reports showing that many rural households quickly took Deng at his word, embracing the traditional Chinese saying that "to get rich is glorious."[64] The new superheroes in China belonged to the *wanyuanhu* (the so-called 10,000-yuan households), many of whom could be identified by new possessions and private homes.

Evaluating the Impact of the HRS Reforms

By most objective standards the rural reforms implemented since Mao's death can be judged as a major success. Yet despite the evidence showing material wealth rising in the countryside, there were some who felt the new reforms were selling out the revolution and that three decades of socialist transformation in the countryside had been for nought. To diehard socialists in the West, as well as to the leftists and the few remaining Mao supporters remaining in government, the dangers inherent in a system that allowed sharp income inequalities to reappear were obvious.[65] They also pointed out the futility of dismantling the organizational system that had taken three decades to build. Such critics were fond of pointing out that many of the recent gains in agricultural productivity were in part the result of earlier collective efforts: the terraced fields, the irrigated lands, and the transportation infrastructure in the countryside—all of which were used successfully by household production units during the reform era.[66] One China scholar has described this as the "mining" of communal capital, which had some obvious short-term benefits but in the long term was associated with infrastructural decay that would seriously hinder local production.[67] In addition, there are concerns that the private plunder of collective capital investment has had some irreversible environmental impacts (see Chapter 16). In a case study conducted in Heilongjiang Province, for example, J.S.S. Muldavin reported that as the collectively built irrigation systems fell into disrepair, villages were left with no protection against the unpredictable rains.[68]

It is relatively easy to appreciate why the post-Mao leadership felt it was important to reform the country's agriculture. Among the most commonly aired problems were consis-

tently low prices in the agricultural sector that resulted in low rural incomes, making it impossible for peasants to spend or to save (thereby limiting rural investment funds); low labor productivity and associated deficient levels of agricultural output; and the need to diversify agricultural production, partly to raise local incomes but also to improve the quantity and quality of Chinese diets.

In objective terms the official data released from China indicate that significant improvements were recorded in these areas by the mid-1980s. The value of agricultural output grew an average of 9 percent per year between 1978 and 1986, although that figure is actually inflated by many farmers' switchover from grains to higher-value crops and to more lucrative sideline activities (which accounted for close to 20 percent of total rural output value by 1984).[69] Higher production meant increased farm incomes, which allowed many peasants to diversify their diets, including foods with more protein and higher fat content.[70] Rural incomes more than doubled between 1979 and 1984, which allowed a 51 percent increase in per capita consumption, reducing—for a short time, at least—the traditional discrepancy between urban and rural wealth.[71]

Although Mao had hoped to eliminate the urban-rural dichotomy, in fact the gap probably expanded during his lifetime. The ratio of urban to rural consumption levels for food and nonfood items increased from 1.9:1 in 1957 to 3.2:1 in 1975, then fell slightly to 3.1:1 in 1979.[72] After a few years of agricultural reform, however, the situation had changed significantly. Between 1978 and 1984 urban sales per capita (a proxy variable for consumption) fell from Y433.7 to Y347.7, whereas sales in rural areas increased from Y102.5 to Y263.4 (see Table 7.2).[73] As promised, peasants had more money to spend and save by the mid-1980s. The rate of commoditization—the proportion of their produce the peasants have left over to sell privately—was nearly 60 percent in 1984; peasant bank accounts increased from 26 percent of the national total in 1978 to more than 36 percent by 1984.[74]

TABLE 7.2   Retail Sales (Total Value and Per Capita) of Consumer Goods in Urban and Rural China, 1978–1987

	1978	*1981*	*1984*	*1987*
Total value of urban sales (billion Y)	74.8	102.6	137.7	247.0
Urban population[1] (millions)	172.5	201.7	330.1	503.6
Per capita urban sales (1978 Y)	433.7	454.1	347.7	490.7
Total value of rural sales (billion Y)	81.0	132.4	199.9	335.0
Rural population (millions)	790.1	799.0	704.7	577.1
Per capita rural sales (1978 Y)	102.5	148.0	236.4	580.5

SOURCE: Adapted from Riskin (1987), Table 12.4, p. 295.

NOTE:[1] There was a rapid urbanization during this time period, but the growth of cities is enhanced artificially by the change in definition of what constitutes a town in 1984 (see Chapter 9).

The productivity of the inputs to agriculture also recorded some impressive gains after 1978 compared to the previous two decades. Whereas labor productivity in the countryside increased only 10 percent from 1957 to 1975,[75] between 1979 and 1983 an annual growth rate of agricultural output per unit of input of 5.7 percent was recorded.[76] There is no doubt that the reforms boosted peasant initiatives, enhanced savings for investment, and expanded the range of lucrative sideline activities. Associated with the HRS reforms was also a reconfiguration of the distribution system, which reinforced regional crop specializations by allowing new peasant-entrepreneurs to sell their products over a wider range of territory.

As with all evaluations, there are many sides to the story, although in the heady days of the early reforms (particularly up to 1984) seriously negative voices were considered to be little more than sour grapes. The remainder of this chapter thus focuses on some of the most significant debates associated with agrarian reform in China. These can be reformulated as several questions:

- What was the role of the HRS in increasing agricultural production, and were any other forces responsible for some of the output and income increases recorded during the reform era?
- Why did agricultural production rates, which had increased so dramatically in the first years of the reform era (1978–1984), begin to slow down in the second half of the 1980s?
- What have been some of the unwanted and unanticipated consequences of the HRS reforms?
- Is it possible to increase farmer investment rates in rural infrastructure in light of the tenuous nature of rural landownership and the much more profitable avenues of rural industry and housing construction?
- Was the rapid adoption and the success of the HRS reforms the result of state-induced (top-down) or peasant-initiated (bottom-up) forces?
- Is it possible to provide a robust theoretical account of the success of the HRS reforms?

What Was the Role of the HRS in Increasing Agricultural Production?

There is no doubt as to the success of China's agricultural reform in quantitative terms. Between 1978 and 1988 the growth in gross value of agricultural output (GVAO) averaged 15 percent per year, compared to 4 percent from 1952 to the late 1970s; this was largely responsible for the doubling of per capita agricultural incomes during the same period. The World Bank's 1997 report on China's food situation, *At China's Table: Food Security Options,* uses a so-called dynamic multisector output response model to estimate how each of many different factors has contributed to the growth in agricultural output rates. The results show that the HRS was among the major contributors to growth, but only during the 1978–1984 period. In southern China, for example, the HRS is estimated to have contributed more than 2 percent per year of the growth rate for rice, other grains, and cash crops; but the contribution to crop growth is estimated to be zero after 1984. In northern China HRS seems to have been a major contributor to growth rates only in wheat production, where it contributed an estimated 3.96 percent per year (out of the total of 7.63 percent) during the 1978–1984 period; HRS made no apparent contribution to corn production growth rates, either before or after 1978. The other major contributor to growth rates was the rate of investment in agricultural research, with a much smaller component contributed by investment in irrigation infrastructure.

It has been suggested that the significant gains recorded in the agricultural sector were the result of factors other than HRS reform. This argument is based on the observation that high rates of growth were first recorded as early as 1978, well before decollectivization had begun in most parts of China. Other factors may have played a major part, including good weather, which allowed bumper harvests, as well as more efficient use of fertilizers and other inputs.[77] Marc Blecher has contended that the rising production statistics during this period were more likely the result of policy changes that accompanied the breakup of the collectives, the most significant of which were increases in procurement prices for grain and other foods, as well as the opening of new retail and wholesale markets.[78] For a short time after the HRS reforms were introduced the increase in agricultural productivity and improvements in food marketing brought substantial gains to many of China's peasants. The introduction of food markets was encouraged by the state because, after the early successes associated with HRS reform, it was considered to be an incentive for peasants to increase output levels of most agricultural products.[79] With easier access to markets the peasants were in a much better position to plan and control their own destinies. They were able to make use of new technologies, especially new seed strains and chemical fertilizers, which led to major increases in productivity.

The extra volume of farm goods produced had to be sold, so markets expanded correspondingly. This in turn encouraged the peasants to branch out into other crops or to focus on specialty lines of production, which generally earned them much higher profits than growing grains. All of this contributed to the breakup of the single-crop pattern of production that had dominated the collective era, and the first years of the reform era saw significant agricultural diversification (as shown in Table 7.3a, with the rising production of cotton and oil-bearing crops).

Why Did Agricultural Production Rates Begin to Slow Down in the Second Half of the 1980s?

After 1985, increases in productivity and income growth were much slower (see Table 7.3b); by comparison, there was an explosion of output from rural industries. The decline in incomes and rural productivity is an indicator that grain prices were not rising much, if at all, during this period, so peasants had little incentive to expand food production. As a result, the government was forced to reassert its control over the grain markets.[80] At this time input prices were rising faster than output prices, which meant that profits were falling and farmers had no surplus funds to try innovations. In addition, the reduction in the average size of plots after the HRS was introduced meant that most farmers had been operating inefficiently. Considering all the evidence that is available, it appears that after 1984 the early gains in agricultural productivity could not be sustained for a number of reasons:

TABLE 7.3a Per Capita Output of Major Agricultural Products (in kilograms), 1978–1996

	Grain	Cotton	Oil-Bearing Crops	Fruits	Meat Products	Fish Products
1978	318.74	2.27	5.46	6.87	8.96	4.87
1985	360.70	3.95	15.02	11.07	12.75	6.71
1990	393.10	3.97	14.21	16.51	22.14	10.90
1994	373.46	3.64	16.69	29.36	30.98	17.98
1996	414.39	3.45	18.16	38.21	39.20	23.10
% increase per year 1978–1985	1.65	9.25	34.40	20.10	23.40	17.20
% increase per year 1985–1990	1.49	−0.08	−0.90	8.18	5.36	10.40
% increase per year 1978–1996	+1.58	+2.73	+2.73	+29.30	+23.00	+24.90

SOURCE: *China Statistical Abstract, 1997,* Table 2.8, p. 41.

TABLE 7.3b Economic Indicators in China's Rural Areas, 1965–1994

Average Annual Growth (%)	1965–1978	1979–1984	1985–1994
Per Capita Grain Production	1.2	3.7	0.4
Cotton Production	−1.9	18.0	0.5
Oil-Bearing Crops	0.6	13.3	2.6
Rural Collective Industry (output value, in constant yuan)	9.2	7.3	23.7
Net Rural Income Per Capita (in constant yuan)	—	9.6	2.4

SOURCES: State Statistical Bureau, *China Statistical Yearbooks, 1989* and *1995.*

- Farm yields, even in China's most fertile areas, were reaching and often surpassing the capacity of the land, and as a result peasants were experiencing diminishing marginal returns;
- with the increased use of chemical fertilizers there was a concern that soils were being "burned" and were unable to produce continually high yields;
- in many areas farmers were beginning to ignore or supplant agriculture for more profitable sidelines, or they were choosing to work in the newly expanding rural industries; and
- farming was being neglected as rural industry received the major share of local investment and agricultural land was being put into industrial, commercial, and residential uses.

After 1984, then, it appears that the agricultural bubble had burst and growth was slowing. One of the problems, in addition to the issues outlined just above, was the state's procurement policies, especially the prices it was paying for grain. Under the new rules the peasants were paid a low price for the first 30 percent of the quota grain; a higher price for the next 70 percent of quota grain; and an even higher price for above-quota grain, which the state was obliged, by contract, to purchase. In bumper years, especially 1984, those commitments became a huge drain on the state's cash reserve, even though the policy had resulted in what the state felt was necessary, which was a significant increase in food output.

Grain production increased significantly between 1978 and 1984, yet sown area decreased from 121 million to 114 million hectares, indicating a significant increase in productivity, some of which was attributable to HRS reform.[81] After 1984, however, agricultural production, particularly of grain crops, went into a general slump, even declining in some years (see Table 7.4).

Increases in GVAO were significantly higher during the 1979–1984 period (averaging 6.9 percent per year) than during the 1984–1988 period (2.8 percent per year). This downward trend was partly a response to the general retrenchments occurring in the economy, especially after the marked bout of inflation during 1986 to 1988. The government's response was to postpone further reforms of the pricing system, recentralize control over the prices of many goods, and tighten the supply of credit.[82]

The 1985 drop in GVAO was a direct result of record harvests in 1984, with bumper crops in cotton and grain, in response to which the state converted the procurement system into a contracted purchasing system, fixing a new, unified price equal to the weighted average of the former quota and above-quota prices.[83] The unified price was obviously lower than farmers had been receiving (35 percent lower for grain), and the peasants responded quickly by reducing the sown area of the two major crop categories: Grain production fell by 7 percent in 1985, cotton by 35 percent. The lower production level was partly due to bad weather, partly because the new proportional prices sent negative signals to producers. Free-market prices rose again in 1985 because of the reduction in grain supply, so many peasants were reluctant to fulfill existing state contracts or sign new ones, knowing they could get higher prices on the open market.[84]

TABLE 7.4   Real Growth Rates (%) of Gross Value of Agricultural Output, 1979–1996

Year	GVAO	Cropping	Sideline Production	Animal Husbandry	Fisheries
1979	7.5	7.2	−3.5	14.6	−3.4
1980	1.4	−0.5	6.1	7.0	7.7
1981	5.8	5.9	24.0	5.9	4.4
1982	11.3	10.3	21.9	13.2	12.4
1983	7.8	8.3	11.6	3.9	8.6
1984	12.3	9.9	33.0	13.4	17.6
1979–1984 Average	7.7	6.9	15.5	7.9	7.9
1985	3.4	−2.0	20.6	17.2	18.9
1986	3.4	0.9	20.0	5.5	20.5
1987	5.8	5.3	15.4	3.2	18.1
1988	3.9	−0.2	12.6	12.7	11.6
1989	3.1	1.8	6.0	5.6	7.2
1990	7.6	8.6	3.8	7.0	10.0
1991	3.7	1.0	0.3	8.9	7.6
1992	6.4	3.5	11.2	8.8	15.3
1993	7.8	5.2	NA	10.8	18.4
1994	8.6	3.2	NA	16.7	20.0
1995	10.9	7.9	NA	14.8	19.4
1996	9.4	7.9	NA	11.4	14.0
Share of GVAO (%)					
1980	100	75.6	3.0	18.4	1.7
1990	100	64.6	6.0	25.7	5.4
1996	100	57.8	NA	30.2	8.6

SOURCE: State Statistical Bureau, *China Statistical Yearbook, 1997*; Table 11-6, p. 369.

Agricultural policies after 1985 primarily involved attempts to tinker with the procurement issue in an attempt to make it work properly. The system for buying grain from peasants broke down in the late 1980s when the Agricultural Bank of China, which handled the business of the state's grain procurement stations, ran out of cash and started issuing IOUs to peasants. Rural policy had become highly politicized and controversial, and without any formal channels of protest some peasants turned to violence against local officials. Some provinces, such as Guangdong, abandoned the enforcement of grain contracts altogether and halted subsidies to urban residents. Private markets emerged quickly to take up the grain supply, and soon such markets were attracting grain suppliers from surrounding provinces, a process that was officially banned yet continued illegally. The state is still expected to play a major role in the supply of grain, oil seed, and cotton—the staples of the agricultural sector—but in 1995, after close to a decade of tinkering, the urban sale of grain was finally taken off the people's food coupons; by this time private traders had stepped in to replace the state as food buyer in many areas.[85]

Unwanted and Unanticipated Consequences of the HRS Reforms

The agrarian reforms were associated with trends that were causing some unanticipated problems for China's leaders. One was inflation, which caused widespread discontent in the cities during the late 1980s and was considered a major factor in the disturbances leading to the 1989 demonstrations. In addition, the experience of the first few years of reform fundamentally altered the balance of power in the rural sector. It was no longer clear that the state could automatically expect or mobilize support from peasants if additional policy shifts were to be announced. In attempting to adapt to the new policies, peasants had learned how to deal with, ignore, resist, and sometimes even cheat the state on matters of policy. For example, at times they refused to sell grain to the state because they felt agricultural input prices were too high; at other times they decided to store grain to wait for better prices.[86]

At a general level, it was becoming more difficult for the central government to impose its political will on local governments during the reform era; this turned out to be an important issue after the Tiananmen tragedy in 1989, when the government acted to cut back the process of rural industrialization. At the same time there is evidence that at all levels the state was becoming increasingly "predatory" or "entrepreneurial" as the economy became more and more market-oriented, and all sectors of the state involved in the rural economy were pursuing their own special interests at the expense of agriculture.[87] As Gordon White has suggested: "Departments in charge of capital investments or materials supply diverted resources to projects from which they could reap quick profits; some commercial departments raised the prices of farm inputs arbitrarily, or sold them elsewhere for a profit or foisted sub-standard products on farmers."[88]

It was widely known that Party officials and leaders tended to underestimate the importance of agriculture in the modernization process, especially compared to industry, in part because the latter tends to produce quick, often substantial profits. Rural leaders were even willing to sacrifice agriculture to strengthen local industry and commerce as a way of expanding their local economies. In the spirit of reform, land was taken out of agricultural use and committed to industrial and residential construction, which produced higher returns in a shorter period. As peasants got richer, more and more agricultural lands were being used for new home building (see Table 7.5). One researcher has reported that the construction of factories, shops, roads, and new housing contributed to a 4.5 percent decline in cultivated land between 1978 and 1994, although the rate of loss slowed somewhat by the mid-1990s.[89]

The tendency to neglect agriculture was also reflected in investment, and data show that the state's contribution to agricultural investment was declining. From 1976 to 1980, for example,

TABLE 7.5   Losses of Agricultural Land to Other Uses, 1978–1995

Year	Decrease in Cultivated Area in the Year*	Capital Construction	Village (Collective) Construction	Peasant Housing Construction
1978	800.9	144.5	—	—
1980	940.8	97.7	—	—
1985	1,597.9	134.3	92.3	97.0
1986	1,108.3	109.6	58.5	84.5
1987	817.5	104.6	52.0	57.5
1988	644.7	87.8	37.4	37.6
1989	517.5	70.1	34.6	27.4
1990	467.4	66.3	30.3	36.7
1991	488.0	71.9	33.4	20.5
1992	738.7	131.7	64.1	23.9
1993	732.3	161.0	86.0	24.0
1994	708.7	132.6	80.2	33.0
1995	621.1	111.9	84.9	31.6
Average Annual Loss/Gain				
1985–1990	858.9	95.5	50.9	567.0
1991–1995	657.8	135.1	69.7	26.6

*1,000 hectares
SOURCE: *China Statistical Yearbook, 1997*, Table 11.5, p. 368.

the state's share of overall capital construction investment was 10.5 percent, but during 1981–1985 it was only 5 percent.[90] It was anticipated that the declining role of the state would be more than offset by increasing private investment in agriculture. Such investment was to be mediated and facilitated by the Agricultural Bank of China, which was accumulating reserves rapidly from the savings made possible by rising peasant incomes in the countryside. It soon became clear, however, that the Agricultural Bank was primarily interested in mobilizing funds for investing in rural industry, which was seen as more profitable than agricultural production.

How to Raise Farmer Incentives and Investment Rates

Another serious problem was the deterioration and declining investment in the collective assets that had been built up during the collective era. This was particularly the case for irrigation structures and waterworks, with the burden of

maintenance shifting from communes to the often cash-strapped township governments. Irrigation systems, for example, are sensitive to lack of maintenance and need to be continually monitored, repaired, and rebuilt.[91] There were similar problems with other collective assets during the HRS era, including schools and health facilities, some of which were closed or suffered extensive budget cuts, which is thought to have contributed to rising illiteracy in the countryside and even rising mortality rates.[92]

State investment in agricultural infrastructure continued to fall throughout the 1980s, and there were fears that the lack of new construction and the declining administrative support for water conservancy contributed to the seriousness of massive flooding in the early 1990s and throughout the decade, leading up to the catastrophic floods experienced in the summer of 1998 (see Chapter 16). Many village and township governments, which during the HRS era became responsible for rural infrastructure maintenance and provision, found they were not only short of cash but virtually bankrupt as a result of failed collective enterprises and financial mismanagement.[93]

After the initial production boom ended by the mid-1980s, the peasants became increasingly unwilling to invest in their farming businesses. By this time the state had all but abandoned its former role as provider for the agricultural sector, and the reforms signaled the demise of the collectively provided infrastructure within the communes.[94] Because prices (and therefore profits) in agriculture were low compared to industry, there was generally less surplus to invest; in addition the average plot size, as a result of the new contracting system, was very small. The state has made some attempts to remedy the situation by setting up county-level centers for agricultural extension, with a new class of highly trained agricultural technicians operating as consultants and disseminating new farming techniques.

The reforms did initiate (or encouraged) a sizeable increase in production, but as one research team has observed, "If the aim is to be development rather than simply [extensive] growth, a new rural strategy [to] promote productive investment is required."[95] Throughout the 1980s and into the early 1990s the bulk of peasant investment went into rural industry and housing construction, though the latter had tailed off significantly by the mid-1990s.[96] The declining rate of investment in the countryside resulted in a steady but significant deterioration of rural infrastructure, particularly irrigation works, that had been built during the collective era. The area under irrigation was almost static (in fact falling slightly from 45 million to 44.5 million hectares) from 1979 to 1989. Bearing in mind falling soil productivity, as well as soil pollution from rural industries and the wholesale destruction of forestlands, there are several grounds for reaching a rather bleak conclusion about the impacts of the HRS reforms, in addition to the economic problems. As Gordon White has noted:

> The early years of spectacular economic progress had been to a considerable degree a "one-off"—the result of institutional and pol-

icy changes, and relying heavily on the accumulated stock of rural [collective] capital, but with the same underlying constraints still in place: including low levels of investment and technology, and the dwindling area of arable land. Agriculture has not [or had not by the early 1990s] reached a point where household farm investment had risen enough to counteract the decline of state investment funds allocated to agriculture.[97]

Another potential contributor to declining agricultural productivity—seen by some to be a major future constraint for Chinese agriculture—is the impermanent nature of most of the land contracts offered to the peasants under the HRS. The loss of agricultural land to nonagricultural uses has been particularly prevalent in the suburban areas outside and between China's major cities, especially in the coastal provinces.[98] China's goals for agriculture (according to recent policy statements) include an attempt to come close to self-sufficiency in food production, which means it is important that farmers should augment their current output per hectare; develop unused land into farmland; and try to halt or slow down the destruction of farmland. A major problem in achieving those goals is the lack of incentive for peasants to work and invest in the land, because there is more money to be made in almost all other (i.e., industrial and commercial) pursuits. In addition, many peasants do not have guaranteed rights to the land they live on and work. With the marginal returns of agricultural production, plus the crippling burden of local taxes and arbitrary fees, there are precious few incentives for farmers to make long-term investments in the land. As a *New York Times* reporter observed in 1996, "The difficulty in making farming pay has discouraged millions of peasants from staying on the land and many have simply fled, leaving behind women and the elderly to till the soil, while the men seek prosperity in China's booming urban centers."[99]

Reform is needed to make clear who owns or has the rights to develop agricultural land. The HRS system gives the peasants no real sense of security about the future, and it is clear that peasants' rights—to improve the land, to invest in it, and to reap the benefits—need to be clarified, written into law, and enforced. It is not unusual for farmers to have their land "reallocated" by local officials, for example, to take into account changes in local circumstances that create new households, which need to have some land allocated to them (the most obvious case being marriage). A survey conducted by the Seattle-based Rural Development Institute found that most peasants had no idea what their land rights were, and as a result they were willing to make investments only if they are guaranteed immediate results. They showed no interest, in other words, in making the badly needed investments such as new irrigation systems, improved seed stocks, and modern farm equipment.[100]

Most observers agree that in general China's rural land is underutilized and yields are far too low. Still, most farmers are reluctant to invest additional money or labor for fear that they might not own the land in the future. Very few peasants have written contracts granting them rights to tend a specific plot, and even when they acquire them the expiration date is often left blank. In many villages the collectives take back the land every three to six years and reallocate it. Larger families usually gain land while smaller families often lose it, which obviously hinders successful household planning. In addition, the state can reclaim land for urban or industrial uses at whim; such "takings" often occur with little warning or compensation and with no means of legal redress. What is needed is a new policy or law requiring companies or institutions wanting to buy land to seek the peasants' consent first and to pay the full market value, with the proceeds going to the individual, not into the collective's coffers, as is most often the case. Most peasants surveyed said they favored land rights that are perpetual, can be inherited, and cannot be reallocated without the farmer having a say in the process. Thus they would be willing to invest if they were assured of permanent access to the land, and researchers have estimated that this could

result in an additional 3.3 million hectares of new land being brought into cultivation. Much of that land is currently judged to be "wasteland" but could easily be put into use for growing grain and more profitable crops. Recommendations for policy changes could include that the government at the county level or above be required to issue uniform land-use certificates and written contracts; these would specify the length of time covered as well as all the rights and obligations of individual land users and collective owners.[101]

Were the HRS Reforms a Top-down or Bottom-up Process?

The rapid shift in the direction of HRS appears to have been at least partly a result of a spontaneous, peasant-initiated movement. One reason for reaching this conclusion is the simple observation that the adoption of the HRS was well under way in many areas before the state officially sanctioned it as a national policy in 1980.[102] Up to that point household contracting was vigorously condemned by state officials, and some local cadres even considered the possible restoration of landlords.[103] There was significant opposition among Party leaders to decollectivization, because "collective agriculture had been the key rural institutional creation of the Maoist period,"[104] and there were some powerful forces within the upper ranks of the Party who were strongly in favor of the status quo (including Chen Yong-Gui, the former Dazhai Brigade leader). There was plenty of opposition among village leaders as well, many of whom felt they would probably lose some of their institutional power base. In addition, there were genuine concerns about the inefficiencies associated with a return to small-scale farming and the waste of infrastructures already erected in rural areas. There was also a fear about the impacts of the responsibility system during poor harvest years, when significant losses would be incurred. Peasant households, in such circumstances, would have to rely on the state for assistance, as was the case during the devastating floods in the summer of 1998.

Given this opposition, how is it possible to account for rapid adoption of the HRS, a policy that was described as "incremental in its execution yet radical in its consequences"?[105] The reforms were much more comprehensive and spread much more rapidly than even the most radical reformers dared hope. Not surprisingly, the opposition was strongest from leaders in areas where agriculture had performed well in the collective era (such as Jilin Province and Shanghai), as well as in places that had acquired a reputation for being hotbeds of radical leftism (for example, Hunan Province, where Mao was born, and Shanxi Province, the site of the Dazhai Brigade). Yet there was a groundswell of support from peasant households desperately in favor of the economic freedoms promised by reform. Support for decollectivization appeared to be greatest in the poorer areas of the countryside (especially in Anhui Province, as well as Gansu, Henan, and Yunan). In fact the reforms were welcomed in areas where collectivization had not been a great success and peasants were in favor of switching back to family farming. All of this represented pressure from below, which was especially strong during 1980–1981, when it was still uncertain how far the reforms would officially be allowed to proceed.

We can point to the emergence of an alliance of sorts between a few reformist leaders and the masses, which outflanked and weakened the position of local officials who stood to lose the most from the introduction of the HRS. Some of the central leaders were probably relieved to find a movement that was peasant-initiated and -supported, unlike many of the coercive mass movements that had been launched in the past. Whatever the causes, once the reform process began the Party-state backed it to the hilt and, in fact, enforced its blanket application regardless of local opposition in some areas.[106] As with earlier movements, the implementation of the HRS became a "one-dimensional political movement that carried all before it."[107] The process of adoption appears to have been incremental and cumulative, moving ahead slowly but surely in line with major increases in food production. As Marc Blecher described the process: "Step by step, villagers and local leaders in various parts of the country moved ahead in developing systems that were more and more comprehensive and individualistic. Each time they were actually crossing the boundaries permitted by state policy at the time."[108] When leaders from Beijing visited the areas recording great HRS successes, they returned with favorable reports, which were used to argue for more and deeper reforms elsewhere. The reformers were eventually successful, and in 1982 "Document No. 1" was released, pronouncing that the HRS was not only permissible but that, amazingly, it was also considered to be "consistent with socialism."[109] At this point, then, what had been a peasant-initiated grassroots movement had become a program actively propagated by the leadership and enforced in all areas.

Some Western scholars have made a significant contribution to this debate with arguments about "peasant power."[110] Daniel Kelliher, for example, has proposed that the peasants did not have any coercive capacity to make the state act against its will but were able somehow to influence, alter, even create what would become fundamental rural policy changes. He has suggested that the strength of the peasantry increased during the reform era because the state was genuinely concerned with balancing economic growth and maintaining social stability.[111] Perceiving that the peasants held the key to rapid agricultural development, the state, Kelliher would argue, was forced to treat the rural sector with unusual respect.[112] According to Kelliher, state socialism had unwittingly created the possibility for mass action in the countryside by forcing millions of previously disorganized and atomized individuals to band together in the collectives.[113] By sheer numbers, in other words, the peasants were able to wield some power, especially at harvest time. For these reasons Kelliher has contended that the state responded to and stitched together a series of diffuse agrarian innovations and made them into its own reform policies; thus peasants effectively invented the reforms, with the state coming into the picture only at a later date.[114]

It is important to point out that China's peasants were allowed no real political power during both the collective era and the reform era. Most of their behavior was unsanctioned, outside the system, often disorganized, and apparently unconscious. The peasants were effectively disenfranchised in the political system, but if Kelliher is correct, then it would appear that collectively they have been able to execute small acts of innovation and disobedience, and, "compounded in countless numbers, countless places and repetitions, these small actions achieved a level of political efficacy unrecognized in any one of them seen alone."[115] That view casts China's peasants as neither victims nor revolutionaries, but their combined power helped to accelerate the push toward family farming, liberalized markets, and privatization.[116]

A more extreme version of this argument is provided by Kate Xiao Zhou in *How the Farmers Changed China*. In that book Zhou agrees with Kelliher that the state acquiesced to the introduction of the HRS, thereby ceding to the peasants the initiative for charting the course of rural reform. Zhou takes Kelliher's point much farther, however, in suggesting that the decollectivization process and the success of the HRS made possible most of the other rural revolutions China would experience under Deng Xiaoping's leadership. At the core was the economic success of the HRS, and with families taking responsibility for all important decisions farm productivity increased enormously in a very short period.[117] The reforms have demonstrated that large and rapid output increases were possible, something China's leaders had wanted but were never able to achieve.

The unanticipated success of the HRS meant that many of the restrictions on private commerce in the countryside were lifted. Markets quickly sprang back to life, and the state relinquished control over them. Price controls were relaxed on most foods, with the major exceptions of grain and cotton. There was also a huge expansion in rural industry of all types, making use of the new mobility associated with the freedom to migrate (see Chapter 15). With HRS, farmers were able to make all the important decisions about producing and selling food, as well as pioneering new sidelines and rural industries. There was also a corresponding depoliticization of the countryside, with class labels such as "capitalist" and "rich peasant" abolished, so that entrepreneurs would no longer be stigmatized as in the past. The state was extricating itself from agricultural decisionmaking as communes lost control over production issues and labor allocation.[118] However, at no time did any group of peasants attempt to seize control or force such a separation. Rather, the peasants effectively "leached" away the government's control. As Zhou has observed:

> Without firing a shot, without raising any placards, without posting any ideological statements on any wall, the farmers . . . moved as silently and unexpectedly as an electric automobile. This silent movement not only restored the position of the family in the Chinese social structure, to some extent it also re-opened the class system and loosened farmers' bonds to cadre lords and to the land. It did this and more without any of the signs ordinarily associated with a "political" movement.[119]

Gordon White has added to this debate by examining the outcomes of the agrarian reforms. In the first seven or eight years (up to about 1985) the pace of reform was more radical and more bountiful than reformers had dared imagine. Even more remarkable, in 1978 the commune system seemed to be entrenched and immovable, and in ideological terms the commitment to collectivization seemed firm. But White offers a largely political account of this phenomenon, based on the evidence that reform leaders at the top and the mass of the peasantry had common goals, perhaps for the first time in many years: to implement institutional reform at the village level. The opponents of that goal—the vast numbers of local cadres and commune officials whose jobs and prestige would be threatened—"found themselves caught in political pincers and [were] forced to climb aboard the policy bandwagon."[120] This reduced the potential for conflict while the remaining Maoists and other potentially influential leftists were either removed or neutralized, which helped strengthen the overall consensus at the center that favored reform.[121]

This was reinforced by the growing evidence of the successes attributed to or coincident with the reforms. Such success was visible in rural construction of homes, factories, and commercial operations, as well as in the exploding rate of consumer durable consumption (see Figures 7.1a, 7.1b, and 7.1c).

Everyone was benefiting, it seemed, and the multiplier effect of new consumption brought forth a virtuous circle of new jobs and further growth. Even those groups who were potential opponents of reform seemed to profit. For example, the state's grain-procurement departments were buying and selling at a much faster rate, and local governments saw their resource bases expanding. White is essentially in agreement here with Zhou, concluding that the HRS "brought about a seemingly irrevocable redis-

tribution of power in favor of the peasant household, both in terms of its relationship with the state and its relation with the collective cadres who had formerly ruled the roost in the village."[122] From this point forward power could no longer simply be mandated downward; there would need to be considerable bargaining and flexibility. The state had lost its ability to push around the peasants, which was probably a new experience for both sides.[123]

Theorizing the Successful Implementation of HRS Reform

Challenging this bottom-up theory of peasant power are two alternative theories to interpret and explain the success of agrarian reform. One is based on the idea that the chaos and catastrophe associated with the Cultural Revolution made the need for change after Mao's death a necessity. As Lucien Pye has noted, for example, "The current reforms and the open-door trade policies could never have come about except for the 'trauma' of the Cultural Revolution."[124]

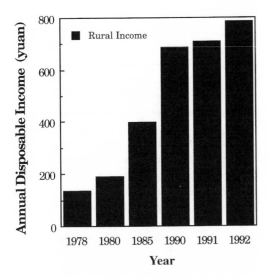

FIGURE 7.1a   Increases in Average Rural Income, 1978–1992

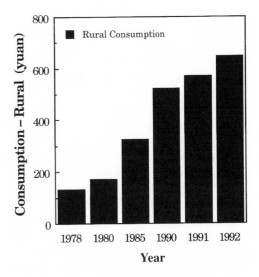

FIGURE 7.1b   Increases in Rural Consumption Rates, 1978–1992

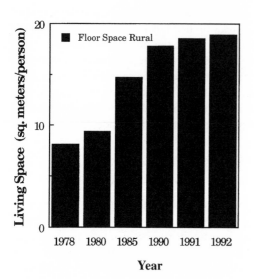

FIGURE 7.1c   Increases in Rural Living Space,
1978–1992

A second plausible theory places the responsibility (and the credit) for the reforms upon the shoulders of China's leaders, notably Deng Xiaoping, who is generally cast (by official Chinese sources and many outsiders) as *zhong shei-jishi* (the architect of the reforms). A number of Western scholars have focused on the way Deng outmaneuvered his political rivals to secure the successful adoption of his reform program.[125]

In the recent book *Calamity and Reform in China*, Dali Yang has offered a different interpretation of events during the reform era. His theory, simply put, is that the post-1978 agricultural reforms were primarily an outcome of the struggle between the state and the peasants, mediated by local and regional leaders and greatly conditioned or influenced by the severity of the famine experienced during the Great Leap Forward. Yang's major hypothesis is expressed succinctly in the following statement: "The Great Leap Famine furnished the structural incentives for peasants and their allies to take advantage of the political opportunity opened up by Mao's death and the succession struggle . . . to pursue liberalization in rural

China."[126] With an intriguing mix of theoretical and empirical analysis, then, Yang would argue that the provinces most enthusiastically embracing the post-1978 reforms were the ones in which people had suffered the most during the 1958–1961 Great Famine.[127] Yang has argued that individual and household contracting was most likely to reappear after 1978 in the areas that were hit hardest during the famine. Adoption of HRS at the time was defined by some as an example of rightist behavior, in the sense that it was opposed to the Maoist (leftist) insistence on collective agricultural production. The best examples Yang points to in support of his theory are Anhui, Henan, Sichuan, and Gansu Provinces, all of which suffered high mortality rates during the Great Famine (see Table 7.6).[128]

A hypothesis like this cannot really be "proved" with aggregate (province-level) data, but Yang argues that his findings clearly support further analysis at the case-study level, that is, at the county, prefecture, and provincial levels, making use of interviews and archival records (similar to the work conducted by Jasper Becker in his book *Hungry Ghosts*). Yang assumes that in the hardest-hit areas some peasants, despite rigid state control in the wake of the famine, retained an "alternative agenda" that was derived from and based on their experiences during the famine years. When Mao died, these peasants realized their opportunity, and the first and most enthusiastic reformers among them—the ones most willing to experiment with reform—were in those areas that had suffered the most.[129]

Yang refines his hypothesis substantially by investigating the political events that took place after Mao's death in 1976. Mao's immediate successor, Hua Guofeng, aided by Chen Yong-Gui, former leader of the Dazhai Brigade, advocated a leftist-Maoist line that was opposed by Deng Xiaoping and others, who argued for pragmatism, moderation, liberalization, and individual-household responsibility. This was the rightist line that eventually succeeded after Deng came to power in 1978. In other words, during the post-Mao interregnum, there were major cleavages in agricultural policy. Yang has argued that

TABLE 7.6 Mortality Rates in Selected Chinese Provinces, 1956–1962 (per 1,000 population)[1]

Province, Autonomous Region, or Special Municipality	Average 1956–1958	Highest Rate 1959–1962	Difference Between Highest 1959–1962 Rate and Average 1956–1958 Rate	Percentage Change[2]
China	11.4	25.4	14.0	122.8
Tianjin	9.0	10.3	1.3	14.4
Shanghai	6.2	7.7	1.5	24.2
Zhejiang	9.3	11.9	2.6	28.0
Beijing	8.0	10.8	2.8	35.0
Guangdong	9.6	15.1	5.5	57.3
Jiangsu	10.9	18.4	7.5	68.8
Hubei	*10.0*	*21.2*	*11.2*	*112.0*
Liaoning	*8.3*	*17.5*	*9.2*	*110.8*
Guangxi	*12.2*	*29.5*	*17.3*	*141.8*
Hunan	*11.2*	*29.4*	*18.2*	*162.5*
Gansu	*14.4*	*41.3*	*26.9*	*186.8*
Henan	*12.8*	*39.6*	*26.8*	*209.4*
Sichuan	*15.9*	*54.0*	*38.1*	*239.6*
Qinghai	*10.9*	*40.7*	*29.8*	*273.4*
Guizhou	*13.6*	*52.3*	*38.7*	*284.6*
Anhui	*11.9*	*68.6*	*56.7*	*478.5*

SOURCE: Modified from Yang (1996), Table 6, p. 38.

NOTES:

[1] The ten provinces shaded are those with the highest mortality rates in China; the six above are selected for comparative purposes.

[2] This is the increase from the average rate for the period 1956–1958 to the highest rate recorded in 1959–1962 (column 4/column *100).

such cleavages at the top indicated a "deconcentration of power and sanctions in the system, which in turn provided political space for some elites to pursue their own policy agendas . . . and for cadres and peasants in some localities . . . to take advantage of the politically ambiguous situation to resurrect and pursue practices such as household contracting."[130]

To return to an important point, we should note that Yang's theory reinforces the importance of history, in this case the effect of vivid memories of past suffering, on current policy. In this sense Yang added support to the work currently being done in societies—including China—that are in the transition away from or out of socialism, arguing for the importance of past events (i.e., the path-dependency approach). According to Yang, "History is path

dependent [which] means that policy outcomes are not merely dependent variables to be explained but are also independent variables constraining the future."[131]

The problem with that hypothesis: It raises more questions than it answers. Granted, Yang has attempted to fill in the behavioral sequences that might put some flesh on the bones of his hypothesis, suggesting that the famine (the result of bad politics) creates serious doubt as to the prevailing political orthodoxy, which included collective control and commandism; this became a powerful agent for constitutional change. Before the famine most Chinese leaders, at all levels within the hierarchy, felt anything was within their grasp, and to prove it they launched some fantastic and outrageous production campaigns (referred to sometimes as output "Sputniks").[132] As Yang suggested: "The famine changed all that. Indeed, one might say that the famine sounded the death knell for the paradigm of collectivization and launched a new paradigm of reform. The famine made people see the world through a different set of lenses and alter their survival strategies. As they did so, the foundations of Chinese politics were transformed."[133]

Peasant Resistance and the Changing Nature of Rural Politics

The unanswered questions center on the relationship between peasants and the state throughout the reform era and the ways that HRS has altered the pattern and content of that relationship. As we have noted earlier, in many rural areas local governments—seeking to replenish their dwindling resources—established a variety of ad hoc levies, fees, and taxes on the peasants.[134] The central government is aware of the grotesque unfairness of many of these new charges and has issued numerous regulations to prevent such behavior, yet it seems virtually powerless to stop the unlawful and exploitive behavior of local government officials. The localities argue that unless they raise revenues in this way they will be unable even to maintain existing levels of agricultural productivity and distribution systems, let alone to repair and rebuild local roads and water conservation structures. The ongoing debate has been acrimonious: Some Party leaders blame farmers, accusing them of being too apathetic, or too greedy, or too corrupt. But a strong case can also be made that the core of the problem lies much more with local and national policies that systematically undermined China's rural collective institutions and are continuing along the same vein in the reform era. Although overall conditions in many rural areas have improved, the problems between peasants and the state have been exacerbated by the absolute success of the HRS reforms, which, by increas-

ing agricultural efficiency, have revealed the extensive problem of underemployment in the countryside. The net effect is that more people than ever are now in need of local support, just as the abilities of the rural collective institutions to provide such support have been undermined and eroded.

As we have seen, after initially opposing HRS reform, the Dengist leadership jumped onto the bandwagon as soon as the results began to look impressive. With the backing of a state mandate, there began what amounted to a program of forced decollectivization; it has gained momentum, even in places where local leaders and peasants were in opposition. The pervasiveness of the reform policies and their impacts effectively destroyed the nature of local politics in the rural collectives, which, according to Marc Blecher, lay "at the center of the participatory, solicitative, and mobilizational mass line politics."[135] Most individuals and households today work primarily as private units or in rural enterprises, no longer interconnected in their workaday lives as in the Maoist era. In addition, the scope of political life has been reduced significantly by the general depoliticization pursued by the Dengist leadership.[136] Political and economic functions are now clearly separable, and the workplace is no longer the site of local politics to the extent it was in the past. Peasants have been squeezed between rising input prices and state demands to grow crops (especially grain) with low selling prices. In many instances peasants are furious about the proliferation of unpredictable taxes and fees; not surprisingly there have been signs of massive rural unrest.

At the end of the 1990s there is little consensus as to exactly what has been achieved in rural China after a decade of reform and almost universal enthusiasm for it. The urban-rural income gap has been rising, and peasants continue to feel they are falling farther and farther behind (see Table 7.7).[137]

There have been some bold steps forward, often followed by swift steps backward. There are still some glaring contradictions, for exam-

TABLE 7.7   Changes in Per Capita Income of Urban and Rural Households, 1978–1996

| Year | Rural | | Urban | | |
	Net Income Per Capita (yuan)	Index (1978=100)	Net Income Per Capita (yuan)	Index (1978=100)	Urban to Rural Ratio
1978	134	100	316	100	2.25:1
1980	191	186	439	127	2.29:1
1985	398	359	685	162	1.72:1
1990	686	416	1,387	198	2.02:1
1996	1,926	559	4,377	297	2.27:1

SOURCE: State Statistical Bureau, *China Statistical Yearbook, 1997.*

ple, in situations where state subsidies are working alongside market incentives. The clash between the state and the peasants over grain and food production has caused some serious problems, as the state experimented, back and forth, with mandatory grain procurement, a process that has been characterized as a "shifting game of cat-and-mouse."[138] The attempts by the state to control what peasants grew and the peasants' natural inclination to favor more lucrative (i.e., nongrain) crops have resulted in several manifestations of peasant resistance that fall short of actual protest, including simply ignoring the quotas; purchasing grain on the free market, then reselling it to the state to meet quotas; and lying to procurement officials about the sizes of harvests.

In addition to rural protests and these forms of "production resistance," many peasants have educated themselves about local taxes and their rights and lodged complaints with local officials; some have gone higher up the ladder, to township and county authorities. Letters to magazines and newspaper editors have been written by the thousand (often using hired writers); sit-ins and sit-downs have been commonplace; and some farmers have gone to court to seek redress for the injustices they feel have been done. All of this represents a new form of peaceful and legalistic activity in China, which in the absence of institutionalized lobbying and protesting can be considered to be a new type of grassroots political participation.

Obviously, the more difficult task—still to be broached—is how to parlay such individualistic micropolitics in the countryside into larger-scale activities and the creation of civic organizations that can advocate and lobby for peasant rights. We shall return to this issue in Chapters 18 and 19.[139]

The post-1978 era in rural China has witnessed the entire range of possible problems, including the stagnation of agricultural production, enduring rural poverty, increasing urban inequality, crumbling infrastructures, and rising rural discontent and protest. Yet it was in that same countryside that the post-Mao reforms achieved their first and perhaps most lasting impacts: Decollectivization was effectively completed within four years; the HRS became firmly entrenched; and marketization emerged in all areas of rural production and distribution. Peasants were for the most part peaceful and passive throughout the tumultuous events of 1989, much to the government's relief, but since then they have increasingly shifted from acquiescence to noncompliance and even armed resistance in the 1990s. As Marc Blecher has warned, the peasants "have become . . . more active and censorious participants in the politics that are portending greater change for China with each passing day."[140] The state can no longer ignore the peasants; in fact it is possible to argue that the countryside is and will continue to be the site of three of China's most urgent problems for the first years of the new millennium: massive unemployment and underemployment; the need for in-situ employment opportunities to stem the already huge exodus to the cities (see Chapter 15); and ensuring the country's food supplies (Chapter 17).

Some China scholars have concluded that the reform era produced an enigma: dramatic change in a sea of continuity.[141] In one sense very little has changed: Agriculture at the local level is still constrained by central and local institutional interests, and there is still a huge rural-urban gap in incomes and living standards. There is, however, a much more rational and informed type of agricultural policymaking today. There are far more experts in the system than ever before, and on the whole the policymaking system is much more complex, with so many new actors and interests involved. The state, still at the center, now has more difficulty keeping an eye on and controlling the whole operation, and it is often forced to rely on desperate bargaining and threats of force (usually referred to as "bluster"). As Gordon White explained it, the state and its agents (i.e., local cadres) "have lost a good deal of their former ability to determine the behavior of the peasantry."[142]

During the collective era the flow of power in rural China was clearly top-down, with only weak channels available for communicating peasant views upward to the leaders. There was a triad of power vested in the party, the state, and the commune, with little separation between the political, social, and economic spheres. Politics, as one China scholar has suggested, "ran like a reed thread through all aspects of rural life,"[143] and the power structure pretty much ensured peasant compliance with official politics. The peasants nominally took part in a participatory process, but their role was most often restricted to supporting political movements of various types that had been initiated higher up the ladder without consultation. Most of the important production decisions were made over the heads of the actual production teams, so even though it seemed like a democratic environment the substance of

rural politics involved the traditional "triple subordination" of peasant households: They were subordinated to the overriding priority of national industrial policies, which resulted in peasants being forced into mandatory procurement quotas at prices that were often unfavorable; they were subordinated to the primacy of accumulation (investment) over current consumption, so they had low incomes and little to spend their money on; and they were subordinated to the production teams, where all of the local investment was channeled.

During the collective era peasants were especially exasperated about the many different mass political movements and the state's exhortation to support them. At every point along the way they were made to feel inferior to city dwellers, which added insult to injury, bearing in mind that the latter were heavily subsidized by the state, mainly on the backs of rural labor and production. Most peasants were prevented from leaving the countryside and from taking better-paying jobs away from the land; for all of these reasons, at the end of the 1970s morale in the countryside was at a low ebb—and productivity was even lower. Realizing the important role of agriculture in the national economy, the post-Mao leadership began to execute some of the changes required in the realm of policy and institutional change in the countryside.[144] Criticisms were leveled at all points in the agricultural system, and the struggle between the state and the peasantry over the agricultural surplus became "a relentless, wearisome game in which both sides expended a lot of unproductive effort."[145]

During the early stages in the process it looked as if the reforms would establish more direct links between the producers (the peasants) and the market, without the interference of village (formerly brigade) cadres. But in reality many village leaders have been able to reimpose some degree of control and have been actively limiting peasant access to the market. The decentralization of power to local areas should have benefited the peasants, but many local authorities, short of cash, have continued to play a significant role. As one team of scholars astutely pointed out, the local cadres "run the only employment agency. . . . They are responsible for distributing land, they still influence access to the use of tractors [and they] play a major part in companies that act as market brokers."[146] In many cases local cadres are still responsible for allocating and rationing farm inputs; and they have considerable latitude in market dynamics (for example, by creating artificial shortages that can raise prices).

Although local officials' roles and their relationships with peasants have certainly changed, it is apparent from most accounts that local officials still exercise considerable power over the peasantry. In addition, evidence suggests that local cadres still provide safety-net functions, for example, for vulnerable households experiencing lean harvests. Rural cadres still shape local economies, albeit via a new form of client-patron relationship, whereby cadres now act as brokers between the state and society. Notwithstanding the obvious benefits to the peasants, the existing power structures are still able to block the emergence of new local organizations to represent peasants' interests, which effectively hinders the emergence of a modern civil society in the countryside.

During the Tiananmen Square demonstrations in 1989 the peasants were largely quiescent, and the protests of the students and workers in the cities fell on largely deaf ears in the countryside. But in the 1990s there have been some significant changes, and in the event of another outburst peasant passivity cannot be guaranteed.[147] When so many peasants act in a certain way at approximately the same time, the government tends to get nervous and pays close attention to what is going on.[148] There is also a structural dictate working on the state, in the sense that to foster development in China's rural areas through industrialization and urbanization it is obliged to protect peasant interests and encourage and endorse their initiatives in rural development. Centuries of inertia, embodied in the mentality of the "moral peasant" engaged in a grim but passive struggle for survival, have come to an end. Today the state is much more likely to encounter the

"rational peasant," who can no longer be relied upon for support and acquiescence.[149]

The new system of agricultural policymaking contains elements of the old ways (the plan) and the new ways (the market), and the state has been moving backward and forward along that continuum. However, it would appear that too much has changed socially, politically, economically, and psychologically to turn back the clock. Yet additional movement toward the new ways could easily unleash forces that the state would be hard-pressed to control.[150] By the mid-1990s the state was in control of less than 20 percent of total grain purchases and 25 percent of sideline produce. Farmers' dreams were expanding exponentially, because as the popular rural saying goes, "One year's hard work in the field is not worth one day in the market."[151] The state has been surprised by the new developments, particularly the vast increase in *jishi* (rural markets) and the sudden rise of *yinjun fujin* (referring to rural industry, the rough translation being "a strange army suddenly appears").[152] There is a new dual economy in China: a nonstate sector operating at full throttle, with a moribund state sector propped up by subsidies. The explosion of rural industry did not (as the Party-state had hoped) prevent rural out-migration, but it did give farmers a vehicle for capital growth, with almost no contributions required from the state. The nonagricultural sector in the countryside was 98 million strong in 1992; and a huge part of total rural production (estimated to be more than 60 percent) came from rural industry. In 1993 only 43 percent of industrial firms were state-owned, compared to 78 percent in 1978, whereas the rural collective sector increased from 7 percent of total industrial output in 1978 to more than 30 percent in 1993.[153]

Kate Zhou has concluded that the "spectacular" agricultural performance in China post-1978 (and especially up to 1985) can be attributed to three factors: the initiative, ingenuity, and greed of farmers; the corruptibility of cadres; and the fact that the central leadership was generally too occupied with other matters to pay attention to events in the countryside. As Zhou has suggested, "The farmers had proved to be alchemists. They had turned their mundane agricultural dross into agricultural, industrial . . . and commercial gold."[154] After almost two decades of reform many things have improved, but there are still multiple sources of rural discontent. However, the difference today is that after the decollectivization process the basic relationship between peasants and the state has been fundamentally altered. Peasants are now able to see routes to economic success, and many have taken bold steps down the capitalist road to make a clean break. They have, individually and in groups, resisted some government policies and supported others. Because of the new and weaker power relationships, the state is now far less likely to mount an effective challenge to peasants who are flexing their muscles.[155]

8

China's Economy in the Transition from Plan to Market

𐃏𐃏𐃏𐃏𐃏𐃏𐃏𐃏𐃏𐃏𐃏𐃏𐃏𐃏𐃏𐃏𐃏𐃏𐃏𐃏𐃏

Along with Adam Smith's invisible hand, we find some evidence of Joseph Berliner's "invisible foot," which administers a sharp rebuke to the backside of unsuccessful firms.

—Barry Naughton, *Growing out of the Plan* (1995)[1]

Introduction: China Catching Up

This reference to hands and feet (the "invisible" influence of the market personified) demonstrates just how far China has traveled down the road to capitalism, albeit with Chinese characteristics. Competition has been the order of the day, and enterprises that failed to make the grade went belly-up. Most China scholars agree, at the end of the twentieth century, that the success of Deng Xiaoping's reforms helped save his government from becoming the next in a long line of socialist casualties during the tumultuous late 1980s. The regime was seriously challenged in the spring of 1989 at Tiananmen Square and in other parts of China, but by 1992, after a brief downturn in the economy, growth rates picked up and began to surpass pre-Tiananmen levels. The benefits of economic growth provided Deng's government with a buffer that managed to keep most of the people either happy or distracted enough to accept the status quo, which gave the Chinese Communist Party some needed breathing space throughout the 1990s.[2]

The acceleration of reform after 1992 allowed mainland China to catch up with its offshore territories in terms of economic development. By the time Mao died in 1976 nearly

three decades of socialism had produced some impressive economic achievements, with industrial production expanding at an average rate of more than 9 percent per year between 1953 and 1980 and gross national product (GNP) growing by more than 6 percent per year.[3] As impressive as these statistics were, the leadership was acutely aware that the economy in the "other" China (i.e., Taiwan, or the Republic of China) was much stronger. Capitalist Taiwan had badly outperformed communist China, and as a result the people of Taiwan were much better off than people in the PRC. Growth of Taiwan's GNP had consistently been close to 50 percent higher than the PRC's GNP, and by the 1980s per capita incomes in Taiwan were more than ten times higher.[4]

Taiwan's economic transformation has been hailed around the world as a miracle of sorts, and the PRC government was forced to recognize that the dynamic partnership between the private and public sectors in Taiwan had produced bountiful results. After consolidating its power, therefore, the post-Mao leadership began to implement dramatic changes in industrial policy to parallel those that had already been introduced in the agricultural sector. In this chapter we investigate and evaluate China's economic restructuring, which some observers have called the "Chinese perestroika" (even though it was occurring before its name-sake in the former Soviet Union). To set the stage for this discussion, and to put the reform era into its historical and political context, it is necessary to describe the socialist transforma-tion of the Chinese economy after 1949.

The Socialist Transformation

After 1949 the CCP moved cautiously toward the transformation of China's industrial sector.[5] The Party had no experience in national government and little in urban administration. China lay pil-laged following four decades of civil, revolution-ary, and foreign wars, and after a century of imperialism the economy was a shambles. Un-employment and inflation were at all-time highs, and there were deep structural defects in the country's economic system, including a chronic shortage of investment in industry, a dearth of skilled labor, and relatively few compe-tent managers. In Canton (Guangzhou), for ex-ample, the new Party-state grappled with the issue of transforming a city famed for small en-terprises into a more efficient system amenable to centralized planning. As Ezra Vogel reported in his book *Canton Under Communism*: "Local officials responsible for planning economic ac-tivities had become painfully aware of the diffi-culty of guiding tens of thousands of private enterprises, each trying to outwit the govern-ment. . . . The task of directing thousands of pushcarts and tiny handicraft shops and mil-lions of tiny farms . . . created headaches for of-ficials everywhere."[6]

Spatial Egalitarianism

In addition to economic and political difficul-ties there was a notorious geographical imbal-ance in China's economy between the developed core along the coast as well as in the northeastern provinces (Manchuria) and the undeveloped periphery in the western, north-western, and southwestern provinces and ARs. The roots of this spatial imbalance were partly environmental, partly cultural, and partly political. In the peripheral regions there tended to be climatic and topographical characteristics unfavorable to agricultural development and dense settlement. Superimposed onto that was the influence of foreign powers during the pre-vious hundred years, as well as the develop-ment of the so-called Treaty Ports in eastern and southern China. In the first tier of such ports to be developed, especially cities like Tianjin, Shanghai, and Canton, Western com-mercial development helped produce bustling economies. Later the northeastern provinces of China were occupied by Japan, and there was considerable investment in mining, industry, and infrastructure.

In the first two decades after the revolution serious efforts were made to counteract regional imbalances by focusing industrial growth in se-lected cities in the interior—including such places as Xian, Zhengzhou, Taiyuan, Chengdu, Yinchuan, and Lanzhou—and by encouraging new industrial development close to resource-rich locations in remoter regions. It was appar-ent, however, that despite the overall commitment to regional equality it made sound economic sense to concentrate development in China's most efficient areas—in other words, in the coastal provinces. In the first two decades the seeds of recovery were sown, largely as a re-sult of careful economic management by the CCP. Industrial output was quickly restored to the level of the 1930s, but it was clear that a ma-jor economic propulsion was still required to bring about socialist transformation.

Nationalization

Unlike the relatively swift dispossession of the landlords in the countryside, many key figures in China's urban bourgeois class were allowed to remain in business after 1949.[7] Nationaliza-tion was carried out only in certain economic sectors, and economic decisionmaking was cen-tralized relatively gradually. The government took over the assets of Nationalist elites, who had fled to Taiwan with Chiang Kai-shek, and of most foreign-owned companies. This represented the industrial core of the economy and accounted for most of the heavy industry and mining and more than three-quarters of fixed capital, but it represented only about a third of the nation's total industrial output.[8]

The bulk of the country's light industry was owned by a group the Communists referred to as the "national capitalists," who had not traditionally been closely allied to the KMT. Instead of expropriating this class, the CCP decided to co-opt them into a newly formed coalition with the understanding that the country needed their technical and managerial skills. The net effect was that China's urban economy came to be dominated, for a short time at least, by petit bourgeois enterprises. By 1953 the number of privately owned firms had increased sixfold, to 150,000, making up almost one-fifth of China's output value.[9] In the second half of the 1950s efforts were made to weed out members of the bourgeoisie who could not be relied upon to support the CCP and the pursuit of socialism, but even those campaigns were mild compared to the assaults aimed at rural landlords.[10]

The development model chosen for reconstructing the Chinese economy was based on the Soviet pattern of Five Year Plans. Although such a strategy was realistic given the need to build up the economy quickly, it represented a fundamental departure from the geographical principles of Chinese socialism. Planning in the new regime was to be highly centralized, effectively reducing the emphasis on local and regional self-reliance that had been so successful in the revolutionary base areas prior to 1949. There was also a marked priority given to industrial development over agriculture, and because the majority of all investment funds were generated by peasant agriculture, it was evident that the countryside was being heavily exploited to support China's industry.[11] This represented a transfer (or appropriation) of resources from the countryside to the cities, which was in direct contradiction to Mao Zedong's rhetoric about balanced economic development. Most of the country's economic growth during this period was to be focused on existing centers of strength, which meant the

urban areas in the northeastern and eastern provinces of China, and their development threatened to further widen the gap between the richest and poorest regions.

During the First Five Year Plan (1953–1957) the state began to speed the pace of nationalization. The previously tolerated bourgeois class was gradually squeezed out, and most of China's private firms came under direct state ownership. At the same time, there was a sharp decline in worker democracy in Chinese industry, as a strictly hierarchical pattern of management was put into place and rigid piece rates and quota systems were instituted.[12] It is not difficult to understand why the CCP moved away from its earlier avowed principles toward the Five Year Plan approach to economic development. The model had worked in the Soviet Union, admittedly under different circumstances, and the Chinese had little experience in directing large-scale industrial development. With significant aid from the Soviets, in the form of both investment funds and technical know-how, the Chinese recorded some impressive results with the First Five Year Plan; for example, the output of heavy industry expanded by 300 percent, that of light industry by 70 percent. The major problem, however, was that agriculture was not growing fast enough to support such a continued rate of accumulation. People in the countryside were, in relative terms, getting poorer while city dwellers were getting richer. The out-migration of peasants from the countryside to the rapidly industrializing cities during the late 1950s put an extra burden on the agricultural sector, and it was becoming difficult to see how the Second Five Year Plan, which would continue to emphasize capital-intensive heavy industry, would be financed.

In political terms this situation was dangerous for the Communists, who were members of a revolutionary organization that had risen to power with the help of the peasants. There was also a natural opposition in the CCP, frequently voiced by Mao Zedong, to the level of bureaucratization and inequality built into Soviet-style economic development. In a now-famous speech in 1956 entitled "On the Ten Major

Relationships," Mao expressed his growing concerns about the dangers of China continuing down a path that would seriously widen existing geographical imbalances among regions and between agriculture and industry.[13] His solution was to push through an ambitious program of forced collectivization.

The Great Leap Forward

Some of the deviations from the Maoist principles of socialism that had occurred in the First Five Year Plan were to be addressed by the Great Leap Forward at the end of the 1950s; in fact to a large extent the previous policies were reversed. The emphasis on heavy industry was to be balanced by the development of both light industry and agriculture. Rural industry and urban agriculture were to be emphasized as twin policies designed to reduce the urban-rural dichotomy. Instead of developing industry at the expense of agriculture, the emphasis for the future was labor, one resource China was well endowed with. Most notably, in geographical terms, there was to be a renewed emphasis on regional equality and local self-reliance, aided by a significant amount of decentralization of economic decisionmaking to the local and regional levels. Provincial and municipal authorities were permitted to keep up to 20 percent of their profits to spend at their discretion, and the relative power of factory workers was increased so they were on more equal footing with management. Incentive systems were shifted more to the collective level, with workers being offered new reasons to work harder. The Great Leap Forward seemed to have been a success quickly, with some major gains in industrial output recorded in 1958, but in terms of efficiency the economy reached an all-time low, mainly the result of fanatical attempts to develop small-scale industry in rural areas.[14]

During this period the issue of decentralization became something of a political football. In the First Five Year Plan the central government established mandatory targets for all industrial sectors, which were passed down in dictatorial fashion to the enterprises. During the Great Leap that vertical structure was altered somewhat, and decisionmakers at the local level were allowed greater independence as to production. Provinces were allowed to plan industrial development on a territorial (i.e., horizontal) basis rather than being told what to do by the central government (i.e., vertical, or functional, coordination).

The Cultural Revolution

After the Great Leap Forward the decisionmaking balance shifted back in favor of centralized economic planning, but during the Cultural Revolution there was a tendency toward decentralization again, with the power of the central (vertical) command structure further damaged by the widespread chaos characterizing that era. In a significant break with the past, even huge firms in key industrial sectors, such as the Anshan Steel Company, were turned over to provincial-level administration. The attempts to restore decisionmaking to the local level at this time were sporadic and were mainly politically driven; they did not represent a coherent strategy designed to bring about greater industrial efficiency through decentralization.

Evaluating China's Industrial Economy at the End of the 1970s

To simplify what was a complex era, the political squabbles over the "best" strategies for economic development had produced a major shift in policy, from the Soviet line associated with the Five Year Plans (1953–1957) to the Maoist line (1958–1961). There was also a series of smaller yet important shifts, either to the right (1961–1965) or left (1966–1976). All of this caused major disruptions to the economy and, more importantly, to the political and social lives of the Chinese people. By the time the post-Mao leadership came to power there had already been several attempts to shift the responsibility for economic planning down to the local level, and in that sense the reforms introduced by Deng Xiaoping were not as difficult to administer as would have been the case in the Soviet Union. As the new leaders surveyed what had happened over the previous two and a half decades, they saw an uneven landscape of achievement. Significant advances had been made, and industrial output had grown considerably (see Table 8.1), but that had been achieved largely by huge investments in fixed capital and by requiring the people to abstain from consumption. To develop China's industry it had always been necessary to devote a relatively high proportion of GNP to investment funds (i.e., accumulation). In the Great Leap years, for example, investment was more than 40 percent of China's GNP, whereas consumption dropped to a rock-bottom (almost starvation) level; even in the most chaotic years of the Cultural Revolution the level of investment remained above 20 percent.[15]

To achieve an accumulation rate of such magnitude, incomes had to be kept low, and the Chinese people had very little money to spend on themselves and their families. After Mao's 1976 death, in fact, Deng Xiaoping was constantly reminding his critics that workers in China's cities had never received a pay raise during three decades of socialism. For mainland Chinese, that harsh reality made the comparison to Taiwan difficult to bear. There is no doubt that the CCP had advanced the cause of

economic development in China, but it had been achieved at the expense of personal consumption. Yet another problem the new leadership faced in 1978 was the imbalance between different sectors of the economy, with agriculture and light industry still, in relative terms, playing second fiddle to heavy industry. Unemployment was also becoming an important concern, and it was recognized in 1978 that focusing more on light industry would create far more jobs in the cities as well as in rural areas.[16] Probably the most consistent concern at this time was the chronically low level of efficiency in China's industry. Although it had proved possible to expand production levels impressively by injecting huge amounts of investment capital, industry still needed to grow "intensively" as a result of technological improvement, innovation at the management level, and greater labor productivity.[17]

The problem was that industrial efficiency had never been the primary goal in communist China's economic policy. Output quotas were set for a given factory without any real consideration of the demand for its product. Quality control was rarely an important issue because the buyer had a contract with the state rather than with the factory, and that made it difficult to seek recourse if the finished goods were

TABLE 8.1   Industrial Output in China, 1952–1978 (1952 = 100)

	Gross Value of Industrial Output	# Workers and Employees (per year)	Fixed and Working Capital	Output per Worker[1]	Output per Unit of Capital[2]
1952	100	100	100	100	100
1957	233.3	146.7	225.6	159.0	103.4
1965	510.1	242.7	705.2	210.4	67.9
1978	1649.2	596.1	2222.0	276.7	74.2
Rates of Growth (% per Year)					
1952	18.0	8.0	17.7	9.7	0.7
1957	10.3	6.5	15.3	3.6	−5.1
1965	9.4	7.2	9.2	2.1	0.7
1978	11.4	7.1	12.7	4.0	−1.1

SOURCE: Adapted from Riskin (1987), p. 264.
NOTES:
[1] Column 1 divided by column 2.
[2] Column 1 divided by column 3.

shoddy. The consideration of profit and loss in a socialist economy also took a backseat to other goals, such as creating full employment and providing worker benefits. A factory in which many workers stand idle for lack of work is obvious inefficiency, but if unemployment is the special local fear, then there is little incentive to make that factory more efficient by laying off unneeded workers.

The traditional explanation for the chronic inefficiency in China's industry during the Maoist period was organizational. Decision-making power at the enterprise level was largely in the hands of Party members, and the enterprises themselves were still mostly controlled from above, at the central or provincial level of government. By the end of the 1970s most factories were top-heavy with administrative and political cadres, many of whom were engaged in control and surveillance functions rather than production activities.[18] The prevalence of appointments based on political considerations—rather than skill and efficiency—was the legacy of the long-standing desire of the CCP to maintain centralized control over the economy. Needed urgently was a set of reform policies to begin making the economy relatively independent from the political leadership at all levels.[19]

The excessively managed administrative structure also contributed to overinvestment. Capital goods were allocated through centralized plans rather than being charged to the individual enterprise, so there was little incentive for managers to limit their requests for raw materials. In fact, to cover for future uncertainties they were wise to request inputs far in excess of current need. The net effect was that in many parts of China there were vast stockpiles of some goods but chronic shortages of others. Central planning also produced the notorious "ratchet effect," which was counterintuitive to overall enterprise productivity. Next year's output targets were based on this year's production, so it became more difficult every year to reach the established quota. The smart (but inefficient) solution chosen by many managers was to slow production this year to ensure

a larger profit margin and greater bonuses for the workers next year.

China Moving Ahead: Decentralizing and Marketizing the Economy

Restructuring China's urban industrial economy would prove considerably more difficult than doing so in the agricultural sector. The major problems were political, in that the move toward expanding market mechanisms would present a direct challenge to the bureaucrats who administered China's industry at all levels. When bureaucrats are faced with a new way of doing things, they are likely to react defensively.[20] The problem was exacerbated by the proliferation of administrators working at both the line and the area levels, which had created myriad constituents, none willing to relinquish any power. Once the new reforms were introduced, however, the initial resistance appears to have been replaced fairly quickly by widespread corruption, bureaucratic "squeeze," and bribery as unscrupulous officials took advantage of the new reforms to line their own pockets. The traditional network of *guanxi*—the connections that open up the back doors for people—would continue to play a central role (see Chapter 3), but in the reform era a new cash nexus would be superimposed onto it. With new opportunities to make and keep the profits from enterprises, many officials found themselves in an excellent position to "get rich" and "glorify" themselves, as Deng Xiaoping had recommended.[21] Even leading cadres in the Chinese government have not been exempt from this sort of corruption, and rumors have circulated about top officials who managed to stash their gains in foreign bank accounts. In her book *The New Chinese Revolution*, Lynn Pan tells a story about a Japanese trader who actually preferred doing business with the Chinese before the reforms, despite all the old inefficiencies. As he reported, business leaders and key officials could easily be satisfied with "bribes" of pocket calculators or radios, but beginning in the 1980s they were more likely to ask for computers and even cars when deals were being made.[22]

In the collective economy, enterprises bought and sold everything through official agents of the state (known as *caigouyuan*). In the reform era they would begin to interact with each other in a predominantly marketlike environment, which generated a new subclass of speculative middlemen (*touji shangfan*) who arrange deals between buyers and sellers for commission. Factories had to negotiate with and, if necessary, bribe the middlemen, a process usually referred to as *yanjiu yanjiu*—which implies wining and dining—to extract the most favorable terms.[23]

At a larger scale, restructuring China's economy brought to the surface the thorny relationship between the center and the periphery. The reform process required some degree of decentralization of economic decisionmaking, but there is no evidence that Party officials (i.e., cadres) were ready to relinquish power. As Chinese leaders would quickly discover, economic reforms intended to allow regions and localities to become more efficient economically were often subverted by greedy and self-serving actions at the local level. After a few years of this, some Party leaders became apprehensive as to the wisdom of continuing with the reform project and began calling for retrenchments (downsizing).

In addition to these difficulties, it was apparent that China's industry simply had far less experience with market mechanisms than did the agricultural sector. Private plots and some private selling had always been a feature of the rural landscape, even in the heyday of collectivization, but urban industry had been pretty much dominated by the centralized control of prices and distribution mechanisms since the 1950s. Despite these difficulties, after 1978 the reforms were advanced along four major axes:

- Decentralization of economic decisionmaking: In a series of stages greater autonomy was granted to regional authorities, as well as to individual enterprises;

- Introduction of market principles into the socialist command economy: This was oriented toward individual workers, who would be offered greater material incentives to work harder, as well as to individual enterprises, which would be allowed and encouraged to become part of the new private sector in the economy; at a larger scale there were some major changes in the centralized system of distribution and, most importantly, in the area of price controls;

- Focus on regional specialization strategies: The traditional Maoist emphasis on regional self-reliance and spatial egalitarianism was pretty much abandoned, as regions and cities were encouraged to expand on their areas of economic strength; and[24]

- Shift toward foreign trade, investments, and financing: Referred to by one scholar as the "Great Leap Westward,"[25] a set of interrelated policies would evolve quickly with the development of "free trade" cities, known locally as Special Economic Zones, in which foreign countries were allowed to take advantage of tax and land concessions to set up industries that could benefit from China's cheap labor.

Decentralization

Experiments with enterprise autonomy had started as early as 1978 in Sichuan Province, when some local industrial enterprises were granted what were known as the "eight rights." The four most important were the right to retain part of their profits; to make their own investment decisions; to produce for outlets other than the state; and to sign contracts with foreign investors. In 1979 these experiments were extended to other provinces, and by 1980 more than 6,000 factories enjoyed such rights. In late 1984 the Party-state officially decided that the gains from the reforms thus far had been too timid and piecemeal, and a new resolution was announced.[26] Henceforth the government would gradually ease out of the business of managing the industrial economy. The experiments with enterprise autonomy were to be extended to the entire country, amounting to an urban economic "revolution" similar to the one that had already occurred in the countryside.[27] Starting in 1985 all industrial enterprises were required to implement a responsibility system under the leadership of the plant manager. With the exception of the basic industries (mining, steel, and energy), enterprises were expected to arrange their own supply of raw materials, set their own output targets, handle their own sales, and schedule their own investments.

Enterprises were also allowed to reward and motivate their workers, and it became clear that the state would no longer be willing to bail out enterprises that continually operated at a loss. Although this at first appeared to be a hollow threat in a socialist economy, some cities introduced bankruptcy laws, and in August 1986 the city of Shenyang announced China's first bankruptcy since 1949.[28] (An instrument factory that had been operating at a loss was actually closed down and its labor force laid off.) Although bankruptcies did not become common until the mid-1990s, the action served notice to China's enterprises that the new reforms would have some real teeth.

To retain some degree of government control over industry and to continue with at least a modicum of central, state-level planning, many factories were allowed to operate along two tracks. They would continue to have an "inside" sector in which production was closely guided by state quotas and controlled raw material prices; but enterprise managers would also be encouraged to operate in an "outside" sector that carried the freedoms—and the risks—of the marketplace. After fulfilling their tax obligations to the state, they could decide for themselves what else to produce, how to produce it, where to sell it, and at what price. With their profits they would also have choices as to how best to allocate the rewards. They could invest in new capital, storage facilities, and services, or they could opt to boost incentives to workers.

Going along with these changes at the enterprise level, provinces and municipalities were also allowed greater authority over the revenues generated within their territory. Beginning in 1982 the provinces were allowed to keep up to 80 percent of revenue generated through taxes on local business. Output and profit levels were generally rising as a result of the enterprise reforms, which meant that some localities had more funds than ever before to invest in local projects. The net effect: Decisionmaking was effectively shifted downward, from the center to the periphery. Localities—provinces, counties, and cities—were encouraged to generate surplus, or "extra-budgetary," funds by increasing taxes, which meant they were generating income that did not have to be returned to the central government. Most provinces and a number of cities were also allowed to contract with foreign enterprises and to keep a share of the resulting profits.

These reforms helped boost industrial output and efficiency in China, but they were also accompanied by the emergence (actually the reemergence) of defensive local behaviors. Although many localities now had newly expanded powers and greater levels of funding, they were nervous about the declining role of central authority, and some began implementing strategies to guard against future downturns in the economy. It was not uncommon for localities to protect their self-interests by pushing their own products and refusing to allow the export of local goods and the import of goods from elsewhere. Others encouraged hoarding of key goods and raw materials, such as steel and cement. As Dorothy Solinger observed, "Localities have used the hoarded supplies to construct new local enterprises, including small, local, duplicative, inefficient, outdated factories known in some quarters as 'local money trees.'"[29]

Thus the national income grew significantly during the early 1980s, yet the balance between center and periphery had changed markedly. As regional authorities grew wealthier, the central government's revenues declined.[30] The major problem was that only part of the economy had been liberalized by the reforms: Whereas enterprises and regions were allowed some degree of autonomy, central control was still exercised over most prices, and there was a centralized distribution and allocation system. If a factory was able to expand production significantly, it would need greater inputs of raw materials like coal and energy; but with the state still largely controlling the pricing and distribution of such resources, it was difficult for enterprises to accumulate the necessary raw materials. This situation obviously caused frustration, and in many cases savvy entrepreneurs managed to find quasilegal ways of acquiring scarce resources, including what amounted to theft of state assets. There have been reports of the removal of railroad sleepers for fuel and entire sections of railroad lines being purloined for steel supplies.[31] In light of such protectionism and corruption, some individuals in leadership roles began to question the wisdom of some of the reform policies, and by the second half of the 1980s some of the regional autonomy was withdrawn, effectively recentralizing the state's economic decisionmaking powers. At the same time, however, there was a contradictory move, as the state began to release its grip over distribution and its domination of the pricing system.

Marketization

China's economic planners realized that additional elements of a market economy were needed to complement the experiments with enterprise and locality autonomy; the most visible new development was the reemergence of private enterprise. As early as 1979 many small businesses started to reappear in Chinese cities, the most common being restaurants, barbershops, photographers, tailors, and street vendors, offering all kinds of goods and services that had previously been scarce or unavailable. In 1981 there were 1.13 million people working in private enterprises, but by 1983 there were 7.3 million, almost 7 percent of the workforce nationwide. By 1987 it was estimated that this

figure had grown to more than 20 million working in businesses with total sales exceeding Y76 billion.[32]

In spite of its long-standing bias against entrepreneurs, the post-Mao leadership encouraged the development of private enterprise.[33] In a landmark 1984 resolution the CCP made that clear, stating that "we should promote [the] individual economy particularly in those economic fields mainly based on labor services and where decentralized operation is suitable [and] we should . . . encourage . . . cooperative management and economic association among the state, collective and individual sectors of the economy."[34] This resolution relaxed constraints on permissible activities and encouraged individuals to overcome fears of embarking on private careers. Contrary to the beliefs of most outsiders, CCP leaders were arguing that such developments would help strengthen rather than damage Chinese socialism. To quote the official language of the resolution: "It is our long-term policy and the need of socialist development to promote diversified economic forms and various methods of operation simultaneously."[35]

About half of all private businesses in 1987 were involved in trading, usually the buying and selling of food, clothes, and other goods. Restaurants, transportation, and miscellaneous services (including hotels) made up another 25 percent of the total.[36] There was also significant growth in private industries during the 1980s, mostly in light manufactured goods and handicraft items (about 10 percent of the total). In spite of such radical developments, the private sector was still a minor component of the national economy: In 1985, for example, the value of industrial output in the private sector was approximately 1.8 percent of the nation's total; the share had doubled by 1987 to 3.6 percent. The total number of privately owned enterprises has increased significantly since then, making major gains in both state and collective enterprises (see Figure 8.1), and by 1996 the industrial output value generated in privately owned enterprises amounted to almost 15.5 percent of the nation's total.[37]

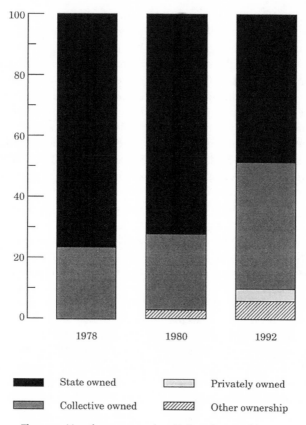

 State owned   Privately owned

 Collective owned   Other ownership

The composition of gross output value of industry by ownership
SOURCE: *China Statistical Yearbook 1993*, p. 470

FIGURE 8.1   Increase in Private Ownership in Chinese Industry, 1978–1992

The growth of private businesses helped generate surplus wealth for spending on additional goods and services, but in the short run—at least until the economy was operating in a higher gear—there was very little to buy. The net effect was a huge growth in savings in urban and rural areas, which increased the total pool of investment funds (see Figure 8.2).

In 1987 bank deposits in cities and towns stood at Y226 billion, an increase of 37 percent over a twelve-month period; rural savings increased during the same period to Y129 billion, an increase of more than 24 percent.[38] By 1996 total (urban and rural) savings amounted to more than Y3.8 trillion, almost thirteen times greater than the 1987 level.[39] As these figures suggest, many Chinese were reaping the benefits of the economic reforms, and at least

some of that wealth was available for new investments.

As private firms became larger and better established they were increasingly able to compete with enterprises in the state and collective sectors, which should have resulted in greater efficiency overall. Most important, from the government's point of view, was the role of the private sector in creating new jobs.[40] The massive threat of rural unemployment, which was becoming a reality as a consequence of the agrarian reforms, called for an expanded private-enterprise sector in small towns and cities all across the countryside, which, for a while at least, helped to reduce the rate of out-migration from the countryside.[41]

The most difficult of the market reforms to achieve in China, and by far the most contro-

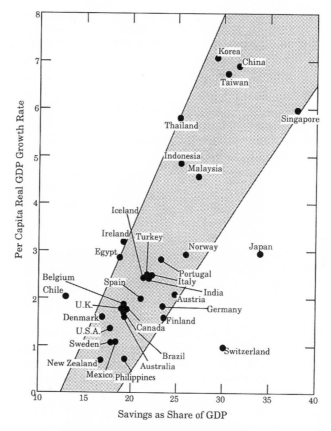

The shaded area indicates a positive correlation
between savings rates and real per capita GDP growth.

SOURCE: *World Economic Outlook* (1995), p. 72.

FIGURE 8.2   Savings and Per Capita GDP Growth: International Comparisons

versial, involved the system of commodity exchange—in other words, the pricing system. The major problem in a command economy, according to the reformers, was that state control of prices reflected planners' ideas of the "exchange value" for particular goods rather than the actual demand, or "use value." This resulted in many irrational prices (i.e., in purely economic terms). The price of steel, for example, was generally kept high and the price of coal low, regardless of changes in the industries' market conditions, technology, and efficiency levels. The reformers argued that until prices were decontrolled it would not be possible to

gauge the efficiency of enterprises. What was needed was a series of additional reforms in which prices would gradually come to reflect changing market circumstances and regional variations and where local authorities would have more authority to set price levels.[42]

Price deregulation was seen as the key to the reform process, the essential component that would make all the other reforms work, but in many areas it proved to be a contentious policy.[43] Probably the most controversial area of price reform was in the market for food. Decontrol of food prices resulted in sharp price increases on many items, and not surprisingly this produced opposition in urban areas. To deal with this potentially explosive situation the government was forced to institute a series of costly urban subsidies, rather than returning to the old price controls.[44] It has been estimated that subsidies to counteract the harsh realities of price increases after deregulation swallowed up about one-third of the state's budget during the early years of reform. This suggested that the government was "caught in a vice between price paralysis on the one side and escalating subsidies on the other."[45]

Because of the difficulties involved and the opposition that had been generated, price reform progressed slowly, cautiously, and unevenly throughout the 1990s; in fact all through the reform era there has been a tendency for market-type reforms to ebb and flow on a periodic basis (the *fang-shou* cycles described in Chapter 4). The first round of market loosening occurred in 1979, but the negative effects resulted in a clampdown by 1981. The second wave of reforms that were started in 1984 also had some disastrous effects, and the result was another period of reassessment.[46] To counteract the inflation caused by price decontrols, reforms were eventually put on hold. The unfortunate part of the cycle, however, was that individual aspirations remained high, so markets were driven underground; there was a renewed surge in the level of economic corruption; and, inevitably, there was a new call for reforms to set the process in motion all over again. Throughout 1988 the issue of price reform remained critical; in fact it was the key to the entire reform movement. The government decided finally to cool its heels, especially in light of the other problems it was then encountering: rising unemployment in the countryside; student protests simmering in the cities; and minority unrest in some of the Autonomous Regions.[47]

Regional Specialization

One aspect of the economic reforms that contrasted particularly sharply with the spatially egalitarian policies of the Maoist period was the focus on regional division of labor, with some parts of the country encouraged to develop economic strengths as fully as possible. This represented a turnaround from the old emphasis in socialist regional development policies, in which all regions were exhorted to become self-reliant and serious efforts were made to reduce the economic gap between the nation's richest and poorest regions.

After 1978 several key economic thinkers began to consider alternative strategies that would involve regional specialization. They argued that the best geographical division of labor was to encourage the traditionally dynamic coastal areas to lead the way by focusing on high-tech growth while the more remote inland regions would concentrate on energy development, raw material extraction, and other local specialties.[48] In 1984 an official statement announced this new emphasis, implying that previous efforts to produce balanced regional growth might actually have detracted from the nation's best interests. It was suggested that "the development of new and outlying backward regions on too large a scale will ... retard the increase of the national income."[49] As this statement suggests, the emphasis of economic development had clearly shifted toward regional specialization, with a declining emphasis on centralized support for deprived regions.[50]

At the same time, a verbal commitment was made to China's poorest regions, but they must have felt increasingly insecure as they anticipated increases in the gap between the richer and poorer parts of the country. Two groups of regions were identified for the task of developing economic strengths. The first included six macroregions, each made up of several provinces; the second was of a group of key cities. In 1984 about a quarter of the nation's suburban counties were assigned to the jurisdiction of nearby cities; in 1987 seventy-two of them were selected as experimental sites for further reforms in enterprise management and new incentive schemes. According to one report, these strategies were immediately successful, with a one-year increase in the value of industrial output in the designated cities of 17.2 percent, far higher than the national average.[51] Several other innovations occurred in these cities at the same time, including the establishment of wholesale markets for capital goods, funds, technology, and even labor. Some of the cities were also able to break down administrative barriers and improve cross-departmental and transregional cooperation, which, it was hoped, would provide valuable role models for other, less well endowed cities and regions in China.

The underlying, usually unwritten principle behind the spatial reforms has been to establish jurisdictions for economic decisionmaking that are based on "natural" economic boundaries rather than on arbitrary administrative and political boundaries, as in the past. Unfortunately, there is evidence that the reforms resulted in more of the predictable rivalry and interregional squabbling that had plagued the reform process from the beginning. There was widespread evidence that local chauvinism and self-interest outweighed regional and national concerns. In the cities, for example, some cadres used their expanded powers over the newly annexed rural counties to further their own political and economic ends exclusively, and to some extent the cities became the new "centers," lording it over and exploiting their suburban "peripheries." Such developments ran counter to the announced goal of reducing the urban-rural dichotomy; they also had serious consequences for the broader issue of regional equality in China (see Chapter 10).

Another group of cities, in fact a specific region of the country, was at the same time targeted for rapid economic development, largely because of its coastal location. These were the much publicized Special Economic Zones, which were opened up as virtual free-trade cities that welcomed foreign investment.[52] In 1979 four SEZs were announced, with the express purpose of drawing in capital, stimulating exports, and gaining access to modern technology and management practices. All four cities are in southern China: Shenzhen, just across the border from Hong Kong; Zhuhai, adjacent to the old Portuguese colony of Macao; Shantou (all three in Guangdong Province); as well as Xiamen (formerly Amoy) in Fujian Province, across the strait from Taiwan. Additional SEZs were opened subsequently, for example, Hainan Island, which was also designated as a new province, and, most notably, Shanghai.

From a purely geographical perspective it was clear that the SEZs were not chosen randomly. The government wanted to encourage investment from traditional (albeit temporarily estranged) Chinese outposts in Macao, Hong Kong, and Taiwan, perhaps as a way to smooth the path for their eventual repatriation. In 1984 it was announced that fourteen coastal ports would also be designated as "Open Cities," with powers to bring in foreign investments. The opening of these new cities and regions can best be understood in the overall context of the larger economic reform movement. One of the bottlenecks in the Chinese economy since the reforms began was a scarcity of raw materials. Opening coastal areas to foreign capital was seen as an obvious way to solve that problem, allowing foreign investment funds and the importation and processing of raw materials from all over the world. The goal was to export high-quality finished products to global markets.[53] The expected advantage accruing from the development of foreign trade in coastal areas would be in the transfer of experience and technology from foreign nations, which would generate additional jobs to employ the surplus labor force in the countryside. True to the spirit of regional comparative advantage, it was anticipated that the growth of economic activity in coastal areas would help generate surplus wealth that would provide a boost, through trickle-down policies, to the economies of China's peripheral and constantly lagging regions.[54]

The Great Leap Westward

The effect of the economic reforms, according to the critics, was that China's economy in the 1980s began to be exposed—some would argue prematurely—to the cutthroat world of international capitalism: "Foreign capital displaces and subordinates . . . important areas of Chinese industry. . . . The restoration of the market mechanism . . . in the context of the 'open-door' to foreign capital . . . is conducive to economic and social polarization, industrial concentration and a tendency toward the technological subordination of Chinese industry to foreign capital."[55] Despite such fears the SEZs were off to a flying start, especially Shenzhen, which grew from a population of 20,000 in 1979 to more than 300,000 by 1984; by the mid-1990s the greater Shenzhen region was home to more than 3 million people from all parts of China. By 1984 Y1.9 billion had been invested in capital construction projects in Shenzhen, and more than 2,500 contracts were signed with foreign investors. This early success led Party leaders to widen their sights, and they came to see open areas as the key to China's economic future. In 1984, for example, then-Premier Zhao Ziyang described their function as follows:

> The special economic zones [and Open Cities] are the bridgeheads in our opening to the outside world, and they should play the role of springboard. On the one hand, they should import advanced foreign technology, equipment, and management . . . absorb and digest them; apply them in innovations; and transfer them to the interior. On the other hand, they should send commodities produced in the coastal areas with foreign technology to the interior, and export the latter's raw materials and produce, with added value after processing . . . to the international market.[56]

Enthusiasm for the SEZs soon waned, however, in spite of the glowing reports of tremendous increases in employment, salaries, and living conditions. The critics pointed out that in Shenzhen, for example, which was originally supposed to focus on imports of high-tech foreign capital to manufacture goods for export, the bulk of "foreign" investment initially came from Hong Kong, and much of the money originated on the mainland. As the critics suggested, this meant that the SEZs were being artificially

supported by domestic "blood transfusions" that drained the rest of the country.[57]

The too-rapid pace of capital construction in the newly opened areas also widened the existing gap between richer coastal regions and the poorer interior regions. The old issue of spiritual pollution from the West was also revived by the critics of the "open-door" policy. Not only had foreign capital been drawn into China; a more insidious result of the "Great Leap Westward" was the encouragement of Western-style consumption habits considered to be wasteful, bourgeois, and counterproductive to the nation's modernization drive. The critics suggested that the open door had in fact become a back door, through which foreign corporations could enter China to exploit its huge markets and cheap supplies of labor.

The rapid population growth of the SEZs, especially Shenzhen, was not accompanied by parallel growth in services, particularly housing, health care, and utilities.[58] There was also an unfortunate political outcome that resulted from the opening of the SEZs: They became destinations for thousands of Chinese unhappy with life in the PRC. It is reasonable to assume that many of the migrants to coastal cities were hoping not only to get rich but also to escape to capitalist Hong Kong and Macao; the SEZs were convenient, accessible jumping-off points.[59]

Assessing the Two Faces of Reform

At the end of the 1990s the socialist market economy had been in place for almost two decades, and in this section we reflect upon the nature of the reforms and evaluate their success. We begin with the Chinese economy, utilizing the most recent empirical data. In a comprehensive review of the reform process, Kenneth Lieberthal concluded that China shifted gradually from a system of central planning to what he calls "indicative" planning and then increasingly toward the market allocation of goods and services. Instead of sweeping out the old centrally planned economy in one stroke, the new elements of market competition were gradually grafted onto the existing structures.[60] In this sense, to use some familiar analogies, the reforms are best likened to the Long March rather than the Great Leap Forward to economic development.[61] The reforms have been composed of many different changes that have been interactive and that in combination have profoundly altered the way the Chinese economic system operates. In many ways the reforms have been successful, so at least one face of the reform process is a positive one.

The Bright Side

Throughout the 1980s China's GDP grew at an average of 9.6 percent per year, putting it ahead of virtually all the major industrial economies in the world, including the other booming nations in Asia, especially Japan and the NIEs (see Table 8.2).

The high growth rates dipped after the disruptions leading up to the 1989 Tiananmen Square incident, but they bounced back to the 12–13 percent mark in the early 1990s, with a drop to 9 percent in 1995 and 9.7 percent in 1996.[62] These rates considerably outpaced the rate of population growth, which averaged about 1.4 percent per year during this period, which means that the annual rate of growth in per capita incomes averaged about 7.3 percent. In the thirteen-year period from 1978 to 1991 average per capita income increased by about 2.5 times, a higher rate than at any time in Chinese history.

With growth rates of such magnitude the reforms have brought unprecedented improvements to the Chinese people in terms of personal income and consumption of goods and services of all types.[63] Economic growth has allowed a significant improvement in living standards for Chinese in the cities as well as the countryside, and it has also allowed them to increase their savings significantly (see Figure 8.2). Even the conservative *The Economist* magazine has concluded that the reform era "has brought about one of the biggest improvements in human welfare anywhere at any time."[64] The Chinese economy is now estimated to be larger than all but those of the United States and

TABLE 8.2   China and the Rest of the World: Comparisons on Key Indicators

	% Increase in GNP per Year 1980–1993	*GNP Per Capita 1993 US$*	*GDP % Increase 1980–1993*	*Service Sector Growth % per Year 1990–1993*	*Energy Use (oil equiv.) kgs. Per Capita 1993*
China	8.2	490	9.6	11.1	NA
Taiwan	6.9	10,200	7.6	13.7	2,662
Hong Kong	5.4	18,060	6.5	NA	2,278
Low-Income Countries (excl. China)	0.1	300	2.9	3.8	83
Middle-Income Countries	0.2	2,480	2.1	2.8	1,531
Upper-Middle-Income Countries	0.9	4,370	2.7	2.9	1,632
High-Income Countries	2.2	23,090	2.9	—	5,245
World Average	1.2	4,420	2.9	—	1,421

SOURCE: Adapted from World Development Report (1995): *Workers in a Integrating World,* Oxford University Press, Tables 1, 2, 3, 5, 13, 26, 27, 28, and 29.

NOTE:

[1] China's GNP is estimated here in standard terms, but using the purchasing power party method estimates places China's GNP much higher, between US$1,000 and $3,000 (see Lardy, 1994).

Japan, and there is a real possibility that it will be the world's largest by the year 2025.[65]

As a result of deliberate attempts to launch China into the global economy, foreign trade has grown at a rate that matches the performance in the domestic economy. By 1993 China had become the world's tenth largest exporter, with exports worth US$195.72 billion, representing a threefold increase in China's share of global exports from 1978 (0.8 percent) to 1993 (2.5 percent).[66] During this period exports and imports grew on average faster than 16 percent each year (see Table 8.3).[67]

It is also important to note that China experienced a significant change in the structure of exports during this period, shifting to a pattern of trade dominated by manufactured goods (82 percent of total exports in 1993, compared to 49 percent in 1982). In some categories recent growth has been truly astounding. In the case of labor-intensive goods, China, by offering cheap but reasonably high-quality products, had come to control a sizable proportion of the world's total exports, including travel goods and luggage (31 percent), toys (22 percent), clothes (14 percent), and shoes (13 percent).[68]

During the later years of reform, especially after 1985, China also increased its foreign debt considerably, with the receipt of loans from international financial organizations such as the World Bank and the Asia Development Bank. The most important rate of growth, however, has been in the area of foreign direct investment (FDI), which increased from US$916 million in 1983 to $25.7 billion in 1993 and $40.9 billion in 1996.[69] However, FDI is highly variable in geographical terms (see Map 8.1); in 1990, for example, 42 percent of all FDI was in Guangdong Province and 8.3 percent went to adjacent Fujian Province, with all inland provinces combined taking only 17.7 percent of the total.[70] This indicates that the lion's share of external investment is targeted toward the Open Cities and the SEZs in China's coastal provinces.[71]

The reforms have shaped and have been shaped by fundamental structural changes in the Chinese economic system. From a state-dominated economy in 1978 there is now about an equal contribution being made by the non-state sector (see Figure 8.1). In 1992, for example, state-owned firms accounted for about 48 percent of the total gross value of industrial output (compared to 81 percent in 1978), but if commercial, agricultural, and foreign-trade business is included, then less than 40 percent of total income originated in the state sectors by the mid-1990s.[72] The evidence demonstrates that in the early 1990s output of foreign and private businesses grew at a rate of 45 percent

TABLE 8.3   Foreign Trade (Exports and Imports), Manufactured Exports, and Terms of Trade, 1980–1996

Year	Exports (billions of US$)	Imports (billions of US$)	Trade Balance	Manufactured Goods as a % of Total Exports	Terms of Trade (1987 = 100)
1980	18.1	20.0	−1.9	49.2	122
1985	27.4	42.3	−14.9	49.5	122
1987	39.4	43.2	−3.8	66.4	100
1990	62.1	53.4	+8.7	74.4	100
1991	71.9	63.8	+8.1	77.5	98
1992	85.0	80.6	+4.4	79.9	97
1993	91.8	104.0	−12.2	81.8	NA
1994	108.0	116.0	−8.0	NA	NA
1995	148.8	132.1	−16.7	NA	NA
1996	151.1	138.8	−12.2	NA	NA

SOURCES: Adapted from Lardy (1994), Tables 2.1 (p. 30), 2.2 (p. 31), and 2.3 (p. 41); latest data (1995 and 1996) from *China Statistical Yearbook, 1997*, Table 3-11, p. 844.

per year, compared to 25 percent for collectively owned businesses and 11 percent for state-owned businesses. This suggests that in relative terms the state sector may have lagged, but that in absolute terms it retains considerable productive capacity.[73]

China also began to develop much of the economic infrastructure needed to support the transition from a centrally planned to a market-dominated economy. When reforms first began in 1978, there were few laws governing economic activities; law firms were practically nonexistent, banks were an administrative arm of the government, and there was no stock market. In these areas major advances were recorded throughout the 1980s and 1990s.[74] There has been genuine competition, a gradual reduction in the degree of state management and interference with economic activities, and the gradual evolution of a buyer's market, as witnessed by the steady decontrol of prices in all aspects of the economy (see Table 8.4). In 1978, for example, 97 percent of retail goods, 94 percent of agricultural goods, and 100 percent of capital goods were sold at fixed prices; by 1993 the figures were 5 percent, 10 percent, and 15 percent respectively.[75]

Such statistics indicate that the commitment to modernization has remained at the top of the leadership's agenda since 1978, but there have been some significant ups and downs throughout the period. For example, there was a significant curb on investment during 1981–1982 and a major stabilization period after the tumultuous events of 1989. Yet there were no major reversals of the economic reforms during the 1990s.[76] The ideology of reform and the commitment to the Four Modernizations have been persistent and pervasive, as one scholar has mentioned: "As with the flow of water, the reforms may vary over time in their speed or extent, yet [they] follow the direction set by the underlying commitment to reforms. . . . Chinese leaders since 1978 have accepted that modernization involves emulation of developed market economies . . . and that it is not possible without the 'open-door' policy, involving extensive reliance on international trade and foreign technology and investment."[77]

In his book *Growing out of the Plan,* Barry Naughton observed that in the early years there was a certain degree of randomness to the reforms, and in many cases the unintended consequences were the most successful.[78] After 1984, however—although there was still no well-articulated, comprehensive reform strategy—there was a consistent trend, made up of incremental measures, pushing the economy

TABLE 8.4   Proportion of Total Output Sold at Fixed, Guided, and Market Prices, 1978, 1990, 1992, and 1993

	1978	1990	1992	1993
Share of Total Retail Sales Sold at:				
State-controlled prices	97.0	29.7	10.0	7.5%
State-guided prices	—	17.2	10.0	7.5%
Market-regulated prices	3.0	53.1	80.0	85%
Share of Total Agricultural Product Sales Sold at:				
State-controlled prices	92.6	25.0	17.0	10%
State-guided prices	1.8	23.4	15.0	10%
Market-regulated prices	5.6	51.6	68.0	80%
Share of Total Industrial Product Sales Sold at:				
State-controlled prices	97.0	44.6	20.0	15%
State-guided prices	—	19.0	15.0	10%
Market-regulated prices	3.0	36.4	65.0	75%

SOURCES: *China Price Yearbook, 1990* (for 1978 and 1990 data); 1992 data from Bell, Khor, and Kochhar (1993), Table 6, p. 27; 1993 data adapted from Lardy (1994), Table 1.2, p. 11.

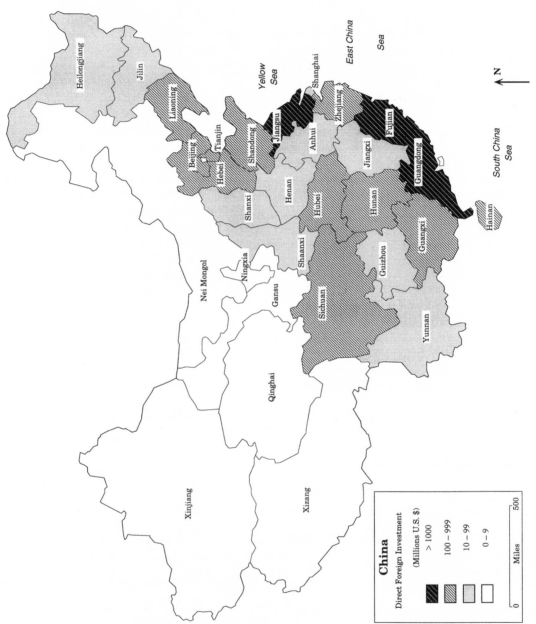

MAP 8.1 Foreign Direct Investment Coming into China, 1993

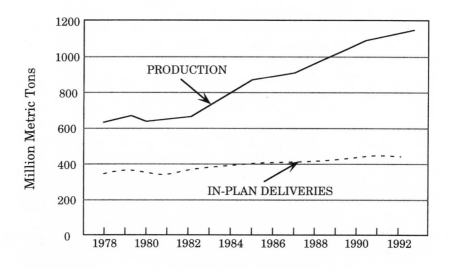

SOURCE: Naughton (1995), p. 225.

FIGURE 8.3a   Coal Industry Production: Market and Plan Target Levels

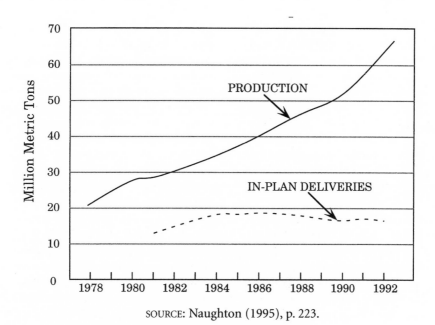

SOURCE: Naughton (1995), p. 223.

FIGURE 8.3b   Steel Industry Production: Market and Plan Target Levels

inexorably toward marketization.[79] The reforms continued to evolve without an overall strategy, and so there was a relentless march forward on a number of fronts. Enterprise reforms were continued and, in some areas, reinforced. For example, the factory management responsibility system was introduced; enterprises were allowed to make their own production decisions; wages were linked more closely to profit margins; and managers were encouraged to negotiate their own long-term contracts rather than making a series of year-to-year contracts specifying output and profit targets (see Figures 8.3a and 8.3b).

The other arm of the reform process was the consolidation and expansion of the dual-track pricing and marketing system. This effectively sanctioned the two distinct spheres of economic activity: the planned sector, with compulsory deliveries at prices fixed by the state; and the market sector, in which prices were freely determined by market forces. Most of the nonstate enterprises operated solely with the market prices, but those in the state sector were free to sell goods and services at market prices after fulfilling their plan responsibilities. As the overall size of the economy expanded, a larger and larger share of output was being marketed outside the plan. The key innovation was that most state-owned firms began to operate with markets and market prices in mind; anything they produced over the state-targeted output level could now be sold freely in the open market.[80]

The Dark Side

Economist Bruce Reynolds has suggested that the trajectory of China's reform process has been uneven:

> It might help to think of the Chinese economy as a water buffalo, which for decades was kept tethered. . . . The system brought fodder at regular intervals; the buffalo grew steadily. But the animal . . . was listless and dispirited; years of inactivity had robbed it of initiative. Why not loosen things, argued the reformers? Remove the stake and let the buffalo forage for itself.

> . . . After ten years, the buffalo has taken on some of the characteristics of a bull. . . . The economy rapidly discovered gaps in the fence. Excessive spending throughout the system, and the resulting breakout of inflation, were too alarming. Back to the tether.[81]

Steps forward were taken, with all systems at full throttle; but at times the government would step in to slow the frenzied pace of development. In aggregate terms the economic achievements of the reform era have expanded human capabilities among Chinese people. The new wealth has been translated into major improvements in standards of living, as measured by traditional social indicators. Compared to many of its Asian neighbors, China has a significantly longer life expectancy, lower rates of mortality, lower fertility, and better access to medical care (see Table 8.5).

China has not suffered, at least to the same extent, the problems that plague most developing nations, such as falling rates of economic growth, declining real wages, nutritional deficiencies, and external indebtedness.[82] Despite all the success, industrial reforms in China were not received with anything like the enthusiasm generated by agricultural reform. In part this is because the urban industrial economy initially proved more difficult to reform. At first the overall impact, at least in terms of industrial output, was not very impressive. Output grew at a slower rate between 1978 and 1982 than between 1965 and 1978 (7.0 percent versus 9.2 percent per year), but that was largely the result of a deliberate shift away from heavy industry, which was de-emphasized relative to both light industry and agriculture. After 1982 light industry growth surpassed that of heavy industry, and consequently total output value began to increase at a faster rate, averaging 10 percent per year between 1982 and 1985.[83]

The reforms have certainly generated enough problems and conflicts to seriously test the government's resolve to stay the course with the ambitious economic programs. Ironically, one of the most serious problems resulted from the absolute success of the reforms, which by 1985

TABLE 8.5 Social Indicators in Asia and Selected Western Countries

Country	Female Life Expectancy at Birth (years)		Maternal Mortality (per 100,000 live births)	Total Fertility Rate	Infant Mortality (per 100,000)	Population per Physician		% in Higher (Tertiary) Education		Daily Caloric Intake Per Capita	
	1965	1993	1980–1993	1993	1993	1965	1984	1965	1992	1965	1992
China	59	71	115[5]	2.0	30	1,600	1,010	0	2	1,931	2,632
Richer Asia:											
Hong Kong	71	82	4	1.2	7	2,520	1,070	5	20	ND	2,699[4]
Taiwan	—	74[1]	ND	ND	ND	1,901	1,318[2]	4	25[3]	ND	ND[3]
Japan	73	83	15	1.5	4	970	660	13	32	2,679	2,848
South Korea	58	75	34	1.7	11	2,680	1,160	6	42	2,254	2,878
Singapore	68	78	11	1.7	6	1,900	1,310	10	12[4]	1,186	2,892
Poorer Asia:											
India	44	61	500	3.7	80	4,880	2,520	5	ND	2,103	2,104
Bangladesh	44	56	600	4.3	106	8,100	6,730	1	5	1,984	1,925
Philippines	57	69	80	3.9	42	ND	6,700	19	28	1,896	2,255
Indonesia	45	65	800	2.8	56	31,700	9,460	1	10	1,796	2,670
Malaysia	60	73	59	3.5	13	6,200	1,930	2	7	2,307	2,686
Thailand	58	72	270	2.1	26	7,160	6,290	2	19	2,134	2,287
Other Countries:											
United States	74	79	9	1.9	9	670	470	40	76	3,236	3,666
Canada	75	81	2	1.7	7	770	510	26	62	3,128	3,447
United Kingdom	74	79	7	1.8	7	870	ND	12	28	3,350	3,252
WORLD AVERAGE	58	68	ND	3.2	54	6,060	4,200	9	16	2,390	2,669

SOURCES: *World Development Report*, 1995, Tables 26, 27, 28, 29 (pp. 212–219); caloric intake data from *World Development Report*, 1991, Table 32 (pp. 266–267).
NOTES:
[1] Statistics for males and females, 1986.
[2] Statistics for 1965 and 1981.
[3] Statistics for 1965 and 1985.
[4] Statistics for 1985.
[5] Based on a study covering thirty provinces.

had helped to overheat the economy. Enterprises all over the country, in their rush to expand output, had launched into heavy capital construction projects, producing a growth rate far higher than the economic planners had bargained for. Much of the growth occurred in the TVEs, which were largely outside the control of state planning and distribution, and at various times it was necessary to shut down the reform plans. For example, in 1983, 1986, and 1988 strict controls were placed on credit and the supply of money, which helped slow industrial growth to more manageable levels.

Even with tightening of this type, investments continued to grow rapidly throughout the 1980s, with vast amounts of public and private money going into building houses and developing the urban-industrial infrastructure, activities that are not directly tied to raising productivity. Investments in fixed assets in the state sector grew by 25 percent in 1984 and 42 percent in 1985, but they slowed to 15 percent in 1986 as a result of retrenchment measures. Yet in the first half of 1987 the investment rate rebounded to 21 percent.[84] With the new profits

being kept by enterprises and the extra money available in consumer pockets, investment and spending veered out of control,[85] and enormous supplies of scarce foreign exchange were used up (see Table 8.6).[86]

One of the major goals of reform was to improve industrial efficiency, and although there is some evidence that labor productivity increased after 1978, by the end of the 1980s there was still much room for improvement.[87] High rates of industrial growth were achieved, but they were accompanied by some very familiar problems: the wasteful use of raw materials; the duplication of product lines; and widespread charges of graft and corruption. A major concern among Party leaders was that some aspects of economic reform were proving difficult to implement, especially price reform. Although some of these problems would have occurred in a fully planned economy, their appearance in China in the 1980s fueled opposition to the reform process; it was clearly time, they could argue, for the free-ranging buffalo to be tethered. The problems were made worse by the incremental and partial nature of reform,

TABLE 8.6   State Revenues and Expenditures, 1978–1996 (billions of current yuan)

	Total Revenue	Total Expenditures	Net Surplus or Deficit	Total Borrowing	Net Deficit Including Borrowing
1978	112.11	111.10	+1.01	0.15	+0.86
1979	110.33	127.39	−17.06	3.64	−20.70
1980	108.52	121.27	−12.75	4.30	−17.05
1981	108.95	111.50	−2.55	7.31	−9.86
1982	112.40	115.33	−2.93	8.39	−11.32
1983	124.90	129.25	−4.35	7.94	−12.24
1984	146.50	157.50	−5.00	7.65	−12.65
1985	186.60	184.48	2.16	8.99	−6.83
1986	226.03	233.08	−7.06	13.83	−20.89
1987	234.67	242.69	−8.03	16.59	−25.62
1990	293.7	308.6	−14.6	37.54	−52.14
1992	348.3	374.2	−25.9	66.97	−92.87
1993	434.9	464.2	−29.3	73.92	−103.22
1994	521.8	579.3	−57.5	117.53	−175.03
1995	624.2	682.4	−58.2	154.98	−213.18
1996	740.8	793.8	−53.0	196.73	−249.73

SOURCES: Adapted from Riskin (1987), Table 14.4, p. 362, and *China: Statistical Yearbook, 1988*, p. 907; 1990s data from *China Statistical Yearbook, 1997*, Table 7.20, p. 256; and Table 7.3, p. 245.

with small changes implemented here and there interspersed with periodic retrenchments—but without any blueprint for the future. For example, reforms in one area—the increase in enterprise autonomy—occurred before the pricing system had been fully reformed, which jeopardized its success.

There remain pressing concerns about some of the direct and indirect results of reform and about areas that are not yet being addressed. Kenneth Lieberthal has divided these concerns into two overlapping groups: those that need to be tackled to make China increasingly efficient and competitive, both at home and abroad; and those that have repercussions for the stability and evolution of the existing political and social systems. It is imperative for China to continue to increase its export sales for the future to help pay for increasing imports of food and energy, which now seem inevitable. This will require a significant effort to continue to rationalize SOEs to make their products increasingly efficient; at the same time, China will be required to import and adapt new technology to make its goods competitive. Wage rates will almost certainly continue to increase, which will begin to erode the competitive edge that China has enjoyed from cheap labor. It is also imperative that China find ways to reduce the amount and extent of local protectionism. Lieberthal noted that "cities, counties, and townships have become bureaucratic entrepreneurs that interfere in the activities of their own enterprises."[88] In this case it has become necessary to clip the wings of the new entrepreneurs—but without damaging their overall drive and profitability.

In addition to these structural constraints on the reform process, there were several less than salutary outcomes. One of the most worrying concerns of the current regime, for example, is the growth of inequalities that have resulted from variations in human, physical, and economic characteristics in different parts of China. There are at least three dimensions of inequality that need to be assessed: gender, geography, and social class.[89] Some people now find that the gains made during the early years of reform are evaporating. Chinese women, for

example, were hoping that they would finally witness some of the gains they had been promised during the revolutionary years (see further discussion in Chapter 13). Although the core regions and the biggest cities have prospered from reform, it is obvious that many areas in the rural periphery have benefited hardly at all (see Chapter 10).

It is also clear that gains in wealth and consumption have been spread unevenly throughout the population. After the first decade of reform, for example, it was evident that even though Chinese people on average had much more money to spend than in 1978, some degree of inequality was reappearing. As one observer has written, the reforms produced "pockets of Western consumption" and a "dual and divided structure of social consumption where a relatively small minority [has] access to higher levels of consumption."[90] As the statistics suggest, there was significant growth in the output of virtually all manufactured goods between 1979 and 1996 (see Table 8.7a), as well as in consumer durables, items considered luxuries just a few years earlier (Table 8.7b).

The rush among the newly rich to spend and consume threatened the essential classlessness of China's social structure. In the countryside as well as the city, a new class of entrepreneurs was emerging: newly rich peasant households, shopkeepers, family-owned small businesses, brokers, and venture capitalists. By the late 1980s some outsiders predicted that if the trend continued, then the newly enfranchised middle class would soon demand some reform to the political system or the leadership would decide to rein in the reform process and forestall such developments. That appeared to have been the policy choice in 1990, following the tumultuous events of the previous year. Although popular calls for political reform were squelched, in the economic realm—as power and decisionmaking diffused downward—monopolistic control from the center became increasingly irrelevant, calling into question whether the CCP could keep up with the pace of change and survive. The situation at the turn of the century was somewhat like rolling marbles down the middle

TABLE 8.7a   Output of Selected Major Industrial (Consumer) Products, 1979, 1983, 1987, and 1996

	1979	1987	1987 as a % of 1979	1996	1996 as a % of 1979
Chemical fibers (10,000 tons)	32.6	117.5	+360%	375.5	+1152%
Machine-made paper (10,000 tons)	493	1,141	+229%	2638	+535%
Synthetic detergents (10,000 tons)	32.4	119.2	+370%	262.2	+808%
Bicycles (10,000)	1,009	4,117	+408%	3361	+333%
Watches (10,000)	1,750	6,159	+349%	47976	+2741%
Canned food (10,000 tons)	50.1	161.5	+322%	282.6	+564%
Beer (10,000 tons)	52	540	+1038%	1682	+3235%
Cigarettes (10,000 cases)	1,303	2,881	+216%	3401	+261%

SOURCES: *China Statistical Yearbook, 1988*, p. 297; 1996 data for 1996 from *China Statistical Yearbook, 1997*, Table 12-20, pp. 443–445.

TABLE 8.7b   Growth Rates (per Year) in Output of Selected Consumer Goods, 1980–1996

	Aggregate Data			Growth Rates (% per Year)		
	1980	1985	1996	1981–1996	1986–1996	1991–1996
Refrigerators (10,000 units)	5	145	980	39.1	19.0	13.3
Color televisions (10,000 units)	3	435	2,538	52.4	17.4	16.2
Washing machines (10,000 units)	25	887	1,075	26.5	1.8	8.4
Cameras (10,000 units)	37	179	4,121	34.3	33.0	63.8

SOURCE: *China Statistical Yearbook, 1997*, Table 2-2, pp. 25–26.

of the street: No one can be certain where the marbles will end up.

In addition to the threat of rising inequality, another concern for the current regime is widespread and growing corruption, which is occurring at all levels of the economy. One of the most publicized negative effects of reform has been clever practices, bordering on outright corruption, that accompanied reforms when they were first being implemented in the early 1980s.[91] To be charitable to the perpetrators, it is perhaps possible to justify their actions as a response to cataclysmic change in operating procedures. Enterprise managers and government bureaucrats, who had worked for years within a centrally planned economy, soon found themselves in a new environment: Whereas the entrepreneur was expected to be bold and adventuresome, the bureaucrat was expected to be obedient and staid. Whereas the former seeks to maximize gain, the latter tries to minimize loss. When they entered this unfamiliar situation, it is not surprising that many went astray. When thrown into a market environment, bureaucrats at first tend to behave not like capitalists, but like black marketeers, lining their own pockets rather than working for the good of society.

It is difficult to determine the extent to which economic crime during the 1980s and 1990s was caused by the reforms and the economic chaos that resulted. It is possible, for example, that corruption is no more prevalent than it ever was in postrevolutionary China but that such crimes are more likely to be reported, perhaps for reasons that are largely political.[92] The issue of corruption associated with the economic reforms has become a significant political and social concern in China, one that has played directly into the hands of reform opponents, as well as those who would like to see changes in the Chinese system of government.

In her book *The Political Economy of Corruption in China*, Julia Kwong has observed that the prevalence of corruption at any given moment is determined by the balance between forces that encourage and discourage it within any given organization, as well as in society at large.[93] That balance obviously fluctuates along with changes in government policy, especially those on the scale that China has been experiencing in its current transition out of socialism. In orthodox socialism (by which Kwong means China during the late 1950s) the emphasis on altruism and faith in socialist ideology worked to reward honesty, discipline, and self-denial among officials; yet there was frequent rule-bending (even outright criminal behavior) in attempting to fulfill organizational targets, as was the case during the Great Leap Forward (see Chapter 7). With a strong attachment to socialist values, there were—or there should have been—all manner of deterrents to corrupt behavior. But it was evident in the 1960s that the commitment to socialism was eroded by the uncertainties and excesses of the political campaigns associated with the Cultural Revolution.

During the reform era the state has officially abandoned the traditional elements of socialism (such as class and class conflict), yet at the same time it has endorsed the contradictory values of capitalism, creating serious dilemmas for administrators and officials. The only ideology currently in fashion is materialism, which

now runs deeply through all of society. Because China still officially holds itself out as a socialist society, state officials are expected to remain altruistic and self-sacrificing, even though almost all the *danwei* and SOEs operate on the profit principle. Officials are expected to live frugally while the rest of society is madly chasing material acquisitions, profits, and success. Kwong has thus argued that disjunctions of this nature tend to undermine officials' commitment to socialism to the extent that they became self-interested and, in their confusion and disillusionment, now seek refuge in the familiar pursuit of financial security and personal comfort, which requires them to explore avenues of corruption.[94] Thus new economic opportunities offer far greater temptations than at any time during the Maoist era. As Kwong explained it:

> In a capitalist society, the striving for individual material gain is regulated by rules of acceptable behavior that are deeply ingrained in the culture. . . . But in China the old rules of behavior became irrelevant, and new formal and informal norms of acceptable behaviors were not clearly defined. In this moral and normative vacuum, the means chosen were often the practical and not those formerly considered permissible or acceptable. As a result, corruption, which had been under control in the fifties, became a serious social problem in the eighties. Money assumed greater importance in these illicit exchanges, and the monetary values involved multiplied exponentially from a few yuan in the fifties to tens of thousands in the eighties. While many of the means administrators used to bilk the government and their clients remained largely the same throughout these forty years, the former became more varied and innovative as they learned to exploit the weaknesses in the socialist system and the loopholes in the capitalist one.[95]

The consensus is that the policies of the reform era have consistently favored urban and industrial China over rural areas, producing what one China scholar has called a "deeply disgruntled countryside," especially in areas that are distant from the most successful urban markets.[96] It is not at all surprising, then, that peasant revolts have been reported in many parts of China. In addition, as we shall examine in Chapter 16, the environmental impacts of China's reforms have resulted in a rapid acceleration of ecological loss and degradation. As the economy grows and the population expands, China will face increasing international pressure to transform production processes to reduce negative environmental impacts, particularly the emission of greenhouse gasses. As a new player in the global market, China will not be able to ignore such demands, which threaten to compromise economic growth, at least in the short term.

It is reasonable to anticipate that some or all of these problems will backfire on the government in the near term. The success of reform was facilitated by shifting a considerable amount of resources and decisionmaking power away from central government. The obvious corollary is that local officials and managers in government departments and enterprises at all levels of the decentralized economy have acquired a great deal of power in a fairly short period. To increase economic efficiency and maintain China's competitiveness in the global economy many officials, as Julia Kwong has observed, have been tempted to maximize short-term economic growth regardless of the impacts to the country's social, macroeconomic, and ecological conditions.

Developing the Socialist Market Economy

The Third Plenary Session of the 14th Party Central Committee calls on the entire Party membership and the people of all nationalities throughout the country to rally more closely around the Party Central Committee with Comrade Jiang Zemin as its nucleus. Under the guidance of Comrade Deng Xiaoping's theory on building socialism with Chinese Characteristics and following the course charted by the 14th Party Congress, let us unite as one and dedicate ourselves

heart and soul to the cause of reform, and, by relying on our own efforts and working diligently, strive to initially build up the structure of the socialist market economy and realize the strategic goals for the second phase of the nation's socio-economic development by the end of this century!

—Decision of the CCP Central Committee, November 14, 1993[97]

One of the major problems in the wake of the Four Modernizations project has been the threat that reform represented to China's cadres. In a market economy there is much less demand for bureaucrats to carry out all of the planning, supervising, enforcing, and surveillance tasks. Not only are these jobs threatened by the reforms; the prestige of politicians and bureaucrats, so long based on political privilege, is challenged in an economy increasingly dominated by hard cash and where status is more likely to be related to wealth than to political position. The reforms also presented a major threat to the ideological principles upon which a Marxist-Leninist state like China had been built. Marxism, especially in the Maoist guise, had strongly espoused such principles as full employment, egalitarianism, and guarantees of food and secure housing. The costs of making such guarantees were high, however, and Chinese citizens had to put up with chronic shortages of many consumer goods, low living standards, little job mobility, and drab surroundings for three decades after the 1949 revolution.[98] With the reforms China's people have been offered a glimpse of change for the better, but as the 1980s and 1990s demonstrated, the rewards would not come without some serious side effects, including rising unemployment, higher food prices, and housing shortages.

In the middle of this tumultuous economic reform process, China's leaders steadfastly maintained that the economic reforms were not capitalist per se and that China was still deeply committed to socialism. In some public pronouncements the reforms were described as an essential part of the "primary" stage of socialism that China was now entering. The trend toward mixed ownership of the means of production, with an increasing role for the private sector, could be justified, according to the top leaders, by the unique economic circumstances facing China in the 1980s. CCP Acting General Secretary Zhao Ziyang explained it in 1987, stating that strict adherence in the past to socialist (read: Maoist) principles meant that attempts to introduce market forces were sharply criticized as capitalist-roader tendencies. The net effect, according to Zhao, was damaging to China's economy and its political system, hindering the drive toward modernization: "Undue emphasis was placed on a single form of ownership [by the state] and a rigid economic structure took shape. . . . This seriously hampered the development of the productive forces and of the socialist commodity economy."[99]

In other words, the economic reforms, in which market principles were being added onto the planned economy, could be justified and defended in the light of the current situation.[100] As Zhao continued, to achieve the Four Modernizations it was necessary for China to take some fairly bold steps away from the orthodox path: "To resolve the principal contradiction of the present stage we must vigorously expand the commodity economy, raise labor productivity . . . and, to this end, reform such aspects of the relations of production . . . as are incompatible with the growth of the productive forces."[101]

Although little progress has been made as to political reform, it appears that some degree of liberalization was being contemplated all through 1987 and 1988, just before the Tiananmen tragedy.[102] The economist most closely associated with the primary-stage-of-socialism theory espoused by Zhao Ziyang wrote in a Shanghai newspaper in 1987 that "no single person or organization can absolutely and completely represent . . . the interests of all people in society. The false impression of no conflict no longer exists. People's interests are no longer monolithic."[103] Whether or not this sentiment reflected the views of a majority of the top brass within the Party will never be known. Even if it did, it seems clear that the events of 1989 moved far too quickly for the CCP. They may

have been considering reforms at the time, but they were certainly not ready to have the details dictated to them by student demonstrators or by world opinion. The suppression of the student demonstrations in 1987 and 1989 and the hard line taken in Tibet show that the discussion about political reform in China was to remain purely theoretical.

It has been difficult for CCP theoreticians to persuade anyone that the economic reforms sweeping China in the 1980s were in any realistic way a part of socialism. Responding to a speech about the "radiance" of the "Great Truth of Marxism," for example, Orville Schell noted that the only radiance he could detect on the streets of China in the late 1980s was that of people making money. Party officials and true believers in socialism could only watch from the sidelines as they became increasingly irrelevant to China's future, at least in economic matters. Schell contended that statements like Zhao Ziyang's are little more than futile attempts "to fit all the incongruities of the new situation into a convincing socialist framework."[104] In reality the Communists were probably not convincing anyone, but their fanaticism is perhaps understandable, in that they are trying desperately to hang onto the legacy of Marxist-Leninist-Maoist thought. For close to half a century this belief system had provided the *guocui* (national essence) of China.[105] Maybe Party leaders were afraid that if China lost touch with that recent incarnation of *guocui*—especially after the pain and humiliation of the century before revolution—the country would "once more become culturally and politically deracinated, and [would] fall into ruin."[106]

The market-socialist project, as represented by the CCP quote at the start of this section, contains an inherent contradiction between economic transformation and political immobility. The success of the Four Modernizations contributed to an undermining of the legitimacy of the current regime, but with hindsight such conflicts seem to be inevitable in light of the new ideas, interests, and forces created by the changing economic conditions and increasingly global interactions China and Chinese people were encountering. Because of the diminishing political legitimacy associated with the Cultural Revolution, the Chinese government had no option but to embark on a reform strategy. The reforms have created the basis for not only a new economic structure but also a new social and political structure (the transformation Mao Zedong referred to pejoratively as the "bourgeois restoration"). Reform leaders are now in a quandary: Should they, or should they not, attempt to craft a new version of the socialist political system that can serve as a viable alternative to both capitalist economics and liberal-democratic politics? As Gordon White has observed in *Riding the Tiger,* this has not appeared to be possible anywhere in the old socialist world, including China. It is difficult to resist his conclusion, therefore, that "Marxist-Leninist socialism has been incapable of reforming itself and that 'market socialism' rather than saving its bacon, cooks its goose."[107] That process may be the result of violent crisis and collapse; perhaps it will be a more or less peaceful transition managed by a reform-minded communist leadership. White was writing at the start of the 1990s, but by the end of that decade we are left waiting to see how all this will turn out. The Party-state remains in command, and the prophets of doom continue to predict collapse at any moment.

9

The World's Most Rapidly Urbanizing Nation

Chinese urbanization is fed not by the collapse of rural agriculture but by rural prosperity ... and the rural urbanization attendant on such prosperity is the linchpin of China's urbanization which is day by day bringing rural dwellers increasingly within an urban lifestyle nexus. As the twenty-first century dawns, we say farewell to peasant China.

—Gregory Guldin, *Farewell to Peasant China* (1997)[1]

Introduction: The End of the Socialist City?

Much has been written about socialist cities, especially the characteristics that differentiate them from capitalist cities.[2] Focusing on cities in the former Soviet Union and Eastern Europe, for example, sociologist Ivan Szelenyi has suggested three sets of characteristics, each of which has been altered by the transition to capitalism. These characteristics are closely related to the characteristics of Chinese cities in the Maoist era, as we shall see later:[3]

1. Socialist cities tend to be underurbanized, are generally smaller, and have lower population densities than capitalist cities; this is usually considered to be a function of repressed demand resulting from the elimination of private property, in addition to specific policies designed to limit the rate of rural-to-urban migration.
2. Socialist cities exhibit fewer qualities of urbanism; for the most part politicians and city planners have chosen to urbanize on the cheap, which means that socialist cities tend to be functional, even Spartan in character: Less physical and human diversity exists than in capitalist cities; there is a dearth of entertainment and

recreational facilities; open space is used more liberally (and thus wastefully) in the construction of huge public squares and monumental structures. In general, however, socialist cities have a lower prevalence of social problems such as crime, prostitution, poverty, and homelessness.

3. Socialist cities have a unique ecological form: The role of the state in the provision of urban housing, and the restrictions placed upon the urban land market, tended to produce an urban form that was clearly different from that found in capitalist cities. Although some degree of spatial inequality is observable, the obvious differences include the absence of a high-rent, high-rise central business district and exclusive, single family–dominated residential suburbs.

During and after the transition period socialist cities witnessed some important changes; in fact Szelenyi concluded that "many features of socialist urban development are now decaying rapidly, and those that still survive are increasingly in contradiction with the emergent socioeconomic reality of the region."[4] To some extent events in Eastern European cities have been mirrored in Chinese cities, although similar outcomes often have markedly different causes. The phenomenon of rural-to-urban migration, for example, has occurred in China, although rather than being a result of rural decline—as in Eastern Europe and Russia—it has been associated with agriculture becoming more efficient and more profitable during the reform era (see Chapters 7 and 15). In other words, in the socialist transition era peasants became redundant in Eastern Europe as well as China—but for different reasons. Moreover, the impact of the new mobility, in terms of the sheer volume of internal migration, has been strikingly different.

The shift toward greater urbanism is also occurring in China's cities, although most of the immigrants (if we can use that term) are ethnic minorities or peasants leaving the land—and both groups are moving about within the same country. Beginning in the late 1980s there was an extraordinary increase in the level of commercial activity on China's city streets, much of it being conducted by former peasants: Everything from food to expensive French wine and Western CDs is on sale, and most any service is available, ranging from shoe-shining to dentistry.[5] There has also been significant suburbanization in China, most of it led by industrial and commercial developments; at present, with the exception of some luxury apartment and housing complexes, residential suburbanization on the Western model has not yet arrived in China.[6] Before investigating the nature of China's socialist cities and exploring the dynamics of the transition period, we should begin with a summary of urbanization in China.[7]

The Chinese City in History

China's urbanization occurred over three historical phases, with the spatial impacts of newer phases being superimposed upon legacies from earlier times. There has been a national urban system in China for nearly 2,000 years, consisting of a national capital, a small number of regional centers and provincial capitals, a network of county towns, and a vast number of villages and hamlets. In geographical terms this was a relatively mature urban system, as there were cities of all different sizes in the urban hierarchy. By contrast, in most other countries the dominant historical pattern of urban development has been a primate system, in which there was one major city and hundreds of villages, with almost nothing of any consequence between them.[8]

In spite of the maturity of China's ancient urban order, it was not a well-connected system. The county towns (*xians*) served as administrative outposts of the national capital, and to some extent they helped hold together the vast territory of China by linking the countryside to the central government. Apart from that function, there was little spatial interaction (i.e., travel and trade) between different regions, making it difficult for the center in Beijing to maintain control over the periphery, sometimes more than 1,000 miles away. The human and physical diversity across the Chinese land has produced some easily identifiable regions, and at many times the forces favoring regional demarcation were an obstacle to national integration. Thus instead of developing into a huge, interacting, interconnected whole, China was subdivided into clearly identifiable, independent regions that tended to interact little. Perhaps the best known of the regional subdivisions are the eight macroregions identified by G. W. Skinner.[9] Although the macroregions' boundaries are drawn largely along physiographic lines such as rivers or mountain ranges, Skinner argued that each macroregion possessed a single, integrated urban system. In other words, there was a mosaic of regional systems, but each system was connected only marginally to its neighbors. This lack of cross-regional interaction was largely a result of the great distances involved and the high costs (in time and money) of long-distance transportation. In the centers of most of the macroregions great markets had emerged, but the pattern of spatial interaction tended to remain largely intra- rather than interregional.

By the nineteenth century this pattern of regionalized urbanization had been altered somewhat by improvements in transportation and industrial development, and in the latter part of the century the development of the so-called Treaty Ports produced even more significant changes in the urban system. In all about a hundred cities were opened up to and partially colonized by Western nations. The influx of new technology, capital, and business acumen meant that the Treaty Ports grew more rapidly than those farther inland. Better transportation links along rivers and coasts meant that these cities began to interact (i.e., trade) with each other more than they had in the past.

It is important not to overstress this point. China's urban system did not suddenly become fully integrated with the emergence of the Treaty Ports; in fact a modern urban system was grafted onto the core of the indigenous system that had been in place for centuries. In some respects the graft was incomplete, resulting in a dual urban system.[10] The new Treaty Ports were connected to each other and also brought China into contact with the global economy; but that development was separate from and had relatively little effect on the old, inland urban system, which remained spatially isolated and poorly integrated with the nation as a whole.

The third phase of urban development after 1949 brought still more change to the Chinese urban system. By 1949 the cities were home to less than a tenth of the total population. Except for the provincial capitals and the larger Treaty Ports, cities never really challenged the rural dominance of feudal China. Under normal circumstances the big push toward economic development after 1949 would have been accompanied by increased urbanization. Such has been the case in most developing nations around the world, but the Party-state in China altered the normal course: actively discouraging growth in the largest cities; encouraging growth in medium and small cities; and for most of the time prohibiting in-migration from the countryside. In these ways urbanization was kept in check, at least until the end of the 1970s, when the current reform era began. Yet the state, for strategic and economic reasons, wanted to foster industrial growth in China's inland cities to counterbalance that in the coastal areas.

As we observed in Chapter 8, under the First Five Year Plan a policy of industrial deconcentration was announced, with development focusing on a series of "cities of pivotal construction" in the interior regions of China, including Lanzhou, Xian, Wuhan, and Zhengzhou.[11] Although the coastal cities would continue to play a major part in the nation's economic growth, the postrevolutionary pattern of urbanization was significantly influenced by the Communists' ideas about egalitarian spatial development.

The theoretical underpinnings of socialism in the writings of Marx and Engels did not provide a complete set of concepts to guide China's leaders on the issue of urbanization. The enormous disparity in wealth between the cities and the countryside was something that socialist theorists and practitioners alike were committed to eliminating, but it was clear to policymakers within the CCP that to develop the countryside at the expense of the cities would be political and economic suicide. Most of China's technology, industrial plant, and skilled labor was concentrated in the cities, and it was obvious to even diehard antiurbanists that national reconstruction would need to rely heavily on the economies of agglomeration made possible in the cities.[12]

In addition, Marxist ideology predicted that it would be in the cities, not the countryside, where the industrial proletariat would rise up to overthrow the capitalists. In other words, communist theory suggested that the cities were needed to help create the right conditions for revolution. Not surprisingly, therefore, there was some ambivalence among CCP leaders toward cities. Some of them, most notably Mao Zedong, had predominantly rural backgrounds, and the Party had spent close to two decades living in exile in the Chinese countryside before reentering the cities in 1949. It is important not to overstress this point, however, because others among the leadership had been born and raised in the cities; some (Zhou Enlai, for example) had even been educated in the metropolitan centers of Europe. After the enforced rural exile of the Party leaders during the 1930s and 1940s, there was a certain amount of antagonism among them toward cities and urban living.

When the Communists finally took control of the cities in 1949, Mao Zedong and many Party leaders were naturally apprehensive about what lay ahead: "In the 1920s [Mao] had turned his back on the cities and discovered revolutionary fires in the countryside. The fires had eventually spread across the lands of China until Mao stood once again facing the cities and once again fearful of them."[13]

Mao was violently opposed to what he felt was the elitism of urban-led socialism, preferring to believe that China should pin its hopes on the sheer mass and strength of the peasantry. The spatial manifestation of Mao's egalitarianism involved an almost fanatic desire to promote a self-reliant agriculture all across China and to direct settlement and industry away from the cities to the countryside. In his written pronouncements Mao was fond of waxing poetic on the wholesomeness of the Chinese countryside. As he said, "Honesty, virtue, hard work, and plain living are to be found primarily among the peasants; it was their revolutionary vision which won the struggle, and which [could] now create a new China."[14]

In Mao's opinion the countryside was untainted by the evils of Western capitalism that had thoroughly besmirched prerevolutionary China, especially in the Treaty Ports. The luxury-loving decadence of Westerners and the Chinese bourgeois class was anathema to the new communist elite. The symbol of everything that was corrupt and evil about city living was exhibited by the city of Shanghai, which was considered by Mao to epitomize Western-inspired degeneration. For Mao, Shanghai exhibited all of the ugliest features of urban capitalism: "Shanghai is a non-productive city. It is a parasitic city. It is a criminal city. It is a refugee city. It is the paradise of adventurers. In a word, Shanghai is a city where consumption is greater than production, indeed . . . where waste is greater than consumption."[15]

Although the writings of Mao Zedong suggest a virulent antiurbanism, some of the subsequent actions taken by the CCP belie that simplistic viewpoint. Despite publicized efforts to hold down growth in China's largest cities, urban growth actually speeded up after 1949, and at least for its first decade the revolution was industrial rather than rural in character. Migration from the countryside to the cities was virtually unchecked, as peasants arrived in search of jobs in the growing industrial sector. Investment in the industrial sector continued to outstrip that in agriculture, to such an extent that in the first three decades of the PRC, growth in industrial output was seven times greater than that in agriculture.[16]

Therefore it is reasonable to question the traditional portrait of antiurbanism among the CCP elite. Rather than antiurbanism per se, it may be more accurate to consider the unique type of urbanism associated with Mao Zedong. Perhaps Westerners cling to the appealing notion of Chinese antiurbanism because we like to believe in the image of Chinese rustic wholesomeness. In reality most Chinese have found rural life dirty, hard, and unrewarding. It may seem attractive to those raised in urbanized societies to consider life without cars, private ownership of homes, and the peculiarly Western sense of individualism expressed in the suburban ideal of single-family residences. The Chinese, however, do not share our enthusiasm at all, as Richard Kirkby has stressed: "If the Chinese are united in one thing, it is in a shared consciousness of struggle against the ravages of nature; it is an irony that we should choose to project onto such a people our own naive rusticism."[17]

Patterns of Urban Growth Since 1949

The ambience of the Chinese city—the apparently gentle pace of life, the throngs of bicycles, the village-like lanes and vegetable patches . . . all contribute towards an anti-urban illusion to which Westerners seem predisposed.

—Richard Kirkby, *Urbanization in China* (1985)[18]

Despite the CCP's avowed antiurbanism and its desire to reduce the urban-rural dichotomy, China's urban population continued to grow after 1949, and in fact it more than doubled between 1950 and 1960 (increasing from 62 million to 130 million). During that period there had been attempts to dissuade peasants from migrating to the cities, as well as efforts to increase opportunities for rural employment by creating industrial jobs in the countryside. At times coercive measures were implemented to discourage urban growth, including the physical deportation of some peasants who had moved to the cities without official permission.

The major economic goal of the Party at this time was to maximize capital investment to increase industrialization. Consistent with this goal was a relative de-emphasis on urban consumption and the provision of public services for city dwellers, including housing, roads, utilities, shops, and public transportation.[19] Critics of the CCP's policies in the cities have argued that this strategy was not so much based on the principle of egalitarianism as on a desire to build cities quickly and on the cheap, in other words, without wasting precious resources on bourgeois trappings of urbanization. The result was that China's city dwellers felt consistently short-changed. Living in a Chinese city meant doing without the small luxuries of everyday life. Scarcity and poor services were the norm, but the official Party line was that going without such luxuries was a virtue that benefited the larger goals of socialism.[20]

The growth of China's cities during the First Five Year Plan (1953–1957) resulted in some demographic headaches for city planners. In addition to absolute growth, cities had to support a larger population of dependents, or people who are unable to support themselves. Declining death rates and increasing birthrates during the 1950s meant that dependent populations were increasing; in fact in China's fifteen largest cities the old and young represented 60 percent of total population in 1957.[21] In addition to the financial burden associated with nonproductive urban residents, industrialization and urban growth meant that the cities were becoming increasingly difficult to manage, and it was clear that more effective planning was needed to head off excessive urban growth.

This was achieved in part by restricting rural-to-urban migration and developing rural industry. Another policy—and certainly the most controversial—was the "sending down" of millions of educated youth from the cities to the countryside, a policy that began in the 1960s. Such exportations were intended to reduce demand for urban jobs and expand the educated workforce in the countryside, thereby helping to eliminate the dichotomy between city and country in China. In the countryside youths were to be "purified" and freed from the "spiritual pollution" surrounding them in the cities. The goal was for the young people to "revolutionize" themselves by first becoming rural laborers: "Going to share the bitter and the sweet with the laboring people in the countryside, educated youths can gradually cultivate the habit of doing labor eagerly, establish a correct attitude towards physical labor [and] reform their nonproletarian thoughts . . . an important guarantee for preventing themselves forever from being corrupted."[22] In the 1960s these measures met with considerable success, at least in statistical terms, and the average yearly rate of urban growth slowed down to about 750,000, compared with 3.4 million in the 1950s.[23]

Beginning in the 1960s and extending through the 1970s there was also a concerted effort to direct growth away from China's largest cities, most of which were on or close to the coast. For example, an attempt was made to encourage growth of medium-sized cities (populations of 200,000–500,000), as well as smaller towns and cities; the success of these efforts can be seen from the data reported in Table 9.1. The absolute numbers and relative shares increased for most categories of cities, but the largest cities (1 million–plus) saw a decline in their overall share of China's total urban population (from 39.3 percent to 36.5 percent), whereas the share in the medium-sized cities increased from 15.9 percent to 22.3 percent.

After a decade of slow urban growth, urbanization began to increase once the economic reforms were implemented in 1978. As one observer has suggested, there were a num-

TABLE 9.1   Urban Population Growth by City Size in China, 1953–1979

	1953			1979		
City Size	# of Cities	Total Pop. (millions)	% of Total	# of Cities	Total Pop. (millions)	% of Total
1 million +	9	17.5	39.3	15	33.9	36.5
500,000–999,999	16	9.4	21.1	28	20.6	22.1
200,000–499,999	28	7.1	15.9	68	20.8	22.3
100,000–199,999	40	5.9	13.5	72	10.1	10.8
50,000–99,999	71	4.6	10.3	147	7.6	8.2
TOTAL		44.5			93.0	

SOURCE: Adapted from Kirkby (1985), p. 271, Table A5.9.

ber of contributing factors to this new urbanization:

> Many of the youth "sent down" during the Cultural Revolution . . . returned to the cities; delayed marriages among those youth [resulted in] higher birth rates; the relaxation of the state controls on urban residence . . . allowed many rural residents to move to cities; there . . . was . . . a massive displacement of peasants who [were considered to be] surplus to the needs of agriculture as a result of the new agricultural reforms in the countryside.[24]

At the time it was not clear how far these developments would be allowed to proceed, but some experts predicted that the agricultural reforms might free up as many as 200 million people, many of whom, it was feared, would want to move to cities for their jobs and housing.[25] That trend continued throughout the 1980s and 1990s (see Chapter 15). In just one year (from 1982 to 1983), China's urban population increased by 14 percent, an explosion compared to the previous slow rates of urban growth (averaging 4.4 percent per year over three decades).[26]

It is difficult to assess urban population growth during any given period because of the frequent changes in the definition of the term "urban." As we saw in Chapter 7, at certain times some cities have been allowed to annex

surrounding rural counties, thereby growing considerably in size virtually overnight. This results in the uniquely Chinese situation in which more than half of a city's population may actually be rural. In Nanjing, for example, which is a city (*shi*) of the second order (after Beijing, Shanghai, and Tianjin in the urban hierarchy), three rural counties were annexed, adding 1.61 million people to the city's population, of which only 100,000 are actually "urban." With an additional 420,000 rural residents living in the city's suburban districts, almost 2 million of Nanjing's 3.74 million residents are essentially rural residents, although for legal purposes they are defined as residents of the city.[27]

Chinese city planners have also exhibited a fondness for creating new urban places. In 1976, for example, there were 189 cities, but by 1986 there were 300 and, by 1987, 381. In 1984 the number of towns (*jizhen*) was doubled, effectively increasing the urban population to more than 330 million, or 31.9 percent of the total population, compared to 20.2 percent in 1981.[28] By 1987, according to the Chinese State Statistical Bureau, the urban population stood at 503.6 million, which was 46.6 percent of the total, surely making China the most urbanized nation in the world in terms of the total number of people living in cities. By 1996, however, the proportion of the population designated as "urban" had been recalculated (see Table 9.2),

TABLE 9.2   China's Urban and Rural Population, 1978–1987

	Urban		Rural	
Year	Population (millions)	% of total	Population (millions)	% of Total
1978	172.45	17.9	790.14	82.1
1979	184.95	19.0	790.47	81.0
1980	191.4	19.4	795.65	80.6
1985	250.94	23.7	807.57	76.3
1990	201.91	26.4	841.42	73.6
1996	359.50	29.4	864.39	70.6

SOURCE: *China Statistical Yearbook, 1988* and *1990*; 1996 data from *China Statistical Yearbook, 1997*, Table 3-1, p. 69.

and the official urban population was given as 359.5 million (29 percent of the total), and the 1985 urban population was given as 277 million (less than 25 percent of the total).[29] In spite of the definitional changes there can be little doubt that China has witnessed a major population increase in its biggest cities in a very short period; for example, by 1986 there were thirty-eight "million cities" and forty-seven more with populations larger than a half-million. Clearly, the so-called Chinese model of urbanization, in which there had been an emphasis on the development of small and medium-sized cities, had come to an end.

To soak up the surplus agricultural population the government has continued to champion the cause of thousands of small towns across the countryside, transforming them into local centers of commerce, trade, and industry.[30] By the middle of the 1980s it looked as though small towns had managed to double the number of manufacturing and processing jobs in small-scale rural enterprises, from 30 million in 1982 to 60 million in 1985.[31] Growth at this level of the urban hierarchy—coupled with the traditional controls on rural-to-urban migration—helped keep China's urban growth to a manageable level. In the three decades after 1950 in-migration made up only about 30 percent of total urban growth, which helped the Chinese to avoid the overcrowding, homelessness, and squalor typical of cities in poor countries around the world.[32] As we shall see,

however, from the late 1980s onward China's cities have been experiencing significantly higher rates of in-migration than at any other time since 1949, largely a result of redundancies in the countryside. Before evaluating this most recent surge of urban growth and its consequences for urban planners, however, it is important to review the legacy that had been left in China's cities by almost thirty years of socialist urban planning.

Maoist City Planning

When the CCP marched victoriously into the Chinese cities in 1949 they faced an uphill task: getting the country back on its feet. In the short run it was clearly necessary for China to develop a strong economy and military to help it regain worldwide respect. China needed to stand up, both internationally and internally, by demonstrating to all that it was finally united and independent, a country that could forever end the crushing poverty under which its people had labored for so long.[33]

In the longer term Mao Zedong predicted that the road to political and economic strength would be littered with a series of contradictions, some of which could only be "correctly" handled rather than solved completely. One of the contradictions Mao continually faced was that between the city and countryside. The assumed policy remained one in which significant attempts were made to reduce the economic disparity between rural and urban workers, but as we have seen, the policies actually implemented were refashioned at various times to meet changing circumstances. With the passage of time there were also changes in thinking about how best to handle the urban-rural contradiction. For purely pragmatic reasons, the early Soviet-style model of economic development heavily favored urban and industrial development over rural and agricultural development, but by the late 1950s that gave way to a pattern of development that improved the terms of trade for agriculture, in which small-scale, decentralized development was emphasized. This demonstrated that Mao's approach to the urban-rural issue was to be pragmatic rather than dogmatic; obviously it would have been a mistake to ignore China's cities in the push for development. Although Mao wanted to see the fundamental disparities between urban and rural life overcome in the first decade after the revolution, he was realistic enough to know that city and countryside alike could make important contributions to development.

The compromise Mao offered was to establish new economic entities—the people's communes—that were not exclusively urban or rural, industrial or agricultural, but contained elements of both. The communes are today largely defunct, but in the countryside the Maoist ideal of rural industrialization transcended even the changing leadership after his death in 1976. By the mid-1980s rural collective industries (i.e., TVEs) made up nearly 80 percent of China's total industrial enterprises and provided 22 percent of the gross value of industrial output.[34] No doubt this contributed greatly to rural incomes and standards of living, thereby helping to narrow the gap.

At the other end of the scale agriculture was successfully brought into the Chinese city, a development that helped to make cities self-sufficient in food production but, more important, brought peasants and workers together, effectively eroding the age-old walls separating

them. As Marc Blecher observed, "Peasants who work the land on the perimeter of the city live in the same urban neighborhoods as factory workers, intermingling with them at markets, political functions, cinemas, clinics and schools."[35] Mao Zedong's solution to the urban-rural contradiction was to tease out what is best from both sides. He declined to make a clear-cut choice between one thing and another, opting instead for a creative synthesis of the two. Mao was aware that the new Chinese society would be shaped by the strategies designed to tackle this and other contradictions that were emerging.

Those contradictions came to a head in the cities. The cities of the past, by definition, were centers of bourgeois activity, but they also contained remnants of the feudal divisions between rich and poor, as well as remnants of the imperialist domination of China. It was in the city, therefore, that the CCP now had to focus its attention, as Mao himself noted in 1949: "The centre of gravity of the Party's work has shifted from the village to the city. . . . We must do our utmost to learn how to administer and build the cities. . . . If we do not pay attention to these problems . . . we shall be unable to maintain our political power, we shall be unable to stand on our feet, we shall fail."[36] After the Communists entered the cities—as soon as the job of wiping out the opposition and pacifying any resistance had been completed—the new elite faced the staggering task of recruiting and training the personnel needed to run all aspects of the urban administration: finance, commerce, industry, transportation, and culture. As Ezra Vogel has described it, the situation in Canton (Guangzhou) when the Communists arrived in 1949 was probably typical of what they encountered everywhere: "When the Communist troops entered Canton, they found the city in turmoil. . . . Some of the lower elements of society . . . were looting deserted homes and the stores and gathering goods abandoned in the streets. Some remnants of the Kuomintang army . . . continued minor sabotage and sniping. . . . Inflation was rampant, the city was filled with transients, and both armies had sorely taxed the local food supply."[37]

In cities like Canton there were essentially two tasks to be carried out, one that was largely physical, the other social. First it was necessary to take immediate action to respond to problems they encountered. The entire citizenry was exhorted to strive for "three years of recovery, then ten years of development."[38] Law and order had to be installed, incomes generated, taxes collected, and education and other collective services provided. Training and organizing the necessary personnel required consolidating the existing Communist supporters and, more important, recruiting and training new ones. The new leaders were convinced that the correct solutions would eventually be found if they could produce a high-quality core of Party officials, that is, the cadres. Like their Confucian predecessors, the Communists believed that the moral qualities of cadres were all-important. They would need to sacrifice private interests for the public good and be able to form effective working relationships with the masses.

Unlike the Mandarins (the top Confucian-educated civil servants in imperial China), however, the new cadres were required to be egalitarian and activist. They would have to lead by example, demonstrating to all that they could resist the temptations of city life and all its comforts and "remain true to the ideal of asceticism, patriotism, and selfless service."[39] According to the Communists, the major difference between themselves and the vanquished Kuomintang was their moral superiority. The people had already made their choice; now it was up to the Communists to make good on their promises.

To examine some of the ways the CCP went about this task, we shall focus on the issues the new elite found most odious and troublesome about the cities they had inherited. The first task was the need to restructure the physical landscape of the city, replacing the legacies of feudalism and imperialism with symbols of the new socialist era. A second was to make China's cities economically self-sufficient, particularly in food production. A third was to bring law and order to the Chinese city and to rebuild it in the image of the new socialist values of moral wholesomeness.

Cities That Erase the Past and Point to the Future

In spatial and architectural terms many Chinese cities had inherited a feudal appearance, symbolizing the inequality that had persisted for centuries. City walls were used to separate town from country and leaders from the masses. Distinct quarters of the city appeared, segregating different categories of the population according to their position in the social hierarchy. In many of the Treaty Ports an imperialist influence was superimposed upon this ancient pattern. In Shanghai, for example, the city was divided into international settlements by the colonizers; in time those areas developed a unique colonial appearance, sharply differentiating them from the ancient Chinese core of the city.

In Shenyang (Mukden), the capital of the Japanese puppet state of Manchukuo, the imperial presence established an extra measure of segregation to land uses. The comprador-bourgeoisie class was encouraged to build up the city's commerce and industry, and a new core area was built adjacent to the old Chinese walled city.[40] That tended to increase the level of segregation within the city, because the new area was dominated by the Japanese and foreign consuls; but it was also laid out along Western lines, with a gridlike pattern, differentiating it sharply from the jumbled Chinese core and its narrow, crooked streets.

Much of what CCP leaders found in the cities in 1949 was loathsome in their view, as they preferred to impose a much more centralized, highly standardized social organization. In social terms many of the Treaty Ports symbolized what the Communists detested most about urban life: They were traditionally inhabited by the literati-intellectual classes, as well as being the focus for investment by the bourgeois class and rapacious foreign businessmen. As Chinese anthropologist Fei Xiaotong has pointed out, both of these urban types were considered by the Communists to be "parasites" living on and off the "real" China.[41]

To transform the cities the Party-state identified three major goals from a larger set of socialist city planning objectives: stimulate industrial productivity; deliver collective services efficiently; and promote socioeconomic equality.[42] The priority given each goal has shifted over time, and of course situations in each city were different, but in general terms the objective was to produce a uniform, largely classless city, one with minimal stratification of urban land uses. Streets were widened, slum areas removed, public housing built, and utilities laid in. In some cases the city centers were rebuilt to cater to the more egalitarian and political functions of a socialist state. That involved the opening of formerly forbidden areas, as in Beijing, as well as the destruction of temples, statues, and other relics of the feudal past.[43] The residential districts were divided into self-contained, largely autonomous units at the ward and neighborhood levels, and the concept of the work unit was strengthened to reduce urban commuting and foster a sense of local community.

In the first decades of the PRC the new socialist cities went through three major phases. The first was during the Soviet-inspired Five Year Plan, when policies favored large-city development and heavy industry. Some so-called New Industrial Districts were built to replace old slum areas, as in Zhabei, in Shanghai; numerous satellite towns were planned to act as industrial and residential countermagnets at the urban fringe. The norm within all newly constructed areas was for uniform public housing on a huge scale, often built in drab, five-story chunks. In some city centers monumental Soviet-style buildings and revolutionary public concourses were constructed, as in Tiananmen Square in Beijing, and new symbols of revolutionary heroism were installed to replace feudal and colonial remnants.[44]

The second phase occurred during the Great Leap Forward (1958–1960), when the Soviet influence on Chinese cities was formally denounced and Chinese, or Maoist, urban development was ushered in. The emphasis at this time was to narrow the so-called three great differences between mental and manual labor, industry and agriculture, and urban and rural standards of living.[45] This era brought a virtual end to most big-city construction projects and brought a new emphasis on urbanization in the countryside.[46]

The third phase of urban development occurred on a very limited scale during the ultraegalitarian phase of the Cultural Revolution after 1966. At this time the strong Maoist emphasis on self-reliance, self-sufficiency, and frugality—combined with the continued desire to reduce the urban-rural dichotomy—produced a unique urban form that was a cross between a rural-style city and an urban-style village.[47] The best example was the oil city of Daqing, Heilongjiang Province, in northeastern China. Daqing had no obvious city center; it intermixed oilfields and cultivated land; industrial facilities were dispersed across the urban landscape; and there was a hierarchy of different-sized residential areas. Daqing essentially became the urban equivalent of the Dazhai Brigade, acting as a model for Chinese urban development: "To symbolize the frugal spirit, earthen houses were built for the people. These embodied the utopian Chinese socialist city: high productivity, hard working spirit, and the integration of industry and agriculture. The principles of uniformity, standardization, and classlessness were all faithfully followed by the city planners."[48]

Cities That Could Feed Themselves

In the decade immediately following liberation the Party-state faced a serious conflict between two of its avowed urban policies: the desire for all administrative units, including cities, to be agriculturally self-sufficient; and the attempt to transform the city into a production-dominated, essentially classless territory. Building the new urban-based factories and the housing necessary for workers would obviously result in competition for valuable cultivable land at the urban fringe. Making matters worse, the Soviet-style urban planning that was adopted in the 1950s was wasteful of urban space. Soviet gigantism emphasized wide boulevards, huge buildings, large public parks, municipal stadiums, and massive public squares—all low-density land uses requiring the demolition of existing (and higher density) land uses, especially housing.[49] The cities expanded outward, and the resulting urban sprawl produced an inevitable conflict with the traditional market-gardening activities that are essential to a city's ability to feed itself. In the eight key cities identified for industrial development in the Chinese interior, for example, 12,900 acres of vegetable fields were lost to city construction projects in 1953 alone.[50] At a national scale this precipitated a steady decline in vegetable production, especially in the cities, which were forced to rely on more distant, and therefore less fresh and more expensive, sources of supply. This became a crisis that stimulated several new policies to increase urban self-sufficiency.[51] It had traditionally been difficult to persuade Chinese farmers to grow vegetables because they were relatively capital-intensive and provided low returns. Bank loans, subsidies, and other incentives were therefore provided to encourage greater vegetable production. New rural collectives were established close to the urban areas in which agricultural activities were switched over from grain and livestock to vegetables. Beginning in 1956 vegetable farmers were allowed to sell their produce at higher prices in free markets in the cities, which increased the desirability of growing vegetables. The problem was that this solution tended to conflict with other policies; for example, the farmers preferred to sell in the free markets, which meant they often had nothing left for the state vegetable corporations.

The ultimate solution to the urban self-sufficiency problem was considered to be the creation of "city-regions" in 1958 and subsequent years. These were large administrative units intended to integrate city and countryside and thereby allow a rational planning solution to the locational conflicts at the urban fringe

between urban and agricultural land use. At first fifty-eight cities were allowed to annex adjacent, largely rural counties, which they would control while resolving land use conflicts. This new phase of urban-rural symbiosis gradually facilitated large-scale conversions of land into vegetable cultivation as close as possible to city centers, thereby allowing peasants to transport produce easily to urban markets.

Immediately adjacent to the built-up area, communes were directed to focus the bulk of their energies on year-round vegetable production, and in many cities these areas were generally able to produce 70–90 percent of the required vegetables. In a zone farther out from the city center, vegetables were to be grown seasonally, which produced the familiar agricultural pattern of decreasing intensity in production, with vegetable cultivation gradually giving way to other crops such as rice and cotton the farther one was from the city.[52]

Since 1958 the city-region concept has been applied to cities of all sizes, and in most cases it has helped formalize what had previously been a chaotic solution to conflicts between urban and rural land uses. It should be noted, however, that the power of cities to annex rural territory was often damaging to the independence of rural communes, effectively subordinating them to the whims of the industrialized urban cores. Thus solving one of the contradictions between city and country caused new contradictions to emerge.

Cities of Tranquillity and Order

The ethnocentricity and morality of the Chinese Communists meant that they were repulsed by what they found in their cities, especially the Treaty Ports, after 1949. In architectural terms, as well as in their economic and social practices, the cities were redolent with foreign, bourgeois, and Nationalist influences. Shanghai, for example, was widely perceived to be "a center of foreign and bourgeois culture. . . . Foreign-owned newspapers, American films, and schools where Chinese pupils were taught in foreign languages were all signs of cultural influences opposed by the Communists."[53] More important, the coastal cities symbolized for the Communists the moral bankruptcy of the Western way of life and the dangers of allowing urbanization to proceed unchecked. The streets were littered with homeless beggars; crime and corruption were rampant; drug abuse was ubiquitous. Shanghai, again acting as the symbol of Western decadence, was reported to have 30,000 prostitutes on its streets in 1949, a higher ratio per capita than in Chicago, Paris, Berlin, and London.[54] As Edgar Snow observed, Shanghai was "a continuous freak circus with all manner of people performing almost every physical and social function in public: yelling, crushing throngs spilling through every kind of traffic . . . past 'honey-carts' filled with excrement [and] past perfumed, exquisitely gowned, mid-thigh-exposed Chinese ladies."[55]

The shameless exploitation of women in pre-liberation Chinese cities was—according to communist lore—the result of a combination of different factors: the obsession with sex and the desire for instant gratification among Westerners; the traditional Confucian bias against women in China and the reluctance to provide education for girls; and the simple fact that Chinese women, partly because of their lack of education, were virtually unemployable and therefore had few options outside the drudgery of home life and domestic service. In the oral history book *Chinese Lives*, the authors interviewed a woman who had been sold as a country girl to the local landlord before the revolution. A year later, in a desperate search for a job, she signed on with a Shanghai labor contractor. Upon arriving at a plush house in the city she was surprised when a woman looked her up and down and agreed to take her in: "She took out a cheongsam and a pair of embroidered slippers and told me to put them on. 'I can't get dressed up like that,' I said. 'I've come to do factory work.' 'I've bought you,' answered the woman with a strange smile. 'There's no factory work here.' I had been sold into a brothel in a well-known red-light district. It was 1933 and I was fourteen."[56]

To reestablish order and purge this sort of degeneracy, the Communists attempted to legislate immorality and crime out of existence, simply sweeping the streets clean. Brothels and opium dens were closed, and prostitutes and addicts were rounded up for rehabilitation. This might have failed but for additional efforts to find a meaningful place for women in the cities: New marriage laws prohibited overt discrimination against women; mass education for the first time meant that girls had the right to go to school on a regular basis; and the drive to push women into the labor force meant that new employment opportunities became available.

The intricate network of social control and surveillance at the street and work-unit levels helped keep out much of the crime and corruption. Delinquents, good-for-nothings, and petty thieves were quickly ferreted out by resident-area guardians, so that "overnight these sons of old Shanghai became living symbols of the city's conversion from adventure to production."[57] In a relatively short time the Chinese city became a purposeful center of socialist production. The prostitutes were gone and the opium dens had disappeared; in fact the new cities were squeaky-clean, and as Ross Terrill described: "You can no more find a singsong girl [or an opium pipe] in [Shanghai] than in a Boy Scout Camp. This is less a result of suppression than of a drastic change in social system. Since there [was] a driving social purpose, the female half of society [was] naturally part of it."[58] Completing the socialist transformation was the effort to eliminate the parasitic consumption characteristic of the old cities. In Nanjing, for example, streets in the old part of the city had been lined with wine shops and restaurants, where close to 100,000 people had once earned a living as waiters, servants, and lackeys to the official and moneyed elite. After liberation, the Communists set out to put the people of the city to more useful work, following Mao Zedong's directive: "From the very first day we take over a city, we should direct our attention to restoring and developing its production."[59]

In Canton, after they had dealt with political opponents, Kuomintang spies, and secret societies, the Communists tackled the city's social problems: prostitution, gambling, opium addiction, and crime. People who committed such crimes were not treated as counterrevolutionaries; they were seen more as feudal remnants who could be reformed through socialist instruction. Instead of being executed like the political prisoners, "all offenders . . . were carefully investigated and then suddenly rounded up. . . . They underwent a program of criticism, self-criticism, labor reform, and retraining. Before being released they were taught a trade and required to sign a statement guaranteeing that they would never again resort to a crime."[60] For the first time in more than a century public morality was restored so that the people of Canton did not have to worry about walking the streets at night. Human nature had not been altered, but tight surveillance and a strongly organized police force operating at the local level went a long way toward wiping out crime. In a symbolic gesture, on June 3, 1951, all the opium and smoking paraphernalia in Canton was rounded up and burned in a huge bonfire. This was exactly 112 years after the Chinese burned the opium they had confiscated from the British, an act that triggered the start of the Opium Wars (which ultimately resulted in the establishment of the Treaty Ports and the cession of Hong Kong to the British). The bonfire was accompanied by patriotic speeches signifying the end to more than a century of oppression by chemicals and foreigners. As Ezra Vogel described it, "In one stroke of political wizardry, local officials appealed to patriotism and promoted the eradication of vices. The obvious hero was the new government."[61]

Instead of idle pastimes and decadent pursuits, the streets of the old Treaty Ports were to be filled with a new breed of politically motivated young workers eager to mobilize for the socialist future.[62] From a Western perspective the new puritanical city was probably a dull place to live, but austerity came to be accepted as a feature of a progressive lifestyle. Western fashions gave way to "cotton clothing and the 'Lenin' suit. . . . Luxurious restaurants [were] closed or converted to cater to a mass clientele, and the conspicuous consumption of automobiles, night life, and fine furnishings decreased."[63] The constant surveillance and close social control brought a chilling vision of big brother to the Chinese city; it would remain that way until well into the 1990s.[64]

As we have seen from this survey of urban life in China after 1949, the cities were largely rebuilt, reorganized, and cleaned up after liberation. Socialist modernity with Chinese characteristics was manifested in a wholesome, efficient, and businesslike urban landscape. The city was wrested from the bourgeois classes, intellectuals, landlords, money lenders, and foreign imperialists and returned to the Chinese. Most important, the city was given to the working classes. The new city was permeated with Maoist puritanism, and a heavy dose of rural values was instilled into all aspects of urban life. After decades of Western exploitation and the subjugation of Chinese women, the city became the bastion of family values, plain living, and hard work: "In the case of Shanghai . . . it appeared that the city had been scrubbed clean and prepared for a new destiny. Shanghai was being stripped for a new existence. Certainly what happened was the very negation of the city's 'raison d'être' [and the message was that] vice will not breed here. Worlds will not meet here."[65]

Chinese Cities at the End of the Millennium

With new leadership safely in place by 1978, the CCP introduced a series of reforms touching all aspects of Chinese life, virtually ending the utopian ideology and the emphasis on class struggle associated with Mao Zedong. From this point on the CCP would focus mostly on economic growth, which produced dramatic change. Under the Four Modernizations the Chinese political economy has been an enigma, characterized variously and ambiguously as a capitalist society espousing socialism; a modern urban-based industrial system with a huge and traditional agricultural sector; and a Third World economy with First World aspirations.[66] The reforms have contributed to what one scholar has referred to as "the return of the god of wealth," making it possible for Chinese people to free themselves from the constraints of collectivization.[67] Once the people were liberated from the bonds of the commune system and other mandatory economic institutions, they "burst out with immense energy and enthusiasm for creating individual wealth and developing the economy."[68] To focus our discussion, we shall consider the impact of two factors of production, both of which have been freed up during the reform era: domestic and foreign capital, which penetrated far into the Chinese mainland; and personal mobility, most clearly manifested in a massive rural-to-urban population transfer (see Chapter 15).

As we observed in Chapter 8, economic reform signaled the abandonment of the autarky principle fundamental to development planning in the Maoist state (1949–1976). China became an open market for investment capital from around the world; in fact by 1995 China was receiving almost 20 percent of all the foreign direct investment going to the world's developing countries.[69] The development strategy of choice in the Dengist era, borrowed to a degree from the Asian NIEs, required rapid growth of export-oriented manufacturing. In geographical terms Maoist egalitarianism was abandoned in favor of spatial comparative advantage, with growth initially focused on the SEZs, which were intended to function as "greenhouses" for domestic and transnational capital, much of which came from overseas Chinese investors in Taiwan, Hong Kong, and Singapore. As we saw in Chapter 8, investment capital has penetrated China unevenly thus far (depicted in Map 8.1).

Another dramatic change associated with reform has been the new population mobility, which set free a huge supply of cheap, highly motivated labor. Since roughly the mid-1980s millions of rural residents have been migrating to the cities, a remarkable turnaround after being kept virtual prisoners in rural production units for three decades. As might be expected, capital mobility and human labor mobility are thoroughly interlinked in contemporary China, because migrants are attracted to places where capital is being invested and where new jobs have become abundantly available. Guangdong Province, for example, especially its Pearl River Delta, is now perceived as a desirable region, a place of wealth and power that many Chinese people have pinpointed as a destination. As the most recent census data demonstrate, millions of Chinese people have been exercising their newfound freedom, with many finding their way to the biggest cities, some of which now have as many as 3 million new residents. In addition, many rural migrants—instead of moving to the largest cities—have been making a series of shorter moves away from their villages into successively larger places in the urban hierarchy.

It is useful to speculate on the urban transformations one might expect when socialist societies begin the transition to capitalism. There is no shortage of literature on this topic, beginning with studies that attempted to characterize the essence of the socialist city.[70] This literature has been enriched by accounts of events in Eastern Europe and the former Soviet Union, as well as by studies conducted in socialist states where market forces have produced significant urban changes, including Cuba, Vietnam, and China.[71] This helps us sketch a general theory of the impacts on urbanization during the transition process, which involves a number of interconnected elements: land use conflicts at the urban fringe; the emergence of commodity housing; and the appearance of new capitalist urban landscapes.[72] As we shall see, some of these processes can be seen in China's cities during the era of reform.

Because China's transition out of socialism has mainly followed the marketization route, its cities have played a key role in the modernization process.[73] As one China scholar pointed out, the "extraordinary productivity of large metropolitan regions, creating agglomeration economies and spillover effects, provides an extremely powerful momentum for economic growth."[74]

In the drive to get rich there was a tendency for land use conflicts to reemerge at the urban fringe, with farmers quickly realizing there were far more profitable and prestigious ways to earn a living and spend money.[75]

Another manifestation of the changing times was the emergence of new housing, evident in two major categories: large single-family homes of newly rich peasants; and suburban developments offering huge and expensive housing, either as apartments or detached units (see Photo 9.1). Although most of the units are targeted for rich "overseas" investors, the wealth and the obvious prestige associated with such developments have acted as an incentive to domestic capitalists who might want to tread a similar path.

One of the first places to exhibit the contrast between the urban landscapes of pre- and postreform China was Tiananmen Square. It is a huge public space, immediately outside the old Forbidden City. Mao Zedong made it clear there would be no more forbidden cities in socialist China, so Tiananmen has significance as a symbol of the new openness and as the place Mao chose to declare the formation of the People's Republic of China in 1949. Tiananmen Square, in other words, was a space of emancipation, representing the liberation of the Chinese people from their traditional oppressors—colonizers, Nationalists, and landlords. In the middle of the square thousands of people line up in any weather to pay their respects at the Mao Zedong mausoleum. As we also know, in spring 1989 Tiananmen Square was the site of the largest public demonstration of resistance ever to be launched by the Chinese people. It is ironic, therefore, that in the southwestern corner China's first Kentucky Fried Chicken opened in the late 1980s, the largest of its kind in the

PHOTO 9.1   Lion Gardens residential development in Panyu, near Guangzhou.

world.[76] Tiananmen is thus one of the most recognizable landscapes in the world and has represented a complexly mixed set of images: the resting place of Mao Zedong; capitalist decadence in the form of poultry consumption, Western-style; the release from oppression; and repression, martial law, and civil disobedience. Today Beijing reflects the new era of economic change despite the ugly face of state power and military excess. Outsiders noticed some shifts in city planning during and after the Dengist era. In line with pragmatic economic reform, it appears that planners, rather than forcing uniform, socialist-style planning, are now more likely to allow individual cities to develop according to their own characteristics. Some cities focus on heavy industry, others on light industry; but many of the fastest growing cities have been able to diversify their employment bases by adding financial services, commercial activities, and tourism facilities. This is a sharp contrast to the Maoist stipulation that all cities be exclusively concerned with production activities. Consistent with the new approach to regional economic development, Chinese cities today focus on whatever they do best, which is dictated by market signs and entrepreneurial endeavor (an urban version of the comparative advantage principle). In Guangzhou (Canton), for example, the city plan of the late 1980s called for "a socialist modern city with well-developed foreign trade and tourism, a center of scientific culture, with a balanced development of raw material . . . and farm produce processing, all built on a light industrial base."[77]

In the 1980s and 1990s city planners have reinforced this new concept of urban diversity, adding genuine concern for environmental degradation and visual appearance. All cities are now required to submit master plans to the central government for approval and are expected to follow the plans faithfully. In the new era it is no longer considered unproductive to plan upgrades of city services such as transportation, housing, and recreation. And the new emphasis on urban beautification not long ago would have been branded as bourgeois and decadent (although most cities have grown so rapidly they resemble permanent construction sites). From the planning perspective, then, there has been a new emphasis on "the individual character of the city, modernity, and the improved livelihood of the people [rather than] the uniformity, frugality, and anti-consumerism objectives of the 1950s and 1960s."[78] From evidence currently available, we can predict that planners will have their hands full trying to orchestrate the spatial structures of contemporary Chinese cities. The new forces of market socialism have altered the use and value of urban land. Thus there is a new "landscape of consumption" in the city, one that may bring back memories of prerevolutionary inequality.[79] As an ever growing number of rural and urban residents gain wealth, they effectively create a new class that probably wants to express its newfound monetary status in material terms. Until the Dengist era the principles of socialist city planning militated against any social or spatial stratification; in fact in the socialist city, with residences traditionally tied to their workplaces, it was rare to see stratification manifested in house size and the amount of living space per family. With the exception of small areas in the largest cities set aside for tourist development and luxury housing for overseas investors, there were few top-value lands dominated by real estate, banking, and other commercial functions.

By the end of the 1990s that situation had changed dramatically. A visitor to Shanghai, for example, can now ride an elevator to the observation lounge near the top of the new radio tower in Pudong or go to the top of the new Jin Mao Hotel and look back across the river on a breathtaking sight: a forest of skyscrapers stretching all directions into the distance. In 1990 there was nothing but paddies in Pudong and no buildings higher than five stories anywhere in Shanghai except along the Bund, the main road running parallel to the Huangpu River.

During the reform era urban populations grew rapidly as restrictions on migration were lifted, sent-down youths were allowed to return, and urban employment opportunities increased. New jobs were created across the industrial, service, and construction sectors, many filled by the floating populations. Somewhat surprisingly, in the early 1980s China's largest cities did not perform or grow in relative terms as rapidly as smaller cities and towns, mainly because the government held down growth in the biggest cities and also because the government was extracting a major chunk of the cities' earnings for the central coffers. As we shall see, that situation changed in the 1990s as most of the biggest cities began to grow again in terms of population, industry, commerce, and services, with much of the new development occurring at the urban fringes and between existing cities.

China's cities have also become increasingly autonomous in administrative and financial terms throughout the period of reform. New policies allowed cities to keep a larger share of their total revenues and greater discretion in spending; this made available more funds for local investment. As Barry Naughton has observed, "With increased [financial] retention and substantially increased autonomy, cities [were] better able to maneuver and [had] more opportunities . . . to cope with the problems of increased growth."[80] It is possible that as the center's control over economic issues weakens, political controls might appear to be more arbitrary and more likely to be contested by city residents and entrepreneurs. In other words, changes in the economic system might contribute to an increase in personal autonomy in the cities.

Whether or not that turns out to be the case, reform has provided urban residents considerably more freedom as to how they live, work, and spend money. Urban incomes are rising significantly, especially in nonstate enterprises in service and production; and the huge construction projects have employed millions of migrant laborers. With the infusion of consumption-oriented goods and services there are now myriad ways to spend money in the city.

Available leisure time has also increased, partly because higher incomes allow workers to spend fewer hours on the job, and partly because many urban residents can afford to hire nannies to look after children and maids to help with housework.[81] On balance the evidence suggests that the Chinese city is becoming an easier place to live: better housing; more interesting diversions; more and better places to eat and drink; more ways than ever before to make a reasonable living; and, sadly, more unemployment and marginal ways of life.[82]

The new urban order is also a result of changing definitions within the urban hierarchy.[83] It became clear to urban administrators early in the reform era that the higher one's town or city was ranked, the greater autonomy it would enjoy. A larger city, officially defined as such, had far more administrative power, greater discretion over investment decisions (including foreign direct investment), better access to financial aid and support from the state, and more control over surrounding rural counties. In other words, as Australian historian John Fitzgerald has pointed out, a higher rank in the urban order would "enhance a city's capacity to take full advantage of the economic reform policies. . . . Hence it is to the advantage of townships to seek classification as towns, for towns to become county-level cities, for county-level cities to seek prefectural status, for prefectural cities to apply for classification as 'separately planned' cities, and for these cities to upgrade to provincial-level cities."[84]

Boundaries between urban and rural areas have also been disappearing, as huge chunks of rural territory are swallowed up by the expanding cities. During the reform era, and especially the 1990s, decentralization has meant that cities challenge provinces as the favored jurisdiction for economic, social, and political decision-making. Thus at least one of Ivan Szelenyi's predictions about urban growth during and after the transition has been borne out: There is a shift from underurbanization toward overurbanization more typical of cities in developing capitalist nations.[85]

An Evaluation:
People and Places in China's
Posttransition Cities

During two decades of transition from socialism, China more than doubled its urban population (see Table 9.2), which now stands at 30–50
percent of the total population depending on
how one defines "urban."[86] Regardless of seman-
tics, in absolute terms China has more city
dwellers than any other country. The remainder
of this chapter will thus focus on three questions
surrounding this transformation. Is it possible
to identify the characteristics of what in the West
might be called the "postmodern" city in China?
To what extent has Chinese traditionalism, expressed in apparently timeless rurality, been
abandoned in the rush to urbanization? And to
what extent is the changing Chinese city providing residents with more space—social and political, as well as physical—in the ongoing struggle
between state and society?

China's Modern and
Postmodern Urban Landscapes

Despite the premodern nature of the rural hinterland, parts of contemporary China are
decidedly modern; some might even be
described as postmodern.[87] The spatial juxtapo-
sition of the premodern and the modern is now
in full view in many larger cities, where remnants of ancient landscapes have been pre-
served for tourists. For example, the former
capital city of Xian, which once rivaled Rome
and Constantinople in beauty and importance,
has a few temples and landmarks that have been
rather crudely restored and repainted. Most of
the city looks like a perpetual construction site,
its gloomy, polluted skyline filled with the sil-
houettes of cranes and towering concrete skele-
tons of high-rises. Ironically the best place to
view the new developments is along the
medieval city walls, which have been restored;
at night they are illuminated by purple spot-
lights and garlanded with Christmas lights,
which, as a recent traveler remarked, "gives the
city a kind of disco feel."[88]

In the transition to capitalism, Xian, like
most big cities in China, is being demolished
and rebuilt at a breathtaking pace. The process
brings to mind an intensification of polarization and privatism, "a mutant money machine"
wired to "a political economy of social dislocation" and driven by "the twin engines of [state]
penetration and [corporate] commodification."[89] Spatial manifestations of Chinese and
global capitalism are clearly evident, for example, in the uneven spread of capital producing a
radically restructured space, dotted with geographical mutations (such as the SEZs). In
other words, China's urban landscape has
become jumbled and fragmented. The areas
generously endowed with capital have followed
a modern, perhaps even postmodern trajectory;
other places, sometimes in adjacent territory,
have been totally passed over and remain
largely unchanged. Another characteristic of
postmodern cities is population diversity,
recalling geographer Edward Soja's description
of Los Angeles as perhaps "the only place where
all places are."[90] With the possible exception of
Shenzhen's theme park (called Windows on the
World; see Photos 9.2a and 9.2b), China's cities
fall far short of such global diversity, but the
unshackling of the peasantry and enormous
population mobility have produced a commin-
gling of epic proportions in statistical terms,
particularly in rapidly growing places like Shenzhen, Shanghai, and Hainan Island.

The Shenzhen SEZ is located at the Hong
Kong border in Guangdong Province. Shenzhen was the flagship for the Four Modernizations throughout the 1980s, becoming one of
the world's fastest growing cities. In the early
1970s it was little more than a village, but now
it is an urban region with more than 3 million
inhabitants, the vast majority being recent
migrants from across China (see Photos 9.3a,
9.3b, and 9.3c).

Shanghai was traditionally the brightest star
in the Chinese economy, but during the first
decade of reform it was overshadowed by Shenzhen and the other SEZs in Guangdong
Province. In the early 1990s, however, bigger
cities shifted into high gear, and Shanghai best

PHOTO 9.2a   Windows on the World theme park in Shenzhen.

PHOTO 9.2b   Another view of Windows
on the World theme park in Shenzhen.

PHOTO 9.3a   Lo Wu (Shenzhen) railway station: the entrance to China from Hong Kong.

PHOTO 9.3b   Shenzhen under construction, 1990.

PHOTO 9.3c   The Marlboro Man in downtown Shenzhen, 1995.

represented Chinese hypergrowth.[91] Of special importance is the district of Pudong, where a new skyscraper was completed virtually every month during the mid-1990s. Pudong is across the river from downtown Shanghai and had long been ridiculed by the urban elite for its lack of modernity; much of the land was still agricultural in the late 1980s. Today Pudong shocks the unprepared onlooker (see Photo 9.4). It quickly became the favored destination for domestic and foreign capital and developed into one of the region's major tourist destinations, in part because it is such an alluring center of wealth and power.

A third new growth zone is Hainan Island, at the extreme southern tip of China, off the coast of Guangdong Province. The island is rapidly being transformed into an export-processing zone, but to make its economy more resilient it is also being developed as a tourist haven. In Hainan the key is its accessibility to the mainland and the rest of Asia, which has been secured by the new joint-venture airport on the island's southern coast. It remains to be seen, however, if Hainan will be able to weather the so-called Asian flu, the late-1990s economic crisis, and the drop in Japanese tourism. These areas represent the restructuring of urban space as new built environments emerge. The restructuring has been completed with mobile capital, from both domestic and foreign sources, as well as huge labor reserves fed by the floating populations. In many instances new developments take the names and to some extent are built along the lines of distant locations. Hainan Island is referred to as "China's Hawaii," and some of its new commercial and residential developments have familiar names: Los Angeles Town, Tokyo Plaza, Hong Kong Towers, and Times Square Gardens (see Photos 9.5a and 9.5b).

These names provide clues as to where the investments originated and illustrate the process of geographical imagination that connects new developments in China with exotic,

PHOTO 9.4   Pudong: the new Shanghai waterfront, 1997.

faraway places that the Chinese associate with wealth, power, and glamour. The adoption of foreign place-names also suggests that capitalist development in areas of hypergrowth is reproducing a standardized image of postmodernity, expressed in the shimmering blue-gray glass towers that dominate urban landscapes around the world.

Changing Urban-Rural Relationships in China

One of the most dramatic outcomes of economic reform has been the rapid industrialization and urbanization of the Chinese countryside. Huge chunks of urban fringe have been transformed in a process of rurbanization, neither urban nor rural but a blend of the two.[92] As Barry Naughton has suggested the fastest industrial and urban growth, from the late 1980s until the end of the 1990s, was taking place just beyond city boundaries, in the coun-

tryside surrounding and between larger cities. This produced a wave of Chinese-style suburbanization, with the emergence of industrial, service, commercial, and residential developments that smudged what had been bright lines between cities and nearby countryside. In this periurban zone most of China's new economic growth has occurred, in part because here "weak surveillance of economic activity intersects with abundant economic opportunity."[93]

In such borderlands it was possible to get almost anything accomplished cheaply and expeditiously. Urban factories were attracted by the lack of crowds, availability of land, and access to cheap labor. Huge new towers sprang up next to mundane warehouses and glitzy restaurants. Some of the most successful TVEs are located here (see Photo 9.6, depicting a refrigeration and air-conditioning factory in Shende, in the Pearl River Delta). For the most part new structures occupy blocks adjacent to major intercity highways, but much of the land

PHOTO 9.5a   Construction work on the new airport in Haikou, Hainan Island.

PHOTO 9.5b   A new development: Times Square Garden, near Shenzhen.

PHOTO 9.6   A TVE producing refrigerators and air conditioners in Shunde, Pearl River Delta.

in between and behind has already been bull-dozed in anticipation of speculative develop-ment.

In a recent volume of case studies conducted in various parts of China, anthropologist Greg-ory Guldin concludes that the majority of China's population can now be defined as "urban" (which includes those living in offi-cially designated urban areas, as well as in urbanized townships and villages). For a nation where identity has been shaped for centuries by the vastness and unchanging character of its rurality, this represents a change of staggering proportions.[94] It is indeed a farewell to peasant China, represented starkly in the Pearl River Delta in southern Guangdong Province, a harbinger of China's future. Here a sprawling new metropolis is emerging: Villages are linking to form new towns; towns are merging into new cities; and cities are developing in the context of the region's twin growth poles—Hong Kong in the south and Guangzhou (Canton) in the north, with Shenzhen in between.[95]

Cities and Breathing Space

The state continues to control most aspects of everyday life through the household registra-tion system, which ties individuals to local work units. As the twenty-first century begins, many Chinese anticipate important gains in their daily lives in addition to the economic oppor-tunities made possible by reform. During the 1980s there was an expectation that the state would continue to withdraw from controlling all aspects of everyday life. It was hoped that the separation between state and society would continue to widen; that there would be an increased tolerance by the state for popular ini-tiatives and organizations; and that ordinary people would be allowed more breathing space.[96] Such dreams were put on hold following the Tiananmen Square tragedy in 1989 and the ensuing crackdowns. There was something of a revival of optimism throughout the 1990s, yet progress remains uneven, and it is worthwhile to consider what the future holds and the role city dwellers are likely to play.

Some China scholars suggest that the reach of the state has been changing, but not necessarily retracting, during the reform era. It appears that control is being relaxed in some domains but tightened in others. Vivienne Shue, for example, finds a spatial analog for this process, describing the irregular ebb and flow of state activity as a process of state "sprawl," which is analogous to the current process of urbanization gobbling the countryside.[97] This creative analogy is based on her observation that both urban sprawl and state sprawl exhibit "a pattern of rather loose, irregular advance."[98] As she observes, state-society relationships in China are entering an uneasy and uncertain phase, with the state not quite able to decide if it should get more or less involved in the business of society. The state, at times, appears to be acting in a consciously self-limiting way; at other times it seems to be operating with new-found enthusiasm. The actions of the state seem to be considerably more selective and reflective than in the past, even though overall its scope is more limited. As Shue noted, the state exhibits "equal measures of avid opportunism and sullen reticence," and Chinese people still have to tread very carefully.[99]

In some contexts there appears to be an expanding breathing space in which human agency can operate; in others, acts of creativity or independence are stamped out.[100] Such indeterminacy sometimes baffles the Chinese, and here is where the sprawl analogy is particularly apt. As urbanization and industrialization advance, modern cities will emerge; as we have seen, however, the bulk of new growth is occurring on the fringes, until very recently predominantly agricultural. The suggestion is that much of new China is in what Sharon Zukin has called a state of liminality: neither urban nor rural but somewhere in between.[101] The same is true of state action, and in both situations people are understandably bewildered. As Shue has suggested, people tend to "lose their breath" with the anticipation and excitement of new possibilities, yet change occurs so slowly, or in such fits and starts, that they get tired of waiting and "lose heart."[102] Perhaps that explains why so many individuals who were committed to democracy in the 1980s abandoned the cause and plunged into business (often referred to as "jumping into the sea").

It is clear that in the 1990s China's city dwellers have been allowed more breathing space in how they spend their free time. This may not be so much the result of the state's retreat as of social forces gnawing away at existing state structures. The Maoist state had always been fanatical in controlling people's leisure time, but today it appears that most anything goes as long as it does not threaten to disturb the social order. Increasing leisure time and greater latitude in spending may not seem like evidence of freedom, but in China it represents a sizeable step forward, at least in symbolic terms. Leisure and free time are things people can realistically expect to claim for themselves, and in doing so they expect the state to look the other way.

The penetration of market forces into all aspects of urban life is the driving force. Just as people were starting to define private territory for themselves, Chinese and foreign entrepreneurs began to take over the recreational and leisure businesses. No longer is the state the only or even the major provider of leisure activities, and profit has now replaced ideology as the primary concern. The net effect has been an explosion of popular culture, bringing new music, film, television programs, and reading materials to the masses, who have eagerly gorged themselves and demanded more.[103] Not surprisingly, new producers have emerged and new distributors have sprung up, both legal and underground, to peddle all manner of cultural and recreational products.[104]

In addition to the new social and cultural spaces, geographical freedom has emerged. There are now far more things to do and places to go in Chinese cities, a stark contrast to the squeaky-clean monotony of Maoist cities. For those with enough cash there are theme parks, karaoke bars, restaurants of all types, as well as vast new department stores and even shopping malls. The new Chinese city, as Vivienne Shue has observed, presents a "jolting cacophony" of new opportunities, which, along with a "jostle of options ... some liberating and others intimidating, was neither known nor knowable just a few years ago."[105] Many Chinese have seen the future; it is Western-style urbanization, and most of them like what they have seen.

10

Inequality and Persistent Poverty in China

𝖗𝖑𝖗𝖑𝖗𝖑𝖗𝖑𝖗𝖑𝖗𝖑𝖗𝖑𝖗𝖑𝖗𝖑𝖗𝖑𝖗𝖑𝖗𝖑𝖗𝖑𝖗𝖑

> *When one turns to the distribution of incomes and capabilities [in China] it is undoubtedly true that spatial differentials ... were much smaller than in many other developing countries, and an unambiguous narrowing of differentials took place.*
>
> —Chris Bramall, *In Praise of Maoist Economic Planning* (1993)[1]

> *Between 1988 and 1995 income inequality increased sharply in China, making it one of the more unequal of Asian developing countries.*
>
> —Azizur Rahman Khan and Carl Riskin, "Income and Inequality in China" (1998)[2]

Introduction: New Wealth and Old Poverty

The reforms implemented during the Four Modernizations have clearly improved living standards for the Chinese people, and the new wealth generated by the reforms has been translated into major improvements in prosperity and well-being, as measured by traditional social indicators (see Table 10.1).

Compared to many of its poorer Asian neighbors, China maintains a significantly higher life expectancy, lower rates of mortality, lower fertility, and better access to medical care. China has not experienced the intractable problems that plague many developing nations, including falling rates of economic growth, declining real wages, nutritional deficiencies, and external indebtedness.[3] The economic reforms also brought on a virtual frenzy of development in China, much of which has been occurring with the help of foreign direct investment. A large proportion of external capital comes from overseas Chinese sources, mainly in Hong Kong and Taiwan, which have been investing heavily in nearby parts of the main-

land.[4] Overseas Chinese are lured by the prospect of huge profits; it is often stated (though rarely documented) that Hong Kong businesses save as much as US$12 billion annually on wages by relocating assembly plants to the mainland. The comparative advantages work strongly in China's favor. The availability of cheap labor, land, and raw materials has helped make China one of the world's most favored destinations for mobile capital.[5]

The constant inflow of foreign capital means that almost everything in China is now for sale, including bridges and highway overpasses, which are sold to multinational companies who are then allowed to advertise their products in busy downtown intersections. Nothing is sacred, as one observer pointed out: "Even the canyon walls in the Yangtze Three Gorges region, soon to be destroyed by the massive dam, are being sold off to potential advertisers."[6] Foreign money is finding its way into all parts of Chinese society, including retail and service activities; the finance and insurance sectors; infrastructure projects; and even educational, recreational, and cultural developments. But the real boom sector in the 1990s has been

TABLE 10.1   Comparing China with Other Countries on Social Well-Being Indicators

Country	Female Life Expectancy at Birth (years) 1965	1993	Maternal Mortality (per 100,000 live births) 1980–1993	Total Fertility Rate 1993	Infant Mortality (per 100,000) 1993	Population per Physician 1965	1984	% in Higher (Tertiary) Education 1965	1992	Daily Caloric Intake Per Capita 1965	1988
China	59	71	115[5]	2.0	30	1,600	1,010	0	2	1,931	2,632
Hong Kong	71	82	4	1.2	7	2,520	1,070	5	20	ND	2,699[4]
Taiwan	—	74[1]	ND	ND	ND	1,901	1,318[2]	4	25[3]	ND	ND[3]
Japan	73	83	15	1.5	4	970	660	13	32	2,679	2,848
South Korea	58	75	34	1.7	11	2,680	1,160	6	42	2,254	2,878
Singapore	68	78	11	1.7	6	1,900	1,310	10	12[4]	1,186	2,892
India	44	61	500	3.7	80	4,880	2,520	5	ND	2,103	2,104
Bangladesh	44	56	600	4.3	106	8,100	6,730	1	5	1,984	1,925
Philippines	57	69	80	3.9	42	ND	6,700	19	28	1,896	2,255
Indonesia	45	65	800	2.8	56	31,700	9,460	1	10	1,796	2,670
Malaysia	60	73	59	3.5	13	6,200	1,930	2	7	2,307	2,686
Thailand	58	72	270	2.1	26	7,160	6,290	2	19	2,134	2,287
United States	74	79	9	1.9	9	670	470	40	76	3,236	3,666
Canada	75	81	2	1.7	7	770	510	26	62	3,128	3,447
United Kingdom	74	79	7	1.8	7	870	ND	12	28	3,350	3,252
WORLD AVERAGE	58	68	ND	3.2	54	6,060	4,200	9	16	2,390	2,669

SOURCES: *World Development Report*, 1995, Tables 26, 27, 28, 29 (pp. 212–219); caloric intake data from *World Development Report*, 1991, Table 32 (pp. 266–267).

NOTES:

[1] Statistics for males and females, 1986.

[2] Statistics for 1965 and 1981.

[3] Statistics for 1965 and 1985.

[4] Statistics for 1985.

[5] Based on a study covering thirty provinces.

real estate. As a result of speculative building, China's urban and suburban landscapes have been transformed, mostly by joint-venture capital. Throughout the 1980s and 1990s construction sites have been appearing almost overnight: Multistory office towers and hotels pop up like mushrooms, and private housing developments spring into life in what used to be rice fields at the urban fringes. In the mid-1980s development was concentrated in the coastal provinces, but the fever soon spread into cities and towns across the country.

Throughout the 1980s the heart of the new China appeared to be in the south, especially the Pearl River Delta in Guangdong Province. There the annual growth rate of the five central cities averaged more than 20 percent in the early 1990s, pushing Guangdong's overall growth rate to 14 percent per year and its industrial output to more than 27 percent per year. Outsiders find it difficult to comprehend growth of such proportions. Orville Schell, for example, remarked that "the Hong Kong–Shenzhen–Guangzhou axis [is] a veritable Ripley's Believe It or Not of growth statistics."[7] The story that best captures the essence of the new economic climate in China is the transformation of the Shenzhen SEZ, just across the border from Hong Kong. Shenzhen was a small village in the late 1970s but is now an urban wonderland of more than 3 million: "Shenzhen was . . . like an enormous intake valve sucking up all kinds of untreated heterodox influences and indiscriminately pumping them not only just across the border . . . but up the hundred miles of hyper-development to Canton [Guangzhou] where almost overnight obscure villages were being transformed into full-blown cities."[8]

In the 1990s, Shanghai, a city unused to playing second fiddle to any other part of China, began to reassert itself as the center of China's modernization drive. In the 1980s Shanghai had fallen behind Guangdong Province and the Pearl River Delta in terms of economic growth. As if to reassert its natural supremacy, however, Shanghai was soon breaking all records in the rush toward modernization. In 1993, for example, US$3.7 billion (half of it overseas investment) went into real estate, and in that same year the value of new foreign investment was equivalent to the combined total during the previous fourteen years.[9] The new SEZ created in Pudong, on the other side of the river from Shanghai (literally, east of the Pu River), is now surpassing even Shenzhen as a growth center (see Photo 10.1).

Dozens of new foreign-funded commercial and residential complexes have appeared; a $100 million radio and transmission tower has been built (Asia's tallest, it is the newest tourist attraction); and the new Shanghai Securities Exchange has been opened. By the end of 1993 Pudong boasted a GDP of Y12 billion, a figure that had doubled in just twelve months. In 1994 six new office high-rises were finished in Lujiazhui, the waterfront area of Pudong; in 1995 another twenty were under construction: "By 1998, according to the master-plan . . . 49 skyscrapers will be jostling for space, dumping onto the Shanghai market some 1.65 million square meters of offices, equivalent to roughly half the total stock of Singapore."[10] Little thought seems to have been given to the long-term consequences of pursuing development of such magnitude. With Shenzhen and Shanghai leading the charge, China has clearly taken the capitalist road so feared by Mao Zedong; to use a contemporary analogy, the Chinese are already a long way down the capitalist superhighway.[11]

It is difficult to predict where it all will end, not to mention the effect it will have on the Chinese Communist Party. The current CCP leadership has accepted the clearly nonsocialist principle that "some people must get rich before others," and many people have taken the plunge into business.[12] Evidence of new wealth is ubiquitous, especially along the so-called golden coastline, with the emergence of five-star hotels, new golf courses, luxury apartment buildings, and a conspicuous fetish for expensive consumer items like French brandy, jewel-encrusted gold watches, and luxury foreign cars (especially from BMW, Mercedes, and Lexus). The opportunities to acquire such items are no longer limited to those few involved in foreign investment ventures but are increasingly

PHOTO 10.1   The waterfront in Pudong, viewed from the Bund.

available to officials and entrepreneurs in the domestic capitalist sector.

In contemporary China reports about lifestyles of the newly rich are matched by others describing a new level of economic desperation: In the cities the poor are panhandling on the streets, the homeless camping outside bus and rail stations; in the countryside millions of peasants desperately wait for salvation from the press of poverty. The massive migration of peasants out of the countryside and the appearance of huge floating populations in the cities provide visible evidence that gaping discrepancies have reopened in Chinese society. In this chapter we shall first explore two dimensions of the new inequality: social class and geography (a third, gender, is fully analyzed in Chapter 13). The discussion begins by looking at how inequality issues were received before economic reform, that is, during the supposedly egalitarian era of Maoist socialism. As the two epigraphs at the beginning of this chapter suggest, before reform serious efforts were made to

maintain a balance between rich and poor in social and spatial terms; with the Four Modernizations, however, it became obvious almost immediately that egalitarianism would be cast aside.

Egalitarianism in Maoist and Dengist China

It is difficult to reach solid conclusions about income inequality in China, partly because of inadequacies in the available data, and partly because the conclusions seem to vary depending on the level of analysis.[13] It would appear, as Carl Riskin has noted, that "China's poor emerged from the Maoist era significantly better off than the poor in most other developing countries," in addition to which personal incomes in China were more equally distributed throughout the urban and the rural populations than was the case in most developing countries.[14] At the domestic level it is gener-

TABLE 10.2   Consumption (Per Capita) of Agricultural and Nonagricultural Populations, 1952–1979

	Per Capita Consumption (1952 = 100Y)		
	National Average	Rural Population	Urban Population
1952	100	100	100
1957	122.9	117.1	126.3
1965	126.4	116.0	136.5
1975	156.9	143.1	181.1
1979	184.9	165.2	214.5

SOURCE: Adapted from Riskin (1987), p. 241, Table 10.8.

ally assumed that during the Maoist era there was some success in achieving spatial equality in China, both at the interregional level and at the urban-rural level; by contrast, after Mao's death the emphasis on equality was relaxed, so the gap between the rich and the poor began to widen.[15]

In fact the situation was not that simple, and one can argue that the Maoist era was not as egalitarian as Mao had hoped or as earlier accounts had indicated. Mao's desire to reduce and possibly eliminate the urban-rural dichotomy inspired several drastic measures. There was a virtual freeze on urban wages, designed to prevent urban-rural inequalities from rising any farther; millions of urban-educated youths were forcibly rusticated, "sent down" to live in the countryside; and severe limitations were placed on rural-to-urban migration. The encouragement of industrial development in the countryside, and deliberate efforts to enhance social and physical infrastructures in rural villages, were intended to prevent some of the traditional patterns of spatial inequality that are common in impoverished countries.[16]

Paradoxically, the evidence suggests that the gap between the cities and the countryside may actually have widened during the Maoist era.[17] Although the Party leaders were focusing their attention on the need to reduce the urban-rural gap in China, there were considerably more words—mostly posturing and propagandizing—than there were actions. During the 1950s industry and the cities were heavily favored over agriculture, and with the brief exception of

a policy reversal immediately after the debacle of the Great Leap Forward, capital investment in industry far outpaced that in agriculture.[18] In other words, in spite of the Maoist rhetoric, investment funds were not shifted toward the countryside in any major way. Not surprisingly, rural incomes and per capita consumption continued to fall farther behind those in the urban sector; in fact the ratio between urban and rural incomes had opened considerably by 1979, with estimates ranging anywhere from 25:1 to 6:1; as the data in Table 10.2 illustrate, the gap in consumption levels has also widened.[19]

During this period rural residents were also deprived of opportunities to supplement meager incomes in the traditional ways, for example, by developing sideline activities, growing commercial cash crops, and selling surpluses in open markets. At the time these activities were considered to be inherently antisocialist, and the majority of agricultural activity was directed toward grain production ("taking grain as the key," as Mao liked to say), in the interests of sustaining local and national self-sufficiency. The net result was that in almost all walks of life China's rural areas lagged behind the cities: health status, nutrition, education, life expectancy, overall living standards, and the enjoyment of "luxury" consumer goods.[20] This conclusion implies a serious discrepancy between the official pronouncements on the issue of urban-rural inequality and reality. Mao Zedong's much-acclaimed "mobilizational collectivism" ended with the rural poor being increasingly disadvantaged.[21] Because some of China's provinces are far more urbanized than

TABLE 10.3   Rural and Urban Ownership of Selected Consumer Durables, 1978–1987

Item	# Owned per 100 Persons (whole of China)			Ratio of Urban to Rural Per Capita Ownership		
	1978	1982	1987	1978	1982	1987
Sewing machines	3.5	6.6	11.0	3.6	3.1	1.8
Wristwatches	8.5	18.8	42.8	7.3	5.5	1.5
Bicycles	7.7	13.1	27.1	5.4	4.1	1.3
Radios	7.8	18.2	24.1	4.0	2.2	1.9
Televisions	0.3	2.7	10.7	13.0	10.2	2.7

SOURCES: Adapted from Trescott (1985), p. 210, Table 3, and also the *State Statistical Bureau* 1988, p. 718.

others, the urban-rural differentials in wealth contributed to income inequality at the regional level as well.[22]

Also contrary to expectations, the first few years of reform turned out to be more egalitarian than either Deng dared imagine or than Mao and his supporters would have predicted.[23] One of the dominant themes during the reform era was the abandonment of the egalitarianism associated with the extreme leftism of Mao Zedong and his supporters. In the old days everyone was exhorted to "eat from the same big pot," but during the reform era that was abandoned in the belief it would likely dampen the enthusiasm of the people and their willingness to work hard. It was possible—in fact it was desirable—for some households to become wealthier than others; that is exactly what happened. In the first years of agrarian reform China's peasants began to enjoy absolute and relative gains vis-à-vis city dwellers. It seems that at least until the mid-1980s—in aggregate terms at least—people living in China's rural areas were able to catch up to some degree. This had a significant effect on consumption in China's rural areas; as shown in Table 10.3 the gap between urban and rural levels of consumption fell significantly from 1978 to 1987.

From that point on, however, there is substantial evidence that inequality at all levels began to increase again and continued to increase throughout the 1990s. In regional terms the reform era has also witnessed a continuation, and in many cases an extension, of spatial inequality. Much of what was achieved at the regional level during the Maoist years was reversed after 1979, resulting in greater divergence between China's most and least productive provinces. In terms of industrial growth and total exports, most of the provinces in the northwest and southwest of China grew at a much slower rate than those in the eastern part of the country; and with the exception of Xinjiang's petroleum boom, industrial output in the peripheral regions has been stagnating, effectively widening the gap between rich and poor regions (see Maps 10.1a and 10.1b).[24] It is also evident that even within the most industrialized provinces industry was still highly concentrated in the biggest cities and in the Special Economic Zones (see Figure 10.1).[25]

Not surprisingly, in the higher tiers of what was still, in name at least, a socialist government, there was a certain amount of anxiety about increasing polarization between rich and poor, and by the second half of the 1980s a great deal of concern was being expressed about rural poverty in China. As Elisabeth Croll noticed in her fieldwork in many rural areas, the rising gap between rich and poor had also become one of the hot topics of peasant debate in villages all over the country.[26]

New Class Contradictions

In the first years of the reforms new economic opportunities became available to rural peasants and urban workers. The reforms were accompanied by the emergence of a new class of people who were upwardly mobile and were

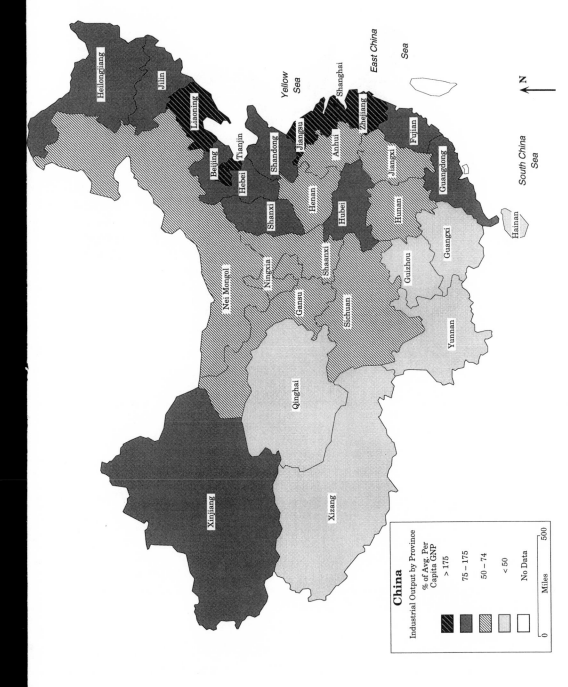

China

Industrial Output by Province

% of Avg. Per Capita GNP

> 175
75 – 175
50 – 74
< 50
No Data

0   500
Miles

MAP 10.1a   Spatial Inequality: Industrial Output by Province, 1996

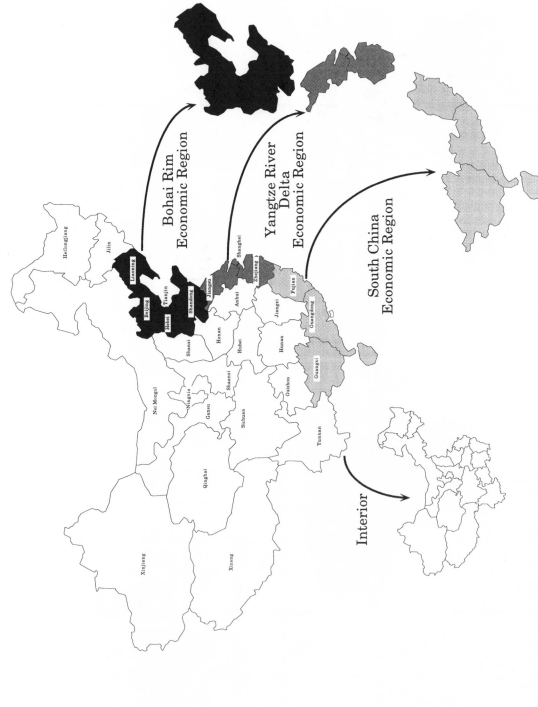

MAP 10.1b China's Major Exporting Regions, Shown with Area Representing Share of Total Exports

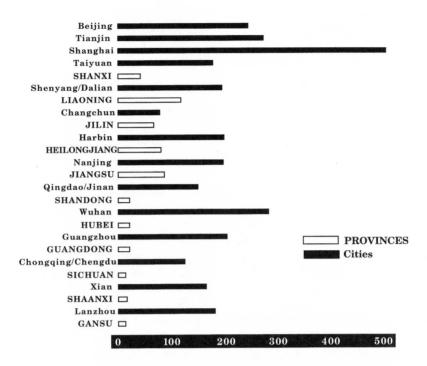

Graph showing provincial and urban gross industrial output and the dominance
of the largest cities despite the attempts to decentralize industry.
    SOURCE: Adapted from J. P. Cole, 1987, "Regional Inequalities in the People's
Republic of China," *Tijdschrift voor Economische en Sociale Geografie* 78,
no. 3, p. 207. Reprinted by permission.

FIGURE 10.1   Industrial Output, Selected Provinces and Cities, 1982

beginning to realize some previously unimaginable freedoms. In the countryside many peasants were able to exploit their comparative advantages to become increasingly efficient producers on the land. Some were able to buy or rent land from other farmers who were less successful and hire contract laborers from other parts of the countryside. Other choices were available: Some opted for local sideline activities; some went to work in rural enterprises; others migrated to the towns and cities in search of jobs. In the richest parts of the country—the suburban villages all along the golden coastline—per capita incomes at the end of the 1980s were many times higher than the national average. Some peasants who had become rich from farming were able to buy more land on which to build relatively palatial homes to symbolize their enhanced economic status.

Some city residents were also moving up in the world as a result of the reforms. A new class of private entrepreneurs emerged in service and consumption activities, and many thousands lined up for jobs as production-line workers in the new export-oriented factories. The net effect of the new opportunity structures was the emergence of a broad-based middle class among the peasants as well as the urban entrepreneurs and workers. They were justifiably enthusiastic about the reform process, and many supported the government's reform policies and called for ever deeper reforms along the road to market socialism. At the provincial level, the new wealth generated by the agrarian reforms was unevenly distributed, with the biggest income gains being reported in the coastal provinces, which widened the gap between the poorest and richest rural areas (see Map 10.2).

In retrospect, it appears that too much may have happened too soon during the first years of reform. Quick and sometimes spectacular gains were recorded, but by 1985 the rate of marginal improvement began to slow considerably. The increase in food procurement prices in the early years of reform (1978–1984) brought unprecedented gains to many peasants, which accounted for the stunning successes associated with the household responsibility reforms in the early 1980s. Real incomes and consumption increased dramatically in the countryside, and there was a sizeable reduction in the proportion of peasants officially defined as living below the poverty line—from 270 million in 1978 to 97 million in 1985—but this was not maintained, and by the early 1990s the incidence of rural poverty was actually increasing again (see Table 10.4).[27]

As these statistics suggest, the early gains brought about by the reforms could not be maintained, and by the middle of the 1980s it was evident that the domestic emphasis of the reforms had to be complemented by new measures. This was the case in the countryside, where the early implementation of the HRS reforms and rural industrialization had been successful; but it was also true in the cities, where enterprise reforms and the growth of urban collectives had produced some impressive growth statistics.[28] For China to compete in the global economy, major industrial restructuring was required; greater economies of scale were called for, through mergers, consolidations, and concentrations. Overall increases in efficiency could be achieved only by a shift away from state ownership toward private, semiprivate, and collective ownership of the means of production. Complementing such trends was a decided shift toward the external sector and the production of manufactured goods for export, much of which was made possible by the infusion of foreign capital and international finance. The fusion of these second-wave reforms resulted in the emergence of a new class of large-scale capitalists, foreign and domestic, who have been "out-maneuvering and encircling the petty-bourgeois class" that rose to early prominence in the reform era.

TABLE 10.4   The Incidence of Urban and Rural Poverty in China, 1978–1990

	1978	*1985*	*1990*
Total Population (millions)	963	1,059	1,143
Urban	172 (18%)	251 (24%)	302 (26%)
Rural	290 (82%)	808 (76%)	841 (74%)
Poverty Line (RMB per year)			
Urban	—	215	319
Rural	98	190	275
Incidence of Poverty (millions)			
Total	270 (28%)	97 (9.2%)	98 (8.6%)
Urban	10	1	1
Rural[1]	260 (33%)	96 (12%)	97 (12%)
Rural[2]	262 (33%)	100 (11%)	121 (13%)

SOURCE: *World Bank,* 1992, Table 1 (Annex 1, p. 140).
NOTES:
[1] Estimates using the planned price of grain.
[2] Estimates using the actual procurement price of grain.

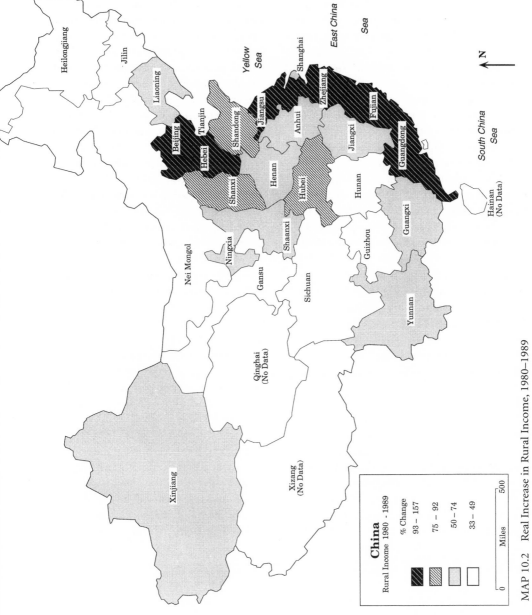

China
Rural Income 1980 - 1989

% Change
93 – 157
75 – 92
50 – 74
33 – 49

Miles
0   500

Heilongjiang

Jilin

Liaoning

Beijing
Tianjin
Hebei

Shandong

Jiangsu

Shanghai

Zhejiang

Anhui

Fujian

Jiangxi

Guangdong

Shanxi

Henan

Hubei

Hunan

Guangxi

Guizhou

Yunnan

Shaanxi

Sichuan

Ningxia

Gansu

Nei Mongol

Qinghai
(No Data)

Xizang
(No Data)

Xinjiang

Hainan
(No Data)

Yellow
Sea

East China   Sea

South China
Sea

N

MAP 10.2   Real Increase in Rural Income, 1980–1989

Robert Weil has noted that other aspects of the reforms have reinforced these trends: "Limits on the hiring of labor . . . allow small producers to compete with larger ones. Thus, from the petty bourgeoisie itself, big new capitalists emerge, to join those already present among the foreign investors and large-scale domestic entrepreneurs, and the officials and managers who are their partners."[29]

The measures that had been successful in the early years of the reforms—the coalition of small-scale private enterprise and socialist leadership and ownership—appeared to be in danger of being pushed aside by the emergence of large-scale industrial enterprises that had global markets.[30] This shift was steering the Chinese economy inexorably farther toward capitalism, regardless of the rhetoric from the leadership about holding fast to socialist principles. In the new mix of public-private-foreign ownership, clear differentials were emerging in wage levels. As shown in Table 10.5, average wages in China's cities vary considerably by ownership: The lowest wages are to be found in enterprises that are domestically owned collectives and state enterprises; the highest are in enterprises that are jointly owned with either domestic or foreign private investors.

In addition to leaving behind the newly created middle classes, the second wave of reforms chipped away at other aspects of the socialist state. The old cradle-to-grave guarantees provided to workers in the countryside were becoming scarce. In the cities traditional welfare benefits associated with the *danwei*, especially those in the SOEs, were rapidly becoming a thing of the past, as the state attempted to

make the SOEs more competitive. In addition, by the mid-1990s the collectively, privately, and foreign-owned enterprises, which offer few if any of the attractive "iron rice bowl" benefits, were beginning to dominate the economy. Weil has argued that the new enterprises acted as a wedge to split apart the existing social relations in China. Workers in new enterprises today are serving as poignant models for the future: No longer are they protected and coddled by the state, as had been the case in the old state work units. The norm today is more likely to be the opposite, in which workers are heavily exploited, often working long hours in dirty and dangerous conditions, and being paid few, if any, of the traditional social wages that Chinese socialist workers had come to expect.[31]

Weil has also used familiar Marxist terminology to describe events in contemporary China: Workers in the new collective and private enterprises are functioning as the "cannon fodder" of the new society, taking part in what Weil has described as a "new class war."[32] The backbone of the old system is being broken, and Chinese workers everywhere are now being forced to accept the conditions made necessary by the new forces of marketization.[33] This is occurring in the most dynamic part of the new booming economy, and although it is still a relatively small sector, it is being viewed by the government and the public alike as the vanguard of the new society. It is expected that the reform of the SOEs, which has been hotly debated throughout the latter part of the 1990s, will follow this model, and that there will be a further dismantling of the traditional social service provisions and job security. The new sector will have

TABLE 10.5   Comparison of Average Wage Levels in Urban Areas, by Ownership (yuan)

Ownership Type	1978	1985	1992
State-Owned	644	1,213	2,878
Collectives	4,676	506	2,109
State/Private Joint Owner	—	2,194	4,311
Collective/Private	—	1,612	4,841
Joint Ventures (with foreigners)	—	2,111	3,973
Run by Overseas Chinese	—	2,500	4,415

SOURCE: *China Statistical Yearbook, 1993*, Tables T4.38, T4.39, T4.40 (pp. 114–116).

higher risks and less secure working conditions, but this will, of course, be countered by the lure of higher salaries in the emerging foreign and private enterprises.[34]

Rising Inequality

Some of the Western research teams working in China have argued that the new wealth in the countryside, combined with the poverty alleviation programs, has kept rural inequality at a minimum in China, at least by international standards.[35] Such conclusions can be challenged, however, on three counts. First, an analysis of increases in rural income at the provincial level indicates significant geographical variation, suggesting that some areas gained during the reform era while others fell farther behind. The gains and (relative) losses have worked to widen an already existing pattern of inequality at the provincial level, in terms of rural incomes.[36] Second, the official data collected by the State Statistical Bureau on rural incomes tend to underestimate inequality, because they do not consider the noncash supplements that are made to peasant incomes, such as cheap housing, in-kind subsidies to poor households, and self-produced farm goods.[37] Studies that include such noncash components report a significant increase in average per capita incomes, which results in considerably higher inequality.[38] The official data also tend to exclude households at the bottom end of the income distribution, because the surveys on which they are based require literacy and arithmetical proficiency that are simply nonexistent among the absolutely poorest households in rural China.[39]

Third, recent statistical evidence suggests that inequality is increasing.[40] Output per capita in many of the inland provinces and Autonomous Regions grew slowly in the early reform period, and in some cases there was even stagnation relative to the national average.[41] In Hunan, for example, output was only 60 percent of the national average in 1980, and that had fallen to 55 percent by 1990. Shanghai, by comparison, had an output level equal to almost 560 percent of the national average in 1980, but that had fallen to 400 percent by 1990, as Shanghai gave up its economic leadership to Guangdong and the Pearl River Delta. At the other extreme, Guizhou and Guangxi AR still had per capita output levels considerably less than 50 percent of the national average, and eleven more provinces had output levels between 50 percent and 70 percent of the average.[42]

In a recent book, Dali Yang has shown how regional economic policies implemented during the Maoist era were intended to favor and support inland provinces, and by the beginning of the reform era that policy was showing some results.[43] In 1984, for example, the coastal provinces had a 51 percent share of total state investment, the interior provinces 49 percent; by 1994 the gap had widened, with the coast having 59 percent and the interior 41 percent.[44] Before 1978 the state was actively engaged in directing economic growth patterns, which included attempts to achieve a more egalitarian regional balance by supporting inefficient industrial plants in the interior. In the Dengist era the state effectively abandoned that role, and development was allowed to proceed wherever the market dictated, which usually meant places that had an indisputable geographical advantage. Political leaders in the inland provinces have attempted to pressure Beijing to correct the worsening imbalance in the 1990s, but Yang has pointed out that with so many Politburo members representing coastal provinces that is unlikely. Interior leaders are doubly distressed about their situation: Not only are their provinces falling behind coastal provinces at an accelerated rate; as they see it, the central government unfairly favors the coastal provinces through preferential policies (for example, to the SEZs) and its distorted pricing system.

Leaders in Beijing realize that geographical imbalance is a sensitive political issue; in fact Jiang Zemin and Li Peng, among others, have publicly discussed the need for action.[45] At present they are pushing hard to fight regional imbalance with a three-pronged attack: increasing the proportion of state investment funds that are targeted for the interior provinces; providing whatever financial support they can to such provinces; and transferring resources from the coastal regions to the interior (for example, resource-intensive and labor-intensive industries are being encouraged to move to new locations on the periphery).[46]

Jiang Zemin is unlikely to do anything to damage the economic interests of the coastal provinces, bearing in mind that his and the Party's mandates are based almost entirely on the continuation of economic prosperity. It is also obvious that the central government is rapidly being marginalized as an economic force in China, in the sense that it has a decreasing share of investment funds to allocate and a serious budget deficit to overcome. At the same time, private and collective sectors are coming to dominate the economy. As Yang pointed out:

> While the regional policy adjustments will placate interior discontents and moderate the rise of regional disparities, they are not designed to fundamentally reshape the regional patterns of economic activity in China . . . Chinese leaders have taken care not to overpromise, conceding that . . . the state will not be able to eradicate coastal-interior inequalities for a long time to come.[47]

Still, Yang has also pointed out the unwritten consensus among Chinese leaders that economic development in the periphery is the best way to go about counteracting secessionist tendencies, especially in volatile regions like Tibet (see Chapter 12), Xinjiang, and Inner Mongolia. It would be reasonable, in other words, to anticipate a continued effort from Beijing to boost the modernization drive in the periphery.[48]

The increases in interprovincial inequality are compounded by intraprovincial polarizations, as the gaps between the richest and poorest counties in each province widen. Using the Gini coefficient as a measure of inequality, 1989 statistics show a low of 0.029 within the Shanghai urban region and a high of 0.356 in Xinjiang AR.[49] Data from the World Bank 1992

report demonstrate that intraprovincial inequality is greatest in the belt of provinces across northern China, from Heilongjiang to Xinjiang, where rural production depends mainly on rain-fed (as opposed to irrigated) agriculture. This means that within a single province some areas are extremely poor compared to others, which appears to be a greater problem in provinces and ARs with the highest overall level of poverty (such as Gansu Province and Ningxia AR); but serious inequality also exists in some of the provinces where income levels are relatively high. Such polarities result from variations in physical and human resources, as well as differences in the way reform opportunities in both agricultural and industrial activities have been seized upon.

Dali Yang would argue that within most of China's provinces geographic disparities were increasing in the late 1980s and early 1990s.[50] The problem is not just the gap between urban and rural areas, or even the coastal-interior differences, but within individual provinces. In general it appears that the provinces that are also able to increase their overall wealth through consistent and significant economic growth are able to reduce intraprovincial inequality. The richer provinces, in other words, have surplus funds available to support their poorer areas. Obviously the opposite is the case in the poorer areas such as Ningxia and Gansu, where even the massive antipoverty programs have not been able to make a dent in inequality (even though the rate of poverty has been reduced significantly). The future does not look very encouraging; in fact Yang notes that "the prospects for alleviating intraprovincial disparities are expected to worsen in the intermediate future."[51] Over the long haul it would appear that the only hope for such places is the promotion of more economic growth.[52]

It is also evident that at the microlevel income differentials within villages have been increasing during the reform era. In 1992 a team of international economists reported a survey they conducted in collaboration with economists from the Economics Institute of the Chinese Academy of Social Sciences.[53] Using its own survey data, the team concluded that incomes had increased much more than was reported by the State Statistical Bureau in its annual reports; they also found that incomes, both urban and rural, were becoming increasingly unequal. The same group conducted a second survey in 1995, reporting a "sharp rise in rural inequality between 1988 and 1995," with the Gini coefficients increasing from 0.24 in 1988 to 0.42 in 1994.[54] Urban inequality also increased during the same period, from 0.23 to 0.33. The researchers found that inequality between China's urban and rural areas dominates the overall pattern of inequality, which led them to the grim conclusion that by 1995 China was "among the more unequal societies in developing Asia,"[55] with a Gini coefficient (for the whole of China) of 0.45, higher than that in India, Pakistan, and Indonesia and equal to the Philippines.

In a recent book, *The Political Economy of Uneven Development*, Shaoguang Wang and Angang Hu reach essentially the same conclusions, noting that "income inequality . . . in China . . . has increased more rapidly and gone further than almost anywhere else. . . . So steep a rise . . . in so short a time is highly unusual in both the historical and comparative perspective [and unless] the trend . . . can be halted or reversed, the glaring inequalities prevailing in Latin America and Sub-Saharan Africa are soon likely to emerge in China."[56]

The research team argued that the growing inequality results from rising wages, which have been made possible, in both urban and rural areas, by reform policies; and it is in this category of earnings (wage levels) that the most inequality is observed. Some people have obviously been following Deng Xiaoping's exhortation to get rich before others. In fact, greater employment opportunities in the cities have sent urban incomes four times higher than rural incomes on average.[57] It appears that the level of inequality in the cities has been made worse by the subsidies provided by the state to many urban residents (the subsidy program was canceled in the mid-1990s, but its effects were still apparent in the 1995 survey). The

researchers also pointed out that the state's current housing policies have been responsible for part of the increase in urban inequality, especially the subsidies it provides to middle-class city dwellers for housing (see Chapter 14). They recommended that a more equitable policy be designed to allow poorer households greater access to the new housing market.

In the countryside, in addition to the higher wages being earned by some individuals and households working in local factories and the service trades, rising inequality has been exacerbated by the state's taxation policies, which are regressive, unfairly draining the resources of the poorer households. The research team concluded that China's rising inequality is not a result of the reforms per se, or the trends toward marketization and privatization (although those factors have accounted for rising wage levels), but is largely a result of what they describe as the "polarizing tendencies" of the state's public policies. As noted above, for the interior provinces the state appears to favor those that are better off, providing subsidies and supports to provinces that are already strongest economically. It would also appear that the state's intervention has similar effects on poor households in China's cities and rural areas.

As the 1995 study pointed out, wealth differentials between rural households in the same village are most likely to be created by wages earned outside the farming sector, particularly in manufacturing and service activities. In a study conducted in Zhejiang Province, for example, the richest households received an average of Y272 per capita from nonagricultural production, compared to the poorest households, which received virtually no income from such sources.[58] In the same study it was found that incomes earned from farming were highly egalitarian (.04 Gini coefficient); income earned from sideline activities such as animal husbandry, fishing, and forestry was more varied between households (0.21); and income earned from manufacturing and service employment was even more unequal (0.43). As might be expected, income earned in joint enterprises, which includes foreign ventures, produced the highest level of inequality (0.50). As this suggests, the growth of nonfarm enterprises, particularly those utilizing foreign capital, has been the key source of rising incomes in the countryside. The downside of this phenomenon during the reform years has been the almost inevitable increase in income inequality.[59]

It is important to add a caveat. As pointed out in Chapter 7, during the first few years of agricultural reform Chinese peasants began to experience significant gains in incomes relative to urban residents. For example, there was an increase in average rural incomes by 1985 to Y463 per year, compared to Y134 in 1978, which meant that many rural households were able to afford some of the "luxury" consumer items they had coveted for so long.[60] In that sense the gains from economic reform in China's rural areas are undeniable. In comparison, life in the cities changed much less than in the countryside during the early 1980s, and the opportunities for dramatic increases in incomes and consumption were nowhere near as great. With the exception of the SEZs, urban workers were unable to increase salaries significantly during the first few years of reform. The result was a reduction in the amount of urban-rural inequality, and although that was a welcome departure, it proved to be only a temporary trend; as many critics have argued, it was only possible after a significant dismantling of China's socialist principles.[61]

The Geography of Poverty

Rural areas in most of the provinces and ARs in northwestern China (Inner Mongolia, Ningxia, and Xinjiang ARs and Gansu Province), as well as in the southwestern region (Guangxi AR and Sichuan, Guizhou, and Yunnan Provinces), had increases in real income below the national average during the 1980s (see Map 10.2), and not surprisingly these regions also had more households on average living below the poverty line.[62] Yet the overall rate of poverty has been reduced considerably, partly due to rising rural production rates and incomes associated with the agricultural reforms, partly due to the state's poverty alleviation programs (see Table 10.4).

The fifteen provinces in these regions contain less than 50 percent of the rural population but 80 percent of rural poverty (representing more than 80 million people). A geographical interpretation of these data indicates that the poverty remaining in China is a result of factors that have hindered the adoption of the reforms and have also made such localities resistant to the beneficial effects of the poverty alleviation programs. Poverty in most cases is concentrated in remote and mountainous areas that are sharply constrained in terms of arable land, transportation, energy, and other basic infrastructural elements.[63] The weakness of local agricultural systems, as well as the poorly developed nature of infrastructure in China's peripheral regions, is well illustrated in the World Bank analysis of poverty in the countryside.[64]

The fragility of agriculture in the poorest regions is invariably reproduced in the human and social infrastructures, as well as the physical infrastructure, including telecommunications and road networks. All this is manifested in generally lower levels of initiative and local enterprise. For comparative purposes it is revealing to consider statistics for Guizhou and Jiangsu Provinces, using mid-1980s statistics, which show the differences in the prevalence of TVEs (see Table 10.6a). In statistical terms it appears that the Four Modernizations project has barely had an effect in the poorer parts of China's periphery, as a team of Chinese economists concluded: "Backward regions are . . . characterized by an unsophisticated economy. The great majority of the rural inhabitants . . . restrict their activities to the home and its surroundings [and] very few community-type economic groupings within the village or township actually cut across the family."[65]

In the case of Guizhou this results in a dramatic difference in the number of employees in collective enterprises; as a result output levels, taxes, and profits are extremely low in comparison to averages in Jiangsu Province. It is also illuminating to note that Guizhou's peasants profited far less from HRS reform and were much less likely to have entered sideline activities than was the case in Jiangsu. As a result, their combined agricultural incomes during the mid-1980s were only 28 percent of those in Jiangsu.[66] It is also evident that the long-term, structural impacts of such inequality are compounded by lower opportunities for education in backward regions (e.g., Tibet and Guizhou; see Table 10.6b). As the statistics indicate, local attainment levels are significantly below the national average. In Guizhou, for example, close to 50 percent of the population over twelve years old is illiterate; for Tibet the figure is roughly 70 percent.[67]

In spite of all the changes brought by reform, in most parts of the Chinese countryside the labor force remains primarily employed in farming activities. The reforms have revolutionized the way things are done in some areas, but in others very little has changed. It is still the minority, in other words, that has taken the opportunity to get rich. Those who have been successful tend to be from one of two groups: former Party officials who have taken advantage of their contacts to gain access to credit, inputs, and business opportunities (including the "nomenklatura capitalists"); or new peasant entrepreneurs—the people with a range of skills and experiences, including doctors, tractor drivers, demobilized soldiers, craftsmen, those formerly classified as having "bad class" backgrounds, and even a few sent-down youths returned from the countryside.[68]

The difference between successful and unsuccessful households lies in the skills and connections (*guanxi*) needed to promote their

TABLE 10.6a   Township and Village Enterprises: Guizhou and Jiangsu Provinces Compared

	# of Enterprises	Employees (10,000)	Output Value (100 m yuan)	Taxes (100 m yuan)	Net Profits (100 m yuan)
Guizhou	13,549	20.9	3.5	0.2	0.5
Jiangsu	70,580	454.1	109.0	12.2	16.7
Guizhou/Jiangsu (%)	19.2	4.6	2.1	1.97	2.8

SOURCE: Adapted from Wang and Bai (1991), Table 3.6, p. 44.

TABLE 10.6b   Educational Levels: Xizang AR (Tibet), Guizhou Province, and the National Average

	Average Level of Education*	Average # of Years in School	University	Education Levels (per 10,000)			Rate of Illiteracy in > 12 Years Old Population
				Senior Middle School	Junior Middle School	Primary School	
Tibet	0.39	2.5	42	121	361	1,677	70.5
Guizhou	0.82	4.0	39	296	1,142	2,878	47.6
China (average)	1.11	5.0	55	660	1,780	3,540	31.9
Tibet/ China (%)	35.1	50.0	76.4	18.3	20.3	46.5	220.0
Guizhou/ China (%)	73.9	80.0	70.9	44.8	64.2	81.3	150.0

SOURCE: Adapted from Wang and Bai (1991), Table 3.8, p. 51.
NOTE: Education level is calculated by assuming university = 4, senior middle school = 3, etc. (illiteracy = 0); average number of years in school calculated by assuming university = 14, senior middle = 10, etc. (illiteracy = 0).

own interests.[69] Elisabeth Croll has noted that a hallmark of financial success among rural families was the placement of at least one (and often several) of their kin in a nearby town or city. That provided extra earning power, but more important it helped provide contacts for family business, as well as go-betweens for selling family-made products.[70] By comparison, those households that did not have well-connected or skilled individuals, have few able-bodied workers, and have a high dependency ratio (many nonworking children and elderly people) were generally unable to take advantage of the new opportunities presented by reform.[71]

This reinforces the idea that the economic reforms have added new layers of inequality in the Chinese countryside, in spite of the inherently egalitarian distribution of land during the decollectivization period after 1978. In the reform era the most enterprising households, realizing that the profits to be made from farming were low, began to devote some of their collective energies to nonfarm production. The proportion of peasant income derived from farming decreased (for example, from 73 percent to 47 percent in Ningxia AR between 1978 and 1986; and from 47 percent to 12 percent in Jiangsu Province). This downward trend continued into the 1990s, and all this points to a considerable amount of socioeconomic mobility in the Chinese countryside, with the emergence of a new class of entrepreneurial peasants and the growth of a sizable income gap between the new rich and the poor.[72] It is apparent that the new wealthy rural households are those that have successfully launched profitable sideline businesses or have become "specialized" households.[73]

Poverty in rural China can be partly explained by geographical factors, in the sense that it occurs as a result of a combination of economic, physical, and human attributes that differ from one location to another. Not surprisingly, the wealthiest rural families in China can be found in the suburbs of the big cities along the eastern and southeastern seaboards, especially in southern Jiangsu Province west of Shanghai. Within individual provinces, however, incomes tend to be strongly correlated with natural endowments, topography, and local soil conditions. In Shaanxi Province, for example, there is an obvious relationship between per capita incomes and residence in the plains, on the hills, or in the mountains (a difference of Y67 on average between the plains and the mountains). The existence of intraprovincial inequality in rural incomes can be illustrated with the data collected in a study of four diverse provinces.[74]

Similar conclusions were reached by Croll in her studies of sixteen villages in different parts of China. Croll noted vast discrepancies in household incomes across the villages. The average per capita cash income was Y85, Y413 per household. At the low end four villages averaged less than Y50 per person; the high end averaged above Y1,500, or thirty times higher. She concluded that the differences between rich and poor households resulted from variations in family labor supplies, physical and mental capacities, education levels, and skills. The dependency ratio was also crucial; having fewer nonworking mouths to feed and a greater supply of able-bodied workers were the most likely predictors of high incomes. Most of the successful households owned livestock and machinery, had access to credit, and, most important, had a source of nonfarm income, often with one or more family members working outside the home in skilled professions such as carpentry or bricklaying.

Poor households have few if any such advantages. In her Sichuan fieldwork, Croll described the characteristics of the poorest households (earning less than Y40 per capita): They were all located in highland villages; they had few workers to send out for extra income; their land was low-yielding; and they had no farm animals. In the richest villages, especially in coastal provinces, successful households are able to hire contract laborers (peasants from nearby villages or even other provinces) to work in the fields, allowing family members to operate sidelines, work in family businesses, or move away from home to work in nearby factories.[75]

The early improvements in equality in the countryside (i.e., during the 1978–1985 period) can be explained in part by the growth of rural industrialization in the first years of reform, as well as the productivity gains made possible by the increases in agricultural procurement prices (in addition to the government's poverty alleviation programs). The subsequent increases in inequality (in some cases more than 2.5 times greater in terms of the coefficient of variation) seem to have occurred in both wealthy and poor provinces. To identify some of the geographical correlates of the rising inequality, one research team looked at a number of indicators in the ten richest and poorest counties in one province (Anhui).[76]

The most decisive factor appeared to be the relative buoyancy of the agricultural sector. The richest counties were located in areas where agricultural prosperity provided the basis for further growth in rural industry and service development, as local savings and investments expanded, and as the overall level of consumption increased. In other words, agricultural success provided the investment capital and the demand level needed to support local industrial and service growth. During the reform era, localities have increasingly been left alone by the central government and have been granted greater fiscal autonomy, which worked to the advantage of localities that had managed to get ahead early. As the researchers observed: "Not only did agricultural prosperity provide local governments with a revenue base from which to invest in infrastructure and non-farm enterprises . . . it also created an enormous increase in disposable incomes [and] a multitude of comparatively small-scale industrial and service enterprises were set up."[77]

Thus in geographical terms there is a correlation between agricultural prosperity and industrial and service prosperity. It is no accident that the parts of rural China enjoying the fastest growth in the reform era are located in the most fertile parts of the country, for example, in the Yangtze Valley around Shanghai and near Nanjing, in the Pearl River Delta in Guangdong Province, and in the Chengdu Plain in Sichuan. Once the initial advantages are manifested in local economic expansion, a "virtuous circle" of growth occurs, and the gap between the richer and poorer localities expands.

What to Do About Poverty?

It can be misleading to compare conditions in China's poorest areas to those in the booming regions near the coast, because it is normal for a country embarking on a modernization drive to encourage its most favored regions to lead the way.[78] It is more illuminating to look at differences between the poorest areas and the average for China as a whole (see Map 10.2). As the gap between rich and poor areas widens, it will become increasingly difficult for any antipoverty program to make an impact. Some researchers have suggested policies that amount to triage, that is, allowing out-migration from the poorest areas to reduce poverty. As noted, one of the most important correlates of the new income inequality at the geographical level is the emergence of a successful rural industrial sector, and rural areas are likely to remain untouched by the reforms if they are unable to set up prosperous local enterprises.[79] To reduce the level of inequality resulting from differentials in local industry there are some obvious solutions. One is to inhibit the overall growth of the rural industrial sector, which would be difficult to do, politically infeasible, and extremely unpopular; a second is to stimulate growth in the agricultural sector, which would help reduce inequality, yet agricultural growth would likely be unable to keep up with the industrial sector.

A third policy option is to remove some of the barriers that inhibit economic (especially industrial) growth in the poorer areas of rural China. In spite of the widespread diffusion of the rural reforms, there remain serious impediments that inhibit the free flow of factors and products in the Chinese countryside. These include artificial barriers such as local taxes, roadblocks, licensing laws, and quotas, all of which restrict the flow of goods into and out of local areas. Many of the poorly developed areas have had limited access to credit and have been penalized by labor policies favoring the hiring of local people rather than recruits from cheaper places. Such barriers are holdovers from the past, when localities felt the need to protect themselves in face of the overall requirement of local self-sufficiency. In the new era of market advantage, however, there are good reasons to enforce the dismantling of such local protectionism in the interests of greater overall economic growth and geographical equality.[80]

At a more general level, a case can be made for researching, in an effort to counteract the impact of rising inequality and growing vulnerability, how poor households can become more economically viable. It is apparent that the Chinese government does not relish the prospect of implementing strategies that would punish or tax those who have been successful during the reform era. In keeping with the general drive toward market socialism, there is a distinct preference to encourage poor households to model their behavior on that of successful households.

As noted earlier, despite the economic opportunities presented by reform, the majority of peasants remain in the business of agricultural production. Of the 431 million in the rural labor force, 342 million are still employed in agriculture. It would be useful, therefore, to open a debate as to the strategies that predict economic success at the household level and that might be adopted by poorer households. To guide such a debate research will need to focus on the dynamics of rural success at the household level; as we have observed, existing studies have suggested that household fortunes are influenced by a number of interrelated factors, including family demographics, connections outside the village, and a combination of geographical advantages.[81]

It has long been recognized that attempts to boost economic development in developing countries are often accompanied by growing inequality along several fronts.[82] The Chinese government has endeavored to implement human development programs to ameliorate the consequences of the new inequalities, but in light of the trends reported here, some policy overhauls might be in order. One of the predictable World Bank recommendations is to introduce user charges for services to help cover the costs of human development programs providing education and health care. Another is to introduce market principles into heavily subsidized social services, such as the commodification of housing currently under way in many urban areas.[83]

The implementation of capitalist-inspired reform in China provides some additional difficulties for the government as it attempts to respond to poverty and inequality in China. First, there has been a tendency to back away from its social responsibilities, for example, universal health care, housing, and education. If that trend continues, the populations that have been hit hardest by reform will be the most vulnerable. Second, success is not guaranteed if the state were to embark on a variety of human development initiatives to enhance human capabilities. Human development programs are usually not "distributionally neutral"; in fact a considerable amount of inequality was noted between the sexes, among regions within the individual countries, between rural and urban areas, and among persons in different economic and social groups.[84]

In spite of the rising wealth in both the Chinese countryside and the cities, access to that wealth is highly uneven. A woman living in a remote rural area, for example, will not be able to live a healthy and fulfilling life if she has no access to education and health care. If she does not have decent food and housing because of discrimination at the household or community level, she is unlikely to receive her entitlements and live up to her capabilities.[85] Similarly, members of the new floating populations may be able to earn an income in the city, but without an urban registration card they have virtually no access to the public supply of housing, education, health care, or education for their children. Even the casual observer can discern signs of economic desperation, with the new poor begging on the streets and rummaging from garbage cans. Such sights haunt the CCP's old-timers, suggesting the dark days before socialist revolution. In the countryside millions of peasants are still mired in poverty, and with the loosening of migration restrictions many are showing up in the cities. From a policy perspective it is clear that the state cannot simply walk away from the distributional impacts of the economic reforms it has developed.

The persistence of poverty and the emergence of new class differentials raises a central question for modernization: How much equity can be traded in the interests of growth and efficiency? One solution in rural China has been to launch widespread efforts to improve the conditions of the poor, without interrupting the incentives for the better-endowed households to continue getting rich. Another solution, made possible by changing government policies since the mid-1980s, has been the lifting of restrictions on labor mobility, which has resulted in mass migrations to the cities. Although that makes sense in theory, there is doubt as to whether the massive departure of peasants from the poorest areas will have a positive or a negative impact.[86]

As the growth zones along the golden coastline reach out to the global economy, many people in China have taken the capitalist road. Many succeeded, yet poverty remains in the interior as well as remote areas within prosperous provinces. This chapter has investigated two dimensions of the new inequality: class and geography. From a policy perspective inequalities in class and geography represent threats to social order that can no longer be ignored. China has succeeded in launching itself into the global economy, but the price has been high. There are signs of division and discontent, the makings of social disruption along the lines of Tiananmen Square. If that in fact surfaced, alienation in the countryside could add the power of the rural masses to the urban workers and students.

11

The Other Chinas:
Taiwan and Hong Kong

*Since the early 1980s China has cherished the hope that
rediscovery of the common Chinese cultural identity and economic
self-interest will automatically create in Hong Kong and Taiwan a
desire for political reunification. Hong Kong has no choice, but in
Taiwan cultural and economic interaction with the mainland has
only strengthened its awareness of being a separate subnation.*

—Willem van Kemenade, *China, Hong Kong, Taiwan, Inc.* (1997)[1]

Introduction: China and Its Offshore Neighbors

China's economic reforms have brought great changes to the mainland, most of them being positive. In its push toward modernization China was able to benefit from the development trajectories of its offshore territories: Taiwan and Hong Kong.[2] Both recorded economic growth rates during the 1980s and 1990s that matched that of China, but for them growth came much earlier than in the mainland. The difference, at least until about the mid-1980s, was the economic and political systems operating in the three Chinas. In the PRC, until the end of the 1970s, economic growth had been led by the command economy, and the living standard of the mainlanders fell far below that of their overseas counterparts.

With the Four Modernizations China has been able to join Hong Kong and Taiwan as a major player in the global economy. By the early 1990s it was apparent that de facto economic integration was occurring between the three societies, fueling dreams about a united economic superpower—"Greater China."[3] Trade and other economic interactions between the three territories increased during the reform years, and by the early 1990s their combined trade with the rest of the world was surpassed

by only five other countries: the United States, Japan, Germany, France, and the United Kingdom. In 1997, as Hong Kong returned to Chinese sovereignty, two-thirds of the triangle was completed.

The core of the new region lies along the golden coastline of the mainland, or China's two southeastern provinces (Fujian and Guangdong). Proximity—in terms of geography and ethnicity—means economic development in this region has been driven largely by direct investment from Hong Kong and Taiwan. Hong Kong has been the major financier, investor, supplier, and provider of technology for Guangdong Province, especially the SEZs in Shenzhen and Zhuhai; a similar argument can be made for Taiwan, particularly in its relationship to Fujian Province. With a much less developed economy in Fujian than in Guangdong, and with Taiwan's huge supply of foreign exchange reserves, the smart money would follow Taiwan's role in the years to come, assuming that peace prevails across the Taiwan Strait.[4]

Before its return to China, Hong Kong had become one of the dominant centers of trade and finance in East Asia. In addition to its traditional role as an entrepôt for trade between China and the rest of the world, Hong Kong's unique combination of advantages helped produce one of the world's most dynamic centers of light industry in the 1960s and 1970s. Economic growth rates averaged more than 8 percent per year for most of the three decades before the handover, boosting per capita income to levels significantly higher than in all countries in Asia except Japan. In more recent times Hong Kong witnessed its industrial competitiveness being eroded, largely because of rising labor costs. The response was swift and decisive: Hong Kong industrialists began investing in mainland China, where labor and land costs were significantly lower; traders increased their imports of Chinese-made goods, finishing and repackaging them in preparation for re-export; and manufacturers who stayed in the territory began to upgrade their production processes to focus more on higher value-added products.

These strategies amounted to a geographical division of labor, with Hong Kong remaining as the investment, commercial, and financial core of the south China region and the mainland's coastal provinces becoming the industrial periphery where most of the actual production occurs.[5] The revitalized manufacturing economy helped Hong Kong maintain its position close to the world's ten largest exporter countries. The development of the financial infrastructure needed to support Hong Kong's role as a global trader, as well as its unique geographical situation in what was at the time the booming East Asia region, established it as a center of international finance. Hong Kong became famous as a place to make and spend money.

Taiwan also became one of the world's fastest growing economies, and its success surprised the rest of the world, beginning soon after the relocation of the exiled Nationalist government in 1949. The economic growth in the early 1950s has been attributed to the interventionist stance of the government in economic affairs, which continued through the 1990s.[6] In this sense Taiwan's path to economic success differed from that of Hong Kong. The emphasis on small and medium-sized enterprises, which have featured significantly in Taiwan's eco-

nomic growth, also differentiates it from the growth strategies of its regional neighbors and competitors—Japan and South Korea.

Perhaps most impressive about modern Taiwan is that it has experienced a twofold revolution, one economic, the other political. Apart from the fact that it was rolling in money by the early 1990s—with foreign exchange reserves of more than US$90 billion in 1993—Taiwan has moved far down the road to democratization. As *New York Times* reporter Nicholas Kristoff has remarked: "Taiwan represents a triumph of Chinese civilization. Other countries from Albania to Paraguay have also cast off their repressive governments, but one would be hard pressed to find any place on earth that has so successfully combined an economic miracle with a political one."[7]

After the reentry of the PRC into the global political scene in the early 1970s, Taiwan was thrust into a period of political isolation. Much of that evaporated, however, as Taiwan's wealth expanded, and Taipei is now being courted by many foreign governments eager to receive some of its rapidly accumulating capital. It is the thirteenth largest trader in the world economy and is spending some of its new wealth to modernize the aging transportation infrastructure and utilities, which ensures that Taiwan will continue to be a popular investment target for international construction companies.

In this chapter we explore the stories behind the development trajectories of the two offshore Chinese territories. This will allow some useful comparisons to be drawn between Hong Kong and Taiwan, as well as between them and the mainland. To begin this discussion it is useful to consider some of the important differences in the means of production in each society. Two key differences are seen in the ownership and control over the production of wealth. *Ownership* involves the question of who (or which institution) has the power to appropriate and dispose of the income that accrues during the production process. In command economies such as the former Soviet Union and Maoist China, that function was performed by the state; in present-day China, and much more so in Taiwan and Hong Kong, it means a combination of public and private ownership. *Control* refers to the power to make production and exchange decisions, for example, about what will be produced, where, in what quantities, and for what price. Again the control dimension varies along a continuum, from socialist command economies to free-trade economies.

For the purposes of conceptual clarity it is useful to employ a two-by-two categorization, based on the ownership and control dimensions (see Figure 11.1). In this simple framework it is possible to locate Taiwan and Hong Kong in Boxes 2 and 4, representing state capitalism (Taiwan) and laissez-faire capitalism (Hong Kong). Chapter 8 examined the development process in China, where the pre-1978 situation represents the command economy category; but after 1978 the term "market socialism" has been widely used to describe the reform era.[8] Here this comparative framework is used as a guide to investigate the extraordinary economic growth that has occurred in Taiwan and Hong Kong and has made them the envy of many developing countries around the world—especially China.

China and Taiwan: Writing the "Brilliant Page" in History

Taiwan and mainland China went their separate ways after 1949, and by most indicators Taiwan can since be judged infinitely more successful (see Table 11.1).

The statistics, definitive as they are, obscure the reality of the common heritage of Chinese on either side of the Taiwan Strait and the genuine desire, among many, to be reunified. Both Taiwan and the PRC share cultural and historical traditions, and in theoretical and sentimental terms both peoples agree that there can only ever be "one China." On the mainland side, for example, Deng Xiaoping declared emphatically that "historians will write better of those people who have strived and worked hard for the glorious task of reunification."[9] On the other side the Taiwan government maintains that "since ancient times, the notion of one unified China has been embedded in the minds of all Chinese. . . . Neither the ROC nor the PRC could dare to deviate from the one-China concept and still claim legitimacy as a Chinese entity."[10] The civil war and the 1949 exile of the Nationalist government to Taiwan artificially separated Chi-

State Ownership of the Means of Production

		Yes	No
State Control over the Means of Production	Yes	**COMMAND ECONOMY** China 1949–1976	**STATE CAPITALISM** Taiwan post-1950
	No	**MARKET SOCIALISM** China 1978–2000	**LAISSEZ-FAIRE CAPITALISM** Hong Kong

FIGURE 11.1   Role of the State in Economic Development

TABLE 11.1   Comparisons Across the Taiwan Strait: China and Taiwan, 1990

	Taiwan	Mainland	Ratio (Taiwan: Mainland)
Relationships Favoring Taiwan			
Per capita GNP (US$)	7,953	321	24.8:1
Exports per capita (US$)	3,322	54.8	60.8:1
Foreign exchange reserves:			
Billion (US$)	72.4	28.6	2.53:1
Per capita power generation			
(kilowatt hrs)	4,224	541	7.8:1
Per capita petroleum products			
(kilograms)	1,027	104	9.9:1
Per capita steel products (kilograms)	366	45	8.1:1
Automobiles per capita	17.7	0.5	39.4:1
Color TV sets per capita	103.8	9.0	11.5:1
Libraries per 100,000 persons	1.25	0.22	5.62:1
Hospital beds per 10,000 persons	43.1	23.1	1.87:1
Population density (pp sq. km)	565.5	119.5	4.73:1
Relationships Favoring China			
Land area (sq. kms)	36,000	9,564,000	1:265.7
Population (millions)	20.4	1,143.3	1:56.2
Population growth rate (%)	11.1	14.4	1:1.30
Doctors per 10,000 persons	10.4	15.5	1:1.50

SOURCE: Adopted from World League for Freedom and Democracy, Republic of China, *Current Situation in Communist China: A Briefing in Chart Form* (Jan. 1, 1992), Table 16, p. 16.

nese citizens, a source of intense sadness and nostalgia to this day. A Kuomintang veteran living in Taiwan wrote a poem to express his feelings when he looked across the water to the other side:

Bury me on a high mountain,
So I can look at the Mainland
Failing to see it still,
I cannot stop my tears.[11]

From the mainland side the message comes that the only possible solution to the Taiwan problem is reunification:

The bright future of our great motherland belongs to us and to you. The Reunification of the motherland is the sacred mission history has handed to our generation. Times are moving ahead and the situation is developing. The

earlier we fulfil this mission, the sooner we can jointly write an unprecedented, brilliant page in the history for our country, catch up with the advanced powers and work together with them for world peace, prosperity and progress. Let us join hands and work together for this glorious good.[12]

The one-China sentiment worked to Taiwan's advantage during the period from 1949 to the early 1970s, when the majority of countries around the world accepted Taipei and the Republic of China (ROC, i.e., Taiwan) as the only legitimate government. Today, however, as most countries recognize Beijing, one China has created a dilemma for Taiwan. Although Taipei still makes the claim for sole legitimacy, in reality it is little more than posturing, which mainland politicians and newspapers refer to as Taiwan's "one-China fiction." The mainland government obviously considers Beijing to be the only legitimate center, with Taiwan being another province within the People's Republic. The problem for Taiwan is that it now has difficulty openly retreating from the one-China position, partly because of the strong sentiments among the people on both sides for reunification as a social, cultural, and economic necessity, partly for reasons of pride. It is also apparent from China's bellicose words and actions, especially in the mid-1990s, that Taiwan risks war if it publicly embraces other alternatives, including independence. Thus although the government in Taipei maintains a theoretical adherence to the one-China principle, in reality it keeps quiet about what and where the China in question is. The result is that Taiwan's people are confused: Are they, or are they not, part of one country that has a 5,000-year history?[13]

Until the mid-1980s such claims stifled debate on the issue, but, as with the Cold War between West and East, standoff also brought a degree of stability. Since then the KMT government in Taiwan has allowed and even encouraged domestic developments that worry the leadership on the mainland and threaten to upset the status quo:

- In the political-military arena a broad consensus has emerged that the status quo—the de facto independence of Taiwan—must be the baseline for future debate. The people of Taiwan, as a result of the gradual democratization and pluralization of their political system, are in no mood to consider anything less. As President Lee Teng-hui said in June 1995, "The most important point is for Taiwan's sovereign existence to be recognized. . . . If we don't have this sovereign status, on what basis can we discuss unification?"[14] In other words, no peaceful settlement of the Taiwan issue is possible unless Taipei is guaranteed at least as much authority as it currently exercises. The situation became infinitely more complex after the emergence of an opposition party that was, at least in its early years, explicitly committed to independence (the Democratic Progres-

sive Party, or DPP). Democratic decision-making and the open discussion and debate of the independence issue now constrain the KMT in its dealings with Beijing, which clearly will not tolerate or take part in any open discussion of independence.[15] To confuse matters even more, the changing composition of the Taiwan elite (with an increasing proportion of Taiwan-born politicians in the KMT government) has produced some important new developments. There are now open discussions, even within the KMT, of alternatives to the one-China scenario, and the long-standing links between the KMT and the military are being eroded.

- In the socioeconomic arena the growing strength and global status of Taiwan's economy are making the government ever more confident about its ability to leverage wealth for international political gain. Recent developments have been eroding the earlier monolithic structure of politics in Taiwan, with the KMT as the sole political party. In the early 1990s even the two-party situation was changing rapidly, as new parties emerged and new ideas about how best to proceed on reunification were openly debated. At the same time, ongoing attempts to restructure Taiwan's economy by replacing labor-intensive industry with more capital- and technology-intensive industries are likely to make the island even more dependent on trade with and investment in the mainland. Any conflict with the PRC over reunification would therefore have a crucial impact on Taiwan's economy, in addition to the massive additional resource allocation that would have to be transferred to the military in the event of armed conflict.

In spite of the uncertainty, a case can be made that such events actually augur well for future stability. In a sense the democratization and pluralization of Taiwan's political system could prevent precipitous decisionmaking on either side. Still, some recent trends are inherently destabilizing, as they signal a clear shift away from a commitment to reunification. Those include the political and social changes associated with the emergence of a distinct and uniquely Taiwanese identity, especially among the young; the Taiwanization of the KMT; and Taiwan's increasing confidence that it can use its wealth and economic strength as a political bargaining chip, even to defy the mainland on important issues.[16]

Observers in the PRC have been intently watching for potentially threatening trends in Taiwan: a gain in political strength for the DPP, a convergence of views between the KMT and the DPP, or the further breakdown of the KMT—any of which would marginalize the remaining one-China adherents in Taiwan, with potentially dangerous consequences. The mainland position on this issue remains as clear as ever: "If we do not quickly set about ending this disunity so that our motherland is reunified . . . how can we answer our ancestors and explain to our descendants? The sentiment is shared by all. Who among the descendants of the Yellow Emperor wishes to go down in history as a traitor?"[17]

Perhaps the best hope for avoiding potential conflict is de facto economic integration, which has been increasing between the mainland and its offshore territories. The desire to continue down the path of mutual economic exploitation, and the concentration of energy and resources in that direction, may deflect attention and priorities away from potential hostility and toward a preservation of the status quo. At the same time, economic cooperation could increase the likelihood of peaceful negotiations to eventually bring about a diplomatic solution.

Such economics-driven rationality is precisely what happened in Taiwan during the period immediately after the forced exile of the KMT in 1949. When Chiang Kai-shek arrived in Taiwan he immediately announced that his goal was to "counterattack and recover the mainland." As he said, in less than three years, he was confident that "we shall make a clean sweep of the Communist bandits."[18] As history demonstrated, Chiang backed down from that aggres-

sive stance quickly, his belligerence channeled into an almost obsessive pursuit of sustained economic development (not unlike Deng Xiaoping after he took power in 1978). In the four decades after the KMT's exile, most of the traditional economic and social indicators suggest it was achieved. In 1951 per capita GNP in Taiwan was under US$100, and international trade stood at $300 million; but by 1990 GNP had reached close to $10,000, and international trade totaled $122 billion, with average economic growth in excess of 8 percent per year.[19] In spite of the growing wealth, income inequality was reduced dramatically in postwar Taiwan, something so rare that it attracted attention from development scholars around the world. In 1953 the ratio between the incomes of households in the top 20 percent of the income bracket to those in the bottom 20 percent was 20.5:1; that had been reduced to 4.2–4.6:1 by the 1970s.[20] (Table 11.2 compares inequality statistics for Taiwan to those in other countries, both developed and developing, from 1964 to 1986.)

Taiwan's economic miracle—rapid economic growth without rising income inequality—has intrigued development specialists who assumed that income equality was not possible during rapid development. It had been assumed that a country (like Taiwan) beginning to pursue development and highly dependent on foreign aid and investment would end up with slow economic growth and significant income inequality.[21] Such has clearly not been the case, and in fact Lee Teng-hui, the Taiwan-born leader who succeeded Chiang Kai-shek's son as ROC president, boasted that "our economic growth rate now surpasses that of capitalist countries, and our distribution of wealth is more even than that of socialist countries"[22] (see Photos 11.1a and 11.1b).

An Interpretation of Taiwan's Economic Transformation

In 1949 the KMT government was defeated by the Communists and, in the euphemistic language of the time, "temporarily moved its

TABLE 11.2   Income Distribution in Taiwan and Selected Countries, 1960s Through 1980s

Country	Year of Data	GNP Per Capita (US$)	Share of Income Earned by:	
			Lowest 40% of Households	Highest 20% of Households
High-Inequality Countries				
Philippines	1971	239	11.6	53.8
Malaysia	1970	330	11.6	56.0
Brazil	1970	390	10.0	61.6
South Africa	1965	669	6.2	58.0
Moderate-Inequality Countries				
Burma	1958	82	16.5	44.8
India	1964	99	16.0	52.0
Netherlands	1967	1,990	13.6	48.5
W. Germany	1964	2,144	15.4	52.9
Sweden	1963	2,949	14.0	44.0
Low-Inequality Countries				
Taiwan	1964	202	20.3	41.1
Taiwan	1972	519	21.9	38.6
Taiwan	1978	1,869	22.6	37.2
Taiwan	1982	—	22.5	37.3
Taiwan	1986	—	23.8	38.2
Korea	1970	235	18.0	45.0
Spain	1965	750	17.6	45.7
Japan	1963	950	20.7	40.0
United Kingdom	1968	2,015	18.8	39.0
Canada	1965	2,920	20.0	40.2
United States	1970	4,850	19.7	38.8

SOURCES: Adapted from Kuo, Ranis, and Fei (1981), Table 2.15, p. 36; and Bello and Rosenfeld (1990), Table 13.2, p. 227.

government to Taiwan," where it could carry on "the struggle against Communist tyranny for a united, democratic China."[23] Taiwan is separated from the mainland's Fujian Province by the Strait of Taiwan, some 130–200 kilometers wide.[24] When President Chiang Kai-shek arrived with 2 million mainland followers, there were only about 6 million Taiwan Chinese in all. By 1990 the population had reached 20 million, all but 325,000 of whom are ethnic Chinese. With more people than Australia and New Zealand combined, living on less than 24,000 square miles of land, Taiwan is one of the most densely populated places in the world.

In light of Taiwan's obvious geographical constraints—the island's terrain is dominated by mountains, and it has virtually no natural resources—the speed and scale of its economic success do indeed suggest that a miracle occurred, although most Taiwan people would insist that hard work was the key. In investigating the path to progress, it is useful to compare Taiwan's situation to that in the mainland. Although there are many obvious differences, especially during the Maoist era (1949–1976), the economic strategies selected by the ROC during the early 1950s are similar to those adopted by the PRC in the late 1970s and early 1980s.[25]

On either side of the Strait the political systems (after 1949 in Taiwan, the late 1970s in the mainland) can be characterized as authoritar-

PHOTO 11.1a   Taipei family in traffic.

PHOTO 11.1b   Digging up the streets in Taipei, building the new subway–light rail system.

ian, in that they were dominated by a single, Leninist-type party. Both governments had recently experienced traumatic events that required them to undertake intensive campaigns to restore political legitimacy: the Cultural Revolution in the mainland, the "Two-Two-Eight" incident in Taiwan. On February 28, 1947, an ethnic conflict emerged between Taiwan natives and the mainland KMT government then on the island. A mainland policeman had shot an innocent Taiwanese bystander, and an uprising spread throughout Taipei and the rest of Taiwan; it was quelled brutally by KMT troops. Estimates vary, but the consensus is that more than 10,000 Taiwanese were killed, and the "Two-Two-Eight" incident left bitterness between Taiwanese and mainland refugees.

The Taiwanese contended that an entire generation of intellectuals and potential civil and political leaders was wiped out, and the event instilled such fear that few dared even to speak about it publicly. The KMT attempted to ignore the incident and was relatively successful in censoring it from the history books. In recent years, however, the incident has been exhumed, and it has become an important rallying point and nationalist symbol for the Taiwan independence movement.[26] Compounding the KMT's difficulties was the continued military threat from the Communists and the temporary abandonment by the United States, a major ally who blamed Chiang Kai-shek for the loss of the mainland to Mao Zedong's Communists.

The ways in which the governments responded to crisis (Taiwan in the early 1950s, the PRC in the late 1970s) were also similar: They embarked on adventurous programs of economic reform, beginning in the agricultural sector. Taiwan's land reform (the "land to the tiller" program) resulted in the government's buying out many landlords and selling the land to tenant farmers. The result was a much more equitable distribution of land, which went far toward promoting income equality among Taiwan's farmers. It also helped create a new entrepreneurial class of former landlords, which was encouraged to open businesses with

the buyout payments they had received from the government. It also established a large number of peasant proprietors farming small holdings. As was the case after HRS reform in the mainland, this proved an enormous incentive to peasants, as earning power and material incentives were transferred to them directly, a powerful force for hard work and efficiency. The land reforms also liberated many of Taiwan's peasants from the land, allowing them to move into towns and cities to find better jobs in industry.

Taiwan during the 1950s and the mainland during the late 1970s faced similar situations in the industrial realm: Production was dominated by state enterprises, many of them under strict government control and chronically inefficient. Despite such similarities, it was in the industrial realm that the governments' reform strategies diverged most. A poor country in the early 1950s, Taiwan faced a balance-of-payments crisis it could ill afford, with imports significantly ahead of exports. To solve the problem it was necessary to embark on a program of import substitution, but during those early years Taiwan did not have the industrial capacity to bring about the required transformation.

The solution adopted in Taiwan thus differed greatly from Deng Xiaoping's actions two decades later. Industrial reform in Taiwan began with the restructuring of ownership, resulting in a rapid expansion of private enterprise. This was considered necessary by the KMT government to help solve the budget deficit; the government simply could not afford the deficit financing that would be required to launch an intensive state monopolization of industry (the route taken in the mainland during the 1950s). As privatization increased, however, the state maintained tight control of the market, thereby defining what was labeled earlier as state capitalism (see Figure 11.1): "Taiwan . . . gradually grew into a private economy, with the means of production mostly in private hands and profits mostly appropriated by private entrepreneurs [but] the state continued to manipulate both administrative and economic levers to guide private enterprises toward goals set by the [government] technocrats. Income power was in private hands but the state exercised great control."[27]

The contrasts with the PRC reform policies during the 1980s are indisputable: The PRC retained a significant amount of socialist ownership of the means of production in all but the most economically advanced coastal provinces while replacing administrative levers increasingly with economic, market-oriented levers. The mainland reforms did not begin with a big push toward privatization, in part for ideological reasons but also because the PRC was not encountering the same balance-of-payments problems Taiwan encountered in the early 1950s. In fact the mainland in the late 1970s and through the 1980s was much less dependent on imports than was Taiwan and was able to increase exports quickly by expanding the capacity of the state-dominated industrial sector. The mainland reforms, in other words, can be characterized as being market socialist in nature; as we saw in Chapter 8, the process of abandoning the plan and gradually letting the market take over is well under way at present.

In Taiwan the industrial reforms began with the process of import substitution, seen as necessary for reducing the budget deficit. In addition to the financial aid received from the United States, Taiwan's reform process was guided by an emerging class of technocratic government officials. Some among these new bureaucrats had been influenced by the Japanese model of combining private ownership with government guidance; many had been educated in business schools in the United States.[28] There was also a highly pragmatic strain running through the KMT government, which allowed a significant amount of policy flexibility. Unlike the much more rigid theorizing conducted in the mainland, ideological principles in Taiwan at that time were loosely based on the so-called Three Principles of the People (nationalism, democracy, and the people's livelihood), established earlier in the twentieth century by Sun Yat-sen. The interpretation of these principles by the KMT was flexible

enough to allow a mixture of state and market roles in guiding the economy.

Taiwan's industrial takeoff began in a small number of industries—textiles, plastics, cement, and pulp and paper—where new private enterprises were created and public corporations were privatized. The state made most of the production decisions and arranged to sell the products while private entrepreneurs kept the profits. In many industries the state prohibited the import of competing finished goods and gave entrepreneurs preferential rates on imported raw materials. The most successful model was the textile industry. With no foreign competition, private companies were able to make huge profits in the domestic market, and Taiwan's now famous textile conglomerates began to emerge.

The principles first applied to the textile industry were extended to other import-substituting industries in the First Four Year Plan (1953–1956). The government typically took care of the preparation work, provided the planning and the capital equipment, then took pains to secure markets for the products. In 1954 the government began to transfer shares of stock in several public enterprises to landlords whose assets had been compulsorily purchased during the land reform period. This enabled many landholding families to transform into successful industrialists. The net result was a rapid increase in the private sector, from 25 percent to more than 50 percent of the total industrial production by 1958.[29] The goal of replacing the import of durable consumer goods with domestic goods was largely achieved during the 1950s. The share of consumer goods in total imports, for example, fell from 20 percent to 6 percent between 1952 and 1957.[30]

During the late 1950s and early 1960s Taiwan's economic planners executed an explicit policy reversal, from import-substitution to export-oriented industrial production. This was a choice largely dictated by necessity, as the size of the small domestic economy could not sustain long-term economic growth. In addition, U.S. aid was coming to an end, and the continuing balance-of-payments crisis called for decisive action.[31] Beginning with a four-year strategy in 1960, Taiwan's bureaucrats drew up plans that would provide incentives for enterprises that produced and marketed export goods. They offered cheap credit and substantial tax breaks, and again the textile industry led the way, creating the "Made in Taiwan" labels that would become known to the world.

With the help of considerable financial support, again provided by the state, as well as fixed exchange rates favoring exports, many small and medium-sized private enterprises emerged in the export sector. Reform measures introduced in the 1958–1961 period helped shift the incentive structure from production for the domestic market to exports; for example, the Taiwan dollar was devalued from NT$25 to NT$40 (new Taiwan dollar) per U.S. dollar, and preferential loans and tax exemptions were offered to tempt industrialists into the export sphere. The result of all of these measures was a sharp rise in the value of Taiwan's export goods, increasing at an average annual rate of 24.5 percent throughout the 1960s, with the export share of GNP doubling from 8.9 percent in 1958 to 19 percent in 1968.[32] Exports crept up gradually throughout the 1960s and skyrocketed during the 1970s and 1980s, with positive implications for the balance of payments.

In a major study of Taiwan's economic miracle the two pillars of economic development were identified as labor-intensive industrialization and export orientation. The labor-intensive strategy helped soak up the surplus rural labor generated by the land reforms and reduced the initial need for capital, which made entry into the production process relatively cheap and easy for small businesses, especially light industry. With such low labor costs Taiwan's export goods were able to compete immediately in world markets, and the growth of the export sector helped generate the foreign exchange needed to purchase the raw materials and equipment for future economic development.[33] The absorption of surplus rural labor also created jobs for the lowest income groups, which contributed significantly to the relatively equitable distribution of income (see Table 11.2).[34]

Despite such success, the researchers warned in 1981 that Taiwan had reached a turning point and that a new economic strategy was needed. The pool of unskilled labor had almost been fully utilized and wage rates were creeping up, which threatened to make Taiwan's exports less competitive in global markets. There was a growing trend toward protectionism all over the world, partly in an attempt by countries, such as the United States, to defend the interests of domestic producers. Competition from other countries with even lower labor costs, as well as the oil crisis, which was continuing to raise production costs in Taiwan, meant that new economic policies were required.

The most obvious switch came in the high-tech sector, with an expansion of automated machinery and a shift toward R&D. That process had begun in the early 1980s as a low-energy alternative to the production of traditional export goods. The plan was to produce goods that created high value and utilized the skills of Taiwan's well-educated and hard-working population.[35] In the late 1970s the government had established the Industrial Technology and Research Institute to train engineers and develop high-tech products, and in 1980 the first of several new science- and technology-based industrial parks was established in Hsinchu, just south of Taipei. This was an attempt to establish a Taiwan Silicon Valley, where high-tech companies can feed off of one another in terms of labor, capital, and ideas. A package of incentives was designed to give tax breaks to computer and telecommunications companies willing to engage in R&D activities, as well as technical training and worldwide brand marketing.

Throughout the 1980s Taiwan's industry became increasingly automated, primarily as a response to rising wages. As the data in Table 11.3 indicate, among the major industrial sectors the ratio of automated to total machines increased significantly from 1982 to 1988.

By the early 1990s Taiwan appeared to be doing well in developing its own R&D systems

TABLE 11.3   Ratio of Automatic Machinery to Total Machines for Selected Industrial Sectors in Taiwan, 1982–1988

	Date			
Industry Group	*1982*	*1984*	*1986*	*1988*
Manufactured Goods	—	66	56	73
Textiles	29	24	55	38
Plastic products	8	10	26	37
Machinery	21	28	36	55
Electronics	27	38	46	59

SOURCE: Chi Schive (1992), Table 5.6, p. 111 (data from *Industrial Automation: A Survey Report,* Taipei: Automation Commission, Executive Yuan; 1982, 1984, 1986, 1988).

and had experienced some success in attracting new technology through strategic alliances with corporations from other countries, most notably Japan and the United States. There were still, however, a number of significant constraints facing Taiwan as it attempted to compete with the United States–Japan–Western Europe triangle of industrial powers.[36]

From the early 1950s to the present the state has continued its important role in directing and shaping Taiwan's economy. It retained control over critical industrial output as well as utilities and services such as energy and water. One of the keys to success has been the separation of the planning role from the implementation role in economic decisionmaking, with decisions about priorities and overall goals being made at the highest level by interministerial councils. The Economic Stabilization Board (renamed the Council for Economic Planning and Development) was primarily responsible for macroeconomic planning and implemented a series of three-, four-, six-, and ten-year development plans outlining broad economic and social goals for the country. Implementation of the plans was left to organizations such as the Board of Foreign Trade, the Industrial Development Bureau of the Ministry of Economic Affairs, and the Council on Agricultural Development.[37]

The government also took pains to create an economic environment that would attract domestic and foreign investors by providing significant incentives and protections to investors; by expanding the country's infrastructure with a huge push on construction projects; by upgrading technology through foreign capital and machinery; by encouraging foreign-educated scientists and engineers to return home; and by establishing industrial parks and export processing zones. The government also provided close regulation of the financial environment to create the stability needed to attract outside investment. This included monetary stabilization policies to curb the rampant inflation characteristic of the late 1940s, as well as the control of interest rates to ensure that savers would not be hurt by inflation. The net result was an extremely high rate of savings, which contributed to the huge monetary surplus made available for capital loans from the banks to local entrepreneurs.

A Civil Society to Replace the Dictatorship?

By the early 1990s no one knew how long the miracle could last, particularly in the face of rising labor costs and growing competition in world export markets. Importantly, the arena for publicly debating such momentous issues was and continues to be widened thanks to the democratization of the political system. That benefit helped further meaningful debate on many issues, including the degradation of the island environment. The increasing crowds and pollution in Taiwan's cities, the toxification of rivers, and the loss of much farmland to urban and industrial land uses had reached crisis pro-portions in the 1990s.[38] By most accounts the frantic pursuit of economic growth, beginning in the 1950s, is fingered as the culprit. The push toward massive industrialization and the encouragement of overseas investment stressed performance measures such as rapid output growth, job creation, and contributions to GNP and exports. Little else was deemed to be as important at that time: "Little if any attention was paid, through formal regulations, laws, or even guidelines, to protecting the quality of the environment. Taiwan became well-known, if not notorious, as a haven for so-called dirty industries such as petrochemicals. As other countries adopted more stringent restrictions on such activities, the attraction of Taiwan increased."[39]

Much of the blame has been attributed to specific strategies within early development plans as well as to the structure of Taiwan's industry. The push toward rural industrializa-tion, for example, helped equalize economic growth in geographical terms and soaked up excess rural labor, but in the process thousands of unlicensed factories and industrial estates appeared, gobbling up scarce cultivable land, damaging riparian networks, and polluting the air. Taiwan's traditional emphasis on small and medium-sized industrial enterprises also con-tributed to the problem, as small factories are generally undercapitalized and operate on low profit and small loss margins. They are the least able and perhaps least inclined to respond to demands for installing antipollution devices or to implement costly regulations on dumping and emissions.

Large-scale infrastructure projects have also contributed to the degradation of Taiwan's environment. Many projects (e.g., the 1973 "Ten Major Construction Projects" and the 1984 "Fourteen Construction Projects") were launched with much fanfare to encourage for-eign and domestic investors. They have helped enormously to expand industrial output but have opened up ever more land to develop-ment, some of it in previously remote and mountainous areas. The impact of road con-struction has also contributed to a huge rise in automobile and motorcycle ownership, with predictable consequences for air quality.

Much of the concern about the growing environmental crisis was expressed in the mas-sive *Taiwan 2000* report, a document published in 1989 by a group of environmentally con-scious scholars. It concluded with cautious optimism punctuated by apocalyptic warnings. In many public pronouncements the govern-ment has committed to dealing with the prob-lem comprehensively and promised that in the near future "Taiwan . . . will live up to its repu-tation of being a beautiful island with blue skies and green meadows, verdant mountains and clear waters."[40] This optimism is similar to that expressed by the World Bank in 1997 on the topic of environmental degradation in the mainland (see Chapter 16), and many critics remain unconvinced, pointing to what is likely to be widespread opposition from Taiwan's business interests.

It is interesting to note that out-migration from Taiwan (especially to North America) continued at a rapid rate into the 1990s. Despite sustained economic growth many well-edu-cated, high-income households decided to start anew elsewhere, sometimes citing Taiwan's growing environmental crisis (in addition to overcrowding, lack of land for recreation, grid-lock, and rising real estate prices). It would seem that many people do not share the gov-ernment's optimism: One of the common com-plaints is that Taiwan may be a good place to make money but the United States is a much better place to spend it. The government must shoulder its share of the blame for the crisis, yet Taiwan's people themselves are not without fault given their fixation with the welfare of families and the desire to get rich at almost any cost. As the *Taiwan 2000* report concluded:

> The forces that pollute and abuse our natural re-sources are strong and, to date largely uncon-strained. They are closely tied to the source of our high incomes, and people and government alike are justifiably hesitant to attempt to con-trol them, for fear that our incomes will decline.

Also, our high standard of living has tended to make us soft, and to reduce our willingness to undertake the often difficult, sometimes expensive, and commonly unpleasant tasks of maintaining the island's resource base.[41]

By the late 1980s an active environmental movement had emerged, partly as a result of growing awareness of the enormity of the problem, partly because of the increasing recognition that environmental abuses were directly influencing health, welfare, and quality of life. All these concerns would be expressed publicly by the end of the decade thanks to the growing liberalization of Taiwan's society and the lifting of restrictions on public dissent and protest. Taiwan now has an active and effective grassroots environmental movement, and in some cases public protests have successfully prevented the opening of new industrial plants and closed down others.[42] What emerged was a multiclass movement that was able to record successes in the face of the business elite and the strong progrowth stance that drove the island's rapid economic growth.

The environmental movement was largely spontaneous in its origins, yet many of the environmental groups allied with the opposition DPP, which has chosen the color green for its flag, symbolically linking the issues of democracy and the environment (see Photo 11.2).

There is a growing consciousness that Taiwan is "home" for the people who live there and that they must now begin to protect it. What is implied here is that Taiwan has been ravaged so seriously by the drive toward modernization because it was, after all, a temporary location, a "colony" of the mainland. As one of the leaders of a grassroots organization put it: "Current policymakers do not love this place as their home since they still operate under the myth of returning to the mainland and have not changed their basic opinion of Taiwan as a temporary stop, a hotel of sorts. After benefiting from the exploitation of the island, they send their children to the States because it's too pol-

PHOTO 11.2   DPP truck cruising the streets of Penghu before an election.

luted here in Taiwan."[43] The notion of Taiwan as a temporary way station or halfway house has been a recurring theme in the growing discourse associated with political pluralization. In the first three decades after the exile of Chiang Kai-shek and the establishment of the new government, the general consensus was that economic development needed to be guided by the strong hand of the state. It is clear, however, that since the mid-1980s there have been some significant social and political changes in Taiwan. As Thomas Gold noted, "A very delicate and protracted renegotiation of the social contract is under way [and] for the first time social forces and not the party/state are determining the agenda and pace of change."[44]

In fact Gold argued that Taiwan is now experiencing the emergence of a "civil society," with the appearance of new political parties and social movements oriented around such issues as consumer protection, environmental awareness, gender concerns, and aboriginal rights. As these movements have expanded their activities and power bases, the people of Taiwan have gradually reshaped their sense of collective identity and developed a new idea of themselves in relation to the state. In contemporary Taiwan, as Gold observes, it is "society at large . . . not necessarily through the organized opposition [which] sets the agenda of political discourse."[45]

An important dimension of this new identity was the development of a strong feeling of rootedness and a sense of place among Taiwan's people. This has been expressed in literature, the arts, and film and is manifested in feelings of nostalgia for the past and a desire for a simpler way of life. There has been a push to emphasize the Taiwanese dialect over Mandarin, and a sincere effort has been made to explore and understand Taiwan's history. In intellectual terms much of this has been concentrated among the student population and the intellectuals and young professionals in urban Taiwan, producing a strong nationalist sentiment as the Taiwan people attempt to define their growing sense of ethnic consciousness: "In a period of extraordinarily rapid transition to the modern world and snubbing by the

outside world, some Taiwanese are seeking anchors, 'unchanging and invariant' parts of social life around which they can build a sense of social cohesion and community."[46]

What is involved here is an attempt to create an "imagined community"—a Taiwan with a separate and independent identity, which has never existed before. The PRC government, of course, continually reiterates that such an entity does not and will not exist.

Postscript, 1995–1999: Changing Fortunes in PRC-ROC Relationships

The new sense of self and identity being expressed in contemporary Taiwan has an overtly political dimension, which has resulted in a smoldering conflict with the mainland. The situation reached a crisis point in the spring and summer of 1995, when President Lee Teng-hui announced plans to visit the United States, and Taiwan demanded to be accepted as a member of international organizations such as the World Trade Organization, the International Monetary Fund, and the United Nations. Throughout 1995 there was increasing evidence of a new spirit emerging in Taiwan. In a review of the daily postings on the Internet, for example, where Taiwan people and mainlanders have been busily exchanging views in recent years, a clear sentiment was emerging: "The time has come to establish a new consciousness, a new identity for Taiwan . . . We've been bearing alien citizenship for more than 400 years. It's very important for us to build a consciousness of being Taiwanese to enhance our own self-confidence."[47]

It was always apparent that Taiwan's increasing democratization and its push to achieve international recognition would put it on a collision course with China. In early 1995, relations across the Strait appeared to be improving: The two sides were talking freely and making counterproposals about how to resolve the conflicts between them. The motivations on both sides were strong, due to their increasing economic interaction. The cooperation and apparent flexibility demonstrated from both sides were the result of a gradual thawing of relationships, which began in

1987 when President Chiang Ching-kuo (the son of Chiang Kai-shek) relaxed the ban on Taiwan citizens traveling to China. Before that date the rigid "three no's" had prevailed—no contact, no negotiations, no compromise—symbolizing Taiwan's determination to stand up to communism. After 1987 the constraints were gradually and informally relaxed: Trade and travel in both directions increased, and Taiwan investors began to seek outlets in the mainland, often through Hong Kong–based intermediaries. Pragmatism on both sides of the Strait appeared; for example, in 1993 the KMT recognized the de facto legitimacy of the Beijing government and publicly announced it had given up on recovering territory lost to the Communists. On the economic side, Taipei partially lifted the ban on direct trade with China in May 1995 and announced plans to create offshore transshipment zones for shipping cargo. It was also thought that direct air travel between Taiwan and the mainland was less than a year away.[48]

The thawing process was interrupted when the U.S. Congress forced President Bill Clinton to grant a visa to Lee Teng-hui to visit the United States as a private citizen in June 1995. At the same time, a visit by Taiwan Premier Lien Chan to Europe was announced. Beijing postponed cross-Strait talks, and the flexibility that had been carefully nurtured disappeared. Harsh verbal attacks were made against President Lee, accusing him of promoting the independence issue and abandoning the commitment to reunification with China. Throughout July and August China conducted a series of aggressive "missile tests" in the South China Sea, with missiles landing harmlessly in the waters just north of Taipei. The verbal attacks against President Lee continued. Beijing was clearly worried about the Taiwan elections in early 1996, in which President Lee, boosted by his new international status, had announced his candidacy. The Chinese feared that the elections would be publicized internationally and that the independence issue would be discussed widely, gaining Taiwan even more sympathy in its struggle with the mainland. From the mainland's perspective the elections were considered

to be something of a time bomb. The Chinese fear is not of democracy per se but the powers and forces that the democratization process is unleashing in Taiwan: the surge of nationalistic hope for the previously marginalized supporters of independence, and the greater "voice" for Taiwan in its attempt to carve out its own "international space."[49]

The Taiwan government would contend that it has shown tolerance and flexibility, believing that the sovereignty dispute should be suspended while the sides cement a more constructive channel for interactions, bolstered by continuing trade and travel freedoms. From Taiwan's perspective China is holding up the process with a blatant exhibition of "narrow-minded nationalistic feelings."[50] At present, uncertainty is widespread: No one can be certain how realistic China's militaristic threats are; it is not known whether the United States would defend Taiwan in the event of military action; and there is little information about how well Taiwan would be able to defend itself in the face of an attack. The Chinese government has called upon Taiwan people to "sweep Lee Teng-hui into the trash bin of history," in a campaign of vilification similar to their treatment of other opponents, including the former Hong Kong governor, Chris Patten; dissident professor Fang Lizhi; and, after the NATO bombing of the Chinese embassy in Belgrade in May 1999, President Clinton.[51]

The Chinese have publicly accused the United States of bolstering Taiwan's confidence and stoking the conflict by granting the visa to President Lee. When President Richard Nixon signed the Shanghai Communiqué in 1972, the United States recognized that there was only one China, with Beijing as its capital. This was reaffirmed by the expulsion of Taiwan diplomats from the United States in 1979. China was clearly worried about the widespread support, both at the highest level and at the grassroots level, demonstrated for President Lee's visit to his alma mater, Cornell University. The sentiment being expressed is not only pro-Taiwan but also deliberately anti-China. The current Republican-dominated Congress has expressed strong anti-China sentiments on several occasions, and many members would like to see U.S. China policies overhauled in light of the recent conflicts over trade, human rights, arms proliferation, and the issue of espionage and the theft of nuclear technology.[52]

The rift between China and the United States was obviously widened by the Tiananmen Square incident in 1989 and by the collapse of the Soviet threat, which had kept the superpowers (China and the United States) in alliance. Throughout the Clinton administration, U.S.-China relationships have been strained, and in spite of the huge amount of trade between the two nations the political conflict continues, fueled by evidence of China's desire to become a military superpower. In 1996 China announced some highly controversial decisions that worried Taiwan and the larger international community: to continue with its nuclear testing; to go ahead with its purchase of vast amounts of military technology from the bankrupt Russians; to build a new squad of jet fighters; and, most recently, to test its mobile intercontinental ballistic missile.[53] As China continues to flex its muscles in the international arena, Taiwan is bracing for the next round of cross-Strait conflict. It is impossible to tell at this juncture how those interactions will be resolved.

Hong Kong: From Remote Colony to Global City to Special Administrative Region

The waters of Yao flow while the sun of Xia prevails,
Doubtless the attire here is also properly Han;
Ascending the stories I see land of our own all around,
But there is no Yellow Dragon insignia to be found.

—Huang Zunxian (1888)[54]

After serving as consul general for China in San Francisco, Huang Zunxian returned to his native Hong Kong in 1888. All around him he saw Chinese land and Chinese people, but his peace was disturbed by the sight of a foreign flag flying in place of the traditional yellow dragon of the Qing Dynasty. Huang would have been happy to know that in 1997 the British Union Jack had been replaced, but this time with the flag of the People's Republic of China.

A Brief History of Hong Kong

In the middle of the nineteenth century an unpromising corner of the Qing Empire off the southern coast of Guangdong Province was used as a pawn in an international power struggle. The territory in question was 1,500 miles from Beijing—two to three weeks' journey even by the fastest courier. In 1840 there were no settlements larger than some market hamlets; the place had precious few resources; and most of the land was too mountainous to farm. The climate was miserably hot and humid most of the year, and diseases like malaria, cholera, and typhoid were endemic. Human life and landscape had changed little for centuries, yet the place was alive with wildlife of all types, as British travel writer Jan Morris wrote: "There were leopards, tigers, badgers, Chinese otters, pangolins, wild cats and boars. . . . There were also crab-eating mongooses, an unusual variety of newt, two hundred kinds of butterfly and thirty-two kinds of snake, including the flowerpot snake, the white-lipped viper and the rock python, which grew up to sixteen feet long and could swallow a dog."[55]

Most people in China, except for the few minority people who called this place home, considered it too peripheral to worry about, and there was scarcely a murmur in 1840 when it was surrendered to the British in a treaty that ended a period of hostilities in Chinese waters. During the next 130 years it would undergo a stupefying transformation from a godforsaken corner of the empire to the world-renowned center known as Hong Kong. By the 1960s it was already a futuristic metropolis—the busiest, the richest, and the most extraordinary of all Chinese cities. This was a remarkable change in such a short time, and today Hong Kong, reunited with

China, has the task of leading China's assimilation into the global economy. Hong Kong was created by the urges of European, Chinese, and American enterprise, and the productive city-state we see today symbolizes the built form of capitalism at its most successful.

Hong Kong is a small island at the mouth of the Pearl River on the southern coast of Guangdong Province. In 1842 it was ceded in perpetuity to the British following China's humiliation in the first of the so-called Opium Wars (1839–1842). In 1860 a 3.5-square-mile piece of the mainland (Kowloon) was added, also in perpetuity, after another British victory. A third and much larger area was added in 1898, but not as a colony. The additional piece of the mainland, known today as the New Territories, was leased to Britain for ninety-nine years, automatically reverting to China in 1997.[56] At that time the lease term probably seemed like a long one, so few people on either side were overly concerned about the wording of the treaties that would hand over Hong Kong to the British. The merchants of Hong Kong made good use of the island's outstanding site and situation, and it became a hugely successful port and financial center.

The people of Hong Kong are well known around the world as hard workers, usually thought to be more interested in making money than in talking politics. In a statement that is typically boorish, author and world traveler Paul Theroux once made this remark about the Hong Kong people he had met on his travels around China:

> They had never before been to China, had never seen snow, their English was poor . . . they did not speak Mandarin. Like most Hong Kongers I had met, they were complete provincials. . . . They were well fed and rather silly and politically naive. In some ways Hong Kong was . . . like Britain itself: a bunch of offshore islands with an immigrant problem, a language barrier and a rigid class system.[57]

With the exception of Paul Theroux, Hong Kong's people had earned respect globally as shrewd operators. Their political naïveté is not surprising, bearing in mind that the British government had kept the vast majority of them disenfranchised for more than a century. Yet during 150 years of British rule the colony had become highly successful. Hong Kong's life expectancy statistics are better than Britain's, and its per capita GDP is catching up fast.[58]

Hong Kong Emerges as a Major Economic Power

For close to a hundred years (1840s–1940s) Hong Kong operated virtually as an autonomous entrepôt, servicing the trade between China and the rest of the world. In 1890, for example, 55 percent of China's imports passed through Hong Kong, and 37 percent of the colony's exports were bound for China. By the start of World War II China still dominated Hong Kong's foreign trade: 59 percent of its exports went to China, and 38 percent of its imports came from China.[59] The entrepôt function was interrupted by the Japanese occupation of Hong Kong from 1942 to 1945 and again by the Chinese revolution in 1949 and the Korean War in the early 1950s. Those international events proved a blessing in disguise for Hong Kong, which was forced to transform its economic base from the entrepôt-trading function to export-oriented manufacturing. Another advantage for Hong Kong at this time was the relocation—in the wake of the communist takeover—of a significant amount of industrial capital and enterprise from the mainland, especially from Guangzhou (Canton) and Shanghai. At the same time, millions of Chinese people fled the mainland seeking safe haven in Hong Kong, producing almost overnight a huge increase in the colony's population and a supply of cheap labor.[60]

A number of historical advantages worked to overcome its smallness and the virtual absence of natural resources. The development of a banking and insurance infrastructure had for close to a century supported the role of the colony as a transshipper of goods into and out of China. Industrial activities had also expanded, based largely on capital and enterprise from China. Hong Kong became famous for shipbuilding, as well as textiles and food production, with much of the productive capacity operating under foreign (mainly British) ownership. In the 1950s Hong Kong emerged from the devastation of World War II and the chaos of Japanese occupation and began to climb back to prewar levels in trade, and industry expanded to produce the consumer goods needed to support a rapidly growing population. Hong Kong's locational advantages, in addition to the supply of cheap labor provided by Chinese immigration and government policies allowing free trade, worked to encourage the inflow of foreign capital and the further development of banking, financial, and shipping services.

The diversification into export-oriented manufacturing was reinforced during the Korean War, the result of the trade embargo imposed on China. As exports from China declined, local industry received a shot in the arm, particularly in textiles, clothing, light metal goods, footwear, plastics, electronics, and optical instruments. During the 1970s, however, Hong Kong's comparative advantage in production was challenged, especially by East Asian nations, some of which had wage levels lower than Hong Kong's. The result was a gradual but perceptible shift toward sophisticated, higher-quality production—but with the clear emphasis still on exports.[61] That shift was demonstrated by the changing structure of exports from Hong Kong: In 1960 clothing represented 29 percent of the total, textiles 23 percent, electronics 2.5 percent, and precision instruments (watches and clocks) 0.7 percent; by 1988 the proportion of clothing was about the same (31 percent), but the textiles sector had fallen to only 7 percent; electronic goods and precision instruments had increased to 22.4 percent and 10 percent.[62] Hong Kong's manufacturing sector, unlike Taiwan's, was still dominated by labor-intensive operations, and the colony was not taking major strides toward high-tech production.

In statistical terms the growth of Hong Kong's export-oriented manufacturing brought about a lengthy period of hypergrowth. During the 1960s, for example, GDP growth exceeded 10 percent each year; the contribution of manufacturing to overall GDP increased from 20 percent to more than 30 percent; and by 1971 47 percent of Hong Kong's labor force were involved in manufacturing. Almost 30 percent of all manufacturing workers were engaged in the production of textiles, popularizing the "Made in Hong Kong" label that became known to the world. The driving force of the economy during the 1960s and 1970s was the export sector, which grew an average 11.5 percent per year, twice the world average. With a few brief exceptions the expansion of the economy generated a demand for labor that guaranteed close to full employment and a healthy annual increase in wages. Inflation remained low (around 4 percent per year) for most of the time, and the economy benefited from healthy injections of foreign capital.

Hong Kong has also made great gains from the huge "invisible" earnings that have come from the growing strength of its shipping, banking, insurance, and real estate activities; and, at least until 1997, Hong Kong was a major tourist attraction, which contributed significantly to the local economy.[63] The colony always maintained a healthy balance of payments, and the currency remained relatively stable. As most outsiders would conclude, Hong Kong was immensely successful, achieving rapid and sustained economic growth with relative price stability, rising real incomes, full employment, and a reasonable degree of income inequality.[64] Hong Kong's extraordinary economic performance from the 1960s through to the 1980s enabled it to catch up to some of the other economic giants around the world, particularly the United States and Britain. By 1988, for example, Hong Kong's GNP was close to 70 percent of that of the United Kingdom, 50 percent of that of the United States; by 1995 Hong Kong's per capita GNP (US$22,990) was in fact higher than Britain's, and 85 percent of that of the United States[65] (see Photos 11.3a and 11.3b).

The structural changes in Hong Kong's economy continued throughout the 1970s and

PHOTO 11.3a   Christmas in Kowloon, Hong Kong.

PHOTO 11.3b   Kowloon street scene.

1980s. The two major trends were toward higher-value-added goods (for example, garments and finished clothing increased relative to unfinished textile goods); and a shift toward the manufacture of electrical goods and appliances, such as watches and clocks. In the 1980s another shift in the labor market became noticeable, this time with a huge increase in the financial services sector, which had overtaken manufacturing as the largest employer group in the Hong Kong economy. The jobs were mainly in banking, investment facilities, insurance, real estate, and corporate services provided to foreign companies based in the colony. By 1991 manufacturing contributed only 15 percent of Hong Kong's GDP and only 33 percent of its workforce (see Tables 11.4a, 11.4b, and 11.4c).

By far the most impressive growth over the decades has come in world trade. In 1960 exports were valued at US$0.69 billion, twenty-seventh in the world; by 1985 exports were valued at $63.17 billion, tenth largest. In the 1950s and 1960s a sharp increase in industrial production meant that the export of domestically made goods began to outstrip the re-export of goods made elsewhere (mostly in China); by 1970 domestic exports outranked re-exports by more than four to one. Throughout the 1980s, however, with increasing economic integration between Hong Kong and southern China, as well as the shift of manufacturing plants to the mainland, re-exports grew rapidly. Much of the re-export business involved the repackaging and improved presentation of goods originally produced in China. By the end of the 1980s re-exports had moved ahead of domestic exports, and by the mid-1990s as much as one-third of Hong Kong's exports were re-exports of goods produced in China, primarily by Hong Kong–based companies.[66]

The traditional explanation for the economic success of Hong Kong—first as an exporter of industrial goods, then as a center for global and regional financial services—has been attributed to three sets of factors:

- the lack of interference by the state in the conduct of industry and commerce;

- the important role of a dynamic indigenous business elite; and
- a long period of relative political stability.[67]

Hong Kong became known as a place where, in economic issues at least, anything goes. *The Economist* magazine, for example, ranked Hong Kong number one in the world on its Economic Freedom Index, which grades countries on the extent to which government policies restrict or interfere with economic activities.[68] To investigate the forces underlying Hong Kong's emergence as an economic giant, it is useful to compare Hong Kong to Taiwan and mainland China. The simple two-by-two framework illustrated in Figure 11.1 shows Hong Kong as a laissez-faire economy, in which the state neither owns nor controls the means of production. It is generally assumed that in Hong Kong the state has deliberately adopted a low-key role in the economy, which serves the best interests of trade and industrial development.

The contrast between Hong Kong and Taiwan is significant, because in Taiwan the state clearly played an active role, particularly in finance and trade. It is important to note that the Hong Kong business elite has performed some of the same functions as the state in Taiwan. For example, local banks that have grown into global giants have effectively guided investment strategies and helped steer the colony toward rapid economic growth. Throughout the period of growth, the government, led by a small cadre of British-trained civil servants, has been able to either co-opt its critics or accommodate them through policy changes.[69] Among economists, the majority view is that the role of the government in Hong Kong throughout the period has been kept to a minimum: providing law and order and supervising land management. Yet throughout the period the government acted in a somewhat authoritarian fashion, with political power highly centralized in the colonial civil service. The net effect was that the people of Hong Kong never really experienced true representation in the political realm. Members of the business elite wanting to expand their influence over policy in their own

TABLE 11.4a Hong Kong: Employed Persons by Occupation (% of total workforce)

Occupation	1982	1987	1992	% Growth 1982–1992
Manufacturing Workers	48.2	47.9	33.3	−30.9
Professional, Technical, and Related Categories	6.6	7.1	9.1	+37.9
Administrative and Managerial	3.9	3.3	4.9	+25.6
Clerical Workers	14.7	17.3	20.4	+38.8
Sales Workers	9.9	11.0	12.8	+29.3
Others	1.6	1.6	0.8	−50.0
Total Employment (1,000s)	2,407	2,681	2,738	+13.8

SOURCE: Hong Kong Census and Statistics Department, 1993.

TABLE 11.4b Hong Kong: Persons Engaged in Selected Industry Sectors (in thousands)

Occupation	1982	1987	1991	% Growth 1982–1991
Manufacturing	847.2	867.9	565.1	−33.9
Building and Construction	82.1	72.5	59.5	−27.5
Wholesale, Retail, and Import/Export, Restaurants and Hotels	517.7	657.4	914.8	+76.7
Financing, Insurance, Real Estate, Business Services	116.1	212.2	314.8	+230.7

SOURCE: Hong Kong Census and Statistics Department, 1993.

TABLE 11.4c Hong Kong: Contribution of Economic Activities to GDP (%)

Occupation	1982	1987	1992	% Growth 1982–1992
Manufacturing	20.7	21.7	15.2	−26.6
Wholesale, Retail, and Import/Export, Restaurants and Hotels	19.1	23.2	25.4	+33.0
Financing, Insurance, Real Estate, Business Services	22.6	18.2	22.7	−0.14
Building and Construction	7.3	4.7	5.6	−23.3

SOURCE: Hong Kong Census and Statistics Department, 1993, Tables 2.3, 2.4, and 3.4, pp. 16 and 26.

interests were able to gain appointments to parliamentary bodies and the Legislative Council and Executive Council, but by the early 1980s Hong Kong could be characterized by a low level of political activism and was far from being a truly representative democracy.

A key advantage during the economic takeoff was access to a large, organizationally weak labor force. The owners of capital could always find people to work long hours in poor conditions for relatively low wages—without much trade union interference. The organizational weakness of the workforce stems from the colony's proximity to China, where a seemingly inexhaustible supply of workers was available. With new workers entering the colony every day as illegal immigrants from the mainland, existing workers no doubt became aware of their vulnerability and expendability. In addition, the majority of Hong Kong's manufacturing occurs in small and medium-sized factories, in which union activity is limited. The unions that do exist tend to operate on a small scale, and their activities have been circumscribed by government legislation.

Another common explanation for the success of Hong Kong's manufacturing-based economy has been the cultural predispositions of a society dominated by Confucian traditions. Until recently it was relatively common to hear arguments about the advantages of the Confucian value system for economic development (see Chapter 3). It was assumed that Confucianism somehow justified the existing hierarchy in society, whether in politics, family life, or the workplace. The net effect was that workers came to accept or believe that those in positions of authority will act with compassion toward them; they in return will work hard to reproduce the status quo without challenging apparent inequities. The stress on respect and loyalty to superiors is translated into an acceptance of conformity and a resignation toward the centralized, meritocratic bureaucracy—which is thus "allowed" to operate in a fairly authoritarian fashion. The Confucian system is also assumed to "breed" a particular type of industrial system that is organized in a community- or family-oriented way, with a strong emphasis on team spirit, mutual respect, and loyalty—all of which translates into a strong work ethic and a sense that labor is in itself a source of satisfaction outside its material benefits.[70] Although there is ongoing debate, some academic writers and journalists have concluded that societies with strongly Confucianist traditions have had a marked edge in the global economy during recent decades: "The Confucian value system encourages hard work, diligence and a reverential attitude toward education, given that such traits are widely perceived to be the most acceptable means of career-progression in a hierarchical system. This in turn implies that Confucianism encourages rapid human capital formation."[71] In an account of the emergence of the NIEs, for example, Simon Winchester portrayed a typically Confucian individual, Mr. Chan, who is an office manager in a company selling business machinery in Hong Kong:

> Mr. Chan comes into the office each morning at a quarter to nine. . . . He is never late, and will accept no excuse from anyone who is. . . . Those who struggle in after the deadline are fined—$50 for the first occasion, $100 for the next . . . and so on. . . . He runs the office along strictly hierarchical lines. Everyone . . . has a rank . . . from tea-boy . . . to section supervisor. . . . He insists on seeing all inbound correspondence, on signing and countersigning all outgoing papers, on approving all decisions. . . . He works unceasingly. . . . He says that to leave the office late gives him considerable status among his superiors. . . . He insists that he has a duty to work as hard as possible [and] to make as much money as possible to spend on the education of his two children. . . . He has taken only one seven-day holiday in the last three years. . . . Mr. Chan thinks of himself and his surroundings as Confucian. . . . He sees his devotion to his aged mother . . . his strict regard for punctuality, order and rank, his pride in his own achievements . . . as firm evi-

dence that he has learned much from the writings of the sage. He does not question the precepts.[72]

Winchester wants us to believe that the values and behaviors of Mr. Chan—and thousands of others like him—go a long way toward explaining the economic success of Hong Kong and its regional neighbors. The first reaction of the outsider, besides questioning the simplified and sweeping generalization, is to ask whether such behavior is indeed Confucian. The way Mr. Chan runs his business is surely far removed from the ideas of the "cultivated man" espoused by Confucius, and adopting some but not all of the Confucian values is arguably a perversion of everything the master stood for.

Although the Confucian model has some appeal, as a way of accounting for the East Asian economic miracles it raises more questions than it answers, especially in the late 1990s, after some of the miracle economies had plummeted. It is not correct, for example, to assume that all of the East Asian NIEs have the family-oriented organization assumed to be dominant in their economies. The model does not explain why economic success only came during the 1960s, after the societies had been dominated by Confucianism for centuries. There is also a problem explaining how economic success occurs in non-Confucian developing societies. On balance, it is perhaps prudent to contend that Confucianism is a contributing factor, one that plays a part in Hong Kong's economic growth, but that a number of other, more causally dominant factors are at work.[73]

Another caveat on the issue of state control and the extent to which it can account for the colony's mercurial rise: No doubt the Hong Kong government has remained in the background; Hong Kong is a free port, there are no exchange controls, no protection of industry, few restrictions on private property, low taxes, and virtually no state-owned enterprises. In this way Hong Kong sidestepped the import-substitution phase adopted in Taiwan and other

NIEs, so it was never necessary for the state to intervene with trade barriers to protect local industries or to make direct investment decisions for high-priority industries. An official statement released by the Hong Kong government in 1973 pointed this out: "Hong Kong is probably the only territory still completely faithful to liberal economic policies of free enterprise and free trade. . . . Economic planning is not a function of the government. . . . The government's role remains one of providing a suitable framework within which commerce and industry can function efficiently and effectively with a minimum of interference."[74]

In spite of such pronouncements the Hong Kong government—before 1997—played a significant role in directing and influencing the economy.[75] One such role, largely hidden, was providing subsidies to workers in the form of relatively low-cost food staples, particularly rice, fish, and vegetables, as well as public housing to a large portion of the population. Such government intervention contributed to Hong Kong's economic success in two ways: First, intervening in the supply and distribution of basic foodstuffs and subsidizing housing costs kept inflation to a minimum, helped stabilize local currency, attracted foreign investors, and boosted the lucrative tourist trade; second, subsidizing the major expenses of working-class households (i.e., food and housing) kept real wages relatively low, which helped Hong Kong's exports compete well in global markets.[76]

The Hong Kong government also provides infrastructure, especially transportation and port facilities, and builds human capital, particularly in education, health care, and social services. This indirect role is thought to have contributed to Hong Kong's overall economic competitiveness by providing a healthy, well-educated, decently housed population—all of which contributes positively to the production process. Expenditures on physical capital (infrastructure) and "social wages" increased significantly from the 1950s through the 1970s as a proportion of total government expenditures. Not surprisingly, government spending accounted for a growing share of Hong Kong's GDP throughout the period, from less than 3 percent in 1950 to more than 10 percent by the mid-1970s.

The Hong Kong government has also intervened directly in the real estate market, which puts it at or close to the center of economic operations. Much of the new development in Hong Kong prior to repatriation was in infrastructure, for example, the reclamation projects in the New Towns and the new airport on Lantau Island (which opened in July 1998). The government controls the supply of land directly through ownership and indirectly through land reclamation and by establishing land use and zoning requirements (see Photo 11.4).

The Hong Kong government is also responsible for constructing apartment housing and relocating industry, mostly in the New Territories since 1980. The government has undertaken to stabilize the financial sector, which helped ensure Hong Kong's attractiveness to foreign investors; it will step in to rescue failing banks, stabilize the Hong Kong dollar, and keep interest rates low. The government plays an active role in monetary matters and has, through its continued watchdog and supervisory activities, created a fiscal environment (i.e., low taxes) conducive to attracting domestic and foreign investment. When all of these subtle but very real contributions are considered, it is appropriate to question the assumption that the Hong Kong government follows the laissez-faire model. As J. R. Schiffer has pointed out:

Non-market forces intervene significantly in all factor markets, having the combined effect of lowering costs of production for small-scale industry, the backbone of Hong Kong's export-led growth. In the labor market, the prices of transport, rice and utilities are regulated; a large percentage of foodstuffs is produced in a centrally planned economy . . . and traded to Hong Kong at something other than free-market prices; health, education and shelter are subsidized. The labor supply is partly determined by regulated immigration from the PRC, labor demand is partly determined by the policies of the Hong Kong government, the largest employer.[77]

PHOTO 11.4   Land being reclaimed for a New Town in the New Territories, Hong Kong.

It is important to stress that before 1997 there were virtually no macroeconomic interventions in the Hong Kong economy, in the sense of development planning and the subsidization of crumbling state-owned industries, as in China and, to a lesser extent, Taiwan. Such activities are effectively ruled out by the nature of Hong Kong's industrial structure, because most enterprises are small-scale and labor-intensive and thus not amenable to economic planning; they also do not need large-scale subsidies and interventions. Yet many subtle and indirect interventions in the Hong Kong economy and a range of microeconomic strategies have been pursued. As one observer concluded, Hong Kong should no longer be championed as the quintessential example of freewheeling market economics: "When one takes all of [this] into account, perhaps it is . . . time to revise our views of this last bastion of unfettered capitalism."[78]

The Struggle for Hong Kong

Our Brother which art in Beijing
Xiaoping be thy name
United Kingdom gone
Thy will be done in here as it is in the
    Forbidden City
Give us this day our daily bet
And forgive us our speculations
As we forgive them that speculate against us
Lead us not into Communism
But deliver us from Gweilos
For thine is the sovereignty, the Power and the
    Territory
Forever and ever, Amen[79]

—Anonymous

As the 1997 handover approached, Hong Kong's people naturally became more sensitive to events occurring within the PRC, as this irreverent version of the Lord's Prayer suggests. It can be argued, however, that during the past decade the process of economic integration with China meant that Hong Kong's influence on the mainland continued to grow and that Hong Kongers thus need not fear that China

would do anything to sabotage or slow down economic growth. As more and more private capital entered southern China, the local economies in Guangdong were increasingly unhinged from the "plan" and were thrust more than ever into regional and global economies. With each passing year Hong Kong and southern China became increasingly interlocked and interdependent, to such an extent that some observers characterized the 1997 handover as a "sideshow"[80] (see Photo 11.5).

By the latest accounting, US$20 billion have been invested each way; it is also rumored that Hong Kong entrepreneurs employ more than 3 million workers in China and that more than one-third of the colony's currency is in common use in the mainland. Guangdong TVEs now invest in some of the choicest properties in Hong Kong's central financial district. Hong Kong businessmen regularly invest in the remotest mainland areas, opening restaurants

PHOTO 11.5   Popular T-shirt for sale in Hong Kong since the late 1980s.

and theme parks, building bridges, and sometimes even restructuring entire cities into small forests of skyscrapers leased as offices, hotels, and apartments.[81] Hong Kong is far and away the biggest "foreign" investor in China (see the discussion on Greater China in Chapter 17) and is China's major trading partner, for exports as well as imports. Much of this new activity began as a response to the transfer of Hong Kong to mainland sovereignty in 1997. It is important, therefore, to review, if only briefly, why and how the transfer was negotiated.

After 1949 the new Chinese government insisted that Hong Kong and the New Territories had been stolen by British imperialists during the nineteenth century. Instead of demanding decolonization, however, which would normally imply sovereignty and freedom for Hong Kong, the PRC tolerated the status quo, albeit reluctantly, until the early 1980s. At that time the British government began to negotiate a settlement, knowing that the expiration date for the New Territories lease was 1997. It was recognized that Hong Kong Island and Kowloon Peninsula depended heavily on the New Territories for food and as places to locate surplus population and industry, so a resolution of the lease issue was of utmost importance.

After protracted and often ill-natured negotiations an agreement was reached in 1984, stipulating that China would regain sovereignty over Hong Kong in 1997, with the British continuing to be responsible for the administration of the colony until then.[82] The Chinese agreed that they would establish the Hong Kong Special Administrative Region (HKSAR) with "a high degree of autonomy," except in the areas of foreign affairs and defense. It was specified that the laws currently in force in Hong Kong would remain unchanged and that the economic system would not be altered for at least fifty years. The Joint Declaration issued by Britain and China put it this way:

> The current social and economic systems in Hong Kong will remain unchanged, and so will one's life style. Rights and freedoms, including

those of the person, of speech, of the press, of assembly . . . will be ensured by law.[83]

The PRC identified its basic policies toward Hong Kong in the Joint Declaration, which provided the blueprint for a miniconstitution (known locally before 1997 as the "Basic Law"). Most worrisome for Hong Kong residents, as well as the British, were and are provisions in the Basic Law that prohibit treason, sedition, subversion, and what is euphemistically referred to as "the theft of state secrets" (Article 23). Another provision allows China, rather than the government of Hong Kong, to declare a state of emergency in the event of threats to local security (Article 18). Although the Joint Declaration guarantees autonomy to the HKSAR, many people are afraid that the Chinese government will renege if a real emergency arises.

Hong Kong's decolonization was destined to follow this unique trajectory. As one observer has pointed out, "There was certainly no precedent for returning close to 6 million people to the rule of those from whom most of them had fled."[84] China had promised Hong Kong that the principle of "one country, two systems" would be resolutely followed (being the same principle Beijing has used to lure Taiwan back into the Chinese world). After Tiananmen Square, however, many people in Hong Kong were anxious, distressed, and uncertain about what they should do. Those who were wealthy enough set out to establish permanent residency and then citizenship in other countries for themselves and their families. Many hoped it would never be necessary to emigrate, but after Tiananmen Square more Hong Kongers than ever began to express such fears by "voting with their feet," with more than 60,000 emigrating every year, mainly to the United States, Canada, and Australia.[85]

In 1992 Chris Patten was appointed the new governor. The arrival of Patten, a close associate of British Prime Minister John Major and the former chair of the Conservative Party, signaled a new direction for British policy; it would also bring Britain and China into direct conflict, which lasted until the very eve of transfer. Wasting no time, Patten set out to broaden the democratic base by expanding the franchise for elections to the Legislative Council, lowering the voting age, and replacing corporate with individual voting. In Patten's own words: "The best guarantee of Hong Kong's prosperity for as far ahead as any of us can see or envisage is to protect our way of life. . . . An integral part of this way of life . . . is the participation of individual citizens in the conduct of Hong Kong's affairs."[86]

Governor Patten attempted to introduce such concepts as accountability and direct representation to ensure that by 1997 a significant amount of democratization would have been imposed. Patten was operating on two major assumptions: First, after 1997 there would be few opportunities to instill democratic changes; second, the process of building democracy would be irreversible by the time the Chinese took over Hong Kong. Patten attempted to implant parliamentary-style government, casting the British as the moral protector of the Hong Kong people and allowing him to preside over the British "exit in glory." During the transition Hong Kongers would be protected, yet Patten also hoped they would become more assertive in demanding and exercising political rights.

The PRC, by comparison, was cast by Patten as the opposition party, constraining or holding up the democratization process. The Chinese government, in response to Patten's proposals, consistently reiterated the themes that were first voiced in Deng Xiaoping's one country–two systems concept.[87] The first theme was the insistence that Patten's proposals "violated" the letter and spirit of the Joint Declaration and ignored the principle of "convergence" with the Basic Law.[88] By introducing his proposals for changes in the 1994 and 1995 elections, Patten's actions (according to the PRC) constituted a unilateral termination of ongoing negotiations; in the PRC's understanding, election issues in Hong Kong were to be negotiated between Britain and China. What followed was a vituperative war of words: Patten was referred to as a "serpent," a "prostitute," and a "criminal down the ages." As one Beijing official put it, "Deep in

his soul are all the deep-rooted bad habits of an extremely arrogant colonist who benefits himself at the expense of others."[89] Ma Yuzhen, China's ambassador to Britain, was certainly not holding back in 1994 when he said, "In the absence of an agreement between China and Britain, China will definitely disband and reestablish Hong Kong's three-tier councils . . . on July 1st 1997. Politically, China will resume the exercise of sovereignty over Hong Kong."[90]

The China threat, which had hung over the negotiations since the mid-1980s, was thus renewed in the early 1990s. The British were warned in no uncertain terms that they needed to back down, and it was implicit that not doing so would be interpreted as deliberately hostile, a direct challenge to Chinese sovereignty. The Chinese threatened to break all contracts pertaining to British business that continued after 1997 and to delay the starting date for construction of the huge new airport (which they did effectively until 1995).[91]

At this point even some British observers felt that Governor Patten was overstepping his powers. Sir Percy Craddock, who had been ambassador to China and was the chief negotiator for the Joint Declaration, felt that Patten's actions represented a real threat to the Chinese and that they, in turn, would take out their resentment on the people of Hong Kong. As Craddock observed: "Heroics are fine when you face the consequences yourself. But heroics at someone else's expense, particularly someone to whom you stand in a position of trust, is another matter."[92]

The second theme evident in the Chinese response to Patten's proposals was an appeal to nationalism. This involved repeating the litany of colonial expansionism of the British, who, it was argued, had plundered China and Hong Kong persistently during the nineteenth century. Party propagandists argued that the PRC needed to act decisively to wipe out the shame of the past and to unify the Chinese by "remapping" Hong Kong as an integral part of China. Interestingly, this form of top-down nationalism was quite different from many of the grassroots movements occurring in other parts of the world, where issues of self-determination and democratization were always close to the surface. As far as Beijing was concerned Hong Kong was an integral part of China, and it was anticipated that the former colony would serve as the gateway for China's ongoing program of modernization. Hong Kong, in other words, would be able to lead the way toward the creation of a Greater China that would eventually include Taiwan as well.[93]

To move toward that desirable future, the Chinese government began to solicit support from the richest and most influential members of Hong Kong society. Members of the business and professional elites were co-opted by being asked to serve as "advisers" to the PRC. They were invited to Beijing, wined and dined, and presented with certificates attesting to their patriotism as Chinese people. Other groups, such as the Hong Kong Federation of Trade Unions and the Democratic Alliance for Betterment of Hong Kong, as well as the Liberal Party (committed to opposing Patten's proposals), were also co-opted by the Chinese. In this way the Beijing government established what amounted to a multiclass bloc of support within Hong Kong, functioning more or less openly as a quasi-governmental alliance of groups acting as an alternative to the Legislative Council, which the Chinese considered to be a tool of colonial administration. Some very important figures in Hong Kong were willing to accept appointments to these Beijing-controlled "advisory" groups because it allowed them to be flexible, in the sense that they were appearing to support China, yet they could wait opportunistically to see which way the wind blew after 1997.[94] Many of them already had citizenship certificates and permanent residency secured in other countries for themselves and their families in the event of a radical decline in Hong Kong's situation after 1997.

As this brief summary indicates, the struggle for dominance in Hong Kong pitted the British and the Chinese against each other, each government attempting to line up allies within the Hong Kong population. Stacked up against the Beijing advisory groups was a multiclass set of

Patten-democratization supporters, including government civil servants, democracy-minded capitalists, and a range of newly formed middle- and working-class groups representing academic social workers, liberal traders and merchants, and workers, as well as the loose-knit Democratic Party (representing liberals wary of China's motives and future actions).

In other words, on the eve of handover Hong Kong was politically divided into two opposing blocs, each seeking its own future for Hong Kong. On one side a collection of groups wanted to keep open the discourse over further democratization, placing them in direct opposition to the PRC government. For its part the PRC was attempting to hold together an opposition bloc by appealing to Chinese nationalism. The outcome depended largely on the balance of forces between and within the alliances that emerged on either side. That balance was tipped one way or the other by the continuing rounds of negotiations between the "conscious agents" (representatives of the British and Chinese governments). The complexity of the debate resulted in a multiplicity of meanings, which "in the short term . . . enable[d] . . . individuals/groups to form new allies and, in the long term, may significantly change the political opportunity structure."[95]

For China Governor Patten represented a "walking nightmare," someone who stirred up ethnic Chinese sentiments on the streets of a city that was supposed to pass peacefully to its rightful owner.[96] It is not clear to outside observers what Patten's (as well as the British government's) goals were throughout this process. Some have suggested that Britain merely wanted to do the right thing by fostering democratization at the eleventh hour in Hong Kong. Others believe that greater freedoms and guarantees did need to be built into the Hong Kong political system before 1997. At present it is too soon to gauge whether Patten's actions succeeded in installing a protective structure that will nurture a democratic system that Beijing would not dare disturb. Patten seemed to genuinely believe that it was immoral to grovel before the Chinese, as he thinks many world governments (including his own) have done in the past. As Patten discovered, dealing with the Chinese is like trying to eat *pao mogu* (Chinese dried mushrooms), which need to soften before cooking and require infinite patience in the kitchen. In spite of this hard-line stance against Beijing, the threats from the Chinese did not materialize. In local parlance, "The skies have not fallen, the stock market has not collapsed, and Beijing will not turn off the water."[97] The risks are great, however, and Patten, if nothing else, proved to be a poker-faced gambler.

In the summer of 1995—with the handover less than two years away—some Patten supporters began to question whether he would be able to stay the course in the standoff. In the case of the agreement to create the Court of Final Appeal, the original stand by Patten and London was that the court must be in place before 1997. In June 1995 the two sides struck a deal that would establish the court on June 1, 1997, the first day of Chinese rule (the court would replace the British Privy Council as the last resort for legal appeals in Hong Kong).[98] In this instance Patten was accused of kowtowing to Beijing by giving the Chinese full control over the court from day one. The fear was that rather than operating according to the principle of international common law the court would embrace what is euphemistically referred to as "common law with Chinese characteristics," a rather worrisome prospect for the rule of law. Patten considered the arrangement to be the only viable possibility and, by reaching the agreement, had hoped that the two sides would be able to reach compromises in other areas.

The last election held before the 1997 handover was scheduled for September 17, 1995. By then the pro-China forces had regrouped (after earlier defeats) to form a party that was officially endorsed by China: the Democratic Alliance for the Betterment of China (DAB). The party did well in municipal elections that March and reportedly was gaining strong support from lower- and middle-income voters as an alternative to the two other parties (the radically anti-China Democratic Party and the business-oriented Liberal Party). The DAB's slogan was "Love Hong Kong, Love China," and its performance in the September 1995 election would be a barometer of overall enthusiasm for Beijing. Even DAB opponents hoped it would show well in the election, as it was feared that a poor showing might prompt China to adopt a tougher approach toward the territory. If the DAB experienced important gains, however, and a large number of pro-Chinese candidates were voted into the Legislative Council, Beijing might—it was argued—be encouraged to allow Hong Kong's "parliament" to continue to exist after 1997 (which it had publicly threatened not to do on a number of occasions). DAB candidates campaigned on general issues—jobs, housing, public services, the environment—in attempting to go beyond the traditionally liberal Hong Kong issues of democracy and human rights. It was hoped that the voters might be more in tune with such everyday concerns. The DAB had strong ties to Hong Kong's largest labor union, the Hong Kong Federation of Trade Unions, which helped curry votes from the working classes. Xinhua, the official Chinese news agency, openly supported the DAB, which rose from eighth to third in popularity in a pre-election poll. The DAB also had the support of the Beijing-controlled Bank of China and had plenty of cash.[99]

The voter turnout at the election was low (less than 40 percent), but in absolute terms the number of voters had increased to 2.57 million (from 1.9 million in 1991, the last election in Hong Kong). The results marked a clear victory for the Democratic Party (DP), which had been formed in 1994 out of the two existing pro-democratic groups: the United Democrats and the Meeting Point. All major leaders of the DP were elected, and as one observer pointed out: "Being a staunch critic of China, particularly of China's policies towards Hong Kong, the D.P.'s victory was generally interpreted as reflecting Hong Kong's defiance vis-à-vis China."[100] The DAB was comprehensively defeated, with even some of its main leaders failing to get themselves elected. It had, however, registered its presence, and along with other pro-Beijing members of the Legislative Council the small number of DAB seats now formed a bloc that could make its presence felt in the future. In terms of overall votes cast, the DAB received more than 40 percent, which indicates a significant level of popular support, making it (DAB) Hong Kong's second largest party. The capacity of the DAB to mobilize at the grassroots level was clearly evident, and in this regard it was well ahead of other parties. Given the fact that Hong Kong would be dominated by China's presence in the run-up to 1997—and certainly after 1997—it was clear that the DAB would be playing a much more prominent role in the future.

Last Words: Predicting and Planning for the Future in Hong Kong

In addition to its striking harbor and dazzling skyline, Hong Kong has been on the cutting edge of modern urban planning for decades. In the early 1970s the government announced a blueprint for the development of New Towns in the New Territories, and to date eight New Towns have been built, located roughly twenty-five kilometers from downtown Hong Kong; a ninth is under construction on Lantau Island adjacent to the new airport at Chek Lap Kok. The planners, borrowing from the model implemented in Britain in earlier decades, envisioned New Towns as self-contained residential, manufacturing, and commercial centers. They were intended to provide decent, inexpensive housing to Hong Kong's crowded population; to alleviate the pressures of high-density living, particularly on Hong Kong Island and Kowloon Peninsula; and to provide ample space for industrial development in open-field sites, which would allow a switch from the traditional high-rise factories in the crowded residential areas of Kowloon and the Central District of Hong Kong Island.[101]

The original idea was to create relatively small communities with adjacent industrial zones to reduce the overall amount of commuting, and since the early 1970s there has been a vast amount of new construction in the New Territories as the New Towns took shape.

Within a decade modern apartment towers had sprung up from what had once been rice fields or on land newly reclaimed from the sea; thousands of families were able to move out of the crowded inner city into reasonably priced and relatively spacious flats. The population of Hong Kong Island remained stable, at 22–23 percent of the total, with a small amount of absolute growth through the 1980s and early 1990s. By contrast the population of Kowloon shrunk considerably, as most of the dilapidated housing areas, including the infamous walled city, were torn down. The proportion of Hong Kong's population living in Kowloon fell from more than 55 percent in 1971 to 34 percent in 1992; correspondingly, the New Territories have experienced massive growth, from 17 percent to almost 44 percent of the total.

The New Towns planning program successfully shifted the population away from crowded core areas, but there has been much less success in attracting jobs to the New Territories, which thwarted the goal of self-sufficiency.[102] Although a subway was built to connect the closer parts of the New Territories, the lack of mass transit into Kowloon and Hong Kong Island means that in the absence of local employment opportunities many inhabitants in more distant New Towns have a torturous daily commute to work. One of the reasons for the failure to expand the employment base of the New Towns has been the overall decline of manufacturing in Hong Kong relative to the growth of its service-based economy. Most new jobs have been in financial and business services, as well as tourism and consumer service, and most have of necessity remained in Hong Kong's traditional business districts rather than move to the New Towns.[103] The most dramatic cause of the problem, however, has been the relocation of hundreds of Hong Kong factories into mainland China. Setting up businesses, particularly in the SEZs and Open Cities, has become much easier. It has been estimated that a half-million blue-collar jobs have been shifted into Guangdong Province alone, jobs that might otherwise have been located in the New Towns.[104] This phenomenon could not have been anticipated in the 1970s, when the original plans for Hong Kong's New Towns were announced.

In response to the problems faced by the 2.5 million people now living in the New Territories, ambitious new infrastructure plans were announced, including a new railway line connecting the New Towns in the western New Territories (Yuen Long, Tuen Mau, and Tin Shui Wai) to southern Kowloon, as well as the extension of a new subway line to Tseung Kwan O in the southeastern New Territories. Such projects will add to vast infrastructural developments currently transforming Hong Kong in association with the building of the international airport on Lantau Island west of Hong Kong. In all, ten projects made up the Hong Kong Airport Core Program, which was, according to one observer, "in scope and price . . . the largest single public works project under way in the world"[105] (see Photos 11.6a and 11.6b). After wrangling back and forth on building of the new airport, the British and Chinese governments reached agreement in summer 1995 to complete the airport.

The new airport will take pressure off the overstrained airport in Kowloon, and because it is several miles offshore and to the west of downtown Hong Kong, it will be able to offer round-the-clock service, thereby vastly increasing international access to Hong Kong. The downside of the project, however, in addition to the enormous environmental impacts, is its distance from the central business districts. This means that the other infrastructure projects are essential to the success of the new airport. For example, the new bridge (the Lantau Fixed Crossing) is the largest suspension bridge in Asia; a new railway has been built to connect the airport with downtown Hong Kong; there is a 12.5-kilometer expressway on the northern shore of Lantau Island, connecting with another new expressway from the bridge to West Kowloon; and there is a six-lane road tunnel (the Western Harbor Crossing) connecting the airport with Hong Kong Island and downtown Kowloon.

Work has also begun on two massive reclamation projects, one developing new land for a container terminal in West Kowloon, the other for new urban developments in the Central District of Hong Kong Island. By 1994 scores of construction contracts worth more than US$8.7 billion had been awarded, mostly to consulting and construction companies from Japan, Britain, and Hong Kong. Seven of the projects were being funded as direct capital works projects and, therefore, did not require loan approval from China. The airport and the new railway, however, needed China's approval, which accounted for the interminable and costly delays throughout the early 1990s.[106] When the new airport finally opened in 1998 there were predictable problems, but once they had been overcome the rail connection began to operate like clockwork, speeding passengers toward the city in air-conditioned luxury.

Despite continued uncertainty as to China's actions toward Hong Kong after 1997, the economic reforms in China are continuing to produce impressive growth statistics. According to many pundits in Hong Kong, China will not want to kill the goose that lays the golden eggs, but Governor Patten, in his usually abrasively cynical fashion, has pointed out that Chinese history is replete with dead geese. As Martin Lee, Hong Kong's leading liberal and a staunch opponent of the PRC, has indicated, "The Chinese are more concerned with control than prosperity. They don't seem to care whether the goose will continue to lay golden eggs. They just want to control the goose."[107]

Before 1997, particularly after the events of 1995 and 1996, there were good reasons to agree with Mr. Lee's gloomy statement. The Chinese government appeared to be making a nuisance of itself globally, with a combination of bullying tactics, aggressively nationalistic sentiments, inappropriate behaviors, and politically incorrect statements. This is occurring in many areas, including intellectual property theft; human rights abuses (worsened by capturing and threatening Harry Wu, a U.S. citizen and former political dissident); aggressiveness toward Taiwan; insensitivity toward women who came to Beijing to attend a United Nations conference on population and development in

PHOTO 11.6a   Plane landing at the old airport in Kowloon.

PHOTO 11.6b   The bridge to Lantau Island and the new airport.

PHOTO 11.7a
Election day in Hong Kong, May 24, 1998.

1995; and harsh treatment of political dissidents, including lengthy jail sentences meted out to individuals attempting to set up the China Democratic Party in December 1998. Despite such public hostility, the prospects for growing economic integration between China and its offshore territories look promising, and there has been an unwillingness to upset the apple cart.

Travelers to Hong Kong since 1997 have been returning with mixed stories. Some are convinced that nothing of significance has changed, although far more people than ever are allowed to vote (see Photos 11.7a and 11.7b).[108] Others, especially those who have spent any time speaking to Hong Kong residents, are telling stories of leaner times.

Hong Kong's economic growth rate is down; unemployment is rising; and demand for consumer goods—in the Mecca of consumption—is falling. Workers in the service industries, including retail and tourism, are noticing a sharp drop in their trade, and many residents are looking for second jobs to make ends meet. Some observers think this is simply a transition phase; others are concerned for the long term. The very rich are not overly concerned, because they have been studiously stashing capital elsewhere. The most likely losers will be the ones unable to leave, as well as those with nobody to arrange visas for them to live in the new subur-

ban "Chinatowns" in Australia, New Zealand, Canada, and the United States. It is still too soon to see which way the wind is blowing, and as we have seen in China before, jumping to conclusions is a hazardous business.

PHOTO 11.7b   Election day in Hong Kong, May 24, 1998.

PART 4

Contested Lives and Landscapes in Contemporary China

12

China's Minorities: Ethnicity, Accommodation, and Resistance

*Transforming Tibet into a modern society is perfectly compatible
with preserving its rich language, culture, and religion, and . . .
it is in the interests of both sides to facilitate such a development.
Political freedom in the Western sense is secondary to preserving
ethnic, demographic, and cultural homogeneity.*

—Melvyn Goldstein, *The Snow Lion and the Dragon* (1997)[1]

Introduction: China's Minority Peoples

As Chinese civilization spread outward from the core region of the Yellow River, many of the minority cultures encountered on the periphery were assimilated. Most outsiders have traditionally considered the Chinese to be a monoethnic people, but there has been considerable ethnic mixing from the earliest times.[2] The resulting ethnic diversity brought vitality and cultural richness to Chinese life, but it has also provided a challenge for the state at various times. In the 1950s the new socialist state, following the precedent set by the Soviet Union, began the process of officially recognizing minority groups. The areas dominated by minority people were designated as "autonomous" units: Autonomous Regions were established at the provincial level, and autonomous counties and prefectures were created at lower levels.[3]

The great majority of the Chinese (more than 90 percent) are known as Han people, a label used by the Chinese to describe themselves since the Han Dynasty (207 B.C.–A.D. 220). In the 1990s there were fifty-six government-recognized minority groups (*minzu*) and

a total population of more than 90 million minority people. Official recognition brings preferential treatment from the government in many areas, including economic aid, educational support, and exemptions from the one-child policy (at least for some groups). Such favorable economic policies are consistent with China's modernization drive, but it is likely that the underlying reasons for these policies are largely geopolitical. Most minority groups are located in borderlands, including some of the largest groups, such as Koreans, Mongolians, Uigurs, Kazaks, and Tibetans. The Chinese government has been keen to appease these groups to counteract nationalist sentiments and calls for secession, an especially sensitive issue in light of the breakup of the Soviet Union. As one observer has pointed out, the government is not likely to enjoy the prospect "that the Uigurs of Xingjiang should threaten allegiance to the [former] Soviet Union."[4] Relationships between the state and the minority groups have often been extremely sensitive, partly because of differences in language, culture, and lifestyle, partly because of sharp discrepancies in wealth between the core and the periphery. Some minority groups have been criticized by the state, even denounced, for being more primitive in their cultural practices than is the norm for China in its current modernizing phase, and they have been encouraged to abandon what the state defines as "feudal" practices.[5]

Some of the borderlands have been contested for decades, as they are of great strategic importance.[6] It is no surprise, then, that the government seeks to ensure that populations in border regions are not antagonistic toward it. Many of the minority-dominated areas are also rich in raw materials: Oil is abundant in Heilongjiang and Xinjiang; tin and copper in Yunnan and Guizhou; uranium in Xinjiang; and the remaining forestlands in the mountainous areas. The minority regions also possess the most precious commodity of all in China—virgin land—which has been used for numerous resettlement projects to ease population pressures in the eastern provinces.[7] There is also a significant public relations dimension in favoring minority groups. The government likes to refer to its minority groups in positive terms, primarily to foster the image of the socialist state as a happy multicultural family that stands in sharp contrast to ethnic strife in many other parts of the world.[8]

In addition to the political argument, many minority groups are clearly in need of economic and other assistance. Most of the minority people live in areas where economic development and living standards are considerably below the norm. In part because they are located in peripheral areas, partly because of a legacy of discrimination, many minority people are significantly poorer than the national average (see Table 12.1, which shows that minority people in three areas are significantly overrepresented in the lowest income groups).

The available evidence indicates that after more than four decades of development under socialism, minority group incomes are still significantly below the average. In part this reflects the centuries of marginalization that minority peoples have encountered. At the start of the twentieth century, for example, the Han majority had already pushed their settlement areas into and beyond lands best suited to arable crop production. This meant that in many instances the minority groups encountered by the Han were forced to retreat to more marginal locations in hilly or arid areas.[9]

After the 1949 socialist revolution the successful extension of public health services, combined with the more liberal birth control policies, resulted in rapid population growth in physical environments that were vulnerable to ecological pressures.[10] With constraints on migration during the first three decades of the socialist era, there were few release valves for population pressures building in the minority areas, many of which had not benefited much from the agricultural and industrial growth experienced in other parts of China during socialist reconstruction.[11]

Thus many of the minority areas were significantly poorer that the rest of China. One researcher has calculated that the rate of poverty in the rural minority areas averaged 20 percent,

TABLE 12.1   Percentage of Minority Groups in the Lowest Income Decile for Selected Regions of China

Minority Group	Province/Municipality		
	Beijing	Guangdong	Liaoning
Hui	29.6	—	—
Manchu	35.7	—	18.3
Li	—	47.7	—
Mongol	—	—	22.8

SOURCE: The World Bank (1992), p. 44 (from State Statistical Bureau Statistics).
NOTE: The Beijing sample was 3.3% Hui and 2.2% Manchu; the Guangdong sample was 2.2% Li; the Liaoning sample was 16.7% Manchu and 2.4% Mongol.

about double the rate for the whole of the country.[12] If that estimate is correct, then some 16 million minority people live in absolute poverty as officially defined by the state. In Yunnan Province, for example, it has been estimated that 9.4 million of the province's 11.4 million minority people live in poverty.[13] The evidence also indicates that human and physical infrastructure is often poorly developed.[14] One of the most disturbing aspects is education, with rates being much lower in minority areas.[15] Compounding language and cultural difficulties, lack of schooling and training puts minority people at considerable disadvantage when seeking jobs and higher education. In this sense, the government's affirmative action policies—including the establishment of minority-only universities—can be interpreted as an attempt to redress the negative effects of past discrimination and inequality.

In recent years there has been marked liberalization of official policy toward minority groups, which has resulted in two significant trends: an increased rate of ethnic identification; and a growing degree of ethnic diversity, particularly in the cities. Recent census data show that the populations of almost all minority groups have grown much faster than the population overall (see Table 12.2).

In fact rapid population growth among minority groups has been occurring for several decades. From 1964 to 1978, for example, the number of minorities increased by almost 70 percent, compared to 43 percent growth for the Han majority. This continued throughout the 1980s, with the number of minorities expanding from 6.7 percent of total population (67 million) to the current 9 percent (91 million).[16]

There are two possible explanations: the growth in birthrates for minorities made possi-

TABLE 12.2   Population of China's Twenty Largest Minority Groups and Growth Rates, 1982–1990

Nationality	1990 Census	% Growth, 1982–1990
Total	1,133,682,501	12.5
Han	1,042,482,187	10.8
Zhuang	15,489,630	15.7
Manchu	9,821,180	128.2
Hui	8,602,978	19.0
Miao	7,398,135	46.9
Uygur	7,214,431	21.0
Yi	6,572,173	20.4
Tujia	5,704,223	101.2
Mongolian	4,806,849	40.7
Tibetan	4,593,330	18.8
Bouyei	2,545,059	19.9
Dong	2,514,041	76.3
Yao	2,134,013	52.6
Korean	1,920,597	8.7
Bai	1,594,827	40.9
Hani	1,253,952	18.4
Kazak	1,111,718	22.4
Li	1,110,900	35.8
Dai	1,025,128	21.9
She	630,378	70.9
Lisu	574,856	19.5

SOURCES: Adapted from *Beijing Review,* December 24–30, 1990, p. 34; and Mackerras (1994), Table 9.1, pp. 238–240.

ble by relaxation of the one-child policy; and an increased rate of self-identification. The census data for 1990 indicate that fertility rates were significantly higher for minority women than for Han women, and in the latter part of the 1980s attempts were made to reduce overall fertility rates in minority areas (see Table 12.3). There is general agreement, however, that attempts to implement the one-child policy were much less stringent among minority populations; most minority families are allowed to have two or more children. As a result, the total fertility rates for many minority groups were above 3; in 1990 nearly 16 percent of all births among minority women were fourth or higher parity births (compared to 6 percent for the Han majority).[17]

Thus for some minority groups the sharp population increase is partly related to differences in the way the one-child policy was administered, yet increases of the magnitude illustrated in Table 12.3 suggest that other forces must be at work. Most observers would agree there is a significantly higher rate of self-identification among China's minority groups.[18] This is an indication of the growing sense of ethnic consciousness in contemporary China, which may be attributable, in part at least, to the desire to take advantage of preferential treatment in labor recruitment, school admissions, university placement, and work assignments.

There is considerable evidence that China's cities, especially in the booming coastal provinces, are becoming increasingly diverse in ethnic terms.[19] This can be explained in part by the huge increase in rural-to-urban migration currently under way in China (see Chapter 15). It is likely that many of the new transients are minority people lured to the cities by the new climate of ethnic tolerance and the opportunity for employment; in the process they identify themselves as minority persons to take advantage of affirmative action policies. Moreover, the economic reforms have resulted in rapid industrialization in coastal areas and growth in private enterprises in the informal urban economy, which has attracted many new entrepreneurs. Some are from minority groups, especially Hui (Muslim) people.[20] Ethnic diversity is also increasing as a result of intermarriage between Han and non-Han people. Some researchers have suggested that the growing pride in announcing membership of a minority group means that people yearn to be viewed as "ethnic," and there is evidence that more young Han people are willing to consider minority spouses.[21]

Surprisingly, until recently the multiethnicity of Chinese society was largely overlooked by outsiders, in part because they represent less than 10 percent of total population, and also because the government has traditionally emphasized homogeneity among Chinese people.[22] Yet in recent years studies of China's ethnic minority groups have been published by outsiders as well as by Chinese scholars.[23] Still, despite the reluctance among foreigners to explore China's minority populations, ethnic

TABLE 12.3   Total Fertility Rates for Minority Women Compared to Han Women in Four Autonomous Regions of China

	Inner Mongolia		Guangxi		Ningxia		Xinjiang	
Years	Mongolian	Han	Zhuang	Han	Hui	Han	Uygur	Han
1970–1974	6.07	5.05	5.54	5.25	6.70	5.48	6.13	5.20
1975–1979	3.68	3.05	5.16	4.26	6.61	4.06	5.87	3.69
1980–1984	3.33	2.43	4.35	3.65	5.45	3.05	6.03	2.77
1985–1987	2.90	1.92	3.94	3.34	3.56	2.57	5.38	2.50

SOURCE: Adapted from Facts on File (1994), *China Facts and Figures Annual*, p. 313 (data from *Population and Economics*, June 25, 1992).

pluralism has consistently been recognized in public pronouncements by leaders. In 1981, for example, Deng Xiaoping told the people how important it was for China to recognize its minorities, stressing that "we must take effective measures to conscientiously strengthen the national autonomous regions of various nationalities."[24]

State Policy Toward Ethnic Minorities

In the spring of 1989 the Chinese government listened sympathetically to a group of young Muslim militants on the streets of Beijing who were protesting the publication of a book they considered slanderous to Islam.[25] As the world witnessed, the government was much less sympathetic to the student protesters in Tiananmen Square a few weeks later, which suggests that at the end of the 1980s it was more acceptable to challenge the state on issues of ethnicity than on issues of democracy and human rights. During the reform era the state has generally been supportive of groups wanting to celebrate ethnic differences, yet there is evidence that gaining ethnic minority status is a public embarrassment and a frustration to some people. Some want to hide their heritage, whereas others want desperately to be officially recognized. This is a recent trend, so it is important to look at it as part of a process whereby people living in society's cultural core attempt to "civilize" those on the periphery. We illustrate this point using case studies that describe the creation and maintenance of ethnic identity in contemporary China.

As might be anticipated in a multiethnic society, the forces of modernization in contemporary China are resulting in a gradual process of assimilation, generally referred to as "Sinicization" or "Hanification."[26] Most of the changes are unidirectional, that is, from the strong (the Han-dominated state) to the weak (the minority groups). The preamble of the 1982 constitution announces unequivocally

that chauvinism would not be tolerated: "In the struggle to safeguard the unity of the nationalities it is necessary to . . . combat local-national chauvinism."[27] Observers may have taken this to mean that minorities would gradually be forced to submit to the wishes of the central government, but it is important to note that the Chinese constitution clearly states that "vigilance" is needed to combat "big-nation chauvinism" (often referred to as "Han chauvinism") to protect the minority groups. Again quoting from the constitution: "The State does its utmost to promote the common prosperity of all nationalities in the country." There are other provisions in the 1982 constitution to safeguard minority rights, for example, in outlawing discrimination against and oppression of any nationality as well as acts that threaten to undermine the unity of the nationalities.[28]

A brief historical analysis reveals that policies toward minority groups in China have passed through several stages. In the formative years of the Chinese Communist Party—the 1920s and early 1930s—Mao Zedong and other top officials openly advocated the right of self-determination and secession for China's minority groups. Those views apparently changed in the years immediately before the Communist takeover in 1949: Party leaders observed the effects of the separation of Outer Mongolia from China as a result of Soviet intervention, as well as the destabilizing influence of a foreign presence in or close to Chinese territory, as in Xingjiang (the Soviets) and Manchuria (the Japanese). From the mid-1930s on, therefore, the Party shifted to more centrist views on minorities, with two principles repeatedly emphasized: All minorities were to enjoy equal rights in self-administration, economics, and cultural issues; and all minorities were to share the unity of the motherland with the Han. Such sentiments reappeared in discourses about minority groups, which generally reiterated that China must be "one state [with] many nationalities" and that there was "unity in diversity." These principles were elaborated upon and codified into law after 1949, emphasizing the equality, autonomy, and freedom of expression in language, religion, and cultural practices.[29]

History since 1949 demonstrates that official minority policy shifted from accommodation, inclusiveness, and ethnic pluralism to forced assimilation. Political scientist Alan Liu has suggested that relationships between the state and minority groups after 1949 can be subdivided into three distinct eras:[30]

- During the "reactive" ethnicity period in the 1950s some minority groups (most notably Tibetans) began to exhibit greater ethnic solidarity, largely in response to actions taken by the state.
- During the "abeyance" period (1958–1977) ethnic opposition was muted, mainly due to the state's repressive activities.
- During the "heterotropic" ethnicity period after 1978, relationships between ethnic groups and the state have taken a number of different forms, including demands for greater ethnic solidarity, calls for ethnic separatism, and state assimilation (or co-optation) of ethnic groups.

During the 1950s two sets of state behaviors were likely to prompt reaction from ethnic groups: the state's "civilizing" work, which involved attempts to establish the so-called autonomous areas; and collectivization of economic life. Although the state viewed these activities as being in the best interests of all Chinese people, including minorities, there were numerous cases of ethnic unrest, sometimes leading to local uprisings, particularly among Hui people in various parts of China and, by 1959, in Tibet.

The leaning toward ethnic pluralism that underpinned new legislation after 1949 was first tested during the Great Leap Forward in the late 1950s. Although the 1954 constitution contained a proclamation against "great-nation (Han) chauvinism," it became clear that in the push to collectivize there would be much less tolerance of minorities. The stated goals of the

Great Leap Forward—increase production, eliminate bureaucratism and red tape, and achieve pure communism—were, according to state discourses, ill served by the proliferation of special accommodations for minority groups. It was no surprise, then, to find that ethnic diversity was rarely an important consideration when the government was creating new communes during collectivization (especially in 1958 and 1959). To oppose or deliberately slow down collectivization policies was seen as tantamount to opposing socialism, so most minority people remained silent. Minority languages were de-emphasized in favor of Mandarin Chinese, and ethnic customs that might hinder all-out production (such as festivals, the ritual killing of valuable animals, and ethnic clothing) were defined as "decadent" habits or "feudal" practices and were discouraged. During the late 1950s and early 1960s some minority areas, especially in Xinjiang and Inner Mongolia, experienced a sizeable influx of Han migrants, many of them fleeing famine areas in the eastern provinces. In protest of Chinese domination (by the state and by Han migrants) there were armed uprisings in many areas in Xinjiang, including the flight of some 60,000 Kazhaks to the former Soviet Union in 1962.[31]

During the Great Leap Forward the state emphasized class and class consciousness over all other issues, including ethnicity. Thus a poor minority peasant was akin to a poor Han peasant, in the sense that what they shared (class consciousness) was more important than their differences (ethnicity). That policy was extended throughout the 1960s, and during the Cultural Revolution there was evidence of severe repression of minority nationalities. Again class struggle was being identified as the key link: "There was no real place for counterpoising the Han and the minorities, but only for struggle between classes within the Han or other nationalities. The poor Tibetan peasant was . . . necessarily the ally of his Han counterpart [and] there could be no antagonism between poor peasants, whatever their nationality."[32] A statement circulated by a group of radical students and workers in Shanghai in

1968 expressed this most clearly: "National struggle is in the final analysis a question of class struggle. The unity of all the nationalities on the basis of the thought of Chairman Mao Tse-tung and the Socialist road should be stressed."[33]

Such views were at the root of marked changes in official policies toward minorities; some observers have described the changes as severe repression. Minority people were forced to behave like Han people, and their traditional festivals and eating habits were prohibited. Restrictions were placed on the most visible representations of minority culture, and as a result Chinese culture temporarily lost much of its rich diversity.[34] Paradoxically, the repression produced greater ethnic solidarity and organization in opposition to Han subjugation; as Alan Liu has pointed out, under this sort of state repression "there was no need to have any special interest group to sustain the will of the minorities to resist Chinese rule."[35]

Minority repression relaxed following Mao's death in 1976 and the fall of the Gang of Four thereafter. A new line on minority policy was specified, not exactly de-emphasizing class struggle but not privileging it to the extent witnessed earlier. The policy trend since then has been to grant greater autonomy to minorities, with more emphasis on preserving and reinforcing minority cultures, customs, and practices. Minority people were expected to contribute their share toward achieving the Four Modernizations, and favorable economic policies were introduced to mobilize economic growth in minority-dominated areas.[36]

The new policy of state accommodation certainly helped increase ethnic identification and consciousness, but from the state's perspective it also heightened ethnic sensitivity and stiffened the resolve of some minority groups to seek greater autonomy. As Liu observed, "All it required for [ethnic mobilization] was a period of reduction in state control," which is what has occurred during the reform era.[37] The state, as part of its new accommodative policies, began to concentrate resources on cultural restoration projects in many minority areas.

Deng Xiaoping had convinced himself (but not necessarily minority people) that economic development was the panacea for China's nationality question, and the state began to pump resources into minority areas. Ironically, even with major cultural and economic development projects under way, the 1980s and 1990s have been marked by separatist activity, especially in Tibet, Xinjiang, and Inner Mongolia.[38]

By the early 1990s affirmative action policies had borne fruit, illustrated by the following achievements:

- Agricultural and industrial output in minority areas has been performing at least as well, and in many cases better than, the national average (see Table 12.4);[39]
- per capita incomes of farmers and herders in minority areas have increased significantly throughout the economic reform years;
- twenty-three of the fifty-six minority groups had their own written language by the 1990s;
- literacy rates went up by almost 10 percent in the 1980s, and the minority peoples made up 6 percent of China's university graduates; and
- there was a significant increase in the number of minority people in government, and in fact the proportion of minority delegates in the National People's Congress (more than 18 percent in the early 1990s) exceeded the percentage of minorities in the population.[40]

Despite the obvious gains, a strong case can be made that economic development is not necessarily the best policy to address ethnicity issues in China. As one scholar pointed out, "Increased national wealth is not all that is needed in dealing with groups that foster separatism; if it were, then the rich nations of Europe would not have separatist movements."[41] At stake is the self-worth and self-realization of minority people, which is likely to require political rather than economic solu-

TABLE 12.4   Selected Economic Indicators for People Living in Minority Nationality Autonomous Areas Compared to National Averages, 1979–1992 (average yearly rates of increase)

Indicators	Minority Rate of Increase (%) (1979–1996 average)	National Average (%) (1981–1996 average)
Gross Output Value of Agriculture and Industry		
Combined	8.8 (11.8)	11.6
Agriculture	5.7 (7.4)	5.9 (6.9)
Industry	11.0 (14.0)	13.2 (15.8)
Output of Major Agricultural Products		
Grain Yield	3.0 (8.1)	2.7 (2.9)
Cotton	18.9 (31.9)	5.4 (2.8)
Output of Major Industrial Products		
Steel	9.8 (18.9)	6.9 (6.5)
Coal	5.5 (11.0)	4.3 (5.2)
Total Value of Retail Sales	13.5 (28.6)	8.5 (9.0)
# Trained Medical Personnel	4.4 (7.6)	3.7

SOURCES: State Statistical Bureau, *China Statistical Yearbook, 1993*, Table T2.44, p. 62; and Table T2.3, pp. 18–20. The statistics in parentheses are for 1996, taken from the *China Statistical Yearbook, 1997*, Table 2-2, pp. 24–31; and Tables 2-26 and 2-27, pp. 57–58.

tions. Developmentalism may benefit some ethnic groups in southwestern provinces and ARs, but it comes with a price: Those ethnic groups are required to speak Chinese and operate in the wider Chinese society—obligations that usually accompany assimilation. Take the cases of Tibet and, to a lesser extent, Xinjiang and Inner Mongolia: Deng Xiaoping's assumption that the state can exchange a higher standard of living for a participatory political system is fundamentally flawed when it comes to minority groups with strong desires for separatism. The Dalai Lama, for example, is no longer insisting on full national independence for Tibet, and he has disavowed violence as a political strategy.[42] He is, however, genuinely concerned about the cultural and social effects of economic development and commercialization, as well as what he considers to be the corrosive influence of continued Han immigration into and development of Tibet. What is needed, as Melvyn Goldstein has observed in *The Snow Lion and the Dragon*, is a compromise between China and Tibet that allows a truly "ethnic" Tibet to exist. This would require China to guarantee Tibetan cultural, linguistic, and demographic integrity while retaining it as a part of China.[43]

Domination of the Periphery by the Core

Current events in China are part of an ongoing process whereby the political and economic core of society, usually concentrated in the cities, is attempting to colonize, or "civilize," those on the periphery. (The Chinese government is by no means the first to address that issue.) According to anthropologist Stevan Harrell, the goal of such "civilizing projects" is usually to help people living on the periphery achieve the supposedly superior cultural, religious, moral, and economic values of the core.[44] Such attempts at civilizing are sometimes successful, for example, when people at the periphery are assimilated into the larger culture, as is generally assumed to be the case for Manchu people. Others, however, remain "barbarians" (to use the language of the core), as is generally assumed to be the case for Tibetans and Uigurs. Not surprisingly, civilizing projects generally work to heighten the sense of ethnic consciousness among peripheral peoples, and in some cases they create a new ethnic identity that was dormant or nonexistent.[45]

After 1949 the Party-state (i.e., the center, or core) faced the task of describing and mapping ethnic characteristics on the periphery so it could define the officially recognized minority groups and establish boundaries between them. This required an objectification of ethnic differences and an attempt to create a scale of "relative backwardness," to determine, as it were, the extent to which specific groups needed to be civilized in order to catch up with the center. This process allowed the center to establish what Harrell has referred to as the "definitions of hegemony." These definitions usually employ metaphors to establish the relationship between the center (traditionally defined as the "strong" party in the relationship) and the periphery (usually defined as the "weak" party). The most common metaphors symbolizing relationships between the center and the periphery are: a sexual metaphor, with the center (male) dominating the periphery (female); an educational metaphor, with the center (adult) teaching the periphery (child); and a modernity metaphor, with the center (modern) modernizing the periphery (feudal). As Harrell has suggested, but without proof, the civilizing projects initiated by the Han in China (as well as European and Japanese colonists earlier) can be characterized in terms of such metaphors: The center has characteristics that are male, adult, and modern, whereas the periphery is attributed the female, juvenile, and ancient characteristics.[46]

During the course of the past few centuries, Harrell suggests, there have been three distinct civilizing projects in China, each one utilizing one or more of these metaphors. The first of these, the Christian project, was primarily directed by foreigners, their fundamental objective being to convert the barbarians (including Han as well as peripheral peoples). The second was the Confucian project, the goal of the elite being to provide moral education and to bring virtue to the periphery. The most recent attempt, of course, is the communist project, which began with an attempt to define and demarcate ethnicity purportedly on a scientific basis. The original set of minority groups was determined by Joseph Stalin's four defining characteristics (common territory, language, economy, and national culture) and, as noted earlier, during the Maoist era, class and the modes of production were generally more important than were ethnic differences.[47]

The communist civilizing project launched with ethnic identification, establishing the original fifty-four minority groups, with two others added later. The goal was to determine exactly where each group fit on the scales of history and to identify how much civilizing was required. Some groups were found to be at a later (i.e., more advanced) stage of development than others who needed special attention, perhaps with affirmative action policies, to speed their development. Once the definitions were complete the center faced the task of doing the actual civilizing work (*minzu gongzuo*), which began with the creation of the Autonomous Regions, counties, and prefectures, then continued with the implementation of educational and economic development strategies, including plans to bring leaders from the periphery into the center. This work would attempt to make good on the promises made by the government to the peripheral peoples that "all *minzu*, equal legally and morally, would march together on the road to historical progress, that is socialism. If some [have] to march further than others, this was because of unequal historical progression up to the time of the Communist takeover."[48]

Harrell believed that the various stages of the civilizing projects in China, particularly

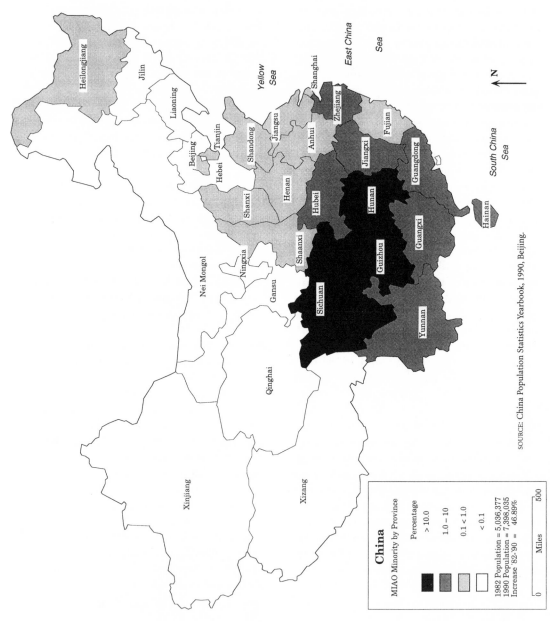

China

MIAO Minority by Province

Percentage

> 10.0

1.0 – 10

0.1 < 1.0

< 0.1

1982 Population = 5,036,377
1990 Population = 7,398,035
Increase '82–'90 = 46.89%

0   Miles   500

SOURCE: China Population Statistics Yearbook, 1990, Beijing.

MAP 12.1   The Miao Minority Group by Province

the communist project, have contributed to a raising of ethnic consciousness. During the process many peripheral peoples came to think of themselves as one unit sharing common land or ancestry. At the same time, they might come to see themselves as clearly different from all other groups. This is illustrated by the case of the Miao *minzu*, more than 7 million people spread across several provinces (see Map 12.1).

A sense of collectivity has developed among Miao groups, based largely on the idea of a common language that has transcended local differences and geographic dispersion. An important contribution to the development of Miao ethnic consciousness has been the globalization of the issue of ethnic solidarity, and in recent years large numbers of Hmong, living as refugees in the United States, have traveled to China to visit the Miao, in recognition of their common ancestral roots.[49] In the following sections we investigate the different experiences of some of China's peripheral peoples, relying on case studies of four peoples: Hui, Mongol, Subei, and Tibetan.

The Hui (Muslim) Minority

At the core of Muslim identity in China is the Chinese translation and interpretation of Islam, in which the notion of *qing zhen* (pure and true) is an essential theme.[50] This has become a "sacred symbol" that implies *qing* (purity), in the sense of ritual cleanliness and moral conduct; and *zhen* (truth), implying authenticity and legitimacy.[51] Implied is a wider meaning than is normally meant by the term *halal*, in that it includes much more than just the ritual preparation of food according to Islamic dietary prescriptions.[52] As anthropologist Dru Gladney has observed: "The concept of *qing zhen* governs all one's life. . . . For the Hui, the two aspects of *qing* and *zhen*, purity and truth, define important tensions for their identity: Islamic moral purity and the authenticity of ethnic ancestry, lifestyle and heritage."[53]

Hui notions of purity and identity define the context and content of their ethnic nationalism,[54] and in China these have been the concepts used to establish boundaries between the Hui and all other groups. There is general agreement that Hui have always been treated with a degree of suspicion by the majority Han, partly because of their foreign origins, partly because of their food preferences. The Hui avoid pork, for example, which most Han people are unable to comprehend; eating pork has become almost ritualistic in Chinese food preparation, and it is the basic source of meat protein and cooking oil.[55]

The centrality of *qing zhen* for the Hui people has been reinforced because their ethnic identity is not as clearly definable by the traditional criteria as is the case for other minorities. Hui people, for example, are scattered all over China, so they have no identifiably common territory; no common language, although the majority of them speak Chinese; and no common economy or culture. The Hui (some 8.6 million according to the 1990 census) are the dominant minority group in the Gansu-Ningxia-Qinghai border area, but they also live in most other provinces, as well as in most cities in northern and northeastern China. They are by far the most urbanized of China's minority peoples, and they usually make up the majority of non-Han people in the bigger cities. Hui people are most likely to be found operating ethnic restaurants and bakeries, working as street traders or in a variety of street-level service activities. They concentrate in small urban enclaves, their "Muslim markets" well known to most city dwellers and tourists.[56] The Hui operate largely in the role of "middleman minority," and they have certainly brought color and diversity to otherwise drab Chinese cities. As Gladney has noted, their "entrepreneurial commitments have enlivened and assisted urban development in cities across China."[57] That has become an important niche for the Hui people, helping them survive in an alien culture; in fact their status as entrepreneurs and traders has become part of the Hui ethnic identity, taking on important symbolic meaning that perhaps even outweighs its economic value.[58]

The only feature held in common by all Hui people in China is their descent from Muslims, but by no means do all Hui practice Islam. In the northwestern regions the issue of common descent has long been a strong ethnic marker, differentiating Hui from Han as well as from the many other northwestern minorities, including Tibetan, Turkic, and Mongol peoples. In some of the southeastern provinces, however, Hui did not claim common ancestry until the communist civilizing project began to impinge on them. During the ethnic objectification-identification project, the work conducted by Chinese ethnologists caused the Hui to reflect upon their ancestry; some groups "discovered" or "rediscovered" their ethnic roots and began to think and act like Muslims. In fact some Hui people gave up eating pork and attending Chinese temples as they began to observe traditional Muslim values. Gladney has identified four distinct strategies whereby Hui people preserve their ethnic integrity:[59]

- In northwestern China the practice of Islam is the fundamental ethnic marker; to be Hui is to be Muslim, and this has been allowed and even encouraged by the state, especially during the reform era;
- in southwestern China Hui people have used genealogical descent as the major ethnic marker, and to be Hui is to be a member of a lineage that traces its descent to foreign Muslim ancestors;
- in many urban areas Hui identity is expressed in terms of cultural traditions, most notably the pork taboo, craft specialties, and entrepreneurship in Hui enclaves; in other words, to be Hui "is to express the purity of one's ancestral heritage through living a Hui lifestyle"[60]; and
- in northern rural areas Hui identity is expressed and perpetuated through strategies of community maintenance, for

example, by marriage to other Hui people (endogamy).

As these examples illustrate, there are different routes to ethnic identification among the Hui, revealing that Hui identity is not fixed in either time or space but is "dynamically involved with and adapted to distinct social contexts."[61] Identity is also shaped by the interactions Hui peoples have with the Chinese state. In the past the state has been known to play minority groups against one another and has specifically defined "local chauvinism" as unacceptable. In the current era, however, the state appears to have concluded that the blossoming of ethnic identification is consistent with the overall goal of building a multinational state.

For the most part Hui people have been able to adapt and manipulate this new acceptance to suit their best interests. For example, the state has realized the benefit of Muslim enclaves and has been active in preserving mosques for the purpose of tourism. Muslim tourists have been invited to visit China from other parts of the world, which has expanded the consciousness of China's Muslims and helped them to think of themselves as part of a global culture. The penchant among Hui people for enterprise has also found a new level of acceptance during the economic reform era, and after being labeled as antisocialist in earlier times, they are now helping to redefine capitalism with Chinese characteristics. Hui businesses have flourished, which has expanded the consumption and service sectors of China's cities while also reviving the sense of ethnic solidarity among the Hui *minzu*. A leading Chinese social scientist, Fei Xiaotong, has remarked on the entrepreneurial talents of the Hui people: "Hui people are very smart traders. They have been blessed with this talent from their ancestors, who nurtured trading skills during centuries-long commercial dealings between farmers and herdsman. This tradition has been developed mainly due to their geographical locations [in the areas between those] inhabited by nomadic groups and the country's farming areas."[62]

Fei's ideas about the cultural roots of the Hui are perhaps too reminiscent of environmental determinism for Western tastes; Gladney, by comparison, has suggested that the Hui concentration in business activities signifies that they have been opportunistic. In the present era of relatively unfettered market operations, the Hui were certainly quick to realize that street-level enterprise was an area in which the power of the state was virtually nonexistent.[63] As China's urban economies expanded, Hui people were more than willing to respond to the almost insatiable demand for new consumer goods and services.[64] In a broader context, the growth of Hui identity illustrates that even though the state in China exerts considerable power, on some issues it cannot push too far in the face of ethnic resistance and resilience. Ethnicity—in China as in most other places—is something that evolves and is reinforced through constant negotiation and renegotiation between the people and the state.

The Mongol Minority

Mongol people thought very little about group identity until the nineteenth century, because these traditional herders and agriculturists were classified by what they did (i.e., ecological criteria) rather than by language and customs (cultural criteria). As traditional pursuits became less dominant, Mongol people attempted to find defining ethnic markers, and many settled on one: common descent. A dimension of this search has been an attempt to position present-day Mongols as figurative reincarnations of Chinggis Khan, who, according to one scholar, has essentially been transformed from an "Imperial Ancestor [into an] ethnic hero."[65] For Mongols living in China, Chinggis Khan has come to be the symbol of ethnic survival in the face of Han domination.

This is the case even within the Inner Mongolia AR. For example, in the capital city, Huhhot, Mongols make up only 20 percent of the population. In a recent study of Mongols in Huhhot, relatively few differences between Han and Mongols could be detected in terms of the traditional ethnic markers, such as food, attitudes, and behaviors.[66] It was evident, however, that Mongols attempted to maintain solidarity through coethnic friendship networks, a traditional behavior for many displaced and dispersed ethnic groups. Not surprisingly, most Mongols in Huhhot reported that their best friends were Mongols and that most of their social ties were with other Mongols. Interview data provide evidence that Mongols have focused on issues such as ethnic-specific celebrations, folk dancing, and sporting activities. Along with efforts to preserve traditional food preferences, such behaviors are examples of what sociologist Richard Alba has referred to as "symbolic" ethnicity.[67] In the Mongol study, for example, one respondent in the city of Huhhot described how he felt about millet tea, a traditional Mongol food: "When I eat this I feel like a Mongol."[68]

Attempts to re-create a sense of group solidarity among Huhhot Mongols have arisen as a result of interactions with the dominant Han. One sensitive issue, for example, has been Han resentment of "preferential" treatment of Mongols in the form of entitlements or affirmative action. In fact during the implementation of HRS reform Mongols were favored in the redistribution of former communal lands by at least two to one. There are ethnic quotas for government jobs and spaces in local and national colleges. In local *danwei* Mongols have been favored for cadre-level jobs and, it is argued by many, are promoted faster than Han colleagues. Perhaps most controversial are the one-child exemptions granted to many minority families. The net effect is that Mongols are now much more likely to identify themselves as Mongols; this stands in stark contrast to the dark days of the Maoist era, when many Mongols, especially those born to mixed-ethnicity couples, would renounce their identity. Today, by comparison, "given the real and imagined perks associated with being a minority . . . they are reverting back to their pre–Cultural Revolution ethnic identity."[69] The government has ruled that anyone with at least one minority parent or grandparent can be reclassified as a minority person.

According to one observer, this has resulted in considerable conflict between Mongols and the Han majority in Huhhot, often manifested in vicious stereotyping based on the perceived cultural habits and customs of both groups. The Mongols, for example, think of Han as "crafty," "cunning," "dishonest," "impolite," "loud," "unkind," "greedy," and even "slippery." They are thought to "speak an ugly language," "eat dogs," and "look like *jiaozi*" (dumplings that are soggy and steamy on the outside, soft on the inside). Han Chinese in Huhhot describe minority Mongols as "simple people," "lazy," "dirty," "not civilized," "stupid," "ugly," "backward", and "ignorant because they eat with a knife." They "don't like vegetables or fruit," they "eat raw meat," they are "drunkards" who "beat their wives," and are "sexual animals who don't know who their fathers are."[70]

Chinese Mongols are similar to Chinese Muslims in that they attempt to define their ethnicity in varied ways depending on local situations. Among young Temut Mongols, for example, a sense of identity was generated through the idea of common descent and a shared experience that results from being born in the countryside. Young pastoral Mongols feel their Mongol identity has been fundamentally shaped by their nomadic way of life and the Mongolian language. Young urban Mongols, by comparison, benefited greatly from the establishment of ethnically oriented boarding schools, where they were first encouraged to focus on ethnic heritage as part of their education.[71] For both groups, however, it appears that Mongolian identity is a relatively recent construction; in fact it was developed only when they found themselves alienated in their own land and unaccepted by the Han society and culture.

Among the Mongols in Huhhot, William Jankowiak has identified four different responses to the issue of Mongol ethnic identity:

- Traditionalists appear to be totally committed to preserving and utilizing Mongol culture and language;
- cosmopolitans emphasize "ethnic pride" but are primarily concerned with individual strategies to promote ethnic solidarity and basically view themselves as modern rather than connected to an ancient Mongol past;
- revisionists are engaged in a militant struggle to achieve a new interpretation of their own ethnic history; and
- assimilationists either deny or are indifferent to their ethnic heritage.[72]

The radicalism of the revisionists appears to have been generated during the oppressive years of the Cultural Revolution, when Mongols were keen to emphasize the centrality of their grassland roots. In comparison, cosmopolitans and assimilationists are not interested at all in grassland roots. Although they may have visited grassland areas, they have no plans to live there, and they express no desire to abandon their urban (and urbane) ways of life. As Jankowiak concluded, Huhhotian Mongols tend to hold "conflicting notions about the 'essence' of Mongolian ethnicity," but in general, he argues, "most Mongols … remain proud of their cultural heritage and enjoy the government benefits."[73] In that sense, then, they can be viewed to some extent at least as opportunists, in that defining and clinging to their ethnic roots have a markedly instrumental component.

Consistent with trends in Chinese society at large, Huhhotian Mongol culture has come to embrace a new set of priorities associated with economic reform. In a 1983 study, Jankowiak identified some of the distinct pathways that Mongol households in Huhhot used to gain prestige in a Han-dominated culture: administrative office (which usually involved becoming a high-level cadre in the Communist Party); knowledge (being a teacher or professor); gentility; and ethics. After replicating his study in 1987, Jankowiak added another pathway to prestige: the acquisition of wealth. Being Party secretary was the number-one choice of profession (in terms of occupational prestige) in 1983, but in 1987 it slipped to eighth. Educational jobs were considered the most prestigious; work on construction sites, as a driver, or in a factory had emerged as respectable jobs in the 1987 survey, primarily because there was good money to be made.

The Subei People of Shanghai

The Subei people of Shanghai are not officially recognized by the PRC government as a *minzu*. Nevertheless, they are a group that has been clearly identified and labeled, largely on the basis of geographic origin and social class. The Subei label is attached to migrants who have, for almost a century, migrated into the city of Shanghai from the impoverished parts of northern Jiangsu Province—literally *su* (Jiangsu) and *bei* (north). The Subei have been continuously and almost uniformly excoriated by the Shanghai elite, mainly because of their poverty: "They [are] laughed at for wearing tasteless, gaudy . . . garments, shunned for the smell of garlic on their breath, and ridiculed for speaking Subei dialect. Subei culture . . . came to be regarded as low-class and despicable. . . . Calling someone a Subei swine meant a person, even if not actually from Subei, was poor, ignorant, dirty and unsophisticated."[74] The label has proved extraordinarily resilient. Even today people are said to be "dirty like a Subei person . . . ignorant like a Subei person [and even] sexually promiscuous like a Subei person." Parents warn children about the Subei, and no one wants their daughter or son to marry into a Subei family.[75]

The stereotype of inferiority foisted upon the Subei is a result of the conditions under which they migrated to Shanghai, as well as the marginal circumstances they have been forced to endure in Shanghai. The irony, as Emily Honig would point out, is that historically many of Shanghai's would-be elite are also migrants, but they tend to be from the southern part of Jiangsu Province (the Jiangnan region), which is generally thought of as richer, more

urbane, and more wholesome. As Honig suggested, the Subei people have achieved (or had ascribed to them) their label as a result of a social construction. Many Subei people are poor, yet the label is applied in blanket fashion to all who look or sound like they migrated from the Subei region.[76]

It is important to point out that Subei people are an ethnic group only in the context of Shanghai, where they coexist with the Jiangnan people. In their hometowns and villages, no one would refer to them as Subei people. Thus we see that ethnicity involves agency, in the sense that one group actively defines, categorizes, and labels another group. Unlike the situation for most of the officially recognized *minzu*, however, being identified as Subei is not usually something to be proud of. In fact most Subei migrants hate to admit their geographic origin and often try to hide their true identity. Unfortunately, they are often given away by dialect and appearance, as well as the jobs they are doing.

As with underclass groups the world over, Subei people have traditionally been associated with the worst jobs in the city: rag picking, cotton waste sorting, pig raising, latrine cleaning, and rickshaw pulling—all referred to as "nuisance and offensive trades" by the Shanghai Municipal Council in 1936.[77] Historically, there are a number of plausible explanations for this concentration in the city's marginal occupations. Subei people likely enter the city without *guanxi* (connections). They are usually poor and invariably have little start-up capital to establish profitable businesses. Linking Subei people with unskilled and physically demanding (coolie) labor has "created and continually reinforced the belief that they were poor, ignorant, dirty and uncivilized."[78] In this way the Shanghai labor market could always find able and willing recruits for the marginal jobs that needed to be done. By defining the Subei people as ethnically distinct (despite the fact they are Han), Jiangnan natives justified to themselves why immigrants from northern Jiangsu were suited for coolie labor. As with all stereotyping, the perceptions one group has of another are distorted and exaggerated. As Honig has suggested, any truth in the stereotype is not important compared to what the elite group believes about the underclass group; they use such beliefs to establish boundary markers to differentiate the "us" from the "other." By necessity, then, Subei people have been forced to live in overcrowded, filthy conditions, occupying temporary huts in shantytowns along creeks at the edges of relatively prosperous areas of Shanghai. In 1949 it was estimated that more than 1 million people— many of them Subei—lived in huts in 322 settlements with populations of at least 200 huts each.[79]

Subei people were also assumed to be responsible for the majority of crimes committed in Shanghai, as well as the vices associated with prostitution and gangs, and the label has stuck. Some Subei people have done well in Shanghai, although no amount of wealth removes the label and what it stands for, as stereotypes are resilient and rarely altered by changing circumstances. Honig concluded that the elite continues to need an "other" to define its own status. Ironically, the arrival of wealthier Subei immigrants from Subei would probably increase intolerance toward Subei in general, as better-off newcomers would represent more of a threat than ever before.

Stereotyping was probably not a deliberate conspiracy by the Jiangnan elite; more likely it was simply the inevitable result of the elites' struggle to define Shanghai culture as their own. In fact the denigration of Subei culture was, from this perspective, a necessary component of Jiangnan culture, "establishing the other against which Jiangnan natives could define themselves and claim, eventually a Shanghai identity." It continues to be necessary, therefore, for Jiangnan people to denigrate Subei culture, just as it had been necessary to destroy Subei huts and shantytowns that had become eyesores and public health hazards. Then, as now, it was important to marginalize the Subei people, both geographically and socially.[80]

Subei identity is also a metaphor for class, in the sense that being poor, living in a paper-and-wood hut, and doing coolie work all defined Subei status. Yet Subei identity is very much a function of geography, in the sense that the label connotes a specific region, the very mention of which identifies the most important (and invariably negative) characteristics of an individual.

Tibet: Modernization and the Struggle for Self-Determination

The Tibetans have already lost their country and much of their heritage, and now they are in danger of being stripped of their spiritual leadership.

—Pico Iyer, *The New York Times* (1995)[81]

In February 1995 a committee of Tibetan monks announced it had found a six-year-old boy who had inherited the Panchen Lama's spirit (the Panchen Lama being the second highest religious authority in Tibet). The Chinese government at first approved the boy, Gedhun Choeki Nyima, who was born in 1989, the year the then-current Panchen Lama had died. He appeared to have all of the required characteristics, but Beijing soon discovered that the committee had secretly conferred with the exiled Dalai Lama for an endorsement, so the boy was placed under house arrest and the search committee's leader was denounced as a traitor. To make matters worse, in late November 1995, Chinese leaders, declaring themselves the sole arbitrators of Tibetan religious customs (which they generally excoriate as "feudal"), supervised a ceremony to announce a rival Panchen Lama, another six-year-old boy, named Guancain Norbu. As Patrick Tyler, the China correspondent for *The New York Times*, observed at the time: "It was as if, after the College of Cardinals chose a Pope, the Italian Prime Minister announced that he would not accept their candidate but would install his own, arguing that he was the final authority of Catholic divination."[82] The Chinese accused the Tibetan-chosen boy of having drowned a dog, which made him unsuitable to replace the Panchen Lama; at the selection ceremony a lottery was conducted among a group of suitable candidates, with names being drawn from a golden urn—as Tibetan lore dictated.

From a political standpoint, the most important aspect of this event was that the Dalai Lama had been accused of making a "preemptive announcement" of his approval before that of the Beijing government.[83] Chinese leaders took that as an act of belligerence intended to embarrass China internationally. Once again, at a critical time, the Party-state deemed that the Dalai Lama had thumbed his nose at Beijing.[84] Although many Tibet supporters around the world considered the Dalai Lama's action to be a victory in that he stood up to China, his actions fueled existing distrust and animosity. Melvyn Goldstein and other Tibet experts argued that it also reinforced the belief among hard-liners in Beijing that the Tibetan government-in-exile, particularly the Dalai Lama, could not be trusted and that Tibet should be dealt with more forcefully in the future. After the debacle, the Chinese government intensified attacks on the Dalai Lama, blaming him for the lack of progress in settling Tibet's future.

In the meantime Beijing continues with an integrationist policy, that is, proceeding at full speed with policies to develop the Tibetan economy and modernize Tibetan society, working from the assumption that improving living conditions is the best way to convince Tibetans it is in their best interests to remain a part of China rather than seek autonomy. The Tibetans are caught in an awkward position, because they realize that economic development at home is much needed, but they fear that China's modernization program will destroy Tibetan culture. For a number of years now, Beijing has been subsidizing major development projects in Tibet to beef up its infrastructure and productive capacity. Such efforts are intended to reduce Tibet's isolation and provide

hard evidence to Tibetans that they have more to gain by working with rather than against China. In 1994 a plan was announced that would increase Tibet's economic growth rate to 10 percent per year, with a doubling of its GDP by the year 2000. This was accompanied by a commitment to invest approximately US$27 million for a whole range of infrastructural projects.[85] Beijing appears to be convinced that the Tibetan people will be grateful to the Chinese government for providing this help and will switch their energies away from political issues to the business of getting rich, effectively falling in line with the rest of China in the reform era.

Unfortunately, from the standpoint of securing a peaceful resolution of the crisis, Beijing's policy has backfired somewhat, stiffening rather than weakening the resolve of those Tibetans pursuing resistance and self-determination. One of the most important issues in the current struggle involves the present and future demographic structures of Tibet. As the Chinese government continues to invest, and as the local economy begins to gain momentum, tens of thousands of Han and Hui people have been attracted to Tibet in search of jobs and to set up businesses. Local Tibetans have reacted with hostility to the newcomers, referring to them as the floating populations stealing their jobs, diluting their culture, and destroying their land.[86] In fact the newcomers have begun to dominate local economies in several areas, and many Tibetans believe they cannot compete with these skilled, aggressive, and industrious outsiders.

The Chinese government refuses to do anything about this problem, believing that population mobility is a good thing, as Tibet has been too sparsely populated for too long. As Deng Xiaoping is reported to have said in his typically pragmatic way, "Two million Tibetans are not enough to handle the task of developing such a huge region. There is no harm in sending Han into Tibet to help."[87] The leaders in Beijing are happy to have more non-Tibetans living in the region, hoping that in addition to speeding up the development process they will ultimately develop into a pro-China constituency. It is also hoped that Han people will export the powerful model of modernity, which will somehow rub off on Tibetans. If we view the situation in terms of the aforementioned civilizing projects, it is possible to interpret the Han migrants as envoys of the core in its attempts at acculturation, whereby more advanced people are poised to open up the less advanced periphery of Tibet. In addition to gaining material benefits, it is assumed that peripheral peoples will learn new ways that replace tradition-bound, religion-based customs.

In addition to the economic policies, Beijing is hoping to modernize Tibetans by enhancing and improving their educational system. There have been some hard-line decisions on cultural issues; for example, the government has decided to backpedal on earlier proposals to mandate the Tibetan language as the standard for government officials in Tibet, many of whom are Han. More ominously, in 1997 there was a reversal on policies intended to expand the use of the Tibetan language in schools. As Goldstein has suggested, the Chinese are attempting to redefine ethnic and cultural autonomy in Tibet. There remain special subsidies, investment programs, and exemptions from the one-child policy, but "the basic policy has moved from the view that Tibet has a special status in China because of its history to the view that Tibet is just another ethnic group in a multi-ethnic state."[88] China's policy toward Tibet is to emphasize the need for modernization rather than focusing on anything that would serve to highlight ethnic differences between Tibetans and the Han. The obvious problem is that such a policy tends to radicalize Tibetan nationalism even more, as it highlights a sense of powerlessness and intensifies hostility toward Beijing. As Goldstein noted, "Beijing has . . . embarked on a high-risk strategy in Tibet that may very well backfire and exacerbate the very violence, bloodshed, and hatred it seeks to overcome."[89] Beijing's policies

have more or less neutralized the Dalai Lama, who remains influential locally as well as globally but possesses virtually no leverage to stop China's new policies. The international community, though supportive of the Dalai Lama, is unwilling or unable to provide much support to Tibet in its struggle against the Chinese; in fact some observers feel that the Dalai Lama's highly publicized international campaign precipitated Beijing's hard-line policy.[90]

The fundamental issue is that Beijing is categorically unwilling even to consider Tibetan self-rule. The Dalai Lama, for his part, has publicly stated he might be able to accept the one country–two systems formula applied to Taiwan and Hong Kong (see Chapter 11), but so far his concession has fallen on deaf ears in Beijing. Thus Tibet seems to have several choices: do nothing, in the hope that the communist regime will disintegrate, either violently or peacefully, which would probably allow the government-in-exile to win independence immediately; continue to drum up international support, which so far has brought plenty of goodwill but no real offers of political or military help; wait for China to democratize, which would not be a sound policy at all (see Chapters 18 and 19), as China's ongoing modernization drive in Tibet may soon become irreversible in terms of the religious, economic, and demographic transformations it produces; or choose a course of violent action, which has significant precedent in ethnic struggles around the world, as well as in Tibet.

For many Tibetans violent uprising would be the disastrous choice. The Dalai Lama insists on a course of nonviolence, and uprising may well cleave the Tibetan independence movement in half:

> The crux of the matter is that Tibetans are unlikely to stand indefinitely on the sidelines watching Beijing transform their homeland with impunity. Nationalistic emotions coupled with desperation and anger make a powerful brew, and there are Tibetans inside and outside

of Tibet who are intoxicated with the idea of beginning ... a campaign of focussed violence—in their view a "war of conscience," a Tibetan-style *intifada*.[91]

To prevent this nightmare, Tibet and China must compromise on a workable solution before other nations are forced to take a stand on a conflict similar to that in Kosovo recently. Needed is an agreement that satisfies China's strategic interests and does not challenge its global prestige while preserving a Tibetan homeland that remains strongly Tibetan in its language, culture, and demographic composition. Given Beijing's stance against independence, the Dalai Lama must accept something less. Goldstein has outlined a compromise solution along such lines: Create a truly "ethnic" Tibet that exists within a framework Beijing can accept, perhaps the existing AR system but with Tibetans eventually heading all government and Party leadership positions. China would have to guarantee that it would restore Tibet linguistically and demographically, so that it could be a nation largely of Tibetans, governed by Tibetans, with Tibetan customs and language in everyday use.

The major stumbling block—assuming that Tibet gives up on self-rule—appears to be the future of "ethnographic Tibet," that is, that portion of China (outside of Tibet proper) where Tibetans are the majority. The government-in-exile and many Tibetans around the world argue that this part of China should be annexed to create Greater Tibet, which Beijing will never consider. A settlement on the Tibetan question might come only after an armed uprising, and even if the Dalai Lama were in support, there would be little chance for success. The armed conflict option, unthinkable to many, may have a useful purpose in the long run. In his magisterial book *Tibetan Nation*, Warren Smith suggests that "the outbreak of violence might be the only way to focus international attention on Tibet and stimulate international efforts to mediate the Tibet issue."[92] Smith reminds us that Tibet

has forced its way into the international spotlight only after violence broke out, for example, in 1950 and 1959 and in a series of demonstrations and riots from 1987 to 1989.[93] China has thus far proved relatively immune to international criticism, so even a violent struggle may not have the desired result. As Warren Smith concluded: "Ultimately, the resolution of the Tibetan issue depends on Chinese political developments, but Tibetans are not totally powerless. ... For Tibetan self-determination to remain an issue confronting China, Tibet must remain a distinctive culture and nation."[94]

The Chinese are not blind to this issue, of course, and are devoting energy and resources to dilute (some would say eradicate) all traces of Tibetan culture and nationalism. As we have already seen in the other case studies, however, the Chinese have succeeded in doing the opposite, and Tibetan resistance to Chinese hegemony continues to be a powerful force.

The Commodification of Chinese Ethnicity

Some China scholars would contend that the 1990s marked the dawn of a new era, a new-found openness in Chinese society in which there has been a rediscovery of ethnic roots. Yet even as the state adopted accommodationist policies toward minorities, there was a tendency for some *minzu* groups to grow increasingly resistant to Chinese rule. It is also likely that the state's interest in promoting ethnic awareness has more to do with the selling of ethnicity and cultural differences than with a genuine concern for ethnic identification. The growing ethnic consciousness has coincided with, and perhaps been reinforced by, the opening of several ethnic theme parks as tourist attractions. The biggest and most significant, the Chinese Folk Cultural Villages, is located in Shenzhen, close to the Hong Kong border (see Photos 12.1a and 12.1b). For the first few years it was a huge financial success, mainly because of its proximity to Hong Kong but also as a

PHOTO 12.1a Minority mannequins at the Folk Cultural Villages theme park in Shenzhen.

PHOTO 12.1b Bai minority house at the Folk Cultural Villages.

result of the economics of "ethnic tourism" and the commodification of Chinese minority groups.[95]

The Shenzhen Folk Cultural Villages opened on October 1, 1991, China's National Day, to emphasize the importance of minority cultures to the definition of the Chinese nation-state. In addition to the usual multitudes of eateries and souvenir shops, the park includes "authentic replicas" of typical dwellings of twenty-one minority groups, all of them peopled by minority persons. These are primarily young men and women recruited from the minority areas to sit around in national costumes, talk to tourists, play ethnic music, dance, and work at local crafts, most of which are available for sale in gift shops inside the replica villages (see Photo 12.1c).

At one level the whole scene can be interpreted as a highly effective tourist trap, especially with McDonald's—the instantly recognizable symbol of global homogeneity—outside the front gate, a stone's throw from carefully crafted examples of local diversity (the individual villages). Domestic tourists have flocked to the park, but the real prize has been the overseas Chinese, mostly from Hong Kong and Taiwan (such "foreigners" pay three times the ticket price of domestic Chinese tourists). Park visitors can wander through the individual villages and behave like other tourists around the world, viewing traditional architecture, eating minority food, and buying minority handiwork. The novel part of the Folk Cultural Villages, however, is that visitors can interact with, probably for the first time, *real minority people*! At another level the cultural park, and others like it, can be interpreted as part of a distinct bow toward the non-Han periphery in China. This represents a deliberate attempt (supported by the government, albeit funded by "foreign," i.e., Hong Kong, capital) to position ethnic minorities and their cultures as a fundamental part of the new China.[96]

PHOTO 12.1c   A minority couple singing and playing music at the Folk Cultural Villages.

Some critics would argue that in the cultural theme parks the ethnic markers used in the Villages are oversimplified and standardized. Using the sorts of descriptions to be found in the traditional government literature on minority groups, the Shenzhen park tries to portray minority people through "typical" clothing, "local" music, and "authentic" products. In other words these ethnic markers are produced according to someone else's vision, and to ensure maximum consumption and enjoyment for visitors the markers have to be kept simple, easily digested, so to speak. In other words, the state allows the park to open and monitors its "products" while the Hong Kong–based company that owns the park defines the ethnic markers. The result is highly selective cultural preservation that arguably ignores local differences while focusing on specific aspects thought to be appropriate and desirable for mass tourism. There is an emphasis on youth and attractiveness, judging by the people hired to work in the Villages: young, attractive, and multiply talented (after talking to tourists all day, some change costume for the glitzy nighttime song-and-dance show). As geographer Timothy Oakes has argued, the Folk Cultural Villages project serves to "fossilize" some aspects of minority traditions, drawing distinct boundaries around local customs, fixing them in time and space, and ensuring that they remain encased as exhibits for the modern metropolitan world to observe and appreciate.[97]

In a similar fashion, the state-sponsored literature describing (or advertising) different minority groups tends to stereotype and simplify ethnic values and traditions. In one such book, the Naxi people from Yunnan Province are described as follows:

> On festivals, Naxi women put on their traditional costumes and wear their favorite accessory—the colorful and exquisite Seven Star Shawl. Made of a whole sheepskin, the shawl is finished with a six-centimeter-wide edge of black woolen cloth round its upper half. On the shoulders, there are two circular cloth pads with a sun embroidered in silk on one of them and a moon on the other.[98]

Of much more interest to many visitors is the Naxi matriarchal marriage system, still practiced in some villages in the Yongning District, Ningliang County, in northern Yunnan Province. The local custom is referred to in the official literature as an *azhu* or *zouhun* marriage (literally a "walking" marriage).[99] *Azhu* refers more to friendship and courting rather than marriage as it is understood elsewhere in China, but the description in the handbook gives the distinct impression that such practices are both "feudal," in the sense of not being modern, and somewhat immoral. The literature mentions that such practices are no longer observed; in other words they are relics of an outmoded past:

> Young Naxi men and women . . . who like each other can start *azhu* relations by exchanging a keepsake [after this] the man can sleep with the woman at her home for the night. . . . This relationship is not permanent [and it] is finished if the woman does not greet the man at the door. . . . They each can [then] seek a new *azhu* lover.[100]

In the official literature it is implied that young Naxi people, because of the *azhu* tradition, have a higher rate of separation than is common for other minority groups and are more promiscuous. For example, it is noted that "at Yongning, Naxi men and women have the custom of associating with several semi-overt, short-term *azhu* lovers, while at the same time keeping an overt long-term *azhu* lover."[101] It is also observed that the children belong to the woman and are brought up by her, with the help of her brothers, who do not take care of their own children because they are likely to be living in another woman's house. The man has no responsibility for the children, so he will have no descendants. As the household is based on the matriarchal system, the property is also inherited by the woman. The net effect is that "there are no grandfathers or fathers [and] some children do not know who their fathers are."[102]

There is an implicit, none-too-subtle message being portrayed: that such practices are considered to be anachronistic; that Naxi people ought to be "modernized" and encouraged to enter into formal marriages. The walking marriage, in other words, "implies widespread, continuous, and nearly indiscriminate sexual promiscuity."[103] What official sources do not divulge to tourists is that the people who practice the *azhu* marriage self-identify not as Naxi people but as Mosou, a group that is not officially recognized as a minority (except in the Folk Cultural Villages at Shenzhen). It is reasonable to hypothesize, therefore, that the Mosou are selected for display in Shenzhen because the walking marriage system is a special attraction intended to titillate weary tourists. It is also consistent, as Stevan Harrell had suggested, with the construction of minority people in China as socially peripheral and exotic, as people who practice odd, anachronistic, and off-color (but still interesting) customs. The Mosou example also fits with the assignation of subjugated people (such as minority groups) as "feminine," and in this sense the Mosou, as well as other groups, are described and figuratively "sold" to the public as erotically interesting and sexually exotic.[104]

This particular case study illustrates some of the shifting dimensions of official policy toward minority groups in China. The state decrees that the Naxi and the Mosou people belong to one group, called Naxizu. Still, the normal criteria used to determine a minority group are those Stalin applied in the former Soviet Union (common territory, language, economy, and national culture).[105] In the last category (national culture) the Naxi and Mosou people are clearly different, as exemplified by the characteristics of the traditional hierarchical society

found among the Mosou in the past. They had aristocratic and commoner (or slave) classes that are not found in other Naxi groups. Added to the mix of sexual and marriage practices, this history of stratification reinforces the argument that the Mosou are—culturally—a distinct group (and, presumably, considered by Chinese to be more "primitive").[106]

When the official recognition of minority groups was under consideration, Chinese ethnologists, for whatever reason, concluded that the Naxi and the Mosou had a common identity, based on antiquity. In other words, they were once the same people, but they had diverged over time. During the 1950s, when the minority boundaries were being defined, there was pressure to emphasize contemporary class relationships over ethnic distinctions, so there was a tendency to amalgamate minority groups wherever possible by reverting to ethnic categories that could be identified in the distant past. In actual fact, one researcher has noted that some of the Mosou people living in parts of southern Sichuan Province (adjacent to Yunnan) have claimed that their lineage actually links them to Mongols from the Yuan Dynasty, on the basis of which they claimed (and won) Mongol ethnic identity—successfully exploiting their status as "living fossils" of past cultures.

As we have seen here, China's official policy toward minority groups has changed over the decades, with the most important being a shift away from class and class conflict and toward ethnic difference and identification. The dominant theme since roughly 1978 has been to denounce Han chauvinism and preserve the idea that China is a "unitary multinational state built-up jointly by the people of all its nationalities."[107] The Chinese state has attempted to solve the minority question by encouraging modernization and economic development. As we have seen in the case of Tibet (and also in Xinjiang), this may have made the situation worse rather than better, indicating, as Alan Liu has argued, that the problem requires a political rather than an economic solution.[108] It is clear that current state policies have not produced the results that were hoped, and there is still a wide gap between the state's desire to preserve the status quo and the demands of minority people to maintain ethnic identity and, in several cases, to carve out some degree of meaningful autonomy. As we have seen in many other parts of the world, particularly in the former Yugoslavia, such demands have the potential to escalate into deadly conflict.

13
Gender Issues in the Transition out of Socialism

To educate a daughter is like watering another man's garden.[1]
—Traditional proverb from rural China

Introduction: Women and Socialism in China

Because I couldn't love our late Premier more
  than I love you
you accused me of being a man without a heart.
There was no use to explain and you
simply swept me away as if I were a weasel.
I never had the good fortune, as you did,
of being chosen from eight hundred students
  in a school
to tie a red scarf around his neck;
besides, he never visited the small town where
  I grew up.
I saw him in the movies and read about him
  in newspapers,
I agree he was a good man working for the
  people day and night.
When he passed away, I also cried like any of
  you,
but still I couldn't love him more than I love
  you. . . .
If only you and I were twenty years younger
or eighty years older, so that
we could love without him

      —Ha Jin, "A Young Worker's Lament
      to his Former Girlfriend" (1990)[2]

Ha Jin's poem expresses the conflicted emotions likely to emerge when people are required to put love of country before personal feelings. The young man despaired of ever being able to compete with the premier (Zhou Enlai) for his girlfriend's heart. The 1949 revolution and Maoist state socialism demanded that considerations of politics and class relationships be privileged in the effort to transform Chinese society. All other issues, including personal relationships and gender, were to play a secondary role. The reforms of the Dengist and Jiangist eras have downplayed class and political issues and have effectively abandoned the goal of state-inspired social transformation altogether, yet the gender issue has still been ignored. As Marc Blecher has pointed out, "Relations between women and men have never been high on the state's political agenda, and significant political and economic resources have never been devoted specifically to attacking the deep patriarchy of traditional China."[3] This chapter reviews some of the events occurring since 1949 to illustrate and evaluate how the gender issue has been addressed.

Gender Issues in the Maoist State

In Socialist China, we have always advocated that husband and wife help each other and work towards a democratic and harmonious way of life within the family. It is necessary to promote communist morality and oppose rash decisions in marriage.

      —Wu Xinya, "Explanatory Notes on the
      Marriage Law" (1980)[4]

In public presentations Mao Zedong claimed to be repulsed by Confucian traditions that had led to the servitude of Chinese women over the centuries. Before he joined the Communist Party he had become outraged over the suicide of a young woman in his home province who had been betrothed by her parents to a much older man—a rich antiques dealer she detested. On the day of the wedding the woman cut her throat just as she was being put into the bridal chair to be carried to her husband's home. Mao was deeply affected by the incident, referring to the bridal sedan chair as a "prisoner's cart," the vehicle that took a young woman away from her own home and planted her in someone else's, usually to live the rest of her life in silent despair as a virtual prisoner. Mao felt that China's young people should have the courage to oppose arranged marriages: "As soon as a person drops out of his mother's belly, it is said that his marriage is settled [but] we must . . . destroy all superstitions regarding marriage, of which the most important is the destruction of belief in 'predestined' marriage."[5]

Mao's prerevolutionary sentiments thus clearly favored equality for Chinese women. He ridiculed the traditional double standard in Chinese society that excluded women from inheriting property and from all important positions yet still required them to behave with utmost propriety. Speaking through a woman's voice, for example, he denounced the ancient Chinese tradition of concubinage, which had survived well into the twentieth century:

> Shameless, villainous men make us their playthings and force us to prostitute ourselves to them indefinitely. Devils, who destroy the freedom of love! Devils, who destroy the sanctity of love! They keep us surrounded all day long, but this "chastity" is confined to us women! Everywhere there are shrines to virtuous women, but where are the shrines for chaste boys?[6]

Mao was considerably ahead of his time, and there is some evidence that as he grew older his championing of women's rights was contradicted by much of his behavior. He was married several times; he had a long-standing reputation as a womanizer; he abandoned his long-term revolutionary partner in Yenan for the urbane charms of a younger woman; and, much later on, it was reported that he developed an appetite for sleeping with younger women, who were brought to his chambers like concubines.[7]

There was some precedent for Mao's views on gender in the socialist literature he was beginning to read in the 1920s and 1930s. It was assumed that marriage and mate selection in capitalist societies were strongly influenced by concerns for material wealth, status, and political power. In the socialist society Mao hoped to see a decline in the functional basis of marriage and a move toward partnering based more on love and personal attraction. As we shall see in this chapter, however, after five decades of Chinese socialism such is still not the case. During the Cultural Revolution, for example, the political acceptability of one's proposed mate was the single most important factor. Divorce and separation for political reasons were commonplace, as were marriages for political convenience, many of which were later dissolved. Rather than following the dictates of the heart, a young couple wishing to marry had to satisfy the Party that they were suitable candidates for marriage.[8]

Chinese women were curtailed in a structural sense as to what they could achieve in the Maoist era for two reasons. The first was the fact that women were not able to form organizations to lobby for women's interests, so any gains made could come only from the initiatives of the Party-state leadership. The second was the state's unwillingness to challenge and replace the centuries-old practice of patrilocal exogamy, which is the direct cause of many forms of oppression aimed at women and girls. Although it was thought that the destruction of such an ancient cultural tradition would have been cataclysmic, in fact it would have been no more radical than other policies attempted after 1949. There are many reasons why patrilocal exogamy was not contested, but as Blecher has observed, a famous opportunity was missed: "in a historical context when many impossibilities and unimaginable transformations occurred, it is hard not to question the state's failure to challenge the status quo."[9]

Engels and Marx, and Mao Zedong after them, had expected that complete equality for women would gradually come about in a socialist society under three conditions:

- the abolition of private property and wealth as the basis for status differentiation and dependency relationships between men and women;
- a gradual shift in the direction of full and equally paid status for women within the labor force; and
- the public provision of the domestic services that are usually the sole responsibility of women, such as cooking, cleaning, and child-minding.

Some progress was made in these directions after 1949, but in the reform era, with the dictates of socialism largely swept aside, additional progress was curtailed.

Gender Issues in the Reform Era

A couple seeking to marry in the 1990s would find a humble, groveling request for betrothal ludicrously outdated. In the new era of materialism, wealth and possessions have once again become the major criteria in the marriage business, and those unable to make an attractive offer may find themselves permanently on the shelf.[10] At the beginning of the reform era it was clear that three decades of collective socialism had brought some considerable gains to Chinese women, but the Dengist state has been disinterested in or incapable of using political power to push through major changes. In fact it seems to be a feature of socialist societies that policies toward women have been forever subordinate to the productivist goals of the state. This means that the perpetuation of female subordination, and the way in which socialist policy condones male-female inequality, is continually postponed:

Every time the issue emerges . . . a new orthodoxy is constructed around it by emphasizing one or the other role of women [reproduction

versus production] rather than a fundamental restructuring of gender relations. This constant displacing of the woman's question is often hidden by the formal equality that women have acquired, and behind the accession of women to previously unconventional occupations.[11]

In other words, the gains since 1949 are used to co-opt women and divert attention away from gender issues. Although the Party-state has successfully smashed some elements of the old patriarchy—by pushing through land reform and changing marriage laws—gender conflict has never really been allowed to emerge as a public discourse. The debate about women's equality, therefore, remained almost entirely within the confines of communist ideology and did not become a public issue that could challenge the various modes of power within Chinese society.[12] The consequence was that despite the strong language often used to criticize discrimination and violence, women have never been able to create the public political space needed to debate and frame their own demands.[13]

It appears that Marxism, at least in its Chinese variant, does not have a conceptual framework to analyze the nature of gender-based hierarchy. The Chinese Communist Party has consistently refused to deal with certain aspects of gender relations, especially the sexual division of labor and the belief that women are naturally suited for certain roles involving reproduction and the family.[14] As a result, contemporary Chinese policy remains a curious mix "of patriarchy and socialism, where the tensions between women's productive and reproductive roles remain unsolved."[15]

It is no surprise to learn that in Party-state discourses women are spoken of as "those who need to be 'protected,' on par with children" and that women's rights are enshrined in the constitution "as a gift of the Party rather than as something won by women through struggle and because women deserve to be equal."[16] This protectionist discourse allowed the CCP after 1949 to suppress the more radical and independent discourses that had emerged decades earlier in the fledgling Communist Party during the May Fourth Movement of 1919. The protective strategy also ensures that women who do act independently outside the state-supported mass organization for women (the All-China Women's Federation) are marginalized and effectively discredited as being divisive. The Party can righteously claim that it *has* established an organization to protect women's interests, and it discourages (in fact prohibits) efforts to set up more radical, autonomous women's organizations.

Harriet Evans, in *Women and Sexuality in China*, has pushed this argument even farther, suggesting that the Party orthodoxy has significant implications for the way Chinese society interprets some of the emerging trends in China that affect women and their sexuality.[17] The Chinese state has managed to control the issue of sexuality as a way of maintaining marital, household, and familial social relationships. By controlling what Evans calls the "technology of sex"—through a variety of medical, pedagogical, social, and political discourses—the state is able to "construct" sex as an issue that requires individuals to place themselves under surveillance, all in the interest of societal harmony.[18] The Party-state seeks, more than anything else, a secure and stable society, and it has appointed itself the guarantor of stability. The assumption is thus that societal stability can be ensured only if there is family stability, which in turn requires the state to control and shape gender relations.

The state today identifies women as the main agents responsible for patrolling general standards of sexual morality and family order. Based on the biological principles of what is considered to be appropriate gender conduct, the "ideal" woman is defined in terms of the private (household-based) sphere of wifely behavior and maternal concern. If she has views about the issue of sexual desire they will, it is assumed, be defined entirely in terms of her conjugal responsibilities, which are necessarily contained within the marital relationship. If a women steps outside that context, her sexuality immediately becomes a source of potential danger, perhaps even contamination and chaos.[19] This produces an attitude in which any woman whose sexual behavior does not conform to societal norms will be marginalized.

Female sexuality is considered to be defined only in terms of complementing the more powerful male drive, and it can only be directed toward the needs of procreation, essentially "ignor[ing] the female subject as an autonomous site of pleasure."[20] To prevent this from occurring the state tries to make sure that women are protected, before marriage, to ensure their virtue, energy, and health for the demands of homemaking and childbirth. During marriage women are expected to be selfless, absolutely faithful and responsive to their husbands' needs, and attendant to all domestic chores and duties. Beyond marriage, widows are expected to remain faithful to deceased spouses, and divorcées are expected to live in celibacy. If a woman performs all of these tasks well, she will be contributing significantly to the state's overall goal of maintaining the moral and social stability of the Chinese family.

In spite of increasing global awareness of women's issues, some Western feminist scholars believe that Chinese women may actually be worse off now than during the Maoist era. In contemporary China it is difficult for women to reconcile the two powerful forces impinging upon them: the naturalized view of gender hierarchy, with women as subservient and primarily responsible for reproduction; and the new but already widespread representation of women as a sexualized object in the commoditized and privatized world of male fantasy. Some Chinese women have successfully managed to carve out a "life of self-mastery" in the very limited new spaces that are becoming available to them. But for the most part women lack autonomous agency in China, and until the dominant discourse is officially challenged—the assumption that women's gender subordination is biologically determined—women's autonomous needs and requirements will not and indeed cannot be addressed.

It is reasonable to point out that the essence of this critique is constructed by Western feminists and thus may not represent the sentiments of Chinese women. It is important to balance the feminist critique, therefore, with an appraisal of some of the gains made by women in postrevolutionary China. To that end it is useful to consider how the subordinate role of women was supported throughout China's history.

The Confucian Heritage: Being a "Proper" Chinese Woman?

A son is born facing in and a girl is born facing out.
A daughter married is like water poured out the door.
Investing in a girl is a loss.
A family with daughters is a dead-end family.[21]

These ancient sayings suggest that the subjugation of women in China has its roots in centuries of Confucian-based oppression. The liberation of women from that oppression was one of the major platforms of the intellectual revolution that began in China in the second decade of the twentieth century; in fact the gender issue provided future leaders like Mao Zedong and other young radicals of the May Fourth Movement with a powerful symbol of everything they loathed about Confucianism.[22] The "woman problem" (*funu wenti*) became one of the most emotionally charged issues of the time, and in fact it has even been suggested that the feminist issue "radicalized many of the future Chinese communist leaders before their conversion to Marxism-Leninism."[23] In this section we consider some of the ways the Chinese state attempted to address the issue of gender inequality. There is no shortage of opinion on this topic, but perhaps it is better to let the facts speak for themselves, focusing on three themes that are most amenable to measurement: educational achievement, status in the labor force, and participation in politics.

Schooling

The gap between the amount of education received by men and women in China declined significantly throughout the twentieth century.

Among a sample of Hong Kong expatriates, for example, for those who began school before 1918 the male-female difference in length of schooling was more than six years; for those who started school after 1958, the difference was less than a half-year.[24] It is important to qualify that observation: In the first place, although schooling opportunities for Chinese women were greater than in other developing countries in Asia at the end of the 1970s, they did not match up well with the countries China sought to be compared with, namely, European socialist states as well as capitalist societies in Europe and North America. The proportion of women in tertiary education in China is significantly lower than it is in most other countries, including the poorest Asian nations, such as India and Bangladesh. It is apparent that there is still nowhere near equal access for women to universities and other institutions of higher learning in China. In 1986, for example, only a quarter of all students in Chinese universities and colleges were women, although the percentage appears to have risen slightly.

At the other end of the academic scale, the evidence is worse. In a study of 416 adults aged between 18 and 39, for example, Margery Wolf reported an illiteracy rate that was ten times higher for women than for men (22 percent versus 2 percent), and only 45 percent of the women in her study reached middle school, compared to 68 percent of men.[25] As would be expected, illiteracy rates were much higher among older people: 75 percent for women, 21 percent for men; only 7 percent of the women over 40 reached middle school. Wolf's data also indicate the existence of a wide gap between urban and rural areas, and the differences there are even greater. This suggests that even though girls in the countryside probably have greater access to schooling now than ever before, their parents are likely to require them to leave school prematurely. One of Wolf's respondents in the countryside told her why this is the case: "With no self-consciousness at all, he explained that girls were simply better at other things, such as cooking and feeding pigs, so their parents preferred to keep them at home. Besides, he said, they marry into other families so people are reluctant to waste too much money educating them."[26]

Labor Force Participation

In absolute terms women have fared much better in the labor force. For younger women there is almost equal participation, although older women, who are less likely to have received training and education, are not as well represented. In total, women constitute 48 percent of the labor force in China, significantly higher than in other poor Asian countries (28 percent), capitalist countries (33 percent), even socialist states (44 percent).[27] Labor force participation rates of this magnitude obviously represent greater opportunities for women, yet working outside the home was more of an economic necessity, not a matter of choice.[28] The result is that most Chinese women find themselves laboring under the double burden: working a job and running a household.[29]

The evidence also shows that urban Chinese women are concentrated in lower-paying jobs than are men, jobs that are generally low in status, with fewer fringe benefits, and considerably less opportunity for upward mobility.[30] Among a sample of Hong King émigrés, for example, women earned 77 percent of what men earned, although that varied by age, with younger women generally earning more. Among Wolf's respondents within the PRC, women earned 72 percent of male wages, averaging Y546 per year compared to Y761 for men.[31] These statistics indicate that Chinese women, at about the time the economic reforms were beginning (late 1970s to early 1980s), were probably no worse off than their counterparts elsewhere. As we shall see, however, in global terms it appears that women in contemporary China have experienced some decline in their incomes relative to those of men.

Politics

It is not uncommon to find women at all levels of the political hierarchy in China, yet with some notable exceptions few women reach the highest positions.[32] That situation is not atypical of socialist countries; for example, 11 percent of CCP Central Committee members in the late 1970s were women, compared to 9 percent in European socialist states.[33] In the mid-1990s only 6 percent of ministerial positions were held by women; they made up only 21 percent of the National People's Congress; and within the CCP as a whole women members represented only 13 percent. Some progress has been recorded. For example in 1994, the official public information branch of the China Organizing Committee for the 1995 UN Fourth World Conference on Women in Beijing reported that there were sixteen women ministers and vice ministers in the ministries and commissions under the State Council; eighteen women governors and vice governors; and more than 300 women mayors and vice mayors.[34] As in the working world generally, Chinese women in political jobs tend to be unevenly clustered at the bottom of the hierarchy. Women have a virtual monopoly over administrative posts in street-level organizations, in heading resident and neighborhood committees, and in policing the birth control policies at the local level. All are important but often intensely unpopular and poorly paid jobs.

Women's Achievements in an International Context

It is useful, if only for illustration, to compare Chinese women to women in other countries by using indices constructed by the United Nations. The UN has assembled a Gender Development Index (GDI), which measures country averages for providing basic human needs and capabilities (see Table 13.1a).[35]

The core measure is the Human Development Index (HDI), which is constructed from statistics on life expectancy, literacy, income, and education; GDI is calculated by applying special weightings on each of the indicators for inequality between men and women. In 1998 (using 1995 data) China had a much lower GDI score than did Asian and non-Asian developed

TABLE 13.1a   Gender Development Index[1] and Its Components for China and Selected Countries (1995 data)

Country	GDI Index	Rank in the World	Female Share of Earned Income (%)	Female Life Expectancy	Female Adult Literacy (%) 1995	Female Combined Primary Secondary Tertiary Education Enrollment Rate
China	0.641	93	38.1	71.3	72.7	61.5
India	0.424	128	25.4	61.8	37.7	46.5
Burundi	0.230	159	42.3	46.1	22.5	20.1
Burkina Faso	0.205	161	39.6	47.4	9.2	14.9
Myanmar	0.478	120	42.3	60.6	77.7	47.5
Sweden	0.932	3	44.7	80.8	99.0	84.0
USA	0.927	6	40.3	79.7	99.0	98.0
Japan	0.902	13	34.1	82.8	82.8	77.0
UK	0.907	11	37.6	79.4	99.0	86.0
Hong Kong	0.836	33	25.6	81.8	88.2	69.9
Singapore	0.848	29	31.9	79.3	86.3	66.6
South Korea	0.826	37	29.2	75.4	96.7	78.4

SOURCE: UNDP, *Human Development Report, 1998*, Table 2, pp. 131–133.

NOTE: [1] The GDI measures each country's average achievement in providing basic human capabilities with special weightings for inequality between men and women. The basic index (HDI) is calculated from measures of longevity, literacy, income, and educational achievements.

states; for example, China's GDI was 0.641 compared to Japan's 0.902 and Sweden's 0.932, which gives it a ranking of ninety-third out of 174 countries for which data were available. Yet China's score is significantly higher than for many Asian and non-Asian developing nations; for example, Myanmar (formerly Burma), 0.478; India, 0.424; and Sierra Leone, at the very bottom, 0.165.[36] In its 1995 report China scored seventy-first on the GDI, considerably higher than the UN's HDI, the more traditional index of development, where China ranked 111th. This suggested that China—and a number of other countries, including Cuba, Malaysia, Thailand, and several Central and Eastern European nations—had made more than average gains in the realm of gender equality. To account for the higher rankings on the GDI, the UN Human Development Report suggested that "these countries have invested in the education and health of their people, irrespective of gender, and as a result [have] achieved much progress in building women's basic capabilities."[37] By 1998, however, China's ranking on the

GDI had fallen to ninety-third and was quite close to its HDI ranking (ninety-eight), so the UN's optimism may have been premature.

China also compares well globally in politics, power, and employment for women. The UN's Gender Empowerment Measure (GEM) is constructed from statistics describing women's participation in economic, political, and professional life. In Table 13.1b the GEM scores for China are compared to selected countries in three other groups: existing and former socialist states; developed states in Asia and elsewhere; and developing states. China's GEM in 1998 was 0.483, ranking thirty-third overall, significantly higher than its rankings for GDI (ninety-third) and HDI (ninety-eighth).[38]

China, like other socialist and former socialist states such as Cuba and Bulgaria, scores well on measures used to calculate the GEM index, which include women holding government positions; women working in administrative, managerial, professional, and technical jobs; and women's share of total earned income. In fact China fares better than the four Asian states

TABLE 13.1b   Gender Empowerment Measure[1] for China and Selected Countries, 1995

Country	GEM	Ranking	Women's Seats in Parliament (%)	Women Administrators and Managers (%)	Women Professional and Technical Workers (%)	Women's Share of Combined Income (%)
China	0.483	33	21.0	11.6	45.1	38
Cuba	0.523	25	22.8	18.5	47.8	31
Bulgaria	0.462	43	10.8	28.9	57.0	41
Sweden	0.790	1	40.4	38.9	64.2	45
USA	0.675	11	11.2	42.7	52.6	40
UK	0.593	20	11.6	32.9	44.2	38
Singapore	0.467	42	4.8	15.4	36.5	32
Japan	0.472	38	7.7	8.9	43.3	34
Pakistan	0.179	100	2.6	3.9	19.5	21

SOURCE: UNDP, *Human Development Report 1998,* Table 3, pp. 134–136.

NOTE: [1] The GEM is a combined empowerment measure of female participation in economic, political, and professional life.

in the table, though not as well as the three non-Asian developed states (Sweden, United States, and the United Kingdom).

These two indices suggest that Chinese women are relatively better off than many women in developing countries as to their standing in society when measured by jobs and earnings. Women in China, however, are underachieving in education and health care. There are also some telling statistics as to the position of women within Chinese society; when considered in absolute terms they call into question the positive picture painted by the UN gender indices. For example, the absolute level of wages earned by women in China in 1995 was estimated to be only 59.4 percent compared to men, far behind many developed nations (75 percent for the United States, 89 percent for Sweden; even in Vietnam it is 91.5 percent).[39] Also disturbing is the percentage of females between ten and fourteen who are economically active in the labor force (22.3 percent in 1990, indicating that more than one in five girls under fourteen were working rather than schooling; it is reasonable to assume that many were in the countryside).[40]

China's women have experienced some important gains in the labor market, but if we use the available data to test the Engels-Marx

hypothesis—that greater participation in the labor force ultimately means complete equality for women—the results are mixed. In relative terms Chinese women are certainly better off than they are in many parts of the world, especially in terms of the jobs they hold (although not necessarily in incomes). They are underachieving in education, and there are some major concerns about women's health and longevity, especially in the Chinese countryside, issues that we shall return to later in this chapter.

As a number of Western feminist scholars have suggested, the CCP, after its radical beginnings, dragged its heels on gender equality. Arguably, the Party was able to use labor force statistics to create an impression that giant steps had been taken, but in fact relatively little was done to improve the status of women in Chinese society. As the earlier discussion has shown, despite some radical feminist roots in the 1920s, the CCP became fairly conservative on women's issues in the 1930s and has remained that way ever since.[41] The result was that although some of the worst aspects of Confucian suppression of women were abolished (such as concubinage and bound feet), the Communists were reluctant to mount serious attacks against the structure of patriarchal authority in rural areas.[42]

Marriage and Family Life in Socialism and Through the Transition

In feudal China, the patriarchal family system went hand in hand with arranged marriages, male chauvinism, and indifference to women's wants and feelings.[43] Marriage and the family were important concerns of the Chinese government after the 1949 revolution.[44] One of the earliest pieces of legislation was the Marriage Law of 1950, which abolished arranged marriages; restricted (but did not eliminate) paying for brides; outlawed much of the ritual and ceremony associated with traditional marriages; prohibited concubinage, footbinding, and child marriages; and provided greater access to divorce for women (see Table 13.2).

The new Marriage Law effectively put an end to the feudal marriage code and provided ground rules for all marriages to be founded on mutual affection.[45] Three decades later, the 1981 Marriage Law retained the basic spirit of the earlier law while extending some of its provisions: Later marriages were to be officially encouraged; men and women were to enjoy equal status in the home; both partners were to share responsibility in caring for parents and children; and divorce was to be granted in cases of "complete alienation" even if only one party felt it was necessary.[46]

As a number of China scholars have noted, the implementation of the new laws was uneven; in fact it has been argued that because Party leaders were so concerned not to alienate their rural power base—the leaders of patriarchal families—they were reluctant to push through many of the new laws. Apologists for the Party have suggested this reluctance was based more on economic concerns than outright hostility toward women. During the civil war Chinese peasants had suffered so badly for several decades—from poverty, social instability, hostilities, and foreign occupation—that Party leaders were not eager to further burden rural patriarchs.[47] They chose instead to focus on promoting female participation in the labor force rather than dealing with other gender inequality issues. Although gender equality has nearly always been on the official agenda and part of government discourse, it has often taken a backseat to other concerns.[48]

As might be expected the new marriage laws were well received by many women: In the first five years, for example, more than half a million women filed for divorce.[49] Yet there was a great deal of resistance: Male peasants threatened women officials attempting to enforce the divorce provisions, and mothers-in-law threw their weight into the conflict, as they too stood to lose if divorces were granted. In 1953 it was reported that 75,000 deaths or suicides each year were directly attributable to marital disharmony and conflict generated or exacerbated by the new laws.[50] The difficulties encountered in enforcement revealed the depth of tradition in rural China and the institutional underpinnings for their acceptance. The traditional family system served important functions for which the Party-state did not offer any viable alternatives."[51]

It is useful to review the progress made in some of the controversial areas associated with marriage and families during the five decades since the revolution.

Divorce and Morality in the New China

The liberalization of divorce in China was considered crucial to the overall effort to improve the quality of women's lives. It represented an acceptance that long-term suffering in unhappy and loveless marriages need not be perpetuated. Yet public opinion has changed slowly, and even today divorced women are treated with contempt. Divorce is seen as the last resort, it is frowned upon and discouraged, and most couples are required to go through mediation beforehand.

The experiences of divorced and widowed women were the theme of new literature produced by Chinese women writers in the 1980s. One of the best known in this genre is Zhang Jie, who has documented the humiliation and constant haranguing that women living alone

TABLE 13.2   Excerpts from the Marriage Law of the People's Republic of China

Article

Chapter I
General Principles

Article 1

The feudal marriage system based on arbitrary and compulsory arrangements and the supremacy of man over woman, and in disregard of the interests of the children is abolished.

The New Democratic marriage system which is based on the free choice of partners, on monogamy, on equal rights for both sexes, and on the protection of the lawful interests of women and children, is put into effect.

Article 2

Bigamy, concubinage, child betrothal, interference in the re-marriage of widows, and the exaction of money or gifts in connection with marriages, are prohibited.

Chapter II
The Marriage Contract

Article 3

Marriage is based upon the complete willingness of the two parties. Neither party shall use compulsion and no third party is allowed to interfere.

Article 4

A marriage can be contracted only after the man has reached 20 years of age and the woman 18 years of age.

Chapter III
Rights and Duties of Husband and Wife

Article 8

Husband and wife are in duty bound to love, respect, assist and look after each other, to live in harmony, to engage in productive work, to care for their children, and to strive jointly for the welfare of the family and for the building up of the new society.

Article 9

Both husband and wife have equal rights in the possession of and management of family property.

Chapter V

Article 17

Divorce is granted when husband and wife both desire it. In the event of either the husband or the wife alone insisting upon divorce it may be granted only when mediation by the district people's government and the judicial organ has failed to bring about a reconciliation.

Article 19

In the case of a member of the revolutionary army on active service who maintains correspondence with his or her family, that army member's consent must be obtained before his or her spouse can apply for divorce.

---

experience in urban neighborhoods.[52] Within the family, considerable pressure is often put on divorcées and widows, who are expected to remain celibate. In Zhang Xian's story "The Widow," the heroine knows that social norms require her to remain faithful to her deceased husband despite her desires. She recalls an ancient tale about the "coins of chastity" that

describes the behavior expected of her by her grown-up children:

> In order to overcome her feelings of emptiness and loneliness, a widow tossed a hundred coins onto the floor every night, then turned out the light and groped around on the floor picking them up one by one. By the time they were all

back in her purse she was finally tired enough to go to bed and fall asleep. And that's how she spent her nights right up till the day she died, letting a hundred coins, shiny from being rubbed countless times, stand as proof of her bitterly attained virtue. She died with a clear conscience and a sense of pride.[53]

The new laws and changing times have produced two distinct patterns of divorce in China since 1949. Immediately after the 1950 Marriage Law, thousands, perhaps millions, of divorces were granted to women married under the old patriarchal system. The divorce rate then slowed to its normal rate, which is much lower than in most Western countries. In the 1980s, especially after the 1981 Marriage Law was passed, divorces rose again.[54] The traditionally conservative, patriarchal response among the Chinese leadership is to assume this is what results from the importation of bourgeois practices from the West.

Part of the rise in divorce rates after 1981 was the result of reapplications from couples who had previously been denied a divorce. In addition, many partners had married in the 1960s and 1970s based on political motivations but now found they were incompatible. Under the new law such marriages could be dissolved much more easily. The changing attitude to divorce in China in the 1980s and 1990s might also be reflecting some of the changes in the economic system introduced by the reforms: "It is not surprising that relations between people are . . . changing, as all seek to maximize the benefits according to themselves personally through this shift in development strategy. In the sphere of divorce this can manifest itself in selfish or mercenary behavior."[55]

Since reform began individuals have been allowed and even encouraged to follow their chosen paths in the economic sphere, and it could be that divorce will increasingly follow suit, interpreted almost as an entitlement. However, regardless of the Marriage Law and its provisions for granting divorces, society and particularly the courts are still biased by a persistent moral double standard. In the past it was easy for a court to define "immoral behavior," as the norms were clearly stated in political terms: Divorce during the Maoist era was most often interpreted as a bourgeois act that threatened the viability of the socialist family.[56]

In the 1980s and 1990s those definitions tended to be more liberal, yet the law is no longer as clear-cut, which may well open the door for antidivorce backlash.[57] It is also reasonable to infer that the political crackdown that reached a head in the wake of Tiananmen Square might have brought a new wave of moral repression, which would set the clock back even farther on women's liberation. This does not appear to have been the case, however, because most reports from China indicate that the divorce rate has hugely increased since roughly 1980. *The Economist*, for example, reported that the divorce rate increased from 4.7 percent in 1981 to 12 percent in 1996, although no source is given for these statistics.[58] The official source of data, the *China Statistical Yearbook*, reports that divorces more than doubled in an eleven-year period (1985–1996), but the rate of divorce was reported as only 1.8 percent in 1996.[59]

The Chinese Family in the 1990s

Family life in China has changed since 1949. Families tend to be smaller, of course, the result of birth control policies as well as trends typical of a society that is modernizing and urbanizing. In China, as in the rest of the world, the conjugal family is gradually replacing the extended family, particularly in the cities. Yet the Chinese would claim with some pride that there is little evidence of the wholesale breakdown of family life so apparent in the developing world and in the inner cities of developed countries. To a large extent this is the result of urban and regional policies implemented in China since 1949.

Yet it may also have something to do with Chinese culture itself, in which patriarchal kinship and the desire to maintain close family ties helped keep Chinese families together through political upheaval and economic austerity. The sociodemographic characteristics of Chinese cities stand in sharp contrast to cities in most other poor nations: the breakdown of family solidarity; early sex and marriage; promiscuity and prostitution; and the prevalence of women-headed households. In China the norm is for the traditional family to remain intact, sex and marriage are delayed, illegitimacy rates are low, and men still dominate family life.[60]

Chinese women probably feel mixed emotions on all this. The strength of the traditional Chinese family, and the continued male dominance in all spheres, has helped maintain social cohesiveness throughout urban and rural China. Although that provides the social stability so important to Chinese politicians, it also suffocates the aspirations of millions of women whose voices have been gagged—their bodies violated as a result. Countless women remain trapped in unhappy marriages with little chance for escaping due to Chinese cultural norms.[61]

It is also possible to argue that the Chinese family has not changed as much as might have been predicted or expected in 1949. For men and the Chinese government, that might be a positive result; for Chinese women—as well as for feminists around the world—it represents a bitter disappointment. The changes that have occurred are best described as evolutionary rather than revolutionary, and the influence of socialism and the Marriage Laws has been much less than was hoped. What still appears to hold the Chinese family together is an unwritten set of ancient cultural traditions that have been left largely intact after fifty years of communist rule.[62]

The government has encouraged family cohesiveness because, in most cases, it has served its purpose, but the state acted swiftly and ruthlessly to break down connectedness among family members. This proved to be particularly useful for isolating counterrevolutionary elements during the Cultural Revolution and for weeding out dissidents on the run after Tiananmen Square. Author Zhang Xianliang, a dissident during the Cultural Revolution, has

pointed out that this is by no means a new tactic for the Chinese state. The long tentacles of the Party-state have torn apart ancient bonds among Chinese people whenever it has suited its purpose. As Zhang put it: "I consider that to be the greatest crime they have perpetrated. They've destroyed a sense of trust among men. Instead of building good intentions and a readiness to help one another, they've made men into wild animals."[63]

Changing Norms for Sexual Behavior: Examining the "Convergence" Theory

It is possible only to speculate whether the changes in law combined with reform-era modernization have prompted changes in the more intimate aspects of male-female relationships in contemporary China. Given the increasing Westernization among young people, we might expect more sexual activity prior to marriage, as well as higher rates of marital infidelity. In the 1990s the state became somewhat fixated with the issue of sexual promiscuity and the erosion of traditional moral values, which it interprets as symptoms of the spiritual pollution creeping in from Hong Kong, Taiwan, Japan, and the West.

It is difficult for outsiders to evaluate the intimate changes in behavior occurring in contemporary China. Much of the evidence about the nature of personal relationships, as well as sexual attitudes and behaviors, is sketchy at best. Several Western observers have described a tendency for greater openness about sex and a greater degree of what the Chinese still refer to as "promiscuity," but it would be unwise to leap to conclusions about morality. As Lynn Pan remarked, "For all these hints of debauchery . . . the Chinese remain a straitlaced people. An open-air dance . . . in Chengdu had a notice at the entrance forbidding couples to dance cheek-to-cheek."[64] Lynn Pan spoke with a Chinese gynecologist, who told her that in his experience the vast majority of young people in

China still had only a dim notion of sex. Pan concluded that even in the late 1980s premarital sex was not allowed and when it did happen it was denounced as immoral.[65] Charlotte Ikels has also written about this in *The Return of the God of Wealth*, which is based on her intensive study of everyday life in the city of Guangzhou.[66] After conducting surveys and in-depth interviews, Ikels concluded that young people in contemporary China generally know little and are confused about sex. Describing China's twenty-somethings, Ikels said they revealed "a shyness, uncertainty, and immaturity characteristic of a much younger age group in the United States."[67]

One thing is certain: There is a far greater exposure to sex and sexual imagery in contemporary China, especially in places like Shanghai and the booming cities along the southeastern coast. The explicit references to and portrayals of sex in books, films, magazines, and advertisements can be interpreted as evidence of changing views on moral issues in China. Literature has seen a major breakthrough, bearing in mind that as recently as the late 1980s some of the pioneering works, such as Zhang Xianliang's *Half of Man Is Woman* and Yu Luojin's *A Chinese Winter's Tale*, were difficult to obtain through normal outlets. Strict censorship continued in the world of literature and art after Tiananmen Square in 1989, which brought forth official criticism of all sources of spiritual pollution from the West. From most published accounts, however, the production and sale of materials with graphic sexual content—including a variety of books, magazines, and videos—are now commonplace, assuming the customer can pay and knows where to look.[68] The government from time to time launches campaigns to drive such materials off the street, but in most cases they simply go underground, reappearing within a few months.[69] The official television networks are still heavily censored, and the film industry is strictly controlled, yet the bombardment of lurid imagery, much of it from Hong Kong and Taiwan, makes a mockery of official puritanical standards.

In a survey of almost 1,000 Beijing families conducted in 1985, there was some quantitative evidence of more liberal, or Westernized, views on sex. Fewer than two-thirds of the respondents said they were opposed to premarital sex, compared to four-fifths in 1982; only one in five respondents under thirty said they considered marital fidelity to be important.[70] And so with the passage of time we can expect to see even more changes in attitudes toward sex. As *The Economist* reported in 1997, there are now many signs that Chinese people are throwing off the sexual repression that has marked much of recent history.[71] That process is being accelerated by increased publicity about sex: rising marital infidelity, premarital sex, pregnancy outside marriage, and rape and sexual violence—all being reported on a regular basis by the media. Prostitution is also flourishing again in China's big cities despite repeated police crackdowns. There are gay bars in some of the big cities, shops that sell everything imaginable, as well as sex hot lines for people to call with stories and problems.[72] *The Economist* suggested that much of it was a function of economic reform and an apparently insatiable appetite for making money: "China's changing attitudes to sex are reflected by the Chinese media. Film and television producers, and their advertisers, are discovering that sex sells [all of which] marks a profound change in the sex life of the nation."[73]

It is not known exactly how *The Economist's* reporter reached those conclusions, but there is some quantitative evidence that attitudes toward sex and sexual behavior are loosening and thus "converging" with those in the West. A report published in 1997, *Sexual Behavior in Modern China,* is based on a nationwide study of 20,000 people.[74] It contains direct comparisons to sexual attitudes and behaviors in Japan and, occasionally, Western countries, especially the United States. In schools the survey found that although boys and girls are maturing earlier in China, they begin to date and usually engage in sexual activities significantly later than in Japan. The survey reports that sex education in schools is rudimentary, and in many

schools sex education is still not part of the cur-
riculum.

Among college students, again the tone is
one of conservatism; Chinese students tend to
be late starters in sexual activities. Less than
two-thirds (63 percent) of male Chinese high
school students said they had masturbated, a
figure the researchers say is much lower than in
Japan and Western societies.[75] Among Chinese
college students, 52 percent said they had never
masturbated; among an adult sample fewer
than one in five in the cities and one in ten in
the countryside reported masturbating before
marriage.[76] These survey results indicated that
Chinese boys and girls, in high school and college, think about sex roughly as often as they do
in the West, but they tend to engage in sex significantly less frequently.

Among married couples the survey over-
sampled for women because it was generally
assumed that Chinese women were significantly more repressed sexually than Western
and Japanese women. In fact, it found that in
many instances such was not the case, with evidence of more progressive views than anticipated. A large majority of women, for example,
felt it was normal for women to take the initiative in sex, although when asked about their
actual experiences, very few of the women (1.3
percent) said they were the initiator in sexual
intercourse (see Table 13.3a), and significantly
fewer women than men reported they were
very satisfied with their sex life (see Table
13.3b).

The researchers concluded that on most
counts Chinese people are similar to Westerners
in their attitudes toward sex and are shedding
the traditional image of passivity, lack of interest, and lack of experience. They also concluded, however, that Chinese tend to be more
conservative when it comes to actual sexual
behaviors. For example, more than half of couples surveyed said they changed their sexual
positions "at least occasionally," and more than
two-thirds said they preferred to be naked during intercourse.[77] Chinese men and women
appear to indulge in premarital sex almost as
much as do Westerners, although it appears
that men in the countryside are much less likely
than urban men to have experienced premarital
sex (Table 13.3c).

There is evidence to support the hypothesis
that Chinese men and women are relatively
inexperienced. For example, the data show that
in the cities and the countryside, for the overwhelming majority of both men and women,

TABLE 13.3a   Who Is the Initiator in Sexual Intercourse? (% of respondents)

Gender of Respondent	Husband	Wife	Both	Not Clear	Total #
Male	63.7	3.4	20.8	12.1	2,052
Female	71.9	1.3	15.4	11.3	5,196

SOURCE: Adapted from Liu et al. (1997), Table 3-113, p. 183, and Table 4-198, p. 298.

TABLE 13.3b   How Satisfied Are You with Your Sex Life? (married couples, % of respondents)

Location and Gender of Respondents		Very Good	Good	Fair	Poor	Very Poor	Total #
City	Male	28.7	48.7	19.2	1.3	0.5	1,503
	Female	17.1	41.8	33.5	2.1	0.4	3,870
Country	Male	47.3	31.9	17.4	0.3	1.0	298
	Female	30.4	33.3	30.7	0.6	0.5	1,083

SOURCE: Adapted from Liu et al. (1997), Tables 4-217 and 4-218, pp. 307–308.

their spouse was their first sex partner; fewer than 10 percent of the respondents, both men and women, reported that they masturbated after marriage.[78] It is also interesting to note that the requirement for chastity in a future spouse is considered very important for women and men. This is revealed in the data collected from a multicountry study.[79] When asked how important chastity was for their future spouse, Chinese respondents scored 2.5 for men and 2.6 for women (on a scale of 0–3, with 0 being irrelevant and 3 indispensable). These scores (which were only slightly lower for men and women in Taiwan) were higher than for men and women anywhere else, with the exception of Iran (see Table 13.4).[80]

One should not read too much into these statistics, given some of the problems the researchers reported in conducting the surveys. Perhaps the most remarkable fact, however, was that the nationwide survey took place at all and that for the first time China has some nonideological and uncensored information about sex and sexuality. There is a much more significant critique, however, of the way such data are interpreted. There is a tendency to evaluate data indicating convergence between Chinese and Western sexual attitudes and behaviors as a positive trend. Similarly, the relatively recent trend toward femininity, and the increasingly pervasive discussions about and images of sex and sexuality in China, are looked upon in the same light. The basis for these evaluations, presumably, is the assumption that the traditional repression of sexuality in China has been abandoned and that the Chinese are now well on the

way toward modernization. This implies both that "they" are normal (or just like us) and that this is a positive, healthy trend. In addition, the new views about sex are thought by some to indicate that Chinese women are being set free from earlier repression.

Such views should not go unchallenged, on a number of grounds. In the first place many feminists argue that the increasing visibility of sex and sexuality in any society exploits rather than liberates women and represents a negative shift away from women's aspirations to be stronger and more independent. In addition, there is evidence that women in China are increasingly being used and are coming to see themselves as commodities. Feminist historian Gail Hershatter has also raised another important consideration about the increasing visibility of sex and sexuality in China.[81] She suggests that evaluating such trends as positive is doing a great disservice to China's women and is missing or ignoring the fundamental cultural importance of sexuality. Hershatter would contend that what makes sex and sexuality in China interesting is not the similarities with the West but the differences.[82]

When we Westerners assume that Chinese are becoming more like us with regard to sex, we are stating, implicitly at least, that our habits are the correct ones to mimic; this would mean that the Chinese are heading down the "correct" path, if indeed they are following the Western example. We are also assuming that the new trends signify modernity, as Chinese men and women finally are able to shrug off their repressive pasts. Hershatter would contend that it is

TABLE 13.3c When Did You First Have Sexual Intercourse?

Location and Gender of Respondents		Male %	Female %	Total #
City	Premarital	24.9	15.7	441
	Wedding Night	62.4	70.8	1103
	After Marriage	12.7	13.5	224
Countryside	Premarital	7.3	17.3	224
	Wedding Night	69.3	62.3	208
	After Marriage	23.3	20.3	70

SOURCE: Adapted from Liu et al. (1997), Tables 4-91 and 4-92, p. 244.

TABLE 13.4   Desirable Characteristics in Your Future Mate (33 countries; 0=irrelevant; 3=indispensible)

	Good Financial Prospects		Ambition and Industriousness		Good Looks		Chastity	
	Male	Female	Male	Female	Male	Female	Male	Female
China	1.1	1.6	2.2	2.6	2.1	1.6	2.5	2.6
Taiwan	1.3	2.2	2.2	2.8	1.8	1.3	2.3	2.2
India	1.6	2.0	1.8	2.4	2.0	2.0	2.4	2.2
Indonesia	1.4	2.6	2.0	2.3	1.8	1.4	2.1	2.0
Iran	1.3	2.0	2.7	2.8	2.1	1.7	2.7	2.2
Israel (Jewish)	1.3	1.8	1.8	2.4	1.8	1.6	0.9	0.6
Israel (Palestinian)	1.3	1.7	2.3	2.6	2.4	1.5	2.2	1.0
Japan	0.9	2.3	1.9	2.4	1.5	1.1	1.4	0.8
Bulgaria	1.2	1.6	1.7	2.2	2.4	2.0	0.7	0.4
Estonian S.S.R.	1.3	1.5	2.3	2.5	2.3	1.6	1.3	0.8
Poland	1.1	1.7	1.9	2.3	1.9	1.8	1.2	1.0
Yugoslavia	1.3	1.7	1.8	2.2	2.2	1.7	0.5	0.1
Belgium	1.0	1.4	1.7	2.0	1.8	1.3	0.7	0.4
France	1.2	1.7	1.8	2.0	2.1	1.8	0.5	0.4
Finland	0.7	1.2	1.4	1.6	1.6	1.0	0.3	0.3
West Germany	1.1	1.8	1.4	1.7	1.9	1.3	0.3	0.2
Britain	0.7	1.2	1.2	1.6	2.0	1.4	0.5	0.5
Greece	1.2	1.9	2.0	2.3	2.2	1.9	0.5	0.4
Ireland	0.8	1.7	1.4	1.8	1.9	1.2	1.5	1.5
Italy	0.9	1.3	1.6	2.1	2.0	1.6	0.7	0.3
Netherlands	0.7	0.9	1.3	1.4	1.8	1.2	0.3	0.3
Norway	1.1	1.4	1.6	1.7	1.9	1.3	0.3	0.3
Spain	1.3	1.4	1.7	1.7	1.9	1.2	0.7	0.4
Sweden	1.2	1.8	2.0	2.0	1.7	1.5	0.3	0.3
Canada (English)	1.0	1.9	1.8	2.3	2.0	1.6	0.6	0.3
Canada (French)	1.5	1.9	1.8	2.1	1.7	1.4	0.6	0.3
U.S. (Mainland)	1.1	2.0	1.8	2.5	2.1	1.7	0.6	0.5
U.S. (Hawaii)	1.5	2.1	2.0	2.2	2.1	1.5	0.9	0.6
Australia	0.7	1.5	1.4	1.8	1.7	1.2	0.7	0.5
New Zealand	1.4	1.6	1.6	1.9	2.0	1.3	0.9	0.7
Brazil	1.2	1.9	1.7	2.2	1.9	1.7	0.9	0.4
Colombia	1.7	2.2	2.4	2.2	1.6	1.2	1.3	0.3
Venezuela	1.7	2.3	2.2	2.4	1.8	1.3	0.9	0.6

SOURCE: Adapted from *Time*, May 1, 1989, p. 67.

wrong to suggest that Chinese discourses about sex can best be understood by characterizing them either as repressed-feudal (in terms of Confucian traditions and by the Maoist state) or liberated-modern (by the May Fourth Movement and by post-Mao market reform). Thinking along these circumscribed paths may cause us to miss or ignore much that is interesting and illuminating about sex and sexuality

among men and women in China. As Hershatter put it: "The meanings assigned to sexual acts by Chinese—indeed the changing definitions of what constitutes a sexual act—suggest a great deal about particular configurations of desire and the ways they interlock with larger social pre-occupations."[83]

Hershatter cautions about trying to typecast Chinese sex and sexuality as modern or just like us. She suggests that it is important to study and think about Chinese sexuality for what it is and what it tells us about the Chinese. This suggestion, of course, runs the risk of exoticising and Orientalizing Chinese sexuality, in the sense that Westerners will be searching to identify an autonomous, native Chinese sexuality. What Hershatter has in mind, however, is that outsiders should try to examine "how, by whom, and to what ends Chinese sexuality has been discussed and reconfigured, particularly in the context of twentieth century conversations about nationalism and modernity."[84]

Sex and Sexuality Discourses in Reform-Era China

As Harriet Evans has observed in *Women and Sexuality in China*, sex, as a topic of conversation and as a commodity, has quite literally taken off since reform began in 1978.[85] As she noted, "Romantic scenes with erotic imagery are a recurring feature of literature and film, despite the watchful eye of the censors."[86] The contrast with the Maoist era is startling, bearing in mind that for the most part sex had been a taboo subject; the only concern of men and women was hard work and frugality and to demonstrate a collective enthusiasm for the future of the "new China."[87] This produced a kind of androgyny, in which female appearance was made to match that of males; all thoughts of sexual activity were supposed to be sublimated and transformed into enthusiasm for the revolution.

Anchee Min, in her novel *Red Azalea*, provides a grim account of how prevailing attitudes impacted young people during the Cultural Revolution.[88] When the heroine of the book is sent down she finds herself at the Red Fire Farm, a rural commune that functions as a military camp. When she discovers that her friend, Little Green, had started a love affair with a local man, she became alarmed because "a good female comrade was supposed to devote all her energy, her youth, to the revolu-

tion: she was not permitted even to think about a man until her late twenties."[89] Little Green and her friend were caught making love by the commune soldiers. The brigade leader (a woman) ordered the soldiers to beat the man, telling them "she would be pleased if the soldiers could make [him] understand that today's woman was no longer the victim of man's desire."[90] Little Green was forced to accuse the man of raping her, and at a kangaroo court he was convicted and sentenced to death. The commune leaders were pleased with the outcome, because "the man was . . . deeply poisoned by bourgeois thoughts [but his death was able] to stop the poison from spreading."[91] After the execution Little Green went into a shell, not bathing or talking. She chopped off her long braids and started mumbling to herself. Eventually she was committed to a mental hospital where she was diagnosed as having had a nervous breakdown: "When [she] returned . . . I did not recognize her. . . . She was fat as a bear . . . she sat quietly most of the day staring in one direction. Her pupils sometimes moved upward into her skull as if to read her own brain."[92]

In spite of the new freedoms experienced by some of the Red Guards during the Cultural Revolution, the era's discourses on the topic of sex were based largely on silence, even denial. Gender neutrality was encouraged by authorities, and "there was virtually no public discussion about [such issues as] women's marital and sexual relationships, unless it was to extol the virtues of socialist comradeship."[93]

Once the free market started to impact the business of selling and representing sexuality, the picture changed. Yet the issue is not only economics: Major social and cultural changes are visible in advertising, literature, music, and film. Within the media women now speak openly about their own sexuality, sexual preferences, and sexual pleasure. Still, most of the public discourses on sex and sexuality still strongly identify the traditional model of sexuality that is based on biological fundamentals. The male is seen as the traditionally strong and active partner, the one with all the urges and drives; the female is considered to be interested in sex only to the extent that it serves reproductive goals.

Events during the 1980s and 1990s highlight a basic paradox in the relationship between women and the state. The latter has intensified its intervention in women's lives (through the operation of the coercive birth control policies; see Chapter 5), yet the state's withdrawal from traditional control over land, labor, and markets has contributed to a marked increase in the commodification of women and sex, often resulting in violent abuse and humiliating exploitation. This trend ranges from relatively bland advertisements depicting women's bodies as a marketing strategy to the sexual violation of women and even murder.[94]

Harriet Evans describes in great detail the flourishing traffic in newly produced pornography; the revival of sex work and prostitution in the biggest cities; the increasing incidence of rape; widely reported stories of the kidnapping and abduction of women and girls;[95] and the rising cost of marriage and brides. As Evans argues, those trends represent women's sexuality being offered as a commodity that is or can be made available to men, either for purchase or for brutalization. The women are seen as hapless victims or as evil, willful sinners. In many rural areas a variety of forces, including out-migration and the missing women phenomenon, have resulted in a chronic shortage of women, which has essentially created a marriage market and driven up bride prices. At the extreme end of the scale are numerous reports of the abduction and transportation of women from the countryside and their sale in coastal cities.[96]

This is considered by some observers to be part of a new social disease related to the reemergence of capitalism and privatization. Most attempts to account for the rise in such disturbing trends highlight the socioeconomic factors, including rural poverty, lack of education and employment opportunities, as well as the marketization of the economy and the appearance of a new underclass. Sometimes the behavior is explained away as a regression to

feudal practices. It is very rare, however, to find an account that considers the hierarchical structure of gender in China and the ideology that allows or condones fundamental abuses of women's rights. Few attempts are made to situate abuses within the context of the gendered power relations that are produced and sustained in the patriarchal structures of Chinese society. In other words, by privileging the socioeconomic causes, or the historical (i.e., feudal) causes, the real issue—which is gender-based subjugation—is being obscured, rarely discussed, and almost never challenged.

Evans applies a similar analysis to the rising incidence of prostitution and sex work in contemporary China. Prostitutes are generally characterized as morally degenerate, sinful pleasure seekers, and the rising prevalence of prostitution is often attributed to the corrupting influence of Western habits (which includes Hong Kong). The prostitute is characterized as a threat to the social order, a symbol of a sick society, something that must be controlled through criminalization, with the state offering "salvation." Woven into this fear of moral turpitude is the more real, physical fear of contamination through the spread of HIV/AIDs and other sexually transmitted diseases. In some ways current public policy toward prostitutes is similar to that in the 1950s, in that the state offers the chance for reform and rehabilitation. But unlike the 1950s, at least according to Evans's argument, the state's current efforts to control and contain prostitution can be interpreted as an official attempt to counter the spread of bourgeois liberalization that has been set loose upon society through reform and openness. The prostitute, in other words, "represents the dangers of Western decadence that economic commercialization has not been able to resist. In this light, the prostitute embodies some of the major contrasts and contradictions inscribed in the reform program. At stake . . . is what modernity looks like and means, as well as what 'women' are and should be."[97]

Evans would suggest that the entire issue of prostitution is a metaphor for modernization, in the sense that marketing sex is consistent with reform. Yet it represents everything that China's leaders feared when and if China opened up to capitalism and the world at large. As Evans pointed out, prostitution "is a symbol of both the possibilities and the dangers of modernity."[98] The same is true of pornography, with the state trying its best to clamp down and destroy all traces, effectively communicating the idea that the naked female body is a corruptive influence, a sign of depravity and danger. Such a view takes no consideration at all of the way pornography is produced; in fact "no comment [is] made about the unequal power relations between men and women that are inscribed in the . . . production of 'yellow' materials."[99] Again this represents the treatment of pornography as an issue of social morality and control rather than as a gender issue, which reinforces the negative attributes associated with female sexuality already widespread in public imagery.

Gender and the Reform Era: An Assessment

If a certain proportion of women were to return home [instead of working] things would be very different. Wives would have enough energy to make their families happy. . . . Husbands freed from household worries, would be able to devote all their energies to their work and study. . . . Very quickly there would be a highly-efficient, trained, disciplined and active work force. Our children would benefit from more maternal care . . . and there would be less delinquency.

—Ma Lizhen, "Women: The Debate on Jobs Versus Homemaking" (1989)[100]

Such a sentiment would probably shock feminists in China and around the world, who have been hoping to celebrate the emergence of a new era of empowerment for Chinese women. Although the policies adopted during reform ought to have benefited women, in many ways expectations have not been realized. In the following sections we examine how reform has impacted women in rural and urban workplaces.

Life in the Cities: Women in the Workplace

Not everyone is happy about the near-full employment that women have access to in China. There are standard arguments, as in the quotation above, to keep women in the home, but another had surfaced by the mid-1980s. To the extent that there were guiding principles behind economic reform, uppermost in the minds of leaders was a desire to make the Chinese economy more efficient. At the end of the 1970s overemployment was extensive all across China. People were going to fields and factories to work, yet many simply did not have enough to do.[101] One response has been a resurgence of discrimination against women in the workplace. Officials are reported to have made such statements as "girls must lower their expectations," and some have even made it clear that women are expected to drop out of the competition for scarce jobs.[102] This is a far cry from the postrevolutionary years, when there were calls for women to step forward to occupy their "half of the sky."[103] By the end of the 1990s that goal has been significantly undermined, to the extent that women are now being excluded from holding even half the jobs and earning half the pay they deserve.

At present the evidence is mainly anecdotal and journalistic, but it appears that discrimination against women in the workplace is increasing. At a jobs fair in Beijing in 1994, more than half the positions were advertised "for men only," and even jobs that are traditionally the domain of women, such as secretaries and teachers, are being taken by men.[104] Women are being passed over in favor of men, who are considered to have fewer home responsibilities to distract them from work responsibilities. It is also being reported that women who do obtain jobs, especially in prestigious foreign enterprises, are chosen for physical attractiveness above all else.

During the reform era the state has encouraged enterprises to be independent and to exercise greater autonomy in all decisionmaking. From the perspective of Chinese women that may have backfired, strengthening the existing sexual division of labor and keeping women in the transient, lower-paying, and subordinate jobs.[105] The availability of new jobs in the export sector and the incentives of the reform era should have increased women's earning power, but in reality both wages and bonuses remain significantly lower for women than for men.[106] Although women in state-owned enterprises cannot be fired, some women have seen their jobs reassigned to those with lower status, and others have been transferred into light industry and service trades or into the traditionally female-dominated occupations such as banking and catering. In the absence of reliable data on this topic, we can only infer that in those jobs women will be paid considerably less than the average for men.[107]

Discrimination has become relatively open in the urban workplace. Increasing competition for jobs in the cities is compounded by reported evidence that almost two-thirds of "surplus workers" in all industries are women. This has resulted in "optimization campaigns" involving layoffs and reassignments, and women are being asked to apply for extended leaves at reduced pay. The reasons put forward to account for rising discrimination among employers are familiar:

- Women workers are thought to take more time off than men;
- it is feared that women will leave to have children; and
- it is thought that welfare provisions for women will be more costly than for men.

In spite of repeated government directives prohibiting such discrimination, women are experiencing real reductions in bargaining power and earned income. Many employers truly believe that women are less efficient in the workplace than are men, and in some cases such assumptions are based on empirical observations:

- Women spend considerably more time than men doing household chores in addition to their professional work;
- they take more time off work to look after sick children and attend to family business; and
- they generally have longer distances to commute because their housing is often assigned according to their husband's work unit.[108]

The outcome has been a widespread call for women to "wait at home." Taking women out of the urban workplace, it is argued, will lessen the stresses associated with the double burden of working at home and outside; support overall social stability; and allow men to work to their fullest capacity.[109] In this sense the reform era represents a decided setback for women and their demands for equality, reinforcing the view that women lack the productivity and efficiency of men. Ironically, the call for women to return to the home has been legitimized by incorporating it into the discourse about supporting the larger goals of economic modernization. Yet from the feminist perspective returning home is seen as a clear step backward,[110] because it is likely to reproduce the traditional subordination of women to men.

There is also increasing evidence that among urban women who are employed, many experience workplace exploitation. Many women, particularly if young, single, or recently migrated from the countryside, have been incorporated into the new export-oriented sectors of the Chinese labor force. This is particularly the case for factories in Open Cities and Special Economic Zones.[111] The new female workforce in booming coastal cities is the most unprotected, least organized element of the Chinese labor force. Young peasant women are particularly vulnerable to abuse and exploitation because many have only temporary work contracts. As transients they are officially unregistered, so they are rarely around long enough to organize for better working conditions. Many new women workers are far from home; often they do not fully understand local dialects; they live in bleak surroundings; and they work in miserable conditions. For the most part they are poorly educated, unsophisticated, and unaware of the social services available, few as they may be.

Young women, especially rural recruits, offer many advantages to the factory managers in growth industries. They can be paid very little, their benefits are usually nonexistent, and if single there are no extra costs associated with day care and family housing. They can be hired and fired at will, which allows the factories to respond flexibly to output changes caused by global demand. Many women leave factory jobs in hopes of finding something better, but some wind up in worse situations or having to return to the countryside. Untold numbers in rapidly modernizing cities like Shenzhen, Guangzhou, and Dongguan land in "barbershops" as "masseuses," walking the streets for sex, or working the pornography trades.[112]

Young women have also become a major component of the labor force in the newly expanded TVEs that have emerged in the suburbs and the countryside. In general, women in rural areas have benefited from the reforms by being allowed to look for work in local factories, as well as in household sideline activities and business enterprises. Although this offers new possibilities, many reports indicate that conditions are similar to those in the coastal factories: low pay, poor benefits, and a lack of job safety and security. A report from two rural counties in Shaanxi Province, for example, showed that despite the new opportunities women's incomes made up less than 28 percent of total household incomes;[113] with some well-publicized exceptions, the gap between women's and men's incomes has increased throughout the reform era.[114]

Somewhat surprisingly, the increase in rural prosperity in the 1980s may have worked against the best interests of women. When a village experiences economic success, for example, the absolute need for women to go out to work (in other words, to leave the home) is reduced. The land is now being farmed by the most efficient households; new village enterprises provide relatively high-paying jobs for male family members; and household sidelines have helped to boost family incomes. In sum, there is now less need for women to go beyond the home in search of work, and the net effect has been a further decline in the independence of rural women.

Several policies implemented since 1978 have threatened some of the long-term aspirations of Chinese people, especially when it comes to women's issues. The family planning program, for example, generally frees women from the onerous responsibilities associated with large families, yet the attempts to enforce compliance with the one-child policy carry odious consequences for women. It reinforced the already dominant pattern of son preference in China, particularly among rural families. In other words, if only one child is allowed, then most people prefer a boy, a sentiment that is still prevalent in the countryside.

Life in the Countryside: China's Women Looking at a Deteriorating Future

In a startling front-page story in *The New York Times* in January 1999, it was reported that the suicide rate in rural China among women aged twenty to forty-five was higher than in any place in the world.[115] It is estimated that of the approximately 500 female suicides per day around the world, more than half (56 percent) occur in China, most of them in rural areas. This report offered some hypotheses to account for this alarming phenomenon, including the traditionally low status of women in the Chinese countryside; the out-migration of many rural men who have moved to the cities in search of work; and the sharp increase in income inequality, which has left the poor increasingly aware of the new wealth they will never be able to attain.[116]

The household responsibility system brought about a redistribution of land in the countryside, with household units achieving virtual ownership of property that had been communally owned.[117] There is some concern among

China scholars that this process will end as a disservice to women for a number of reasons.[118] In the first place, the individual registered by name on the HRS contract with local authorities is usually the senior male of the household. As household-based production increases, it seems likely that the traditional authority relationships within the household will once again be centered on the household's men, with women having less overall bargaining power and independence.[119] There is also the concern that with all production decisions now more firmly fixed inside the household, men will continue to assume most decisionmaking. Under HRS, the household as a unit contracts with the collective or the production team, and invariably the contract is negotiated by the husband. The result is that "instead of reporting to the team leader for job assignments ... a woman will be under the supervision of the male head of household. He will decide when she works, what she does, and whether she can take time off."[120]

In addition, in HRS all transactions and payments are calculated on the basis of total output quotas, with no recognition of family members' individual contributions to production. It is likely under such circumstances that the individual contributions of women to the household budget will become less evident than before, when women and men were counted equally in the collective production system. As contributors to the household production unit, some women may now find they have fewer opportunities to work and socialize away from the home, which further isolates them from society. In some cases women have assumed major roles in their household's newly developed sideline production activities, but often the work is monotonous and unrewarding and ties them permanently to the home. If the men in the household have left home to seek higher-paying jobs, the women may be required to stay behind to tend to unglamorous and less rewarding tasks associated with caring for young and old dependents, as well as farming. Although the reforms may have opened up new avenues for ambitious households, for the majority of women this has often meant the opportunity to work harder than ever before.

In China, as Nobel Prize–winning economist Amartya Sen has suggested, an individual's status in the countryside depends largely on the perception of who is doing the "productive," or "gainful," work.[121] For a woman that perception is influenced by the proportion of household income that she has clearly earned on the outside and is seen to be making a significant contribution to the household budget. There is some concern that during the reform era the HRS has made it more difficult for a rural woman to identify household income attributable to her efforts. Without a source of outside income, women have less independence, which may mean they receive less respect and are more vulnerable to abuse and neglect. The net effect is a shrinkage in the pool of income earned by women, as well as a reduction in what Sen has referred to as their "entitlement"—the measure of their perceived value within the home. As Sen has suggested, that can be manifested in many different ways, including worsening nutrition, poorer health care, and the manipulation of the birthrate through the abortion of female fetuses and female infanticide.

Before the reforms, women working in the collectives had some control over sideline activities, such as raising chickens or pigs and working private plots for vegetables. Although the income derived therefrom in most cases is small and was not theirs alone, they did have the power to organize and regulate such activities. By comparison, in family enterprises today women may be little more than hired hands working in male-controlled contexts. Not only are women thus likely to lose decisionmaking powers; in the new cooperative and private economy they are also likely to lose individual paychecks, as well as health care benefits and pensions.[122]

Reports from all parts of the Chinese countryside show that women are not benefiting from reform as much as anticipated, and in some areas the news is much worse. One of the most disturbing aspects of persisting rural poverty is the apparent correlation between female-headed households and poverty. In Guangxi Autonomous Region, for example, the World Bank reports that 61 percent of poor households (some 2.02 million households overall) were "female-managed," meaning that men were absent or unable to work productively.[123] Besides income, education is unevenly distributed in the countryside. It is well known, for example, that in many rural areas girls are not encouraged to stay in school, because their parents—in the knowledge that they will almost certainly leave home after getting married—consider it to be a less profitable investment. This accounts for the well-known epigraph that begins this chapter: "To educate a daughter is like watering another man's garden." As a consequence, girls in the countryside are more likely to enter the workforce earlier than are boys and are much more likely to be illiterate.[124]

Rural women also have less access to health care services than do rural men; that problem becomes particularly serious for prenatal care. In one study, for example, surveys showed that in many poor areas little or no prenatal care was available, with less than 20 percent of births being attended by qualified doctors or nurses.[125] Expectant mothers encounter other problems associated with poverty, including lack of hygiene and excessive work demands both inside and outside the home. The net result is higher average rates of cervical and bladder infections among poor women and a greater chance of prolapsed uterus, in addition to the adverse effects associated with birth control devices, particularly IUDs. A survey conducted in 1991 showed that maternal mortality in China's poor counties averaged 202 per 100,000, more than ten times the figures for Beijing and Shanghai and twice as high as the national average. Two-thirds of the women who die during childbirth die at home or while being transported to the hospital; 45 percent of the deaths occur with no health worker in attendance.[126]

The state's desire to control birthrates has, in general, resulted in significantly better birth control practices and maternal health care in China. The problem, as we saw in Chapter 6, is that the actual level of health care varies from one area to another, especially now that the state has withdrawn much of its support. As a result women are increasingly at risk and vulnerable to violence, disease, and discrimination. As one scholar has suggested, women's health and their quality of life are threatened more than ever, the result of the interaction of the economic reforms and the one-child policy, all of which are operating within the context of enduring social and cultural prejudices against women.[127]

Women and Population Policy: Enduring Contradictions

The contradictions of reform are especially well illustrated by population policy. When the HRS economy allowed greater prosperity and greater independence from collective authorities, the response was a rise in birthrates. In other words, a pronatalist economic policy was implemented almost simultaneously with the widespread introduction of antinatalist birth control policies. The new population policy brought into the open some of the most egregious discrimination against women, especially in rural China. At the same time, the government and the male hierarchy at all levels of administration assumed an unprecedented increase of social control over the lives and reproductive actions of individual families, the burden of which falls most heavily on women.

Boy Preferences and Continuing Gender-Based Discrimination

Perhaps the most worrisome aspect of gender-based discrimination in the countryside is the persistent preference for boys over girls.[128] The household responsibility system has reinforced the preference for boys in the countryside, mainly because sons promise greater labor power and will bring additional workers into the family when they marry and have their own children. Daughters, in contrast, usually leave home when they marry, depleting the family labor force and failing to contribute to the future welfare and security of parents.[129] The result is further deterioration in the woman's position within the family. Baby girls are poorly treated, assuming they are allowed to survive. The ideas underlying son preference have been heavily criticized by the state, but as traditional beliefs they prove to be resilient. In Mo Yan's book *The Garlic Ballads*, for example, we find a father waiting anxiously at the commune clinic as his wife delivers their baby. Eventually, the doctor emerges wearing elbow-length rubber gloves, dripping with blood. On hearing that he had a baby daughter,

> the man rocked a time or two, then fell over backwards, cracking his head resoundingly on tile, which he apparently smashed. "What's *that* all about?" the doctor remarked. "Times have changed, and girls are every bit as good as boys. Where would you males come from if not for us females? Out from under a rock?" Slowly the man sat up, trancelike. Then he began to wail and weep, like a crazy man, punctuating his cries with reproachful shouts of "Zhou Jinhua, you worthless woman, my life's over, thanks to you!"[130]

The man gradually manages to pull himself together, and later that evening he bumps into the doctor as he is leaving with his baby daughter:

> "Doctor," he said as he paused in the doorway, "do you know anyone who'd like a little girl? Could you help us find her a home?" "Do you have a stone for a heart?" the doctor asked angrily. "Take your baby home and treat her well. When she's eighteen you can get at least ten thousand for her."[131]

In a series of reports from village studies conducted over some two decades, anthropologist Elisabeth Croll shed considerable light on this issue. She observed that in the 1980s and 1990s, perhaps more than ever before, peasant ideas about what the future will bring for their household (what Croll calls their "dreams of heaven") are cast very much in terms of the birth of sons.[132] Daughters, by comparison, signify a questionable future for the household. The most obvious contributing factor to boy preference has been the one-child policy, and the data indicate that in the early years of reform infant mortality for girls increased significantly. It is also possible that the dismantling of rural health facilities in the reform era, and the corresponding cutbacks in medical services, could have contributed to the rising mortality rates for women in the Chinese countryside.

In addition to the consequences for adult women, gender-based inequality has sinister implications for the human development prospects of Chinese girls. The countryside provides a grim reminder of cultural constraints, poignantly illustrated by the tragedy of female infanticide and sex-selective abortion. In terms of human development, however, even girls lucky enough to survive can expect a diminished quality of life, denied entitlements, and lowered capabilities. If the current trends continue, girls in the countryside can look forward to lives dominated by continued discrimination. For many poor peasant families reform has required them to choose between educating their girls or sending them off to work. For many the choice has been clear, and as Croll has observed, the typical attitude in the countryside is that "while farming makes money, schooling takes money."[133] Peasant girls are often encouraged to leave school prematurely and are thus more likely to be illiterate, which means they run a greater risk of being exploited in the workplace, whether in the factory or on the farm.[134] After putting in more than their share of work as children, in their teens many girls will be required to go out to find jobs, either in rural factories or in the cities. If they look for alternatives to factory work they will probably find that they are only qualified for jobs as shop assistants, nannies, and domestic helpers.

At this point Amartya Sen's argument can be related directly to events occurring during the reform era.[135] In spite of the slow economic growth associated with the Maoist era, health care and nutritional improvements produced sharp decreases in overall mortality rates, especially for women. The reforms brought expanded prosperity and more and better food to almost all of China's people, so it would have been normal to anticipate even further reductions in the death rates after 1978. What is perplexing is that, at least according to Sen, there has actually been a slight increase in overall mortality rates in China throughout the 1980s and 1990s, and as shown in Table 13.5; by the early 1990s they were higher than in 1978, particularly in the countryside. Sen is suggesting that part of the reason for the static death rates is that women have been experiencing a worsening of their relative survival rate. This can be measured in two ways: the decline in the ratio of women to men in the population, from 94.3 in 1979 to 93.4 in 1986; and falling life expectancy, now lower than that for men.[136]

China's Missing Women

At present it is not possible to support Sen's argument fully because there appear to be divergent trends in rural households in China.[137] In some villages women are clearly emerging with the upper hand in the household economy; in others such has not been the case. Whether or not the entitlement theory is correct, excess female mortality in China is an established fact, producing the well-known phenomenon of the missing women.[138] The absence of women on a huge scale is no longer in contention; the only debate is about the causes, and the actual numbers of the missing. Estimates vary from 60 million to more than 100 million worldwide, with about half assumed to be missing from China (see Table 13.6). The sex ratio at birth reported in Chinese

TABLE 13.5 China's Death Rates, Total and Rural Areas (numbers per 1,000 of the population)

Year	Total		Rural Areas	
	# per 1,000	Index 1979=100	# per 1,000	Index 1979=100
1978	6.3	102	6.4	100
1979	6.2	100	6.4	100
1980	6.3	102	6.5	102
1981	6.4	103	6.5	102
1982	6.6	106	7.0	109
1983	7.1	115	7.7	120
1984	6.7	108	6.7	105
1985	6.6	106	6.7	105
1986	6.7	108	6.7	105
1987	6.7	108	—	—
1988	6.6	106	—	—
1989	6.5	105	6.8	107
1990	6.7	108	7.0	109
1991	6.7	108	7.1	112
1992	6.6	106	6.9	108
1993	6.6	106	6.9	108
1994	6.5	105	6.8	107
1995	6.6	106	7.0	109
1996	6.6	106	6.9	108

SOURCE: State Statistical Bureau, *China Statistical Yearbook 1990, 1993*; 1996 data from Table T3.3, p. 67.

TABLE 13.6   Missing Women Around the World[1]

Country	Expected Sex Ratio	Actual Sex Ratio	No. of Women (millions)	% Missing	# Missing
China	**0.993**	**1.066**	**548.7**	**7.32**	**40.14**
India	0.990	1.077	406.3	8.83	35.87
Pakistan	1.002	1.105	40.0	10.23	4.09
Bangladesh	0.969	1.064	42.2	9.78	4.13
Nepal	0.980	1.050	7.3	7.13	0.52
West Asia	1.005	1.060	55.0	5.47	3.01
Egypt	0.996	1.047	23.5	5.12	1.20
Total Number of Missing Women (millions)					**88.96**

SOURCE: Adapted from Klasen (1994), p. 1067.

NOTE: [1] Other estimates, using different methods to calculate the number of missing women, put the number at anywhere from 60 million (Coale, 1991) to 107 million (Sen, 1989).

fertility surveys rose markedly from 1.082 during 1977–1981 to 1.128 during 1985–1989. In addition to general male bias in China's sex ratio at birth (SRB), it is evident that the bias gets larger with increasing birth order. Among firstborns the ratio remains low (for example, 103.0 in 1996; see Table 13.7a). However, at each successive increment in birth order the ratio increases; for fourth-order births in 1989 the ratio was 131.7. This implies that second and subsequent births are either not reported or that female fetuses are being aborted.

Of several possible explanations, two are fairly benign: nonreporting (or underreporting) and adoption. Two other explanations are female infanticide and sex-selective abortion. Demographers are in disagreement as to which factor is most responsible for China's rising SRBs. Some have argued that underreporting cannot be a major factor, as unreported girls should show up in later censuses, yet they do not. Adoption is similarly discounted as a major cause.[139] The leading candidates, therefore, appear to be female infanticide (or abandonment) and sex-selective abortion. As a number of researchers have noted, the rapid diffusion of ultrasound B technology means that even in the remote countryside it has been possible, at least since the beginning of the 1990s, to determine the sex of children in utero. In spite of the government's denial, there is some empirical work supporting the sex-selective abortion hypothesis. One research team, for example, looked at SRBs among hospital births in twenty-nine provinces, working on the assumption that because hospital births rule out both underreporting and infanticide, a high and increasing ratio of males to females must be the result of sex-selective abortion. Their findings tend to support this view, with overall male-to-female SRBs of 108.0 in 1988 and 109.7 in 1991.[140]

Another study, focusing on more than 10,000 abortions, was conducted in southern Zhejiang Province, where the local SRB was 120. The results showed that overall more girls than boys were aborted (the sex ratio of aborted fetuses being 86.7; see Table 13.7b). This is especially the case if daughters already existed in the family. For example, if one girl was already at home the SRB of the fetuses was 51.0; with two it was 56.7; and with three or more it was 36.4. If mothers already had sons, however, the SRBs were close to parity. The authors of this study argued, based on these data, that sex-selective

TABLE 13.7a   Reported Sex Ratio at Birth by Birth Order, Selected Years, 1982–1996

Year	First	Second	Third	Fourth +	All Births
1982	106.5	105.0	109.4	111.9	107.2
1984	102.1	113.6	112.6	122.2	108.3
1986	105.2	116.8	123.2	124.7	112.1
1989	104.9	120.9	124.6	131.7	113.8
1990	—	—	—	—	114.7
1991	—	—	—	—	116.1
1993	—	—	—	—	114.1
1996	103.0	—	—	—	—

SOURCES: Adapted from Zeng et al., 1993, Table 1, p. 284; 1996 data from *China Statistical Abstracts,* 1997, p. 73. Data on all births SRB for 1990–1993 from Gu and Roy (1995), Table 1, p. 20.

TABLE 13.7b   Sex Ratios of Aborted Fetuses, by Number and Sex of Surviving Children, Southern Zhejiang Province, 1993

Gender and # of Surviving Children		Total # Aborted	Male Fetuses	Female Fetuses	Sex Ratio of Aborted Fetuses
Male	Female				
0	0	4518	2345	2173	107.9
1	0	2559	1329	1230	108.0
0	1	3124	1055	2069	51.0
2+	0	81	40	41	97.6
0	2	105	38	67	56.7
0	3+	15	4	11	36.4
1+	1+	380	196	184	106.5
Total		10,782	5007	5775	86.7

SOURCE: Adapted from Gu and Roy (1995), Table 5, p. 29.

abortion was common in the area of the study, and it appeared to be a major contributor to the extremely high male-to-female birth ratio.[141]

Life for women in the Chinese countryside promises to be filled with anguish. There are frequent stories of wives being beaten and harshly criticized for their failure to deliver sons; personal lives are subject to intensive surveillance and scrutiny; and in many cases they are coerced into terminating pregnancies and undergoing sterilization. As the evidence builds, a crucial question needs to be answered: Should the Chinese government do more to reduce the overwhelming preference for sons in the countryside, which has already derailed the one-child policy and continues to cause misery for millions of women? At present the govern-

ment has focused much of its attention on simply trying to wipe out the resistance to the birth control policy rather than make fundamental changes to bring about full gender equality. A few lame arguments have been made in favor of matrilocal marriages to replace the ancient custom of female exogamy. And publicly current leaders deplore beating and infanticide, but in practice they are loathe to consider major structural changes in rural society.

Recently the government categorized these practices as feudal remnants, yet if the one-child policy is to remain it may, in the long run, force the CCP to return to the agenda of women's liberation in China to finally carry out the goals of the May Fourth Movement. At present, however, rural women remain desperate and continue to "carry the hoe outdoors, handle the pot indoors, and take a back seat in a meeting."[142] In addition, they have to deal with the humiliating consequences of a birth control policy that is sharply at odds with the dictates of a patriarchal system that appears to be as dominant as it has ever been.

Women of the World
Come to Beijing

For women who have benefited from reform—generally urban women—the present and the future look promising. With greater purchasing power, more openness to the outside world, and far higher access to material goods and services, who could blame contemporary Chinese women if they decide to question the benefits of working or studying and stop pushing for greater equality? As soon as they were able, many women began to focus attention and resources on consumption, spending money for clothes, cosmetics, styling, and fashion magazines. Associated with the increasingly common use of female images in advertising, despite superficial appearances, this may be nothing more than a process of cultural homogenization, but it might also reflect a more fundamental shift in attitudes:

> The revival of feminine interests, set against the awareness of fewer educational and employment opportunities and the official stress on women's domestic role, has strengthened the traditional female vision of a desirable personal future: not one's [personal] socio-economic advancement but marriage to a man who is on the pathway to success. . . . Indeed a higher education might be positively detrimental to a young woman's marriage prospects.[143]

Newfound wealth among HRS families in rural China could also have benefited women greatly as a result of the new inheritance law that became effective in 1985.[144] As a result of

rising incomes, the possessions of many families are now more extensive: Houses are larger and families can build up their supply of capital, including animals, machinery, labor, and land. The new law appeared to promise women an equal share of this greater wealth, but in reality a woman who survives her spouse has to share the inheritance with her children and his parents. Under the law, an individual's claim to the inheritance is dependent on the role that individual played in the family economy. Thus children who supported their parents would be well rewarded, and in China these are most often sons. In addition, a woman's rights to the household's means of production are lost if she leaves her spouse through divorce. Clearly this works to discourage divorce even more than is normally the case in rural China.

When Beijing was chosen as the site for the 1995 Fourth World Conference on Women, the United Nations and the Chinese government publicly announced they would focus special attention on the "woman question." To the outside world China claimed that it had consistently promoted women's participation in the country's development and that it could boast a record of actively pursuing gender equality. To back up these claims a new law was adopted in 1992 (formally the Law Protecting Women's Rights and Interests), intended to improve the status of China's women. The new Women's Law went much farther than earlier attempts in several ways:

- It was comprehensive, establishing new laws on marriage, divorce, and voting rights—all designed to guarantee equality between men and women and prohibit discrimination and abuse against women;
- it specified punishment for those who violate the law and abuse the rights of women;
- it sought local input in the drafting of the new laws; and
- it was intended to demonstrate China's international commitment to improving the status of women.

The Women's Law was to be implemented amid publicity campaigns; special programs on, about, and for women were arranged; and specific cases in which the laws were broken were publicized. In one case, six men were executed in Beijing in July 1992 and three others received life in prison for killing, raping, or injuring women. At present it is too soon to evaluate how effectively the new laws are being implemented. One observer, however, is pessimistic, based on contemporary attitudes and behaviors.[145] As she noted, discrimination against women is deeply rooted in Chinese society, and the existing network of *guanxi* is proving impossible for women to penetrate. It appears that China's ruling oligarchy is resistant to giving up any rights, either to men or women, and in her own research she found that 90 percent of women she interviewed questioned the effectiveness of the Women's Law "and doubted that the Chinese leadership would allow implementation of provisions guaranteeing political rights . . . if receiving these rights challenged the rule of the CCP."[146] The suspicion is that the Women's Law was little more than a showcase for the UN, intended to impress visiting foreign dignitaries and allow China to fulfill its obligation as a signatory member state to the conference.

The 1995 Fourth UN Conference on Women in Beijing was attended by some 17,000 delegates from 187 countries.[147] One of the obvious benefits to Chinese women was the global attention it drew to their situation. For a few days, at least, the gaze of the world was officially focused on gender relationships in China.[148] Unfortunately for the organizers the conference was controversial from the beginning, and the Chinese government was accused by many delegates of public boorishness and even deliberate sabotage. Many delegates complained of being spied upon, tailed, photographed, and even roughed up by Chinese security agents.[149] In violation of UN rules for such conferences, agents confiscated handouts, disrupted meetings, and blocked protest demonstrations. The major meeting site was actually located in a distant suburb (Huairou), where poor facilities and transportation, in addition to torrential rain, hampered conference activities.[150] Within the overall structure of the conference there were many subthemes deserving of public attention. The official Chinese government's Tibetan delegation showed up for a photo opportunity session, but the real Tibetan delegates were nowhere to be found. The Hong Kong delegates came wearing high heels and blue blazers, exhorting their "inland" compatriots to support their three-pronged recipe for political participation: "First, be a wonder woman, receptive to grass-roots input; second, be a super-woman, able to balance the needs of public and domestic life; third, be a pretty woman, decorously groomed so as not to turn off constituents."[151]

The conference theme was intended to focus on the impacts of rapid economic development, so China was in many ways the ideal host, and it is interesting to speculate on the impact the conference had on women in China. There is some evidence that women, at least those living in and around Beijing, were aware of the conference; and in one study it was reported that two-thirds of those interviewed were able to name the main theme, which was "Equality, Development, Peace." At present, however, there is little evidence that the agenda established by the conference's Programme of Action will have any immediate impacts on China's women.[152]

The keynote address in downtown Beijing was given by Hillary Rodham Clinton, a knowledgeable and formidable figure. After thanking the Chinese people for hosting the conference she was able to direct pointed criticism at the Party-state, in reference to the decision not to grant visas to the Tibetan and Taiwan delegates. It is indefensible, she said, "that many women in non-governmental organizations who wished to participate have . . . been prohibited from fully taking part."[153] Yet the most significant aspect of all this is the fact that a conference of this nature actually took place in Beijing. Some observers have suggested it demonstrated courage on behalf of the Party-state, which was willing to expose the country to potentially enormous criticism about the way Chinese women are treated. Hosting the conference was, perhaps, a symbol of acknowledgement that China now regards itself as part of the world and no longer as a world within itself.[154]

Conclusion

The 1949 communist takeover certainly brought changes to the traditional attitudes and behaviors toward Chinese women. It is equally true, however, that events since 1978 illustrate other dramatic changes. Reform has brought far-reaching economic changes and a transformative agenda in social relations (see Table 13.8, which compares prerevolutionary China and the Maoist and Dengist eras).[155]

How and in what ways has modernization had an impact on women's lives? Certainly the reforms have benefited Chinese women. Bearing in mind the economic and cultural restrictions of the Maoist era, including the continued subordination of women, the market reforms have brought choice, mobility, some extra autonomy, as well as the hopes of a functioning civil society to China's women.

The counterargument, which might be referred to as the reformist argument, suggests that in comparison to gains made during the Maoist era the reform era has been marked by

TABLE 13.8   Family and Gender Relationships Through Time

	Traditional, Feudal China (pre-1949)	*The Maoist State (1949–1976)*	*The Dengist/ Jiangist Market Socialist State (post-1978)*
Gender Relationships	Male dominant, women financially, politically, and socially dependent	Equality among sexes, women equally independent in many aspects	Mix of new and old gender relations, some women prefer to be dependent economically
Marriage	Arranged, class background, weddings elaborate and manifest cultural domination	Free choice, political correctness and class background, simple wedding, forming new revolutionary units	Mix of free choice and money-oriented marriages, weddings become more elaborate, increasing divorce rate
Child Rearing	According to grandparents' wishes, biased toward boys	According to wishes of the Party, contribution to the revolution	Parents' wishes must be subordinated to the state: one-child policy
Family Lifestyle	Live well, honor the lineage, respect wealth as a blessing, effort devoted to improving the quality of life for the whole family and kinship network	Important to live simply, be thrifty, honor egalitarianism, despise capitalistic tendencies of consumption; people dare not improve their homes or acquire luxury consumables	Recognition of the need to consume, enjoyment is acceptable, growing inequality, efforts in improving quality of life for nuclear family

SOURCE: Adapted from Cecilia Lai-Wan Chan (1995), p. 210.

serious setbacks for Chinese women, which would include the following:

- lack of collective support for women's education, welfare, and health care;
- implicit support for restricting women's access to workplaces outside the home;
- the threat to women's autonomy and ability to participate in the public domain; and
- a range of negative and often violently brutal consequences of the commoditization of women and sex, including exploitation in the labor market (see Table 13.9, evidence that the proportion of school-age girls in the labor market is among the world's highest).

It would be unwise to support either position definitively, bearing in mind that elements of truth can be found in both. Yet it is clear that during the Maoist and post-Maoist periods the Party-state remained largely gender-blind. The regimes did not challenge the patriarchal foundations of gender-based discriminations against women. In the 1990s some women have finally been able to find some autonomous space in the emerging civil society, but as long as the regime refuses to give up its monopoly of political power, and its insistence on monitoring the public sphere on its own terms, it will continue to be "difficult for women to organize in their own interests, other than at peripheral levels."[156]

Thus, even though women have made significant gains they have done so as "subordinate daughters" rather than as "equal sisters of fraternal Communist men."[157] Depending on which measures we survey, Chinese women have managed to achieve at least as much if not more than women have achieved elsewhere in the world: greater labor force participation; less occupational segregation; and higher representation in politics. The gains in these areas are significant achievements for a country that has been dominated for so long by traditions of male superiority. There is still a feeling, however, that the revolution—which promised women so much—has actually delivered them very little. Even if the Chinese had been able to bring about total income equality between men and women, female subordination, especially in the countryside, would not have been changed very much. The reason is that subjugation of women in the Chinese countryside rests on ancient principles of kinship organization and family formation. Even after five decades of socialism there is no real evidence that patri-

TABLE 13.9 Female Children (Aged 10–14 Years) Economically Active in the Labor Force for China and Selected Countries

Country	1970 %	1990 %
China	38.0	22.3
All Developing Countries	22.6	12.3
All Developed Countries	1.5	—
Latin America	6.0	2.1
South Asia	16.7	—
Sub-Saharan Africa	28.3	19.6
USA	1.2	—
UK	0.1	—
Nordic Countries	0.3	—
Hong Kong	8.3	2.5
Singapore	2.9	0.5
South Korea	3.6	0.7
Japan	1.0	—

SOURCE: United Nations Development Programme, *Human Development Report, 1995*, Table A2.5, pp. 63–65.

archy is losing its grip, because in China "a woman's life is still determined by her relationship to a man, be he father or husband, not by her own efforts or failures."[158]

The leaders of the CCP may have genuinely wanted to relieve women of this patriarchal burden, but they were and still are unable to do so, largely because of their own patriarchal biases. Women have always been defined as a commodity in China, and in the reform era the price of and the profit to be made from such commodities have increased exponentially. The official response to the upsurge of female infanticide after the introduction of the one-child policy illustrates the extent of the patriarchal bias in China. The newspaper *China Youth News*, for example, reported that "if female infanticide is not stopped quickly, in twenty years a serious social problem may arise."[159] It was clear from the report, however, that the "problem" in question was not that baby girls were being murdered but that there would not be enough women around to be wives! We are reminded here that Chinese women over the centuries have been defined, and have come to define themselves, by their relationships with and their status relative to men.

The revolution has not brought China's women to where they had hoped to be by the turn of the century. The more optimistic Western feminists, like Margery Wolf, suggest that the gender revolution has only been "postponed" and that the path toward liberation can once again be cleared, perhaps after the economic reforms have solidly placed China on the road to modernization. As she put it, "Revolutions are made, not delivered in a package; women must make their own revolution."[160] It is difficult to imagine how women can go about this task at the present time, especially in light of some of the economic reform policies that have worked, inadvertently or otherwise, to close the door to women's liberation. As Wolf herself pointed out, even in the 1980s a Chinese woman was still expected to be "the good wife and devoted mother," roles she has played for centuries.[161]

14

Serving the People? Private Versus Public Provision in China's Cities

⌐⌐⌐⌐⌐⌐⌐⌐⌐⌐⌐⌐⌐⌐⌐⌐⌐⌐⌐⌐⌐⌐⌐⌐⌐

> *The first generation of the single-child consumer, or the s-genera-*
> *tion, is now entering adulthood and assuming . . . real life*
> *responsibilities. . . . What sort of world will these children make?*
> *A survey of 400 urban children aged 7–12 showed that 81.3 per-*
> *cent dreamed of international travel, 61.9 percent wanted space*
> *travel, 60.2 percent wanted to be more beautiful or handsome, and*
> *almost 90 percent wanted to be more intelligent.*
>
> —Conghua Li, *China: The Consumer Revolution* (1998)[1]

Introduction: Collective Consumption and State Legitimacy

In this chapter we shall examine the provision of services in China's cities, focusing on the impact of the Four Modernizations project on the pattern of service delivery. In the reform era the state has been shedding its responsibility for providing urban services, and the development of markets has made far more goods and services available to all urban residents. At the same time, privatization began to appear on the scene as an alternative and, in many ways, became a far more efficient alternative to public provision. After introducing the fundamentals of collective service provision in postrevolutionary China, and briefly looking at some of the factors influencing the quality of life in the socialist and the postsocialist city, we discuss two new developments that have changed lives and landscapes in Chinese cities: expanded consumption of all types of goods and services; and commodity housing.

Until relatively recently, even in most market-oriented societies, responsibility for basic urban services lay almost entirely with govern-ment. It was assumed that without direct state intervention there could be no guarantee that housing, health care, education, services for the elderly, and the whole range of urban support services such as public transportation, roads, parks, trash removal, and utilities, would be provided. Because of the scale of the operations involved, the importance of the services provided, and the need to keep costs as low as possible, the general consensus was that the private sector either could not be trusted to provide such services equitably or would not be interested in doing so. As a result, a sizable portion of collective service provision, for better or worse, became the responsibility of the state, especially in socialist societies.

In recent years we have witnessed an erosion in the arguments favoring public service provision in capitalist societies around the world.[2] The "commodification" of the services involved, as well as the "privatization" of their delivery, have become standard practice. In noncapitalist societies the role of the state in providing public services remained dominant until relatively recently, because in most cases there were few alternatives. This is beginning to change slowly, and in China the examples from overseas and the ongoing experiment with economic reform have helped generate lively debates over privatization. Progress down the private path has thus far been limited, and, as with all reform in China, the momentum was slowed somewhat by the political crisis in 1989 and by the regular oscillations of policymaking.

The standard argument in socialist societies is that the legitimacy of the government is largely dependent on its ability to ensure an equitable distribution of goods and services to its people. In other words it was essential for the Chinese Communist Party from the very beginning "to devise a system of distribution that would enable even poorer families to get reliable access to the food, housing, schooling, health care, and other resources needed for a decent life."[3] When the Communists entered the cities after the 1949 victory, a priority was to restore a semblance of order. Food had to be put on the table regularly; the people had to have decent and safe housing; and access to education and medical services had to be assured. After several decades of struggle, a sufficient number of people had cast their lot with the CCP, and now it was important for local Party organizations to prove to them they had made the correct choice. In Canton (Guangzhou), for example, as Ezra Vogel has indicated, the Communists took over a city that was in tremendous disarray after the departure of the Nationalists: "Some of the lower elements of society, taking advantage of the hasty departure of the 'bourgeois opportunists' were looting deserted homes . . . and gathering goods abandoned in the streets. . . . Inflation was rampant, the city was filled with transients, and both armies had sorely taxed the local food supply."[4]

The immediate task of the Communists was to win the cooperation of local residents. On a day-to-day basis the goal was simply "to keep the schools in session, the factories in operation [and] the government offices open."[5] To ensure that goods and services were equally available to all people, the CCP followed a course that would gradually result in the abolition of market forces in the cities, replaced by a system of centralized allocation.

At this point the Chinese government encountered a dilemma. National defense and the reconstruction of the war-ravaged economy dictated an emphasis on production first, both in the cities and the countryside. It was essential to get the economy back into action quickly, so relatively little consideration and few resources were devoted to collectively consumed services. Vogel argued that the CCP was walking a tightrope by ignoring service provision and stifling consumption, because before too long the people would be certain to register their widespread dissatisfaction; but it was in the cities that the CCP felt it most urgent to effect a swift transformation over to production. Canton was a prime example. The city was seen by the Communists as a hotbed of bourgeois corruption that needed to be swept clean: "Books, magazines, and newspapers had been geared to the bourgeois audience; the Communists wanted to remold them for workers and peasants. Intellectuals had been pursuing personal ends, but now they were to be reformed to serve societal goals."[6]

Mao Zedong had warned the Chinese people that they should expect a lengthy struggle even after the revolution had been won, and many were prepared to make sacrifices. By the time of Mao's death in 1976, however, the credibility of such a request had been sorely stretched. Consumption of essentials such as food and clothing and the delivery of all services had been sorely neglected for more than twenty-five years. In spite of determined efforts to increase the supply of basic urban utilities there were shortages of almost everything that helped ease daily life: consumer goods, housing, transportation, libraries, cinemas, and parks (see Table 14.1). In most cases the quality of what was available was questionable and access to it was tortuous. Food was available, but the quantity and quality were variable; there were buses, but they were decrepit, crowded, and dangerous; there was housing, but it was cramped, poorly designed, and often impossible to get into.

Just making a telephone call—say, before about 1990—was difficult. In one report, an old man, after trying unsuccessfully at several phone booths in his neighborhood, eventually

TABLE 14.1 Growth in Urban Services and Utilities, 1980–1996

	1980	1985	1990	1996	% Growth per Year		
					1981–1996	1986–1996	1991–1996
Volume of Tap Water Supply (100 million tons)	88.3	128.0	382.3	466.1	11.0	12.5	3.4
Length of Sewer Pipelines (kms)	21,860	31,556	57,787	112,812	10.8	12.3	11.8
Volume of Coal Gas and Natural Gas Supply (10,000 cubic meters)	254,428	411,853	2,389,354	1,985,908	13.7	15.4	Negative
Numbers of Public Buses	32,098	45,155	62,215	148,109	10.0	11.4	15.6
Length of Paved Roads (kms)	29,485	38,282	94,820	132,583	9.9	12.0	5.7
Areas of Green Land (hectares)	85,543	159,291	474,613	665,119	13.7	13.9	5.8

SOURCE: *China Statistical Yearbook, 1997*, Table 2-2, pp. 30–31.

admitted defeat. Philosophically, he recalled the ancient folktale about the "Old Fool Who Moved the Mountain" and resigned himself to the problem: "What does it matter if it is difficult for me to make a telephone call? When I shall die, my son will try. When he shall die, my grandson will continue to try."[7] The implication here, of course, is that everything comes to him who waits—but very slowly—and anyone who has tried to place a telephone call (at least until recently) in China will appreciate the irony in this situation. Fox Butterfield, a reporter for *The New York Times*, gathered some amusing anecdotes describing the difficulties of everyday life in the prereform Chinese cities. A newlywed couple discovered some of the trials and tribulations that would never occur to Westerners:

Buying furniture, taking a bath, finding a house—require all the connections, luck, and artifices that [the] Chinese can muster. . . . To purchase three of the most essential items, a double bed, a folding dinner table, and a dresser cabinet, you had to have a special ration coupon issued only to newly married couples. To prevent cheating, you also had to present your marriage certificate, which the furniture shop stamped on the back. Even so, it took a six-month wait to get a bed.[8]

It comes as no surprise to find that many city dwellers resigned themselves to purchasing from the black market; otherwise they were required to stretch their personal web of *guanxi* as far as it would go: "In this environment many began to lose faith in the distribution system and to feel that one had to pursue special angles to get your needs met. One had to cultivate special ties with gatekeepers guarding access to various goods and services or with truck drivers or others who were able to go around the barriers in the system."[9]

The long-term consequences of such activities were serious. Time and energy were needed to keep attuned to the underground economy, which acted as a drain on the production work that was supposed to be the focus of life in socialist society. Naturally people became cynical about the long-term benefits of socialism, because it appeared that in order to survive it was necessary to bend the rules. In circumstances such as these who could blame people for thinking only of their own needs rather than the overall good of society?[10]

It is not surprising, then, that by the end of the 1970s, after three decades of deprivation, many city dwellers were ready to demand changes. It is generally accepted that the new regime headed by Deng Xiaoping correctly perceived the level of discontent and committed to providing the long-suffering Chinese people access to the stuff of their dreams. Deng and his practical-minded colleagues understood better than Mao that centuries of living with scarcity in China had bred "a strong strain of materialism . . . a craving only intensified by the shortages of recent years."[11] It was in this context that Deng and his supporters announced that economic development and modernization would be major goals for China, and it became clear that the legitimacy of the regime would stand or fall on the achievement of those goals. In many ways the reforms have been successful, and life in China's cities by the end of the 1990s is much different—and for many much better—than at any time in the recent past.

China's Socialist Cities: Overcoming Scarcity, Providing Security

When the CCP began to plan China's economic and political recovery, it approached the cities with some trepidation. Triumphant as they were in 1949, the Communists found chronic food shortages in the cities, poor or nonexistent services, and a chaotic administrative system. After an initial period in which the major focus was to establish military control, concerted efforts were made to install a working civil administration in each city. In pushing toward that end the CCP began implementing a new pattern of spatial organization in all of the larger cities. The Communists had a utopian view of the city they wanted, a view sharply in contrast to the teeming decadence they could see in the Western-influenced Treaty Ports along the eastern coast. To organize the necessary changes and maintain tight control over the population, the Communists implemented a system of spatial organization that made it possible to administer the policies of the central government all the way down to the household level.

The Spatial Organization of Urban Service Delivery

To begin building the new socialist cities, it was important to ensure that all individuals and families were functionally connected to a tightly knit organizational structure that was subordinated to the CCP. No one was to be isolated: Each individual and family was to become part of a local community of citizens. Such arrangements were not unfamiliar to the residents of China's cities; in fact in the past many people had belonged to autonomous guilds or neighborhood associations, but in most cases such groups had been established by local activists to perform certain tasks, with membership usually being voluntary.

The new system of urban spatial organization was different, as it was created deliberately from above and was meant to be a fully integrated network of local territories at different levels in the hierarchy. Life was to be organized vertically.[12] The fundamental goal of the new urban structure was to assist the government in establishing law and order and to carry out its policies. It was also hoped that the new structures would provide a vehicle for mobilizing the population and raising political consciousness at the local level, as well as providing an outlet for the people to express their views about the government's policies and help them develop their own initiatives. This was, in theory at least, how a socialist democracy was intended to function, with information and ideas flowing upward from the people all the way to the highest echelons of state government.[13] In addition to the primary law-and-order function and the implementation of central policy, of most interest here is the role the new neighborhood-level organizations played in providing a variety of local services.[14]

From the beginning the activities of the new neighborhood organizations overlapped significantly with those of the police; in fact the first organizations began by expanding the role of local police stations to take on civil administrative functions. In the early 1950s there were experiments in Tianjin and Shanghai to create totally new organizations. Residents' committees were established to supplement the activities of both the local police station and the various local ad hoc groups. The new committees were intended to assist the city's district-level operation of government, thereby providing a more uniform and integrated pattern of service delivery.[15] After a few years of experimentation, residents' committees were extended to all cities in 1954 by government directive.

The new system of spatial organization greatly facilitated the tasks of urban governance. At first the residents' committees, with the help of local police stations, were involved with mediating disputes between residents and providing local security. Over time, however, the committees have taken on numerous other functions, for example, local cleanups, tree-planting campaigns, and, beginning in the 1970s, family planning activities.[16] The spatial organization of a typical Chinese city would involve the following hierarchy (for the specific example of Beijing in 1980, see Figure 14.1):

- a small number of very large urban districts, each with several hundred thousand residents (with ten in Beijing and six in Guangzhou, for example);
- each district to be divided into urban neighborhoods, with anywhere from two to 10,000 families, with officials in the two top levels appointed from above;

- each neighborhood to be divided into residents' committees, which could include anywhere from 100 to 800 families;
- each committee to be further subdivided into residents' courtyards or residents' buildings, usually containing some fifteen to forty families; and
- small residents' groups at the lowest level, with eight to fifteen members working on specific tasks.

With slight variations to the basic model, the Chinese city came to have a highly structured spatial organization, strengthened by the affiliation with local police. In many cases the neighborhood affairs office was located close to, and sometimes even next door to, the Public Security Bureau (the police station). The police are usually local residents well-known to everyone in the neighborhood. They maintain up-to-date records and keep active dossiers on everyone legally registered to live in the neighborhood; more importantly, they know who does not belong in the neighborhood.[17] A policeman or -woman may be designated to supervise one or two residents' committees: Jobs might include keeping the register up to date; watching out for suspicious characters and activities; and generally keeping their ears close to the ground.

The neighborhood structures were intended to function as conduits for information in both directions. Officials at all levels of the hierarchy report back (upward) to the next highest level; for example, the director of the neighborhood office would report to the city mayor, who would report to a provincial head, and so on, all the way to the top. In the other direction, once a decision is made at the top it can be executed immediately downward through all levels of the hierarchy. In this way the Party-state was able to strengthen its hold over the cities; at the same time, local organizations offered a mechanism for people at the street level to get involved in running their own affairs.

The new structures were also to play an important social-control function, providing constant surveillance. With urban space divided

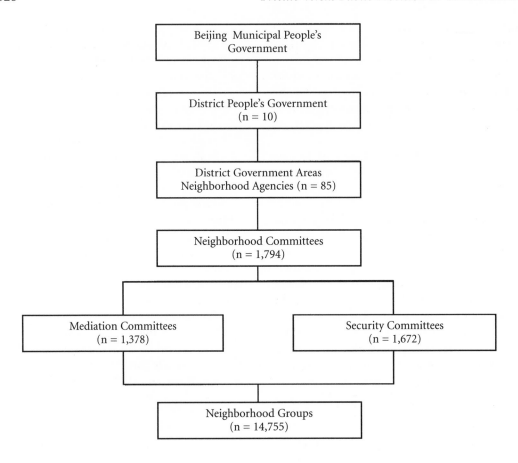

FIGURE 14.1   Spatial Organization of the City of Beijing

into small and manageable chunks, there is literally nowhere for potential outcasts and deviants to hide. At the street level there would always be many pairs of eyes and ears, all finely tuned to monitor anything untoward, and this constant scrutiny ensured there were few surprises in the neighborhood. The presence of a newcomer or someone doing something out of the ordinary quickly became common knowledge through the local information network, and preventive or preemptive actions could be taken in response. It is no surprise to find that such constant surveillance is generally unpopular with the residents, with the brunt of hostil-

ity usually borne by the individuals selected to act as spies and busybodies for the neighborhood and courtyard groups.[18]

It is probably safe to conclude that most city dwellers harbored ambivalent feelings toward their neighborhood organizations. Some of the local activities were clearly beneficial: Constant surveillance allowed committee members to monitor family dynamics extremely closely, which provided information that can be used to intervene in egregious cases of wife beating and child abuse. In such instances the costs of gathering the information are high, but the benefits are considerable.[19] Yet neighborhood committees have been actively administering and enforcing unpopular policies that probably could not have been performed without the constant, face-to-face interaction and surveillance made possible by this mosaic of local-level organizations. In the 1960s and 1970s, for example, they were called upon to recruit local educated youths to be sent down to the countryside. The unpopularity of that campaign is easy to comprehend, in the sense that residents were being required to send their own children away from home, often permanently, and it is understandable that many corrupt practices emerged as families tried to circumvent their responsibilities.[20]

As we saw in Chapter 5, the one-child policy has been one of the most unpopular in the five decades of the PRC, and a large part of the success in implementing the policy in urban areas must go to neighborhood committees. In addition to providing contraceptives and access to birth control clinics, the residents' committees conduct much of the propaganda work. Elisa-

beth Croll has studied the operation of birth control policies in urban Beijing at the neighborhood level (see Figure 14.2, an illustration of the organization of local family planning agencies).[21]

In one residents' committee, for example, there were 735 households and 408 women of childbearing age. Within the neighborhood a six-person "leading group" was responsible for family planning issues. This group trained 113 "propagandists" who visited all households to "explain" the ramifications of the new policies. In 1983 they reported a 100 percent success rate in "persuading" couples to sign a one-child certificate, although in some cases they reneged on their contracts.

The story of one of these propagandists, herself the mother of two children, is illuminating. She kept a detailed record of all the relevant facts on the women to whom she was assigned, including the method of contraception being used and the date they were officially permitted to become pregnant. She checked the regularity

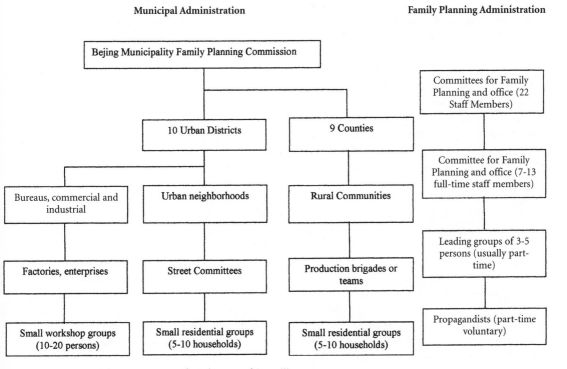

FIGURE 14.2   Spatial Organization of Birth Control in Beijing, 1984

of the women's monthly cycles and any changes in their contraceptive plans. As Croll reported, "Anything out of the ordinary will be reported to the health station."[22] The whole system is based on regular contacts and face-to-face interaction, and "since [the] propagandist . . . resides so near to the women for whom she is responsible, she is in frequent informal doorstep contact with them."[23] As this suggests, even the most unpopular policy has a human face at the grassroots level, without which it could not possibly be effective. In most instances urban couples have been prepared to accept the policy as inevitable, and many have even come to defend it as being essential for the good of the nation.

In addition to the services provided by neighborhood-based organizations, many of China's city dwellers have access to services provided by their work unit. Units associated with large urban factories, state-operated enterprises, universities and colleges, and government agencies were usually able to offer a range of services to workers as fringe benefits, some of which—housing, for example—are highly prized. The largest units are actively involved in almost all aspects of their workers' lives:

> [They] . . . may run nurseries, clinics, canteens, and recreational facilities; they convene employees to hear government decrees and for political study; they organize campaigns for birth control . . . they approve marriages and divorces and mediate disputes; they hold meetings to discuss crimes and misbehavior . . . by their members; they distribute rations and carry out cleanliness campaigns; they supervise untrustworthy employees and organize patrols to guard the area; and they may employ family members of employees in . . . small workshops or vegetable farms.[24]

To the average Westerner who is accustomed to returning from work to complete independence and privacy at home, the all-embrasiveness of the *danwei* would be difficult to stomach. Yet the advantages are substantial. Not only are crucial services provided, such as housing, utilities, health care, nurseries, primary schools, and stores; the *danwei* also provides some identity and a sense of community within the alienating context of urban life. The *danwei* is also the major point of contact between the people and the state. The dictates of the state—for example, production drives and new political campaigns—are interpreted and administered at the *danwei* level, which helps to reduce the anonymity of the Chinese bureaucratic machine. A person responds to his or her work unit rather than to the state per se, which is presumably a more human (and humane) level for interaction.

The *danwei* provides a tightly knit social grouping, fostering cohesive patterns of social interaction. In spite of these benefits, and the considerable advantage of reduced commuting time (as a result of living and working at the same location), a life spent almost entirely within a walled compound, with a gate for exit and entry, is extremely restrictive.[25] Thus although the *danwei* offers stability and security, it can also be a dangerously parochial community.[26] The Big Brotherism of life in the *danwei* reached a head during the Cultural Revolution, when the work unit was often the scene for the humiliating struggle sessions, in which politically suspect workers were interrogated, humiliated, and often tortured. Anne Thurston, in her book *Enemies of the People*, has assembled many individual accounts of inhumanity almost beyond belief during the Cultural Revolution.[27] The personnel department of the *danwei*, whether it was a factory, an office, or a university, kept detailed dossiers on everybody in its employ, which could be used as evidence against almost anyone at any time.

In the universities, which were well known as (or believed to be) the home of "stinking" intellectuals and as hotbeds of counterrevolutionary thought, the struggle sessions often became grotesque public spectacles. Attendance was encouraged by local Party officials, but Thurston argued that the events actually became quite popular with students and workers, who often appeared to treat them as a form of spectator sport. When asked why people appeared to enjoy such appalling brutality, one of her respondents suggested that it was part of the Chinese character to love excitement, a commodity that was usually in extremely short supply in the Chinese city of the Maoist era. Everyday life for the vast majority was excruciatingly boring, with routine events punctuated only by tedious delays and frustrating ineptitude in most areas of service provision. For all but the top cadres the possibility for a little rest and recreation, for example, at the seaside or in the country, was a distant dream. After the rigors of work and managing family life, there was precious little time or energy left for socializing outside the unit. As macabre as it may seem, a public argument on the street, a traffic accident, or even the torture session of a workmate might have helped provide some much needed entertainment.

One reason so many people want to live in the cities has been the prized status of having an urban *hukou* (residence card). Although the new employment patterns generated by the economic reforms are altering the picture considerably, until recently, at least, an urban *hukou* brought with it the promise of employment, housing, medicine, and entertainment—usually at significantly subsidized prices.[28] The lure of the city acted as a strong magnet for peasants who had been made redundant or were desperate to leave the countryside, but until the regulations were changed in the mid-1980s the desire to move to the city was constrained by the need to have an urban *hukou*. This presented a familiar catch-22: Peasants wanted to move to the city to try to make a decent living, but before they could do so they had to be rich enough, or have the connections needed, to obtain a residence permit.[29]

The attraction of an urban *hukou* for those without one, and the determination of those who have them to hold onto them, means that very few were willing to leave the cities voluntarily, and during the reform era the city has in fact become "an overloaded machine with an influx but no exodus."[30] To obtain a valid *hukou*, some people are willing to pay almost any price.[31] A doctor living in an urban work unit in

Henan Province, for example, had been trying for years to acquire residence cards for his wife and three children. In the new materialist economy he discovered that the cards could be bought easily, so he borrowed from the factory and used all his savings. He was broke, but he had no regrets. As he said, "Although I've lost my family fortune, I feel very happy at heart, for I'll have bequeathed to my three children a most precious legacy—the urban residency booklet."[32]

For those lucky enough to hold urban residency cards there is a hierarchy of neighborhood organizations responsible for delivering a range of urban services. This is especially important for people who are not connected to a specific work unit, but in fact there is some overlap between what is provided by the neighborhood and the *danwei*. In some ways the operations of local organizations represent state socialism at its best. Through the local structures help can be provided to families in financial need; old people are cared for; teenagers are counseled; criminals are excluded; and friendship networks and supports are available. At the other extreme the neighborhood surveillance system is an example of socialism at its worst, in the sense that the neighborhood committees were sometimes "turned into organs of petty harassment against any persons or family not thought to be going along enthusiastically enough."[33]

As we have seen, the most important functions of the neighborhood organizations are related to the maintenance of order and local cohesiveness, expressed largely through the security committees. In a fine piece of socialist understatement, a *Beijing Review* reporter observed how the local security forces helped implement the new emphasis on law and order in China by "explaining the newly enacted laws to the local populace so that everyone knows their content."[34] In addition to the police function there is a strong emphasis on prevention at the neighborhood level, and efforts are made to mediate personal disputes before they escalate. In 1980 the mediation committees in Beijing reportedly handled more than 43,000 civil disputes, five times the number of cases in the district people's courts. Whether that activity is interpreted by residents as excessive intrusion or as a real contribution to local problem-solving is impossible to determine.

From the 1980s onward city dwellers began to experience greater independence from work units and neighborhood associations. In the new era of urban economic reform, the growth of smaller collective and private enterprises has been rapidly breaking the monopoly of the *danwei*, with more people having to make their own living arrangements and organize services for themselves. State enterprises have also been pruning the quantity and quality of the services they offer, primarily in the interests of cost-cutting and the need to be competitive with collective and private enterprises. As food and goods and services of all types began to become available in the cities, the entire organization of urban service delivery, what political scientist Dorothy Solinger has referred to as the "urban public goods regime," has been fundamentally altered.[35]

Fighting Crime and Establishing Social Control

By killing the most serious opposition and intimidating the rest in a well-organized campaign, the Communists produced more fear than love, but their campaign was the vehicle for establishing a greater sense of public security throughout the province than the people had ever previously known in their lives.[36]

—Ezra Vogel, *Canton Under Communism* (1969)

In general the state's performance in providing services in China since 1949 leaves much to be desired. The story from one city to another is a familiar one: Services are basic at best, shoddy and dangerous at worst. There are constant shortages, delays, and frequent opportunities for graft and corruption, in many ways a deliberate policy of state planners as a way of "urbanizing on the cheap."[37] In one area of service provision, however, the state has spared no expense and left no stone unturned. This is the police function of the state—providing services to control the actions and perhaps even the thoughts of the Chinese people.

As Ezra Vogel has explained, when the Communists first occupied the cities in 1949, their primary goal was to restore law and order.[38] In Canton the most urgent threat perceived by the Communists was the continued presence of counterrevolutionaries, which at the time meant soldiers of the recently surrendered Kuomintang who had not fled to Taiwan. Rather than trying to kill off their enemies immediately, the Communists went about their task stealthily. For years the Communists had been actively engaged in sabotage and disruption, but now it was their turn to put an end to such activities. Ironically, the tactics they employed were borrowed largely from their old adversaries in the KMT. They began by seizing all available weapons; they required all KMT members to register with public security officials; they put pressure on citizens to report all known members and associates of the KMT; and they employed counteragents to infiltrate KMT hiding places. In a strategy that would become one of the hallmarks of the Chinese Communists in later years, they also set about restricting human movements; in this case the most important action was to close off the border between Guangdong Province and Hong Kong.

From an initial kid-glove approach the Communists quickly shifted to a more brutal regime. They guaranteed clemency to all people who had been registered as spies and KMT sympathizers, but they were sufficiently worried about the security risk to countermand their previous position by arresting and executing men who had been promised leniency. This was not interpreted by the Communists as a breach of faith; it simply meant that circumstances had changed, necessitating a new strategy. This symbolized a streak of cynicism that would become commonplace during the next five decades—saying one thing but doing another. It seems that denying something will happen virtually guarantees that it will happen.

Novelist and travel writer Paul Theroux has observed, only partly with tongue in cheek, that we should "never believe anything [about the actions of the Chinese government] until it has been officially denied."[39]

After an immense roundup, the Communists executed more than 28,000 enemies in a ten-month period beginning in October 1950, representing one out of every 1,000 people in Guangdong Province.[40] To explain the need for such brutal measures, mass rallies and exhibitions were staged and radio programs aired. Running the risk of alienating the citizens of Canton before they had embarked upon the process of rebuilding the city, the Communists had learned a very important lesson about how to get results by using brutal tactics. In these early activities the Communists revealed much about the strategies they would continue to employ in their attempts to restore and maintain order in China's cities. People from all walks of life were labeled, sometimes almost indiscriminately, as "fascists," "feudal remnants," "counterrevolutionaries," and "imperialists." These were people who had opposed the new government in some way and thus needed to be "struggled against" and flushed out of the system. To discredit them, the entire artillery of the propaganda machinery was mobilized.

The overall success of the CCP in bringing about order in the first years after 1949 can, from Vogel's account, be attributed to disciplined organization, careful planning, and the cultivation of mass support from the people. Although all of it was backed by threat of force, the CCP soon realized that in peacetime the best strategy was to be patient and selective. As Vogel described the situation: "They first built up their own organizational support and struck at a few key targets while assuring others they had nothing to fear. By careful selection of targets they removed potential rivals for power and influence and obtained a modicum of compliance from others, thus consolidating their own control."[41]

The crime rate in China's cities, at least during the Maoist era, was much lower than in most other parts of the world, partly a result of constant fear among the Chinese, at least until the mid-1970s.[42] Naturally the Party-state would prefer outsiders to believe that low crime rates resulted from the replacement of materialistic motives with communistic and socially responsible behavior; Party members would also be quick to point out that a great deal of internal social control was achieved through the development of a collective social conscience that made criminal behavior less likely to occur. Yet there is no doubt that effective social control in China has been achieved, at least partly, through external means, in the shape of the deterrent effect associated with brutality and fear of punishment.

Somewhere between these two poles is the rather simplistic, even deterministic view that the new administrative structures put in place in China's cities after 1949 helped keep down crime.[43] The spatial organization of everyday life in China, particularly in the cities, was more than anything else an attempt to achieve order, which meant compliance with the law. Contributions to this effort have been made in two major ways: First, there has been the implementation of what Richard Kirkby called "passive control structures," or mechanisms that directly or indirectly reduce crime; second was the "active control structures," or the deliberate attempts to change individual thoughts and behaviors on the issue of crime.[44]

The passive control structures are features of the Chinese city that contribute to crime reduction and are best illustrated through comparison to U.S. cities. In sharp contrast to U.S. cities, the post-1949 Chinese city had far fewer "danger spots" where crimes are likely to be committed. The bars, clubs, parking lots, and empty alleys of the U.S. city did not exist in the Spartan cities of Maoist China. There were fewer breeding grounds for the development of criminal subcultures, a phenomenon that has typically been associated with high-rise slums. In social terms the absence of an obvious, visibly marginalized underclass, found in most U.S. cities, simply did not exist in Maoist China. There was very little job or residential mobility, which helped to foster local cohesiveness, mutual helping, and a strong presence of neighborhood watch–type surveillance. Many of the discontented youth and undesirable elements were sent down to the countryside, thereby eliminating them and their potential influence on others. In addition, the general level of equality within the Chinese city meant that no specific group considered itself to be relatively more deprived than any other.

There are many other characteristics of Chinese urban life before the reform era that we in the West would consider to be healthy, in the sense that they help keep down crime rates. There has been a very low incidence of problem drinking, alcoholism, and drug abuse in China; a virtual absence of handguns; a low rate of divorce and marital instability; a very limited autonomous youth culture; a strong sense of intergenerational family cohesiveness; very little ethnic or racial tension (at least at the intracity level); generally low rates of unemployment (a situation that changed significantly in the 1990s); and a high degree of citizen involvement in both surveillance and mediation functions. The net effect was that the Chinese city, at least during the 1949–1980 era, was for the most part a safe and orderly place in which to live, and the prevalence of crime was extraordinarily low by international standards.

The net effect of passive and active control structures is, in theory at least, a city in which there were no hot spots or dead corners, and very few parts of the city were unpatrolled or unsurveyed. When the new neighborhood structures were first established in the 1950s, the goal to create an environment in which criminals were unwelcome, and if they showed their faces they would be chased away: "We should create an atmosphere in which the black sheep [criminals] find themselves like rats scurrying across the street with everyone yelling 'kill them, kill them' so that they can find no market and no hiding place."[45]

From the late 1980s onward there have been some interruptions to this idyllic picture of the low-crime Chinese city. One contributor was the return of millions of youths who had been sent down to the countryside. Many returned illegally, with no jobs, no residence cards, and with their education disrupted. Some were bitter and resentful of the system that had exiled them, and it has been suggested that many among this population were forced into or attracted to criminal activities, including dubious private businesses (which were illegal until the late 1970s), picking pockets, gambling, and black marketeering. As sociologists Martin King Whyte and William Parish have suggested, as a group they "had no real stake or responsibility in the city. They saw themselves as living by their wits outside . . . the system, and they were not easy to shame into repentance and good behavior."[46]

During the mid- to late 1980s the vast influx of unemployed peasants from the countryside began to stretch the social control capacities of Chinese cities. With a limited number of jobs to go around, and with city services such as transportation and water provision already stretched to the bursting point, the Chinese city was beginning to face a potential crisis in the not-too-distant future. On the basis of their research with Hong Kong émigrés, Whyte and Parish characterized this crisis as one in which city dwellers, especially youths, have few legitimate opportunities available to them and simply were not able to look to the future with much optimism:[47]

> Urban youths no longer [were able] to see clear strategies for planning their futures, and had neither predictable rewards for good behavior presented to them, nor certain penalties for getting in trouble. . . . This . . . dismantling . . . of the urban opportunity structure was sufficient to offset the solidarity and sanction mechanisms fostering urban orderliness.[48]

Daily Annoyances in City Life: Transportation, Traffic, and Solid Waste

The trappings of urban prosperity are highly sought, but there is always another side to the picture. Surely a major consequence of economic reform was soaring inflation, especially in food prices. The government response was to provide cash subsidies to many city residents, a policy that helped divert the crisis but had a disastrous effect on the economy.[49] Another feature associated with a bustling economy and rising incomes has been an increase in motor vehicles on the roads, with consequences familiar to Westerners. Because motor vehicle use was low for so long, the increase from the mid-1980s onward has been dramatic, with 16 percent more vehicles each year in Beijing, 20 percent in Guangzhou.[50] The private ownership of passenger vehicles in China increased by 45 percent each year in the decade 1985–1995; the number of privately owned trucks increased 17 percent per year.[51] Total vehicular traffic on city streets is still low by international standards; for example, the rate of car ownership in Beijing in 1996 was 24 per 1,000; in Shanghai it was 15, and in Guangzhou 21; but by the year 2010 it is estimated that these three rates will have increased to 96 per 1,000 in Beijing, 105 in Shanghai, and 116 in Guangzhou.[52] The impacts of a fourfold increase are potentially serious for a number of reasons:

- The number of vehicles of all types has grown and will continue to grow at a far faster rate than the mileage of urban roads on which they can travel;
- the announcement in 1994 that the production of automobiles was to become a "pillar" industry, expected to play a key role in China's modernization program;[53] and
- the official encouragement, by the state, of private car ownership as a way of providing a market for China's budding automobile industry.

The most disturbing aspect is that such growth can only continue and will probably increase exponentially, especially in light of the currently low level of private car ownership in China. As incomes rise the Chinese will probably be quick to realize the enormous personal benefits—not to mention status enhancement—to be gained by having their own cars. At present most vehicles are still imported, but production plans called for an increase in domestically produced cars from 20,000 in 1987 to 159,000 by 1995, with another big push announced for the late 1990s. The traditionally low level of spending on roads means that vehicles are jammed together with the growing army of bicycles, buses, and commercial vehicles. The result has been a frenzy of highway construction and plans to build subways in some cities (currently they are in existence only in Beijing, Tianjin, and Shanghai).

As cities become increasingly congested, buses, the only viable method of traveling long distances, become even more crowded and less punctual. In 1983 the average commute times for the inner city and suburbs of Beijing were 44 and 66 minutes; by 1986 these had increased to 60 and 90 minutes respectively.[54] In 1985 the death toll from traffic accidents rose by almost 20 percent over the previous year, claiming 12,043 lives, more than all deaths resulting from crime in China in that year.[55] The major problem is lack of space on roadways that were not designed for motor vehicles. The annual growth rate for bicycles and cars has been on the order of 10 percent per year since 1949, compared to a 5 percent growth rate in total road mileage. The result is that in comparison to large cities around the world China's urban areas have a very small proportion of their total land area devoted to roads.[56] Although the congestion is part of the problem (in terms of noise and air pollution), it actually helps to keep down the death and injury rates by ensuring that traffic continues to move slowly. One estimate is that the average traffic speed in Chinese cities in the late 1980s was below 10 miles per hour, compared to 15 miles per hour in the 1960s. As recent visitors to China can attest, the average standard of the major roads has increased very substantially in recent years, especially with the profusion of expensive toll roads.[57]

A sure sign that times are changing is the shortage of parking spaces. Along the fifteen kilometers of Shanghai's main shopping street, Nanjing Road, there is virtually nowhere to park. It is difficult to imagine what China's cities will look like when car ownership rises significantly from the current level, which is less than 1 percent. Major efforts have been made to reduce the demand for private transportation, for example, by planning for workers to be closer to their companies; by encouraging enterprises and offices to relocate outside city centers; and by requiring city planners to generate master plans with strong public transportation components.[58] Once again we see evidence of a contradiction between the different branches of government policy. The natural consequences of rising personal wealth are the demand for more travel and a greater level of private car ownership, but these will conflict with the logic of Chinese city planning, as well as continued efforts to limit urban growth.[59]

Another unwelcome side effect of the new prosperity and population growth is the problems associated with solid waste and garbage. In Shanghai and Beijing, for example, in the inner cities alone there are 5,000–6,000 tons of household garbage and trash to be disposed of each day, or about 2 million tons per year for each city.[60] As per capita incomes rise, so do the consumption of luxury items and the use of prepackaged goods—including millions of plastic water bottles—all of which generate extra waste. The time, energy, and resources needed to deal with garbage in a city of 10 million–plus is enormous. In Beijing, for example, in the late 1980s the sanitation bureau had 2,466 vehicles, including 466 refuse trucks, 55 sprinkler vehicles, and 36 scavenging cars; even so, less than 35 percent of the job was done by machines.[61] In many cities the streets are meticulously swept every day, sometimes several times a day, often by middle-aged and elderly women scratching away at the sidewalks with handmade brooms. The intent is not so much to make the streets clean but to strip them bare and render them desertlike and dusty. Most Westerners conclude that the goal of this activity has little to do with cleanliness but is simply to keep the sweepers busy; as curmudgeon Paul Theroux observed, "Sweeping doesn't freshen a city. It gives it a disconcerting baldness."[62]

The combination of population growth and an increase in the per capita amount of garbage generated has placed a considerable strain on the available dumping sites, the majority of which are located in the predominantly agricultural suburbs. The city's garbage trucks have to travel farther and farther out to find suitable sites. The long-distance travel into the heart of the suburban agricultural districts represents an obvious traffic and health hazard, as does the search for new sites. In the early 1990s there was a proposal to construct three new mountains out of garbage on the outskirts of Beijing, but the city's sanitation bureau faced stiff opposition from farmers who objected to dumping in their vicinity.[63]

Quality of Life in the Socialist City

As we have seen in earlier chapters, economic reform quickly brought relief to the long-suffering city dwellers in the 1980s, but for many city life remained tedious and trying. It is reasonable to predict that the perceived quality of life for urban residents is quite low. In the late 1980s some Western journalists reported that the level of discontent with city life had contributed to political disruption among students and workers in 1989. In spite of the benefits of reform, life in the city for many people was deteriorating as more and more people competed for a fixed supply of services and urban resources.[64] All of this was made worse by the drabness of the urban landscape in China. To outsiders, in particular, the Chinese city is an exceptionally grim place. Arriving by train in Changsha, near Mao's birthplace in Hunan Province, Paul Theroux must have been pining for his native Boston when he wrote: "The words 'a Chinese city' had acquired a peculiar horror for me, like 'Russian toilet,' or 'Turkish prison.' In the cold rain of winter, with the cracked and sooty apartment houses, the muddy streets, the skinny trees and dark brown sky, Chinese cities are at their very worst."[65]

Moving beyond such generalizations it proves difficult to make valid assessments of something as subjective as quality of life, but

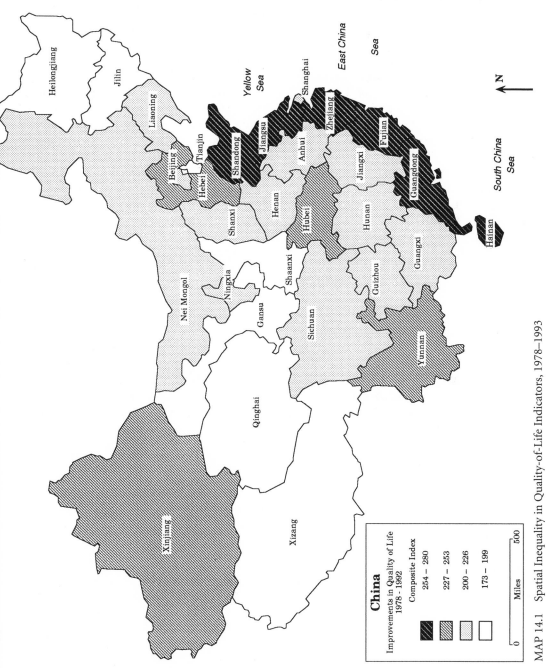

MAP 14.1   Spatial Inequality in Quality-of-Life Indicators, 1978–1993

there have been two approaches to the topic within the social sciences. The first approach uses objective data to measure the availability of facilities and services that are thought to contribute to a person's overall quality of life.[66] At the provincial level, for example, it is possible to gather data on a number of variables that are thought to influence the quality of life, which would presumably include increases in personal income, consumption rates, and housing quality. In 1994 the official news agency Xinhua produced an index of quality of life in China (see Map 14.1). Although no information was provided to describe how the composite index was calculated, from the map it looks as though quality of life is correlated with economic growth indicators: Coastal provinces, from Shandong southward, all score in the top category, suggesting that China's golden coastline is the most desirable part of the country in which to live.

At the scale of cities and urban regions, quality of life studies involve city comparisons on such measures as schools, hospitals, and parks per capita; and we can assume that for most people city A is a better place to live than city B if its per capita rates, overall, are higher. Obviously this is a reasonably crude measure of quality of life, and there are many dangers

inherent in such a simplistic method of assessment; but at least it provides a rough guide for comparing relative livability in places. Data of this type can be used to compare quality of life in cities of different sizes and to test the general assumption that Chinese people prefer to live in larger rather than smaller cities.

This issue can be boiled down to two questions: Do larger cities offer greater access to urban services than smaller cities? Does greater access result in higher levels of satisfaction for residents? The first question is easier to answer than the second, especially for the year 1984, when the State Statistical Bureau produced some useful data on quality of life–related issues, broken down by city size (see Table 14.2).

If we focus on the variables that are traditionally thought to influence quality of life in the city, we see that with a couple of critical exceptions (for example, "living space" and "cinemas/theaters") there is a roughly linear relationship between city size and the per capita availability of urban services. If we are correct in assuming that a greater availability of such services contributes positively to urban livability, then it would seem that life may be more acceptable in China's larger cities than it is in the smaller cities.[67] Clearly this would help

TABLE 14.2   Indicators of Quality of Life in Chinese Cities, 1984 (# of services per 10,000 people)

		City Size			
	China Avg.	2 mill.+	1–2 mill.	$\frac{1}{2}$–1 mill.	200–500,000	<200,000
Books in public libraries	0.91	1.63	1.65	1.07	0.65	0.35
Clinics/hospitals	3.94	5.30	4.21	4.65	3.76	2.79
Hospital beds	46.0	49.3	55.9	57.9	46.5	33.9
Doctors	34.8	49.2	46.1	41.4	30.9	22.0
Medical personnel	83.1	112.9	109.7	102.8	74.8	52.6
Cinemas/Theaters	0.19	0.13	0.13	0.19	0.21	0.23
Telephones per 1,000 persons	1.58	2.96	2.24	1.76	1.24	0.73
Public buses per 10,000	2.20	4.93	3.66	2.44	1.40	0.65
Paved roads (kms) per capita	1.76	2.14	2.64	2.11	1.66	1.12
Sewage lines (length per 10,000)	1.54	2.37	2.54	1.86	1.34	0.72
Green space (m²)	0.23	1.88	3.21	0.40	0.25	0.07
Living space	4.89	4.84	4.95	4.89	4.86	4.97
Electricity	106.0	193.0	154.0	133.0	78.0	45.0

SOURCE: State Statistical Bureau, 1985.

explain why so many Chinese people express a preference for living in larger cities, and, of course, why they have continued to grow rapidly in spite of the persistent attempts made by the government to restrict growth.[68]

To answer the second question it is necessary to explore the other major branch of quality-of-life studies: subjective assessments of satisfaction and dissatisfaction with urban living. To tap that, we rely heavily on journalistic accounts and individual case studies, although in recent years several large-scale surveys have been conducted in various cities. Another important source of data has been the publication of personal narratives, in which ordinary people tell their life stories to Chinese or Western scholars. Such books have provided revealing snapshots of everyday life in China.[69] As one might expect, the more the Chinese learn about life outside China—not only in the West but also in other Chinese communities such as Taiwan, Hong Kong, and Singapore—the more they come to realize the extent of their relative deprivation. One woman complained about the pains associated with her daily routine. In the Maoist city the search for what Westerners would consider the most mundane of services was an ongoing nightmare, and she illustrated hers in describing what happens when a Chinese woman becomes pregnant:

> Although you get free medical care you have to worry about finding a good doctor. . . . After the baby is born, you have to look for nutritious foods. . . . Even ordering milk is difficult, because you need a hospital certificate. . . . After that you have to find a babysitter you can trust [then] a good nursery. Most nurseries will only take fifty children, and usually there are 400 people who want to get their babies in.[70]

In the prereform era the legal response to shortages was an elaborate network of rationing, but the Byzantine complexity of the rationing schemes often served only to frustrate people even more. Coupons were needed for almost everything; if you lost your coupons you could go hungry. If you needed a new lightbulb

you had to turn in the broken one to the authorities to get a new one: "Each bulb bears a serial number—those used in factories are different from those intended for home uses, and those sold in Peking are marked with a different sequence from those in other places. That way, you can't cheat and bring in a light bulb from anyplace but your home. If your bulb is stolen, you have to get a letter from the police before you can replace it."[71]

Another source of information about quality of life has been short stories and novels, which proliferated in the post-Mao era. In contrast to the unbearably patriotic "socialist realism" literature that was commonplace (in fact mandated) during the early years of the PRC, many new authors in the 1980s and 1990s felt freer to describe details of everyday lives—the houses they live in, the places where they work, and the harrowing details of trying to make ends meet.[72]

All these disparate sources present a picture of dissatisfaction. One worker reported, for example, that dealing with life from one day to the next was like planning out a battle strategy: "One family member goes out to buy rice, another coal, another vegetables, another meat."[73] By the end of the week they were all too jaded, physically and mentally, to enjoy their one day off. With a fine sense of irony this person asked how, after getting through such a week, "can we possibly have the strength to think of the four modernizations or carry them out" during the weekends?[74] It was not unusual for people who had to face the extraordinary difficulties of everyday life in urban China to become passively resigned to adversity. A worker riding on a crowded train expressed an air of helplessness when he said, "Life's like this train. If the station it gets to is Beidaihe [a popular seaside resort near Beijing] you can have a great time. But if the station's just a hall in the desert with nothing to eat, nothing to drink and nobody around it's still your station. We didn't lay the track and we can't choose where to stop."[75]

Straddling the objective and the subjective approaches are some recent attempts to conduct survey research. Although such studies have been common in the West for years, they came into fashion in China in the late 1980s. As with all survey data it is difficult to gauge the reliability of the results, and that is a problem with most of the Chinese studies, where survey methods are not described in detail. It is also difficult to account for political bias, as most official publications are unlikely to criticize urban governments by reporting that city dwellers are dissatisfied with local services.

Many surveys have been conducted to determine how urban residents feel about their lives and whether their lives have improved as a result of economic reform. The consensus has been that people support the reforms but feel that change was too slow in coming. A popular complaint has been about the inadequate and corrupt responses of mid-level officials and bureaucrats to changes. All of these are "safe" responses, and (probably not coincidentally) also reflect the government's concerns.[76] Longitudinal surveys conducted among urban families show that greater wealth has allowed higher levels of consumption and savings, as well as an overall improvement in living standards.[77] Again it is difficult to assess how representative such conclusions are, and there is little or no information on the respondents' subjective evaluations of their lives. One of the potential uses of such survey research is to influence municipal policy as to service provision. In the city of Tianjin, for example, 1,000 families have been surveyed at random every year since 1983. The city government pledged to respond to the enduring issues. In 1983, for example, 680 families asked for better access to gas for cooking. That became a priority item, and by 1985 680,000 families (70 percent of the city's total) were cooking with gas. In 1986 there was extensive criticism of the state and collectively run vegetable stores in the city, and the response was to allow private enterprise a larger share of the business.[78]

In the two following sections we shall explore some of the more tangible benefits of the reform era: consumption of goods and services, and housing and housing markets.

Urban Goods and Services: The New Consumption in China

In 1992 a team of Chinese economists attempted to assess how far China had gone down the path to modernization, analyzing the actual achievements in relation to desired goals. Standards were established for the year 2000, and the goals were subdivided into three categories: objective economic conditions; quality-of-life measures; and effectiveness-of-life indicators. The authors intended to compare China's achievements with those in countries defined in 1988 terms as lower-middle-income societies, with per capita GNPs in the range of US$600–2,000 (which in Asia would include the Philippines, with a GNP of $630; Thailand, $1,000; and Malaysia, $1,940).[79] The reforms implemented in the cities as well as the rural areas had obviously contributed to wealth and well-being to such an extent that in some categories China had already surpassed the desired goals by 1990, for example, in the reduction of poverty, expanding and improving the daily food intake, and raising the average life expectancy (see Table 14.3).

Despite such achievements, in other areas, notably the desire to reduce regional inequality and increase per capita incomes, attainment was considerably below expectations.[80] It is important to note that the attainment levels in 1990 were significantly higher in China's cities, where the overall attainment index—which might serve as an indicator of quality of life— was 65.2 percent, compared to 50.6 percent in the countryside. In the cities high attainment has been recorded in several categories, including middle school attendance rates and average life span; but performance was judged to be poor on indicators such as the amount of protein being eaten and the ratio of tertiary employment in urban labor markets. In the countryside there were significant concerns in the areas of food and clothing, as well as safety and security issues and the availability of safe drinking water.[81]

In the two decades after the reforms began in 1978, real per capita consumption has

TABLE 14.3   Progress Toward "Being Well-Off": Indicators and Estimates for China, 1989–2000

Categories and Indicators	How Measured (Goal for 2000)	1980 (A)	1990 (B)	Desired Level for 2000 (C)	Weighting (% of total)	1990 Attainment Index[1]
Objective Economic Conditions						
Per Capita GNP	Rmb per capita (1990 prices goal = Y2,400)	735	1,558	2,400	15	49.4
Industrial Structure	% of tertiary employment (goal = >36%)	20.5	27.2	36	8	42.9
Poverty	% living in poverty (goal = <58%)	33	8	5	5	89.3
Income Inequality	Gini coefficient: Lorenz curve measuring income dispersion (goal = 0.3–0.35)	0.28	0.36	0.32	9	93.0
Quality of Life Measures						
Per Capita Income	Rmb per capita (Y2,380— cities, Y110—rural areas)	320	970	1,400	14	51.1
Food Intake	Calories per capita (goal = >2,600 kcals. per day)	2,400	2,550	2,600	4	75.0
Protein Intake	Protein per capita (goal = >75 grams per day)	50	35	75	5	60.0
Housing Space	Square meters per person (goal = <15.5m²)	4.7	11.0	15.5	10	58.3
Calorie Consumption	Engel coefficient: (goal = 44–46% cities, 50% = rural areas)	60	54.5	48	8	45.8
Culture/Education	Share of culture and education of total consumption (goal = >16%)	6	11.2	16	5	52.0
Effectiveness of Life Indicators						
Life Expectancy	Life span >70 years	67	70	70	10	100.0
Education Level	Middle school attendance 55–60%	35	50	57	6	68.2
Overall Index					100%	57.4%[2]

SOURCE: Adapted from Yabuki, 1995, Tables 21.1, 21.2 (pp. 230–232).
NOTES:
[1] The 1990 attainment index is calculated as $(B-A) + (C-A)$ u 100.
[2] The cumulative index is calculated by the weighting (%) multiplied by the individual attainment indices.

grown at an annual rate of 7 percent, almost four times higher than in the previous two decades.[82] The result, not surprisingly, is that the standard of living in China in quantitative terms is more than twice what it was before the reform era began. Yet growth has been variable over time and across space. In the first seven years of reform (1978–1985) there was across-the-board growth in consumption levels, with all subgroups enjoying the benefits. After 1985 and through the early 1990s, consumption levels slowed considerably and certain subgroups of the population began to fall behind (see Chapter 10). In the 1990s, once the Four Modernizations project was back on track, the average rate of increase in consumption was again very high, increasing at about 8–9 percent per year.

In terms of disposable incomes the same pattern has been observed, with a rapid increase from 1978 to 1985, slowing significantly in the late 1980s, then rising again through the 1990s.[83] In quantitative terms, at least, China's urban residents and their rural counterparts have seen great improvement in the reform years as incomes have, in most years, grown at a faster rate than prices, which has meant a general improvement in consumer satisfaction.

There is a downside, as some dimensions of urban life have clearly not been improving to the same extent. In the 1990s, for example, there has been a much greater concern with job security and unemployment in the cities. This is in part associated with the relative decline of the state sector, where employment and benefits were generally guaranteed on a cradle-to-grave basis, vis-à-vis the private sector, where benefits are marginal or nonexistent, with job security dependent upon the whims of the market. In addition, city dwellers in the 1990s had to compete for jobs with the floating populations, who were employed in jobs that permanent city residents usually would not take for one reason or another. There is also the concern over growing inequality of access to health care, increasing rates of illiteracy, and rapid urbanization. The problems associated with growing urban populations are familiar to Westerners and include long lines, crowded buses, non-availability of potable water, and air pollution.

During the reform era the fundamental structure of urban consumption in China has been changing gradually. Food remained the largest drain on the pocketbooks of city dwellers, but the proportion of total income spent on food fell from an average of 57 percent in 1981, to 47 percent in 1990, and 45 percent in 1996 (the reduction spread about equally between staple and nonstaple foodstuffs).[84] China's city residents have also been spending more on consumer goods, including clothing and the items that used to be considered luxuries, and they have been paying more for basic services such as utilities, transportation, education, and health care. Interestingly, the expenditure on housing doubled during the 1980s, but the increase was from an average of 1.4 percent per household in 1981 to 2.7 percent in 1990.[85]

There has also been a major expansion of basic urban services (see Table 14.1). On a yearly basis, for example, during the 1981–1996 period great improvements were recorded (in the official statistics, at least) in the volume of tap water supplied, the amount of sewer pipelines laid, and the number of households gaining access to natural gas. Similar expansion was reported in the number of public buses and the amount of paved roadway. Somewhat surprisingly, all these achievements have been accompanied by a major increase in the acreage of green land, which in the absence of a better definition we can assume to be open space usable for urban recreation.[86] Again we might be running into a reliability problem with official data sources. It should also be noted that increases in urban services illustrated in Table 14.1 are absolute numbers, not rates per capita, and as we saw in Chapter 9 the percentage of China's population living in cities almost doubled during the period in question, so the improvements in service provision must be considered in the context of growing levels of demand.

It would be useful to compare the new patterns of consumption in China to those elsewhere. One of the obvious problems in such comparisons is purchasing power parity, which is very difficult to calculate because of China's constantly undervalued currency (i.e., Chinese prices are difficult to compare on an international basis). Another problem is the issue of state subsidies to urban residents, which were provided until the second half of the 1990s, as well as price controls and rationing, which have been common practice.[87] One researcher has concluded that consumption levels in China were significantly lower than those in Taiwan and Japan at similar times in their development (1969 for Taiwan, and 1955–1960 for Japan).[88] Overall food consumption was higher than Japan's, although the amount of protein eaten in China (1985–1990) was lower. Housing conditions seemed better in China than they were in Japan in the 1960s, although the general quality of housing (piped water and flushing toilets) was significantly worse.

The most obvious difference in consumption between China in 1985 and Japan in 1960 was in services, with Chinese households spending less than one-third of the amount spent in Japan, partly because of state subsidies but also because of the traditionally low level of service provision in urban China. In spite of the significant absolute improvement in urban services (see Table 14.1), China's cities are still a long way from providing what would be considered a moderate comfort level. In the consumption of other items, however, including nonstaple foodstuffs, consumer durables, clothing, and luxury items, the 1990s have been a godsend for many of China's city dwellers, with real consumption standards close to doubling by the end of the decade. Still, the future of consumption and service provision in the cities is unpredictable, given that the state is withdrawing from its provider role. With the added insecurity of a declining pool of investment funds, the Chinese government may be forced to restrain consumer demand, either by allowing significant price increases (which would be extremely unpopular), or by slowing down economic expansion to constrain incomes (which would be suicidal). In its usually pragmatic fashion the state may choose neither option, preferring a third strategy: al-

lowing and encouraging a major increase in the private sector's participation in the production of consumer goods and providing collective services. By the end of the 1990s it has become clear that the latter option has been dominant, and in cities across China there has been a huge increase in private service provision. One example is transportation, with an explosion of new private providers at all levels, from multiseater buses to smaller vehicles, which are usually more expensive but quicker and more comfortable (with heat for winter driving and air-conditioning for the summer). The most pervasive example of privatization in urban service delivery in the 1990s was in the realm of housing.

Home and Housing in the New Chinese City

Housing in China is not equitably provided:

> Those with power . . . [government officers] . . . those with money [merchants and traders] those with materials [distributors of production goods] and those with connections get to live in large places, while people with little power and workers in small enterprises . . . have to live in cramped housing. . . . In Beijing, while the average living area is 3.6 square meters per capita, employees of the government . . . enjoy an average of over 7 square meters.[89]

After 1949 there was far less emphasis on personal consumption than in most Western societies. This has been especially evident in housing and the creature comforts we take for granted.[90] After 1949 the CCP deliberately steered away from personal consumption, which was partly intended to conserve resources and ensure rapid development of the productive forces, partly to denigrate the decadent consumption habits typical of the West and the old Treaty Ports.[91] In Mao Zedong's China, private home ownership was not officially encouraged or facilitated as in most capitalist societies.[92]

In the austerity of the first decades after the revolution, and the all-out drive toward national reconstruction, the de-emphasis of private home ownership was a valuable way to conserve scarce resources. A low rate of private home ownership also facilitated the social control functions that were considered to be necessary in a totalitarian state. As we have already seen, in China (as in most countries with one-party systems of government) there has been an almost fanatical concern with security, law and order, and compliance with Party-state dictates.[93]

Most Chinese city dwellers have never been able to think of their home as exclusively their own: It was something they rented from the state, from which they could be moved at any time if others' needs were greater, and over which they had little individual control. In Mao's China, therefore, the role of the home as the bulwark against the state was virtually nonexistent, and by Western standards one's home was certainly not a castle. Although there was some private home ownership, until the 1980s the home itself was rarely considered to be a major source of investment; equally rarely was it a showplace for personal consumption. The socialist city was intended to be a place that would no longer privilege the rich and exclude the poor; in fact the goal was to provide cheap and affordable housing for all residents; even the poorest people would have their material needs provided for by the "iron rice bowl" guarantee of public service provision.

By Western standards the post-1949 Chinese city was an austere place, certainly not something to behold in the traditional Western sense of the "city beautiful." The Communists hoped to build cities that would contribute usefully to China's modernization rather than providing an arena for what they considered to be the wasteful and decadent practices of privatized consumption and the luxurious enjoyment of visually pleasing environments. For most ordinary Chinese people this sort of socialist city proved to be functional but probably unlovable. It is difficult to compare the standard of living from one country to another, but there can be little doubt that the average Chinese home was (certainly until reform) far less spacious and more sparsely furnished than those in most Western capitalist countries. In addition, it was common for Chinese families to share basic private facilities such as toilets and kitchens, and many even had to double up, providing permanent homes for newly married sons and daughters. In general, the housing problem has been worse in the cities than in the countryside, where households usually have more space and there is better access to building materials.

By the end of 1970s the post-Mao leadership was beginning to seriously consider overhauling housing policies. It was still rare for citizens to openly criticize government policies. By the end of the 1970s, however, long-standing public resentment about the housing situation (among other things) briefly surfaced in a new literature of dissent, some of it highly critical of government policies in providing urban services. One poet, signing only as a "revolutionary citizen," was bold enough to point out some of the glaring inequalities in the way different sectors of the population were housed in socialist China:

There's a housing shortage in Beijing,
But in Zhongnanhai new buildings are built.
When Chairman Mao and Premier Zhou were
    still alive,
Was there that kind of extravagant spending?
Sites of culture and history are completely
    demolished,
Really it is not just absurd but gross!
There's a forest of building cranes which daily
    revolve,
And the lorries come and the seasons go,
Still half the city's construction force is
    employed here
If local authorities thus break the view, they
    should
be severely punished,
For when those above behave unworthily,
    those below will do the same.
Premier Zhou's attitude to the masses should
    be copied

Rather than Qin Shihuang's when he built the
  Afang palace.
Think carefully Vice-Chairman Wang
We lesser mortals only live in two square
  meters each.[94]

As the poem suggests, despite Maoist aspirations for classless cities there were inequalities in the housing allocation system that were particularly hard to swallow among ordinary people. The furious new construction in Zhongnanhai, the CCP headquarters on the western side of the Forbidden City, tended to increase public resentment. The evidence suggests that government officials and other well-placed individuals were much better housed than others. In the mid-1950s, for example, a survey had shown that class differences were reflected in significantly greater amounts of living space for party officials and white-collar workers.[95] The low cost of public housing in China was considered to be necessary as a subsidy to urban residents in light of low wages and the relative absence of consumer goods and garden plots. In fact even the subsidies contributed to inequality, as the low cost of housing meant that the better-paid workers had more money to spend on food and consumer goods. When some families started to get rich as a result of economic reform in the 1980s, the effect of this subsidy was increased, which continued until the mid-1990s, when the newly rich began to spend more on commodities they had been deprived of for so long.[96]

As bad as it was at the start of the 1980s, China's housing situation would have been much worse but for persistent efforts to slow growth in the largest cities. The net effect of antigrowth policies was to reduce the pressure on the urban infrastructure, especially housing.[97] There had also been a major drive to expand the industrial base in the countryside, which increased the supply of local jobs and thereby reduced the rate of rural out-migration. These and other policies had reduced the existing urban population in absolute terms and resulted in a lower demand for new homes in the future.

The statistics themselves can tell only part of the story. Most homes had access to kitchen, toilet, and bathing facilities, but the commonplace sharing meant frustration and conflict.[98] Public control of housing and the bureaucratic method of allocation also resulted in widespread claims of slowness, ineptitude, and corruption. The housing stock varied in quantity and quality from one work unit to another; if you were not connected to a specific unit, you were placed on the interminable waiting lists of city housing bureaus.[99]

By the early 1980s, after three decades of relatively austere state socialism, the urban housing situation had reached crisis proportions. Although compared to others in poor nations the Chinese were relatively well housed, Chinese leaders by this time preferred to make comparisons to developed nations. From that perspective the housing situation was deplorable; on that even official Party sources were in agreement. In 1980, for example, *People's Daily* estimated that 20 percent of urban residents were slum dwellers.[100] The final ignominy came with the realization that socialist China had not even been able to improve upon the housing situation that existed in 1949. As a result of general population growth, by the late 1970s the absolute amount of living space per person in China's cities had actually fallen below the 1949 level (from 4.5 to 3.6 square meters; in the largest cities the average was considerably lower).

During the reform era the new leadership was eager to lay some of the blame for the housing crisis on Mao Zedong and the recently vanquished Gang of Four. One of the contributing causes, they argued, was the "excessive egalitarianism" in Maoist philosophy that resulted in a desire to provide everyone with equal access to extremely cheap housing. With rents pegged at an artificially low level, there were few opportunities to increase the supply of housing because virtually no revenue was being generated. In most cases the revenue collected from rentals barely covered the repair bills, so ongoing maintenance and new construction were continually falling behind demand levels.[101] The shortage of funds for housing construction became especially serious during the push for industrial expansion that began in the late 1970s and continued through the 1990s.

The persistent tendency to shortchange the public in housing, particularly compared to collectivized education and health care, has also been observed in the former Soviet Union and Eastern European states.[102] The norm in socialist societies, as in China, is for housing that is functional, cheap, and usually in poor condition. It is difficult to avoid the conclusion that the trappings of luxury to be found in homes in capitalist societies are considered too bourgeois for socialist countries, although there is no indication that this reflects the preferences of residents. During the Cultural Revolution, when all facets of inequality came under attack, the most vulnerable areas were housing and bourgeois possessions such as books, art collections, furniture, and musical instruments, particularly pianos—all of which became popular targets for the Red Guards' truncheons.[103]

The housing crisis at the end of the 1970s was also interpreted as one of the negative outcomes of Maoist investment priorities. The push to develop the forces of production rather than allowing higher levels of consumption and service provision meant that the amount of investment in so-called nonproductive categories had always been extremely low, especially during the first Five Year Plan.[104] The proportion of housing investment fell to as low as 4 percent during the early radical years of the Cultural Revolution (1966–1970), with the average being significantly lower than 10 percent during the entire 1950–1978 period.

In the reform era significant efforts were made to change investment priorities, which had resulted in chronic neglect of all aspects of the urban infrastructure, especially housing. The plan for the seven-year period beginning in 1979 called for a housing construction boom that would generate more living space than during the previous thirty years combined (a total of 550 million square meters).[105] This effectively required tripling the investment allo-

cated to housing, from less than 7 percent in 1977 to 22 percent in 1984; in physical terms this represented an astonishing increase in new floor space from 28.3 million to 100 million square meters.[106] It was clear that such an ambitious plan would overstretch the economy, already struggling by the end of the 1970s, so it had to be accompanied by radical thinking and policymaking at the highest levels of government. To generate the revenue surplus needed to free investment funds for new housing construction, it would be necessary to allow individuals and enterprises to expand their incomes considerably, both in the countryside as well as in the cities. This would boost the level of savings and thus the supply of credit. It would also be necessary to allow people to move freely off the land and into the cities to help feed the vast labor needs for constructing all the new housing. In addition, the state's monopoly over commodity distribution would need to be loosened, and the rigid price system would have to be deregulated, to facilitate huge increases in needed building supplies. Thus the proposed expansion in housing construction was an integral part of the overall restructuring and marketization of the Chinese economy that had begun in earnest after 1978 and continued throughout the 1980s and 1990s.[107]

To construct new housing at the level specified in the plan, it was necessary to build highrise towers. There has also been strong criticism of the overall low quality of the new construction, the lack of landscaping, and the inadequate ancillary facilities for shopping and social services.[108] Even in Beijing, with dozens of highrise apartment towers across the city, many residents found themselves without basic utilities such as electricity, water, heat, and sewage disposal, the result of scarce building materials and overeager construction by work units, many of which ran out of money before basic services had been installed. An official survey conducted in 1985 showed that more than 3.2 million urban families were still living in nonhousing spaces such as corridors, cubby holes, and offices; 13 percent of families had less than four square meters per person, which was half the new standard; and 10.5 percent were living in one room.[109]

In addition, what little progress had been made since 1978 was offset by population growth. Thus despite the urban building boom the average amount of floor space per person increased only marginally in the cities, from 5.2 square meters in 1977 to 6.3 in 1982 (it rose to 6.7 square meters in 1990 and 8.5 in 1996). The official estimate of families living in poor housing was unchanged since 1978, about 20 percent of the total, but the pool of families in 1982 had increased from around 6–7 million to about 11 million. By 1987 the average amount of floor space per person in China's cities varied from 6.0 to 7.2 square meters, usually with less space available in the largest cities.[110]

Despite the turnaround in investment priorities, the housing crisis by the early 1980s prompted key CCP thinkers to prepare a radical shift in housing policies. The preferred solution was a headlong confrontation with the ideology underlying Maoist social and economic policies. It had already been considered necessary to introduce market-oriented principles into the economy as a whole, and that had helped to generate investment funds to build new houses; but it also stimulated demand for more and better housing. It was now clear that market-oriented principles would have to guide the housing industry itself.

The solution was a move toward commodification of housing, meaning a greater emphasis on private home ownership; the acceptance of the user-pays concept for rent; and the introduction of market principles into the business of housing construction. In the tradition of previous plans, the government set a goal of housing all citizens by the year 2000 based on an average of 8 square meters per person. In the mid-1980s the average monthly rent for a two-room apartment was less than Y4 (slightly more than US$1 at that time), but the cost of new construction averaged Y300–500 per square meter of floor space. Obviously, the state and collective units needed to charge much more for housing to meet the established goal. That in itself would allow cities and enterprises to speed housing construction as rental revenues begin to approximate construction costs. At the same time, families with enough funds were encouraged to purchase their homes.

Experiments began in various cities in the mid-1980s, with house buyers paying up to a third of total costs. Those early experiments were immensely successful, with demand almost constantly outstripping supply, especially as family and individual resources continued to rise at unprecedented rates. An experiment conducted in the city of Yantai in 1987 was recommended as the basis of urban housing reform planned for 1988. The proposal would increase rents up to Y1.56 per square meter per month. This meant that families wanting more space could be accommodated as long as they were able to pay for it. For example, a family in Yantai with 60 square meters now had to pay Y25 per month, which was more than 10 percent of their salary, about three times the proportion they had been paying. To ease the transition to this user-pays system, the government started to issue housing allowance vouchers, amounting to as much as 25 percent of the families' income, which could only be used for rent. The vouchers meant that most families that could tolerate living in small houses or were too poor to consider moving were not seriously affected by the higher rents.[111]

Among CCP leaders it was not a simple or unanimous decision to move toward commodifying housing. Even raising housing prices to the level of the total value of the labor embodied in the construction process proved to be controversial. There was a natural hesitancy among many old-timers in the Party, as well as among the relatively few who harbored ideas of returning to Maoist egalitarianism. After three decades of almost constant propaganda and mass movements to continue the class struggle, the remaining leftists were naturally hesitant about producing a new class of property owners in the cities, a process that was already well developed in the countryside. Nevertheless, the process continued to gather momentum throughout the 1980s, and by 1987 official survey data published by the State Statistical Bureau showed a significant improvement in the urban housing situation compared to the early 1980s (see Table 14.4a). Unfortunately there are no details about how or where the sample was compiled, or how some of the categories were defined. Still, it is interesting that a considerable proportion of city dwellers were still living in units officially defined as "crowded" or "inconvenient" in 1987. Although the debate was finally settled in favor of com-

modification, ambivalence about the whole process slowed it to a far more moderate level than had first been envisioned. Housing sales continued to expand into the late 1980s and throughout the 1990s while housing prices have increased steadily but not dramatically (see Table 14.4b).

Bearing in mind the increasing consumer prices that accompanied economic reform, the government prudently prevented housing prices from rising too rapidly. Public outcry

TABLE 14.4a   Housing Conditions: Urban and Rural Residents Compared (1981–1987)

	1981	1985	1987
Rural Areas			
Average living space per capita (square meters)	9.40	14.70	16.00
Average number of rooms per family	4.06	5.11	5.36
Urban Areas			
Average living space per capita (square meters)	5.2	7.46	8.47
Average number of rooms per family	NA	2.24	2.39
Urban households with no housing			
(% of total in each year)	3.22	1.50	0.48
Crowded households	24.6	12.5	7.9
Inconvenient households	9.7	8.7	7.6
<6 square meters per person	31.3	19.4	19.1
6–8 square meters per person	17.7	22.6	22.2

SOURCE: State Statistical Bureau, 1988, p. 746. Based on survey data (definitions not provided).

TABLE 14.4b   Urban Housing in the Reform Era: Private and Public Provision

Year	Annual Rent (yuan/person)	Rate of Private Ownership	Living Space (m²/person)		Public NBSF (100 m.sq.)	Private NBSF (100 m.sq.)
			Rural	Urban		
1978	NA	NA	8.1	3.6	0.38	NA
1980	NA	NA	9.4	3.9	0.92	NA
1985	6.48	24.9	14.7	5.2	1.25	0.63
1990	9.43	24.2	17.8	6.7	1.07	0.65
1991	10.66	30.2	NA	NA	1.17	0.68
1992	14.33	NA	NA	NA	1.46	0.86
1993	22.00	NA	NA	NA	1.78	0.98
1994	37.44	NA	NA	NA	2.14	1.23
1995	NA	NA	21.0	8.1	2.42	1.33
1996	NA	NA	21.7	8.5	2.48	1.46

SOURCES: State Statistical Bureau, China Statistical Yearbook, 1997, 1994, 1992, 1987, 1985; and Chen (1996), Tables 1 and 2, pp. 1079–1081.
NBSF = newly built floor space

resulting from inflation can easily transform into calls for retrenchment and a slowing of the entire reform process. Some observers have argued that the success of economic reform called for housing commodification at a much faster pace just as the government was beginning to slow down. The reforms resulted in higher family incomes all through the 1980s, so that even with the new higher rents, the proportion of the average family income spent on housing actually decreased, from 2.3 percent in 1979, to 1.5 percent in 1983, and to 1.2 percent in 1985; in the 1990s the average percentage spent on rent continued to be fairly small.[112]

The first Five Year Plan for housing, implemented in 1988, set an ambitious agenda to bring all cities and towns into the reform programs. Although many cities had produced local housing reform plans, only a few had put them into practice before the 1990s. There were different strategies, some of them following the Yantai model of balancing total rent with coupon-subsidies, others favoring incremental rent increases without coupons. Many cities began to provide housing at discounted rents to privileged households (i.e., those with members working in SOEs or the Party). For example, in Ruxian County, Henan Province, Party members who joined before 1949 were given a 1 percent per year discount; in Taiyuan, the capital of Shanxi Province, the discount was as much as Y50 for each year of service.[113]

In 1991, Shanghai, usually at the forefront of economic reform, began to implement a comprehensive housing reform program with the following characteristics:

- a compulsory housing savings system with both employers and employees putting 5 percent of their salary into a special housing account for future use (either for repairs or to build or buy a new house);
- rents rising by as much as 100 percent of the 1991 rent, with an additional 2 percent added to the existing (25 percent of salary) housing coupons;
- new public housing tenants paying a large deposit, Y20–80 per square meter of hous-

ing, which went into the Shanghai Housing Savings Management Center, which would repay tenants over five years with interest;
- discounts, especially to tenants able to buy rather than rent housing (i.e., tenants who could afford it received up to 20 percent of the sale price; others were allowed to pay for their housing with what was effectively a mortgage, payable over five years); and
- local housing committees were to make proposals about future reforms, organize and arrange new construction plans, raise and control housing investment funds, and make housing distribution policies.

Using the Shanghai plan as a model, the Urban Housing Reform Resolution of 1991 updated the 1988 resolution. The major goals were to alter the low-rent and free-distribution characteristics of China's housing system, with rents being restructured to generate additional funds for new housing construction. The resolution also updated the minimum standards, with floor space per person raised to 7.5 square meters by 1995 (the end of the eighth Five Year Plan). The resolution proposed that rents in the public sector should be increased to cover basic construction and maintenance costs.

Inequality and Housing Affordability

Following the Urban Housing Reform Resolution of 1991, another round of housing reform was implemented in many parts of China, with some cities selling off most (in some cases more than 90 percent) of public housing.[114] Clearly the new housing policies, especially with coupon subsidies, were benefiting households that were doing well in the reform era. By the end of the 1980s the richer households had already bought most of the consumer goods they needed and were starting to save and invest their incomes, and new houses seemed to be an excellent investment. Subsidized house sales were particularly attractive to individuals whose job-related entitlements gave them additional perks. In fact the new housing system tended to widen urban inequality by providing the most benefit to those with the highest incomes, as well as those who were working in prestigious work units or as Party officials (see Photos 14.1a and 14.1b).

In 1994 a new housing resolution was published, announcing the intent to deepen the housing reform program. On balance, the reform policies have produced important developments in the business of housing provision: They have significantly changed the public perception of state housing provision and have introduced a range of new policies, including rent increases, sales of public-sector housing, compulsory housing savings schemes, and commercial house building and distribution. The net effect has been diversification and expansion in the housing market. With additional foreign investments in new housing developments in the bigger cities, overall residential floor space increased every year during the 1990s, with more and better housing being added to every city's housing stock.

At the start of the 1980s the average floor space in China was about 3 square meters per person; by 1993 it was around 7.5 square meters.[115] According to the State Statistical Bureau it had increased to 8.5 square meters by 1996, with a significant rate of yearly increase of 4 percent in the 1990s (see Table 14.4b).[116] Many urban families have been able to acquire better housing either by improving their existing space or buying a new home. Still, younger lower-income families remain on the outside, facing higher rents and sale prices, as the state slowly backs out of its provider role (by 1994 the central-local government share of housing investment was only 23 percent, compared to more than 90 percent in 1979). In 1994 SOEs and work units financed close to 70 percent of housing investments, with the remaining 17 percent being directly financed by individual households.[117]

One of the major problems with housing reform is affordability. According to a news-paper report, in 1996 there were 60 million square meters of unsold housing despite 4.16 million households with per capita living space of less than 4 square meters in China's cities.[118] Obviously for many urban households the real problem is the inability to generate enough surplus funds to buy a house, and many new housing developments have not sold very well because it is still much more affordable to rent. Another problem has been the continued involvement of enterprises and work units in the business of housing provision. As noted, most public housing stock is owned by enterprises, which also have to pay employee wages as well as price subsidies, benefits, and pensions. Thus most housing reform measures such as rent increases and housing sales represent little more than an internal circulation of funds—from the employer to the employee and back again—with no real incentive for enterprises to push for more reforms. The stumbling block has been the continued existence of the old system. Most families that cannot afford a new house simply wait in line for employer-provided housing (costing, on average, 1–3 percent of their income). Thus the best option is to rent; in 1983, for example, the rent-sale price ratio for an apartment in public housing was about 1:120, which had increased to 1:140 in 1996.[119] Obviously, as long as the old system exists, with housing still being provided cheaply by the government and other enterprises, complete commercialization cannot occur.[120]

The most significant change has been a public recognition that housing is no longer an entitlement but is something that can be bought and sold, with the old state support system reduced to a onetime purchase subsidy. There is also an open supply of housing, as all manner of local governments, work units, and individuals are allowed to raise funds to construct housing. With the continued existence of coupons and subsidies, given only to households that can afford to buy their own housing, this system of allocation remains highly inegalitarian.[121] Oddly enough, many observers would suggest that the only solution to the current

PHOTO 14.1a
New housing in Zhongshan City,
Pearl River Delta.

PHOTO 14.1b
Old housing in Zhongshan City,
Pearl River Delta.

housing problem is a more thorough set of reforms that would completely alter the way housing is produced and distributed. As two scholars have recently noted, for example:

> The shift from a centrally controlled housing finance system to one based on local government and enterprise autonomy has brought about rapid housing development during the reform decade. Having achieved earlier success, this partially reformed system has already begun to stall as a victim of its own essentially unaltered redistributive logic. The new but diminishing housing investment will have decreasing economic returns, if it is not recovered through more extensive privatization of housing ownership and complete commercialization of housing sales and rents.[122]

This suggests a shift away from the practice of local governments and work units controlling the supply of housing to a practice in which the housing market and individual households gain control. This would be a difficult step, as it involves households facing up to the reality of paying full costs for housing without the redistributive help from local governments and work units.

The steps to commodify urban housing in China thus far can be interpreted as just one component of the overall economic reform process, which in the long term has caused major ideological shifts within the CCP. The inherent danger has always been that reform might generate additional demands for ideological shifts. The newfound wealth and the highly prized possession of land, housing, and capital will continue to produce wider disparities within Chinese society, and it is possible that the new gentry will soon demand political powers to match their wealth. Many Westerners view the events that occurred in China during the 1980s and 1990s as a triumph of capitalism over socialism, and it is intriguing to speculate whether the market solution to the housing crisis—along with all the other economic reforms—helped destabilize the system of government in China by the end of the 1980s. By attempting to respond to the people's call for a greater share of national wealth, the government may have unwittingly contributed to the tumultuous events of the late 1980s.

15

Market Forces
and the New Population
Mobility in China

🮐🮐🮐🮐🮐🮐🮐🮐🮐🮐🮐🮐🮐🮐🮐🮐🮐🮐🮐🮐🮐🮐🮐

*[In] . . . the reform era, China's cities came to appear more and
more similar to those . . . in the third world.*

—Dorothy Solinger, *Contesting Citizenship in Urban China* (1999)[1]

Introduction:
The Geography of China's
New Population Mobility

*In an attempt to curb the tidal wave of temporary
rural-urban migration, China has kept the basic elements of the household registration system in place.
The large "floating population," however, has already
begun to weaken the "urban public goods regime" of
the entitled population based on household registration, as urban bureaucrats try to balance their loyalty
to the old system and established habits against the
promotion of markets by allowing rural migrants into
cities and reducing entitled urbanites' welfare benefits.*

—Xiangming Chen and William Parish,
"Urbanization in China" (1996)[2]

China's economy heated to the boiling point
with the introduction of market-oriented
reforms, which began to have an effect in the
early 1980s. At the same time, the power of the
collectives and their stranglehold over the peasants was gradually being relaxed. The net effect
was an unprecedented increase in population
mobility across China, including the movement
of peasants to urban areas. Between 1978 and
1993 an average of one-fifth of new entrants
into the urban labor force (those in nonagricultural employment living in cities and towns)
came from rural areas. The actual rates varied

from year to year, with the pace of out-migration accelerating in the economic liberalization
years (1985–1989), slowing with the retrenchments at the end of the decade, then increasing
again after the economic recovery in 1992.[3]

In official terminology most migrants are
defined as "temporary" urban residents, regardless of length of time spent away from home.
The new transients vastly increased the supply
of cheap labor in China's cities, which helped
power the reform economy, yet they put extra
burden on the already stretched infrastructures
in the biggest cities. Migrants are not entitled to
the subsidies and benefits that come with the
possession of an urban *hukou* (registration
card), but the fact that so many are able to survive without one indicates that the state's
monopoly over public service provision in the
cities (i.e., the urban public goods regime) has
effectively been ended.

Longtime city dwellers and newspaper
reporters most often refer to the new transients
as *liudong renkou* (floating population), a label
describing those who are not permanently registered in their current place of residence. Many
of the floaters find that life in the cities is not all
they had imagined, and they are forced to
occupy marginal spaces in housing and labor
markets. This marginalization has created a new
underclass population comparable to ethnic
minorities and immigrants in Western cities.

The major difference, however, is that in China the new underclass is not defined in racial, religious, or national terms but by class status and geographical origin within China. The new transients are as Chinese as everyone else, but their minority status is ascribed to them largely because they are poor and from the countryside—in other words, because they are peasants.

The 1990 population census provided the first official estimate of the new mobility. Two types of movement were counted: permanent and temporary. A permanent migrant is someone whose move is officially sanctioned as to origin and destination and is granted a *hukou* in the new place of residence. The census data show that this category remained stable throughout the 1980s, at about eighteen per 1,000. Thus most of the new mobility in China has involved temporary migrants: individuals who have lived in a place where they were not registered for more than a year or had been away from home, living in different places, for more than a year.[4] By this definition the 1990 census counted 21.3 million temporary migrants, an increase of 325 percent over 1982.[5] If we add the estimated 50 million people who were not counted by the census because they were away from home for less than a year, the total number of migrants in 1990 was probably some 70 million, more than 6 percent of the total population.[6]

The rate of migration varies geographically (see Map 15.1a). In 1990 the highest in-migration was recorded in the territory along the coast, stretching from the northeast to the southeast, where the prospect of employment has attracted peasants searching for better lives. In-migration is also high in the provinces and Autonomous Regions in the border areas, where the government has been officially encouraging economic development and resettlement (including Heilongjiang, Jilin, Inner Mongolia, Ningxia, Gansu, Xinjiang, Qinghai, Yunnan, and Tibet). Interprovincial migration was also an important component of the new mobility in the 1990 census, with the nation's largest provinces being the major attractions (see Map 15.1b); close to half the total number of officially counted migrants (16 million) moved from rural areas to urban areas (see Table 15.1).[7]

At the provincial level Guangdong was the nation's leading destination for in-migrants in

TABLE 15.1   Migrants by Origin and Destination in China, 1985–1990

	Number	*% of Total*
Interprovincial migration	10,836,260	100.0
urban to urban	3,752,030	34.6
urban to rural	492,930	4.6
rural to rural	1,760,280	16.2
rural to urban	4,831,020	44.6
Intraprovincial migration	23,004,350	100.0
urban to urban	7,504,080	32.6
urban to rural	910,400	3.9
rural to rural	2,997,610	13.0
rural to urban	11,592,260	50.4
All migration	33,840,610	100.0
urban to urban	11,256,110	33.3
urban to rural	1,403,330	4.2
rural to rural	4,757,890	14.1
rural to urban	16,423,280	48.5

SOURCE: Adapted from State Statistical Bureau (10 Percent Sampling Tabulation on the 1990 Population Census of the PRC).

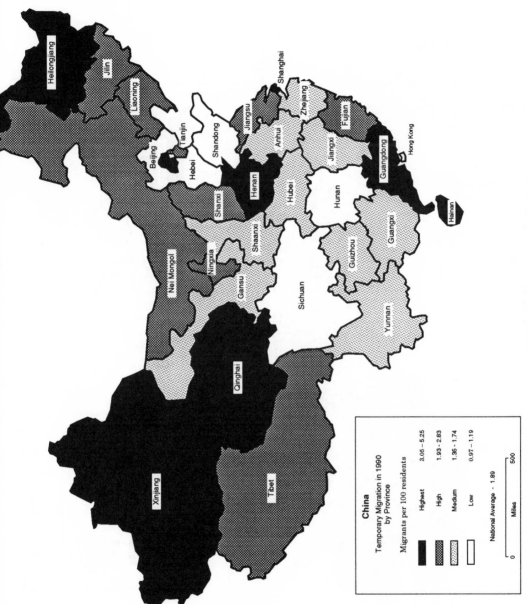

MAP 15.1a   Temporary Migration by Province, 1990

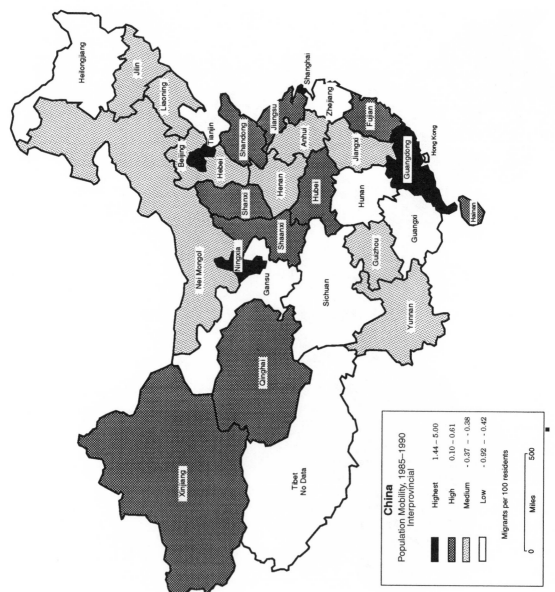

China

Population Mobility, 1985–1990
Interprovincial

■	Highest	1.44 – 5.00
▨	High	0.10 – 0.61
▨	Medium	– 0.37 – – 0.38
□	Low	– 0.92 – – 0.42

Migrants per 100 residents

0   Miles   500

MAP 15.1b   Interprovincial Population Mobility, 1985–1990

1990, with more than 3.3 million newcomers, representing more than 5 percent of its total residents.[8] A marked "distance decay" effect was evident in the pattern of migration, with the majority of migrants moving from elsewhere within the same province or adjacent provinces. Of the 33.8 million total migrants who moved between 1985 and 1990, for example, more than 23 million (68 percent) went to destinations in the same province. This was the case in all of the provinces that experienced significant amounts of net in-migration.[9] One of the strongest attractions has been employment opportunities created by new economic reform and development, which in Guangdong has been strongest in the Pearl River Delta, centered on the cities of Guangzhou, Foshan, Zhongshan, Dongguan, Shenzhen, Zhuhai, and Jiangmen, as well as in some of the adjacent coastal counties to the south and southwest of Guangzhou.[10] During this period the Pearl River Delta accounted for more than 43 percent of the province's fixed capital investment and attracted almost 90 percent of its foreign direct investment, and not surprisingly the region received more than 80 percent of the province's migrants, making it China's major migrant destination in 1990.[11] In-migration throughout the latter part of the 1980s contributed to rapid urbanization; in Guangdong, for example, the percentage of the population officially designated as urban almost doubled, from 18.6 percent in 1982 to 36.8 percent in 1990.[12]

The typical rural-to-urban migrant in a developing country is the single man; in light of China's many urban construction sites, one might assume that to be the case in China as well. Yet the official census documents that the rural-to-urban flow is heavily feminized, with many women drawn to the cities for work. Women are more likely to choose some destinations over others, as shown in the male-to-female ratios for cities in the Pearl River Delta (see Table 15.2); it is reasonable to hypothesize that more women will go to cities where a high proportion of new jobs are made available to women. Many migrant women enter the urban labor markets in the service trades, as wait-resses, hair stylists, maids, and nannies. Women are also attracted to (and are recruited for) work in export-oriented factories, especially those in the Pearl River Delta and the Shenzhen and Zhuhai SEZs. In the city of Guangzhou, for example, men and women migrants are about equally represented in manufacturing jobs, but overall there are significantly more men than women in the migrant labor force (see Figure 15.1a); the ratio will vary significantly from city to city (see Figure 15.1b; Dongguan City has many factories where women workers predominate).

The Great Escape from the Countryside: Causes and Consequences

The reforms paved the way for economic growth on an unprecedented scale in China, with growth rates in many coastal provinces exceeding 10 percent per year; in some localities 20 percent has been the norm. After three decades of socialist austerity, Chinese people were finally experiencing a true great leap forward in living standards. Transients from the countryside began moving in unprecedented numbers, due to the surplus of labor in rural areas. Agrarian reforms resulted in new economic efficiency in the countryside, including a significant reduction in the average person-hours devoted to cultivating various crops. It is important to remember, however, that the surplus labor in the countryside was not caused by reform per se but was a structural feature of China's rural commune system. The "iron rice bowl" security provided by communes effectively guaranteed jobs for everyone, but it also created massive hidden underemployment. With the reforms, peasants were lured by the profits to be realized by selling at higher procurement prices; and they were able to offer their products much more easily than in the past in the newly emerging free markets in small towns and cities. The reforms gave peasants tangible incentives to work more efficiently on the land, and within a relatively short period

TABLE 15.2   Floating Population[1] in the Cities of Guangdong Province, by Gender, 1990

	Total Population	Gender Ratio (men/women)
Total, Guangdong Province	3,314,656	100.34
Guangzhou	486,983	128.50
Shaoguan	132,889	145.05
Shenzhen	1,022,723	97.21
Zhuhai	160,474	114.64
Swatow	65,798	82.91
Foshan	278,276	112.40
Jiangmen	87,869	95.07
Zhanjiang	91,126	86.69
Maoming	50,043	46.26
Zhaoqing	86,055	93.39
Huizhou	158,008	103.86
Meizhou	54,108	130.09
Shanwei	30,583	78.75
Heyuan	15,326	147.23
Yangjiang	20,576	111.38
Qingyuan	31,871	111.58
Dongguan	439,777	73.62
Zhongshan	96,673	97.78
Chaozhou	5,498	85.93

SOURCE: Guangdong Population Census Office, 1990, Table 2, pp. 14–22.
NOTE: [1] Floating population here is defined as individuals who are away from their official place of residence (where their *hukou* is registered) for more than twelve months.

higher output levels were being achieved by fewer agricultural workers than had been possible during the collective era.

The profits earned during the early years of agrarian reform also allowed rural households to mechanize production in the fields, which meant that sons, daughters, and other members could search for work.[13] Some went to nearby villages, others to the nearest big city; the most adventurous set their sights on newly booming cities along China's golden coastline. At harvesttime they would be recalled, if necessary, to share the extra burden; in some cases households simply hired replacement laborers, either from poorer villages nearby or adjacent provinces. Once a few local residents had tried their luck, others followed, and in some areas the idea of migration spread rapidly from household to household, village to village. Although very few households have given up

their land completely, it is not unusual to come across villages populated only by children and grandparents, with most able-bodied adults working elsewhere. In many instances elders stay at home to look after grandchildren on a semipermanent basis.

In addition, environmental, technological, and demographic forces contributed to the growing labor surplus in the countryside. The amount of rural land available for farming declined steadily throughout the 1980s, partly due to overcropping and soil exhaustion, partly due to urban and industrial encroachments.[14] Combined with the introduction of machinery and other technological innovations in agriculture, this resulted in a significant reduction in the amount of labor needed to get crops to market. It was reported, for example, that rice production required 22 percent less labor between the years 1978 and 1985; for wheat the

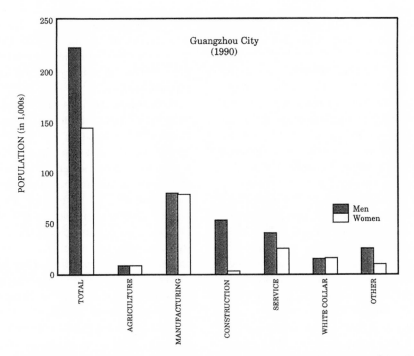

FIGURE 15.1a   Guangzhou's Floating Population: Employment by Sector and Gender

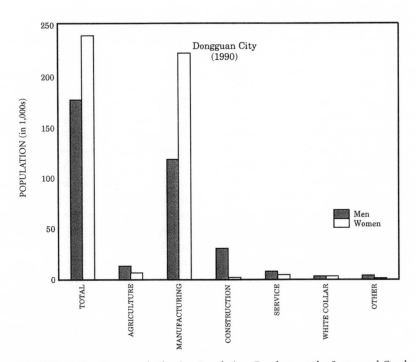

FIGURE 15.1b   Dongguan's Floating Population: Employment by Sector and Gender

figure was 53 percent.[15] In addition, beginning in the late 1970s an increasing cohort of rural dwellers who were born in the high-fertility period of the 1960s reached working age in the countryside, just as all of these other changes were starting to have an influence. The net effect: A significant proportion of the rural workforce (15–40 percent, or 60–156 million people, depending on calculations) became surplus to requirements during the 1980s.

The government's initial response was to encourage growth in nonagricultural employment in rural areas to absorb local surpluses of labor. Peasants were now allowed to "leave the land but not the countryside," which quickly became a popular option for those who wanted to try their luck in other lines of work, especially in the new enterprises. This strategy proved successful, and the Chinese countryside saw increases in industrial and service jobs. In little more than a decade (1978–1989), non-agricultural employment increased from 10 percent of the total rural labor force to 21 percent. Another 13 percent of the rural workforce was employed in nonfarm activities within the agricultural sector, so by the end of the 1980s more than a third of those employed in rural areas did not directly work in farming.[16]

The program of rural industrialization soaked up some of the surplus labor, but it was not a long-term solution, partly because of fuel and raw material shortages, partly because rural industry and services are less labor-intensive than is agriculture. It soon became obvious that there were too many surplus workers, and by the early 1980s other solutions would become necessary. The central authorities thus loosened restrictions on rural-to-urban migration.[17] In 1984 60,000 small and medium-sized market towns were opened to peasants, either to start their own business or to work in industry and service jobs. Peasants were also allowed to move away from the areas in which they were permanently registered and take up residence in urban areas with only a temporary registration permit.[18] This was accompanied in 1985 by a new system of national identity cards, which meant that permission to move from one's res-

idence was no longer necessary. These two new policies allowed peasants to "leave the land and the countryside" on the understanding that they would arrange their own food supplies and support themselves.[19]

With the restrictions thus lifted, peasants were free to move into nearby towns and cities to work on construction sites (or whatever job they could find) and to set up small businesses, mostly as traders and service providers. More than a release valve for pent-up mobility, liberated peasants would provide cheap labor needed to speed construction and production in urban areas, helping to raise tax revenues and contributing to the overall process of economic reform and modernization. They would also contribute indirectly as cash-paying consumers of the new goods and services being produced, which would speed the circulation of capital.

Rural migration gained momentum, and by the early 1990s some larger coastal cities had transient populations in excess of 1 million. At times the police would attempt to control the flow of illegal migrants by removing obvious offenders, particularly at key holidays such as the Spring Festival or, in the case of Guangzhou, before the semiannual international trade fair. In reality, it proved impossible to stem the flow of temporary migrants into cities the size of Guangzhou and Shenzhen, given the many points of entry and many places to live and work.[20] Illegal city dwellers can stay out of sight by moving to the anonymity of the suburbs, which now extend into what were recently farmlands.[21] The few who are sent home by authorities are quickly replaced by newcomers. The chain migration effect has worked to speed up the movement from the countryside, and by the early 1990s the transient population was increasing by as much as 10 million every year.[22] Small towns, especially in coastal provinces, experienced huge population increases and increasing industrialization. The Pearl River Delta saw rapid growth rates in the nonagricultural populations of small towns in peripheral counties. By comparison, growth rates in the larger central cities—Guangzhou, Foshan, Dongguan, and Zhongshan—were lower (though still considerable in absolute terms).[23]

During this period rural-to-urban migration followed the government's preferred policy, which was to control growth in large cities and allow growth in smaller cities and towns. Still, the attraction of larger cities remained strong; as the census data demonstrated, the Delta cities experienced substantial absolute increases in "temporary migrant" populations by 1990.[24] It appears that the relaxations in migration policies have allowed many peasants to bypass small towns and move directly to the cities, where the lure of better-paying jobs and the attraction of superior urban amenities continually act as a strong "pull" factor.[25]

Migration and Its Impacts

It is apparent that an interaction of market and state forces has brought about the new population mobility. Government policy allowing rural out-migration was the crucial factor; but the underlying forces were the direct and indirect effects of economic reform. Nevertheless, planners and politicians expressed concerns that the strain was being placed on city governments by the new transients, who are perceived as freeloaders (or, in economists' terms, "free riders" who are overburdening city governments). In Guangzhou, for example, the official 1990 census placed the floating population at close to a half-million; and for the entire province of Guangdong it was estimated at 3.5 million. As already noted, the official census undercounts transient populations, by defining temporary migrants only as those who have been away from home for more than one year.[26] Including migrants who have been away from home for shorter periods, the total number for Guangdong Province could be closer to 10 million; for Guangzhou alone it would be more than 1.5 million.

To explore some consequences of the new population mobility it is helpful to begin with a conceptual model of the migration process. Within the last two decades academic debates about migration have been influenced by structural theories that have their roots either in Marxist writings, dependency and world systems theories, or labor market segmentation theories.[27] These approaches assume that labor migration should be considered within the context of global economics, with less developed (peripheral) regions functionally linked to more highly developed (core) regions. In the new conceptualizations it is not automatically assumed that geographic mobility produces gains for all of the involved actors; in fact the core regions usually profit at the expense of the periphery (clearly the case in China; see Chapter 10).

Several structural forces currently influence the spatial context of migration in China, both in the core (urban) areas and in the periphery (rural) areas (see Figure 15.2). These forces have changed the balance of traditional behavior patterns in urban and rural areas—the urban and rural control mechanisms that once acted as constraints on migration. From among the pool of potential migrants some become actual migrants who move into the towns and cities; although the numbers involved are large, it is important to recall that the vast majority of peasants stay at home in the countryside. The empirical evidence also shows that for a number of reasons most of the original migrants return home, either permanently or on a circulating basis.

The following sections explore the role of migration as an agent of change in contemporary China, focusing on four issues: spatial integration of rural and urban territory; the process of economic development; the phenomenon of cultural change; and the contest for position and power in the city.

Migration and Spatial Integration

The new mobility in China began with the industrialization of the rural areas, which offered the peasants their first taste of nonfarm employment opportunities. It continued with the urbanization of the countryside, as peasants were allowed to move away from the land com-

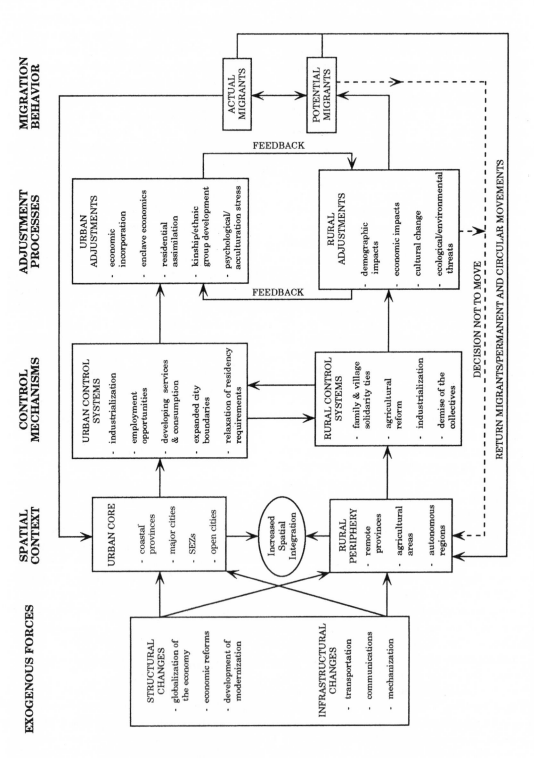

FIGURE 15.2   A Model of Internal Migration in China

pletely, to live in expanded and newly defined towns, the majority of which were close to their homes. The process has now reached a final stage, in which the biggest cities have been the most desirable destinations for peasants arriving from all parts of China. Their presence in the cities is immediately obvious: They congregate conspicuously on the streets; outside the railway stations; in construction sites and factories; in the free markets; and in all other places where jobs are to be found and money is to be made (see Photos 15.1a and 15.1b). They are

PHOTO 15.1a   Migrants waiting for work in a Guangzhou street market.

PHOTO 15.1b
Migrants rummaging in the
trash for recyclable waste.

easily identifiable by their dialects, by their appearance, and by the jobs they are doing (usually characterized as the "three D's"—dirty, dangerous, and difficult).[28]

In human and economic terms the new migration has contributed to greater integration between city and countryside. The freedom given to the peasants to trade, work, and live away from home, and to move freely between the countryside and the city, has helped blur distinctions between urban and rural China that had been hardened by three decades of collectivism. Along with urbanization, new corridors of mixed agricultural-nonagricultural activities fill in the spaces between larger cities, characterized by complex back-and-forth flows of people and commodities. Geographer Terry McGee has labeled these zones in China and other parts of Asia "desakota" regions, using an Indonesian word that denotes a mix of town and village characteristics. The best example of this is to be found in the Pearl River Delta.[29]

Although a dramatic shift from recent decades, this is consistent with Chinese patterns centuries before the Communists' 1949 takeover. Based on what had happened in other parts of the world, industrialization in China might have resulted in an increased rate of urban concentration, with polarizations between the growing urban core and the declining rural periphery. This pattern did not occur in China to anything like the extent it did in the West, and in fact by the mid-nineteenth century a large number of roughly equal-sized urban settlements were spread across China, producing an evenly distributed pattern of urbanization, at least in the eastern provinces. Urban historians have also pointed out that China's cities were composed largely of migrants with close ties to the countryside; intense spatial interaction between city and countryside has been the norm for centuries.[30]

The result was that for 2,000 years there had been relatively little differentiation and conflict between town and country.[31] Rural people transplanted in the cities were able to maintain their roots through the cultural systems that dominated Chinese life, namely, ancestor worship and strong patrilineage systems.[32] In geopolitical terms China's bureaucratic system has historically involved strong leadership at the center, with a significant amount of autonomy in the regions; the net effect was "overarching unity" between city and countryside in traditional China.[33] Thus China rarely experienced the urban-rural differentiation and antagonism characteristic of the West. Power in the hands of the elite classes was not as concentrated in the cities; there were few architectural or design differences between city and countryside; and cultural and economic life flourished in the rural areas to an extent unknown in many other parts of the world.[34]

There is a general consensus that the urban-rural unity of the past was one of the earliest casualties in China's search for modernity, beginning as early as the latter half of the nineteenth century (in other words, after China was introduced to capitalism and global trade, and with the growth of the Treaty Ports; see Chapter 9). At this time a much sharper urban-rural gradient began to emerge. Peasants living in the countryside were clearly assigned underclass status because they were considered part of the decidedly antimodern (read: anti-Western) periphery. Modernization brought increasing specialization into Chinese society, as the Western-dominated coastal cities became centers of production and trade, relegating the countryside to second-class status. What was emerging in China was a greater antagonism between town and country, along the lines that Marx had characterized as the "feudal" mode of production.[35]

These new urban trends undermined the distinctive characteristics of China's cities, and some observers have suggested that this may have sown the seeds of the urban problems that would emerge in the early decades of the twentieth century, as the cities, swollen by the in-migration of desperate peasants, became repositories for poverty, homelessness, and crime. The Communists came to power in 1949; deeply suspicious of the Western-influenced cities, they talked about trying to restore some of the ancient unity between city and countryside. Interaction between the rural areas and the cities was reduced during the Maoist era, and city and countryside became increasingly separate and unequal. In the cities workers were guaranteed jobs, wages, fringe benefits, and subsidized food as entitlements; but in the countryside no such guarantees were available. The urban and rural spheres "became increasingly different from one another, with very different political and economic structures, leading to very different social consequences."[36]

Communist rhetoric about the rural roots of the revolution must have sounded like so much hot air to the peasants, who experienced a marked deterioration in living standards during the Maoist era.[37] The increasing gap between urban and rural dwellers was measurable in all regions and across all indicators, including income, education, and health. The deepening divide translated into negative views expressed by city dwellers.[38] This situation was not altered significantly during Mao's lifetime, one reason why in the late 1970s the government was willing to experiment with radical economic reform in the agricultural sector.[39]

There was significant movement from the countryside to the cities at the end of the 1950s, but by the early 1960s migration out of the countryside slowed to a trickle. As one observer remarked, the peasants at the time "lived a life of enforced separateness . . . effectively tied to the land."[40] Imprisonment on the land secured their identity as peasants, which became the "first and last fact of their social existence."[41] With so little interaction between city and countryside, the traditional links of urban dwellers to their rural native places began to atrophy, as city dwellers were increasingly drawn into the all-encompassing embrace of their work units.[42]

It should have come as no surprise, therefore, that when the constraints were lifted in the mid-1980s Chinese peasants literally burst out of the countryside and headed for the cities. They arrived in huge numbers, and the cities were once again exposed to rural people and their ways. This was how life had always been in China, with the relatively brief exception of the Maoist years. In that sense, then, increasing integration between the city and countryside that resulted from the new population mobility was reproducing traditional patterns rather than creating new ones. Yet in the 1980s and 1990s the cultural, social, and economic differences between peasants and city dwellers in China were probably greater than ever. The countryside had indeed come to the city, but the primitiveness of rural ways of life and the peasants' unpreparedness for city living were cruelly exposed. The reforms had brought geographical freedom to peasants, but getting to the cities turned out to be the easy part. Once they had arrived the real struggle for survival began.

Migration and Development

In much of the literature about population mobility, there are assumptions regarding the relationship between levels of development and migration. Development studies traditionally focus on spatial variations: income and factor productivity, rates of industrialization, and growth of trade. Migration involves population movements occurring within and between places, presumably in response to variations in such factors as employment opportunities, wage levels, and living standards. Migration can be interpreted as a response to development, in the sense that regularities in the patterns of mobility can be correlated with different levels of development. It is generally assumed that in their premodern, or traditional, phases societies encounter little mobility; at the other extreme, modern or postmodern societies are associated with migrations on a previously unimagined scale. This observation is the basis of the mobility transition hypothesis, and one of its intermediate stages involves widespread internal migration.[43] In this stage a massive transfer of population from rural to urban areas occurs, along the lines of what has long been observed in developing countries (and in China since the early 1980s).

We can interpret the new patterns of mobility in China using the mobility transition hypothesis. First we must establish where China is situated within the transitional model compared to other developing and developed countries. The massive rural-to-urban migration in China throughout the 1980s and 1990s has contributed to a sharp increase in urbanization, depending on how the term "urban" is defined.[44] The penetration of capitalism during the reform era has set in motion a radical transformation of Chinese society that has resulted in massive rural-to-urban migrations. In other words, the changing patterns of mobility can be viewed as a response to China's entry into the global economic system. Changing patterns of international investment bring about shifts in the international division of labor, which, as Ronald Skeldon has written, "can be expected to alter the spatial structure of mobility, with the forms of mobility on the semi-periphery gradually changing to those of the core, and those on the periphery changing to those of the semi-periphery as development occurs."[45]

As the China case illustrates, the type of population mobility experienced in a specific society is closely related to the overall process of development. It is important to note, however, that the changing patterns of mobility observed from one country to another are by no means identical. In China temporary movements from rural to urban areas still dominate the migration streams and have not yet been replaced (as the mobility transition hypothesis would suggest) by permanent migration or by commuting.[46] Yet the continued emphasis on temporary migration (or circulation) has not been a matter of choice for China's peasants: It is primarily the result of the *hukou* policy, which assigns most of the new transients to "permanent temporary" status in the cities, regardless of how long they have been away from home. This strategy has allowed China to urbanize and industrialize without the state having to invest significantly in the urban infrastructure and the urban public goods regime. Demographer Sidney Goldstein has argued that circulation helps adjust the demand for and the supply of labor

on a regional basis, without the social dislocation that large-scale, permanent migration would produce and without placing an undue strain on the cities. He also has suggested that other developing societies might be able to fashion their development and population distribution policies on the Chinese model.[47]

This implies that temporary migration contributes to the expansion of manufacturing and services in the cities (by providing a cheap source of labor) while allowing individuals the flexibility to return to home villages to take back their earnings and knowledge (see Figure 15.3).

In this way migration serves as a "modernizing force in both the cities and the rural areas."[48] In the China context, however, that conclusion can be challenged by two counterarguments: First, many temporary migrants in the largest cities are already behaving like permanent migrants, even without receiving an urban *hukou*; second, the costs to China's cities of allowing mass in-migration from the countryside have already reached crisis proportions. The first policies that allowed movements away from the land into small towns whetted peasants' appetites for mobility and for living in urban places. As a result they are now seeking to become de facto permanent city residents. Because of the size of the flows, many of China's cities are now reportedly overburdened by the recent influx.[49] It appears that many cities are now approaching one of the worst nightmares for China's urban planners: uncontrollable urban growth and its negative consequences. Xiangming Chen and William Parish, for example, have predicted that with the new transients working in the most dynamic sectors of the economy (urban and rural collective and private enterprises) China's cities might soon take on the much more disorderly appearance of cities in other developing societies, where a highly heterogeneous informal sector makes up for many of the deficits in the formal sector of employment: "Barring drastic changes in unemployment insurance, old age assistance, and other service delivery programs, Chinese . . . cities will become highly fragmented, with

A.   MOBILITY PATTERN DOMINATED BY
      PERMANENT/LONG-TERM MIGRATIONS

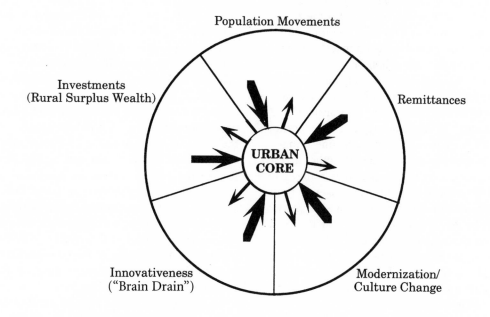

B.   MOBILITY PATTERN DOMINATED BY
      TEMPORARY AND CIRCULATORY MIGRATION

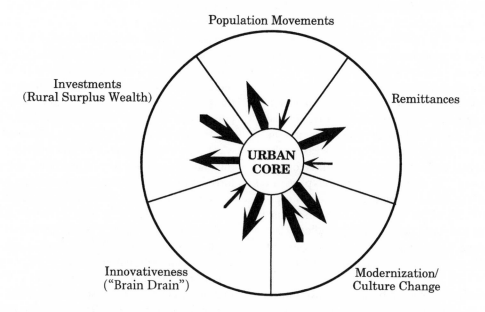

FIGURE 15.3   The Impact of Permanent and Temporary Migration Compared

different workers and citizens subject to very different life chances."[50]

Dorothy Solinger, in *Contesting Citizenship in Urban China*, has also predicted some rather disturbing trends as a result of continued rural in-migration.[51] She has argued that the competition for jobs and urban services between migrants and natives was heating up at the end of the 1990s. This competition, she suggested, depends on two conditions: "rivalrousness" and "elasticity." In rivalrousness, if one group, migrant or native, gets more of one thing—such as jobs or services—then the other necessarily gets less. Solinger argues that in the early 1990s migrants were not taking away jobs from natives, because they were employed primarily in the so-called three D's, which for the most part natives refused. At the end of the decade, however, as the number of migrants expanded and the total pool of jobs was shrinking, migrants and natives were likely to be more involved in competition with each other, even for the worst jobs. The concept of elasticity implies a situation in which the supply of a particular service or set of goods in the city—water, for example, or jobs—can easily be expanded in response to increased demand. In many areas elasticity has been high in the 1990s, but it is now beginning to fall, which promises to produce new urban tensions in the short term.

It is also possible to conceive of the relationship between development and migration working in the other direction. In traditional societies, for example, migration accelerates the process of class differentiation and weakens the traditional solidarity and immobility of the peasantry.[52] In this way migration plays an important role in the global extension of capitalism, both within and between specific countries of the world. In China, the landlord class had been removed as an obstacle to peasant mobility soon after the revolution, but for most of the next three decades the peasants were effectively immobilized by specific government policies. Industrialization on the scale envisaged by Deng Xiaoping is strongly correlated with urbanization, and that required the geo-

graphic concentration of labor power in the towns and cities. It was fortuitous, therefore, that reforms and the changing migration policies made this possible within a miraculously short time period.[53] After little more than a decade the peasants were freed to move to the cities; wealth generated in the countryside was being made available as a source of investment for urban industrialization; and a surplus of relatively cheap food was being produced for urban consumption.[54] China's peasants have thus been liberated from the traditional mode of production in the countryside and are now free to declare themselves for hire as wage workers (proletarianization), or to set themselves up as private traders (bourgeoisification). The events occurring in China are similar to what has happened elsewhere, as rural-to-urban migration reinforced the transformation of traditional societies by speeding up the spread of industrial capitalism.[55]

Once the movement out of rural areas begins, the migrants also become agents of economic change in villages, with the most common vehicle for change being extra income (remittances) that becomes available for local investment. As in almost all circumstances, "money is a great polarizer,"[56] in the sense that households with successful out-migrants will be more likely to create surplus wealth and raise more educated children, which will then increase the likelihood of further out-migrations. Other households will become relatively poorer, and they may also be required to send out family members as a desperate measure to ward off poverty. As polarization increases in the village economy, some households will be forced into reckless acts: going into debt to purchase food and raw materials; hiring themselves out as contract laborers; or, in extreme cases, selling their land—all of which threatens to erode their ties to the village and makes subsequent out-migration more likely.[57]

Perhaps the most significant point is that migration creates an industrial labor force. In the short term the agricultural surplus helps hold down wages, thereby allowing industrialization to occur cheaply.[58] It also provides a source of geographically flexible labor able and willing to move quickly into new growth areas.[59] In addition, the overall size and ready availability of surplus labor reduce the likelihood of industrial action among workers, who are forced to accept low wages and miserable working conditions. For this reason—although rural migrants remain agents of change in an aggregate, economic sense—they are unlikely to become a revolutionary group, preferring to compare themselves with the people left behind in the villages rather than with the urban elites they encounter.[60] The situations confronting new transients are made worse by a lack of formal integration into urban society, which is manifested in the inability to acquire urban *hukous*. Many new transients are destined to remain clustered in the most marginal, highest-risk, and lowest-paying sectors of the urban economy.

Migration and Sociocultural Change

Many academics, journalists, and politicians fear that the new mobility will contribute to the demise of normative behaviors and community solidarity that characterized urban life during the Maoist era.[61] Arguably, what is happening in the Chinese city, in sociological and cultural terms, is a convergence with trends in Western societies. One dimension is the increasing sense of disorder and the rising prevalence of social problems.

Compared to the collective era, migration in the 1980s and 1990s has been more spontaneous and less susceptible to state influence.[62] The state has allowed, even encouraged greater mobility, but there are concerns that the resulting transformations, occurring within such a short period of time, will have negative consequences. The transformations are similar to what Durkheim called the shift from "mechanical" to "organic" solidarity, a process that was experienced over many decades in Western societies but that in China is occurring much more rapidly.[63] As Chinese society becomes more open, the traditional group solidarity and cohesiveness that used to exert powerful informal social controls will be subjected to dramatic changes. It is often assumed that a more mobile population and a more open society will be accompanied by a rising incidence of social pathologies. The transformation accompanying the shift from a rural, closed, homogenous society to an open, urban, heterogeneous society could, according to this line of reasoning, be the widespread breakdown of existing norms and values.

Arguably this represents a transitional period between the disintegrating old order and the emerging—but as yet unknown and unknowable—new order. In the interim prophets of doom, with very little hard evidence, predict widespread social breakdown. Lurid newspaper stories are reinforcing public suspicions that some of the worst aspects of the new normlessness—the erosion of solidarity, the increasing sense of fear and insecurity, and the widespread public disobedience and lack of compliance with official public policy—are associated with the arrival of the new transients. Stories connect specific criminal events to known transients and point out that many female migrants are forced into prostitution. Despite a lack of comprehensive studies, it has become widely accepted that the rising prevalence of deviant behavior is causally related to the increasing presence of the floating populations.

No doubt some migrants have been involved in criminal activities.[64] One study reported that more than 30 percent of the crimes in Shanghai were committed by nonregistered residents.[65] Migrants are also accused of contributing to the general urban malaise by their constant disregard for official state policies, such as the birth control laws. In a small town in the Pearl River Delta, the locals are convinced that "temporary migrants are often engaged in moral and economic crimes such as selling pornographic material and selling vice, cheating and swindling, or engaging in house break-ins, robberies and petty theft."[66] In a more sweeping indictment, one research team noted that "in the busiest districts of Beijing, 80 percent of criminal offenses were committed by them [migrants]. In other big and medium sized cities and in the open coastal zones, the migrant population committed 40–60 percent of all criminal offences."[67] It has also been suggested that the presence of so many transients, mostly young singles, erodes the traditional sense of community and the strength of the extended family in the cities. Many permanent residents of China's cities, though obviously benefiting indirectly from the presence of the transients, conclude that migrants are responsible for everything that is wrong in urban China.

In official discourse migrants are often referred to as that portion of the urban population that is "mobile" or "temporary." In popular discourse, however, opinions about the new transients have been influenced by another frequent label: *mangliu renkou*, which translates roughly as the "blindly floating" population. In comparison to the relatively neutral terms "mobile" and "temporary," this is a more pejorative label, implying a degree of randomness of movement and even vagrancy; in fact 5–8 percent of temporary migrants were officially classified in the census as "vagrants." Describing the entire floating population as such implies they are lost souls wandering blindly into the cities looking for ways to make a living, whether legal or illegal. This may well be the case for some, but most migrants arrive with a clear purpose in mind; many have signed (or been signed up for) existing employment contracts; and many live in dormitory-style residences constructed by their employers (Photos 15.2a and 15.2b).

As with other immigrant and ethnic minority groups in cities around the world, public perceptions of the new transients are often shaped by ignorance and discrimination. In the minds of many city dwellers in China the new migrants are the embodiment of the great rural wasteland. They are peasants; they look and behave differently; they are unsophisticated; and for the most part they are poor, uneducated, often dirty, and appear dangerous.[68] In light of the increased competition for urban jobs, such assumptions become the basis for sweeping assertions about the moral character of all floaters. It has even been suggested that this negativism has a profound feedback effect

on the transients themselves, causing them "to lack the identity and responsibility of city residents"; as a result "they are prone to feel that they are treated unequally and are relatively deprived, and they resent this." Negative views are only reinforced by public depictions of floating populations, for example, the image of huddled masses outside the railway stations, sleeping on their luggage and picking their way through mountains of garbage (see Photos 15.3a and 15.3b). Yet in reality far more floaters earn their keep quietly and painstakingly in the factories and on construction sites (see Figure 15.4, showing employment categories for the official floating population in Guangdong Province). Unfortunately, the success stories are rarely reported, and the image of squalor, disorder, and crime endures in the public eye. Once formed, such labels are resilient and will persist even in the absence of incriminating evidence.

Migration and the Contest for Power in the City

The processes that have marginalized transients in Chinese cities are similar to those in cities around the world, as large numbers of newcomers (internal migrants and international immigrants) challenge existing city residents for jobs, housing, and other resources.[69] In many cases such challenges are resolved in favor of long-term residents and established elites, but even then minority groups may be strengthened in the process (for example, by an affirmation or rediscovery of a collective ethnic identity).[70] In fact the new mobility in China is producing urban populations that are considerably more diverse and colorful. This has become a popular research theme in the West and has generated many studies of the relationships between majority and minority groups. Similar studies are appearing in China as researchers explore the lives and experiences of minority groups.[71]

At present very few such studies have been extended to Han population groups, which make up the majority of the new urban tran-

PHOTO 15.2a
Floating population's temporary
housing on construction site, Panyu.

PHOTO 15.2b   Dormitory residences for construction workers at a Guangzhou hospital.

PHOTO 15.3a Guangzhou railway station, where thousands of migrants arrive daily.

PHOTO 15.3b Migrants outside the station, waiting for trains, hoping to hear about jobs.

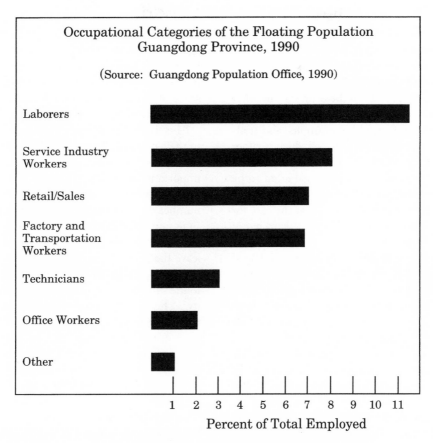

FIGURE 15.4   Employed Migrants by Category, Guangdong Province, 1990

sients. There is, however, some precedent for including Han migrants from specific localities as members of ethnic groups, and migrants have clustered in specific neighborhoods and occupations. As William Skinner has observed:

> There is no difficulty whatsoever in viewing the "colonies" of extraregional traders in Chinese Cities as ethnic minorities. . . . The Cantonese is as much an alien in Shanghai . . . as the Portuguese was in Spain. . . . Anhwei merchants in Chungking, Ningpo merchants in Peking, Hokkien merchants in Hankow . . . all spoke languages unintelligible to the natives and practiced customs that appeared outlandish.[72]

Skinner is suggesting that ethnicity in China can be attributed without using traditional markers such as nationality, religion, and race. In fact, as he noted, "slight accents and even minor mannerisms may serve as ethnic markers if either side finds it advantageous to maintain or erect ethnic boundaries."[73]

In her study of the Subei people in Shanghai, Emily Honig has taken up this argument and has made a powerful case for the creation of ethnic identity (see Chapter 12); there are several similarities between the situation of the Subei people and that of the new transient populations.[74] Both concentrate in the most marginal residential areas; they work in the dirtiest, lowest-paying, least prestigious occupations; and they are viewed in a negative way. The Subei people and the floating populations are also considered to be decidedly antimodern. The modern international sector dominated the Shanghai economy in the 1930s and 1940s, when the majority of Subei migrants arrived; this is also the case today in such places as Guangzhou, Shenzhen, and Shanghai. Elite status is claimed in part by an association with the most advanced sector of the economy, in other words, the financial sector: banking, real estate, stock markets, financial institutions, and trading companies—the majority of which is either controlled by or is in frequent interaction with foreigners. Subei were thus considered to be backward because they had no knowledge of or contact with foreigners; this is also the case for most peasants currently living and working in China's biggest cities.

Thus the ethnic identity of a group is shaped by structural forces such as urbanization, in-migration, industrialization, and international-ization. Almost by definition, then, the places that attract large floating populations are undergoing major restructurings along these dimensions. The furious pace of economic development in China's coastal cities (much of it funded by foreign investment), as well as the powerful forces unleashed by China's own agricultural and urban reforms, has produced an inevitable clash of cultures as members of the urban elite are thrown into contact with new-comers on a daily, ever-changing basis. Migration effectively brings the periphery to the core, and it is within this dynamic that the ethnic status of China's newest urban residents is being shaped. In this sense, ethnicity is an example of what Michel Foucault called a "meta-power," something that is constantly being negotiated and renegotiated between the powerful and the weak (in this case, the state and the ethnic groups). The dialogue is ongoing and regularly being redefined in changing social contexts.[75]

Negotiations and power struggles between the state and the transients, as well as between transients and native population groups, are already under way.[76] There is some evidence that in the largest cities the floating populations are starting to sort themselves out, spatially and occupationally, to provide jobs, social networks, and places to live for members of their own "ethnic" groups, most of which are based on geographic origins. This process of ghettoiza-tion, or enclavization, represents a tried and tested mechanism for the survival of minorities in an alien setting. Their efforts also work to preserve or, perhaps more accurately, to create a sense of group identity, which is an early stage in the process of ethnogenesis.

The ability of migrants to adapt successfully to their new situations is also a function of the context in which the migration occurs. One important dimension of success is their ability to find good jobs, which will depend on the number of other migrants arriving at the same time and the health of the local economy. In Mao's China only a select few were allowed to leave the countryside. This shift from a trickle to a flood of migrants is a geographical analogy to the shift from sponsored to contested mobil-ity.[77] Thus the "sponsored" migrants of the past were able to adjust successfully to life in the cities, whereas new migrants must enter a "con-test" of sorts in which only a few are expected to succeed.

The two mobility situations (prereform and postreform) are fundamentally different in the ways the state is able to maintain social control over the disadvantaged classes. In the collec-tivist era, rural to urban migration was largely "sponsored," in the sense that recruits for the elite were chosen from above (by the Party). It was made clear to the masses that they were either too incompetent or too uneducated to have access to elite status, so only the cream of the crop was selected and indoctrinated in advance. In the situation that has prevailed since the 1980s, however, it is made clear to all, both by government edicts and by chain migra-tion stories and networks, that the system is now wide open. Everyone has a chance, so peas-ant "dreams of heaven" can be kept alive.[78] Acquiring official status as an urban resident and being economically successful in the city are, at least theoretically, open to all who enter the "contest." Hope, and the dream of success, keeps people actively involved, and as long as some models exist to demonstrate that success is possible, others will continue to try their luck by moving to the city.[79]

Conclusion: Mass Migration in Contemporary China

Mass migration is a powerful force of change and includes geographical, economic, social, and political impacts. Events in one region are rarely applicable to other regions, and development in post-Mao China has been extremely uneven geographically. In some parts of China very little has changed, and the press of poverty has barely been reduced by out-migration.

In the developing world in the late twentieth century, it has been estimated that more than 100 million people are on the move, either within their own countries or from one country to another,[80] due to geopolitical events and socioeconomic circumstances. Technology allows the exchange of information and facilitates human movement, providing potential migrants a much greater range of aspirations and opportunities than ever; at the same time, global and national policy changes, for example, in the definitions of refugee status and in immigration laws, have rewritten the definitions for who can leave and who can enter.

As for China, the sheer size of the migrant pool is remarkable: It may be as large as all others combined. The scale and the speed of the new mobility in China, and its causes and consequences, require reflective thought on some of the most fundamental issues involved in migration research, particularly as to how to draw the line between voluntary and involuntary population movements. The recent mass migrations in China and elsewhere force us to look for explanations beyond the simplistic "push" and "pull" formulations common in the literature. There is no doubt that in many parts of China, especially in places like the Pearl River Delta, outflows from the countryside to the towns and cities have been driven primarily by the availability of economic opportunities in the nonfarm sector. But for millions of others, in China and other poor countries, migration is part of the daily struggle against debilitating poverty. Many geographical moves are involuntary: In China, for example, in some regions it is impossible for people to remain in the face of life-threatening poverty and environmental crises.

One author has recommended using the term "forced ecomigration" to describe what is currently happening in China and many other parts of the world, where out-migration "is propelled by economic decline and environmental degradation to the extent that local conditions become immediately life-threatening."[81] In the past, groups fleeing environmental degradation have been able to settle in less inhabited areas with better resources, but in China such places have long since been settled. At the same time, some of the more accessible places suffer from a combination of ecological threats: low soil fertility, lack of water supplies, deforestation, and soil erosion. It is impossible to say with certainty to what extent the combination of economic and environmental threats is responsible for the current mass out-migration from the Chinese countryside. Government policies and the trickle-down effect from rapid economic growth during the early years of reform have helped reduce poverty, but as we saw in Chapter 10 the absolute numbers living in poverty have hardly declined at all since the mid-1980s.[82] The largest concentrations of poverty are in the northwestern and southwestern provinces and the borderland Autonomous Regions. They are also found among places with the most fragile environmental conditions: Gansu, Qinghai, Inner Mongolia, Shaanxi, Yunnan, Xinjiang, Ningxia, Guizhou, and Shanxi—all remote and inaccessible.

Economic and environmental circumstances are contributors to out-migration even in prosperous coastal provinces. In a study conducted in a Guangdong village, where the majority of the migrants had moved from other parts of the same province, it was reported that "thirty-eight subjects [in the study] came because ... their home villages suffered from poor soil, mountainous topography, natural disasters, high population density, or low standards of living; the infrastructure, communication system, and collective industry in their villages are poorly developed; their families had too many mouths to feed."[83]

To draw attention to the seriousness of the situation, a group of Chinese scientists in the late 1980s focused on the destructive relationship that exists between population growth, economic growth, and environmental concerns.[84] During the reform era the development drive has resulted in significant increases in production and consumption, which, combined with population growth, are further depleting already scarce natural resources and degrading the environment. This is creating problems everywhere in China, especially in places with existing environmental problems (as we shall examine in Chapter 16). Significant population increases have been recorded in several arid inland provinces where vegetation and water resources are extremely limited. In Gansu Province, for example, population density now exceeds eighty persons per square kilometer in eighteen arid and semiarid counties, compared to the reasonable maximum of seven for arid areas and twenty-five for semiarid areas. One of the few solutions to a problem of this scale is out-migration on a large scale.

The long-term effects of continued economic and population growth in fragile regions include accelerated and irreversible environmental degradation. In provinces that are delicately balancing marginal environments and large population densities, the consequences

are grave. As a leading environmental scholar has warned, "The reality for tens of millions of Chinese in the worst affected areas will be a desperate effort to survive."[85] This desperation is illustrated in a discussion of peasants living in Shangzhuang, which is less than forty kilometers from Lanzhou, the capital of Gansu Province. The average per capita income in 1983 was less than Y40, and the wealth of the local people is measured not by the number of television sets or tractors they own but by the number of blankets they have to sleep on and the padded jackets they wear to keep warm in the winter.[86] One-third of the households had less than Y30 in total possessions, which would typically include a worn-out quilt, a roll of tattered cotton wadding, a few cooking pots, bowls, and chopsticks.

There is some evidence that migrants are now beginning to leave the absolute poorest and ecologically threatened regions, adding to the estimated 2 million who will be forcibly removed when the Yangtze River floods once the Three Gorges Dam is completed (see Chapter 16). The implications of these trends are that in spite of the already vast numbers of people on the move in China there are still millions more who could benefit, and perhaps who can only survive, by moving away from their existing homes. Under such circumstances it is not unreasonable to predict further increases in forced ecomigration undertaken in response to life-threatening circumstances.

PART 5

State and Society in China at the End of the Millennium

16

Saving the Bad Earth?
China's Environmental Crisis

卍卍卍卍卍卍卍卍卍卍卍卍卍卍卍卍卍卍卍卍卍卍卍卍

New policies and careful investments made today mean China's children and grandchildren would also enjoy clear water and blue skies.

—The World Bank, *Clear Water, Blue Skies* (1997)[1]

Introduction: Environmental Degradation in Contemporary China

When the sun is up, everything goes rotten, everywhere. The vegetable mound in front of the market steamed in the sun. Its yellow drainage ran to the corner of the street. Every household hung last year's rotten fish and meat in the sun. White maggots crawled all over. Tap water became undrinkable, also. It was said that a decomposing corpse had blocked the pump. For days, people had been drinking "corpse water." They feared it might cause an epidemic. Stinking water oozed from the aged putrid ulcers on their shanks. Several people almost a hundred years old rolled their pants high to display their wounds at the doorway, letting passersby enjoy the cracked red flesh. A postal vehicle paused in Yellow Mud Street for only half an hour before one of its tires decomposed. When they checked, they found the inner tube had turned to a lump of paste. One day, Wang Si-ma, who lived at the corner of the street, suddenly lost one ear. When people asked them where his ear had gone, he treated them to a supercilious look and said, "Of course it rotted off during the night. It's as simple as that." Looking at his "ear"—a naked and almost invisible little hole running with yellowish pus— people felt uncomfortable, afraid their own ears might rot off. What would they do if that happened?

—Can Xue, *Yellow Mud Street* (1991)[2]

Vaclav Smil, in the 1993 book *China's Environmental Crisis*, paints a devastating picture of

China's current environmental nightmare.[3] Although life is not yet as horrific as Can Xue suggests in her surreal description of Yellow Mud Street, the real China is probably closer to it than it is to the World Bank's depiction of "clear water and blue skies." Smil documented the seemingly insurmountable problems associated with the loss of cultivable land and declining soil quality; quantity and quality of water supplies; massive deforestation; and the chronic and growing shortage of energy. As he concluded:

> With per capita availability of arable land ranking among the lowest . . . worldwide, with only marginal opportunities remaining for the extension of productive farmlands, with astonishingly large losses of fields to growing settlements and industries, with widespread qualitative degradation of soils, with deforestation depressing the country's tree cover to little over one tenth of all land, and with grasslands desertifying and overgrazed, China's land resources offer increasingly precarious support even for mere continuation of the recent demands, and they will pose a clear check on the ambitious modernization plans.[4]

The costs of environmental degradation are difficult to estimate, though some researchers have made honest efforts. Smil suggested that environmental degradation added up to about 5 percent of China's GDP in 1990, the major

377

shares being the overcutting of forestlands (60 percent) and soil erosion (20 percent).[5] Another way to assess the costs is to calculate the extra mortality and morbidity associated with pollution. The World Bank researchers used two estimates: the so-called willingness to pay method, which estimates the cost of avoiding a premature death (about US$60,000 for urban areas, $32,000 for rural areas) and is a scaled-down version of a methodology used in the United States; more common is the human capital approach, which bases calculations on wages lost as a result of premature deaths ($4,000 in urban areas, $4,800 in rural areas).[6] The two methods reveal the overall costs of air and water pollution to be $24–54 billion, or 3.5–7.7 percent of China's current GDP (see Table 16.1).

The World Bank researchers also attempted to estimate the costs of not doing something to prevent or reduce air pollution. Based on their estimates, without "assertive" policies to tackle combustion emission, air pollution could result in 600,000 premature deaths by the year 2020 (corresponding to 9 million life-years lost); 5.5 million cases of chronic bronchitis; more than 5 billion "restricted activity days"; and 20 million cases of respiratory illness each year.[7] The report concludes that "at current income levels the health care costs of this increased disease burden will reach $98 billion, or 13 percent of GDP."[8]

As alternative scenarios to this bleak picture, the World Bank suggests two policy mixes: a medium-cost scenario, in which the cost of pollution abatement investments would be dou-

TABLE 16.1   Costs Associated with Air and Water Pollution in China: Two Costing Methodologies (in billions of US$)

Problem Area	"Willingness to Pay" Valuation	"Human Capital" Valuation
Urban Air Pollution	32.3	11.3
Premature deaths	10.7	1.6
Illnesses (morbidity)	21.7	9.7
Restricted activity days	3.8	3.8
Chronic bronchitis	14.1	2.1
Other health effects	3.7	3.7
Indoor Air Pollution	10.7	3.7
Premature deaths	3.5	0.5
Illnesses	7.1	3.2
Lead exposure (children)	1.6	0.3
Water Pollution	3.9	3.9
Health care costs	1.9	1.9
Agricultural & fishery losses	1.2	1.2
Water shortages	0.8	0.8
Acid Rain	5.0	5.0
Crop and forest damage	4.4	4.4
Materials damage	0.3	0.3
Ecosystem damage	0.4	0.4
Total Costs	US$53.6 billion	US$24.2 billion
% of China's GDP	7.7	3.5

SOURCE: World Bank, 1997, p. 23 (Table 2.4).

bled, from the existing 0.5 percent to about 1 percent of GDP; and a high-cost scenario, in which investments represented 2 percent of GDP (with the state responsible for two-thirds). Both alternatives would result in significant reductions in emissions, with major savings in health-related costs. The World Bank also attempted to estimate costs for policies to control and reduce water pollution, as well as sulfur dioxide emissions (primarily responsible for worsening acid rain in China). The World Bank is optimistic, suggesting that as long as China follows the suggested strategies it can continue on an environmentally sustainable pattern of economic growth that can increase incomes and living standards and also improve environmental quality. Moreover, in typical World Bank language, the report concluded that every single yuan invested in the medium-

cost scenario "will yield 3 yuan in reduced pollution damages."[9]

Smil is not so optimistic and would contend that pollution is not the major environmental problem facing China (see Figure 16.1a). Of more serious concern is the gradual degradation of environmental resources: the erosion of soils by wind and water; the decline of nutrient content and organic material in agricultural soils; the salinization and alkalization of irrigated farmlands; the overdrawing of groundwater; and the continuing advance of deforestation and desertification (see Figure 16.1b). As Smil points out, most forms of pollution can be dealt with, given the right amount of government determination, capital investment, and technical know-how, much of which can be borrowed from other parts of the world or brought in as foreign direct investment.[10]

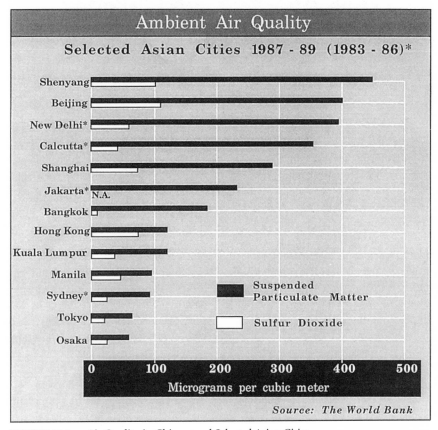

FIGURE 16.1a   Air Quality in Chinese and Selected Asian Cities

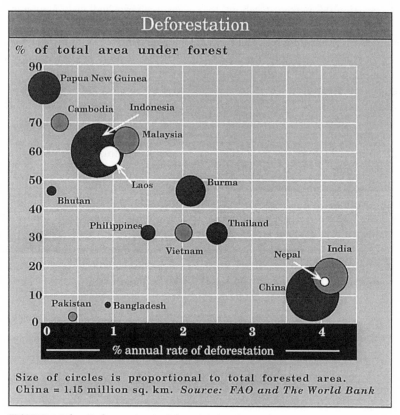

FIGURE 16.1b   Deforestation in Selected Asian Countries

The processes of degradation, however, can be overcome only in the long term with a significant slowdown in both economic and population growth.

Yet in contemporary China the notion of slowing economic growth is a nonstarter, as the current regime has tied its legitimacy to improvements in the people's well-being, which can realistically be achieved only by furthering the current push toward modernization. It is assumed that this will speed environmental degradation. As Smil observed:

> Attainment of modernization goals . . . would require emplacement in just one decade of a variety of productive capacities equivalent to total national outputs of such populous nations as India or Indonesia, or such industrial economies as Japan or Canada. . . . The

environmental implications of these enormous gains will be far-reaching as the additional demand for living space, water, food, energy, and raw materials will accelerate ecosystemic degradation and inexorably diminish the per capital availability of already strained or restricted resource utilization.[11]

China has managed to limit population growth to an extent, but further reductions have met resistance, particularly in the countryside. The problem for China today is the unenviable task of not only maintaining and enhancing living standards for the current population but also catering to about 125 million additional people during the 1990s, which is the equivalent of Japan's current population or half that of the United States. In another generation—say, by the year 2025—there will most likely be another 200 million people in China, more than Indonesia's population in 1990. Given such parameters, Smil concluded that China has three possible choices.[12] The first choice is to do without economic growth and quality-of-life improvements. That might be feasible for Japan and rich Western nations that already have an excess of energy, food, wealth, and educational opportunities and can theoretically absorb some declines in per capita consumption; but it is certainly not an option for the current leadership or for the Chinese people. The second choice is to follow the World Bank's recommendations to restructure the entire industrial system, introducing new, expensive, high-tech production methods, which are available but far too costly to be implemented in the near future.

The only real choice, then, is to continue down the current path: attempting to make improvements at all possible points. For example, China can realistically expect to improve the efficiency of its energy utilization from the current 30 percent level to at least 50 percent—as Japan did—which would reduce demand for primary fuels and electric power. However, the modernization push and the additional demands resulting from population growth are, as Smil observed, likely to go up by about 40 percent in just ten years, which will cancel out the effects of increased efficiency.[13]

Efforts to enhance the supply of food by market transformations and higher efficiency, particularly in the use of irrigation water, would make a significant contribution to resource conservation. The problem, however, is that the current regime is determined to push forward with the twin goals of food self-sufficiency and agricultural sustainability (see Chapter 17). Yet the continuing decline of cultivable land, resulting from both actual land losses and population growth, makes it especially difficult to achieve these twin goals. This "will prevent the two agronomic practices essential in sustaining agriculture . . . [the] cultivation of green manures and complex crop rotations including leguminous species."[14] In an effort to increase grain yields, China's farmers will be forced to intensify the use of inputs such as chemical fertilizer, which will further weaken the soil's capacity to sustain long-term productivity.

Richard Edmonds, the current editor of *The China Quarterly*, has concluded that China is able to support about 950 million people at a reasonable standard of living based on the existing resources, a figure that was reached and surpassed quite some time ago. Even with the continuation of stringent birth control policies, it is likely that China's population will rise to 1.5–1.6 billion by the year 2025. The saturation point at which such a number of people could be supported—assuming only a low standard of living and that resources would be used to their fullest capacity—might be reached as early as the year 2015.[15] Stating the problem this way stresses that in addition to its population problem China has a dangerously low per capita supply of many critical natural resources, especially land, forest cover, and water.[16] Its coal reserves are less than half the world average; other energy sources (oil, gas, and hydroelectric power) are even less available (see Table 16.2). In addition, China's energy efficiency is poor, even compared to many developing countries.[17]

Thus most observers have concluded that China will not be able to halt environmental degradation. As Edmonds predicted, for example, "while we can expect some progress in environmental control in certain places over the next decade, the overall trend will be for

TABLE 16.2 China's Per Capita Energy Reserves Compared to the Rest of the World and the United States

Country	Raw Coal	Crude Oil	Natural Gas	Hydropower
China	95 tons	3 tons	1,416 cubic meters	1,603 kilowatt hours per year
Rest of the World	209 tons	28 tons	28,400 cubic meters	2,909 kilowatt hours per year
United States	962 tons	15 tons	18,400 cubic meters	1,504 kilowatt hours per year

SOURCE: Adapted from World Bank, 1997, p. 49, Table 4.3.

environmental conditions to continue to worsen."[18] The continuing emphasis on economic growth, in addition to the decentralization of decisionmaking to the local level, seems likely to steer events in this direction. One viable alternative, therefore, is to follow the World Bank guidelines and implement significant price increases for resource inputs such as water, timber, and coal, which are currently artificially underpriced.[19] The increase in prices should have positive consequences, forcing polluters to invest in cleaner, more efficient technology. There is evidence that market forces have already had some positive effects in state-run enterprises, providing some support to the World Bank's optimism about China's ability to keep urban pollution levels down.

The problem remains, however, with resource degradation, particularly in rural areas, where the bulk of industrial enterprises are small and privately or locally operated. The rural industrial sector has been growing in leaps and bounds throughout the 1990s and is now estimated to be producing close to half of China's total industrial output. Many enterprises can ill afford to spend for pollution abatement or pay the fines that would be levied if the current laws were implemented properly. The most serious pollution problem in the countryside and the cities seems likely to be the degradation of water quality, which will ultimately require massive state and private investment to provide equipment, as well as a huge state commitment to enforcement.

The prognosis for resource depletion looks bleak; as water sources are used up and as rates of soil erosion, deforestation, and desertification increase, it seems overly optimistic to assume that everything can be solved with World Bank recipes based on economic efficiency and market mechanisms. There needs to be greater control over the way pollution abatement equipment is installed, used, and maintained, as well as a continuing requirement for greater environmental education and awareness among the public and, more important, at the enterprise and local-government levels. In this chapter we shall attempt to outline some of the

dimensions of a political economy approach to China's environmental crisis and explore some problems in environmental policymaking. Before that, however, we consider the current crisis from a global perspective, as events in China can no longer be considered in isolation.

Global Concerns

How China tackles the environmental crisis is important because the scale and speed of Chinese industrialization and urbanization will compound the existing global ecological crisis. As one journalist has observed, the real problem is the accelerating rate of environmental degradation associated with the push toward modernization:

> China's huge population and grand economic ambitions make it the most important environmental actor in the world today. . . . China could all but single-handedly make climate change, ozone depletion, and a host of other hazards a reality for people all over the world. What happens in China is therefore central to one of the great questions of our time: Will human civilization survive the many environmental pressures crowding in on it at the end of the twentieth century?[20]

Environmentalists and political leaders have realized China's potential role as environmental spoiler and have undertaken to persuade China to sign multilateral agreements. Chinese leaders have thus far been relatively cooperative and have certainly learned to say the right things; for example, China was an enthusiastic participant in the 1992 UN Earth Summit in Rio de Janeiro. Yet it is obvious that China and the global community cannot afford to enforce such agreements, so words are not being matched by deeds. And the China environmental effect continues apace: Within twenty years China will be the world's largest emitter of greenhouse gases (which contribute to global warming), mostly from the use of coal in homes and factories in addition to methane emissions from wet rice paddies.[21] China is also the world's third largest user of commercial energy.[22]

The environmental crisis also threatens social stability in China and could even derail the modernization program. The most serious threats are the shortage of water, especially in and around some of China's largest cities in the northeast of the country;[23] health hazards, measured in rates of illness and mortality, associated with lung disease and cancer, in addition to lead poisoning from motor vehicle emissions; and the combination of desertification, loss of forest cover, and the shortage of water, which will make it necessary for many people to migrate from certain areas just to stay alive (adding to large floating populations and promoting urban conflict).[24] All of these issues could plunge the nation into political chaos.

China's reliance on coal is unique among the largest economies in the world; in fact it has risen from 74 percent in 1980 to 78 percent in 1995 (compared to less than 20 percent in Japan and the United States; India is the only large economy that comes close).[25] There is some evidence that China has been using its energy more efficiently since 1980, and its "energy intensity" has fallen by more than 50 percent; although this is still much higher than in the United States and Japan, a rate of decline of this magnitude is unprecedented for an industrializing economy. Most of the improvement has been achieved through efficiency gains in industry, as well as the gains made as overall industrial output switched to less energy-intensive or more energy-efficient sectors. There have also been changes in the implementation of cleaner technologies. Prices for energy, always very low in socialist China, have been raised, which has helped somewhat by requiring greater efficiency in production processes.[26]

Unless China continues its success in these areas, it will experience coal-related health consequences. The World Bank researchers calculated that the cost of coal would have to be doubled in order to cover health-related impacts (from Y200 to Y400 per ton, about US$48).[27] The World Bank report suggested that taxes be levied on coal to defray health costs and, more important, lead the way toward lower emissions through more efficient and cleaner technology. The report also favored taxing coal emissions, but that would be virtually impossible (in both economic and enforcement terms) for small enterprises and residential users to enforce or afford. The tax, however, could be phased in over time, effectively doubling the cost of coal over three to five years to convince home owners and enterprise managers to invest in new boilers and space heaters.

During the 1990s there was an enormous increase in environmental awareness at the global level, especially on the issue of global warming, with the accords reached in Kyoto (1994) and Buenos Aires (1998). The Kyoto treaty was implemented in Buenos Aires, when some 160 countries signed an action plan, complete with deadlines.[28] A key issue, which almost derailed the Buenos Aires talks, was whether and when the world's developing nations should be made to comply with the emission standards negotiated in Kyoto. At present, only developed nations are required (with penalties for noncompliance) to implement policies that will produce major reductions by the year 2010.

In the United States it is anticipated that treaty ratification in the U.S. Senate will be difficult, primarily because some of the largest industrializing (and thus emitting) countries, particularly China, were not required to comply. Some developing nations agreed in principle to honor the Kyoto recommendations; some global energy corporations and industrial giants, notably British Petroleum, have voluntarily agreed to reduce their emissions. Other countries, however, have sought to trade in "emission credits," whereby they can keep higher emissions at home if they agree to invest in "clean" technology abroad. Environmental critics used the evidence of such horse-trading to downplay the seriousness and likely success of the agreement. As a member of Friends of the Earth International put it, the meeting was in effect "a trade fair [with] wrangling over how to keep the fossil fuel industry alive and burning," and most critics are convinced that the

Kyoto Accord will mean little improvement to global warming.[29]

The concerns of some developed nations and environmentalists as to China's role are grounded in reality. China is already the second largest producer of commercial energy and the second largest emitter of carbon dioxide (CO_2), in spite of its low overall per capita energy consumption.[30] China currently accounts for about 11 percent of global CO_2 emissions, even though its emissions per capita are only about one-tenth as high as those in the United States. All these concerns have been reinforced by China's sky-high industrial growth, and because China has been the recipient of foreign direct investments (particularly from Hong Kong, Taiwan, South Korea, and Japan), there is a fear that it is being used to provide a home base for heavily polluting industries. The Taiwan Plastics Corporation, for example, contemplated a US$7 billion investment in petrochemicals facilities in Fujian Province, mainly because the combination of local corruption and lax enforcement of environmental standards made it look like an excellent opportunity (similar, in fact, to the situation existing in Taiwan in the 1950s and 1960s).[31]

In the long run China's apparent willingness to accede to international accords to implement environmental regulations bodes well. Yet such commitments mean China must eventually invest heavily in the abatement of environmental degradation, much like Taiwan in the 1990s and Japan since the 1970s.[32] That point has not yet arrived, and most policymakers in China are convinced that incomes and living standards are too low to consider steps that might damage industrial growth. As political scientist Kenneth Lieberthal pessimistically concluded:

> The prognosis therefore, is for sharply increasing environmental damage . . . as fast GNP growth, rapid urbanization, and growing use of environmentally damaging conveniences such as personal motor scooters produce escalating environmental degradation. Such damage may become severe enough to limit sharply the

country's ability to sustain rapid economic growth.[33]

Another new problem is the rising personal automobile ownership, especially in light of the 1994 announcement that automobile production was to become a pillar industry of the economy.[34] At present the number of cars in Beijing is only about a tenth of that in Los Angeles or Tokyo, but evidence shows that vehicular emissions (mostly of ambient hydrocarbons, carbon monoxide, and ozone concentrations) are about the same.[35] If incomes continue to rise and urban densities fall, along with a decline or worsening of public transit systems, automobile ownership in China could reach 100–130 vehicles per 1,000 people by the year 2010, perhaps double that rate by 2020 (see Photos 16.1a and 16.1b).[36]

Assuming that the demand for private automobiles will remain high, China must act immediately to reduce skyrocketing oil demand and auto emissions, to develop and follow master plans that minimize commuting distances, and to provide viable public transportation systems. This will help reduce emissions and conserve scarce oil resources, a cleaner alternative than coal for home and commercial heating.[37]

Domestic Politics and the Environment

Chinese history demonstrates that relations between people and their environments are often contradictory, in that the environment is both a resource for and a constraint to development. In the struggle to solve that contradiction, humans usually manage to defeat the environment.[38] A tree is generally seen as wood for either fuel or furniture, yet when a tree is cut down its ability to provide shelter against wind and water erosion is lost forever; and it no longer returns nutrients to the soil. In the twentieth century, especially after 1949, it appears as though the Chinese state has adopted a domineering, almost tyrannical attitude toward the

PHOTO 16.1a   Guangzhou traffic, with motorbikes.

PHOTO 16.1b   Bicycle parking in Guangzhou.

environment, suggesting it must always be subservient to human need. It is important to recall, however, that such a view was by no means new with Mao Zedong or the Chinese Communists; in fact the Chinese have historically gone in for spectacular transformations of nature, as in the case of the Great Wall and the Grand Canal (and, in the late 1990s, the Three Gorges Dam, which will create a new reservoir more than 400 miles long).[39]

Since the Stone Age Chinese peasants have "struggled to transform nature and remove mountains, not to mention forests," and in the process they have produced what must surely be the most transformed landscape on earth. As geographer George Cressey pointed out in *The Land of Five Hundred Million*:

> The . . . history of Chinese civilization is one of continuous intensification of field farming. . . . The sum of these actions is a landscape refashioned by the human hand to an extent unparalleled in other . . . cultures: virtually complete deforestation . . . garden-like cultivation extending uninterrupted . . . over the space of mid-size European countries; and the relentless displacement of all natural ecosystems by a mosaic of fields and settlements.[40]

Over the centuries there has always been a conflict between environmental ideals and the harsh realities of housing, feeding, warming, and clothing a huge population. Whenever it was necessary the environment had to be subordinated to the requirements of everyday life, and after the 1949 revolution the conflict was solved through the dictates of socialist ideology. Concern for beautification and aesthetic appreciation of landscapes were interpreted as bourgeois values, and the proper use of the environment was above all else to serve the people, implying the masses rather than a relatively small group of privileged artists and intellectuals. The environment, therefore, was considered to be a resource that could be used to create value. A tree was seen not so much as something to look at, or even as an essential component of the delicate ecological balance, but

rather as the source of timber to construct homes, feed fires, and power factories.

The ancient reverence of the Chinese gentry for the landscape contrasts with this utilitarian view. In the Maoist version of Marxism, the Chinese were embroiled in a constant struggle to transform nature through their own labor, either to make it work for them or to make themselves safe from its ravages. Mao was convinced that Chinese people could, if they were sufficiently motivated and effectively organized, move their own mountains, accomplish miracles, and remake their own history.[41]

In the countryside the Maoist exhortation to "take grain as the key link" resulted in the exclusive production of wheat and rice in the interests of local self-reliance, often in areas totally unsuited to intense cultivation. The effects in many regions were disastrous. In some of the northern provinces, for example, entire areas of grassland were destroyed in futile efforts to grow wheat, but in this and many other instances the damage inflicted on the land could be justified by the potential benefits flowing to society at large. In addition, without private ownership of land and environmental resources, there was no one (acting either as individuals or on behalf of activist groups) to represent the interests of the environment. Collective land, in other words, belonged to everyone; therefore it belongs to no one; and there is no one to speak out when it is mistreated.

Thus socialism might well represent a more serious threat to the environment than does capitalism, but as the Industrial Revolution demonstrated in Europe and North America capitalist development can match socialist development blow for blow in its ability to destroy the environment. There is evidence the world over that ecological plunder associated with atmospheric pollution, rain forest encroachment, and oil spills is as likely to occur in capitalist as in socialist societies. Moreover, despite the overall perception that centrally planned economies have inflicted serious environmental damage, some research points in the other direction. In one study, for example, researchers reported that regulation of state enterprises is associated with success in implementing wastewater controls, even with rising output figures.[42] We have no evidence that early socialist theoreticians thought much about environmental degradation; if they did, we can assume they considered pollution to be a negative by-product of greed and wasteful production within the capitalist economy. It has also been suggested that an authoritarian and centrally planned system of government is better able to control and regulate economic behaviors—making full use of its inherently hierarchical organizations, in addition to its threatened use of force—to ensure that its policies are implemented. The state is able to process and control information, issue regulations, and enforce compliance,[43] so in this sense an authoritarian government has a comparative advantage in the realm of administering and regulating environmental policies. In the face of environmental threats, the centralized nature of socialist planning should allow the state to act in the best interests of society as a whole, rather than pandering to special interests or to certain classes within the population. In other words, compared to capitalist societies a socialist society ought to exhibit higher levels of environmental concern, as well as a greater ability and willingness to respond to environmental threats.

Sadly, the experiences of China since 1949, the former Soviet Union, and communist satellites in Eastern Europe prove such was not the case.[44] In China, as in most socialist societies, there has been fanatical concern with industrial and agricultural production, and during the development push the environment has taken a backseat; resources are seen primarily as inputs to the production process, with little or no concern given to their long-term survival and replenishment. In addition, widespread inefficiency, waste, mismanagement, corruption, and laziness associated with socialist command economies have, arguably, led to a cavalier environmental attitude.[45]

From a purely ideological perspective, concern over environmental issues might have been interpreted as irrelevant to egalitarianism, perhaps even part of the spiritual pollution threatening to drift over China from the West (the moral equivalent of acid rain?). For a country struggling to modernize, however, concern for aesthetics, clean air, and potable water would normally be low priorities, luxuries that China could ill afford.[46] Thus the Western environmental movement of the 1960s and early 1970s swept past China, largely because of its self-imposed isolation and its mistrust of such bourgeois values. Few major industrial projects during the Soviet era of economic development in the 1950s or later in the 1960s demonstrated any sensitivity to effects on the environment. The only priority was economic development.

China returned to the world community in the late 1970s, and as the magnitude of its own looming environmental crisis became increasingly apparent, researchers began to study it and the environment gradually became an important political issue. During the early 1970s several pilot projects were introduced; an emission control project in Shanghai was funded, and a water quality improvement project began in Beijing's Guanting Reservoir.[47] Yet the physical environment had suffered greatly in the relentless pursuit of economic development. In the cities, in particular, years of neglect and the fanatic concentration on production resulted in a decayed and poisoned environment. In Shanghai, Westerners found that the city "had been run into the ground, its housing dilapidated, its waters befouled, its traffic a torment, and its resources milked to the point of exhaustion."[48]

At first the new concern for the environment was restricted, as might be expected in a Leninist society, to ensuring that environmental concerns were built into centralized planning agendas while avoiding anything that might inhibit economic growth. In 1974 the central Environmental Protection Office was established, with branches in each of the provinces, but its status (as an office rather than a ministry or bureau) indicated its advisory capacity and tenuous position. The government was distracted by bitter infighting among the leadership, with the Gang of Four enforcing the primacy of leftist (Maoist) politics within the context of class conflict.

After the demise of the Gang of Four, environmental issues returned to the political agenda, and in 1979 an environmental protection statute established a basis for future governmental action.[49] The new law provided a basic structure for environmental monitoring and protection, including a statute requiring environmental impact assessments for all new construction projects; a new environmental bureaucracy; the rudiments of sanction-reward and enforcement procedures; and a schedule of effluent charges and fines for excessive discharge of pollutants.[50] The major problem remained enforcement. Lacking teeth, the Environmental Protection Office, although promoted to bureau status within the Ministry of Urban and Rural Construction and Environmental Protection, was still perceived as a peripheral agency. But in 1984 the Environmental Protection Commission (EPC) was established to coordinate all environmental activities, with Li Peng (the future premier) as its chairman. Later that year the EPC became an independent state bureau, breaking away from its parent ministry.

Despite EPC's pronouncements on pollution, it still had no formal authority and, more important, no influence over the budgets of any agencies. It functioned in a largely persuasive role, but it appeared to be receiving strong moral and vocal support from Party leadership. This was especially the case during retrenchment in the late 1980s, when efforts were made to slow the construction boom generated by economic reform. In a roundabout way stricter environmental controls were helping to enforce policies designed to cool the overheating economy, thereby also contributing to attempts to control inflation and budget deficits. For that reason, and somewhat paradoxically, new environmental laws were likely to be supported by conservative elements within the Party leadership, even though actual environmental concerns were secondary. The irony of this situation was that "environmental protection, which first blossomed in a period of liberalization, remained a

priority item in . . . a more budget-conscious and politically conservative phase."[51]

By the mid-1980s environmentalists within the leadership had won an important moral victory. In the past it was made clear that environmental policies must not interrupt economic progress in any way, but that situation had been reversed, and it was now clear that the economy would not be allowed to expand without due consideration of environmental impacts. Although funding for environmental protection remained at the local and enterprise levels rather than at the central level, the greater commitment was beginning to bear fruit in financial terms. In 1980 environmental protection expenditures totaled Y1.8 billion, but by 1985 they had increased to Y5.4 billion, representing 0.5 percent of the country's total output value, a figure that was scheduled to increase to more than 1 percent by 1990.[52]

In the reform years the desire to increase output at almost any cost meant that environmental concerns were often sacrificed, something that was effectively institutionalized thanks to the lower status of China's environmental agencies vis-à-vis its production ministries.[53] Yet recent trends in policy implementation might well favor environmental regulation despite the continuing commitment to economic growth. There has, for example, been enhanced support of the National Environmental Protection Administration (NEPA) by China's top leaders, and other institutional changes, such as a wastewater discharge permit system[54] and the devolution of regulatory powers to local Environmental Protection Bureaus (EPBs), which reflects a new level of concern for environmental issues, as well as some marked changes in behavior. Recent trends are encouraging; emissions have increased, but at a slower rate than industrial output, and higher proportions of wastewater are now being treated before discharge. Chinese leaders seem intent on continuing the trend toward environmental control, combined with specific links between economic processes and environmental outcomes. There is still a long way to go, but perhaps there is some justification in concluding, as the World

Bank has, that China's children and grandchildren will be able to enjoy clear water and blue skies.[55]

What could derail this scenario, however, is the continuation of current market forces, which threaten to have disastrous effects on the environment. Problem areas include the fundamentally unregulated status of China's burgeoning TVE sector; the absence of meaningful hazardous waste regulations; and growing environmental stresses in rural areas. Some critics have suggested that the shift back to the individual ownership of land and resources and the lure of material incentives in the reform era have resulted in unprecedented environmental degradation, even when compared to the three decades of collectivism. William Hinton, for example, has observed the changes in the rural economy and has been a critic of agricultural reform: "It is doubtful if in history there has ever been such a massive, wholesale attack on the environment as is occurring in China now. . . . By atomizing landholding and making each family responsible for its own profits and losses, this regime has virtually guaranteed such destruction. Neither regulation nor exhortation will stop it."[56] Behind Hinton's rhetoric are three lines of reasoning:

- Environmental degradation is a function of the level of economic activity, and with the economy expanding at the rate it has been during the 1980s and 1990s, the environment has been under attack on all sides;
- pollution and a lack of concern for the environment are considered to be the result of the amoral behavior associated with the individual desire to get rich in the environment of market socialism, which is now relatively unfettered by central planning or the decrees of the government; and
- the critics argue that the government is currently in cahoots with industry, prosperous households, and foreign investors to push forward the economy as rapidly as possible, without any serious consideration for the effects on the environment.[57]

The relationship between politics and environmental degradation is complex, and it is impossible to determine definitively whether one form of political economy causes more damage to the environment than another. Critics of the new regime in China (William Hinton, for example) have warned about the environmental impacts of privatization in the countryside; others, like Vaclav Smil, have argued that doctrinaire socialism and the CCP's historic approach to environmental issues had been disastrous. Smil pointed out some of the "towering inconsistencies" and the "pervasive mismanagement" that brought about unprecedented environmental degradation (which prompted his 1984 book, *The Bad Earth*).

Chinese leaders are now fully aware that the sort of economic growth needed to maintain the Four Modernizations project is certain to increase pollution levels per capita unless additional resources are devoted to neutralizing the polluting effects of the industrial processes. This is especially important when the industrial processes require increased utilization of energy and chemical production, as is the case in much of rural China. Under the umbrella of protection mechanisms and in light of the ongoing discourse about environmental protection, the current leaders will likely continue to privilege economic development over environmental protection, with some exceptions, beyond the 1990s until per capita incomes have increased substantially.

Some critics contend this is a dangerous policy for several reasons.[58] It ignores the damage to human health that arises from polluted environments.[59] Privileging economic growth will cause short-term damage to soils, forests, and fisheries that provide the basis for many production activities and promises long-term degradation associated with the loss of soils and forests. The least convincing critique centers on the damage to the aesthetic and recreational values of the physical environment. Yet the logic in these sorts of arguments has captured the attention of Chinese leaders, and so there has been a flurry of activity in recent years, with numerous new policy bundles and plans announced to address different aspects of environmental degradation (see Table 16.3).

Implementing the New Environmental Laws

Leaders today are fully aware of the price to be paid if they fail in a united effort to overcome the looming environmental crisis. In a speech made in 1993, for example, Premier Li Peng remarked:

> We clearly are aware that the situation of the environment in our country is still quite severe. Since China is now still at the stage of rapid industrialization and urbanization, the intensity of exploitation of natural resources rises continuously. In addition, because of the extensive mode of economic growth and backward technological and managerial levels, emissions of pollutants increase continuously. Environmental pollution in center cities is worsening and is extending into rural areas, and the scope of ecological damage is increasing.[60]

In addition to the concern at the very highest level, there has been a gradual buildup of environmental knowledge and expertise to match the burgeoning environmental laws and regulations already in place. There has certainly not been a lack of effort and attention paid to environmental issues, in light of the significant increase in the number of personnel working in the environmental field; continuing education about environmental issues; and the state signaling its intent by directing more funds to pollution treatment.[61]

China's environmental controls will be implemented along three policy paths: the establishment of standards for ambient conditions and polluting behavior, along with environmental impact statements for all economic development projects; directions given to SOEs through the overall economic planning process, stressing that environmental goals should be synchronized with production at each stage of enterprise activity; and tighter regulation of

collectively and privately owned production units.[62]

This third policy will be implemented in light of the growth of nonstate enterprises during the reform era. Unlike the controls placed on the SOEs, however, this implies the operation of environmental authorities that are independent of the administrative structure of production. This has usually resulted in a type of command-and-control policy, with local environmental authorities imposing regulations directly on polluters. In general, Chinese standards for such pollutants as sulfur dioxide (SO_2) and total suspended particulates tend to be lower than those in OECD countries, which need not be a problem if they are rigidly enforced, but such is clearly not the case. The major problem in enforcing environmental laws is China's "generally amorphous" legal system and weak juridical institutions.[63] Legal sanctions are usually the last resort, and adherence to environmental regulations is most often simply expected of enterprise managers, who are required or exhorted to follow the examples expounded by the country's leaders.[64]

In the beginning it was especially difficult to achieve compliance, a situation that has improved over time, especially given the resources specifically set aside for pollution abatement and the like. Gradually environmental issues have been taken more seriously and are beginning to receive more backing from powerful institutions such as the State Planning Commission and the State Science and Technology Commission. There has also been an evaluation of local government officials based, at least partly, on environmental conditions within their jurisdiction; administrative units in direct contact with enterprises (the local, city, or county EPBs) have also received increasing powers to deal with industrial enterprises.

The guiding principle of environmental regulation is that the "polluter pays," and enterprises are required to pay fines if and when they do not follow regulations. The data show some inconsistent trends in the environmental charges being imposed, with a significant increase in the overall number of enterprises

TABLE 16.3   Key Environmental Initiatives and Policy Documents, 1992–1996

Programs and Plans	*Approving Agencies and Dates*	*Details*
Ten Countermeasures in China's Environment and Development	Central Committee of CPC, State Council, August 1992	A program document guiding China's environment and development
China's Environmental Protection Strategy	NEPA, SPC, 1992	A policy document about environmental protection strategies
China's National Program for Gradually Phasing out Ozone Layer Depleting Substances	State Council, January 1993	A program for implementing the Montreal Protocol
China's National Environmental Protection Plan (1990–2000)	State Council, September 1993	Ten-year action plan on China's environmental protection in different fields
China's Agenda 21	State Council, March 1994	White Paper on national pollution, environment and development at a national level
China's Biodiversity Conservation Action Plan	State Council, 1994	An action plan implementing the Convention on Biodiversity
China's Urban Environmental Management Study (Sewage and Garbage)	NEPA, MOC, 1994	A study on environmental management focusing on urban sewage and garbage
China: Issues and Options in Greenhouse Gas Emissions Control	NEPA, SPC, 1994	An analytical study on greenhouse gas emission inventories, with suggested control measures and costs
China's Agenda 21 for Environmental Protection	NEPA, 1994	A ministry-level iteration of China's Agenda 21
China's Agenda 21 for Forests	MOF, 1995	A ministry-level iteration of China's Agenda 21
The Ninth Five-Year Plan and Long-Term Program Compendium by 2010 for National Environmental Protection	July 1996	A plan guiding national environmental protection in the coming five and fifteen years

SOURCE: National Environmental Protection Agency, *Executive Summary of China's Trans-Century Green Plan* (Beijing: 1997), from Tremayne and de Waal (1998), Table 1, p. 1017.

charged; still, the average fee has declined, from just more than Y8,000 in 1985 to Y4,133 in 1993, indicating that the fines for noncompliance are not very significant, in addition to the difficulty local EPBs have in collecting fees.[65]

Kenneth Lieberthal has remarked on the most obvious problems in implementing China's new environmental laws.[66] In the semireformed state of the Chinese economy, most of the responsibility for steering economic growth lies with local (township and county) governments. Naturally such entities want to encourage as much growth as possible to extend their local employment base and maximize tax-based local revenues. Under such circumstances there may be a reluctance to penalize enterprises for "minor" infractions; and in some instances local authorities even provide grants and tax abatements to enable enterprises to maintain optimal production and employment levels.

There are also problems with the regulations per se. In the case of water pollution charges, for example, the polluter pays only for the one pollutant that dominates the local water system, with all other pollutants essentially being dumped for free. The fees charged to polluters are small relative to the cost of reducing the offending discharge by installing newer and cleaner technology, so in many cases fees are simply built into production costs—a minor irritant, not a deterrent. In addition, the fee system does not allow charges across jurisdictions; in some cases big polluters will locate at the borders of the next-door jurisdiction, effectively exporting their pollution problems with impunity. To prevent such corruption it would be necessary to shift the power of regulation upward to regional authorities; unless all counties are made to comply, there will always be free riders operating without any sanctions.

Another problem is the status of the National Environmental Protection Administration, ranking lower on the bureaucratic ladder than the production ministries that control the enterprises. As an administration (rather than a ministry), it can raise issues and draft regulations but cannot publish binding orders and enforce compliance. This is also true for the commissions charged with designing integrated development plans for the major river basins (such as the Yangtze and Yellow Rivers), as they are subordinate to the production ministries as well as provincial authorities. Lieberthal would agree with the World Bank researchers that further market reforms are needed to create greater incentives for enterprises to develop and invest in cleaner technology, particularly in the case of coal use and water. Yet the power of regulation is inevitably weakened by locating regulation authority at the local level. As Lieberthal noted, "Because most enterprises are either

state or collective bodies, their profits still depend more on negotiations with the administration for favorable policies than on maximizing efficiency and improving technology in production."[67]

It is generally assumed that such problems will become less of an issue with the expansion of TVEs, which are often smaller and more independent of political authorities; they also tend to be concentrated in the less polluting industries.[68] To some extent this optimism is well founded: Although the TVEs contribute 25–30 percent of total industrial output, they contribute less than 10 percent of air emissions. Still, the very existence and ubiquitous nature of TVEs make them difficult to regulate, especially because control over TVEs is shared by NEPA and the Ministry of Agriculture.[69] In addition, because the TVEs in many rural areas contribute up to 80 percent of local revenues, it is unlikely they will be forced to clean up operations for fear that production and the local economy will fall off. In addition, the small size of many TVEs and their sheer number mean that environmentally efficient technology may be economically unrealistic, with detection and monitoring well-nigh impossible. Not surprisingly, then, TVEs are becoming an increasing environmental problem. To make matters worse, the World Bank data show that water pollution, smoke dust, processing dust, and sulfur dioxide levels in the nonstate sector have increased significantly in recent years.[70]

The local EPBs are limited in their ability to monitor polluters effectively due to lack of finances and personnel. As the World Bank report indicates, "Medium-size and large enterprises are monitored by the bureaus once or twice a year. Small enterprises are monitored less often, and continuous monitoring of wastewater flows and smokestack emissions occurs rarely, if ever."[71] This problem, in addition to the obvious absence of public awareness and involvement, all point up the leniency in China's environmental policy enforcement.

Despite all the difficulties, the government has started to get tough on polluters; in 1996 it ordered some 60,000 heavily polluting factories—including many TVEs—to close, although that represented only about 1 percent of the total number of industrial enterprises operating in China.[72] The closings demonstrate that the government means business. But the real problem lies with the SOEs. As the state begins to sell off many SOEs, it is reasonable to assume that some will be either closed or forced to install clean technology at considerable cost.

The World Bank report contends that SOEs are still China's biggest pollution concern, mainly because they generally operate less efficiently than nonstate enterprises and are less likely to be able to lower the amount of pollution they generate during production.[73] This is partly because SOEs are concentrated in some of the most heavily polluting industries. Their machinery and pollution control devices are generally older or nonexistent, and they tend to be less responsive to price signals or the implied cost of paying discharge fees. In dealing with SOEs, then, the state has the unenviable task of trying to reconcile environmental control with increased economic growth:

> [China's leaders] can, in the name of economic growth, leave the big factories and other environmental hazards essentially undisturbed and hope that the resulting pollution and ecological destruction do not trigger either unmanageable popular protest or long-run economic stagnation; or they can clamp down, clean up and face the double short-term risk of a stalled economy and a wrathful proletariat.[74]

At present most decisions appear to favor the first option. As one official was reported to have said, "Heavy pollution may kill you in a hundred days, but without enough heat and food you die in three."[75] In spite of the greater enthusiasm for new environmental laws, there have been some setbacks, especially with the new burst of economic activity that followed Deng Xiaoping's visit to the southern provinces in 1992. From that time onward Chinese environmentalists once again realized they were fighting an uphill battle. As one scholar pointed out, "the ethos of the reforms and the political econ-

omy constructed to support reform goals are antithetical to solving China's environmental problems."[76]

The current consensus is that although policy formulation appears to be on track, policy implementation has lagged. In the first years following the adoption of the new laws, EPBs had difficulty trying to implement regulations in the face of strong opposition from growth-conscious local governments and enterprise managers. Although it looked like those problems were being overcome in the early 1990s, new and worrisome problems have arisen since. For example, there is evidence that city governments started to use collected discharge fees to pay salaries and build roads instead of controlling future sources of pollution. Enterprises, not surprisingly, are becoming more reluctant to pay the fees that are assessed. One researcher found that enterprise managers, particularly in the rapidly expanding TVE sector, interpret the fees as a hindrance to their profitability and thus resisted, either by refusing to pay or dragging their heels.[77] Local government leaders have often supported enterprise managers in this respect. Most of the local EPBs are small and thinly staffed; they are not recognized as authoritative governmental bodies; and there is rarely any legal recourse to enforce compliance by local enterprises. These problems were partly corrected after the late 1980s, when EPBs began to make arrangements with local banks to have the pollution fees transferred directly from enterprise bank accounts, but that occurred primarily in the state-owned sector, especially in the cities; rural TVEs remained largely outside the net of the new laws. As one county-level EPB official explained: "You don't know when [the TVEs] set up and you don't know when they switch trades or when they are not working. It's very difficult to collect money from them because their money is not in the bank. . . . They don't have an environmental protection division . . . and they are often located in places that are difficult to reach."[78]

In the early 1990s some Chinese banks decided to discontinue arrangements whereby EPBs could seize discharge fees; if this continues it will signal a further setback, reducing the leverage critical to ensuring compliance. There is also evidence that most of the collected fees are not being used to install pollution reduction equipment. Once the funds are returned to the enterprise, they are often used to pay bonuses to workers, erect new buildings, open stores, and build dormitories. To solve this problem a subsidy or loan arrangement began to appear in the 1990s, whereby the money collected by an EPB is returned to the enterprise as a low-interest loan, to be used only for installing pollution control devices, with the interest rates dropping significantly once the new investments are finished. Yet the pollution discharge fee system has largely failed to address the problem and to make matters worse, in 1994 county and township EPBs were reduced to second-tier status, diminishing their authority vis-à-vis other local government authorities and enterprises.

Most important, the discharge fee system has failed in its original intent: to create economic incentives to encourage enterprises to reduce original pollution rates and use the collected and returned funds to invest in new and cleaner technology. The major problem seems to be that fees are set lower than the cost of the equipment needed to control pollution and lower even than the cost of operating such equipment. In many cases enterprises that had pollution control equipment elected not to use it, choosing to pay the fee instead.[79] It also appears that a certain amount of "goal displacement" has occurred in environmental policy. The poorly staffed and often underresourced EPBs now see the collection of discharge fees as an essential component of their budget, which must be kept level; in many instances that has become the sole rationale for their activities. Some EPBs have even switched to an organizational version of the contract responsibility system, whereby they are required to meet previously established fee collection targets, with rewards paid to collectors who are able to exceed targeted levels.[80] In other words the discharge fee system is now assuming the function of a tax, effectively downgrading its initial goal of effluent reduction.

Thus EPBs need to be strengthened vis-à-vis local government bodies, with the central government requiring all local bodies to establish EPBs of first-tier status, fully funded and with adequate trained personnel. As Jahiel suggested, "Only a central level financial commitment . . . can remove local EPB's from the financial grips of local governments. And only such financial assistance can free EPB's from the temptation to generate their own funds at the expense of pollution reduction and environmental cleanup."[81]

Although China is certainly aware of the magnitude of the problem, the political will to implement laws already on the books may be lacking. No single solution seems to be on the horizon, as the issues are too large and complex; what is needed is a multifaceted ongoing strategy. As Richard Edmonds pointed out, feeding, clothing, and keeping the people warm, as well as satisfying their desires to get rich, will require some consistency and creativity; ultimately, he suggests, the problem is political: "To tackle this gigantic problem, China needs strict population control, a rise in the education and consciousness level, an increase in wealth and infrastructural investment, stability and *a more open society where information can be obtained and opinions freely expressed.*[82]

To illustrate just how far China has to travel in the direction Edmonds suggests, it is useful to look at the likely consequences of building what will be the world's largest dam, in the Three Gorges region of the Yangtze River.

Thinking Like a State: The Three Gorges Dam Project

Five mu of new land in the mountains is not worth one mu of land near the river.

> —A farmer facing resettlement in the Three Gorges region of the Yangtze River[83]

The first villagers to be resettled in anticipation of the Three Gorges Dam project were moved to new homes in September 1998. Their county will be one of eleven counties that will become submerged when the middle reaches of the Yangtze River upstream from the new dam are transformed into a huge reservoir. Among those who were resettled, farmers were quick to discover that the higher land was nowhere near as productive as the riverside land they left behind. In all, more than 1.8 million people will be resettled, at a total cost of US$4.8 billion by the time the project is completed in the year 2009. The cost of the relocations will eventually be reimbursed by a levy on the electric power to be produced by the new dam.[84] There are reports that resettlement efforts have thus far been plagued by corruption, falsified statistics, and inadequate resources. Many villagers fear they will not be adequately compensated, critics argue that too much arable land will be lost to the new reservoir, and prospects for agriculture and industry are bleak in the upper areas of the gorges.[85] Until the late 1990s villagers in the Three Gorges region were able to supplement their incomes through tourism, but once the reservoir is completed most of the original beauty and scenic value of the Three Gorges region will be lost.

Many local people seem resigned to their fate. They recall the story of Qu Yuan, a poet and minister of the State of Chu, whose temple can be found in the town of Zigui, Hubei Province, one of the picturesque towns that will be inundated. The town is scheduled to be moved sixty kilometers downstream (closer to the dam), but the temple built to Qu Yuan (who died in 280 B.C.) is to be moved only thirty kilometers to an isolated tourist attraction. Qu Yuan had committed suicide by drowning himself in the river after being falsely accused of wrongdoing. His death is commemorated locally by a dragon boat festival, which reenacts the search for his body in the river. When asked if they think a modern-day Qu Yuan would drown himself to protest the new dam, locals laughed and shook their heads collectively, observing that "Qu Yuan couldn't do anything about it, neither can we, so what's the point of protest? What they order above, we just have to carry out."[86]

The Three Gorges project has a long history, going back to 1919, when Sun Yat-sen originally suggested the idea of building a dam to prevent the floods that frequently inundated the huge agricultural area in the middle and lower reaches of the Yangtze. The river had been known to flood more than 200 times before the twentieth century, representing one serious flood event roughly every ten years. That has continued during the twentieth century, but the civil war and the Japanese invasion pushed back any realistic discussions about the dam, and it was not until Mao Zedong resuscitated the idea that people began to seriously consider the project, and feasibility studies were launched.[87] Because of Mao's support for the project, opponents were labeled as rightists, their political consciousness inadequately developed.

Despite Mao's support the project was not started for another four decades, primarily, one assumes, because China did not have the resources to complete so large a construction project. Some of Mao's advisers, including Li Siguang, minister of geological resources, were opposed to the project.[88] When interest was renewed in the 1980s, critics were silent or had been silenced; Li Peng, then one of China's up-and-coming technocratic leaders, made the dam his pet project.

There is an interesting story concerning Mao Zedong and his championing of the Three Gorges project. In 1958 Mao undertook three of his now famous swims across the Yangtze River at Wuhan. He had been advised by his doctor not to make the swim, because even as far down as Wuhan the Yangtze was known to have dangerous whirlpools. But Mao triumphed over the water, which some people interpreted as a symbol of his and China's determination to transform the environment to serve society. After the third swim, Mao wrote the poem "Swimming," which many people (mostly critics) have subsequently interpreted as his strong endorsement for building the dam at that time.[89] In the poem Mao describes how the Chinese in 1958 were planning to build a bridge across the Yangtze at Wuhan, and he insinuated that the next great step should be to build the great dam:

> *Great plans are being made;*
> A bridge will join north and south,
> Turning the deep chasm into a thoroughfare;
> Walls of stone will stand upstream to the west
> To hold back Wuhan's clouds and rain,
> Till a smooth lake rises in the narrow gorges.
> The mountain goddess if she is still there
> Will marvel at a world so changed.[90]

The "smooth lake" Mao wrote about will be almost 400 miles long, enveloping two cities, eleven counties, 140 towns, and 1,351 villages—all of which will disappear as the water level rises more than 175 meters (see Photo 16.2). As one U.S. observer remarked, the environmental and symbolic effects on the displaced people, the Chinese landscape, and the region's ecological balance will be "comparable to those of damming the Grand Canyon or diverting Niagara Falls."[91] Once the chaos of the Cultural Revolution was over and the economic reform process under way, an agreement was reached on the site; final approval was delayed several times throughout the 1980s, arguably because of concerns over the overheating economy.[92]

Numerous reports and counterreports appeared throughout the 1980s, and by the end of the decade a stalemate had been reached. Li Peng, who had cut his political teeth as deputy minister of energy and headed the State Council's Three Gorges committee at the time, announced he strongly favored going ahead with the dam project.[93] In the early 1990s another feverish push was launched in an effort to get the go-ahead, with 350 members of the National People's Congress (NPC) taking all-expenses-paid trips to the Three Gorges region to "inspect" the plans. Then, in the summer of 1991, there was a catastrophic flood in the lower Yangtze Basin. More than a million families in nine provinces became homeless due to the flooding; "the pro-dam lobby seized the ... flood as a clinching argument even though it had been most severe on the Huai River and

further downstream on the Yangtze in Anhui province."[94] By early 1992 heavy pressure was being put on the NPC to approve the project and silence the critics. Finally, Mao's dream of a "smooth lake" in the high gorges of the Yangtze Valley was to be realized.[95]

Arguments regarding flood control and sedimentation have dominated the discourse. Supporters insisted that China needed to focus on the vulnerable middle section of the river below the Three Gorges. The dam, if built to the height specified, should be able to guard against huge, 100-year flood events. They also pointed out that since there had not been a huge flood since 1954, many of the retention pools had been filled up with houses and fields, and that the dikes had been built as high as possible. Only a dam with the projected capacity could save the middle and lower reaches of the valley, they argued. The critics have tirelessly pointed out that the causes of flooding in the region are too diverse to be solved by just one dam; and that as much of the flood danger can come from below the dam as above it. A good case can be made, in other words, for focusing attention on smaller flood prevention schemes on tributary rivers. One critic pointed out that the Party-state should delay work on the construction of the 175-meter-tall dam until they had heard from specialists who would, it was suggested, point out the defects of the proposed plan. As he noted, "Please pay careful attention to their opinions, and excuse me for using an old saying, 'Listen to both sides and you will be enlightened.'"[96]

Historian Jonathan Spence put the Three Gorges project into historical context, noting that the celebrated Chinese folk hero Yu the Great had devoted much of his energies to hydraulic engineering projects. Emperor Yu, it was said, had traveled to more than fifty rivers and numerous mountains to tame the floods, cutting dikes and ditches and even changing the course of some rivers, laboring so hard that he was away from home for more than ten years, literally working his fingers to the bone.[97] From Yu's time onward, many of China's rulers have seen the

PHOTO 16.2   Tributary of the Yangtze River, in the Three Gorges region. After the dam is built, the water level in the river will rise to above the point where the bridge is now.

need to control flooding and the construction of canals for irrigation and transportation as central to their life's works: "More than a millennium ago, Chinese engineers had solved the hydraulic problems of running a south-to-north canal link across the eastward flowing Yellow River and the Yangtze, enabling the food deficit regions of northern China to draw on the rice resources of the lush southern paddy fields and making Beijing a viable capital."[98] Spence observes that even though the current leaders may turn out to be disastrously wrong in gambling on the huge dam project, "at least their grandiosity has impeccable historical credentials."[99]

The opprobrium heaped upon the project by international environmental experts has been matched by the eagerness of industrialists to get in on one of the world's largest construction jobs. At home, with the exception of a very vocal minority, few ordinary Chinese even have the opportunity to learn about the dam and its implications; even fewer have been able to air opinions on the subject. In the mid-1990s, with the construction of the dam already under way, peasants living in the areas to be inundated were concerned as to how they would make a living after resettling on the higher land. The peasants also expressed resentment about being forced to leave their homes and communities. They were asked if they thought the government would be able to complete the dam successfully; despite their concerns about their own futures, almost half of the respondents surveyed in the area said they were confident the government would be able to complete the dam successfully and that it could achieve its goals.

In one of the rare opportunities to express their views, the potential resettlees expressed an unusual amount of faith in the state and its abilities to care for them. A typical comment from the people to be impacted was, "The central government would never have planned the dam if there were many difficulties."[100] At other levels more uncertainty was expressed; for example, in the NPC, where deputies met to discuss and vote on Party proposals, about a third of the deputies registered reservations in

1992 when the project was approved. In fact, of the 2,588 deputies present, 1,767 voted in favor, 177 were opposed, and 644 abstained. Most observers agree this represents a highly unusual amount of opposition from the NPC, which until recently was considered to be a rubber stamp.[101]

Thus there has been little debate within China. Much has been written about the many unsolved problems, refuting the government's estimates of the benefits and suggesting alternative projects. Accordingly, in the Chinese government's fascination with the huge dam, we can discern some of the benefits:

- flood control and prevention; the new reservoir will be hold 22.2 billion cubic meters of water, which will be held in place by a dam wall 175 meters tall;
- electric power generation; the world's largest power station would be capable of producing 84 billion kilowatt-hours of electricity per year (ten to fifteen times greater than other large dams built in China) in "clean" energy;
- improved navigational capacity; the reservoir will be almost 400 miles long and 600 feet deep, inundating the existing shoals and rapids that currently make journeys through the Yangtze River treacherous; the lake will allow heavy-laden boats, including oceangoing freighters, to penetrate 1,500 miles inland, to the city of Chongqing in Sichuan Province; and
- water conservancy; the dam will improve the supply of water in a huge area of central China, by channeling water from the Yangtze Basin to chronically water-deprived areas in northern China.

One of the most conspicuous and vociferous opponents in China is writer-journalist Dai Qing, who has argued that the state's confidence in the project—which includes both the ability to construct the dam and that the dam can fulfill its goals—represents a socialist regime's "blind faith" that engineers and technicians can solve any problem. She argues that such confidence in technology and progress, coupled with a decisionmaking system that is autocratic, means the state has ignored or refuted a series of devastating environmental consequences. Key decisions have been based only on what is technically possible in terms of building the dam and the turbines, without any serious consideration of the hydrological, environmental, and human problems likely to develop during and after construction.

The government's decision to push ahead implies the same sort of reasoning that created the Great Leap Forward project at the end of the 1950s. As we saw in Chapter 7, the Great Leap became one of the great tragedies in human history, with millions of people starving. What we are witnessing again in the 1990s is an authoritarian government intoxicated by its belief in itself and the power of technology, determined to push forward with a controversial, unusually huge project in the absence of viable opposition from society.[102] Anthropologist James Scott would argue that such reasoning has launched many projects that became disastrous failures. This argument seems to be especially pertinent in the case of massive dams, which were at one time very much in vogue but are no longer being built anywhere in the world, mainly because of the questions raised about whether they can achieve what is intended, in addition to the externality effects on local environments and human populations.

In China there are additional reasons for the state to exercise caution. One is the failure of China's most recent megadam project, on the Yellow River at the Three Gate Gorge (*Sanmenxia*), which began operating in 1962 after huge controversy about its effects and costs. By the third year of operation the reservoir had accumulated a dangerously high level of sediment (some 5 billion tons) that polluted the river upstream and dangerously raised the water level. Despite a media blackout, it has also become known that two of China's largest dams, both of them in Henan Province, were destroyed on the same night in August 1975 by

rains produced by a powerful typhoon. The exact number of deaths resulting from the disasters is not currently known, but estimates range from the official count of 55,000 to unofficial estimates as high as 230,000.[103]

As it turned out, sixty other dams were destroyed at this time in various parts of the country, many of which had been referred to as indestructible "iron dams" but appear to have been hastily and shoddily constructed during the high tide of socialism, especially during the Great Leap years.[104] Jonathan Spence is essentially in agreement with Scott, observing that "the leadership's fascination with the immense dam can be seen as a final gesture by an aging Stalinist-style Chinese Communist [Party] infatuated with an outmoded concept of huge engineering projects that can be used to cement their power and prove their indispensability."[105]

Dai Qing and her supporters have been asking for an open debate about the issues, and in her most recent book she lines up some of the opposing voices to summarize the major problems she claims the government is trying to hide, deny, or disguise from the people. In her view the Three Gorges project has become a metaphor for China's changing society:

> The politicians who support it have all the characteristics of the old society: authoritarianism, central economic control and the dictatorship of one person. They have no regard for the individual and allow no democratic discussion. . . . Those opposing the dam represent the new society. They are the majority of intellectuals, who oppose it for scientific, financial and ecological reasons as well as human rights and the preservation of cultural relics. So one can actually study China through this case—the whole of society and contemporary Chinese affairs.[106]

According to Dai Qing the most contentious issues can be grouped into six categories:

1. Flooding and major dam disasters. Critics have pointed out that China should by now have learned a hard lesson regarding the dangers of flooding caused by weather- or earth-

quake-related events. The almost yearly trauma of flooding means that this issue is constantly in public awareness—no more so than in the summer of 1998, when floods were estimated to have left 14 million people homeless (mainly in two areas along the Yangtze River in central China and the Songhua River in Heilongjiang Province, in the northeast), claimed more than 3,000 lives, and caused more than $36 billion in damage, about 4 percent of China's current GDP.[107] Opinions are mixed about the effect of the Three Gorges project and the severity of floods. Some critics have suggested that maintenance of other flood management systems has been neglected by the government's obsession with the new dam.[108]

2. Forced resettlement. The government argues that the numbers are smaller than opposition groups suggest, that there will be minimal disruption during the resettlement process, and that most people will be given compensatory land that will soon support them economically.[109]

3. Irreversible environmental damage. One of the major concerns is with the quality of the water in the Yangtze River, which is already known as "the biggest sewer system in China"; more than 3,000 industrial and mining enterprises near the new reservoir already pump more than 1 billion tons of polluted wastewater every year.[110] With the creation of the new lake, the river's flow will be greatly reduced, which will result in a significant slowing and reduction of the river's flushing capacity, which could create massive algal blooms that deplete the oxygen from the deeper water, making it more acidic and toxic, killing all life. In addition, opponents claim that sedimentation will result in higher concentrations of toxic elements such as mercury, cadmium, chromium, arsenic, phenol, lead, and cyanide; as well as major increases in the chemical oxygen demand, a measure of the extent of oxygen depletion in the water. This will be particularly damaging for the city of Chongqing, at the western end of the new reservoir.[111]

4. The ability of the environment to sustain huge numbers of resettled people. As the critics point out, the region is already strained, and the resettlement projects will add to the concerns of extra population pressures, overploughing, deforestation, and soil erosion. Much of the land to which the people will be resettled is at higher altitudes, where it will not be flooded, and it is considered too steep for building homes and farming.[112]

5. Loss of cultural relics. The inundation will result in the loss of important architectural sites (mostly temples), many world-renowned wall carvings in caves along the banks of the river, as well as important archaeological sites that are already below the ground but not yet fully excavated (sites related to the so-called Ba-Shu culture, 2,000–220 B.C., have been discovered close to the river).[113]

6. Vulnerability to military attack. The location of the huge dam in central China in the middle of a highly populated, industrial, and agricultural region could be a prime target in the event of military conflict. Attacks on the dam would result in widespread flooding, with a wall of water rushing out at 400,000 cubic yards per second, potentially affecting more than 200,000 people on the river's southern bank alone.[114] The critics have argued that in light of this threat the state should seriously consider building a new series of smaller dams.

Clear Water, Blue Skies— Green Politics?

China has an unprecedented opportunity to increase its environmental quality of life. Rapid economic growth makes cleaner waters and bluer skies more attainable. High rates of investment can be used to develop cleaner, more energy-efficient industries. Policies that channel investment into cleaner production, encourage material and energy efficiency, and encourage conservation of scarce resources could reduce emissions in 2020 below today's levels, improve air and water quality, and lower pollution and related health costs by 75 percent—even as China quadruples its output.

—The World Bank, *Clear Water, Blue Skies* (1997)[115]

Considering Richard Edmonds's call for greater openness and sharing of information, the recent history of the Three Gorges project does not give cause for optimism. Yet there is a rapidly developing body of research in environmental sciences in Chinese universities and research institutes; one result has been the development of a new, clean-burning coal compound that is beginning to replace highly polluting soft coal currently in use.[116] The World Bank, at least, is convinced that with these sorts of innovations, as a base and example, China will be able to tackle its environmental problems successfully. To back up such astounding optimism, the World Bank lists some of China's achievements:

- The rate of pollution in 1995, in terms of both air quality (measured by SO_2 levels and total suspended particulates) and water quality (measured by chemical oxygen demand) is still growing but at a significantly slower rate than GDP. In the cities this is due to the reduction in coal usage, taller stacks on industrial boilers, and urban planning policies that have moved some industries away from residential areas.
- China's energy demand in recent years has been growing at only half of GDP, primarily a result of significant reductions in "energy intensity," which has fallen 4–5 percent per year since 1980—very impressive for an industrializing economy. The World Bank attributes this primarily to the economic reforms, which have "spurred investment in more efficient production technologies" and increased economic competition;[117] as well as more realistic (that is, higher) energy prices, which have resulted in more parsimonious usage and increased conservation; in addition to the implementation of the government's energy conservation policies, requiring enterprises to adopt new and cleaner technology and to pay the price for being polluters.
- There has also been a significant fall in the size and output of those industrial sectors that are the heaviest polluters, a result of gradual structural shifts in the economy toward cleaner sectors. The five worst polluting sectors are chemicals, pulp and paper, nonferrous metals, ferrous metals, and nonmetallic minerals (mostly cement). There has been a net increase in the rate of imports of goods produced in these sectors, which means that other countries are assuming the pollution burden.[118] Other side effects of the economic reforms that have helped to lower China's "energy intensity" include the gradual shift toward larger enterprises, which tend to be more efficient (and less polluting per unit of output); and the declining share of state-owned enterprises in China's total industrial output.

As the World Bank study pointed out, much of the benefit or improvement registered thus far can be attributed directly to state environmental policies or indirectly to the reform process (which in this case the state is happy to take the credit for). The report concluded, therefore, that the strategies for future environmental policies should not focus only on the issues of cleanup or the old command-and-control measures of the past;[119] instead they should take advantage of China's strengths. Thus future environmental policies should harness three characteristics of the contemporary situation:

- attempt to make the market work for the environment rather than against it (harnessing the market);
- investments should be pursued that have the highest environmental benefits for future generations (harnessing growth); and
- there must be more effective administration of environmental policies and planning, including setting national standards for emissions and energy efficiency, as well

as stronger efforts at enforcement (harnessing administrative capacities).

Much of this is already occurring, including a unique ability in the absence of a fully functioning civil society to regulate and control potential environmental degradation. Throughout the report, however, the researchers focused much more on what Vaclav Smil has described as the more easily solvable problems of pollution to air and water;[120] but they focused much less on longer-term issues and the much more difficult problems of environmental degradation: reducing resource usage; preserving and using resources more efficiently; and suggesting patterns of industrial and urban growth that will, in the long term, help to direct China toward sustainable development. According to *Clear Water, Blue Skies*, the keys are the adjustment of resource prices to cover the economic costs of utilization and the taxation of pollution and other externalities. Both, it is claimed, will result in more efficient usage of energy and raw materials in all spheres of economic and social life.[121]

Harnessing growth implies securing investments from all sectors of the economy and abroad in equipment that is more efficient and cleaner, thereby conserving scarce resources and resulting in less pollution. The World Bank also recommends increased investment in natural gas to replace coal as a fuel used in homes and increased investment in research and development intended to bring cleaner industrial technology into use. In addition, investments in public transit systems would help avoid or reduce the impact of the inevitable increase in the use of private automobiles, which will otherwise have a damaging effect on congestion and air pollution.

As to regulation and administration, the World Bank recommends the introduction of serious regulations that are effective at the level of TVEs, as well as the establishment of national emissions standards (for example, for cars and motorbikes), and the phasing out of leaded gasoline. The report recommends that

environmental master plans at the city and regional levels should be implemented, with a focus on removing polluting industries from downtown and residential areas and improving public transportation. All of this, in addition to massive public education campaigns, comes with a high price, and the report recommends a significant increase in government spending on pollution control investments (in fact a doubling, to about 1 percent of GDP).

One of the most serious constraints on China's modernization is the per capita availability of energy resources, which is estimated to be only about 3 percent of what is available to the average American. This tells us a great deal about the current standard of living in China and helps explain why Chinese leaders are so obsessed with the need to raise industrial output. In addition, China's GDP quadrupled in the fifteen-year period 1980–1995, but its energy demand only doubled (reaching 1,240 million tons of coal equivalent, which still makes it second only to the United States).[122] The comparisons illustrated in Table 16.2 are startling in comparing energy supplies in China to other countries. One of the consequences is that China will probably have to continue its currently high and environmentally disastrous use of coal, although some new hydroelectric power is anticipated, as well as some expansion of natural gas reserves. Statistics show that coal reliance has increased since economic reform began. A partial solution, in addition to bringing new power sources on line (hydroelectric power, oil, and gas), is to import more fuel, especially oil and gas. But in the immediate future it is essential for China to continue investing in clean coal technologies, especially for power generation and its largest industrial enterprises. There are numerous new technologies available; for example, coal gassification plants are cost-effective and promise considerably lower emission rates.[123]

When we think about the enormity of the environmental crisis we should remember that China suffered by having a very late start. It was not until the late 1970s, in fact, that the first signs of Western-style environmental consciousness began to surface, with the publication in Chinese of *Only One Earth: The Care and Maintenance of a Small Planet*, by Barbara Norton and Rene Dubos. The growth of an environmental movement, which had begun in some parts of the world as early as the 1960s, did not make its mark in China until recently. And in the much more open climate of Deng Xiaoping's reform era, the topics of economic modernization and democracy were much more likely to be heard in public and private discourses.

Many outsiders have been surprised by the general lack of awareness about the dangers of environmental degradation; some have even suggested that the Chinese have been forced to ignore so many injustices and irrational events over past decades, that avoiding or not recognizing the seriousness of environmental problems is an adaptation, rather like burying one's head in the sand. There is a saying in China that is often used to question the motives of would-be environmentalists—"Is your stomach too full?"—implying that the people have become so well-off they can afford the luxury of attempting to save the environment.[124]

Building an environmental awareness movement has been difficult in light of this apparent apathy, in addition to the Party-state's natural suspicions about such activities. China's only nominally independent environmental group, Friends of Nature, for example, was initially registered as a cultural rather than a political organization. Friends of Nature is still small and has chosen deliberately not to challenge state authority, like international organizations such as Greenpeace and Friends of the Earth. Friends of Nature focuses mainly on raising environmental awareness among the public and encouraging Chinese journals to carry stories about environmental issues. Fortunately, since about 1985 the government has pushed environmental issues to the forefront, especially with the creation of NEPA; as long as the government remains active in this way, newspapers and organizations like Friends of Nature will feel more justified in pressing their concerns.

Friends of Nature was formed in the Beijing suburbs in 1992 under the stewardship of Liang Congjie, a former member of the Chinese People's Consultative Conference. There are currently about 500 members, mostly in and around the capital. They tend to be elite individuals, including intellectuals, journalists, and some entrepreneurs. They have deliberately set modest targets for their immediate agenda: educational awareness activities and programs; surveys about environmental awareness; a campaign to free caged birds; and a tree-planting project in Inner Mongolia.[125] Friends of Nature has also put forward a proposal to relocate the gigantic Shougang steel plant, located about a half-hour west of central Beijing; it is a huge consumer of energy and water and a great polluter of the air and the local drainage network. The group has proposed that the plant gradually be moved, starting with the dirtiest components—the iron-smelting, coking, and steel-rolling plants.

It is abundantly clear that in China environmental awareness and activity are of a different order of magnitude than that in the West. The only nongovernmental organization currently in existence (Friends of Nature) is very much under the control of the government, precisely because it is an NGO and thus inherently a source of suspicion. There, is, however, some cause for optimism in the sense that in the absence of laws and the political will to protect the environment, the growing awareness of China's environmental problems may generate enough public pressure to allow citizen groups to take a more proactive stance than is currently possible. As one Chinese scholar suggested, "In the post-Deng era, it is possible that policies concerning environmental protection will be the next to be liberalized [which would] serve as an experimental or transitional stage for the liberalization of China's political life."[126]

At present that might sound hopelessly romantic, yet environmental awareness and political activities associated with environmental causes have been instrumental in the push toward democratization in Taiwan.[127] In fact, in Taiwan, concern for the environment has become so strong that industrial enterprises realize that by getting involved in environmentalist causes will improve everyone's quality of life and that a growing proportion of consumers will look more favorably upon such industries and will be more likely to buy their products or use their services. In other words, environmentalism has become good for business: "The benefits include an increase in sales, a reduction in pollution-control costs and an improvement in the enterprise's international competitiveness [which is] essential if an enterprise wants to tap into international markets."[128]

Some observers have warned China's budding environmentalist movement against moving too rapidly and suggest that for the time being activists should avoid aligning too closely with the democracy movement. A safe strategy would be to remain in the domain of generally popular public issues, such as preserving natural resources and wildlife and fighting industrial waste and pollution. In other words the environmental movement should be trying to improve people's lives rather than winning political power.[129]

Many would prefer that the movement focus on local concerns rather than mega-issues like the Three Gorges Dam, on the assumption that "all environmental issues are local," thus leaving nationwide movements to be developed only after solid grassroots movements are established in specific communities. China's environmental movement has much work to do: The legal system cannot be utilized to force the closure of certain factories or to prevent the building of roads and other potentially damaging structures. Popular protests against specific polluters have, on occasion, been successful, but that is rare; at present there is only the faintest glimmer of a trend toward rising environmental consciousness.[130]

Support for the new environmental laws throughout the 1980s can be interpreted as part of a general pattern of liberalization in all walks of life, including the new respectability afforded

to intellectuals, scientists, city planners, and environmental researchers.[131] After the purges of 1989 and the retrenchments of the early 1990s, there was a fear that the new status afforded to intellectuals and scientists in China would again evaporate.[132] Some observers felt that after the events in the spring of 1989 it would be a long time before people would be willing to stick their necks out again—on any issue—and as we have seen in many chapters of this book, most people, as well as the state, have been concentrating exclusively on economic issues in the 1990s. By the end of the decade, however, it is fair to say that some progress has been made, as illustrated by the new environmental programs and policies that have been implemented (see Table 16.3, above). The regime had been more tolerant of outbursts of popular dissent during the 1980s. Pollution from factories, for example, had become a major source of local discontent in China's cities, often leading to plant shutdowns, letters to newspaper editors, even neighborhood protests. In some instances the government supported such protests, if it helped them to gain important leverage over recalcitrant local agencies and their officials.

We can assume that a society is more likely to adopt major policy reforms, such as environmental protection, if it has an open political system, in the sense of being receptive to new ideas from the outside and within.[133] In addition, any new policy is far more likely to be implemented if the system of government is conflict-oriented rather than operating under the so-called consensus politics of a one-party system. From this observation it is possible to construct a two-by-two matrix to represent the variations in China's responses to the problem of environmental degradation during the last five decades and also to compare what has happened in other societies. As illustrated in Figure 16.2, under a closed-consensual situation, such as the pre-Gorbachev Soviet Union and Mao's China, as well as immediately post-1989 China, a country is not open to external political influence or, in fact, to any new ideas, and little change can be anticipated.

OPENNESS TO EXTERNAL AND INTERNAL INFLUENCES

		OPEN	CLOSED
TYPE OF POLITICAL SYSTEM	**CONFLICTUAL**	United States	Cultural Revolution China
	CONSENSUAL	Pre-1989 China Gorbachev's USSR	Pre-Gorbachev USSR Maoist China (pre-Cultural Revolution)

A matrix of potential policy outcomes. SOURCE: **Adapted from L. Ross, 1988,** *Environmental Policy in China* **(Bloomington: Indiana University Press), pp. 148–149, Figure 2.**

FIGURE 16.2   Political Systems and Openness to External Influences

At the end of the twentieth century it is no longer appropriate to describe China as a closed society, as witnessed by the embryonic growth of its green movement and the range of new environmental policies—all of which indicate that China is closely watching events elsewhere and taking the problem seriously. In the post-Mao era, therefore—prior to 1989 and after about 1995, at least—China could perhaps be placed in the open-consensual category, implying that leaders were and are increasingly receptive to ideas from abroad about how to solve China's environmental crisis and tolerate a diversity of views. In light of China's willingness to be involved in international discussions of environmental issues, we can assume that the door that was closed in 1989 is now at least slightly ajar. Still, there is little room to maneuver for domestic environmental groups, and the vast majority of China's people are either too afraid to act independently on environmental issues or too busy with other concerns.

Conclusion

In the twentieth century political forces have contributed to the widespread destruction of China's environment, in addition to its ever increasing population. The most significant event was the socialist construction that transformed China's agriculture and industry beginning in the 1950s.[134] During the reform era there has been some mitigation of the damage to the environment, for example, by changing the industrial mix to feature more light industry and nonpolluting forms of production. At the same time, the gradual shift from the centrally planned economy should prove beneficial, in the sense that industrial ministries are no longer as prominent as they once were. The new emphasis on profitability and markets, with natural resource prices rising to reflect more closely their relative scarcity, has provided a powerful incentive to improve technical efficiency and employ cleaner technology (in addition to the extra threat of government regulations and fines).

China's opening to the global economy has also had a major impact on environmental consciousness, as many outside experts have studied China's environmental problems. In 1991 China signed the Montreal Protocol to end the use of chlorofluorocarbons by developed countries by the year 2000, developing countries by 2010. Its commitment, however, was made on the assumption of foreign aid and technology, particularly clean technology to replace the ozone-destroying gas freon, which was still being used in millions of newly produced Chinese refrigerators in the mid-1990s. The Montreal signing made China eligible for aid from a United Nations fund of up to US$2 million, but the government has calculated that it will need closer to US$5 billion just to control existing environmental problems and another US$200 billion to clean up past pollution problems.[135]

In spite of the positive aspects of economic reform, there is great concern about many problems, not the least of which is the continuing loss of agricultural land to urban and industrial land uses, as well as the decline in the amount of forested land. As most observers have noted, the continuation of economic growth at anything like the levels attained in the early 1990s (9–12 percent growth per year in GDP) will represent a huge threat to China's environment.[136] In the cities there are concerns about the growing density of motor vehicle traffic, bringing extra pollution to the air as well as increased noise levels. Perhaps the greatest concern, however, has been in the Chinese countryside, where the breakup of the communes has been associated with profligate use of the land, in addition to the rapid growth of rural industry, much of which is in small and difficult-to-regulate industries.

In his case study based on research in southwestern Heilongjiang Province, geographer Joshua Muldavin provided a detailed, distressing account of environmental impacts, which he has categorized into three distinct groups.[137] One is the intensification of land use, which has resulted in damage to and depletion of croplands, grasslands, soils, and forests. In the case of grasslands, for example, Muldavin observed how agricultural production had extended into land that was simply not optimal for growing crops, and grazing had been intensified in the remaining pasture areas, which resulted in a significant degradation of all local lands. As he pointed out:

> It is impossible to travel through Zhaozhou County without being struck by the immensity of environmental decline due to ... alkalization. ... One sees large white plains of salt-encrusted soil. ... As the water [from recent storms] evaporates, it draws more of the killing salts to the surface ... where they mix with the rainwater and flow into other areas, stunting the growth of grass and crops.[138]

The second major impact is agroindustrial pollution, mainly caused by unregulated TVE activities, which are posing a serious health threat, especially through the contamination of groundwater. In Hesheng village, for example, the local noodle factory empties its effluent into dirt-lined ditches alongside roads. The factory uses a purple-colored chemical to process potatoes into starch, and when "families began drawing violet water from their household wells" it was clear that the chemical had contaminated the local groundwater.[139]

The third impact is what Muldavin refers to as the "mining" of communal capital. As noted in Chapter 7, the sharp decline in state investment in agricultural infrastructures, combined with the diversion of most local funds into rural industry, means that there has been a reduction in the provision of new infrastructure and a rapid increase in the deterioration of existing facilities. As Muldavin observed, in the entire area in which his fieldwork was conducted, "reservoirs, dikes, irrigation canals, tube wells, erosion control, tree planting—all critical to sustaining and increasing production—receive little investment for maintenance, let alone improvement or expansion."[140]

Environmental degradation can be seen throughout the countryside. There is a danger that the new agricultural and industrial practices associated with the reform era are contributing to a problem that is probably uppermost in the minds of the Chinese people—the fear of flooding. One of the worst-hit areas during the disastrous floods of the summer of 1998, for example, was in Heilongjiang Province, particularly along the course of the Songhua River, which flows through the region where Muldavin has been working. As he observed in 1997, the increased prevalence of flooding can be directly related to the new practices he had chronicled: "Raised silt loads and deposits in lower reaches of the major rivers threaten dike systems weakened by lack of repairs and investments. Reservoirs are rapidly silting up, undermining water conservancy efforts, decreasing both flood control and the electricity-generating potential of the large-scale hydro-electric projects on [the] major rivers."[141]

Recent research has uncovered some of the negative impacts of air and water pollution of agricultural and forestry practices. Acid rain, for example, is associated with the acidification of soils, with resulting damage to vegetation, including food crops and trees; the eutrophication of surface waters that have an excessive nitrogen content; and the direct impact on vegetation associated with greater exposure to SO_2 and nitrogen oxides close to the major emitting areas. In an attempt to document these impacts, the World Bank researchers described three serious trends:

- Almost 10 percent of China's total land is exposed to sulfur deposition in excess of 1,000 milligrams per square meter;
- about 1 percent of the land area, particularly close to the largest cities, especially in Sichuan Province and in the Shanghai region, has depositions in excess of 5,000 milligrams; and
- in and around the city of Chongqing, there are depositions in excess of 11,000 milligrams.[142]

The World Bank's attempts to provide cost estimates of the damage of such emissions to farming and forestry suggest that in some areas more than 5 percent of the food output is damaged, amounting in total to US$4.36 billion, which does not take into account any of the health-related costs associated either with eating the produce from lands polluted in this way or breathing the local air.

In another study, focussing on crop yields, researchers observed that environmental stress had adversely affected food production in many areas.[143] This is particularly the case where, because of rising food demands and diminishing land supplies, marginal land has been drawn into production and existing cultivated areas are overworked. This research team estimated that between 1983 and 1989, grain yields should have increased by nearly 160 kilograms per hectare; as a result of environmental stresses, they believe there has been a loss of as much as 5.7 million metric tons in the early 1990s, close to one-third of the grain China needed to import at a cost of about US$700 million at 1990 prices.[144] As the researchers pointed out, the monetary value of this lost production is roughly equal to China's entire annual budget for agricultural infrastructure investment. They recommend major policy efforts to protect land resources, particularly in southwestern China, the Loess Plateau, and Xinjiang AR, where rising population rates have resulted in the conversion of land to cropping that is highly inappropriate. Effective environmental pollution measures are taking hold much more slowly than is required, in part because local leaders do not have sufficient incentives to carry out drastic implementations in the face of strong progrowth local forces. As the research team noted, marginal lands should be restored to their original use, with a considerable amount of land reverting to grassland and forest. Areas prone to salinization, such as those studied by Muldavin, need to be treated or fallowed; irrigation and drainage infrastructure must be rebuilt and maintained; and erosion-prone areas must be terraced or contoured.

A program called the Comprehensive Agricultural Development Program, which began in 1987, has been one attempt thus far to address some of these problems by diverting central and local funds into specific projects for land improvement, irrigation, afforestation, and farm technology—all intended to increase per-unit crop output and raise peasant incomes. Again, however, such programs require considerable motivation and effort by township and village leaders, whose priorities may lean more toward industrial production than to environmental protection and agricultural conservation.

17

China and the Global Economy at the Century's End

The rise of pro-market sentiments among the political and administrative elite represents the biggest feedback [effect] of all. In the early 1990s these reactions coalesced into a stunning reversal of deep-seated attitudes. Ideas that only ten years earlier stood outside the limits of permissible discussion now took center stage. Ambitious bureaucrats began to resign their official posts to pursue private business careers. China's Communist Party formally announced a national goal of creating a decentralized market economy. This remarkable change in outlook, combined with intense fiscal pressures, has sparked a series of policy innovations aimed at relieving governments of the burden of supporting loss-making enterprises. Although official documents avoid terms like "ownership reform" or "privatization" to describe these changes, recent initiatives amount to a policy of gradual and induced privatization.

—Thomas Rawski, "Implications of China's
Reform Experience" (1996)[1]

Introduction: "Market Socialism" and Its Discontents

Thomas Rawski aptly described what has been happening to China's economy during its transition from plan to market. The process of transition ushered in a new era—market socialism—and most of this book focuses on the impacts of that transition upon the lives of Chinese people and the landscapes they inhabit. Yet the success of reform has been marred by negative externalities, and it can be argued that market socialism has been tearing the fabric of Chinese society throughout the late 1980s and 1990s. One of the most worrying concerns has been the growth of inequalities, both social and geographical. Even during the Maoist era inequality was by no means eradicated, but the danger in the expansionary 1980s was that the gap between China's richest and poorest regions was widening to unacceptably high levels. We also saw that the gap

between men and women, which had substantially diminished during the Maoist era, also widened after 1978.

The economic impact of reform has also been eroded significantly by high rates of inflation, particularly for foodstuffs, which by the mid-1990s had reached critical levels (in excess of 25 percent per year). In spite of the dangers involved in trying to explain events in contemporary China, it is reasonable to assume there has been a connection between the pervasive discontent within society and popular uprisings—the events of 1989 serving as the most obvious example. Adding to the equation, the 1990s witnessed a significant increase in rural unrest. The consensus is that the policies of the reform era have consistently favored urban and industrial China, and it is not surprising that peasant revolts are reported in many parts of the countryside.

The problems associated with reform are serious and potentially deeply divisive. Population pressures have created severe unemployment in some cities, made worse by massive rural-to-urban migrations and the emergence of floating populations competing for jobs and services. In addition, the environmental impacts of reform point toward a rapid acceleration of ecological loss and degradation. As the economy grows and population expands, China will face increasing international pressure to transform its production processes to reduce negative environmental impacts, particularly the emission of greenhouse gases. As a new player in the global market China will not be able to ignore such demands, which threaten to compromise economic growth, at least in the short term.

The success of the reforms was facilitated by shifting a considerable amount of resources and decisionmaking power away from the central government. The obvious corollary was that local officials in government departments and enterprise managers have acquired a great deal of power in a short period. Accompanying that newfound power has been corruption at all levels. In short, to increase economic efficiency to maintain China's competitiveness in the global economy, local officials and enterprise managers have been tempted to maximize short-term economic growth regardless of the impacts it has on the country's social, macroeconomic, and ecological conditions.

As Kenneth Lieberthal concluded pessimistically, this combination of circumstances could be explosive for the current regime in China: "domestic unrest, growing out of some combination of a political stalemate at the apex, major economic setbacks . . . tensions over corruption and inflation, fears of unemployment, a ballooning of the 'floating population,' and rural discontent, resulting in social upheaval that in turn produces a violent, repressive political response."[2]

Because of the diminishing political legitimacy associated with the Cultural Revolution, the Chinese government had no option but to embark on a reform strategy after the death of Mao Zedong in 1976, and in some ways that strategy has brought too much success too quickly, requiring society to make a series of adjustments in a short time. China scholars and foreign journalists anticipated that some or all of these problems would backfire on the government, but as the decade and century drew to a close, that had yet to materialize. The reforms have created the basis not only for a new economic structure but also a new social and political structure (the transformation Mao referred to as the "bourgeois restoration"). Reform leaders are now in a quandary: Should they craft a new version of the socialist political system that can serve as a viable alternative to both capitalist economics and liberal-democratic politics?

China's shift toward market socialism contains an inherent contradiction between economic transformation and political immobility. The avowed purpose of reform was to transform China's economy to guarantee significant and lasting economic growth, and the regime pinned its hopes—and legitimacy—on its ability to bring about that transformation. As things turned out, economic success alone has not prevented a long-term erosion in the Party-state's legitimacy, exploding at Tiananmen Square in 1989.

In retrospect, many commentators have suggested that conflicts were inevitable in light of the ideas, interests, and forces created by changing economic conditions and increasingly global interactions. As political scientist Gordon White has noted in *Riding the Tiger*, these conflicts appeared almost everywhere in the old socialist world, and it is difficult to resist the conclusion that "Marxist-Leninist socialism has been incapable of reforming itself."[3] The consequences might be a violent crisis and collapse or a more or less peaceful transition, managed by a reformist communist leadership (see Chapters 18 and 19).

This chapter endeavors to place recent economic developments in China in their international context. We first consider the actual and potential impact of events in contemporary China on the rest of the world; then we compare what has happened in reform-era China with events elsewhere. We shall return to agricultural reform and the argument that despite extraordinary agricultural efficiency China cannot feed itself and will soon have to become a major food importer. The discussion then focuses on the strategies China adopted for modernization, comparing strategies and outcomes with events in other societies making the transition out of socialism, especially the former Soviet Union and its Eastern European neighbors. The second half of the chapter attempts to put China's reform experience into a regional context, comparing the poorer parts of the Asian continent as well as richer countries, especially the newly industrializing economies that China now emulates. Finally, we look at the process of economic integration in southern China, as the economies of China, Hong Kong, and Taiwan become increasingly interconnected and as a new economic region—"Greater China"—emerges as a significant actor in the global economy.

Global Agriculture: Will China Be Able to Feed Itself in the New Millennium?

Despite extraordinary changes in the Chinese countryside, everyday life is much the same. Collectives still play economic, political, and social roles; in fact as one China scholar has observed, the grip of the Party-state may have been loosened, but the "apparatus of authority and control is still in place."[4] Thus the market does not dominate China's rural economy, and the public sector is still strong in many areas. At the national policymaking level, rural issues are still subordinate to urban issues, and Party leaders are still very concerned about the need to keep the peasants under control, bearing in mind what happened in the cities in 1989.

In other ways rural China has changed a great deal. Agricultural production is now undertaken largely by peasant households, and the private sector has expanded greatly into distribution, including marketing, transportation, and financing.[5] Peasants have thus largely been freed from the "triple subordination" of the collective era.[6] Policymaking has become more

rational, with a much greater role for technical expertise and information.[7] The process of policymaking is also more transparent, with greater openness and more discussion and debate on the key issues. Indeed the business of agriculture has become complex, and with so much power being passed downward to the peasants and localities it is more difficult for the state to maintain its control: "The state [and its former agents, the village cadres] have lost a good deal of their former ability to determine the behavior of the peasantry. . . . To a . . . considerable extent, central policy-makers are the prisoners of [the new] over-arching political network of social and institutional interests and pressures."[8]

On balance, what has emerged in the countryside is a hybrid system reflecting many deficiencies in both the plan and market approaches to agricultural development. A reversal to the old system of state control and central planning is well-nigh impossible at this point. Still, it is generally agreed that moving ever farther toward marketization would require reform in basic rural economic institutions, including the system of landownership and the role of collective organizations. Gordon White believes that if a move in this direction is made too quickly "it may unleash forces which it [the state] will be hard-pressed to control."[9]

The two years after the 1989 crackdown were a period of retrenchment. Many rural industries were ordered to close or went bankrupt due to tighter credit and taxation policies.[10] More attention was paid to agriculture, the result of the Party-state's fear of rising rural discontent. The situation was made worse by the state's fiscal crisis, particularly by the continuation of urban subsidies; in many instances there were simply not enough funds to buy the contracted grain without resorting to the odious practice of distributing IOUs.[11]

The major government concern in the 1990s was to ensure the supply of food grain and other agricultural commodities. One approach was to unhinge the price of grain, allowing it to rise (or fall) to market levels. As it turned out, in some years even the incentive of significantly higher procurement prices was not enough to convince many peasants to return to grain production. As one observer remarked, "Almost anything the rural household chose to plant . . . would yield a better income than grain."[12] This suggested the state could not bring urban inflation under control while also raising grain prices to a level that made it profitable for farmers to produce more.[13]

Another 1990s concern was the loss and destruction of agricultural infrastructure, a problem the state had to address without returning to the old collective solution. A fierce debate is raging about whether (and by how much) the state needs to supplement investment in the rural sector to make up for a 50 percent–plus reduction between 1970 and 1990.[14] As to land contracting and its long-term implications, many people are not receiving land that should be allocated to them (for example, newly married couples and women moving by marriage into other families). For many there is simply no land available, and the recent response has been out-migration, which will continue to rise unless rural industry is able to provide enough new jobs.[15]

Faced with the enormity of such problems the state has attempted or permitted additional agricultural liberalizations in certain regions, including Guangdong Province. The ultimate goal according to state pronouncements was to eliminate mandatory quota deliveries of grain to the state, in the realization it was an implicit tax on farmers, discouraging them from producing grain. In 1993, after the regional experiments, the government announced a new grain policy intended to free the price while fixing the quantity: Farmers still had to sell quota amounts of grain and oil seed to state granaries, but now the procurement price would be determined by the market.[16]

These problems notwithstanding, during the 1990s there have been some major benefits from the agricultural reforms, not the least of which has been significant growth in per capita incomes in many rural areas. Yet due to even greater gains in the urban areas the ratio of urban-to-rural incomes increased from 1.72:1

in 1985 to 2.27:1 in 1994.[17] There has also been an expansion of periodic markets in rural China, with the number of markets growing by nearly 10 percent between 1990 and 1992; the value of goods traded rose by more than 25 percent.[18] The success of the reforms was soon forgotten, however, when food prices began to rise rapidly in 1993, with the price of rice increasing as much as 80–90 percent in some major cities, with wheat and other grains close behind. This continued into 1994, when grain prices shot up by about half, causing another huge jump in the inflation rate. Opponents of reform argued that the new liberalizations had caused the rising prices and that the government had effectively lost control of the food economy.

With food still representing more than 50 percent of the average urban household's expenditures (60 percent for rural households), there was a fear that rising prices would threaten social stability, so policymakers began to consider applying price caps to urban grain markets. Again the state faced a quandary: Should it press forward with deeper reforms or start to implement retrenchment plans?[19] In fact fixed procurement prices were reintroduced for grain and cotton in 1994; price caps on other food products were installed; and exports of rice and corn were reduced in a comprehensive attempt to control prices. Market deregulation, in other words, which had appeared to be well under way, was experiencing major setbacks; in 1994 the state had to release 2.5 million metric tons of grain from its reserves to make up for the shortfall in production.

The rising price of grain in 1994 created global concern about China's ability to produce enough food to feed its people. When grain imports increased, beginning in the early 1990s, there was a strong hint that China was losing its traditional comparative advantage in agriculture, especially for land-intensive crops such as wheat and rice. The task of ensuring a reliable food supply for the future depends on the numerator of the food supply fraction, which is the supply of food, and the denominator, which is the size of the population. The latter must be kept as low as possible, the former increased as much as possible.[20] As we have seen, the household responsibility system contributed to near-miraculous output increases in the first years after 1978, but the rate slowed considerably in the late 1980s.

Over the long haul it appears the major problem has been maintaining an adequate supply of grain in the face of rising farmer expectations and their desire to diversify into other crops or engage in more lucrative sidelines. At the same time, the supply of cultivable land was decreasing, with a net annual loss averaging about 1,600 square miles; in fact from 1978 to 1996 the total amount of cultivable land fell from 99.39 billion hectares to 94.97 billion, a 4.4 percent decrease.[21] As we saw in Chapter 5, tremendous efforts have been made to slow the growth of China's population, and there have been major successes, at least in the cities. The problem persists, however: If we assume a continuation of population growth at the current rate, and if changes in dietary preferences are maintained (including the demand for more meat), by the year 2030 it is estimated that China will need to produce more than 600 million tons of grain per year.[22] This implies an increased production rate of about 2.74 million tons of grain per year.[23]

At this point we can only speculate, as some agricultural experts concluded that grain outputs will continue to decline over the next thirty years. This debate expanded into a full-blown controversy in 1994 thanks to a report written by Lester Brown under the auspices of the Worldwatch Institute. Concern was first raised in the early 1990s, when it appeared that grain production in China had stabilized or was increasing only slightly.[24] From 1992 to 1995 China became a net importer of grain, buying more than 15 million tons per year, which had some important impacts on world grain markets, raising average prices. Lester Brown and his colleagues interpreted this as the first sign of major crisis—for China and the world. The amount of cultivable land was stable or falling; demand for meat consumption (which is very grain-intensive) was rising; and investment in agriculture had been declining for more than a decade.[25]

The Worldwatch report attracted global attention with predictions that by the year 2030 China's grain production would fall by about 20 percent, primarily from lost cropland and the growing scarcity of water. That would result in a grain deficit of some 300 million tons by the year 2030, assuming a total population of 1.5 billion. The Worldwatch researchers estimated China's grain consumption based on two scenarios: One assumed consumption would stay as it was in the early 1990s, about 300 kg per person per year; in the second, demand increased to 400 kg, which would assume a significant increase in consumption. The status quo scenario would require grain production of some 497 million tons by the year 2030 (about where it was in the mid-1990s); the growth scenario would require a production level of about 645 million tons. In either case there would be a serious grain shortfall in the future, anywhere from 200 to 370 million tons, which would presumably have to be made up by imports. The world's grain surplus in 1993 was only about 220 million tons, so Brown expressed concern as to where the additional food would come from. The higher estimate, which Brown suggested was realistic bearing in mind China's current trajectory, meant China's demand would be almost double the current total of world grain exports. With its newfound wealth, China would probably be able to buy virtually all of the available grain from the global markets, even if market prices increased; the implications would be serious for less wealthy nations experiencing food shortages, which would be priced out of the global market.[26]

Such gloomy projections and scenarios produced predictable reactions in China, as well as negative responses from food experts around the world. Most of the criticism has been directed at Brown's method of extrapolating from current production and consumption trends without building in corrective responses—either production capabilities or global activities. One obvious omission is Brown's inability or refusal to think along the lines of the World Bank's "market triumphalism." Brown, in other words, was accused of failing to account for the power of market forces in the new China. For example, if grain prices were to rise significantly, it is possible that China's farmers would be drawn back into production in significant numbers. It would also alter the calculus of decisionmaking in the countryside, because if agriculture were to become a more lucrative activity, lands would remain in or be returned to agricultural use.

Many experts—and this includes indignant Chinese agriculture officials—claim that Brown's predictions were based on a substantial underestimation of available cultivable land in China.[27] It is widely believed, for example, that many peasants underreport the size of their property in order to pay lower taxes; the government also underestimates the amount of cultivable land so that output per acre will appear high. Satellite imagery and detailed sample surveys show that there may be as much as 140 million additional hectares of land, 45 percent more than official reports. Brown is also accused of failing to recognize that China could increase agricultural productivity by adopting new seed strains and other technological innovations, and some experts suggest that China's agricultural efficiency could be improved through better management and increased innovation and investment, both of which might result from a more realistic pricing system for grain. There is enormous potential for improving irrigation methods and, as Vaclav Smil has argued, as much as two-thirds of China's irrigation water is being wasted, mainly because it is priced too low and applied inefficiently.[28]

In addition to the role of market forces in solving China's food crisis, it is possible that land could be saved and productivity increased with low-tech solutions: matching crops more closely to local terrain and climates; using low-cost sensors to limit excessive water flow and leakage; and installing better linings in the canals to reduce seepage—all of which might increase water availability by more than 40 percent.[29] In addition, an unknown portion of China's grain crop is being lost or wasted in the transportation, storage, and distribution processes. Smil estimated that as much as 50 million tons of grain are squandered through inefficient storage facilities, animal feeding, and grain fermentation processes.[30] Beginning in 1995 the government directed provincial leaders to coordinate a major effort to increase grain production, primarily by contracting with households for increased grain output and regulating more tightly the process by which agricultural land is turned over to residential, commercial, and industrial uses. By 1996 it seemed these policies were working, as grain output rose to more than 500 million tons, and the plan is for such increases to continue by making use of close state surveillance, increasing investment levels, protecting farmlands, and adjusting grain prices.[31] It is difficult to determine how much of this response has been sparked by Brown's initial predictions; although it is interesting to note that after some early anger directed at him and other "meddling," Westerners, Brown has, at the very least, prompted some thought and action on the looming grain crisis. Whether or not their forecasts are accurate, most would agree that China must continue to be a net grain importer rather than attempting to be self-sufficient. In a direct response to Brown's challenge, the PRC issued a statement describing why and how China should be able to achieve grain self-sufficiency.[32]

There are many possible improvements in production, distribution, and consumption of food in China, which will require extensive reforms. As Smil suggested, "none seems beyond the capabilities of the Chinese"[33] and in his opinion China "has at least a plausible hope for a well-fed future."[34] It is also possible that if China's demand for additional food imports does continue to raise prices, as seems likely, farmers in other parts of the world might benefit even though some countries will be too poor to compete in the game of world grain production. In this sense Smil is in line with the official Chinese government position.[35] The Chinese believe the solution is to push harder for market reform and to improve technological efficiency and capability in production and distribution processes. In spite of the pungent rhetoric, Brown has provided a useful service by pointing out some of the structural problems of Chinese agriculture. Yet China's official response to the suggestion that it has or will soon have a food crisis is entirely consistent with the actions of an aggressively nationalistic state that is hell-bent on a course of modernization.

It is worthwhile remembering, however, that forty years ago the Chinese state also insisted it could solve the food problem through a combination of hard work, technological innovation, and collective organization—the typical modernizer's solution. Although the two situations are very different, the issue is the same: The state is convinced it can avoid major food shortages by implementing what appears to be a well-intentioned, well-designed plan. During the Great Leap Forward (see Chapter 7) the state appealed to the efficiency of collective farming and relied on the wisdom of Soviet science and technology. Today's leaders pin their hopes on the marketplace and the promise of technology. Yet the planned goals of Mao Zedong and his followers did not materialize, and because they discounted the gravity of their failure, China experienced one of the greatest tragedies in human history.

In his book *Seeing Like a State* James Scott has suggested that such disasters (he mentions the Great Leap Forward specifically) originate in the destructive combination of four elements:

- the administrative ordering of nature and society to create legible road maps for the future, which, when allied with state power, causes a regime to think it can achieve almost anything;
- "high-modernist" ideology, which provides a strong sense of self-confidence about technical and scientific progress and what it can achieve, for example, in the area of increased production or increased living standards (an ideology that is usually uncritical and hopelessly optimistic);
- an authoritarian state willing and able to use the full weight of its coercive powers to

bring high-modernist ideas into being, particularly in times of war, depression, or continued struggle; and
- a weak or incompletely formed civil society that essentially lacks the ability or capacity to resist implementation of the great blueprints for the future.

As Scott concluded, "The legibility of a society provides the capacity for large-scale social engineering, high-modernist ideology provides the desire, the authoritarian state provides the determination to act on that desire, and an incapacitated civil society provides the leveled social terrain on which to build."[36] As for contemporary China, it would be reassuring to know officials have learned a lesson from history's grandiose planning, but the official vehemence directed at Lester Brown and other meddling Westerners suggests otherwise.

One team of researchers recently concluded that the most likely scenario—even if all of these reforms are implemented—is that China will remain a grain importer into the new century, though not at the level predicted by Brown.[37] This team predicted that China may import about 24 million metric tons of grain by the year 2000, about 25 percent more than the highest level of the mid-1990s; thereafter China's insistence on self-sufficiency should result in declining imports. These researchers did not focus so much on technological and managerial improvements but rather on external factors, such as the rising price of imports (which should lower demand) and limits on how much grain can be moved through China's inefficient ports and transportation networks.

China's angry posturing is worrisome because it represents a dangerous discourse of aggressive nationalism (how dare the West even assume China will not be able to feed itself?); socialist developmentalism (big plans are needed for a big country, like the Three Gorges Dam); Stalinist efficacy and self-belief (the Party and the proletariat can change the world); and modernist optimism (science and technology are the solution to China's food shortage and most other problems). None of this should come as a surprise to outsiders, but perhaps we should worry that China's leaders are so uncritical in regard to the power of technology and planning that they actually believe their own outlandish claims. In 1997, for example, Vice Minister of Agriculture Wan Baorui, speaking at a conference in the United States, stated:

> Presently, the share of agro-science and technology in helping to boost farm production is only 35 percent, and it will reach 50 percent by the end of the century. This share in the countries with developed agriculture has surpassed 60 percent. . . . China's agro-science and technology development still lags behind. . . . Apart from that there are still over 20 million hectares of barren land suitable for agriculture, and we shall reclaim this land in a planned way.[38]

All of this can be achieved, Mr. Wan assured his audience, while protecting natural resources and achieving sustainable agricultural development:

> We shall carry out large scale water and soil conservancy activities, try to address the soil erosion problem in small watershed areas, prevent land and pastures from desertification and degradation, protect existing vegetation, configure our national afforestation campaign to increase forest coverage and bring environmental pollution caused by industrialization under control through legal, administrative and economic measures.[39]

Just over a year later, in the summer of 1998, the disastrous floods hit many parts of China, illustrating the enormity of the task China faces with the loss of farmland and harvest crops and showing exactly how difficult it will be to achieve the goals the Chinese have set for themselves.

The World Bank researchers concluded that China should aim for and can achieve 90 percent self-sufficiency (rather than the 95 percent currently being touted by China's leaders).[40] Yet the World Bank recommendations look omi-

nously similar to those of Mao and his followers in the late 1950s: enhance agricultural research capabilities; improve the application of fertilizer; improve the efficiency of water distribution and irrigation; go ahead with hugely ambitious plans to transfer water supplies from the Yangtze to the Yellow River basin; reclaim and develop new land for increased arable activity; and invest in massive improvements in transportation and port facilities to accommodate increased grain imports. There is more than a hint of capitalist science fiction here, and it should be no surprise that the World Bank, an agent of global capitalism and unrestricted free markets, suggests that China can achieve these goals only if it joins the World Trade Organization and relies on market forces, particularly global forces, to trigger investment, production, and consumption decisions. Only in this way—the World Bank argues—will China be able to benefit, through lower production costs and higher farm incomes, as each country's comparative advantage is exploited. If agriculture develops in this way, the World Bank suggests that China will also be able to attract more FDI and import more technology into the agrarian sector to balance what it has already received in the industrial sector.

In general, the World Bank supports Chinese leaders' confidence in their ability to solve or prevent a food crisis—and their contempt for interfering outsiders. As might be expected, the World Bank believes the necessary improvements are well within reach and that China has simply to increase efficiency in agricultural production and distribution. China must also abandon current policies that increase state control over grain production pricing and marketing and continue to control food stocks and international trade.[41] The World Bank has no doubt that global grain markets can easily supply China's needs, based on the evidence that world trade in grain in 1995 was slightly more than 200 million tons compared to total world output of 1,760 million tons.[42] In addition, domestic consumption in the major producing countries (United States, 42 percent; European

Union, 22 percent; Canada, 11 percent; Australia, 7 percent; Argentina, 6 percent) is relatively low, and population growth is slow, so they could all increase their exports significantly if necessary.[43] The World Bank agreed that significant increases in grain imports by China could push up world prices but is convinced that if imports were gradually increased, over several years, the price impact would be marginal.

At home, the World Bank assumes China can improve its food security and market efficiency by reducing state intervention and allowing the market to determine prices of inputs and outputs (in addition to major changes in land allocation policy). It recommended that rural residents be allowed to lease their cultivation rights to others and that the private sector be allowed to invest in land reclamation.[44] All in all, the World Bank predicts a healthy future for China and its ability to feed itself, concluding that "investment in agriculture will enable China to increase its domestic food production, and investments in infrastructure mean that food surpluses and food imports can be efficiently transferred. . . . Expanded options for food security will mean greater variety and abundance at China's table."[45]

Comparative Transitions: Assessing the Uniqueness of China's Reforms

The economic reforms made it possible for Chinese people to feel they had been freed from the constraints of collectivization and the centrally planned economy. They wasted no time taking advantage. As one observer remarked, "Liberated from the bonds of the commune system and free from other forms of mandatory economic institutions, people burst out with immense energy and enthusiasm for creating individual wealth and developing the economy."[46] With economic reform ongoing for more than two decades (with some periods of

retrenchment), it is remarkable that there have been no major reversals of the overall development trajectory. In fact after Deng Xiaoping's now-famous tour of the south and his speech in Shenzhen in January 1992, reform shifted into overdrive.[47] The ideology of reform and the commitment to modernization have been persistent and pervasive, as one observer remarked:

> As with the flow of water, the reforms may vary over time in their speed or extent, yet [they] follow the direction set by the underlying commitment to reforms . . . Chinese leaders since 1978 have accepted that modernization involves emulation of developed market economies . . . and that it is not possible without the "open-door" policy, involving extensive reliance on international trade and foreign technology and investment.[48]

China's Innovative Route out of Socialism?

In the early years of reform there was a certain randomness and groping about, and in some cases the unintended consequences were the most successful.[49] The turning point, however, came in 1985. Although there was no well-articulated and comprehensive strategy to reform, there was a consistent trend of incremental measures, pushing the economy inexorably in the direction of marketization.

First there was an overall expansion of market forces, achieved by limiting the scope of state planning and encouraging the entry of new enterprises, both domestic and foreign-owned. Second, there were attempts to extend greater autonomy to state-owned enterprises and to allow them to respond to market incentives with increasing effectiveness. The reforms continued to evolve without an overall strategy, but there was a relentless march forward along a number of fronts. Enterprise reforms were introduced; for example, the factory management responsibility system was introduced; enterprises were allowed to make their own production decisions; wages were linked more closely to profit margins; and managers were encouraged to negotiate their own long-term (rather than year-to-year) contracts specifying output and profit targets.

The other arm of the reform process was the consolidation and expansion of the dual-track pricing and marketing system. This effectively sanctioned two distinct spheres of economic activity: the planned sector, with compulsory deliveries at prices fixed by the state; and the market sector, with prices freely determined by market forces. Most nonstate enterprises operated solely with the market prices, but those in the state sector were free to sell goods and services at market prices after meeting their plan responsibilities. As the overall size of the economy expanded, a larger and larger share of output was being marketed outside the plan (see Figures 8.3a and 8.3b, illustrating the cases of the steel and coal industries). The key innovation was that most state-owned firms began to operate with markets and market prices in mind; anything they produced over the state-targeted output level could be sold freely on the open market. Although this system has experienced problems, the consensus is that the reforms of the late 1980s were accompanied by rapid output growth and improved productivity, the result of greater competition from new firms. State-owned firms were required to respond to the new competition by increasing efficiency so they could compete at market prices.[50]

After 1978 the economic reforms proceeded in a series of steps. The early years (1978–1984) were marked by domestic policy initiatives: Agricultural reforms swept through the countryside, and in the industrial sector import substitution was introduced on a wide scale. Many of the early reforms were focused in the countryside, and a significant amount of rural industrialization occurred. In this era the government maintained its deep-rooted and pragmatic reform ideology and sustained its commitment to political and macroeconomic stability. Also during this era a large-scale transfer of resources occurred from the state sector to the nonstate sector, most notably through a system of differential taxation, with the state sector consistently being taxed at the highest rate (see Table 17.1). This helped create a competitive economy through the back door without the need for a crash program of privatization. As some observers have suggested, in fact, the resource transfer helped to beef up the nonstate sector by creating some genuine competition.

In the late 1980s and 1990s, by comparison, domestic policies were continued, but more attention was focused on external policy initiatives to develop the labor-intensive production of manufactured goods intended for export. In this sense China was emulating the export orientation that had worked so well for Japan and, later, for Hong Kong, South Korea, Taiwan, and Singapore. In geographical terms the policies adopted in this era encouraged the development of cities and towns in China's best endowed regions along the golden coastline. These external strategies have been complemented and reinforced by growth in FDI and foreign borrowing, as well as by a series of currency devaluations that made Chinese goods increasingly competitive in global markets.

TABLE 17.1   Enterprise Taxation Rates in China, 1991

Type of Enterprise	Taxation Categories			% of Profit to Be Retained by Enterprises
	Sales Tax as % of Profits	Profit Tax	Depreciation Allowance Rate	
State-owned	89.3	49.6	4.3	17.4
Collectives	5.3	29.3	6.4	19.2
Township and village	5.0	25.7	6.8	20.9
Other nonstate-owned	4.5	31.2	6.4	20.0

SOURCE: Adapted from Jia (1994), Table 1, p. 13.

The obvious successes make it likely that economic reform will continue, but some significant changes are anticipated. Further price reforms are being implemented, and extended debates are occurring as to how best to reform the SOEs. One area of focus has been wage-setting, the immediate goal being to create pay scales that reward individual effort and skill rather than length of service and political connections. There are also continuing plans to provide welfare independent of benefits provided by state enterprises, especially for insurance, social security, health care, and housing. This would reduce the overall costs and responsibilities of SOEs, allowing them to concentrate on economic issues and to use hard-budget constraints—such as bankruptcy and unemployment—in the drive for increased efficiency. Reforms of enterprise finances are also planned, with proposals for SOEs to issue shares for purchase by the general public. Foreign investment is to be allowed in new sectors of the economy, particularly in the service sector; for example, the first joint venture involving the insurance industry has been opened in Shanghai, and foreign banks will be allowed entry, including some from Taiwan.[51] There are plans to expand the range of foreign investments into the interior of China through tax breaks and other preferential terms offered to foreign investors, even in the peripheral borderlands near Central Asia and the former Soviet Union.

Accounting for China's Success: An Institutional Analysis

When we look at events in the former Soviet Union and Eastern Europe, the most obvious difference is that the communist superstructure in China has not been dismantled by reform; in fact the Chinese Communist Party was not required to surrender much power at all. The Chinese experience demonstrates that it is indeed possible to move from a command economy to market competition without changing the fundamental character of the political system. As political scientist Susan Shirk has suggested, "Communist rule in and of itself is not an insuperable obstacle to economic transformation."[52] Two obvious questions emerge. Why have China's economic reforms been so successful compared to the former Soviet Union and its Eastern European allies? And how was it possible for the CCP to stay in power amid all of the economic and social changes that have accompanied the reforms?[53]

The models used to gauge economic success and failure in Europe and Russia do not apply to China. The two simplest explanations of China's successful transition are the privatization account, which considers privatization to be essential for kick-starting and maintaining the economic reforms, and the competition account, which argues that the introduction of real competition encourages both state and nonstate enterprises to become more efficient.[54] There are obvious merits to both accounts, but neither can explain China's remarkable record of economic growth that has been sustained for more than two decades. Privatization per se is not a guarantee of economic success, as poor economic performance has been registered in all types of economies (those with primarily private ownership, as well as those dominated by public ownership, for example, Cuba and the former Soviet Union). We need more clues telling us how the transition from a centrally planned economy to a market economy occurs, and the privatization model fails on that score. Even though China's private sector has grown rapidly during the reform years, it has remained relatively small until recently and is still highly concentrated geographically. The public sector, by comparison, has remained large; although it is inefficient in many ways, it cannot be written off. Competition has only recently become a feature of the Chinese economy, and using it to explain the success of the economic reforms begs an obvious question: How did competition come about in the first place? For the most part, the competition between state and private sectors has been unfair, as the public sector has been heavily and artificially supported by the state and, in fact, has been allowed to compete on a playing field that is far from level.

The privatization and the competition models also tend to ignore the political dimensions of the reform strategy, assuming politics to be a constant factor. In a country as large and underdeveloped as China, one that is also undergoing a generational change of leadership, this is a naïve assumption. On reflection, it is also clear that China's reforms are more complex than is assumed in the purely economic models. China, as Susan Shirk pointed out, has been encountering several different "revolutions" at the same time, including a rapid process of modernization, a major transformation of the economic system, and a significant change in leadership. Any one or a combination of these could generate a major political or economic crisis, as they could threaten the material interests of many individuals and constituencies.

To construct a politically realistic account of the economic reform process, then, it is helpful to consider Shirk's institutional analysis of policymaking.[55] Studies of communist systems—and again this has all been analyzed in great detail in the Russian and European contexts—generally do not consider such notions as pluralism, institutional rules, and lines of authority. It is assumed that all decisions are made at the top by the leader or a small clique. It follows that the policies adopted by communist leaders are designed to address specific issues, such as dealing with a specific economic problem, or pursuing the ideological vision of the party. Shirk would contend, however, that policymaking in China is nowhere near that simple; in fact it has become a pluralistic process that involves negotiations between hundreds of Party officials and the government departments. Although the power of the leader is formidable, formal rules shape policy outcomes. Deng Xiaoping acted to further this process when in 1980 he set out to institutionalize the Chinese political process, transforming the system from the personalistic, or charismatic, realm under Mao to one that was more institutionalized. This should not be taken to mean that the Chinese political system was democratized. Yet a clear set of rules, lines of authority,

and decisionmaking institutions emerged to replace the concentration of power and patriarchal rule that typified the Maoist era.[56]

The major problem in economic reform is that the institutions at the center (in this case, the Party and the government bureaucracies) have so much to lose that reformers must ensure that an effective counterweight to the center emerges. The transition from a centrally planned to a market economy will result in a major redistribution (i.e., decentralization) of funds and power. Reformers, therefore, must mobilize those groups who will benefit from the redistributions into an effective coalition to support reform and win over (or neutralize) those groups who stand to (or fear they will) lose.

In the former Soviet Union a decision was made to create the counterweight to the center by opening up the political system to mass participation and competition, which eventually led to the dismantling of the Communist Party and its loss of power. Deng Xiaoping chose a different strategy, electing to maintain the traditional communist political system in the belief that he could make use of newly empowered local officials as an effective counterweight to resistance at the center.[57] He set out to steer the economic reforms through the old decisionmaking apparatus rather than risk a complete opening up of new channels. In fact, as Shirk has argued, the Chinese political and economic systems were already considerably more decentralized than was ever the case in the Soviet Union; in fact she suggests that three decades of Maoist rule had not managed to alter the ancient traditions of decentralized power in China. Central planning in China was considerably less inclusive and more primitive than in the Soviet Union, and a substantial share of economic activity had always occurred outside the national plan and was administered at the provincial level.[58]

The net effect was that in China the central Party-state bureaucracies were a less formidable barrier to reform, and provincial politicians stepped into the limelight to act as the reformist counterweights to the more conservative center. With provincial support, Deng was able to push his reform program through without risk of changing the political rules completely (as Gorbachev did in the Soviet Union). Thus a series of nonthreatening reformist steps were undertaken: decollectivizing agriculture; expanding foreign trade; encouraging private enterprise; allowing localities to keep a share of their profits—all of which worked to change the economic and career incentives of thousands of bureaucrats and managers, giving them reasons to support the existing reforms and demand further reforms. In addition, the gradual expansion of private enterprise demonstrated to state bureaucrats and managers the real advantage of breaking free of the plan. All this worked to sustain the momentum of reform throughout the 1980s and 1990s, despite periodic setbacks (especially Tiananmen Square in 1989) and retrenchments (post-Tiananmen). The reform process proceeded largely through a series of consensus decisions, which by necessity tended to be incremental and gradual, not sweeping and revolutionary.

A package of successful reforms was crafted, consisting of strategies that were appropriate to and realistic for the existing political system.[59] This helps explain why many of the attempts to deviate from the path of incrementalism—for example, by instituting widespread price decontrols or tax overhauls—were destined to fail. "Communist institutions proved their flexibility as the bureaucratic support for economic reforms snowballed over the decade."[60] In other words, the communist bureaucracy proved flexible enough to allow and participate in a set of incremental changes that would over fifteen years come to be relatively radical. Provincial officials managed, supported, and carried through the reforms, acting as the buffers to some of the naturally more conservative elements. Throughout the 1980s support for the reforms broadened, and living standards noticeably improved for many.

The challenge for the reformers, therefore, was to build new constituencies among the groups likely to benefit: provincial officials, light-industry bureaucrats, local leaders in rural areas, and new entrepreneurs in the cities and the countryside. Their support would counterbalance opposition within the command economy, such as heavy industry and the state sector. The desired approach was thus to transform the economy not by abolishing the plan but by "allowing markets and nonstate firms to grow out of the plan."[61]

The nonstate sector was easily co-opted, and it showed the way for others to follow, especially true of the privately and collectively owned enterprises in China's rural areas (the TVEs). State-owned firms saw the benefits, and they could opt to become more efficient or use the dual-track system, selling above-quota output on the open market, which allowed them to keep some profits for future investment or to reward workers. Barry Naughton has concluded that by the end of the 1980s many managers and bureaucrats in the SOEs had changed their views about which was best—the security of the plan or the lure of the market; and after watching the nonstate sector prosper even during periods of economic retrenchment when state industry suffered, they concluded they could do better by escaping from the plan rather than clinging to it.[62] In this way the nonstate sector effectively became a magnet for growth, "drawing state industry away from the plan and toward the market [and] the higher prices in the market leached the best produce, labor, and managers out of the plan."[63] In some cases enterprise managers began to lease parts of their operations to collective owners (a trend referred to as "one factory, two systems").[64] This represents an inexorable movement away from state ownership, especially toward collective ownership, which is generally more palatable in China because it represents a form of social ownership rather than the more starkly capitalist option of private ownership.[65]

China's Uniqueness?

In the former Soviet Union and Eastern Europe, reforms tended to be dramatic and widespread, often described as "big bang" experiments, whereby the move toward the market was made with "one cut of the knife." In China the reform process was described as "touching stones to cross the river."[66] This produced a hybrid of market socialism, neither capitalist nor socialist, in which market reforms occurred while the state remained heavily involved in regulating and controlling the economy. The economic crisis before and after Tiananmen Square appeared to signal that reform had failed, but in retrospect that proved not to be the case. The reforms have certainly faltered at several points in time, but since 1978 the new hybrid economy has continued to perform well.

That success has puzzled international economists advising societies through the transition from socialism. Many economists had concluded that market socialism could only work under certain conditions: Clearly defined property rights need to be fully established; prices should be completely freed from government control; and there must be a full process of integration into the global econ-omy. All these changes, it was argued, needed to be implemented rapidly and at the same time. It was also assumed that democratic political institutions and successful economic reforms were interrelated: In the case of the former socialist nations it was expected that political reform would precede economic reform; in other societies, notably the Asian NIEs (especially Taiwan and South Korea), democratization has followed (and to a large extent has been a result of) significant economic success.

China confounded such expectations. Throughout the reform period the CCP remained on solid ground. Public ownership, state planning, and socialist values remained central to socioeconomic life, at least in the minds of Party leaders. Whether or not the West buys into the official line—that Chinese-style capitalism is a primary stage of socialism—the Chinese reform strategy continues to combine the strengths and virtues of the market and the plan. This stands in sharp contrast to events in Eastern Europe and the former Soviet Union, where the role of the state in the economy was viewed with hostility from the moment the ruling Communists were ousted.

It is difficult to explain why the Chinese economic reforms have performed so well against all expectations. Perhaps China entered the reform era with relative advantages, including:

- a low level of international debt;
- a special relationship with capital- and enterprise-rich societies (especially Hong Kong and Taiwan);
- a long tradition of petty capitalism stretching back more than a thousand years; and[67]
- a low-income, mainly rural society that has been able to provide a huge supply of cheap and geographically mobile labor.

It is also reasonable to infer that the incremental approach was the only one that could have succeeded, as it provided a stable transition through a period of major structural upheaval and great uncertainty. It is plausible, in other words, that a strong state is required for transition to occur: to maintain national unity; to ensure political stability; and to place the overall national interests ahead of those of the powerful vested interest groups. Whatever the explanation, it is evident that a mix of economic and political forces shaped what appeared to be a chaotic and inconsistent set of policies into a coherent process.

China's Transition in the Asian Context

As we saw in Chapter 8, China's rate of economic growth throughout the 1980s and 1990s has outperformed almost all of its Asian neighbors (see Table 17.2).

In fact China has undergone a two-sided revolution. One side has involved its economic growth, which has averaged around 10 percent per year during the 1990s; China's economy is now surpassed in size only by the United States

TABLE 17.2   Comparisons of Economic Performance: China and Its Regional Neighbors, 1980–1991

Indicators 1980–1991	China	Hong Kong	Taiwan	Singapore	South Korea	Japan	India	Thailand
Average Annual Growth Rate of GDP (%)	9.4	6.9	7.6	6.6	9.6	4.2	5.4	7.9
Agricultural Growth (%)	5.7	NA	4.7	−6.6	2.1	1.2	6.3	3.8
Industrial Growth (%)	11.0	NA	11.7	5.8	12.1	4.9	6.3	9.6
Services Growth (%)	11.2	NA	13.7	7.3	9.3	3.7	6.7	8.0
Savings as a % of GDP	39.0	32.0	27.3	47.0	36.0	34.0	19.0	32.0
Average Growth in Exports (%)	11.5	4.4	14.3	8.9	12.2	3.9	7.4	14.4
Average Growth in Imports (%)	9.5	11.3	14.5	7.2	11.1	5.6	4.2	11.1
Per Capita GNP[1] (US$)	370	14,430	8,788	14,210	6,330	26,930	330	1,570

SOURCE: *Asia 1996 Yearbook*, pp. 14–17.

and Japan, and it may well be the world's largest by 2025.[68] The other side of China's revolution has been its demographic transition, with fertility declining to levels in some of Asia's most highly developed countries. Yet China still faces the problem of absolutes. In per capita terms its economy, although growing rapidly, remains underdeveloped, with income levels closer to those in India than in Taiwan and Hong Kong. In demographic terms China has managed to slow down its rate of growth, but the sheer size of its population remains a major obstacle to long-term development.

Economic growth has allowed a significant improvement in living standards in the cities and the countryside, which can be measured quantitatively by looking at consumption and savings rates.[69] In the first decade of reform it was evident that the Chinese economy was not taking off as expected, especially in the cities. In absolute terms production grew throughout the 1980s, but per-worker and per-machine levels of productivity remained chronically low, particularly in comparison to the East Asian NIEs. One of the major disappointments for the Chinese government was that even after the hard-won gains of the collectivist period were abandoned, the economy remained far behind the rest of the region. Thus it is useful to compare the PRC experience to the NIEs and espe-

cially the overseas Chinese territories—Hong Kong and Taiwan. In his study of the reform process in Guangdong Province, Ezra Vogel pointed out that the NIEs, particularly Japan, South Korea, and Taiwan, shared a number of characteristics that contributed toward their economic development.[70] Most notable among them were:

- the successful borrowing and application of technology from developed nations;
- close contact with and major economic support from an advanced economic power (usually the United States and/or Japan);
- a powerful national drive to succeed in the global economy;
- a stable authoritarian system of government willing to combine strong central guidance with a high level of private initiative (the developmentalist state concept);
- an early emphasis on import substitution, usually followed by the rapid development of manufactured goods for export in markets all over the world (export-oriented industrialization);
- a willingness to invest significantly in human resources, especially in education and job-skills training; and

- an apparent willingness to work hard and forego consumption in the early stages of development.

It can be argued that China shares some of these advantages, particularly the so-called Confucian work ethic, the strong and stable government, and the willingness to forego consumption in the interests of long-term economic growth. Yet some features of state socialism initially inhibited the prospects that China could become the next Japan or the next Taiwan. Even in Guangdong Province, which has always been "one step ahead" (to use Vogel's phrase), there were many obstacles, including "a bloated, poorly trained bureaucracy, a rigid system of planning, and no experience in guiding a market economy. Its intellectuals were disaffected, its workforce poorly disciplined [and the economy was] subject to far more political and economic constraints."[71]

By the time China began to experiment with its own brand of capitalism (i.e., market socialism) at the end of the 1970s, the world was saturated with manufactured goods from cheap-labor countries. This meant that China did not have the same access to the enormously profitable markets that Hong Kong, Taiwan, and the other NIEs had been exploiting during the two previous decades and which had been so instrumental to their economic miracles. Still, Guangdong was successful in launching its economic takeoff and in achieving explosive economic growth by the mid-1980s, much of it based on an ability to produce cheap goods for export to world markets. As the evidence in Table 17.3 indicates, Guangdong's contribution showed the way for the rest of China, with the result that exports grew rapidly all through the 1980s and 1990s.

In Guangdong, and later in other parts of China, there was a significant break from the stultifying traditions of state socialism. As the reforms continued through the 1990s, however, China's economic successes continued to amaze the rest of the world, and as a consequence there is now a much closer comparison

between economic performance in the PRC and the Asian NIEs (see Table 17.2). In addition, there is a clear gap between China and the poorer countries in Asia, such as India, the Philippines, Bangladesh, and Pakistan—all of which show a combination of lower economic growth and higher population growth (see Figure 17.1).

Greater China: A New Global Giant?

Success in Guangdong Province did not come by accident, as reforms were carried out more comprehensively and more ambitiously compared to elsewhere in China. There was a swift and painless transition to a commodity economy and a much lower rate of state involvement in economic decisionmaking.[72] Perhaps Guangdong's single greatest advantage has been geography. Proximity to Hong Kong allowed new entrepreneurs in Guangdong to seek economic support and the transfer of technology from the colony, prompting a massive inflow of foreign direct investment. Hong Kong also provided a powerful example to the people and the political leaders of Guangdong, encouraging them to push hard for material success and end three decades of socialist austerity. As Vogel argued, "By flaunting the benefits of their economic progress, Hong Kong made people in Guangdong acutely dissatisfied with their state of backwardness, mobilizing them to pursue what their brethren across the border had achieved."[73]

Guangdong's economic takeoff in the 1980s showed the way for the rest of China, although there were some initial fears that Guangdong might consider a radical break with China if it became necessary to slow down the reform juggernaut. By the end of the 1980s it was obvious that the economic integration between the mainland and Hong Kong had taken on a life of its own to such an extent, in fact, that some observers were convinced the 1997 handover of Hong Kong to China was little more than a

TABLE 17.3   Guangdong Province's Exports, Compared to Other Regions, 1994–1996

	Year					
	1994		1995		1996	
Region	$US Billions	% of total	$US Billions	% of total	$US Billions	% of total
Guangdong	50.19	41.5	56.57	38.0	59.34	39.3
Shanghai	9.16	7.6	12.96	8.7	13.03	8.6
Beijing	8.34	6.9	10.25	6.9	8.13	5.4
Jiangsu	6.68	5.5	9.79	6.6	11.60	7.7
Fujian	6.43	5.3	7.91	5.3	8.38	5.5
Zhejiang	6.08	5.0	7.69	5.2	8.04	5.3
Shandong	5.86	4.8	8.16	5.5	9.18	6.1
Shaanxi	0.96	0.8	1.27	0.9	1.08	0.7
Gansu	0.35	0.3	0.36	0.2	0.27	0.2
Guizhou	0.30	0.2	0.44	0.3	0.36	0.2

SOURCE: *China Statistical Yearbook, 1997,* 16-10, p. 602.

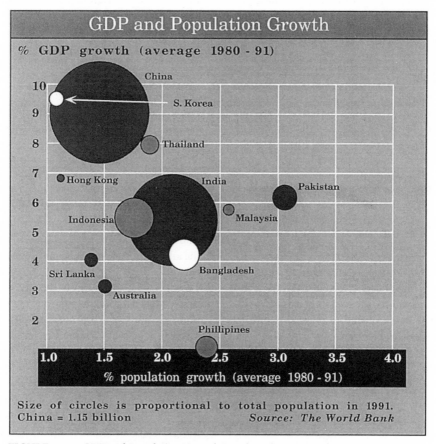

FIGURE 17.1   GDP and Population Growth in Selected Asian Countries

symbolic sideshow. Certainly the economic success made possible by reform meant that the entire process had become irreversible.

The increasing evidence of informal economic cooperation between South China and Hong Kong (and, to a lesser extent, Taiwan) invited discussion about the emergence of a new de facto region. The names vary: the Chinese Economic Area, the Greater South China Economic Zone, and the South China Economic Community. But the most frequent name is Greater China.[74] It is important to recall that economic interactions among the mainland, Hong Kong, and Taiwan (i.e., Greater China) predated formal political integration (although that changed in 1997). The growth of trade and investment between Taiwan and the mainland remains a sensitive issue, especially in light of the frequent quarrels in the 1990s over reunification, the one-China issue, and Taiwan's growing status in the global economy. Until recently, much of the economic interaction between Taiwan and the PRC remained informal or passed through Hong Kong.

The emergence of Greater China can be attributed to market forces mediated through geographical proximity and facilitated by the existence of a shared culture and common language.[75] The gradual growth of trade and investment among the three Chinese territories can be attributed to a realization of their respective comparative advantages:

- China has huge reserves of raw materials, virtually unlimited supplies of cheap labor, and (at least potentially) considerable amounts of land that can be converted from agricultural uses, assuming the food supply issue can be settled satisfactorily.
- Hong Kong has the necessary international financial services and is the transportation hub of the region (air, shipping, telecommunications, banking, and finances).
- Taiwan has huge supplies of capital and the required manufacturing technology.

The two most visible indicators of a growing Greater China are trade statistics and foreign direct investment. As illustrated in Figure 17.2, the total value of three-way trade in 1993 amounted to US$119.4 billion. The largest share involved trade between China and Hong Kong (exports to Hong Kong from China totaled HK$402 billion; imports to China's represented more than 36 percent of Hong Kong's total trade in 1992, representing US$40.1 billion). China is Hong Kong's major trading partner, receiving 28 percent of its exports and 33 percent of its re-exports, mostly finished goods produced elsewhere. The growth in trade within the last decade has been significant. In 1984, for example, China's total trade with Hong Kong (exports and imports) was valued at US$8.9 billion, but in 1992 it was $40.1 billion, a fivefold increase. During that nine-year period the share of Hong Kong's total domestic exports (goods made in Hong Kong) exported to China increased from 8.2 percent to 28 percent, with corresponding reductions in the share of exports to most other regions, especially North America, Europe, and Japan. Likewise, the share of Hong Kong's imports from China increased from 25 percent in 1984 to 37 percent in 1993, with corresponding reductions in imports from Japan and the United States.

In comparison to the Hong Kong–PRC trade, the other flows within Greater China are smaller, yet the absolute growth has been significant. In 1984, total trade between Taiwan and the mainland was US$553 million; by 1993 it was valued at US$8.5 billion. In relative terms Taiwan's trade with China represents only 3.6 percent of China's exports and 3.5 percent of its imports, but the yearly rates of growth, especially in the 1990s, have been extraordinary; from 1991 to 1992 China's imports from Taiwan grew by almost 50 percent and by 100 percent from 1992 to 1993, when they were valued at US$6.3 billion. The third link in the triangle, between Hong Kong and Taiwan, has also seen a significant amount of growth during the 1990s. Imports to Hong Kong from Taiwan, for example, stood at HK$94 billion in 1993 but

Greater China Trade, 1993
Total Value = Hong Kong $919.4 Billion
(U.S. $119.4 Billion)

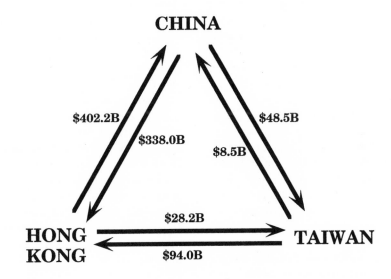

FIGURE 17.2   Internal Trade in Greater China: PRC, Hong Kong, and Taiwan

had grown only marginally from 7.8 percent of the total in 1984 to 9 percent in 1993. Exports from Hong Kong to Taiwan of domestic goods in 1993 were valued at HK$6.3 billion; re-exports were valued at HK$21.9 billion.

It is clear that the greatest change in the flow of trade within Greater China has been the result of China's entry into global markets since 1978 as an exporter and importer. Foreign trade increased so dramatically that it has started to represent a rapidly growing share of China's GDP.[76] This has been a result of the decentralization of China's foreign trade system during the reform era. Throughout the 1980s and 1990s an increasing number of enterprises have been allowed to produce directly for export. Factories and TVEs are now permitted to keep a greater share of foreign exchange earnings, and provincial and municipal governments have been granted greater autonomy in approving imports from abroad.[77] The net effect has

been a huge increase in the volume of exports and imports; for example, exports grew from US$26.1 billion in 1984 to $108 billion in 1994; imports grew from $27.4 billion to $116 billion. Manufactured goods have figured largely in the export trade, rising from less than 50 percent of the total in 1980 to 82 percent in 1993.[78] In geographical terms the major change in China's external trade was the increasing importance of Hong Kong. In the 1980s, for example, the share of Chinese exports bound for Hong Kong doubled, and most of these goods are subsequently re-exported from Hong Kong–based enterprises that have moved into China to produce goods more cheaply.[79]

This brings us to the second indicator of growing economic integration within Greater China—foreign direct investment. China, particularly during the second stage of reform, began to welcome almost all forms of investment from around the world, including wholly owned subsidiaries of foreign firms, equity joint ventures, and even foreign purchases of stock.[80] Foreign investors who once had to produce only for export are now allowed to market their products in China and are able to keep a greater share of their profits. Entrepreneurs from Hong Kong and Taiwan, realizing that their own rising labor costs were making them less competitive in an increasingly protective world economy, were quick to spot the opportunities in China, both as a market for their exports and as a site for investment. Once China opened its door to foreign investment, capital began to pour in, and by 1990, for example, an estimated US$25 billion had come in from Hong Kong alone (to the extent that Hong Kong manufacturers were employing more workers in the mainland than they were at home).[81] Taiwan was initially much slower to invest, but the dictates of competition in world markets and the desire to improve relations across the Taiwan Strait resulted in a gradual erosion of the restrictions on cultural and commercial exchanges. Taiwan's investment in China became possible only after 1986, by which time trade had become significant. It has been estimated that Taiwan investment in the mainland increased from US$100 million in 1987 to $1.3 billion in the early 1990s (see Table 17.4).

Investments of such magnitude provide a stronger mechanism than trade alone for integrating the three economies, because factories are built and formal financial and administrative arrangements are made. Most FDI in China goes to the coastal provinces, especially Guangdong and Fujian, which is not surprising, as nearby Hong Kong and Taiwan are the major sources. In 1991, for example, approximately 70 percent of the capital coming into Guangdong came from Hong Kong; in Fujian about 60 percent came from Taiwan—it has been estimated that more than one-third of Taiwan's investment in China is in Fujian Province—although with the ban on direct investment in the mainland Taiwan enterprises have had to go through Hong Kong to get into China.

The latest statistics show that FDI actually used (as opposed to agreed upon) increased from US$11 billion in 1992, to $25.72 billion in 1993, and to $41.73 billion in 1996.[82] Since the mid-1980s Hong Kong's share of that total has increased from 60 percent to 70 percent; Taiwan's share was close to 10 percent in 1992. In other words, 80 percent of China's FDI was coming from the two other Chinese territories; the U.S. share fell from 17 percent to less than 5 percent (1986–1992), the Japan share from 11 percent to 6 percent. By the early 1990s Taiwan

TABLE 17.4   Foreign Direct Investment in China from Hong Kong and Elsewhere

Country	Number of Contracts		
	1990	*1991*	*1992*
Hong Kong	4,751	8,502	8,358
Taiwan	1,103	1,735	1,702
Japan	341	599	571
Germany	13	24	33
United States	357	694	815
	Total Value (US$ millions)		
Hong Kong	3,833	7,215	9,703
Taiwan	900	1,389	1,320
Japan	457	812	826
Germany	46	558	36
United States	358	548	809

SOURCE: *The Other Hong Kong Report, 1993*, Table 3.

had become the second largest investor in the PRC.[83]

Greater China had also become a major player in world trade by the early 1990s (see Table 17.5). Only five countries (the United States, Germany, Japan, France, and the United Kingdom) had larger shares of total world trade by the early 1990s. The proportion has increased significantly, from just over 1 percent in 1970 to 1.75 percent in 1980, 4.17 percent in 1989, and more than 8 percent in 1993. Trade within Greater China grew from about 10 percent of total trade in East Asia to more than 35 percent in 1990, which exceeds that of all free trade arrangements outside the OECD area. In other words, even without a free trade arrangement (such as exists between the ASEAN nations) the Greater China region has already developed extremely strong intraregional trade flows.[84]

Two other key issues in the increasing economic integration of Greater China are economic reform on the mainland, which has allowed and encouraged foreign trade and overseas investment; and the pivotal role of Hong Kong, which serves not only to make connections between the former colony and the mainland but also as a go-between for trade and investment from Taiwan to the mainland. It is obvious that Hong Kong and China are highly significant to and for each other, and this became increasingly the case after the Joint Declaration, when the "China factor" became of increasing importance to the future of Hong Kong. From the other side of the fence, however, Hong Kong is also extremely important to China; in fact, the two have a symbiotic relationship. Because of the growth of trade between the two Hong Kong supplied a large chunk of China's imports and an even larger share of its exports, which means that Hong Kong is responsible for much of China's supply of foreign currency. With its nonconvertible currency, China has relied heavily on its earnings through the Hong Kong trade to pay for imports. This may help explain why China has always left Hong Kong alone, and promised to do so after 1997.

China also provides commodities that are essential to Hong Kong, including water (which means China, if necessary, could take Hong Kong simply by closing the pipeline). China provided 64 percent of Hong Kong's water, as well as a major share of its food, particularly fruit, vegetables, meat, seafood, dairy products, and rice. China is also the source of much of Hong Kong's imports of industrial and agricultural inputs, including unprocessed materials such as textile fibers, yarns and fabrics, heavy building materials, metals, coal, and chemicals.

Hong Kong also has the business skills essential to mainland China's modernization. Its well-developed offshore banking industry and stock market are the best place to raise money

TABLE 17.5   Intra- and Interregional Trade as a Percentage of Total World Trade

Trade Between	1970	1980	1989	1993
China and Taiwan	NA	NA	0.03	—
China and Hong Kong	0.08	0.12	0.52	—
Hong Kong and Taiwan	0.03	0.05	0.12	—
China and the Rest of the World	NA	1.14	1.27	2.5–2.6
Hong Kong and the World	0.72	0.76	1.06	3.67
Taiwan and the World	0.47	0.99	1.83	2.16
Greater China and the Rest of the World	1.19	1.75	4.17	8.43

SOURCES: 1970, 1980, and 1990 data adapted from Jones, King, and Klein (1992), Figs. 2a, 2b, 2c (pp. 33–35). 1993 data from *World Development Report* (1995), Table 13, pp. 186–187. Lower estimates for China trade with rest of world, from Lardy (1994), p. 2.

NOTE: Hong Kong trade figures for 1993 based on statistics from *World Development Report* (1995). Total trade value = $273,906 (U.S. millions) and total world trade = $7,480,192 (U.S. millions). The discrepancy/difference with 1989 statistics may be because the earlier statistics do not include re-exports from Hong Kong.

through syndicated loans and securities. Chinese exporters also rely on Hong Kong for repackaging, advertising, and marketing their products—without which Chinese goods would not be able to compete nearly as well in world markets. The pivotal role of Hong Kong involves four major components, with Hong Kong acting as financier, trading partner, middleman, and facilitator (see Table 17.6). "The Chinese giant reaches out to the world on the back of the Hong Kong midget, and the Chinese leadership value Hong Kong so much that they have promised, in a formal agreement with Britain, that they will preserve the capitalist system in Hong Kong for fifty years after 1997."[85]

The emergence of Greater China as a de facto economic region will have consequences for the Pacific Rim and the rest of the world. By the early 1990s, some estimates placed total GDP for the Greater China region as high as US$2.9 trillion, 13–15 percent of world GDP.[86] In 1997 China and Hong Kong switched from being de

facto to de jure partners. In addition to combining the joint wealth of the two Chinese territories, the reunification with Hong Kong will gradually erode any existing barriers to the cross-fertilization of investment and initiative. China harbors plans to reunify Taiwan, of course, which would add significant wealth and technological know-how to the regional alliance. At the end of the 1990s the prospects for reunification did not look promising in spite of the cross-Strait talks between Koo Chen-Fu and Wang Daohan in late 1998.[87]

What was taking place even before 1997 has been described as a "reverse takeover,"[88] and as 1997 drew closer Hong Kong looked more likely to change China than the other way around. The relationship between Hong Kong and China appears to some to have been made, if not mandated, in heaven, in the sense that Hong Kong can be seen as China's window on the world. "By the year 2000," said one investor, "I can see clearly that Hong Kong will be like

TABLE 17.6   Hong Kong's Role in China's Modernization–Open Door Policy

Major Role	Components	Subcomponents
Financier	Direct investment Indirect investment Loan syndication	
Trading Partner	Commodity trade Services trade	
Middleman	Commodity trade	Entrepôt trade Transshipment Brokerage in direct trade
	Services trade	Tourism Loan syndication Business consultancy Financial services
Facilitator	Contact point Conduit of information and technology Training ground	Marketing Advertising Production Presentation Public relations

SOURCE: Adapted from Sung (1991), Table 2.1, p. 17.

Tokyo, the business headquarters and financial center of China; while Guangdong, Fujian and the other coastal provinces will be the workshop."[89]

Conclusion

Throughout the reform era problems with the economy have tended to recur on a regular basis: spiraling inflation rates; the threat of massive rural unemployment; double-digit industrial growth rates; a credit explosion; and a boom in investment. Some Western academics are optimistic about the future, suggesting that the reforms will continue to create some winners and some losers, but in the long run things will come out right for China.[90] The problem with this argument is that the growing pie of economic wealth generated by reform is not being split equitably among the losers, and no significant attempts are being made to defuse political tensions. The high hopes of the late 1980s were dashed by the events of 1989, leaving only dyed-in-the-wool optimists confident that the CCP could successfully regain legitimacy.

As we review the many achievements of economic reform since Mao's death, we would do well to recall Simon Leys's evaluation during the Cultural Revolution in the early 1970s. As Leys said then, "We must acknowledge the considerable material improvements in many areas of Chinese life since 1948." This is still the case at the end of the 1990s, and few would argue with the proposition that overall the Chinese people are better off in the year 2000 than they were in 1949 and 1978. In the political realm, however, change has been much slower. In the 1970s Leys concluded that "it is a fantastic imposture to present the regime as socialist and revolutionary when in fact it is essentially totalitarian and feudal-bureaucratic."[91] After two decades of embracing capitalism there are now visible changes in the relationship between the people and the state, and although it would be foolish to attempt to predict the future, a return to the far left now seems extremely remote.

In spite of the rising wealth in the countryside and the cities, access to that wealth is uneven. A woman living in a remote rural area, for example, will not be able to live a healthy and fulfilling life if she has no access to education or health care. If she does not have decent food and housing, because of discrimination at the household or community level, she is unlikely to be receiving her "entitlements" and she will be unable to live up to her "capabilities," to use economist Amartya Sen's terms.[92] Similarly, a peasant living in one of China's big cities as a member of the new floating populations may be able to earn an income, but without an urban registration card he or she has virtually no access to the city's public supply of housing, education, and health care.

Even the casual observer can witness a new level of economic desperation in China. In the booming cities panhandlers work the streets, and the homeless are camping outside bus and rail stations. These are sights that haunt the old-timers in the Communist Party, reminiscent of the bad days before the revolution. In the countryside millions of peasants remain caught in the trap of poverty; with the loosening of migration restrictions, many are now showing up in cities in search of jobs, housing, and food. There are reports that women are being shut out of the workplace, both in the cities and the countryside, and that their value as contributors to the rural household economy is coming under assault. The newly emerging middle classes who had stood to gain so much from the reforms now face the prospect of being left behind in the full-throttle drive toward prosperity from export-oriented industrialization. The state has played a major role in setting these trends in motion, and although it is now attempting to extricate itself as much as possible, the distributional impacts of the economic reforms require a continued state presence.

Yet there is an obvious vitality to the Chinese economy, particularly in comparison to other societies making the transition out of socialism. Some Western and Chinese observers have, in fact, argued that rising inequality is a normal part of the development process, even a stimu-

lus to more rapid economic growth. That sentiment was expressed best by Deng Xiaoping,
when he said that "some people will have to get
rich first" in the drive to modernization. Still,
inequalities are increasing unreasonably, and
reaching a level far above what Deng had in
mind when he made that now-famous statement. With the emergence of new super-rich
capitalists, the gap between the richest and the
poorest sectors has widened; those in the middle
are also being hit hard, and in both the cities and
the countryside they are rapidly being left
behind.

Even some leaders are convinced that the
new economic distress is reaching a crisis
point.[93] Premier Jiang Zemin, for example, publicly talked about the "new and unfairly wide
gaps in the social distribution"; he suggested
that if left unattended they might lead "to
widespread concern in society and strong dissatisfaction among the laboring people."[94]
Jiang's fears have already become a reality, with
reports of numerous peasant disturbances in
the early 1990s. Some reports reinforce the
belief that the traditional social order is breaking down in many parts of the countryside.
There are potentially many causes for this,
including a resentment about the spread of
crime and corruption, as well as an awareness
among peasants that their incomes and pur-

chasing power are declining in both absolute
and relative terms.

A similar level of resentment is smoldering in
the cities, with reports of riots and strikes in
industrial enterprises. Such disturbances can be
interpreted as evidence that class polarization in
China has been elevated to dangerous levels by
economic reform. Pessimists are drawing analogies with the corruption, colonialism, and warlordism of the Nationalist era. As one reporter
noted, "After fifteen plus years of reform . . .
China is again at the brink, facing a fundamental choice as to which path [to] take."[95] As growth
zones along the golden coastline reach out to the
global economy, many people have "jumped
into the sea"—taking the capitalist road to
riches. Many have succeeded; but poverty
remains a real threat to millions of peasants in
the vast interior, as well as in the more remote
parts of prosperous provinces. From a policy
perspective the rising inequality represents a
threat to the social order in China that can no
longer be ignored. China has been successful in
its attempts to launch itself into the global economy, but the price has been high. There are now
signs of division and discontent that could create another Tiananmen Square. The difference
this time is that alienation in the countryside
could add the power of the rural masses—and
we saw what they accomplished in 1949.

18
State-Society Relationships in the Post-Utopian Age

☙❧☙❧☙❧☙❧☙❧☙❧☙❧☙❧☙❧☙❧☙❧☙❧

The ideological debate in the post-Tiananmen phase has been muted somewhat by the partial silencing . . . and exile of the most strident . . . voices for radical reform. However, apprehensions regarding an ideological vacuum and the search for . . . some sort of coherent framework for beliefs and values to unify and guide the society and state through a crucial phase of transition continue with the same urgency.

—Kalpana Misra, *From Post-Maoism to Post-Marxism* (1998)[1]

Introduction: Jiang Zemin Solidifies His Position

In the . . . two years [before his death] the abiding presence of Deng had seemed to lend a sort of imprimatur to [Jiang's] efforts. To have attacked corruption in the Beijing municipality, lobbed missiles at Taiwan, or articulated a range of new theories after Deng's death would have been seen as a brazen attempt to fiddle with the patriarch's legacy and heartlessly take advantage of his departure. With the old man still around, Jiang's claim to be merely marching the next step down the Dengist path was more credible. It was no wonder that he had said back in 1989 that the "health and longevity of Comrade Xiaoping are of great significance to the smooth development of the work of the party and state."

—Bruce Gilley, *Tiger on the Brink: Jiang Zemin and China's New Elite* (1998)[2]

Although no giant steps have yet to be taken toward democracy in China, some small but important political reforms were introduced during Deng Xiaoping's stewardship. Some have been reinforced by Jiang Zemin as part of his efforts to consolidate his leadership position.[3] Jiang has been especially concerned with strengthening specific institutions and reducing the infighting within the leadership that char-

acterized the Maoist and Dengist eras. In the early 1990s, long before Deng's death, Jiang embarked on three strategic missions:

- to strengthen his support from the armed forces, especially the People's Liberation Army, which he did by replacing many long-serving officers with his own appointees and by allowing the PLA to expand its nondefense-related commercial activities;[4]
- to appoint his key political associates to leadership positions in the central Party apparatus, including the promotion of the Shanghai party secretary, Huang Ju, which brought to four the number of former Shanghai leaders on the Politburo (including himself, Zhu Rongji, and We Bangguo); and
- to launch a series of high-profile campaigns to tackle official corruption and profiteering, a strategy that was likely to garner some support, even if little was achieved.[5]

Jiang was determined to be seen as a man with a plan, unlike Hua Guofeng, Mao's successor, who was always accused of sticking too closely to the old Maoist line. It is reasonable, in

433

fact, to suggest that Jiang wanted to put some distance between himself and Deng (who was actually still alive but no longer mentally competent). Jiang was trying to demonstrate his independence and courage, which, as Richard Baum sarcastically observed, was quite an achievement for a man "with a reputation as a weak and windblown sycophant."[6] He was also setting himself up as a man of the people, publicly attacking crime and corruption—nonpartisan activities that everyone could support.

There were murmurings, even evidence, of another Beijing Spring in 1995, and the backstage gossip began to focus on a possible reversal of the 1989 Tiananmen verdict that the Party-state was justified in its actions. After a six-year silence, intellectuals and dissidents began to make their voices heard again through petitions, both on the verdict itself and to request the release of still-jailed Tiananmen leaders. There were also proposals for multicandidate elections for cabinet-level positions; some interesting votes were taken in the National People's Congress (for example, 30 percent of the delegates voted against Jiang's candidate for vice-premier, Jiang Chunyun; 33 percent voted against Zhu Rongji's proposal for a semi-independent central bank). This confirmed a growing split within the leadership, between a "rule by law" clique and an older, more conservative group referred to as a "rule by core" group, which included Jiang Zemin, Li Peng, and Zhu Rongji. In late May 1995, however, close to the anniversary of the Tiananmen, the bubble of expectation was burst with a new round of detainments and arrests of dissidents, effectively shutting down any debate on political reform and reversing the verdicts. The rule-by-core group appeared to have gained the upper hand, and they appear to still be in control at the end of the 1990s.[7]

In fall 1995 Jiang made a speech at the Fifth Plenary Session of the Fourteenth Central Committee, calling for a combination of development and modernization—with stability as a major goal—and promising an enhanced role for the state. As one scholar has noted, the speech "was intended to present Jiang as a thoughtful leader, cognizant of the difficulties

facing China and reasonable in his approach to problems. . . . It was . . . an agenda-setting speech intended to lay the foundation for Jiang Zemin's leadership."[8] There had been a marked change in Party leadership, with the old left-versus-right alignments no longer dominant. Deng Xiaoping and Chen Yun, the venerated leaders of the two cliques, were now out of the picture and had been replaced by new faces.[9] The newcomers ruled a China that was rapidly becoming "more complex and less statist," with the emergence of a new entrepreneurial class and an increasing association among entrepreneurs, the new bourgeoisie, and the state—a new form of corporatism.[10] As for the intellectuals, the virtual abandonment of ideology in favor of an all-out drive for wealth banished them even farther outside the state's orbit:

> The commercialization of Chinese society . . . and the bureaucratization of the Chinese state . . . have left Chinese intellectuals far less able to play their traditional role of social conscience. To the dismay of some, Chinese intellectuals are themselves jumping into the sea of commerce, taking up . . . jobs as outfitters for popular literature and soap operas.[11]

It appears that many Chinese were pleased to see the demise of the old guard, the poorly educated revolutionaries; but their replacements—skilled technocrats and well-educated bureaucrats—were a colorless bunch with no apparent ideology (see Tables 18.1a and 18.1b).

The new leaders, including Jiang himself, were destined to confront the negative by-products of the reforms, as well as their own lack of revolutionary legitimacy. Many conflicts remain unresolved, including the tense relationships between the center and the localities; increasing peasant rebelliousness; and a range of potentially dangerous social problems associated with the floating populations. The pseudonymous author of the popular book *Viewing China Through a Third Eye* characterized China as a country lurching dangerously out of control, the result of what has been described as "the adverse destabilizing conse-

TABLE 18.1a Profile of the CCP Central Committee

Year	1982	1987	1992	1997
Average Age	59.1	55.2	56.3	55.9
College Educated (%)	55.4	73.3	83.7	92.4

SOURCE: Pei (1998), p. 71.

TABLE 18.1b Profile of Provincial Leaders

Year	1982	1983	1988	1996
Average Age	62.0	55.0	53.0	55.0
College Educated (%)	20.0	43.0	62.0	79.0

SOURCE: Pei (1998), p. 71.

quences of unbridled reform, the loss of central ideological and political control, and the alarming decline of public morality."[12] In this chapter we investigate some of the political dimensions of the reform era, focusing on changes that have been introduced, then consider some of the choices that are in store for China's new leaders. We begin by looking at changes in the way class and class conflict have been de-emphasized and the fluid nature of state-society relationships.

Class, Class Conflict, and Socialism in Post-Mao China

In the Maoist era much was made of the notion of egalitarianism, but it was primarily an economic concept; in the political realm egalitarianism was rarely in evidence. There was instead a system of permanent discrimination based on the production of class labels; the worst fate of all was to be assigned a "bad" class label. Once such a label was pinned upon a person or family, they (especially the children) became outcasts, subject to violence in times of mass campaigns, denied career and educational opportunities, and denied the right to equal treatment in the courts.[13] Mao frequently referred to the need to unite 95 percent of the population to struggle against the other 5 percent at any given time, suggesting there may have been more than 50 million people being

"struggled against" at the height of a campaign (see Photo 18.1).

In the reform era class labels have been removed for most designated "class enemies," and the legal system no longer recognizes class as a consideration in determining guilt and in sentencing. The major exception is the counter-revolutionary label: The state has power to incarcerate people who cause, or are accused of causing, political disturbances. The demise of class labeling meant that talent and performance could once again rise above class background and considerations of parentage to become the basis of a reward system in the new China. Political scientist Marc Blecher described the Maoist use of class labeling in terms of the ideas about hegemony associated with Italian Marxist thinker Antonio Gramsci. A social group or a particular class has hegemony over others when it has succeeded in persuading them to accept its political and cultural beliefs. Hegemony, in other words, involves the rules that run society, and in post-1949 China attention was paid not so much to *what* people thought as to the *way* they thought. The Chinese Communist Party undertook a project of counterhegemony, in which it attempted to transform and re-create China's political culture.[14] In the Maoist era this was achieved by the Party's manipulation of the concept of class, which had not been used either as a term or in reality in pre-1949 China.[15]

PHOTO 18.1   Mao Zedong salutes the nation.

In political movements and during the many campaigns such labels became the basis of conflict, which was, at heart, a struggle to punish and, if possible, eliminate the bad classes. In addition, class was at the core of the economic struggle, as socialism was defined as the form of social organization most favorable to the peasants and workers. In reality, the CCP, as the sole party in power, represented these classes and acted on their behalf; this explains why other classes (for example, capitalists) are not permitted and why no other autonomous political associations and interest groups are allowed to exist. In this way the CCP guarantees its monopoly of power and ensures that its power will be reproduced, as it is unopposed and unchallenged—all in the interests of preserving socialism. In Gramscian terms, the CCP was conducting a counterhegemonic strategy, in which all of Chinese society was seen through the lens of class, with all political conflict interpreted in class terms. Cultural hegemony is achieved when all members of the society interpret politics and societal activities in terms of the specific definitions of class as dictated by the ruling party.

During the Cultural Revolution, Maoists altered the theory by interpreting bureaucratic state socialism (what the CCP had become) as a new source of class conflict. The bureaucracy was now seen as a class, and some individuals within that class needed to be struggled against and, if necessary, expelled. Such was particularly the case for Party persons in authority taking the "capitalist road," which at that time meant people like Liu Shaoqi and Deng Xiaoping, who opposed the policies of the ruling faction under Mao Zedong. The problem was that such definitions of class, as opposed to materially based labels like "landlord" and "peasant," were vague and subjective. In reality it was easy for the Red Guards—Mao's "little soldiers"—to examine an individual's dossier and reach the conclusion that he or she should be defined as a new class adversary, or an enemy of the people.

After Mao's death, formal class categories were abolished, and the Party more or less stopped talking about class altogether. By abolishing the notions of class and class conflict, the reformers effectively removed the core of Maoist socialism but replaced the class system with "nothing less than a new hegemonic project."[16] The central problem for China was to be redefined: No longer was there any need to perpetuate class struggle; now it was the need to eradicate poverty and push rapidly toward modernization. Blecher argues, however, that only the definition and content of the hegemonic project have changed: There is now a new ideological tenet at the core of Party politics, and it is being used in much the same way as the Maoists had used the concept of class (in other words, to justify monopolistic CCP rule and restructure the economy). Socialism has been retained as a formal goal, but with a new core definition: It was now seen as something for which, or for the achievement of which, economic modernization was a necessary precondition. The CCP is still in power for two reasons: There is still a need to make sure that capitalist devices (such as markets and material incentives) do not themselves become hegemonic; and it is still necessary to keep the goal of socialism clearly in view as the modernization project moves forward.[17]

After the chaos of the Cultural Revolution, and realizing the level of poverty to which the Chinese people had almost become accustomed, the post-Mao leadership was faced with some agonizing choices. How can a poor country solve its poverty problem yet still retain its socialism? Should it give up entirely on such an effort, deciding instead to "become just one more playground for the powers of international capitalism," as Robert Weil has suggested?[18] To outsiders it surely looks as though China opted for the latter route and has become a true believer in the notion of "capitalist triumphalism." Oddly, China's leaders are convinced, and have tried to convince anyone who would listen, that the route China has followed since 1978 has not been capitalist. As we shall see, that required redefining key terms and issues, a process that one scholar has referred to as "linguistic copulation."[19]

Deng Xiaoping argued that capitalist icons—like markets and stock exchanges and even such get-rich-quick havens like Hong Kong and Macao—could be considered socialist. As he pointed out, "socialism has markets, too. Plans and markets are simply economic stepping stones ... to universal prosperity and richness."[20] Using such extraordinary fancy footwork Deng was able to suggest that even expanding regional inequality could be tolerated, because eventually the richer regions would help to pull along the backward regions by the process of trickle-down.

At the end of his tour of the south in 1992, Deng came up with what would later be referred to as his "brilliant thesis," which involved shifting China from a "socialist planned commodity economy" to a "socialist market economy" (see Photo 18.2).[21] This shift was officially proclaimed in a published statement adopted at the Third Plenary Session of the Fourteenth Central Committee of the CCP in November 1993.[22] In that statement, the following was set forth:

FIGURE 18.2   Deng Xiaoping salutes the nation; a Guangzhou billboard.

The socialist market economy structure is linked with the basic system of socialism. The establishment of this structure aims at enabling the market to play the fundamental role in resource allocations under macro-economic control by the state. To turn this goal into reality, it is necessary to uphold the principle of taking the publicly owned sector as the mainstay, while striving for a simultaneous development of all economic sectors.[23]

This shift in terminology legitimated the abolition of traditional mechanisms of central planning in favor of the introduction of state macroeconomically regulated market competition. Without direct central state planning, the socialist component of the socialist market economy was now limited almost exclusively to the public ownership of productive property (land, labor, capital, and infrastructure). That was to be the predominant form of ownership for the foreseeable future.

Through the second half of the 1990s there was extensive debate about state-owned enterprises. Some of the leaders—for example, economics czar Zhu Rongji—tried to just push SOEs into the market; others, including Jiang Zemin, preferred to shore up the inept SOEs beforehand. As Premier Li Peng said in 1994, "Without solid state-owned enterprises, there will be no socialist China." As a result reforms were introduced in 1995 and would continue for several years with pilot projects intended to establish a new corporate structure in the SOEs.[24]

It should be clear, of course, that the new definition of "socialist" required some sleight of hand (i.e., linguistic copulation), because to claim that most of the productive property was publicly owned flew in the face of reality by the mid-1990s. By that time the private and collective sectors of the economy, which had been growing far faster than the state sector for more than a decade, were coming close to parity in terms of ownership. It is apparent that to make this statement the leaders had lumped together the collective sector (which by 1992 accounted for about 33 percent and, by 1998, about 40 percent of the country's total industrial output) *and* the traditional state sector, to create a new fictitious category of "public ownership."[25] In fact, most of the collective sector, defined by the state as "public," consisted of the booming township and village enterprises, which operated as semiprivate firms set up by local communities and governments, usually run by local entrepreneurs almost entirely along market lines.[26]

The notion of the primary stage of socialism was laid out in detail by Zhao Ziyang as early as 1987. As Zhao noted, the major contradiction at that time was no longer class and class struggle but China's relative economic backwardness and the need for material improvements in people's lives. Zhao suggested that China was in the primary stage of socialism in 1987 and "must . . . never deviate from it [and should not attempt to] jump over this stage."[27] It was suggested that the doubters—people who thought it was impossible to reach socialism by going through a phase of full-blown capitalism—were thinking too mechanistically, a common failing of the rightists. Yet to assume that China could simply jump over the primary stage of socialism—during a period of reform when productive forces were to be highly developed—was to take an overly utopian view of society, a common leftist mistake. In Zhao's words:

> Because our socialism has emerged from the womb of a semi-colonial, semi-feudal society, with the productive forces lagging far behind those of the developed capitalist countries, we are destined to go through a very long primary stage (of socialism). During this stage we shall accomplish industrialization and the commercialization, socialization and modernization of production, which many other countries have achieved under capitalism.[28]

Deng Xiaoping–style socialism could be maintained, but modernization, specifically the Four Modernizations, would be the vehicle for achieving socialism. In other words, socialism could be almost anything as long as it promoted the socialist economy. Both the plan and the market qualified, as both were simply economic methods rather than the quintessential delimiters of socialism and capitalism.

A disbelieving Hong Kong press jumped all over this new example of dogma, referring to it as the "new cat thesis."[29] More importantly, critics within the top leadership dismissed it as simplistic theorizing the notion that anything that improves the economy is automatically socialism.[30] Song Ping, for example, criticized Zhao and Deng in 1988, effectively questioning Deng's notion that the "color of the cat" is irrelevant. Song was suggesting that such ideas were "absurd theories" that were the result of "bourgeois liberalization" associated with China's entry into the global economy and too much proximity to the decadent ideas of the West.[31] In response to outsiders' observations that China had turned to capitalism, Deng and others were vigorous in their denials, stating that it was their intent to create "socialism with Chinese characteristics," which was never properly defined but was always complemented by referring to the so-called Four Principles: accepting the leadership of the CCP; adhering to Marxism–Leninism–Mao Zedong thought; practicing democratic socialism; and following the socialist road.[32]

By 1992 Deng Xiaoping, in public pronouncements, had abandoned the earlier habit of asking whether China was practicing socialism or capitalism, one of the key themes of his conservative critics. From that time forward no mention was made of whether a policy was socialist or capitalist: It was simply stated that the reforms and the open policy were examples of China's firmly adhering to "the socialist course and uphold[ing] the dominant role of public ownership."[33] In future debates Deng declared that instead of defining socialism it was necessary only to ask if a particular policy could help to produce one of the following: Was it advantageous to the development of the socialist productive forces? Did it enhance the overall strength of the socialist state? And did it help improve the people's living standards?[34]

The Individual, the Party, and the State in China's Transitional Phase

Historical studies suggest that the state has always dominated the individual in China. That was certainly the case in Confucian China, and it has been true of the post-1949 period—so much so that it makes little sense to speak of state-society relations in contemporary China. Apart from their government, the Chinese have had no established institutions with what Lucien Pye would call "authoritative reach." As Pye suggested, "It was always an imperial or a national government confronting local communities, fragmented interests, parochial private groupings, or semi-illegal societies."[35] Chinese culture is generally considered to have always been group-oriented and essentially hostile to the individual and individualism; in fact the individual has been seen as merely a disciplined member of a larger group. At the core of Chinese ethics and morality is the ideal of rejecting self-interest in favor of glorifying self-sacrifice for the collectivity.

After 1949 the CCP essentially redefined the status of the individual, beginning with a direct attack on the family system and asking for greater loyalty to the collective (the urban *danwei* or the rural brigade) than to the family. The goal was to control not only the individual physically but also their thoughts and thought processes. As we saw earlier, this was achieved by establishing a sort of caste system of class labels and by requiring a household registration book with the "five red types" of class labels (those destined for social mobility), the "five black categories" (those who were not), and the "bad elements" (who had no future at all). Dossiers were kept on all individuals and updated with any new "evidence" that was collected or concocted. At the bottom of the heap, and in most urgent need of being reformed,

were the intellectuals, who were known as the "stinking ninth category."

In the contemporary era there are signs that all this is changing. In the past, whenever the state was weakening, the people would usually look to other primary groups for support and sustenance—including the family, the clan, the guilds, and secret societies—so there was still no advance in individual autonomy. Today, as we shall explore below, China's leaders are clearly encountering a crisis of "governability," and the Party-state has lost much of its legitimacy. Just as this is happening, however, China is experiencing a loosening of institutional subgroups and a strong search for individual freedom and autonomy.[36] As Pye explained, Chinese culture demands conformity, humility, and selflessness, so it is difficult for individuals who want to assert their independence to find a suitable outlet. Individuals may want to receive emotional support from their different groups—the sort of team spirit common in Western societies—but in China that can rarely be achieved.[37] Pye insists that Chinese people become inured to the fact that intimacy is not attainable and, consequently, are rarely able to "let go" in public. Yet during the 1990s, even though Chinese culture systematically denies the legitimacy of individualism, under the sorts of social changes and cultural constraints currently being experienced, there were some strong urges for individuals to assert their autonomy. As new outlets emerge for this purpose (both legal and illegal) there are usually many people willing to explore such possibilities.[38]

As we have seen elsewhere, there have been consistent zigzags in policy, both in the long term (e.g., the Great Leap Forward and the Cultural Revolution) and in the short term (e.g., the *fang-shou* cycles). The cumulative effect, in addition to public weariness, has been the gradual erosion of the state's moral authority. This came to a head during the Tiananmen Square tragedy, when it became obvious that the state had little more than coercive powers to exercise social control over the people. The state is no longer capable of terrorizing its people the way it once did, so we are now witnessing a dual process of what Pye called "ritual behavior."[39] The state's actions have become less formalistic and less substantial while the people's responses to authority have become increasingly cynical. There is a thin veneer of acceptance, with private reservations and more than a hint of anger close beneath the surface.

The state is now "paralyzed," according to Pye, somewhere between its Confucian and Leninist traditions: It would like to think it can uphold moral order and that its ranks are filled with morally upstanding cadres; but the people, who know this to be untrue, think of the state as corrupt and illegitimate. The disease of cynicism is spreading, and the state has (according to Pye, at least) all but lost its ability to control and mobilize the people. He even suggests that when the state issues orders it no longer checks to see if anyone complies. The state, in other words, is simply going through the motions, carrying out a ritual rather than governing. What is implied here is a halfhearted and weaker state—similar in some ways to the highly ritualized Confucian state during the Ming Dynasty—compared to the state in the Maoist era.[40] The state is effectively at a standstill, paralyzed, ignored by the people. Pye uses the analogy of the traffic light to illustrate what he means: "When the red light is on, they . . . [the people] . . . make a detour and proceed the same way they were going; when the yellow light is on, they ignore it and keep going at the same speed; and when the green light is on, they rush straight ahead at full throttle."[41]

Pye insists that contemporary Chinese have learned the art of "feigned compliance" to the state, appearing to accept its authority but going their own way regardless. This has been strengthened by the open-door nature of reforms, meaning that many Chinese have come into contact with foreigners and their ways. The foreign influences, especially from Hong Kong and Taiwan, are quickly taken aboard, and the appearance of compliance is tempered by a willingness to stand out as an individual. This apparent split between public and private actions is accentuated by the blatant corruption evident at all levels of government, which effectively forces the people to cheat and lie, as if that were the natural thing to do.[42] In contemporary China many people are shaping who they are (or who they want to be) less in accordance with their primary group—the *danwei*, or the brigade—and more with their broader stratum of society. They are now much more likely to identify themselves as workers, or students, or migrants, or intellectuals, or women—or a combination of these—rather than as part of a rural brigade or urban *danwei*.[43] We have already seen one result: a veritable blossoming of artistic and literary creativity (although primarily in the realm of popular culture).

Another trend has been the proliferation of voluntary and independent associations. The growth of such groups can be interpreted as the early sprouts of civil society, which Chinese people might eventually be able to use to counterbalance state power and to make effective demands for change. In theory, at least, this should not be seen as a challenge to the state because it represents "a strengthening of both the autonomy of individuals and the authority of the state."[44] In other words, by allowing such groups to function the state would be, and would be perceived as, responsive to the needs and preferences of society, not just a tool of the ruling elite.

At present this is happening in fits and starts, and many Chinese remain ambivalent about where such developments might take them. On the one hand they crave freedom, but on the other they have a deep-seated need for security and dependency, producing a basic conflict between conformity and self-assertion. If the demands for autonomy turn extreme, the more likely it is that the state will repress them, given its fundamental distrust of individualism and the fear of events in the former Yugoslavia and in parts of the former Soviet empire throughout the 1990s. The Chinese are obsessed with the need for stability and the fear of chaos, and the state has, for the time being at least, decided to hitch its wagon to the star of economic progress, not political liberalization.

As many of the old controls erode or vanish, Chinese society has become much more fluid.[45] Urban workers have left their jobs in the public sector to go into business; peasants have left the land to work in industry, on construction sites, and in services; officials and professionals have left their jobs to plunge into the sea of business; and people from poor regions have been moving, voluntarily and involuntarily, to richer regions. As a result, new forms of association have sprouted, rather like mushrooms in the early morning. Many of these represent the interests and aspirations of evolving social forces seeking greater autonomy and influence over the Party-state.[46] The state has added momentum to this process by introducing some new and newly empowered institutions of government intended to adjust to societal changes. In other words, change is occurring under both societal and state-initiated forces.

In China's transitional period there has been a fundamental shift between state and society that has not come about through democratic politics—as was the case in Eastern and Central Europe—but through the growth of economic freedom, made possible by reform. In this sense the reform era can be seen as a societal revolution as well as an economic revolution, in that there has been a marked erosion, limitation, and decentralization of the state and its power.[47] This has been, in Minxin Pei's words, a process in which "societal revolutionaries" have set out to extricate the power and influence of the state from society and to entrust society with the task of remaking itself. In China, the majority of this activity has not been undertaken by a particular group or social class but by the members of many groups—the intelligentsia, students, peasants, entrepreneurs, and minorities—those members of society who have long been dominated by the state and have little else in common with each other.

Some China scholars argue against making too much of this argument. For example, Brantly McCormick has noted that despite tremendous economic growth the only real evidence of political change is the steady erosion of the old political order, not the rise of any new form of organizational framework.[48] Deng Xiaoping and especially Jiang Zemin worked hard to staff the Party with younger, more technically competent leaders, and they both called for increasing separation between the Party and government bureaucracies. Yet both consistently supported the principle of exclusive Party leadership. Thus despite the decentralization and radical restructuring of economic organization, the various attempts to revitalize the legal system, the emergence of new parliamentary organizations, and the declining reach of the state, the fact remains that all key decisions are still made by a small group of leaders in Beijing.

Marc Blecher would point out a fundamental difference in state-society relations in the Dengist-Jiangist era compared to the Maoist era.[49] In Mao's time the state certainly controlled most aspects of social life through coercive power and surveillance. The state did not demand mere obedience from the people—it insisted that they actively believe, not just consent—and in that sense Maoism opposed the state being too autonomous from society. Unfortunately for the Maoist state—with the exception of a few years in the 1960s and 1970s—the people often did not share the same enthusiasm for the state's utopian vision.[50] In the Dengist and Jiangist eras the state has attempted to extricate itself from such a tightly enmeshed relationship with society, effectively depoliticizing social and economic life and becoming increasingly indifferent to what the people do—as long as they do not challenge the status quo.[51]

In truth the state no longer cares much about ideology, or class, or class struggle; it has given up trying to run the economy or people's lives; and it permits far more cultural and social variety than in the recent past. All these trends have been reinforced by the material benefits of the new market economy because, as Blecher has suggested, "marketization and privatization force people to be intensely preoccupied with procuring and advancing their material lives."[52] In general Chinese people now see state officials much less often and from a much farther distance than they did during the Maoist period.

Formerly virtual prisoners in their work units and production brigades, Chinese people now enjoy a markedly different life. Lieberthal has described the major components of such new lives in terms of three sets of changes in state-society relationships:[53]

- the resurgence and reappearance of non-state sources of moral authority and spiritual well-being (in the absence of moral stewardship by the state, and the almost ubiquitous adoption of get-rich-quick values throughout society), including religious activity, with Buddhism and Daoism flourishing and Christian churches springing up in many places;
- the emergence of new, emotionally charged, quasi-religious activities, such as *qigong* exercises (including the cultlike activities of such groups as Falun Gong);[54] and
- a proliferation of a variety of groups, including professional organizations, sports clubs, and charitable organizations, most of which are local, small, and must be registered with the government—in fact many are disbanded quickly if the state is suspicious of their activities.

In addition, there are millions of individuals who are now effectively able to skirt state authority to pursue their own agendas, including the floating populations, although at present they appear to be politically quiescent—more concerned with earning a living than trying to change the political system.[55] There is more "space" in the semireformed political and economic environment of contemporary China, which means that there is now (in relative terms) plenty of room for individuals and associations to "breathe" and realize some of their ambitions—all of which represents a decline in the authority of the center vis-à-vis the periphery. This is perhaps what Minxin Pei meant when he spoke about a new social contract "whose essence is the redefinition of the scope of the state's power and of citizens' freedom. Although never explicit articulated, the new so-cial contract abolished most curbs on the personal and economic freedom of ordinary citizens in exchange for their tacit acceptance of the CCP's authority."[56]

Evaluating Chinese Politics in the Reform Era

Chinese society prior to 1978 was similar to any less developed country in the Third World: overwhelmingly rural, with most people involved in manual labor, and a geographically stratified (urban-rural) society. The society was homogenous, with little opportunity for advancement in social and spatial mobility. It was a vertical society, in which each individual was incorporated into a hierarchically organized system rather than being a member of a social institution organized horizontally by members. This was the centralized bureaucratic system organized on the branch principle (e.g., in the work units). Such verticality tended to produce individuals who were virtually imprisoned within their own systems and units, and were highly segregated from other systems and units. Verticality was reinforced by the official prohibition of spatial mobility; most of the power relationships in such a system worked from the top downward. At the ground level, as we have seen in Chapter 3, power is maintained and ties between people are determined primarily by networks of personal relationships (*guanxi*).

The economic reforms began within this cultural environment of verticality and immobility, and it is hardly surprising that they have had some major impacts. The reforms were specifically intended to foster economic diversification, for example, in the types of ownership and the dominant economic activities. They encouraged increasing inequality; they rewarded hard work; they encouraged greater occupational, sectoral, and geographical mobility; and, perhaps most important, they called forth increasingly horizontal relationships between economic actors operating in market contexts.

In general terms the reforms have made Chinese society considerably more complex, with all types of new strata and classes emerging and interacting with each other in ever more complex relationships; vastly more diverse types of enterprise and ownership; and of course greater opportunities than ever before for personal advancement—which has created a lot of what the Chinese jokingly refer to as "red-eye disease" (social envy or jealousy). Capital and labor mobility have increased significantly and individuals have grouped together to form "economic associations" of numerous types. There have been all manner of joint ventures, often on an interregional basis, with rural enterprises and urban companies teaming up, using subcontracting to spread wealth out over an ever wider swath of territory. All of this new horizontal ("market") activity has been superimposed onto the old ("plan") arrangements of work units and villages—which are still in existence, but in a much weakened form.

As would be expected within such economic dynamism, the strata within society have fared differentially well throughout the reform era. At the bottom of the social ladder are the peasants and workers, now joined by a huge group of transients seeking jobs in small, medium, and large towns and cities all over China (and within this group the new wealthy rub shoulders with the miserably poor). New opportunities have arisen for entrepreneurs, whether they are former Party officials (so-called nomenklatura capitalists) or private entrepreneurs with foreign backing. Some members of the intelligentsia were willing to support reform in return for being left alone while others became a sort of counterelite, especially in their calls for free speech and democracy leading up to the tumultuous events of 1989.

Women have in theory had more economic opportunities than at any time in the past, and many have become entrepreneurs, sideline producers, and factory workers. There is still a general sentiment, however, that rural women have not done as well as they would have expected under the new system of contract farming (the HRS); and in the cities there is considerable evidence that women are increasingly being squeezed into "female" occupations—with lower pay, lower status, and fewer benefits—or out of the labor market altogether. Women are being discriminated against in hiring and firing and are now more likely to be asked or told to return home.

In sum, there are some groups that have benefited greatly from the reforms and others that have done much less well. Among the potentially threatened groups, such as state officials and state workers, many have managed to improve their situations; other groups have seen their interests ignored or jeopardized by marketization. These would include women; the elderly and the disabled; peasants in labor-poor households or in remote areas; and the unemployed and floating populations. Gordon White concluded that among such groups the level of discontent had escalated to alarming heights by the end of the 1980s, and by most accounts the same sources of discontent are present at the end of the 1990s:

> Fear of threats to status, power or income; disappointment because the reforms were delivering less than they had promised; disgruntlement arising from the "red-eye disease"; concerns that gains already achieved were in danger of erosion (through inflation and leadership mismanagement); contrarily, impatience at a deceleration of the reforms and anxiety at an acceleration.[57]

In political terms it is important to assess what has changed and what has stayed the same, as well as what still needs reforming. There is a new set of leaders who were less ideological and more progressive, and some new institutions, but much remains to be done to bring about the political part of the transition away from socialism. There is an urgent need to reappraise the role of the Party and to renegotiate relationships between central and local governments, with the new power of the latter being recognized and formalized. Also, some of the blossoming social groups need to be accommodated, to allow more social and political autonomy, by expanding civil liberties and giving them more access to the policy process.

Institutional "Decay" and the "Predatory" State

In the 1990s the Party-state has found itself mired in a process of institutional "decay," already in evidence in 1978 but becoming much worse in the reform years.[58] As White suggested, "The Party [is] more divided, less disciplined, more demoralized, less prestigious, more alienated from society and less capable of implementing its policies."[59] By most accounts the decay has traditionally been caused by dissent and conflict among the different leadership factions, particularly between the leftists, who wanted more power over society, and the rightists, who were more likely to be technocrats and professionals.[60] Individuals within the latter group—the reformers—saw themselves in a nonideological role, the managers and coordinators willing to an extent to share power with other groups and institutions. White likened the Party in this era to a halfway house in which new tenants have arrived but the old ones are refusing to leave. Similar to Mao Zedong's "struggle between two lines within the Party," there is now a "struggle between two Parties within the Party."[61] The record throughout the 1990s suggests that the leftists have been largely silenced and marginalized, with the rightists—the proponents of reform and moderation—well on the way toward consolidating their power.

Minxin Pei has focused on the declining capacity of the Party-state to govern China and the fact that dysfunctional political institutions and procedures have not been adequately offset and replaced by new institutions. Institutional decay manifests itself in various ways, including the loss of government authority and the rising incidence of sometimes violent antiregime activities. The major indicators of institutional decay, many of which have been witnessed throughout the 1990s, have included the declining effectiveness of the CCP and the government, indicated in many surveys conducted at all levels, showing that the people's evaluation of the Party has declined to an all-time low level;[62] the unprecedented commercialism and corruption within the vital organizations of the state, especially the military; and the large numbers of reported cases of official corruption, especially prevalent in law enforcement agencies.

Decay at these levels, Pei would suggest, makes it more and more difficult for the state to govern, partly because it produces a deteriorated level of performance or effectiveness in service delivery.[63] As he noted, "Whether a state can provide an adequate level of public goods is one of the most rudimentary measurements of a country's governability," and the obvious lack of that ability is easily recognizable in the currently high level of public discontent.[64] The decay of key political institutions also erodes the government's capacity to build and maintain social support and solve social problems through peaceful means. The consequence is that when problems do arise the state may find it has to resort to more coercive, invasive, more expensive methods of political repression.

Again we come across Deng Xiaoping's legacy, in which the long list of economic benefits attributed to reform is countered by his regime's major failing: an inability to construct durable political institutions that can safeguard its economic legacies.[65] As Pei notes, a crisis of governability stems from the decay of key political institutions and an erosion of the state's capacity to solve problems and meet the needs of its citizens. In the early 1990s a number of centrifugal tendencies were visibly eroding Beijing's authority and its ability to carry out the work of government. The center's share of total GDP had dropped drastically with increasing decentralization (only 12.2 percent of GDP in 1994). There was widespread rural discontent, rising crime, and a growing fear among the population that the Party-state was losing control and that chaos and social disorder were imminent.

Institutional decay is also apparent when the ruling elite abuses its power (backed by the state's coercive powers) to such an extent that the state is visibly "preying" on society to extract resources for personal gain rather than for the nation's benefit. In this sense China is becoming a "predatory" state as state corruption and predation reach alarming heights.[66] One measure of state predation is evidence that even as state revenues decline as a percentage of GDP the size of the bureaucracy has grown.[67] The contradiction is that even though the state is collecting and generating much less revenue than before, many state functions are still growing, and these trends provide clear indicators of increasing state predation (see Table 18.2).[68] It is evident that as the state's administrative expenditures (as a percentage of the total) have increased, investment in other important areas has been declining, for example, in agricultural infrastructure, social service provision, and research and development activities.

State predation in the cities and the countryside is one of the major sources of public corruption and has fueled enormous popular dissent, especially as most of the extrabudgetary revenue goes toward government employee benefits, bonuses, administrative expenses, as well as banquets and expensive hotels for meetings and conferences.[69] The most revealing measure of the state's parasitism is the sum of money reportedly spent by Communist Party organizations, government agencies, and SOEs on what is euphemistically referred to as "privatized public consumption": expensive Japanese and German automobiles, air conditioners, cellular phones, color televisions, and stereos, as well as opulent multicourse banquets, with each course accompanied by a toast with top-of-the-line French brandies or single-malt scotch—all paid for with public monies but enjoyed only by the elite.[70]

Institutional "Renewal": Light at the End of the Tunnel?

On a more optimistic note, there is some evidence of institutional "renewal" in contemporary China, providing some hope that evolutionary change might prevent the need for violent change.[71] There are some signs, for example, of the state's attempts at institutional "deepening" by providing (or allowing) new economic, social, and political institutions designed to safeguard the achievements of economic liberalization. The best examples are the strengthening of the National People's Congress; the enhancement of the legal system; and the introduction of free elections in village governments in many parts of the countryside.[72] The NPC, for example, has evolved from little more than a symbolic institution to a potential challenger to the Party's monopoly,

TABLE 18.2   Selected Central Government Expenditures in China, 1978–1994 (as a percentage of the total)

Year	Administrative Expenditures	Investment in Agricultural Infrastructure	Expenditures on Pensions and Social Welfare	Research and Development Expenditures
1978	4.76	4.59	1.62	4.76
1980	6.22	3.96	1.65	5.33
1982	7.87	2.42	1.82	5.66
1984	9.04	2.13	1.61	6.13
1986	9.40	1.84	1.50	4.83
1988	10.03	1.44	1.51	4.48
1990	12.00	1.91	1.59	4.03
1992	10.54	1.93	1.50	—
1994	14.02	1.84	1.64	—

SOURCE: Pei (1997), Table 1.2, p. 23 (data from *China Statistical Yearbooks*, various years, and *China Finance Statistics, 1950–1991*).

and in recent years it has asserted its prerogatives as China's supreme lawmaking body. Members of the NPC now sponsor their own bills, actively debate and amend proposed legislation, and will even hold up or vote against important bills. In March 1995, a third of the deputies refused to approve the nomination of a Politburo member for vice premier; and in an attempt to register their concern about crime and corruption, 32 percent of NPC deputies voted against the annual report of the Supreme Court.[73] A 1994 poll conducted by *Far Eastern Economic Review* showed that a majority of citizens saw the NPC as an effective vehicle for expressing some of their grievances.

The progress in village democracy has also been a source of satisfaction to the beleaguered peasantry, who suffered from the decline and decay of local Party organizations. Partly as a response to that, partly to express resistance to increasing Party tyranny and predation, self-governing local bodies have been emerging, at first spontaneously; then in 1982 the amended constitution gave legal recognition to village committees as a form of local civic organization. By 1985 nearly 1 million village committees had been formed.[74] In 1995 a U.S. mission sent to investigate the situation reported that more than 90 percent of existing village committees had been formed through local elections in the 1990s, a trend supported by the government.[75] Village representative assemblies, adopted to extend political participation in rural China, have also been expanding in recent years, and although it is too soon to evaluate these new trends, they represent a bold and historic step toward rural self-government in China. Significantly, many of the candidates for election are not Party members. The trend toward village self-government may already be irreversible, even though at present in many villages there is little true freedom of choice.[76]

On balance, there is evidence of parallel decay and renewal, and renewal encourages some cautious optimism for a "managed gradual transition to a relatively consolidated soft-authoritarian system based on a market economy."[77] These trends point toward a solution for the long-term problem of institutional decay, in that some of the new institutions may become political buffers able to shield the regime from the powerful and potential uncontrollable social and political pressures that have been unleashed by the dramatic transformation in post-Mao China. In Chapter 19 we shall take a more detailed look at these new trends and attempt to assess the likelihood of radical political change in the immediate future.

19

Utopia and "Dreams of Heaven" in the New Millennium?

꧁꧂꧁꧂꧁꧂꧁꧂꧁꧂꧁꧂꧁꧂꧁꧂꧁꧂꧁꧂꧁꧂꧁

> *The real malaise of Beijing [is] its domination by an ideology so all-pervading, so arbitrary . . . so inconstant [it] can change the way the nation thinks from one year to another. Today it is liberal and welcoming, Chinese tradition is honored, people are free to wear what they like, consort with foreigners if they will, sell their ducks in a free market and even build themselves houses with the profits. Yesterday it was puritanically narrow, the revolutionary condition was permanent, aliens were devils, Mao caps and floppy trousers were de rigueur. . . . And tomorrow, when another generation succeeds to domination, everything may be different again, and all the values so painstakingly absorbed into the public consciousness may have to be ripped out of mind once more.*
>
> —Jan Morris, *Journeys* (1984)[1]

Introduction: Looking Forward, Looking Backward

After everything that happened in China during the 1980s, particularly 1989, followed by the extraordinary renewed push toward modernization throughout the 1990s, it is wise to be circumspect about making any prediction for the future. China scholars find themselves in an awkward predicament. They can jump to conclusions about what is likely to happen in China in the near future, only to be proved wrong by the latest extraordinary turn of events; or they can sit tight-lipped, waiting to see what happens next. An ancient Chinese folktale comes to mind: The simpleminded youngest son of a poor peasant family was sent into the wilderness to forage for food. At the end of a fruitless day he sat down to rest, and shortly afterward a rabbit flashed by; in a panic it crashed into a nearby tree, knocking itself unconscious. The boy brought the rabbit home and the family feasted, convinced their fortunes had changed and that their son was not as dim-witted as they

had thought. The next day the parents again sent the boy in search of food. Still knowing nothing about how to hunt wildlife, he returned to the scene of his earlier triumph, sat down, and waited for another rabbit to bump into a tree!

When studying contemporary China, Western academics by necessity are often forced to resort to the gray areas of guesswork and hunches based on past observations. So in that sense we often find ourselves waiting for a rabbit to bump into a tree! It is difficult to evaluate the official data released by the government, and it is practically impossible to decipher or believe many of the public pronouncements made in the regular media channels. As suggested in Chapter 2, social scientists are usually uncomfortable with the easy and sweeping generalizations of travel writers and journalists. Not only are they considered to be unscientific; they also require us to rely too heavily on intuition. From a cognitive perspective, successful intuitiveness means leaping to the correct conclusions in the absence of sufficient empirical evidence. Using our intuition to predict what will happen in China in the new millennium is thus a hit-and-miss prospect. This point was brought home dramatically by the events of 1989, especially the aftermath, the course and outcome of which were predicted very inaccurately by many China watchers.

At the end of the 1980s it was difficult to interpret the round of economic retrenchments that had occurred in 1988 and 1989 and that would continue into the early 1990s. From the vantage point of the late 1990s it would now appear that they represented a relatively minor reversal in what has been described as the gradual transition from plan to market. Bearing in mind the hazards associated with making predictions, political scientist June Dreyer has been bold enough to imagine four scenarios for China's political future in the new millennium:[2]

- The Party-state will remain in power and be able to stem the "decay" of political institutions while providing the guiding hand needed for continued economic development (which will need to be done gradually and carefully to prevent further inequality). This would presumably be a "neoauthoritarian" regime that would continue to reject demands for political liberalization.
- The current government will be overthrown and replaced by a popularly chosen reformist regime, although at this point there are no indications who that might involve, or how it will be able to organize.
- There will be a peaceful evolution toward a more liberal regime that is market-oriented and tolerant of a variety of political views. This evolution would probably be accompanied by frequent and sometimes major social disruptions.[3]
- The Party-state will stand by in a kind of paralysis as power continues to devolve to provinces and regions.

Dreyer has pointed out that by the mid-1990s the state had no blueprint for what to do next, even though it regularly proclaimed the importance of continued reform.[4] As many China scholars would agree, there has been a marked decrease in the state's ability to exact compliance from society in the 1990s, which has worked to blur and soften the differences between state and society. Instead of increasing and sharpening the gap between the two, we now have all sorts of hybrid situations, such as new ties between merchants and entrepreneurs, cadres and bureaucrats.[5] At the macro level this could have a positive outcome, with a loose-knit federation of competing and quite autonomous provinces and cities, all coordinated from Beijing; but it could easily slide into a situation of "state impotence, confusion, and disarray," in which the center is able only to react and suppress activities rather than create and inspire new ones.[6]

Other analysts agree in principle with the sorts of scenarios Dreyer offers. Marc Blecher, for example, has suggested four basic scenarios, two of which assume the collapse of the state in its current form:

- A new and weaker state emerges, based on elections, as in Russia and some states in Eastern and Central Europe;
- the state collapses into competing, maybe even warring provinces, as in Yugoslavia;
- the state survives and evolves into a gradual, elite-led liberal regime, along the lines of what happened in South Korea and Taiwan in the 1980s and 1990s; or
- the state survives and evolves into the most likely scenario: a "muddling through" era, with the same combination of economic inducements and hard-line politics, a combination Blecher refers to as "market Stalinism."

Table 19.1 reflects Blecher's basic outline, suggesting some of the possible scenarios under the heading "The Existing State Survives," which could range from the status quo (most likely) to a new pluralist state (perhaps most unlikely).

It is easier to interpret the past than to predict the future, and as we look back on the 1980s and 1990s there are two ways to characterize the flow of events in contemporary

TABLE 19.1 Alternative Political Scenarios for China in the New Millennium

	State Type	Models	Characteristics	Comments
	Market Stalinism	China, 1978–1999	Developmentalist state, status quo muddling through Brezhnevism	Most likely, but how long can it survive the contradictions?
	Corporatist State	Singapore	Decentralization to lower-level economic and political decisionmaking; linkages between entrepreneurs and bureaucrats	High likelihood of conflict; society is incorporated, not liberated; the central state is impotent
The Existing State Survives	**Liberal State/Civil Society**	Taiwan, S. Korea, 1990s	Evolution of existing regime, with either gradual or sudden political change	Can China be democratic? What happens in economic downturns? What to do with the CCP?
	Revolutionary State	Late 1950s China	Return to mass line politics and grassroots democracy; recollectivization; increasing state provision	Seems extremely unlikely to happen
	Pluralist State	Eastern Europe, Russia post-1990	Peaceful transition (e.g., Czech Republic) or violent revolution (e.g., Romania)	Can the CCP be defeated, challenged, replaced?
The Existing State Collapses	**Warring States**	Yugoslavia, former Soviet Union	Political collapse, violent civil war, ethnic cleansing	Is it unthinkable? High-level ethnic tension in far west of China (Tibet, Xinjiang, etc.)

SOURCE: The author.

China. The first emphasizes the amount and speed of changes that have occurred in Chinese society; from that perspective the 1990s can be viewed as an extension of the 1980s, exhibiting a series of dramatic, often cataclysmic policy reversals (reflected in the Jan Morris quote that opens this chapter). Throughout this book we have examined the extraordinary changes occurring since 1978. Policy reversals caused new patterns of everyday life for Chinese people, as well as dramatic transformations in the character of the places where they live and work. Many of these changes occurred rapidly, with the effects of one program being swept up and overturned by the effects of new programs fast on its heels. In addition to the sheer speed of the process, many changes occurred in pendulum fashion, as Morris would suggest. The trends of one decade were dramatically reversed in the next decade; but in fact the changes were even quicker than that, taking place in one or two years, or months, or even days.

After the chaos of the Cultural Revolution, the Chinese people hoped they had seen the last use of inhumane tactics to sweep away political enemies, and throughout the 1980s it looked as though that would be the case. By the end of the decade, however, particularly after the Tiananmen demonstrations, it was clear that some of the old practices had been brought back into regular use. After reading about the inhumanities that occurred during the Cultural Revolution, Chinese people and Westerners alike were horrified to hear about a return of purges, self-criticisms, mobilization campaigns, and public excoriation sessions. In the 1990s, as prosperity increased and China continued its meteoric rise, such tactics were gradually de-emphasized again, and the nation was able to settle down and concentrate on the major task of making China richer. It was assumed again that the old tactics and bullying had been left behind for good. But at the end of the 1990s the Chinese government outdid itself yet again, leaving Western journalists and politicians flabbergasted by the harsh treatment of the so-called dissident groups that had been trying to legally register an alternative political party.[7]

Returning to events in the 1980s, we can discern a pattern of contradictions that resulted from the state's implementation of fundamentally opposing policies. In the Chinese countryside, for example, the goals and impacts of agricultural reform clashed with several modernization policies in Dengist China. As we reviewed in Chapter 7, the conflicts between the agricultural production policy inherent in the new household responsibility system and reproduction policy designed to lower the birthrate damaged the effectiveness of both policies. As sideline activities opened up, and as jobs in rural enterprises became more easily available, many parents in rural China realized that future earning potential could be increased considerably by having more children. The agricultural reforms also made it difficult for city planners to go about their business in a logical fashion (see Chapter 9). Greater agricultural efficiency on the land meant that the surplus rural population grew rapidly in the 1980s, and many of the people displaced from the land began to move into the cities—with more waiting at home for their turn to do the same. As that happened it became increasingly difficult for cities to avoid problems associated with rapid urbanization, in addition to having to provide the extra services to support a growing population of poor and dependent people.

Increases in crime and corruption have become one of the most serious threats to the legitimacy of the current regime, another negative externality effect of economic reform in the 1980s. Western and Chinese criminologists agree that higher crime rates might be attributable to the new level of material concern and avarice that accompanied reform. As the drive to get rich took hold in the 1980s, the economy took a step forward, yet embezzlement, tax evasion, theft, and large-scale corruption became everyday media events. The new wealth also upset the Chinese model of urbanization, in which the prevalence of social problems was kept low, at least compared to cities in the West, particularly in the United States. As a result of the agricultural reforms it is likely that the growing "reserve army" of unemployed (and perhaps unemployable) peasants will want to leave the land and seek work elsewhere. The newly dispossessed will look enviously upon families that have become wealthy and longingly at those lucky enough to be able to live in the cities. It remains to be seen what consequences such unfulfilled aspirations will have for patterns of crime and other social problems in contemporary urban China.

Despite the turmoil and frequent contradictions, in some ways China has changed very little or not at all. Simon Leys, for example, has suggested that in many instances outsiders have focused on the shadows rather than the substance.[8] The evidence may have fooled us into thinking that major changes were afoot and that the pace of change would continue to accelerate; but as the sobering events of 1989 demonstrated, it was apparent that in the most important areas very little had changed. This is illustrated in the largest cities, where by the end of the 1990s a new landscape of capitalism has thoroughly transformed the austerity of the Maoist city. There has been a huge increase in vehicular traffic; new highways have been built, some of which allow traffic to roar through the center of large cities, as in the case of Shanghai and Shenzhen; new hotels have been built for Chinese and foreign tourists; restaurants and shops cater to the new wealthy; and billboards and advertisements for all manner of consumer goods sprang up overnight. In spite of such changes the decision to hand out hefty jail sentences to the would-be founders of the new Democratic Party demonstrated that in politics, at least, little had changed.

As to culture a great deal has changed yet much has stayed the same. Old Confucian values have faded somewhat, but they have certainly not withered away. There is ample evidence of the cultural legacies that dominated lives and landscapes for centuries. This is particularly true for women, especially in the male-dominated countryside. It is also still obvious that the norm for most Chinese people, both in the cities and the countryside, is to be told what to do by the Party. After five decades of socialism and freedom from the landlords, there is still evidence of widespread passivity and acceptance of one's station in life, a cultural trait that is usually associated with Confucian values in China and other traditional Asian societies. There is some empirical evidence to suggest that many people in contemporary China are thinking of themselves and their lives

primarily in individual rather than collective terms, but it is important not to overemphasize this point. In the aftermath of the Tiananmen Square incident, for example, we saw that the Chinese family was still of critical importance, mainly because it is virtually the only source of protection for the individual from the pervasive reach of the state.

A detailed look at the Chinese economy at the end of the millennium also reveals that despite the enormous successes reported from all parts of China, there is still plenty of evidence of issues that have been persistent for centuries. Among the most obvious is the fundamental disparity of wealth between the cities and the countryside as well as between the eastern and southeastern provinces and the interior. As has always been the case, there are pockets of desperate poverty in rural China, and as some of the better-endowed areas become richer, the gap will widen.

The events of 1989 represented to the Chinese government a uniquely threatening combination of students and workers, and although the government considers its actions to have been successful, the brutality of the crackdown has given all future popular rebellions in China an incredibly powerful symbol around which to rally.[9] Many Western observers believe, however, that the key to the future may lie not with the students or the workers or the peasants but in a disaffected elite within the Party. If that represents the necessary condition for political reform in China, the sufficient condition could be the actions of the ordinary citizens: on the streets, in the workplace, even in the countryside. From that perspective a prolonged economic downturn could become a dangerous trend, as Andrew Walder has noted: "Any future economic stagnation will once again make this group [the workers] available for political mobilization. In a situation of heightened political repression, through slowdowns and isolated walkouts, workers will have more effective means of political leverage than students and intellectuals."[10]

The prospect of further economic austerity could, therefore, represent political dynamite for the Party, and a combined rebellion by the workers and the peasants would be a much more serious threat than could ever be mounted by the students.

Problems and Prospects for Civil Society and Democracy

In his book *The Democratization of China*, Baogang He defines the term "civil society" as a political space that cannot be controlled by authorities and can be used by the people to deal with the authorities with some additional leverage and support.[11] He suggests that the Tiananmen Square demonstrations represented a demand for this type of space from students, intellectuals, and workers in what amounted to "an attempt to institutionalize the political opposition movement."[12] As we now know, the events were interpreted by the CCP as a serious threat, even though none of the demonstrators were audibly calling for the overthrow of the regime; and significantly, the phrase "civil society" was not in common usage at the time.[13]

Space for the People: The Emergence of a Civil Society in China?

Most definitions of the term "civil society" describe it as the existence and operation of "de facto autonomous organizations that are independent of direct political control by the state and the party."[14] In general there are three spheres in which "civil society" operates:

- economic—autonomous organizations and entrepreneurial activities;
- political—opposition organizations and social movements; and
- cultural—the discourse of civil society and the various groups and associations formed to further individual and group cultural and recreational interests.

In the broadest terms, then, civil society includes formal and informal social networks, which would include nongovernmental organizations, economic interests operating free of state control, as well as free media operations and even public houses and cafés that are used for debate and discussion. In China there have traditionally been significant obstacles standing in the way of the evolution of civil society.[15] The productive forces, for example, have mainly (and certainly until very recently) been publicly owned; and the workforce, both urban and rural, has traditionally been publicly (and vertically) organized, which makes the creation of horizontal linkages with the outside difficult to arrange.[16] Beginning in 1978, however, Chinese cities first witnessed the mushrooming of various types of societies, associations, and salons.[17] Unofficial journals started to appear, private bookshops opened and thrived, and "roadside cafes provided meeting points for the local populations, as well as for the increasing migrant populations."[18] The economic reforms also spawned a variety of new socioeconomic organizations and associations, and all of this new activity helped to fuel rising expectations for the future growth of China's civil society. In the absence of any significant plurality in the realm of party politics, this associational growth was virtually the only way in which the public space for political participation could be expanded.

Two caveats are important at this point. First, no political parties are yet allowed to operate independently of the CCP; in fact in 1998 after numerous attempts were made to register such groups, the door was slammed shut with the jailing of those involved.[19] The implication of these actions is that if the term "civil society" is meant to signify the sphere of independent political action taken by groups that have the social standing, legal status, and power to assert themselves by influencing policymaking, then it certainly does *not* exist in China today. What does exist are a mélange of "illegal" political organizations demanding democracy; some semi-independent organizations that are academic, religious, and professional but limited in the scope of their actions; and a variety of secret societies, brotherhoods, and sects that are often officially banned and engaged in criminal activity. Most of the official organizations are not autonomous of state controls, and many other organizations, although legal and officially registered, have leaders and members recruited from the Party-state system.

The second caveat is that although this heterogeneous group certainly does not yet amount to a civil society, it does amount to something, which perhaps needs to be given another name to capture the essence of its essentially hodgepodge, semiofficial, and ragged activities. Some China scholars would argue that the concept of a civil society, as it is used in the West, is simply not appropriate for present-day China. In the West, the term refers to the oppositional role that civil society plays in relation to the state, and the rise of civil society is assumed to have emerged gradually and naturally from the introduction of a market system. In China there has been no similar emergence of class-based oppositional politics; there has also been no long-term evolution of capitalism. In addition, although there has been considerable associational activity in China's cities, no similar phenomenon has yet occurred in the rural areas.[20] It is also apparent that the idea of a civil society as an oppositional space to the power of the state (a political definition) may not be appropriate to the current Chinese situation, whereas a more sociological definition may be closer to the mark. In reform-era China, the new economic and social climate created by the economic expansion has produced many demands that the Party-state has not been able to respond to within its current institutional and organization structure. As a partial and temporary measure, a limited sphere of autonomous social space has been created (or, more accurately, it has been allowed), and in this limited sense the use of the term "civil society" is appropriate.[21]

As we have reviewed throughout this book, especially in Chapter 18, China's state apparatus no longer dominates all aspects of society, as was the case during the Maoist era. The evidence suggests that Chinese society at large is "stirring," even though it is still locked in the "embrace of local officialdom, including local unit leaders of state organizations."[22] The central state is no longer so tightly in control, and local officials are often able to negotiate with higher authorities. The strong vertical element of control over social life in China, in both the cities and the rural areas, used to have a near lock on society. The reality is that many peasants and workers are now totally free of such organizational control and are able to establish horizontal ties by migrating and looking for jobs in other economic sectors.

Also breaking with the old model is the huge proliferation of private enterprises, joint ventures, and private schools, all of them offering services, making products, and creating jobs totally independent of the state. In fact, the state is reinforcing this trend by shifting the role of service delivery from the old work units to city-wide or countywide organizations, so that the delivery of urban goods and services (including social security, insurance, health care, housing, and education) is increasingly being provided outside the work-unit system, often on a private basis, or not at all—which is one of the dangers inherent in the contemporary era.

As noted above, there are essentially two spheres of activity that civil society can operate within. One is political, in which activities take on the form of resistance to state control on the part of societal organizations that have explicitly political agendas. In socialist states the best recent example would be the Solidarity movement in Poland. In China since 1949 there have been some limited occurrences, most recently with the two Tiananmen Square movements (in 1978–1979 and 1989). Although only a partial movement against the state was launched, both events represented an ideological challenge to the regime, as well as a cultural challenge, mainly directed against official corruption within the Party-state. At neither time was there much evidence of the "highest" form of challenge to the state—the call for the creation of new political institutions to replace existing ones.

The second sphere of operation is the market, where civil society can be interpreted as the result of a redistribution of social power away from the state to a new set of influential actors: individuals and groups that have been successful in the reform era. In the case of Hungary, for example, in the 1970s and 1980s, a "second economy" emerged that was eventually able to challenge the state.[23] Although that has not yet occurred in China, a "new sphere of social association" has emerged to alter the balance of power between the state and society, to such an extent that China has moved away from its system of total state control to one in which social organizations are able to "represent the interests of their social constituencies rather than the control imperatives of the state."[24]

Gordon White has argued that there has been some degree of political relaxation, evidenced by the depoliticization of everyday life and the expansion of areas of activity—cultural, economic, and professional—that are now relatively free of state controls. In this sense the political and market dynamics of civil society are "interactive and reinforcing," with the latter impinging on the former by weakening its ability to repress alternative political activities.[25] The new institutions of the market society attract recruits and resources that are able to nurture some forms of political opposition, in addition to providing safe havens to retreat to in the event that such activities fail or backfire. The market expansions, therefore, offer potential political opponents a new home base from which to launch their activities. From all accounts it appears that increasing numbers of intellectuals and former dissidents are now entering the economic sphere. At present we have no way of knowing how much of this activity is intended solely for material gain, how much a cover it is for individuals and groups who might at some later date want to make a preemptive strike against the state. Perhaps more modestly, patiently, and in the spirit of gradual and small-scale change such activities can at least be used as a stepping-stone for future political activity.

In response to all of the economic and social changes being witnessed in China, there has been a two-pronged impetus. Chinese society has developed independently, with new associations and organizations emerging; but at the same time the state has responded by making some changes of its own, for example, by opening new avenues for political participation and attempting some limited institutional reform. In many instances the state has moved either to repress such activity, if it arose "naturally" from the people, or to incorporate it and regulate its activities.[26] This observation enables us to characterize China's civil society by the extent to which the state tolerates or accepts the different associations and organizations that have been emerging, and also by the extent to which such entities are old and traditional or newly formed (see Figure 19.1). White has suggested that all of these different examples embody, to varying degrees, "the associational characteristics of civil society," and from that perspective it is possible to identify four broad categories of civil society in contemporary China:[27]

- The "caged" sector. These are the old-style mass organizations of the pre-reform era, such as the Women's Federation, the All-China Federation of Trade Unions, and the Young Communist League—all of which are officially backed and controlled by the state, with no real organizational autonomy, and where attempts to become more assertive are generally restrained by the state. White suggests that the trade unions, for example, "struck a Faustian bargain with the Party whereby they sacrificed greater autonomy for greater access to and influence over official policy-making at both national and local levels."[28] These organizations are like caged birds that would probably like to escape but do not, partly because the cage is too strong, but also because they have grown accustomed to the comforts of caged life.
- The "incorporated" sector. This is a new stratum of officially recognized social organizations, operating both nationally and at the local level, including business and trade organizations; professional organizations; academic societies; and sporting, recreational, and social clubs. By

Stability/Longevity

	Old	New
High	**CAGED SECTOR** e.g., mass organizations— WF; ACFTU	**INCORPORATED SECTOR** e.g., new social organizations in business, trade, professions, academic, sports, recreation, etc.
Low	**UNDERGROUND SECTOR** e.g., All China Qigong Association, Democracy Movement	**INTERSTITIAL SECTOR** e.g., salons of intellectuals pre-1989, homosexuals, semiformal and loosely connected

Level of State Tolerance (left axis)

FIGURE 19.1   Categories of Civil Society in China

1993 there were a reported 1,460 such groups registered nationally, 19,600 provincially, and 160,000-plus at the county level.[29] Such organizations represent a unique combination of newly influential social actors and still-powerful state institutions, effectively creating a new hybrid form of organization that "braids" state and society in new and different ways.[30] Some are totally controlled by the state, but others (mostly small organizations) are not considered important enough to be controlled.

- The "interstitial" (limbo) sector. In the late 1980s there was growth in a new sphere of activity, with urban associations that were still embryonic and not officially recognized—including the expansion of "salons" of intellectuals—that were influential in the years leading up to the Tiananmen incident. They operated mainly informally and intermittently, conducting conferences and seminars. After 1990 some remained in existence, but new groups have emerged, composed of networks of like-minded, usually nonpolitical individuals connected horizontally to one another (including lawyers, journalists, artists,

homosexuals, martial-arts specialists, and women). In many cases such groups operate under a cloak of respectability, such as the Women Journalists Association, the Women Entrepreneurs Association, and the Women's Mayors Association, all of which are "second-level associations" providing shelter for women through their link to the officially recognized Women's Federation. In the 1990s there has also been new growth of informal women's groups that do not have official sponsors, as well as environmental organizations such as the Green China Association. As the reforms were accelerated throughout the late 1990s, all sorts of new organizations were emerging, and although some of them have been watched closely by the state, it would appear that the growth trend is now irreversible.[31]

- The "suppressed" or "underground" sector. Most of these groups are under constant surveillance by the state, and suppression is a possibility at any time. They include such varied organizations as the All-China Qigong Association, the National Alliance of Demobilized Servicemen of the Rural Areas, the Association of

Urban Unemployed, and the Association of Individual Households. At the extreme end of the scale are the officially banned political groups associated with the 1989 democracy movement.[32] Groups in this category stretch from the extreme left of the political spectrum, for example, relics of the Maoist era such as the Jiangxi Red Uprising Column; to ethnic and religious groups such as the Xingiang Justice Party, which advocates ethnic self-determination and freedom of expression.[33] At the end of the 1990s the state is caught in a bind: The growth of such groups shows that the state simply cannot control them; but to ban them outright would be difficult and unpopular (especially in the case of the more politically oriented groups), whereas to tolerate them could encourage the growth of other such groups.

All of this demonstrates "a burgeoning sphere of intermediate social association in China which embodies, in different ways and to different degrees, the basic characteristics of a 'civil society'—voluntary participation, self-regulation, and separation from the state."[34] Relatively few of the organizations meet that definition fully, so it is indeed a partial and incipient civil society, with all sorts of associations, old and new, urban and rural, political and nonpolitical, ultra-left to liberal, open and underground. There is, in fact, a continuum of groups, from the huge "caged" associations close to the core to the new, small, relatively disorganized associations at the periphery.[35] As social pressure increases in China, and without adequate outlets or political institutions, the "force of incipient civil society" has increasingly been, and will probably continue to be, manifested in spontaneous and sporadic activities, including demonstrations, riots, protests, sit-ins, beatings, and fighting in rural and urban areas.[36] It looks as though it will be a long uphill struggle, but it appears to be a movement that can no longer be kept in check.

From a societal perspective the most important concern is to continue pressuring the state

to provide some sort of institutionalized guarantee for such organizations to exist and operate autonomously. In 1998 there were reports of numerous attempts to register (and therefore to legitimate) a democratic opposition party in Shandong Province, with reports suggesting that the proposal was being considered by the local Civil Affairs Bureau. This group, if approved, would be called the Shandong Preparatory Committee of the China Democracy Party (CDP), and its consideration appears to have been associated with the visit of UN human rights chief Mary Robinson to China.[37] Other reports are more mixed, however, with unsuccessful attempts to register the CDP in Wuhan; but more positive signs were reported in Beijing.[38] The state (at least in response to the applications made in Shandong and Hubei Provinces) initially announced that the new groups could be registered as long as the following conditions were met: They paid the Y50,000 registration fee and they provided particulars of their headquarters, the names of the organizers and at least fifty members, and details of the group leaders. The state appeared to be wavering, blowing hot and cold on this issue, and the potential leaders were reported to be "cautiously optimistic."

In some areas newspaper reporters felt there was no way the CCP would allow such an opposition party to register; other reports provided details of the attempts to start a branch of the CDP in Shanghai, arguing that "the current political system is not organized enough to sustain the demands of economic development. The system needs a fundamental change to a multi-party one, so we therefore lodge this application."[39] The individual submitting the application was detained for several hours, and a sum of Y8,000, reportedly supplied by human rights groups based in the United States, was confiscated. Most similar applications have been turned down, but others have been accepted "provisionally." Later reports indicated that many of the organizers and petitioners were being detained, confirming the announcement that attempts to register opposition parties are still illegal; and in December 1998 several key leaders of the movement were in fact tried and sent to prison with lengthy sentences.[40]

The image here is of a pressure cooker that will sooner or later heat to such an extent that some of the steam will have to escape. The problem (from the societal perspective) is that China's existing civil society is diverse, fragmented, and politically anarchic; there is no consensus of what is needed or how to achieve it. Also, as White has suggested, some of the most powerful new constituencies, such as the entrepreneurial classes, have no real interest in major political change, because they have done so well in the current circumstances. In fact, civil societies have many different goals and outcomes, of which democracy is only one. Gordon White has warned that we should not idealize the politics of civil society and that it might not be the right path for China to take in the current circumstances. All of the different groups have different ideas of what the outcome should be, and in that sense civil society in its current manifestation might be more of an obstacle rather than an impetus to democratization.[41] White also suggested that political reform, as in Russia, might have to wait to be sponsored by a reformist clique from within the current political elite.[42]

The Prospects for Democracy in China?

Of yore, the Duke Huan of Qi appreciated the color purple only. As a result, there was no cloth of other colors for sale within his state. The King Zhuang of Chu appreciated slim beauties. As a result, the women all over his country looked hungry. Thus, once the superiors set an example, the inferiors will follow, and herein lies the line of demarcation between order and disorder.

—Ancient Chinese maxim[43]

As this ancient Chinese maxim suggests, the tradition in China has been for the emperor to inform the masses about how to behave, where-

upon they will follow, sheeplike. In contemporary discussions about the prospects for democracy, arguments of this sort are still commonplace, with the implication that the status quo should remain as it is because the Chinese people have had no experience in democracy. In his discussion of China's prospects for democratizing, Minxin Pei observed that the evidence of institutional "renewal" in China (see Chapter 18), both in the cities and in the countryside, suggests the existence of a new social contract in which there has been to some extent at least a redefinition of the scope and extent of the state's power in relation to society and to individuals: The state will relax many of the restrictions on personal and economic freedom in exchange for "their [the people's] tacit acceptance of the CCP's authority."[44] One limited piece of evidence of this is the overall reduction of political repression, with the focus now mainly concentrated on a relatively small community of dissidents.[45] There is also evidence that the state has shifted somewhat in the direction of what can be called a kinder and gentler politics, which has involved a determined effort to make sure that old and corrupt cadres were removed from office, a move that has stabilized the government and reduced dissension.[46]

In spite of the successes China's government has had in overseeing some degree of institutional renewal and directing a significant response to crime and corruption, so far it has strongly resisted democratic reforms. Most scholars would agree that China's leaders fear that opening up the political process to mass democratic participation will lead to chaos. They are convinced that Gorbachev's greatest error in the 1980s was to open up the political system before beginning any significant economic reform. More specifically, Pei suggested, the former Soviet Union opened up democratic participation before any constitutional reforms were implemented to create the institutions needed to govern and rule by democratic methods.[47] What happened in the Soviet Union was that as soon as democratic reform came, the existing system was overthrown—exactly what Chinese leaders fear. This is especially a concern in light of the obvious decline of the CCP, both in organizational and institutional terms.[48] The CCP is also dealing with a radically changed society and a bolder citizenry less fearful of bullying by the state. The people have been exposed to new values and many of them are no longer susceptible to—in fact many are openly hostile to—orthodox Party ideology.[49]

To govern effectively, then, the state needs to have a solid base of support somewhere within society. In China this has traditionally come from the peasants, and until the 1990s the state had been able to mobilize them to resist, challenge, or ignore potential democratic opposition in the urban areas.[50] In the long run, without that type of support the CCP cannot even begin to think about implementing democratic reforms; we can only assume, therefore, that the leadership will continue to resist any efforts in that direction. Party leaders have chosen to try to strengthen the Party, with some cautious political reforms intended mainly to support and manage China's rapid economic development—such as reforms in the legal system and in its representative institutions.[51] This seems to be what Jiang Zemin had in mind when he proclaimed that "rule according to law" should be expanded.[52] Perhaps it is unrealistic to expect too much progress too quickly in the realm of democracy. China's leaders, after all, are by no means confident about the durability of their political system, and they are unlikely to open it up to popular participation, over and above the small-scale democratic experiments already in existence at the grassroots level.

The issue of whether and in what form democracy might come to China has obviously attracted a great deal of attention from outside observers, especially in the West, where the small steps taken thus far are not considered to amount to much. Gordon White, playing the devil's advocate, asks whether democracy is necessary in China, to which he responds that it is not (and it would be very damaging) if it meant a rapid shift of the type attempted by Gorbachev in the Soviet Union.[53] Reviewing the manifold obstacles to democracy, as well as the usual arguments favoring a strong state in China, White has concluded that the immediate introduction of a multiparty system would be "highly problematic."[54] In general, it is assumed that given the formidable tasks needed to launch a modernization project, states need to be strong enough to restrain population growth and prevent or contain regional inequality.[55] Issues like these require the state to make strategic decisions that will necessarily be imposed in the face of popular inertia or resistance from powerful social forces.[56] A too-rapid transition to democracy could weaken the developmental state, opening it up to special interests, political demagoguery, or the multifarious schisms of civil society—all of which have occurred in the former Soviet Union.[57]

This argument notwithstanding, on balance most of the assertions explaining why China is not yet a candidate for democracy are unconvincing. One such argument—that China has no historical experience of a functioning democracy and is simply not ready—is far too static and demeaning, and we only need to recall that China was also judged to be not ready for capitalism. So much change has already occurred that more movement in the direction of democracy would not be unreasonable to anticipate.[58] Another argument holds that China is too deeply rooted in a cultural tradition of authoritarianism based on popular obedience to authority to provide fertile ground for democracy.[59] This line of reasoning also misses the mark. The assumption that Chinese people are simply not interested in democracy is patently false, as recent events in Hong Kong have shown, particularly in the June 1998 elections, where 60–70 percent turnout was recorded despite a howling thunderstorm that lasted the entire day. There are some economic arguments against democratization, however, that appear to have some merit. Democracy is indeed difficult to imagine or impose when so many people are still engaged in a daily struggle for existence and survival. There is a fear that China's democratic opening-up might be taken over by powerful new elites, made up of private entrepreneurs, probably with foreign support, with the vast majority of the urban and rural poor people still effectively disenfranchised.[60]

In addition, there are powerful social reasons to question whether China is indeed ready for democratization. As we have seen, during the reform era China has become a much more complex and potentially conflictual society, with so many new sources of power, making it virtually ungovernable, even by so vast a state apparatus as the CCP.[61] Power has been dispersed to bureaucratic institutions and local governments, as well as to thousands of emerging enterprises; rural inequality has created so many points of potential resistance and class differentiation that the prospects for democracy being able to function seem remote. As Gordon White observed:

> There is potentially destructive antagonism between the "wooden soldiers" of the [Stalinist] status quo and the new social and political forces emerging under the impact of economic reform [that are] powerful enough to impose severe strains on any set of political arrangements, particularly one that is designed to express rather than control social conflicts, such as a multi-party system.[62]

White concluded that any move toward democracy in China should be made very cautiously.[63] The current regime, he would argue, has clearly lost its legitimacy, and as we have seen there has been a steady erosion of state socialism and its core institution, the CCP. These circumstances indicate that reconstitution of the political order is required to accommodate the scale of change in the economic, social, and political character of the new China, with its growth of markets, the pluralization of interests, the growth of civil society, and the massive changes in attitudes and beliefs.

The only remaining question, then, is what form the democratic transition should take. Is it possible for the regime to achieve reform itself, or are we more likely to see a political paralysis and collapse, as was the case in a number of European nations and the Soviet Union? Will the transition be peaceful and slow or rapid,

chaotic, and violent? It seems obvious to many observers that to avoid a potentially disastrous rapid shift to democracy China needs a dual transition: first from a totalitarian to an authoritarian form of state socialism; then from that to a liberal-democratic polity presiding over a basically private enterprise economy.[64] The first stage would involve the CCP keeping a dominant though diminished position (similar to the KMT in Taiwan today). This makes good sense, because at this time the CCP has ensured that there is no viable political alternative on the horizon.[65]

If the second stage—the transition from authoritarianism to full democracy—is to occur, there are several prerequisites, some of which are already in place:

- a change in the leadership of the Party to bring in younger, better educated, less political-ideological–minded and more pragmatic-reform–minded members;
- a compromise between Party reformers and activists in the democracy movement, which is now factionalized, especially with so many representatives living in exile (obviously this would require a skillful and broadly popular leader);[66]
- constitutional changes to guarantee basic citizen and economic rights and the ability to enforce them, itself a prerequisite for a renewed commitment to further economic reforms;
- institutional changes to redefine the position of the CCP (which would presumably be just one dominant party among others) and to ensure the passing of some power to other institutions, such as the Chinese People's Political Consultative Conference, or to local communities in both the cities and the countryside; and
- an expansion of civil society along with greater freedom of ideological and cultural expression and the establishment of a more autonomous mass media.[67]

In the short term the resulting political system would be a hybrid, much like in contemporary Singapore, Taiwan, and South Korea, where elements of single-party dominance are still visible. A two-stage move like this might be able to break the deadlocks that have inhibited political reforms throughout the 1980s and 1990s, manifested in the *fang-shou* cycles of conflict and policy oscillation (see Chapter 4). A total Party collapse, as in some Eastern European countries, is unlikely in China because the Party is indigenous, and by virtue of its size it simply cannot just disappear overnight. Unlike the situation in Eastern Europe, China does not yet have a strong civil society to speed the demise of the CCP or the sort of ethnic conflict that is evident in the former Soviet Union and Yugoslavia.[68]

White would argue that the primary obstacles to democratization are political, including the lack of skilled and charismatic leadership; the need for a coherent political alliance between reformist elements inside and outside the Party; the need to neutralize the views and actions of the hard-liners and their allies in the armed forces; and the challenges from radical elements in society that want to see a faster pace of political reform. Even if all of these problems can be overcome the new form of polity would still need, as it were, to live by its results. If it could not deliver on promises of political stability, transformation of the economic system, and improvements in material welfare, then "the prospect of a radical, possibly violent, political break becomes more likely."[69]

Conclusion

In an analysis that many China scholars will no doubt evaluate as hopelessly idealistic, Robert Weil has suggested that contemporary China still has the potential to produce a new form of democratic socialism.[70] He suggests that a "turning back" or a rediscovery is still possible, along the lines of what was being attempted during the Cultural Revolution, without the attendant chaos and with a significant amount of institutional change. In this sense Weil is echoing the sentiments of several Marxist sym-

pathizers who refuse to accept that the current situation is the best China can achieve, including such scholars as Araf Dirlik, Hill Gates, and Maurice Meisner.[71] What Weil is hoping for is a return to something like a grassroots type of socialism, working from the assumption that the mass power of the state is mutually exclusive of the level of marketization and privatization currently in evidence in China.

In this sense, Weil is hoping that China will be able to achieve what Deng Xiaoping wrote about early in his leadership period: a situation in which true socialism would emerge at the end of a long phase of capitalism. Weil is visualizing China as perhaps the only country able to stand up against global capitalism and return to what he refers to as its "revolutionary past" as a viable alternative.[72] Weil is fairly vague about how all this would work out, but he is talking about a bottom-up struggle on a mass basis, in which "every worker, peasant, and intellectual is encouraged to confront the forces of exploitation and oppression . . . and to take a direct role in running society at all levels."[73] Weil is convinced this would have all sorts of positive outcomes for China, including "a moderate rate of growth on a sustainable basis . . . while strengthening egalitarianism between social strata and economic and geographic regions [which] may well help provide a guide to the future, as peoples of the world strive for development without class polarization and environmental disaster."[74]

These are grand thoughts with noble ideals, but the fact that Weil's "solution" seems to most observers to be patently ridiculous is evidence enough that it could probably never come to pass. This does not mean, of course, that we should dismiss his ideas outright: It may be a good idea—and for many of the same reasons discussed in this book—to consider alternatives to global capitalism for China. At present China is a society under great strain, with inequalities widening rapidly and potential conflicts simmering dangerously. The economic and political problems China has faced during its transition away from orthodox socialism have not yet come close to the depredations witnessed in some of the European states, but it would be arrogant of the Chinese to assume that they are immune to such a turn of events.

There is a consensus that in the current era the government has lost something that had always seemed to be of crucial importance in traditional and Maoist China: the expectation of the people that their government would provide and nurture a compelling moral framework as a prerequisite to social and economic well-being. Today, it is clear that few people in China see the state being able to provide any sort of exemplary leadership. Amid the new fluidity and restructuring in contemporary China, the only idea that seems to be widely accepted among the people is that "money and improving one's standard of living are important."[75] Although Russians, Ukrainians, and certainly Kosovars may have good reason to be jealous, China's dilemma in the post-utopian age is unenviable: It remains to be seen how the state can continue to buy social peace and order with economic success alone; yet if the economic modernization project is damaged or diverted, the consequences are unthinkable.[76]

NOTES

ᓄᓄᓄᓄᓄᓄᓄᓄᓄᓄᓄᓄᓄᓄ

Chapter 1

1. L. Kolakowski, 1990, *Modernity on Endless Trial.* Chicago: University of Chicago Press, p. 143.

2. See, for example, Minxin Pei, 1998, *From Reform to Revolution: The Demise of Communism in China and the Soviet Union.* Cambridge: Harvard University Press.

3. See C.G.A. Bryant and E. Mokrzycki (eds.), 1994, *The New Great Transformation: Change and Continuity in East-Central Europe.* London: Routledge; see also K. Polanyi, 1944, *The Great Transformation: The Political and Economic Origins of Our Time.* Boston: Beacon. Its central feature was the self-regulating market, guided by economic rationality; in other words it was the beginning of the era of economic liberalism, which had to be counterbalanced by what Polanyi referred to as "social protection" for the economically less privileged groups.

4. For a discussion of these issues, see M. Burawoy and K. Verdery, 1999, *Uncertain Transitions: Ethnographies of Change in the Postsocialist World.* Lanham, MD: Rowman and Littlefield. In the China context, see, for example, the special issue of the journal *boundary 2* entitled *Postcolonialism in China*, Vol. 24, No. 3 (Fall 1977), coedited by Arif Dirlik and Zhang Xudong.

5. Along these lines Stephen Kotkin has attempted an analysis of the way Stalinism was lived on a day-to-day basis in the gigantic new steel factory built in Magnitogorsk in the early 1930s. Under appalling physical conditions, freezing weather, and close surveillance and control of the Stalinist state, the people who were constructing and working in the new city–cum–steel plant somehow managed to make life bearable for themselves. As Kotkin observes, "in Magnitogorsk there were many creative people, the definition of which might be an individual who manages to discover, even invent, room to maneuver. Beyond individual virtuosity, even ordinary human actions undertaken as part of daily life

had the effect of realigning . . . what might be called the landscape of possibility, opening up some options and closing off others." See S. Kotkin, 1995, *Magnetic Mountain: Stalinism as a Civilization.* Berkeley: University of California Press, p. 155. In this book I shall be considering these "landscapes of possibility" in contemporary China. For a more recent review of the way Soviet citizens coped with the harshness of everyday life in the Stalinist city, see Sheila Fitzpatrick, 1999, *Everyday Stalinism: Ordinary Life in Extraordinary Times—Soviet Russia in the 1930s.* New York: Oxford University Press.

6. Spence suggests that China has been on a quest for modernity for more than three centuries, pointing out that as early as the end of the sixteenth century the Chinese people "seized their own fate [and] threw themselves against the power of the state." See J. D. Spence, 1990, *The Search for Modern China.* New York: W. W. Norton, p. xxi. For a fascinating account and the interactions that took place between Chinese people and Westerners, see F. Wood, 1998, *No Dogs and Not Many Chinese: Treaty Port Life in China, 1843–1943.* London: John Murray.

7. P. Duara, 1995, *Rescuing History from the Nation: Questioning Narratives of Modern China.* Chicago: University of Chicago Press. See also A. Anagnost, 1997, *National Past-Times: Narrative, Representation, and Power in Modern China.* Durham: Duke University Press.

8. D. Harvey, 1989, *The Condition of Postmodernity: An Enquiry into the Origins of Cultural Change.* Oxford: Blackwell. As Lisa Rofel (1999) has defined it, the term "modernity" "encompasses the invention of humanism, the secularization of society, and the emergence of technical reason. It is taken to mean a belief in the triumvirate of truth, reason, and progress, whose singular subject for grasping the world in these terms is Man—a subject free of located interests with a will and agency that originates

463

from within himself. In short, it is identified with the European Enlightenment project"; see Rofel's 1999 book, *Other Modernities: Gendered Yearnings in China After Socialism.* Berkeley: University of California Press, p. 10.

9. M. Blecher, 1997, *China Against the Tides: Restructuring Through Revolution, Radicalism, and Reform.* London: Pinter.

10. G. White, 1993, *Riding the Tiger: The Politics of Economic Reform in Post-Mao China.* London: Macmillan, p. 233.

11. K. Lieberthal, 1995, *Governing China: From Revolution Through Reform.* New York: W. W. Norton, p. 239.

12. Ibid., p. 239. Some Western socialists look back nostalgically to earlier times in China, when there was really something approximating the "democratic socialism" of the early Maoist period. But as others like Maurice Meisner have suggested, there really was never any such thing, and to speak of it as having existed is to create an imaginary past. See Meisner, 1996, *The Deng Xiaoping Era: An Inquiry into the Fate of Chinese Socialism, 1978–1994.* New York: Hill and Wang.

13. Minxin Pei, op. cit., for example, argues that China's route to transition can be described as the "evolutionary authoritarian" route, because it is gradual, and at the end of the day an authoritarian party (the CCP) is still in command. There are two other obvious alternative routes to transition. The "double breakthrough" route is where democratization is followed by economic transformation on a large and rapid scale, as happened in Poland, Czechoslovakia, and East Germany. The third route, as yet not taken by any regimes, is the "single-breakthrough" shortcut, where the two processes occur simultaneously, the closest example being Hungary in 1988–1989.

14. Deng Xiaoping, 1990, *Deng Xiaoping on the Development of the Party.* People's Publishing House, p. 262; see Pei, op. cit., p. 20.

15. In fact, the first reforms to be launched were in China's urban areas, but for a variety of reasons it proved very difficult to implement such reforms successfully. The reforms attempted in the rural areas, by contrast, were much more successful much sooner; such success meant the reforms were pushed further than anticipated, even by the most optimistic of reformers (see Blecher, op. cit.).

16. As we have already seen, the CCP was able to remain firmly in control, although some political scientists argue that the prolonged success of the

reforms will continue to generate resistance that will eventually pressure the regime into allowing more political openness. See, for example, Lieberthal (op. cit., 1995).

17. This comparison should probably begin with the most obvious observation: that economic and social conditions in China have at no time reached the low points being reported from Russia throughout the 1990s. See P. Nolan, 1995, *China's Rise, Russia's Fall: Policies, Economics, and Planning in the Transition from Stalinism.* New York: St. Martin's.

18. See M. K. Whyte, 1996, "The Social Roots of China's Economic Development," pp. 37–47 in A. G. Walder (ed.), *China's Transitional Economy.* Oxford: Oxford University Press, p. 45. I am using the term "short" here in relative terms, in comparison to the seven decades of socialism in the former Soviet Union. My usage follows that of Eric Hobsbawm in the subtitle of his masterly book about the twentieth century (*The Age of Extremes*), which for him was "short" because it included only the years between 1914 and 1991. I do not intend to imply that the three decades of socialism were an easy or necessarily a pleasant period for the majority of the Chinese people.

19. Nolan (1995), op. cit.

20. Q. G. Jia, 1994, "Reform Ideology, Political Commitment, and Resource Transfer: An Alternative Model for the Explanation of China's Economic Reform," *Journal of Contemporary China,* No. 5 (Spring), pp. 3–24.

21. China's route to transition in the arena of economics has been described as "touching stones to cross the river," which was significantly different from what took place in many of the European states, where the move toward the market was made with one drastic cut of the knife. It is also apparent that China's route to transition and its outcomes have been determined by the unique nature of the preexisting (socialist) society; to use Stark's (1992) term, it is "path dependent." D. Stark, 1992, "Path Dependence and Privatization Strategies in East Central Europe," *East European Politics and Societies,* Vol. 6, No. 1, pp. 17–54. As Michael Watts (1998) has observed, it is evident that the reform process involves a significant amount of mixing of old structures and new ideas, in "an interplay between national reform policy and local socio-cultural dynamics." M. J. Watts, 1998, "Recombinant Capitalism: State, De-Collectivization and the Agrarian Question in Vietnam," pp. 450–505 in J. Pickles and A. Smith (eds.), *Theorizing Transition: The Political*

Economy of Post-Communist Transformations. New York: Routledge, p. 452. Although Watts is speaking mainly about Vietnam, the similarities with China are striking. In Vietnam Watts describes the emergence of an assertive class of farmers, operating "on top of a weak and often ineffective constitutional base." As we shall see in Chapter 7, this is similar in many ways to what occurred in China, as documented very forcefully by Kate Xiao Zhou (1996) and Daniel Kelliher (1992), both of whom have argued strongly for a power-to-the-peasants account that attributes relatively little importance to the state as the architect and driving force of the reforms. Kate Xiao Zhou, 1996, *How the Farmers Changed China: Power of the People.* Boulder: Westview Press; D. Kelliher, 1992, *Peasant Power in China: The Era of Rural Reform; 1979–1989.* New Haven: Yale University Press.

22. This expectation was primarily for societies that began the transition with socialist governments. It is important to recall that in other societies, most notably the Asian NIEs (Hong Kong, Singapore, Taiwan, and South Korea), democratization has followed (and one could argue was a result of) significant economic success. As already noted, it was also assumed that political reform would necessarily occur before economic reform. Moreover the communist superstructure in China was not dismantled by the reforms, demonstrating that it was possible to move from a command economy to market competition without changing the fundamental character of the political system.

23. It is difficult to explain why the Chinese reforms have performed so well against all expectations. One possible answer is that China (compared to the other transitioning socialist states) entered the reform era with some significant advantages: a low level of international debt; a special relationship with capital, and enterprise-rich societies (especially Hong Kong and Taiwan); a long tradition of (petty) capitalism stretching back more than a thousand years as noted by H. Gates, 1996, *China's Motor: A Thousand Years of Petty Capitalism,* Ithaca: Cornell University Press; and a low-income, mainly rural society that was able and more than willing to provide a huge supply of cheap and geographically mobile labor. It is also plausible to suggest that the incremental approach was the only one that could have succeeded in China by providing a stable transition through a period of major structural upheaval and great uncertainty. It may be that a strong state is required for such a transition to occur: to maintain national unity; to ensure

political stability; and to place the overall national interests ahead of those of the powerful vested interest groups. This is precisely the explanation selected by Manuel Castells (1998), who uses the term "developmentalist" to characterize the action of the state in Japan and the Asian NIEs. See M. Castells, 1998, *End of Millennium.* Oxford: Blackwell. Whatever the explanation, it is clear that events in China have been markedly different from those witnessed elsewhere, and the differences are not just related to the speed of the process. It is evident that a mix of economic and political forces shaped what appeared to be a chaotic and inconsistent set of policies into a coherent process; see B. Naughton, 1995, "Cities in the Chinese Economic System: Changing Roles and Conditions for Autonomy," pp. 61–89 in D. S. Davis et al. (eds.), *Urban Spaces in Contemporary China: The Potential for Autonomy and Community in Post-Mao China.* Washington, DC: Woodrow Wilson Press, especially pp. 472–475.

24. Blecher, op. cit., p. 109. As Blecher points out, this term was first used by White in *Riding the Tiger,* op. cit., p. 256.

25. G. Veeck (ed.), 1991, *The Uneven Landscape: Geographical Studies in Post-Reform China.* Baton Rouge: Geoscience Publications, Louisiana State University.

26. Premodern China was always a place of remarkable diversity, but the modernization project, rather than homogenizing China, has actually served to reinforce some of the existing differences. In a single day's outing, for example, starting at the coast in one of the southern provinces and driving inland, a traveller can leave behind the brightness of the city and its glittering postmodern towers and enter the darkness of what are essentially premodern landscapes in the countryside.

27. J.S.S. Muldavin, 1996, "The Political Ecology of Agrarian Reform in China," pp. 227–259 in R. Peet and M. Watts (eds.), *Liberation Ecologies: Environment, Development, Social Movements.* London: Routledge, esp. pp. 228–229. See also J.S.S. Muldavin, 1997, "Environmental Degradation in Heilongjiang: Policy Reform and Agrarian Dynamics in China's New Hybrid Economy," *Annals of the Association of American Geographers,* Vol. 87, No. 4 (December), pp. 579–613. A similar argument (about a place being "all things to all people") can be made for Taiwan, although the components are obviously different. For an excellent treatment of this issue, see W. M. Tu, 1996, "Cultural Identity and the Politics of Recognition in Contemporary Taiwan," *The China*

Quarterly, No. 148 (December), pp. 1115–1140. An NIE in the Asian context is usually taken to mean the four "developmentalist" economies of Hong Kong, South Korea, Taiwan, and Singapore; see Castells, op. cit.

28. See Rofel, op. cit., p. 13. See also L. Rofel, 1992, "Rethinking Modernity: Space and Factory Discipline in China," *Cultural Anthropology*, Vol. 7, No. 1 (February), pp. 93–114.

29. Pei, op. cit.

30. M. Elvin, 1997, *Changing Stories in the Chinese World*. Stanford: Stanford University Press. In fact, as Elvin notes, one of the defining characteristics of the modern age is that it "creates" or "gives a voice" to people who are able to "live in more than one [story] at the same time." Ibid., p. 177.

31. See Peet and Watts, op. cit.

32. T. G. Rawski, 1996, "Implications of China's Reform Experience," pp. 188–211 in A. G. Walder (ed.), *China's Transitional Economy*. Oxford: Oxford University Press, p. 188.

33. The term "capitalist revolution" is borrowed from Pei, op. cit.; see esp. chap. 3, pp. 85–117.

34. At the end of the millennium it is clear that we in the West have many questions to ask China, especially concerning its position in the global community. At the time of writing (late 1999) China appears to be (or as many Chinese would prefer to say, China is being made out to be) the next global aggressor, largely on account of increasingly bellicose attitudes and behaviors and a general tendency to go its own way regardless of protests from other major powers. The new, muscular China, complete with the latest nuclear weapons technology, is certainly giving the United States and other Western nations plenty to worry about for the next few decades. Although it is reasonable to worry about China being too strong, an equally important consideration is, as President Bill Clinton observed in 1999, that the United States probably has as much to fear from a weak China, whose ailing banks and bankrupt enterprises could threaten to undermine the world economy. In a recent *New York Times* article David Sanger quoted the president on this issue: "As we focus on the potential challenge that a strong China could present to the United States in the future, let us not forget the risk of a weak China, beset by internal conflicts, social dislocation and criminal activity, becoming a vast zone of instability in Asia." "When Allies Are Fierce Competitors," *New York Times*, May 2, 1999, sec. 4, p. 1. At present another question, also with global ramifications, involves the impacts of a fur-

ther deterioration of China's current ecological problems. Environmentalists from around the world are increasingly concerned about China's role in the deterioration of air quality, noting that China is already the second largest producer of commercial energy and the second largest emitter of carbon dioxide; it is also leading the world in methane gas emissions, most of which come from wet rice cultivation and the burning of low-grade coal. All of these concerns are exacerbated by China's big push toward accelerated growth in what are considered to be heavily polluting industries (see Chapter 16 for a detailed discussion of these issues). At the global level there have also been some recent concerns about China's ability to feed what amounts to more than a fifth of the world's population (see Chapter 7 for a discussion of Lester Brown's now-famous publication on this topic). This became a particularly important question after the security of the collective provision of food was abandoned in favor of privatized agriculture in the Chinese countryside, at which time farming became an even more unglamorous occupation than was ever the case in the past. If the Chinese are not able to feed themselves they may need to import massive quantities of food, which, according to some experts, would raise prices globally and create food shortages for poorer countries. Insecure and dwindling food supplies could have potentially devastating consequences, especially in parts of the world that are already teetering on the brink of ecological exhaustion.

35. M. Blecher, op. cit., p. 212.

36. M. Elvin, op. cit., p. 177.

37. K. Saunders, 1996, *Eighteen Layers of Hell: Stories from the Chinese Gulag*. London: Cassell, pp. 233–234.

38. In fact, Deng survived until 1997, although by that time Jiang Zemin had already taken what he considered to be the necessary precaution of having Deng declared mentally incompetent—a step he took in February 1994, before moving to indict some of the Deng family members and associates in his widespread (and popular) anticorruption campaign. See R. Baum, 1996, *Burying Mao: Chinese Politics in the Age of Deng Xiaoping*. Princeton: Princeton University Press, p. 387.

39. Just as Deng Xiaoping was giving his blessings to an acceleration of the reforms in 1992, two events occurred in the summer and fall that made his opponents and supporters nervous about the future. One was the riot at the Shenzhen Stock Exchange in August, followed by disastrous market plunges in

both the Shenzhen and Shanghai exchanges; the other was a new round of rapid overheating in the economy. Fixed capital investments, responding to Deng's relaxation of the government's austerity measures, rose by 32 percent in the first half of 1992; industrial output had also risen by 19 percent, overall economic growth by 16 percent. See Baum, ibid.

40. By 1993 inflation had reached 16 percent in the biggest cities; as Marc Blecher (op. cit., p. 11) has observed, "With inflation and crime soaring, and significant parts [especially in rural areas] of society going ballistic, the leadership [saw the need for] forceful measures to maintain social and political stability." By the end of summer 1993, banks were ordered to call in loans, interest rates were raised, and infrastructure projects were abandoned; in spite of these measures both growth and inflation continued to grow into the next year and beyond.

41. To improve its own image the state announced two new campaigns designed to appeal to the masses, under the assumption they would be safe and popular. One was another round of crackdowns on official corruption; the other was the state's affirmation of an increasingly hostile and belligerent line on issues of nationalism, with warnings issued to those parts of China where the people might be considering the struggle for increased autonomy. See Blecher, op. cit., p. 113.

42. In addition, after the death of Chen Yun, an old hard-liner who had been one of Deng's most ardent opponents throughout the reform period, a continuation of the bitter power struggles between the leftist and rightist cliques within the Party leadership seemed to be unlikely. See ibid., p. 114.

43. Ibid.

44. Baum, op. cit., p. 378.

45. Ibid., pp. 381–382.

46. In addition to events in China at this time, there was publicity about the declining fortunes of many of the states in the former Soviet Union and Eastern and Central Europe that were experiencing the transition out of socialism. With this as extra fuel, the debate—about whether or how soon China would collapse—continued throughout the 1990s.

47. See, for example, N. C. Hughes, 1998, "Smashing the Iron Rice Bowl," *Foreign Affairs,* Vol. 77, No. 4 (July/August), pp. 67–77.

48. The book, which appears not to have been published yet in the West, is reviewed in B. Y. Liu and P. Link, 1998, "A Great Leap Backward?" *New York Review of Books,* Vol. 65, No. 15 (October 8), pp. 19–23, 19.

49. Ibid., p. 20, quoting from He's book.

50. Hughes, op. cit.

51. This is compared to bad debt ratios of about 3 percent in most modern international banks; see P. Chan and M. O'Neil, "Asia Woes Spur Beijing to Act," *South China Morning Post,* May 14, 1998.

52. For example, in the huge and inefficient state enterprises, managers have effectively become what He calls "semiowners" who can operate with impunity as long as they have their superiors in their pockets (i.e., through bribery). Once the manager has ensured his superior's loyalty, "He or she has all the powers of an owner while remaining free of all the responsibilities." See Liu and Link, op. cit., p. 20.

53. Ibid., op. cit., p. 22. What is perhaps most amazing of all, however, is how the book was ever published in China. Liu and Link suggest that *China's Pitfall* was deemed acceptable because it will allow Jiang Zemin, in time, to distance himself from Deng Xiaoping and his legacy, just as Deng had been able to use the scar literature written about the Cultural Revolution chaos to distance himself from Mao Zedong.

54. Ibid., pp. 212–213. For a discussion of Chinese people's "dreams of heaven," see E. Croll, 1994, *From Heaven to Earth: Images and Experience of Development in China.* London: Routledge. For other, equally damning accounts of corruption in contemporary China, see M. Meisner, 1996, *The Deng Xiaoping Era: An Inquiry into the Fate of Chinese Socialism, 1978–1994.* New York: Hill and Wang; and R. Weil, 1996, *Red Cat, White Cat: China and the Contradictions of "Market Socialism."* New York: Monthly Review Press.

55. This was the case over the issue of the U.S. sale of military aircraft to Taiwan. The war of words with Britain was intensified during the last years of the Patten governorship before the handover of Hong Kong in 1997. In spring 1999 these aggressive stances were accentuated (arguably with some justification) by the bombing of the Chinese embassy in Belgrade by NATO planes in the struggle with the Serbs over Kosovo.

56. Liu and Link, op. cit., p. 23.

57. As He observes, "The preponderance of new wealth . . . was gained illegally" and China "is [now] headed toward joint rule by the government and a mafia." See Liu and Link, p. 23. To scholars working in Eastern and Central Europe, as well as Russia, this situation must sound familiar, in the sense that with so much newfound wealth just around the corner, corruption and graft were almost inevitable during

the transition years. He's reports from China are reminiscent of what happened in Poland during the great privatization rush in the 1990s; in fact the definition of "privatization" in former socialist economies, according to Janusz Lewandowski, former minister of property transformation in Poland, is a situation in which "someone who doesn't know who the real owner is and doesn't know what it's really worth sells something to someone who doesn't have any money!" See K. Verdery, 1996, *What Was Socialism, and What Comes Next?* Princeton: Princeton University Press, p. 210.

58. Baum, op. cit., p. 392. By the end of 1999 the disintegration has still not occurred, although the prophets of doom are at the door constantly. It appears that Jiang Zemin has safely navigated through the succession period, during which time he has strengthened his position and conducted two highly successful "summits" with the United States, one in the fall of 1997, when he visited the United States, the other in spring of 1998, when President Clinton went to China. Jiang had very carefully prepared the way for the succession by bolstering his own position, beginning as early as 1993.

59. Verdery, op. cit., p. 227.

60. Ibid., pp. 227–228.

61. Vladimir Tismaneanu, *Fantasies of Salvation: Democracies, Nationalism, and Myth in Post-Communist Europe.* Princeton: Princeton University Press, p. 29.

62. For example, in March 1998 China's leaders announced a series of plans to transform the SOEs and pay their debts; to cut government employees by 50 percent; and to reform the financial system. All were, by the summer of 1998, receiving strong opposition, with critics suggesting that even these drastic measures were a case of too little, too late. From this perspective, as He Qinglian points out, Deng Xiaoping's legacy is clear: He aborted the reforms in 1989, deciding in 1992 to buy stability for the regime by pursuing rapid economic growth, the price of which was sharply increased corruption, financial deception, and the erosion of the moral basis of China's society. See Liu and Link, p. 23.

63. This paradox—which may still prove to be based on faulty reasoning—is similar in some ways to Hong Kong's dilemma during the 1990s, when its demise as a colony was already assumed to have occurred well before the actual handover in 1997. Hong Kong was suffering from or experiencing a syndrome that Ackbar Abbas has referred to as "deja disparu," meaning, literally, "already disappeared" or

"already gone." In some ways this is exactly what has been occurring in China throughout the 1990s—the assumption that the political transition has already taken place. See A. Abbas, 1997, *Hong Kong: Culture and the Politics of Disappearance.* Minneapolis: University of Minnesota Press, esp. chap. 2, "The New Hong Kong Cinema and the Deja Disparu," pp. 16–47.

64. Tismaneanu, op. cit., p. 29.

65. As a *New York Times* reporter described the situation in early May 1999 (just before the abortive attempt of parliament to impeach Boris Yeltsin), the Russians have been following U.S. advice about how to become capitalists for almost a decade: "They followed American foreign-policy handouts urging that Russia be 'integrated into Euro-Atlantic and global communities' and built into 'a modern, market-based economy.' They gave up on empire, cut up their missiles and ceded three of their clients to NATO. And for what? More than $60 billion in new debt. A beggar, rubble-trouble economy. A skeletal military. A short lease held tight by the International Monetary Fund. And now, the leveling of their one remaining friend in all Europe, Yugoslavia." Michael Wines, "Straining to See the Real Russia," *New York Times,* May 2, 1999, sec. 4, p. 1.

66. In his obituary for Galina Staravoitova, one of the intellectuals who had contributed to the construction of democracy in Russia, Adam Michnik suggests that her murder in November 1998 was symptomatic of the lawlessness in Russia at the end of the millennium. He also observes that in the democratic spirit she had helped to establish it was by no means unusual to listen to the new dialogues about freedom being openly matched by such events as "the Russian national Communist Makashov openly calling for anti-Jewish repression." Michnik believes that the malevolence of such oratory is not directed primarily at the Jews; in fact, as he suggests, "they were at most a bait for the mob [while] the real target was Russian democracy and Russian democrats, such as Galina Staravoitova." Adam Michnik, "Death in St. Petersburg," *New York Review of Books,* January 14, 1999, p. 5. Michnik explains that the so-called Black Hundreds see the world very simply: with the global/Jewish mafia and its democratic agents in Russia lined up against Russian national Communists and Russian Orthodox-monarchist patriots. As he puts it, "they reject the West as the seat of evil and the ruin of Russia [and] they aim at the annihilation of Russian democracy, in which they see the fifth column of Western

democracy" (ibid.). In addition to such disturbing developments in the new Russia is the terrible possibility of the emergence of new fascist groups. See, e.g., Martin Malia, 1999, *Russia Under Western Eyes: From the Bronze Horseman to the Lenin Mausoleum.* Cambridge: Harvard University Press. Malia argues that contemporary Russia is going through a period that is very similar to the Weimar period in Europe when the party that became the German Nazis was being born. In Russia, it appears there is no shortage of ultranationalist groups proposing dictatorship as a means of restoring law and order and national self-respect. The two strongest among these are led by Vladimir Zhirinovsky and his Liberal Democratic Party of Russia, and Gennady Zyuganov and his Communist Party of the Russian Federation, both of whom are described as "united in nostalgia for Stalinism, hostility to liberalism and parliamentarianism, and a fondness for xenophobic rhetoric and conspiracy theories." See the review of Malia's book in Aileen Kelly, "The Russian Sphinx," *New York Review of Books*, May 20, 1999, pp. 7–10.

67. Tismaneanu, op. cit., pp. 12–13.

68. Kolakowski, op. cit., p. 139.

69. Tismaneanu, op. cit., p. 14.

70. Ibid., p. 39 (emphasis added).

71. Ibid., p. 61.

72. Burawoy and Verdery, op. cit., p. 14.

73. Ibid., p. 15.

74. Ibid., p. 7.

75. It is important to recognize here, however, that freedom can be a two-edged sword: A peasant is now free to leave the countryside to look for work in the city; but that same peasant is also free to die in the squalor and poverty of a city that does not provide for him/her (see Chapter 15).

76. Burawoy and Verdery, op. cit., p. 14.

77. It is important to bear in mind, however, that the socialist state in China has not collapsed to the same extent as it has in Europe and that economic conditions are for the most part considerably healthier; see Pei, op. cit.

78. As Derek Gregory points out, "geography . . . is not confined to any one discipline. . . . It travels instead through social practices at large and is implicated in myriad topographies of power and knowledge." D. Gregory, 1994, "Geographical Imagination," pp. 217–218 in in R. J. Johnston, D. Gregory, and D. M. Smith (eds.), *Dictionary of Human Geography,*. 3d ed., p. 11. Gregory is concerned with bridging the enormous gap between the sociological and the geographical imagination, to make sure that space gets at least some consideration in discussions of social theory. David Harvey's work, perhaps more than any other, has helped to do this. As Gregory notes, "A series of changes in the organization and experience of social space (sometimes called the 'culture of space') have been registered not only in the academy but also in the media and through an explosion of interest in travel writing and 'traveling theory' which has also had a major impact on social thought and cultural criticism." See ibid., p. 218.

79. In the spring of 1996 China took offense to what it perceived to be Taiwan's aggressive posturing in the international arena, whereas Taiwan perceived China's hostile words and deeds to be reflective of its combative nationalism on the issue of reunification. The event blew over, but not before a show of thuggish force, involving the launching of Chinese missiles in the general vicinity of Taipei.

Chapter 2

1. C. Mackerras, 1994, *China's Minorities: Integration and Modernization in the Twentieth Century.* Hong Kong: Oxford University Press, pp. 266–267.

2. M. Selden, 1988, *The Political Economy of Chinese Socialism.* Armonk, NY: M. E. Sharpe, p. 144.

3. See S. W. Toops, 1999, "China: A Geographic Preface," pp. 11–28 in R. E. Gamer (ed.), *Understanding Contemporary China.* Boulder: Lynne Rienner.

4. This explains why the book does not include such standard geographical themes as physical geography, including climate, geomorphological features, and soils; or transportation geography; or distributional studies of production facilities and capabili-

ties. These topics *are* obviously important to an understanding of contemporary China, but in this book, largely in the interests of saving space, they are excluded. For an excellent coverage of such themes, see Gamer, cited above, especially the chapter by Stanley Toops.

5. This is, of course, not the case for travel writers and novelists, who often paint superbly detailed pictures of places with words alone. The British travel writer Colin Thubron is in a class of his own in this respect. He was astounded by the differences he encountered between northern and southern China when he first crossed the Yangtze River. As Thubron

writes: "The Yangtze ... marks the immemorial divide between a soldierly, bureaucratic north, and the suave, entrepreneurial south. Men dwindle in size and integrity as they go south (say the northerners) and the clear-cut Mandarin of Beijing becomes a slushy caress. The dust of the wheat and millet-bearing plains dissolves to the monsoons of paddy fields and tea plantations. The staple of noodles becomes a diet of rice, and the low cabbages and symmetrical northern streets twist and steepen into labyrinths of whitewashed brick." As a master craftsman with words Thubron is able to characterize these differences in a simple but richly evocative manner. Unlike travel writers, social scientists are rarely comfortable making such sweeping generalizations about people and places. See C. Thubron, 1987, *Behind the Wall: A Journey Through China.* London: Heinemann, p. 88.

6. M. C. Goldstein, 1997, *The Snow Lion and the Dragon: China, Tibet, and the Dalai Lama.* Berkeley: University of California Press, pp. xi–xii.

7. See Toops, op. cit., p. 14

8. J. K. Fairbank, 1987, *The Great Chinese Revolution, 1800–1985.* New York: Harper and Row, p. 7.

9. This aggressive behavior has been particularly evident over the issues of Hong Kong and Taiwan, as we shall see in more detail in Chapter 11. China's relative isolation guaranteed that when the time finally came for modernization it would be a peculiarly torturous experience. It is important to point out here that modernization in the United States was a relatively painless process forged by recent immigrants who had already shed the tough skins of their cultures. In China, by comparison, modernization has required the moving of a veritable mountain of cultural baggage that had been sitting in one place for thousands of years. To quote Fairbank again, modernization for the Chinese amounts to the moral equivalent of Americans rejecting "the Virgin Mary and the Founding Fathers [and] a denial of the values of one's grandfather." See Fairbank, op. cit., p. 7. In the early 1980s it was a particularly cruel punishment for the Chinese to accept their economic backwardness relative to many of their East Asian neighbors, particularly in the Chinese territories of Hong Kong and Taiwan. The Chinese have clearly enjoyed the new level of attention lavished upon them in the 1990s as their powerful economic growth dazzled the world and even surpassed that of regional competitors.

10. China Statistical Publishing House, 1998, *China Statistical Yearbook 1997*, No. 16, p. 69, table 3-1.

11. R. Fuson, 1999, *Fundamental Place-Name Geography*, 9th ed. Boston: McGraw-Hill.

12. *China Statistical Yearbook 1997*, op. cit., p. 55, table 2-24.

13. D. Gregory, 1994a, *Geographical Imaginations.* Oxford: Blackwell, p. 217. There is an analogy here with C. Wright Mills's discussion of the sociological imagination in the sense that Mills was concerned not solely with the academic discipline of sociology but with what he referred to as "habits of the mind" that could be located throughout the human and social sciences.

14. At first, one might assume this division implies the usual dualities in China, such as the urban-rural divide or the separation between the coastal and the interior provinces; in fact the trajectory of development in China has produced a more complex pattern than this. As we shall see, there are large pockets of poverty even in the rich coastal provinces like Guangdong, as well as regions of relative wealth in some of the interior provinces. See C. C. Fan, 1995, "Of Belts and Ladders: State Policy and Uneven Regional Development in Post-Mao China," *Annals of the Association of American Geographers*, Vol. 85, No. 4, pp. 421–449; and E. Vogel. 1979: *One Step Ahead in China: Guangdong Province Under Reform.* Cambridge: Harvard University Press. It is also important to point out that the sum of the places involved in China's current rush toward modernity, and those not involved, amounts to *all* places in China, so no places can be excluded. From another viewpoint *all* places are, by definition, involved in a relational sense, because *any* places are involved.

15. In addition, the Chinese have during the past two centuries spread themselves very widely around the world. The term "place," as used here, can be thought of as a "between" concept in the sense that most geographers choose to situate themselves between two apparently opposed definitions of place. At one end of the scale is the notion of a science of place(s), which puts place in the realm of a decentered universalism (as opposed to a more humanistic view of geography, in which place is the unique space where a person is "situated"). The humanistic definition offers the notion of place as a form of centered particularism, which, during the so-called quantitative revolution in geography, or the era of spatial science, was generally considered to be a provincial or parochial concept, something that ought to be relegated to the background, outdated, as it were, by the forces of modernity. These ideas are

discussed by J. N. Entrikin, 1991, *The Betweenness of Place: Towards a Geography of Modernity*. Baltimore: Johns Hopkins University Press; and also by D. Massey, 1984, *Spatial Divisions of Labour: Social Structures and the Geography of Production*. New York: Methuen. As Entrikin notes, many contemporary geographers prefer to situate themselves between these two extremes in their attempts to conduct "contexualist" studies in the so-called new regional geography. Doreen Massey, for example, argues that "local uniqueness matters. Capitalist society . . . develops unevenly. The implications are twofold. It is necessary to unearth the common processes, the dynamic of capitalist society, beneath the unevenness, but it is also necessary to recognize, analyze and understand the complexity of the unevenness itself. Spatial differentiation, geographical variety, is not an outcome: it is integral to the reproduction of society and its dominant social relations. The challenge is to hold the two sides together; to understand the general underlying causes while at the same time recognizing and appreciating the importance of the specific and the unique." Ibid., pp. 299–300.

16. G. B. Cressey, 1955, *Land of Five Hundred Million: A Geography of China*. New York: McGraw-Hill, p. 3.

17. As French philosopher Gabriel Marcel has observed: "There is virtually for everyone a deep association with and a consciousness of the places where we were born and grew up, where we live now, or where we have had some particularly moving experiences. This association seems to constitute a vital source of both individual and cultural identity and security, a point of departure from which we orient ourselves in the world." Marcel summarized this simply with the following statement: "An individual is not distinct from his place; he is that place." Quoted by Edward Relph, 1976, *Place and Placelessness*. London: Pion, p. 43.

18. In his travels across China in the late 1940s American journalist Jack Belden found some surprising pockets of isolation, even in the densely populated provinces of the North China Plain. He asks the outside reader to consider what life must have been like in such an area: "Almost completely outside the influence of modern science and twentieth century culture, the peasant was a brutal, blundering backwoodsman. He had never seen a movie, never heard a radio, never ridden in a car. He had never owned a pair of leather shoes, nor a toothbrush and seldom a piece of soap. And if he was a mountain man, he perhaps

bathed twice in his life—once when he was married and once when he died—not because he so much enjoyed wallowing in the dirt, but because water was scarce and could be spared only for drinking." See J. Belden, 1949, *China Shakes the World*. New York: Monthly Review Press, p. 129. The situation for women was much worse than it was for men, because they were rarely allowed to leave their husband's village once they had married. Missionary Arthur Smith met a woman who told him that in her next life she wanted to be a dog, because she would have more freedom. As Smith wrote, "Most Chinese girls [at the end of the nineteenth century] never go anywhere to speak of, and live what is literally the existence of a frog in a well. Tens of thousands of them have never been two miles away from the village." A. N. Smith, 1899, *Village Life in China: A Study in Sociology*. New York: Fleming H. Revell, p. 262. The strong sense of attachment to locality has contributed to the centrifugal tendencies within China over the centuries. For the relatively few people who did travel beyond their homes, this attachment provided them with an identity. Two people meeting for the first time would introduce themselves by ascertaining each other's native place, which was usually more important than their surnames. If a person moved away from home, it was taken for granted that he would sooner or later return to his native place. "The normative pattern was clear: a young man who left to seek his fortune elsewhere was expected to return home for marriage, to spend there an extended period of mourning on the death of either parent, and eventually to retire in the locality where his ancestors were buried." G. W. Skinner, 1977, "Introduction: Urban Social Structures in Ch'ing China," pp. 522–553 in G. W. Skinner (ed.), *The City in Late Imperial China*. Palo Alto: Stanford University Press, p. 539.

19. See ibid., pp. 545–546. In life the strength of the attachment to home place was equally strong. For example, among the businessmen from Ningbo who had moved to Shanghai in the nineteenth century and experienced great financial success, hiring practices were based predominantly on geographical principles. The first to be hired would be kinsmen from Ningbo (sons first, then nephews, then other relatives); next would be people from the same city; then the same county; then the same region of the province. See Y. Shiba, 1977, "Ningpo and Its Hinterland," pp. 391–440 in ibid., p. 437. The businessmen were also likely to endow their home place with some of the profits they had amassed: "Successful emigrants were expected to expand their family estates back home, to endow their lineages, and to invest in

community property. [Many] also retired to their native places, having ensured the continuity of their businesses abroad by grooming kinsmen or fellow natives for management." See Shiba, op. cit., p. 438.

20. See Zhang Xinxin and Sang Ye, 1987, *Chinese Lives: An Oral History of Contemporary China*. New York: Pantheon Books, p. 124.

21. The length of time spent away from one's "true" home may not be important. Arthur Smith, for example, told of a man who had been gone from his native village for twenty years. He finally returned unannounced and immediately went about his business as if he had never been away: "[He] enters his house, throws down his bundle and without a question or a greeting to anyone, proceeds to take a solacing smoke. He may have been away so long that no one recognizes him, and perhaps he is taken for a tramp. . . . But he merely replies 'Why should I not make myself at home in my house?' and resumes his smoking, leaving [the] details to be filled in later." See Smith, op. cit., p. 319.

22. From all accounts the traditional strength of the attachment to place in China was reinforced in the postrevolutionary era, both in the cities and in the countryside. Although we would normally expect the process of modernization to result in a weakening of traditional ties to localities, in China after 1949 the opposite appears to have been the case. In spite of the liberating principles of the Chinese revolution, the cooperatives, and later the communes, actually worked to increase the bondage of peasants to the land. In feudal China the peasants had always been poor, but they were never serfs. They could walk off their land to seek work, and throughout history there is evidence that many of them chose such a path whenever conditions in the countryside became intolerable. As American journalists like Graham Peck, Edgar Snow, and Jack Belden reported, the prerevolutionary countryside was often overrun by itinerant hobos, medicine men, tinkers, and small-time traders from all parts of China. After land reform and the early cooperative movement (see Chapter 7) every peasant was firmly tied to the land, and it became much more difficult to opt for a life on the road. The peasants were secure as long as the harvests were bountiful, but in the bad years, for example, during the Great Leap Forward (1958–1961), they all suffered together, but they could not leave the land because they had nowhere else to go.

23. One answer to these questions is that the task of organization is indeed too substantial, as witnessed by the considerable inefficiency in many walks of life and the trials and tribulations average Chinese citizens have to face as they go about their everyday tasks. This would appear to be increasingly the case in the new era of privatization and markets, with all of the additional complexities involved in making a living, finding a place to live, and surviving on a daily basis—all of which used to be taken care of by the state by the "iron rice bowl" provision of services, mostly organized and accessed from within the work units (*danwei*).

24. E. Hobsbawm, 1994, *Age of Extremes: The Short Twentieth Century*. London: Michael Joseph, p. 465.

25. In addition to the work units, in China's cities the system is complemented by small-scale geographical units at the neighborhood level, especially in the residents' committees (see Chapter 14). For a good discussion of this, see G. White, 1993, *Riding the Tiger: The Politics of Economic Reform in Post-Mao China*. London: Macmillan, esp. pp. 223–225.

26. Ibid., pp. 200–201.

27. M. Dutton, 1998, *Streetlife China*. Cambridge, UK: Cambridge University Press, p. 21. Dutton also observes that to "float" without a work unit is to be an outsider, a stranger, a vagrant—a source of danger, captured by the use of the Chinese character *liu*, as it used in the terms *liumang* (hoodlum) and *liudong renkou* (floating population).

28. In a discussion of the peasant reactions to collectivization in the Chinese countryside, political scientist Edward Friedman launched a vitriolic attack on collectivization and the tyranny of party rule in communist China, drawing an analogy with religious fundamentalism rather than utopian socialism: "The language of communist fundamentalism and the policies it legitimated are more in line with the telos of Ayatollah Ruhollah Khomeini than with the human solidarity and harmony envisaged by Peter Kropotkin." See E. Friedman, 1989, "Decollectivization and Democratization in China," *Problems of Communism*, Vol. 38, No. 5 (September/October), pp. 103–107.

29. White, op. cit., pp. 225–232.

30. See D. Gregory, 1994b, "Contextual Theory," pp. 90–93 in Johnston et al. (eds.), op. cit., p. 90. Geographers usually refer to such an approach as a "contextual approach." Sociologists, by comparison, might be more likely to utilize a compositional th ory in which human activity is divided up (or broken down) into general categories based on

principles of similarity—usually social class, gender, age, and ethnicity—which are then recombined to constitute an explanation of social life. From a geographical point of view a contextual theory seems to be more appropriate, and from this perspective, place is the location where social structure and human agency might meet each other. See N. Thrift, 1983, "On the Determination of Social Action in Space and Time," *Environment and Planning D: Society and Space*, Vol. 1, pp. 23–57. The place, in other words, is substantive and material enough (in its spatial qualities) to be the generator and conductor of structure; but it is also human enough (in its social qualities) to ensure that the intimate and corporeal dimensions are catered to. A key role in this contextual theory can be found for the situated life story, a biography in time and space that is able to tell us about the identity of the people in question. Perhaps the leading figure in the geography literature associated with this contextual theory is Swedish geographer Torsten Hägerstrand. See, for example, T. Hagerstrand, 1973, "The Domain of Human Geography," in R. J. Chorley (ed.), *Directions in Human Geography*. London: Methuen; and also Hagerstrand, 1974, "Commentary," pp. 50–54 in A. Buttimer, *Values in Geography*. Association of American Geographers, Commission on College Geography, Resource Paper No. 24. Hagerstrand (1973) has written that "being a geographer basically means to appreciate that when events are seen located together in a block of space-time they inevitably expose relations which cannot be traced any more, once we have bunched them into classes and drawn them out of their place in the block" (quoted in Gregory (1994b), op. cit., p. 90).

31. Ibid., p. 91.

32. See, for example, the work of Edward Soja, particularly his 1989 book, *Postmodern Geographies: The Reassertion of Space in Critical Social Theory*. London: Verso.

33. Among the best of the recent works are the following edited collections: L. McDowell (ed.), 1997, *Undoing Place: A Geographical Reader*. London: Arnold; T. Barnes and D. Gregory (eds.), 1997, *Reading Human Geography: The Poetics and Politics of Inquiry*. London: Arnold; and S. Pile and M. Keith (eds.), 1997, *Geographies of Resistance*. London: Routledge. See also E. W. Soja, 1996, *Thirdspace: Journeys to Los Angeles and Other Real-and-Imagined Places*. Oxford: Blackwell; A. Pred and M. J. Watts, 1992, *Reworking Modernity: Capitalisms and Symbolic Discontent*. New Brunswick, NJ: Rutgers Uni-

versity Press; S. Corbridge and J. A. Agnew, 1995, *Mastering Space: Hegemony, Territory, and International Political Economy*. New York: Routledge.

34. D. Gregory, 1994c, "Spatiality," pp. 582–585 in R. J. Johnston et al. (eds.), op. cit., p. 584.

35. Ibid., p. 583.

36. It is important to note that the issue of subjection involves the double meanings of the word "subject": in addition to the sense of being subjected to the power of others, the term refers to an assertion of identity and self-knowledge. Soja (1996, op. cit.) also argues that the struggle against subjection has become the most prominent issue in the new cultural politics of difference, or the struggle to determine who defines the individual or collective subject. Soja suggests that geographers, by privileging space and spatiality, might be able to contribute usefully to this debate.

37. Rofel, 1999, *Other Modernities: Gendered Yearnings in China After Socialism*. Berkeley: University of California Press, p. 13.

38. Spatial structure in this example is the articulation of the spatialities at each of these different levels. As Gregory (1994c) observes, spatial structure is both "a reflection of different systems of social practices and a constraint upon them" (p. 583). Manuel Castells takes this even farther, arguing that "there is no space (a physical quantity yet an abstract entity) [only] an historically defined space-time, a space constructed, worked, practiced by social relations." In other words, "socially speaking, space, like time, is a conjuncture, that is to say, the articulation of concrete historical practices." See Gregory (1994c), op. cit., p. 583, quoting Castells.

39. Soja, (1996) op. cit., p. 34.

40. Gregory (1994a), op. cit., p. 262.

41. Harvey, op. cit., p. 306.

42. Yet others like Frederic Jameson (1988) would argue that the spatial peculiarities of postmodernism involve our insertion as individual subjects into a multidimensional set of radically discontinuous realities, whose frames range from the still-surviving spaces of bourgeois life all the way to the unimaginable decentering of global capitalism. See Harvey, op. cit. p. 351. Harvey thinks Jameson is exaggerating the shock effect of the processes that he believes are simply continuations of trends that have been observable for more than a century.

43. See, for example, *China's Pitfall* (so far only published in China and Hong Kong), by Q. L. He, 1998, Hong Kong: Mingjing Chubanshe. It was reviewed by Liu Binyan and Perry Link, 1998, "A

Great Leap Backward?" *New York Review of Books*, Vol. 65, No. 15 (October 8), pp. 19–23.

44. An important distinction can be made here between three different meanings of the term "post-modernism": One is a postmodern *style*, which is most visibly present in postmodern works of art and architecture; another is a postmodern *method*, which is a form of critical interpretation, or deconstruction; and the third is a postmodern *epoch*, which is an era in which changes in culture and ways of thinking are themselves located in geopolitics and the evolution of the global economy. See M. Dear, 1986, "Postmodernism and Planning," *Environment and Planning D: Society and Space*, Vol. 4, pp. 367–384; see also C. Calhoun, 1995, *Critical Social Theory: Culture, History, and the Challenge of Difference*. Oxford, UK: Blackwell.

45. The geographer, in this case, might claim that attachment to a specific place is a good way to go about this. Harvey, for example, notes that if no one "knows their place" in this anonymous and alienating world, "how can a secure social order be . . . sustained?" Harvey, op. cit., p. 302.

46. Rofel (1999), op. cit., p. 31.

47. Ibid., p. 32.

48. Ibid., p. 221.

49. In a very different context, Nigerian Poet Laureate Wole Soyinka has assessed the possibilities of his people openly resisting the tyranny of the Nigerian state. Solinka believes that one day soon this will happen, simply because humans are political animals who eventually must stand up to their oppressors: "We must insist that man is indeed a political animal if only to give dictators sleepless nights, in order to remind them that they hold sway over a restless breed of their own kind, whom they have deprived of their animal rights and who will one day challenge them . . . as usage dictates within the animal kingdom. When, as the fable teaches us, the king of the forest loses all measure of self and demands that its daily prey deliver itself up to him in meek obedience to an agreed-upon roster of consumption, it is time

to confront him with the fathomless resources of alternative power and drown him in the arrogance of a delusion." W. Soyinka, 1997, *The Open Sore of a Continent: A Personal Narrative of the Nigerian Crisis*. New York: Oxford University Press, pp. 128–129. By the end of the 1990s it looked as if Nigeria was finally headed toward political plurality and stability, with a much diminished role for the military.

50. Describing this critique, Araf Dirlik quotes Cornell West, who argues that the goal is to "trash the monolithic and homogenous in the name of diversity, multiplicity, and heterogeneity; to reject the abstract, general, and universal in light of the concrete, specific, and particular; and to historicize, contextualize, and pluralize by highlighting the contingent, provisional, variable, tentative, shifting, and changing." A. Dirlik, 1994, *After the Revolution: Waking to Global Capitalism*. Hanover, NH: Wesleyan University Press, pp. 95–96.

51. H. A. Giroux, 1992, *Border Crossings: Cultural Workers and the Politics of Education*. New York: Routledge, p. 21.

52. This can, of course, happen under socialism as well; in fact in Maoist China there was considerable unevenness resulting from geographical and historical forces, interwoven with the outcomes of seemingly endless contests between state and society. In Deng's and Jiang's Chinas, however, such contests have been joined by Chinese and "foreign" capitalists—many of them from different parts of the Chinese diaspora—who are acting as the new purveyors of power. These are the people Rupert Hodder has called the "merchant princes." See, for example, R. Hodder, 1994, "State, Collective, and Private Industry in China's Evolving Economy," pp. 116–127 in D. Dwyer (ed.), *China: The Next Decade*. Harlow, Essex, UK: Longman Scientific and Technical. See also R. Hodder, 1993, *The Creation of Wealth in China: Domestic Trade and Material Progress in a Communist State*. London: Belhaven Press.

53. X. L. Zhang, 1988, *Half of Man Is Woman*. New York: W. W. Norton, p. 264.

Chapter 3

1. D. Davin, 1997, *Mao Zedong*. Stroud, UK: Sutton Publishing (Pocket Biographies), p. 107.

2. One of the urban myths that became well known in China involves the story of a man who avoided injury in a deadly traffic accident because, he claimed, he had a picture of Mao on his dashboard. Somehow,

the Chairman's presence had saved him! See G. R. Barmé, 1996, *Shades of Mao: The Posthumous Cult of the Great Leader*. Armonk, NY: M. E. Sharpe, p. 22.

3. Ibid.

4. Ibid. For a description of the *qigong* phenomenon in China, see N. N. Chen, 1995, "Urban

Spaces and Experiences of *Qigong*," pp. 347–361 in D. S. Davis et al. (eds.), *Urban Spaces in Contemporary China: The Potential for Autonomy and Community in Post-Mao China*. Cambridge, UK: Cambridge University Press. In the late summer of 1999 *qigong* received international attention when the Chinese government banned the nationwide organization known as Falun Gong, which practiced *qigong*, among other things. The government appeared to be worried about the vast growth in the membership of Falun Gong, perceiving it to be a threat to national security.

5. Barmé, op. cit., p. 18.

6. Ibid., pp. 18–19.

7. As we shall see in Chapter 4, this has a parallel with the way some Westerners managed to create a favorable image of Mao and Maoism, one that would fit with what they wanted him to represent rather than the actually existing Maoism, which was in many ways much more brutal.

8. Z. S. Li, 1994, *The Private Life of Chairman Mao: The Memoirs of Mao's Personal Physician*. London: Arrow Books. Doctor Li's book was controversial, to say the least, and many reviewers argued that much of what appeared in the book was either trumped up completely or vastly overexaggerated. A much more balanced account of Mao's later years is provided in Philip Short, 1999, *Mao: A Life*. London: Hodder and Stoughton; see esp. chap. 16, "Things Fall Apart," pp. 586–626. It is clear, however, that many people simply refused to believe some of the stories Doctor Li told about Mao's sexual exploits. Others, who maybe accepted the stories as true, preferred to believe that they provided further evidence of Mao's superhuman energies and abilities. There is, of course, a parallel to be drawn here between Mao Zedong and many other leading political figures. Beginning in early 1998 President Clinton found himself mired in the controversy arising from an admitted sexual affair with Monica Lewinsky, which eventually led to full-blown impeachment proceedings in the U.S. Senate. It is clear that in Mao's China the leader was able to keep sexual activities hidden in a way that is simply no longer possible.

9. Ibid., p. 21.

10. Ibid., p. 47. Barmé even goes so far as to draw an analogy between Mao Zedong and Elvis Presley, in the way they have been posthumously lionized. See, for example, G. Marcus, 1991, *Dead Elvis: A Chronicle of a Cultural Obsession*. New York: Doubleday.

11. S. Boym, 1994, *Common Places: Mythologies of Everyday Life in Russia*. Cambridge: Harvard University Press.

12. M.M.H. Yang, 1994, *Gifts, Favors, and Banquets: The Art of Social Relationships in China*. Ithaca: Cornell University Press, p. 86.

13. Y. X. Yan, 1996, *The Flow of Gifts: Reciprocity and Social Networks in a Chinese Village*. Palo Alto: Stanford University Press.

14. As Yan indicates, a person who has built an extensive network of *guanxi* is referred to (in her case-study village) as "a person in the society"; one who is not successful is likely to be called a "dead door" (*si menzi*). Ibid., p. 222.

15. Yan offers three senses in which *renqing* is understood in contemporary China. First, it is seen as part of the intrinsic character of human nature, that which differentiates us from animals; second, it can mean the "proper" way of conducting oneself in social relationships, e.g., by giving a gift when needed and appropriate; third, it refers to the bond of reciprocity (*bao*) and mutual aid that exists between two people, in the sense of an emotional attachment such as an obligation or a sense of indebtedness. Ibid., pp. 67–69.

16. As Yan puts it, "*guanxi* and *renqing* are characterized by moral obligations and emotional attachments in interpersonal relations and by the stable mutuality between people within networks over a long period." Ibid., p. 226.

17. Ibid., p. 227. In this sense, *renqing* becomes part of an individual's moral world. A person is tied to others in the village by various role relations, which are differentiated depending on the degree of intimacy involved. This is part of what anthropologists refer to as the "cultural construction of personhood," which individuals learn to do over time through the practice of giving and receiving gifts. In many instances, for example, in the case of villagers who give gifts to local officials, the gifts are not necessarily reciprocated—implying that the gift does not change the hierarchical relationship between the two. See Yan, p. 14–15.

18. See Yang, op. cit., p. 1. In Yang's words, "social connections" implies "dyadic relationships that are based implicitly . . . on mutual interest and benefit." Ibid., p. 1.

19. Ibid., pp. 91–108. There are numerous ancient Chinese sayings to express the meaning of *guanxi*. For example: "a command of mathematics, physics, and chemistry is not worth as much as having a good father (with connections)," and also "an official seal is not as good as a fellow from the same hometown." See esp. pp. 8 and 115.

20. For a more detailed discussion of *li* and the other fundamentally Confucian values, see C. J.

Smith, 1991, *China: People and Places in the Land of One Billion*. Boulder: Westview Press.

21. The operation of *guanxi* in Chinese society involves a fairly specific vocabulary. If a relationship exists between an individual and either a household or a corporate group, e.g., in a work unit, then that household is referred to as the *guanxihu*. A person of whom one can ask a favor in that network is a *shouren* (familiar person), and the process of doing this is called *la guanxi* (literally, pulling off a relationship, or pulling strings). If one "goes through the back door" (*zou houmen*), it is usually a semilegal or irregular process, though it may just be a very exclusive or particularistic tie; for example, if one has a close relative in a factory, he/she might be able to use the "back door." Those very effective at the *guanxi*-building process (*guangxixue*) are sometimes called *you*—implying that they are "oily" or "greasy" and probably have *shiliyan*, or an "eye for power." Such a person may be referred to as *lao youtiao* (which is a long strip of fried dough, a common breakfast food in many parts of China); or as *hua*, which means "slippery"—people who know how to behave in order to best serve their own ends. As Yang's uncle related to her, "people who are *hua* know how to talk in front of leaders (cadres). . . . If a leader likes to be flattered, they'll 'pet the horse's ass' (*paimapi*)." See Yang, op cit., p. 66. In contrast, the term *laoshi* refers to someone who is very upright and honest, perhaps even naive or simpleminded. Such a person would not usually get involved in *guanxixue*. It is important to note here that another key concept associated with *guanxi* is *li*, which traditionally means "ritual," implying the correct way to do things, according to the Confucian value system. *Li* is part of the word *liwa*, which is a "gift." See Yang, op. cit., pp. 64–74.

22. Yan, op. cit., pp. 208–209, argues that this is not really a return to feudal or traditional patterns. As she notes, by the early 1990s "new and unconventional items have become targeted [as] betrothal gifts . . . such as a plot of farming land . . . a factory, or a dairy cow." Ibid., pp. 205–206. Such gifts are to be used in rural production and the generation of wealth, but they are no longer given and received by the parents. They are now equally likely to be asked for by the groom. As Yan says, "It is now quite common for the groom to encourage his bride to request a higher 'bridewealth' from his family, in the hope of extracting more family wealth for [their] conjugal family" (p. 206). As such, gifts can be interpreted as a form of "wealth devolution" (p. 208) for the groom, or as a "down payment" on his inheritance rights.

23. Table 3.1, which is adapted from Yan (p. 84), shows that this individual spent more than Y520 (yuan) on gifts in the first half of the year, with the busy part of the season (engagement rituals and weddings) still to come, after the autumn harvest. This amount does not include the more than Y200 he spent on gifts for visiting relatives during the lunar new year celebrations. It is also informative to note that twenty-three of the twenty-eight people he gave gifts to had attended a birthday ceremony he held, for his father, the previous year. Each of some 129 guests at the ceremony gave gifts of at least Y10, or its equivalent in goods. The family received a total of Y1,470 in cash, plus some gifts of wine, canned food, fruits, and cookies. As this example shows, the whole process of gift-giving is a ritual of reciprocity. As the man in question told Yan, "Some of the guests [at his father's party] came because I had given them gifts before. . . . You can see it from my record. We just exchange things" (p. 83). The record he keeps of outgoing gifts serves as a credit list for incoming gifts. If someone does not reciprocate, they assume there is either something wrong with their relationship, or the person was ill. Yan estimates that in 1990 more than half the residents in the village she studied spent more than Y500 on gifts; and 30 percent spent from Y300 to Y500. The average household income in the village that year was Y2,650 (p. 77). In 1999 the exchange rate was Y8.1 to US$1.

24. Ibid., p. 238.

25. Ibid., p. 226.

26. This is the way *guanxi* is normally used to enter the back door, which implies that *guanxi* is the process, but *renqing* is the exchangeable resource (with the gift acting as the "vehicle"). In these circumstances, the *renqing* in question need not be sentimentally or morally based (as between lovers or close neighbors) but is almost purely instrumental. See Yan, ibid.

27. Yang, op. cit., p. 320.

28. M.M.H. Yang, 1989, "The Gift Economy and State Power in China," *Comparative Studies in Society and History*, Vol. 31, No. 1, pp. 25–54, 38.

29. Yang, op. cit., p. 311.

30. Ibid., p. 311. Yang is suggesting here that *guanxixue* can serve as the basis for the reweaving of an emerging *minjian*, which she describes as "a web of kinship in which personal networks of guanxi do not yet form clear contours . . . but stretch out indefinitely, and result in a kaleidoscopic fluidity of social relations." The civil society she is envisioning would be based on *guanxi*, which, as she argues, is charac-

terized by two "between" statuses: between the individual and a society as a whole; and between the individual and formal, voluntary associations (pp. 295–305).

31. In the United States, for example, as Orville Schell suggests, "There is a constant, pervasive innuendo of sexuality in almost all of our relationships. . . . We are exhorted to define and perceive ourselves through a sexual image; through clothes, manner, body shape, facial features. . . . We are a nation slavishly devoted to sexual success and failure." O. Schell, 1979, "Private Life in a Public Culture," pp. 23–36 in R. Terrill (ed.), *The China Difference*. New York: Harper Colophon Books, p. 29.

32. Ibid., pp. 29–30.

33. L. Pan, 1988, *The New Chinese Revolution*. Chicago: Contemporary Books, p. 141. See also J. Wen, 1995, "Sexual Beliefs and Problems in Contemporary Taiwan," in T. Y. Lin, W. S. Tseng, and E. K. Yeh (eds.), *Chinese Societies and Mental Health*. Hong Kong: Oxford University Press.

34. See, for example, A. Kleinman and T. Y. Lin, 1981, *Normal and Abnormal Behavior in Chinese Culture*. Dordecht, Holland: D. Reidel Publishing; W. S. Tseng and D.Y.H. Wu, 1985, *Chinese Culture and Mental Health*. Orlando, FL: Academic Press; and also M. H. Bond (ed.), 1986, *The Psychology of the Chinese People*. Hong Kong: Oxford University Press.

35. G. C. Chu, 1985, "The Emergence of the New Chinese Culture," pp. 15–28 in Tseng and Wu, op. cit.

36. Wei-Tsuen Soong and Ko-Ping Soong, 1981, "Sex Differences in School Adjustment in Taiwan," pp. 157–168 in Kleinman and Lin, op. cit.; F.M.C. Cheung, 1986, "Psychopathology Among Chinese People," pp. 171–212 in Bond, op. cit.; see also D.H.F. Ho, 1986, "Chinese Patterns of Socialization: A Critical Review," pp. 1–37 in Bond, op. cit.

37. Kuo-Shu Yang, 1986, "Chinese Personality and Its Change," pp. 106–170 in Bond, op. cit.

38. D.Y.H. Wu and Wen-Shing Tseng, 1985, "Introduction: The Characteristics of Chinese Culture," pp. 3–13 in Tseng and Wu, op. cit. In assessing such conclusions we need to remember that until recently most studies using "Chinese" respondents had to be conducted exclusively in Hong Kong or Taiwan, partly because psychology as an individually oriented discipline was held in low esteem in socialist China. It is difficult to say how accurately the results of such studies can be generalized to the mainland. With psychological testing still in its infancy in the PRC, cultural bias is also a problem, because most of the tests being used in the earliest

studies were prepared by Westerners for use with Western respondents. A specific personality trait may measure what it purports to measure in the United States, but in China the concept may have an entirely different meaning. This was evident with the McClelland achievement tests measuring "nAch" (pronounced *en atch*; the need for achievement) using schoolchildren's books in the PRC. The tests showed that Chinese children scored significantly higher than the world average, which contradicts the usual assumption that compared to Americans Chinese children would be low in nAch. Part of the discrepancy here is a result of the political propaganda found in children's books after liberation depicting heroic revolutionary struggles to overcome all manner of adversity. In addition to this, achievement tests are probably biased by a Western view of what nAch means (in other words, individual as opposed to group or social achievements). It follows, therefore, that the results of any tests should be interpreted with great caution. See D. C. McClelland, 1963, "Motivational Patterns in Southeast Asia, with Special Reference to the Chinese Case," *Social Issues*, Vol. 19, pp. 6–19.

39. G. Hofstede, 1980, *Culture's Consequences: International Differences in Work-Related Values*. Beverly Hills, CA: Sage Publications. Additional work by Hofstede is discussed in his 1991 book, *Cultures and Organizations: Software of the Mind*. London: McGraw-Hill.

40. Follow-up studies conducted in the PRC have basically reproduced these findings for residents of the mainland. See Yang (1986), op. cit.

41. Chinese Culture Connection, 1987, "Chinese Values and the Search for Culture Free Dimensions of Culture," *Journal of Cross-Cultural Psychology*, Vol. 18, No. 2 (June), pp. 143–164.

42. This finding is essentially replicated by Hofstede in some of his later work. See, for example, op. cit., esp. pp. 164–173.

43. G. Hicks and S. G. Redding, 1983, "The Story of the East Asian Economic Miracle: II. The Cultural Connection," *Euro-Asian Business Review*, Vol. 2, pp. 18–22. It is important to note that by 1999 many of these Asian economies were suffering from serious economic problems, particularly South Korea, Japan, and, to a lesser extent, Hong Kong. Such cyclical trends tend to make something of a mockery of serious attempts to draw general conclusions about national character from survey-based data (or any other type). They also show how dangerous it is to reach conclusions about the importance of Confu-

cianism to the so-called Asian miracles. By 1998 we could just as easily reach the opposite conclusion—that Confucian traits are correlated with economic downturns!

44. H. Kahn, 1979, *World Economic Development: 1979 and Beyond.* London: Croom Helm, p. 122.

45. See S. H. Schwartz, 1994, "Cultural Dimensions of Values: Toward an Understanding of National Differences," pp. 85–119 in U. Kim et al. (eds.), *Individualism and Collectivism: Theory, Method, and Application.* Thousand Oaks, CA: Sage Publications; and S. H. Schwartz, 1992, "Universals in the Content and Structure of Values: Theoretical Advances and Empirical Tests in 20 Countries," in M. Zanna (ed.), *Advances in Experimental Social Psychology,* pp. 1–65. New York: Academic Press. See also S. H. Schwartz and W. Bilsky, 1990, "Toward a Theory of the Universal Content and Structure of Values: Extensions and Cross-Cultural Replications," *Journal of Personality and Social Psychology,* Vol. 58, pp. 878–891.

46. This is reported in the 1996 edition of the book edited by Michael Bond, op. cit., which has been retitled *Handbook of Chinese Psychology.* Oxford University Press, pp. 216–217.

47. Schwartz (1994), op. cit., p. 111.

48. At another scale entirely, it is also possible to generalize about the impact of Confucian values on spatial attitudes and behaviors in China. Based on the work of such authors as Robert Sommer, Edward T. Hall, and Erving Goffman, it would appear that there are clear-cut cultural differences in the way people from different societies organize themselves in space and respond to the world around them. For examples of such studies, see the collection of articles in H. M. Proshansky, W. Ittelson, and L. G. Rivlin, 1970, *Environmental Psychology: An Introduction.* Englewood Cliffs, NJ: Prentice-Hall. The way the Chinese behave territorially, however, may be more a matter of necessity than a conscious choice or preference. As noted, over the centuries it is reasonable to expect that the Chinese people developed an impressive array of strategies to cope with adversity. In modern times they appear to have drawn deeply from this cultural reservoir to help them survive the austerity of the socialist transformation period; the years of economic disaster during the Great Leap Forward; and the political chaos during the Cultural Revolution. In geographical terms Confucian values of restraint might have contributed to the tolerance the Chinese appear to have for living at high densities, far higher in cities like Shanghai, Guangzhou,

and Hong Kong than most Westerners would find acceptable. Confucian values about individualism may have contributed to the abilities of the Chinese to live collectively in the cities and the countryside and to share territory, possessions, and even everyday household facilities such as kitchens and bathrooms. Traditional Confucian acceptance of the status quo and the lack of concern with individualism may also have helped the Chinese adjust to the surveillance and invasion of privacy that have been the norm since 1949. This should not, of course, be taken to mean that the Chinese necessarily like such practices, just as they probably do not like to live in crowded cities. Evidence from novels and from the more explicit outpourings from the democracy movement suggests that the Chinese, like people everywhere else in the world, loathe the invasion of privacy they have to endure.

49. One consequence of this is that places only take on an importance for the Chinese when they are significantly bound up with human relationships. For a place to mean something to a particular person, it must be where he or she has ancestors, or at the very least they must know someone who lives there, or have been there with someone else who is important to them. This might help to account for the tendency among the Chinese to eschew scenes that are, to Western eyes, of great beauty. Observing crowds of Chinese tourists, one might be forgiven for concluding that they prefer a crowded pavilion to a lonely vantage point and that for them a landscape is not complete until it has somebody important sitting or standing in its midst. The author, for example, recalls trying to take a picture of a statue of Buddha in a cave in Yenan. Chinese onlookers kept insisting that the photograph should have a human being in the foreground; in fact one woman physically picked up one of my children and sat her on a ledge next to the statue so that my photograph would be complete! The ever-observant Colin Thubron commented on this phenomenon at Confucius's birthplace in Qufu: "The flurry of Chinese snapshots was directed not on this beautiful [place] but exclusively at one another. A place seemed to take its meaning only from a person's presence there. Sometimes I received the overwhelming impression that these snapshots were really statements of identity, and that to be commemorated with a famous site was to be touched by its manna." C. Thubron, 1987, *Behind the Wall: A Journey Through China.* London: Heinemann, p. 63. Travellers often remark that Chinese people are puzzled by Westerners who choose to

travel alone, automatically assuming that being on one's own is the same thing as being lonely. It is almost as if they find it difficult to accept that anyone would choose to be alone rather than be part of a group, in addition to worrying about how people traveling alone are able to take satisfactory photographs!

50. A number of scholars interested in this issue have attempted to outline cultural-ecological models for this purpose. See, for example, M. H. Fried, 1969, *The Fabric of Chinese Society: A Study of Social Life of a Chinese County Seat*. New York: Octagon Books; W. LaBarre, 1946, "Some Observations on Character Structures in the Orient: The Chinese," *Psychiatry*, Vol. 9, pp. 215–237. See also the chapters in Bond, op. cit.

51. Yang (1986), op. cit.

52. Ibid., p. 153. Of course such an assumption involves all sorts of traps and pitfalls, because it assumes that "our" behaviors and values are somehow the correct ones and that the Chinese are doing the right thing to follow in our footsteps. It is also implicit in such statements that our values are symbols of our version of modernity and for that reason China, a backward and poor country, ought to be following us in the same direction. This issue has been discussed in recent years by many China scholars; see, for example, the work of Gail Hershatter, 1997, *Dangerous Pleasures: Prostitution and Modernity in Twentieth-Century Shanghai*. Berkeley: University of California Press; and Ann Anagnost, 1997, *National Past-Times: Narrative, Representation, and Power in Modern China*. Durham: University of North Carolina Press; see also the discussion about sex and modernity in Chapter 13 of this book.

53. D. Yang et al., 1996, "Psychological Transformation of the Chinese People as a Result of Societal Modernization," pp. 479–498 in Bond, op. cit.

54. Ibid., p. 481. Specifically, Yang notes that most of the four major dispositions of Chinese social orientation are now visibly decreasing under conditions of societal modernization: familistic orientation, orientation toward the "other," relationship orientation and authoritarian orientation. Most of the characteristics that appear to be increasing among Chinese people are in four other groups, self-orientation, independent orientation, competitive orientation, and egalitarian orientation.

55. Ibid., p. 482.

56. Ibid., p. 489.

57. Ibid. During the modernization process, some of the traditional characteristics that were functional and useful to people in the past will be lost or will weaken. There will still, however, be some traditional characteristics that will remain, coexisting with modern characteristics. Among these modern characteristics, Yang hypothesizes that those that prove to be useful or functional will increase in strength over time, so on the whole there will be movement in the direction of further modernization.

58. See R. Weil, 1996, *Red Cat, White Cat: China and the Contradictions of "Market Socialism."* New York: Monthly Review Press, p. 41.

59. O. Schell, 1984, *To Get Rich Is Glorious: China in the 1980s*. New York: Pantheon Books.

60. O. Schell, 1994, *Mandate of Heaven: A New Generation of Entrepreneurs, Dissidents, Bohemians, and Technocrats Lays Claim to China's Future*. New York: Simon and Schuster.

61. As Thomas Gold has pointed out, "The emphasis on income tied to efforts, productivity, efficiency, and specialization is establishing new hierarchies, occupational and economic strata, as well as a division of labor that will reinforce instrumental relationships." See T. B. Gold, 1985, "After Comradeship: Personal Relations in China Since the Cultural Revolution," *The China Quarterly*, No. 104 (December), pp. 657–675, esp. 671. It is ironic that two such different eras in China's recent history—the Cultural Revolution and the period of economic reforms—have in a number of ways produced similar results. They have both reinforced a tendency for the Chinese to put the clock back in terms of the conduct of personal relationships. Ties between people in the current era of freewheeling capitalism are more than ever based on considerations of "who can do the most for me?" This is essentially what was happening in the Cultural Revolution years, with the only difference being that in the 1980s and 1990s the majority of new relationships are cash-based, as opposed to earlier times of scarcity, when power and influence were all that were available to be traded. Once again Chinese society has produced a marked social hierarchy, but this time the wealthy are on the top and the poor on the bottom. During the Cultural Revolution the politically connected were able to lord it over the rest, whereas in feudal China the Confucian intellectuals had been the elite group. The value systems have changed, but the results have stayed very much the same.

62. J. Y. Zha, 1997, "China's Popular Culture in the 1990s," pp. 109–150 in W. A. Joseph (ed.), *China Briefing: The Contradictions of Change*. Armonk, NY: M. E. Sharpe.

63. From his extensive observations of the Chinese countryside, William Hinton has suggested that the enthusiasm with which the peasants embraced the new responsibility system can be traced to their deep resentment of the commune cadres and the tight control under which they were kept in the collectives. As he notes, "Functionaries in China just assume that they have a right to run everything, down to the smallest details of people's lives. This tradition is deeply 'feudal.' It is . . . resented down below and that is one of the reasons for the extraordinary attraction that a free-market economy . . . has for ordinary Chinese citizens. For people suffering under feudal restraint, the cash nexus seems to promote a radical liberation where ability and not influence . . . counts." See W. H. Hinton, 1989, "A Response to Hugh Deane," *Monthly Review*, Vol. 40, No. 10 (March), p. 18. After the landlords were removed from the scene, control over the peasants had been passed on to the collectives and the Party cadres. In this sense the peasants saw the post-1978 agrarian reforms as a sort of "second liberation." In the 1950s they had managed, with the help of the Communist Party, to rid themselves of the landlords; and in the 1980s, as Hinton reports, "They were absolutely delighted to get the cadres off their backs." Ibid., p. 19.

64. Gold, op. cit., has noted that brides today are likely to ask for much more than just the traditional "three things that go round" (watches, bicycles, and sewing machines) and are now expecting anything with "legs" (furniture); everything with *ji* (machinery, tape recorders, televisions, and refrigerators); and anything with *ya* (duck down, as in bedclothes). Again, it is important to note that it is only the medium of the relationship that has been changed. In the reform era it is cash and expensive gifts; in the Cultural Revolution "political correctness" was all-important. A survey conducted in Jiangxi and Fujian of newlyweds in small county towns revealed the average cost of weddings in 1988 to be Y3,000 and could be as high as Y7,500 (one-fifth of this was generally spent on the wedding banquet, the rest on outfitting the new home). See Pan, op. cit., p. 146. Lynn Pan tells the story of a Shandong woman who conducted open competitive examinations to help her find a suitable husband. The winner was a soldier who averaged 94 percent on all of the tests that were set for him. Ironically, as Pan notes, this represents a return to the ancient methods of selecting mates, but with a slight twist, in that "in Chinese stories the happy ending only comes with the groom passing the imperial examinations" (p. 40).

65. Mo Yan, 1995, *The Garlic Ballads* (translated from the Chinese by Howard Goldblatt). New York: Penguin Books, p. 216.

66. The shift from "friendship" to "comradeship" (to use Ezra Vogel's terms) was at best only a partial shift. See Gold, op. cit. It is clear, for example, that life in the Chinese socialist city was certainly not always comradely, and during the Cultural Revolution matters would get much worse. Personal relationships began to turn away from the universal comradeship that Vogel had predicted and back toward individual friendships. The Cultural Revolution was an attempt to overhaul the socialist experiment that had begun with liberation in 1949. Mao Zedong believed that the socialist revolution had strayed badly off course, and he was desperate to get it back on track. During this period (1966–1976) the attempts to transform social relationships and to create a wholly new "socialist man" were pushed to the extremes. At the best of times life was chaotic, with shortages of everything—jobs, food, housing, and services. At the worst of times people were disappearing, bundled off in the night for interrogation, sometimes not to be seen again for months or even years. Others began to fear for their safety and waited apprehensively for the knock on the door.

67. Gold, ibid., p. 671. According to Gold the expression commonly used for the term "a bit of prosperity" to which many Chinese now aspire is an ancient Confucian term, *xiao kang*.

68. As noted earlier in this chapter the *guanxi* system is as important as ever, because in the current situation what makes you important to someone else in a business relationship is not who you are but how much you earn and own, as well as who you know. As Lynn Pan has observed, for example, "In China one is always having to use irregular channels, because the regular ones are so clogged by red tape and bumbledom. . . . Although many a guanxi rests on bonds of true friendship, one is often left wondering how far one is valued for oneself, and how far for one's power or usefulness." See Pan, op. cit., p. 175. A survey recently conducted among Chinese college students confirms some of the trends referred to here. The values traditionally associated with China, such as having a great concern for others and a reverence for the elderly, appear to be in decline; whereas values China shares with the West, such as the desire to work hard to get ahead and the importance of

money, are increasing. See Zhao Wen, 1989, "New Times, New Values: Changes in Social Ethics," *Nexus—China in Review* (Summer), p. 30.

69. J. Y. Zha, 1995, *China Pop: How Soap Operas, Tabloids, and Bestsellers Are Transforming a Culture.* New York: The New Press, p. 4. See also Zha (1995), op. cit.

70. Ibid., p. 4.

71. Ibid., p. 19.

72. Ibid., p. 3.

73. Ibid., p. 10.

74. Ibid., p. 12. For more than a decade—in fact from 1978 until 1989—there had been a steady but fragile growth of some of the components of what appeared to be an incipient Chinese civil society: with the publication of magazines; lively discourses occurring in democracy "salons"; and endless debates and public ruminations about the future. In retrospect, it now appears that all of this activity culminated in the widespread public demonstrations in Beijing and other cities in the spring of 1989. As people around the world saw, this trend was crushed by the army tanks on the night of June 4, and many of the persons involved subsequently gave up on democracy, opting instead for what Zha calls the "spring wind of marketization." After Tiananmen Square, Zha argues, Chinese people didn't just sit around complaining and blaming the government; instead they decided to take the future into their own hands in the only way possible—which was through the workings of the marketplace.

75. S. G. Wang, 1995, "The Politics of Private Time: Changing Leisure Patterns in Urban China," pp. 149–172 in D. Davis et al. (eds.), *Urban Spaces in Contemporary China: The Potential for Autonomy and Community in Post-Mao China.* Cambridge, UK: Cambridge University Press.

76. Zha (1995), op. cit., p. 23.

77. Ibid., p. 202. In a recent book (*China: The Consumer Revolution.* Singapore: John Wiley, 1998), author Conghua Li uses the term the "s-generation" to refer to this group, who are the recipients, or the products of, China's one-child birth control policy. They have been "showered with [the] care, attention and financial means of up to ten adults . . . raised in peaceful, prosperous times [and who] continue to receive, even as they grow into adulthood, the financial support of doting parents, grandparents, aunts and uncles" (p. 6).

78. Zha (1995), op. cit., p. 207.

79. Wang, op. cit.

80. Z. D. Pan et al., 1994, *To See Ourselves: Comparing Traditional Chinese and American Cultural Values.* Boulder: Westview Press.

81. Ibid., pp. 211–212.

82. Ibid., p. 212.

83. The survey results indicated that both chastity and wifely obedience were considered to be more important by the respondents from Taiwan and Korea than was the case for those from China. It is important to stress that the findings here are very different from those reported in the Buss et al. (1990) study, which is reported in Chapter 13, where great importance appeared to be placed on the requirement of chastity in one's future spouse. D. M. Buss, 1990, "International Preferences in Selecting Mates," *Journal of Cross-Cultural Psychology,* Vol. 21, pp. 5–47. The survey data in the 1994 study also showed that contrary to expectations the Chinese respondents were less likely to endorse "traditional family values" than were Americans. The Chinese appear to be more ready to accept divorce than Americans and less likely to accept the need for families to have "benevolent fathers," "filial sons," and "a houseful of children and grandchildren." On items intended to assess support for hierarchical relationships, the results showed that the Chinese respondents were less likely than the Americans to want to please their "superiors."

84. M. H. Bond, 1996, "Chinese Values," pp. 208–226 in Bond, op. cit.

85. D.Y.F. Ho, 1996, "Filial Piety and Its Psychological Consequences," pp. 155–165 in Bond, op. cit.

86. Pan, op. cit., p. 109.

87. Wang, op. cit.

88. Ibid., p. 172.

89. R. Kraus, 1995, "China's Artists Between Plan and Market," pp. 173–192 in D. Davis et al. (eds.), *Urban Spaces in Contemporary China: The Potential for Autonomy and Community in Post-Mao China.* Cambridge, UK: Cambridge University Press, p. 183.

90. S. Wei and W. Larson, 1995, "The Disintegration of the Poetic 'Berlin Wall,'" pp. 279–296 in D. Davis et al., op. cit.

91. Ibid., p. 282.

92. Ibid., p. 293. This comment clearly attributes such work to the "skeptical" wing of postmodernity rather than the "affirmative" (see Chapter 2).

93. Ibid., p. 292.

94. J. F. Andrews and M. L. Gao, 1995, "The Avant-Garde's Challenge to Official Art," pp. 221–278 in D. Davis et al., op. cit. For a more complete discussion of

Chinese art in the Maoist period and the economic reform era, see the lavishly produced volume edited by J. F. Andrews and Kuiyi Shen, 1998, *A Century in Crisis: Modernity and Tradition in the Art of Twentieth-Century China*. New York: Guggenheim Museum Publications, esp. pp. 228–275 (by Andrews), "The Victory of Socialist Realism: Oil Painting and the New Guohua," and also pp. 278–323 (by Andrews and Shen), "Chinese Painting in the Post-Mao Era."

95. Charlotte Innes, 1991. Foreword in Can Xue, 1991, *Old Floating Cloud: Two Novellas*. Translated by R. R. Janssen and J. Zhang. Evanston, IL: Northwestern University Press, p. xii.

96. In the foreword Innes suggests that her work should not be taken too literally and that close readings are unlikely to "yield a literal description of current events in China." In fact, to read Can Xue "is more like falling asleep over a history book and dreaming a horribly distorted version of what you've just read" (p. xvii). Can Xue has herself written that she deliberately tries to make her stories "run counter to reality," a result of what she describes as occasional "attacks of madness." Innes comments that this "unreadability" may well have its benefits, in that the government has been slow to condemn her work. For the same reason Innes expects that Western readers will be able to appreciate Can Xue's work, because, she suggests, we are more used to such "exploring" and (virtually) unreadable fiction. See Innes, p. xii.

97. Ibid., p. 48. In another of her short stories, entitled "Soap Bubbles in the Dirty Water," Can Xue offers a frightening allegorical tale that deals with a topic close to the heart of many contemporary Chinese families: marriage and matchmaking. The story is about a crotchety old woman who was constantly badgering her thirty-three-year-old son to marry. She went so far as to set up meetings with the assistant section chief from her workplace, who happened to have an eligible daughter. The mother offered dried bamboo shoots to the chief as a gift, but no deal could be struck on the topic of marriage. One day, the son fixes a hot bath for his mother, into which she sank, never to be seen again. As the main character in the story says: "My mother has melted into a basin of soap bubbles. Nobody knows what happened. I would be called a beast, a contemptible, sinister murderer, if anyone knew " (p. 34).

98. Having said this, however, the new emphasis on mass domestic tourism has involved a very considerable commodification of temples of all types (as well as Confucian and other traditional Chinese artifacts, including bell and drum towers and impressively gated walls). Observing the way people flock to such sites might lead one to assume that there is a resurgence of religious belief, at least as indicated by the reverence shown to the statues and the actual evidence of praying behavior.

99. A. F. Thurston, 1988, *Enemies of the People: The Ordeal of the Intellectuals in China's Great Cultural Revolution*. Cambridge: Harvard University Press.

100. This is a quotation from T. Terzani, 1986, *Behind the Forbidden Door: Travels in Unknown China*. New York: Henry Holt, p. 20. Terzani was an exceedingly bitter reporter on contemporary China; he was finally expelled from the country for his extremely negative views on the current regime and its policies.

Chapter 4

1. *Chinese Maxims: Golden Sayings of Chinese Thinkers over Five Thousand Years*. Sinolingua Press, 1994, maxim no. 6495, p. 197.

2. M. X. Pei, 1998, *From Reform to Revolution: The Demise of Communism in China and the Soviet Union*. Cambridge: Harvard University Press. Pei uses this theme as the title for his book, arguing that China's route to transition can be described as the "evolutionary authoritarian" route, because it is gradual, and at the end of the day an authoritarian party (i.e., the CCP) is still in command.

3. See, for example, Kenneth Lieberthal, 1995, *Governing China: From Revolution Through Reform*. New York: W. W. Norton.

4. M. Blecher, 1986, *China: Politics, Economics and Society: Iconoclasm and Innovation in a Revolutionary Socialist Country*. London: Frances Pinter.

5. Pei, op. cit.

6. Pei argues that this economic transformation contributed to the significant erosion, limitation, and decentralization of the state's power, although other China scholars are not quite as sure as he is on this issue. For different views, see B. Naughton, 1995a, "Cities in the Chinese Economic System: Changing Roles and Conditions for Autonomy," pp. 61–89 in D. S. Davis et al. (eds.), *Urban Spaces in Contemporary China: The Potential for Autonomy and Community in Post-Mao China*. Washington, DC:

Woodrow Wilson Press; see also, in the same volume, V. Shue, "State Sprawl: The Regulatory State and Social Life in a Small Chinese City," pp. 90–112. Pei (op. cit.) notes that there were diverse social groups working to split apart state and society in China. Some had been newly enfranchised by the reforms (the peasants); others had been encouraged to resist by close to a decade of relative peace and prosperity, after the chaos of the Cultural Revolution (the intelligentsia); and still others, who had objected strongly to the continued lack of political freedom and the widespread nature of corruption in Chinese society finally saw their opportunity emerging at the end of the 1980s (the students). Pei also argues that in addition to the absolute and relative decline in the resources the state was able to control (as a result of the reforms), the deciding factors in pushing the reforms toward a societal revolution were what he calls the "institutional decay" of the regime: the state's inability to compete with and respond to new economic, social, and cultural forces; as well as its own lack of adaptability and inability to change and deal with contemporary forces and pressures; and the continued evidence of widespread corruption, increasing cynicism, and loss of ideological faith among the people—all of which resulted in a crisis of "governability." See also M. X. Pei, 1997, "Racing Against Time: Institutional Decay and Renewal in China," pp. 11–50 in W. A. Joseph (ed.), *China Briefing: The Contradictions of Change.* Armonk, NY: M. E. Sharpe. This institutional decay, according to Pei, contributes to what amounts to a "takeover" of society (by societal forces rather than by the state), because the state is increasingly unable to demonstrate that it can absorb and control the new economic forces and resources. All of this undermines the cohesiveness of the ruling elite and its ability to govern and deprives the regime of its capacity to monitor and contain newly activated societal groups. Some might think Pei is being far too optimistic here, projecting what he would like to see happening. By the end of the 1990s China's people still seem to be embracing capitalism and getting rich, with no obvious political challenge coming up over the horizon. This argument is well stated in Jianying Zha, 1995, *China Pop: How Soap Operas, Tabloids, and Bestsellers Are Transforming a Culture.* New York: The New Press.

7. This quote is attributed to Deng Xiaoping. See "Deng Xiaoping Leads a Far-Reaching, Audacious but Risky Second Revolution," *Time,* January 6, 1986, pp. 24–40.

8. D. Wilson, 1979, *The People's Emperor: Mao, A Biography of Mao Tse-tung.* New York: Lee Publishing Group.

9. K. Marx, 1935, *Class Struggles in France.* London: Lawrence and Wishart, p. 173.

10. L. Bianco, 1971, *Origins of the Chinese Revolution, 1915–1944.* Palo Alto: Stanford University Press, p. 74. For a further discussion of Stalin's brutality toward the kulaks (and others), see R. Medvedev, 1989, *Let History Judge.* New York: Columbia University Press; as well as Sheila Fitzpatrick, 1994, *Stalin's Peasants: Resistance and Survival in the Russian Village After Collectivization.* New York: Oxford University Press.

11. H. Feis, 1953, *The China Tangle.* Princeton: Princeton University Press, p. 140.

12. Bianco, op. cit., p. 59.

13. For details of this event, see Bianco, op. cit., and J. K. Fairbank, 1987, *The Great Chinese Revolution, 1800–1985.* New York: Harper and Row, especially chap. 12, "The Nationalist Revolution and the First KMT-CCP United Front," pp. 204–216.

14. Mao Zedong, March 1927, "Report on an Investigation of the Peasant Movement in Hunan." Reprinted in *Selected Readings from the Works of Mao Tse-tung.* Beijing: Foreign Languages Press, 1971, pp. 23–39.

15. The best exposition of this argument is provided by Chalmers A. Johnson, 1962, *Peasant Nationalism and Communist Power: The Emergence of Revolutionary China, 1937–1945.* Stanford: Stanford University Press. See also M. Meisner, 1979, "Marxism and Chinese Values," pp. 99–116 in R. Terrill (ed.), *The China Difference: A Portrait of Life Inside the Country of One Billion.* New York: Colophan Books. Manuel Castells also favors this argument in his treatment of China as part of his analysis of global economics and politics. See M. Castells, 1998, *End of Millennium.* Oxford: Blackwell.

16. The best account of China's centuries-long embrace of petty capitalism is provided by Hill Gates, 1996, *China's Motor: A Thousand Years of Petty Capitalism.* Ithaca: Cornell University Press.

17. For an excellent account of why this was the case, see Blecher (1986), op. cit. Blecher argues that the landed elite continued to dominate the economic landscape at this time, in addition to which much of the industry remained in the hands of the Western capitalists and was concentrated in the eastern coast's so-called Treaty Ports.

18. As British historian R. H. Tawney described the situation in the early 1930s, "over a large area of

China, the rural population suffers horribly through the insecurity of life and property. . . . There are districts in which the position of the rural population is that of a man standing permanently up to the neck in water, so that even a ripple is sufficient to drown him." See R. H. Tawney, 1932, *Land and Labour in China.* Boston: Beacon Press, pp. 73–77. The devastating poverty Tawney observed can be attributed partly to politics and partly to geography. China had been overrun for more than a century by imperialist powers. Superimposed onto that was almost constant civil strife: first to remove the dynastic legacy, then between the regional warlords. In addition to this perpetual chaos, life in rural China, which was marginal at the best of times, was prone to seasonal disasters brought on by floods and droughts, as well as the occasional earthquake. Due to topography and climate much of China's territory was unusable for agriculture.

19. K. Buchanan, 1970, *The Transformation of the Chinese Earth.* London: G. Bell and Sons, pp. 35–36.

20. Mao Zedong's views on the struggle between people and the environment were illustrated in his version of the ancient fable of Yu Kung, the "Foolish Old Man Who Removed the Mountain." Mao altered the original story to apply it to the class struggle of the Chinese proletariat. The physical environment (to be struggled with) represents the two "mountains" of feudal and capitalist opposition. The Old Fool, in spite of being ridiculed by his neighbors, finally managed to move the two mountains outside his home, through his incredible determination. As he said, "When I die, my sons will carry on; when they die, there will be my grandsons, and then their sons and grandsons, and so on to infinity." Mao was suggesting that the Chinese people could, if they were sufficiently motivated and effectively organized, move their own mountain, accomplish miracles, and remake their own history. This story is repeated in M. J. Coye, J. Livingston, and J. Highland (eds.), 1984, *China: Yesterday and Today,* 3d ed. Toronto: Bantam Books, p. 289. It is significant that at the end of his version of the Old Fool story Mao modified the original to read as follows: "We must work persistently, work ceaselessly, and we too may be able to touch God's heart." As this suggests, Mao knew that the Chinese people would need some help from higher sources. In light of his revulsion toward Christianity, it is ironic that Mao should include in his version of the story the reference to God in the traditional folktale. Bearing in mind some of the often violent opposition to communist principles

among Christians in the West (and vice versa, i.e., the opposition of Communists in China to Christianity in the West), it is interesting to note some of the parallels between Maoism and Christianity. M. Meisner, 1979, "Marxism and Chinese Values," pp. 99–116 in R. Terrill (ed.), *The China Difference: A Portrait of Life Inside the Country of One Billion.* New York: Colophan Books. For example, the values of Mao's new "communist man" were similar in some ways to the asceticism—the so-called Protestant ethic—that followed the Protestant Reformation, and which were associated with the rise of capitalism. Both the Protestant ethic and Mao's call for self-discipline focused on hard work and self-sacrifice among the populace.

21. Meisner, op. cit., p. 108.

22. Ibid., p. 103.

23. For a discussion of the Confucian value system, see C. J. Smith, 1991, *China: People and Places in the Land of One Billion.* Boulder: Westview Press. The term "feudal" is used in quotation marks to signify prerevolutionary China, but the term is in fact a misnomer. Most historians use the term to describe the serf-and-manor system characteristic of medieval Europe. In China the peasants were not serfs or slaves, but in fact they were so closely tied to the land that they were little better than serfs. The term "feudal," therefore, is used loosely to describe a society in which a ruling class owned most of the land and lived off the surplus produced on that land by the peasants, who were actually a "propertied proletariat" (see Tawney, op. cit., p. 73).

24. Meisner, op. cit., p. 107.

25. This is essentially what was meant by the term "better red than expert," which is often associated with Mao and Mao Zedong thought. See, for example, Blecher, op. cit. The Communists probably also blamed the Confucian value system for the stultification of Chinese economic development and the stagnation of its culture. Unlike the utopian socialists, traditional Confucian scholars had very little to say about the future. They emphasized social harmony but basically accepted the world as it was. Confucius himself had no concept of a paradise that could be attained on earth, although he did yearn for a return to the peace and plenty of the so-called Golden Age of China during the Zhang and Zhou Dynasties. See J. K. Fairbank, 1967, "The Nature of Chinese Society," pp. 34–66 in F. Schurmann and O. Schell (eds.), *Imperial China: The Decline of the Last Dynasty and the Origins of Modern China—the Eighteenth and Nineteenth Centuries.* New York: Vin-

tage Books. Even in this belief, however, Confucius did not suggest that ethical and moral behavior should be practiced because it could produce a better world—simply because it was in man's nature to behave that way.

26. In the Dengist era, of course, many people were able finally to experience what they considered to be the good life, but as noted in Chapter 3, in the 1990s China's pervasive materialism has dominated cultural and social life, leaving little space for any traditional values, including those associated with Confucianism.

27. This is reported to be a Shandong peasant saying, quoted in T. Terzani, 1986, *Behind the Forbidden Door: Travels in Unknown China*. New York: Henry Holt, p. 128.

28. See Blecher, op. cit., pp. 190–192. It is important to recall that at this time (the prereform era), although many areas in the countryside looked urbanized, they were still classified as rural areas. As Barry Naughton has observed, there was a clear-cut marker between the cities and the countryside (which Naughton refers to as a "hard-edge"). By comparison, and as we shall see later in Chapters 8 and 9, much of the new industrialization and urban growth would appear on the fringes of the existing cities, that is, in the suburbs; this had the effect of obliterating the "hard-edge" to the extent that the cities appeared to stretch for many miles into the countryside. See B. Naughton, 1995a, "Cities in the Chinese Economic System: Changing Routes and Conditions for Autonomy," pp. 61–89 in D. S. Davis et al. (eds.), *Urban Spaces in Contemporary China: The Potential for Autonomy and Community in Post-Mao China*. Cambridge, UK: Cambridge University Press.

29. This is well documented by Naughton (ibid.) and also by G. Guldin, 1997, *Farewell to Peasant China: Rural Urbanization and Social Change in the Late Twentieth Century*. Armonk, NY: M. E. Sharpe.

30. Blecher, op. cit.

31. The phrase "forces of production" usually refers to the means of production or the factors of production; in other words the land, technology, tools, raw materials, and capital that are used to produce goods and services. Obviously, in China in 1949 the only sector in mass supply was the huge labor force, hence the importance of efforts to improve the value of labor through education, training, and, most important, attempts to increase revolutionary consciousness. The phrase "relations of production" refers to the relationship between people in the pro-

cess of production. At that time, most of the means of production (especially land and capital) was in the hands of an elite group of landlords and lenders; the mass of the peasants essentially worked at subsistence level to support that group. Thus the relations of production effectively define the class system in a society, which is usually translated into wealth and well-being that can be handed down to later generations, thereby "reproducing" the existing system of class relationships into the future. See J. A. Gurley, 1970, *China's Economy and the Maoist Strategy*. New York: Monthly Review Press; and also V. D. Lippit, 1987, *The Economic Development of China*. Armonk, NY: M. E. Sharpe, esp. chaps. 1 and 4, pp. 3–34, 78–102.

32. See W. Hinton, 1984, *Shenfan: The Continuing Revolution in a Chinese Village*. New York: Vintage Books, pp. 63–67.

33. Bianco, op. cit., p. 190.

34. Gurley, op. cit.

35. This is the concept of "continuous revolution" that is generally associated with Mao Zedong thought. See, for example, L. Dittmer, 1987, *China's Continuous Revolution: The Post-Liberation Epoch, 1949–1981*. Berkeley: University of California Press.

36. Deng Xiaoping died in 1997, and Jiang Zemin took over the reins of the Party and state in the mid-1990s.

37. Although as Blecher suggests, more realistic evidence available much later would place this estimate at closer to 15 percent growth per year. See M. Blecher, 1997, *China Against the Tides: Restructuring Through Revolution, Radicalism, and Reform*. London: Pinter. We should also note that China's industrial capacity was so weakened by civil war and other strife that in the early 1950s even small amounts of absolute growth added up to large proportionate increases.

38. V. Shue, 1980, *Peasant China in Transition: The Dynamics of Development Towards Socialism, 1949–1956*. Berkeley: University of California Press.

39. See, for example, A. G. Walder, 1986, *Communist Neo-Traditionalism: Work and Authority in Chinese Industry*. Berkeley: University of California Press, esp. chap. 6, "Maoist Asceticism," pp. 190–221.

40. Mao Zedong, 1977, *Selected Works*, Vol. 5. Beijing: Foreign Languages Press, p. 134.

41. This era is generally referred to as the "Yenan period," after the style of politics and mass-mobilization campaigns developed in the communist-based area that was centered in rural northern Shaanxi

Province. For details, see M. Selden, 1971, *The Yenan Way in Revolutionary China*. Cambridge: Harvard University Press.

42. See Blecher (1986), op. cit., esp. chap. 2, pp. 42–92; and also Gurley, op. cit., chap. 5, pp. 236–263.

43. An excellent introduction to the chaotic situation that prevailed during the Cultural Revolution is provided by W. A. Joseph in the foreword to Gao Yuan, 1987, *Born Red: A Chronicle of the Cultural Revolution*. Stanford: Stanford University Press. The period is also discussed by P. Van Ness and S. Raichur, 1983, "Dilemma of Socialist Development: An Analysis of Strategic Lines in China, 1949–1981," pp. 77–89 in the Bulletin of Concerned Asia Scholars (eds.), *China from Mao to Deng: The Politics and Economics of Socialist Development*. New York: M. E. Sharpe.

44. One of the best descriptions of this process is provided in Barry Naughton, 1995b, *Growing out of the Plan: Chinese Economic Reform, 1978–1993*. Cambridge, UK: Cambridge University Press.

45. The events in Beijing during April–June 1989 dominated the world's media headlines for many weeks. Much was written on the background to the demonstrations, and there was extensive coverage of the events up until the imposition of martial law in May and the crackdown and purging that began in early June. From the massive number of newspaper and magazine articles that were generated, a representative sampling would include the following: S. WuDunn, "Hu's Death Stirs Up Political Unrest," *New York Times*, April 16, 1989, p. 1; the obituary column on Hu Yaobang written by Nicholas D. Kristoff on the same day (p. 38); and the article by W. R. Doerner, "Come Out, Come Out: Mourning for a Fallen Leader Erupts into Defiant Demands for Political Change," *Time*, May 1, 1989, pp. 24–25. These articles describe the outpouring of student emotions when former CCP chief Hu died in April 1989. Hu had been ousted in 1987, supposedly for supporting the students in the earlier demonstrations during the winter of 1986–1987. Another symbolic figurehead, and now perhaps China's most famous dissident, is Fang Lizhi, who was also pinpointed by the CCP as an instigator of the demonstration in 1986–1987 and again in 1989. The buildup to the May and June activities in Tiananmen Square, and Fang's importance in the minds of both the Party and the students, have been nicely described by Orville Schell, 1989, "An Act of Defiance," *New York Times Magazine*, April 16, 1989, pp. 27–30, 43. One of the best reviews of the entire

buildup, attempting to account for the students' discontent, was provided by Nick Kristoff, 1989, "China Erupts: The Reasons Why," *New York Times Magazine*, June 4, 1989, pp. 26–29, 85–90. Later in 1989 and in early 1990 a series of books began to hit the presses, most written by journalists. Among the best: S. Simmie and B. Nixon, 1989, *Tiananmen Square*. Seattle: University of Washington Press; Yi Mu and M. V. Thompson, 1989, *Crisis at Tiananmen: Reform and Reality in Modern China*. San Francisco: China Books and Periodicals; and M. Fathers and A. Higgins, 1989, *Tiananmen: The Rape of Peking*. London: The Independent. Some important information is also available in the Amnesty International report of October 1989, *People's Republic of China: Preliminary Findings on Killings of Unarmed Civilians, Arbitrary Arrests and Summary Executions Since June 3, 1989*. New York: Amnesty International.

46. See *Chinese Maxims: Golden Sayings of Chinese Thinkers over Five Thousand Years*. Beijing: Sinolingua Press, 1994, maxim no. 6497, p. 189.

47. After such a sweeping statement we should remember that there have been periods of starvation in the postrevolutionary era, most notably the so-called three disastrous years following the Great Leap Forward in 1958. It is also clear that most evaluations of food output levels and incomes are based on nationally aggregated statistics, and there are still considerable pockets of poverty in many areas throughout China. See E. B. Vermeer, 1982, "Income Differentials in Rural China," *The China Quarterly*, No. 89 (March), pp. 1–33. On the three disastrous years, see J. A. Jowett, 1989, "Mao's Man-Made Famine," *Geographical Magazine*, Vol. 61, No. 4, pp. 16–19; and J. A. Jowett, 1987, "Famine in the People's Republic of China," Department of Geography, University of Glasgow, Occasional Paper Series, No. 21. See also Chapter 7 of this book for a detailed discussion of the Great Famine.

48. Extending the comparison to the global level, the evidence also suggests that in the 1970s and especially in the 1980s, in terms of absolute growth rates, industrial and agricultural outputs were higher than in most other countries of the world; see B. Reynolds, 1989, "The Chinese Economy in 1988," pp. 27–48 in A. J. Kane (ed.), *China Briefing, 1988*. Boulder: Westview Press.

49. For what amounts to a deconstruction of the Maoist legacy, see C. J. Smith, op. cit. See also Chinese Communist Party, 1981, "Resolution on Certain Questions in the History of Our Party, 1949–1981,"

Authoritative Assessment of Mao Zedong, The Cultural Revolution, Achievements of the People's Republic. Beijing: Foreign Languages Press; R. J. Thompson, 1988, "Reassessing Personality Cults: The Cases of Stalin and Mao," *Studies in Comparative Communism,* Vol. 21, No. 1 (Spring), pp. 99–128; T. P. Bernstein, 1985, "How Stalinist Was Mao's China?" *Problems of Communism,* Vol. 34, No. 2 (March/April), pp. 118–125; and A. G. Walder, 1987, "Actually Existing Maoism," *Australian Journal of Chinese Affairs,* No. 18 (July), pp. 155–166.

50. Blecher (1997), op. cit., pp. 164–167.

51. R. Baum, 1996, *Burying Mao: Chinese Politics in the Age of Deng Xiaoping.* Princeton: Princeton University Press, p. 5.

52. Ibid., p. 6.

53. S. L. Shirk, 1993, *The Political Logic of Economic Reform in China* (Berkeley: University of California Press.

54. Baum, op. cit., p. 51.

55. Ibid., p. 10.

56. It is important to recall that "leftism" in post-Mao China has the opposite connotation from what we would typically understand. Leftists in China at this time might be allied with Maoism but more generally would be considered conservative in the sense that they are concerned with restoring traditional orthodox communist values and CCP institutions. On the other side, represented by Deng and his clique, were the rightists, who were committed to liberalism, implying support for market reforms and (sometimes) political reforms, including a greater role for societal forces in the face of state actions. Only a few, perhaps only Hu Yaobang, were openly willing to consider democratization; see ibid., pp. 11–15.

57. Ibid., p. 16.

58. This process was often referred to as "crossing the river by groping for stepping stones."

59. Baum, op. cit., pp. 17–18.

60. At that time (the late 1980s) there was also some evidence that a small amount of political reform was under way, which was not followed up, probably for the same reasons.

61. Again this is an issue on which a great deal has been written already; see C. J. Smith, 1991, *China: People and Places in the Land of One Billion.* Boulder: Westview Press, esp. chap. 15, "Human Rights and the Crime of Dissent in China," pp. 259–272.

62. Baum, op. cit., p. 18.

63. See Lowell Dittmer, 1990, "China in 1989: A Crisis of Incomplete Reform," *Asian Survey,* Vol. 29, No. 1 (January), pp. 25–41.

64. J. T. Dreyer, 1996, *China's Political System: Modernization and Tradition,* 2d ed. London: Macmillan, p. 134.

65. See Chapter 8 and also Shirk, op. cit. In addition, new constituents were created among all of the newly rich Party officials, China's so-called nomenklatura capitalists; see M. Meisner, 1996, *The Deng Xiaoping Era: An Inquiry into the Fate of Chinese Socialism, 1978–1994.* New York: Hill and Wang.

66. Blecher (1997), op. cit.

67. Ibid., p. 224.

68. By the end of the 1990s there clearly appears to be more political stability at the top, especially after Jiang Zemin strengthened his position in the post-1997 era (after Deng's death).

69. See J. Fewsmith, 1997, "Reaction, Resurgence, and Succession: Chinese Politics Since Tiananmen," pp. 472–531 in R. MacFarquhar (ed.), *The Politics of China: The Eras of Mao and Deng,* 2d ed. Cambridge, UK: Cambridge University Press, p. 473. Fewsmith also notes that international events have continued to exert an influence in China, especially the political collapses in Eastern Europe and Russia and the rise and subsequent fall of the economically powerful Asian economies.

70. Ibid., pp. 483–484.

71. Ibid., pp. 472–473.

72. Ibid., pp. 522–533.

73. See Pei (1998), op. cit.

74. This fear of chaos is what Baum (op. cit.) refers to by recalling Deng Xiaoping's paraphrasing of Madame de Pompadour's expression "Après moi, le déluge."

75. See L. W. Pye, 1996, "The State and the Individual: An Overview Interpretation," pp. 16–42 in B. Hook (ed.), *The Individual and the State in China.* Oxford: Clarendon Press.

76. Pei (1998), op. cit.

77. See, for example, Philip Cunningham, 1999, "Reaching for the Sky," available online through the International Online Library. On the occasion of the tenth anniversary of the Tiananmen Square massacre, an event that was well covered in the Western press but downplayed in China (except in Hong Kong), the issue has been rekindled; see, for example, Ian Buruma, "Tiananmen, Inc.," *The New Yorker,* May 31, 1999, pp. 45–52; and also Jonathan Mirsky, "Holding out in Hong Kong," *New York Review of Books,* July 15, 1999, pp. 33–35. See also *June Fourth Massacre: Testimonies of the Wounded and the Families of the Dead* (Human Rights in China, June 1999), URL: hrinchina@igc.org.

78. Interestingly, this action of Deng's was the reverse of his actions in April 1976, after the first Tiananmen incident, when he requested the offenders be exonerated. As Baum notes, however, there is a good deal of overlap between the two Tiananmen events: They both began with peaceful demonstrations mourning a deceased leader (Hu Yaobang in 1989, Zhou Enlai in 1976); each culminated in the purge of a popular leader who was blamed for inciting a counterrevolutionary riot (Zhao Ziyang in 1989, Hu Yaobang in 1976); and both events escalated when party hard-liners impugned the motives of the participants in an attempt to delegitimize the demonstrations. Baum, op. cit., p. 391.

79. R. Evans, 1995, *Deng Xiaoping and the Making of Modern China*. London: Penguin.

80. Baum, op. cit., p. 391.

81. Evans, op. cit., p. 329.

82. A few olive branches were offered to society at this point, with martial law being lifted and Fang Lizhi allowed to leave for Britain; but as Marc Blecher (1997, op. cit.) observes, no one really mistook any of this for a change in the Party's commitment to holding on to political control.

83. See Blecher, ibid., p. 110. There were some attempts to do internal housecleaning, and one of the most popular campaigns at this time was the renewal of the anticorruption drive, which was almost universally supported throughout society. Yet at about the same time many intellectuals were being subjected to ideological study campaigns and were reminded of their obligations to serve the state—again suggesting the state's ambivalence toward the intellectuals as a class and the need to keep liberalizations in check by balancing them with frequent retrenchments, effectively extending the familiar *fang/shou* cycles.

84. Ibid., p. 110.

85. Ibid.

86. One very popular strategy, one that would generally receive nonpartisan support, was to launch a campaign against pornography, which the Party insisted was obviously a Western-influenced source of spiritual pollution; but it was not really close to the central ideological issues that his opponents, the conservatives, wanted to pursue. See Baum, op. cit., p. 477.

87. Ibid.

88. Fewsmith, op. cit., p. 494.

89. Ibid., p. 495; the quote is attributed to Yang Shangkun.

90. This was reminiscent of the old arguments about whether economics or politics should be in command, and it also required a continued emphasis on the importance of adhering to the four cardinal principles, i.e., mandating unwavering devotion to socialism, the people's democratic dictatorship, the Communist Party leadership, and Marxism–Leninism–Mao Zedong thought.

91. Baum, op. cit., pp. 350–351.

92. Ibid., p. 351.

93. Ibid., p. 344.

94. Dreyer, op. cit., notes that in fact the differences between the two groups was not very large, and historically many people had jumped the fence, one way or the other, at particular times (p. 121).

95. Baum, op. cit., p. 358.

96. Baum, op. cit., p. 392.

97. Fewsmith, op. cit., p. 529.

98. Ibid.

99. Ibid., p. 530.

100. Ibid., pp. 530–531.

101. Ibid., p. 531.

Chapter 5

1. Xinhua News Agency, April 28, 1991. Reprinted in L. R. Sullivan (ed.), 1995, *China Since Tiananmen: Political, Economic, and Social Conflicts*. Armonk, NY: M. E. Sharpe, p. 225.

2. Mao Zedong, 1956. *Mao Tse-tung: Selected Works*. Vol. 4: *1941–1945*. New York: International Publications, p. 454.

3. H. Y. Tien, 1973, *China's Population Struggle: Demographic Decisions of the People's Republic, 1949–1969*. Columbus: Ohio State University Press, p. 179.

4. L. Pan, 1988, *The New Chinese Revolution*. Chicago: Contemporary Books, p. 152.

5. Mao Zedong, 1960, *On the Correct Handling of Contradictions Among the People*. Beijing: Foreign Languages Press, pp. 46–47.

6. E. J. Croll, 1985a, "The Single-Child Family in Beijing: A First-Hand Report," pp. 190–232 in E. J. Croll, D. Davin, and P. Kane (eds.), *China's One Child Family Policy*. London: Macmillan.

7. New World Press, 1983, *China ABC*. Beijing: New World Press.

8. In announcing this new development in 1979 the government looked for moral support in the writings of the major socialist theoreticians; see Croll (1985a), op. cit. In the nineteenth century, Engels had written about the twofold nature of production, suggesting that one of the unique strengths of a socialist system was the state's ability to include both production and reproduction within its planning domain.

9. Ibid., p. 196. Again it appears that the birth of a second child produced some ambivalence in official responses. The vast majority of penalties to date have been directed toward the families that have had three or more children, particularly if they happen to be political leaders, who are expected to set a good example to others.

10. Critics of the policy also pointed out that if a one-child policy was adopted for two decades, China's population structure would become fundamentally unbalanced, with each able-bodied person having to support two parents and four grandparents. The prospects for a nationwide pension system did not look good, so it was not surprising that most people in the countryside felt it would never be possible for them to support a one-child policy, because there would not be enough younger people around to support them after retirement.

11. Jinghua Shou, 1979, "Interview with a Specialist on Population," *Beijing Review*, Vol. 22, No. 46, pp. 20–21. See also G. T. Wang, 1999, *China's Population: Problems, Thoughts, and Policies*. Aldershot, UK: Ashgate, esp. chaps. 1–2, pp. 1–52.

12. C. W. Pannell. and L.J.C. Ma, 1983, *China: The Geography of Development and Modernization*. London: V. H. Winston.

13. See Wang, op. cit., and also P. Woodruff, 1981, "A Historical Survey of Population in China," pp. 1–8 in *Teaching About China*. Washington, DC: U.S.-China Peoples Friendship Association, No. 9 (Summer/Fall).

14. E. J. Croll. 1985b. "The Single-Child Family: The First Five Years," pp. 125–139 in N. Maxwell and B. McFarlane (eds.), *China's Changed Road to Development*. Oxford: Pergamon Press. In some provinces there is even less cultivable land per person; for example, in Zhejiang the figure is closer to 0.05 hectare per person. Throughout the 1980s the loss of arable land averaged about 7 million mu per year, whereas the population was growing by more than 13 million each year. Grain output, although growing steadily until 1984, was matched by the growth of population, so that in 1987 China's per capita grain

availability was only slightly higher than in 1952, and in many provinces the per capita share of grain had actually fallen. See Zhing Qing, 1989, "1.1 Billion and Rising: The Population Problem Still Dominates China's Future," *Nexus—China in Focus* (Summer), pp. 4–6.

15. The land shortage was considered most critical in and around China's biggest cities. Beijing, for example, had a population of 2.03 million people in 1949, with 0.3 hectare per person on which to grow food; but by the early 1980s Beijing had almost 9 million people and only 0.05 hectare of farmland per person. The population growth meant that the per capita amount of land available to grow food in the city had been reduced sixfold. See V. Smil, 1984, *The Bad Earth: Environmental Degradation in China*. Armonk, NY: M. E. Sharpe, p. 70.

16. Secondary population concentrations are evident in several other parts of South China, especially along the coast, the Songliao River basin in northeastern China (former Manchuria), the Hexi corridor in Gansu Province, and the Wei River valley in Shaanxi Province.

17. K. Buchanan, 1970, *The Transformation of the Chinese Earth*. London: G. Bell and Sons, p. 26.

18. Population pressures in such areas did not generally result in a mass migration to the higher lands or to the unpopulated areas; rather there would be a spreading out into neighboring river basins. The net effect was that the existing areas of the "good earth" would fill up, with densities getting higher and higher, but with the relative distribution of population remaining relatively static for hundreds of years. It was not until the Party-state began some major resettlement projects in the 1960s that any attempts were made to fill in some of the more sparsely populated lands. See ibid., p. 28.

19. X. X. Zhang and S. Ye, 1987, *Chinese Lives: An Oral History of Contemporary China*. New York: Pantheon Books.

20. This argument has been made strongly by many observers. See, for example, G. P. Qu, 1989, "Over the Limit," *Earthwatch*, Vol. 34, p. 2; and the book written by Qu and his colleague J. C. Li, 1994, *Population and the Environment in China*. Boulder: Lynne Rienner. They point to the excess amounts of ecological destruction and environmental pollution that will result from the absolute size of China's population and its rate of increase. They argue that a sustainable population for China, bearing in mind the relatively small amount of cultivable land that is available, is about 700 million, which will be

exceeded by 500 million by the end of this century. This argument is also made forcefully by Vaclav Smil (1993), as we shall see in greater detail in Chapter 16. Some observers have, often on ideological grounds, challenged this notion of crisis, in part to support their criticism of China's coercive birth control program. It is simply wrong, as Wang (1996) points out, to suggest that there is a relationship between population size and the chronic shortages in China's cities (housing, for example). F. Wang, 1996, "A Decade of the One-Child Policy: Achievements and Implications," pp. 97–122 in A. Goldstein and F. Wang (eds.), *China: The Many Facets of Demographic Change.* Boulder: Westview Press. The shortage of housing in China, as we shall see in Chapter 14, is the result of too little investment by the state. During the Maoist era, for example, from 1952 to 1978 the average annual share of state spending on housing was 6.2 percent, compared with 25 percent in the 1980–1985 period. This argument has been made strongly by some U.S. demographers, such as John Aird and Nicholas Eberstadt, who were invited to testify at the 1995 congressional hearing on China's coercive population control methods. Eberstadt, in fact, has argued that the term "overpopulation" is a myth, that it is unscientific, poorly defined, and often grotesquely overused. He argues that it is just too simplistic to suggest that overpopulation causes or exacerbates poverty. In his testimony before Congress, for example, Eberstadt argued that setting population targets, as has occurred in China, is a troubling procedure because targets almost always result in coercion and the implementation of antinatal family planning programs, which restrict free and open choices. As he says, "free peoples and open societies should have no use for, or tolerance of . . . population targets." U.S. House of Representatives, 1995, *Coercive Population Control in China.* Washington, DC: Hearings Before the Subcommittee on International Operations and Human Rights of the Committee on International Relations, May 17, June 22 and 28, and July 19, 1995. The submission by Nicholas Eberstadt can be found on pp. 96–108. He ends with a strong piece of advice for China: "I submit that the American imprimatur should not grace or legitimize . . . efforts to imprint population targets on other lands" (p. 107).

21. See Deng Shulin, 1989, "Sounding the Alarm on Population Growth," *China Reconstructs*, Vol. 38, No. 7 (July), pp. 30–33. A new and largely unanticipated nightmare for Chinese family planners at the end of the 1980s was the problem of the "floating populations" that have fled to the cities in the wake of the agricultural reforms. There may be as many as 100 million surplus workers in the countryside (see Chapter 15). With attachment to neither work nor residence units, it is very difficult for family planners to institute birth control strategies among this population, and the average number of children per family is thought to be consequently far higher than government regulations allow. Another major problem is the illegal trading in second-child birth certificates, costing anywhere from Y800 to Y2,000.

22. Zhang and Sang, op. cit., p. 132. To press home the importance of continuing the fight to lower the birthrate, the government has continually bombarded the people of China with masses of data about the drastic consequences of allowing things to continue unchecked. There is, of course, much information available, and the government does not need to exaggerate the seriousness of the situation. For example, in the mid-1980s the cost of raising a child in a Chinese city averaged Y18,740, 64 percent of which was borne by the state (compared to Y6,695 in the countryside). The babies born each year consumed about 20 percent of the country's increase in national income, e.g., 49 percent of the increased grain harvest and 46 percent of the increased meat production. Some economists have predicted that with a population of "only" 1.2 billion in the year 2000 (which will be surpassed easily), every increase of 10 million babies will lower the per capita share of the national income by Y10, and in the middle to late 1980s at least 15 million babies were being born every year. See Wang (1999), op. cit.

23. As might be expected, for the policy to be effective, it involved a considerable invasion of personal privacy: "Every woman of childbearing age is monitored by Family Planning representatives. . . . Her work or neighborhood unit . . . will have a dossier on her reproductive history, and will know what contraceptive method she is using. If a woman already has a child, it will not take many missed periods to set off an official reaction. Every kind of pressure, from interminable nagging to downright arm-twisting will be exerted." Pan, op. cit., p. 153.

24. In 1986 the birthrate in China's cities averaged 17.4 per 1,000, compared to 21.9 for rural areas. The variations from the highest to the lowest areas were from 15.3 per 1,000 in Shanghai (highly urbanized) to 27.3 per 1,000 in Xinjiang (mostly rural); see China Statistical Publishing House, 1988, *China Statistical Yearbook 1987*, pp. 76–77. There has also been a marked discrepancy between individual

cities. In two of China's largest cities, Shanghai and Chengdu, for example, by 1986 the growth rate had been brought down to the level required to set the entire country on the path toward zero population growth; but the growth rate in two other big cities, Beijing and Tianjin, was twice as high. See *China Daily*, March 14, 1987. There was also considerable variability *within* the countryside, from one rural area to another. An official survey conducted in Jiangsu Province reported that 43 percent of the couples interviewed said they wanted to have only one child, and 57 percent said they wanted no more than two children. See *China Daily*, March 25, 1986. Such statistics may appear suspect in a country where children are so highly treasured, but the evidence suggests that (in Jiangsu, at least) the provincial government was able to coordinate production and reproduction plans very successfully in the 1980s. From 1981 to 1986 the population in the province grew slowly (averaging 0.83 percent per year), and 670,000 fewer babies were born than in the previous five-year period. Industrial and agricultural output was reported to be eighteen times higher than the population growth during this period, and according to official sources that has allowed the people of Jiangsu to experience some major improvements in their living standards. In contrast to the report from Jiangsu, a survey conducted in rural Hubei Province showed that only 5 percent of the families interviewed said they were willing to limit themselves to one child, whereas 51 percent said they wanted to have two and 43 percent wanted three or more. The percentage wanting to have at least three children appears to be a function of the degree of isolation and the physical hardships of the region in question. In the hilliest parts of southern Hubei, far from the cities, more than 70 percent of the families expressed a preference for three or more children. This reinforces the belief among many rural Chinese people that their best security blanket for the future is to have as many children as possible, in the hope that at least some of them will stay close to home in order to take care of them in their old age.

25. Croll (1985b), op. cit.

26. See ibid.

27. In Guangdong Province, which is close to Hong Kong and generally considered to be one of the most Westernized parts of China, the population growth rate in the 1990s was still significantly higher than the national average. This can be explained in part by exemptions, which have allowed couples in rural areas to have a second child in any of a number of circumstances, including if their first child was handicapped with a nongenetic disease and unable to work as an able-bodied person; if they were married for a second time and only one of them had a child in the former marriage, or if both had children being raised by their former spouses; if they had adopted a child after one of them was incorrectly diagnosed as sterile; if both of them were only children; and finally, if either or both of them had worked for more than five consecutive years underground. See *China Daily*, May 6, 1986.

28. B. Robey, 1985, "Sons and Daughters in China," *Asian and Pacific Census Forum* (East-West Center), Vol. 12, No. 2 (November), pp. 1–5. See also J. L. Li and R. S. Cooney, 1993, "Son Preference and the One-Child Policy in China," *Population Research and Policy Review*, Vol. 12, No. 3, pp. 277–296.

29. *China Daily*, May 21, 1986.

30. An analysis of the exemptions in different parts of the country reveals that second children were generally allowed under two major categories, one of which is cultural, the other geographical or economic. The first set of exemptions exists to preserve the patrilineal family—for example, if the first child was a girl, or if only one son in the family had been able to procreate. The second set of exemptions was intended to reduce gross spatial inequalities by giving special dispensations to underprivileged groups and families in deprived areas (generally minority areas and very remote rural counties). See L. Bianco and Chang-ming Hua, 1988, "Implementation and Resistance: The Single-Child Family Policy," pp. 147–168 in S. Feuchtwang, A. Hussain, and T. Pairault (eds.), *Transforming China's Economy in the Eighties*. Vol. 1: *The Rural Sector, Welfare, and Employment*. Boulder: Westview Press; and D. Davin, 1985, "The Implementation of the Single-Child Family Policy in the Chinese Countryside," in E. Croll (1985b), op. cit.

31. S. Greenhalgh, 1986, "Shifts in China's Population Policy, 1984–1986: Views from the Central, Provincial, and Local Levels," *Population and Development Review*, Vol. 12, No. 3 (September), pp. 491–515. See also S. Zhong, 1991, "Propaganda Work Is Still a Weak Link in Rural Family Planning," *Renkou Xuekan* (translated), No. 1 (February), pp. 63–64 (Popline: CD Rom Search).

32. To account for variations such as these it would be necessary to look in detail at what was happening at the grassroots level (in other words at the county level), where national and provincial regula-

tions are further modified to fit local conditions. A preliminary review of these local variations shows that fertility policies are generally designed to match local conditions according to the level of economic development, existing population density, and the carrying capacity of the cultivable land. In Emei County in Sichuan, for example, the following rules pertain: in larger urban areas, one child only; in plains townships, one child only; in hilly areas (500–1,000 meters above sea level), two children if the first was a girl; in mountainous areas (1,000–2,000 meters), two children permitted; in ethnic minority areas, no rules implemented. See R. Freedman et al., 1988, "Local Area Variations in Reproductive Behavior in the People's Republic of China, 1973–1982," *Population Studies*, Vol. 42, No. 1 (March), pp. 39–57, 48. In addition to rules like these, implementation methods vary considerably from one area to another. In some places gross mismanagement and excessively high-handed local cadres have alienated the local populations; in others educational campaigns, effective distribution of contraceptives, and the application of scientific management techniques have produced some remarkable results. See Greenhalgh, op. cit.

33. Some foreign journalists have capitalized on this to produce lurid stories, such as a piece entitled "The Best Baby Is a Dead Baby," in which a peasant from Shangdong Province drowned his four-year-old daughter after being assured by a fortune-teller that his next child would be a boy. T. Terzani, 1986, *Behind the Forbidden Door: Travels in China*. London: Allen and Unwin.

34. A. J. Coale and S. L. Chen, 1987, *Basic Data on Fertility in the Provinces of China, 1940–1982*. Honolulu, HI: East-West Center; see also Y. M. Shen, 1987, "Selected Findings from Recent Fertility Surveys in Three Regions of China," *International Family Planning Perspectives*, Vol. 12, No. 3 (September), pp. 80–85.

35. Although the percentage of all births that were first births varied greatly across China, in many areas the figure approached that in more developed countries (for example, in Taiwan it was 38 percent in 1982; in the United States it was 43 percent in 1981). See Freedman et al., op. cit.

36. In fact fertility was slightly higher in 1990 (2.31) than it had been in 1980. This issue is discussed by G. Feeney, 1994, "Fertility Decline in East Asia," *Science*, Vol. 266, No. 5190, pp. 1518–1523; see also N. Riley and R. W. Gardner, 1997, "China's Population: A Review of the Literature" (unpublished

manuscript); and G. Feeney and F. Wang, 1993, "Parity Progression and Birth Intervals in China: The Influence of Policy in Hastening Fertility Decline," *Population and Development Review*, Vol. 19, No. 1, pp. 61–101.

37. Although fertility decline slowed down in the 1980s (and in some years fertility actually increased), the program was tightened up in the early 1990s and the fertility rate again began to drop, reaching a level of 1.96 by 1992 and 1.8 by 1996 (for the 1996 statistic, see Population Reference Bureau, 1997, *World Population Data Sheet*). In response to the suggestion that the one-child policy was not responsible for the decline in fertility, a reasonable counterargument has been made, namely, that without the restraining effect of the one-child program China's fertility rate would have certainly rebounded back up to the pre-1979 level. See Alice Goldstein, 1996, "The Many Facets of Change and Their Interrelations, 1950–1990," pp. 3–20 in A. Goldstein and Wang F. (eds.), *China: The Many Facets of Demographic Change*. Boulder: Westview Press. Although we will never know, this counter-scenario seems rather unlikely, bearing in mind the overwhelming evidence from around the world concerning the drop in fertility that generally accompanies greater economic wealth, which is certainly what China experienced throughout the 1980s. It also appears that major fertility declines are common in societies in which families have traditionally expressed a strong preference for having large families (with an emphasis on boys), such as Taiwan and South Korea. For data to illustrate this, see B. C. Gu and K. Roy, 1995, "Sex Ratio at Birth in China, with Reference to Other Areas in East Asia: What We Know," *Asia-Pacific Population Journal*, Vol. 10, No. 3, pp. 17–42.

38. In formulating the program, China's demographers had assumed that because fertility rates had halved from the 1950s to the 1970s they would continue to decline at the same speed after 1979. As demographer Wang Feng has recently suggested, that flew in the face of reality for rural families in China, partly because it misinterpreted the reasons for the sharp drop in fertility in the 1960s and 1970s, and partly because it ignored the needs, or rather the strong preferences, of China's peasants to have large families. Wang argues that most of the fertility decline occurred because women were getting married later and, as a result of better education and improving economic circumstances, were choosing to have fewer children.

39. *China Daily*, April 18, 1987. The statistics here are from Guo Xiao, 1989, "The Population Threat," *Nexus—China in Focus* (Summer), pp. 2–3.

40. See S. Greenhalgh, 1994, "Controlling Births and Bodies in Village China," *American Ethnologist*, Vol. 21, No. 1, pp. 1–30.

41. There are many stories of women who refuse to be sterilized when ordered to do so by local officials. Although it takes tremendous courage to stand up to the state, in many cases these acts of resistance prove to be a two-edged sword, in both physical and social terms. This issue is discussed by Ann Anagnost, 1997, *National Past-Times: Narrative, Representation, and Power in Modern China*. Durham: Duke University Press; and by Harriet Evans, 1997, *Women and Sexuality in China*. Cambridge, UK: Polity Press.

42. In actual fact, the 1.2 billion figure had almost been reached by April 1989, and the government began to circulate some strongly worded propaganda about the importance of staying with (or close to) the original goals of the population policy.

43. Greenhalgh (1986), op. cit.

44. The phrase "fertility transition" refers to the phenomenon of a developing nation significantly reducing the fertility rate to almost the level attained in developed countries. See F. Arnold and Z. X. Liu, 1986, "Sex Preference, Fertility, and Family Planning in China," *Population and Development Review*, Vol. 12, No. 2, pp. 221–246. The assumption here is that couples who already have a boy are more likely to be persuaded to abort "out of plan" pregnancies than couples who have a girl. See *China Daily*, April 18, 1987. One hypothesis to account for the reversal by the mid-1980s is the effect of a larger than ever number of so-called baby boomer families, people who were born in 1963 and 1964, when population growth was largely unchecked, and who were getting married and having children in the early and mid-1980s. If this is true, the reductions in birthrates achieved in the early 1980s were in fact only partly a result of the one-child policies. An equally important component might have been the gap that occurred in the Chinese population pyramid around 1982 as a result of the famine that followed the disastrous Great Leap Forward in 1958–1960. In other words, a smaller-than-average twenty- to twenty-four-year-old cohort in those years (a cohort that accounts for more than half of all births) could have resulted in lower birthrates in the early 1980s. By the end of the 1980s, however, the cohorts getting married were much larger, and in 1987 it produced 1.2 million more babies than in 1986, helping to swell the population growth for 1987 to 15.9 million (compared to 14 million in 1986).

45. E. Salem, 1987, "Procreating for Profit: China's Population Growth Threatens Economic Reforms," *Far Eastern Economic Review*, Vol. 136, No. 26 (June 25), pp. 56–57.

46. B. C. Gu, 1997, "China's Population Grows Despite Fertility Decline," *Forum for Applied Research and Public Policy*, Vol. 12, No. 2, pp. 41–45.

47. J. L. Li, 1995, "China's One-Child Policy: How Well Has It Worked? A Case Study of Hebei Province," *Population and Development Review*, Vol. 21, No. 3, pp. 563–585.

48. These policy shifts had some important effects, most notably a sharp drop in the number of official complaints made to family planning agencies; a significant increase in the adoption of "voluntary" contraception methods; and an increase in the number of families wanting only one child even among families officially allowed to have two children. This has been achieved by persuading families that having one child (or small families in general) will improve their chances for social mobility, help to provide them with greater levels of consumption, and give them more leisure time. At the same time, the economic reforms contributed significantly to the attainment of such aspirations.

49. In 1995, according to the statistics in the 1998 United Nations *Human Development Report*, China's birthrate had fallen to 17.7, its death rate to 7.2. By comparison, among other developing countries both rates are significantly higher; for example, in the group of countries described in the UN report as being at the high end of the development scale, the average birthrate was 21.5, the death rate 6.3; whereas in those countries grouped at the bottom end the numbers were 32.7 and 11.2.

50. The major diseases such as malaria and schistosomiasis were eliminated, and many of the others—including dysentery, typhoid, and tuberculosis—were substantially brought under control. In addition to the mass campaigns designed to eliminate and control these diseases, the reduction in prevalence rates can also be partly attributed to an overall increase in the standard of living in the Chinese countryside. There have also been major campaigns to provide improved sanitation and better water supplies in both town and country; mass-immunization programs; elimination of the "four pests" (mosquitoes, flies, rats, and sparrows); and large-scale training of rural medical personnel (see Chapter 6).

51. C. N. Milwertz, 1997, *Accepting Population Control: Urban Chinese Women and the One-Child Family Policy.* London: Curzon Press (Nordic Institute of Asian Studies, Monograph Series, No. 74), p. 189. Milwertz claims she heard this statement frequently from the respondents she interviewed in the city of Shenyang. Another commonly heard statement was "family is the small issue, society is the big issue" (p. 195).

52. Ibid., p. 81.

53. Ibid., p. 81.

54. A. I. Hermalin and X. Liu, 1990, "Gauging the Validity of Responses to Questions on Family Size Preferences in China," *Population and Development Review,* Vol. 16, No. 2, pp. 337–354.

55. Milwertz, op. cit., pp. 113–114.

56. As we shall see in Chapter 15, however, it is by no means clear that the floaters use their freedom in the cities as a license to have the children they are not allowed to have in the countryside. What little work has been conducted on this issue currently suggests the opposite, i.e., that the migrants are more likely to model their own child-rearing behavior on that of city residents rather than their own rural norms.

57. In Chinese this would be *xisheng xiaowo, wancheng dawo.* See Milwertz, op. cit., p. 189.

58. As Wang Feng (1996), op. cit., has observed, "from the standpoint of the individual, a whole generation of adults without siblings is unprecedented. No society has ever experienced such a radical change." Interestingly, Wang uses this point to argue that the failure of the one-child policy, in the countryside at least, can actually be considered a blessing in disguise, because if the policy had succeeded in the countryside, the consequences by the second decade of the twenty-first century would have been disastrous. He points out, with a nice touch of black humor, that this may be "another instance in which Chinese peasants have saved China from disaster." See Wang, op. cit., p. 116.

59. See China Statistical Publishing House, 1998, *China Statistical Yearbook 1997,* table 3-5, p. 73.

60. See R. D. Strom, S. K. Strom, and Q. Xie, 1995, "Traditional Expectations and Emerging Views of Raising Children in Urban China," *Scientia Paedagogica Experimentalis,* Vol. 32, No. 2, pp. 333–352.

61. E.N.L. Chao and S. M. Zhao, 1996, "The One-Child Policy and Parent-Child Relationships: A Comparison of One-Child with Multiple Child Families in China," *International Journal of Sociology and Social Policy,* Vol. 16, No. 2, pp. 35–62.

62. D. L. Poston Jr. and T. Falbo, 1990, "Scholastic and Personality Characteristics of Only Children and Children with Siblings in China," *International Family Planning Perspectives,* Vol. 16, No. 2, pp. 45–48.

63. This is also the case for firstborn children in families with more than one child, so the higher achievement does not appear to be necessarily related to being an only child. See ibid.

64. Much of the worst in this whole story can be found in Human Rights Watch/Asia, 1996, *Death by Default: A Policy of Fatal Neglect in China's State Orphanages.* New York: Human Rights Watch, p. 33.

65. See Bruce Shu, "Population Minister Defends Abortion Policy," June 9, 1991. Agence France-Presse. Hong Kong, *Foreign Broadcast Information Service,* June 13, 1991. Reprinted in L. R. Sullivan (ed.), 1995, *China Since Tiananmen: Political, Economic, and Social Conflicts.* Armonk, NY: M. E. Sharpe, pp. 227–230, 229.

66. Arnold and Liu (1986), op. cit.

67. Greenhalgh (1986), op. cit.

68. Terzani (1986), op. cit.

69. See U.S. House of Representatives, op. cit.

70. *China Daily,* March 16, 1987.

71. Arnold and Liu (1986), op. cit.

72. Bianco and Hua (1988), op. cit., pp. 151–152.

73. *China Daily,* January 28, 1987.

74. C. Tietze, 1983, *Induced Abortion: A World Review, 1983.* In China, as we might expect from the earlier data on contraception, there are some major differences in the abortion rates from place to place. In the four provinces in which the fertility survey was conducted, abortion rates were significantly higher in cities than in the rural areas (with percentages ranging from 38 percent to 68 percent in the cities, from 9 percent to 41 percent in rural areas). Again, it is no surprise to find that existing family structure also influences abortion rates; thus for families who already have a daughter, the abortion rate was 22.8 percent, compared to 35.9 percent for families with a son. See Arnold and Liu (1986), op. cit., p. 241. The assumption here is that couples who already have a boy are more likely to be persuaded to abort out-of-plan pregnancies than couples who have a girl.

75. See H. Yuan Tien et al., 1992, "China's Demographic Dilemmas," *Population Bulletin,* Vol. 47, No. 1 (Population Reference Bureau), esp. pp. 20–21.

76. See ibid., fig. 7, p. 21.

77. United Nations, 1991, *The Sex and Age Distribution of Populations, 1990 Revision.* New York: United Nations, pp. 132–133.

78. *China Statistical Yearbook 1997*, op. cit., table 3.7, p. 76.

79. This issue is discussed by S. Harper, 1994, "China's Population: Prospects and Policies," pp. 54–76 in D. Dwyer (ed.), *China: The Next Decade*. London: Longman. See also J. Jowett, 1990, "People: Demographic Patterns and Policies," pp. 102–132 in T. Cannon and A. Jenkins (eds.), *The Geography of Contemporary China: The Impact of Deng Xiaoping's Decade*. London: Routledge.

80. Life expectancy has increased by more than a third since 1960. See C. W. Harbaugh and L. A. West, 1993, "Aging Trends—China," *Journal of Cross-Cultural Gerontology*, Vol. 8, pp. 271–280. See also J. Lin, 1995, "Changing Kinship Structure and Its Implications for Old Age Support in Urban and Rural China," *Population Studies*, Vol. 49, No. 1 (March), pp. 127–145; and J. Lin, 1994, "Parity and Security: A Simulation Study of Old Age Support in Rural China," *Population and Development Review*, Vol. 20, No. 2 (June), pp. 423–448.

81. See J.C.B. Leung and R. C. Nann, 1995, *Authority and Benevolence: Social Welfare in China*. Hong Kong: The Chinese University Press, p. 105.

82. S. Harper, 1992, "Caring for China's Aging Population: The Residential Option—a Case Study of Shanghai," *Aging and Society*, Vol. 12, pp. 157–184.

83. Zeng Yi, 1991, *Family Dynamics in China: A Life Table Analysis*. Madison: University of Wisconsin Press.

84. For a discussion of this, see J. K. Kallgren, 1992, *Strategies for Support of the Rural Elderly in China: A Research and Policy Agenda*. Hong Kong Institute of Asia-Pacific Studies. Hong Kong: Chinese University Press; L. C. Yu, Y. J. Yu, and P. K. Mansfield, 1990, "Gender and Changes in Support of Parents in China: Implications of the One-Child-Policy," *Gender and Society*, Vol. 4, No. 1 (March), pp. 83–89; W. McGurn, 1994, "The Grandfather Trap: China's Rapidly Greying Population," *Far Eastern Economic Review*, Vol. 157, No. 49, pp. 47–48; and K. S. Chang, 1993, "The Confucian Family Instead of the Welfare State: Reform and Peasant Welfare in Post-Mao China," *Asian Perspectives*, Vol. 17 (Spring/Summer), pp. 169–200.

85. It should be noted here, of course, that the overall proportion of urban workers supported by work-unit pension schemes will decline as the reforms take a stronger hold and the share of collectively and privately owned enterprises increases. In addition, the vast majority of the migrants getting jobs in the cities, or working for themselves, is unlikely to be receiving any benefits such as health care and pensions.

86. See Harper (1994), op. cit.; see also D. Davis, op. cit., and L. Wong, 1993, "Slighting the Needy? Social Welfare Under Transition," pp. 23.1–23.25 in C.Y.S. Cheng and M. Brosseau (eds.), *China Review 1993*. Hong Kong: The Chinese University Press.

87. Wong, op cit., p. 23.16.

88. See G. Feeney and J. H. Yuan, 1994, "Below Replacement Fertility in China? A Close Look at Recent Evidence," *Population Studies*, Vol. 48, No. 3, pp. 381–394; and Li, op. cit.

89. S. Greenhalgh, C. Z. Zhu, and N. Li, 1994, "Restraining Population Growth in Three Chinese Villages, 1988–1993," *Population and Development Review*, Vol. 20, No. 2, pp. 365–395.

90. Ibid., p. 389.

91. U.S. House of Representatives, op. cit.; see also Gu and Roy, op. cit.

92. The two featured were John Aird and Nicholas Eberstadt. Aird is perhaps best known for his 1990 book, *Slaughter of the Innocents*. Washington, DC: AEI Press; see also J. S. Aird, 1978, "Fertility Decline and Birth Control in the People's Republic of China," *Population and Development Review*, Vol. 4, No. 2, pp. 225–252.

93. S. H. Potter and J. M. Potter, 1990, *China's Peasants: The Anthropology of a Revolution*. Cambridge, UK: Cambridge University Press.

94. This issue—the existence of a population crisis in China—is one area the two U.S. demographers who testified at the 1995 congressional hearings were attacking. They suggested that the term "crisis" has to some extent been manufactured by the state to get the people to support the new birth control policies. See U.S. House of Representatives, op. cit.

95. See A. Anagnost, 1995, "A Surfeit of Bodies: Population and the Rationality of the State in Post-Mao China," pp. 22–41 in F. Ginsburg and R. Rapp (eds.), *Conceiving the New World Order: The Global Politics of Reproduction*. Berkeley: University of California Press; and also A. Anagnost, *National Past-Times: Narrative, Representation, and Power in Modern China*. Durham: Duke University Press.

96. See Anagnost (1995), p. 27.

97. M. Selden, 1985, "Income Inequality and the State," pp. 193–218 in W. L. Parish (ed.), *Chinese Rural Development: The Great Transformation*. Armonk, NY: M. E. Sharpe. Selden shows convincingly that the best predictor of which families

become "rich" is family size; in other words, more children means more production, which means higher incomes.

98. To help solve the contradiction between the production and reproduction policies, new regulations have been announced in some areas, intended to link the distribution of contracted land and the setting of output quotas more closely to family size, with larger families being assigned smaller plots of land and larger production quotas, and vice versa. This, of course, may prove to be administratively problematic in the future because to make the responsibility system work it is necessary to guarantee a family a specific plot of land for a fixed number of years. If the family grows, it will be difficult to reduce the size of the plot without jeopardizing the intent of the new incentive system.

99. N. Kristoff, "China's Crackdown on Births: A Stunning, and Harsh, Success," *New York Times*, April 25, 1993.

100. One research team placed the figure at 1.96 in 1992, and by 1996 fertility had dropped even farther, to 1.80 (see Table 5.1). This was reported in a study conducted in central Shaanxi Province by Greenhalgh, Zhu, and Li (1995), op. cit. As we have already discussed, the major problem in evaluating the birth control policies is that it is virtually impossible to

separate out the effects of the policies from the effects of China's rising wealth and economic security.

101. Croll (1985a), op. cit.

102. M. Wolf, 1985, *Revolution Postponed: Women in Contemporary China*. Stanford: Stanford University Press.

103. S. Greenhalgh and J. Bongaarts, 1987, "Fertility Policy in China: Future Options," *Science*, Vol. 235 (March 6), pp. 1167–1172.

104. J. Bongaarts and S. Greenhalgh, 1985, "An Alternative to the One-Child Policy in China," *Population and Development Review*, Vol. 11, No. 4, pp. 585–617.

105. D. G. Johnson, 1994, "Effects of Institutions and Policies on Rural Population Growth with Application to China," *Population and Development Review*, Vol. 20, No. 3, pp. 503–531.

106. S. Greenhalgh and J. L. Li, 1995, "Engendering Reproductive Policy and Practice in Peasant China: For a Feminist Demography of Reproduction," *Signs*, Vol. 20, No. 3, pp. 601–641, esp. 627.

107. See Arnold and Liu (1986), op. cit., pp. 229–230; son preference is quantified as the percentage difference between couples with sons who have signed the one-child pledge compared to couples with daughters.

Chapter 6

1. R. Dubos, 1959, *Mirage of Health: Utopias, Progress, and Biological Change*. New York: Doubleday Anchor Books, p. 177.

2. See, for examples of such literature, works written by Jamison and his colleagues: D. T. Jamison, 1985, "China's Health Care System: Policies, Organization, Inputs, and Finance," pp. 21–52 in S. B. Halstead, J. A. Walsh, and K. Warren (eds.), *Good Health at Low Cost*. New York: Rockefeller Foundation; D. T. Jamison, J. Evans, I. King, N. Porter, N. Prescott, and A. Prost, 1984, *China: The Health Sector*. Washington, DC: World Bank; and D. T. Jamison, A. Piazza, J. P. Gittinger, J. Leslie, and C. Hoisington (eds.), 1985, *Food Policy: Integrating Supply, Distribution, and Consumption*. Baltimore: Johns Hopkins University Press. See also R. J. Blendon, 1979, "Can China's Health Care Be Transplanted Without China's Economic Policies?" *New England Journal of Medicine*, Vol. 300, pp. 1453–1458; and G. L. Albrecht and Tang Xiaoyin, 1990, "Rehabilitation in the People's Repub-

lic of China: A Reflection of Social Structure and Culture," *Advances in Medical Sociology*, Vol. 1, pp. 235–267.

3. Liu Xingxhu and Cao Huaijie, 1992, "China's Cooperative Medical System: Its Historical Transformations and the Trend of Development," *Journal of Public Health Policy*, Vol. 13 (Winter), pp. 501–511.

4. See, for example, C. E. Taylor, R. L. Parker, and S. Jarrett, 1988, "The Evolving Chinese Rural Health Care System," pp. 219–236 in *Research in Human Capital Development*, Vol. 5. Greenwood, CT: J.A.I. Press. For another perspective, see *China Business Review*, 1992, "China's Health Care Sector," Vol. 19 (July–August), pp. 18–23; and some of the reports produced by the Hong Kong–based *China News Analysis* on health and health care issues, for example, *China News Analysis*, "Health Care: Old Problems and New Challenges," Vol. 1415 (August 1, 1990); and also *China News Analysis*, "A Diet with

Chinese Characteristics for the Year 2000," Vol. 1427 (January 15, 1991).

5. A statement often attributed to Mao Zedong, and quite appropriate for this discussion, is "When shall we truly obtain deliverance from the Kingdom of necessity?" The issue of the political economy of health care has been discussed by R. C. Hsu, 1977, "The Political Economy of Rural Health Care in China," *Review of Radical Political Economics*, Vol. 9 (Spring), pp. 134–140. For an account written by a geographer, see M. Turshen, 1978, "Women and Health: Lessons from the People's Republic of China," *Antipode*, Vol. 10, No. 1 (March), pp. 51–63. For a general introduction to the political economy account of health and health care issues, see L. Doyal, 1980, *The Political Economy of Health*. London: Pluto Press.

6. This interpretation is provided by the Western academics who were, at the time, convinced of the superiority of the Maoist approach to development in China; see, for example, J. A. Gurley, 1970, *China's Economy and the Maoist Strategy*. New York: Monthly Review Press.

7. This issue is discussed in more detail in Chapter 10. See also C. Riskin, 1987, *China's Political Economy: The Quest for Development Since 1949*. New York: Oxford University Press; and M. Selden, 1988, *The Political Economy of Chinese Socialism*. Armonk, NY: M. E. Sharpe.

8. Mao Zedong, 1971, *Selected Readings from the Works of Mao Zedong*. Beijing: Foreign Language Press, p. 51.

9. Ibid., p. 52.

10. For example, Gurley and writers like William Hinton, who was a longtime supporter of the Maoist model of development; see his most recent book in which he discusses the failures of the reform era: W. Hinton, 1990, *The Great Reversal: The Privatization of China, 1978–1989*. New York: Monthly Review Press.

11. The revisionist critiques of the Maoist era have been popular in the recent literature. For a selection of such works, see K. C. Tan, 1993, "Rural-Urban Segregation in China," *Geography Research Forum*, Vol. 13, pp. 71–83; P. Kane, 1988, *Famine in China, 1959–1961: Demographic and Social Implications*. New York: St. Martin's Press; Cheng Tiejun, 1991, "Dialectics of Control: The Household Registration (Hukou) System in Contemporary China." Ph.D. dissertation, Department of Sociology, SUNY at Binghamton; and S. W. Mosher, 1990, *China Misperceived: American Illusions and Chinese Reality*. New York: Basic Books.

12. See R.J.R. Kirkby, 1985, *Urbanization in China: Town and Country in a Developing Economy, 1949–2000 A.D.* New York: Columbia University Press; and K. W. Chan, 1994, *Cities with Invisible Walls: Reinterpreting Urbanization in Post-1949 China*. Hong Kong: Oxford University Press.

13. See Tan, op. cit.

14. Perhaps the best example of the pro-Maoist scholarship on the issue of urbanization and urban planning in China is provided by R. Murphey, 1980, *The Fading of the Maoist Vision: City and Country in China's Development*. New York: Methuen.

15. For a very brief discussion of Mao Zedong as a modernist, see D. Harvey, 1989, *The Condition of Post Modernity: An Enquiry into the Origins of Cultural Change*. Oxford: Basil Blackwell.

16. P. U. Unschuld, 1987, "Traditional Chinese Medicine: Some Historical and Epistemological Reflections," *Social Science and Medicine*, Vol. 24, No. 12, pp. 1023–1029.

17. See Hou Zhaotang, 1986, "Traditional Chinese Medicine Making Its Mark on the World," *Beijing Review*, No. 20 (May), pp. 15–20. See also Cai Jingfeng, 1988, "Integration of Traditional Chinese Medicine with Western Medicine: Right or Wrong?" *Social Science and Medicine*, Vol. 27, No. 5, pp. 521–529; M. M. Rosenthal and D. Frederick, 1987, "Physician Maldistribution in Cross-Cultural Perspective: United States, United Kingdom, Sweden, and the People's Republic of China," *Research in the Sociology of Health Care*, Vol. 5, pp. 101–136; and P. Wilensky, 1976, *The Delivery of Health Services in the People's Republic of China*. Ottawa: International Development Centre, Monograph No. 56E.

18. S. C. Leng and H. Chia, 1985, *Criminal Justice in Post-Mao China: Analysis and Documents*. Albany: State University of New York Press.

19. See, for example, the writings of Mao Zedong himself: Mao Zedong, 1977, *On the Ten Major Relationships*. Beijing: Foreign Languages Press; and also the interpretation of the self-sufficiency issue by Rupert Hodder: R. Hodder, 1993, *The Creation of Wealth in China: Domestic Trade and Material Progress in a Communist State*. London: Belhaven Press.

20. For examples, see: J. T. de Haas and J. H. de Haas-Posthuma, 1973, "Socio-medical Achievements in the People's Republic of China," *International Journal of Health Services*, Vol. 3, No. 2, pp. 275–294; and J. Horn, 1969, *Away with All Pests: An English Surgeon in People's China*. New York: Monthly Review Press. The work of Victor and Ruth Sidel has contributed

greatly to Westerners' understanding of the Chinese health care system. See R. Sidel and V. W. Sidel, 1973, *Serve the People: Observations on Medicine in the People's Republic of China.* Boston: Beacon Press; R. Sidel and V. W. Sidel, 1982, *The Health of China.* Boston: Beacon Press; and other papers and book chapters, including: V. W. Sidel and R. Sidel, 1975a, "The Health Care Delivery System of the People's Republic of China," pp. 1–12 in K. W. Newell (ed.), *Health: By the People.* Geneva: World Health Organization; R. Sidel and V. W. Sidel, 1975b, "Health Care in the People's Republic of China," in V. Dukanovic and E. P. Mach (eds.), *Alternative Approaches to Meeting Basic Health Needs in Developing Countries.* Geneva: World Health Organization; and V. W. Sidel and R. Sidel, 1981, "The Delivery of Medical Care in China," pp. 597–612 in P. Conrad and R. Kern (eds.), *The Sociology of Health and Illness: Critical Perspectives.* New York: St. Martin's Press.

21. See Sidel and Sidel (1975a), op. cit.

22. The emphasis on service provision at the local level was different from what was happening in the Soviet Union at a similar stage in its development; see, for example, A. E. Joseph and D. R. Phillips, 1984, *Accessibility and Utilization: Geographical Perspectives on Health Care Delivery.* New York: Harper and Row. This difference can be largely attributed to the Maoist variant of socialist political economy, with its emphasis on local self-reliance and the importance attributed to mobilizing the energy and imagination of the Chinese peasants; see Gurley, op. cit., and D. M. Lampton, 1977, *The Politics of Medicine in China.* Boulder: Westview Press.

23. G. Henderson and M. S. Cohen, 1984, *The Chinese Hospital: A Socialist Work Unit.* New Haven: Yale University Press.

24. See S. M. Huang, 1988, "Transforming China's Collective Health Care System: A Village Study," *Social Science and Medicine* Vol. 27, No. 9, pp. 879–888; and also W. C. Hsiao, 1984, "Transformation of Health Care in China," *New England Journal of Medicine,* Vol. 310 (April 5), pp. 932–936; and W. C. Hsiao, May 1988, "The Incomplete Revolution: China's Health Care System Under Market Socialism." Unpublished manuscript, School of Public Health, Harvard University. See also Yang Honglian et al., 1991, "Multi-Sectoral Approach to Primary Health Care in Fujian, China," *Health Education Quarterly,* Vol. 18, No. 1 (Spring), pp. 17–27.

25. Sidel and Sidel (1982), op. cit.

26. See S. Hillier and Z. Xiang, 1994, "Rural Health Care in China: Past, Present, and Future," pp. 95–115 in D. Dwyer (ed.), *China: The Next Decades.* Harlow, Essex, UK: Longman Scientific and Technical.

27. G. Henderson, 1989, "Issues in the Modernization of Medicine in China," pp. 199–221 in D. F. Simon and M. Goldman (eds.), *Science and Technology in Post-Mao China.* Cambridge: Harvard University Council on East Asian Study, Contemporary China Series, No. 5.

28. See S. Feuchtwang, A. Hussain, and T. Pairault (eds.), 1988, *Transforming China's Economy in the Eighties.* Vol. 1: *The Rural Sector, Welfare, and Employment.* Boulder: Westview Press.

29. P. K. New and M. L. New, 1975, "The Links Between Health and the Political Structure in the New China," *Human Organization,* Vol. 34, pp. 237–251.

30. See K. Lieberthal, 1995, *Governing China: From Revolution Through Reform.* New York: W. W. Norton.

31. For a discussion of the benefits brought to the Chinese people in this period, see M. Selden, 1998, *The Political Economy of Chinese Socialism.* Armonk, NY: M. E. Sharpe.

32. See Turshen, op. cit.

33. V. L.Wang, 1976, "Food Distribution as a Guarantee for Nutrition and Health," *Milbank Memorial Fund Quarterly.* Vol. #, pp. 145–165. See also Hillier and Xiang, op. cit.

34. R. H. Gray, 1988, "Fundamentals of the Epidemiologic and Demographic Transitions, pp. 25–42 in *Research in Human Capital Development,* Vol. 5. Greenwood, CT: J. A.I. Press.

35. These ratios had declined slightly by 1992, but the urban/rural gap was still wide—3.3:1 for hospital beds, and 3.6 for doctors.

36. See Sidel and Sidel (1982), op. cit. In the face of such levels of inequality it is disconcerting to note that there had actually been vast improvements, in absolute terms, in the access to health care in the Chinese countryside after 1949. The number of beds increased from fewer than 20,000 to 1,140,000 in 1978; and the number of doctors almost doubled, from 297,000 to 591,000 (see *State Statistical Abstract,* 1984). In per capita terms these improvements were wiped out by the sharp population increases in the countryside during this period. As far as hospital beds are concerned, the gap between the cities and the countryside had been reduced, but it remained significant. In 1949 there were 0.63 beds per 1,000 in the cities compared to only 0.05 in the countryside. By 1978, the situation in both the cities and the countryside had improved dramatically, but

beds in urban areas were still almost four times more available than in rural areas (4.85 per 1,000 versus 1.41 per 1,000). The availability of doctors in the countryside had fallen even further behind that in the cities by 1978. There had been a fourfold increase in the cities, from 0.70 to 2.99 doctors per 1,000 of the population; but in the countryside the ratio barely improved at all (from 0.66 to 0.73 per 100).

37. In 1979 the ratio of the highest to the lowest province in terms of health care personnel per 1,000 was 4.6:1; and for hospital beds it was 3.22.

38. See M. K. Whyte and W. L. Parish, 1984, *Urban Life in Contemporary China.* Chicago: The University of Chicago Press.

39. For a discussion of the services provided by state-owned work units (*danwei*), see Y. T. Bian, 1994, *Work and Inequality in Urban China.* Albany: State University of New York Press; and also A. G. Walder, 1986, *Communist Neo-Traditionalism: Work and Authority in Chinese Industry.* Berkeley: University of California Press; and A. G. Walder, 1991, "Workers, Managers and the State: The Reform Era and the Political Crisis of 1989," *The China Quarterly*, No. 127 (September), pp. 447–453.

40. See S. Harper, 1994, "China's Population: Prospects and Policies," pp. 54–76 in D. Dwyer (ed.), *China: The Next Decade.* London: Longman; and also J.C.B. Leung and R. C. Nann, 1995, *Authority and Benevolence: Social Welfare in China.* Hong Kong: The Chinese University Press.

41. D. Davis, 1989, "Chinese Social Welfare: Policies and Outcomes," *The China Quarterly*, Vol. 119 (September), pp. 577–597, 581.

42. See Walder (1986), op. cit.

43. R. Smith, 1993, "The Chinese Road to Capitalism," *New Left Review*, No. 199 (May–June), pp. 55–99, 73.

44. See, for examples, Murphey, op. cit.; and Gurley, op. cit.

45. Davis, op. cit.

46. Wang Bingqian, 1982, "Report on the Final State Accounts in 1981," *People's Daily* (Renmin Ribao), August 24; and also, by the same author, "Report on the Execution of the 1986 Budget and the Draft Budget of 1987," *People's Daily* (Renmin Ribao), June 14.

47. Hsueh Tien-tung and Ouyang Xiaoming, 1993, "Pattern of China's Public Expenditure and Revenue: An International Comparison," pp. 17–41 in Hsueh Tien-tung et al. (eds.), *Studies on Economic Reforms and Development in the People's Republic of China.* Hong Kong: The Chinese University Press.

48. Chen Pichao and Tuan Chihsien, 1983, "Primary Health Care in Rural China: Post 1978 Development," *Social Science and Medicine*, Vol. 17, No. 19, pp. 1411–1416.

49. Liu Xingzhu and Wang Junle, 1991, "An Introduction to China's Health Care System," *Journal of Public Health Policy*, Vol. #, pp. 104–116.

50. For discussions of recent developments, see Hou Ruili, 1992, "Can or Should China's Free Medical System Survive?" *China Today*, Vol. 61, No. 4, pp. 25–28; and also A. S. Bhalla, 1991, "Access to Health Services," *Journal of International Development*, Vol. 3, No. 4, pp. 403–420.

51. See Huang, op. cit.

52. Taylor et al., op. cit.

53. This issue is dealt with in a recent report about human rights in China. See *Human Rights Tribune*, 1991, "Health Care for All: Miracle of Mirage?" Vol. 11, No. 5 (November), pp. 13–14. See also He Bochuan, 1991, *China on the Edge: Crisis of Ecology and Development.* San Francisco: China Books; and the chapter dealing with the elderly in China, written by Sarah Harper, in Denis Dwyer's volume, op. cit. In spite of the rapid growth of the private sector in the provision of social services, the underlying system of economic and political control in China has remained largely intact, which will work to slow down the rate at which further privatization can occur. In the cities, for example, the large state-owned enterprises still account for a major though declining share of the nation's industrial output. Many such enterprises are plagued by low levels of productivity and massive overstaffing, but it is difficult to imagine that the managers of such enterprises will choose to rationalize the workforce by firing inefficient and excess workers; and they are even less likely to attempt belt-tightening by cutting off welfare (including health) benefits. The reason is that in a state-owned enterprise the state pays the workers' salaries as well as a variety of other noncash benefits, including housing, utilities, education, and health care. Such payments are made directly to the individual through the *danwei* (work unit); added together they represent more than half of the worker's total wages. In this system the social costs of reproducing the labor force cannot be passed off from the employer to the state as they would be in a capitalist system, because in China the employer and the state have until recently been the same entity. Downsizing the workforce and eliminating the social wage component would amount to throwing the workers out of their homes and into the streets, cut-

ting off food subsidies and social security payments, and eliminating medical benefits. In addition, the state would still have to provide unemployment benefits and the full range of social services to former workers or face the prospect of massive social upheaval. Recent reports show that a growing number of urban workers has been voluntarily giving up state-sector jobs, with the accompanying social benefits, to take a chance in private industry and commerce. With the higher wages they can usually earn in the private sector, they hope to be able to buy social services, including health insurance, at market rates. With the exception of such voluntary transfers, the state is still wary about attempting any drastic reductions in the scale of its social costs payments.

54. Song Fujian, T. Rathwell, and D. Clayden, 1991, "Doctors in China from 1949 to 1988," *Health Policy and Planning,* Vol. 6, No. 1 (March), pp. 64–70. The transfer-of-technology issue is described in the work of Henderson and her colleagues: G. Henderson, Liu Yuanli, Guan Xiaoming, and Liu Zongxiu, 1987, "The Rise of Technology in Chinese Hospitals," *International Journal of Technology Assessment,* Vol. 3, pp. 253–264; and G. Henderson, E. A. Murphy, S. T. Stockwell, Zhou Jiongliang, Shen Qingrui, and Li Zhiming, 1988, "High-technology Medicine in China: The Case of Chronic Renal Failure and Hemodialysis," *New England Journal of Medicine,* Vol. 318 (April 14), pp. 1000–1004.

55. R. Delfs, 1990a, "Pay as You Go: Improved Health Care Means Higher Costs," *Far Eastern Economic Review,* Vol. 149, No. 30 (July 26), pp. 222–223.

56. Henderson et al. (1987), op. cit.

57. For discussions on this topic, see A. Lucas, 1980, "Changing Medical Models in China: Organization Options or Obstacles?" *The China Quarterly,* Vol. 83, pp. 461–488; and Qui Ren-Zong, 1989, "Equity and Public Health Care in China," *Journal of Medicine and Philosophy,* Vol. 14, No. 3 (June), pp. 283–287.

58. Henderson (1989), op. cit., p. 216.

59. P. K. New, 1986, "Primary Health Care in the People's Republic of China: A March Backward?" *Human Organization,* Vol. 45, No. 2 (Summer), pp. 147–153.

60. Liu and Wang, op. cit.

61. See Hsiao, op. cit. A World Bank report published in 1997 shows that 64 percent of rural residents were uninsured in 1993, compared to 15 percent in urban areas; see World Bank, 1997, *Financing Health Care: Issues and Options for China.* Washington, DC: World Bank, p. 3.

62. See *China News Analysis* (1990), op. cit.

63. Liu and Wang, op. cit., pp. 109–110.

64. This is discussed in two articles written by N. Prescott and D. T. Jamison, 1984, "Health Sector Finance in China," *World Health Statistics Quarterly,* Vol. 37, pp. 397–402; and 1985, "The Distribution and Impact of Health Resources Availability in China," *International Journal of Health Planning and Management,* Vol. 1, pp. 1–12.

65. Henderson (1989), op. cit., p. 206.

66. Y. Shao, 1988, *Health Care in China.* London: Office of Health Economics.

67. Bhalla, op. cit.

68. See World Bank (1997), op. cit.

69. Although this charge is generally denied by Chinese government officials, it is widely reported by Western visitors. See, for example, H. R. Rosemont Jr., 1991, *A Chinese Mirror: Reflections on Political Economy and Society.* La Salle, IN: Open Court Books. The story about the unregistered doctors is taken from an editorial article in *People's Daily,* July 12, 1990, p. 5.

70. *China News Analysis* (1990), op. cit, p. 7.

71. See Jamison et al. (1985), op. cit., and A. Piazza, 1986, *Food Consumption and Nutritional Status in the PRC.* Boulder: Westview Press.

72. The per capita consumption of grain, for example, was 205 kg in the rural areas in 1957 and 225 kg in the cities; meat consumption was much lower in the countryside (4.77 kg per capita as opposed to 7.92 in the urban areas). See C. Aubert, 1988, "China's Food Take-off?" pp. 101–136 in S. Feuchtwang, A. Hussain, and T. Pairault (eds.), *Transforming China's Economy in the Eighties.* Vol. l: *The Rural Sector, Welfare, and Employment.* Boulder: Westview Press.

73. See *China News Analysis* (1991), op. cit.

74. Ibid.

75. This is discussed in the multination longitudinal study conducted in China in the late 1980s; see Chen Junshi et al., 1990, *Diet, Life-Style and Mortality in China: A Study of the Characteristics of 65 Chinese Counties.* Oxford: Oxford University Press.

76. *China News Analysis* (1991), op. cit. In this context it is instructive to recall Joseph Eyer's hypothesis of "prosperity as a cause of death." Eyer's powerful argument linked elevated mortality statistics in advanced capitalist countries to the behavioral and dietary changes that are associated with increasing societal wealth. In China during the reform era, it is plausible that rising death rates may be one of the costs associated with the successful adoption of capitalism (or market socialism); see J. Eyer, 1977, "Pros-

perity as a Cause of Death," *International Journal of Health Services*, Vol. 7, No. 1, pp. 125–150. The work of Amartya Sen is also interesting in this respect, as discussed later in this chapter and in Chapter 10. Sen has suggested in many of his recent writings that the successes of the reform era have not necessarily translated into better health and lower mortality among the Chinese people.

77. E. Vartiainen et al., 1991, "Mortality, Cardiovascular Risk Factors, and Diet in China, Finland, and the United States," *Public Health Reports*, Vol. 106, No. 1, pp. 41–46.

78. *China News Analysis* (1990), op. cit.

79. Chen et al., op. cit.

80. Population data from the China Statistical Publishing House, 1998, *China Statistical Yearbook 1997* (table 3-2, p. 69) shows that death rates in China have actually increased slightly throughout the 1980s and 1990s from the all-time low of 1978 (6.34 percent), rising to 6.72 percent in 1987, and then 6.70 percent in 1991; but falling again in the 1990s (6.56 percent in 1996).

81. A. Sen, 1989, "Food and Freedom," *World Development*, Vol. 17, No. 6, pp. 769–781. This argument is also made by J. Knight and L. Song, 1993, "The Length of Life and the Standard of Living: Economic Influences on Premature Death in China," *Journal of Development Studies*, Vol. 30, No. 1 (October), pp. 58–91. It is argued that after the first rapid increase in rural incomes in the early 1980s, subsequent gains were minimal, and in fact the urban-rural income gap increased. Between 1985 and 1989, for example, real peasant incomes grew at an average of 4 percent per year, but that had declined to 1–2 percent in the early 1990s, and the ratio between urban and rural incomes widened from 2.0:1 in 1987 to 2.2:1 in 1990. See L. Wong, 1993, "Slighting the Needy? Social Welfare Under Transition," *China Review 1993*, edited by J.Y.S. Cheng and M. Brosseseau. Hong Kong: Chinese University Press, p. 15.

82. P. Nolan and J. Sender, 1992, "Death Rates, Life Expectancy, and China's Economic Reforms: A Critique of A. K. Sen," *World Development*, Vol. 20, No. 9, pp. 1279–1303.

83. This issue is discussed by G. Henderson, 1993, "Public Health in China," pp. 103–123 in W. A. Joseph (ed.), *China Briefing, 1992*. Boulder: Westview Press. As Henderson notes, "Dietary patterns have shifted to higher consumption of fat and protein, and major health problems now consist of the diseases associated with higher levels of economic development [such as] cancer, stroke, respiratory

disease, heart disease, and accidents [that are] now the five leading causes of death" (p. 112). Henderson also observes that risk factors associated with chronic diseases are also on the rise, including dietary change, creating more obesity; high blood pressure; increased cholesterol; decreased exercise and higher everyday stress levels; and, most significantly, smoking (pp. 112–113). It is also clear that the urban-rural gap for both health indicators and levels of service are increasing: for example, in life expectancy (four years higher in cities) and deaths from respiratory diseases (16 percent of all city deaths, 25 percent in the countryside).

84. Ibid., p. 114.

85. See World Bank (1997), op. cit.

86. Henderson (1993), op. cit., p. 111.

87. World Bank, 1992, *China: Strategies for Reducing Poverty in the 1990s*. Washington, DC: World Bank, pp. 90–107, 93; the immunization in this case is for measles, pertussis, diphtheria, and polio. See also Nolan and Sender, op. cit. In spite of the encouraging downward trend for infectious diseases (see World Bank [1992], op. cit., pp. 94–95), there is a concern that endemic diseases and micronutrient deficiencies (such as schistosomiasis, iodine deficiency, and iron and vitamin A deficiencies) are still highly prevalent in the poorest areas.

88. E. Croll, 1994, *From Heaven to Earth: Images and Experience of Development in China*. London: Routledge.

89. World Bank (1992), op. cit., pp. 99–100.

90. Ibid., p. 100. There is also evidence suggesting rising prevalence rates for some diseases in the poorest areas, which had previously been all but eradicated, including tuberculosis and schistosomiasis.

91. Croll (1994), op. cit., pp. 86–87.

92. Ibid., p. 87. From the results of preliminary fieldwork being conducted in Ningxia Hui Autonomous Region, the author is able to reinforce some of Croll's observations. In some of the very poor mountainous regions in the southern areas, which have no access to irrigation-based water supplies, poverty and a lack of iodine in the local wells are thought to have contributed to a high prevalence of birth defects and developmental disabilities.

93. Croll et al. (1994), p. 93.

94. Ibid., p. 111.

95. Ibid., p. 111.

96. See Yang Peilin and J. S. Lawson, 1991, "Health Care for a Thousand Million," *World Health Forum*, Vol. 12, pp. 151–155; and Yang Peilin, V. Lin, and J. Lawson, 1991, "Health Policy Reform in the

People's Republic of China," *International Journal of Health Services,* Vol. 21, No. 3, pp. 481–491.

97. For data and a discussion of this issue, see Zhu Ling, 1991, *Rural Reform and Peasant Income in China: The Impact of China's Post-Mao Rural Reforms in Selected Regions.* New York: St. Martin's Press. On the peripheral regions, see the discussion in Wang Xiaoqiang and Bai Nanfeng, 1991, *The Poverty of Plenty.* London: Macmillan.

98. See Hinton, op. cit., and P. Howard, 1988, *Breaking the Iron Rice Bowl: Prospects for Socialism in the Chinese Countryside.* Armonk, NY: M. E. Sharpe.

99. This is discussed in many recent papers written about the spatial impacts of the reforms, particularly in the Pearl River Delta. See, for example, C. P. Lo, 1989, "Recent Spatial Restructuring in Zhujiang Delta, South China: A Study of Socialist Regional Development Strategy," *Annals of the Association of American Geographers,* Vol. 79, No. 2, pp. 293–308; T. G. McGee, 1991, "The Emergence of Desakota Regions in Asia: Expanding a Hypothesis," pp. 3–26 in N. Ginsburg, B. Koppel, and T. G. McGee (eds.), *The Extended Metropolis: Settlement Transition in Asia.* Honolulu: University of Hawaii Press; and P. B. Prime, 1991, "China's Economic Reforms in Regional Perspective," pp. 9–28 in G. Veeck (ed.), *The Uneven Landscape.* Baton Rouge: Louisiana State University Press.

100. The rate of population growth in China's rural areas continued to be higher than was the case in the cities, and as a result the per capita availability and staffing of rural health care facilities also declined appreciably during the 1980s. Ministry of Public Health statistics show that the number of health care personnel assigned to rural areas (those at the township and village levels in the hierarchy) fell from more than 1 million in 1980 to 873,323 in 1989. See R. Delfs, 1990b, "Stress Symptoms: Changing Health Needs Undermine Medical System," *Far Eastern Economic Review,* Vol. 149, No. 30 (July 26), pp. 21–22. The number of hospital beds per 1,000 in the cities was 4.02 in 1980 but had increased to 4.71 by 1992; the figure for rural areas was 1.53 per thousand in 1980, declining to 1.44 by 1992. There had also been a flip-flop in the provision of both hospital beds and total medical personnel in favor of the urban areas. In 1992 the cities provided 55.5 percent of the total beds (compared to less than 40 percent in 1975) and 58 percent of all medical personnel (compared to 41.9 percent in 1975).

101. M. M. Rosenthal and D. Frederick, 1987, "Physician Maldistribution in Cross-Cultural Per-

spective: United States, United Kingdom, Sweden, and the People's Republic of China," *Research in the Sociology of Health Care,* Vol. 5, pp. 101–136.

102. Henderson (1993), op. cit.

103. In spite of the evidence of growing inequality in the provision of health care, there is anecdotal evidence that the overall quality of rural health care increased during the 1980s, largely as a result of improved training programs and more rigorous examinations; see Bhalla, op. cit. Journalistic evidence also suggests that technological capability has been improved in many rural health care facilities; see Delfs, 1990a, op. cit. In the countryside many patients can now be treated with radiological diagnostic techniques and operated upon if necessary. Again it is important to stress that access to high-technology medical equipment varies considerably from one area to the next, largely as a function of local wealth. The areas that have benefitted most from the economic restructuring in the Dengist era are also likely to have the most technologically advanced health care facilities.

104. According to Bhalla, op. cit., the number of barefoot doctors fell from 1.6 million in 1975 to 905,800 in 1985.

105. Lewis and Diamond-Kim, op. cit.; see also M. E. Young, 1989, "Impact of the Rural Reforms on Financing Rural Health Services in China," *Health Policy,* Vol. 11 (February), pp. 27–42.

106. This is discussed in an editorial in *People's Daily,* September 27, 1991; see China New Analysis (1991), op. cit.

107. Davis, op. cit.

108. See R. Smith, op. cit., and Riskin, op. cit.

109. This statement was made in the official magazine *Outlook,* No. 37 (1989), p. 14. See also Wang and Bai, op. cit.

110. China New Analysis (1990), op. cit., p. 2.

111. See the World Bank's 1997 report, op. cit., p. 32. The statistics on venereal disease were provided in *Outlook* (overseas ed.), No. 10 (1989), pp. 11–12 and 15–16. On the smoking issue in China, see D. Tomson and A. Coulter, 1987, "The Bamboo Smoke Screen: Tobacco Smoking in China," *Health Promotion,* Vol. 2, No. 2, pp. 95–108.

112. See, for example, Chen Yue, L. L. Pederson, and N. M. Lefcoe, 1992, "Father's Education Level, Adult's Smoking Status, and Children's Smoking Behavior in Shanghai," *Health Values,* Vol. 16, No. 2 (March–April), pp. 51–56. The smoking issue has presented a dilemma for the government throughout the reform era, as the obvious health hazard of smok-

ing conflicts with the economic reality that China is the largest cigarette producer in the world. In 1988 tobacco production generated revenues of Y21 billion, amounting to 10 percent of the government's total revenues. *Nanfang Daily*, July 1, 1989, p. 6.

113. This is discussed by J.B.R. Whitney, 1991, "The Waste Economy and the Dispersed Metropolis in China," pp. 177–192 in N. Ginsburg, B. Koppel, and T. G. McGee (eds.), *The Extended Metropolis: Settlement Transition in Asia.* Honolulu: University of Hawaii Press. See also Chen et al., op. cit.

114. Hou, op. cit.

115. Yang Lin and Lawson, op. cit.

116. This is covered in detail by Selden, op. cit., and also by Davis, op. cit.

117. M. K. Whyte, 1986, "Social Trends in China: The Triumph of Inequality?" pp. 103–124 in A. D.

Barnett and R. Clough (eds.), *Modernizing China.* Boulder: Westview Press.

118. One final caveat is in order. Bearing in mind the size and diversity of China, it is easy to overemphasize the extent of the changes in the health care system and the degree to which the new ways of providing health care have surpassed and supplemented the old ways. In many parts of the Chinese countryside, it is likely that very little change has occurred in the way things are done. In a peculiarly Chinese makeshift fashion, the new system of health care has been grafted onto the old one, rather than the old one being entirely replaced. There are stories, some of which may be apocryphal, of expensive new imported machines being operated in rural health clinics by untrained operators who cannot afford to wear rubber gloves.

Chapter 7

1. For the quote, see W. Hinton, 1984, *Shenfan: The Continuing Revolution in a Chinese Village.* New York: Vintage Books, p. 80. In the 1950s the peasants took the collective road, and together they managed to do the impossible, unlocking the riches of the barren wastelands and steep slopes of Dazhai. From that time onward the Dazhai miracle was used across China as the model of "socialist efficiency," and peasants everywhere were urged to "learn from Dazhai" and follow its example.

2. *Daily Telegraph*, February 10, 1961, cable message from the Chinese Red Cross Society to the League of Red Cross Societies in Geneva, rejecting all offers of food assistance. See J. Becker, 1996, *Hungry Ghosts: China's Secret Famine.* London: John Murray, p. 297.

3. Ibid.

4. Ibid., p. 282.

5. See Chu Han, 1996, *A Documentary of the Three-Year Natural Disaster Period.* Chengdu: Sichuan Renmin Chubanshe. The book is reviewed by Shuping Chen, 1998, "Starvation and Victimization in China," *China Strategic Review*, Vol. 2, No. 2, pp. 98–113. In the review Chen notes that the author chooses to accept Liu Shaoqi's observation that natural disasters (floods in some areas, droughts in others) were responsible for 30 percent of the catastrophe, with human factors, mostly in the form of policy errors, making up the other 70 percent.

6. The basic premise of the Great Leap Forward was an all-out attempt to speed up production in all spheres of activity, but mostly in the area of food

supply and industrial output; see K. Lieberthal, 1997, "The Great Leap Forward and the Split in the Yan'an Leadership, 1958–1965," pp. 87–147 in R. McFarquhar (ed.), *The Politics of China: The Eras of Mao and Deng*, 2d ed. Cambridge, UK: Cambridge University Press.

7. Quoted in Becker, op. cit., p. 284.

8. Ibid., p. 284.

9. There are some major exceptions, however, such as the 1996 publication of the Chu Han book. The book provides an accounting of the strategic errors made in both industrial and agricultural policy areas. For example, the industrialization push resulted in too large a share of total investment going into industry, with a consequent reduction in agriculture; at the same time, the increase in the urban population meant that there were far more people in the cities who needed to be fed and subsidized by the state. All was made worse by the drastic decline in food production throughout the three-year period (Chen, pp. 106–108).

10. As Jasper Becker writes, "No monuments commemorate the victims and some Chinese are still not willing to believe that a famine costing so many lives ever took place." Becker, op. cit., pp. 285–286.

11. See J. Banister, 1987, *China's Changing Population.* Stanford: Stanford University Press.

12. According to Becker, op. cit., what sets the Great Leap famine apart from other similar events in history (for example, the potato blight famine in Ireland in 1845 and the famines in India in 1896 and

1897) is that it was entirely "man-made." By the end of the 1950s China was at peace; no blight had destroyed the harvest; and there were no unusually severe floods or droughts. The granaries were full, and other countries were ready to send grain if supplies ran out. In addition to the general lack of concern about why the tragedy occurred, China's collectivization program, which appears to have been largely responsible for the tragedy, was being described throughout the 1960s and 1970s as a model that other developing countries might consider following. Leaders and future leaders of several Third World nations at that time were being advised by China's top agricultural strategists, and some were even following China's lead in their own agricultural policies. Communist Party officials from North Vietnam, North Korea, and Cambodia visited China to learn more about the commune system. The Great Leap Forward was intended to be China's big push toward full communism and the withering away of the state, which, in the late 1950s, was assumed to be only a few years away.

13. One leader described what the new future might be like: "What does Communism mean? . . . First, taking good food and not merely eating one's fill. At each meal one enjoys a meat diet, eating chicken, pork, fish or eggs . . . delicacies like monkey brains, swallow's nest, white fungi are served to each according to his needs." This quote is attributed to Tan Chen Lin, minister of agriculture in 1958, reprinted in a Red Guard magazine and quoted in R. MacFarquhar's *The Origins of the Cultural Revolution*; see Becker, op. cit., p. 59. From our vantage point at the end of the century, it is almost unthinkable that Mao could have been so easily hoodwinked by the promises of Stalin's "miracle science," which he then set about applying to both food and steel production during the Great Leap Forward. In the agricultural sector, Lysenko's ideas led Mao and others to believe that crop growth could be radically modified by changing the way plants were cultivated and that such modifications could be transmitted to the next generation. In spite of the abject failure in the Soviet Union, China's chief Lysenkoist, Luo Tianyu, worked with Mao to draw up an eight-point blueprint to be applied by all peasants in the new collectives. This amounted to a new agricultural "constitution" for China, calling for the popularization of new breeds and seeds; close planting methods; deep ploughing; increased fertilization; the innovation of farm tools; improved field management; pest control; and increased and improved irrigation. Many of these practices made sound agricultural sense, but others were taken to ridiculous extremes. The idea of pest control, for example, resulted in bizarre episodes of mass bird-killings, after which the people were ordered to catch their quota of flies, which had become more prevalent because the bird population had been decimated! See Becker, op. cit.

14. One of the long-term consequences of Mao's faulty logic at this time, in addition to the deaths that would occur as a result of starvation, was his belief that it would not be necessary for China to restrict its population growth because food supplies were in abundance (Becker, p. 81). It appears that Mao and his supporters had convinced themselves they were not bound either by human laws or by the laws of nature. They thought that with the benefit of their willpower, hard work, "scientific" agriculture, and a superior ideology, "the rules of biology, chemistry and physics could be rewritten: according to their bizarre world view, infant piglets could be made to spawn litters, broken glass could fertilize crops and earthen embankments could be put to the same exacting use as concrete dams." N. Eberstadt, "The Great Leap Backward," *New York Times Book Review*, February 16, 1997, pp. 6–7.

15. Eberstadt, op. cit., p. 6.

16. It was in Henan, in fact in Xinyang Prefecture, that the first commune had been formed in April 1958, setting off waves of enthusiasm for mass collectivization. The Party's provincial secretary in Henan, Wu Zhifu, was a fanatical Maoist who was eager to please the Great Leader and advance his own career (Becker, op. cit.). Becker also describes similarly chilling stories from his fieldwork elsewhere in China, including Anhui and Sichuan Provinces, as well as Tibet.

17. Becker, op. cit., p. 113.

18. A competition was organized to see which of the counties in the Xinyang Prefecture could find the most "hidden" grain. As Becker tells the story, to get peasants to toe the line, officials "created a nightmare of organized torture and murder" (ibid., p. 115).

19. Ibid., p. 117.

20. When family members died their bodies were often hidden so the rest of the family could feed from the corpse while still claiming the deceased's food ration. "In Guanzhou county, one woman with three children was caught after she had hidden the corpse of one of them behind the door and then finally, in desperation, had begun to eat it." Ibid.

21. J. Jowett, 1989, "Mao's Man-Made Famine," *Geographical Magazine*, No. 4 (April), pp. 16–19.

22. R. L. Edmonds, "Land of Hungry Ghosts," *Times Literary Supplement*, October 25, 1996, pp. 3–4.

23. Jowett, op. cit., p. 18.

24. Ibid., p. 18.

25. Becker, op. cit., p. 152.

26. Ibid., pp. 153–154. There were many grim stories coming from various points in the countryside. One involved the experimentation with various unlikely food substitutes, which involved sawdust and wood pulp, marshwater plankton, straw, and even soil, in addition to a range of wild grasses, weeds, leaves, and the bark from trees. Many people suffered intestinal problems and even died from eating such indigestible items, and others died from eating poisonous mushrooms or berries they foraged in the woods.

27. This almost unthinkable notion—that slaves are somehow willing participants in their enslavement—has recently been explored by Kevin Bales in his disturbing book about the prevalence of what he calls the "new slavery." In the case of the sex trades in the cities and towns of Thailand, for example, Bales observes that many of the female workers, who have been sold into virtual slavery by their parents, come to depend upon and even support their pimps, somehow managing to rationalize their enslavement. This explains, in part (according to Bales), why the girls do not attempt to escape and, in some cases, do not choose to leave even when their "debt bondage" has been paid off. See K. Bales, 1999, *Disposable People: New Slavery in the Global Economy*. Berkeley: University of California Press.

28. Becker, op. cit., p. 310.

29. Ibid., pp. 311–312.

30. Chen, op. cit., for example, argues that the rapid shift toward collectivization in the late 1950s resulted in a huge amount of wasteful investment in large-scale irrigation and dam-building schemes, highway construction, and industrial projects, all of which not only required massive capital inputs but also took away large numbers of peasants from the land and their agricultural duties (p. 108).

31. A. P. Liu, 1986, *How China Is Ruled*. Englewood Cliffs, NJ: Prentice-Hall.

32. For a scathing critique of the Maoist drive toward large-scale collectivization, see M. Selden, 1988, *Chinese Political Economy*. Armonk, NY: M. E. Sharpe.

33. This point was reinforced in the 1980s when private farming returned very rapidly in many parts of the countryside in the 1980s, indicating that the "capitalist" tendencies among the peasants had never fully been eradicated. See, for example, Kate Xiao Zhou, 1996, *How the Farmers Changed China: Power of the People*. Boulder: Westview Press. For other examples of this argument, see "Whither China's Agricultural Reforms: An Interview with William Hinton," *Contemporary Marxism*, Vols. 12–13 (Spring 1986), pp. 137–143; and also P. Howard, 1986, "Some Comments on China's Controversial Rural Economic Reforms," *Contemporary Marxism*, Vols. 12–13 (Spring), pp. 163–201. Perhaps the most polemically negative critique of the agricultural reforms has been provided by M. Chossudovsky, 1986, *Towards Capitalist Restoration? Chinese Socialism After Mao*. London: Macmillan, p. 25. At the time (1986), most China scholars considered Chossudovsky's argument to be too far-fetched; but time has shown that he was in fact prophetic, and much of what he predicted would happen in the mid-1980s has actually happened by the end of the 1990s.

34. Hinton, op. cit., p. 78.

35. C. W. Pannell and L.J.C. Ma, 1983, *China: The Geography of Development and Modernization*. London: V. H. Winston.

36. V. Smil, 1984, *The Bad Earth: Environmental Degradation in China*. Armonk, NY: M. E. Sharpe.

37. By comparison, the United States, with only a quarter as many people, has half as much cultivable land again (156 million hectares). The only solution to this age-old dilemma was to increase the productivity of the land that was available. This was possible by the use of irrigation, greater quantities of chemical fertilizers, the use of higher-yielding strains, and a significant increase in the effective amount of cultivable land by multiple cropping. This was easy to achieve in the subtropical areas of South China, where three crops a year were possible, and even in some parts of northern China, where winter wheat could be planted after the summer crop had been harvested; but in many areas climate and soil constraints made multiple cropping impossible. Although multiple cropping has always been a feature of Chinese agriculture, it was stepped up significantly after 1949, to such an extent that the regional cropping index increased from 130 (for the whole of China and where 100 equals one crop per year) to 150 in 1979 and was in fact as high as 200 in some parts of the Yangtze Basin. The geographic pattern of grain yields reveals the extent of the underlying variations in the productivity of the Chinese land. The basic pattern of grain yield is one in which output declines sharply as one moves north, northwest, and

west from the most productive areas in the Yangtze Valley and South China.

38. M. Blecher, 1986, *China: Politics, Economics, and Society: Iconoclasm and Innovation in a Revolutionary Socialist Country*. London: Frances Pinter, pp. 43–49, 45. In spite of the obvious advantages, there were two major problems associated with the process of land reform. First, the poorest peasants, many of whom were given land, were often the worst farmers, in addition to which they were usually too poor to invest in the land they were granted. Second, the relatively small number of well-off farmers who managed to hold on to their land lost all interest in doing well for fear of political reprisals.

39. Hinton, op. cit., p. 65.

40. See ibid., p. 71. One such family in Long Bow village was headed by Li Chuan-chung, known locally as Li-the-Fat. He did so well with new animals and new land, which were bought with his newfound prosperity, "that he was soon in a position to buy more houses. He bought six sections in his home courtyard from a poor peasant . . . who could not make ends meet [and he] continued the expansion of his holdings by setting up a small flour mill." Ibid., p. 72.

41. Most CCP leaders agreed on collectivization as the goal for Chinese agriculture, but they disagreed on the pace of the program and the best way to achieve it. Mao Zedong was eager to push the process along rapidly by establishing huge communes, both as a way to increase production and to centralize power in the countryside. This was the leftist flank of the Party, and opposing it was a more pragmatic group (the rightists) favoring small collectives over mass organizations and allowing production to be guided by some degree of material incentives for individual peasant families (for example, the right to maintain small, "private" plots on which to grow a few subsistence crops). In the short run Mao's views predominated, and the mutual aid teams were intended to be the first step in the continuing effort to eliminate class exploitation of the poor by the rich peasants. The successful production teams, such as the ones in Dazhai, were used as models in propaganda efforts to encourage others to raise their own productivity. Rich peasant households were excluded from the teams in an attempt to isolate and destroy them as a class. At the same time, state monopolies unifying the purchase and distribution of grain were introduced, so that peasant families were protected by the state from the vicissitudes of a private market in grain. This, in addition to the establishment of rural credit cooperatives, helped the poorer peasants to avoid becoming dependent on their richer neighbors.

42. Mao's concerns are expressed in Mao Zedong, 1977, *Selected Works*, Vol. 5. Beijing: Foreign Languages Press, p. 206. In spite of the push toward collectivization, class differences, at least in monetary (income) terms, remained. For example, Vivienne Shue (1980) has shown that a group of "rich" peasants living within her study area earned a combined family income that was twice the average in 1954— Y861 compared to Y421. The average for the families in cooperatives was Y466, and for "poor" peasants the average was Y272. It is interesting to note that the average income of former landlords was only Y286 at that time. See V. Shue, 1980, *Peasant China in Transition: The Dynamics of Development Toward Socialism, 1949–1956*. Berkeley: University of California Press, p. 283.

43. The new cooperatives were much larger than their predecessors, and they were fully socialist in the sense that distribution was based solely on work done rather than previous ownership of land and capital. The richer peasants were dealt another blow, because those who were allowed to enter the new cooperatives lost their land forever and were reclassified as ordinary peasants. By this time many infrastructural improvements had already been carried out in the Chinese countryside. Average field size had been increased, making economies of scale and the efficient use of tractors possible. New water conservancy projects were constructed, and a small amount of the cooperatives' resources was being set aside for agricultural risk-taking and investment projects. Supporters of the cooperatives argued that none of this could (or would) have occurred to the same extent under an individual household economy. In Long Bow village, for example, the cooperative was able to borrow Y8,000 to buy a waterwheel, which irrigated vast stretches of land that could never have been reached in the old days. See Hinton, op. cit.

44. Ibid., p. 133.

45. Liu, op. cit., p. 198.

46. With the advent of the higher-stage cooperatives a new tier of cadres forced the grassroots leaders who had emerged during land reform to take a backseat. In addition, all buying and selling were now done in the cooperatives, and this largely eliminated the independence of individual families. Many peasants felt that the cooperatives offered them the worst of all possible worlds: making excessive demands on them in terms of output, but rewarding them so

poorly that they were not inclined to work as hard as if they owned the land or had the rights to market their own produce. It had also proved difficult to come up with an equitable system of work points to remunerate peasants with different levels of skills and abilities. The basic principle was "he who works more gets more," but at the end of each day it was difficult to reach agreement on this. In Long Bow, for example, there was an argument about a peasant who had been dragging his heels in the fields all day: "If we allow this then everyone will start to dawdle. We must give him less [work points]. . . . He came out late and he never caught up with the rest of the group all day." Hinton, op. cit., p. 128.

47. The brief experiment with the larger communes and with rewards allocated entirely according to needs was generally judged to have been a mistake. See Blecher (1986), op. cit.

48. Ibid., p. 71.

49. C. Aubert, 1988, China's Food Take-Off?" pp. 101–136 in S. Feuchtwang, A. Hussain, and T. Pairaullt (eds.), *Transforming China's Economy in the Eighties*. Vol. 1: *The Rural Sector, Welfare, and Employment*. Boulder: Westview Press.

50. William Hinton, op. cit., has also described another problem that began with the cooperatives and worsened with the communes, namely, the bondage of the peasants to the land. In "feudal" China the peasants had been dirt-poor, but they were not actually serfs. They were bound to the land, but only by debt, not by contract. They could and did walk off their land to seek work whenever it seemed to be available, and preliberation China was in fact a land of itinerant hobos, but after about 1953 every peasant was firmly tied to the land. They were secure as long as the crops grew well, but they could not leave because they had nowhere else to go. Their bondage was confirmed with the formation of the State Grain Company in 1954. The state would now buy and distribute all grain, and it established a rationing system that split the Chinese population into two groups. In the cities people received ration books, which were linked to urban residency; in the countryside the peasants were not allowed to have urban permits to live in the cities; therefore, they had no access to grain rations. In other words, unless they could somehow secure urban residence permits, they were tied to their communes as the only source of food. The desire to live in the cities was very strong among the peasants, as it is in all developing countries with an impoverished countryside, but in China rural-to-urban mobility was effectively blocked, because "to make the leap one had to acquire a ration book, a book that could not be obtained without an urban residency permit. Without a ration book one could not buy grain and therefore one could not survive away from home for very long." Ibid., p. 107. This policy, as we shall see in later chapters, helped to keep down rural-to-urban migration, thereby helping to control the size of China's cities; as a result it helped to reduce the problem of urban unemployment and associated social problems. But it was also a harsh sentence to foist upon the peasants. It is precisely because they had no viable options that the peasants' problems could be ignored by a cynical and self-satisfied middle tier of officials. Thus, the peasants were kept on the land, and to survive they had to stay busy. As the old Chinese proverb implies, "When the peasants are content the empire is stable." See T. Terzani, 1986, *Behind the Forbidden Door: Travels in Unknown China*. New York: Henry Holt, chap. 6, p. 104. But as the famine began in 1960, and as millions of peasants died of starvation, it was clear that all was not well on the Chinese land. As Hinton says, the situation actually gave the administration complete control over the rural population, which was something the old elites had always wanted but could never actually achieve. Elsewhere Hinton (in the 1986 interview, op. cit.) has expanded this idea and brought it forward into the 1980s. He argues that there was in the 1950s, and still today, a basic contempt for the peasants among China's bureaucratic elite—the cadres—signaling an effective return to the old Mandarin mentality. In this sense, then, both the green revolution (the increasing mechanization of agriculture) and the new household responsibility system (in which some peasants could get rich again, so to speak) would represent a serious challenge to the cadre class: "As long as the peasants are down there endlessly laboring with their hoes, the official in his office feels secure. Why should we do anything to rock the boat?" (p. 142).

51. Shuping Chen (1977), op. cit., for example, reports from the book written by Chu Han that food grain production fell by 26 percent from its 1957 level to 287 billion jin (one jin equals 0.5 kg), increasing only slightly to 295 billion jin in 1961 (p. 100). By 1984 a new record-high level of 405 million tons was reached, largely as a result of new agricultural reforms since 1978. Production of grain fell in 1985 to 379 million tons, largely as a result of adverse weather conditions and a reduction in the amount of land cultivated, and partly because many farmers decided to spend their surplus not on more produc-

tion but on consumption goods. In Shanxi Province, for example, farmers' spending on consumption goods increased by 5.4 percent in 1986, but investment for production fell by 11.2 percent. *China Daily*, February 28, 1987.

52. Aubert, op. cit., p. 107.

53. See chap. 3 in C. J. Smith, 1991, *China: People and Places in the Land of One Billion*. Boulder: Westview Press.

54. A. Piazza, 1986, *Food Consumption and Nutritional Status in the PRC*. Boulder: Westview Press. Incomes in the countryside increased fourfold between 1957 and 1983, although the most dramatic changes did not occur until after the reforms began in 1978. In 1957 the per capita net income in the countryside was Y72.9. By 1978 it was Y133.6, and by 1987 it was Y462.6. China Statistical Publishing House, 1989, *Chinese Statistical Yearbook 1988*, p. 732.

55. Howard, op. cit.

56. The collectives themselves did not totally disappear. In many areas they still own and operate local enterprises, as well as schools and local social services. In the realm of agricultural production, however, the collectives are no longer dominant in rural China. There are no work points to be decided, and most of the peasants—at least among those who have remained on the land—spend most time working on their own plots. There was no longer any need for collective meetings for production purposes; but collective politics still dominates some aspects of rural life, such as dispute mediation. For historical reasons collective debate is common in the Chinese countryside, and to some extent this is to be expected because the land contracted out to individuals and families was in fact property that had been developed as a result of several decades of collective effort.

57. Liu, op. cit.

58. A. Watson, 1983, "Agriculture Looks for 'Shoes That Fit': The Production Responsibility System and Its Implications," *World Development*, Vol. 11, No. 8 pp. 705–730, 706. In fact it has been suggested that the original intent of the reforms was nowhere near as radical as things actually turned out. Elizabeth Croll, for example, has argued that the individual household economy was never intended to expand at anything like the scale that ultimately occurred. According to Croll, the production team was expected to continue to be in control of the bulk of production activities in the countryside. See E. Croll, 1988, "The New Peasant Economy in China," pp. 77–100 in S. Feuchtwang et al. (eds.), op. cit.

59. Peasants were required to sell their mandated quota at the fixed (lower) price, but after that they could dispose of what was left to the highest bidder. In the years after 1979 further price increases were allowed; the price increases for farm goods were 7.1 percent in 1980, 5.9 percent in 1981, 2.2 percent in 1982, 4.4 percent in 1983, and 4.0 percent in 1984. C. Riskin, 1987, *China's Political Economy: The Quest for Development Since 1949*. London: Oxford University Press, p. 285. Since then food price increases have been even higher; in fact the rate of inflation has become a major problem, holding back further aspects of the reform program.

60. It is worthwhile to point out that the agricultural reforms did not really represent a planned sequence of reforms. As we shall see later in this chapter, to a large extent the Party and the government were passive reactors to the dynamic economic pressures and the enthusiasm for the reforms at the local level. Thus the new contracting system resulted in greater production levels, which contributed to the growth of free markets. This then challenged the state monopoly over prices and distribution networks, so in time changes were also made in those directions.

61. Many different types of contracts were signed after 1978, and that diversity was intended to match contract systems with local conditions. At first small groups of peasants, even single families, could contract with the production team to fulfill specific tasks, and they would be repaid in work points, with bonuses for overfulfilling their contracts. This was only a minor break with the past, and it kept the essential ingredients of collectivism intact: The machinery and animals and, most importantly, land, remained collectively owned by the production team; in addition, all local planning remained at the collective level. The major innovation was that a closer link had been established between work done and rewards received. Although this appeared to be a new system, similar arrangements had in fact already appeared in the 1960s as a result of peasant opposition to collectivization and the disastrous harvests during and after the Great Leap Forward. Later, contractual developments would allow families to use a particular piece of land to produce their output. In these arrangements production was privatized, but distribution remained collectivized. Households contracted a fixed amount of their output to the production team for an agreed-upon number of work points. Although they could dispose of their surplus any way they chose, the actual value of their work

points was still dependent on the total output of the production team. Planning and the ownership of machinery and animals also remained in the hands of the collective.

62. For details, see Riskin, op. cit., and Croll, op. cit. Croll has pointed out that the HRS needs to be put into its historical context, in that the household peasant economy had always been an important element in the Chinese countryside. Even during the heyday of collectivization, the household was expected to remain as the fourth tier in the rural production system, subservient to the communes, brigades, and teams, yet still an important element. In a similar way, there had always been opportunities for "sideline" activities in the countryside. In 1978, before the reforms were started, 5.7 percent of all arable land in China was allocated to private plots; by 1980 this had increased to 7.1 percent; and in 1981, a provision was made for this portion to increase to 15 percent. Jonathan Unger has also suggested that the shift over to the HRS was probably not as much of a voluntary process as the Chinese press (and the government) would like the rest of the world to believe. In Unger's survey of twenty-eight villages, for example, the shift had been mandated from above in twenty-six of them, and it is certainly not true to say that all villages were equally enthusiastic about the reforms. Unger also points out that the *baogan daohu* system was originally only intended for the very poorest areas, but the early successes resulted in a very rapid spread to villages of all types. Again, according to Unger, the entire reform process was probably not a well-thought-out master plan for a newly efficient system of agriculture: It was partly the result of planning but mostly a piecemeal process that spread in an almost contagious fashion after the early successes. See J. Unger, 1985–1986, "The Decollectivization of the Chinese Countryside: A Survey of 28 Villages," *Pacific Affairs*, Vol. 58, No. 4, pp. 585–606. See also two other more recent sources: Jean C. Oi, 1999, *Rural China Takes Off: Institutional Foundations of Economic Reforms.* Berkeley: University of California Press; and Tamara Jacka, 1997, *Women's Work in Rural China: Change and Continuity in an Era of Reform.* Cambridge, UK: University of Cambridge Press.

63. Chossudovsky, op. cit., p. 50. Croll, op. cit., has shown that the families who were most likely to get rich were the largest ones, i.e., those with access to the greatest supplies of labor. In her study area, for example, Croll reported that 31 percent of the richest families had more than six members, whereas only 8 percent had one to two members. This is exactly the relationship between production and reproduction that we saw in Chapter 5 interfering with the anticipated outcome of the birth control policies in the countryside.

64. O. Schell, 1984, *To Get Rich Is Glorious: China in the 1980s.* New York: Pantheon Books.

65. See, for example, W. Hinton, 1988, "Dazhai Revisited," *China Now,* No. 126, pp. 23–27.

66. See, for example, S. Wittwer, Yu Youtai, Sun Han, and Wang Lianzheng, 1987, *Feeding a Billion: Frontiers of Chinese Agriculture.* East Lansing: Michigan State University Press; see also Oi, op. cit. Probably the most significant impact of the HRS has been the creation of a new balance of power between the individual households (the private economy) and the villages (the collective economy). The village now has, in most cases, a subordinate role in the production process, and its role is for the most part restricted to that of servicing the private economy, through the provision of technology, capital, transportation, and so on (in addition to the welfare function). There was a certain amount of contagiousness in this transformation, in that the individual households found that they liked their newfound independence, and they naturally wanted to extend it to other areas of their lives, most notably into the area of birth control (see Chapter 5). Unger, op. cit., has commented on this new independence at the household level, noting that it had extended into both the political and the economic realms: "Before, brigade and team cadres had had the authority . . . to bring pressures to bear against ordinary peasants; now the system . . . would entirely eliminate the cadres' daily supervision and, by pulling the land and other resources out of their control, would severely curtail their powers over the peasants. Under the collectives, the peasantry had been required to devote most of their days to raising low-priced grain on the collective fields; now many peasants foresaw that, by controlling the use of their own time, they would be able to put their spare hours into endeavors that paid better" (pp. 592–593). As one of Unger's respondents said, "We felt like birds freed from a cage."

67. J.S.S. Muldavin, 1997, "Environmental Degradation in Heilongjiang: Policy Reform and Agrarian Dynamics in China's New Hybrid Economy," *Annals of the Association of American Geographers*, Vol. 87, No. 4, pp. 579–613.

68. See ibid. There was also more than a hint of irony in the reforms, because in the 1980s actions that were officially sanctioned by the state had been

illegal only a few years earlier. What once was rewarded with harsh criticism, imprisonment, and even worse was now helping to elevate individuals and households to the status of local heroes.

69. Riskin, op. cit., table 12.1, p. 291, and table 12.2, p. 292. This, of course, was one of the major benefits of the HRS, in that it allowed a relaxation of the very restrictive Maoist focus on growing grain everywhere ("taking grain as the key link"). In the reform era the emphasis has been on the "all-round development of agriculture" (Croll, op. cit., p. 81). The essence of the new policy was to allow a basic free-for-all, in which each family (and presumably, therefore, each area) would specialize in whatever it could produce most efficiently. Agricultural output slowed down a little after the mid-1980s; in fact the rate of growth in output had been 14.4 percent each year between 1980 and 1984, slowing to 10.9 percent after that and reaching a new low in 1988 of only 3 percent growth. More seriously, the production of three major crops declined in 1988: grain by 2.2 percent, cotton by 1.1 percent, and edible oil seeds, so important in Chinese cooking, by 13.3 percent. There are a number of possible explanations for these slowdowns, the most obvious being the apparent lack of interest many farmers had in growing crops for which the sale price (set by the government) was fairly low. They were choosing either to move into other crops that fetch higher prices or out of agriculture altogether, either into sideline activities or, more likely, into rural industries where the wages are considerably higher. See B. L. Reynolds, 1989, "The Chinese Economy in 1988," pp. 27–48 in A. J. Kane (ed.), *China Briefing, 1988*. Boulder: Westview Press.

70. The consumption of edible oils grew by 14 percent per year and meat output by 9 percent. See Riskin, op. cit.

71. Ibid., p. 292; note that a significant proportion of this increase—estimated to be as much as a fifth—is the result of agricultural price increases.

72. D. Perkins and S. Yusuf, 1984, *Rural Development in China*. Baltimore: Johns Hopkins University Press.

73. It is important to point out that a large part of the per capita reduction in sales during 1978–1984 was the result of the increase in the urban population—a large part of which resulted from the annexation of rural counties in the nation's biggest cities. See Chapter 9.

74. Howard, op. cit., p. 181.

75. T. G. Rawski, 1979, *Economic Growth and Employment in China*. New York: Oxford University Press, pp. 119–121.

76. Reynolds points out that the output for rural workers in China increased by a staggering 250 percent between 1978 and 1987. Most of this, however, can be accounted for by growth in village and township enterprises, as an estimated 85 million people were soaked up from the land into rural industries. Rural enterprises increased their share of the nation's total output from 5 percent to 21 percent in these nine years (op. cit., p. 37). Nevertheless, agricultural output increased significantly during this period; for example, grain production increased by 43 percent overall, cotton by 93 percent (p. 35).

77. B. Brugger and S. Reglar, 1994, *Politics, Economy, and Society in Contemporary China*. London: Macmillan, p. 65.

78. M. Blecher, 1997, *China Against the Tides: Restructuring Through Revolution, Radicalism and Reform*. London: Pinter, p. 195. The price increases were first implemented in 1978 to encourage the production of grain (there was an increase of 20 percent in 1978, and an additional 50 percent increase for "above-quota" grain). Once the basic quota was filled, peasants could sell to the state at the above-quota price, which was sometimes higher than the market price. At the same time, however, the state increased prices on agricultural inputs (such as fertilizer and pesticides), offsetting the gains made (see also Zhou, op. cit., pp. 78–79). Overall, higher prices for agricultural produce meant that farmers' incomes benefited significantly, and they were encouraged to increase output. In some years (for example, 1983), when grain production was high, the market price fell below the state's agreed-upon above-quota price, so peasants were eager to sell to the state granaries. Throughout the 1980s the state continued to be a major player in the grain business: In 1993, for example, the state bought 72 percent of the total grain produced, compared to 32 percent in 1978 (Zhou, op. cit., p. 79). It has been suggested that some of the great jumps in productivity were essentially onetime gains, caused by rising prices and improved marketing; but continued growth required significant technical change (for example, developing new strains of seeds), which did not occur.

79. An unanticipated result of the production increases was a fall in market prices, and because of its contracts with the farmers the state was obliged to buy the grain at the agreed-upon (higher than mar-

ket) price. The state fairly quickly learned that this anomalous situation—in which the more grain the state bought from the farmers, the more money it lost—could be prevented by allowing a further opening of the markets (see Zhou, op. cit., p. 81).

80. Zhou, op. cit.

81. Brugger and Reglar, op. cit., p. 73.

82. This was part of the so-called rectification program, which ended in 1992, when the market reforms were reaccelerated; see also Chapter 4 for a discussion of the alternating tightening and letting-go policies.

83. The government's response was to abolish the distinction between quota and above-quota prices for grain, establishing a new "proportional" price that was equal to 70 percent of the old above-quota price plus 30 percent of the old quota price, with regional variations. The new system was intended to curb speculation and remove the inequalities caused by uneven quotas. The state also removed mandatory grain quotas and began to contract with peasants for grain supplies, requiring the agricultural tax to be paid in cash (not grain). A safety net was set up: If the market price fell below the basic state procurement price, the state would buy the contracted amount at the set price.

84. There were many years in which the GVAO of other agricultural products and sideline activities increased substantially (see Table 7.4), as the incentives provided by the HRS and access to the new marketing outlets resulted in a significant diversification into crops other than grain, as well as into non-agricultural pursuits. As a result, compulsory quotas were reimposed in 1986, effectively postponing the marketization of grain. For several years the state wavered between de facto direct procurement and indirect controls; but with gradually freer prices and intermittent controls, grain production has risen in some, but not all, years with very large gains in 1990 (from 407 million to 446 million tons) and in 1996 (466 to 504 million tons). See China Statistical Publishing House, 1997, *China Statistical Yearbook 1996*, table 11/18, p. 383. China has, in other words, already reached (in fact it has surpassed) the grain production target, set for the year 2000, of 500 million tons, although population increases mean that per capita grain production (and consumption) will remain about the same.

85. F. Christiansen and S. Rai, 1996, *Chinese Politics and Society: An Introduction*. London: Prentice-Hall/Harvester Wheatsheaf, pp. 222–223.

86. G. White, 1993, *Riding the Tiger: The Politics of Economic Reform in Post-Mao China*. London: Macmillan, p. 111.

87. See M. X. Pei, 1997, "Racing Against Time: Institutional Decay and Renewal in China," pp. 11–50 in W. A. Joseph (ed.), *China Briefing: The Contradictions of Change*. Armonk, NY: M. E. Sharpe.

88. White, op. cit., p. 112.

89. In the 1990s the government was forced to intervene by introducing a new Land Administration Bureau empowered to allocate licenses for nonagricultural land uses, which were subject to a special tax, with the revenues earmarked for the development of new land. See Blecher (1997), op. cit., p. 196. See also Christiansen and Rai, op. cit., p. 222.

90. Brugger and Reglar, op. cit., pp. 127–128.

91. As Christiansen and Rai have suggested, and as Muldavin (op. cit.) has shown in his fieldwork, conducted in Heilongjiang Province.

92. Brugger and Reglar, op. cit., p. 129.

93. Blecher, op. cit., p. 197.

94. Christiansen and Rai, op. cit., p. 224.

95. Brugger and Reglar, op. cit., p. 84.

96. Ibid., p. 84. As the statistics in Table 7.5 show, the amount of land being used in the countryside for both capital construction and collective construction has remained high, but the amount used for housing construction has fallen, from 97,000 hectares in 1985 to 32,000 hectares in 1996. During this period the amount of land lost to cultivation remained high, peaking in 1985, when 1,597,900 hectares were lost; the figure stood at 621,100 in 1995, still high but lower than ten years ago (see *China Statistical Yearbook*, table 11.5, p. 368), which reflects the new policies implemented in the late 1980s to help save rural land from being transferred to nonagricultural uses.

97. White, op. cit., p. 109.

98. See B. Naughton, 1995, "Cities in the Chinese Economic System: Changing Roles and Conditions for Autonomy," pp. 61–89 in D. S. Davis et al. (eds.), *Urban Spaces in Contemporary China: The Potential for Autonomy and Community in Post-Mao China*. Washington, DC: Woodrow Wilson Press; and G. E. Guldin, 1997, *Farewell to Peasant China: Rural Urbanization and Social Change in the Late Twentieth Century*. Armonk, NY: M. E. Sharpe.

99. P. E. Tyler, "No Rights Mean No Incentive for China's Farmers," *New York Times*, December 15, 1996, p. 20.

100. Local officials are apparently able to ignore central policy directives at will, so mandates to

improve and extend the land rights of peasants have generally not been implemented, mainly because such reforms would seriously diminish the power of local officials. Among the peasants surveyed by the Seattle team, it was common to find that many of them no longer wanted to be involved in agricultural production. Compared to the collective years, when peasants spent an average of 250 to 320 days a year in the fields, the average is now between sixty and ninety days on the same amount of land. This has been achieved by making some fundamental changes in agricultural techniques, which have resulted in dramatic increases in productivity (for example, using better weeding methods, better seeds, more careful applications of fertilizer, and irrigation). As noted already, though, these gains soon reached their limit, and long-term investments are now long over-due for more effective drainage systems, better irri-gation facilities, improved land terracing, and soil upgrading. See R. L. Prosterman, T. Hanstad, and L. Ping, 1996, "Can China Feed Itself?" *Scientific American,* Vol. 275, No. 5 (November), pp. 70–76.

101. The state is now making plans to run some pilot projects along these lines, as well as promising to implement reforms that will inform farmers of their rights and obligations. In some of the pilot projects, land use rights are extended to seventy-five years for farmland, 100 years for usable wasteland; and there is a provision to terminate the process of readjusting land plots for changes in household size. In the late 1980s land rights were extended to fifteen and in some cases thirty years, but in many cases these contracts were ignored by local officials. In 1995, therefore, land rights were extended for up to thirty years, according to an announcement by the Chinese State Council, with strict punishment to be meted out to local officials who illegally attempt to terminate or alter the new contracts. Ibid., p. 75.

102. Brugger and Reglar, op. cit., p. 64.

103. Ibid., p. 64.

104. Blecher, op. cit., pp. 93–94.

105. White, op. cit., p. 104.

106. There is reason to believe that, given the choice, villages in many areas would not have decol-lectivized voluntarily. Unger, op. cit., p. 593.

107. White, op. cit., p. 105. Some China scholars believe to this day that it might have been better to allow certain areas to opt out rather than impose an across-the-board decollectivization, which produced significant unhappiness and opposition in some areas.

108. Ibid., p. 94.

109. Ibid., p. 94.

110. D. Kelliher, 1992, *Peasant Power in China: The Era of Rural Reform; 1979–1989.* New Haven: Yale University Press.

111. In fact with the abandonment of Marxist ide-ology, particularly as manifested in class struggle, improving economic achievements and keeping order were the only ways the state could uphold its legitimacy; see Blecher (1997), op. cit.

112. Kate Zhou (1996), op. cit., in contrast, believes that the state effectively ignored the peas-antry during this time.

113. See Kelliher, op. cit., pp. 252–253.

114. Kelliher's work suggests that peasants were able to influence political outcomes in at least four ways. First, by manipulating policy, which means not merely resisting policy (a passive act) but actually reshaping it into something new. This took place in numerous ways, such as the deliberate misconstruing of policy and finding weaknesses in the new roles to favor themselves, which were especially prevalent in the area of price manipulation. Second, by creating original policies, which occasionally happened, including illegal experiments that were hidden from view until the results showed success. Third, through aggressive productivity, in which peasants throw their energies into policy alternatives banned by the state, which then won official approval. And fourth, by inflating the cost of state preferences; this is the least creative and active and is, in Kelliher's view, a piece of simple resistance, including passivity, sabo-tage, and lethargy, which undermined the state's efforts to keep the collectives functioning. None of these has any real, coercive power, and each one is, strictly speaking, illegitimate. In concert, however, they were successful because in its desire to foster balanced economic growth the state was eager to have the peasants' agreement and cooperation, oper-ating as a united front.

115. Kelliher, op. cit.

116. The peasants were, to use Eric Hobsbawm's term, "prepolitical" people, and this, according to Kelliher, means that most people consider them to be without power—at least after the revolution had been attained. Most of the time, peasants in China are seen as victims, helpless sufferers in the successive transformations that come their way. Kelliher believes that this view—of peasants being swallowed by fate—is not historically correct. Much of their activity necessarily has always and perhaps will con-tinue to fall below the threshold of what is described as "political." This may be true of individuals and

even whole communities, but, Kelliher argues, the real strength of the Chinese peasantry lies in their vast numbers and their strength as a class, which opens up the possibility of the "cumulative power of small acts" (p. 252).

117. Real incomes increased threefold in an eight-year period; see *The Economist*, "When China Wakes: A Survey of China," November 28–December 2, 1992, p. 4.

118. Blecher, op. cit., p. 95. Fei Ling Wang argues that in the last two decades the allocation of labor in China has shifted over from what he calls an "authoritarian state" labor allocation pattern to one that is increasingly dominated by both "community-based" labor markets (especially in the rural TVEs) and a "national" labor market, created largely by private and foreign enterprise. Fei Ling Wang, 1998, *From Family to Market: Labor Allocation in Contemporary China*. Lanham, MD: Rowman and Littlefield.

119. Zhou, op. cit., p. 71. Zhou's enthusiasm for this argument perhaps leads her to some leaps of faith: She is convinced, for example, that China's farmers have been primarily responsible for (in addition to the revitalization of agricultural production) the huge proliferation of rural markets (see her chapter 4); the development of rural industry (TVEs) and private enterprise in the countryside (chapter 5); the freeing-up of labor and choice about where to live (chapter 6); the rural resistance to the one-child policy (chapter 7); and bringing equality to China's rural women (chapter 8). Zhou also claims that the peasants were successful because the state was not inclined to stop the process, either because it could not be bothered or because it was looking the other way—not paying attention—at the time. She describes the peasant-initiated process as a special kind of movement, which she refers to as "SULNAM," "a spontaneous, unorganized, leaderless, non-ideological, apolitical movement" (p. 1; see p. 17 in Zhou for a further explanation of each term). Her argument is perhaps too far-reaching, but it makes for exciting reading, with the sweep of some of her suggestions. This type of focus puts Zhou's work in the category of research that has investigated "sites of resistance," with an emphasis on the creativity of peasant (or worker) movements, along the lines of that described by James C. Scott in his book *Weapons of the Weak*. For Scott, however, the peasants occupy the margins of the political arena and have very limited power: They do not make great changes or lead revolutions. Zhou suggests that China offers a very different case, because the individual actions of half a billion peas-

ants push the situation far past that being made in *Weapons of the Weak* (see Zhou, p. 16). As Zhou says, this was a "political" movement because it has had far-reaching implications for the structure of governance in China. But it is important to recall that "the farmers who did these things wanted to be left alone, left to their own devices. They did not seek out any Tiananmen" (p. 16).

120. White, op. cit., p. 108.

121. See R. Baum, 1996, *Burying Mao: Chinese Politics in the Age of Deng Xiaoping*. Princeton: Princeton University Press. Baum describes how Deng went about this process; see both his introductory chapter ("The Age of Deng Xiaoping," pp. 3–23), and chapter 14 ("Deng's Final Offensive," pp. 341–368).

122. White, op. cit., p. 107.

123. Kate Zhou actually claims that the farmers essentially pulled a fast one on the leaders, who cared so little about agricultural issues that they didn't notice what was happening: "The central government; which literally had . . . control of virtually everything in China, really did not think much about the farmers. They thought about heavy industry and the urban sector, so what took place among the farmers slipped right out from under them, caught them unawares, until the results were so widespread and powerful in terms of a double-digit real growth rate that officials were more likely to claim credit than to interfere." Zhou, op. cit., p. 101. Although this is an interesting idea, it seems highly unlikely that the state simply failed to notice what was going on in the countryside.

124. D. L. Yang, 1996, *Calamity and Reform in China: State, Rural Society, and Institutional Change Since the Great Leap Famine*. Stanford: Stanford University Press, p. 4.

125. See, for example, S. Shirk, 1993, *The Political Logic of Economic Reform in China*. Berkeley: University of California Press.

126. Yang, op. cit., p. 121.

127. Yang (ibid.) measures famine-related suffering in two major ways: One is the level of resistance and refusal encountered locally when the state began to procure grain compulsorily after 1957, effectively beginning the famine era; second is the mortality rate, measuring the number of excess deaths presumed to be a result of the famine.

128. It is interesting to note that these provinces were the ones featured as case studies in Becker's 1996 book, *Hungry Ghosts*, although neither one references the other, so their conclusions appear to be

independent of each other; see also Domenach's 1995 study conducted in Henan Province; J. L. Domenach, 1995, *The Origins of the Great Leap Forward: The Case of One Chinese Province.* Boulder: Westview Press.

129. Yang measures the extent of "liberalization" after 1978 by a measure called the "brigade accounting rate" (BAR), which indicates the extent to which a province adhered to the radical (leftist or Maoist) line, with the production brigades still responsible for agricultural accounting. A lower BAR rate presumably indicated a higher proportion of accounting done at the individual or household level; see Yang, op. cit., p. 131.

130. Ibid., p. 130. Yang tests his hypothesis against the idea that increasing distance from Beijing, and consequently a lower density of party members per capita, would be related to a higher degree of innovativeness in adopting the HRS. This idea is reinforced, Yang suggests, by the evidence that in general communism spread from the north to the south of China (see his p. 143). This hypothesis was proved to be statistically significant, using province-level data, whereas a third hypothesis, related to differences in provincial income levels, could not be supported. It is perhaps significant that in a statistical analysis involving both the "distance" and the "severity of famine" variables, the latter proved to be the most important predictor of post-1978 agricultural innovation (in terms of the adoption of HRS).

131. Ibid., p. 143.

132. Becker, op. cit., pp. 121–122.

133. Yang, op. cit., p. 242.

134. Blecher, p. 197.

135. Ibid., p. 216.

136. Ibid., p. 217.

137. Brugger and Reglar, op. cit., p. 136.

138. Blecher, p. 194.

139. According to Blecher there has been a great deal of violence in China's rural areas, with farmers locking horns with state officials and public security forces as they protest against continually rising input costs and government exactions in the face of declining crop revenues. See Blecher, p. 219, for different examples of rural violence: for example, the killing of tax collectors, looting of state warehouses, and armed clashes with police.

140. Ibid, p. 198.

141. White, op. cit., pp. 115–116.

142. Ibid., p. 116.

143. Ibid., p. 97.

144. Ibid., p. 99.

145. Ibid., p. 99.

146. Brugger and Reglar, p. 131.

147. See W. X. Chen, 1997, "Peasant Challenge in Post-Communist China," *Journal of Contemporary China,* Vol. 6, No. 14, pp. 101–115, 107; see also J. B. Starr, 1997, *Understanding China: A Guide to China's Economy, History, and Political Structure.* New York: Hill and Wang. Starr observes (p. 133) that in 1994 the Chinese press reported more than 1,000 instances of protest demonstrations in rural areas across China. China's leaders fear (with good reason) the impact of a volatile peasantry. A few isolated demonstrations are not a major concern, but as Kelliher (op. cit.) points out, the numbers involved are so vast that the government has to keep a close watch.

148. The potential political power of the peasantry became evident in the early 1990s, when, according to Chinese press sources, at least 830 incidents of rural rebellion, each involving more than 500 people, were reported in 1993, twenty-one of which had involved crowds of larger than 5,000. See Kelliher, op. cit., and Zhou, op. cit.

149. Chen (1997), op. cit., p. 108.

150. Ibid., p. 117. In the collective era, as Zhou notes (p. 232), the cadres controlled the peasants like feudal lords in everything but inheritance; local (village) cadres, who often lacked agricultural experience, directed agricultural operations; and *hukou* restrictions and the grain rationing system kept the peasants virtually imprisoned. The changes, post–1978, have been enormous: As Zhou notes (p. 233): "Chinese farmers are no longer 'collective peasants' . . . because of the rapid increase in market activities, rural industries, and migration. They are now, increasingly, independent producers and managers [they] have wrested initiative for themselves. Their horizons for material betterment have expanded, explosively. The sky's the limit for economic productivity and diversification, if only the cadres leave them alone."

151. Zhou, op. cit., p. 233.

152. Ibid., p. 234.

153. Ibid.

154. Ibid., p. 243.

155. In the second half of the 1980s the reforms were starting to go awry. In many areas the peasants were humiliated by and enraged about being "paid" with IOUs in lieu of cash for their mandated produce quotas. Peasant households were experiencing difficulty coping with such cash-flow problems, coupled with the instability of new market pricing and the

rising costs of agricultural inputs such as fertilizer, plastic sheeting for winter coverings, and pesticides. Not surprisingly, the post-1986 period saw a rising tide of peasant discontent as the war between them and the state continued. In surveys conducted in the countryside, peasant dissatisfaction was being quantified: The peasants reported being unhappy about rising prices, government policies, and (perhaps most of all) the predatory and corrupt practices of local government and village-level cadres. At the same time, peasants were learning about how to conduct business from their new involvement in private production and marketing, and they were realizing they could and should make their voices heard. Gradually they realized they had the power to strike out on their own whenever the need arose, even if it involved acting contrary to the law.

Chapter 8

1. B. Naughton, 1995, *Growing out of the Plan: Chinese Economic Reform, 1978–1993*. Cambridge, UK: Cambridge University Press.

2. M. X. Pei, 1998, *From Reform to Revolution: The Demise of Communism in China and the Soviet Union*. Cambridge: Harvard University Press, p. 44.

3. See J. Domes, 1985, *The Government and Politics of the PRC: A Time of Transition*. Boulder: Westview Press, esp. chap. 12, "Economic Development," pp. 195–210.

4. For a description of the Taiwan "miracle," see R. G. Sutter, 1988, *Taiwan: Entering the 21st Century*. New York: University Press of America; T. B. Gold, 1986, *State and Society and the Taiwan Miracle*. Armonk, NY: M. E. Sharpe; and the special issue of *The China Quarterly*, No. 94 (October 1984), "Taiwan Briefing."

5. According to Ezra Vogel, the phrase "socialist transformation" refers to the "transfer of economic ownership from private to public hands." See E. F. Vogel, 1969, *Canton Under Communism: Programs and Politics in a Provincial Capital, 1949–1968*. Cambridge: Harvard University Press, p. 125.

6. Ibid., p. 132.

7. Ibid., chap. 4.

8. T. Cannon and A. Jenkins, 1986, "Freeing the Market Forces," *Geographical Magazine*, Vol. 58, pp. 566–571. See also M. Blecher, 1986, *China: Politics, Economics, and Society: Iconoclasm and Innovation in a Revolutionary Socialist Country*. London: Frances Pinter, p. 509.

9. M. Chossudovsky, 1986, *Towards Capitalist Restoration? Chinese Socialism After Mao*. Hong Kong: Macmillan, esp. chap. 4.

10. The campaigns are described in detail by Vogel, op. cit., esp. chap. 4, pp. 125–180; see also J. Gardner, 1972, "The Wu-Fan Campaign in Shanghai: A Study in the Consolidation of Urban Control," pp. 477–539 in A. D. Barnett (ed.), *Chinese Communist Politics in Action*. Seattle: University of Washington Press.

11. V. Shue, 1980, *Peasant China in Transition: The Dynamics of Development Towards Socialism, 1949–1956*. Berkeley: University of California Press.

12. This process is described by Vogel, op. cit., esp. pp. 173–180.

13. Mao Zedong, 1977, *Selected Works*, Vol. 5. Beijing: Foreign Languages Press, pp. 284–307.

14. See Blecher, op. cit., pp. 73–74.

15. Ibid. In 1959, for example, the accumulation rate was 43.8 percent; it was 39.6 percent in 1960. In the early 1970s the rate averaged around 33 percent, 31 percent in the early 1980s. In 1987 it was 34.7 percent. See China Statistical Publishing House, 1989, *China Statistical Yearbook 1988*, p. 50.

16. A survey conducted by the Chinese Ministry of Light Industry in 1980 showed that a Y10,000 investment would create only ninety-four jobs on average in heavy industry, compared to 257 in light industry and 800 in handicraft sidelines. See F. Gipouloux, 1988, "Industrial Restructuring and Autonomy of Enterprises in China: Is Reform Possible?" pp. 107–117 in S. Feuchtwang, A. Hussain, and T. Pairault (eds.), *Transforming China's Economy in the Eighties*. Vol. 2: *Management, Industry, and the Urban Economy*. Boulder: Westview Press. The different emphasis on heavy as opposed to light industry reflects some important changes in economic philosophy. For example, in 1952 65 percent of total output value in China came from heavy industry; but this had been reversed by 1982, when the figure was only 47 percent. By 1987 the balance was almost equal, with 48 percent being heavy and 52 percent light industry. See China Statistical Publishing House, 1988, *China Statistical Yearbook 1987*, p. 37.

17. This issue is discussed by L. Pan, 1988, *The New Chinese Revolution*. Chicago: Contemporary Books, 1988, p. 50. As the statistics in Table 8.1 illus-

trate, there was a significant increase in the value of industrial output between 1952 and 1978 (more than a sixteenfold increase). But this was achieved mainly by a massive (x 22) increase in the investment of fixed capital rather than a more efficient usage of inputs. The statistics also suggest that the increase in labor productivity (nearly threefold) was also achieved in this way, and in fact the level of output per unit of capital dropped after 1957, to 67.9 in 1965 and 74.2 in 1978. Part of the explanation for this lies in the structural imbalance in Chinese industry toward heavy industry; but part stems from "deficiencies in the system of economic organization, planning and management that are rather deep-rooted." See C. Riskin, 1987, *China's Political Economy: The Quest for Development Since 1949.* Oxford, UK: Oxford University Press, p. 265.

18. Gipouloux, op. cit., p. 114. Probably the best account of authority relationships in Chinese industry has been provided by A. G. Walder, 1986, *Communist Neo-Traditionalism: Work and Authority in Chinese Industry.* Berkeley: University of California Press.

19. Chinese industry was excessively overmanaged, with a complex and unyielding system of administration. Most enterprises belonged to two different sets of administrative hierarchies: one was the so-called line organization, in which a local factory came under the auspices of one of the central industrial ministries; and the other was the area, or block, organization at the territorial level. It proved enormously difficult to coordinate the area and line proposals into one coherent plan for all regions and sectors of the economy. To complicate matters even further there were several tiers to the regional administrative structure—at the provincial, county, and city levels—all of which produced a hopelessly complex chain of command. Enterprises found themselves in a maze, with a baffling array of agencies and bureaus to respond to. There were simply too many chiefs in the system, or, as the Chinese might prefer to say, factory managers had too many mothers-in-law looking over their shoulders. See Pan, op. cit., p. 52. There are many examples of the counterproductive effects of the byzantine administrative complexity of Chinese industry. In a Qingdao factory, for example, the managers received conflicting output targets. In 1982, the county included the factory in its annual plans and recommended an output level of Y19 million; but the city Machine-Building Bureau set the output level for the same year at Y13 million.

20. Pan, op. cit., pp. 219–241. It is interesting to note that a large part of the criticisms leveled at the government during the waves of student demonstrations in 1986, 1987, and 1989 were focused on the extent of corruption in China, especially among high-level Party officials. See, for example, O. Schell, 1989, "An Act of Defiance," *New York Times Magazine,* April 16, 1989, pp. 27, 43; and S. WuDunn, 1989, "Hu's Death Stirs Political Unrest," *New York Times,* April 15, 1989.

21. O. Schell, 1984, *To Get Rich Is Glorious: China in the Eighties.* New York: Pantheon Books.

22. Pan, op. cit., p. 223.

23. Schell, op. cit., p. 84. Schell notes that there is actually a double entendre involved in the terms *yanjiu yanjiu,* which means "to make a study of a situation" but also means "wine and cigarettes."

24. The old idea of balanced growth gave way to the notion of regional comparative advantage, which meant that some localities, like some individuals and enterprises, would be encouraged to get rich at a quicker rate than others. It was expected that the less well-endowed regions would eventually benefit from this strategy, through the process of trickle-down.

25. The phrase is used by Jurgen Domes, op. cit., pp. 197–202.

26. *Decision of the Central Committee of the Communist Party of China on Reform of the Economic Structure.* Beijing: Foreign Languages Press, 1984.

27. Riskin, op. cit., p. 342. For a discussion of this "revolution," see *Time,* "China: Deng Xiaoping Leads a Far-Reaching Audacious but Risky Second Revolution," January 6, 1986, pp. 24–40.

28. "Chinese Experiments with Allowing Enterprises to Go Belly Up," *Christian Science Monitor,* Friday, August 8, 1986. See also Da Chen, 1988, "Labour Combination System Practiced in Qingdao," *Nexus—China in Focus* (Winter), pp. 29–31.

29. D. J. Solinger, 1987, "Uncertain Paternalism: Tensions in Recent Regional Restructuring in China," *International Regional Science Review,* Vol. 11, pp. 23–42, 32. The Chinese press quickly picked up on such practices, and newspapers began to report stories of local protectionism. A township in Anhui Province, for example, imported cheap tractors from another province rather than buying more expensive tractors produced locally. In a retaliatory move, the county authorities responded by refusing to allocate diesel fuel, so the tractors sat idle. See Pan, op. cit., p. 60. The worst and most visible effects of local protectionism involved wasteful duplication of productive capacity, as each level of the administrative

hierarchy (regional, county, and municipal) continued to protect its own interests. Barriers and blockades were established to regulate local trading practices, and in some areas toll gates were installed on public roads. There were even stories of what amounted to highway robbery, as peasants physically forced vehicles off the road, making them pay local taxes and repair fees. See W. Zafonelli, 1988, "A Brief Outline of China's Second Economy," pp. 138–155 in S. Feuchtwang, A. Hussain, and T. Pairault (eds.), *Transforming China's Economy in the Eighties.* Vol. 2: *Management, Industry, and the Urban Economy.* Boulder: Westview Press, pp. 148–149. Some local authorities exercised tighter control over the enterprises within their jurisdiction, effectively negating many of the benefits that could have accrued from the greater autonomy at the enterprise level. In addition, locally self-serving strategies in some cases thwarted the flow of capital, commodities, and information between China's regions, thereby damaging the overall growth potential of the country. The result is that in spite of the boost in efficiency stimulated by the reforms, the benefits to the economy as a whole were mixed.

30. Solinger, op. cit., p. 40.

31. Zafonelli, op. cit., p. 149.

32. S. Q. Gong, 1988, "Economic Features of the Primary Stage of Socialism," *Beijing Review*, No. 7 (February 15–28), pp. 18–20. According to the State Statistical Bureau, in 1996 there were more than 23 million people in urban China who were employed either in private enterprises or were self-employed, with an additional 38 million in those categories in the rural areas. China Statistical Publishing House, 1998, *China Statistical Yearbook 1997*, No. 16, table 4.4, pp. 96–97.

33. The tolerance, and to some extent the promotion, of private ownership produced some understandable feelings of ambivalence in a country that had so recently been committed to socialism. Obviously the idea of private business is closely affiliated with preliberation China and with some of the despised "capitalist roader" tendencies that were so abhorrent to the left wing of the Communist Party. Even before the revolution there had been a long-standing prejudice against self-employment, which was assigned low status in comparison to the more worldly values of Confucianism to be found among intellectuals and civil servants. The result was that the operators of private businesses inhabited a twilight zone of low and uncertain status. In Mao's China private enterprise had been a particularly dangerous choice to make, but even in the more liberal (pragmatic) climate of the 1980s it was still considered desirable to seek employment in the more secure realm of state and collectively owned businesses. As prosperous as the new private sector was proving to be for many Chinese citizens, it did not offer the "iron rice bowl" type of security provided by the work units (see Chapter 14), in terms of either job security or welfare benefits. Another advantage of the state and collective work units is that they provided access to the Communist Party, with all of the attendant privileges and avenues for social and political advancement. It was probably clear to many of the individuals who took the private road that they were running the risk of being branded as capitalist roaders if the reform process were suddenly to be reversed. In light of such fears, it is interesting to speculate on the causes of such a rapid growth rate of private enterprises. It is obvious, for example, that the private economy helped to supplement the state and collective sectors by providing goods and services that would otherwise not have been available. In addition, most of the smaller private enterprises could be established with relatively little capital, which represented a major gain to the state in terms of the circulation of capital needed to keep the economic machine healthy.

34. *China Daily*, "Decision on Reforms of Economic Structure," October 23, 1984, pp. 9–12, 11.

35. Ibid., p. 11.

36. *Far Eastern Economic Review*, "Peddling the Private Road," October 8, 1988, pp. 106–108.

37. It is important to note that throughout the 1990s industrial output continued to grow rapidly, with the proportion contributed by state enterprises increasing in absolute terms but declining in relative terms; the share contributed by collectively owned enterprises increased dramatically, surpassing even the state's share by 1996. In addition to the huge increase in the share of industrial output value coming from privately owned enterprises in the 1990s, an even larger share came from enterprises under "other" types of ownership, which presumably include those owned by foreign companies, especially those from Hong Kong and Taiwan. The data reported here are from table 12.6 in the *State Statistical Yearbook 1997*, p. 415.

38. The Economist Intelligence Unit, 1988, *China and North Korea: Country Report, Analysis of Economic and Political Trends Every Quarter*, No. 3. London: The Economist Intelligence Unit, pp. 24–25.

39. See *China Statistical Yearbook 1997*, table 9.3, p. 293.

40. J. P. Emerson, 1983, "Urban School-Leavers and Unemployment in China," *The China Quarterly,* No. 93, pp. 1–16.

41. The post-Mao leadership was also eager to see some reform in the way goods were distributed in China. The distribution system in the old command economy consisted of a centralized system of materials supply that allocated raw materials and capital to enterprises; a commercial network to handle retail and wholesale transactions; and a system of rural supply and marketing cooperatives to distribute industrial goods to the countryside and farm produce to the cities. By all accounts this system was unproductive and cumbersome, and reformers had suggested several measures of deregulation. Centralized allocation was to be scrapped for many goods; private traders were introduced into the system; and enterprises were allowed to bypass the state channels to market a part of their output directly. This produced significant growth in private retail and wholesale markets in both cities and the countryside during the 1980s. In conjunction with the rapid expansion of collective and private service establishments—such as restaurants, repair shops, clothing outlets, and food stalls—such changes have contributed to a major increase in the level of retail sales throughout China, and as early as 1984 collective and private units accounted for almost half of all such sales. As a result, employment in the tertiary sector (including retail, catering, and service trades) tripled between 1978 and 1983, and the majority of this growth was in the private domain.

42. In spite of the trend toward price deregulation, it was assumed that for the foreseeable future the state would continue to fix prices for strategic goods and consumer items such as food.

43. In actuality, price reform proved to be an extremely complex task—and highly controversial for a number of reasons. In the first place, if prices were to accurately reflect market conditions, they would need to be realigned frequently, but during the early 1980s China lacked the computer technology required to do that on a daily basis. With up to 1 million prices to be manipulated, and an infinite number of sectors in all corners of the country needing to be consulted, there was a simple technological constraint on what could be achieved. More important, perhaps, was the political problem inherent in the old system of controlled prices. Each price controlled by the state created a constituency that came to see price control as an entitlement. If coal prices were not allowed to rise past a certain point, this acted as a powerful subsidy to the users of coal; if food prices were kept low this would benefit millions of nonagricultural households in the cities.

44. *Far Eastern Economic Review,* "Let Them Eat Cash: China Tries to Scrap Food-Price Controls," May 26, 1989, pp. 72–73.

45. G. White, 1988, "Evolving Relations Between State and Markets in the Reform of China's Urban-Industrial Economy," pp. 7–25 in Feuchtwang et al., op. cit. As we have seen elsewhere, the reforms were associated with a number of economic problems during the last years of the 1980s, and the sharp increase in food prices rubbed salt into the wounds of the already overstretched citizenry. The government was faced with a challenge: At first it looked as though the leadership was willing to ride out the impacts of price reform, to make sure the overall trajectory of economic reform could be maintained. By that time about a third of all agricultural and retail commodity prices were determined entirely by market forces, and in May 1988 the prices of four major food items were decontrolled (eggs, vegetables, sugar, and pork). For an account of this, see *Far Eastern Economic Review,* "A Hunt for Economic Steroids," October 20, 1988, pp. 100–101. In the end, the government lost its nerve, and according to economist Bruce Reynolds, by September 1988 "the five-year plan to . . . decontrol prices was dead . . . the government . . . [re]imposed direct administrative quotas and controls over the spending of all state units (and collective and township enterprises as well). New bank lending was simply frozen." B. L. Reynolds, 1989, "The Chinese Economy in 1988," pp. 27–48 in A. J. Kane (ed.), *China Briefing, 1989.* Boulder: Westview Press; see p. 45. The effects were dramatic. Within a matter of weeks food prices shot up, anywhere from 30 percent to 60 percent, and Chinese families found themselves paying out more than half of their income for food alone. In May, June, and July the inflation rate reached 36 percent, three times higher than it had been in the first three months of that year. This caused a panic among China's consumers: Millions of people rushed to the banks to withdraw their hard-earned savings, and others decided to spend what they had on consumer goods of any type, figuring that spending was better than saving during an inflationary period. On September 12, 1988, the government announced that the price reform program was to be shelved for the time being. Controls reappeared on a nationwide scale and economic decisionmaking was recentralized to a level close to the pre-1979 situation. *Far Eastern Economic*

Review, "Toughing Out Price Reforms," July 21, 1988, pp. 19–20. There are some rather ludicrous stories about the panic buying that occurred during 1988. One man in Wuhan went out and stocked up on salt—enough for ten years! The sales of refrigerators and other "luxury" items shot up by close to 100 percent compared to 1987. At this point Deng Xiaoping is reported to have said, "We have been bold enough; now we need to take our steps in a more cautious way."

46. The retrenchment process usually begins with much publicized complaints about the economic chaos and corruption that have been a by-product of the economic reforms. At this time, for example, it was argued that many enterprises had used the price decontrols as an excuse to gouge the public, with no increase in commodity quality.

47. Reynolds, op. cit., pp. 45–46, gives three major reasons for the failure of the price reforms: First, the rate of inflation killed off the enthusiasm, among both the public and the government, although, as Reynolds argues, that was entirely predictable given the rate of growth in China's productive capacity during the 1980s; second, China's workers, long starved of material benefits, pushed very hard for pay raises and were often successful, with the costs being shifted on to the prices of finished goods and services; and third, it appears that the Chinese government made some serious mistakes in announcing the price decontrols before they happened, which resulted in panic spending, and by not allowing the interest rate for savings to rise with the inflation rate, which would have reduced the rate of panic withdrawals.

48. Solinger, op. cit.; see also Riskin, op. cit., chap. 9, pp. 201–222.

49. *Foreign Broadcast Information Service* (*FBIS*), February 8, 1984, p. 20 (quoted in Solinger, ibid., p. 29).

50. An important part of the new regional development plans was a mandatory form of cooperation between the richer and the poorer regions of China. In the tradition of trickle-down economics, it was felt that if the coastal regions could get rich first, then the whole country would ultimately benefit. To make sure this process worked, there were to be trading arrangements, joint investment ventures, and technology transfers between regions—all of which amounted to so-called core-periphery transfer relationships. In many cases these arrangements were not voluntary, and the officials in the richer areas were often unwilling to participate, preferring to build up their home economies rather than risking faraway ventures.

51. Ge Wu, 1988, "Urban Reform Experiment Goes in Depth," *Beijing Review*, Vol. 31, p. 7.

52. For a detailed discussion of China's Special Economic Zones, see Chossudovsky, op. cit., especially chaps. 7–9, pp. 132–190.

53. Rong Ye, 1988, "Foreign Economic Cooperation in the Coastal Areas," *China Reconstructs*, Vol. 37, pp. 8–10. Although few people in the PRC leadership would be willing to admit it, the phenomenal success of Taiwan on the world trade markets probably provided an important model and a powerful incentive to the CCP's plans for modernization; see Sutter, op. cit.

54. The parallel between the new SEZs and Open Cities and the nineteenth-century Treaty Ports is an obvious one, and to many Chinese people the concept of an open door to foreign capital was a painful reminder of the humiliation of foreign exploitation. See J. Fewsmith, 1986, "Special Economic Zones in the PRC," *Problems of Communism*, Vol. 35, pp. 78–85. Although the economic power is now much more solidly in China's hands than it was in the last century, to some the new policy still had an ominous ring to it, because it invited foreigners to launch an attack on China's independence and self-reliance. This was also a blow to the few remaining Maoist sympathizers within China, who argued that the open-door policy, in conjunction with the economic reforms, could have disastrous consequences for China. Some critics have suggested that the SEZs would essentially create "little Hong Kongs"—small areas of foreign imperialism, where outside capital could legally exploit cheap Chinese labor. Of course, the supporters of the new policies could counter such attacks by arguing that the creation of little Hong Kongs was extremely desirable, i.e., exactly what was needed in China after three decades of socialist economics.

55. Chossudovsky, op. cit., p. 131.

56. Zhao Ziyang, 1984, *FBIS*. Daily Report: China (December 26), pp. k/1–3 (quoted in Fewsmith, op. cit., p. 79).

57. Another criticism leveled at the SEZs was that although they appeared to be able to assemble goods using foreign parts they were far less effective in producing goods from scratch. Another problem was that most of the goods produced with foreign capital were being sold in the PRC, which was not one of the original goals of the SEZs. The upshot was a sharp rise in imports, which soaked up much of China's

supply of foreign exchange resources without the expected rise in exports to rebuild that supply. As a result, China's foreign exchange reserves plummeted, dropping at one point by a third in 1985 in just six months. See Pan, op. cit., p. 122. This produced stringent measures to control foreign exchange, and in 1985 free trading activities were sharply curtailed in all but four of the Open Cities. This is reported in Huan Guocang, 1986, "China's Opening to the World," *Problems of Communism*, Vol. 35, pp. 59–77.

58. D. R. Phillips and A.G.O. Yeh, 1987, "The Provision of Housing and Social Services in China's Special Economic Zones," *Environment and Planning: Government and Policy*, Vol. 5, pp. 447–468.

59. Highly publicized scandals in the SEZs contributed to the mounting criticisms, and none was more serious than what happened on the island of Hainan. The freedom to import foreign goods had been granted as part of the push to develop the island's weak economy. In actual fact the supply of scarce foreign exchange was used largely to import foreign cars and televisions cheaply, then to resell them to eager customers in the mainland for a healthy profit. This was used by the critics of the reform movement as an example of the practices employed by localities to line their own pockets at the expense of the national economy. Criticisms of this sort produced some tightening of the policies toward the SEZs, as well as an attempt to get them to focus more on the production of goods for export (outside the PRC) than had previously been the case. See Reynolds, op. cit., pp. 46–47.

60. See K. Lieberthal, 1995, *Governing China: From Revolution Through Reform*. New York: W. W. Norton. The notion of a gradualist approach to reform is stressed by many of the researchers writing about China in the mid-1990s. See, for example, S. L. Shirk, 1993, *The Political Logic of Economic Reform in China*. Berkeley: University of California Press; and H. Wang, 1994, *The Gradual Revolution: China's Economic Reform Movement*. New Brunswick, NJ: Transaction Publications. The gradual nature of the reform is also stressed in recent international reports; see, for example, International Monetary Fund (by M. W. Bell, H. E. Khor, and K. Kochhar for the IMF), 1993, *China at the Threshold of a Market Economy*. Washington, DC: IMF; and the report prepared for the Organization for Economic Cooperation and Development (by K. Fukusaku, D. Wall, and M. Y. Wu), 1994, *China's Long March to an Open Economy*. Paris: OECD. It is important to note, however, that the term "gradual" is not especially helpful

or interesting in this context, because all economic transitions tend to be gradual and because much of the gradualness results from timidity and vacillation on behalf of the leadership. What makes the Chinese case interesting is the unique set of characteristics that have shaped the reform policies; see B. Naughton, 1994, "What Is Distinctive About China's Economic Transition? State Enterprise Reform and Overall System Transformation," *Journal of Comparative Economics*, Vol. 18, No. 3 (June), pp. 420–490.

61. See Fukusaku et al., op. cit.; also A. Hussain, 1994, "The Chinese Economic Reforms: An Assessment," pp. 11–30 in D. Dwyer (ed.), *China: The Next Decades*. Burnt Mill, Essex: Longman Scientific and Technical, p. 12.

62. The latter two statistics are from table 2.9 of the *China Statistical Yearbook 1997*, p. 42.

63. At the same time, savings have reached an all-time high, averaging close to 40 percent of China's total GDP, which is higher than in the Asian NIEs, with the possible exception of Singapore. Hussain, op. cit., pp. 12–13, argues that in absolute terms the reforms have not brought economic hardship to any significant segment of the population. In other words there have been few if any losers, the exception being the summer of 1988, when inflation rose from 7 percent to almost 20 percent. Even after accounting for inflation, the growth in incomes was 5.9 percent per year during the 1981–1990 period, slowing down to about 5 percent during the early 1990s. From 1978 to 1992 China's national income increased by 225 percent, an average of 8.8 percent per year; see *China Facts and Figures Annual*, Vol. 17, 1994. New York: Academic International Press, p. 111.

64. *The Economist*, "China: The Titan Stirs," November 28, 1992, p. 3.

65. See N. R. Lardy, 1994, *China in the World Economy*. Washington, DC: Institute for International Economics, table 1.3, p. 15. These predictions are elaborated in a report prepared by the International Monetary Fund, 1993, *World Economic Outlook*. Washington, DC: IMF. The different estimates of China's total GNP result from the different methods used. The lower rates (under US$400 per capita) are calculated from the official exchange rate, but the higher estimates are based on the actual purchasing power of the Chinese currency. They have produced per capita estimates as high as $2,598, which, multiplied by China's population, means a total GDP of $2.90 trillion, about 15 percent of the world's GDP.

66. By 1996 China's exports had increased to US$289.9 billion, an increase in just three years of 67

percent; see *China Statistical Abstract 1997*, table 16.1, p. 587.

67. In addition, the "openness" of China's economy, measured by the ratio of its international trade to its overall GNP level, increased from slightly more than 10 percent in 1980 to 37 percent in 1991; the terms of trade (prices received for exports as opposed to prices paid for imports) improved from 122 in 1980 to 97 by 1992. See Lardy, op. cit., table 2.3, p. 41.

68. Ibid., p. 41.

69. See *China Statistical Abstract 1997*, table 16.1, p. 587.

70. These figures are tabulated by C. Chen, L. Chang, and Y. M. Zhang, 1995, "The Role of Foreign Direct Investment in China's Post-1978 Economic Development," *World Development*, Vol. 23, No. 4, pp. 691–703. There is some evidence that by the middle of the 1990s foreign direct investment in China was being spread around significantly more than was the case at the start of the decade. Guangdong's share of the total, for example, dropped to 27 percent by 1996, but Fujian's increased to 9.7 percent; see *China Statistical Abstract 1997*, table 16.16, p. 608.

71. For a detailed discussion, see the IMF report by Bell, Khor, and Kochhar, op. cit., especially sec. 5, pp. 46–57.

72. Quoted from Q. G. Jia, 1994, "Reform Ideology, Political Commitment, and Resource Transfer: An Alternative Model for the Explanation of China's Economic Reform," *The Journal of Contemporary China*, No. 5 (Spring), pp. 3–24, 4.

73. These estimates are provided by J. McMillan and B. Naughton, 1992, "How to Reform a Planned Economy: Lessons from China," *Oxford Review of Economic Policy*, Vol. 8, No. 1, p. 132. It is important not to overstate the extent to which China's economy has shifted toward the private sector; in fact many SOEs have performed reasonably well during the reform era, although many are also extremely inefficient and act as a drain on the central government's resources and contribute to inflation. It is also clear that the shift toward the private sector has been much more rapid in Guangdong and Fujian Provinces, largely as a result of "foreign" investment from Hong Kong and Taiwan. For detailed discussions of this issue, see P. Bowles and X. Y. Dong, 1994, "Current Successes and Future Challenges in China's Economic Reforms," *New Left Review*, No. 208 (November–December), pp. 49–76; and Naughton (1994), op. cit. See also R. Hodder, 1994, "State Collective and Private Industry in China's Evolving Economy," pp. 116–127 in D. Dwyer (ed.), *China: The Next Decades* (Harlow, Essex, UK: Longman Scientific and Technical), p. 124. Hodder uses this argument to make a much broader point, namely, that economic progress *is* compatible with a continuation of the existing regime in China. In fact, as he points out, a greater fear is that the continued push for democratic reforms and political freedom in China will ignore and perhaps destroy (as in the former Soviet Union) the industrial progress and economic success that have been achieved. For a more detailed exposition of this argument, see R. Hodder, 1993, *The Creation of Wealth in China: Domestic Trade and Material Progress in a Communist State*. London: Belhaven Press.

74. Although as many observers have reported, much still needs to be done. Some of the continuing problems that are hindering the development of the Chinese economy are detailed by Lieberthal, op. cit., and also by Hussain, op. cit. As one research team has reported, there are still innumerable problems: "The financial system misdirects funds, with state banks being unable to refuse loans to state enterprises, however unproductive, and non-state firms having restricted access to credit; agricultural production is distorted by the continuing state regulation of grain output; government policy keeps urban incomes artificially high and rural incomes artificially low; labor markets are inadequate or non-existent; the lack of basic laws of exchange and contract is a hindrance to both state and non-state firms; and property rights are ill-defined." See McMillan and Naughton, op. cit., p. 142.

75. See Lardy, op. cit., table 1.2, p. 11.

76. See Hussain, op. cit., p. 24.

77. Ibid., p. 24; see also Jia, op. cit.

78. Naughton (1995), op. cit.

79. As suggested earlier in this chapter, the reforms occurred in a number of disctinct groupings. Naughton suggests they can generally be subdivided into two interdependent categories: First, there was an overall expansion of market forces, achieved by limiting the scope of state planning and encouraging the entry of new enterprises, both domestic and foreign-owned; second, attempts were made to extend greater autonomy to the SOEs, allowing (or requiring) them to respond to market incentives with increasing effectiveness.

80. Although this system has not been free of problems, the consensus of opinion is that the reforms were accompanied by rapid output growth and improved productivity resulting from the

greater competition infused into the economy by the entry of new firms. State-owned firms were required to respond to the new level of competition by increasing their efficiency in order to compete at market prices. As Naughton has observed, both state-owned and nonstate firms responded to the dictates of the market, demonstrating that they were sensitive to both the invisible hand and foot of competition; see Naughton (1995). Naughton also mentions some of the problems associated with the dual-track pricing system: It inhibited attempts to implement more comprehensive reforms of China's pricing and taxation systems; it encouraged widespread corruption, as enterprises were allowed to buy materials at (low) state prices and sell at (higher) market prices; and it generated a significant amount of local government intervention and "protectionism." Ibid., esp. pp. 228–233.

81. Reynolds, op. cit., pp. 447–468.

82. See K. Griffin and J. Knight, 1996, "Human Development: The Case for Renewed Emphasis," pp. 610–639 in K. P. Jameson and C. K. Wilbur (eds.), *The Political Economy of Development and Underdevelopment*, 6th ed. New York: McGraw-Hill. Yet China lags behind the developed Western countries and the NIEs on many social indicators; in some areas, most notably education, China is behind even its poor Asian neighbors.

83. Riskin, op. cit., table 14.8, p. 369. This growth rate has continued. For example, 1987 output statistics show that light industry grew by 18.6 percent in 1986, heavy industry by 16.7 percent. *China Statistical Yearbook 1988*, p. 267. This, of course, is a mixed blessing, because growth rates of these proportions have inevitably led to some very serious problems usually associated with an overheated economy, most notably, inflation. The growth rate in China's GDP was higher during the first six years of the 1980s than it was in any other country in the world, averaging 10.5 percent per year, compared to South Korea's 8.2 percent and Japan's 3.7 percent. Reynolds, op. cit., suggests that it was only growth of this magnitude that enabled China to cope with its devastatingly high rate of inflation in 1987 and 1988, which was close to 20 percent.

84. Far Eastern Economic Review, *Asia Yearbook 1988*. Hong Kong: Review Publications, 1988, p. 120. Investments in fixed assets in 1987 were up by 16 percent over 1986. *China Statistical Yearbook 1988*, p. 499.

85. *Far Eastern Economic Review*, "China's Spending Frenzy," Vol. 141 (August 4, 1988), p. 48.

86. To purchase foreign-made goods, such as Japanese radios, tape recorders, and motorcycles, Chinese people (until the early 1990s) had to use foreign exchange certificates (FECs, or *waiweichuan*). They were not allowed to use the people's money (RMB, or *renminbi*). Because of the attractiveness of FECs and their relative scarcity, a black market developed in which Chinese people did everything to increase their holdings, hence the near-constant demands made on tourists to "change money" as they wandered through the streets of China's cities. After FECs were abandoned, this was very rarely heard.

87. Riskin, op. cit., pp. 368–371.

88. See Lieberthal, op. cit., pp. 259–265.

89. Another dimension of increasing inequality in China is along ethnic lines. From most accounts the minority populations encounter significant poverty and deprivation (see Chapter 12).

90. Chossudovsky, op. cit., pp. 124, 126. In the late 1980s not only did this raise the level of resentment among the have-nots; it also encouraged extra demands for consumer durable goods. The production of such goods, to meet the new level of demand, threatened to detract further from the production of what were initially considered to be more "necessary" consumer goods, such as basic housing, clothing, and food. The problem, as the Chinese leaders saw it at the time, was that too much money was being spent on the wrong items, eating up resources that should have been saved and used for more balanced economic growth. A study conducted by the Chinese Academy of Social Sciences in 1987 pointed out that too many Chinese families had been spending their newfound surpluses on "deviant" consumables, notably the so-called four new essentials: color televisions, refrigerators, washing machines, and tape recorders (for which sales increased by more than 50 percent between 1984 and 1986). A similar trend can be detected in the production of consumer goods in China throughout the 1980s and 1990s, with preferences shifting toward different items, including VCRs and karaoke equipment. This trend continued into the 1990s. For example, by 1996 there were 93.5 color TVs per 100 urban households, compared to 17.2 in 1985. For refrigerators the figures are 69.7 in 1996 and 6.6 in 1985; for washing machines, 90.1 and 48.3; and for tape recorders, 46.2 and 22.3. See *China Statistical Abstract 1997*, table 9.7, p. 295.

91. See, for example, O. Schell, 1988, *Discos and Democracy: China in the Throes of Reform*. New York: Pantheon; and P. B. Prime, 1988, "Low Expectations,

High Growth: The Economy and Reform in 1987," pp. 19–30 in A. J. Kane (ed.), *China Briefing, 1988*. Boulder: Westview Press.

92. Zafonelli, op. cit.; see also M. Findlay and T. Chiu, 1989, "Sugar-Coated Bullets: Corruption and the New Economic Order in China," *Contemporary Crises*, Vol. 13, No. 2 (June), pp. 145–162.

93. J. Kwong, 1997, *The Political Economy of Corruption in China*. Armonk, NY: M. E. Sharpe.

94. Ibid., p. 147.

95. Ibid., pp. 147–148.

96. K. Lieberthal, op. cit., p. 273.

97. This decision is printed in full in ibid., p. 440; Lieberthal's discussion of the reforms is found in chapter 9, "Economic Development," pp. 243–275.

98. M. K. Whyte and W. L. Parish, 1984, *Urban Life in Contemporary China*. Chicago: University of Chicago Press.

99. Zhao Ziyang, 1987, "The Primary Stage of Socialism," pp. 20–25 in *The 13th Party Congress and China's Reforms*. Beijing: Beijing Review Press, p. 24.

100. Qian Jiaju, 1988, "The Primary Stage of Socialism," *China Reconstructs*, Vol. 37, pp. 15–18.

101. Zhao Ziyang (1987), op. cit., pp. 24–25. With a statement like that it is easy to see how Zhao would be in trouble within the Party long before he was accused of siding with the student demonstrators in 1989. It seems likely that his thinking on the economic issue was too far ahead of the events, and he was treated as the scapegoat when things began to go wrong.

102. The massive student demonstrations in April and May 1989 received front-page and prime-time coverage around the world. In spite of repeated calls for greater freedom of speech, freedom of the press, and freedom to travel, few visible signs of compromise by the CCP were in evidence. See, for example, *Schenectady Gazette*, "Chinese Students March, Break Police Barricades," April 28, 1989.

103. This quote was attributed to Su Shaozhi, 1987, "Ideological Inconsistencies: Attacks on Reforms Force Leadership to Redefine Socialism," *Far Eastern Economic Review*, Vol. 138 (October 8), pp. 50–52. One can only wonder about Su's fate after the crackdown of 1989, because he appeared to be saying pretty much the same things as most of the student demonstrators.

104. Schell, op. cit., p. 105.

105. Ibid., p. 107.

106. Ibid.

107. G. White, 1993, *Riding the Tiger: The Politics of Economic Reform in Post-Mao China*. Stanford: Stanford University Press, p. 12.

Chapter 9

1. G. E. Guldin, 1997, *Farewell to Peasant China: Rural Urbanization and Social Change in the Late Twentieth Century*. Armonk, NY: M. E. Sharpe, p. 274.

2. For an excellent recent summary of this work, see G. Andrusz, M. Harloe, and I. Szelenyi (eds.), 1996, *Cities After Socialism: Urban and Regional Change and Conflict in Post-Socialist Societies*. Oxford: Blackwell.

3. I. Szelenyi, 1996, "Cities Under Socialism—and After," pp. 286–317, in ibid.

4. Ibid., p. 288. After the collapse of collective agriculture in the old European socialist states, many rural areas went into a steep decline, resulting in an increase in rural out-migration and a small but significant increase in urbanization. The character and quality of urban life have also changed significantly with the reintroduction of capitalism. City centers now are now bustling with traders, small-scale service providers, and immigrants from across Europe and beyond; and there has been a rising prevalence of Western-style urban social problems. There have also been changes in the urban structure of former socialist cities, including some degree of suburbanization among the wealthier groups, as well as an abandonment of many of the massive apartment complexes that were built to house the middle classes. New shopping malls are emerging in some of the richer suburbs; and there are numerous examples of inner-city decay, as city dwellers trapped by poverty are left behind in the least desirable areas.

5. P. R. Gaubatz, 1996, *Beyond the Great Wall: Urban Form and Transformation on the Chinese Frontiers*. Stanford: Stanford University Press.

6. See B. Naughton, 1995, "Cities in the Chinese Economic System: Changing Routes and Conditions for Autonomy," pp. 61–89 in D. S. Davis et al. (eds.), *Urban Spaces in Contemporary China: The Potential for Autonomy and Community in Post-Mao China*. Cambridge, UK: Cambridge University Press.

7. For a detailed introduction to the topic of the Chinese city in history, see G. W. Skinner (ed.), *The City in Late Imperial China*. Stanford: Stanford University Press. Perhaps the most impressive work on this topic is Paul Wheatley's magisterial history of the

city in ancient China. P. Wheatley, 1971, *The Pivot of the Four Quarters*. Chicago: Aldine. Another useful source on the topic of historical urban geography is Gaubatz, op. cit. For a recent treatment of China's urbanization, see K. W. Chan, 1994, *Cities with Invisible Walls: Reinterpreting Urbanization in Post-1949 China*. Hong Kong: Oxford University Press.

8. For more detailed discussions of the history of Chinese urbanization, see C. M. Nelson, 1988, "Urban Planning in Pre-industrial China," *U.S. China Review*, Vol. 12, pp. 17–21; and C. W. Pannell and L.J.C. Ma, 1983, *China: The Geography of Development and Modernization*. London: V. H. Winston.

9. See G. W. Skinner, 1977, "Introduction: Urban Social Structures in Ch'ing China," pp. 522–553 in G. W. Skinner, op. cit.

10. R. Murphey, 1980, *The Fading of the Maoist Vision: City and Country in China's Development*. New York: Methuen.

11. K. Buchanan, 1970, *The Transformation of the Chinese Earth*. London: G. Bell and Sons, p. 233.

12. Murphey, op. cit.

13. J. G. Gurley, 1976, *China's Economy and the Maoist Strategy*. New York: Monthly Review Press, p. 81.

14. Murphey, op. cit., p. 35.

15. R. Gaulton, 1981, "Political Mobilization in Shanghai: 1949–1951," pp. 35–65 in C. Howe (ed.), *Shanghai: Revolution and Development in an Asian Metropolis*. Cambridge, UK: Cambridge University Press, p. 46. All of this and much more is addressed in a marvelous new book about Shanghai by Leo Ou-fan Lee, 1999, *Shanghai Modern: The Flowering of a New Urban Culture in China, 1930–1945*. Cambridge: Harvard University Press.

16. This observation is made by R.J.R. Kirkby, 1985, *Urbanization in China: Town and Country in a Developing Economy, 1949–2000 A.D.* New York: Columbia University Press. Kirkby estimates that industrial output in China grew twenty-one times between 1952 and 1982, compared to a threefold growth of agricultural output.

17. Ibid., p. 18.

18. Kirkby (1985), op. cit., p. 18.

19. Ibid., p. 19.

20. This point is elaborated by M. K. Whyte and W. L. Parish, 1984, *Urban Life in Contemporary China*. Chicago: University of Chicago Press. It is important to point out that we have no evidence to indicate that this norm was shared by the majority of the urban population or whether it was simply a piece of communist fiction.

21. Kirkby (1985), op. cit.

22. T. P. Bernstein, 1977, *Up to the Mountains and Down to the Villages: The Transfer of Youth from Urban to Rural China*. New Haven: Yale University Press. Between 1968 and 1975 an estimated 12 million youths (about 10 percent of the existing urban population) were dispatched to the countryside. The "sending down" process has recently been illustrated for Westerners by Joan Chen's 1998 film, *Xiu Xiu: A Sent-Down Girl*. In general terms the sending-down rate varied with city size, the degree of industrialization, and the extent of Westernization, which would indicate a city greatly in need of revolutionary purification. Cities like Shanghai obviously led the others in this category. Assuming that one of the major goals of the sending-down policy was to provide a stimulus for rural development, we would expect to find that the majority of youths in question was sent to the most remote and poorly developed parts of China. This happened in many cases, and modern Chinese literature is filled with stories about the plight of youths eking out miserable existences in faraway places and squabbling with local peasants (who were usually no happier to receive them than the youths were to be sent). The evidence provided by Bernstein, however, suggests that the majority of sent-down youths did not end up going to the areas most in need of development. On the contrary, the areas most likely to receive them were those closest to provincial capitals and generally the richest and most modernized counties; they also tended to be counties at lower altitudes and with good railway connections. In other words these were not the remote and mountainous areas of China. Overall, there was a clear tendency for the sent-down youths to end up in nearby destinations, and perhaps this was a compromise that resulted from the overwhelming unpopularity of the policy. Instead of sending youths where they were most needed, many of them were allowed to go to places where they could keep in touch easily with their families. For vivid accounts of the experiences of sent-down youths in the Chinese countryside, see Liang Heng and J. Shapiro, 1984, *Son of the Revolution*. New York: Vintage Books; and Lo Fulang, 1989, *Morning Breeze: A True Story of Chinese Cultural Revolution*. San Francisco: China Books and Periodicals. In some cities—Shanghai, for example—government decrees dictated that if families had more than one educated child, at least one of them would have to be sent down. This resulted in some excruciating choices. Some families believed that if they lacked *guanxi* (see Chapter 3), a failure to vol-

unteer early might result in their children being sent off to outlandishly remote places such as Xinjiang, Tibet, or Inner Mongolia—places that for most urban Chinese people were literally foreign countries. There is also some evidence that certain classes of educated youths (or their parents) were willing to act in a fully revolutionary (red) way, by volunteering to go off to such remote places, regardless of their education levels or class backgrounds. These and other situations are brilliantly depicted in Wang Anyi, 1988, *Lapse of Time*. San Francisco: China Books and Periodicals.

23. Fifteen cities increased in population by 70 percent between 1953 and 1956, during which time productive employment increased by only 28 percent and service employment increased by 5 percent. Kirkby (1985), op. cit.

24. P. C. Chen, 1972, "Overurbanization, Rustication of Urban-Educated Youths, and the Politics of Rural Transformation," *Comparative Politics*, Vol. 4, pp. 381–386. Chinese cities continued to grow until 1959, after which they declined both in relative and absolute terms. See C. P. Cell, 1979, "Deurbanization in China: The Urban-Rural Contradiction," *Bulletin of Concerned Asia Scholars*, Vol. 11, pp. 62–72. This trend, and in fact the relatively slow rate of urbanization during the entire history of the PRC since 1949, suggest a pattern of underurbanization in China—a situation in which the actual rate of urbanization remains significantly below the expected rate. In general this is found to be the case in most of the world's socialist nations (as Szelenyi has observed; see earlier in this chapter). See M. X. Ran and B.J.L. Berry, 1989, "Underurbanization Policies Assessed: China, 1949–1986," *Urban Geography*, Vol. 10, pp. 111–120.

25. C. Riskin, 1987, *China's Political Economy: The Quest for Development Since 1949*. Oxford: Oxford University Press.

26. C. P. Lo, 1987, "Socialist Ideology and Urban Strategies in China," *Urban Geography*, Vol. 8, pp. 440–458.

27. Kirkby (1985), op. cit., pp. 93–99.

28. L.J.C. Ma, 1986, "Chinese Cities: A Research Agenda," *Urban Geography*, Vol. 7, pp. 279–290. According to China Statistical Publishing House, 1989, *China Statistical Yearbook 1988*, in 1987 there were 381 cities; 632 out of the total number of 1,986 counties were directly under the administration of cities.

29. This is a complex problem that has received much attention from urban geographers and other scholars. Rather than review this material here, the reader is directed to Kam Wing Chan's 1994 book, op. cit.; and a recent overview by Li Zhang and Simon Zhao, 1998, "Re-examining China's 'Urban' Concept and the Level of Urbanization," *The China Quarterly*, No. 154 (June), pp. 330–381.

30. D. Zweig, 1987, "From Village to City: Reforming Urban-Rural Relations in China," *International Regional Science Review*, Vol. 11, pp. 43–58.

31. R. R. Kirkby, 1988, "China Goes to Town," *Geographical Magazine*, Vol. 58, No. 10 (October), pp. 508–511, 510.

32. Kirkby (1985), op. cit.

33. Gurley, op. cit.

34. It is important to point out that the TVEs, although rurally located, were not an outgrowth of the communes. See M. Blecher, 1986, *China: Politics, Economics, and Society*. London: Frances Pinter.

35. Ibid., p. 162.

36. Mao Zedong, 1956, "Report to the Secondary Plenary Session," *Selected Works of Mao Tse-Tung*, Vol. 4. New York: International Publications, pp. 363–364.

37. E. F. Vogel, 1969, *Canton Under Communism: Program and Politics in a Provincial Capital, 1949–1968*. Cambridge: Harvard University Press, p. 46.

38. Ibid., p. 51.

39. Ibid., p. 44.

40. C. P. Lo, C. W. Pannell, and R. Welch, 1977, "Land Use Changes and City Planning in Shenyang and Canton," *Geographical Review*, Vol. 67, pp. 268–283.

41. Fei Xiaotong, 1953, *China's Gentry: Essays in Rural-Urban Relations*. Chicago: University of Chicago Press. In addition to the intra-urban patterns of inequality, the CCP inherited an extremely uneven pattern of economic development at the regional level, with urbanized and Westernized coastal areas sharply differentiated from the largely rural and premodern interior. This issue will be addressed in more detail in Chapter 10.

42. W. T. Rowe, 1984, "Urban Policy in China," *Problems of Communism*, Vol. 33, pp. 75–80.

43. This rather sad chapter of socialist city planning, in which the Chinese destroyed much of their urban heritage, has been well documented by Chinese urban scholars and foreign observers. For different views, see Hou Renzhi, 1986, "Evolution of the City Plan of Beijing," *Third World Planning Review*, Vol. 8, No. 1, pp. 5–17; and T. Terzani, 1986, "Death by a Thousand Cuts: The Destruction of Old Peking," pp. 22–59 in his *Behind the Forbidden Door:*

Travels in China. London: Allen and Unwin. The land use of the ancient Chinese city often followed religious and geomantic considerations. There was a preoccupation with nature's dominance over man and the Confucian belief in the merits of order, symmetry, and hierarchy. The Communists rejected this in favor of a more pragmatic approach to planning, in which man was to conquer nature. See Nelson, op. cit. For a detailed discussion of what happened in Beijing, see V.E.S. Sit, 1995, *Beijing: The Nature and Planning of a Chinese Capital City.* Chichester, UK: John Wiley and Sons.

44. For a detailed discussion of the rebuilding of Beijing, see Sit, op. cit.

45. Rowe, op. cit., p. 77.

46. The experiment with and failure of the urban communes are discussed by J. Salaff, 1969, "The Urban Communes and Anti-City Experiments in Communist China," *The China Quarterly,* No. 70, pp. 82–110.

47. Lo, op. cit., p. 446.

48. Ibid., p. 446.

49. K. I. Fung, 1980, "Suburban Agricultural Land Use Since 1949," pp. 156–184 in C. K. Leung and N. Ginsburg (eds.), *China: Urbanization and National Development.* Chicago: University of Chicago, Dept. of Geography Research Paper No. 196. In 1956 alone, for example, Fung estimates that 2.48 million square meters of housing were demolished in 175 cities.

50. See Fung, ibid.; in Harbin, between 1954 and 1956, the population increased from 1.21 million to 1.47 million, but the acreage growing vegetables fell from 4,980 hectares to 2,662 during the same period.

51. See, for example, G. W. Skinner, 1978, "Vegetable Supply and Marketing in Chinese Cities," *The China Quarterly,* No. 76, pp. 733–793. It is important to point out that the goal of urban self-sufficiency represented much more than simple Maoist egalitarian dogma. In addition to the obvious geographical advantages, growing vegetables within the city made good ecological sense, in that it helped to provide labor and technology from the cities, as well as local sources of fertilizer, including night soil and ash from domestic fires. In organizational terms the propinquity of production and consumption also made things much easier. Most importantly, however, self-sufficiency would help to lower China's dependency on imported food, and it would help to establish the independence of the interior cities from the traditionally dominant cities on the eastern coast. In economic terms local self-sufficiency helped the government to hold down food prices, which was essential in its quest for legitimacy in the first decade after liberation. By maintaining peasant incomes and smoothing out fluctuations in the demand for agricultural labor throughout the year, urban self-sufficiency also helped to prevent unemployment and the inevitable urban unrest it could bring.

52. Skinner (see ibid.) has shown that in spite (or perhaps because) of the intensity of agricultural production in the inner production zone, relatively little of the actually available land in this zone is devoted to agriculture—16 percent in Shanghai and 28 percent in Guangzhou (Canton). He also notes that the size and width of the zone required to make a city self-sufficient are a function of spatial variations in productivity and, of course, city size. By assuming an annual vegetable yield of sixty tons per hectare, and using an average of 20 percent of the available land, Skinner estimated that the vegetable zone would need to be close to ten kilometers wide for a city of 6 million people but only 2.8 kilometers wide for a city of half a million.

53. Gaulton, op. cit., p. 40.

54. L. W. Snow, 1981, *Edgar Snow's China: A Personal Account of the Chinese Revolution Compiled from the Writings of Edgar Snow.* Boston: Little, Brown, p. 47.

55. R. Terrill, 1975, *Flowers on an Iron Tree: Five Cities in China.* Boston: Little, Brown, p. 47.

56. X. X. Zhang and Y. Sang, 1987, *Chinese Lives: An Oral History of Contemporary China.* New York: Pantheon Books, 1987, pp. 31–38, 32.

57. Terrill, op. cit., pp. 82–83.

58. Ibid., p. 85. The former prostitute interviewed in *Chinese Lives* was certainly grateful to the Communists for providing her with a new start in life. As she said, "The new society allowed us to be human beings for the first time." In 1949 she had syphilis and was wasting away as a result of her opium addiction. She was sent to reform school and was forcibly cured of her sickness and vices. Later on she managed to find a job, and in 1958 she found a husband and settled down.

59. See "The New Conquers the Old in Nanking," *China Reconstructs,* No. 22 (March 1973), pp. 21–26.

60. Vogel, op. cit., p. 65.

61. Ibid., pp. 65–66.

62. As Vogel has written, these were probably the most exciting times these youths had ever seen or were likely to see again: "Their idealism and optimism was at a peak, and they eagerly debated their views of the ideal society and how to realize that soci-

ety. . . . As talented young individuals with a long future, they looked forward to great career opportunities. . . . They did not need or demand material rewards. . . . Their own sense of satisfaction, the respect of peers, the praise of superiors . . . were more than adequate." Ibid., p. 56.

63. In keeping with the Maoist obsession with reducing the dichotomy between city and country, the new values to be inculcated into China's urban youths would be largely rural values. In 1958, for example, Miss Yao Feng-chu became the model for revolutionary commitment in Shanghai. It was not a bourgeois beauty contest that she had won but the All-City Pig-Feeding Championship: "She awoke each day at 4:30 A.M., to prepare several thousand catties of hog feed, fetch 60 to 70 buckets of water and wash the sties. Such an excellent worker could maintain almost 100 collectively owned hogs, plus three privately on the side. Few urban youths had Yao's rural competence, but many studied it." See Gaulton, op. cit., p. 61.

64. Ibid.

65. L. Pan, *Old Shanghai: Gangsters in Paradise.* Hong Kong: Heinemann, p. 236.

66. J.S.S. Muldavin, 1996, "The Political Ecology of Agrarian Reform in China," pp. 227–259 in R. Peet and M. Watts (eds.), *Liberation Ecologies: Environment, Development, Social Movements.* London: Routledge, p. 228; see also Muldavin, 1997, "Environmental Degradation in Heilongjiang: Policy Reform and Agrarian Dynamics in China's New Hybrid Economy," *Annals of the Association of American Geographers*, Vol. 87, No. 4 (December), pp. 579–613.

67. C. Ikels, 1996, *The Return of the God of Wealth: The Transition to a Market Economy in Urban China.* Stanford: Stanford University Press.

68. S. G. Wang, 1995, "The Politics of Private Time: Changing Leisure Patterns in Urban China," pp. 149–172 in D. S. Davis et al. (eds.), *Urban Spaces in Contemporary China: The Potential for Autonomy and Community in Post-Mao China.* Washington, DC: Woodrow Wilson Press, p. 156.

69. See P. Dicken, 1998, *Global Shift: Transforming the World Economy*, 3d ed. New York: Guilford Press, p. 47.

70. For examples of this work, see J. H. Bater, 1980, *The Soviet City: Ideal and Reality.* London: Edward Arnold; and Bater, 1986, "Some Recent Perspectives on the Soviet City," *Urban Geography*, Vol. 7, pp. 93–102. For more general studies of Eastern European cities, see D. M. Smith, 1991, "The Socialist City," pp. 70–99 in G. Andrusz et al., op. cit.; and

D. M. Smith, 1989, *Urban Inequality Under Socialism: Case Studies from Eastern Europe and the Soviet Union.* Cambridge, UK: Cambridge University Press.

71. For an excellent summary of the situation in Russia leading up to the fall of communism, see M. Castells, 1998, *The Information Age: Economy, Society, Culture.* Vol. 3: *End of Millennium.* Oxford: Blackwell. Studies of cities experiencing the transition in socialist states include R. Segre, M. Coyula, and J. L. Scarpaci, 1997, *Havana: Two Faces of the Antillean Metropolis.* New York: Wiley; K. Barry (ed.), 1996, *Vietnam's Women in Transition.* Basingstoke, UK: Macmillan. For discussions about China's transition, see P. Nolan, 1995, *China's Rise, Russia's Fall: Politics, Economics, and Planning in the Transition from Stalinism.* New York: St. Martin's Press; and P. R. Gaubatz, 1995, "Urban Transformation in Post-Mao China: Impacts of the Reform Era on China's Urban Form," pp. 28–60 in D. S. Davis et al. (eds.), *Urban Spaces in Contemporary China: The Potential for Autonomy and Community in Post-Mao China.* Cambridge, UK: Cambridge University Press; specifically dealing with Beijing, see Sit, op. cit.

72. For a collection of essays on the topic of urban transformations in socialist cities, see Andrusz et al., op. cit.

73. The alternative route is via democratization, which was the way the former Soviet Union elected to go under the leadership of Michael Gorbachev; see M. X. Pei, 1998, *From Reform to Revolution: The Demise of Communism in China and the Soviet Union.* Cambridge: Harvard University Press.

74. B. Naughton, op. cit., pp. 88–89.

75. This process, where the peasants switched from agricultural to industrial and service activities, has been excellently recorded by Kate Xiao Zhou, 1996, *How the Farmers Changed China: Power of the People.* Boulder: Westview Press, chap. 7.

76. O. Schell, 1988, *Discos and Democracy: China in the Throes of Reform.* New York: Pantheon.

77. Y. T. Sun, 1988, "Shock Wave of Unemployment in Qingdao City," *Nexus—China in Focus* (Winter), pp. 27–28.

78. Lo, op. cit., p. 449. This indicates a sharp reversal from the days of Maoist populism, in which most experts and technicians—including city planners—were considered suspect. In the 1980s the greater focus on living conditions within China's cities, on environmental protection, and on the need for carefully considered urban plans pointed to a new lease on life for urban planning as a profession.

79. This argument has probably been made most forcefully by M. Chossudovsky, 1986, *Towards Capitalist Restoration? Chinese Socialism After Mao.* Hong Kong: Macmillan.

80. Naughton, op. cit., p. 88.

81. This has been discussed by Chan (1994), op. cit.; also by Wang, op. cit. Wang reports, for example, based on survey data, that the average amount of leisure time in Chinese cities was 2.1 hours in 1980; this had increased to 3.59 hours in 1986 and to 4.48 hours in 1991 (see Wang, p. 158).

82. Access to the good life in China's cities is highly uneven. The floating populations are helping to improve the quality of urban life—by working on the construction sites, selling on the streets, waiting tables in the restaurants, cutting and styling hair in the barbershops, and looking after the children in people's homes—but they are not yet sharing fully in the new wealth (see Chapter 15). Most migrants are still treated as second-class citizens and are forced to live and work at the urban margins, in places that long-term residents would never tolerate. The emergence of a new underclass population is a stark reality of the reform era, and it is widely believed that the new urban poor are contributing to rising crime rates and other social problems in China's biggest cities.

83. See, for example, Chan (1994), op. cit.; Zhang and Zhao, op. cit.; and also L.J.C. Ma and C. S. Lin, 1993, "Development of Towns in China: A Case Study of Guangdong Province," *Population and Development Review,* Vol. 19, No. 3, pp. 583–606.

84. See J. Fitzgerald, 1998, "What Is a Province? Or an Institutional History of Provincial Separatism in Twentieth Century China." Paper presented at the international conference "Imagining China: Regional Division and National Unity," Taipei, Taiwan (March), p. 18. As Fitzgerald observes, the most extreme case of this occurred in 1997 when the city of Chongqing in Sichuan was declared a provincial-level city, independent of the province of Sichuan and answering directly to Beijing. In effect a new province had been created, but it was called a city. In size Chongqing is two to three times the size of the average of China's provincial-level cities (Shanghai, Tianjin, and Beijing) combined, and its population is about 30 million, placing it at about the mean population for all provinces in China. More than 80 percent of the city's population is classified as rural. It is anticipated that Chongqing will serve as a model for the rest of China by showing the way toward further integration between urban and rural areas. As Fitzgerald notes, "This experiment will explore new ways for China to urbanize, industrialize and modernize the rural areas in the midwest region, and provide a demonstrative role to third world countries facing similar tasks and difficulties." See Fitzgerald, op. cit., pp. 19–20.

85. The increase in China's level of urbanization is easily measurable from the statistics (see earlier in this chapter).

86. See Zhang and Zhao, op. cit.

87. As noted in Chapter 2, the spatial and cultural consequences of contemporary capitalism have been described as the "condition of postmodernity," the features of which are its "excessive emphemerality and fragmentation in the political . . . private [and] social realm." D. Harvey, 1989, *The Condition of Postmodernity: An Enquiry into the Origins of Cultural Change.* Oxford: Blackwell, p. 306. For a discussion of postmodern architecture and urbanization in China, see Wang Mingxian, 1997, "Notes on Architecture and Postmodernism in China," pp. 163–175 in *Postmodernism and China,* a special issue of the journal *boundary 2,* Vol. 24, No. 3 (Fall).

88. See A. Stille, 1998, "Faking It," *The New Yorker* (June 15), pp. 36–42, 38. In fact, as Alexander Stille observed, nighttime is probably the best time to see the new Chinese cities, because, as he writes, "almost all the new buildings in Xian—and, indeed, in almost all of China—are simply reinforced-concrete boxes covered with the kind of industrial white tile you might find in a gas-station restroom. . . . As a guilty afterthought on the part of the architect, many of these . . . buildings have been capped with upturned Chinese eaves, which perch on the buildings like ill-fitting wigs" (pp. 38–39). Stille makes a more general point that is worth considering here, that is, about the tendency of the Chinese to be what we might think of as careless when it comes to preserving aspects of their culture. As he notes, in the case of buildings, works of art, and historical monuments, they are more likely to copy and remake facsimiles of the originals than to attempt to preserve what was originally there. This is often disconcerting to Westerners, either as tourists or as art and culture appreciators. According to Stille, this tendency has something to do with the Chinese sense of time, which is cyclical rather than linear, with the clock restarting for each new emperor. It is not surprising, Stille argues, that "in a world that was both eternal and ever-changing, rebuilding monuments made perfect sense. Similarly, copying an existing work of

art was seen as a sign of reverence rather than as a lack of originality" (p. 37).

89. M. Dear, 1986, "Postmodernism and Planning," *Environment and Planning: Society and Space*, Vol. 4, pp. 367–384, 380.

90. E. Soja, 1989, *Postmodern Geographies: The Reassertion of Space in Critical Social Theory*. London: Verso.

91. See Y. M. Yeung and Y. W. Sung (eds.), 1996, *Shanghai: Transformation and Modernization Under China's Open Policy*. Hong Kong: Chinese University Press, esp. pp. 273–298 therein, "Pudong: Remaking Shanghai as a World City," by A.G.O. Yeh.

92. This new territory is similar to what the Japanese call *konjuka*, or what Terry McGee has labelled *desakota* or *kotadesasi*, using Indonesian terms for the almost continuous urbanization to be found in many parts of Indonesia, including most of the southern part of Bali. See G. E. Guldin, 1997, *Farewell to Peasant China: Rural Urbanization and Social Change in the Late Twentieth Century*. Armonk, NY: M. E. Sharpe.

93. Naughton, op. cit., p. 83.

94. Accompanying the material side of the rural urbanization process has been the deagriculturalization of the workforce. By 1995 more than a third of the rural workforce was employed in the nonfarm sector (see Guldin, op. cit.). In the newly integrated rural-urban areas, we now see the odd phenomenon of what Guldin (1997) calls "amphibianized" peasants, who are neither urban nor rural (op. cit., p. 273). It is important to note that in describing all of this activity none of the authors in the Guldin volume envision any serious problems associated with the process of rural urbanization. Neither, as Guldin observes (op. cit., p. 268), is the process being precipitated by the collapse of rural agriculture, which is what has been observed in some of the transitioning state in Eastern Europe (see, for example, Szelenyi, op. cit.). In fact, the most rapidly urbanizing areas in contemporary China are those where agricultural productivity has been strongest.

95. For a comprehensive overview of development in the Delta, see George C.S. Lin, 1997, *Red Capitalism in South China: Growth and Development of the Pearl River Delta*. Vancouver: University of British Columbia Press.

96. This is a phrase used by Deborah Davis in her 1995 edited volume, cited above.

97. V. Shue, 1988, *The Reach of the State: Sketches of the Chinese Body Politic*. Stanford: Stanford University Press; and see V. Shue, 1995, "State Sprawl: The Regulatory State and Social Life in a Small Chinese City," pp. 90–112 in Davis et al. (eds.), op. cit.

98. Shue, op. cit., p. 111.

99. Ibid., p. 90.

100. In this respect it is interesting to speculate on what appeared to be widespread and spontaneous demonstrations in Beijing and other cities after the bombing of the Chinese embassy in Belgrade during the NATO airstrikes against Serbia (*New York Times*, May 9, 1999). Within hours of the bombing there were violent scenes outside the U.S. embassy in Beijing, with demonstrators throwing rocks and making ugly threats toward all American (and, to a lesser extent, British) nationals, for what was assumed to be a deliberate attack. NATO spokespersons insisted the bombing was a failure of CIA intelligence. Some U.S. newspapers suggested that the demonstrations were probably staged or encouraged by the government (bearing in mind that at this time the United States and China were locking horns over many issues, not the least of which was the "theft" of state secrets by the Chinese). Whether or not this turns out to be the case, it is worthwhile noting that demonstrations on the scale and with the speed that was observed are highly unusual events in China; it is possible that the phenomenon was in equal parts a manifestation of the new level of openness and freedom of expression being enjoyed by the Chinese people, and a symbol of China's new agressive nationalism.

101. S. Zukin, 1992, "Postmodern Urban Landscapes: Mapping Culture and Power," pp. 221–247 in S. Lash and J. Friedman (eds.), *Modernity and Identity*. Oxford, UK: Blackwell; and also S. Zukin, 1991, *Landscapes of Power: From Detroit to Disney World*. Berkeley: University of California Press. Zukin (1992) has argued that the key factor defining postmodern spatiality is the quality or the situation of liminality. She suggests that specific locales within the postmodern world are liminal spaces, i.e., sites of activity that are in transition from one status to another; or they are perceived as being one thing and another at the same time. Thus, the sleek new towers of the postmodern city are juxtaposed with red brick originals or reconstructions of past eras, such as Faneuil Hall in Boston and the South Street Seaport in New York. Liminality, described in this way, complicates the residents' efforts to construct a spatial identity. Because they mix functions and histories, liminal spaces are ambiguous: They combine profit-making with nonprofit activities, leisure spaces with

workplaces, and residential neighborhoods with commercial centers. They can be places of commerce, residence, and entertainment—all at the same time—and represent the erosion of local distinctiveness.

102. Shue (1995), p. 90.

103. See, for example, J. Y. Zha, 1997, "China's Popular Culture in the 1990s," pp. 109–150 in W. A. Joseph (ed.), *China Briefing: The Contradictions of Change.* Armonk, NY: M. E. Sharpe; and J. Y. Zha, 1995, *China Pop: How Soap Operas, Tabloids, and Bestsellers Are Transforming a Culture.* New York: The New Press.

104. To give just one example: The sale of books has increased dramatically in recent years, especially for titles the state considers to be unhealthy or immoral, including martial arts, romance, fashion, violence, and, particularly, sex. The state cracks down at intervals, and the books disappear for a time, but within months they reappear as if nothing had happened and the whole process rolls onward. See S. G. Wang, 1995, "The Politics of Private Time: Changing Leisure Patterns in Urban China," pp. 149–172 in D. S. Davis et al. (eds.), op. cit.

105. Shue (1995), op. cit., p. 90.

Chapter 10

1. C. Bramall, 1993, *In Praise of Maoist Economic Planning: Living Standards and Economic Development in Sichuan Since 1931.* Oxford: Clarendon Press.

2. A. Khan and C. Riskin, 1998, "Income and Inequality in China: Composition, Distribution and Growth of Household Income, 1988 to 1995," *The China Quarterly,* No. 154 (June), pp. 221–253.

3. See K. Griffin and J. Knight, 1996, "Human Development: The Case for Renewed Emphasis," pp. 610–639 in K. P. Jameson and C. K. Wilbur (eds.), *The Political Economy of Development and Underdevelopment,* 6th ed. New York: McGraw-Hill.

4. Discussions of the ups and downs of the investment cycles in contemporary China are provided in some of the reports of the *Far Eastern Economic Review.* See, for example, "The Fever Cools," August 31, 1995, pp. 43–45. On the issue of the growing connection between Taiwan and the mainland, especially Fujian Province and the Xiamen SEZ, see "Southern Cooking," May 25, 1995, pp. 22–24.

5. These estimates are discussed in two articles by Robert Weil, 1995, "China at the Brink: Class Contradictions of "Market Socialism." *Monthly Review,* December 1994, pp. 10–55 (Part 1); and January 1995, pp. 11–43 (Part 2).

6. Ibid., p. 15.

7. See O. Schell, 1994, *Mandate of Heaven: A New Generation of Entrepreneurs, Dissidents, Bohemians, and Technocrats Lays Claim to China's Future.* New York: Simon and Schuster, esp. pt. 5, "The Boom," pp. 331–442; quote from p. 338. For another recent view of the frenzied development in the Pearl River Delta, see P. Theroux, 1993, "Going to See the Dragon," *Harper's* (October), pp. 33–56.

8. Ibid., p. 337.

9. Weil, op cit., p. 14.

10. See *The Economist,* "City of the Plain," Vol. 334, No. 7906 (1995), p. 18.

11. Movement in this direction is marked by the most telling symbol of modernization, the appearance of often foreign-funded superhighways connecting the southern metropolises, for example, the road from Guangzhou to Shenzhen, and the newest: from Shenzhen to Zhuhai (and, therefore, to Macau, the newest Special Administrative Region).

12. Weil, op. cit., p. 13.

13. For a review of the issues and a look at some of the data, see C. J. Smith, 1991, *China: People and Places in the Land of One Billion.* Boulder: Westview Press.

14. Riskin, op. cit., p. 250.

15. Bramall, op. cit.; see also Selden, op. cit., p. 175.

16. C. T. Wu and D. F. Ip, 1980, "Structural Transformation and Spatial Equity," pp. 56–88 in N. Ginsburg and C. K. Leung (eds.), *China: Urbanization and National Development.* Chicago: University of Chicago, Department of Geography, Research Paper No. 146.

17. D. Zweig, 1987, "From Village to City: Reforming Urban-Rural Relations in China," *International Regional Science Review,* Vol. 11, No. 1, pp. 43–58. As we saw in Chapter 7, and as reiterated later in this chapter, the urban-rural gap appeared to have narrowed to some extent during the first decade of the post-Mao agricultural reforms, perhaps as a result of rural industrialization or a onetime absolute gain in efficiency in farming activities.

18. See Riskin, op. cit., p. 238.

19. The income inequality estimates are provided in Selden, op. cit., p. 162. The higher estimates are obtained by considering the effect of the massive

subsidies on food in China's cities. There is a general consensus in the literature that the gap between urban and rural incomes probably doubled between 1952 and 1979, partly as a result of the food, housing, and other subsidies offered to city dwellers, but also as a result of absolute gains in urban residents' incomes and the lack of investment and low productivity in the agricultural sector.

20. Ibid., pp. 169–170.

21. In the 1950s the average ratio of per capita consumption between urban residents and peasants was 2.8:1 (Y188 per year in the cities, compared to Y73 in the countryside). By the 1960s the ratio had been lowered to 2.5; but in the 1970s it was 2.6. Part of the inequality was a result of the so-called scissors effect of agricultural pricing policies in China, which guaranteed city dwellers cheap food by keeping agricultural prices, and therefore rural incomes, artificially low. In addition to the monetary differentials in wealth, city dwellers generally had far greater access to services such as education, health care, recreation, and transportation—all of which tended to enhance the quality of life for China's city dwellers, effectively widening the urban-rural gap even more. See Trescott, op. cit., table 2, p. 207.

22. In 1979, for example, it was estimated that the ratio of the richest to the poorest regions (Shanghai versus Tibet) was 16:1, and the next nearest poor relation to Tibet, Guizhou Province, had a per capita industrial output level that was only 39 percent of the national average. In Shanghai, by comparison, the industrial output level was more than five times higher than the national average. Even excluding the urban areas there were some major discrepancies in income levels among the regions of China by the end of the 1970s. Collective incomes per commune member varied from Y139 in Jilin Province in the industrial northeast, to Y56 in Guizhou and Y68 in Gansu in 1979 (with Y100 as the national average). To a large extent such variations reflected geographical and ecological variations within the Chinese countryside (climate, soil quality, topography, proximity to urban areas, and the availability of transportation), in addition to differences in administrative efficiency and management practices, which were more difficult to assess. See Riskin, op. cit., table 10.2, p. 230. It is important to point out that in addition to the spatial sources of inequality in China, there are significant sources of inequality between individuals, for example, between the crippling workload of peasants laboring in the rice fields or porters carrying heavy loads up mountainsides and the relatively cushy life

of many office workers. Gender inequality, as we shall see in Chapter 13, is still widespread in China, as are some of the discrepancies in power and status generally associated with Party membership. See Trescott, op. cit., pp. 207–209. In light of the socialist commitment to spatial equality, the size and persistence of these income discrepancies are puzzling. It has been suggested by Dorothy Solinger that in China there is an almost fatalistic acceptance of the traditional differences in physical endowment between rich and poor regions. This fatalism, arguably, can be explained in part by Confucian paternalism, which would condone the continued dependence of localities (siblings) on the central government (parents); and the continued existence of inequalities between richer provinces (elder brothers and husbands) and poorer ones (sisters and wives). The inequality, in other words, is accepted as a fact of life rather than something that must be eliminated: "A rich elder brother is expected to take care of poorer, younger brothers out of benevolence, but the latter are obligated to respect the oldest regardless of his behavior. Any demand to be equal would be regarded as a transgression." See D. J. Solinger, 1987, "Uncertain Paternalism: Tensions in Recent Regional Restructuring in China," *International Regional Science Review*, Vol. 11, No. 1, pp. 23–42.

23. See M. K. Whyte, 1986, "Social Trends in China: The Triumph of Inequality," pp. 103–123 in A. Doak Barnett and R. N. Clough (eds.), *Modernizing China: Post-Mao Reform and Development*. Boulder: Westview Press.

24. In 1984, for example, Guizhou's per capita industrial output was 46 percent of the national average. Although this represented an increase for Guizhou from 39 percent in 1979, at the same time Shanghai's output had increased to 654 percent of the national average (compared to 516 percent in 1979). In spite of the efforts made to boost industrial growth in China's peripheral regions, industry remained heavily concentrated in certain provinces, mainly those in the northeast, along the east coast, and in the southeastern part of the country. See J. P. Cole, 1987, "Regional Inequalities in the People's Republic of China," *Tijdschift Voor Econ. en Soc. Geografie*, Vol. 78, No. 3, pp. 201–213.

25. Ibid., fig. 2, p. 207.

26. E. Croll, 1994, *From Heaven to Earth: Images and Experience of Development in China*. London: Routledge.

27. The estimated number of people living below the poverty line varies according to how such calcu-

lations are made. The numbers living in poverty in China's rural areas estimated by the PRC government, for example, appear to be impossibly low: For example, it estimated that by 1988 the number of people living in poverty was between 27 million (1988) and 39 million (1989). Western researchers have concluded that these figures are much too low, probably because they are based on an unrealistically low level of household income unadjusted for inflation. The calculations made by researchers working for the World Bank place the late 1980 figures close to 100 million, with higher estimates, based on actual procurement prices for grain, in the 120 million range. See World Bank, 1992, *China: Strategies for Reducing Poverty in the 1990s.* Washington, DC: World Bank, esp. annex 1, "Incidence of Absolute Poverty," pp. 137–155, executive summary, pp. ix–xviii, and chap. 1, "Incidence and Correlates of Absolute Poverty," pp. 21–48. A similar trend toward greater levels of inequality can be observed in the official statistics recording per capita changes in income and consumption rates from 1978 to the early 1990s. In absolute terms China's rural residents did well, with increases in real income from Y134 in 1978 to Y398 in 1985 and Y784 in 1992. In terms of actual consumption rates, however, the statistics are not as impressive: Rural residents experienced an increase from Y132 per capita in 1978 to Y648 in 1992, whereas their urban counterparts saw an increase from Y383 to Y1,983 in 1992. This means that the ratio of urban to rural consumption fell during the first seven years of the reform period, from 1:2.9 in 1978 to 1:1.22 in 1985; but by 1992 the ratio had increased again to 1:3 and continued to rise throughout the 1990s. These statistics are reported in China Statistical Publishing House, 1998, *China Statistical Yearbook 1997.*

28. It was obvious that the small-scale commodity production that was dominant in both the rural and urban parts of China was not sufficient to support the massive modernization being planned in Beijing. Many of the new private and collective enterprises were relatively efficient, but they were often small in scale; the state enterprises, although much larger, were usually more inefficient. The problem of the small size of China's industrial sector is seen by some Chinese and Western observers as a crucial concern. In China's iron and steel industry (which is mostly state-owned), the thirty-eight largest enterprises account for less than 50 percent of total output, compared to the much more efficient structures of countries like Japan (where the twenty largest enterprises account for 84

percent of total production) and the United States (where the seven largest companies account for 83 percent of production). See R. Hodder, 1994, "State, Collective, and Private Industry in China's Evolving Economy," pp. 116–127 in D. Dwyer (ed.), *China: The Next Decades.* Harlow, Essex, UK: Longman Scientific and Technical, esp. table 7.2, p. 123.

29. Weil, op. cit., p. 26.

30. Ibid., p. 26. Kenneth Lieberthal has discussed the need for Chinese industry to increase efficiency and further technological achievement. See K. Lieberthal, 1995, *Governing China: From Revolution Through Reform.* New York: W. W. Norton, esp. pp. 259–265.

31. See A. Chan and R. A. Senser, 1997, "China's Troubled Workers," *Foreign Affairs,* Vol. 76, No. 2 (March–April), pp. 104–117. Anita Chen has recently published a book dealing with the issue of the work conditions that have been underlying the Chinese economic miracle. See A. Chen, 1999, *China's Workers Under Assault.* Armonk, NY: M. E. Sharpe.

32. See Weil, op. cit., and M. Meisner, 1996, *The Deng Xiaoping Era: An Enquiry into the Fate of Chinese Socialism, 1978–1994.* New York: Hill and Wang.

33. See Weil, op. cit., p. 29.

34. Unsafe and hazardous working conditions in the newly emerging private and foreign-owned enterprises have become a major public concern in recent years, most famously as a result of the disastrous fire in a Shenzhen toy factory that killed eighty-one workers in 1993; Guangdong Province alone reported 836 industrial accidents in 1997, a 63 percent increase over the previous year; there were a staggering 15,000 industrial deaths in total, increasing in 1993, when over a nine-month period there were 60,000 deaths, many of which are considered to have resulted from the eager pursuit of profits causing lax security and health conditions. See, for example, Weil, op. cit., pp. 16–17. Weil also observed that in a number of ways this new economic sector has become a geographical magnet for the entire country. Enterprises have been physically relocating to the areas dominated by the new sectors, especially along the golden coastline; and workers from all over the country have been streaming in to fill the jobs on the shop floors. There has also been a mental reorientation on behalf of those who have not yet relocated but who have accepted that the way of the future has been clearly indicated. Enterprises in this sector can make it on their own in the global economy, but in what must appear to be adding insult to injury they are also benefiting from the preferential

policies, especially tax breaks, that were still (until the late 1990s) being given to manufacturers in the SEZs and Open Cities. These benefits are largely unavailable to the SOEs and small collective enterprises, which, in their desire to compete, face the unsavory task of following the model established in the new sectors.

35. See, for example, T. McKinley, 1996, *The Distribution of Wealth in Rural China*. Armonk, NY: M. E. Sharpe.

36. See Riskin, op. cit.

37. See C. Bramall and M. E. Jones, 1993, "Rural Income Inequality in China Since 1978," *Journal of Peasant Studies*, Vol. 21, pp. 1–70.

38. A. R. Khan, K. Griffin, C. Riskin, and R. W. Zhao, 1992, "Household Income and Its Distribution in China," *The China Quarterly*, No. 132, pp. 1029–1061.

39. The surveys also focus only on farm households, thereby excluding those that rely almost entirely on nonfarm activities—such as household industrial production—where incomes are generally much higher. Using survey data that sample a wider range of households, there are striking differences in the estimated extent of inequality, and on balance it appears that the Chinese countryside is considerably less egalitarian than the official data suggest. See Bramall and Jones, op. cit.

40. At the provincial level statistics measuring industrial output and total output per capita (which includes agricultural, construction, and commercial output) point to an increase in equality since the reforms began in 1978. This occurred because output growth in the traditional industrial core regions was relatively slow, especially during the early reform years. This was clearly so in the three special urban municipalities (Beijing, Shanghai, and Tianjin) and in the northeastern industrial provinces (Liaoning, Heilongjiang, and Jilin), which combined represent the traditional industrial cores of China. As geographer Cindy Fan has shown, during the 1980s output trends in these regions were "converging downward" toward the national average. C. C. Fan, 1995, "Of Belts and Ladders: State Policy and Uneven Regional Development in Post-Mao China," *Annals of the Association of American Geographers*, Vol. 85, pp. 421–449. At the same time, output was increasing quite significantly in some of the northern interior provinces and ARs, such as Inner Mongolia, Gansu, Qinghai, Ningxia, and Shaanxi, as well as Hubei and in some of the booming coastal provinces (Jiangsu, Zhejiang, Fujian, and Shandong), where output

trends were converging upward. This suggests that at the provincial level, at least, China's interior regions were beginning to build up their industrial strength. See Fan, ibid., p. 429, and table 1, p. 430.

41. Output in Hunan Province, for example, was only 60 percent of the national average in 1980, but that had fallen to 55 percent by 1990 (see China Statistical Publishing House, 1994, *China Statistical Yearbook 1993*).

42. These large regional discrepancies are also evident in per capita investment rates: In the early 1990s Guizhou, with 29 percent of the national average, and Guangxi (33 percent) were again at the bottom, with Beijing (378 percent) and Shanghai (363 percent) at the top (see *China Statistical Yearbook 1993*).

43. D. Yang, 1997, *Beyond Beijing: Liberalization and the Regions in China*. London: Routledge.

44. The gap was even wider in terms of the share of industrial output: In 1981 the coast had 60 percent of the total, the interior 40 percent; in 1994 the coastal provinces had 67 percent of the total. See ibid., table 2.6, p. 35.

45. During the reform era economic policies have favored the coastal provinces because of their superior assets. In other words, they were able to cash in on their comparative advantages. After 1985 selected locations within these areas have received preferential status, which resulted in a rapid influx of domestic and foreign investment. In other words, the coastal areas have received double benefits: As well as being naturally selected by market forces, they have been favored by the government's open-door policies. The interior areas, by comparison, have been told to wait their turn and eventually it is hoped some of the enormous new wealth will start to come their way. There is some recent evidence of a diffusion of FDI into the Chinese interior, as foreign investors realize there are healthy profits to be made in such capital-starved locations, so the trickle-down is clearly under way, but it is occurring slowly and unevenly, and in the meantime the investment gap between the coast and the periphery is still wide. See ibid.

46. Yang also notes that Beijing has been pushing the regional cooperation programs, whereby rich areas team up with poorer areas to provide technical and financial support, as well as attempting to make more investment capital available through the state banks and encouraging foreign investors to consider opening up branch plants in the interior provinces. Even with the best will in the world it is difficult to imagine this policy being very successful, bearing in

mind the real economic and geographical disadvantages of the interior provinces.

47. See Yang, op. cit., p. 134.

48. See A. P. Liu, 1996, *Mass Politics in the People's Republic: State and Society in Contemporary China*. Boulder: Westview Press, esp. chap. 5, "Ethnic Separatism," pp. 189–222. Melvyn Goldstein also discusses the role of modernization in the ethnicity issue in Tibet-China relations; see M. C. Goldstein, 1997, *The Snow Lion and the Dragon: China, Tibet, and the Dalai Lama*. Berkeley: University of California Press. The interprovincial gap is even more striking when we look at the map of FDI per capita, which has been the engine of economic growth during the post-1985 reforms. As Map 8.1 shows, the majority of FDI continues to find its way into the coastal areas that have Open Cities and SEZs, with a sharp drop-off with distance from the coast. Interior provinces and ARs such as Gansu, Ningxia, Henan, Inner Mongolia, Shanxi, Guizhou, and Shaanxi all had FDI levels under 10 percent of the national average in 1990 (compared to 618 percent for Beijing, 409 percent for Shanghai, and 505 percent for Guangdong Province). For a discussion of this issue, see Fan, op. cit., table 3, p. 433.

49. World Bank (1992), op. cit., pp. 35–37.

50. Yang, op. cit.

51. Ibid., p. 160.

52. The booming economic climate in the coastal provinces has obviously not solved the problem of intraprovincial inequality completely, which is true even in Guangdong Province, which has benefited most from the new open-door policies. It is clear that sharp polarities exist between the rich and the poor areas of the province, with the poorer regions concentrated in Guangdong's mountainous northern counties. The forty-seven counties usually described as the most mountainous have 34 percent of the total population but contribute less than 10 percent of the gross value of production and only 5 percent of the basic capital investment. See E. Vogel, 1989, *One Step Ahead in China: Guangdong Province Under Reform*. Cambridge: Harvard University Press. A recent analysis of intraprovincial inequality in the more prosperous parts of China concluded that in a number of regions, Guangdong particularly, spatial inequality increased significantly during the reform era, largely as a result of the uneven penetration of FDI. See Fan, op. cit., pp. 434–442.

53. Khan et al., op. cit.

54. Khan and Riskin, op. cit., p. 238.

55. Ibid., p. 246.

56. See S. G. Wang and A. G. Hu, 1999, *The Political Economy of Uneven Development*. Armonk, NY: M. E. Sharpe, p. 201.

57. In fact, as the World Bank has noted, "In China the gulf between rural and urban residents explains 60 percent of the overall income inequality." See World Bank, 1997, *China 2000: Development Challenges in the New Century*. Washington, DC: World Bank, p. 8.

58. See Bramall and Jones, op. cit. The official statistics indicate that the share of rural income earned in nonagricultural production increased from less than 10 percent in 1978 to 44.5 percent in 1992. As a result of the reforms the production process in many of China's rural areas is being dramatically restructured. In 1978 almost 70 percent of the total value of production in rural areas came from agriculture, with less than 20 percent coming from industry. By 1992 the industrial portion had risen to 50 percent and the agricultural portion had shrunk to half of its earlier share. The official data also show that working in nonfarming pursuits is considerably more remunerative than working on the land; in fact wages in industry and construction jobs are more than 50 percent higher than in agriculture.

59. As we saw in Chapter 7, agricultural reform in the post-Mao era brought relative prosperity to many poor households, especially in the early 1980s. Although some people feared that would result in larger gaps between the rich and the poor households, the evidence suggests otherwise: In fact a survey conducted in 1984 showed that inequality fell during the period 1978–1984 but began to increase again after 1984.

60. Data provided by the Chinese State Statistical Bureau; see *China Statistical Yearbook 1993* and *1997*.

61. It is evident, for example, that the incentives provided by agrarian reform contradicted some of the other policies that were important components of China's modernization drive. For example, the financial gains to be realized in sideline enterprises and rural industries encouraged many peasant families to allow children to drop out of school and enter the labor force as soon as possible, thereby rejecting the nationwide call to emphasize higher education and the development of human capital. This and other issues are discussed by J.S.S. Muldavin, 1996, "The Political Ecology of Agrarian Reform in China," pp. 227–259 in R. Peet and M. Watts (eds.), *Liberation Ecologies: Environment, Development, Social Movements*. London: Routledge. The reforms in the countryside also encouraged many families to ignore

the birth control policies in their desire for extra family income (see Chapter 5). Perhaps the most threatening aspect of the agricultural boom was the cutback that occurred in investments in agricultural infrastructure, a trend that was accelerated by the demise of the collectives. According to Mark Selden the government cutback in agricultural investment came in response to the threat of alienating urban workers, who were seeing the advantages of the countryside stacking up against them. The state was afraid of creating or exacerbating a politically explosive situation in which workers and intellectuals might unite to demand political reforms, along the lines of the Solidarity movement in Poland (Selden, op. cit., p. 180). It is clear that in the reform era nobody, including the state, has shown great enthusiasm for investing in agriculture, and the enormous infrastructural gains made during the collectivization years—terracing, irrigation networks, and the economies of large-scale farming—were negated during the rush to privatize the countryside. What was involved here has been described as the exploitation, plunder, and "mining" of what had been communal capital, mainly for private gain. See Muldavin, op. cit. (1996).

62. World Bank (1992), op cit., annex 1, p. 142, and table 2.2, p. 37.

63. These areas are also likely to have a higher-than-average proportion of minority people and are more likely to have households disadvantaged by lack of education, illiteracy, ill health, and other disabilities. In Yunnan Province, for example, 9.4 million of the 11.4 million minority people lived in households with incomes below Y120 per year, compared to only 8.4 percent of the Han population. Similar evidence is available elsewhere; for example, the dominant ethnic group in any province or municipality tends to be overrepresented in the poverty statistics. Thus in Beijing 30 percent of the Hui and 36 percent of the Manchu people were in the lowest 10 percent of the population in terms of income; in Guangdong this was the case for 48 percent of the Li people; and in Liaoning 18 percent of the Manchu and 23 percent of the Mongol people were in this category. See World Bank (1992), op. cit., p. 44. A book recently published by two Chinese scholars has focused on the east-west divide in terms of incomes and human well-being, and the authors have concluded that much of the lack of economic development and failure to exploit local natural resources results from the inferior "quality of human resources," which inhibits the development of a viable commodity economy; in fact the problem is worse than it appears from the usual economic indicators (e.g., output value) because many of these regions are propped up by government aid and imports from the coastal regions, which mask the inferiority of their infrastructures and the marked weakness of their local economic systems. See X. Q. Wang and N. F. Bai, 1991, *The Poverty of Plenty.* London: Macmillan. It is noted in the preface that focusing on the poor quality of human resources is a thinly masked version of Han chauvinism, because many of the poorest areas are dominated by China's minority peoples.

64. See World Bank (1992), op. cit., pp. 72–79. The report focused on three typically poor counties in the loess plateau region in northwest China. This region suffers greatly from fragile and degraded soils, steep slopes, and erratic and insufficient rainfall. Many communities suffered greatly during the Maoist era of grain self-sufficiency, when local farmers were required to switch from pastoralism to grain-growing, with disastrous consequences for the land and its carrying capacity. Although the amount of land per person in all three counties is far greater than the national average, the irrigation capacity is limited. As a result, multiple cropping is rare, and the application of fertilizer is low. Not surprisingly, output is constrained, which means that incomes are low (less than 50 percent of the national average). Significant land rehabilitation programs are under way, and attempts are being made to terrace the land, to transfer land over to pasture plants, to plant trees and shrubs to prevent erosion, and to import improved agricultural technology, including new fertilizers, improved crop strains, and more efficient water conservation methods. As the report indicated, such efforts have started to show some local successes, but even with the rehabilitation programs it is recognized that many residents in the most constrained areas will need to be resettled. By 1990 320,000 upland farmers from the region had been moved to newly irrigated lands in adjacent regions; in Ningxia Hui Autonomous Region it is estimated that about 200,000 people have been relocated in similar resettlement schemes. Surveys indicate that many of them are content with the move and have no plans to return because they are now earning up to three times as much as they did before.

65. Wang and Bai, op. cit., p. 44. Zhu Ling and Jiang Zhongyi have also documented some of the poverty alleviation programs in China's poorest regions, focusing on what they describe as *yigong-*

daizhen programs that are intended to create the conditions for economic growth rather than simply offering relief from poverty. See L. Zhu and Z. G. Jiang, 1996, *Public Works and Poverty Alleviation in Rural China*. New York: Nova Science Publishers.

66. Wang and Bai, op. cit., p. 49.

67. Ibid.

68. In fact both groups could be made up of peasant entrepreneurs, an argument that is made most persuasively by Kate Zhou, 1996, *How the Farmers Changed China: Power of the People*. Boulder: Westview Press.

69. As Elisabeth Croll observed, the highest rural income earners are usually well connected to the world outside the village. They are, in other words, individuals in a position "to cultivate relations and alliances outside of the village which gave them privileged access to raw materials, markets, and market information." See Croll, op. cit., p. 176. Another group of successful households is described by Croll as "aggregate families." They may be composed of several separate households, usually consisting of brothers, fathers' brothers, and fathers' brothers' sons; in other words, households dominated by males descending from a common antecedent. Such households have been able to operate in a collective and mutually reinforcing manner during the reform era by pooling resources, sharing labor, and helping out poorer relatives.

70. Ibid., pp. 172–177, "Inter-Household Relations."

71. Discussions of the characteristics of peasants who have become rich, either through sideline activities or new business enterprises, are provided by D. R. Kelliher, 1992, *Peasant Power in China*. New Haven: Yale University Press, and O. Odgaard, 1992, *Private Enterprises in Rural China*. Aldershot, UK: Avebury Press.

72. In 1988, for example, it was estimated that nonagricultural activities were four times more profitable than grain farming on a per day–per laborer basis.

73. The data collected in a rural survey in the mid-1980s demonstrate, for example, that only 20 percent of the total income of the richer specialized households was derived from field cultivation, compared to 67 percent for the households classified as poor; see Croll, op. cit.

74. As the data reported in Bramall and Jones, op. cit., demonstrate, there is a significant inequality in the four provinces, as measured by the coefficient of variation; it is also clear that inequality was

increasing throughout the 1980s. See pp. 58–65. For purposes of illustrating the differences between provinces, two prosperous (in aggregate terms) provinces were also selected, Guangdong and Jiangsu; one that was middle-ranking, Anhui; and one that was extremely poor, Guizhou. The study looked at the per capita value of agricultural and industrial production and estimated the net domestic material product as a proxy for GDP (which does not suffer from the limitations of the official survey data published by the State Statistical Board and the Ministry of Agriculture).

75. Croll, op. cit., pp. 141–142, 164.

76. Bramall and Jones, op. cit.

77. Ibid., p. 64.

78. See Wang and Hu, op. cit., esp. chap. 3, "Changes in Regional Disparity Since 1978," pp. 41–77.

79. Ibid.

80. These issues are discussed in detail in S. Rozelle, 1994, "Rural Industrialization and Increasing Inequality: Emerging Patterns in China's Reforming Economy," *Journal of Comparative Economics*, Vol. 19, pp. 362–391. See also Wang and Hu, op. cit., chap. 7, "Confronting Inequality in China," pp. 199–219.

81. See World Bank (1992), op. cit.; Wang and Bai, op. cit.; and Croll, op. cit.

82. See, for example, R. Peet and M. Watts, 1993, "Introduction: Development Theory and Environment in an Age of Market Triumphalism," *Economic Geography*, Vol. 69, No. 3 (July), pp. 227–253. In socialist societies the harsh effects of these inequalities should have been ameliorated by social planning and human resources development. This was certainly the expectation in China during the Maoist era, although the actual achievements may have been considerably less than was originally claimed; see Riskin, op. cit.; Griffin and Knight, op. cit.; and Wang and Hu, op. cit.

83. Although, as noted earlier, this is likely to increase income inequality even further. Another option is for the state to change the structure and composition of its social programs. In the health and education fields, for example, that could be done by switching resources away from such facilities as urban hospitals and universities and toward primary health care and education in rural areas. The recent evidence is not encouraging; in fact there are reports that the gap between urban and rural areas in health and education expenditures is increasing, with the poorest parts of the countryside

being especially hard-hit. In their 1999 book, Wang and Hu, op. cit., argue that although increasing inequality is normal during rapid economic development, it is not inevitable, and it can be reversed or ameliorated. In chapter 7 (see pp. 212–217), they recommend the following policies: redressing coastal bias, which they describe as "morally outrageous"; rebuilding a system of interregional fiscal tranfers; eradicating poverty; ensuring a minimum level of essential public services; improving infrastructure in poor regions; and facilitating "factor mobility." As they note, "The pith and marrow of the above proposals can be summarized in one word: *empowerment*. . . . The emphasis should be on enhancing the long-term development capabilities of backward regions . . . by pushing and pulling production factors into areas where they can be more fully and efficiently utilized."

84. See Amartya K. Sen, 1999, *Development as Freedom*. New York: Alfred A. Knopf. Human development programs tend to reproduce and sometimes even exacerbate existing inequalities. There are a number of possible causes. One is the often reported "urban bias" in the provision of services, which in China is especially prominent in health care and education. It is also possible that the intended recipients fail to make adequate use of the services provided due to cultural, geographical, or social reasons. This may be the case for women in China, who are unable to participate in human development programs that are provided for their benefit. In this case it is imperative that the government pays close attention to reports of discrimination against women and children in the workplace and in society at large. Legislation exists in China to protect vulnerable populations, but the means and determination to enforce the law are often missing at the local level.

85. See, for example, A. K. Sen, 1984, *Resources, Values, and Development*. Cambridge: Harvard University Press; for a more specific emphasis on China, see A. K. Sen, 1989, "Food and Freedom," *World Development*, Vol. 17, No. 6, pp. 769–781, as well as A. K. Sen, 1990, "More Than 100 Million Women Are Missing," *New York Review of Books*, Vol. 37 (December 20), pp. 61–66.

86. The potential role of out-migration in the reduction of poverty in China is discussed by P. Nolan, 1993, "Economic Reform, Poverty, and Migration in China," *Economic and Political Weekly*, Vol. 28 (June 26), pp. 1369–1377. See also Chapter 15 in this book.

Chapter 11

1. Willem van Kemenade, 1997, *China, Hong Kong, Taiwan, Inc.: The Dynamics of a New Empire*. New York: Alfred A. Knopf, p. 159.

2. It is important to mention Macao here, the Portuguese colony that is being handed back to China in 1999. Although we shall not focus on Macao at all here, the reader is advised to look at Jonathan Porter, 1996, *Macao: The Imaginary City: Culture and Society, 1557 to the Present*. Boulder: Westview Press.

3. This issue is discussed in more detail in Chapter 17. The emergence of the Greater China region is discussed more fully in R. Jones, R. King, and M. Klein (eds.), 1992, *The Chinese Economic Area: Economic Integration Without a Free Trade Agreement* (Paris: Organization for Economic Cooperation and Development). The phrase "Greater China" has been used frequently in journalistic reports of the recent developments, as well as in some other accounts. See, for example, W. H. Overholt, 1993, *The Rise of China: How Economic Reform Is Creating a New Superpower* (New York: W. W. Norton), esp. pp. 183–247, 326–332; and O. Schell, 1994, *Mandate of Heaven: A New Generation of Entrepreneurs, Dissidents,* *Bohemians, and Technocrats Lays Claim to China's Future*. New York: Simon and Schuster, esp. chap. 30, "Greater China," pp. 331–340. It has been estimated that by the year 2000 Greater China's collective domestic product will surpass that of the United States (Schell, p. 333).

4. See Jones et al., op. cit., p. 5; also *Far Eastern Economic Review*, "Southern Cooking: Coasts' Hot Economies Find Centre Distasteful," May 25, 1995, pp. 22–24.

5. George C.S. Lin, 1997, *Red Capitalism: Growth and Development of the Pearl River Delta*. Vancouver: University of British Columbia Press, esp. chap. 8, "Influence of Hong Kong," pp. 148–169.

6. For an excellent review of the role of the developmentalist state in in both Hong Kong and Taiwan (as well as the other Asian NIEs), see Manuel Castells, 1998, *The Information Age: Economy, Society, and Culture*. Vol. 3: *End of Millennium*. Oxford: Blackwell. Castells uses the term "developmentalist" to describe societies (like Taiwan and Hong Kong) where a clear decision has been made by the state to pursue rapid economic development and where the

success of such development serves as the primary indicator of its own legitimacy.

7. N. D. Kristoff, "A Dictatorship That Grew Up," *New York Times Magazine,* February 16, 1992, sec. 6, pp. 16–21, 53–57. For detailed discussions of the democratization process, see T. B. Gold, 1994, "Civil Society and Taiwan's Quest for Identity," pp. 47–68 in S. Harrell and C. C. Huang (eds.), *Cultural Change in Postwar Taiwan.* Boulder: Westview Press. For a more comprehensive treatment of this topic, see J. J. Wu, 1995, *Taiwan's Democratization: Forces Behind the New Momentum.* Hong Kong: Oxford University Press; and also E. A. Feigenbaum, 1995, *Change in Taiwan and Potential Adversity in the Strait.* Santa Monica, CA: RAND Institute/National Defense Research Institute.

8. As a simple model of reality, the illustration requires the suspension of real-life complexity, as well as the changing situations in the economies in question. Hong Kong, for example, has been moving closer to state control and ownership of some of the means of production and is likely to move even farther in that direction, following its return to Chinese sovereignty in 1997. The opposite has been happening in Taiwan, however, with greater market control of its economy in the late 1980s and 1990s. As we have already seen, the situation in contemporary China has also been changing rapidly, as the state sector shrinks in face of growing competition from private and foreign ownership, particularly in the coastal provinces. This framework is based on that described by Y. S. Wu, 1994, *Comparative Economic Transformations: Mainland China, Hungary, the Soviet Union, and Taiwan.* Stanford: Stanford University Press, esp. chap. 1, "Introduction," pp. 1–16, and chap. 5, "The ROC and the PRC," pp. 139–197. For more discussion of the different roles of the state in Taiwan and Hong Kong, in comparison to those in the PRC, see Castells's *End of Millennium,* op. cit., chap. 4, pp. 206–309.

9. Deng Xiaoping, "Message to Compatriots in Taiwan," *Beijing Review,* January 5, 1979, p. 16. For a simplified and extremely PRC-focused view of the Taiwan situation, see *China in Focus,* 1987, *The Taiwan Issue: Its History and Resolution.* Beijing: Beijing Review Publications, esp. "Taiwan: Prospects for Reunification," pp. 42–50.

10. Yu-Ming Shaw, 1985, "Taiwan: A View from Taipei," *Foreign Affairs,* Vol. 63, No. 5 (Summer), pp. 1053–1054.

11. The poem is attributed to Yu Youren; see *China in Focus,* op. cit., p. 54.

12. This was the National People's Congress Standing Committee's 1979 "Message to Compatriots in Taiwan," reprinted in ibid., pp. 93–99.

13. For a discussion of Taiwan's dilemma, see H. H. Wu, 1994, *Bridging the Strait: Taiwan, China, and the Prospects for Reunification.* Hong Kong: Oxford University Press, esp. pp. 65–73. For a discussion focusing more on the issues associated with democratization in both Taiwan and China, see Bruce J. Dickson, *Democratization in China and Taiwan: The Adaptability of Leninist Parties.* Oxford, UK: Clarendon Press.

14. Quoted in *Far Eastern Economic Review,* June 22, 1995, p. 17.

15. Throughout the early 1990s the evidence suggested that only one political party in Taiwan (the DPP) made the independence issue an explicit part of its agenda, which would probably provoke China into a threatening stance. In fact such an outcome seems unlikely at the end of the decade because of the perceived danger of the threat, bearing in mind the strength of the Chinese military. Only full control by the DPP of both the executive and legislative branches of the government would make an independence declaration compelling, but as opinion polls have shown, the public considers it too great a risk to even consider declaring independence. For example, polls conducted from 1989 through 1993 show that only between 12 and 24 percent of the population polled approves of the independence issue. See table 3 in Feigenbaum, op. cit., p. 39. The drift away from KMT dominance in Taiwan politics was evident in the December 1992 election, in which nearly a third of the seats in the legislature were occupied by opposition members. The KMT won merely 53 percent of the popular vote, the lowest ever recorded, whereas the DPP won 31 percent of the vote and controlled fifty-one seats of the 161-member parliament. In the middle of 1992 a KMT stronghold in Penghu (the Pescadore Islands) was won by the DPP. See Far Eastern Economic Review, 1994, *Asia 1994 Yearbook.* Hong Kong: Far Eastern Economic Review, "Taiwan," pp. 207–213. On the issue of independence for Taiwan, see P. Ferdinand, 1996, *Take-off for Taiwan?* Chatham House Papers, The Royal Institute of International Affairs. London: Pinter.

16. The most significant and dangerous example of this occurred in the summer of 1999, when President Lee Teng-hui publicly stated that Taiwan and the Chinese mainland have a "special state-to-state relationship." This remark (made on June 9) natu-

rally infuriated the Beijing government. See the lead article by Myra Lu in *Free China Journal*, "ROC Emphasizes No Change to Its Mainland Policy," Vol. 16, No. 28, July 16, 1999, p. 1. In the ensuing war of words, Taipei maintained a hard-line stance, and on August 2, for example, Sheu-Ke-Sheng, chairman of the Mainland Affairs Council, noted that Taiwan "cannot accept mainland China's hegemonic version of the 'one-China' concept"; see Frank Chang, 1999, "ROC Reiterates Its Position on Relations with Mainland," *Free China Journal*, Vol. 16, No. 31, p. 1.

17. NPC Standing Committee, op. cit., p. 94.

18. Quoted in H. H. Wu, op. cit., p. 65.

19. These statistics are taken from ibid., p. 67. For substantive discussions of the so-called Taiwan economic miracle, see T. B. Gold, 1986, *State and Society in the Taiwan Miracle*. Armonk, NY: M. E. Sharpe; see also S.W.Y. Yuo, G. Ranis, and J.C.H. Fei, 1981, *The Taiwan Success Story: Rapid Growth with Improved Distribution in the Republic of China, 1952–1979*. Boulder: Westview Press; D. F. Simon and M.Y.M. Kau (eds.), 1992, *Taiwan: Beyond the Economic Miracle*. Armonk, NY: M. E. Sharpe; and Yu-ming Shaw, 1988, *Beyond the Economic Miracle: Reflections on the Developmental Experience of the Republic of China on Taiwan*. Taipei: Kwang Hwon.

20. See Kuo, Ranis, and Fei, op. cit., pp. 33–35. It has been observed that after further reductions in the income gap in the early 1980s the switchover from labor-intensive to capital-intensive industries has produced a widening, from 4.33:1 in 1981 to 4.73:1 in 1988. This issue is discussed at length in the chapter on Taiwan in W. Bello and S. Rosenfeld, 1990, *Dragons in Distress: Asia's Miracle Economies in Crisis*. San Francisco: Institute for Food and Development Policy, pt. 2, "Taiwan in Trouble," pp. 175–286. See also R. G. Sutter, 1988, *Taiwan: Entering the 21st Century*. Lanham, MD: University Press of America for the Asia Society; and S. Ogden (ed.), 1993, *China*, 5th ed. Guilford, CT: Dushkin Publishing Group, Global Studies Series, "Taiwan: A Dynamo in East Asia," pp. 48–71.

21. See R. E. Barrett and M. K. Whyte, 1982, "Dependency Theory and Taiwan: Analysis of a Deviant Case," *American Journal of Sociology*, Vol. 87, No. 5, pp. 1064–1089.

22. Quoted in H. H. Wu, op. cit., p. 69. The unique features of Taiwan's pattern of economic development are also discussed by A. Leonard, "Taiwan Goes Its Own Third Way," *The Nation*, April 13, 1992, pp. 482–484.

23. See *Questions and Answers About the Republic of China*, 1987. Taipei: Kwang Hwo Publishing Co., p. 13.

24. Taiwan was formerly known as Formosa, the name given to it by the Portuguese. In fact the island has had many different names throughout history. During the Warring States period (475–221 B.C.) it was called Daoyi; during the Han Dynasty (206 B.C.–A.D. 220) it was Dongjun; during the Three Kingdoms Period (A.D. 220–280) it was Yizhou; and during the Sui and Tang Dynasties (until A.D. 907) it was called Liuqia. The name Taiwan was first used during the Ming Dynasty (A.D. 1368–1644). China's administration of the island began more than 1,700 years ago, when the Three Kingdoms' emperor sent an exploratory force of 10,000 men to Taiwan in A.D. 230. Military forays were repeated in later centuries, but it was not until the Tang and Song Dynasty periods that people began to emigrate from the mainland, mostly from Guangdong and Fujian Provinces, to Taiwan and the offshore islands known as Penghu (renamed by the Portuguese as the Pescadore Islands). The island was "discovered" by the Portuguese in 1590, and Dutch as well as Spanish settlers followed. Most of the current inhabitants (with the aboriginals numbering less than 350,000, mostly pushed into the remote mountain areas and offshore islands) are descendants of the south coast (mainland) emigrants, who, although they originated in China, are usually referred to as "Taiwanese," as distinct from the "Mainlanders," who make up fewer than 20 percent of the population but who have dominated the political system until recent years. See J. J. Wu, op. cit. The Manchus from the north overthrew the Ming Dynasty rulers in Taiwan in 1568, but little formal government authority was exerted over the island, which remained largely underdeveloped. After the Chinese defeat in the Sino-Japanese War (1894–1895) the Manchus were forced to cede Taiwan to the Japanese, who remained until 1945. The Japanese kept Taiwan as a colony, but during that time they built up the country's agricultural system and laid the foundations of its modern transportation system and the rudiments of an industrial infrastructure—all of which were greatly beneficial to economic development in the post-1949 period. Chiang Kai-shek set up his government-in-exile in 1949, with full support from the U.S. government, which was deeply distrustful of the new communist regime on the mainland. For a more detailed discussion of these events, see Ogden, op. cit., esp. pp. 48–51; and H. H. Wu, op. cit., pp. 64–65. A useful brief discussion of the history and settlement of Taiwan is also provided in a Taiwan document entitled *The Republic of China Yearbook, 1995*. Taipei: Gov-

ernment Information Office, esp. chap. 3, "People,"
pp. 29–41.

25. This argument is developed more fully by Y. S.
Wu, op. cit., esp. chap. 5, "The ROC and the PRC,"
pp. 139–197. See also Dickson, op. cit.

26. The 2–2–8 Incident, its causes, and its aftermath have been described in detail in a book published in 1991 by Ramon Myers, an American scholar
at the Hoover Institution, with two Taiwanese scholars. See T. H. Lai, R. H. Myers, and W. Wei, 1991, *A
Tragic Beginning: The Taiwan Uprising of February
28, 1947.* Stanford: Stanford University Press. The
only other book written about the incident (in
English) is G. Kerr, 1965, *Formosa Betrayed.* Boston:
Houghton Mifflin. Both books agree that the KMT
was largely responsible for the incident, but Myers
and his colleagues put to rest the (unfounded) claim
that the Communists instigated the uprising. See, for
example, the reviews of the book, including P.
Mooney, "Taiwan Temporized," *Far Eastern Economic
Review,* February 27, 1992, pp. 50–51; and in the
same issue J. Baum, "Look Back in Anger," pp. 48–49;
see also J. Baum, "Unfinished Business: KMT Still
Evasive over Role in 1947 Massacre," *Far Eastern Economic Review,* March 19, 1992, pp. 30–31.

27. Y. S. Wu, op. cit., p. 162.

28. Y. S. Wu has noted that between 1951 and 1965
the United States provided more than $4 billion in
grants, loans, and military equipment, the nonmili-
tary share of which amounted to 6 percent of Taiwan's GNP and was able to finance about 40 percent
of the country's investments and imports during that
period. See ibid., p. 164.

29. See Kuo, Ranis, and Fei, op. cit., p. 60. By 1964
more than 60 percent of Taiwan's manufacturing
production was in privately owned enterprises (table
38, pp. 60–61).

30. Y. S. Wu, op. cit., p. 167.

31. In spite of the rapid growth of the import-
substitution industries, Taiwan's trade deficit
remained burdensome, at about 5 percent of total
GDP in the 1950s, mainly because of the continued
need to import capital and intermediate (nonfin-
ished) goods and raw materials. Taiwan's primary
export products (rice and sugar, 70 percent of total
exports in 1958) could not be expanded as a result of
international quotas and land constraints as the
cities increasingly encroached on the rural areas. In
this sense the expansion of the export-oriented sector was a structural necessity, prompted by the small
size of the domestic market (small in terms of population numbers and low incomes for consumption).

Taiwan's economic planners saw no alternative but to
enter the world of exports, even though that meant
they would be gradually less and less able to direct
and control the market, as they were able to do at
home. See Y. S. Wu, op. cit., pp. 169–170. Wu notes
that Taiwan rejected the strategy of secondary
import substitution (domestic production of previously imported capital goods such as consumer
durables and the processing of intermediate goods)
that had been followed in other developing countries, largely because of the lack of expandable primary exports and the small size of the domestic
market (p. 170). In addition, Taiwan in the late 1950s
had a labor surplus, produced by high population
growth and its successful land reform process that
released people from the need to work on the land.
The expansion of labor-intensive industrialization,
geared mainly to export goods, was intended to solve
an already existing unemployment problem (p. 171);
see also Kuo, Ranis, and Fei, op. cit.

32. For details, see Kuo, Ranis, and Fei, op. cit.,
esp. chap. 4, "Economic Policies in the 1960s," pp.
73–83. Kuo et al. show that the structure of Taiwan's
exports changed considerably during this period. For
example, in 1953 exports were dominated by pro-
cessed agricultural products (78 percent of the total
value), with industrial products making up only 8
percent. By 1979, industrial products were 91 percent
of Taiwan's exports, agricultural products only 9 percent (fig. 2.8, p. 24).

33. Ibid., pp. 144–145. It is important to point out
that the export-oriented push was accelerated in
1966 with the creation of the first Taiwan export-
processing zone (EPZ) in the southern port of Kaoh-
siung, which has subsequently become the world's
third busiest port; see Leonard, op. cit., p. 484, and
H. S. Wu, op. cit., pp. 192–195. In the EPZs the state
manipulated all the economic levers by providing
lower tax rates, duty-free imports, and the like to
assure private entrepreneurs, both domestic and foreign, that they would make huge profits. They carefully selected the best types of industries and took
pains to ensure that no portion of the production
output was sold domestically (with high walls,
watchtowers, and police patrols). This was another
clear-cut example of state, or developmental, capitalism, in that, as H. S. Wu notes, "the State set profit
parameters and directed private enterprises toward
targetted industries and markets" (p. 104). It is interesting to observe that when the mainland began its
experiments with special economic zones, they were
modeled largely after Taiwan's EPZs. The Chinese

were copying the practices of state capitalism, Taiwan-style, rather than laissez-faire capitalism, Hong Kong–style. H. S. Wu, op. cit., p. 194.

34. As the data in Table 11.2 illustrate, Taiwan's income distribution compares favorably with many other developing countries, particularly those with low incomes that are embarking on economic development strategies. As the data show, the ratio of the richest to the poorest categories fell through the 1960s and 1970s but increased slightly during the 1980s. Comparing the top and bottom 20 percent income groups, for example, the ratio in Taiwan increased from 4.18 in 1978 to 4.60 in 1986 (8.9 percent lowest, 37.2 percent highest in 1978; and 8.3 percent lowest, 38.2 percent highest in 1986). It has been suggested that this was the inevitable result of economic success, which had allowed the emergence of a new category of the super-rich in Taiwan, with a resulting decline in income equality.

35. See Kuo et al., op. cit., p. 146.

36. See Leonard, op. cit., p. 484. The shift to high-tech industry in Taiwan is also discussed by Bello and Rosenfeld, op. cit., pp. 251–277, 279–285. The data on automation in the 1980s are provided by C. Schive, 1992, "Taiwan's Emerging Position in the International Division of Labor," pp. 101–121 in D. F. Simon and M.Y.M. Kau (eds.), *Taiwan: Beyond the Economic Miracle.* (Armonk, NY: M. E. Sharpe). In the Simon and Kau edited volume there is also a useful discussion of the problems and prospects facing Taiwan in the area of high technology and R & D systems. See D. F. Simon, "Taiwan's Emerging Technological Trajectory: Creating New Forms of Competitive Advantage," pp. 123–147.

37. See R. M. Selya, 1995, *Taipei.* New York: John Wiley and Sons, esp. chap. 1, "From Colonial Backwater to World City," pp. 1–18.

38. See ibid., pp. 14–16; and Bello and Rosenfeld, op. cit., esp. chap. 12, "The Making of an Environmental Nightmare," pp. 195–214.

39. J. F. Williams, 1992, "Environmentalism in Taiwan," pp. 187–210 in Simon and Kau, op. cit.

40. "Privatizing by the Year 2000," *Free China Journal,* November 2, 1989, quoted in ibid., p. 207.

41. Steering Committee for the Taiwan 2000 Study (ed.), 1989, *Taiwan 2000: Balancing Economic Growth and Environmental Protection.* Taipei: Institute of Ethnology, Academia Sinica, p. 40.

42. See Williams, op. cit., and Bello and Rosenfeld, op. cit.

43. A quote attributed to Hsu Shen-Shu, founder of the New Housewives Association, one of the grass-

roots organization attempting to link the emerging feminist and environmentalist movements in Taiwan. See L. A. Simpson, 1988, "Shu Shen-Shu of the NEHA," *Bang,* March 1988, p. 10, Quoted in Bello and Rosenfield, op. cit., p. 214.

44. Gold's 1986 book, *State and Society in the Taiwan Miracle,* emphasized the role of the state in Taiwan's early development after 1950, but in a later publication he looks at some of the recent changes and the emergence of what he refers to as "hegemonic challenges in the form of . . . new political parties, social movements and a quest for identity." See T. B. Gold, 1994, "Civil Society and Taiwan's Quest for Identity," pp. 47–68 in S. Harrell and C. C. Huang (eds.), *Cultural Change in Postwar Taiwan.* Boulder: Westview Press. Robert Marsh has also documented some of this in R. Marsh, 1996, *The Great Transformation: Social Change in Taipei, Taiwan, Since the 1960s.* Armonk, NY: M. E. Sharpe.

45. Gold (1994), op. cit., p. 66.

46. Ibid., p. 64. It is likely that this new feeling is in part, at least, what President Lee Teng-hui has in mind when he describes his idea of the "New Taiwanese," who are "his fellow citizens who are willing to fight for the prosperity and survival of their country." See Allen Pun, 1999, "Lee Explains That Taiwan's Interest Must Be Foremost," *Free China Journal,* Vol. 16, No. 43, p. 1.

47. "Don't Tread on Me: China's Bullying Brings out Steel in Taiwanese," *Far Eastern Economic Review,* September 14, 1995, pp. 22–23. For a well-reasoned account of Taiwan-PRC relationships, see Tse-Kang Leng, 1996, *The Taiwan-China Connection: Democracy and Development Across the Taiwan Straits.* Boulder: Westview Press.

48. J. Baum. "Frankly Speaking: Pragmatism Increasingly Determines China Policy," *Far Eastern Economic Review,* June 15, 1995, p. 24.

49. J. Baum. "Lee's Challenge," *Far Eastern Economic Review,* September 14, 1995, pp. 20–22.

50. A quote from Vincent Siew, chair of Taiwan's cabinet-level Mainland Affairs Council; see ibid., p. 22.

51. J. Baum, "Up and Running," *Far Eastern Economic Review,* September 7, 1995, pp. 14–15. The complexities of the reunification issue and some of the obstacles (perceived and real) on both sides are discussed by H. H. Wu, op. cit.

52. See N. Chanda, "Winds of Change," *Far Eastern Economic Review,* June 22, 1995, pp. 14–16. Taiwan's international success in the Lee Teng-hui issue was matched by a humiliating defeat in another

realm of global politics, when the bid to host the 2002 Asian Games was rejected, largely, it was suggested, as a result of member nations' refusal to antagonize Beijing by voting in favor of Taiwan. See J. Baum, "Journey to the West," *Far Eastern Economic Review,* June 8, 1995, p. 16. In spite of the continued bad feeling and negative rhetoric between the two sides, the United States successfully negotiated a major trade agreement with China in November 1999, which was interpreted at the time as a success for President Clinton in face of the anti-China sentiments in Congress.

53. Ibid.

54. The poem is reproduced in *The Other Hong Kong Report* (1993) published by the Chinese University Press. See "Introduction," by Choi Po-king, p. xxiii. The economic development of Hong Kong (and Taiwan) is discussed in all of the growing number of books written about, and comparing the causes and consequences of, economic growth in the newly industrialized countries. Among the most useful of these works are Bello and Rosenfeld, op. cit.; A. Chowdhury and I. Islam, 1993, *The Newly Industrializing Economies of East Asia.* New York: Routledge; S. Chan, 1990, *East Asian Dynamism: Growth, Order, and Security in the Pacific Region.* Boulder: Westview Press; S. M. Goldstein (ed.), 1991, *Mini-Dragons: Fragile Economic Miracles in the Pacific.* Boulder: Westview Press; H. C. Tai (ed.), 1989, *Confucianism and Economic Development: An Oriental Alternative?* Washington, DC: Washington Institute Press; R. Wade, 1990, *Pathways to the Periphery: The Politics of Growth in the Newly Industrializing Countries.* Ithaca: Cornell University Press; and A. Dirlik (ed.), 1993, *What Is in a Rim? Critical Perspectives on the Pacific Region Idea.* Boulder: Westview Press. For straightforward introductions to the region and the trajectory of development over the past decade, see R. Hodder, 1992, *The West Pacific Rim: An Introduction.* London: Belhaven Press; G. P. Chapman and K. M. Baker, 1992, *The Changing Geography of Asia.* London: Routledge; and R. Elegant, 1990, *Pacific Destiny: The Rise of the East.* London: Headline Books. In a more journalistic style, see S. Winchester, 1991, *Pacific Rising: The Emergence of a New World Culture.* New York: Prentice-Hall. Another book dealing with the NIEs, China, and Japan, with a very useful accompanying video series, is M. Borthwick, 1992, *The Pacific Century: The Emergence of Modern Pacific Asia.* Boulder: Westview Press. From a reading of this literature it is important to point out some of the most obvious and significant differences between

Hong Kong and the other NIEs. One obvious factor is that unlike administrations in Taiwan, South Korea, and Singapore, Hong Kong's government has not had to allocate a large proportion of its overall revenues to the defense budget. Another obvious difference is that the Hong Kong government has not attempted to intervene by identifying the strategic high-tech industries on which to base future economic development, largely the case in Taiwan, South Korea, and Singapore. The Hong Kong model has been to stick with its own comparative advantage, which has been in labor-intensive industry (much of which has now largely shifted to the mainland) and in the financial services sector, the consumption industry, shipping, and tourism—all of which have been highly lucrative for the colony.

55. J. Morris, 1988, *Hong Kong.* New York: Random House, p. 8.

56. The history of Hong Kong has been told many times, but two recent books stand out as among the best and most readable: F. Welsh, 1994, *A Borrowed Place: The History of Hong Kong.* Hong Kong: Kodansha; and Jan Morris, op. cit.

57. P. Theroux, 1988, *Riding the Iron Rooster: By Train Through China.* New York: Ivy Books.

58. To provide a North American analogy, Hong Kong can be compared to Puerto Rico, which became an American colony in the same year the New Territories were ceded to Britain. On most of the traditional quality-of-life indicators, Hong Kong would be rated far higher than Puerto Rico. Infant mortality is much lower and life expectancy much higher in Hong Kong; crime is significantly lower; literacy is almost universal; and the quality of public transportation is far superior. J. Mirsky, "The Battle for Hong Kong," *New York Review of Books,* April 7, 1994, pp. 16–20. The comparison with Puerto Rico is made by Welsh, op. cit. See also R. Terrill, 1991, "Hong Kong: Countdown to 1997," *National Geographic* (February), pp. 101–139.

59. For a detailed account of this period, see J. P. Burns, 1991, "Hong Kong: Diminishing Laissez-Faire," pp. 104–143 in Goldstein, op. cit. A valuable study of Hong Kong was also conducted by the Economist Intelligence Unit and published in 1990 under the title *Hong Kong to 1994: A Question of Confidence,* by Ken Davies, Special Report No. 2022. London: Economist Intelligence Unit; see esp. chap. 3, "The Hong Kong Economy Since 1984," and chap. 2, "The Industrial Revolution: From the 1950s to the 1970s." The tone of the report, highly pessimistic, is a result of its publication immediately after the

Tiananmen Square incident in 1989. If a new report had been written in the mid-1990s it would no doubt have drawn some very different conclusions about the relationship between China and Hong Kong.

60. See Chowdhury and Islam, op. cit., esp. chap. 2, pp. 28–41. Hong Kong's population increased from 600,000 in 1945 to 1.6 million in 1948, largely as a result of in-migration from China, but in 1949 another 330,000 immigrants arrived from the mainland, at a rate of 10,000 or more each week; see Burns, op. cit.

61. These developments are discussed in I. Kelly, 1986, *Hong Kong: A Political-Geographic Analysis*. Honolulu: University of Hawaii Press; see esp. chap. 2, "Evolutionary Developments," and chap. 3, "Landscape Evolution." The trade embargo on China that began during the Korean War cut significantly into the entrepôt function of Hong Kong. In 1952, for example, the value of exports to China was HK$1.6 billion, but this fell to $520 million in 1953 and $136 million by 1956. As a result, Hong Kong's economic base was forced into a shift away from trade toward manufacturing (although most of that was intended ultimately for export). Note that in comparison to Taiwan, Hong Kong did not go through an intermediate stage involving import substitution, mainly because the domestic market was too small to support such a phase. See Burns, op. cit. A detailed account of the transformation of Hong Kong's economy is provided by Y. P. Ho, 1992, *Trade, Industrial Restructuring, and Development in Hong Kong*. Honolulu: University of Hawaii Press. The transformation (trading up) in Hong Kong's manufacturing has been accompanied by (or accelerated by) the shift of some of the lower-level production activities to factories in the mainland. This is clearly the case for such operations as textile production, shoes, plastic toys, and luggage. There is now practically no heavy industry in Hong Kong. See Economist Intelligence Unit, op. cit.

62. Ho, op. cit., table 4.1, p. 76.

63. The sharp drop-off in tourism after the 1997 handover has been very worrying to Hong Kong's people and its business elite. It is hypothesized that the huge growth in tourism during the late 1980s and early 1990s was based, at least in part, on a desire to visit Hong Kong "one last time" before it reverted to Chinese rule—and now that phase has clearly peaked. At least one of the local airlines (Cathay Pacific) has been advertising heavily to help turn the tourism trend around, offering cheap package deals for tourists who want to travel to the region, using Hong Kong as a base for visiting other countries in Asia.

64. Burns, op. cit. The development of Hong Kong's economy during this period is also discussed by K. W. Li and K.W.K. Lo, 1993, "Trade and Industry," pp. 109–126 in *The Other Hong Kong Report*, op. cit. Some of the statistics quoted here are taken from J. R. Schiffer, 1991, "State Policy and Economic Growth: A Note on the Hong Kong Model," *International Journal of Urban and Regional Research*, Vol. 15, No. 2 (June), pp. 180–196. Incoming tourists to Hong Kong increased from 2.6 million in 1982 to 8 million in 1992, and although average length of stay remains short, per capita spending by tourists increased until 1997, especially in the case of visitors from Japan and Taiwan.

65. See United Nations Development Program, 1998, *Human Development Report, 1998*. New York: Oxford University Press, pp. 184, 125.

66. See Hong Kong Census and Statistics Department, 1993, *Hong Kong Social and Economic Trends, 1982–1993*. Hong Kong, esp. chap. 2, "Labour," pp. 12–20. The relative (and absolute) decline in the importance of manufacturing vis-à-vis services in the Hong Kong economy can be explained as a result of a number of forces that were at work throughout the 1980s, one of which was the growth of protectionism around the world (particularly in the United States), which made Hong Kong–produced garments and textile goods less competitive. As noted, one response to rising wage and land costs in Hong Kong had been for manufacturers to shift an increasing proportion of their production activities into the mainland, particularly to Guangdong Province. The rise of the financial and business service-sector activities also occurred in part as a support for the growing trade with China throughout the 1980s and the sharp increase in foreign investment by Hong Kong capitalists in the mainland; see Burns, op. cit. The trade statistics are provided by Y. P. Ho, op. cit., table 1.1, p. 11. The statistics on the changing balance between domestic exports and reexports come from the Economist Intelligence Unit 1990 report, op. cit., pp. 15–16.

67. These three factors are discussed by Burns, op. cit. The Hong Kong government objects to the term "laissez-faire," preferring instead "positive nonintervention," which indicates that the government invests significant resources toward the development of Hong Kong's physical and human capital infrastructure. This contributes significantly to improving the efficiency of its economy and continues to

make it attractive to foreign investors. As the Economist Intelligence Unit 1990 report noted, "noninterventionism" means that anyone with enough money to invest in a small factory could "do business freely with minimum encumbrance: low taxes, free trade, good communications, weak trade unions, minimal or no training costs, and no risk of confiscation. Hong Kong has been a free port since it was founded. . . . Manufacturers have benefitted from duty-free raw materials. . . . Free trade has also boosted re-exports and tourism, since the colony is widely regarded as a huge duty free shop" (op. cit., pp. 5–6). Hong Kong's low taxes are the envy of the world. There is no capital gains tax, and inheritances are taxed at a very low rate. Economic Intelligence Unit, op. cit., p. 6.

68. The indicators used to make up this index were trade policy, taxation rates, monetary policy, the banking system, foreign investment rules and regulations, property rights, the proportion of economic output consumed by the government, regulation policy, the size of the black market, and the extent of wage and price controls. From these indicators, each country is assigned a score ranging from 1 (most free) to 5 (least free). Hong Kong scores 1.25, Singapore 1.30, and Bahrain 1.70. The United States ranks seventh with a score of 1.90; the UK scores 1.95. At the bottom end of the index are Ghana and Algeria, at 3.25. See *The Economist*, 1997, *World in Figures, 1997*. London: The Economist Press, p. 27.

69. Burns notes that the image of uninterrupted economic growth in Hong Kong has been punctuated by some periods of crisis and recession; for example, there was a banking crisis in 1965 and a series of riots and disturbances among dissatisfied (predominantly working-class) groups in 1966 and 1967. In response, the government set up new consultative institutions, with local citizens and workers appointed to advisory boards and committees, as well as an ambitious program of social welfare service delivery. A huge public housing program was launched, compulsory education was initiated, and steps toward expanded welfare and health service provision were taken. The impressive New Town redevelopment schemes were introduced, mainly as a way to decentralize housing and industrial development away from the crowded urban core areas of Hong Kong (Central) and Kowloon and toward the New Territories. Those actions were complemented by significant infrastructural developments, including the construction of a subway, a light rail system,

and port developments. See Burns, op. cit., esp. pp. 135–136.

70. The advantages of the Confucian value system for industrial development have been stressed by numerous observers as a way of attempting to account for the economic miracles witnessed in the Asian NIEs. See, for example, Goldstein, op. cit., and Chowdhury and Islam, op. cit.

71. Chowdhury and Islam, op. cit., p. 33.

72. S. Winchester, op. cit., quotes from pp. 233–236.

73. For a discussion of the critique of Confucian-dominated economic success, see, for example, L. Pye, 1988, "The New Asian Capitalism: A Political Portrait," pp. 86–92 in P. L. Berger and H. M. Hsiao (eds.), *In Search of an East Asia Development Model*. New Brunswick, NJ: Transaction Books.

74. Quoted in Burns, op. cit., p. 132.

75. This argument is made very convincingly by Manuel Castells, op. cit., who concludes that Hong Kong is as "developmentalist" a state as the other NIEs, although in a very different way.

76. This point is stressed by Schiffer, op. cit., pp. 182–188.

77. Ibid., p. 194.

78. Ibid., p. 195. A similar argument has also been made by Burns, who subtitles his chapter on Hong Kong "Diminishing Laissez-Faire" to account for the subtle growth of government interventions. For similar accounts, see M. Castells, L. Goh, and R. Y. Kwok, 1991, *The Shek Kip Mei Syndrome: Economic Development and Public Housing in Hong Kong and Singapore*. London: Pion; and A. R. Cuthbert, 1991, "A Fistful of Dollars: Legitimation, Production, and Debate in Hong Kong," *International Journal of Urban and Regional Research*, Vol. 15, No. 2 (June), pp. 234–247. The role of the state in the reproduction of the labor force and state intervention in the provision of wage subsidies, particularly for the semiconductor industry in Hong Kong, are discussed in J. Henderson, 1989, "The Political Economy of Technological Transformation in Hong Kong," pp. 102–155 in M. P. Smith (ed.), *Pacific Rim Cities in the World Economy: Comparative Urban and Community Research*, Vol. 2. New Brunswick, NJ: Transaction Publishers.

79. This poem is reprinted in Frank Ching, 1985, *Hong Kong and China: For Better or Worse*. New York: China Council of the Asia Society, p. 48. *Gweilo* is the mildly derogatory term the Chinese, in Hong Kong and elsewhere, often use to describe foreigners.

80. I attribute this opinion to Ronald Skeldon, former professor of geography at Hong Kong University (personal communication, 1995).

81. See Mirsky, op. cit., pp. 17–18. There is also an ugly precedent being set by the huge transfer of manufacturing jobs from Hong Kong to the mainland, involving the export of dirty and heavily polluting industries. Although this solves the pollution problem for Hong Kong, it is extremely damaging to China in the long run. Of particular concern are the production processes making printed circuit boards for computers, which use significant amounts of ozone-depleting CFCs as a cleaning solvent, and the huge new development of styrofoam production, which is being transformed in China by its use for disposable lunch boxes, made, literally by the million for China's hungry workers. See C. Goldstein, "Pollution Exporters: Hong Kong's CFC Uses Shift to China," *Far Eastern Economic Review,* May 14, 1992, p. 54.

82. See G. Segal, 1993, *The Fate of Hong Kong.* New York: St. Martin's Press, esp. chap. 3, "Negotiating the End of Empire," pp. 31–51. The full story of the negotiations leading to the Joint Declaration is laid out by Robert Cottrell, 1993, *The End of Hong Kong: The Secret Diplomacy of Imperial Retreat.* London: John Murray. It is clear that among all of the British colonies, Hong Kong was in a unique position in the sense that the British did not grant independence but arranged for it to be returned to "another country." The consequence of this arrangement was that unlike the other colonies there was no gradual struggle for independence, which meant that no strong leaders or political movements emerged. Most historians, including Welsh, op. cit., argue that the British were never very interested in Hong Kong, finding it to be more of an annoyance and an embarrassment than anything else. Welsh reports that during World War II the British Foreign Office considered Hong Kong as a thorn in the side and wanted it returned to China. Welsh suggests that it was not until Prime Minister John Major made his political ally and personal friend, Chris Patten, governor of Hong Kong that Britain made Hong Kong a real priority, realizing that it had become an extremely valuable property. Margaret Thatcher (in charge of the 1984 negotiations) was concerned about the future of Hong Kong but was not about to push the issue of democratization with the Chinese. She realized that (in the early 1980s) Britain, with its own unemployment and economic problems, would not and could not welcome having 6 million Chinese from Hong Kong lobbying for their rights to enter Britain. She

strove, therefore, for "convergence" with the mainland. According to Cottrell, Hong Kong was not an issue that "captured her imagination" (op. cit., p. 63). On the other side of the equation, it is generally agreed that China did not push hard to have Hong Kong returned immediately after the 1949 revolution because they needed the colony as a trading (entrepôt) center linking them to the outside world. A more significant explanation is that China did not want to diminish its chances of reunification with Taiwan, which was a much greater prize, in political terms, in the 1950s. By the late 1970s, however, Hong Kong was seen by Deng Xiaoping as the key component in China's drive toward modernization. It is important to note, however, that the negotiations leading to the 1984 Joint Declaration were initiated by the British, who were keen to protect their own business and commercial interests. China, it is suggested, was willing to be moderate in the negotiations, to demonstrate to the outside world that it was sincere in its proclamation that any reunification with Taiwan could be done peacefully. See Economist Intelligence Unit, op. cit., p. 65.

83. See Cottrell, op. cit., p. 206.

84. Segal, op. cit., p. 52.

85. These issues are discussed in Mirsky, op. cit. The issue of out-migration from Hong Kong is dealt with in a recently edited volume: R. Skeldon (ed.), 1994, *Reluctant Exiles: Migration from Hong Kong and the New Overseas Chinese.* Hong Kong: Hong Kong University Press, esp. pt. 1, "Setting the Scene," pp. 3–20, and "Migration from Hong Kong: Current Trends and Future Agendas," pp. 325–332.

86. This quote is provided in N. L. Sum, 1995, "More Than a 'War of Words': Political Reform Period in Hong Kong," *Economy and Society,* Vol. 24, No. 1 (February), pp. 67–100.

87. This concept began in reference to Taiwan in 1978 and was applied to Hong Kong in 1982. The idea was that China was to continue to practice socialism and Hong Kong be allowed to retain its capitalist institutions for at least fifty years after 1997. See Sum, ibid., note 2, p. 96.

88. See *Beijing Review,* January 3–9, 1994, p. 17 (quoted in ibid., p. 73). From 1984 until Patten's appearance in 1992, the British government had not overly emphasized the issue of increasing the level of democracy in Hong Kong, preferring instead to adopt a policy of convergence with the PRC. This meant that Britain basically accepted a very slow move toward democratization, allowing a smooth transition to Chinese rule in 1997. Arguably the

events of 1989 demonstrated to the British, and to many others around the world, that China might not be trustworthy and might quickly change its mind about Hong Kong, in spite of the spirit of the Joint Declaration. The Chinese, for their part, worried by what happened in 1989, wanted to slow down the pace of democratization in Hong Kong (as well as at home). See Economist Intelligence Unit, op. cit., pp. 75–76.

89. *Beijing Review,* January 10–14, 1994, p. 22. The quote about Patten is taken from N. D. Kristof, 1993, "British-Chinese Rift Stirs Anxiety in Hong Kong," *New York Times,* November 10.

90. Mirsky, op. cit., p. 16, quoting *Hong Kong Sunday Morning Post,* February 13, 1994.

91. The Chinese carried out this threat and, contrary to Patten's wishes, the delays meant that the new airport did not open until after the British had left, thereby thwarting any plans Patten had of making his personal "exit with glory" from the new airport he had personally engineered. As Jonathan Mirsky notes, "Under no circumstances . . . will Beijing permit the airport's opening day to be early enough for the hated Patten to cut the ribbon" (ibid., p. 20).

92. Quoted in ibid., p. 16.

93. For a more detailed discussion, see Sum, op. cit.

94. See Mirsky, op. cit., and Sum, ibid. In the appointment of these "advisory" groups, the New China News Agency (Xinhua) has played a major role, effectively operating in Hong Kong as the unofficial embassy for the PRC. Two of the leaders of the Democratic Party (Martin Lee and Szeto Wah) remained unco-optable in their opposition to the advances of Xinhua and Beijing. In the elections of 1994 and 1995, the Democrats did well in the elections in which voters, for the first time, had the opportunity to elect, either directly or indirectly, all sixty members of the Legislative Council. See *The Economist,* "China's Magic Tool for Hong Kong," March 18, 1995, pp. 35–36, and also a story reprinted in the *China News Daily* (available on the Internet) entitled "Patten Seems to Lose Ground as China Stalemate Drags On," November 24, 1995. In the March 1995 elections, for example, Mr. Szeto, a strong Patten supporter, soundly defeated Elsie Wu (known locally as "Beijing Elsie"), who was an open supporter of Beijing; see *The Economist,* "Tears for Tu," March 11, 1995, p. 34.

95. Sum, op. cit., p. 95. For a discussion of the confrontation between the two blocs, see *Far Eastern Economic Review,* 1994, *Asia 1994 Yearbook.* Hong Kong: FEER, pp. 123–126, "Politics/Social Affairs."

96. Mirsky, op. cit., p. 18.

97. Ibid., p. 20. The last issue refers to Hong Kong's dependence on the mainland for most of its drinking water, some of which can be seen flowing through a huge pipeline that runs parallel to the rail line from the Chinese border at Lo Wu (Shenzhen) to Hong Kong.

98. The issue of the court is discussed in L. Do Rosario, "A Court Too Far," *Far Eastern Economic Review,* June 22, 1995, p. 20.

99. See L. Do Rosario, "Between Two Stools: Pro-China Party Wants to Play Middleman's Role," *Far Eastern Economic Review,* September 14, 1995, pp. 26–28.

100. K. S. Louie, 1996, "Election and Politics," pp. 51–66 in Ngaw Mee-kau and Li Si-ming (eds.), *The Other Hong Kong Report, 1996.* Hong Kong: Chinese University Press, p. 57.

101. See Kelly, op. cit., esp. chap. 4, "Existing Trends," pp. 76–95. The New Towns issue is also discussed in Castells, Goh, and Kwok, op. cit., and in J. Henderson, 1991, "Urbanization in the Hong Kong–South China Region: An Introduction to Dynamics and Dilemmas," *International Journal of Urban and Regional Research,* Vol. 15, No. 2 (June), pp. 169–179. In actual fact, the government's ambitious housing developments began earlier than that, in the mid-1950s, after a disastrous fire left 53,000 people (mostly poorly housed and squatters) essentially homeless. A newly established housing authority launched a huge rebuilding program, and by 1964 some 240 new tower blocks had been built, providing subsidized small apartments for some 84,000 families. In subsequent developments, more substantial housing blocks have been built, both in Kowloon and on Hong Kong Island. By 1992, 45 percent of Hong Kong's population was living in subsidized public housing. See also Economist Intelligence Unit, op. cit., p. 11.

102. The planning concepts lying behind the Hong Kong New Towns are discussed in detail in R. Bristow, 1984, *Land Use Planning in Hong Kong: History, Policies, and Procedures.* Hong Kong: Oxford University Press. For more recent accounts, see D. R. Phillips and A.G.O. Yeh (eds.), 1991, *New Towns in East and Southeast Asia.* Hong Kong: Oxford University Press; and A.G.O. Yeh, X. Q. Qu, and X. P. Yan, 1997, *Urban Planning and Education Under Economic Reform in China.* Hong Kong: Center of Urban Plan-

ning and Environmental Management, University of Hong Kong.

103. During the period 1990–1994, for example, there was a 20 percent growth in the number of people employed in the finance and insurance business, and it is estimated that two-thirds of the local workforce worked in only 10 percent of the colony's total 1,050 square kilometers. See L. Do Rosario, "New Towns, Old Problems," *Far Eastern Economic Review*, June 15, 1995, p. 60.

104. Ibid.

105. M. Bociurkjw, "Building Boom Transforms Colony," *Toronto Globe and Mail*, October 4, 1994.

106. It had been estimated that every delay of six months added about $685 million to the total cost of the project; see ibid.

107. Patten is quoted in Mirsky, op. cit.; Lee is quoted in Terrill, op. cit., p. 108.

108. The fact that so many more are now allowed to vote is a result in part of Governor Patten's hurried reforms before his exit in 1997. As the campaign advertisements demonstrate (see Photos 11.7a and 11.7b), Hong Kong now has elections that are similar to those conducted in most other democracies; and as the official poster notes, they are "fair, open, and honest." At the election on May 24, 1998, the first since the handover, there was a record turnout, in spite of a daylong thunderstorm caused by a typhoon. Almost 60 percent of the electorate came out to vote, most of them voting for the Democrats and their allies, to such an extent that, as Jonathan Mirsky notes, "if Hong Kong were a true democracy, Martin Lee [the well-to-do lawyer who heads the Democratic Party] would be Hong Kong's Chief Executive." Mirsky points out that to prevent such a thing from happening the existing Beijing-appointed chief, Tung Chee-hwa, had already installed election laws to ensure that fewer than a third of the Legislative Council's seats would go to the Democrats. The high turnout rate is even more remarkable in the sense that the electorate knew in advance that this would be the case. See J. Mirsky, "Holding out in Hong Kong," *New York Review of Books*, Vol. 46, No. 12, July 5, 1999, pp. 33–35.

Chapter 12

1. M. C. Goldstein, 1997, *The Snow Lion and the Dragon: China, Tibet, and the Dalai Lama*. Berkeley: University of California Press, pp. 127–128.

2. Perhaps the most comprehensive treatment of China's minority groups is Colin Mackerras, 1994, *China's Minorities: Integration and Modernization in the Twentieth Century*. Hong Kong: Oxford University Press.

3. Some of the newly created Autonomous Regions were dominated by minority people; for example, 96 percent of Tibet's population and 62 percent of Xinjiang's were minorities. In the other ARs the percentages were lower; for example, in Guangzi the figure was 39 percent, Ningxia 33 percent, and Inner Mongolia 19 percent.

4. C. Mackerras, 1985, "The Minority Nationalities: Modernization and Integration," pp. 237–266 in G. Young (ed.), *China: Dilemmas of Modernization*. London: Croom Helm.

5. This has been a particularly important component in the ongoing conflict between the Chinese state and Tibet; see Mackerras (1994), op. cit., and J. T. Dreyer, 1993, "China's Minority Peoples," *Humboldt Journal of Social Relations*, Vol. 19, No. 2, pp. 321–358. See also a number of recent books written on the Tibet issue: T. Grunfeld, 1996, *The Making of Modern Tibet*. Armonk, NY: M. E. Sharpe; W. W. Smith Jr., 1996, *Tibetan Nation: A History of Tibetan Nationalism and Sino-Tibetan Relations*. Boulder: Westview Press; M. Goldstein, W. Siebenschuh, and T. Tsering, 1997, *The Struggle for Modern Tibet: The Autobiography of Tashi Tsering*. Armonk, NY: M. E. Sharpe; and Cao Changching and J. Seymour, 1997, *Tibet Through Dissident Eyes: Essays on Self-Determination*. Armonk, NY: M. E. Sharpe.

6. This is particularly the case for the territory in Kashmir that is held by the Chinese. This area, indeed the whole of that region, is at the center of an ongoing and troublesome relationship between India and Pakistan, the latter being China's ally (China providing Pakistan much of its nuclear capability).

7. See C. W. Pannell and L.J.C. Ma, 1983, *China: The Geography of Development and Modernization*. London: V. H. Winston. The sensitive nature of the border areas means that the minority groups assume a special significance. Mackerras (1994), op. cit., points out the discrepancies in wealth between the minority areas and most of the rest of China, and this has been a particularly important component of the ongoing conflict between the state and Tibet.

8. It is important to point out that for many of the minority people geographic isolation meant that they were practically unaware of their minority status. In a recent research study, for example, Dai has shown that among the young people recruited to work in the Folk Cultural Villages theme park in Shenzhen, many did not know they were minority people until they arrived in Shenzhen. F. Dai, 1996, *Internal Migration in the Reform Era in China: With Case Studies in Guangdong Province.* Unpublished M.A. thesis, Department of Geography and Planning, State University of New York at Albany. It is generally thought that the situation of many of China's minority people is different from that of the African and Latin American minorities in the United States, for example, because they are not as easily identifiable as minorities. Although this is the case in terms of visible characteristics, it is important to point out that their dialects are easily identifiable in most parts of China and clearly mark them as outsiders.

9. World Bank, 1992, *China: Strategies for Reducing Poverty in the 1990s.* Washington, DC: International Bank for Reconstruction and Development. In fieldwork conducted in Ningxia Hui AR, for example, the author and his collaborators observed that although the minority people in the region represent only about 30 percent of the total population, they make up a disproportionate share of those living in poverty, often in the most mountainous areas and areas with no river-irrigated lands.

10. See, for example, V. Smil, 1993, *China's Environmental Crisis: An Inquiry into the Limits of National Development.* Armonk, NY: M. E. Sharpe.

11. As the World Bank report on poverty in China pointed out, for example: "The process of agricultural innovation . . . favored the best endowed agricultural lands, and industrial development has occurred fastest in areas with low cost transportation and better developed markets" (op. cit., p. 43).

12. Ibid.

13. The official statistics show that industrial and agricultural ouput value in minority areas is significantly below the norm (Y1,328 versus Y2,586); see ibid.

14. X. Q. Wang and N. F. Bai, 1991, *The Poverty of Plenty.* London: Macmillan.

15. This is clearly not the case for some of the minority groups; in fact for Korean and Manchu people the reverse is true.

16. Mackerras (1994), op. cit.

17. These data were reported by a team of demographers from China led by H. Yuan Tien, a well-known demographer from Ohio State University. See H. Y. Tien et al., 1992, "China's Demographic Dilemma," *Population Bulletin,* Vol. 47, No. 1 (June), published in Washington, DC, by the Population Reference Bureau.

18. The fate of the Manchu people in northeastern China provides a good example of the trend toward population growth as a result of increasing self-identification. They more than doubled their size from 4.3 million in 1982 to 9.8 million in 1990. This could not have resulted from extra births, because the Manchu people do not receive exemptions from the one-child policy. Until the 1980s the Manchus, although dominant in some regions, had no autonomous geographical units, but three were established subsequently, and many villages have recently declared themselves to be Manchu villages. See D. Gladney, 1991, *Muslim Chinese: Ethnic Nationalism in the People's Republic.* Cambridge: Council on East Asian Studies, Harvard University, p. 317.

19. The issue of the new multicultural city in China is taken up by several authors: G. Guldin and A. Southall, 1993, *Urban Anthropology in China.* Leiden, Netherlands: E. J. Brill; see esp. Zhang Conggen, "The Impact of Cities on the Development and Prosperity of Minority Nationalities," pp. 247–256, and Ma Guoqing, "Cities, Urbanization and Cultural Change: The Tumote Region of Inner Mongolia," pp. 308–315.

20. Hui people are the predominant ethnic group in virtually all of China's biggest cities, especially in areas that are dominated by Han people. In Beijing, for example, they represent 57 percent of the minority population; in Shanghai 89 percent; and in Tianjin 87 percent. Hui people are also significantly more concentrated in commercial, service, and factory jobs than are ethnic minority people in general. See D. Gladney, op. cit., table 2, p. 28. Gladney also demonstrates the occupational differences between Hui people and other minority groups. For example, the Hui have significantly fewer workers in agriculture (61 percent compared to 84 percent for all minority people); and far more in commerce, service industries, and factory jobs (30 percent compared to less than 10 percent for all minority peoples). See ibid., table 4, p. 32.

21. Ibid., p. 331; see also D. Gladney, 1993, "Hui Urban Entrepreneurialism in Beijing: Ethnoreligious Identity and the Chinese City," pp. 278–307 in Guldin and Southall, op. cit.

22. It is also possible that the invisibility of China's minority people is a result of biases among foreign-

ers, who prefer to think of the Chinese per se as the "other," ignoring the increasingly visible evidence of so many additional "others" inside China.

23. Several studies of minority (*minzu*) groups are provided in Stevan Harrell (ed.), 1995, *Cultural Encounters on China's Ethnic Frontiers*. Seattle: University of Washington Press, and Guldin and Southall, op. cit. Other useful recent studies of individual minority groups include J. N. Lipman, 1997, *Familiar Strangers: A History of Muslims in Northwest China*. Seattle: University of Washington Press; J. J. Rudelson, 1997, *Oasis Identities: Uyghur Nationalism Along China's Silk Road*. New York: Columbia University Press; A. Hali, Z. X. Li, and K. W. Luckert, 1998, *Kazakh Traditions of China*. Lanham, MD: University Press of America; L. Benson and I. Svanberg, 1998, *China's Last Nomads: The History and Culture of China's Kazaks*. Armonk, NY: M. E. Sharpe; A.D.W. Forbes, 1986, *Warlords and Muslims in Chinese Central Asia*. Cambridge, UK: Cambridge University Press; P. K. Crossley, 1990, *Orphan Warriors: Three Manchu Generations and the End of the Qing World*. Princeton: Princeton University Press; and B. Pasternak and J. W. Salaff, 1993, *Cowboys and Cultivators: The Chinese of Inner Mongolia*. Boulder: Westview Press. Also helpful are the general surveys of China's ethnic groups: L. J. Moser, 1985, *The Chinese Mosaic: The Peoples and Provinces of China*. Boulder: Westview Press; and T. Herberer, 1989, *China and Its National Minorities: Autonomy or Assimilation?* Armonk, NY: M. E. Sharpe. For descriptive purposes, although obviously biased and in some places extremely thin on detail, are some of the Chinese works on the minority groups: Fei Xiaotong, 1981, *Toward a People's Anthropology*. Beijing: New World Press; Ma Yin (ed.), 1985, *Questions and Answers About China's National Minorities*. Beijing: New World Press; and Zhang Weimen and Zeng Qingman, 1993, *In Search of China's Minorities*. Beijing: New World Press. For a discussion of ethnicity in a different context, see Emily Honig's book about the Subei people in Shanghai: E. Honig, 1992, *Creating Chinese Ethnicity: Subei People in Shanghai, 1850–1980*. New Haven: Yale University Press.

24. Gladney (1991), op. cit., p. 320.

25. The Western media paid little attention to the protests of a number of Muslims who were noisily denouncing the publication of a book called *Sexual Customs*—an event referred to as the Chinese version of the Salmon Rushdie incident. The Chinese government acceded to the demands of the protesters: The book was removed from circulation, and the violence associated with the protests was for the most part ignored. After the dust of protest had settled, it was surprising to learn that one of the leaders in the Tiananmen Square demonstrations in 1989, Wu'er Kaixi, was a Muslim—a Uighur student from Xinjiang Autonomous Region. He became the darling of the Western press. He was photogenic, had undeniable stage presence, and was brave enough to challenge the Beijing authorities; but his ethnic background was never mentioned in public. When he reached the safety of the United States he told reporters he had been afraid that he would not have been taken seriously if his "barbarian" background was revealed. Yet he claimed that his experiences as a member of one of China's oppressed minority groups had helped to formulate his opinions and strengthen his character. Other minority students, both leaders and followers, joined Wu'er Kaixi in Beijing in 1989, and many of them also knew about oppression. One of the students on the infamous most-wanted list in the summer of 1989 was Wang Zhengchun, identified as a member of the Ku Cong minority group from the forests of Yunnan Province in southwest China. This group has never been officially recognized by the state; in fact the Ku Cong are designated as a subbranch of the Lahu minority group (the so-called Yellow Lahu). When he was arrested Wang had listed the name of his minority group on his identification papers as a mark of protest. For a short time, while Wang was on the most-wanted list, his people received official recognition as a minority group. As soon as the mistake was realized, however, Wang was reclassified and listed as a Ju Cong person affiliated with the larger Lahu group. This story is reported in Gladney (1991), op. cit., esp. chaps. 1 and 7.

26. This term is used by Lynn Pan, 1988, *The New Chinese Revolution*. Chicago: Contemporary Books, chap. 12, "Minorities," pp. 267–291.

27. Quoted in Mackerras (1985), op. cit., p. 243.

28. It is recognized that "the people of all nationalities have the freedom to use and develop their own spoken and written languages, and to preserve or reform their ways and customs." These provisions of the 1982 constitution are discussed by Jiann Hsieh, 1984, "China's Policy Toward the Minority Nationalities in an Anthropological Perspective," Alumni Working Paper No. 1, East-West Center, University of Hawaii, Honolulu, p. 11. These provisions were included in the 1982 constitution to redress some of the injustices done to minorities during the extreme leftist era of the Cultural Revolution (see later).

29. Ibid., p. 7.

30. A.P.L. Liu, 1996, *Mass Politics in the People's Republic: State and Society in Contemporary China*. Boulder: Westview Press, esp. chap. 5, "Ethnic Separatism."

31. Ibid., pp. 203–205.

32. Mackerras (1985), op. cit., p. 241. For the Cultural Revolution, see Dreyer, op. cit., pp. 321–358. In a detailed discussion of state policy toward minorities during the Great Leap Forward and the Cultural Revolution, Dreyer notes that in some instances the policies designed to increase the rate of assimilation of minorities actually had the opposite effect, by driving opposition underground and increasing the resistance to state policies, especially in places such as Xinjiang and Tibet.

33. Quoted in J. T. Dreyer, 1968, "China's Minority Nationalities in the Cultural Revolution," *The China Quarterly*, Vol. 35 (July–September), p. 109. For a more detailed discussion of the evolution of policies toward minority groups, see J. T. Dreyer, 1976, *China's Forty Millions: Minority Nationalities and National Integration in the People's Republic of China*. Cambridge: Harvard University Press.

34. During this period culture and the expression of the visual and written arts were dominated by what came to be known as "socialist realism," expressed most vehemently by Jiang Qing's (spouse of Mao Zedong) model operas, which "dominated the stage at the expense of traditional dances of the nationalities." Mackerras (1985), op. cit., pp. 241–242.

35. Liu, op. cit., pp. 204–205.

36. The emphasis on new rights and freedoms was even granted (in theory at least) to Tibet. In 1980, for example, Premier Hu Yaobang announced that "full play must be given to the right of national regional autonomy [and] all principles, policies and regulations not suited to Tibetan conditions are to be rejected or modified." Ibid., p. 242. As we shall see later in this chapter, these principles were often abandoned or ignored.

37. Ibid., pp. 204–205.

38. Ibid., pp. 206–212.

39. The official data, in this case shown in Table 12.4, are from the China Statistical Publishing House, 1998, *China Statistical Yearbook 1997*. The numbers are suspect, to say the least. There is no way to determine how they were calculated or why the statistics for the two time periods are in some cases so wildly different.

40. Liu, op. cit., pp. 205–206. See also Xiaowei Zang, 1998, "Ethnic Representation in the Current Chinese Leadership," *The China Quarterly*, No. 153, pp. 107–127.

41. Liu, op. cit., p. 216, quoting Elise Boulding, 1979, "Ethnic Separatism and World Development," p. 277 in L. Kriesberg (ed.), *Research in Social Movements Conflicts and Change*. Greenwich, CT: JAI Press.

42. Liu, op. cit., p. 216.

43. Goldstein, op. cit., pp. 127–128.

44. The term "civilize" here is taken from Stevan Harrell in his edited volume entitled *Cultural Encounters on China's Ethnic Frontiers*; see esp. "Introduction," pp. 3–36. Harrell prefers to use the term "peripheral peoples" because he wants to avoid the term "minorities," which refers to a subset of peripheral peoples—those found in a modern nation-state with boundaries and citizenship papers; and also the term "indigenous peoples," which implies that the Han are not indigenous, which they are. The term "peripheral" is less connotative and implies that these are people who are geographically distant from the centers of institutional and economic power (see Harrell, op. cit., note 2, p. 3).

45. See ibid., pp. 3–36, for a discussion of ethnogenesis. Some researchers have argued that the attempts to create new ethnic groups and ethnic awareness are examples of what Benedict Anderson calls an "imagined community," a process that is occurring all over the world, as witnessed by the rising power of nationalism and the conflicts it has brought. The term "imagined" here is the key, in the sense that (as the Chinese government would claim) Tibet, for example, has never actually been a state and is only a nation in the eyes (or minds) of Tibetan people. See B. Anderson, 1983, *Imagined Communities: Reflections on the Origin and Spread of Nationalism*. London: Verso Press. Another example is the situation of the Mongols of Inner Mongolia who were able to transform the folkloric belief that they were the actual descendants of Chinggis Khan into an ethnic marker. In recent times some Mongols have referred to themselves as the "sons and grandsons of Ghinggis Khan," which is an all-inclusive description transcending differences in descent, class, and tribal or regional affiliation. See A. Khan, 1995, "Chinggis Khan: From Imperial Ancestor to Ethnic Hero," pp. 248–277 in Harrell, op. cit., p. 266. It is important to note that interactions between the core and the periphery can also produce some changes in the core. In China this has been the case for the Han people during the past few decades, as they have been forced to become more aware of their own identity and conscious of the dif-

ferences between themselves and the people on the peripheries.

46. See Harrell, op. cit., pp. 8–17.

47. Stalin's requirements were that to be included as an official nationality a group needed to have a common territory, a common language, a common economy, and a common national culture. Harrell has suggested that one of the major theoretical differences between the communist and the Confucian and Christian projects is that no moral differences were assumed between the center and the periphery: In other words, all people were considered to be equal, and no attempts were made to replicate the values of the center in the periphery; the goal was simply to modernize the periphery. As Harrell notes, "The goal is not ostensibly to make the peripheral peoples more like those of the center, but rather to bring them to a universal standard of progress or modernity that exists independent of where the center might be on the historical scale at any given moment." Ibid., p. 23. It is by no means clear, however, that the people on China's periphery, especially those in Tibet, would agree with these sentiments. For a discussion of the Tibet situation, see, for example, Mackerras (1994), op. cit., and Dreyer (1993), op. cit.

48. Harrell, op. cit., p. 24.

49. The Hmong people once lived in southwestern China as part of the larger Miao group, but they migrated as a result of oppression during the Qing Dynasty and settled in the mountainous regions of northern Burma (Myanmar), Thailand, Laos, and Vietnam. The story of the Hmong is told in Sucheng Chan, 1994, *Hmong Means Free: Life in Laos and America*. Philadelphia: Temple University Press.

50. See C. Geertz, 1968, *Islam Observed: Religious Development in Morocco and Indonesia*. London: University of Chicago Press, p. 79.

51. This issue is discussed in detail by Gladney (1991), op. cit., pp. 7–15.

52. Ibid.

53. Ibid., p. 13.

54. Ibid., p. 15.

55. In China, pork has been the basis of meat protein for centuries and was regarded by Mao Zedong as a "national treasure." See M. Harris, 1968, *The Rise of Anthropological Theory*. New York: Crowell, p. 78.

56. See Gladney (1993), op. cit.

57. Ibid., p. 279.

58. Ibid.

59. These strategies are explained by Gladney (1993), op. cit., pp. 321–322.

60. Ibid., p. 322.

61. Ibid., p. 323.

62. Ibid., p. 331.

63. This issue is discussed more fully in Chapter 15; see also D. J. Solinger, 1999, *Contesting Citizenship in Urban China: Peasant Migrants, the State, and the Logic of the Market*. Berkeley: University of California Press.

64. As Gladney notes, "For the Hui the market provides a public sphere for autonomous expression within the hegemony of the Chinese State" (ibid., p. 331).

65. This argument is made by Khan, op. cit., pp. 248–277 in Harrell, op. cit. See also P. Crossley, 1990, "Thinking About Ethnicity in Early Modern China," *Late Imperial China*, Vol. 11, No. 1 (June), pp. 1–34; and W. Borchigud, 1995, "The Impact of Urban Ethnic Education on Modern Mongolian Ethnicity, 1949–1966," pp. 278–300 in Harrell, op. cit.

66. See W. R. Jankowiak. 1993a. *Sex, Death, and Hierarchy in a Chinese City: An Anthropological Account*. New York: Columbia University Press.

67. In a study of white Europeans in the United States, Alba has noted that similar activities have been observed in the context of declining ethnic solidarity. Alba refers to this as the "twilight" of ethnicity, which involves the gradual disappearance of "traditional" ethnic markers among white European groups in the United States and their replacement with "symbolic" markers. See R. D. Alba, 1990, *Ethnic Identity: The Transformation of White America*. New Haven: Yale University Press.

68. W. R. Jankowiak, 1993b, "Urban Mongols: The Search for Dignity and Gain," pp. 316–338 in Guldin and Southall, op. cit., p. 320.

69. Ibid., p. 321–322.

70. Ibid., p. 322.

71. See Borchigud, op. cit., pp. 298–300.

72. See Jankowiak (1993a), op. cit., pp. 40–48.

73. Ibid., p. 50.

74. A fascinating and detailed study of the Subei people is provided by Emily Honig, op. cit.; the quote here is on page 2.

75. An elderly women now living in New York explained that whenever she wants to complain about the behavior of African Americans she simply refers to them as "Subei people," avoiding the possibility of being called a racist. See ibid., p. 2, and E. Honig, 1990, "Invisible Inequalities: The Status of Subei People in Contemporary China," *The China Quarterly*, No. 122 (June), pp. 273–292.

76. It is interesting to note that in spite of the ubiquity of the label, there is in fact no actual place called

Subei; it is a catch-all geographical label attached to all people who are (or might be) from the towns and rural areas in the northern parts of the province. The constructed label—Subei—has emerged over time as a result of a set of relationships between one group with power and status (the Jiangnan people) and another group fighting to survive in a hostile environment (the Subei people). As the example of the Subei people demonstrates, ethnicity is not an objective fact based on racial, national, or religious characteristics. It has been created by the members of one group to differentiate themselves from an "other" group they consider to be inferior; see Honig (1992), op. cit.

77. Honig (1992), op. cit., p. 43.

78. Ibid., p. 76.

79. Ibid., p. 47.

80. Ibid., p. 57.

81. P. Iyer, "China's Buddha Complex," *New York Times*, December 3, 1995.

82. P. Tyler, "Tibet's Ultimate Political Comeback," *New York Times*, December 3, 1995.

83. See Goldstein, op. cit., pp. 106–109.

84. Ibid., p. 108.

85. Ibid., p. 93.

86. The term "floating population" is a pejorative applied in blanket fashion to migrants, who are usually recently arrived from the countryside; see Chapter 15.

87. Goldstein, op. cit., p. 95.

88. Ibid., p. 98.

89. Ibid., p. 98.

90. This is the opinion of Tom Grunfeld, outlined in a public lecture he gave in Albany in December 1998. See also T. Grunfeld, 1987, *The Making of Modern Tibet*. London: Zed Books; and the 1996 expanded and updated edition of the same book.

91. Goldstein, op. cit., p. 116.

92. W. W. Smith, op. cit., p. 692.

93. This issue has been well covered in Liu's *Mass Politics in the People's Republic*, op. cit. In chapter 5 ("Ethnic Separatism," pp. 189–222), Liu discusses some of these events, although he focuses on the ethnic strife in Xianjiang AR more than in Tibet.

94. Smith, op. cit., pp. 693–694. The issue of Tibetan self-determination is also covered in a recent book edited by Changching Cao and James D. Seymour, op. cit., made up of pieces written by Chinese writers, the majority of them dissidents living in exile.

95. For discussions of Chinese tourism in general, see A. A. Lew and L. Yu, 1995, *Tourism in China: Geographic, Political, and Economic Perspectives*. Boulder: Westview Press; specifically on ethnic tourism, see T. S. Oakes, 1992, "Cultural Geography and Chinese Ethnic Tourism," *Journal of Cultural Geography*, Vol. 112, No. 2, pp. 3–17; see also D. MacCannell, 1984, "Reconstructed Ethnicity," *Annals of Tourism Research*, Vol. 11, pp. 375–391.

96. This argument is made by T. S. Oakes, "Tourism in Guizhou: Sense of Place and the Commerce of Authenticity." Paper presented at the annual meeting of the Association of American Geographers, Chicago, March 1995.

97. Ibid., p. 5.

98. This description is provided in Zhang and Zeng, op. cit., p. 200.

99. See C. F. McKhann, 1995, "The Naxi and the Nationalities Question," pp. 39–62 in Harrell, op. cit.

100. Zhang and Zeng, op. cit., p. 202.

101. Ibid.

102. Ibid.

103. McKhann, op. cit., p. 43.

104. See Harrell, op. cit., "Introduction," pp. 3–36; see specifically the section "The Sexual Metaphor: Peripheral Peoples as Women" at pp. 10–13.

105. See Hsieh, op. cit., p. 4.

106. See McKhann, op. cit.

107. Ibid., p. 243. The statistics on minority achievements in the 1980s are from Dreyer (1993), op. cit., esp. pp. 349–350. Dreyer ends, however, on a decidedly pessimistic note, arguing that the minority peoples still face some very serious obstacles, particularly in the realm of academic achievements and economic prosperity, as well as the ongoing issue of religious persecution, especially in Tibet. With the dissolution of the Soviet empire, many of China's minority groups have been contemplating the issues of independence and secession.

108. Liu, op. cit.

Chapter 13

1. Traditional saying from rural China, quoted in Shirin M. Rai, 1995, "Gender in China," pp. 181–203 in R. Benewick and P. Wingrove (eds.), *China in the 1990s*. Basingstoke, UK: Macmillan Press, p. 181.

2. "A Young Worker's Lament to His Former Girlfriend," Ha Jin, 1990, *Between Silences: A Voice from China*. Chicago: University of Chicago Press, p. 54.

3. M. Blecher, 1997, *China Against the Tides: Restructuring Through Revolution, Radicalism, and Reform*. London: Pinter Press, p. 151.

4. Wu Xinya, September 2, 1980, "Explanatory Notes on the Marriage Law." Excerpts given at the Third Session of the Fifth National People's Congress, reprinted in Wu Xinya, 1987, *New Trends in Chinese Marriage and the Family*. Beijing: Women of China, p. 17.

5. Quoted in D. Wilson, 1979, *The People's Emperor: Mao—a Biography of Mao Tse-tung*. New York: Lee Publishers, p. 75.

6. Quoted in ibid., p. 74.

7. For a discussion of Mao and his views about and behavior toward women, see R. Terrill, 1984, *The White-Boned Demon: A Biography of Madam Mao-Zedong*. New York: William Morrow. For a sampling of Mao's behavior toward women in his later years, it is illuminating to read the book written by his former personal doctor, Li Zhisui, 1996, *The Private Life of Chairman Mao: The Memoirs of Mao's Personal Physician*. London: Arrow Books. In his old age Mao's sexual appetites expanded and diversified, at least if we are to believe even half of what was recently revealed in Doctor Li's book. According to Li, Mao became an adherent of Daoist sexual practices, in which older men are recommended to supplement their fading *yang* (male essence, the source of power and strength) with *yin shui* (the water or vaginal secretions of young women). The more *yin shui* absorbed, the more male essence is strengthened. This gave him the perfect excuse to pursue sex not only for pleasure but also to extend his life expectancy: "He was happiest and most satisfied with several young women simultaneously sharing his bed." He encouraged his sexual partners to introduce him to others for shared orgies, allegedly in the interests of his longevity and strength. When his wife, Jiang Qing, was out of town, Mao would have his current favorite stay with him, "sleeping with him when he slept and waiting on him when he was awake—serving him meals and tea, sponging him down with hot washcloths" (p. 361). Mao became careless about personal hygiene, unaware or not bothered by the prospect of sexually transmitted diseases and totally oblivious to outsiders' opinions about his activities. Doctor Li even claims that the young women he selected were proud to be infected, thinking of the disease transmitted by Mao as "a badge of honor, testimony to their close relations" (p. 363). Mao did not care if the women he was romancing were married; in fact he used his power to over-

come any such obstacles. Li also suggests that a cuckolded husband usually did not feel disgraced if his wife consorted with Mao: "Indeed, he considered it an honor to the Chairman—and a stepping stone to . . . promotion" (p. 362). It is important to note that the Li book was extremely controversial, because many critics suggested that he had concocted many of the stories; in fact most of the book is recorded from memory, with no corroboration from other sources.

8. The letter to the local officials asking for permission to marry might have read as follows: "The farm-worker Zhang Youglin, male, age thirty-nine, marital status: never before married, and the farm-worker Huang Xianglu, female, age thirty-one, marital status, divorced, hereby apply to get married. Both parties . . . guarantee that after marriage they will continue to remake themselves, will receive supervision and re-education under the leadership of the Party Branch and the Lower Middle Farming Class, and will do their best to aid in the construction of a socialist society." See Zhang Xianliang, 1988, *Half of Man Is Woman*. New York: W. W. Norton, p. 125.

9. Blecher, op. cit., p. 156.

10. One of Zhang and Sang's respondents in their book *Chinese Lives* faced just such a prospect. As he said: "My biggest headache is finding a wife. My job's nothing great. Even with bonuses and extras the best is a little over seventy yuan a month. . . . The girls I go for wouldn't give me a second glance. . . . If I had 3,000 yuan I could buy a colour TV, a sofa and a fridge, and they'd all be after me." Xinxin Zhang and Sang Ye, 1987, *Chinese Lives: An Oral History of Contemporary China*. New York: Pantheon Books, p. 138.

11. See R. Thakur, 1997, *Rewriting Gender: Reading Contemporary Chinese Women*. London: Zed Books, p. 6.

12. Rai, op. cit., p. 184.

13. As a consequence, some Western feminists contend that the CCP colluded with China's patriarchal system in order to gain peasant support for the revolution, both before and after 1949. See, for example, E. R. Judd, 1994, *Gender and Power in Rural North China*. Stanford: Stanford University Press.

14. J. Stacey, 1983, *Patriarchy and Socialist Revolution in China*. Berkeley: University of California Press, p. 263. There has never been a problem mobilizing women for tasks that are seen to be an extension of their familial roles, and it is important to note that many women have been keen to join and support the Party, even with the implicit understanding that gender-specific interests would always be subor-

dinated to the larger issues of national and class liberation.

15. Thakur, op. cit., p. 62.

16. Ibid.

17. H. Evans, 1997, *Women and Sexuality in China: Dominant Discourses of Female Sexuality and Gender Since 1949.* Cambridge, UK: Polity Press.

18. The terminology here is adapted from the works of Michel Foucault in ibid., p. 217.

19. Ibid., p. 218.

20. Ibid., p. 219.

21. According to Elisabeth Croll, all of these are commonly heard in the Chinese countryside. See E. Croll, 1994, *From Heaven to Earth: Images and Experiences of Development in China.* London: Routledge, p. 198 and chap. 9 generally.

22. S. W. O'Sullivan, 1958, "Traditionalizing China's Modern Women," *Problems of Communism,* Vol. 34, No. 6 (November–December), pp. 58–69.

23. Stacey, op. cit. This would, of course, also include Mao Zedong.

24. M. K. Whyte and W. L. Parish, 1984, *Urban Life in Contemporary China.* Chicago: University of Chicago Press, p. 198.

25. M. Wolf, 1985, *Revolution Postponed: Women in Contemporary China.* Stanford: Stanford University Press, pp. 124–125. National data for 1987 show that 26.8 percent of China's population over twelve years old are either illiterate or semiliterate; for females this figure was 38.1 percent, for males 15.8 percent. See China Statistical Publishing House, 1989, *China Statistical Yearbook 1988,* p. 91; the statistics on women in college are from the same source, p. 793. Although women represent about 50 percent or more of the student population in low-status teaching colleges, they form only 16.5 percent of the students at the nation's top technological institution, Qinghua University in Beijing. Of seventy-two students sent from the China University for Science and Technology to the United States to study for a Ph.D. in the early 1980s, only three were women. Of China's first group of Ph.D. recipients in 1983, only one (out of eighteen) was a woman. See B. Hooper, 1985, *Youth in China.* London: Penguin Books.

26. Wolf, op. cit., p. 128. It is important to point out that in China the cost of educating a child is not just the money needed to buy books and pay fees but the loss of potential income to the family. As we have seen in Chapter 10 there is a marked fear that the economic reforms in the countryside will work to discourage parents from keeping their children, especially their daughters, at school. The tradition of patrilocal exogamous marriage customs—whereby girls go to live with their husband's parents—has been continually supported by the Chinese government, both before and after 1949. This was one way of stabilizing local communities and rural family life, but it also helped to garner support for the Communists among the largely patriarchal structure of village life in the countryside. The tradition of girls moving away to marry perpetuated the rural habit of denying education to girls, thereby reducing their overall opportunities. This has been described in detail by K. A. Johnston, 1983, *Women, the Family, and Peasant Revolution in China.* Chicago: University of Chicago Press. Johnston argues that the tradition of exporting girls supported "male supremacist attitudes, which favor sons over daughters [and] community power structures which . . . discriminate against women and exclude women from public authority, and to family practices which continue to assign subordinate traditional roles and obligations to women" (p. 216).

27. Whyte and Parish, op. cit., table 23, p. 202. For China as a whole, based on the 1 percent sample survey conducted in 1987, 69.2 percent of women over the age of fifteen are in the labor force. See *China Statistical Yearbook 1988,* p. 92.

28. There is some evidence that in the 1990s many urban families in China were finding they had more leisure time than in the past, presumably because higher incomes allow them to work fewer hours, in addition to the new time-saving cleaning and cooking technologies that are becoming universally available. It has also been popular for urban families to hire rural women and girls as maids and child caretakers, which has further liberated adults, especially women. See S. G. Wang, 1995, "The Politics of Private Time: Changing Leisure Patterns in Urban China," pp. 149–172 in D. Davis et al. (eds.), *Urban Spaces in Contemporary China: The Potential for Autonomy and Community in Post-Mao China.* Cambridge, UK: Cambridge University Press.

29. It is obvious that the public provision of child care, cooking, cleaning, and other household services has not emerged to liberate women from the drudgery of housework. Women in rural areas, for example, spend an average of 3.5 hours each day simply buying and preparing food. See E. Croll, 1983, *Chinese Women Since Mao.* Armonk, NY: M. E. Sharpe, p. 61. As Whyte and Parish show, there is no evidence to suggest that Chinese men (husbands) are any more likely than men in other countries around the world to share the burden with their wives (op.

cit., p. 217). There is some evidence that in the 1990s women and men were experiencing some of the benefits of the economic reforms in terms of increased leisure time, but this is a very recent phenomenon and probably applies only to the wealthier urban households; see Wang, op. cit.

30. Whyte and Parish's data show a fairly high inverse correlation between jobs with high status and high salaries and the proportion of the labor force that is female. Among the top four occupations in terms of salary (and presumably status)—college professors, engineers and technicians, doctors, and government administrators—between 22 percent and 39 percent of the labor force is women; compare that to the the bottom four occupations: preschool teachers (100 percent women), nursemaids and servants (93 percent), temporary workers (75 percent), and street cleaners (86 percent). See Whyte and Parish, op. cit., table 24, p. 204. In addition, the jobs many women find are more likely to be in collective or private enterprises rather than in state enterprises. This has serious implications for women, because these jobs are less likely to carry the sorts of benefits provided in the state sector, such as health care, insurance coverage, retirement benefits, and so on.

31. Wolf, op. cit., p. 66.

32. Whyte and Parish suggest that the average women's wage in capitalist countries ranges from 50 to 80 percent of men's wages; in socialist countries it ranges from 63 to 84 percent (op. cit., p. 207).

33. The official media made available in the English language is fond of printing stories about women who have done well in traditionally male strongholds; see, for example, the story about Wan Shaofen, who is Party secretary for Jiangxi Province: "Party's Woman at the Top," *China Daily*, March 3, 1987, as well as the story about a well-known woman pilot, Xue Wenshu: "Xue's 3000 Hours Aloft," *China Daily*, March 11, 1987. For an entire story written about successful women, see Tan Manni, 1987, "Vast Sky, Heavy Wings," *China Reconstructs* (March), pp. 13–18.

34. See Internet URL: http://solar.rtd.utk.edu/.

35. The index is constructed so that a high score, indicating high equality for women, is closer to 1.0, with lower scores indicating more inequality. See United Nations Development Program (UNDP), 1995, *Human Development Report, 1995*. New York: Oxford University Press.

36. Ibid., pp. 17–18.

37. Ibid., p. 78.

38. Again it is important to note that China's ranking on the GEM fell from twenty-third in 1995 to thirty-third in 1998, which suggests either that other nations are catching up or that China is slipping; see UNDP, *Human Development Report, 1995*, op. cit. The changes that occur in just a few years on these indices are alarming, implying perhaps that they are not very robust measures, or that the data from which they are constructed are unreliable.

39. Ibid., p. 36.

40. It should be noted that this figure has fallen considerably since 1970, when it stood at 38 percent, and it may well have fallen even farther by the end of the 1990s. However, as some of the text in this chapter suggests, there are reasons to believe that girls are likely to be even more under pressure to enter the workforce in the reform era than was the case earlier. See Croll (1994), op. cit.

41. Stacey, op. cit. The usual explanation for this is that the Party did not want to do anything that would damage its support in the countryside. That support was strongest among the rural patriarchs who dominated village life all across China.

42. The net effect was that even after the revolution in 1949 the two major stanchions of local authority structure—patrilocal marriages and the entrenched division of labor—have never been substantially challenged. For a discussion of this, see Blecher, op. cit., and O'Sullivan, op. cit.

43. Lei Jieqiang, 1987, *New Trends in Chinese Marriages and the Family*. Beijing: Women of China, pref., p. i.

44. See Wolf, op. cit.

45. Lei, op. cit.

46. R. Sidel and V. W. Sidel, 1982, *The Health of China*. Boston: Beacon Press, chap. 6, "The Family and Child Care."

47. N. E. Riley, 1997, "Gender Equality in China: Two Steps Forward, One Step Back," pp. 79–108 in W. A. Joseph (ed.), *China Briefing: The Contradictions of Change*. Armonk, NY: M. E. Sharpe, p. 84.

48. Ibid., p. 86.

49. M. J. Meijer, 1971, *Marriage Law and Policy in the Chinese People's Republic*. Hong Kong: Hong Kong University Press, pp. 112–114.

50. P. Andors, 1983, *The Unfinished Liberation of Chinese Women*. Bloomington: Indiana University Press, p. 35.

51. K. S. Tsai, 1996, "Women and the State in Post-1949 Rural China," *Journal of International Affairs* (Winter), p. 4. See Internet URL: http://www.columbia.edu/cu/sip/PUBS/Journal/Tsai.html.

52. Zhang Jie's story "Love Must Not Be Forgotten" deals with the nearly taboo topic (at that time) of marital infidelity, although in the case of this story the couple in question had never even held hands. The issue of loveless marriages, arranged by parents in the prerevolutionary era, came to a head after the new Marriage Law, because couples were now free to get divorced. In another story, "The Ark," Zhang describes the constant vigilance and oppression experienced by three divorced women who lived together and were constantly accused by vicious neighbors of immoral behavior. See Zhang Jie, 1986, *Love Must Not Be Forgotten*. San Francisco: China Books and Periodicals, pp. 113–202 ("The Ark"). According to Lynn Pan, the official disapproval of divorce results in less than half of the petitions ending with actual divorce. The rest of the couples are talked into a settlement of some sort, usually as the result of mediation (op. cit., p. 183). For an interesting perspective on divorce in China and a look at the way the divorce court handles cases that come before it, see T. K. Haraven, 1987, "Divorce, Chinese Style" *Atlantic Monthly* (April), pp. 70–76; see also K. S. Kerpen, 1987, "Divorce and Custody in China," *US-China Review*, Vol. 11, No. 4 (July–August), pp. 5–8.

53. Zhang Xian, 1987, "The Widow," *China Now*, No. 122 (Autumn), pp. 31–35.

54. Pan, op. cit., pp. 182–183.

55. R. Conroy, 1987, "Patterns of Divorce in China," *Australian Journal of Chinese Affairs*, No. 17 (January), pp. 53–75. Conroy estimates that the divorce rate in China in the late 1970s and 1980s was roughly 3–4 percent, compared with the estimate in the United States, which is closer to 50 percent.

56. Ibid., p. 73.

57. Tamara Jacka, for example, observes that the increased prices being paid for brides make it more difficult for women to seek divorce, because parents are demanding the dowry be repaid. See T. Tacka, 1997, *Women's Work in Rural China: Change and Continuity in an Era of Reform*. Cambridge, UK: Cambridge University Press, p. 63.

58. Ibid.

59. China Statistical Publishing House, 1998, *China Statistical Yearbook 1997*, table 19-33, p. 739.

60. Whyte and Parish, op. cit., pp. 191–194.

61. Until very recently the stresses of life, particularly in the cities, have worked to increase the double burden under which women have been living: the high population density at which most urban families live; the lack of labor-saving devices in the home that have come to be standard equipment elsewhere; and the pressures of promoting their children's welfare in an overcrowded and overcompetitive educational system. All add to the strains placed on women, for whom work at home only begins after a full day in the factory or at the office.

62. There is one significant way in which socialism has made a contribution (albeit negative) to family life in China. The modern Chinese family, especially the urban family, had to be strong and resourceful in the face of the privations of life in communist China in the prereform era. Family members clung to each other tenaciously in an effort to cope with the austerity of the socialist city and the oppression of the Chinese bureaucracy. For many people the state became the enemy, which made it increasingly important to maintain kinship and family ties as a way of surviving. In the future Chinese families will have to stick together, not so much because they want to but because they need to in the face of continued austerity and the renewed threat of repression. The current situation is far removed from the romantic view of socialist family life that Marx and Mao had hoped for. The Chinese family today is still intact because it has to be: "Families may not provide a peaceful haven or a warm nest of human feelings for their members, but they are still the primary resources urbanites turn to for the cooperative efforts needed to cope with urban life." See Whyte and Parish, op. cit., p. 194.

63. Zhang, op. cit., p. 267.

64. L. Pan, 1988, *The New Chinese Revolution*. Chicago: Contemporary Books, p. 177. When asked whether China's prim attitude toward sex is a remnant of feudal tendencies, one student answered, "No. . . . It is a socialist attitude. Dissolute behavior between the sexes is a phenomenon of capitalist society." Quoted in Hooper, op. cit., p. 183, from Zhang Xian, 1983, "The Corner Forsaken by Love," in H. F. Siu and Z. Stern (eds.), *Mao's Harvest: Voices from China's New Generation*. New York: Oxford University Press.

65. Pan, op. cit., p. 176. Pan does note, however, that there is substantial journalistic evidence of higher rates of illegitimate births, sexual offenses, rape, and prostitution in China's cities.

66. C. Ikels, 1996, *The Return of the God of Wealth: The Transition to a Market Economy in Urban China*. Stanford: Stanford University Press.

67. Ibid., p. 12.

68. See, for example, Wang, op. cit.

69. J. Y. Zha, 1997, "China's Popular Culture in the 1990s," pp. 109–150 in Joseph, op. cit., pp. 136–143.

70. Sha Yin, 1987, "A Survey on Marriage and the Family in Beijing," pp. 106–119 in Lei, op. cit.

71. *The Economist*, "China Rediscovers the Joy of Sex," October 4, 1997, p. 10.

72. S. Faison, "Behind a Great Wall of Reticence, Some Sex Toys," *New York Times*, March 5, 1998.

73. *The Economist*, op. cit., p. 2.

74. D. L. Liu, M. L. Ng, L. P. Zhou, and E. J. Haeberle, 1997, *Sexual Behavior in Modern China: Report on the Nationwide Survey of 20,000 Men and Women* New York: Continuum.

75. It is interesting to note, however, that among the Japanese high school girls surveyed, only 10.7 percent report they have masturbated, which is only one-seventh of the rate for boys; ibid.

76. Ibid., p. 141.

77. Ibid., p. 266; on the nudity issue, see p. 274. The data provide an interesting piece of geographical information, in that on many of the questions the Guangzhou respondents turned out to be the most sexually active and innovative. For example, it was reported that Guangzhou respondents were more likely to be naked during intercourse (table 4-152, p. 274); that they had intercourse more frequently than other respondents (table 4-106, p. 252); and that Guangzhou women were more likely to initiate sex than women elsewhere (table 4-199, p. 298). These results may not be statistically significant and they are difficult to interpret, but it is possible that the proximity to Hong Kong and the level of economic development and modernization in Guangzhou have something to do with this. It is rather surprising that the Shanghai respondents were generally less active and innovative in their sexual behaviors, although when this survey was conducted (1991) Shanghai's big economic push was not yet fully under way.

78. Ibid.

79. These data are from D. M. Buss et al., 1990, "International Preferences in Selecting Mates," *Journal of Cross-Cultural Psychology*, Vol. 21, pp. 5–47. The table reproduced here was from an earlier paper published by the same authors and reproduced in *Time*, May 1, 1989, pp. 66–67.

80. On the same question, women and men in the United States scored 0.9 and 0.5, showing a major difference in the requirement for virginity among future spouses in the two countries. In some of the European countries reported in the study, even lower scores (in the 0.2–0.3 range) were recorded on this item (see Table 13.4). In spite of the stated aims of the Marriage Laws, there is also evidence provided in this study that mate selection in China is still governed by instrumentalist considerations, especially wealth, security, and status. As the statistics indicate, "good financial prospects" for a future husband were rated 1.6 by women in China, 2.2 by women in Taiwan. When asked how important it was for their future spouse to be "ambitious and industrious," women in mainland China scored 2.6 and in Taiwan, 2.8, which were higher scores than in any of the other countries surveyed.

81. G. Hershatter, 1996, "Sexing Modern China," pp. 77–96 in G. Hershatter et al. (eds.), *Remapping China: Fissures in Historical Terrain*. Stanford: Stanford University Press.

82. In addition, there are reasons to question the traditional view that Chinese attitudes to sex have generally, and always, been repressive—as opposed to the presumably more liberal views in the West. For most of China's history, Confucian and Taoist writings and teachings have viewed sex as a natural and highly beneficial activity. In other words, natural sexual urges were not repressed but were institutionally circumscribed: to the right place, at the right time, and with the right person. See Internet URL: http://www.arts.unimelb.edu.au/Dept/Russ Cent/Chang.html.

83. Hershatter, op. cit., p. 78.

84. Ibid., p. 81. This issue is also very much the subject of some of Ann Anagnost's work; for example, see A. Anagnost, 1997, *National Past-Times: Narrative, Representation, and Power in Modern China*. Durham: Duke University Press.

85. Evans, op. cit.

86. Ibid., p. 1.

87. This is what was implied in the notion of the "dreams of heaven" in the collective era. See Croll (1994), op. cit.

88. Anchee Min, 1994, *Red Azalea*. New York: Pantheon Books.

89. Ibid., p. 58.

90. Ibid., p. 60.

91. Ibid., p. 60–61.

92. Ibid., p. 62.

93. Evans, op. cit., p. 8.

94. A survey conducted in Beijing in 1994 showed that 21 percent of husbands admitted to beating their wives; also, more than a fourth of divorces in China are a result of family violence; see Blecher, op. cit., p. 157. The incidence of rape has been increasing rapidly (see Liu et al. [1997], op. cit.) and by the late 1980s was second only to robbery in crime rates.

95. In 1991 and 1992 alone, police statistics reported that 50,000 cases of the abduction of

women and children were solved, with 75,000 people arrested. See Evans, op. cit., p. 170. In 1993, 33,000 women were abducted and sold between mid-1993 and early 1995 (ibid., p. 120). There are reports of young girls being kidnapped and lined up against a wall, stripped to their underwear, with prices (between Y2,000 and Y3,000) written on their clothing (ibid., p. 171).

96. Evans raises an important point about this issue that brings up the economic and social dichotomy between the city and the countryside in China. Most of the women being abducted are poor, innocent girls from the countryside, who are passive victims in a chain of crime that invariably ends up in the city. Here is a metaphor commonly reiterated in China, comparing the backwardness of the rural and the modernity of the urban. In other words, the young female victims are being defined as the "others" to the urban, which is assumed to be the place at the opposite end of the spectrum from the countryside—where people are wealthy and well educated. In this sense, Evans suggests, "The abduction of women . . . appears as a metaphor for the need for urban-oriented development of the countryside" (op. cit., p. 173). An interesting twist on this theme is offered in Zhang Yimou's film *The Story of Qiuju*, in which a peasant woman persistently attempts to challenge the patriarchal and urban hierarchy—and systematically refuses to be categorized as a simple, poor, wretched individual in need of education and modernization in the city. The main character, Qiuju (played by Gong Li), challenges the formidable labyrinth of Chinese bureaucracy to get some redress against the chief of her village, who had kicked her husband below the belt. Intriguingly, a further subplot of the film unfolds when it turns out that the village chief has four daughters but has been unable to sire a son. The kicking episode occurred after Qiuju's husband had questioned the chief's masculinity, and the kick to the testicles was, therefore, a retaliation to render him as impotent as he was himself. A startling turn in the story occurs when, finally, long after the two men had resolved their dispute, a ruling is made in favor of Qiuju, and the village chief is arrested for his part in the original kicking incident. The peasant woman, in other words, had successfully challenged the patriarchal bureaucracy and had asserted her agency. For a deconstruction of the film, see Ming-Bao Yue, 1996, "Visual Agency and Ideological Fantasy in Three Films by Zhang Yimou," pp. 56–73 in W. Dissanayake (ed.), *Narratives of Agency: Self-Making in China, India, and Japan*. Minneapolis: University of Minnesota Press. Ann Anagnost also devotes a chapter in her recent book *National Past-Times* (op. cit.) to analyzing the story of Qiuju; see "Chili Pepper Politics," pp. 138–160.

97. The quote here is from Hershatter, op. cit., p. 171; see Evans, op. cit., p. 178.

98. Evans, op. cit., p. 176. She also argues that sex work is rarely, if ever, considered as a legitimate form of employment, even though for some women it may be the only job possible, and for others, in fact, it is seen as a relatively good job.

99. Ibid., p. 181.

100. Ma Lizhen, 1989, "Women: The Debate on Jobs Versus Homemaking," *China Reconstructs*, Vol. 38, No. 3, pp. 66–68; the quote is from p. 68 (a letter written to the author by Jian Shufan, a woman).

101. Ma estimated that 20 million employees, 60 percent of them women, had paid jobs but little work to do (ibid., p. 67).

102. See R. Weil, 1994, "China at the Brink: Class Contradictions of 'Market Socialism': Part 1," *Monthly Review* (December), pp. 10–55; and also R. Weil, 1995, "China at the Brink: Class Contradictions of 'Market Socialism': Part 2," *Monthly Review* (January), pp. 11–43.

103. Wolf, op. cit.

104. This was reported in a story in the official English-language newspaper, *China Daily*, March 29, 1994, p. 3.

105. Events in China are consistent with the worldwide trend toward the feminization of the workplace, as employers strive to reduce labor costs and increase flexibility; see G. Standing, 1996, "Global Feminization Through Flexible Labor," pp. 405–430 in K. P. Jameson and C. K. Wilbur (eds.), *The Political Economy of Development and Underdevelopment*, 6th ed. New York: McGraw-Hill.

106. X. X. Gao, 1994, "China's Modernization and Changes in the Social Status of Rural Women," pp. 80–97 in C. K. Gilmartin, G. Hershatter, L. Rofel, and T. White (eds.), *Engendering China: Women, Culture, and the State*. Cambridge: Harvard University Press; and X. J. Li, 1994, "Economic Reform and the Awakening of Women's Consciousness," pp. 359–382 in ibid. See also B. J. Nelson and N. Chowdhury (eds.), 1987, *Women and Politics Worldwide*. New Haven: Yale University Press.

107. T. E. Barlow (ed.), 1994, *Gender Politics in Modern China: Writing and Feminism*. Raleigh: Duke University Press.

108. *Women's International Network News*, Vol. 15, No. 1 (Winter 1989), and No. 4 (Autumn 1989). It

has been estimated that women in Tianjin spent an average of 444 minutes each day on household and child-care duties, compared to 144 minutes for men. See Y. J. Bian, 1987, "A Preliminary Analysis of the Basic Features of the Life Styles of China's Single-Child Families," *Social Sciences in China*, Vol. 8, pp. 189–209.

109. P. D. Beaver, L. H. Hou, and W. Xue, 1995, "Rural Chinese Women: Two Faces of Economic Reform," *Modern China*, Vol. 21, pp. 205–232.

110. As one Chinese woman has written, "The suffocation of women's individual self-worth is the price paid for men's realization of their greatest social value" (Li [1994], op. cit., p. 364). She argues that for educated women who have experienced the independence of being wage-earners a return to the run-of-the-mill life at home—cooking, cleaning, and child care—is asking too much (or, rather, too little) of them; see also Beaver et al., op. cit.

111. Because young women are willing to work for low wages and in poor conditions in the new industrial jobs, the gender ratio in some of the more advanced cities, for example, the SEZs, has already exceeded the 50:50 mark, with marked surpluses of women. The products made in these areas are often in light industry, and the jobs are considered to be highly suitable for women: making clothes, electronic goods, travel bags and luggage, and toys. In the export-processing zones the gender ratio among the newly imported transient workers is often on the order of two women to each man. In some cases it is higher; for example, in a plastic handbag processing factory, the ratio was as high as 50:1. Gao, op. cit., pp. 92–93.

112. In a recent report, Weil (op. cit.), for example, observes that in 1993 a two-month police crackdown in Guangzhou rounded up more than 30,000 prostitutes.

113. Croll (1994), op. cit., p. 94.

114. N. D. Kristoff and S. Wu Dunn, 1994, *China Wakes: The Struggle for the Soul of a Rising Power*. New York: Times Books/Random House.

115. E. Rosenthal, "Suicides Reveal Bitter Roots of China's Rural Life," *New York Times*, January 24, 1998. The study on which the report was based was conducted by the World Bank, Harvard University, and the World Health Organization.

116. The report also places considerable emphasis on the easy availability of bottled pesticides, which are ubiquitous in rural homes and provide a simple and very effective route to suicide. This is apparently the method of choice among China's rural women,

but it has been suggested that many of the suicides are accidental, in the sense that the women perhaps did not want to die, but the pesticides are so strong that it is unavoidable.

117. The household responsibility system was the first of the agricultural reforms to be implemented widely in the Chinese countryside after 1978, replacing the collective (commune) system of agricultural production (see Chapter 7). In the HRS, households or groups of families entered into a contractual arrangement for their quota of land. On that land households could produce whatever they wanted; they were also allowed to market surplus products in the emerging retail markets. Household members were free to work on the land, at sideline activities, and in nearby industries. See K. Lieberthal, 1995, *Governing China: From Revolution Through Reform*. New York: W. W. Norton.

118. See Croll (1994), op. cit.

119. This would not be the case in households where women control the majority of the sideline activities, which may be a fairly large group. A survey conducted by the All-China Women's Federation in 1987 showed that 35–40 percent of all specialized households, and up to 55 percent in the more developed regions, were operated by women. Ibid.

120. Wolf, op. cit., pp. 268–269. The hidden impacts of this new situation could be enormous. Young women (daughters) will be less able to go out to meet people, which could increase the parental role in the area of matchmaking. The safety rules of the workplace may be abandoned in the home. Women could be seriously overworked, with no one to report their husbands to. Urban and rural women alike are also much more likely nowadays to work at home in the rapidly growing putting-out system, in which they contract with local enterprises or cooperatives to work at home. This could result in women becoming increasingly isolated from the wider community and more subject to family (male) authority, in addition to the threat of working under sweatshop conditions, with no adequate fringe benefits and the normal protections of the state workplace.

121. Sen's work has been published in various guises. For the best sources, see A. K. Sen, 1984, *Resources, Values, and Development*. Cambridge: Harvard University Press; and Sen, 1989, "Food and Freedom," *World Development*, Vol. 17, No. 6, pp. 769–781. More specific to the issue of women in China are Sen, 1990, "More Than 100 Million Women Are Missing," *New York Review of Books*, Vol. 37 (December 20), pp. 61–66; Sen, 1992, "Life and

Death in China: A Reply," *World Development*, Vol. 20, pp. 1305–1312; Sen, 1994, "The Causation and Prevention of Famines: A Reply," *Journal of Peasant Studies*, Vol. 21, pp. 29–40. Sen has spent a great deal of his time defending himself and his work from rather vicious attacks from Peter Nolan, an economist from Cambridge University, who appears to have some doubts about how Sen's theories can be applied to the case of China. In a recent volume, Sen reviews much of his earlier work; see A. Sen, 1999, *Development as Freedom*. New York: Alfred A. Knopf. It is interesting to note that Sen has recently been appointed to Cambridge University and is now master of Trinity College.

122. D. Davin, 1988, "The Implications of Contract Agriculture for the Employment and Status of Chinese Peasant Women," pp. 137–146 in S. Feuchtwang, A. Hussain, and T. Parrault (eds.), *Transforming China's Economy in the Eighties*. Vol. 1: *The Rural Sector, Welfare, and Employment*. Boulder: Westview Press, p. 140.

123. World Bank, 1992, *China: Strategies for Reducing Poverty in the 1990s*. Washington, DC: International Bank for Reconstruction and Development. One particularly vulnerable group of rural women includes widows. In Liaoning and Beijing, for example, 21.2 percent and 19.4 percent of widows are in the bottom decile in terms of income. The World Bank report also indicates that rural women often have unequal access to household resources such as food, clothing, and shelter.

124. The decline in collectively funded schools has hit women hard, and the percentage of girls attending primary school fell by 9 percent from 1978 to 1994; in 1993 70 percent of China's illiterates were women; see Blecher, op. cit., p. 157.

125. See Sen (1990), op. cit.

126. World Bank (1992), op. cit., pp. 45–47.

127. V. Pearson, 1996, "Women and Health in China: Anatomy, Destiny, and Politics," *Journal of Social Policy*, Vol. 25, No. 4 (October), pp. 529–542.

128. Boys are preferred in many countries (including China) because it is expected that they, and only they, will be able to take care of their parents in their old age. If the status of women in the labor force, and correspondingly in the household, improves, then it is possible that female children would receive more attention and care after they are born; indeed, more of them may actually be born; Croll (1994), op. cit. A more extensive discussion of the topic of boy preference can be found in Chapter 5.

129. The HRS threatens the population policy in a number of ways. The amount of land allocated to each family is determined by family size, which encourages parents to go against the plan. In addition, some local officials have been neglecting their birth control duties to take care of their own plots. The HRS also diminishes the pool of local welfare funds, which means less funds are available locally to pay the rewards to compliant (i.e., one-child) families. It is also much more difficult to extract penalties from deviant families under HRS, in comparison to the old work-point system, because it is difficult to determine incomes that are earned largely outside the collective unit. For a discussion of these issues, see T. Whyte, 1987, "Implementing the One-Child Population Program in Rural China: National Goals and Local Politics," pp. 284–317 in D. M. Lampton (ed.), *Policy Implementation in Post-Mao China*. Berkeley: University of California Press; see esp. pp. 308–309. There is some evidence that the successful implementation of the HRS is associated with greater son preference. For example, the male-to-female survival rate for children appears to be highest in those parts of China that have implemented the HRS most completely—for example, in Anhui Province, where the male-to-female ratio for infants is 111:100; see O'Sullivan, op. cit., pp. 67–68.

130. Mo Yan (trans. Howard Goldblatt), 1995, *The Garlic Ballads*. New York: Viking Penguin, p. 252.

131. Ibid.

132. Croll (1994), op. cit.

133. Ibid., p. 165.

134. In Hebei Province an investigation conducted in nine prefectures and cities found 7,400 child laborers illegally employed by township enterprises. Most of the children were girls as young as eleven. A spot-check conducted in Guangdong Province found that only 70 percent of the children aged six to seventeen were in school, and only 54 percent of those aged between fifteen and seventeen. Croll (1994), op. cit., p. 166.

135. Whether or not Sen's entitlement theory is correct, there is no doubt that there is excess female mortality in China, producing the disturbing phenomenon of the missing women (see later). See, for example, S. Harper, 1994, "China's Population: Prospects and Policies," pp. 54–76 in D. Dwyer (ed.), *China: The Next Decade*. London: Longman.

136. It is important to point out that this is only a hypothesis and that Sen's argument has been questioned, especially by Peter Nolan; see, for example,

P. Nolan and J. Sender, 1992, "Death Rates, Life Expectancy, and China's Economic Reforms: A Critique of A.K. Sen," *World Development*, Vol. 20, pp. 1279–1303. One of the critical issues in this debate is the accuracy of the data that are being used to assess the death rate in China. Both Sen and Nolan have been able to produce statistics that support their own side of the argument. It is difficult to reach any firm conclusions on this topic without more definitive data. See also P. Nolan, 1993, "The Causation and Prevention of Famines: A Critique of A.K. Sen," *Journal of Peasant Studies*, Vol. 21, pp. 1–28.

137. See Croll (1994), op. cit.

138. J. S. Coale and J. Banister, 1994, "Five Decades of Missing Females in China," *Demography*, Vol. 31, pp. 459–479; and also S. Klasen, 1994, "Missing Women Reconsidered," *World Development*, Vol. 22, pp. 1061–1071.

139. T. H. Hull and X. Y. Wen, 1992, "Recent Trends in Sex Ratios at Birth in China," *Population and Development Review*, Vol. 16, No. 1 (March), pp. 63–83; on the adoption issue, see S. Johansson and O. Nygren, 1991, "The Missing Girls of China: A New Demographic Account," *Population and Development Review*, Vol. 17, No. 1 (March), pp. 35–51.

140. Y. Zeng et al., 1993, "Causes and Implications of the Recent Increase in the Reported Sex Ratio in China," *Population and Development Review*, Vol. 19, No. 2, pp. 283–302. Another study reported in *The Economist*, "The Lost Girls," September 18–24, 1993, p. 38, showed that in hospitals in China, where the sex ratio at birth should be 100.0, it was 105.6 for firstborn children. For mothers who already have one girl child, however, the ratio was 149.4; and for those with more than two girls it was 224.9. See also X. S. Ren, 1995, "Sex Difference in Infant and Child Mortality in Three Provinces in China," *Social Science and Medicine*, Vol. 40, No. 9 (May), pp. 1259–1269.

141. Yet they also point out that it is not *only* the one-child policy that has created such a situation. In Taiwan and South Korea, for example, where no such policies have been implemented, SRBs are also very high: 116.9 in Korea in 1990, 110.2 in Taiwan. A possible explanation in these cases is that both Taiwan and South Korea have experienced major declines in total fertility (1.81 and 1.60 respectively in 1990), largely as a result of improving economic circumstances. With fewer children being born overall, families in Taiwan and South Korea are choosing to abort females, indicating that they, like the Chinese, have a strong boy preference. See B. C. Gu and K. Roy, 1995,

"Sex Ratio at Birth in China, with Reference to Other Areas in East Asia: What We Know," *Asia-Pacific Population Journal*, Vol. 10, No. 3, pp. 17–42.

142. O'Sullivan, op. cit., p. 69.

143. See Hooper, op. cit., p. 109. A survey conducted in 1983 found that only 28 percent of the current male university students wanted their wives to be university graduates, compared to 80 percent of the women in universities. There is also some evidence that traditional patterns of patriarchal kinship are being strengthened by the household responsibility system in the countryside. In many rural areas the private plots allocated to the newly contracting households were predominantly in small, scattered strips, and cooperation within the village was still necessary to manage crop rotations, irrigation, and pest control. This has produced a greater degree of mutual aid than might have been expected, but much of it tends to be along kinship lines, thereby strengthening the male-based lineage associated with village life in the countryside, a development that is not likely to further women's interests. See M. Palmer, 1988, "China's New Inheritance Law: Some Preliminary Observations," pp. 169–197 in Feuchtwang et al., op. cit.

144. See Whyte, op. cit.

145. C. L. Brown, 1994, "The Rights and Interests of Women in the People's Republic of China: Implementation of a New Law," pp. 116–123 in D. K. Vajpeyi (ed.), *Modernizing China*. Leiden, Netherlands: E. J. Brill.

146. Ibid., p. 122.

147. See C. A. Traut, 1997, "China and the 1995 United Nations Conference on Women," *Journal of Contemporary China*, Vol. 6, No. 16 (November), pp. 581–589.

148. Hall, op. cit., p. 176.

149. *Far Eastern Economic Review*, "Much Ado: Women Meet, Educate, Get Spied on, Protest," September 14, 1995, pp. 17–18.

150. *Far Eastern Economic Review*, "To Bear Any Burden: Asia's Women Pay a Disproportionately High Price for the Region's Economic Boom," September 7, 1995, pp. 42–43.

151. *Far Eastern Economic Review*, September 14, 1995, op. cit., p. 18.

152. Hall, op. cit., p. 177.

153. *Far Eastern Economic Review*, September 14, 1995, op. cit., p. 18.

154. Hall, op. cit., p. 177.

155. Table adapted from Cecilia Lai-Wan Chan, 1995, "Gender Issues in Market Socialism," pp.

188–215 in L. Wong and S. McPherson (eds.), *Social Change and Social Policy in Contemporary China.* Aldershot, UK: Avebury Press, p. 210.

156. F. Christiansen and S. M. Rai, 1996, *Chinese Politics and Society: An Introduction.* London: Prentice-Hall.

157. Stacey believes that the CCP could only keep its support base among the vastly partriarchal countryside by keeping its promise not to alter the status quo in any significant way. She suggests that during the Great Leap Forward the CCP violated this unwritten pact with the male-dominated villagers by pushing forward too rapidly with antipatriarchal policies, particularly the socialization of domestic work and the concept of family production units. According to Stacey, opposition to these policies at the village level was one of the major causes of the disasters following the Great Leap Forward (op. cit., pp. 212–213). In spite of the strength of patriarchal traditions in the countryside, there are some historical examples in which women have temporarily been able to break free. In the silk factories of Guangdong Province, for example, the largely female workforce in the late nineteenth century offered serious resistance to local (and Chinese) customs. Among their strategies were to pledge themselves to celibacy and to refuse to join their husband's family after marriage by binding themselves on their wedding night. After two nights without consummation they were allowed to return home to live as spinsters. See A. Y. So, 1986, *The South China Silk District: Local Historical Transformation and World System Theory.* Albany: State University of New York Press, esp. pp. 123–131.

158. Stacey, op. cit., p. 256. Hooper has suggested that the absence of a strong women's movement in China is a result of the weakness of the Women's Federation, which was intended to look after females' interests but actually does little more than parrot the government's line on all issues. Basically the government believes that male-female inequality is not a gender issue at all but a class issue; and as class differences are eliminated, so will gender differences be eliminated. As a result the government condemns independent feminist organizations as "women's rights movements of the bourgeoisie"; see Hooper, op. cit., p. 111.

159. Wolf, op. cit., p. 261. The contributors to a book of personal stories related by Chinese women in 1988 reinforce this depressing conclusion. The 1982 census in China showed that 70 percent of Chinese illiterates or barely literates were female, and the gap appears to be increasing. Although girls are told to study hard at school, many articles in the press promote "scientific conclusions that boys are superior to girls intellectually." Three out of five couples in the countryside still meet through matchmakers; and the phenomenon of childhood betrothals is reappearing. The reports demonstrate that many of the oppressive and patriarchal aspects of traditional Chinese family life have not only survived but have taken on modern, respectable forms. See E. Honig and G. Hershatter, 1988, *Personal Voices: Chinese Women in the 1980s.* Stanford: Stanford University Press.

160. Wolf, op. cit., p. 271.

161. Ibid., p. 261.

Chapter 14

1. C. H. Li, 1998, *China: The Consumer Revolution.* Singapore: John Wiley and Sons (Asia); see pp. 6, 57.

2. J. LeGrand and R. Robinson, 1984, *Privatization and the Welfare State.* London: George, Allen and Unwin.

3. M. K. Whyte and W. L. Parish, 1984, *Urban Life in Contemporary China.* Chicago: University of Chicago Press, p. 57

4. E. F. Vogel, 1969, *Canton Under Communism: Programs and Politics in a Provincial Capital, 1949–1968.* Cambridge: Harvard University Press, p. 46.

5. Ibid., p. 44.

6. Ibid.

7. T. Terzani, 1986, *Behind the Forbidden Door: Travels in China.* London: Allen and Unwin, p. 53.

8. F. Butterfield, 1983, *China: Alive in the Bitter Sea.* Toronto: Bantam Books, p. 108.

9. Whyte and Parish, op. cit., p. 102.

10. The inadequacies of the distribution system also had an indirect influence on patterns of social interaction, and sometimes it was necessary to tolerate disagreeable people. One family in Cheng Naishan's story, called "No. 2 and No. 4 of Shanghai," had a tiresome uncle whom they would rather have nothing to do with. The problem was that this uncle had extraordinarily good *guanxi*, and if they were to live well they simply could not manage without him: "This in-law . . . was a real nuisance, yet the painful truth was that [he] was indispensable. From big things like plane and boat tickets to little things like movie tickets or a TV purchase coupon, not to men-

tion arranging hotel dinner parties or even getting a taxi, without Ahwei none of this was possible. So [he] made himself completely at home. . . . He even addressed the family . . . with glib intimacy." See Cheng Naishan, 1989, "No. 2 and No. 4 of Shanghai," pp. 1–116 in *The Piano Tuner*. San Francisco: China Books and Periodicals, p. 84.

11. Butterfield, op. cit., p. 102.

12. This pattern of spatial organization was very different from the sort of bottom-up structure that would typically be found in Western cities. In the United States, for example, we might expect to find a loose collection of grassroots local groups, usually operating at the neighborhood level, each one focusing on a specific task. By comparison, the local organizations in the communist city were mandated from above; they did not emerge naturally from the desires of the people.

13. In actual fact this sort of decentralization was rarely possible, and for most of the time since 1949 the flow of information and the chain of command have remained solidly unidirectional (downward).

14. For a further discussion of the original structure and purpose of the neighborhood organizations, see J. A. Cohen, 1968, *Criminal Process in the People's Republic of China, 1949–1963: An Introduction*. Cambridge: Harvard University Press, esp. pp. 106–112.

15. See F. Schurmann, 1968, *Ideology and Organization in Communist China*. Berkeley: University of California Press.

16. For an illustration of the services provided at the neighborhood level in one Beijing district, see Luo Fu, 1980, "City Dwellers and the Neighborhood Committee," *Beijing Review*, No. 44 (November 3), pp. 19–25.

17. It is this local level of record-keeping and surveillance that makes it extremely difficult for anyone on the run to remain at large from the government, as the dissident students in Beijing found after the crackdown in 1989.

18. The way the system works is described beautifully in Zhang Jie's short story "The Ark," which revolves around the lives of three divorced women who live together in an apartment. Partly because they have politically questionable backgrounds, but also because they are divorcées, they find themselves constantly under the watchful eyes of Mrs. Jia, the head of their courtyard committee. One day she pays the divorcées a visit, on the pretext of looking for her cat, but probably just to snoop around to see if they are doing anything she should know about. During the conversation it becomes clear that she suspects the divorcées of some (unspecified) immoralities: "'Has our cat by any chance come over to your place?' [Mrs. Jia asks]. 'No' [one of the divorced women] replied quickly. 'Why should it come here?' 'Oh dear, Comrade Cao. Don't you know? Your cat has been playing court to all six of our toms.' And she tittered sarcastically. Could single cats really evoke the same disapproval as single women? Perhaps they ought to marry Maotou [the cat] off as quickly as possible!" At this point Mrs. Jia retreated, unable to find any evidence to put into the files. She is, of course, more convinced than ever of the lax moral standards of the single women, so lax that their behavior could even rub off onto their cat! See Zhang Jie, 1986, *Love Must Not Be Forgotten*. San Francisco: China Books and Periodicals, pp. 113–202 ("The Ark"); quote from pp. 122–123.

19. It is one thing to have such information, of course, but quite another thing to do anything about it. The evidence is widespread that spouse abuse remains at an unacceptably high level in China. See Whyte and Parish, op. cit., chap. 7, pp. 195–228. Some of the benefits of neighborhood committee work in this area are illustrated by the results of surveys conducted in specific locations. See, for example, "Neighborhood Findings," *China Daily*, March 10, 1987.

20. It is likely that the invasiveness of the residents' committees today is but a shadow of what it was during the prereform era, especially during the Cultural Revolution. At that time residents lived in constant fear. A knock on the door could be the local official, sometimes referred to within the neighborhoods as the "policemen with small feet," who have extensive powers to search and seize. No one was safe: The police could enter people's homes at any time to ask what was cooking in the pot or to look under the bed, allegedly to check whether the family abides by the rules laid down by the hygiene campaign; but actually to check whether anything or anybody is hiding underneath.

21. E. Croll, 1985, "The Single-Child Family in Beijing: A First-Hand Report," pp. 190–232 in E. Croll, D. Davin, and P. Kane (eds.), *China's One-Child Family Policy*. London: Macmillan.

22. Ibid., p. 209.

23. Ibid.

24. Whyte and Parish, op. cit., p. 25.

25. The *danwei* is parallel in a symbolic way to the binding of a woman's feet in prerevolutionary China, in the sense that it keeps people at home, where they

can be kept under close scrutiny, and it restricts their interaction with the outside world. All visitors can be screened by the officials working at the gates of the unit; if necessary, undesirables can be prevented from entering.

26. E. M. Bjorklund, 1986, "The Danwei: Socio-Spatial Characteristics of Work Units in China's Urban Society," *Economic Geography*, Vol. 62, No. 1 (January), pp. 19–29.

27. A. F. Thurston, 1988, *Enemies of the People: The Ordeal of the Intellectuals in China's Great Cultural Revolution*. Cambridge: Harvard University Press, pp. 124–125.

28. For purposes of maintaining public support, most charges for urban services have remained extremely low. Bus fares in Shanghai, for example, were four, seven, and ten fen for several decades (10 fen equals Y0.1; Y3.7 yuan equaled US$1 in the 1980s). Tickets to urban parks, zoos, museums, and galleries cost next to nothing (a few fen, but often several yuan for foreigners). It has been estimated that what is collected at the gates of such entertainment facilities does not cover even 1 percent of the wages for the workers involved. See Tian Bingxin, 1988, "A Tragicomedy Concerning Residence Cards," *Nexus—China in Focus* (Winter), pp. 24–26.

29. For a detailed discussion of the significance of urban residence cards, see L. T. White, 1977, "Deviance, Modernization, Rations, and Household Registers in Urban China," pp. 151–171 in A. A. Wilson, S. L. Greenblatt, and R. W. Wilson (eds.), *Deviance and Social Control in Chinese Society*. New York: Praeger. The net effect of the huge flow of migrants out of the countryside is that the cities have had to shoulder an increasingly heavy burden to provide the services and subsidies required by the expanding urban population. It has been estimated that for every extra 10,000 migrants to the city of Shanghai there is an exponential increase in the cost of providing additional services. The costs are already sky-high: Y3.5 million each year for infrastructure including roads, buses, and utilities; Y6.4 million for new housing; Y1.2 million in food subsidies; and Y2.3 million for education and health care. To meet the needs of the floating populations of Guangzhou (those without residency cards, estimated at 880,000 in 1988 and more than 1.3 million in 1993) an investment increase of between Y4.4 and 6.2 billion is needed, along with a daily increase of 440,000 kilowatts of electricity, 270,000 tons of tap water, and 1,000 tons of grain and vegetables. See Tian, op. cit., p. 26.

30. Ibid.

31. As we saw in Chapter 9, however, attempts are ongoing to encourage both enterprises and people to move to medium-sized and smaller cities, where urban services are cheaper to provide and less in demand. Of course, they also tend to be less plentiful in smaller cities. The irony of this situation is that in spite of the great desire to obtain residency cards urban and rural dwellers alike realize the mixed blessing the cards represent. The card ties a family down to a specific city, making any voluntary movement—for example, to seek a new job or to get married—extremely difficult. Yet most city residents realize they must acquire a card and hold onto it at all costs. The only exception here is some of the new breed of peasants involved in commodity production in the countryside, who are free to go where they please in search of profitable work. Included therein are the itinerant tribes, so to speak, of construction workers, cobblers, housemaids, and tailors that began to appear in most cities across China in the mid- and late 1980s. Ibid., p. 26.

32. Ibid., p. 24.

33. D. Bonavia, 1989, *⊥he Chinese*, rev. ed. London: Penguin, p. 24.

34. Luo Fu, 1980, "City Dwellers and the Neighborhood Committee," *Beijing Review*, No. 44 (November 3), pp. 19–25, 20. According to a *China Daily* report, Beijing neighborhood committees provided 13,600 clues, which led to the solution of 1,500 criminal cases in 1986. Interestingly, however, the same article noted that more than half of the committees had never reported any criminal cases, implying the importance of prevention and mediation activities. See "Committees Play Vital Roles in Urban Areas," *China Daily*, March 13, 1987.

35. D. J. Solinger, 1999, *Contesting Citizenship in Urban China: Peasant Migrants, the State, and the Logic of the Market*. Berkeley: University of California Press, p. 101.

36. Vogel, op. cit., p. 64.

37. K. W. Chan, 1994, *Cities with Invisible Walls: Reinterpreting Urbanization in Post-1949 China*. Hong Kong: Oxford University Press.

38. Vogel, op. cit., esp. chap. 2, "Local Urban Control: Takeover and Consolidation, 1949–1952," pp. 41–90.

39. P. Theroux, 1988, *Riding the Iron Rooster: By Train Through China*. New York: Ivy Books, p. 273. To make sure there is no national or ethnic bias here, it is probable that the Chinese say the same thing about Americans or Europeans, especially in times of con-

flict. When a U.S. plane bombed the Chinese embassy in Belgrade in May 1999, for example, the swift denials—often contradicting each other—must surely have given the Chinese reason to suspect the worst intentions of the NATO allies.

40. Vogel, op. cit., p. 64.

41. Ibid., p. 89.

42. See Whyte and Parish, op. cit., pp. 246–261.

43. In other words the reduction in the level of crime has been the result of specific activities that have either prevented opportunities for crimes to occur or have militated against the concentration of large subcultures of criminally inclined people. Although this is in itself an impressive achievement, it is not really a result of the switch over to socialism per se, in the sense of "producing" a new type of person (the "new communist man") who is presumably less likely to commit crimes.

44. This conceptualization is based on a discussion by R.J.R. Kirkby, 1985, *Urbanization in China: Town and Country in a Developing Economy, 1949–2000 A.D.* New York: Columbia University Press.

45. Whyte and Parish, op. cit., p. 247. This raises the now familiar theme of "defensible space," which is part of a broader area of study, environmental criminology. The defensible-space idea implies that crime rates can be lowered if there are fewer open and unwatched spaces, such as parks, empty lots, parking garages, and hallways. The solution, according to this theory, is to redesign urban and residential spaces to eliminate or reduce the amount of nondefensible space. The obvious counter to the theory is that criminals will simply shift their activities elsewhere, implying that the solution is little more than a cosmetic activity that does little to deal with the root causes of crime. See, for example, O. Newman, 1972, *Defensible Space.* New York: Macmillan.

46. Whyte and Parish, op. cit., p. 257.

47. Ibid., p. 234.

48. Ibid., p. 258. It is essential to note that the 1980s also offered many people in China, both urban and rural, a dream of, or at least a hope for, a new future, one that would involve a certain amount of prosperity they had been denied in the past. The new population trends need to be considered, therefore, within the context of rising aspirations nationwide, which strengthens the blocked opportunities hypothesis.

49. *Far Eastern Economic Review,* "Let Them Eat Cash: China Tries to Scrap Food-Price Controls," May 26, 1988, pp. 72–73. The inflation of food prices throughout 1985 and 1986 continued into 1987. Vegetable prices, for example, increased by 25 percent in the summer months and more than 50 percent in the winter months. Poultry and egg prices increased at an average of 20 percent in 1987, and the urban retail price index rose by 10 percent. The trend continued into 1988, and in the first quarter food prices rose by 24 percent, with vegetable prices going up by more than 50 percent.

50. T. M. Cheung, 1988, "Road Works Ahead: Traffic Congestion Is Choking China's Cities," *Beijing Review,* Vol. 141, No. 27, July 7, 1988, p. 79. The demand for travel among the Chinese, and particularly among tourists, with such antiquated road systems, slow and decrepit buses, and a virtual absence of urban trains, has meant a bonanza for taxis in China's cities. See, for example, "Guangzhou's 6,000 Taxis Hustle for Fares," *China Daily,* March 7, 1988. Orville Schell estimates that in the mid-1980s there were 14,000 cabs in Beijing, 3,000 more than in New York City. See O. Schell, *Discos and Democracy: China in the Throes of Reform.* New York: Pantheon Books, p. 65.

51. See World Bank, 1997, *Clear Water: Blue Skies.* Washington, DC: World Bank, p. 78.

52. Ibid., p. 79.

53. Ibid., p. 85.

54. "Traffic Rethink Needed," *China Daily,* March 31, 1987.

55. "Road Death Toll Rises 20 Percent in 1985," *China Daily,* June 14, 1986. The rising rates have been blamed on growing populations, including the influx of rural migrants; streets that are too narrow; too many bicycles; poor driving habits; and a shortage of road-traffic controllers.

56. It is estimated that Beijing's vehicle numbers have expanded 100 times since 1949, Shanghai's thirteenfold, compared to twelve- and fivefold increases respectively in the total road mileage in each city. See Cheung, op. cit., p. 79.

57. "Vehicle Increase Causes More Accidents," *China Daily,* April 10, 1987.

58. See World Bank, op. cit., chap. 6, pp. 73–85; see also Chapter 16, on the environmental issues associated with increasing car ownership in China.

59. Schell, op. cit., p. 66. The appearance of fleets of Japanese taxis and even Mercedes and Cadillac limousines aimed at the high end of the tourist market has symbolized the end of a chapter in China's recent history. In the not-too-distant past virtually the only cars on the streets of Beijing were the chunky old Red Flag limousines that were domesti-

cally made and sported the Chinese characters for "Red Flag"—written in Mao's own hand—affixed to their trunks.

60. Hu Sigang, "City Bids to Fight Garbage Problem," *China Daily*, December 11, 1986.

61. Shen Ji and Si Jiuye, "Making Mountains out of Rubbish," *China Daily*, April 24, 1986.

62. Theroux, op. cit., p. 389.

63. See Shen and Si, op. cit. The Beijing Sanitation Bureau paid Y2,500 for one mu of land to dump garbage. In 1985 the bureau spent Y150,000 for land for dumps. Obviously the loss of arable land in the suburbs is a major concern, as is the pollution of local air and water sources. These problems have prompted a considerable amount of research into viable options to dumping, including incineration, biodegradation, and irradiation treatment. The problem is that 50 percent of China's waste tends to be inorganic and is therefore difficult to dispose. The only solution, therefore, is the landfill method, which will cost an estimated Y300 million, a staggering amount in comparison to the bureau's current budget of Y40 million, already one-third of the city's total maintenance expenses.

64. An editorial in *China Now*, for example, published in London before the 1989 demonstrations, predicted some of the later events. The major problem appeared to be the grimness of the economic picture throughout 1988, exacerbated by skyrocketing inflation rates and energy shortages. The editorial reported on several calls for Zhao Ziyang to resign, presumably for his role in creating the economic crisis. The influx of unemployed peasants—2.5 million in Guangdong coastal cities alone—has seriously stretched the employment and service capabilities of many cities. Rising crime rates are being reported, as well as new record levels of unemployment. See "Sinofile," *China Now*, No. 129 (Summer 1989), pp. 3–5.

65. Theroux, op. cit., p. 275.

66. For a discussion of quality-of-life studies, see P. Knox, 1988, *Urban Social Geography: An Introduction*. London: Wiley.

67. These data were gathered from *China: Urban Statistics* (1985), compiled by the State Statistical Bureau of the PRC and published in London by the Longman Group. The data presented do not, of course, necessarily mean either that the people in the largest cities have better access to such services or that they make use of or appreciate them any more than do residents of smaller cities. We also have no indication of the quality of the services in question;

it could be, for example, that the greater level of usage in larger cities may result in lower quality or slower access (e.g., longer lines, worse roads, buses in worse condition, etc.). It is also impossible to locate comparable statistics for rural areas, but in general it is assumed that many of the services and facilities in question are less likely to be available than they are in cities. See, for example, Kirkby (1985), op. cit.

68. For a discussion of recent urban population trends, see S. Goldstein, 1985, *Urbanization in China: New Insights from the 1982 Census*. Honolulu: University of Hawaii, Papers of the East-West Population Institute, No. 93 (July).

69. Among the best examples are Zhang Xinxin and Sang Ye, 1987, *Chinese Lives: An Oral History of Contemporary China*. New York: Pantheon Books; and E. Honig and G. Hershatter, 1988, *Personal Voices: Chinese Women in the 1980s*. Stanford: Stanford University Press.

70. S. Peck (ed.), 1985, *Halls of Jade, Walls of Stone: Women in China Today*. New York: Franklin Watts, p. 266.

71. Cheng, op. cit., p. 55.

72. Another way for outsiders to get a feel for everyday life for the Chinese city dweller is to ride on the public buses. The jostling, the dirt, the noise, and the intense discomfort of bus travel can provide, in small doses, a culturally rewarding experience. For the tourist it can be fun riding cheek-by-jowl with so many others for a short time, but on a daily basis, through winter and summer, with neither heat nor air-conditioning, the experience is probably less than enchanting. There should be no doubt in anyone's mind, therefore, that most people would prefer to slip into the warmth, privacy, and security of their own car and drive themselves to work, if that were possible. It has been estimated that in China the ratio of people to buses was on the order of 2,640:1, compared to a worldwide average of around 1,000:1; see R. Kojimo 1987, *Urbanization and Urban Problems in China* Tokyo: Institute of Developing Economies, Occasional Paper Series No. 22. The major problem with the bus situation in most of China's large cities is the decrepit state of the buses themselves. The estimated depreciation time for buses in China is twenty-seven years, about five times longer than in Japan and the United States. The low fares, offered as a government subsidy, barely contribute to operating expenses.

73. Whyte and Parish, op. cit., p. 99.

74. Ibid., p. 99.

75. Zhang and Sang, op. cit., p. 156.

76. Li Ping, 1987, "Opinion Poll: How People Feel About Urban Reform," *China Reconstructs* (January), pp. 55–57.

77. Sheng Huochu and Liu Hongfa, 1986, "Resurvey of Workers' Living Standards in Tianjin," *Beijing Review* (December), pp. 29–32.

78. "Polls Help to Improve Tianjin," *China Daily*, January 8, 1987.

79. Note that in 1988 China's GNP was estimated at US$330, although it was probably (in real terms) much higher than that, bearing in mind the lower prices for most commodities in China. The issue has been discussed in detail. N. R. Lardy, 1994, *China in the World Economy*. Washington, DC: Institute for International Economics, pp. 14–18. See also V. Smil, 1993, *China's Environmental Crisis: An Inquiry into the Limits of National Development*. Armonk, NY: M. E. Sharpe, chap. 3, "China's Modernization," pp. 67–98, esp. 69–75. The work on levels of well-being is reported in State Statistical Bureau, 1992, *The Standard for China's Being Well-Off*. Beijing: Chinese Statistical Press; the same is summarized in S. Yabuki, 1995, *China's New Political Economy: The Giant Awakes*. Boulder: Westview Press, chap. 21, "Charting China's Development to the Year 2000," pp. 229–242, esp. tables 21.1–21.4 and figs. 21.1–21.3.

80. It is important to note that the standards by which the attainment levels of 1990 have been assessed are highly subjective and are based on data that are probably very questionable. For example, it is estimated that the proportion of people living in poverty decreased from 33 percent in 1980 to 8 percent in 1990. This conclusion, of course, depends largely on what level of income is used to assess poverty; as Nolan (1993) has observed (see also Chapter 10 of this book) there are reasons to question such estimates and to think that poverty has not been reduced in anything like the proportions claimed by the Chinese government, even with the extensive programs set in place since the mid-1980s. See P. Nolan, 1993, "Economic Reform, Poverty, and Migration in China," *Economic and Political Weekly*, Vol. 28 (June 26), pp. 1369–1377.

81. See Yabuki, op. cit., pp. 231–234.

82. See China Statistical Publishing House, 1998, *China Statistical Yearbook 1997*, and its various tables; see also Chapters 8–10 in this book for other discussions on the growth in consumption of urban goods and services. The material consumption index (with 1978 set to 100) reached 184 by 1985, 225 by 1990, and 362 by 1996. The average growth per year from 1978 to 1988 was 9.1 percent, only 4.1 percent

from 1985 to 1990. See J.C.H. Chai, 1996, "Consumption and Living Standard in China," pp. 247–276 in R. F. Ash and Y. Y. Kueh, 1990, *The Chinese Economy Under Deng Xiaoping*. Oxford: Clarendon Press, table 1, p. 248.

83. The consumption index grew from 221 in 1990 to 362 in 1996, which represents an annual growth of 9.1 percent, showing that consumption is clearly back on track. *China Statistical Yearbook 1997*, table 9-2, p. 292. The statistics also show that the annual growth rate was in fact slightly higher in the rural areas than in the cities (8.5 percent versus 7.9 percent).

84. See Chai, op. cit., table 6, p. 527; and also *China Statistical Yearbook 1997*, table 2-3, p. 35.

85. To most Westerners the proportion of total income spent on housing in China seems to be preposterously small, although there are some indications, as we shall see later in this chapter, that the price of housing is rising quite significantly in the 1990s. In 1990 the proportion of urban household income spent on housing (or residence) was reported to be 7.7 percent of disposable income; but there appears to be a major discrepancy here between the data reported by Chai (op. cit.) and those of the *Yearbook*. For example, in 1985 Chai reported that only about 1.7–1.9 percent of urban incomes was spent on housing, whereas the *Yearbook* shows a figure of 4.8 percent. Obviously there is a different definition in use, but the percentage spent on residence in 1990 did increase significantly in the 1990s, from 4.8 percent in 1990 to 7.7 percent in 1996 (see *China Statistical Yearbook*, table 2-3, p. 35).

86. It is possible that this enormous increase in green space in China's cities (see Table 14.1) is largely an artifact of the way the term "urban" is defined. As we noted in Chapter 9, the reform era has seen some major redefinitions of what is considered to be urban, with significant annexations of areas in the peri-urban fringe that are largely agricultural, which implies they do not have a high proportion of urban land uses. If this is the case, then it may not be correct to think of this as recreational space.

87. In a 1991 study reported by Chai, op. cit., direct subsidies amounted to almost 11 percent of the average urban household's expenditures, in addition to the indirect subsidy provided by the state in the form of significantly below-cost services, especially housing.

88. Ibid.

89. This is a direct quotation from Lin Zhiqun, in R. Kojima, 1987, *Urbanization and Urban Problems in*

China. Tokyo: Institute of Developing Economies, Occasional Paper Series, No. 22, p. 38.

90. D. R. Phillips and A.G.O. Yeh, 1987, "The Provision of Housing and Social Services in China's Special Economic Zones," *Environment and Planning C: Government and Policy*, Vol. 5, pp. 447–468. It is useful to remember that in the early 1990s there were still an estimated 35 million Chinese people living in caves, ranging from the luxurious to the squalid. See, for example, "Living in a Cave Has Its Own Charm," *China Daily*, August 19, 1987. In many cases cave dwellers reckon that their homes are larger than the average city dweller's home and easier to keep warm during winter and cool during summer.

91. R. Murphey, 1980, *The Fading of the Maoist Vision: City and Country in China's Development*. New York: Methuen.

92. The housing that was owned privately was usually old and generally a remnant from before liberation. Much of it has been passed from parents to children and does not generally enter into a commodity-like housing market. It is important for Westerners to avoid the trap of assuming that the lack of luxury or apparent comfort in the Chinese home necessarily assumes a lack of attachment. For most outsiders the typical "room" that is home to many Chinese people appears to be cramped, hopelessly ill-equipped, and relatively unadorned by such basics as carpet and wallpaper. Many young families with only one room have to cook in the hallways or on balconies and share toilets and even water outlets. By Western standards such homes would be intolerable, but it is clear that real attachments can develop even to the most basic spaces. See R.J.R. Kirkby, 1988, "Urban Housing Policy After Mao," pp. 227–244 in S. Feuchtwang, A. Hussain, and T. Pairault (eds.), *Transforming China's Economy in the Eighties*. Vol. 1: *The Rural Sector, Welfare, and Employment*. Boulder: Westview Press.

93. As noted earlier in this chapter, to maintain order in the city the state established a hierarchical system of organization that made sure the policies of the central government could be administered effectively at the local level. The lowest tier in this hierarchy operated on the streets and in the courtyards—almost at people's back doors, in fact—where locally appointed resident-officials could keep a close watch on the comings and goings of everyone within their domain. Unlike an American family, therefore, an urban Chinese family was rarely able to use the home to close itself off from the outside world. Neighborhood security officials considered

homes within their jurisdiction to be in the public rather than the private domain. See Terzani, op. cit., p. 53.

94. D.S.G. Goodman, 1981, *Beijing Street Voices: The Poetry and Politics of China's Democracy Movement*. London: Marion Boyars, p. 94. According to Goodman the main target of this poem is Wang Dongxing, vice chairman of the Chinese Communist Party at that time and the person in charge of the administrative offices in Zhongnanhai—the Politburo and State Council headquarters—where the nation's leaders were reportedly living comfortably in spacious surroundings. This, of course, is the source of the poet's discontent, in that it symbolized the corruption and inequality in contemporary China. Qin Shihuang, China's first emperor, was justifiably considered to be a tyrant, the creator of the first totalitarian state. We can assume that the poet implied an analogy here with Mao Zedong, who was often referred to as the "people's emperor." See D. Wilson, 1979, *The People's Emperor: A Biography of Mao Zedong*. New York: Lee Publishing.

95. Kirkby (1988), op. cit.

96. Although these sorts of differences were persistent, there is little evidence that class variations in housing standards in China had any spatial pattern to them, as they typically might in a North American metropolis, with high-quality and more spacious housing in the suburbs and poverty in the city centers. In the socialist cities of Eastern Europe, housing inequalities have also been persistent, and although there is a spatial pattern to such inequality, it is generally not as simply observable as it usually is in capitalist cities. In the Chinese city, by comparison, housing inequality was more likely to occur at the micro scale and within the confines of each individual work unit, for example, where the top administrators and party officials lived. In recent years there had also been a boom in private housing construction, especially in the small towns and rural counties administratively attached to the larger cities, as a result of new levels of affluence among peasants and so-called specialized households. Many peasants have built themselves relatively luxurious homes that now stand as examples of conspicuous consumption for others to see and admire. See, for example, O. Schell, 1984, *To Get Rich Is Glorious: China in the Eighties*. New York: Pantheon Books. There is also some evidence of housing inequality emerging as a result of recent government experiments with providing housing for sale in various cities. In Changzhou, for example, there is a three-tier devel-

opment of new housing; the first offers relatively luxurious and spacious apartments and detached units, averaging more than 100 square meters per person and usually only affordable by overseas Chinese from Taiwan or Hong Kong. The other two tiers of housing, still relatively spacious, are intended for new wealthy families. See "Apartments for Sale in Changzhou," *China Daily*, February 2, 1987. A similar hierarchical structure also has been developed in Shanghai. See "Shanghai Savers Buy Homes," *China Daily*, May 19, 1986. In addition to the obvious problem of lack of space, China's urban housing stock was in a poor state of repair. Years of neglect and the shortage of building materials resulted in a hodgepodge of dilapidation, with many of the older structures crumbling, patched up, and dangerous. See C. Riskin, 1987, *China's Political Economy: The Quest for Development Since 1949*. Oxford: Oxford University Press. At the interurban scale there were also some significant variations in the standard of housing. The country's largest cities were usually the most crowded. In Shanghai, for example, almost one-fifth of the 5 million inner-city inhabitants were encountering severe housing problems by the end of the 1970s, living at an average density of less than two square meters of floor space per person, which is about the space taken up by a twin bed. See Kirkby (1988), op. cit., p. 230; see also Kojima, op. cit., esp. chap. 3, "Urban Housing." In the back streets of Shanghai and Beijing, and in fact in all Chinese cities, decrepit ancient buildings invariably coexist with a jumble of newly built structures.

97. C. P. Lo, 1987, "Socialist Ideology and Urban Strategies in China," *Urban Geography*, Vol. 8, No. 5 (September–October), pp. 440–458.

98. "Housing Policy Changes Rushed," *China Daily*, June 30, 1987.

99. One innovative and logical solution to the chronic housing shortage in China's largest cities has been a system of housing exchanges. This began informally but soon blossomed into a semiofficial and computerized service. The usual reason for wanting to exchange was to avoid a lengthy journey to work, a chronic problem in the absence of rapid transit systems in China's hugely overcrowded cities. See "Beijing Fair Busy with House-Swappers," *China Daily*, August 22, 1986, and "Exchanging Homes Is Popular in Beijing," *China Daily*, February 28, 1987.

100. Whyte and Parish, op. cit., p. 78.

101. "Too Low Rents Cause Housing Shortage," *China Daily*, March 21, 1987; see also Riskin, op. cit., and M. Chossudovsky, 1986, *Towards Capitalist Restoration: Chinese Socialism After Mao*. Hong Kong: Macmillan.

102. There are many observers, both foreign and Chinese, who argue that the acclaimed excellence of the Chinese health care delivery system is a well-maintained myth (see Chapter 6) and that China's education system is certainly not as effective as many outsiders had originally thought. See, for example, S. Pepper, 1990, *China's Education Reform in the 1980s: Policies, Issues, and Historical Perspectives*. Berkeley: Center for Chinese Studies, University of California. For examples from Eastern European countries, see I. Szelenyi, 1983, *Urban Inequality Under State Socialism*. London: Oxford University Press. Housing and housing policies in the Soviet Union are well described by G. Littlejohn, 1984, *A Sociology of the Soviet Union*. London: Macmillan; by J. H. Bater, 1980, *The Soviet City*. Beverly Hills, CA: Sage Publications; and by V. George and N. Manning, 1980, *Socialism, Social Welfare, and the Soviet Union*. London: Routledge and Kegan Paul.

103. For a fascinating account of the attitudes toward such bourgeois home fittings as pianos, see R. C. Kraus, 1989, *Pianos and Politics: Middle-Class Ambitions and the Struggle over Western Music*. Oxford, UK: Oxford University Press. The most terrifying of the accounts, all of which are provided from actual interviews, are available in Anne Thurston's *Enemies of the People*, op. cit. In recent years many accounts have been written, in short-story and novel formats, by Chinese people who lived through the Cultural Revolution. See, for example, Gao Yuan, 1987, *Born Red: A Chronicle of the Cultural Revolution*. Stanford: Stanford University Press; Liang Heng and J. Shapiro, 1984, *Son of the Revolution*. New York: Vintage Books; and Lo Fulang, 1989, *Morning Breeze: A True Story of China's Cultural Revolution*. San Francisco: China Books and Periodicals. As we see in a beautifully told story by Wang Anyi entitled "Lapse of Time," during the Cultural Revolution rich families were often under constant scrutiny from the Red Guards. The family in Wang's story had had all of their expensive possessions commandeered and placed in storage in the ground floor of their house. At irregular intervals, totally unannounced, groups of Red Guards would back up trucks to the front door and cart off varying amounts of the family's belongings. The family, too terrified to respond, was totally passive in the face of what amounted to theft of their possessions. One day the rest of their belongings were moved out and a poor (working-class) family was moved in, effec-

tively to live as squatters but with the sanction of the local Party and the Red Guards.

104. This generally refers to investments in the area of urban utilities, education, social services, cultural facilities, recreation, transportation, and housing. In the national construction period during the early 1950s, investment levels in these areas were relatively high. See J. Domes, 1985, *The Government and Politics of the PRC: A Time of Transition.* Boulder: Westview Press.

105. "How to End the Shortage of Housing, *China Daily,* March 6, 1987.

106. Kirkby (1988), op. cit.

107. See Riskin, op. cit., and Chossudovsky, op. cit. An all-out attempt to solve the housing crisis not only represented a serious pragmatic problem; it also required a major ideological shift in the direction of an increasingly market-oriented economy. As we saw in Chapter 4, the Party leadership was divided in its commitment to the reform goals, with serious infighting between the two major cliques on either side of the left-right political continuum. As noted earlier, the housing crisis at the end of the 1970s was associated with the overall austerity of Mao's China. Mao had convinced himself (but not all of the CCP leaders) that China's people should not anticipate any major improvements in their living standards in the near future. It was Mao's belief that the struggle aspect of the revolution had not ended in 1949, and in fact class struggle would continue until the persistent remnants of the old bourgeois society had been permanently exorcised. Consistent with this belief was Mao's assertion that self-sacrifice was required of Chinese people. Instead of aspiring to the consumption standards of the West, they should accept the need for frugality, hard work, and the ascetic lifestyles of a new socialist order. In the home this translated to the rejection of luxury and comfort and the tolerance of extremely basic living quarters. It is unlikely that this revolutionary commitment was still widespread during the 1980s, as incomes began to rise in both the cities and the countryside and as more and more consumer goods began to be easily available. In fact some Western scholars argue that this sort of commitment was never widespread among the ordinary people, except in propaganda documents.

108. See Phillips and Yeh, op. cit., and L.J.C. Ma, 1981, "Urban Housing Supply in the People's Republic of China," pp. 222–259 in L.J.C. Ma and E. W. Hanten (eds.), *Urban Development in Modern China.* Boulder: Westview Press. See also R.J.R. Kirkby, 1987,

"Housing the Masses," *China Now,* No. 120, pp. 28–30.

109. "New Housing Criticized by Residents," *China Daily,* March 13, 1987. The survey results and the proposed housing reform plans are discussed by Liu Hong, 1989, "Housing Construction and Reform," *China Reconstructs,* Vol. 38, No. 8 (August), pp. 8–11; see also Mou Zhentou, 1989, "Housing Reform in Yantai," *China Reconstructs,* Vol. 38, No. 8 (August), pp. 12–13.

110. As implausible as it may have seemed at first, the vast exodus from the countryside to the cities during the 1980s produced some of the homelessness problems so common in U.S. cities beginning in the late 1980s. Unemployed peasants were reportedly squatting in Chinese cities all across the country, sleeping in the streets and any available spaces they could find. At present there is very little information on the extent of actual homelessness in China, but in the absence of very harsh prohibitions on rural out-migration, it is difficult to see how China's already overstretched cities will be able to house the influx in the future; see "Too Low Rents Cause Housing Shortage," *China Daily,* op. cit. For evidence of the rising prevalence of unemployment and homelessness in some of China's cities, see Sun Yuntao, 1988, "Shock Wave Unemployment in Qingdao City," *Nexus-China in Focus* (Winter), pp. 27–28. In a 1989 editorial, *China Now* reported that the official newspaper *Economic Daily* considered the rural surplus/redundant population to be China's most serious problem for the 1990s and estimated that by the year 2000 there could be as many as 260 million surplus laborers in China. See Angela Knox, 1989, "Sinofile," *China Now,* No. 129 (Summer), p. 5. This issue is addressed in more detail in Chapter 15.

111. Riskin, op. cit. Richard Kirkby has estimated that the state subsidies for housing amounted to Y3.5 billion. See Kirkby (1988), op. cit., p. 234. Such subsidies aggravated the already serious problem of the state's budget deficit. There had been a significant decline in state revenues as a result of the decision to allow individual enterprises and localities to keep a larger portion of their own profits. In addition, as part of the agricultural reforms, the state had started to decontrol food prices, which meant the government was paying far more for food than it had been in the recent past. The success of China's new SEZs had also produced a sizeable increase in foreign imports, which had helped to drain the country's scarce reserves of foreign exchange (see Chapter 8). So, in addition to catering to the absolute need for

additional housing in China, and also providing a viable outlet for consumption among the newly wealthy, the commodification of housing had actually become a financial necessity by 1980. In 1979 China experienced, for the first time since 1949, a significant budget deficit, amounting to Y17 billion. For details of the Yantai experiments, see Mou, op. cit.

112. "Housing Policy Changes Pushed," *China Daily*, June 30, 1987.

113. See Y. P. Wang and A. Murie, 1996, "The Process of Commercialization of Urban Housing in China," *Urban Studies*, Vol. 33, No. 6, pp. 971–989.

114. Ibid., p. 981. In Liaoning, for example, 96 percent of the city's public housing was offered for sale—and sold—within three months at an average price of Y100 per square meter.

115. See C. H. Sun, "Urban Housing and Reform in China." Paper presented at the Sixth International Research Conference on Housing, Beijing (September 21–24, 1994).

116. State Statistical Publishing House, 1998, *China Statistical Yearbook 1997*, table 2.2, pp. 30–31.

117. See Wang and Murie, op. cit.

118. A. Chen, 1996, "China's Urban Housing Reform: Price-Rent Ratio and Market Equilibrium," *Urban Studies*, Vol. 33, No. 7, pp. 1077–1092. In fact, this author observes that there were more than

320,000 urban households that still had less than 2 square meters per capita.

119. Ibid.

120. See M. Xhou and J. R. Logan, 1994, "Market Transition and the Commodifications of Housing in Urban China." New York: Russell Sage Foundation, Working Paper #59. One useful policy would be to establish a cap on the price of open-market housing. At present the ratio of income to housing prices in China is roughly 1:13, a result of China's low average household incomes (compare 1:2.8 in the United States, 6.7 in Japan, and 2.4 in the United Kingdom). See United Nations Development Program, 1998, *Human Development Report*. New York: Oxford University Press.

121. See A. Khan and C. Riskin, 1998, "Income and Inequality in China: Composition, Distribution, and Growth of Household Income, 1988–1995," *The China Quarterly*, No. 154 (June), pp. 221–253. They report that housing policies, especially subsidies and coupons, have made a significant contribution to the rising inequality in Chinese cities. See also Chapter 10 in this book.

122. X. M. Chen and X. Y. Gao, 1996, "China's Urban Housing Development in the Shift from Redistribution to Decentralization," *Social Problems*, Vol. 40, No. 2 (May), pp. 266–283.

Chapter 15

1. D. J. Solinger, 1999, *Contesting Citizenship in Urban China: Peasant Migrants, the State, and the Logic of the Market*. Berkeley: University of California Press.

2. See X. M. Chen and W. L. Parish, 1996, "Urbanization in China: Reassessing an Evolving Model," pp. 61–90 in J. Gugler (ed.), *The Urban Transformation of the Developing World*. London: Oxford University Press, p. 76.

3. The statistics here are provided by Y. M. Siu and S. M. Li, 1993, "Population Mobility in the 1980s: China on the Road to an Open Society," pp. 1–31 in J.Y.S. Cheng and M. Brosseau (eds.), *China Review, 1993*. Hong Kong: Chinese University Press.

4. It is apparent that definitions of the floating population may differ depending on who is doing the counting. The Ministry of Public Security, for example, includes all migrants, whereas the official census counts only those who cross city or county lines. The larger estimates of the floating population also include individuals who are away from home

but will not be seeking work and accommodation in the new locality, including such categories as visiting relatives, seeking hospital treatment, attending meetings, tourists, and students. In theory, all of these people, as well as longer-term migrants, are required to get a temporary residential registration card from the Public Security Bureau if they are away from home for more than three days, but in fact many do not. There is also another category, known as "vagrants," who are people wandering around with no fixed abode and who do not register with the local Public Security Bureau office, even temporarily. See *China News Analysis*, "From and in the Villages: New Migrants and Old Clans," No. 1462 (January 1, 1991), pp. 1–2.

5. Another way to calculate the number of temporary migrants is to aggregate from the more than 8 million estimated to be living in the eleven largest cities in 1990. See M. B. Li and Y. Hu, 1991, *Impact of Floating Population on the Development of Large Cities and Recommended Policy* (in Chinese). Beijing:

Jingi Ribao Chubanshe. This produces an overall estimate of about 70 million. Other estimates are lower; for example, the *Foreign Broadcast Information Service* (hereafter *FBIS*) in Washington, DC, in 1990 estimated 50 million. See *FBIS*, "Floating Population Exceeds 50 Million," January 19, 1990. In fact it is almost impossible to count the "temporary" migrant population accurately because of the vast numbers involved and the rates at which new migrants enter and leave cities. There is general agreement, however, on two major points: The official census seriously undercounts the total number of migrants; and the overall number of migrants is increasing every year.

6. The 1987 sample census collected similar data, but migration was defined differently, so the two databases are not comparable. See Siu and Li, op. cit.

7. See Guangdong Population Census Office (hereafter GPCO), 1990, *The Floating Population Census in Guangdong Province, 1990.* Guangzhou, Guangdong Province: Guangdong Population Census Office. The next most popular destinations were the nation's biggest cities: Beijing had an in-migration rate of 4.8 percent, Shanghai 4.1 percent.

8. As the attempts to exclude outsiders from other provinces increased during the 1990s, it was likely that an increasing share of the temporary migrants would be coming from the same province; see, for example, L. Wong, 1994, "China's Urban Migrants: the Public Policy Challenge," *Pacific Affairs*, Vol. 67, No. 3 (Fall), pp. 335–355. Wong discusses the attempts to make employees in the Pearl River Delta cities hire workers from only Guangdong Province.

9. The migration into Guangdong Province requires a little more interpretation, because it appears to be significantly different from migration patterns in other parts of China. In the first place, as Siu and Li, op. cit., point out, Guangdong led the nation with intraprovincial migrants (3.99 per 100 residents), but its interprovincial net immigration rate was 1.44, significantly lower than the corresponding rate for the three special metropolitan regions—Beijing, Tianjin, and Shanghai—magnets for migrants in China. Although Guangzhou is considerably smaller than those three cities, until recently it had been the clear leader in the pace of economic development; thus in relative terms, at least, it was a bigger attraction for people on the move. See E. F. Vogel, 1989, *One Step Ahead in China: Guangdong Under Reform.* Cambridge: Harvard University Press. Guangdong's temporary migrant population in 1990 was 486,983. Of Guangdong

Province's total migrants (inter- and intraprovincial, permanent and temporary) more than two-thirds (68.3 percent) originated in rural areas, and 93.2 percent had destinations in urban areas (the corresponding figures for the whole of China were 62.5 percent and 81.8 percent). In total, the province increased its population (in-migrants minus out-migrants) by 2,572,000 in the five-year period 1985–1990, which was the highest rate for any province in China; the rate of in-migration increased 6.6 times from 1982 to 1990 (compared to 1.6 times for China as a whole and 2.54 times for Beijing, the second fastest growth rate). These and other data about Guandong are provided by L. Li, 1993, *Migration, Urbanization, and Urban Planning in Guangdong Province.* Working Paper No. 8, Center for Urban and Regional Studies. Guangzhou: Zhongshan University. Because of the frantic pace of economic development, Guangdong generally receives a much higher proportion of migrants seeking employment opportunities than all other provinces; see H. Y. Hu and M. K. Ng, 1993, *Population Distribution Within a Socialist City.* Working Paper No. 7, Center for Urban and Regional Studies. Guangzhou: Zhongshan University. In addition, compared to the national statistics, Guangdong receives more than the average proportion of women as temporary migrants, many of whom are attracted to (or are recruited into) jobs in the heavily feminized manufacturing sector, especially factories making textiles, clothing, and electronic products. The gender ratio in the province varies significantly from city to city. In the city of Guangzhou, temporary migrants are considerably more likely to be men (gender ratio: 128.5 men per 100 women); but in other cities, such as Shenzhen and Dongguan, the ratio reflects considerably more women than men in the working transient populations. See also D. M. Zhou, 1993, "An Approach to the Problem of Population Movement and Cultural Adaptation in the Urbanizing Pearl River Delta," pp. 205–215 in G. Guldin and A. Southall (eds.), *Urban Anthropology in China.* Leiden, Netherlands: E. J. Brill.

10. See Li, op. cit., p. 6. Again it is important to point out that the estimate for Guangdong Province includes only those people who have been away from home for more than a year. If we apply the same weighting as indicated earlier, assuming that the number of migrants who have been away for less than a year is about 2.5 times as large, then Guangdong's total floating population is closer to 10 million. This in fact is the estimate made by the

province's Ministry of Public Security. By the same reasoning, the city of Guangzhou's floating population is thought to be in excess of 1 million and probably closer to 1.5 million in 1990. In fact the most attractive city for migrants has consistently been the SEZ city of Shenzhen, which in 1990 recorded more than 1 million temporary migrants. See GPCO figures for 1990, op. cit. In this case, however, the weighting we applied earlier to the national and Guangdong temporary migrant statistics may not apply, because as an SEZ Shenzhen requires that most migrants obtain a special permit to live there. In other words the official census statistic may be closer to the real size of Shenzhen's floating population than is the case for Guangzhou and other cities.

11. It is important to point out that the definition of "urban" in China is frequently being changed (see Chapter 9); see, for example, Li, op. cit. The old prefectures were reclassified as cities or municipalities (*shi*), and many of the former communes were redefined as market towns or townships (*zhen*). Li has estimated that as many as 45 percent of the additional 2.6 million urban dwellers in Guangdong between 1985 and 1990 resulted from new definitions. This still leaves about 41 percent of the urban increase in Guangdong Province accounted for by in-migration, most of which came from the rural areas, with the balance (14 percent) made up by natural increase of the population. For a detailed discussion of the definitional issues, see K. W. Chan, 1994, *Cities with Invisible Walls: Reinterpreting Urbanization in Post-1949 China.* Hong Kong: Oxford University Press. It is important to add a caveat about the definitional changes that have contributed to the rapid increase in the rate of urbanization during the last decade. In a number of provinces (including Guangdong) prefectural centers and county seats have been redefined as cities (*shi*), with jurisdiction over a number of surrounding counties, many of which are largely rural in character. Many small towns have been upgraded into cities; and in some cases township boundaries have been expanded beyond the built-up area to provide leadership for the small towns within the jurisdiction. See K. C. Tan, 1993, "Rural-Urban Segregation in China," *Geography Research Forum*, Vol. 13, pp. 71–83. The goal of these strategies was to bring about greater integration in terms of economic and demographic interaction between the urban and rural areas. To some extent these were artificial changes, producing unrealistically large jumps in the rate of urbanization. But it is also evident that many of the towns selected for upgrades had indeed experienced significant population growth, often fueled by in-migration from the surrounding countryside, which reflects a bona fide increase in the rate of urbanization. See Chan, op. cit.

12. O. Schell, 1994, *Mandate of Heaven: A New Generation of Entrepreneurs, Dissidents, Bohemians, and Technocrats Lays Claim to China's Future.* New York: Simon and Schuster, p. 387.

13. For a detailed discussion of this process, see the case studies reported in E. Croll, 1994, *From Heaven to Earth: Images and Experiences of Development in China.* New York: Routledge.

14. The environmental degradation issue is discussed in detail by V. Smil, 1993, *China's Environmental Crisis: An Inquiry into the Limits of National Development.* Armonk, NY: M. E. Sharpe; and R. L. Edmonds, 1994, *Patterns of China's Lost Harmony: A Survey of the Country's Environmental Degradation and Protection.* London: Routledge. For a Chinese view, see B. C. He, 1991, *China on the Edge: Crisis of Ecology and Development.* San Francisco: China Books and Periodicals.

15. See J. R. Taylor, 1988, "Rural Employment Trends and the Legacy of Surplus Labor, 1979–1986," *The China Quarterly*, No. 116, pp. 736–766; and also J. R. Taylor and J. Banister, 1991, "Surplus Rural Labor in the People's Republic of China," pp. 87–120 in G. Veeck (ed.), *The Uneven Landscape: Geographic Studies in Post-reform China.* Baton Rouge: Louisiana State University Press, GeoScience Publications, Vol. 30.

16. Taylor and Banister, op. cit., p. 98. Mao Zedong had anticipated this phenomenon as early as the 1930s, when he realized that a mass exodus from the countryside was part of a long process of transformation in which the rural population become residents of the cities. See R.J.R. Kirkby, 1985, *Urbanization in China: Town and Country in a Developing Economy, 1949–2000 A.D.* New York: Columbia University Press. This is exactly what happened during the first decade after the communist takeover in 1949; but after 1958 a series of restrictive measures was implemented to keep the peasants from leaving the land. Going back even farther in time it is evident that the Chinese countryside has traditionally had an underemployment problem. A survey of rural households conducted in the later 1920s, for example, showed that only 35 percent of able-bodied men in the Chinese countryside worked full-time. See Taylor and Banister, op. cit., p. 94.

17. D. Solinger, 1985, "Temporary Residence Certificate Regulations in Wuhan, May 1983," *The China Quarterly*, No. 101 (March), pp. 98–103.

18. Zhou, op. cit., p. 208.

19. Wong, op. cit.

20. See S. Goldstein and A. Goldstein, 1991, "Permanent and Temporary Migration Differentials in China," Papers of the East-West Population Institute No. 117. Honolulu: University of Hawaii.

21. See *FBIS*, January 19, 1990, "Floating Population Exceeds 50 Million."

22. See Li, op. cit.

23. See GPCO, op. cit.

24. L.J.C. Ma and C. S. Lin, 1993, "Development of Towns in China: A Case Study of Guangdong Province," *Population and Development Review,* Vol. 19, No. 3, pp. 583–606, table 10.

25. Dorothy Solinger has written a series of penetrating papers on the floating population issue, including the following: D. Solinger, 1993, "China's Transients and the State: A Form of Civil Society?" *Politics and Society,* Vol. 21, No. 1, pp. 91–122; D. Solinger, 1994, "China's Urban Transients in the Transition from Socialism and the Collapse of the Communist Urban Public Goods Regime," *Comparative Politics,* Vol. 27, No. 2, pp. 127–146; and D. Solinger, 1994, "The Floating Population in the Cities: Chances for Assimilation?" pp. 113–142 in D. Davis et al. (eds.), *Urban Spaces in Contemporary China: The Potential for Autonomy and Community in Post-Mao China.* Cambridge, UK: Cambridge University Press. Solinger has also addressed the issue of whether floaters represent a serious drain on urban resources and services, focusing on their excess consumption of food, grain, electricity, water, and transportation. She concluded that the floaters are perhaps being used as a scapegoat for everything that is going wrong in contemporary Chinese cities, as they are transformed from the old planned economy to the new market economy. See D. Solinger, 1996, "The Impact of Migrants on City Services," *Chinese Environment and Development,* Vol. 7, Nos. 1 and 2, pp. 118–143. Solinger in 1999 published a book on this topic: See *Contesting Citizenship in Urban China,* op. cit.

26. This issue has been discussed in a number of articles circulated by *China News Digest.* See, for example, Lena H. Sun, "With Millions of Underclass Migrants, Will China's System Collapse?" *China News Digest* from *Washington Post,* October 9, 1994; Rone Tempest, "Government Begins Counting 'Floating Population,'" *China News Digest* from *Los Angeles Times,* November 19, 1994; and Uli Schmetzer, "Corrupt Officials, Foreign Businesses Spell Doom for Workers: Profit-First Mentality Overlooks Safety Needs," *China News Digest* from *Chicago Tribune,* October 5, 1994.

27. See, for example, J. J. Macisco Jr., 1992, "International Migration: Issues and Research Needs," pp. 229–248 in C. Goldscheider (ed.), *Migration, Population Structure, and Redistribution Policies.* Boulder: Westview Press; and A. Portes and R. Manning, 1986, "The Immigrant Enclave: Theory and Empirical Examples," pp. 47–68 in J. Nagel and S. Olzack (eds.), *Comparative Ethnic Relations.* Orlando, FL: Academic Press.

28. See Solinger (1999), op. cit.

29. G. E. Johnson, 1993, "The Political Economy of Chinese Urbanization: Guangdong and the Pearl River Delta Region," pp. 167–204 in Guldin and Southall, op. cit. See also the recent volume edited by Guldin, 1997, *Farewell to Peasant China: Rural Urbanization and Social Change in the Late Twentieth Century.* Armonk, NY: M. E. Sharpe.

30. G. W. Skinner (ed.), 1977, *The City in Late Imperial China.* Stanford: Stanford University Press.

31. F. W. Mote, 1977, "The Transformation of Nanking, 1350–1400," in G. W. Skinner (ed.), *The City in Late Imperial China.* Stanford: Stanford University Press. See also M. K. Whyte, 1993, "Adaptation of Rural Family Patterns to Urban Life in Chengdu," pp. 358–380 in Guldin and Southall, op. cit.

32. This is discussed in detail in E. Friedman, P. G. Pickowitz, and M. Selden, 1991, *Chinese Village, Socialist State.* New Haven: Yale University Press.

33. See Skinner, op. cit. See also Chapter 9 in this book for a more detailed discussion of the history of urbanization in China; see also A. Southall, 1993, "Urban Theory and the Chinese City," pp. 19–40 in Guldin and Southall, op. cit. The unity broke down periodically, for example when specific rulers attempted to increase their powers and the dominance of the center over the periphery, which usually led to rural revolts and the overthrow of the ruling elite. What Southall is describing is consistent with Marx's theories about the historical emergence of cities as centers of power and production. Marx described the traditional Chinese urban system as part of the "Asiatic" mode of production.

34. M. K. Whyte and W. L. Parish, 1984, *Urban Life in Contemporary China.* Chicago: University of Chicago Press, p. 361. These ideas about rural and urban unity in China are certainly not shared by all historians. J. D. Spence, 1990, *The Search for Modern China.* New York: W. W. Norton, for example, focuses on the harshness of life in the countryside compared to the cities, arguing that city dwellers have always

been contemptuous of the peasants and their lifestyles. Some urbanists have drawn attention to the long-standing feeling of antiurbanism among the elite in China, which increased considerably after Western contact and industrialization began in the mid-nineteenth century.

35. A. Southall, 1993, "Urban Theory and the Chinese City," pp. 19–40 in Guldin and Southall, op. cit.

36. Whyte and Parish, op. cit., p. 361. This, of course, is precisely the fear of many people in contemporary China, i.e., that the floating populations will plunge China back into its nightmarish past, with a return to problems that were once rampant but had been well under control during the relative tranquillity and orderliness of the Maoist city.

37. Tan, op. cit.

38. The orthodox view of the peasants by the Party elite was consistent with those of Engels, who wrote that "the first major division of labor, that is the separation of city from country, enable(d) the rural population to remain in a foolish state for thousands of years"; quoted in S. H. Potter and J. M. Potter, 1990, *China's Peasants: The Anthropology of a Revolution.* Cambridge: Cambridge University Press, p. 300. These attitudes were reproduced by Party members in their daily dealings with the peasants (see F. Butterfield, 1982, *China: Alive in the Bitter Sea.* Toronto: Bantam Books) and also by many of the youths who were sent down to the countryside during the 1960s and 1970s; see T. P. Bernstein, 1977, *Up to the Mountains and Down to the Villages.* New Haven: Yale University Press. It was generally accepted among the urban elite that "to live like a peasant was a punishment." Potter and Potter, op. cit., p. 303.

39. M. Selden, 1988, *The Political Economy of Chinese Socialism.* Armonk, NY: M. E. Sharpe. Several forces were contributing to rural stagnation: The rural population almost doubled between the 1950s and 1970s; peasants were barred from migrating or going into private business to improve their life chances; and the state was continually extracting more from the countryside than it was returning. As a result many poor, marginal, and peripheral rural communities experienced long-term income stagnation at bare subsistence levels; as a result millions of peasants living in rural collectives were left with scant prospect of improving their livelihood or their conditions of work.

40. D. Kelliher, 1992, *Peasant Power in China: The Era of Rural Reform, 1979–1989.* New Haven: Yale University Press, p. 103.

41. Ibid.

42. Patrilineal organization principles remained strong in the countryside but were breaking down in the cities. Other traditions were also being forgotten: Cremations replaced burials, traditional Chinese festivals were outlawed, and in the 1970s having large families started to become an issue of critical concern. See Friedman, Pickowitz, and Selden, op. cit.

43. The so-called mobility transition hypothesis is described by W. Zelinsky, 1971, "The Hypothesis of the Mobility Transition," *Geographical Review,* Vol. 61, pp. 219–249. Zelinsky originally envisaged an irreversible progression of stages through which societies modernized; as urbanization increased, the role of circulation and temporary migration diminished, to be replaced by longer-distance and more permanent migrations. From this fundamental premise it has been noted that mobility (defined as the combination of circular and one-way movements between places) does not occur as a random process but has clear, identifiable spatial patterns; in other words, as countries modernize it is possible to detect changes in the type of migration they are associated with. See ibid.

44. From studies conducted in developing societies around the world, it appears that events are not occurring as Zelinsky had predicted, and several modifications of the original hypothesis have appeared. This is discussed by R. Skeldon, 1990, *Population Mobility in Developing Countries: A Reinterpretation.* London: Belhaven Press; and also by L. A. Brown, 1991, *Place, Migration, and Development in the Third World: An Alternative View.* London: Routledge. One of the most significant modifications has followed from the observation that rather than being a transitional stage of mobility, circulation appears to be an enduring pattern of geographical behavior in many different cultures and at all stages of development. As many recent studies of both internal and external migration have demonstrated, migration streams typically encompass a broad spectrum of mobility behaviors: from those who move on a seasonal, sporadic, and short-term basis all the way to permanent migrants who will never return to their homes. See, for example, D. S. Massey et al., 1987, *Return to Aztlan: The Social Process of International Migration from West Mexico.* Berkeley: University of California Press; and D. S. Massey and F. G. Espana, 1987, "The Social Process of International Migration," *Science,* Vol. 237, No. 4816 (August 14), pp. 733–737. What appears to vary from one society to another is not the variety of forms of movement that

are observed but the particular mix of alternatives and the conditions under which one or another alternative dominates. See S. Goldstein, 1987, "Forms of Mobility and Their Policy Implications: Thailand and China Compared," *Social Forces,* Vol. 65, No. 4 (June), pp. 915–942.

45. Skeldon, op. cit., p. 150.

46. *FBIS*, op. cit.; see also S. X. Gui and X. Liu, 1992, "Urban Migration in Shanghai, 1950–1988: Trends and Characteristics," *Population and Development Review,* Vol. 18 (Spring), pp. 533–548; R. Ma, 1992, "Town Residents and Rural-Town Migration in Inner Mongolia, PRC," pp. 91–116 in C. Goldscheider (ed.), *Migration, Population Structure, and Redistribution Policies.* Boulder: Westview Press; and L.J.C. Ma and C. S. Lin, 1993, "Development of Towns in China: A Case Study of Guangdong Province," *Population and Development Review,* Vol. 19, No. 3, pp. 583–606.

47. Goldstein, op. cit., p. 921. This appears to make sound economic sense. It has been demonstrated, for example, that when short-term and circular movements dominate the mobility patterns, migrants tend to provide more support for the sending areas, producing a reverse flow of wealth, progressive attitudes, and technical skills to the peripheral areas. With migration streams dominated by permanent moves, wealth is more likely to flow away from the countryside to the cities and is unlikely to return (see Figure 15.3). If Zelinsky is correct, and a switch from circulation to permanent migration occurs, it would represent a significant threat to the continued economic and social survival of out-migration areas in the countryside. The downward spiral in such areas may be accelerated by increasing rates of out-marriage, which makes it less likely that migrants will return to their original homes. If wealth stays at the destination rather than being sent back, there is also an overall cost to the household members living at home, which will ultimately result in lower fertility rates and smaller families, signaling a further decline of rural communities. From this perspective continued emphasis on circulation would contribute to the positive development of both sending and receiving areas. This argument does not consider, of course, the difficulties involved in attempting to implement a set of policies that have been successful in one place (i.e., China) in other places.

48. See Chen and Parish, op. cit., p. 85; *China News Digest* articles, op. cit.; and White, op. cit.

49. Solinger (1999), op. cit.

50. Chen and Parish, op. cit., p. 85.

51. See Solinger (1999), op. cit.

52. See also G. Standing, 1981, "Migration and Modes of Exploitation: Social Origins of Immobility and Mobility," *Journal of Peasant Studies,* Vol. 8, pp. 173–211; and G. Standing (ed.), 1985, *Labour, Circulation, and the Labour Process.* London: Croom Helm.

53. The assumption here, as noted in Chapter 7, is that the reforms were *not* part of an overall plan that had been debated and deliberated but were the result of a combination of forces, including what might be called "peasant power," as well as good luck and perhaps even opportunism among the leadership, in the sense that they realized the agrarian reforms were very successful very quickly, so they did everything in their power to extend and reinforce them.

54. This is a controversial statement, of course, bearing in mind the sharp inflation that has been experienced in food prices in China's cities during the later years of the reforms. It is important to point out, however, that food prices in China began at an artificially low level and in many years have risen at a rate slower than increases in earnings and other prices. See Solinger, op. cit.

55. M. H. Dobb, 1963, *Studies in the Development of Capitalism.* London: Routledge and Kegan Paul.

56. Standing (1981), op. cit., p. 195.

57. In addition to the material changes, migration transforms rural areas by its effect on the attitudes and behaviors of the peasants. Migration stimulates "the 'taste' for commodities produced by capitalist industry"; ibid., p. 198. But it also generates a desire among the previously immobile to experience the world beyond the village walls. See K. Gardner, 1995, *Global Migrants, Local Lives: Travel and Transformation in Rural Bangladesh.* Oxford: Clarendon Press.

58. See Chan, op. cit., and Solinger (1993), op. cit.

59. See Zhou, op. cit.

60. In addition to their unwillingness to demand better working conditions the surplus labor force is usually superexploited, i.e., paid survival wages; see C. Meillassoux, 1981, *Maidens, Meal, and Money: Capitalism in the Domestic Economy.* Cambridge: Cambridge University Press.

61. Whyte and Parish, op. cit. Obviously, one retort to this claim is that the Maoist era was characterized by unhealthy amounts of social control, surveillance, and browbeating and that these prices were too heavy to pay for the tranquillity of the period. From that perspective, the loosening that

is currently under way can be seen as a healthy breath of fresh air providing extra vitality and spark to China's cities, which had become staid and boring.

62. As Croll, op. cit., has suggested, this has involved a shift from "instructed" to "self-initiated" actions, although in many cases peasants moved in response to involuntary "pushes" from state enterprises or collectives who made urban jobs available.

63. Siu and Li, op. cit.

64. Whyte and Parish, op. cit.

65. White, op. cit.

66. Y. F. Woon, 1994, "Circulatory Mobility in Post-Mao China: Temporary Migrants in Kaiping County, Pearl River Delta Region," *International Migration Review*, Vol. 27, No. 3, pp. 578–604, esp. 591–592.

67. S. Tan and D. Li, 1993, "Urban Development and Crime in China," pp. 345–352 in Guldin and Southall, op. cit.

68. See *China New Digest*, "With Millions of Underclass Migrants," op. cit. Dorothy Solinger (personal communication) has offered an explanation for the assumption that the floating populations are responsible for the increase in crime in China's cities. She suggested that one reason why so much of the new urban crime is linked to the migrants is that there is indeed an increase in urban crime rates and that many of those involved are on the run from the authorities. When (or if) they are apprehended, they are likely to be located in and among the residential and employment places frequented by migrants; the most obvious connection—that they are in fact all migrants—is made in error.

69. S. Castles and M. J. Miller, 1993, *The Age of Migration: International Population Movements in the Modern World*. New York: Guilford Press.

70. A. Portes and R. G. Rumbaut, 1990, *Immigrant America: A Portrait*. Berkeley: University of California Press.

71. One significant exception is the excellent piece of research recently reported about the growth of residential and commercial peasant enclaves in the city of Beijing; see L.J.C. Ma and B. Xiang, 1998, "Native Place, Migration, and the Emergence of Peasant Enclaves in Beijing," *The China Quarterly*, No. 155 (September), pp. 546–581.

72. Skinner, op. cit., p. 544.

73. Ibid.

74. Honig (1992), op. cit.

75. For a more extensive discussion of this issue, see Chapter 6 of this book; see also Gladney (1991), op. cit., and Harrell, op. cit.

76. See Solinger (1999), op. cit.; as well as Ma and Xiang, op. cit. For examples in other parts of the world, see Portes and Rumbaut, op. cit.

77. Whyte, op. cit.

78. See Croll, op. cit.

79. This discussion has been focused on the migrant receiving regions, but it is clear that negotiations between the strong and the weak are also occurring in the sending areas, producing new (although not "ethnic") stratifications. In the regions that have high rates of out-migration, local empowerment often comes to individuals and households who have access to foreign countries. In Nigeria, for example, Hannerz refers to the "been-tos" (those who have "been to" other places) and the "bush" people (who have not been anywhere); see U. Hannerz, 1992, *Cultural Complexity: Studies in the Social Organization of Meaning*. New York: Columbia University Press. In Bangladesh access to foreign countries has become a source of local power that differentiates migrants (*bidesh*) from people who only have access to the the home region (*desh*); see Gardner, op. cit. Access to migration, therefore, "has increasingly become the pole around which inequalities are clustered. . . . Power relations . . . in part a result of migration . . . are intimately connected to the production, and reproduction, of local culture" (ibid.). As this suggests, it is class differences—in this case defined in terms of access to migration—that shape local culture and local power relationships. As Gardner has observed, migration results in "the emergence of a new axis of differentiation, based around people's access to places. Power relations are increasingly expressed geographically [but] places are not simply sources of income, they are also idioms for power relations, ways of declaring oneself and one's household more sophisticated, more knowledgeable, and more wealthy than others" (ibid., p. 213). In the case of the new transients moving out of the countryside into China's cities, it is reasonable to suggest that a similar transformation of local (i.e., home) culture is being renegotiated. Going "out" to work to a nearby town, or to one of China's bustling new urban areas, is seen as the route to power at home. The out-migrants are the new sophisticates. As Hannerz has observed, "to have wealth and power is to have easy access to the metropolis . . . and it is through one's relationship to the metropolis that one

... gains wealth and power in the periphery" (Hannerz, op. cit., p. 242).

80. See Castles and Miller, op. cit.

81. W. B. Wood, 1994, "Forced Migration: Local Conflicts and International Dilemmas," *Annals of the Association of American Geographers,* Vol. 84, No. 4, pp. 607–634, 617.

82. Ibid.; P. Nolan, 1993, "Economic Reform, Poverty, and Migration in China," *Economic and Political Weekly,* Vol. 28 (June 26), pp. 1369–1377.

83. See Woon, op. cit., p. 586.

84. See Smil, op. cit.

85. Ibid., p. 192.

86. These observations here are reinforced by the author's recent fieldwork in Ningxia Hui AR, where as many as 200,000 people have already been moved (i.e., resettled) from the arid regions in the south to the irrigated lands of the north, allowing them to escape the grinding poverty of the type discussed here.

Chapter 16

1. World Bank, 1997, *Clear Water, Blue Skies: China's Environment in the New Century.* Washington, DC: World Bank, p. 3.

2. Can Xue (trans. R. R. Janssen and J. Zhang), 1991, *Old Floating Cloud: Two Novellas.* Evanston: Northwestern University Press, pp. 19–21.

3. V. Smil, 1993, *China's Environmental Crisis: An Inquiry into the Limits of National Development.* Armonk, NY: M. E. Sharpe. Smil is certainly not the only researcher stressing this issue; see, for example, Bochuan He, 1991, *China on the Edge: The Crisis of Ecology and Development.* San Francisco: China Books and Periodicals. See also the special issue of *The China Quarterly* ("China's Environment," December 1998).

4. Smil, op. cit., p. 53.

5. V. Smil, 1996, "Environmental Problems in China: Estimates of Economic Costs." East-West Center Special Report, No. 5. Honolulu: University of Hawaii, quoted in World Bank, op. cit., p. 15.

6. World Bank, op. cit., p. 23.

7. The World Bank's calculations assumed that the assessed costs could be reduced by the immediate implementation of these "assertive policies," which would include the substitution of cleaner fuels, investments in cleaner industrial air pollution technology, and favoring public over private forms of transportation. Ibid.

8. Ibid., p. 37.

9. Ibid., pp. 39–40.

10. In a study of industrial pollution conducted in five provinces, the World Bank researchers have been able to shed some significant light on the changing dynamics of pollution. The provinces involved in the study were Sichuan, Guangdong, Liaoning, Beijing, and Shanghai; the data used were from regulated enterprises. There is a sharp variation in the level of pollution: measured for the air by sulfur dioxide emissions and total suspended particulates; and for water by chemical oxygen demand. The highest pollution levels were recorded in Sichuan, followed by Guangdong, then Liaoning, Beijing, and Shanghai. As the World Bank suggests, such variation can be accounted for by three sets of variables: the effectiveness of the environmental regulations in each province; the amount and intensity of community participation, which tends to be strongest in the wealthier locations (Shanghai and Beijing), where education levels are highest and the local populations more willing and able to complain and confront local authorities; and industrial and plant characteristics, with industrial emissions generally greater in provinces that have a higher proportion of polluting industries, with the worst offenders being coal mining, metals (including steel) production, chemicals, cement, and petroleum. See ibid., pp. 59–62.

11. Smil, op. cit., pp. 193–194.

12. Smil's pessimism here is quite different from what he says in 1996 while reviewing Lester Brown's book, *Who Will Feed China?* In 1996 Smil launched an attack on what he calls the "doomsayers." See V. Smil, "Is There Enough Chinese Food?" *New York Review of Books,* February 1, 1996, pp. 32–34. He actually refers to Brown as one of the major "catastrophists" (a term he also uses in his 1993 book, op. cit., p. 7).

13. Smil (1993), op. cit., pp. 198–199.

14. Ibid., p. 198.

15. See R. L. Edmonds, 1994, "China's Environment: Problems and Prospects," pp. 156–185 in D. Dwyer (ed.), *China: The Next Decades.* Harlow, UK: Longman Scientific and Technical, p. 156. Edmonds (1998) also stresses this issue in an editorial for *The China Quarterly,* No. 156 (December), pp. 725–732. See also Edmonds's contribution to a recent volume: R. L. Edmonds, 1998, "China's Environmental Problems," pp. 237–266 in Robert E. Gamer (ed.), *Under-*

standing Contemporary China. Boulder: Lynne Rienner.

16. China's land, forest, and water resources are only 36 percent, 13 percent, and 25 percent, respectively, of the average levels around the world; see Edmonds (1994) op. cit., p. 156.

17. The 1997 World Bank report, op. cit., for example, estimates that if China were able to increase its technology level to the best that is currently available, then it would be able to reduce its coal consumption by close to 250 million tons, about 20 percent of the current level (see table 4.2, p. 49); researchers reported that in 1996 China's energy reserves were significantly below those in other parts of the world. This is an issue that Vaclav Smil also discusses in the December 1998 issue of *The China Quarterly*, op. cit., "China's Energy and Resources: Continuity and Change," pp. 935–951.

18. See Edmonds (1994), op. cit., p. 180. Fortunately, as editor of *The China Quarterly*, Edmonds is in an excellent position to make sure that the environmental issue is kept at the forefront of academic attention, something he appears to have achieved given the publication of a number of individual papers in the last few years. In addition, an entire special issue of the journal focused on environmental issues in December 1998.

19. World Bank, op. cit.

20. M. Hertsgaard, 1997, "Our Real China Problem," *Atlantic Monthly* (November), pp. 97–114, 100. The Hertsgaard article is reprinted (pp. 377–389) in O. Schell and D. Shambaugh (eds.), 1999, *The China Reader: The Reform Era.* New York: Vintage Books.

21. According to Kenneth Lieberthal, China is the leader of methane production globally, with 16 percent of the world's total. K. Lieberthal, 1995, *Governing China: From Revolution Through Reform.* New York: W. W. Norton, p. 189.

22. World Bank, op. cit., pp. 46–47.

23. Ibid., pp. 88–90.

24. This is the process referred to as "forced ecomigration" in Chapter 15; see W. B. Wood, 1994, "Forced Migration: Local Conflicts and International Dilemmas," *Annals of the Association of American Geographers,* Vol. 84, No. 4, pp. 607–634.

25. World Bank, op. cit., fig. 4.1, p. 46.

26. See ibid., table 4.4, p. 53, for comparisons of energy prices globally. Crude oil, for example, costs $105 per ton in China (1995 statistics), $126 in the United States, and $118–135 from OPEC. Even with these gains, however, there is still room to improve in the field of energy efficiency within industry, as well

as in residential and building usages. The World Bank, for example, recommends that China continue to develop new technologies for making coal more efficient to use and less polluting, including coal-washing and the implementation of high-efficiency dust precipitators; continue ongoing attempts to replace coal with oil and gas for home heating and cooking; and place more emphasis on imports of both oil and gas; ibid., p. 53.

27. Ibid.; see box 4.3, p. 54.

28. *Washington Post*, "160 Nations Endorse Pact on Global Warming Compliance," November 15, 1998, pp. A6–A7.

29. Ibid., p. A7.

30. See Z. X. Zhang, 1998, *The Economics of Energy Policy in China: Implications for Global Climate Change.* Cheltenham, UK: Edward Elgar, p. 240.

31. Lieberthal, op. cit., p. 289.

32. Ibid., p. 290.

33. Ibid. Lieberthal, in other words, is invoking the vicious circle situation sometimes referred to as the "population (or production) resources trap."

34. World Bank, op. cit., p. 85.

35. M. P. Walsh, 1996, "Motor Vehicle Pollution Control in China: An Urban Challenge," pp. 139–158 in S. Stares and Zhi Liu (eds.), *China's Urban Transport Development Strategy.* Washington, DC: World Bank.

36. World Bank, op. cit., p. 73.

37. Ibid., p. 84.

38. Of course, in China—perhaps more so than in most other countries—the environment has also made its mark over the centuries, particularly droughts in northern China and floods in South China and along the Yangtze River; note also the Three Gorges Dam project, which is expected to solve all of the problems associated with the irregular flow of the Yangtze River (see below).

39. Ironically it seems that Mao's views toward nature may have stemmed from his intellectual roots in Confucian reformism rather than communism. Most Westerners associate Confucianism with the well-documented, esoteric reverence for and stewardship of the environment; but there was a more practical side to Confucianism in the nineteenth century, one that involved an attempt to promote modernization and national integration. It was from that second branch of Confucianism that Mao received his early inspiration, long before he had even heard of Marxism. See M. S. Samuels, 1978, "Individual and Landscape: Thoughts on China and the Tao of Mao," pp. 283–296 in D. Ley and M. S. Samuels (eds.),

Humanistic Geography: Prospects and Problems. Chicago: Maaroufa Press.

40. G. B. Cressey, 1955, *Land of Five Hundred Million: A Geography of China.* New York: McGraw-Hill, p. 1.

41. R. Murphey, 1976, "Man and Nature in China," *Modern Asian Studies,* Vol. 1 (October), pp. 313–333. Mao Zedong's views on the struggle between people and the environment were illustrated in his own interpretation of the ancient fable of Yu Kung, "The Foolish Old Man Who Removed the Mountain." Mao altered the original story to apply it to the class struggle of the Chinese proletariat: The physical environment (to be struggled with) represents the two "mountains" of feudal and capitalist opposition. The Old Fool, in spite of being ridiculed by his neighbors, finally managed to move the two mountains outside his home, through his own hard work and determination. As he said, "When I die, my sons will carry on; when they die, there will be my grandsons, and then their sons and grandsons, and so on to infinity." See M. J. Coye, J. Livingston, and J. Highland (eds.), 1984, *China: Yesterday and Today,* 3d ed. Toronto: Bantam Books, p. 289.

42. See R. Lotspeich and A. M. Chan, 1997, "Environmental Protection in the People's Republic of China," *Journal of Contemporary China,* Vol. 6, No. 14 (March), pp. 33–60.

43. Ibid., p. 49.

44. See, for example, C. W. Pannell and J.L.C. Ma, 1983, *China: The Geography of Development and Modernization.* London: V. H. Winston, pp. 7–8. For evidence of environmental pollution and policy in the Soviet Union, see T. Gustafson, 1981, *Reform in Soviet Politics: Lessons of Recent Policies on Land and Water.* Cambridge: Cambridge University Press. For a more recent review, see M. Feshbach, 1995, *Ecological Disaster: Cleaning Up the Hidden Legacy of the Soviet Regime.* New York: Twentieth Century Fund Press.

45. See Smil (1984), op. cit.

46. Some people in the West are convinced that this is a very short-sighted view, and by the late 1970s some of the Chinese were beginning to see this clearly for themselves.

47. L. Ross, 1988, *Environmental Policy in China.* Bloomington: Indiana University Press, p. 137.

48. L. Pan, 1988, *The New Chinese Revolution.* Chicago: Contemporary Books, p. 62.

49. Ross (1988), op. cit., pp. 139–140.

50. L. Ross and M. A. Silk, 1985, "Post-Mao China and Environmental Protection: The Effects of Legal and Politico-Economic Reform," *UCLA Pacific Basin Law Journal,* Vol. 4, Nos. 1–2 (Spring–Fall), pp. 63–89.

51. Ross (1988), op. cit., pp. 142–143.

52. Ibid, p. 144. An example of the workings of environmental policy is provided by the efforts made to reduce pollution by steel factories. In the late 1980s the Ministry of Metallurgical Industry was conducting research and planning for its new plants to adopt advanced antipollution devices. The ministry allocated 10 percent of total investment in new blast furnaces to environmental protection. The ministry also reported that the amount of recycled water in steel plants was rising yearly, reaching 79 percent by 1987. See "Steel Makers Bid for Less Pollution," *China Daily,* February 7, 1987. The overall achievements in the area of environmental protection have been described by Qu Geping, director of the State Environmental Protection Bureau. See Qu Geping, 1987, "Urban Environmental Protection Well Under Way," *Beijing Review,* No. 2 (January 12), pp. 20–21. For a description of some of the attempts being made to pursue, arrest, and fine polluters, see Chaozhong Chen and Wang Geng, 1987, "Luoyang Arrests the 'Yellow Dragon,'" *Beijing Review,* No. 2 (January 12), pp. 22–23.

53. Ross and Silk, op. cit., pp. 45–46. These authors also report that the efficacy and implementation of environmental regulations are greater in industries that are more geographically concentrated, such as metals production (especially iron and steel), as opposed to more dispersed industries such as chemicals, food processing, and coal mining; see ibid., pp. 46–47 and table 5 therein.

54. A. R. Jahiel, 1997, "The Contradictory Impact of Reform on Environmental Protection in China," *The China Quarterly,* No. 149 (March), pp. 81–103.

55. World Bank, op. cit., p. 3.

56. In recent times the strongest case against Maoist socialism and its utter disregard for the environment has been made by V. Smil, 1984, *The Bad Earth: Environmental Degradation in China.* Armonk, NY: M. E. Sharpe; as well as his 1993 book, *China's Environmental Crisis,* op. cit. Smil was convinced quite early on that the return to market socialism offered the only ray of hope for the Chinese environment, in sharp contrast to the ideas expressed by W. H. Hinton, 1989, "A Response to Hugh Deane," *Monthly Review,* Vol. 40, No. 10 (March), pp. 10–36. The price of progress is recorded by teams of outsiders visiting China; see, for example, D. Elsom and M. Haigh, 1986, "Progress and Pollution," *Geographical Magazine,* Vol. 58, No. 12, pp. 640–645. In addi-

tion to the impact of industrial development, another major dimension of environmental degradation, associated with the opening-up of China, has been tourism's impact on the landscape. In Tibet, for example, evidence that foreigners are interested in Buddhism, temples, minority people, and remote scenery prompted a major phase of hotel development in Lhasa. In 1985 the modern Lhasa Hotel opened, and in the following year the Holiday Inn chain opened a new Y100 million hotel. A special hillside is planned to allow tourists to view by telescope the "sky burial" rituals, the age-old practice of dismembering the dead and feeding them to the vultures to hasten their reincarnation. As Lynn Pan has observed caustically, "The authorities have not grasped how corrupting tourism can be. . . . Economics has overtaken politics, and as buildings go up and more scenic areas open, it is difficult to avoid the conclusion that Tibetan culture, which has survived the worst that Maoism and force could do to stamp it out, has been left to be killed by tourism" (Pan, op. cit., p. 281).

57. In face of such arguments some observers have pointed out that the rate and the level of environmental degradation in China have been reduced since 1978. This is partly a result of new laws to force compliance from potential polluters. The general line from critics of the Maoist era is that the Chinese economy has become considerably more efficient as a result of the reforms, with positive environmental results. A major impact, for example, has been felt from the system of charging potential polluters fees to make them realize the potential social costs of their behavior. For a discussion of this argument, see Ross, op. cit., chap. 4 ("Pollution Control"), pp. 131–175; see also L. Ross, 1998, "China: Environmental Protection, Domestic Policy Trends, Patterns of Participation in Regimes, and Compliance with International Norms," *The China Quarterly,* No. 156 (December), pp. 809–835.

58. See Lotspeich and Chan, op. cit., p 34. For another recent discussion of this issue, see A. R. Jahiel, 1998, "The Organization of Environmental Protection in China," *The China Quarterly,* No. 156 (December), pp. 757–788.

59. As noted earlier in this chapter, such effects are notoriously difficult to estimate, but in its recent report the World Bank has estimated that urban air pollution in China in 1995 was responsible for 178,000 premature deaths, with indoor air pollution responsible for a further 110,000 premature deaths; 134,000 deaths were related to drinking polluted water. These additional deaths are mostly due to diarrhea and hepatitis; see World Bank, op. cit., table 2.3, p. 21. It is important to remember that these are just the deaths involved. The World Bank also provides estimates for the numbers of hospital visits and admissions and a range of symptoms associated with polluted air and water, as well as an estimate of workdays lost as a result of such ill effects; see ibid., table 2.1, p. 19. Implied is that this number of deaths could have been avoided if China reached the level recommended by the World Health Organization; see ibid. on deaths; fig. 1.1, p. 6, on standards. Most of China's biggest cities were exceeding the air quality standards by two to five times in 1995, and the World Bank claims that in some parts of China indoor pollution exceeds that in the cities, with suspended particulate levels sometimes reaching 1,000 micrograms per cubic meter in people's kitchens; the air in places like Taiyuan in Shanxi Province is about 600 micrograms (see ibid., pp. 19, 6). The pollution comes mainly from the use of biomass and low-grade coal for heating and cooking in most homes.

60. This quote is attributed to Li Peng in a 1996 speech to the Fourth National Environmental Conference. See World Bank, op. cit., p. 7.

61. Although, as Lotspeich and Chen show, as a proportion of GNP this amount has declined from 0.26 percent in 1985 to 0.22 percent in 1993, although the actual amount spent increased considerably from Y1.7 billion to Y2.72 billion; Lotspeich and Chen, op. cit., table 9, p. 55.

62. These are the so-called three synchronizations of the planning, construction, and operation phases; ibid., p. 50.

63. Ibid.

64. See *China News Digest,* "Paper Mill Manager Receives First Jail Sentence for Pollution," October 9, 1998.

65. Lotspeich and Chan, op. cit., p. 56.

66. See Lieberthal, op. cit., p. 286.

67. Ibid., p. 287.

68. In fact the 1984 regulations covering TVEs specifically prohibit them from engaging in production that generates environmental hazards at the risk of being shut down. See ibid.

69. By the end of the 1980s few of the TVEs were in compliance with local wastewater regulations; Lotspeich and Chan, op. cit., p. 57, estimate less than 15 percent.

70. See World Bank, op. cit., table 5.1, p. 59. There are some inherent problems associated with the process of pollution levy charges, which involve two

components: One is noncompliance; the fees are assessed on pollution levels above the emission (air) or effluent (water) standards, plus fines and other charges assessed for observed violations of local regulations. The fees collected mainly go back to the enterprises in the form of loans from the local Environmental Protection Bureaus to pay for pollution control projects, with about 20 percent kept back for administrative and monitoring costs. In addition to the low level of the fines, they have not been indexed to inflation, so the "real" costs have declined in the 1990s (ibid., p. 58). The second problem is that levies are also charged only on pollution levels above the standards, so there is no incentive to decrease pollution rates below that level.

71. Ibid., p. 59.

72. Herstgaard, op. cit., p. 104.

73. World Bank, op. cit., pp. 62–63.

74. Herstgaard, op. cit., p. 105.

75. Ibid. The implementation of policies has also been affected significantly by the decentralization of environmental regulations: A provision in the new (1984) environmental laws allowed provinces to set more stringent emission standards than those established centrally, which had the advantage of greater flexibility, but it also resulted in problems. For example, the devastating effect of the floods of 1991 were made worse because there was no coordination of prevention activities, with each area showing concern only for its own needs. See J. T. Dreyer, 1996, *China's Political System: Modernization and Tradition*, 2d ed. Basingstoke, UK: Macmillan, p. 251.

76. Jahiel (1997), op. cit., p. 81.

77. Ibid.

78. Ibid., p. 88.

79. Ibid., p. 94.

80. Ibid., p. 97.

81. In spite of the criticisms, the discharge fee system has served at least one extremely important function, that is, familiarizing the Chinese people with the concept of environmental protection at the local level. It has also generated a vital though small source of funds to be used (if only partly) for environmental protection. This is important because the funding for environmental protection in China is so limited, because neither the Ministry of Finance nor NEPA itself is able or willing to provide local EPBs with enough funding to do their work properly. The funds collected have been put toward pollution monitoring and control efforts and, to a lesser extent, to fund environmental education efforts. See ibid., p. 103.

82. Edmonds (1994), op. cit., p. 182 (emphasis added).

83. This is a quote from a farmer facing resettlement in the Three Gorges region of the Yangtze River. See Ding Qiyang, 1998, "What Are the Three Gorges Resettlers Thinking?" pp. 70–89 in Dai Qing, *The River Dragon Has Come: The Three Gorges Dam and the Fate of China's Yangtze River and Its People*. Armonk, NY: M. E. Sharpe, p. 83.

84. Supporters have pointed out that the World Bank has approved China's methods for handling large-scale resettlement projects in other regions, such as Gansu (readers are directed to the Chapter 10 discussion of the 1992 World Bank report on reducing poverty in China). But the critics reply that since Beijing is the World Bank's largest customer, it is generally inclined to view China's progress in such processes in a favorable light, as we have clearly seen in the 1997 report on China's environmental problems, *Clear Water, Blue Skies*, op. cit.

85. *China News Digest*, "Floods Update: Jiang Zemin Asserts Party Has Proved Right to Rule," September 28, 1998.

86. J. Gittings, 1996, *Real China: From Cannibalism to Karaoke*. London: Simon and Schuster, esp. pp. 110–111.

87. Mao is quoted as saying, "The Socialist Three Gorges Dam project should excel other major projects in Chinese history such as Qin Shi Huang's Great Wall and Shui Yang Di's Grand Canal." See C. Li, 1997, *Rediscovering China: Dynamics and Dilemmas of Reform*. Lanham, MD: Rowman and Littlefield, p. 168.

88. Li is reputed to have told Mao that he would commit suicide if he could not prevent the construction of the dam; see ibid., p. 168.

89. Gittings, op. cit., p. 98.

90. Ibid.

91. See A. R. Topping, 1994, "Ecological Roulette: Damming the Yangtze," *Foreign Affairs*, Vol. 74 (September/October), p. 133, quoted in Li, op. cit., p. 166.

92. As John Gittings has suggested, as industry boomed in the 1980s and power shortages grew increasingly serious, the dam's potential for power generation began to seem more attractive. In the 1950s the critics argued the dam would produce more power than would possibly be needed: "Now they could only cast doubt on its ability to produce enough power"; op. cit., p. 102.

93. Li Peng's support of the Three Gorges Dam project has been interpreted as a way for both himself and the Party-state to rebuild its image after the

Tiananmen Square massacre, in which he was seriously implicated as a supporter of the hard-line policy that was adopted.

94. Gittings, op. cit., p. 104.

95. In spite of the trend working toward acceptance of the dam project, there were some voices of protest; for example, Dai Qing was sent to prison for a year after the 1989 publication of *Yangtze! Yangtze!* (Guizhou People's Publishing House), a volume of essays criticizing the dam. This book was republished under the coeditorship of Patricia Adams and John Thibodeau, 1994, *Yangtze! Yangtze! Debate over the Three Gorges Project.* Toronto: Probe International and Earthscan. As we have suggested here, there were still some serious misgivings about the project. One critic, for example, wrote that "if a decision was taken on undemocratic and unscientific grounds, then the laws of nature will mercilessly punish us, and we will have to pay even more dearly"; ibid., p. 105.

96. This was Li Rui, who had been Mao Zedong's secretary of industrial affairs and a vice minister in the Ministry of Water Resources and Electric Power. See L. R. Sullivan (ed.), 1995, *China Since Tiananmen: Political, Economic, and Social Conflicts.* Armonk, NY: M. E. Sharpe, pp. 115–119, "Letter to the Leadership of the CCP in 1992."

97. Gittings, op. cit., p. 114.

98. J. Spence, "A Flood of Troubles," *New York Times Magazine,* January 5, 1997, sec. 6, pp. 34–40.

99. Ibid., p. 39.

100. See Ding, op. cit., p. 74, in Dai Qing's book *The River Dragon Has Come,* op. cit. Unfortunately, such survey results may conceal as much information as they reveal. For example, is such blind faith in the government truly representative of the people whose homes are to be inundated by the Three Gorges project? What do the other half of the respondents think about losing their homes (those who do not think the dam will be successful, or are not willing to criticize their government and its wisdom)?

101. See Dai, op. cit., pp. 7–8, and Li, op. cit., p. 170.

102. J. C. Scott, 1998, *Seeing Like a State: How Certain Schemes to Improve the Human Condition Have Failed.* New Haven: Yale University Press, Yale Agrarian Studies.

103. See F. Shui, 1998, "A Profile of Dams in China," pp. 18–43 in Dai, op. cit.; see also the foreword to the Dai Qing book: Audrey Topping, "Foreword: The River Dragon Has Come," Dai, op. cit., pp. xv–xxix.

104. See "The Three Gorges Dam in China: Forced Resettlement, Suppression of Dissent, and Labor Rights Concerns," *Human Rights Watch/Asia,* Vol. 7, No. 2 (February 1995), app. 3, "The Banqiao and Shimantau Dam Disasters."

105. Spence, op. cit., pp. 38–39.

106. See Topping's "Foreword" in Dai, 1998, op. cit., p. xx; and also Spence, op. cit.

107. *China News Digest,* "Jiang Zemin Declares Victory over Flood Fighting," September 8, 1998.

108. Proponents of the dam, however, are quick to point out that the severity of the 1998 floods reinforces the need to control the river's water supply and reduce the likelihood of floods; but as others point out, most of the 1998 floods occurred in the lower reaches of the Yangtze, an area that is fed by tributary rivers that will not be controlled by the new dam. In fact some critics argue that the presence of a huge new dam may, by creating a false sense of security, attract more development to flood-prone areas, taking even more agricultural and forest land out of circulation, increasing the speed of soil erosion and runoff, and resulting in reduced investments in dikes downstream. Many outsiders are now in agreement, in fact, that the megadams, once so popular, especially in the American West and developing nations, are now considered to be only marginally effective for flood control; if water levels are kept full to maximize power generation, the dam may not be able to accommodate surging water levels during a flood. Recommended instead are comprehensive policies to restrict agricultural and especially industrial and residential development in flood-prone areas; the creation of additional overflow areas for floodwaters; the rebuilding of existing dikes; and attempts to make existing buildings more resistant to flood damage. All would make better economic sense than building a new megadam; see *New York Times,* August 23, 1998, p. 14. The Indian novelist Arundhati Roy (author of *The God of Small Things*) has brilliantly argued this case in the context of India's megadam-building projects. See A. Roy, 1999, *The Cost of Living.* New York: Modern Library.

109. See R. Qu, 1998, "Discussing Population Resettlement with Li Boning," pp. 39–49 in Dai Qing, op. cit.

110. Jin Hui, 1998, "Water Pollution in the Three Gorges Reservoir," pp. 160–170 in Dai Qing, op. cit.; see p. 160.

111. The critics point out that there is already a lack of political will and funding to deal with the existing problem of polluted wastewater being

dumped into the river. So how can there be optimism about the future when the problem looks like it is being magnified several times? This implies a lack of logic in building a dam that will cost more than Y100 billion yet not being willing to pay the currently estimated Y2.8 billion to treat wastewater in the Three Gorges area—or even the Y650 million to mitigate pollution made worse by the dam! See ibid., p. 168.

112. This argument is based on the state's own definitions of land that is too steep to be cultivated, enacted into law in the Water and Soil Protection Act of 1984; see World Bank, op. cit.

113. Thus far, although generous funding has been promised to speed up the evacuation process, much of it has not yet been forthcoming, and it looks certain to not be enough. In addition it is virtually impossible, given existing money and manpower, to conduct so much excavation and preservation work within the time remaining (approximately ten years after the project began in earnest).

114. See Da Bing, 1998, "Military Perspectives on the Three Gorges Project," pp. 171–176, in Dai Qing, op. cit. Short of talking about lowering the water level in the dam during a crisis, diverting water into the lower reaches, and reinforcing the coffer constructions in front of the dam, the Chinese government recognizes that it could not realistically defend against an air attack, which would result in water rushing hundreds of miles to inundate the city of Nanjing (p. 175).

115. World Bank, op. cit., p. 2.

116. J. B. Starr, 1997, *Understanding China: A Guide to China's Economy, History, and Political Structure*. New York: Hill and Wang, p. 172.

117. Ibid., p. 63.

118. Ibid.

119. World Bank, op. cit., p. 2.

120. Smil (1993), op. cit.

121. In addition to the measures that are specific to the use of environmental resources and pollution charges, the World Bank report recommends the acceleration of more general economic reforms, including the massive overhaul of SOEs, which are generally considered to be very inefficient at using resources, as well as the major polluters. This will require making SOEs considerably more responsive to market signals, which will include effective pollution taxes and regulatory penalties. Reform of the price system and of trading methods would also ensure the survival and growth of the most efficient industries, which, it is claimed, will also be the least pollution-intensive. The World Bank also recommends the deepening of capital markets and "establishing a framework for private participation in infrastructure" (op. cit., p. 105) that would open up new ways for municipalities to finance their investment in such projects as water supply and sanitation. This would also facilitate investments in energy-efficient equipment with the most up-to-date abatement technology. Such reforms, the report claims, not only benefit the overall pattern of economic growth but also help to "reduce the cost of cleanup and rapidly improve China's environmental living standards" (ibid., p. 105).

122. Ibid., p. 46.

123. Ibid., p. 51.

124. Hertsgaard, op. cit., p. 112.

125. Hao Bing, op. cit.

126. H. C. Qi, 1997, "From Concept to Social Action: The Green Movement in China," *China Strategic Review*, Vol. 2, No. 3 (May/June), pp. 39–49.

127. See, for example, D. Lin, 1998, "Environmentalism Support Flowering in Greener Taiwan," *Free China Journal* (February 13), p. 7.

128. Ibid.

129. Qi, op. cit., p. 48.

130. This observation is made by Lotspeich and Chan, op. cit., table 6, p. 48.

131. D. D. Buck, 1986, "Changes in Chinese Urban Planning Since 1976," *Third World Planning Review*, Vol. 6, No. 1, pp. 5–26.

132. As the purges continued throughout the summer of 1989, the news from China slowed to a trickle, but what little there was confirmed the impression that intellectuals were increasingly feeling the weight of the new era of oppression. In August, for example, two of the country's leading social scientists at the Chinese Academy of Social Sciences in Beijing were ousted from the Party, and warrants were issued for their arrests. One of them, Yan Jiaqi, reportedly escaped China; the other, Bao Zunxin, disappeared after being arrested. See "China Expels Two Social Scientists from Party for Opposing Li Peng," *Schenectady Gazette*, August 10, 1989, p. 47. Although Mao Zedong's role had been critically assessed, in the early 1990s there was some evidence of his resurgence (see Chapter 3), and there was a fear that the purges following the Tiananmen Square incident were an indication that China was entering yet another era in which political "redness" was preferred to "expertness." By the end of the 1990s this no longer seemed to be a possibility, with the leftist clique apparently a spent force.

133. L. J. Lundquist, 1980, *The Hare and the Tortoise: Clean Air Policies in the United States and Sweden*. Ann Arbor: University of Michigan Press.

134. The Maoist system, as Lieberthal has observed, "sowed the seeds of tremendous environmental injury through its emphasis on heavy industry, its adoption of wasteful technologies for production, its pricing policies that systematically encourage waste of natural resources, and its conscious focus on maximizing industrial output without regard for environmental impact." Lieberthal, op. cit., p. 282.

135. Dreyer, op. cit., p. 252.

136. Smil (1993), op. cit.

137. J.S.S. Muldavin, 1997, "Environmental Degradation in Heilongjiang: Policy Reform and Agrarian Dynamics in China's New Hybrid Economy," *Annals of the Association of American Geographers*, Vol. 87, No. 4 (December), pp. 579–613.

138. Ibid., p. 597.

139. Ibid., p. 598.

140. Ibid., p. 600.

141. Ibid., p. 603.

142. World Bank, op. cit., map 1, p. 57.

143. S. G. Rozelle, G. Veeck, and J. K. Huang, 1996, "The Impact of Environmental Degradation on Grain Production in China, 1975–1990," *Economic Geography*, Vol. 73, No. 1, pp. 44–66.

144. Ibid., p. 62.

Chapter 17

1. T. G. Rawski, 1996, "Implications of China's Reform Experience," pp. 188–211 in A. G. Walder (ed.), *China's Transitional Economy*. Oxford: Oxford University Press, pp. 192–193.

2. K. Lieberthal, 1995, *Governing China: From Revolution Through Reform*. New York: W. W. Norton, p. 340.

3. G. White, 1993, *Riding the Tiger: The Politics of Economic Reform in Post-Mao China*. Stanford: Stanford University Press, p. 12.

4. White, op. cit., p. 102.

5. Kate Xiao Zhou, 1996, *How the Farmers Changed China: Power of the People*. Boulder: Westview Press.

6. White, op. cit., p. 98.

7. See World Bank, 1997, *At China's Table: Food Security Options*. Washington, DC: World Bank; in contrast to the past, there is now universal agreement that technical expertise is far more important than political correctness, or "redness."

8. White, op. cit., p. 116.

9. Ibid., p. 117.

10. One of the results of this was a sharp increase in the number of peasants who were willing (in fact being driven) to leave the land in search of job opportunities in the cities; see R. Baum, 1996, *Burying Mao: Chinese Politics in the Age of Deng Xiaoping*. Princeton: Princeton University Press.

11. Baum refers to this process as "beggaring the peasants" (ibid., p. 378); see also M. Blecher, 1997, *China Against the Tides: Restructuring Through Revolution, Radicalism, and Reform*. London: Pinter. Blecher claims the IOU problem is not just a simple matter of cash flow but is a structural problem of the reforms, in which the state does not have the funds to pay peasants for the grain it demands they grow.

12. J. B. Starr, 1997, *Understanding China: A Guide to China's Economy, History, and Political Structure*. New York: Hill and Wang, p. 124.

13. As we shall see later, the working of the market is one of the solutions the state describes for the problem of food supply, raised by Lester Brown. See L. R. Brown, 1995, *Who Will Feed China? Wake-Up Call for a Small Planet*. New York: W. W. Norton. The experiences of the early 1990s do not seem to support such an assumption.

14. White, op. cit., p. 91; and also B. Brugger and S. Reglar, 1994, *Politics, Economy, and Society in Contemporary China*. London: Macmillan, p. 134.

15. A plan was announced in the early 1990s to create another 100 million jobs in the countryside, but most observers question whether this is a realistic goal. See Brugger and Reglar, op. cit., p. 135.

16. White, op. cit.

17. China Statistical Publishing House, 1998, *China Statistical Yearbook 1997*.

18. Ibid.

19. The old pattern of *fang* (letting go) and *shou* (tightening) was being raised again; see Chapter 4 and Baum, op. cit., pp. 5–9.

20. Starr, op. cit., p. 123.

21. See *China Statistical Yearbook 1997*, table 11.5, p. 368; in 1996 the amount of cultivable land was approximately 80 percent of what it was in 1950. See also Starr, op. cit., p. 124.

22. This is compared to the output level of 504 million tons in 1996, which represented a significant increase over the previous year, when total produc-

tion was 466 million tons; see *China Statistical Year-book 1997*, table 2.2, pp. 26–27.

23. Starr, op. cit., p. 125, estimates an annual increase of 4.4 million tons, using a lower figure for 1996 of 480 million tons.

24. A total of 446.24 million tons was produced in 1990, 466.62 million tons in 1995; see *China Statistical Yearbook 1997*.

25. It is important to recall that Lester Brown has made a name for himself as both a publicity seeker and, as one expert reviewing the book concluded, a "professional catastrophist" who has been turning out forecasts of food shortages, crippling energy crises, and planetary collapse since the early 1990s. See V. Smil, "Is There Enough Chinese Food?" *New York Review of Books*, February 1, 1996, pp. 32–34. Smil argues that Brown and the other prophets of doom, like Paul Ehrlich, are usually proved wrong, as they were in the early 1970s, when they predicted the world would soon run out of fuel.

26. Global grain prices increased significantly in the mid-1990s, partly in response to China's increased imports. Between 1994 and 1996, for example, wheat prices doubled, to US$7 per bushel; corn prices went up to $4.43 per bushel. The ratio of grain to meat used in the production of beef in China stood at 7:1; pork, 4:1; chicken, 2:1. China's meat consumption increased by 12 percent in 1995, compared to an over-all consumption increase of 4 percent (in 1977 China's mean consumption per capita was 8 kg; in 1994 it was 32 kg). It is important to observe that in contemporary China only about 20 percent of grain currently goes to feed animals, compared to about 70 percent in the United States. Imports of grain doubled between 1994 and 1995, totaling US$3.5 billion in value. In 1995–1996 China imported 11–12 million tons, which could go as high as 17–20 million tons by 2000 according to Brown's estimates. Unlike the situation in grain production, China has a comparative advantage in export-oriented manufacturing and in growing cotton. The textile industries contribute about 30 percent of China's foreign exchange reserves and employ more than 15 million people, so China should focus on this rather than trying to raise its own beef according to the Worldwatch researchers. The Chinese response to Lester Brown's scenarios involves plans to grow "miracle" strains of rice that can yield 10 tons per hectare, and "superhybrid" rice capable of producing 13 tons per hectare (conventional rice yields average 3.5 tons).

27. See Smil (1996), op. cit.; and also P. B. Prime, 1997, "China's Economic Progress: Is It Sustainable?"

pp. 51–77 in W. A. Joseph (ed.), *China Briefing: The Contradictions of Change.* Armonk, NY: M. E. Sharpe. Some estimates indicate there may be as much as 40 percent more land available.

28. See Smil, op. cit., p. 33.

29. Ibid., p. 34.

30. Smil also thinks that animals in China could be raised and fed more efficiently, allowing them to get to market weight much more quickly; the current average for pigs, for example, is about twelve months, compared to six months in the United States (see ibid.). It is also possible that Chinese consumers could make what Smil calls "more intelligent nutritional choices" by eating less beef and pork and more chicken, which is less grain-intensive to produce. In general, fish are more efficient at converting grain to meat than are warm-blooded animals; and more high-quality protein could come from increased fish consumption, although Lester Brown reported that increases in fish production are not very likely in most areas. Smil also argues that the Chinese could benefit by consuming more milk products as a source of protein, especially yogurt, skim milk, and hard cheeses, which would avoid the problem of lactose intolerance among a population that is unaccustomed to drinking milk. This has occurred in Japan, where per capita dairy consumption increased from close to zero in 1945 to 50 kg in 1996, compared to China's current consumption of about 2 kg per capita. The official statistics show that the average consumption of fresh dairy produce in urban areas was 4.83 kg, plus an additional .41 kg of dried milk products, with a range from 2.52 kg in the poorest to 7.9 kg in the wealthiest households; see *China Statistical Yearbook 1997*, table 9.10, p. 298.

31. See Prime, op. cit., p. 57. Although these reports are unsubstantiated, stories carried in *China News Digest* have indicated that grain production remained high in 1997, at around 490 million tons; see *China News Digest*, "China's Grain Production Remains High Despite 1998 Floods," October 15, 1998. In 1998, in spite of the tremendous losses incurred in the summer floods, output was expected to be 492.5 billion tons, mainly as a result of expanding the autumn and winter crop acreage by more than 115 million acres over the previous year; see *China News Digest*, "China Expands Autumn and Winter Crop Planting," November 4, 1998.

32. A number of foreign agricultural experts have pointed out that such a path would be counter to China's best interests and would be ignoring its comparative advantage, which is clearly in manufactured

products. As Prime has observed, "Since China's low percentage of arable land area means its global comparative advantage is most likely not in agricultural products, a trend toward increased food imports is not necessarily a bad development" (op. cit., p. 58). For comparative purposes, it is interesting to note that in the United States each person is supported by about 5,200 square meters of cultivable land, as opposed to 1,320 square meters in China; and Japan has only 373 square meters per person. This process is to be expected in modernizing and developing nations, where it is normal for agriculture's comparative advantage to decline. The official response argued that "on the eve of the founding of the New China some Westerners predicted that the Chinese government would not be able to solve the problem of feeding the country's population. History has already shown the futility of a such a prediction. In the coming decades, though China will be confronted with the reality of less cultivated land, a large population and great demand for grain, there exists huge potential for development. The Chinese government has experience and has developed methods for solving the grain problem, and the peasants have a vast reservoir of enthusiasm for production. It can be believed with full reason that the Chinese government and people have the ability to solve the problem . . . by relying on their own efforts. Practice will prove to the world: the Chinese people can not only feed themselves, but also make their quality of life better and better year by year. Instead of being a threat to the world's grain supply, China will make even greater contributions to it." Information Office of the State Council of the PRC, 1996, *White Paper: The Grain Issue in China.* Available on the Internet. URL: http://www.prchina.net/Press/wpgrain.html. According to the report, China is planning to be more than 95 percent self-sufficient in grain, leaving no more than 5 percent or less to imports (ibid., p. 4). The report lists a large number of factors to support this claim, including increasing output, saving and marketing more of the harvested crops, and increasing nongrain food resources, including fish. All of this can be achieved, it is claimed, without further excess damage to the environment and within the context of sustainable agriculture.

33. The Chinese estimate that of the 400 kg–per–person output (projected for the year 2030), 50 percent would go toward staple foodstuffs and 50 percent to animal feed to produce meat. Those estimates require China to increase its grain output by 1 percent per year to 2010, 0.7 percent per year thereafter until 2030. This is low compared to the average per annum increase of 2.3 percent during the period 1950–1996. Most of these statistics are from the White Paper issued by the Information Office of the State Council of the PRC in October 1996 (op. cit.).

34. V. Smil, op. cit., p. 34.

35. See also V. Smil, 1984, *The Bad Earth: Environmental Degradation in China.* Armonk, NY: M. E. Sharpe.

36. See J. C. Scott, 1998, *Seeing Like a State: How Certain Schemes to Improve the Human Condition Have Failed.* New Haven: Yale University Press, Yale Agrarian Studies, p. 5.

37. International Food Policy Research Institute (IFPRI), 1997, *IFPRI Report/Newsletter,* "Study Projects China Will Remain a Grain Importer," Vol. 19, No. 1. Internet. URL: http:/www.cgiar.org/IFPRI/reports/0297RPT/0297RPTE.HTM.

38. B. R. Wan, "China's Food and Agriculture: Development Prospects and Policies," Statement delivered at the National Agricultural Forum, Des Moines, Iowa, March 3, 1997.

39. Ibid.

40. World Bank, op. cit.

41. In its unique way, the World Bank suggests that "reducing government control and permitting more reliance on competitive market forces for determining prices would allocate resources more efficiently and improve long-term food security." Ibid., p. 4. The World Bank bases some of its predictions and policy recommendations on the data it presents, which show that China's cereal yields per hectare are roughly on par with the average for Asian countries but much lower than the average among the top-ranking cereal producers, demonstrating that there is considerable potential for improvement. Much of the improvement can come, the World Bank argues, from increased and improved fertilizer use, which is a direct rejection of Lester Brown's assertion that there is very limited potential for increasing yields any further and some considerable dangers in terms of destroying the soil. The World Bank suggests three areas in which improvements are possible: changing the nutrient balance of the fertilizers in use; improving the quality of the fertilizers and increasing the quantity; and applying fertilizers more efficiently. On the issue of water availability and irrigation, the report continues: "To improve the efficiency of water use, including irrigation, the government must raise prices. Low prices encourage overuse and contribute to low efficiency and to scarcity" (pp. 4–5). The World Bank suggests a num-

ber of investments that would improve water supplies and delivery systems, as well as better methods
of water conservation. According to the report, the
state's existing grain procurement policies represent
a major burden to farmers and discourage them
from increasing food (especially grain) production
and investing in long-term infrastructure improvements. In 1995, for example, 142 million tons of
grain (30 percent of total production) were marketed
outside the village of production. Of that amount, 65
percent was procured by state grain enterprises at
either the quota price (averaging 60 percent of market price) or the negotiated price (90 percent of market price). According to World Bank calculations this
represents a loss (or a tax, if you like) of Y40.7 billion
to grain producers (i.e., by selling to the state rather
than on the market); see p. 23.

42. Ibid., p. 31; see table 4.2.

43. The report also indicates that in the early
1990s as much as 35 million hectares of land per year
globally was being taken out of grain production as a
result of shrinking demand, which implies that
another 115 million tons of grain could be produced.
See ibid., p. 31.

44. The World Bank warns, however, that the agricultural investment needed will be costly in terms of
water supplies, irrigation facilities, fertilizer production plants, agricultural research, and transportation
improvements. The estimates, for example, between
1995 and 2020 could amount to the equivalent of
US$96 billion, which includes $25 billion for water
transfer from the south to the north, $39 billion for
irrigation improvements, and $26 billion for
research. As might be expected, the World Bank recommends that private investors and international
companies (for example, seed producers, transportation providers, and fertilizer manufacturers) be
encouraged to invest significantly in the business of
China's agriculture.

45. Ibid., p. 29.

46. S. G. Wang, 1995, "The Politics of Private
Time: Changing Leisure Patterns in Urban China,"
pp. 149–172 in D. S. Davis et al. (eds.), *Urban Spaces
in Contemporary China: The Potential for Autonomy
and Community in Post-Mao China*. Washington,
DC: Woodrow Wilson Press.

47. A. Hussain, 1994, "The Chinese Economic
Reforms: An Assessment," pp. 11–30 in D. Dwyer
(ed.), *China: The Next Decades*. Burnt Mill, Essex,
UK: Longman Scientific and Technical, p. 24.

48. Ibid., p. 24; see also Q. G. Jia, 1994, "Reform
Ideology, Political Commitment and Resource

Transfer: An Alternative Model for the Explanation
of China's Economic Reform," *Journal of Contemporary China*, Vol. 5, pp. 3–24.

49. B. Naughton, 1995, *Growing out of the Plan:
Chinese Economic Reform, 1978–1993*. Cambridge,
UK: Cambridge University Press, esp. chap. 5, "Refor-
mulation and Debate: The Turning Point of 1984,"
pp. 173–243. A similar periodization is also described
by the IMF report written by M. W. Bell, H. E. Khor,
and K. Kochhar, 1993, *China at the Threshold of a
Market Economy*. Washington, DC: International
Monetary Fund. These authors identified four
phases: 1978–1984, 1984–1988, 1988–1991, and 1992
to the present. The issue of resource transfer from
the state to the nonstate sector is also discussed by
Jia, op. cit.

50. Naughton discusses three serious problems
associated with the dual-track pricing system: It
inhibited attempts to implement more comprehensive reforms of China's pricing and taxation systems;
it encouraged widespread corruption, as enterprises
were allowed to buy materials at (low) state prices
and sell at (higher) market prices; and it generated a
significant amount of local government intervention
and protectionism; see op. cit., esp. pp. 228–233.

51. Some of the new reforms are described in
G. H. Jefferson, 1993, "The Chinese Economy: Mov-
ing Forward," pp. 35–54 in W. A. Joseph (ed.), *China
Briefing, 1992*. Boulder: Westview Press. See also
Lieberthal, op. cit., for a discussion of the new
reforms that are both planned and needed.

52. S. L. Shirk, 1993, *The Political Logic of Eco-
nomic Reform in China*. Berkeley: University of Cali-
fornia Press, p. 334. This is also the opinion of
geographer Rupert Hodder. See, for example, R.
Hodder, 1993, *The Creation of Wealth in China:
Domestic Trade and Material Progress in a Communist
State*. London: Belhaven Press; and R. Hodder, 1994,
"State Collective and Private Industry in China's
Evolving Economy," pp. 116–127 in D. Dwyer, op. cit.

53. In attempting to answer these questions it is
helpful to clarify some of the issues. Economist Barry
Naughton, for example, warns against making comparisons that are too simplistic. As he suggests, characterizing the old command economy (the "plan") as
a "dinosaur"—which is perceived to be "big, clumsy
. . . unable to adopt . . . [and therefore] . . . fated to
become extinct"—is only partly true and not very
helpful. Similarly, to picture the market economy as
a group of emergent mammals, which are thought of
as "small, plucky, and intelligent, they scurry about
the floor preparing for their eventual hegemony," is

equally misleading. See op. cit., p. 471. In fact, neither of these models is very helpful, and as stereotypes they tend to cloud reality, presenting some of the truth but not enough.

54. Jia, op. cit.

55. Shirk, op. cit.

56. Shirk, ibid., p. 9. Shirk discusses five features of the Chinese communist system that worked to shape the behavior of officials who were responsible for crafting and implementing the economic reform policies. The five areas are authority relations—who has the power and who carries out policy?; leadership incentives—how are leaders selected and to whom are they accountable?; bargaining arenas—where are the policies made and by whom?; enfranchised participants—who sits around the bargaining table?; and decision rules—what are the rules of collective choice, and how are they reached and carried out?

57. Deng's strategy and the differences between the Chinese case and that in the Soviet Union are discussed by R. MacFarquhar, "The Anatomy of Collapse," *New York Review of Books,* Vol. 38, No. 15, September 26, 1991, pp. 5–9.

58. Shirk also argues that the Cultural Revolution worked to weaken and disrupt China's central institutions and created a constituency for the economic reforms. The political and economic chaos experienced at all levels in that period (1966–1976) made China's leaders and citizens alike ready and willing to consider a radical change; op. cit., pp. 13–14; for a similar argument, see MacFarquhar, op. cit.

59. It is important to note, as the discussion in Chapter 7 makes clear, that the idea that Deng Xiaoping and the government were responsible for initiating the reforms (especially in the countryside) is only one of a number of possible hypotheses. As we saw in the discussion of agricultural reforms, there are powerful arguments on the other side, including the ideas associated with the power of the peasants; see, for example, the works of Kate Xiao Zhou and Daniel Kelliher. See Kate Xiao Zhou, 1996, *How the Farmers Changed China: Power of the People.* Boulder: Westview Press; and D. Kelliher, 1992, *Peasant Power in China: The Era of Rural Reform, 1979–1989.* New Haven: Yale University Press.

60. Shirk, op. cit., p. 17.

61. Ibid., p. 335. This is similar in some ways to the thesis put forward by Barry Naughton, op. cit. There were some disadvantages to the system as described; for example, transferring power to the lower levels and allowing those at the lower levels to keep more of their profits works well to build up the

needed constituencies and to stimulate rapid growth, but it does not necessarily guarantee industrial efficiency. In fact it tended to encourage extensive rather than intensive growth, and this now represents a major challenge for future reforms, especially if China is to continue to compete with and perform well in a highly competitive global export market. In addition, in many cases there was no real incentive for those who had benefited from the piecemeal and particularistic reforms to think about more significant and comprehensive reforms; the net effect was that many of the reforms have a half-completed quality to them. Nevertheless, the reform drive was kept alive, mainly as a result of the dynamism of the nonstate sector, which had the dual-track economy to fall back on. Even when no one could agree on how to bring about reform of the SOEs, those enterprises themselves, as a result of having to coexist in a competitive market economy, were changing themselves and were drawn toward the attractive models set by nonstate enterprises. Another possible criticism of Shirk's analysis is that it required opportunism, skill, and more than a modicum of sensitivity on behalf of top Party strategists—all or any of which may not be present. Another line of criticism, although not necessarily of Shirk's analysis, is that the chosen strategy of gradual incrementalism has left a weak and inefficient state sector still in place, which would not have been the case with a more comprehensive reform package that radically restructured the price and taxation systems. The advantage of the incrementalist approach was that it reoriented the preferences of officials, managers, and even workers in the SOE sector. They came to appreciate that market competition had plenty of risks but also offered major rewards. If they succeeded, they tended to support the reforms and looked for more; in other words they learned from the nonstate sector how to operate successfully in market conditions.

62. Naughton, op. cit.

63. Ibid., p. 343.

64. Ibid., p. 344.

65. See J. McMillan and B. Naughton, 1992, "How to Reform a Planned Economy: Lessons from China," *Oxford Review of Economic Policy,* Vol. 8, p. 132; and also B. Naughton, 1994, "What Is Distinctive About China's Economic Transition? State Enterprise Reform and Overall System Transformation," *Journal of Comparative Economics,* Vol. 18, pp. 420–490. The importance of collective ownership, especially in the rural areas (the TVEs), is discussed in detail in P. Bowles and X. Y. Dong, 1994, "Current

Successes and Future Challenges in China's Economic Reforms," *New Left Review,* Vol. 208, pp. 49–76.

66. See P. Nolan, 1994, "The China Puzzle: Touching Stones to Cross the River," *Challenge,* Vol. 37, No. 1 (January–February), pp. 25–31.

67. H. Gates, 1996, *China's Motor: A Thousand Years of Petty Capitalism.* Ithaca: Cornell University Press.

68. See N. Lardy, 1994, *China in the World Economy.* Washington, DC: Institute for International Economics, p. 15 and table 1.3. In a more recent book Lardy has expanded on many of the same ideas; see N. Lardy, 1998, *China's Unfinished Economic Revolution.* Washington, DC: Brookings Institution Press. These predictions are elaborated in an IMF report: International Monetary Fund, 1993, *World Economic Outlook.* Washington, DC: IMF.

69. *The Economist,* "China: The Titan Stirs," November 28, 1992, p. 3.

70. E. Vogel, 1989, *One Step Ahead in China: Guangdong Province Under Reform.* Cambridge: Harvard University Press.

71. See ibid.

72. See, for example, B. Hook (ed.), 1996, *Guangdong: China's Promised Land.* Vol. 1 of the Regional Development in China series. Hong Kong: Oxford University Press; and S. Yusuf and W. P. Wu, 1997, *The Dynamics of Urban Growth in Three Chinese Cities.* Washington, DC: Oxford University Press for World Bank.

73. See Vogel, op. cit., p. 437. Closeness to capitalist Hong Kong was initially a mixed blessing from the perspective of the Chinese government, because of the sharp income gradient across the international border at Shenzhen. Hong Kong in 1990 had a higher GNP than the whole of Guangdong Province, with less than one-tenth its population. In spite of the obvious dangers, this has generally been an advantage for Guangdong, because it shows what can be achieved in China. Still there was a certain amount of danger involved in the proximity of Hong Kong. As Vogel notes, "It was one thing for the people of Guangdong to hear that people somewhere in the world had access to [material possessions], and quite another to learn that their own friends and relatives, less than a hundred miles away had them" (ibid., p. 74).

74. Perhaps the best and most comprehensive study of Greater China is Willem Van Kemenade, 1997, *China, Hong Kong, Taiwan, Inc.: The Dynamics of a New Empire.* New York: Alfred A. Knopf. The

phrase "Greater China" is also used as the title for an edited volume; see D. Shambaugh (ed.), 1995, *Greater China: The Next Superpower?* Studies on Contemporary China. London: Oxford University Press. Going back even farther is H. Harding, 1992, "The Emergence of Greater China: How U.S. Policy Will Have to Change," *American Enterprise* (May/June), pp. 46–55. See also W. H. Overholt, 1993, *The Rise of China: How Economic Reform Is Creating a New Superpower.* New York: W. W. Norton. The term "Greater South China Economic Zone" is used by X. M. Chen, 1993, "China's Growing Integration with the Asia-Pacific Economy," pp. 89–120 in A. Dirlik (ed.), *What Is in a Rim? Critical Perspectives on the Pacific Region Idea.* Boulder: Westview Press. "Chinese Economic Area" is used by R. Jones, R. King, and M. Klein, 1992, *The Chinese Economic Area: Economic Integration Without a Free Trade Agreement.* Paris: Organization for Economic Cooperation and Development; "South China Economic Community" is used by S. Stewart, 1992, "The Latest Asian Newly Industrialized Economy Emerges," *Columbia Journal of World Business* (Summer), Report No. 27230, pp. 31–37. The Greater China region referred to here includes Guangdong and Fujian Provinces in South China, as well as Hong Kong and Taiwan. It is not, of course, a closed system. For example, there is a significant amount of external investment coming into China from outside the region, especially from Singapore, Japan, the United States, and Europe; Hong Kong's entrepôt role brings in trade from outside the region and, in fact, from all over the world.

75. It is important to recall that before 1949 most of Taiwan's inhabitants had migrated to the island from Fujian Province, and today they speak either Fujianese or Mandarin, which is the official language of Taiwan; both are also distinct from Cantonese, the major dialect spoken in Hong Kong and Guangdong Province. In spite of the dialect differences, the written language is the same in all three parts of the Chinese territory. The issue of common language and its importance is setting up trade, and investment linkages cannot be overstated. As one researcher has observed, direct communication in a common language helps to prevent misunderstandings, but perhaps even more important is the role of indirect communication—the understanding of hidden messages shared by people who speak the same language—and the crucial issue of what is not said, as well as what is said. See, for examples of the role of

language in trade negotiations, Y. T. Hsing, "Linking up from the Bottom: The Role of Local Chinese Governments in Taiwanese Investment in Southern China," Paper presented at the Fourth Asian Urbanization Conference, January 1994, Taipei. See also Y. T. Hsing, 1998, *Making Capitalism in China: The Taiwan Connection.* London: Oxford University Press.

76. Lardy (1994), op. cit., esp. chap. 2, "China and the World Trading System," pp. 29–48.

77. Harding, op. cit., p. 47.

78. Lardy (1994), op. cit., pp. 30–31. As Lardy noted, China's share of the world's total trade has increased from less than 1 percent in the early 1980s to 2.5 percent in 1993, with a combined value in excess of US$200 billion (p. 2). Among the manufactured goods exported from China, the most rapid growth was in the area of electrical equipment, which increased its share of total exports from 2 percent to 11 percent between 1985 and 1990 (p. 32). Most of this growth involved the export of televisions, radios, telephone equipment, washing machines, air conditioners, and refrigerators. The growing independence of trade-oriented manufacturing has been largely responsible for the decline in the share of the central government's total revenues of China's overall GNP, which fell from 38.7 percent in 1978 to 16.6 percent in 1990, a figure that is lower than that for the United States, and just above that for Hong Kong (both of which are capitalist societies). See Overholt, op. cit., pp. 48–49.

79. The role of Hong Kong in the growth of China's export trade is discussed in detail in Y. W. Sung, 1991, *The China–Hong Kong Connection: The Key to China's Open-Door Policy.* Cambridge: Cambridge University Press, esp. chap. 1 ("The Open-Door Policy"), pp. 1–21, and chap. 2 ("The Pivotal Role of Hong Kong") pp. 22–43. See also R.Y.W. Kwok, "The Formation of Hong Kong–Guangdong Metropolitan Region: Transnational Investment in South China," Paper presented at the Fourth Asian Urbanization Conference, January 1994, Taipei.

80. Overholt, op. cit., esp. chap. 3, "The Emergence of Capital Markets," pp. 147–182.

81. Harding, op. cit., p. 49.

82. See *China Statistical Yearbook 1997*, table 16-13, p. 605.

83. These statistics, as well as a detailed discussion of the reasons for and the patterns of the growing amount of Taiwan investment in the mainland, can be found in an OECD report written by K. Fukasuki, D. Wall, and M. Y. Yu, 1994, *China's Long March to an Open Economy.* Paris: Development Centre, The Organization for Economic Cooperation and Development, pp. 78–84. This is also discussed by H.H.M. Hsia and A. Y. So, 1993, "Assent Through National Integration: The Chinese Triangle of Mainland–Taiwan–Hong Kong," pp. 133–150 in R. A. Palat (ed.), *Pacific Asia and the Future of the World System.* Westport, CT: Greenwood Press.

84. Jones, King, and Klein, op. cit.

85. Sung (1991), op. cit., pref., p. xi; see also Y. W. Sung, 1992, "The Economic Integration of Hong Kong, Taiwan, and South Korea with the Mainland of China," pp. 149–181 in R. Garnaut and G. E. Liu (eds.), *Economic Reform and Internationalization: China and the Pacific Region.* Canberra, Australia: Allen and Unwin Publishers.

86. See Lardy (1994), op. cit., pp. 14–18, 15. The high figures (US$2.56–2.90 trillion) for China's GDP are provided in R. Summers and A. Heston, 1991, "An Expanded Set of International Comparisons, 1950–1988," *Quarterly Journal of Economics,* Vol. 106, No. 2 (May), pp. 327–368; and the *Asian Wall Street Journal,* May 31, 1993, p. 21.

87. See, for example, "Koo's Coup," a commentary in *Free China Review,* Vol. 48, No. 12 (December 1998), p. 1.

88. L. Kroar, "A New China Without Borders," *Fortune,* October 5, 1992, pp. 124–127, 125. China's changing role in the Pacific Asia region is also discussed by Chen (1993), op. cit. See also G. Boyd, 1992, "China in the Pacific Regional Economy," pp. 147–176 in R. H. Brown and W. T. Liu (eds.), *Modernization in East Asia: Political, Economic, and Social Perspectives.* Westport, CT: Praeger Publishers.

89. Kroar, op. cit., p. 126. See also the IMF report by Bell, Khor, and Kochhar, op. cit.

90. B. Reynolds, 1989, "The Chinese Economy in 1988," pp. 27–48 in A. J. Kane (ed.), *China Briefing, 1988.* Boulder: Westview Press.

91. S. Leys (pseud. Pierre Ryckmans), 1978, *Chinese Shadows.* London: Penguin Books, p. xi.

92. Sen won a Nobel Prize in 1998. His work on poverty and inequality has been widely published, including the following key references to the topic at hand: A. K. Sen, 1984, *Resources, Values, and Development.* Cambridge: Harvard University Press; Sen, 1992, "Life and Death in China: A Reply," *World Development,* Vol. 20, pp. 1305–1312; Sen, 1994, "The Causation and Prevention of Famines: A Reply," *Journal of Peasant Studies,* Vol. 21, pp. 29–40.

93. See Lieberthal, op. cit.

94. C. Bramall and M. E. Jones, 1993, "Rural Income Inequality in China Since 1978," *Journal of Peasant Studies*, Vol. 21, pp. 1–70.

95. R. Weil, 1995, "China at the Brink: Class Contradictions of 'Market Socialism': Part II." *Monthly Review*, January 1995, pp. 11–43.

Chapter 18

1. K. Misra, 1998, *From Post-Maoism to Post-Marxism: The Erosion of Official Ideology in Deng's China*. London: Routledge, pp. 207–208.

2. B. Gilley, 1998, *Tiger on the Brink: Jiang Zemin and China's New Elite*. Berkeley: University of California Press, p. 289.

3. This is the argument made by M. X. Pei, 1998a, "Is China Democratizing?" *Foreign Affairs*, Vol. 77, No. 1 (January/February), pp. 62–82.

4. R. Baum, 1996, *Burying Mao: Chinese Politics in the Age of Deng Xiaoping*. Princeton: Princeton University Press, p. 384.

5. This campaign was generally popular, even though it represented quite a risk for Jiang to be taking, in the sense that he could end up biting the hand that fed him. See Baum, ibid., p. 387. In fact there have seen some major breakthroughs and well-publicized successes in the fight to eradicate corruption; as Baum has observed (p. 385), including efforts to investigate the reputedly illegal activities of some of Deng's family members and close associates.

6. Ibid., p. 387.

7. Ibid., p. 390. The hard line on political reform and dissidents was never so clear as in September 1998, with the arrest and sentencing of the individuals who had been leading the attempt to register the China Democratic Party. See *China News Digest*, "Dissidents Hope to Establish Legal Opposition Party," September 18, 1998, and "Dissidents Warned Against Attempts to Register Opposition Party, Two Detained in Beijing and Shanghai," September 17, 1998.

8. J. Fewsmith, 1997, "Reaction, Resurgence, and Succession: Chinese Politics Since Tiananmen," pp. 472–531 in R. MacFarquhar (ed.), *The Politics of China: The Eras of Mao and Deng*, 2d ed. Cambridge: Cambridge University Press, p. 521.

9. See Pei (1998a), op. cit.

10. Fewsmith, op. cit., p. 524.

11. Ibid., p. 525.

12. This quote is from Misra, op. cit., p. 210. The *Third Eye* author, a "Doctor Leninger," is widely thought to be the neoconservative CCP cadre Wang Shan; its ideas, although generally written off as "self-serving neoconservative polemic," attracted a great deal of attention in 1993 (see Baum, op. cit., p. 393). Since then, a number of other similar polemical publications have appeared, with very similar messages, including the 1998 book *China's Pitfall*, which was reviewed for *New York Review of Books* by Liu Binyan and Perry Link. B. Y. Liu and P. Link, 1998, "A Great Leap Backward?" *New York Review of Books*, Vol. 65, No. 15, pp. 19–23; see also Chapter 1 of this book.

13. K. Lieberthal, 1995, *Governing China: From Revolution Through Reform*. New York: W. W. Norton., p. 311.

14. M. Blecher, 1997, *China Against the Tides: Restructuring Through Revolution, Radicalism, and Reform*. London: Pinter, p. 210.

15. In Confucian times there had been hegemony, in the sense that many ordinary people came to think and act in a Confucian way; but there were also, concurrently, many other belief systems, involving local and popular cultures. In other words there were multiple worldviews. The difference, according to Blecher, however, is that there was no concept of class or class conflict. Some people had more power than others, but this was not considered to be the result of exploitation or political usurpation: It was simply in the natural order of things. See Blecher, ibid., p. 211. There was discontent about and resistance toward individuals and groups, such as landlords and local leaders, but such actions were seen mainly as attacks on people who had lost the moral and natural right to rule and collect rent, not as a process of overthrowing a class of exploiters and despots. Both before and after 1949 the CCP started to try to convince the people (mostly the peasants) that the gentry elite was rich and powerful because it had systematically kept them (the peasants) poor and weak. This became the Party's claim to legitimacy—the fact that it represented the interests of the poor peasants and workers against the landlords and capitalists. To do this the Party had to make "the language of class and class conflict a part of everyday discourse." See ibid., p. 211. In addition to the obvious objective class categories (such as peasant, landlord, worker, capitalist) there were subjective categories—"good" and "bad" classes; to carry out the major campaigns, such as land reform and the

Great Leap Forward, people had to be sorted into classes defining exactly where they stood in the local hierarchy of power.

16. Ibid., p. 212.

17. Interestingly, modernization per se is not, according to Party propaganda, to be considered capitalist, even though it employs capitalist-type strategies.

18. R. Weil, 1996, *Red Cat, White Cat: China and the Contradictions of "Market Socialism."* New York: Monthly Review Press, p. 263.

19. The quotation is from M. J. Watts, 1998, "Recombinant Capitalism: State, De-Collectivization, and the Agrarian Question in Vietnam," pp. 450–505 in J. Pickles and A. Smith (eds.), *Theorizing Transition: The Political Economy of Post-Communist Transformations.* New York: Routledge, p. 450.

20. Baum, op. cit., p. 342. Deng suggested, in fact (after his 1992 tour of the south), that China should strive to create "several Hong Kongs" within its borders (ibid., p. 343).

21. Ibid., p. 360.

22. Lieberthal, op. cit., pp. 419–440.

23. Ibid., p. 420.

24. N. C. Hughes, 1998, "Smashing the Iron Rice Bowl," *Foreign Affairs*, Vol. 77, No. 4 (July/August), pp. 67–77.

25. See ibid. and also He's book, *China's Pitfall.*

26. Jiang Zemin, who in the early 1990s was making his bid for the leadership, had managed to cover the apparently blatant shift toward the market with a "veil of conventional socialist respectability." Baum, op. cit., p. 361. This was entirely consistent with his unflagging pragmatism and opportunism, as witnessed in his public pronouncement that all Party members and leaders should "break the shackles of traditional conceptions and subjective prejudices. . . . We must not simply cling to certain Marxist principles . . . or to ideas that are wrong because in the primary stage of socialism they are premature." See ibid., p. 361. The Jiang quotation is taken from *Beijing Review*, Vol. 35, No. 42 (October 19–25, 1992), pp. 29–30.

27. F. Christiansen and S. Rai, 1996, *Chinese Politics and Society: An Introduction.* London: Prentice-Hall, p. 78.

28. Ibid. Zhao hinted that the primary stage of socialism could last as long as a hundred years after the socialist transformation of the late 1950s (p. 79).

29. Fewsmith, op. cit., p. 487. This refers to the frequently quoted Dengism that it did not really matter what color a cat was, as long as it catches mice—

implying that almost any policies could be implemented as long as they advanced the developmental goals of the Four Modernizations.

30. Ibid., p. 476.

31. Ibid.

32. J. T. Dreyer, 1996, *China's Political System: Modernization and Tradition*, 2d ed. London: Macmillan, p. 117. There are some obvious problems with this definition; for example, much of what is implied in following the road to the "four modernizations" ran directly counter to Maoist thought. As Dreyer notes, "how . . . could one follow the socialist road when many of the directional signals appeared to be written in capitalist language?" (op. cit., p. 117).

33. Fewsmith, op. cit., p. 494.

34. Ibid., p. 497. This was also reproduced in the decision of the CCP Central Committee announced in November 1993; see Lieberthal, op. cit., p. 420.

35. L. W. Pye, 1996, "The State and the Individual: An Overview Interpretation," pp. 16–42 in B. Hook (ed.), *The Individual and the State in China.* Oxford: Clarendon Press, pp. 16–17.

36. In part this can be seen as a reaction to what Pye describes as a source of ambivalence: Groups and collective organizations in China provide a source of security for individuals, who in fact get very little out of the relationship. Individuals are expected to be self-sacrificing, including giving up their material well-being, in return for which they can expect, at best, only symbolic or ritualistic support. Similarly, children are expected to be disciplined by socialization and not to show their emotions publicly. All of the sacrifices are made by the individual, which makes for an inherently unequal relationship.

37. However, in July 1999 the world was quite impressed by the Chinese women's World Cup soccer team, which appeared to have no problem at all exhibiting this sort of team spirit, even in defeat.

38. Pye, op. cit., p. 24.

39. Ibid., p. 31.

40. As Pye suggests, "It is better to uphold stability by concentrating on the rituals of governance, arguing about orthodoxy, and scheming to ensure that any misguided attempts at a policy by another faction will be doomed" (ibid., p. 33). In sharp contrast to Pye's views on this issue, other China scholars, including Maurice Meisner, are convinced that the state still has not only the power but also the will to intimidate the people. After the jailing and sentencing of the individuals attempting to register the China Democratic Party in December 1998, there are reasons to indicate that this is indeed still the case.

41. Ibid., p. 32.

42. It is commonly argued that these tendencies are being exaggerated by the massive increase in the floating populations in the cities, and many people see the new armies of transients as a major threat to stability and security. The peasants on the move are certainly willing to take risks by going into business, becoming peddlers, repairers, shoe-shiners, and ragpickers; but in fact there is little real evidence to connect migrants with crime (see Chapter 15). Interestingly, permanent residents of the city were until recently subsidized by the state, but the much poorer floaters have never been considered for such support, which Pye refers to as one of the "great reversals." The other reversal is the evidence that the new wealthy private entrepreneurs are now earning far more than people on fixed incomes like teachers, doctors, scientists, and other professionals. In other words, much of what is observable in contemporary China is reversed: The more knowledge and training one has, the less one earns, as exemplified by the popular saying that "wages are hanging upside down" (*gongzi daogu*). Ibid., p. 38.

43. A similar point is also made by Alan P.L. Liu, 1996, *Mass Politics in the People's Republic: State and Society in Contemporary China.* Boulder: Westview Press.

44. Pye, op. cit., p. 39.

45. G. White, 1996, "The Dynamics of Civil Society in Post-Mao China," pp. 196–221 in B. Hook (ed.), *The Individual and the State in China.* Oxford: Clarendon Press, p. 204.

46. The state responds to societal forces in a number of ways, the most obvious being repression and incorporation, in which different associations and interest groups are licensed and recognized by the state in return for observing controls over their behavior (in other words co-optation). New associations may be allowed to exist, but they must agree to being regulated. This issue is taken up in more detail later in the next chapter.

47. M. X. Pei, 1998b, *From Reform to Revolution: The Demise of Communism in China and the Soviet Union.* Cambridge: Harvard University Press, p. 44.

48. See B. L. McCormick, 1996, "Concluding Thoughts: Reforming Socialism in China—Another New Dragon?" pp. 203–214 in B. L. McCormick and J. Unger (eds.), *China After Socialism: In the Footsteps of Eastern Europe or East Asia?* Armonk, NY: M. E. Sharpe, p. 212.

49. Blecher, op. cit., p. 212.

50. Some China scholars (for example, Alan Liu, op. cit.) argue that although the leaders, especially Mao Zedong, liked to believe that the state and society were of a like mind on most policy issues, this was most often not the case, because in fact no one had ever asked the "people" what they wanted.

51. Blecher, op. cit., p. 221.

52. Ibid.

53. Lieberthal, op. cit., p. 297.

54. N. N. Chen, 1995, "Urban Spaces and Experiences of *Qigong*," pp. 347–361 in D. S. Davis et al., *Urban Spaces in Contemporary China: The Potential for Autonomy and Community in Post-Mao China.* Cambridge: Cambridge University Press.

55. Lieberthal, op. cit., p. 299.

56. Pei (1998b), op. cit., pp. 77–78.

57. G. White, 1993, *Riding the Tiger: The Politics of Economic Reform in Post-Mao China.* London: Macmillan, p. 217.

58. See Pei (1998b), op. cit.

59. White (1996), op. cit., p. 196.

60. In the language of the post-1949 revolutionary era, this division is similar to that between the politically reliable "reds" and the better-trained "experts." In the arena of health care, for example (see Chapter 6), those doctors who were trained in the West or in Western medicine would be the "experts," as opposed to the more politically motivated and revolutionary "reds," medical workers, and the so-called barefoot doctors.

61. White (1993), op. cit., p. 197.

62. See Baum, op. cit., p. 294.

63. Pei (1997), op. cit., illustrates this in the provision of education and health services, the provision of law and order, and the chronic lack of rural infrastructure.

64. Ibid., p. 30.

65. Ibid., p. 20.

66. A relatively recent and comprehensive treatment of the growth of corruption in reform-era China is provided in J. Kwong, 1997, *The Political Economy of Corruption in China.* Armonk, NY: M. E. Sharpe. For a fascinating discussion of the "predatory" nature of states in sub-Saharan Africa, see M. Castells, 1998, *End of Millennium,* Vol. 3 of *The Information Age: Economy, Society, and Culture.* Oxford, UK: Blackwell.

67. The central government's revenues have been falling, from 40 percent of GDP in 1978, to 31 percent in 1980, 18 percent in 1993, and only 12 percent in 1994. See Pei (1998b), op. cit. Another contribut-

ing factor has been the reform measures that have allowed the SOEs to keep more of their earnings and pay less to the state; see, for example, He's book *China's Pitfall,* op. cit.

68. The state's labor force has grown significantly, from 13 million in 1980 to 31 million in 1990, many of whom, Pei reports, are "excess personnel"; Pei (1997), op. cit., p. 22. Also, the state has been claiming a progressively larger share of dwindling state resources for its own consumption (for example, in administrative expenditures, which includes office salaries, benefits, capital costs for new buildings and official vehicles, operating expenses, and, of course, meetings and entertainment, which increased from 4.76 percent of the total state budget in 1978 to 14.62 percent in 1994; compared with falling shares of investment in agriculture, pensions and social welfare, and R&D expenditures); see ibid., Table 18.2, p. 23. Pei calculates that government expenditures— in other words the maintenance of the state apparatus—increased eightfold between 1978 and 1990. There has been a proliferation of arbitrary fees and other informal levies; for example, courts, police departments, and customs agencies charge public fees for services that used to be provided free. Even though overall taxation has declined during the reform years, state predation has taken on a new but no less "rapacious" form (p. 24). These new charges fall into the general and rapidly growing category of "extrabudgetary revenues," which increased from 30–35 percent of official tax revenues in 1978 to almost 97 percent in 1992.

69. Pei discusses a central government document that disclosed that "most (off-budget) revenues

have gone into cash slush funds—used to finance automobile purchases, bonuses, wasteful consumption, and expansion of employee benefits" (ibid., p. 25).

70. One news report in an official publication estimated that in 1992, automobile purchases and related expenses accounted for Y60–70 billion, about 70 percent of "social group consumption" (purchases of consumer goods by government agencies and SOEs), which is equivalent to the total amount of foreign and domestic debt borrowed by the government that year. Pei, ibid., p. 26. Pei argues that this sort of evidence is the symptom of the decay of the state's ruling institutions. As Pei notes, the most striking example in contemporary China is the "systematic and unrestrained abuse of power for private gains which has become a pervasive feature of the Party-state" (ibid., p. 27). An internal document reported the following reasons for the decay of the CCP: erosion of the official ideology; loss of faith in communism; the rising gap between a rapidly changing society and a slowly changing Party; cadres' weakening identification with the Party; low sense of Party discipline; rising localism; and decreasing frequency of organizational activities within many of the Party cells (ibid., p. 28).

71. Ibid., p. 12.

72. Ibid., pp. 37–48.

73. Pei (1998a), op. cit., p. 75.

74. Ibid., p. 45.

75. Pei (1997), op. cit., p. 46.

76. Ibid., p. 48.

77. Ibid.

Chapter 19

1. Jan Morris, 1984, *Journeys.* New York: Oxford University Press, pp. 152–171 ("Very Strange Feeling: A Chinese Journey"), p. 167.

2. See J. T. Dreyer, 1996, *China's Political System: Modernization and Tradition,* 2d ed. London: Macmillan, p. 335.

3. See G. White, 1993, *Riding the Tiger: The Politics of Economic Reform in Post-Mao China.* London: Macmillan. White suggests that the increasing prevalence of the rudiments of a civil society does not automatically point toward a desirable outcome of this type.

4. Dreyer, op. cit.

5. As Dreyer suggests, this is not necessarily a recipe for the liberation of society but its incorporation; see ibid., p. 338.

6. Ibid.

7. The following reports, all written in the late summer of 1998, describe the early stages of this process, when the attempts were being made to register the new China Democratic Party in various locations. All appeared in *China News Digest*: "Dissidents Hope to Establish Legal Opposition Party," September 11, 1998; "Dissidents Warned Against Attempts to Register Opposition Party, Two Detained in Beijing and Shanghai," September 17,

1998; "Shanghai Dissidents Submit Opposition Party Application," September 18, 1998; "Released Dissident Says One-Party Policy Is Not Changing," September 19, 1998; and "More Dissidents Detained for Registering Opposition Party," September 21, 1998.

8. S. Leys (pseud. Pierre Ryckmans), 1978, *Chinese Shadows.* London: Penguin Books.

9. A. G. Walder, 1989, "The Political Sociology of the Beijing Upheaval of 1989," *Problems of Communism*, Vol. 38, No. 5 (September/October), pp. 30–40. In 1989 David Zweig also argued that the Chinese peasants, although not as involved in the uprisings of 1989, were anything but passive in the face of contemporary events. According to Zweig, "At no time since the great famine of the early 1960s has the potential for rural instability been greater. . . . The recent return to power in Beijing of aging conservatives, many of whom were the architects of the unpopular and unproductive agricultural policies of earlier decades, makes widespread rural unrest and violence more likely in China in the near future." D. Zweig, 1989, "Peasants and Politics," *World Policy Journal*, Vol. 6, No. 4, pp. 633–646, 633.

10. Walder, op. cit., p. 40.

11. B. G. He, 1996, *The Democratization of China.* London: Routledge.

12. Ibid., p. 177.

13. As He concludes, "The 1989 Chinese Democratic Movement is best understood as the expression of fundamental conflict between a state with totalitarian intentions and an emerging civil society" (ibid., p. 177).

14. Ibid., p. 176.

15. F. Christiansen and S. Rai, 1996, *Chinese Politics and Society: An Introduction.* London: Prentice-Hall, p. 14.

16. For example, workers in one work unit had difficulty interacting with those of another unit, because most of their social interactions occurred within the walls of their own unit; see Chapter 14.

17. For example, see J. N. Wasserstrom and X. Y. Liu, 1995, "Student Associations and Mass Movements," pp. 362–393 in D. S. Davis et al., *Urban Spaces in Contemporary China: The Potential for Autonomy and Community in Post-Mao China.* Cambridge: Cambridge University Press; in the same volume, see M. Sidel, 1995, "Dissident and Liberal Legal Scholars and Organizations in Beijing and the Chinese State in the 1980s," pp. 326–346.

18. Christiansen and Rai, op. cit., p. 124.

19. See the various reports from *China News Digest*, op. cit.

20. This, of course, does not mean that there has been no political activity in the countryside; in fact nothing could be farther from the truth; see Chapter 7. It does mean, however, as Alan Liu points out, that most of the activity in China's rural areas has been isolated and unorganized, with groups acting to deal with their own specific problems rather than forming an area-wide or regional network of groups, ultimately forming a social movement. Alan P.L. Liu, 1996, *Mass Politics in the People's Republic: State and Society in Contemporary China.* Boulder: Westview Press.

21. See Christiansen and Rai, op. cit., p. 126. The division here corresponds to White's twin definitions of "civil society." G. White, 1996, "The Dynamics of Civil Society in Post-Mao China," pp. 196–221 in B. Hook (ed.), *The Individual and the State in China.* Oxford: Clarendon Press. One definition is sociological—in which there is an "intermediate associational realm situated between the state [and] society . . . populated by social organizations which are separate from the state, enjoy some degree of autonomy from it, and are formed voluntarily by members . . . to protect or extend their interests or values" (p. 198). A political definition, by contrast, equates civil society with political society in the sense of a "particular set of institutionalized relationships between the state and society based on the principles of citizenship, civil rights, representation, and the rule of law" (p. 198). As White notes, much analysis of the civil society issue in China tends to fuse the two definitions, linking the emergence of civil society to pressures for liberal democratization. This results in an evaluation of the possible elements of civil society in China by determining the extent to which each different organization is truly civil or uncivil—with the "leading to democratization" criterion uppermost. White argues that this approach is not very helpful in assessing events in contemporary China, so he offers a third notion of civil society that is unhinged from any specific tradition of political thought and ideology. Also, White notes that the emergence of a functioning civil society is only one route to liberal democracy. In Gorbachev's Soviet Union, for example, it was the party-state apparatus that provided the thrust in that direction, not the workings of civil society. There are also international pressures and the workings of domestic elites located within the state. So it is important to unhinge the two ideas, looking at and for evidence of an "in-

termediate stratum of social organizations [that have] emerged and changed the relationship between state and society" (pp. 199–200). Thus the search is for social organizations that demonstrate spontaneity, voluntariness, and autonomy in the way they were formed and how they operate (p. 200).

22. K. Lieberthal, 1995, *Governing China: From Revolution Through Reform*. New York: W. W. Norton, p. 302.

23. See White (1996), op. cit., p. 201, and also M. X Pei, 1998a, *From Reform to Revolution: The Demise of Communism in China and the Soviet Union*. Cambridge: Harvard University Press.

24. White (1996), op. cit., pp. 201–202.

25. Ibid., p. 202.

26. Ibid., pp. 205–206. Such repression occurred when the Falun Gong movement was judged to have grown to an unmanageable and unwarranted size in the summer of 1999. Although the leaders of the movement argue it is not a political organization, its huge size and ability to mobilize its members to demonstrate against the state have clearly represented a threat to the regime, causing a predictable response. See Ian Buruma, 1999, "China in Cyberspace," *New York Review of Books*, Vol. 46, No. 17 (November 4), pp. 9–12.

27. White qualifies this remark by adding that it is a very partial and patchy civil society made up of "a complex and rapidly changing social constellation with many layers and many different types of relationships with the party/state" (ibid., p. 207).

28. Ibid., p. 208.

29. Ibid.

30. As Dreyer, op. cit., points out, they are sometimes referred to as examples of a new state "corporatism."

31. There is also some new growth in rural areas of semi-informal and informal associations, often based on kinship, religious belief, or ethnicity, and some of which have attracted state attention and have been closed down; see Liu (1996), op. cit. For example, in remote western areas, local Muslim leaders promote the growth of religious revival groups that are being approved by the state and are making links with Islamic nations in the Middle East, which might lead to lucrative investments and perhaps even to calls for secession sometime in the future.

32. In 1993 an official report claims to have banned some 1,370 illegal organizations, but they are still reported to be spreading rapidly; see White (1996), op. cit.

33. There have been reports of increases in religious groups, as well as secret societies, criminal fraternities, and criminal gangs. In fact a 1992 report listed some 1,830 underworld organizations, with more than 30,000 members, organized nationally and with global linkages; ibid. The banning of Falun Gong in 1999 has been publicized internationally and has resulted in a considerable amount of criticism directed at the Chinese government; see Buruma, op. cit.

34. Ibid., p. 217.

35. "Core-periphery" here implies political relationships, not necessarily geographical ones.

36. See Liu (1996), op. cit., and White (1996), op. cit., p. 219.

37. *China News Digest*: "Dissidents Hope . . . ," September 11, 1998, op. cit.

38. *China News Digest*, "Dissidents Warned . . . ," September 17, 1998, op. cit.

39. *China News Digest*, "Shanghai Dissidents . . . ," September 18, 1998, op. cit.

40. *China News Digest*, "More Dissidents Detained . . . ," September 21, 1998, op. cit.

41. This argument is also made by Alan Liu. Liu suggests that the fragmented nature of the new associations, and their inability to coalesce or unite to act together (which he refers to as the problems of "occasionalism" and "sectionalism"), result in the "heterotropic" character of social change in post-Mao China, which he likens to a scene from *Alice in Wonderland*, where the individual "rode off furiously in several directions" (p. 226).

42. White (1996), op. cit., p. 221.

43. *Chinese Maxims: Golden Sayings of Chinese Thinkers over Five Thousand Years*, 1994. Beijing: Sinolingua Press, maxim no. 6546, p. 218.

44. Minxin Pei (1998b), "Is China Democratizing?" *Foreign Affairs*, Vol. 77, No. 1 (January/February), pp. 62–82, 78.

45. Pei argues that this has not won China much support internationally, because this antidissident coercion is now so widely publicized that the whole world, it seems, is watching their every move—not that this makes any apparent difference to the regime; see ibid.

46. There has also been the apparent failure of many of the children of first-generation leaders—the princelings—to get "elected" to key positions in the leadership, thereby reducing the amount of family-based patronage; ibid., p. 73.

47. See Pei (1998a), op. cit.

48. This is the case even though the CCP is still the world's largest political party, with 58 million members and 3.4 million grassroots party cells; Pei (1998b), op. cit., p. 79.

49. This argument is made very well by Alan Liu (op. cit.), who suggests that four groups in particular have effectively created mass public opinion and possibly also a new political culture that is often hostile to and in opposition to the state: the peasants, the urban-based workers, students and intellectuals, and ethnic minority groups.

50. In other words if there were to be open elections, such mass support would provide the Party with the legitimacy it needs to win, which would prevent the need to use force to suppress the opposition. Perhaps this is overstating the case. At the very least the state would hope that the peasants would be (again) apathetic about an urban-based uprising and refuse to join it.

51. These reforms, as we have seen, include the changes in the workings of the National People's Congress and the spread and popularity of rural elections. See Alan Liu, op. cit., who has described some of the political-legal reforms implemented or overseen by the state that might, he suggests, end up challenging the regime.

52. The new tax system, implemented in 1994, is a move in this direction because it establishes new and legal relationships between the central government and the provinces.

53. White (1993), op. cit.

54. Ibid., p. 242.

55. As in the case of the Asian NIEs, or the "developmental states" such as South Korea and Taiwan, which remained very authoritarian and very much in control of the economic development process, at least until recently. See, for example, M. Castells, 1998, *The Information Age: Economy, Society, and Culture*. Vol. 3: *End of Millennium*. Oxford, UK: Blackwell.

56. White (1993), op. cit., p. 242.

57. See Castells, op. cit.

58. This argument is now particularly interesting in light of the enthusiastic way that Chinese people in Hong Kong (as well as Taiwan) appear to have embraced democracy; see Chapter 11 and the *China News Digest* articles, op. cit.

59. He, op. cit., also rejects the three traditional explanations given to justify China's inability to democratize, including the so-called cultural explanation, which assumes there can be no change in Chinese political culture. He argues in fact that a new

Chinese political culture is already emerging; see also Liu (1996), op. cit. The second is the argument that China lacks a pluralist and self-organizing civil society independent of the state. He in fact agrees (p. 224) with White (1996), op. cit., that a civil society is emerging and in fact did play a key role in the Tiananmen incident in 1989. Third is that the Chinese state is totalitarian with a self-enforcing power structure that cannot be reformed or transformed or cannot democratize itself from within. Again He argues that this need not be the case; as Pei (1998b), op. cit., argues, there are already some hopeful signs, e.g., in the increased importance of the NPC. In short, He argues that China already has the "bones" of a democratic culture, in the form of an emerging civil society, and reform factions within the Party that will be able to play the democratic card when the time comes. The main question is how these factors can interact at a favorable time so as to break the current deadlock; see He, p. 225.

60. Countering this argument are those who suggest that the peasants can and already do exert some degree of power and often have major influence. See, for example, the arguments put forward in Chapter 7 by such scholars as Kate Zhou and Daniel Kelliher. See Kate Xiao Zhou, 1996, *How the Farmers Changed China: Power of the People*. Boulder: Westview Press; and D. Kelliher, 1992, *Peasant Power in China: The Era of Rural Reform, 1979–1989*. New Haven: Yale University Press. In addition, and as Marc Blecher warns, it could be a mistake to think that either the poor (who are assumed to be too busy) or the rich (who are assumed to be too corrupt) are not interested in democracy. See M. Blecher, 1997, *China Against the Tides: Restructuring Through Revolution, Radicalism, and Reform*. London: Pinter.

61. This is the argument put forward by Minxin Pei; see M. X. Pei, 1997, "Racing Against Time: Institutional Decay and Renewal in China," pp. 11–50 in W. A. Joseph (ed.), *China Briefing: The Contradictions of Change*. Armonk, NY: M. E. Sharpe; see also Pei (1998a, 1998b), op. cit.

62. White (1993), op. cit., p. 245.

63. However, Blecher warns against using such fears to justify the continuation of an authoritarian regime legitimating itself purely through economic liberalization, which is precisely what the existing regime has been doing now for more than a decade; see Blecher, op. cit.

64. This, of course, does not mean that this process is likely to happen anytime soon; in fact White (1993), op. cit., p. 248, considered China's democra-

tization to be as unlikely to happen as it was to succeed, and at the turn of the century we cannot say much more than this.

65. It can be argued that China was moving in this direction in the late 1980s before the tragedy of Tiananmen Square, with steps being taken gradually to limit the power of the Party by separating it from state administration; by reducing the power of Party secretaries and committees in relation to professional managers in state enterprises; and by allowing such political institutions as the NPC to have more power. According to Minxin Pei (1998b), op. cit., this could be achieved by abolishing leading Party member groups in governmental bodies and reducing the incidence of interlocking directorates, whereby the same people hold both Party and government posts; see also Pei (1997), op. cit.

66. At present it is too early to judge whether Jiang Zemin is, or could be, that person; see B. Gilley, 1998, *Tiger on the Brink: Jiang Zemin and China's New Elite.* Berkeley: University of California Press.

67. See White (1993), op. cit., pp. 252–253, and Pei (1998a), op. cit.

68. See Castells, op. cit. This is a contentious issue, of course, because there are some signs of major ethnic unrest in many parts of China, especially in Tibet and the far west (see Chapter 12); see also Liu (1996), op. cit.

69. See White (1993), op. cit., p. 255.

70. See R. Weil, 1996, *Red Cat, White Cat: China and the Contradictions of "Market Socialism."* New York: Monthly Review Press.

71. See, for example, A. Dirlik, 1994, *After the Revolution: Waking to Global Capitalism.* Hanover, NH: Wesleyan University Press; and also A. Dirlik, 1996, *The Postcolonial Aura: Third World Criticism in the Age of Global Capitalism.* Boulder: Westview Press.

Meisner's work is well summarized in his recent book: M. Meisner, 1996, *The Deng Xiaoping Era: An Inquiry into the Fate of Chinese Socialism, 1978–1994.* New York: Hill and Wang. See also Hill Gates, 1996, *China's Motor: A Thousand Years of Petty Capitalism.* Ithaca: Cornell University Press.

72. The most important questions, of course, are whether China would want to do either of these, and at present there are few indications that it does.

73. Weil, op. cit., p. 270.

74. Ibid.

75. Lieberthal, op. cit., p. 313.

76. Following this lead, it is useful to speculate on what the future might bring, politically speaking, in China. The current situation can be likened to what Samuel Huntington has described as a "praetorian" society, that is, one that lacks effective political institutions but where power comes from multiple sources and is highly fragmented and there are no agreed-upon, nonviolent ways of resolving conflicts (such as elections or examinations). In a praetorian society each group uses or attempts to use whatever means it can to make its point: bribes, riots, demonstrations, or brute force. In contemporary China, the key to the future, as June Dreyer, op. cit., argues, is the extent to which the state will be able to use the countryside to contain, pacify, or neutralize the ever-expanding and unruly cities. In 1989 the peasants remained passively neutral—not joining with the students, workers, and intellectuals—but not actively supporting the government. As we have seen throughout this chapter and others (see especially Chapters 7 and 10), China's rural areas have multiple problems, including what one scholar has called the enforced "marginalization and pauperization" of the countryside; Liu (1996), op. cit.

INDEX